THE ESSENTIALS OF
REAL ESTATE LAW

THIRD EDITION

THE ESSENTIALS OF

REAL ESTATE LAW

THIRD EDITION

LYNN T. SLOSSBERG

 CENGAGE

Australia • Brazil • Mexico • Singapore • United Kingdom • United States

**The Essentials of Real Estate Law,
Third Edition**
Lynn T. Slossberg

Vice President, Skills Group: Dawn Gerrain

Senior Director of Development, Skills: Marah Bellegarde

Senior Product Development Manager: Larry Main

Senior Product Manager: Shelley Esposito

Content Developer: Mary Clyne

Product Assistant: Diane Chrysler

Marketing Manager: Scott Chrysler

Market Development Manager: Jon Sheehan

Senior Production Director: Wendy Troeger

Production Manager: Mark Bernard

Content Project Management: S4Carlisle

Art Direction: S4Carlisle

Text and cover design: S4Carlisle

Media Editor: Deborah Bordeaux

Cover Image: © shippee/ Shutterstock.com
© Andy Dean Photography/ Shutterstock.com
© Mark Winfrey/Shutterstock.com

For product information and technology assistance, contact us at
**Cengage Customer & Sales Support, 1-800-354-9706
or support.cengage.com.**

For permission to use material from this text or product, submit all requests online at **www.cengage.com/permissions.**

Library of Congress Control Number: 2013945839

ISBN-13: 978-1-133-69357-4
ISBN-10: 1-133-69357-1

Cengage
20 Channel Street
Boston, MA 02210
USA

Cengage is a leading provider of customized learning solutions with employees residing in nearly 40 different countries and sales in more than 125 countries around the world. Find your local representative at: **www.cengage.com.**

Cengage products are represented in Canada by Nelson Education, Ltd.

To learn more about Cengage platforms and services, register or access your online learning solution, or purchase materials for your course, visit **www.cengage.com.**

Notice to the Reader

Publisher does not warrant or guarantee any of the products described herein or perform any independent analysis in connection with any of the product information contained herein. Publisher does not assume, and expressly disclaims, any obligation to obtain and include information other than that provided to it by the manufacturer. The reader is expressly warned to consider and adopt all safety precautions that might be indicated by the activities described herein and to avoid all potential hazards. By following the instructions contained herein, the reader willingly assumes all risks in connection with such instructions. The publisher makes no representations or warranties of any kind, including but not limited to, the warranties of fitness for particular purpose or merchantability, nor are any such representations implied with respect to the material set forth herein, and the publisher takes no responsibility with respect to such material. The publisher shall not be liable for any special, consequential, or exemplary damages resulting, in whole or part, from the readers' use of, or reliance upon, this material.

Printed at CLDPC, USA, 12-18

In loving memory of my uncle, William Cooper

Brief Contents

Contents

Preface

The Essentials of Real Estate Law, Third Edition, embraces a systems approach. This text first provides a basic foundation of legal concepts necessary for an understanding of real estate transactions. The text then guides the student by providing not only procedural checklists the paralegal may utilize daily in the law office but also hypothetical client scenarios worked through each step of the way, resulting in a final product that shows the paralegal how to handle various client matters. Finally, the text involves the student by placing him or her in a virtual law office in the accompanying CourseMate, thus building proficiencies in real estate management that range from handling closings from start to finish to handling common real estate litigation.

I believe students learn most effectively by doing. The process of involving students in the course materials by mimicking their functions in the legal environment serves three purposes. The first is the creation of excitement in the material presented. This is a constant challenge for both student and instructor. Faced with a lengthy narrative of new legal concepts followed simply by questions geared toward memorization rather than assimilation, the student tends to lose interest. Active participation with practical applications speeds and reinforces the assimilation process.

The second purpose is increase in self-esteem. Traditional examinations are limited in the way they test learning. Because of this, the student is not certain that examination results truly reflect performance capability on the job. By performing typical paralegal tasks first in the receptive environment of the classroom, the student receives helpful feedback and reassurance that he or she is leaving the course with the requisite knowledge to do the job demanded of him or her.

The third purpose is competitive edge. Utilizing these materials, the student will be able to compile a portfolio of work at the completion of the course that may be used to great effect in the employment interview. Most students taking a basic real estate law course will lack prior law office experience and will need a marketing tool in "selling" their skills to attorneys. Indeed, most attorneys I know are "show me" people, more interested in the efficient output of quality product than in examination results. By completing paralegal tasks for "clients" in the virtual law office, a student can compile a portfolio of "experiences" to bring to an interview and is more likely to become a desired employee.

Although this text addresses itself to the entry-level paralegal, more experienced paralegals may benefit from its contents. Each chapter sets forth clear objectives that are reinforced at the end of the chapter in a chapter summary. After the presentation of major concepts, most chapters include hypothetical client scenarios illustrating the application of these concepts by showing a real estate paralegal performing the responsibilities discussed in the chapter. Additionally, each chapter includes review questions, discussion questions, an ethical question related to real estate practice, and Web resources. Most chapters also include case law and case questions.

The text is divided into four major sections: Part I, Fundamental Concepts of Real Estate Law; Part II, The Closing: Residential and Commercial Closings; Part III, Landlord/Tenant Law; and Part IV, Real Estate Litigation.

Part I provides the foundation for the rest of the text. In this section, the basic principles of real estate law are set forth. The section begins with a chapter on ethics and real property practice that first outlines basic ethical principles and then discusses potential ethical problems that may arise in real estate practice. The next chapter introduces the student to the concept of real property, basic ownership rights, estates and tenancies, and methods of title holding. This is followed by a chapter on various categories of real property, both residential and commercial. Subsequent chapters include governmental and private ownership restrictions, legal descriptions of property, real estate brokers, the basic real estate contract, deeds, liens on property, real estate financing, and title examination and insurance. The chapters on real estate contracts, deeds, financing, and title examination include hypothetical client scenarios highlighting paralegal responsibilities in these areas.

Part II of the text concentrates on the closing. The first chapter in this section is an introduction to the closing process, concentrating on the opening of a client file and its management, preclosing arrangements, document preparation for closing, real estate closing software, the closing itself, postclosing matters, tax matters, and escrow closings. The next two chapters are devoted to different closing situations: a residential real estate closing and a commercial real estate closing. Included in each of these chapters is a discussion of special considerations pertaining to that type of closing, checklists, and a hypothetical client closing showing a paralegal in each step of the process.

Part III centers on landlord/tenant law. It covers the basic area of residential and commercial leases and includes a chapter on eviction procedures. Each of the chapters in this section includes a hypothetical client matter, covering such matters as drafting leases and preparing documents for an eviction proceeding.

The focus of Part IV is real estate litigation, a topic too often overlooked in real estate texts. The section explores many common litigation situations, including breach of a sale contract, actions by real estate brokers, partition of property, and mortgage foreclosures. Each chapter in this section includes checklists, an explanation of pleadings to be filed, and a hypothetical client lawsuit.

A multitude of exhibits illustrates the text. These exhibits make reference to a fictional city, county, and state. Therefore, no zip code has been included in addresses. Readers should be aware that zip codes should be included on all correspondence and other pertinent documents. Please note as well that interest rates have been inserted in various exhibits for illustrative purposes and do not reflect prevalent interest rates at any given point in time. Similarly, the year included as part of the date in exhibits was inserted for illustrative purposes and chosen arbitrarily.

The student has an opportunity to apply his or her knowledge in the Slossberg Virtual Law Office in which a fictional law firm is created: Hernandez, Sanders, and Norris, P.A. Here, the student works as a fourth paralegal hired by the firm and is assigned to work with real estate attorney Deborah Sanders. The materials include an introduction to the firm and a policies and procedures manual for the firm.

Each module corresponds to a chapter in the text. Within each module, the student will be provided with instructions by the supervising attorney, ticklers stating the tasks to be completed, client files containing the requisite information to complete the tasks, interactive forms in the form file, and mentor tips from a senior paralegal in the firm to aid in the completion of the tasks. The student is asked to keep track of time spent on time sheets. The documents produced through working on client files in the virtual law office can then be compiled into a portfolio of final work product that can serve the student as sample work to be provided in an interview process and then, later, as a resource tool that may be referred to on the job.

Lynn T. Slossberg,
Esquire

Acknowledgments

This text would not be possible without the assistance of others. First, I would like to thank all those at Delmar Cengage Learning who believed in this project for their guidance and patience. Special thanks to Shelley Esposito, Senior Acquisitions Editor; Melissa Riveglia, Senior Product Manager; Diane Chrysler, Editorial Assistant; and Betty Dickson, Senior Content Project Manager.

Cases appearing in the publication were obtained from Westlaw and used with permission. Additional thanks to Attorneys' Title Insurance Fund, Inc. for its assistance with materials for the chapters on legal descriptions and title examinations and to Elayne Prince for her input on commercial leases.

Thanks also to Landtech Data Corporation for permission to use forms generated by Landtech software in the chapters on real estate closings. I would like to thank The National Conference of Commissioners on Uniform State Laws for permission to reproduce sections of various uniform acts.

Finally, special thanks to the reviewers of this book for their invaluable input, including:

Linda Cames Wimberly
    Eastern Kentucky University

Jay Strike Carlin
    Grantham University

Sheila Foglietta
    Schenectady County Community
    College

Sally Bisson
    College of Saint Mary

Bob Diotalevi
    Florida Gulf Coast University

Ancillary Materials

Paralegal CourseMate

The Essentials of Real Estate Law, Third Edition, has a Paralegal CourseMate available.

Paralegal CourseMate includes:

- An interactive eBook, with highlighting, note-taking, and search capabilities
- Interactive teaching and learning tools, including:
  - Quizzing
  - Case studies
  - Chapter objectives
  - Flash cards
  - Web links
  - Crossword puzzles
  - PowerPoint® presentations
  - Slossberg Law Office
  - And more!
- Engagement Tracker, a first-of-its-kind tool that monitors student engagement in the course

To learn more about this resource and access free demo CourseMate resources, go to **www.cengagebrain.com**, and search by this book's ISBN (9781133693574). To access CourseMate materials that you have purchased, go to **login.cengagebrain.com**, enter your access code, and create an account or log into your existing account.

INSTRUCTOR RESOURCES

Instructor Resources

Spend Less Time Planning and More Time Teaching. With Delmar Cengage Learning's Instructors Companion Website, to Accompany The Essentials of Real Estate Law, preparing for class and evaluating students has never been easier! This invaluable instructor resource allows you on-line access to all of your resources:

- Written by the author of the text, the **Instructor's Manual** contains chapter overviews; answers to the review questions, discussion questions, and ethical questions; useful websites; and a test bank and answer key.
- The **Computerized Testbank** powered by Cognero makes generating tests and quizzes a snap. With many questions and different styles to choose from, you can create customized assessments for your students with the click of a button. Add your own unique questions and print rationales for easy class preparation.
- Customizable **PowerPoint® Presentations** focus on key points for each chapter.
  PowerPoint® is a registered trademark of the Microsoft Corporation.

To access additional course materials (including CourseMate), please go to **login.cengage.com**, and use your SSO (single sign-on) login to access the materials.

Web Page

Come visit our website at **www.paralegal.delmar.cengage.com**, where you will find valuable information such as hot links and sample materials to download, as well as other Delmar Cengage Learning products.

SUPPLEMENTS AT A GLANCE

SUPPLEMENT	WHAT IT IS	WHAT'S IN IT
Paralegal CourseMate CourseMate	Online interactive teaching and learning tools and an interactive eBook, all accessible at **login.cengage.com**	Interactive teaching and learning tools, including: • Quizzing • Case studies • Chapter objectives • Flash cards • Web links • Crossword puzzles • PowerPoint® presentations • Slossberg Law Office • Interactive eBook • Engagement Tracker
Online Instructor Companion	Resources for the instructor accessible via Cengage SSO	• Instructor's Manual with chapter overviews, answers to text questions, and test bank and answer key • Computerized Testbank powered by Cognero, with many questions and styles to choose from to create customized assessments for your students • PowerPoint® presentations

Table of Exhibits

PART I

Fundamental Concepts
of Real Estate Law

1

Ethics and Real Property Practice

CHAPTER OBJECTIVES

Upon completion of this chapter, the student will:

- Understand the ethical principles governing both lawyers and paralegals
- Know the various billing methods utilized by law firms to bill clients
- Know how to open a new client file
- Understand the ethical problems that are particular to real property practice

Introduction

Real estate law offers you, the paralegal, a richly satisfying and challenging experience. It requires knowledge of a wide array of subjects: contracts, mortgages, surveys, and title insurance, just to name a few. It puts you in contact with an equally wide array of people: buyers and sellers, real estate brokers, mortgage brokers, bankers, lawyers from various firms, and others. The first exposure many individuals have to the legal profession occurs when they contact a law firm to aid them in a real estate transaction. The person with whom they are most often in contact throughout the transaction process is the real estate paralegal. The professionalism you exhibit through your knowledge of the law, your personal skills, and, most important, your ethics can profoundly influence the way these individuals feel about the legal system and, specifically, your firm.

This chapter begins broadly, expounding upon basic ethical principles governing all legal practice. It then focuses on the role the paralegal plays in the first meeting with the client, from the first telephone contact to the processing of a new client file. Finally, potential ethical problems that often surface in real estate matters are addressed.

Basic Ethical Principles

Professional ethics are governed by various regulations establishing guidelines for acceptable and unacceptable conduct within a particular profession. The legal profession abounds with such regulations to ensure that the profession responsibly serves the society in which it practices. These regulations take into consideration the interests of the general public; clients; the lawyer; nonlawyers working in legal environments, including paralegals; and the legal system as a whole. Further, these regulations come from state statutory and case law, rules of court, and codes of ethical conduct adopted by the American Bar Association (ABA) as well as state bar associations. In addition, professional paralegal associations provide guidelines for the ethical conduct of their members.

The ABA Model Code of Professional Responsibility, created in 1969, was adopted by most states' bar associations as the official standard for legal conduct. In 1983, the ABA's House of Delegates approved a revised code, combining the prior rules with a set of ethical considerations clarifying and, in some instances, imposing more stringent restraints on legal conduct. This revised code was named the **ABA Model Rules of Professional Conduct,** and it has, since its adoption, undergone various amendments. At the time of this writing, apart from California, all states and the District of Columbia have rules of professional conduct that follow the ABA Model Rules. Although these rules speak to a lawyer's conduct and responsibilities, paralegals must be acquainted with them because the supervising attorney is responsible for all actions of the paralegal.

The two largest voluntary national associations of paralegals are the **National Association of Legal Assistants (NALA)** and the **National Federation of Paralegal Associations (NFPA).** Each of these associations has adopted standards of ethical conduct for paralegals. NALA adopted its Model Standards and Guidelines for Utilization of Paralegals in 1984 (at that time referred to as the Model Standards and Guidelines for Utilization of Legal Assistants), taking into consideration provisions of the ABA Model Rules of Professional Conduct as well as ethical promulgations of various state bar associations and state courts. NFPA adopted its Model Code of Ethics and Professional Responsibility in 1993 and its Model Disciplinary Rules to enforce this code in 1997. They were subsequently combined and are now known as the Model Code of Ethics and Professional Responsibility and Guidelines for Enforcement. The emphasis of the ethical guidelines set forth by each of these associations is to clarify the role the paralegal plays in a legal environment, noting the tasks that may and may not be undertaken by the paralegal and stressing lawyer supervision and ultimate responsibility for the work product.

Ethical guidelines in statutes, court decisions, and association rules all state that paralegals must not engage in the *unauthorized practice of law*. This includes such practices as advising a client of his or her legal rights and remedies, representing a client in court, making strategy decisions in client matters, negotiating settlements, accepting cases, and setting fees. Each state has a statute that defines the practice of law, and many states have an "unauthorized practice of law" statute, the violation of which results in the imposition of sanctions. Although it is generally the law firm, not the transgressing paralegal, that incurs civil liability for any damage to a client resulting from the violation, the end result for the paralegal is often termination of employment. In some states, the unauthorized practice of law is considered a criminal offense, and the offender may suffer fines or possible imprisonment.

Paralegals may engage in many aspects of legal work as long as the work is performed under the direction and supervision of an attorney. This means that the attorney maintains direct contact with the client and that all paralegal tasks are delegated by the attorney, who personally examines, ultimately approves, and assumes full responsibility for the work product.

In supervising a paralegal, an attorney should give consideration to the paralegal's knowledge, training, and experience and delegate responsibilities accordingly. Within these parameters, paralegals may perform a multitude of functions such as conducting client interviews, locating and interviewing witnesses, conducting

ABA Model Rules of Professional Conduct: Model rules for the regulation of the ethical conduct of legal professionals that have been adopted by state bar associations.

National Association of Legal Assistants (NALA): A voluntary national paralegal association. It lists among its goals working to improve the quality of the delivery of legal services.

National Federation of Paralegal Associations (NFPA): A voluntary national paralegal association. It lists among its goals advancing the paralegal profession through strategic alliances and promoting regulation and educational standards for the paralegal profession.

factual and legal research, drafting legal documents and correspondence, and assisting at depositions, hearings, trials, and real estate closings.

When a paralegal is first introduced to a client, his or her nonlawyer status must be made clear. Similarly, when communicating with persons outside of the law firm, including other attorneys, a paralegal must disclose his or her status. Many states allow paralegals to carry business cards as long as their status appears next to or under their name. Many states also allow a paralegal's name to appear on law firm letterhead, again as long as he or she is listed as a paralegal or support staff. Letters signed by paralegals must indicate their status and must not contain legal advice.

Both attorneys and paralegals should assist in maintaining integrity and **competence** in the legal profession. An attorney must act competently in the representation of a client, which means that he or she not only must have the necessary legal skill required but also must devote adequate time and thorough preparation to the client matter. In like manner, a paralegal must be competent in fulfilling tasks delegated by the attorney. Competency is of particular concern in real estate practice because so many areas of the law may have an influence on any given real estate transaction. If asked to handle a responsibility totally outside his or her capabilities or experience, a paralegal must admit that the responsibility is beyond his or her present skills. The attorney will then determine whether the matter is one in which there is adequate time for the paralegal to become competent in the skill area or whether the matter is best handled by another staff member.

Incompetent representation includes not only taking on a legal matter one is not competent to handle but also neglecting a client matter. Failure to handle a client matter in a timely fashion is one of the most frequent complaints heard before a state bar's grievance committee. Promptness and **diligence** (attentiveness and care) are as important in real estate practice as they are in any other area of law. Although real estate lawyers usually do not deal with court dates or **statutes of limitations** (statutes indicating the time period within which suit must be brought or be forever barred) as often as civil trial lawyers, real estate contracts and closing documents do contain numerous deadlines that must be met.

Paralegals often are responsible for keeping track of all deadlines in each assigned client file and are involved directly in managing the workload. A good **tickler system** is crucial to prevent missed deadlines. A tickler system is a method of keeping track of priorities and deadlines. Implementing a tickler system may be as simple as listing daily tasks on a calendar or as sophisticated as utilizing one of the many docketing software programs on the market. Many insurance companies require that law firms use at least two different systems as a condition for providing legal malpractice insurance.

Clients deserve attention. Communication is central to client satisfaction. Clients must be kept informed of the status of their legal matter on a regular basis. This task usually falls into the lap of the paralegal. Telephone calls should be returned promptly, preferably on the same day on which the original call was made. Many times the client simply wants a progress report. If this is the case, the paralegal may be in a better position to provide such a report than the attorney because the managing of client files is his or her domain. There are times, however, when the client will raise a question a paralegal may not ethically answer, even if the paralegal believes he or she knows the proper answer, because the answer necessarily contains legal advice or legal judgment (for example, rendering an opinion of title or the tax consequences of a particular real estate transaction). These matters must be addressed by the attorney, and if the

competence: Having the necessary legal skill to perform a given task and devoting the requisite time to that task to do a thorough job for the client.

diligence: Attentiveness and care.

statute of limitations: A statute indicating the time period within which a suit must be brought or be forever barred.

tickler system: A method of keeping track of priorities and deadlines.

attorney is not presently available, the client should be informed that the matter will be forwarded to the attorney, who will return the client's call promptly.

Sacrosanct in the practice of law is the concept of **confidentiality.** All persons working in a law firm must preserve the confidences of clients. This rule pertains to potential clients who decide not to engage the firm, current clients, and former clients. Note that confidentiality is a different concept than **attorney-client privilege.** Attorney-client privilege is a rule of evidence law that prevents a court from compelling the revelation of communications between attorney and client. The privilege belongs to the client, not the attorney, and only the client may waive it. Confidentiality is an ethical concept and is considerably broader in scope than attorney-client privilege. It prohibits an attorney, and others in the legal environment, from voluntarily disclosing information about a client matter. It covers not only direct confidential communications between client and attorney but also any other information the attorney obtains during representation of the client from whatever source. Further, it pertains to both the disclosure of this information and the use of it, which prevents an attorney and his or her support staff from using confidential information without the client's consent.

The most complex ethical issues are found in the context of **conflicts of interest,** particularly in the field of real estate law, as discussed in a later section of this chapter. In general terms, situations giving rise to conflicts of interest are set forth in the ABA Model Rules of Professional Conduct as well as each state's adopted code of professional responsibility. A basic definition of a conflict of interest is any situation in which an attorney's professional judgment might be affected because of business or personal interests. Taking on a new client who wishes to sue a current client is an obvious example of a conflict of interest inasmuch as an attorney in this situation is prevented from properly representing one party without adversely affecting the other. If the conflict is apparent before the attorney takes on a matter, the attorney must not represent the conflicting client. If the conflict becomes apparent only after the attorney has taken on the matter, the attorney must withdraw from the representation of one or both clients.

The ABA Model Rules of Professional Conduct state that an attorney cannot represent a client if to do so would adversely affect the interests of another *unless* the attorney informs the parties of the conflict and each party consents after consultation. The problem here is that consultation necessarily includes the disclosure of all relevant facts. If the attorney were to disclose these facts, he or she could very well be breaching the duty of confidentiality.

A subtler but equally discomfiting situation pertains to third parties. Sometimes the attorney's compensation will come from a third party. However, the attorney's ethical responsibilities are to the client. The client is the individual or entity requiring the legal representation, not the individual or entity paying the legal fees. If the attorney believes that the third party's interest will prevent proper representation of the client (for example, it might conflict with the interest of the client, or the third party might request that the lawyer violate the duty of confidentiality), the attorney must address these issues before assuming representation.

In real estate practice, third-party issues often surface in other ways, usually through a real estate broker, title agent, or lender who refers business to the attorney in anticipation that the grateful attorney will act as a "deal maker." In order to properly represent the client, the attorney may be forced to disappoint the third party who referred the matter. The loyalty must always be to the client.

confidentiality: An ethical concept prohibiting a lawyer and others in a law firm from voluntarily disclosing information about a client matter.

attorney-client privilege: A rule of evidence law that prevents a court from compelling the revelation of communications between lawyer and client.

conflict of interest: A situation in which a lawyer's professional judgment might be affected because of business or personal interests.

Initial Meeting with the Client

As a paralegal, you may become involved with your firm's clients as early as the initial client meeting. Law firms today realize that under the direction and supervision of an attorney, a knowledgeable paralegal can competently and cost-effectively provide many services for the client and, as noted earlier, is often the client's major contact in the firm. Clients who understand the role a paralegal plays in a law firm welcome the assistance of a paralegal with their legal matters, especially when apprised of the fact that paralegal services are billed at a lower rate than attorney services.

When a potential client telephones the law firm to make an appointment, the receptionist will turn the call over to you. Be sure to check your attorney's calendar for availability and to obtain certain basic information, such as the date and time of the call, the client's name and telephone number, and a brief description of the client matter. Before ending the telephone conversation, give the client precise directions to the office and inform him or her of appropriate documents to bring to an initial meeting. For example, the attorney may need the client to bring a real estate contract, existing title policy, surveys, or other pertinent documents. Once you have concluded your telephone conversation with the client, note the date, time, client's name, and telephone number directly on the attorney's calendar. This provides both you and the attorney immediate access for reviewing the client schedule for the day first thing in the morning as well as for quick rescheduling of appointments.

The new client's name should be checked against the firm's current client case listings for a conflict of interest before the initial meeting with the client. If your law firm has more than one attorney, you must check not only your own attorney's client list but also the case listings for all attorneys in the firm. Under the **doctrine of imputed disqualification,** the entire body of attorneys in a firm is treated as one for conflict of interest purposes. Conducting such a check may reveal, for instance, that another attorney in the firm is representing an established client in a matter directly in conflict with the matter of the person for whom you set up an initial appointment, in which case the conflict of interest must be brought to your supervising attorney's attention.

A conflict of interest can also arise when an attorney or paralegal leaves a law firm, government agency, title company, bank, or mortgage company for other employment. If the new firm, agency, or company represents a client whose interests are adverse to those of a party represented by the old firm, agency, or company, a conflict of interest exists. If the new firm has yet to agree to represent the client, the firm may decline representation. Alternatively, the new firm may agree to representation and isolate the attorney or paralegal from the old firm from all contacts with the client's case. This tactic of isolation is sometimes referred to as a **Chinese Wall.**

When checking for conflicts of interest, even though a business client will be the business entity and not the individual who represents the entity, both names must be checked. For example, if the new client is Douglas Harrington of Country Estates Development Corporation, a thorough check would include both names. A corporate client may conduct business under a **fictitious name,** a name other than the corporation's legal name on the articles of incorporation. If this is the case, the fictitious name would need to be checked as well.

Once you are assured that no conflict appears, your next step is to open a file for the new client. To initiate this procedure, many firms use a new client data sheet, such as the one provided in Exhibit 1–1. Basic background information on the client, such as the nature of the client matter, the name of the individuals to be handling the matter, and the pertinent billing information, is included on this

doctrine of imputed disqualification: A doctrine that provides that the entire body of lawyers in a firm is treated as one for conflict of interest purposes.

Chinese Wall: A situation in which an attorney or paralegal is isolated from a client case for conflict of interest reasons.

fictitious name: A name other than one's legal name under which one operates a business.

New client data sheet — **EXHIBIT 1–1**

NEW CLIENT DATA SHEET

DATE: _____

REFERRED BY: _____

INITIATING ATTORNEY: _____

ASSIGNED ATTORNEY(S): _____

ASSIGNED PARALEGAL(S): _____

CLIENT NUMBER: _____

MATTER NUMBER: _____

TYPE OF CASE: _____

(Supply one of the following):

01 Real estate closing
02 Real estate litigation
03 Commercial litigation
04 Probate
05 Divorce
06 Medical malpractice
07 Other professional malpractice
08 Personal injury
09 Contracts
10 Corporate
11 Bankruptcy
12 Trusts and estates
13 Workers' compensation
14 Other

BILLING METHOD: _____

(Supply one of the following):

01 Hourly fee: standard rate
02 Hourly fee: special rate
03 Contingency fee: standard rate
04 Contingency fee: special rate
05 Flat fee: (supply fee in special rate line below)

SPECIAL RATE (Please describe in detail): _____

RETAINER FOR COSTS: _____

BILLING FREQUENCY: COSTS: _____ FEES: _____

(Supply one of the following):

01 Annually
02 Semiannually
03 Quarterly
04 Monthly
05 End of case
06 Other

CLIENT NAME: _____

CLIENT BILLING ADDRESS: _____

CLIENT PHONE: HOME: _____ OFFICE: _____ FAX: _____ CELL: _____

CLIENT E-MAIL ADDRESS: _____

CASE NAME: _____

OPPOSING PARTY (PARTIES): _____

ADDRESS OF OPPOSING PARTY (PARTIES): _____

OPPOSING COUNSEL: _____

ADDRESS OF OPPOSING COUNSEL: _____

OPPOSING COUNSEL'S PHONE: _____ FAX: _____

CASE NUMBER: _____ COURT: _____

JUDGE: _____ JUDICIAL ASSISTANT: _____

form. After the form is completed, it will be forwarded to the legal secretary for data entry, assigned a client number and matter number, forwarded to the billing department, and placed in the client file.

Every new client is assigned his or her own client number, which may be numeric (for example, 4839) or alphanumeric (for example, T4839). If an alphanumeric system is used, the letter may refer to the client's name or the responsible attorney's name. The assignment of a client number helps not only to organize office files but also to preserve the confidentiality of a client. The names of clients are as confidential as any other client information and must not be revealed to others coming into the law office. Attorneys and paralegals often have several client files stacked on their desks or elsewhere in their offices. If a client's name appeared on the outside of the file and another client entered the office, this could present an ethical problem. The use of client numbers prevents a breach of confidentiality.

It is common for an attorney to handle several different matters for a client, so a client matter number must be assigned to each matter. This number is added to the end of the client number; for example, in 4839.0001, the 0001 refers to the first client matter the firm is handling for this client.

In addition to the new client data sheet, a **retainer agreement** should be placed in the file. A retainer agreement is a contract spelling out the fee agreement reached between the attorney and the client should the client decide to hire the attorney after the initial consultation. The retainer agreement will reflect a billing method utilized by the law firm that best suits the tasks to be handled.

One type of fee arrangement common in real estate practice is the charging of **flat fees,** which are sometimes referred to as fixed fees. These fees make the most sense when dealing with routine legal matters in which the amount of work involved is fairly easy to determine. In real estate, flat fees may be used in simple closings, the preparation of a title opinion letter, or the preparation of a residential lease.

In handling other matters such as a mortgage foreclosure or other types of real estate litigation in which the amount of time required on the matter is difficult to determine, the **hourly fee** agreement may be more appropriate. Here the client pays for the attorney's services based upon the amount of time spent on the client matter. A hierarchical fee structure typically prevails in law firms, with a client paying more per hour for the services of a senior partner than for those of an associate, and still less for those of a paralegal.

Contingency fees are not used in standard real estate practices. They are used most commonly in personal injury cases and certain other tort matters. The fee for the attorney's services, set forth as a percentage of the judgment or settlement, is contingent upon the client settling the case or winning in court. Caps are set by statute on the percentage that may be charged in contingency fee cases in many states. Additionally, clients often are given the right to cancel the contingency fee agreement within three business days from the date they signed it. It is important to note that the contingency fee refers only to payment to an attorney for the time spent on the case and does not include any costs incurred on behalf of the client (for example, filing fees and expert witness fees). The client is responsible for these costs whether or not the client settles, wins, or loses.

Recently, some law firms have offered clients additional alternative fee arrangements. One such arrangement is for **unbundled services.** In some legal matters, clients do not want to (or cannot afford to) pay for a full array of legal services offered and may want to hire an attorney to handle only specific aspects of a legal matter or transaction. In a residential real estate transaction, for example, a client

retainer agreement: A contract between an attorney and a client that sets forth the manner in which the client will be billed for the attorney's work.

flat fee: An attorney's fee set forth as a sum certain for the performance of a specified task.

hourly fee: An attorney's fee based upon the amount of time the attorney spends on a client matter.

contingency fee: An attorney's fee that is contingent upon the client reaching settlement or winning in court. The payment the attorney receives is set forth as a percentage of the settlement or court award.

unbundled services: A fee arrangement in which the attorney handles only specific aspects of a legal matter or transaction.

may want to hire an attorney to review a real estate contract or a closing statement but may not want to pay for an attorney to accompany him or her to a closing. Often, these services are bundled together in a flat fee arrangement. However, a firm that offers unbundled services may allow a client to choose "à la carte" the services for which the attorney is responsible and bill the client accordingly.

A less-often-used alternative fee arrangement is a **subscription.** Whereas a flat fee arrangement is used for a single task or transaction, such as those mentioned previously, subscriptions provide clients with a special rate for certain types of ongoing tasks. For example, if an attorney is representing a large developer and is in communication with the developer's office routinely, the developer may not want to be billed for each telephone call. The attorney and the developer may work out a subscription price for unlimited telephone calls per month. Similarly, a landlord who owns a large rental complex may want to hire an attorney at a subscription rate for a regular, periodic review of all tenant leases.

Understandably, it is imperative to keep track of time meticulously when working on a client matter. Many law firms bill in tenths of an hour (six-minute intervals). Each attorney and paralegal is required to record the time he or she spends on each client matter. A proper timekeeping system specifies the time each task was started and completed and contains a description of the work done. These timekeeping systems may be manual forms, or they may be computerized programs.

An attorney may require a retainer to be paid upon the signing of a retainer agreement. This sum must be deposited in the firm's **client trust fund account,** which is an account separate from the firm's regular business account. This retainer amount may be put toward fees, costs, or both, according to the terms of the retainer agreement, with withdrawals made in installments as the costs are incurred or the fees are earned. Any unearned portion of the retainer must be refunded to the client. In addition to retainer fees, any deposit money, closing proceeds, or escrowed funds must be deposited in the client trust fund account. State professional codes of ethics impose very strict rules for the handling of client trust accounts; therefore, it is crucial to understand the manner in which your firm's accounts are administered.

Finally, the new client file should contain an interview information worksheet to be used during the initial client conference. The client will have provided you with a basic summary of his or her legal matter when speaking with you to set up the appointment. This information will enable you to select the appropriate specialized worksheet to aid in preparing the initial client documents (for example, a specialized worksheet for a residential real estate closing or for a commercial real estate closing). Numerous specialized worksheets are provided throughout this text. Such worksheets aid significantly in ensuring that all details are addressed. A well-organized paralegal will have the new client file containing these basic contents sitting on the attorney's desk prior to the initial client meeting.

An initial conference with a client will start with a discussion between the client and the attorney. The attorney should introduce the client to all staff members who will be working on the client matter and may ask you to attend. Your status as a paralegal, as well as the status of all other staff members, should be clearly indicated to the client. The consultation fee, if any, may have been discussed by the attorney and client over the telephone. The attorney should explain to the client that all fee arrangements will be discussed thoroughly before the client must pay any additional amounts.

The attorney also should indicate to the client that both the attorney and the client are free to withhold judgment on representation until the end of the consultation. The attorney may spend enough time in this initial conference to assess the client's

subscription: A special billing rate for certain types of ongoing tasks.

client trust fund account: An account separate from the law firm's regular business account in which fee advances, deposit money, closing proceeds, and/or escrowed funds are placed.

legal matter and then turn the client over to you, asking you to take the client into a conference room to obtain further detailed information.

Should the client decide to hire your firm to represent him or her in a particular transaction, the attorney and client will sign the retainer agreement before the client leaves the office, and the client will receive a copy of the agreement for his or her files. If a retainer fee is required, it will be collected at this time.

Before the client leaves the office, you or your supervising attorney should review with the client any additional information the client must provide before the client matter can proceed further. Additionally, a follow-up letter should be sent to the client as a reminder. If the client was unable to provide all of the information required on the worksheet, make a photocopy of the partially completed worksheet, and give it to the client to complete at home, together with an addressed, stamped envelope for return to your office. Again, a reminder letter should be sent.

The importance of a reminder letter cannot be stressed too strongly. The letter serves not only as a common courtesy but also as protection against miscommunication between attorney and client and possible malpractice. Without a reminder letter, a client may assume that his or her legal matter is progressing when, in fact, the client file has remained inactive awaiting further information from the client. It is advisable to follow up the reminder letter with a telephone call to motivate the client to return papers or provide necessary information promptly.

In some instances, the client may not be certain that he or she wants to proceed after the initial meeting with the attorney, and the results of the consultation may be unclear because the client has neither accepted nor declined legal representation. If this happens, rather than closing the file, it should be retained as an inactive file for a prescribed period of time (for example, 90 days or 120 days). Prior to the expiration of this time period, a letter should be sent to the prospective client, informing him or her that the firm will be closing the client file if it does not hear from the client by a set date.

Should the client decide not to hire the firm or the attorney decline representation for any reason, the file should be closed, but not without first sending the client a letter confirming that the client met with the attorney and declined representation, such as the sample letter found in Exhibit 1–2. Although paralegals are allowed to draft these letters, the ethical code prohibits paralegals from signing them; such a letter must be signed by the attorney.

Some firms may allow correspondence with clients to be sent by electronic means. This may include the letters mentioned above. Prior to sending any correspondence by electronic means, be certain to check your firm's policies and procedures. Each firm should set up policies regarding not only the sending but also the receiving of correspondence by electronic means. This includes e-mail, cell phones, and texting. It is incumbent upon the law firm to advise clients regarding the protection of confidentiality of communications and, when necessary, to tailor communications accordingly, particularly when the correspondence may be sent from or delivered to a client's workplace or transmitted through an electronic device provided by the client's employer.

Even if your firm does allow correspondence by electronic means, communicating with clients by means of text messages can be problematic. Text messages generally tend to be shorter than other written means of communication and therefore may not be the most appropriate method to convey complex information. Although one can make notations to a client file pertaining to a text message, a text message is not as easily preserved as traditional or e-mail correspondence. Therefore, there is greater likelihood for a misunderstanding or even a dispute to arise. The best practice

May 1, 2015

CERTIFIED MAIL #P112264551
RETURN RECEIPT REQUESTED

Madeline Stevenson
22 Granville Terrace
Any City, Any State

Re: Stevenson v. Dutton Construction Company

Dear Ms. Stevenson:

Thank you for consulting our office concerning your legal matter. It is my understanding that as a result of our meeting on April 28, 2015, you have decided to decline our services with respect to your proposed lawsuit against Dutton Construction Company for breach of a construction contract.

Should you choose to pursue this matter further, I advise you to consult another attorney immediately. There are certain statutory time periods during which lawsuits must be filed and claims must be made. Any delay could prevent you from exercising your rights.

Sincerely,

Ava Ross, Esquire

is to include all information pertaining to the firm's communications policies in either the retainer agreement or a supplemental document that is signed by the client.

Potential Ethical Problems

The majority of ethical problems confronting the real estate attorney fall within the realm of conflict of interest. Problems occur because real estate attorneys commonly are requested to take dual representation in several scenarios. One such scenario involves a seller who hires an attorney to represent him or her in a closing and a buyer who requests that the attorney represent both the buyer and the seller. Sometimes the attorney is hired by one party and agrees to prepare closing documents for the other party for a small fee. Another scenario is one in which one party retains the attorney and then enters into an agreement with the other party to split the fee. Still another dual representation scenario occurs when a buyer or seller retains the attorney, who is then requested to represent the lender financing the transaction.

Although the ABA Model Rules of Professional Conduct allow dual representation in a transaction if the parties are informed of the potential conflict and agree to the dual representation after full disclosure, the better practice is to decline such representation, suggesting that either the buyer or the seller seek independent counsel. If the attorney believes, in his or her own professional judgment, that multiple-party representation will adversely affect his or her legal judgment, then the attorney must decline such representation, even if the parties consent to it.

Special problems are presented in the area of title examination. An attorney must be able to exercise fully his or her independent professional judgment when rendering an opinion of title. This judgment is easily challenged when the attorney takes on any form of dual representation. If an attorney representing a seller provides a title insurance policy to the buyer at the seller's expense, no problem presents itself. If the buyer pays for the policy, however, the ethical question arises. Many real estate attorneys become title insurance agents with commercial title companies. If the attorney providing the title examination of a property is an agent and is charging a party for the title work separately from the charges for other real estate services, the attorney must disclose his or her interest in the title insurance company.

Often, one party to a real estate transaction will choose to forego legal representation and the other party's lawyer will draft all necessary closing documents. Dealing with unrepresented parties poses its own problems. The unrepresented party may seek legal advice from the attorney or may assume that, because the attorney is drafting all of the documents, the attorney is a disinterested party. The attorney should guard his or her conduct carefully in these situations, declining to provide legal advice and clarifying his or her role in the transaction. Some courts have held that when a party is unrepresented at a real estate closing, the attending attorney must not only disclose to the unrepresented party that he or she is representing an adverse interest but also explain the material terms of all closing documents to the unrepresented party so the party understands the effect of signing the documents. The better practice is to provide a form to the nonrepresented party advising him or her that the attending attorney represents the seller (or buyer, as the case may be) and that he or she should consult his or her own counsel. The following case provides a dramatic example of problems that can arise when one party is not represented by counsel.

CASE: *The Florida Bar v. Belleville*

591 So. 2d 170 (Fla. 1991)

PER CURIAM.

We have this case on complaint of the Florida Bar for review of a referee's report recommending that Walter J. Belleville, an attorney licensed in Florida, be found not guilty of alleged ethical violations. We have jurisdiction. Art. V §15, Fla. Const.

In the summer of 1988, Belleville was retained as counsel for Bradley M. Bloch. Bloch had entered into an agreement with James F. Cowan to purchase property owned by the latter. Cowan was an elderly man, eighty-three years of age, who had a third-grade education. While the evidence showed that Cowan had substantial prior experience in selling real estate when he was younger, neither party to this cause disputes that the various written documents alleged to constitute the agreement overwhelmingly favored the buyer, Mr. Bloch. Cowan, in fact, has subsequently disputed that he ever agreed to some of the terms embodied in these documents.

Although Cowan and Bloch had negotiated only for the sale of an apartment building, the documents stated that Cowan was selling both the apartment building *and his residence,* which was located across the street from the apartments. The referee specifically found that Cowan had no intention of selling his residence and did not know

that it was included in the sale. The record substantially supports this finding, which accordingly must be accepted as fact by this Court. *The Florida Bar v. Bajoczky,* 558 So. 2d 1022 (Fla. 1990).

It is unclear whether Belleville knowingly participated in his client's activities or merely followed the client's instructions without question. Whatever the case, Belleville drafted the relevant documents to include the legal description of Cowan's house in the instruments of sale. Cowan then apparently signed the documents without realizing he was transferring title to his house. No one at the closing explained the significance of the legal description to him. Belleville only sent a paralegal to the closing and did not attend it himself. In fact, he never met Cowan to this point in time.

In exchange for the apartment and his residence, Cowan received only a promissory note, not a mortgage. The loan thus was unsecured. This note provided for ten percent interest amortized over twenty-five years. However, the first payment was deferred for four months with no apparent provision for interest to accumulate during this time, and the note by its own terms will become unenforceable upon Cowan's death. Finally, the documents called for Cowan to pay the closing costs, which Bloch and Belleville construed as including Belleville's attorney fee of $625.

(continued)

When Cowan received the promissory note and closing documents, he realized that their terms varied from the agreement he thought he had entered. Cowan contacted an attorney, who wrote a letter to Belleville explaining the points of disagreement. The next day, Bloch attempted to evict Cowan from his home.

The referee recommended no discipline based on his conclusion that Belleville owed no attorney-client obligation to Cowan. The Board of Governors of The Florida Bar voted to appeal this decision, and the Bar now seeks a thirty-day suspension.

*   *   *

Based on the facts, we cannot accept the referee's recommendation about guilt and punishment. The referee's factual findings established that Cowan had negotiated to sell the apartment, that he did not intend to sell anything other than the apartment, and that he did not know that the documents of sale would result in the loss of his residence. It also is clear Belleville should have harbored suspicions about the documents he was preparing, because the documents established on their face a transaction so one-sided as to put Belleville on notice of the likelihood of their unconscionability.

When faced with this factual scenario, we believe an attorney is under an ethical obligation to do two things. First, the attorney must explain to the unrepresented opposing party the fact that the attorney is representing an adverse interest. Second, the attorney must explain the material terms of the documents that the attorney has drafted for the client so that the opposing party fully understands their actual effect.[1] When the transaction is as one-sided as that in the present case, counsel preparing the documents is under an ethical duty to make sure that an unrepresented party understands the possible detrimental effect of the transaction and the fact that the attorney's loyalty lies with the client alone. *R. Regulating Fla. Bar 4-1.7.*

*   *   *

For the foregoing reasons, we adopt the referee's findings of fact but reject the recommendations regarding guilt and discipline. . . . Accordingly, we grant the request of The Florida Bar. Walter J. Belleville is suspended from the practice of law for a period of thirty days. . . .

It is so ordered.

Case Questions

In the above case, the Florida Supreme Court sets forth various facts concerning this real estate transaction that are particularly troubling, giving emphasis to the fact that the seller's deed conveyed property (the seller's private residence) that was not part of the negotiated transaction. Additionally, as you will learn in subsequent chapters, the financing documents were problematic as well.

Typically, when a buyer finances a purchase of real property, whether the financing is handled through a financial institution or is seller-financed, as is the situation in the *Belleville* case, the buyer signs two important documents that provide protection to the lender. The first is a mortgage instrument that secures the purchased property as collateral for the loan. Should the buyer default on the loan, the mortgage instrument allows the lender to foreclose on the property. The second document that is signed by the buyer is a promissory note whereby the buyer promises to pay back the loan amount (plus agreed upon interest). Should the buyer default on the loan, the lender will first look to foreclose on the collateralized property. However, should a foreclosure sale fail to cover the amount of the loan and costs incurred by the lender, the promissory note allows the lender to sue the buyer for the deficiency and look to all of the buyer's nonexempt property (real or personal) wherever located to cover the deficiency judgment.

Most institutional loans are twenty- or thirty-year loans (although this is not a requirement, as lending institutions offer loans for longer or shorter durations), whereas most seller financing is for a shorter duration. With both institutional and seller financing, the financing documents typically bind not only the buyer/borrower to the terms of the documents but also the buyer/borrower's heirs, successors, and assigns. Thus, should the buyer/borrower die before the loan is paid off, the loan becomes a debt of his/her estate.

1. Noting the above, what problems do you find with the financing documents in this transaction? If you were Mr. Belleville's paralegal and were asked to draft these documents, what would you do?

2. In the *Belleville* case, the real property to be conveyed, according to the agreement between the buyer and seller, was an apartment building. Mr. Belleville did not attend the closing; instead, he sent a paralegal to conduct the closing. Do you think a paralegal should be allowed to conduct a closing on an apartment building? Why or why not? Are paralegals allowed to conduct this type of closing in your state without the presence of a supervising attorney?

3. Assume you were Mr. Belleville's paralegal and you were permitted by law to conduct this closing. How would you proceed? What would you say to Mr. Cowan? What questions could you answer? What questions would you not be allowed to answer?

---

1. We limit this holding to the facts of this case. We have no intent to mandate that an attorney who has prepared documents for a real estate closing always must be present at the closing to explain the documents to the respective parties.

The situation of unrepresented parties may arise not only in cases in which the attorney represents the buyer or the seller but also in cases in which the attorney represents the lender in the real estate transaction. In such a situation, the buyer (borrower) may be unrepresented, yet may be contributing to the payment of the lender's attorney fees as part of the loan costs. If the attorney representing the lender has any direct dealings with the buyer, the attorney may have certain disclosure duties, such as disclosing any title defects to the buyer.

Due to the recent economic downturn in the real estate arena, more attorneys have been approached to assist in loan modifications. This has led to a number of potential ethical issues that have received increased attention from state bar ethics committees. The first pertains to an attorney who partners with a loan modification company. Such a company may inform homeowners that it is "working with" an attorney and may refer clients to that attorney. An attorney may not pay a referral fee to the loan modification company in such an instance, nor may the attorney split a fee with the company. The second situation arises when a loan modification company hires an attorney to serve as in-house counsel. If the attorney provides legal advice to the company's clients, the attorney may be deemed to be forming a legal business relationship with a nonlawyer, assisting a nonlawyer in the unauthorized practice of law, and/or allowing a nonlawyer to control an attorney-client relationship. A third situation occurs when an attorney hires nonlawyers, such as mortgage specialists, to work with the law firm's clients. In such a situation, the client has hired the attorney directly, and the attorney is utilizing the expertise of a nonlawyer to assist the client. This generally is permissible if the attorney obtains the client's consent, retains responsibility for the client's file, and properly supervises the work. The compensation paid to the nonlawyer must be handled in a manner that cannot be construed as fee sharing.

Many real estate transactions are considered "routine," while others may be quite complex. An attorney must educate himself or herself on the law pertaining to aspects of the transaction with which he or she is unfamiliar. The complexities of the transaction may require the hiring of additional counsel specialized in other areas such as federal and state tax laws, securities regulations, or environmental law. The client must be informed of and agree to the hiring of additional counsel. Further, nonlegal experts may be required to ensure a successful transaction. No experts should be retained without the informed consent of the client. The client should be informed not only of the costs of employing experts but also of the potential detriment to the client if the expert is not employed.

CHAPTER SUMMARY

1. Almost all state bar associations have adopted the American Bar Association (ABA) Model Rules of Professional Conduct. Although this code addresses the ethical conduct of attorneys, it pertains to paralegals as well. Additionally, the National Association of Legal Assistants (NALA) and the National Federation of Paralegal Associations (NFPA) have adopted ethical standards to clarify the role of the paralegal in legal transactions.

2. Paralegals may avoid the unauthorized practice of law by following certain guidelines: (1) accept only tasks delegated by a supervising lawyer, (2) alert

clients and third parties to one's paralegal status, (3) avoid any request for legal advice, and (4) make certain that the lawyer personally examines and approves of the work product produced.

3. A paralegal's ethical duties include preserving clients' confidences, alerting attorneys of potential conflicts of interest by conducting a conflict of interest check prior to opening a new client file, and ensuring that clients are routinely updated on the status of their cases.

4. An initial client folder should be prepared prior to the client's first conference at the law office. This folder should include a new client data sheet, a retainer agreement, and a client interview worksheet. Each new client is assigned a client number, and each client project is assigned its own matter number. These numbers are assigned to promote efficiency in handling client files as well as client confidentiality.

5. The three most common types of retainer agreements are flat fee, hourly fee, and contingency fee agreements. Many routine real estate transactions are handled on a flat fee basis, while most real estate litigation is billed at hourly rates. Recently, some law firms have utilized other alternative fee arrangements, such as fees for unbundled services and subscription rates.

6. Upon the completion of the initial consultation, the client file may be given an active, inactive, or closed file status. If the client hires the attorney, the client will receive a copy of the retainer agreement. Before leaving the office, additional information to be provided by the client should be reviewed, followed by a reminder letter. If the client remains undecided about representation, the file is labeled inactive and remains so for the firm's prescribed inactive period. At the close of this period, a letter is sent to the client indicating the firm's intentions to close the file. The file will be closed if the client declines representation, and a letter is sent to the client confirming the client's decision. If a letter is to be sent by electronic means, the firm's policy guidelines should first be checked.

7. The most common ethical problems facing real estate attorneys occur in one of three contexts: (1) dual representation, (2) the unrepresented party, and (3) the pairing of lawyers with nonlawyers to perform services.

8. Dual representation may arise when (1) a buyer or seller hires a lawyer and the lawyer is later asked to represent both, (2) buyers and sellers decide amongst themselves to split a lawyer's legal fees, (3) a lawyer represents one party and also prepares documents for an unrepresented party for a small fee, and (4) a buyer or seller hires a lawyer and the lawyer is later asked to also represent a lender. The best practice is to decline dual representation, suggesting that all parties obtain independent counsel.

WEB RESOURCES

http://www.abanet.org/

This is the site of the American Bar Association (ABA), where you can access a variety of resources, including the ABA Model Rules of Professional Conduct as well as links to state ethics rules.

http://www.nala.org/

This is the site of the National Association of Legal Assistants, Inc. (NALA). Among other things, you can access the NALA Model Standards and Guidelines for Utilization of Paralegals at this site as well as the NALA Code of Ethics and Professional Responsibility.

http://www.paralegals.org/

This is the site of the National Federation of Paralegal Associations, Inc. (NFPA). Along with other resources, the NFPA Model Code of Ethics and Professional Responsibility and Guidelines for Enforcement can be accessed at this site.

http://www.legalethics.com/

Although this site's primary focus is on legal ethics issues related to the use of technology, it also provides a wealth of other legal ethics resources.

REVIEW QUESTIONS

1. Which of the three billing options (flat fee, hourly fee, contingency fee) would be most appropriate in the following situations?
   a. Preparing a residential lease
   b. Representing a client in a construction litigation lawsuit
   c. Handling a complex commercial closing
2. Distinguish between the concept of attorney-client privilege and the concept of confidentiality.
3. How may a paralegal avoid the unauthorized practice of law?
4. What are the most common ethical problems facing real estate attorneys? What should be done when confronted with these situations?
5. What items should be included in an initial client folder?

DISCUSSION QUESTIONS

1. Do you believe paralegals should be allowed to provide certain services directly to the public without attorney supervision? Why or why not? If yes, which services do you think should be permitted? Would a residential real estate closing be included in these services? Why or why not?
2. Does state licensing of the profession (or lack thereof) impact your answer to the above question? Why or why not?
3. What measures would you suggest a law firm implement to ensure that a Chinese Wall truly prevents conflict of interest issues? Do you believe it is possible to ensure proper protection?
4. As a real estate paralegal, you will be handling numerous real estate files at the same time, all of which contain a multitude of deadlines (for example, deposit deadlines, inspection deadlines, loan approval deadlines, and title work deadlines). You may be handling twenty to fifty files at the same time, representing the buyer in some transactions and the seller in others.

This chapter noted the importance of acting with diligence and keeping tickler systems. What system would you set in place for yourself to ensure that no important deadlines are missed?

5. As a real estate paralegal, you will be handling numerous checks. If your firm is acting as escrow agent for a real estate transaction, you will be receiving deposit checks, and if a problem should occur at closing, funds may be escrowed to cover the cost of repairs yet to be completed. Your firm also may be acting as closing agent and thus will have the responsibility of disbursing funds to realtors, lenders, title companies, and so forth. Noting that these funds are not to be commingled with regular office funds and that you will be handling numerous transactions at the same time, what is the best way to assure that all incoming checks and all disbursements are handled properly?

ETHICAL QUESTION

Your supervising attorney is representing client CBH Properties, Inc. CBH Properties is in the business of buying and selling real property for investment purposes and has found a commercial property it would like to obtain. Rather than purchasing the property, CBH Properties wants to do a like-kind property exchange, exchanging one of the commercial properties it presently owns for the one it wants. Your supervising attorney hands you some notes pertaining to the two properties in question and asks you to research the relevant tax laws to determine whether the proposed transaction will satisfy the statutory criteria to defer the paying of capital gains taxes on the transaction. Your supervising attorney wants you to provide her with a memorandum and copies of all relevant statutes. She needs an answer by this afternoon. You have no experience with tax law, and once you begin your research, you realize you are in over your head; yet you do not want to disappoint her. What should you do?

Slossberg Law Office on CourseMate

Please go to www.cengagebrain.com to log into CourseMate, access the Slossberg Law Office, and open the Introduction file. Be sure to review the firm's policies and procedures manual before you proceed to the first module. Each module corresponds to a chapter in the text. Within each module, you will be provided with instructions by the supervising attorney. You are asked to keep track of time spent on time sheets. The documents produced through working on client files in the law office can then be compiled into a portfolio of final work product.

CourseMate

The available CourseMate for this text has an interactive eBook and interactive learning tools, including flash cards, quizzes, and more. To learn more about this resource and access free demo CourseMate resources, including the Slossberg Law Office, go to www.cengagebrain.com, and search for this book. To access CourseMate materials that you have purchased, go to login.cengagebrain.com.

2

Basic Principles of Real Estate Law

CHAPTER OBJECTIVES

Upon completion of this chapter, the student will:

- Know the classifications of real property

- Understand the legal bundle of rights one possesses when one becomes an owner of real property

- Know the primary methods of acquiring real property

- Understand the distinctions between various types of estates

- Understand the similarities and differences between the three basic methods of concurrent ownership

Introduction

Property is a broad term, encompassing everything subject to ownership. There are various ways of classifying property, some of which necessarily overlap. One classification is tangible property. *Tangible property* is property that can be touched. The intrinsic value of tangible property is embodied in the physical subject matter itself. Examples abound everywhere: a desk, a plate, an office building, a boat, a tree. All of these are examples of tangible property.

Juxtaposed to tangible property is *intangible property,* which is property that has no intrinsic value in and of itself but that represents something of value. For example, checks, stock certificates, and patents are intangible property. Their value is found not in the physical slips of paper but in what the slips of paper represent.

Real property is a type of tangible property comprised of land and all things affixed to it, such as apartment buildings, shopping centers, and single-family homes as well as natural objects on or growing on the land. **Personal property** includes everything that is not considered real property.

This chapter begins with a discussion of classifications of property, concentrating on the physical components. The chapter continues with an explanation of basic ownership rights and the methods of acquiring these rights. As a real estate paralegal, you will be called upon to draft numerous documents exchanged by parties in a real estate transaction, such as deeds, financing instruments, and bills of sale, just to name a few. In order to draft these and other documents properly, it is important to understand the types of interests that can be conveyed and the various methods of holding title to property, so the chapter details these issues. The chapter concludes with special spousal rights that may impact the title to and transfer of real property.

Classifications of Property

Real Property

Real property, also referred to as *real estate* or *realty,* is a general term pertaining to land and all things permanently attached to the land. It also refers to a composite of physical components, including surface, subsurface, and air space, and the rights attendant to each.

Surface Rights. Surface rights in property may be divided into land rights and water rights. *Land rights* are those one ordinarily presumes to have and enjoy when one purchases real property. They are defined as property rights in all land contained within specified boundaries, plus everything permanently attached to the land, including natural elements such as trees, shrubs, and other foliage, as well as man-made elements such as buildings and other artificial constructions. Certain items growing on the land are deemed part of the real property, and others are considered personal property. The determining factor is whether the item is the result of cultivated labor, as in the case of farming crops. In such a case, the item is considered personal property. If the item is naturally growing, requiring no annual cultivation, it is considered real property.

Water rights are those rights pertaining to property covered by water on or adjacent to a landowner's boundaries as well as rights in the use of the water itself. Water has always been considered a scarce and prized resource in this country—valuable for consumption, recreation, and industry. Because of this fact, a landowner's rights in a body of water adjacent to his or her property are an important factor in assessing the value of that property. Factors determining the extent of the landowner's rights in water are (1) the source and (2) the characteristics of the water.

One source of water is groundwater, found below the surface of the land. It may be created by underground streams or by the accumulation of rainwater that has penetrated the soil. Groundwater is considered part of the property on which it is found and therefore belongs to the property owner to use as he or she deems fit as long as that use does not divert water away from or harm an adjoining property owner. The same is true of surface water formed by rainwater accumulating on the surface of the land. In neither case may the property owner divert the natural flow of the water.

Natural bodies of water, such as rivers, lakes, and streams, are governed by one of two doctrines: the riparian doctrine or the appropriation doctrine. The word *riparian* derives from the Latin *ripa,* meaning "river." The *riparian doctrine,* dating back to ancient times, is premised on the theory that citizens should share water rights equally for their daily needs. This doctrine divides water rights into riparian rights and littoral rights.

Littoral rights are those pertaining to a landowner whose land abuts a lake, ocean, or sea. Littoral rights give the landowner access to and use of the water, but the landowner owns only up to the high-water line.

Riparian rights are those pertaining to a landowner whose land abuts a river, stream, or similar watercourse. To determine the extent of a landowner's riparian rights, one must look to the body of water and first determine whether it is navigable or nonnavigable. If the water adjacent to a landowner's property is deemed navigable, it is considered a public waterway, and the submerged land underneath this waterway is owned by the state. Therefore, the landowner may use the water

real property: Property comprised of land and all things affixed to it as well as natural objects on or growing on the land.

personal property: All property that is not considered real property.

littoral rights: Water rights pertaining to a landowner whose property abuts a lake, ocean, or sea.

riparian rights: Water rights pertaining to a landowner whose property abuts a river, stream, or similar watercourse.

just as a member of the public may, with the landowner's property rights extending only to the water's edge. Nonnavigable waters generally are shallow lakes, small ponds, and rivulets. A landowner whose property is adjacent to nonnavigable water owns the submerged land up to the center of the water.

Under the riparian doctrine, a landowner whose property abuts a natural body of water may make use of the water as long as he or she does not preclude a neighboring landowner's use of it. Additionally, this doctrine affords the landowner ingress and egress between the property and the water as well as the right of view from the property to and over the water.

The *appropriation doctrine* developed out of necessity as American settlers moved west to claim homesteads at the same time that a new mining industry was expanding. Increasing conflict over the scarce water supply resulted in a doctrine of first in use, first in right. In order to substantiate a claim under this doctrine, a landowner must be able to show diversion of the water with the intention to use it in a beneficial manner. Those states that still follow this doctrine (primarily western states) issue water permits to landowners who can show valid appropriation.

The understanding of a few other terms is necessary to round out this discussion of surface rights. They are *accretion, erosion, avulsion,* and *reliction.* Accretion and reliction pertain to the addition to land, whereas erosion and avulsion pertain to the loss of land.

Accretion is the addition to land by the gradual and seemingly imperceptible deposit of waterborne material, called *alluvium,* on the shore. The landowner who has riparian rights continues to own the land up to the edge of the water, thus owning this addition to his or her property.

The process of **reliction** works differently. Instead of materials washing up on shore and adding to the property, water gradually recedes and dries up, uncovering land. The same rule applies, however, when applying riparian rights. The landowner, owning to the water's edge, has gained the additional land uncovered by reliction.

Erosion, sometimes referred to as *submergence,* is the opposite of accretion. In this instance, material is gradually washed away from the shore by tides or currents. Erosion causes the owner of riparian rights to lose portions of property that are submerged by this process.

Avulsion is the result of a sudden or violent natural disturbance, such as a tropical storm or hurricane, that causes a loss of property bordering on the water. When avulsion occurs, unlike erosion, the landowner retains ownership of the now-submerged property lost during the upheaval.

Air Rights. In addition to owning the surface of his or her parcel of property, the landowner owns the air space above the parcel extending up to heights established by law. Up to these legal limits, the property owner has *private air rights*. Above the legal limit, the air space necessarily is subject to *public air rights* to allow use for communications technology and aerial transportation. Local government regulates air rights near airports.

Depending on the location of the parcel, the value of private air rights may be insignificant or quite high. In congested cities, buildings have been constructed on the air space of another's property. The Merchandise Mart in Chicago is an example of a landmark structure built on a private air "lot," located in a strategic city center. In recent years, air rights transactions have increased. Government-owned or nonprofit organizations, such as Grand Central Station and the Church of the

accretion: The addition of land by the gradual deposit of waterborne materials on shore.

reliction: The gradual drying up of water, resulting in the addition of uncovered land.

erosion: The gradual washing away of land from the shore by tides or currents.

avulsion: The loss of land bordering water as a result of a sudden or violent natural disturbance.

Epiphany in Manhattan, have sold air rights. In the latter instance, air rights were sold to build condominiums above the church property. Additionally, local authorities in some areas, such as Manhattan, have created *transferable development rights* (*TDRs*), which permit property owners to transfer their air rights to owners of adjacent properties for the purpose of constructing larger buildings. This sometimes is referred to as *lot-merging.*

Air space also is important to a property's value if the property is in a scenically desirable location. In this situation, one wants to prevent another from building a structure that would obstruct the view. A possible solution to ensure a continued view would be to buy the air space of adjoining properties.

Subsurface Rights. *Subsurface rights,* sometimes referred to as *mineral rights,* are rights in land extending from the surface boundaries of a parcel of land downward, toward the center of the earth, and include oil, gas, ore, and other minerals but not water. When a purchaser purchases a parcel of land, subsurface rights generally are included with the surface rights to the property unless they have been previously severed or the real estate contract for sale and purchase provides otherwise.

In some instances, the subsurface rights may be more valuable than the surface rights, such as in the case of property located in areas rich in mineral, gas, or oil resources. Under such circumstances, the property owner may choose to sell or lease subsurface rights to another, allowing the purchaser or lessee of such rights to enter the property to extract the natural resource, while keeping the surface rights for himself or herself.

Personal Property

Personal property, also referred to as *chattels* or *personalty,* is a catch-all term referring to all property that is not real property and the basic characteristic of which is movability. Whereas real property is transferred legally by deed (discussed in detail in Chapter 8), personal property is transferred by a document called a **bill of sale,** or *receipt.* Although a real estate contract for sale and purchase may contain a personalty provision that itemizes any personal property (for example, a dining room set, patio furniture, area rugs) sold to the buyer of a residential property, most attorneys also prepare a bill of sale.

In assisting your supervising attorney in preparation for a real estate closing, you may be asked to draft this document. The bill of sale may include items that are being sold outside of the real estate contract for sale and purchase. Additionally, the bill of sale may state the condition the personal property must be in at time of sale. A bill of sale is signed by the seller(s) and, depending on state law, may be witnessed and notarized. A sample bill of sale is found in Exhibit 2–1.

If a real estate transaction involves both real and personal property and financing is involved, a lending institution may require the pledging of personal property as part of the collateral for the loan. In this situation, it is important for the lending institution to *perfect* its security interest in the personal property. Perfecting a security interest is a way of indicating priority status among creditors. This is done by filing a **UCC-1 financing statement,** sometimes referred to as a *filing statement* or *financing statement,* in the same office in which mortgages on real property are recorded.

The abbreviation UCC refers to the Uniform Commercial Code, which is a uniform set of laws drafted by the National Conference of Commissioners on Uniform

bill of sale: A document that transfers title to personal property.

UCC-1 financing statement: A document filed in the public records that perfects a security interest in personal property.

BILL OF SALE

KNOW ALL MEN BY THESE PRESENTS that ROBERT PRENTISS and REBECCA PRENTISS, Husband and Wife, Parties of the First Part, for and in consideration of the sum of Ten and No/100 Dollars ($10.00) lawful money of the United States, paid by JOHN HALL and JUDITH HALL, Husband and Wife, Parties of the Second Part, the receipt whereof is hereby acknowledged, have granted, bargained, sold, transferred and delivered, and by these presents do grant, bargain, sell, transfer and deliver unto the said Parties of the Second Part, their heirs, executors, administrators and assigns, all those certain goods located at 22 King's Court, Any City, Any State and described as follows:

> Imported crystal chandelier in dining room, black-out draperies in master bedroom, mahogany Empire-style bedroom set in master bedroom, tan leather sofa and loveseat in family room, cream brocade sofa and loveseat in living room, glass and marble coffee table in living room, and etched glass mirror in foyer

TO HAVE AND TO HOLD the said personal property unto the said Parties of the Second Part, their heirs, executors, administrators and assigns forever.

AND we do, for ourselves and our heirs, successors and assigns, covenant to and with the said Parties of the Second Part, their heirs, executors, administrators and assigns, that we are the lawful owners of the said goods and chattels; that they are free from all encumbrances; that we have good right to sell the same aforesaid, and that we will warrant and defend the sale of said personal property hereby made, unto the said Parties of the Second Part, their heirs, executors, administrators and assigns against the lawful claims and demands of all persons whomsoever.

IN WITNESS WHEREOF, the Parties of the First Part have hereunto set their hand this 5th day of May, 2015.

Signed, sealed and delivered in the presence of:

_____   _____
                                                          Robert Prentiss

_____   _____
                                                          Rebecca Prentiss

STATE OF ANY STATE
COUNTY OF ANY COUNTY

The foregoing instrument was acknowledged before me this 5th day of May, 2015 by ROBERT PRENTISS and REBECCA PRENTISS, Husband and Wife.

Witness my hand and official seal at Any City, County of Any County, State of Any State, this 5th day of May, 2015.

_____
Notary Public, State of Any State
My commission expires:_____

State Laws. The UCC has been adopted by every state except Louisiana. It governs commercial transactions, including sales of goods and secured transactions. By filing a UCC-1 financing statement, the lender is giving notice to third parties of its security interest in the personal property described in the statement.

If your law firm represents a lending institution, you may be asked to prepare a UCC-1 financing statement. If you assist legal counsel of a title company, you may be asked to conduct an online search to determine whether any UCC-1 filing statements have been filed in connection with particular property. An example of a UCC-1 financing statement can be found in Exhibit 2–2.

EXHIBIT 2–2

STATE OF FLORIDA UNIFORM COMMERCIAL CODE FINANCING STATEMENT FORM

A. NAME & DAYTIME PHONE NUMBER OF CONTACT PERSON
Brian Munden, Esquire, (000) 111-2222

B. SEND ACKNOWLEDGEMENT TO:
Name Brian Munden, Esquire

Address Munden and Anderson, P.A.

Address 600 Bushnell Street, Suite 201

City/State/Zip New City, Florida 00000

THE ABOVE SPACE IS FOR FILING OFFICE USE ONLY

1. DEBTOR'S EXACT FULL LEGAL NAME – INSERT ONLY **ONE** DEBTOR NAME (**1a OR 1b**) – Do Not Abbreviate or Combine Names

1.a ORGANIZATION'S NAME
MRT Properties, Inc.

1.b INDIVIDUAL'S LAST NAME	FIRST NAME	MIDDLE NAME	SUFFIX

1.c MAILING ADDRESS Line One
260 Norbrook Drive — This space not available.

MAILING ADDRESS Line Two Suite 350	CITY New City	STATE FL	POSTAL CODE 00000	COUNTRY U.S.A.

1.d TAX ID# 99-999999	REQUIRED ADD'L INFO RE: ORGANIZATION DEBTOR	1.e TYPE OF ORGANIZATION Corporation	1.f JURISDICTION OF ORGANIZATION Florida	1.g ORGANIZATIONAL ID# ☑NONE

2. ADDITIONAL DEBTOR'S EXACT FULL LEGAL NAME – INSERT ONLY **ONE** DEBTOR NAME (**2a OR 2b**) – Do Not Abbreviate or Combine Names

2.a ORGANIZATION'S NAME

2.b INDIVIDUAL'S LAST NAME	FIRST NAME	MIDDLE NAME	SUFFIX

2.c MAILING ADDRESS Line One — This space not available.

MAILING ADDRESS Line Two	CITY	STATE	POSTAL CODE	COUNTRY

2.d TAX ID#	REQUIRED ADD'L INFO RE: ORGANIZATION DEBTOR	2.e TYPE OF ORGANIZATION	2.f JURISDICTION OF ORGANIZATION	2.g ORGANIZATIONAL ID# ☐NONE

3. SECURED PARTY'S NAME (or NAME of TOTAL ASSIGNEE of ASSIGNOR S/P) – INSERT ONLY **ONE** SECURED PARTY (**3a OR3b**)

3.a ORGANIZATION'S NAME
Occidental Bank

3.b INDIVIDUAL'S LAST NAME	FIRST NAME	MIDDLE NAME	SUFFIX

3.c MAILING ADDRESS Line One — This space not available.

MAILING ADDRESS Line Two 500 Main Street	CITY New City	STATE FL	POSTAL CODE 00000	COUNTRY U.S.A.

4. This **FINANCING STATEMENT** covers the following collateral:

All furniture, equipment, and other tangible personal property of any kind attached to or located at TRIDENT INDUSTRIAL PARK NO. 2, according to the plat thereof recorded at Plat Book 70, page 15, Middle County, Florida.

5. ALTERNATE DESIGNATION (if applicable)
☐ LESSEE/LESSOR ☐ CONSIGNEE/CONSIGNOR ☐ BAILEE/BAILOR
☐ A G.LIEN ☐ NON-UCC FILING ☐ SELLER/BUYER

6. Florida DOCUMENTARY STAMP TAX – YOU ARE REQUIRED TO CHECK **EXACTLY ONE** BOX
☐ All documentary stamps due and payable or to become due and payable pursuant to s. 201.22 F.S., have been paid.
☑ Florida Documentary Stamp Tax is not required.

7. OPTIONAL FILER REFERENCE DATA

STANDARD FORM - FORM UCC-1 (REV.01/2009)   Filing Office Copy   Approved by the Secretary of State, State of Florida

Fixtures

A **fixture** is an object that at one time was personal property but that has, through the process of attachment to real property, become part of the real property. Examples of fixtures are gasoline pumps installed on the real property on which a gasoline station is located, bathtubs installed in a bathroom, and customized built-in wall units installed in a family room. Each of these items started out as personal property but, after being affixed to the real property, may be seen as part of it.

Are fixtures legally treated as real property or personal property that may be removed by the owner when the owner sells the real property? What about the situation in which a tenant of an apartment or office installs items that are affixed to the real property? May the tenant remove the items at the end of the lease?

The answer to these questions depends first and foremost upon the intentions of the parties involved. Unless a contract indicates otherwise, an item that is determined to be a fixture is considered part of the real property and therefore stays with the real property. However, real estate contracts and leases are governed by contract law, and the terms of the contract, as long as they are not illegal, govern the transaction between the parties. Contracts are negotiable and, therefore, a buyer and seller may decide between themselves whether the gas pumps or the bathtub or the wall units "go with" the property or may be removed by the seller. If the intentions of the parties are clear from a reading of the contract, the resolution of these matters is equally clear.

Fixture Provisions. From the previous discussion, one can gather how important it is to carefully draft the fixtures provision of a real estate contract or a lease. Nothing should be assumed. The buyer may assume that the wall-to-wall carpeting in the living room will remain in the living room after closing on the property, while the seller may intend to use that carpeting in his or her next home. Fixtures are deemed part of the real property, but if there is a question, these matters should be determined at the time of negotiating the contract. Misunderstanding may forestall the closing or prevent it from taking place at all. If the parties fail to include a fixtures provision when negotiating the contract, they should include one in a later addendum that can be attached to it.

As a real estate paralegal, you may be asked to draft or review real estate contracts for sale and purchase or leases. The fixtures provision should be as specific as possible. Anything that is not structurally part of the house, apartment, or office (for example, anything other than the walls, ceiling, floors, or stairways) should be addressed in this provision. Thus, floor coverings, window treatments, air-conditioning units, appliances, lighting fixtures, and the like should be addressed. The provision should indicate whether the items are considered personal property that will be removed by the seller or whether they are considered fixtures that will be included with the real property. Additionally, these items should not only be named but also, if possible, be described. For example, the dishwasher should not be described simply as a dishwasher but rather as the "stainless steel GE Profile™ dishwasher," or at least as the "existing dishwasher."

This may seem excessive, but numerous lawsuits abound where a seller has switched appliances from superior to inferior ones before a closing, taking the superior appliances with him or her. This drafting method may appear time-consuming and premised on lack of trust between the parties, but one must remember that the

fixture: An object that at one time was personal property but that has, through the process of attachment to real property, become part of the real property.

primary aim of both buyer and seller is a problem-free closing, and a well-drafted fixtures provision helps the parties meet their goal. A real estate contract for sale and purchase also may include a provision pertaining to personal property in which the parties describe furniture, paintings, or other items of personal property that may be sold together with the real property.

In drafting a lease, a fixtures provision should indicate what items may be attached to the real property and whether the tenant has the right to remove them upon termination of the lease. If removal is allowed, the lease should stipulate that the tenant agrees to return the real property to the condition it was in before the item was attached.

Judicial Tests for Fixtures. In the event that the parties to a real estate contract for sale and purchase or a lease fail to include such provisions, how do the courts settle disputes that arise? Over the years, courts have devised various tests to aid them in determining whether an article is a fixture that must remain with the real property. The courts generally look at four things: (1) the intention of the parties, (2) the method of annexation of the item to the real property, (3) the adaptation of the item, and (4) the relationship of the parties involved.

The intention of the parties is of primary importance in determining whether an item is a fixture if there is some way in which this intention can be shown. It is possible a court will allow and consider evidence of an oral agreement if no provision is contained in the written contract stating whether the attached items are to be sold to the buyer along with the house. If no oral agreement can be proven, the courts consider the intention of the party who attached the item to the real property. Did this party intend the item become a fixture? How did he or she intend to use the item? Did this party say anything to a third party such as a real estate agent to indicate his or her intent? Although the "intention test" is an important criterion because the courts wish to enforce the intentions of the parties when they enter into a voluntary agreement rather than rewrite the contractual terms of the parties, the courts do utilize other tests when the intentions of the parties cannot be ascertained.

One such test is the "annexation test," in which the courts look to see how the item was annexed, or attached, to the real property. The more permanent the method of annexation—as in the case of central air conditioning, for instance—the more likely the courts will determine that the item can no longer be considered personal property and must be considered a fixture. Using this test, the courts also consider the amount of damage resulting if the item were to be removed. The more potential damage to the real property, as in the case of ripping out kitchen cabinets, the more likely the courts will consider the item a fixture that must remain with the real property.

Some courts have stretched the concept of annexation to include not only actual annexation but also "constructive annexation," where the courts will construe annexation has occurred because of the relationship between the item and the real property, even if the item has not been attached in any manner that may be considered permanent or damaging if the item were to be removed. In some instances, courts have determined that items customized to fit into or onto real property, such as window screens or storm shutters, are fixtures even though they could easily be removed.

A third test that courts utilize in determining whether an item is a fixture is the "adaptation test," looking at the manner in which the item has been adapted for use with the real property. For example, the gasoline pumps mentioned earlier may be considered fixtures if a court determines that they have been adapted for use with the rest of the gasoline station and that the pumps are necessary for the continued use of the real property as a gasoline station and therefore are considered intrinsically part of the purpose or use the previous and new owners have made of the land.

The fourth test is the relationship between the parties involved in the transaction. Is the relationship that of a buyer and seller of real property or that of a landlord and tenant? And if it is that of a landlord and tenant, is it one concerning a residential lease or a commercial lease? Over the years, special statutory and common law principles have evolved in the area of tenants' fixtures.

Domestic Fixtures. It is quite common for a residential tenant to want to improve the leased premises by installing built-in bookshelves or ceiling fans, for instance. Items installed by residential tenants to make the premises more attractive or more functional are called *domestic fixtures*. While many states treat domestic fixtures as the personal property of the tenant, some states do not and, instead, maintain that anything a residential tenant annexes to the leased premises must remain with the premises. Therefore, state statutes should be checked carefully.

Trade Fixtures. Commercial tenants often need to install certain items before they can open their doors for business. A tenant in the retail clothing business needs to install display counters, garment racks, and mirrors. A dentist renting space in a professional building needs to install dental chairs and cabinets for dental equipment. Those items used in carrying out a trade or business are called *trade fixtures*. Absent a fixtures provision in the lease, most courts routinely allow removal of trade fixtures as long as (1) they are installed by the tenant, not the landlord; (2) they are removed prior to or at the expiration of the lease (any fixtures remaining after the expiration of the lease become the property of the landlord except in the circumstance of eviction, which is discussed in later chapters); and (3) the premises are restored to their original condition.

Basic Ownership Rights

Now that the classifications of property have been established, it is important to understand the legal rights that go along with real property ownership. When one acquires real property, one acquires both the real estate and certain legal rights in that real estate. These legal rights are sometimes referred to as a "bundle of rights."

The first of these rights is the **right of disposition,** which is the right to "dispose" of one's property by transferring rights to the property or any portion of it during one's lifetime or at time of death. One may do this through sale, lease, gift, or will. It is possible to lose this right by operation of law in certain circumstances, such as the nonpayment of property taxes, the failure to pay a mortgage loan, or criminal forfeiture.

The second of these rights is the **right of use,** which is sometimes referred to as the *right of enjoyment* because it allows one to use one's property in any manner one sees fit as long as that use is lawful, or to give a general or limited right of use of the property to another. Until the mid-nineteenth century, this right was virtually

right of disposition: The right to dispose of one's property by transferring rights to the property during one's lifetime or at time of death.

right of use: The right to use one's property in any lawful manner or to give a general or limited right of use of the property to another.

absolute. As the population grew and density increased, however, so did the restrictions placed on the use of one's property. (These restrictions are addressed in Chapter 4.) Nonetheless, the legal concept of right of use remains intact.

The third of these rights is the **right of possession,** which allows a property owner to occupy his or her property in privacy. Unauthorized entry onto the property by others constitutes trespass that can be stopped by requesting injunctive relief from the court as well as money damages for violation of this right.

The last of these rights is the **right of exclusion,** which is a means of exercising control over one's property. This right has been limited through the introduction of fair housing laws (discussed in Chapter 4) that disallow most forms of discrimination in the sale or lease of one's property.

Rights to real property are transferred by sale, gift, inheritance, or operation of law. Real property rights may be transferred voluntarily and deliberately, as in the basic real estate transaction in which property is bought and sold, a person makes a gift of real property to another, or a person dies and leaves a will specifying to whom real property is to pass. In other circumstances, property rights may pass by operation of law. This may occur when a property owner dies without a will indicating the intended beneficiary, which requires the real property to pass according to state inheritance statutes. Property rights also may arise by operation of law when a property owner "sleeps" on his or her rights and neglects to enforce them, as in the case of adverse possession, which is discussed in the following text. Further, state statutes may give special rights to certain categories of people, such as surviving spouses and dependent children.

Methods of Acquiring Real Property

Purchase

The sale and purchase of property is the most common way in which property changes hands. The agreement between the buyer and seller is reduced to writing by the drafting of a real estate contract for sale and purchase, which is signed by the parties. If a real estate broker was instrumental in bringing the parties together, another contract, generally known as a *listing agreement,* is involved as well. The listing agreement specifies the terms under which the seller "lists" his or her property with the broker as well as the circumstances under which the commission will be paid and the amount of commission to be paid to the broker. If financing is required by the buyer, a separate contract, such as a *mortgage agreement* or a *deed of trust,* must be signed by the buyer and the lender. This contract will specify the conditions under which the financing will be arranged, the amount of financing, and the terms for repayment. Each of these contracts is discussed in detail in later chapters. As a real estate paralegal, you may be involved actively in the drafting of these contracts.

Devise and Descent

Another common way to acquire property is by inheritance. Upon the death of a real property owner, the manner in which his or her real property will pass depends upon whether he or she died *testate* (with a valid will) or *intestate* (without a will). The person executing a valid will is called a *testator.* When a valid will exists, real

right of possession: The right to occupy one's property in privacy.

right of exclusion: The right to exercise control over one's property.

property passes according to the terms of the will. A gift of real property made to a beneficiary in a will is called a *devise,* and the recipient is known as the *devisee.*

Generally, the devisee will take the real property subject to all encumbrances and liens. If the testator intends for the real property to pass clear of any liens, then he or she must make provision elsewhere in the will for any mortgages to be paid off and must indicate the source of funds from which the mortgages are to be paid. A general provision in a will that all debts are to be paid from the *residue* (remainder of an estate after specific gifts have been distributed) is not sufficient to pass title of the property without encumbrances. The primary family residence must pass according to state statutory law pertaining to homestead property, which is discussed further in the following text. When a person dies intestate, his or her property passes according to the *intestacy laws,* sometimes referred to as the *laws of inheritance* or *laws of descent,* of the state in which the property is located. For example, if Fred Franklin dies intestate leaving real property in New York and in California, the intestacy laws of New York will govern how the New York property passes, and the intestacy laws of California will govern how the California property passes.

Gift

A person may also obtain title to real property by *gift.* The person making the gift of real property is called the *donor,* and the recipient is called the *donee.* A gift of real property generally is revocable prior to the execution and delivery of a deed indicating transfer of title from the donor to the donee. Should the donor change his or her mind prior to delivering a deed, the donee rarely has legal grounds to bring suit to enforce the gift.

In most states, the oral gift of real property is not legally enforceable. However, some states have provided that the oral gift may be enforced if the donee can prove the donor's intent to give the land and can show that the donee took possession of the land in reliance upon the gift and that the donee made permanent and valuable improvements upon the land. Other states will allow the donee to recover the costs of any detrimental reliance (for example, purchasing insurance, payment of taxes, repair costs) but will not enforce the gift of real property.

Adverse Possession

Acquiring title through **adverse possession** means acquiring title through taking possession of land that belongs to another without the owner's consent and retaining possession for a statutory period of time. This statutory period varies from state to state from a period of several years to a period of a few decades. Many states have statutes prohibiting individuals from acquiring state land through adverse possession.

The principle behind adverse possession is an English common law principle that land is of value and should be put to use. Thus, if the legal owner of the property does nothing to enforce his or her rights to the property within the statutory time period, the owner may lose title. The property in question may be a few feet, as in the case where a neighbor installs a fence a few feet beyond his or her property boundaries, or several acres, as in the case where a cattle farmer grazes his or her stock over a large acreage and extends the grazing into acreage belonging to another.

adverse possession: The acquisition of title to real property through taking possession of land that belongs to another without the owner's consent and retaining possession for a statutorily prescribed period of time.

Adverse possession must be *hostile,* meaning it must be without the owner's consent. It must be *actual,* meaning there must be physical dominion and control exerted over the property. Although there is no requirement that the adverse possessor live on the property, in some states the adverse possessor must pay the real property taxes on the land for the statutory time period to be said to have actual possession.

Adverse possession must be *open and notorious,* meaning anyone would be able to determine that possession was taking place through inspection of the property. This does not mean that the owner actually is aware that possession has taken place, only that the owner could find out if he or she made proper inspection.

Many states require the adverse possessor to take possession *under claim of right,* meaning the adverse possessor has the intent to claim the land as his or her right. In most states, however, the physical possession meets the intent requirement, and there is no additional requirement that the adverse possessor subjectively intend to lay claim to the land of another.

Taking possession under claim of right is not synonymous with taking possession *under color of title.* In the latter instance, the adverse possessor possesses documentation that is in some way defective (for example, the deed may be lacking witnesses or notarization or may fail to meet some other statutory requirement for validity) but that allegedly gives title to the property to the adverse possessor. In this situation, the adverse possessor truly believes he or she is the title owner of the property. Many states shorten the requisite time period for the person who takes possession under color of title and give him or her title to the entirety of the property described in the defective document rather than giving title only to the actual property possessed.

The adverse possessor must be in *continuous* possession for the entire statutory period. However, most states apply the concept of *tacking* to adverse possession. Tacking allows one adverse possessor to "tack on" the time periods of previous adverse possessors if there is privity of contract or a blood relationship between them. For example, suppose the state of Any State has an adverse possession statute permitting tacking and setting the statutory time period of possession for seven years. If adverse possessor A continuously used the property in question for five years and then the property was taken over by his son, the son would be allowed to "tack on" his father's five years to the amount of time the son had been in possession of the property to meet the statutory requirements.

Finally, the adverse possession must be *exclusive.* This means the adverse possessor cannot share use of the land in question with its title owner. Generally, possession by only one co-owner of property in which title is held jointly (joint ownership is discussed in detail later) does not constitute adverse possession unless the other co-owners are excluded from possession through *ouster.* In that event, the ousted co-owners must bring suit to regain possession within the statute of limitations for adverse possession or else lose all rights to the property to the ousting co-owner.

The volume of foreclosed properties in recent years has led to an increase in adverse possession claims across the country. In some instances, without notification, individuals have simply moved into properties allegedly abandoned by their owners. In many states, notification to the property owner of record is not required by state statute. In other instances, the adverse possessors have made their claims known to the property owners of record, the owners' lenders, or both.

Estates and Tenancies

When one acquires real property by one of the methods discussed previously, one is acquiring an interest in the land and the improvements thereon. This interest may include full or limited property rights. The interest a person receives in real property is based on the type of *estate* or *tenancy* conveyed. These terms are used to denote the nature, extent, and duration of a person's interest in the property.

The concept of estates and tenancies derives from feudal English law. Feudal law was pervasive throughout Europe between the twelfth and the fourteenth centuries. It was introduced in England in the early twelfth century during the Norman Conquest and has formed the basis of all real property law in England until very recently. Certain feudal concepts, particularly the concept of freehold and leasehold estates, still survive and were incorporated into American real property law. Exhibit 2–3 diagrams the most common freehold and leasehold estates.

Freehold Estates

A **freehold estate** is an estate of indeterminate duration. If ownership rights are granted for a period of time capable of being accurately fixed and determined at the time of granting, the estate is not a freehold estate. Thus, freehold estates last indefinitely, either for the lifetime of an individual (and who is to say what the duration of that lifetime may be) or continuously as the property is passed from one

freehold estate: An estate of indeterminable duration.

EXHIBIT 2–3   **Types of estates**

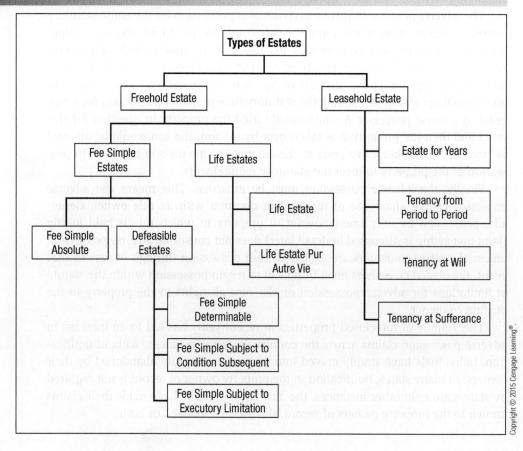

generation to the next. A freehold estate is created through the combination of *words of purchase* (indicating the party to be granted the estate—for example, "To Hilary Hodgson") and *words of limitation* (indicating the extent of the estate created—for example, "to have and to hold for her lifetime").

Fee Simple Estates. The greatest estate one may hold is a **fee simple absolute,** also known as a *fee simple* or a *fee*. A fee simple absolute grants to the owner each of the four basic ownership rights. The estate is generally conveyed through the words "To . . . and his/her heirs forever." Thus, the owner may dispose of the property in any manner he or she chooses during his or her lifetime and may leave the property to whomever he or she chooses upon death. The majority of real property transactions convey a fee simple absolute to the grantee unless words to the contrary appear in the deed.

A property owner may also convey property with conditions attached. When this occurs, the owner is creating a **defeasible estate** through the use of words of duration, such as "until," "as long as," or "while used for." If the condition occurs or the condition is breached, the grantee's ownership rights may be divested either automatically or through the grantor's exercise of the right of re-entry. There are three types of defeasible estates: (1) a fee simple determinable, (2) a fee simple subject to condition subsequent, and (3) a fee simple subject to executory limitation. With the first two defeasible estates, a future interest in the grantor is created, whereas with the third defeasible estate, a future interest in a third party is created.

A **fee simple determinable** is a fee simple estate that will terminate automatically upon the occurrence of a condition or event, at which point the estate reverts back to the grantor or the grantor's estate. Suppose Natalie wants to give a parcel of real property to her church and she wants the church to have ownership of the property as long as it is used for religious purposes. At such time as it no longer is so used (for example, if the church attempts to sell it), Natalie wants the property automatically to revert to her or her estate. The church's ownership of the property continues indefinitely, but there is a possibility of the property reverting back to grantor should the condition attached be breached. This condition creates a future interest in the grantor (Natalie) that is referred to as the *possibility of reverter*.

The wording of a conveyance is of paramount importance. Continuing with the example of Natalie's intention to convey property to her church, if the conveyance states a condition ("on condition it is used for religious purposes") and further states that upon breach of this condition the grantor has the right to enter and take back the property, Natalie has created a **fee simple on a condition subsequent.** In this case, Natalie must perform an overt act to exercise her rights to recover the property. The conveyance creates in Natalie a future interest that can be exercised through the *power of termination* or *right of entry*.

The third type of defeasible estate is a **fee simple subject to executory limitation,** referred to in some states as a *fee on limitation*. If Natalie conveys property with a condition and, upon the occurrence of that condition or event, the property is to go to a third party (for example, another named church or religious organization) rather than reverting back to Natalie or her estate, a fee simple subject to executory limitation has been created. The future interest is held not by Natalie but by the third party she has named in the conveyance.

fee simple absolute: An estate that grants the property owner each of the four basic property rights.

defeasible estate: A fee simple estate in which the grantor conveys property with conditions attached that may, upon the occurrence or breach of the condition, divest the grantee of ownership of the property.

fee simple determinable: A fee simple estate that will terminate automatically upon the occurrence of a condition or event, at which point the estate reverts back to the grantor or the grantor's estate.

fee simple on a condition subsequent: A fee simple estate in which the grantor has the power of termination upon the occurrence of a condition or event.

fee simple subject to executory limitation: A fee simple estate that will terminate upon the happening of an occurrence or event, at which point the rights to the property will vest in a third party.

Life Estates. Another type of freehold estate is a **life estate.** As the name implies, the owner (the grantor) gives title to the property to another (the grantee, also referred to as the *life estate holder*) for a period of time measured by someone's life, which can be the life of the grantee, the life of the grantor, or the life of a third party. Words creating a life estate are "To . . . for [some person's] lifetime, then to. . . ."

If the owner does not specify who takes title to the property once the lifetime ends, the grantor retains a *reversionary interest* in the property. This means that upon termination of the lifetime specified, the property reverts back by operation of law to the grantor, if still alive, or to his or her estate, if the grantor is deceased at that time.

If the grantor does specify to whom title to the real property passes upon termination of the life estate, the person so indicated is referred to as a *vested remainderman*. This person has a present interest in the property but will not get the right to exercise his or her interest until the life estate ends, at which time he or she receives a fee simple absolute.

For example, suppose Paul Peterson had a daughter, Pamela, from his first marriage. Paul is presently married to Priscilla. Paul and Priscilla live a lavish lifestyle, spending time in various properties Paul owns in Manhattan, Boulder, and Palm Beach. The primary domicile of the Petersons is located in Palm Beach, and they hold title to the property jointly. Paul would like Priscilla to retain her present lifestyle after he dies but would also like his daughter to eventually inherit the properties he holds in his own name. In his will, Paul might devise the Manhattan and Boulder properties "to my wife, Priscilla Peterson, for her lifetime, then to my daughter, Pamela." Thus, Priscilla would get a life estate, and Pamela would be a vested remainderman. This means that a present interest in the properties would pass to Pamela but she would not get the right to exercise it until Priscilla's death, at which time Pamela would get title to the properties in fee simple absolute, as illustrated in Exhibit 2–4. If, instead of

> **life estate:** An estate in which the grantor conveys title to real property to another for a period of time measured by somebody's life.

EXHIBIT 2-4   Interest of a life estate

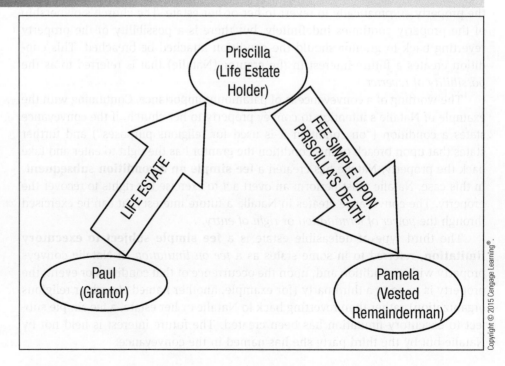

giving the remainder to Pamela, Paul wanted his yet-to-be-born grandchild to have it, the grandchild would be a *contingent remainderman,* whose interest in the properties would be contingent upon being born.

When a life estate is granted for the lifetime of someone other than the grantee, it is called a **life estate pur autre vie.** For example, parents of an adult child with severe mental disabilities might want to leave a life estate to the child's caretaker for the life of the child and then have the property revert back to the parents' estate. The life estate is given to the caretaker, but another person's life—in this instance, the life of the adult child—is the measuring life.

The owner of a life estate enjoys the same rights of use, possession, and exclusion as the owner of a fee simple absolute, but usually not the right of disposition. However, the life estate holder may rent out the property and keep all income from the rental. The life estate holder may use the property in any manner not contrary to law as long as the life estate holder does nothing to diminish the value of the property—that is, the life estate holder cannot commit *waste.* The law recognizes three types of waste: (1) permissive, (2) voluntary, and (3) ameliorative (also known as ameliorating). **Permissive waste** occurs when the life estate holder fails in the upkeep of the property (for example, fails to make necessary repairs or to keep the grounds in good condition). **Voluntary waste** occurs when the property is actively used in a manner that reduces its market value. **Ameliorative waste** is, in many respects, a misnomer because it increases the property value. It occurs when the original condition of the property is altered by improvements (for example, tearing up the back lawn to install a swimming pool). A life estate holder may commit ameliorative waste because it actually improves, rather than reduces, the value of the property.

Life estate holders have various obligations as well as rights. State law may require them to pay all real property taxes. Additionally, they may be required to obtain adequate insurance on the property and keep any mortgage payments current.

The question of whether the holder of a life estate may ever be entitled to sell the property is an interesting one and can often depend on the wording used in the conveyance of the life estate, as is the situation in the following case.

> **life estate pur autre vie:** A life estate granted for the lifetime of someone other than the grantee.
>
> **permissive waste:** The diminishment of the value of property when a life estate holder fails in the upkeep of the property.
>
> **voluntary waste:** The active use of property by a life estate holder in a manner that reduces its market value.
>
> **ameliorative waste:** The alteration of property through addition of improvements by a life estate holder that increase the value of the property.

CASE: *In Re Estate of Sauer*
194 Misc. 2d 634, 753 N.Y.S.2d 318 (2002)

JOHN B. RIORDAN, S.

This is a proceeding pursuant to §§ 1901, 1902(7) and 1918 of the Surrogate's Court Procedure Act by the decedent's surviving spouse to dispose of the decedent's interest in real property in which the petitioner has a life estate. The decedent, Sally E. Sauer, died on August 24, 2001. She was survived by a spouse, Arthur W. Sauer, Jr., the petitioner herein. The decedent was also survived by three children from a previous marriage—Kathleen Siracusa, Arthur Caddigan, and James Caddigan. The decedent's daughter, Kathleen Siracusa, was appointed executrix of her mother's estate on December 5, 2001. The executrix opposes the application.

The decedent and her husband owned a home in Garden City as tenants-in-common. Pursuant to Article Tenth of the decedent's Last Will and Testament, the decedent provided the following: "my husband, Arthur W. Sauer, shall continue to live, for his lifetime should he so choose, in our marital residence and he shall not be asked, forced, nor required in any manner to sell the premises until he so desires as long as the maintenance is paid by my husband, including all taxes and insurance thereon."

The petitioner has asked the court for permission to buy the real property for $161,264.08. The aforesaid amount represents the decedent's one-half of the home based on an appraisal of $575,000 less one-half of the outstanding mortgage less the value of petitioner's life estate. The petitioner received an offer to buy the house for the amount of $605,000. When the contract was drafted and sent to the executrix to sign, the executrix was made

(continued)

aware, apparently for the first time, that the petitioner would seek the value of his life estate. The executrix refused to sign the contract. As a result the petitioner has now asked the court for permission pursuant to §§ 1901 and 1902 of the Surrogate's Court Procedure Act to buy the property himself since presumably the buyer may no longer be interested. The petitioner has further asked the court to value his life estate pursuant to Section 1918(2) of the Surrogate's Court Procedure Act.

The question thus becomes, can the holder of a life estate force the sale of the real property and collect the value of his life estate over the objections of the remaindermen, or can the remaindermen simply wait for the death of the life tenant, and collect the full value of their interest in the real property upon his death.

Although not in dispute, the threshold question is whether the petitioner holds a life estate in the home or whether the petitioner is merely allowed to occupy the house. Traditionally, the "descriptive words denoting a life tenancy are 'use and occupation'" (*Warren's Weed New York Real Property, Life Estates* § 1.01(2), [4th ed.]). The distinction is critical as a right of occupancy is a personal privilege only (*Matter of Cimino*, NYLJ, Aug. 2, 1995 at 25, col. 6). Where an agreement was drawn by an experienced lawyer and the "usual words denoting a life tenancy 'use and occupation' were not used," the court found the party had "merely a right to occupancy" as opposed to a life estate (*Rizzo v. Mataranglo*, 16 Misc.2d 20, 135 N.Y.S.2d 92), *aff'd*, 16 Misc.2d 21, 186 N.Y.S.2d 773, *lv. denied* 285 A.D. 814, 137 N.Y.S.2d 837. Similarly, when the wife of the decedent was "permitted to occupy, rent free, for her residential purposes," the wife was found to have a "mere right of occupancy" as the bequest was carefully drafted to avoid giving the "use" of the premises (*Matter of Stokes*, NYLJ, Dec. 29, 1995 at 31, col. 5). Further indicia of a right of occupancy can be found where there is "no language from which the added rights and responsibilities of a life estate can be implied" and no right exists to lease or collect rents and the responsibility for maintenance falls upon someone other than the life tenant (*Stokes, supra*).

*   *   *

In the instant proceeding, the petitioner was given the right to live in the premises for his lifetime and was directed to pay the maintenance, including the insurance and taxes thereon. Further, the petitioner has an apparent power of sale as he can be neither forced nor required to sell "until he so desires." Finally, all of the parties conceded that the petitioner has a life estate in the home. Clearly, even though the traditional "use and occupancy" words were not used, the petitioner has a life estate in the real property.¹

*   *   *

Pursuant to SCPA § 1904(1), "any person interested" can petition for authorization to dispose of the decedent's real property (SPCA §§ 1904(1) and 1901). Any person interested includes a life tenant (*Matter of Bolton*, 79 Misc.2d 895, 362 N.Y.S.2d 308). Moreover, where a party to a proceeding pursuant to Article 19 of the SCPA has a life estate, the "court must determine whether the interests of all the parties will be better protected or a more advantageous disposition can be made of the real property by including such right or interest . . ." (SCPA § 1918[1]).

Section 1602 of the Real Property Actions and Proceedings Law, in turn, provides that "[w]hen the ownership of real property is divided into one or more possessory interests and one or more future interests, the owner of any interest in such real property . . . may apply to the court designated in § 1603 for an order directing that said real property . . . be . . . sold." An application may be granted if the court is satisfied that the "act to be authorized is expedient" (RPAPL § 1604). Although § 1603 of the RPAPL provides that the application be made to the Supreme Court, the Surrogate's Court has concurrent jurisdiction pursuant to SCPA § 1902(7) to grant the relief (*Gardiner v. U.S. Trust*, 275 A.D.2d 413, 712 N.Y.S.2d 873). SPCA § 1902(7) provides that real property may be disposed of "[f]or any other purpose the court deems necessary."

As the courts have noted, "[t]here is a dearth, if not total absence, of reported cases dealing with the subject" of the sale of life estates over objection of a party to the proceeding (*Matter of Perkins*, 55 Misc.2d 834, 837, 286 N.Y.S.2d 586; *see also, Matter of Bolton, supra* at 901, 362 N.Y.S.2d 308). To justify a sale, pursuant to Section 1902(7) of the SCPA, "some estate purpose must be served, the action must serve to carry out the provisions of the will *or* be of benefit to those interested in the estate" (*Matter of Perkins, supra; Matter of Bolton, supra,* emphasis added).

Where a life tenant brings a proceeding to compel the sale of real property pursuant to Section 1602 of the RPAPL, the life tenant must show that the act is expedient. Expedient is defined as "characterized by suitability, practicality, and efficiency in achieving a particular end; fit, proper or advantageous under the circumstances" (*Webster's Third New International Dictionary*, at 799 [1966]). A petition was granted as expedient where the purchase price was well in excess of the appraised value; the rent was insufficient to pay the taxes; the house was unoccupied; and the life tenant would have to expend a considerable sum of money for taxes, insurance and maintenance of the house (*Matter of Gaffers*, 254 A.D. 448, 450, 5 N.Y.S.2d 671).

In the instant proceeding, the life tenant's purported reasons for selling the real property are that the real estate market is high and he desires to relocate. The will provides that the life tenant cannot be forced to sell the

(continued)

property "until he so desires." The life tenant now desires to sell the property. The only way to carry out the provisions of the will is to allow the life tenant to sell the property. Granting the application is expedient, as well as suitable, practical and efficient in reaching the end which is to allow the life tenant to sell the property, the power of which he was given pursuant to the decedent's will.

The final question that remains is what value shall be given to the life estate and in what form does the life tenant take the proceeds. Section 1918(2) of the Surrogate's Court Procedure Act sets forth the following: "[t]he provisions of law in relation to the right of . . . estates for life . . . so far as applicable, shall govern and control the distribution of moneys realized on such disposition. . . ." The provisions of law relating to life estates are found in the Real Property Actions and Proceedings Law which provides that anyone who is a "tenant for life or for years, in or of an undivided share of the property sold . . . is entitled to have a proportion of the proceeds of the sale invested, secured or paid over, in such a manner as the court deems calculated to protect the rights and interests of the parties" (RPAPL § 967). Moreover, § 968 of the Real Property Actions and Proceedings Law sets forth that the "power to determine whether the owner of the particular estate shall receive, in satisfaction of his estate or interest, a sum in gross or shall receive the earnings, as they accrue, of a sum invested for his benefit in permanent securities at interest, rests in the discretion of the court. . . . The application of the owner of any such particular estate for the award of a sum in gross shall be granted unless the court finds that unreasonable hardship is likely to be caused thereby to the owner of some other interest in the affected real property." As this issue has not been fully addressed, the parties are directed to file memorandums of law in support of their position that the petitioner is either entitled to the gross amount of the value of the life estate or whether said amount must be invested for his benefit.

* * *

Case Questions

In the above case, the Surrogate's Court in New York looked at two issues pertaining to life estates: (1) whether the holder of a life estate can force the sale of property over the objections of the remaindermen and (2) the value to be given to a life estate and how the proceeds should be distributed to the life tenant.

1. In looking at the first issue, the court placed a lot of importance on the actual wording of the conveyance and made a distinction between a life tenancy and the mere right of occupation. Does your state's law make such a distinction? If so, is there particular wording that must be used to convey a life estate? If there is no particular wording, what wording would you use to convey a life estate that would avoid any possible ambiguities?

2. Based on the wording of the conveyance in the above case, do you believe the decedent wanted to give her husband the right to sell the property? Do you think she anticipated potential problems between her husband and her adult children? What might she have done when drafting her will to prevent the situation presented in the above case? Do you believe life tenants should be allowed to sell a life estate over the objections of the remaindermen? Why or why not? What circumstances might influence your decision?

3. Does your state's law provide guidelines for valuation of the interest of the holder of a life estate in the property conveyed? If so, do you believe the law on this matter to be fair to both the holder of the life estate interest and the remaindermen? If your state's law does not provide such guidelines, how would you propose to calculate a just valuation of a life estate interest when a property is sold, as in the above case?

1. The conveyance of the life estate coupled with a power of sale may in some cases convey fee absolute. In New York, however, there must be some language in the will which indicates that the interest in the property is greater than the life estate or that the testator intended that the power of sale benefit the holder of the life estate (*Matter of Hayes*, 114 N.Y.S.2d 87; *Weinstein v. Weber*, 178 N.Y. 94, 70 N.E. 115).

Leasehold Estates

A **leasehold estate** is an estate of determinable duration. This estate conveys the rights of use, possession, and exclusion, but not disposition, and is initially created by a lease agreement between a landlord and a tenant. There are four basic leasehold estates: (1) an estate for years (sometimes referred to as a *tenancy for years*), (2) a tenancy from period to period, (3) a tenancy at will, and (4) a tenancy at sufferance.

Estate for Years. An **estate for years** is a tenancy that continues for a designated period, be it three months or longer than the average lifetime (for example, ninety-nine years), the estate automatically extinguishing upon a fixed date. If an estate for

leasehold estate: An estate of determinable duration.

estate for years: A tenancy that continues for a designated period.

years is created for a period of more than one year, the lease conveying the interest must be in writing in order to be enforceable. An estate for years does not convey actual title that allows the estate holder to sell the real property (although the estate holder may be able to rent out the property) but simply conveys for a temporary period the rights of possession, use, and exclusion.

Tenancy from Period to Period. A **tenancy from period to period** is a tenancy that continues for successive intervals until one party to the agreement provides the other party with notice of termination of the tenancy. The agreement between the parties may be *express* (reduced to words, either oral or written) or *implied* (created by the actions of the parties—for example, a landlord accepting monthly payments of rent may imply a tenancy from month to month).

Tenancy at Will. A **tenancy at will** is similar to a tenancy from period to period. The primary distinction is that a tenancy at will typically begins as an estate for years and then converts to a tenancy at will once the estate for years expires and the tenant remains on the property by agreement with the landlord. Originally, a tenancy at will meant exactly what its name implies, that the tenancy could be terminated at the will of either party, by the property owner's sale of the property, or by the death of one of the parties. However, most state statutes now require appropriate notice by the terminating party. Appropriate notice generally is determined not by the notice requirements of the original written or oral lease but by the intervals between rent payments. For example, if the tenant had a two-year lease that expired and under that lease he or she made monthly rental payments, then the applicable notice requirements are those pertaining to a month-to-month lease (for example, fifteen days). Some state statutes distinguish between the notice requirements for residential leaseholds and those for commercial leaseholds.

Tenancy at Sufferance. At common law, a **tenancy at sufferance** did not create any rights in the tenant. This situation occurred when a tenant remained on the leased premises after the lease expired without the agreement of the landlord. Under these circumstances, the landlord could choose to "suffer" the party's presence and treat the party as a tenant at will or choose to evict the party. No notice was required to remove the party from the property. Today, most state statutes disallow this common law principle, requiring statutory notice prior to termination of a tenancy.

Methods of Title Holding

Title to real property may be held in the name of a single owner, or it may be held jointly by two or more persons in one of several types of *joint* or *concurrent ownership*. Each method of concurrent ownership confers different rights on the titleholders. Title to real property also may be held in the name of a business entity such as a partnership, corporation, or limited liability company. As noted at the beginning of the chapter, title to real property typically is obtained through a *conveyance* (for example, through the conveyance of a deed granting title). Additionally, title to real property may come about through operation of law, such as in the case of community property shared equally by husband and wife in community property states, or by statutory rights afforded a surviving spouse in a percentage of a deceased spouse's real property.

tenancy from period to period: A tenancy that continues for successive intervals until one party to the agreement provides the other party with notice of termination of the tenancy.

tenancy at will: A tenancy that begins as an estate for years, with the tenant remaining on the property by agreement with the landlord after the estate for years expires.

tenancy at sufferance: A tenancy occurring after the expiration of a lease, in which a tenant remains in possession of the property without the landlord's consent.

Individual Ownership

An individual may hold title to real property in his or her own name as a single owner. This method of ownership is termed **ownership in severalty.** The individual taking title in fee simple absolute has the right to use and ultimately dispose of the property in any manner he or she chooses, subject to law. Additionally, the individual is personally liable for all real property taxes, income taxes arising from any income produced by the property (for example, rents or sale of the property), and any claims made against the property.

Although it usually is a single person who takes title in this fashion, a married or widowed person also may take title as a sole owner. It is necessary to indicate the sole owner's marital status after his or her name on the deed (for example, "Greg Grayson, a single man"; "Nancy Nelson, a married woman") because of special rights afforded widows and widowers in some states. These are the rights of *dower,* which allows a widow a certain percentage of her deceased husband's property, and *curtesy,* which allows a widower a certain percentage of his deceased wife's property. A few states afford married persons *community property rights,* which are rights to share equally in property acquired during marriage. Many states also afford spouses special rights in *homestead property,* which is the primary domicile of the family. Dower, curtesy, community property, and homestead rights are discussed in detail later in the chapter.

In states that afford special spousal rights, Nancy Nelson's husband would have to join her as a grantor on a deed granting title to a buyer should Nancy decide to sell her property, even though title to the property is held in her name, to indicate his relinquishment of any curtesy, community property, or homestead rights he may have in the property.

Types of Concurrent Ownership

Joint or concurrent ownership of real property occurs when more than one individual (or entity) holds title to the same property at the same time. The joint owners are termed *co-owners* or *co-tenants* in the real property. Co-owners share certain rights, such as the right to enjoy possession of the entire property and the right to their proportionate share of any rents or profits derived from the property. Further, they share certain responsibilities with regard to the real property. Co-owners cannot commit waste that reduces the market value of the property, and each is responsible to the other(s) for any contribution toward the maintenance of the real property. The most common forms of concurrent ownership are a tenancy in common, a Joint Tenancy, and a tenancy by the entirety.

Tenancy in Common. **Tenancy in common** is the most commonly used method of concurrent ownership because, if two or more persons are co-owners of real property and there is no indication to the contrary, the law in most states presumes they are tenants in common. This may vary in some states where the co-owners are a husband and wife.

Any number of persons may own property together as tenants in common and need not acquire title at the same time. Each co-owner may have obtained separate title from the same or from different grantors. Further, they may own equal or unequal shares in the real property. For example, Eve Enderby, Joyce Johnson, and

ownership in severalty: Ownership of real property in one's own name as a sole owner.

tenancy in common: A form of concurrent ownership in which two or more persons have undivided interests in property but which does not confer the right of survivorship.

Henry Hickson may be tenants in common, with Eve owning a one-half interest in the real property and Joyce and Henry each owning a one-quarter interest in the real property. Nonetheless, tenants in common share *unity of possession,* which is the right each has to possession of the entire property. Additionally, each co-owner is said to own an *undivided interest* in the real property, which means that the interests of the co-owners, although fractional interests, are not physically separate. If the fractional shares of each co-owner are not documented, the law presumes that each co-owner owns an equal share in the real property.

This method of concurrent ownership does not confer *right of survivorship,* the right of the co-owners to inherit a deceased co-owner's share in the real property. Thus, each co-owner's share passes to his or her heirs or to beneficiaries designated in a will. In addition, each co-owner has the right, during his or her lifetime, to mortgage or convey his or her undivided interest in the real property without obtaining the consent of the other co-owners unless there is an agreement to the contrary. Should a co-owner transfer his or her interest, it may be necessary for that co-owner to have his or her spouse join in the execution of the deed for the same reasons indicated in the previous discussion of transfer of property in severalty.

Should a dispute arise among tenants in common over the use of the property or any other rights associated with it, any of the co-owners may file a legal action requesting *partition* of the property, which is the division of real property into distinct portions so that co-owners may hold them in severalty. In granting partition, a court will divide the real property into parcels according to the percentage owned by each co-owner. If this is not possible for some reason, then the court may order the property sold and the proceeds of the sale allocated proportionately. Partition of property is discussed in detail in Chapter 18.

Joint Tenancy. A **Joint Tenancy** is sometimes referred to as a *Joint Tenancy with right of survivorship.* The most striking characteristic of a Joint Tenancy is the right of survival each co-owner has in the undivided interests of the other co-owner(s). For example, assume Burt Bryant, Patrick Pickering, and Lisa Lawson are co-owners in a Joint Tenancy. Should Burt die, his heirs will not inherit his undivided share in the real property; rather, it will pass to Patrick and Lisa. Should Patrick then die, Lisa will own the real property in severalty. Because of this feature, many states presume that co-owners are tenants in common unless the words "as joint tenants with right of survivorship" appear on the deed to indicate the contrary.

Another characteristic of a Joint Tenancy is the presence of the *four unities:* (1) unity of possession, (2) unity of interest, (3) unity of time, and (4) unity of title. As in a tenancy in common, each co-owner in a Joint Tenancy has the right to enjoy the use of the entire property. Unlike a tenancy in common, however, in a Joint Tenancy each co-owner's interest is identical. Further, for a Joint Tenancy to exist, each co-owner must take title under the same deed at the same time. If one or more of these unities is not present, the co-owners are deemed tenants in common.

Even if the four unities are initially present, the sale or mortgage of a co-owner's interest will sever the Joint Tenancy. Using the above example, should Burt sell his interest to Richard Runnells, Patrick and Lisa remain joint tenants with respect to each other and become tenants in common with Richard. Therefore, Richard's heirs may inherit his interest; however, Patrick's heirs will not receive Patrick's interest, which will pass to Lisa.

Joint Tenancy: A form of concurrent ownership in which two or more persons have undivided interests in property with right of survivorship.

Tenancy by the Entirety. A **tenancy by the entirety,** sometimes referred to as a *tenancy by the entireties,* is a distinct form of joint ownership that can occur only when property is owned by a husband and wife. This form of ownership has its origins in the early English common law principle that a husband and wife are one person and that their joint ownership could be divided only by the death of one or the other spouse. If state law provides, neither spouse has an individual interest in the property to convey and, therefore, neither can mortgage or convey the property without the consent and signature of both parties. Each spouse owns a 100 percent interest in the property, preventing the creditors of one spouse from obtaining a judgment against property held in this fashion. If a debt is owed jointly by the spouses, however, a creditor may obtain judgment against tenancy by the entirety property. Because right of survivorship exists in this form of joint ownership, neither spouse may dispose of the property by will; the property instead passes automatically to the surviving spouse upon the death of the other.

Although this form of joint ownership is not recognized in all states, some states that do recognize it will presume a tenancy by the entirety, unless there is evidence to the contrary, any time a conveyance is made to a husband and wife, even if the words "as tenants by the entirety" do not appear on the deed. In a minority of states, the words "as tenants by the entirety" must appear on the deed. Should the spouses divorce, a divorce decree terminates the tenancy by the entirety, and the ex-spouses become co-owners in a tenancy in common.

Exhibit 2–5 provides a chart indicating the characteristics of each type of concurrent ownership.

Ownership by a Business Entity

The manner in which title to real property is held by a business is determined by the laws governing the particular business structure. There are seven basic business structures: (1) sole proprietorships, (2) general partnerships, (3) limited partnerships, (4) limited liability partnerships, (5) limited liability limited partnerships, (6) corporations, and (7) limited liability companies.

tenancy by the entirety: A form of concurrent ownership by husband and wife in which each spouse has an undivided interest and right of survivorship.

Characteristics of concurrent ownership   EXHIBIT 2–5

Characteristics	Tenancy in common	Joint Tenancy	Tenancy by the entirety
Owners	Two or more persons	Two or more persons	Husband and wife only
Nature of interest	Undivided	Undivided	Undivided
Right of survivorship	No	Yes	Yes
Right of partition	Yes	In some states	Only in event of divorce
Quantity of interest	Equal or unequal shares	Equal shares	Each spouse has 100% interest
Co-owner's right to sell interest	Yes	Yes	No

Copyright © 2015 Cengage Learning®.

Sole Proprietorships

The most common business structure in the United States continues to be the sole proprietorship, although it is the least likely to acquire substantial real estate holdings. A *sole proprietorship* is exactly what the term implies, an unincorporated business owned and operated by a single individual. The inclusion of the term *unincorporated* is important because many states allow incorporation of a business with a single shareholder. The central concept is one-person ownership. A sole proprietor may hire employees but may never share ownership of the business with someone else. If this happens, the business ceases to be a sole proprietorship.

A sole proprietorship cannot be separated from the identity of its owner. Therefore, any real property acquired by the sole proprietor is acquired in his or her name, and the sole proprietor is personally responsible for the mortgage note.

Partnerships

There are four types of partnerships: general partnerships, limited partnerships, limited liability partnerships, and limited liability limited partnerships. A *general partnership* is the voluntary association of two or more individuals or entities, acting as co-owners of a business for profit. Profits and losses, as well as management responsibilities, are shared among the partners according to the terms of a partnership agreement. Each partner in a general partnership is personally responsible for the financial obligations of the general partnership.

Each partner has a *partnership interest* in the general partnership, usually proportionate to his or her capital contribution, which is considered a personal property right. This partnership interest does not entitle any partner to particular partnership property; instead, it typically reflects that partner's equity interest in the business. Therefore, although real property may be acquired or conveyed either in the partnership name or in the names of the partners, it is the partnership that holds title to real property, not the individual partners. Additionally, because the real property owned by a partnership is owned by the business, not the partners themselves, spouses of partners do not have dower, curtesy, or community property rights in the real property.

A *limited partnership* is similar to a general partnership, requiring the joining of two or more individuals or entities to run a business based on the terms set forth in a partnership agreement. In a limited partnership, however, there must be at least one general partner and at least one limited partner. The limited partner is limited in terms of both personal liability (he or she is liable personally for business losses only up to the amount of his or her capital contribution) and managerial responsibility (he or she may not actively participate in the running of the business).

Limited partnerships require more formalities in formation than do general partnerships. They do not officially exist until a *certificate of limited partnership* is filed with the appropriate state authority, usually the secretary of state. If a limited partnership wishes to expand operations outside of the state of its creation, it must apply to do so as a foreign limited partnership. With regard to the sale and acquisition of real property, conveyance to or from a limited partnership is similar to that of general partnerships.

A *limited liability partnership* combines aspects of both general and limited partnerships. All partners may act as general partners and partake in the everyday running of the business, yet all receive liability protection from certain debts and obligations of the partnership. The extent of that protection is governed by state statute. As with limited partnerships, there are formalities that must be met to create a limited liability partnership, including the filing of documents with the appropriate state authorities. The document that creates a limited liability partnership is referred to, in some states, as a *statement of qualification*. The newest form of partnership is the *limited liability limited partnership*. It offers protection against personal liability to both the general and the limited partners. Many states that recognize this form of partnership include provisions for its governance in their limited partnership acts. Regarding the sale and purchase of real property, conveyance to or from either a limited liability partnership or a limited liability limited partnership is similar to that of the other two partnership forms discussed.

A *joint venture* is similar to a partnership but is established to create a relationship between the parties only for a single transaction or business venture. Joint ventures are often chosen as the preferred business structure for the acquisition and development of real property. A joint venture is not considered a separate legal entity in many states and, therefore, real property acquired by a joint venture is considered the real property of the joint venturers, who hold title as tenants in common. Because the property is considered the property of the individual joint venturers, conveyance of the property may require the signatures of any spouses.

Corporations

A *corporation* is a business structure that is a legal entity separate from the owners of the business and is created according to the dictates of statutes. It does not exist until a document called *articles of incorporation* is filed with the secretary of state or other designated authority. The owners of a corporation are called *shareholders,* and their shares of the profits are apportioned by the number and types of shares of stock they hold in the corporation. An important feature of a corporation is the shielding from personal liability of the owners for the debts of the corporation.

All corporations are managed by a board of directors, elected by the shareholders. The board of directors, in turn, appoints corporate officers who oversee the daily affairs of the business. A document called the *bylaws* serves as a procedural guide for the running of a corporation. It specifies voting procedures, meetings to be held, and the powers of the board of directors and of the officers as well as the procedures for removal of directors and officers.

The bylaws typically indicate that the officers of the corporation, acting on behalf of the board of directors, may enter into contracts for the purchase or sale of real property. Such a contract would have to be ratified by the board of directors. The board of directors does this by passing a resolution adopting the actions of the officer. An example of such a resolution is found in Exhibit 2–6. Because a corporation is a separate legal entity, title to real property of a corporation is held in the name of the corporation, not in the name of its shareholders.

Limited Liability Companies

A *limited liability company* encompasses characteristics of a partnership as well as characteristics of a corporation. The formation of a limited liability company originally required at least two owners, called members. Now, most states allow a

EXHIBIT 2–6   **Board of directors resolution to purchase real property**

BOARD OF DIRECTORS RESOLUTION TO PURCHASE REAL PROPERTY

RESOLUTION OF BOARD OF DIRECTORS
OF AMERICAN LAND ACQUISITIONS, INC.

WHEREAS, CONTINENTAL DEVELOPMENT CORP., owner of the land located in Any City, Any County, Any State, has offered to sell certain real property to this Corporation for the sum of ONE MILLION FIVE HUNDRED THOUSAND DOLLARS ($1,500,000.00), upon the terms hereinafter set forth, and

WHEREAS, the Board of Directors deems it advisable that the Corporation acquire said land from CONTINENTAL DEVELOPMENT CORP. for the price aforementioned, be it

RESOLVED, That this Corporation purchase from CONTINENTAL DEVELOPMENT CORP. the land more specifically described as follows:

Tract 16 of KENSINGTON MANOR ESTATES, 2nd Edition, according to the plat thereof recorded at Plat Book 56, page 23 of the public records of Any County, Any State.

RESOLVED, FURTHER, That the President and Secretary of this Corporation are hereby authorized to enter into an agreement on behalf of this Corporation with said Seller to purchase the above described property pursuant to agreement annexed.

RESOLVED, FURTHER, That the President and Secretary of this Corporation are hereby authorized to execute all instruments and make all payments necessary to carry the foregoing resolution into effect, and to accept all documents, duly executed, which may be necessary for the transfer and conveyance of the land to this Corporation.

I do hereby certify that I am the duly elected and qualified Secretary, and that the above is a true and correct copy of a resolution duly adopted at a meeting of the Board of Directors thereof, convened and held in accordance with law and the Bylaws of said Corporation on May 5, 2015, and that such resolution is now in full force and effect.

IN WITNESS WHEREOF, I have affixed my name as Secretary and have caused the corporate seal of said Corporation to be hereunto affixed, this 5th day of May, 2015.

A True Record
Attest

AMERICAN LAND ACQUISITIONS, INC.

_____
Secretary

limited liability company to comprise only one member. A creature of state statute, a limited liability company comes into creation when *articles of organization* are filed with the appropriate state authority. The document governing the daily operations of a limited liability company is the *operating agreement,* a hybrid between a partnership agreement and corporate bylaws. The company may be manager-managed or member-managed. A limited liability company, as its name implies, provides its members with limited liability for business debts and, in so providing, is similar to a corporation. A limited liability company acquires title and conveys title to real property in the name of the company.

Dower and Curtesy

dower: The provision the law makes for a widow to lay legal claim to an interest in her deceased husband's real property.

Dower is an old legal right that used to exist in the majority of states. It still survives intact in a few states but has been considerably altered in others. **Dower** is the provision the law makes for a widow to lay legal claim to an interest in her deceased husband's real property (that is, in property he held in severalty). Traditionally, the claim could be made only by a widow with children by the deceased husband. The widow was entitled to a life estate in one-third of the deceased husband's real property, the children being the vested remaindermen, with the remainder of the property passing to the children outright. This entitlement was given to the widow so she had property upon which to bring up the children and from which she could support herself. Because of this rationale, the widow's rights to the property took precedence over those of the husband's creditors.

Some states have retained the concept of dower but have allowed widows with no children the same right. In some other states, the widow, with or without children, is entitled to a one-third interest, or some other fractional interest, in fee simple rather than simply a life estate in the property.

Until the death of a husband, a wife's dower rights are *inchoate,* meaning that they are contingent upon her outliving her husband and will vest only upon his death. Nonetheless, because this inchoate right exists in states that continue to recognize dower rights, a husband cannot sell real property without his wife's signature accompanying his own on a deed. Her signature acts as a release or satisfaction of her inchoate interest in that particular real property.

In a number of states, if the buyer accepts the deed without the signature of the grantor's wife, the buyer risks the chance that the wife may make a claim against the property after her husband's death. In the event that she does so, her claim may be found to be superior to that of the buyer. This would not be the result in other states in which the widow has dower rights only in real property that the husband owned at the time of his death.

Should a husband and wife divorce, her dower rights terminate. In the event the wife predeceases her husband, his property passes to his heirs; her heirs have no legal claim to a one-third share of the real property because the deceased wife's inchoate rights never vested.

In some states, a similar right is given to a widower in his deceased wife's real property. This right is known as **curtesy.** Traditionally, the widower's curtesy rights were not limited to a fractional share; instead, he was given a life estate in all real property his wife owned during their marriage, provided that there were children born from the marital union. Most states have forfeited the requirement that there be children from the marriage, and a number of states have reduced the widower's curtesy rights to an interest in a fractional share of the deceased wife's property, similar to dower rights. As with dower, some states recognize rights in all lands owned during the marriage, while others recognize rights only in lands owned at the time of the wife's death. Thus, it is safe practice to require the husband's signature on all conveyances of real property by the wife.

Most states have abolished the concepts of both dower and of curtesy in favor of gender-neutral statutes that allow the surviving spouse to choose between taking the property passed to him or her by the deceased spouse's will or taking an **elective share,** sometimes referred to as a *marital share,* which is a fractional share of the property (usually both real and personal) in fee simple owned by the deceased spouse at the date of death. This guarantees the surviving spouse a certain interest in the deceased spouse's property should a will leave the surviving spouse less than he or she would be entitled to under state intestacy statutes. In states providing for an elective share, the surviving spouse is entitled to take that share even if he or she contests the will and the deceased spouse's will provides that the surviving spouse is to receive nothing if the will is contested.

curtesy: The provision the law makes for a widower to lay legal claim to an interest in his deceased wife's real property.

elective share: A spouse's statutory right to a fractional share of real and personal property owned by the deceased spouse at the date of death.

Community Property

Community property law developed in certain, but not all, states that were founded under Spanish or French rule. The states with community property systems are Louisiana, California, Nevada, Arizona, Idaho, New Mexico, Washington, and Texas. In 1986, Wisconsin adopted a concept called *marital property* that is very similar to community property. All other states follow a common law system of real property in which each spouse owns whatever he or she earns or has rights to by conveyance. Under the community property law system, all property falls within one of two categories: separate property and community property.

Separate property is (1) all property acquired by a spouse prior to marriage, (2) all income from property acquired by a spouse prior to marriage unless commingled in such a manner that it is difficult to separate it from community property, (3) property acquired solely through separate funds, and (4) all property acquired by gift, will, or descent unless the gift or will clearly indicates that the property is given to both husband and wife.

Community property is all property, both personal and real, acquired during marriage by either spouse. It pertains only to marital relationships. Community property is owned equally by the spouses, regardless of each spouse's contribution to the acquisition of the property (indeed, it applies even if one spouse makes no financial contribution) or the manner in which title to the property is held.

Thus, if Monica Montrose purchases a vacation home in her own name during her marriage to Martin Montrose, there is a legal presumption in community property states that the vacation home is community property by operation of law, regardless of the fact that only Monica is listed on the deed as grantee, unless she can show that the vacation home was purchased entirely from funds legally considered her separate property. If Martin contributed anything to the purchase of the vacation home or if community property was used in part to purchase the vacation home, apportionment would take place, and a proportionate percentage of the vacation home would be considered Monica's separate property, while the remaining percentage would be considered community property owned equally by Monica and Martin. Because community property cannot be sold by one spouse without the other spouse's consent, if the vacation home was deemed community property, even though Monica's sole name appeared on the present deed, both Monica and Martin would have to sign a new deed as grantors when the home was sold.

Most community property states honor *prenuptial agreements*. Therefore, spouses in community property states may desire to determine among themselves what property is to be considered separate property and what property is to be considered community property. Prenuptial agreements must be in writing in order to be enforceable. As with any other type of contract, consideration must be given on both sides for a prenuptial agreement to be valid, but in this circumstance, the exchange of mutual promises to marry may be determined to be sufficient consideration. Further, each party must make full financial disclosure to the other prior to signing the agreement. It is advisable that each spouse seek advice of separate counsel prior to signing a prenuptial agreement.

Absent a prenuptial or *postnuptial agreement* (an agreement made during the marriage; if made in contemplation of separation and divorce, it is called a

separate property: Property that is (1) acquired by a spouse prior to marriage, (2) income from property acquired by a spouse prior to marriage unless commingled in a manner that makes it community property, (3) acquired solely through separate funds, or (4) acquired by gift, will, or descent unless the gift or will clearly indicates that the property is given to both husband and wife.

community property: All property, both real and personal, acquired during marriage by either spouse, in states that recognize this concept.

separation agreement) to the contrary, community property is divided equally should a husband and wife divorce. Community property to be divided in this fashion is considered all property acquired during the marriage, and the time period of the marriage, for purposes of division of property, typically is calculated until the time the petitioner files a petition for dissolution of marriage with the court, not the time at which the divorce is granted. Once the spouses are divorced, they hold title to the property as tenants in common.

The intestacy laws of each state govern the manner in which community property passes upon the death of a spouse who dies intestate. In some community property states, the surviving spouse receives his or her one-half of the community property plus the deceased spouse's half and additionally, as an heir, may be entitled to all or a portion of the property the deceased spouse held as separate property. In others, the surviving spouse receives his or her one-half share and the deceased spouse's share passes to his or her heirs.

Homestead Property

Homestead property is defined as the primary dwelling house or residence of the head of household plus adjoining land. Although a person may own many properties, he or she may have only one domicile qualifying as homestead property. The concept of homestead property is important in three contexts: (1) the probate laws pertaining to homestead property, (2) the property tax exemption laws pertaining to homestead property, and (3) the homestead right of protection against claims of creditors. Some states limit the statutory homestead by size restrictions (for example, a certain amount of acreage outside city limits and within city limits), while others limit it to a certain dollar amount.

Traditionally, one had to be head of a family in order to reap the benefits accorded to homestead property, which meant that one had to be the primary supporter of a spouse and minor children. In many states, the "head of family" has been broadened to include unmarried, divorced, legally separated, or widowed persons who provide support of a child or other dependent, and in certain contexts, a single person with no dependents may claim his or her primary residence as homestead property for specified purposes, such as the property tax exemption.

Probate homestead refers to the right the surviving spouse and minor children have in homestead property. When a husband or wife dies leaving a surviving spouse and minor children, the homestead property passes automatically to the surviving spouse and children. This is the case even if the deed to the homestead property is solely in the name of the deceased spouse. Under state statutory law, the surviving spouse may receive a life estate with the minor children as vested remaindermen, or the surviving spouse may receive a fee simple in the homestead property. Because of this statutory right, homestead property cannot be sold or mortgaged without the signatures of both spouses on the deed or mortgage documents.

Many states provide *homestead property tax exemptions* on real property taxes levied. The term *exemption* is a misnomer, for most states do not exempt homestead property entirely from real property taxes. Rather, the majority of states that provide these statutory exemptions allow a set dollar figure (for example, $50,000) to be subtracted from the assessed value of the homestead property before real

homestead property: The primary dwelling house or residence of the head of household plus adjoining land.

property taxes are calculated. For example, in a state that allows a $50,000 tax exemption on homestead property, a homestead property that has an assessed value of $300,000 will be taxed on $250,000 of the property value.

In states that allow such exemptions, there is usually the prerequisite that a formal homestead declaration be recorded, often in the property appraiser's office or in the clerk's office where the deed is recorded. Typically, there are statutory deadlines for the recording of such declarations before one may take advantage of the exemption (for example, the declaration must be recorded by March 1 of the year in which the exemption on real property taxes is claimed). In some states, verification of this declaration must be made each year if the exemption is to remain in force, while in others the exemption is automatic after the initial filing of the declaration.

Homestead property also is afforded certain protection against the claims of creditors under the doctrine of *homestead rights*. Homestead rights may prevent a forced sale of the primary residence to satisfy creditors or may protect a certain dollar amount of equity in the primary residence should the residence be sold. The rationale behind homestead rights is that of providing the members of a struggling family with a roof over their heads or at least a minimum amount of capital to prevent them from living on the streets.

Until recently, a few states, such as Florida, were known as a bankruptcy debtor's paradise because homestead property could not be sold to pay off creditors as long as any mortgage payments on the homestead property were current. Thus, in Florida (and other select states with similar statutes) one could conceivably declare bankruptcy and still keep a million-dollar homestead property out of the hands of creditors as long as the homestead property met statutory size restrictions (in the case of Florida, 160 acres of contiguous land and improvements if located outside a municipality or one-half acre of contiguous land and improvements if located within a municipality). Federal bankruptcy exemptions allowed protection of a specified dollar amount for equity in the bankruptcy petitioner's homestead property. Some states allowed a bankruptcy petitioner to choose between federal and state bankruptcy exemptions, while others permitted only the use of state exemptions.

On April 20, 2005, President George W. Bush signed into law Senate Bill 256, known as the Bankruptcy Abuse Prevention and Consumer Protection Act of 2005, considered to be the most widespread revision of the bankruptcy law since the 1978 Bankruptcy Code. This revision has impacted various aspects of real estate, including homestead. Section 322 of the Act placed a cap on the value of the homestead exemption for those filing for bankruptcy that applies unless the homestead property owner has owned that property or other homestead property in the state during the 1,215 days (forty months) preceding the filing of the bankruptcy petition. If the bankruptcy petitioner has owned homestead property in the state for forty or more months prior to filing, then this limitation does not affect him or her, and state homestead exemptions apply. Thus, if someone filing a Chapter 7 bankruptcy petition in Florida had owned homestead property in Florida for at least forty months prior to filing (and had kept current on mortgage payments), the homestead property would be exempt from the reach of creditors, regardless of the value of the property or the amount of equity the owner had in the property. Other states with liberal homestead rights, including but not limited to California and Texas, are most strongly affected by these changes in the bankruptcy law.

CHAPTER SUMMARY

1. *Property* is a generic term used to describe anything that can be owned. Property can be divided into various classifications. For the purpose of the study of real property law, the two most important classifications are *real property* (land and any permanent attachment thereto) and *personal property* (everything else).

2. Surface rights in real property are divided into land rights and water rights. Land rights include rights to all land contained within specified boundaries and permanent attachments to that land, be they manmade or natural elements. Water rights pertain to the right to use water adjacent to one's land as well as the right to possess property covered by water adjacent to one's land. Air rights may be classified as public air rights, which allow use for aerial transportation and communications technology, and private air rights owned by real property owners, which extend from the surface of an allotted parcel of land up to a statutorily specified height. Private air rights are valuable in congested metropolitan areas where they may be sold as air "lots" upon which buildings may be built. They also are of value on properties located in scenically desirable spots where they may be purchased to ensure an uninterrupted view. Subsurface rights also can be of considerable value should the subsurface contain hard minerals or oil and gas deposits.

3. A fixture is an item of personal property that, through the process of attachment, is transformed into real property. To determine whether an item is a fixture that must remain with the real property, the intention of the parties is of primary concern. Cautious parties include a carefully drafted fixtures provision in their real estate contract or lease. In the absence of this, the courts must decide the matter should a dispute arise. The courts have several tests at their disposal. First, they attempt to determine the intent of the parties. If this cannot be ascertained, they may look at the method of annexation, the adaptation of the item, and the relationship of the parties.

4. The basic ownership rights acquired when purchasing real property include the right of disposition (which allows one to freely transfer all or any portion of one's property by sale, lease, gift, or will), the right of use (which allows one to use one's property in any manner one chooses as long as such use is consistent with local laws), the right of possession (which allows one privacy on one's property), and the right of exclusion (which allows one to control entry upon the land).

5. Although the most common method of acquiring title to real property is by purchasing it, one may acquire it by other means. A real property owner's heirs may take title to property through the right of descent should the owner die intestate. If a real property owner dies leaving a will, the named beneficiaries in the will are the devisees and take title by devise. Property also may be acquired by a gift of real property by a donor to a donee. For the gift to be valid, a deed of conveyance must be executed by the donor and delivered to the donee. Absent such evidence of conveyance, an oral promise to convey real property usually will not be upheld, although some courts have upheld such a promise where the donee could show evidence of intent on the part of the donor, possession of the property in reliance on the promise, and improvements made upon the property.

6. The largest estate one may acquire is a fee simple absolute, the ownership of which confers all the legal rights to real property: the right of disposition, the right of use, the right of possession, and the right of exclusion. A fee simple absolute passes by descent to the property owner's heirs or by will to the owner's named beneficiaries. Defeasible fees place conditions on a conveyance and create future interests, either in the grantor or in a third party, should a condition occur or, alternatively, should a condition be breached. A life estate is a freehold estate that is conveyed for the lifetime of the grantee or the lifetime of some other person. The life estate holder may enjoy full use of the property and may keep any income derived from the property. While in possession, the life estate holder must do nothing to devalue the market value of the property. He or she must pay all real property taxes, insurance, and other maintenance costs.

7. Leasehold estates exist either for a definite period of time, as in the case of an estate for years, or for successive intervals, as in the case of a tenancy from period to period. Upon the expiration of a lease, a tenancy at will can be created if the tenant remains on the property by agreement with the landlord and continues to pay rent. Under common law, should the tenant continue in possession without agreement by the landlord, the tenant becomes a tenant at sufferance and may be evicted without notice.

8. There are three basic methods of concurrent ownership: a tenancy in common, a Joint Tenancy, and a tenancy by the entirety. Co-owners in a tenancy in common may dispose of their interest in the property in any manner they choose, and upon their death, their interest in the property will pass to their heirs or beneficiaries. Both a Joint Tenancy and a tenancy by the entirety share the characteristic of right of survivorship, with a co-owner's interest automatically passing to the surviving co-owner(s). Although any number of persons may be co-owners in a tenancy in common or a Joint Tenancy, only a husband and a wife may take title to property as tenants by the entirety.

WEB RESOURCES

http://www.lawchek.net/

Lawchek provides various resources and information for legal professionals. Its "Legal Forms" section provides a glossary of real estate terms, answers to commonly asked real estate questions, and free sample legal forms.

http://publicrecords.onlinesearches.com/

This site provides access to various public records. You can search by choosing either the type of record or the state. Among other options, the site provides links to each state's online database to search UCC filing records.

http://www.abiworld.org/

This is the site of the American Bankruptcy Institute. It provides detailed information on the Federal Bankruptcy Code, including the Bankruptcy Abuse Prevention and Consumer Act of 2005. This site also provides access to other online resources, such as bankruptcy statistics, court opinions, and legislative news.

http://realestate.findlaw.com/

FindLaw is a general site that links to primary legal sources, government resources, and related FindLaw pages. This site provides easily understandable overviews of real estate principles. By going into the "Legal Help and Resources" section, you can access state property and real estate laws.

http://www.law.cornell.edu/

This is the site of the Legal Information Institute (LII)., You can access LII's legal encyclopedia, which provides articles and definitions pertaining to various real property subjects. The site also links to state property law statutes.

REVIEW QUESTIONS

1. Distinguish between the following:
   a. Littoral rights and riparian rights
   b. Separate property and community property
   c. Freehold estates and leasehold estates
2. Explain how one determines whether an item is a fixture.
3. List and explain the basic ownership rights acquired when purchasing real property.
4. Distinguish among (a) a tenancy in common, (b) a Joint Tenancy, and (c) a tenancy by the entirety.
5. List and explain the four basic leasehold estates.

DISCUSSION QUESTIONS

1. What do you think of the concept of adverse possession? Do you agree with those who advocate that those who sleep on their rights should lose them? Why or why not?
2. In community property states, each spouse owns one-half of property acquired during marriage and from the efforts of either spouse. With property held as tenants by the entirety, each spouse owns 100 percent of the property and has right of survivorship. Which form of spousal property ownership do you think is more appropriate? Why?
3. Mary is the mother of two adult children, Ann and Bill. She wants her house to pass to them outside of probate, so she decides to deed her house to herself and Ann and Bill as joint tenants with right of survivorship. Ann is engaged to be married, and Bill currently is single. What problems can you foresee with this arrangement?
4. As noted in this chapter, most states have abandoned the concepts of dower and curtesy and have instead adopted the concept of the spousal elective share, which permits a surviving spouse to elect to take a statutorily set percentage of a deceased spouse's property rather than what was left to the surviving spouse in a will. Do you agree with this concept? What if the deceased spouse preferred to leave property held in severalty to other family members? Shouldn't the

deceased spouse be allowed to dispose of his or her own property as he or she deems fit? Why or why not?

5. As its name implies, the Bankruptcy Abuse Prevention and Consumer Protection Act of 2005 attempts to address abuses of the legal system by bankruptcy filers and hold them more accountable for their financial responsibilities. The Act has provisions pertaining to various areas of real estate, including homestead. What impact, if any, do you see this having on real estate sales throughout the country?

ETHICAL QUESTION

Client Marjorie Greenway recently purchased a house, and your supervising attorney handled the closing. Marjorie telephones to say that she wants to file for your state's homestead tax exemption. She asks you where she must go to file and the procedures she must follow to file for the exemption. You are thoroughly familiar with the procedure. May you answer her question?

Slossberg Law Office on CourseMate

Please go to www.cengagebrain.com to log into CourseMate, access the Slossberg Law Office, and work on your client files. Each module corresponds to a chapter in the text. Within each module, you will be provided with instructions by the supervising attorney. You are asked to keep track of time spent on time sheets. The documents produced through working on client files in the law office can then be compiled into a portfolio of final work product.

CourseMate

The available CourseMate for this text has an interactive eBook and interactive learning tools, including flash cards, quizzes, and more. To learn more about this resource and access free demo CourseMate resources, including the Slossberg Law Office, go to www.cengagebrain.com, and search for this book. To access CourseMate materials that you have purchased, go to login.cengagebrain.com.

Categories of Real Property

3

CHAPTER OBJECTIVES

Upon completion of this chapter, the student will:

- Understand the distinctions between a condominium and a cooperative
- Know the major documents required for creating a condominium
- Understand the concept of planned unit developments
- Know the factors that must be considered when purchasing various types of residential and commercial property

Introduction

Real property may be purchased for residential use, for commercial use, or for a combination of these. As a paralegal, you may be called upon to assist in a variety of real estate transactions that require knowledge of the special factors influencing the sale and purchase of different categories of real property. The concerns of a prospective purchaser of a single-family home will differ from those of a prospective purchaser of a strip center. The sale of a condominium will require different procedures than the sale of a cooperative.

This chapter introduces you to various types of real property, both residential and commercial. It focuses on the factors that must be considered in each type of transaction, an understanding of which will aid you in drafting or reviewing the contract for sale and purchase. Additionally, this chapter discusses the mechanics of creating and operating certain types of residential communities: condominiums, cooperatives, and planned unit developments.

Knowledge of the manner in which these communities are created and operated is important for several reasons. Your law firm may represent a developer who is developing a condominium project, and your supervising attorney may require your assistance in drafting the documents used in creating and operating the condominium. Your law firm may represent a condominium association, the body of which oversees the operation of a condominium and enforces its rules, in which instance knowledge of your state condominium statutes will enable you to assist your supervising attorney in addressing the client's objectives. On the other hand, your firm may be representing a purchaser who is planning on buying a condominium or home in a planned unit development. You may be asked by your supervising attorney to review the requisite documents to determine whether there are any restrictions that would impinge on his or her enjoyment and use of the property.

Residential Property

In General

American families are more transient than they were several decades ago. When considering the purchase of a residential property, purchasers must take into account not only their immediate personal needs but also the resale potential of the real property in question. Residential real estate includes single-family homes in traditional suburban neighborhoods, houses in planned unit developments, condominiums, and cooperatives. The purchase of each of these types of properties has distinct advantages and disadvantages. There are some general considerations, however, for the purchase of any type of residential property.

The purchase of a home is a major commitment and responsibility. The ability to obtain satisfactory financing for the purchase is a primary concern, and prior to undertaking a serious search for residential property, prospective purchasers should take steps to prequalify for a mortgage loan. No prospective purchaser should enter into a contract for sale and purchase without ensuring the inclusion of a provision that makes closing on the property contingent upon the obtaining of satisfactory financing. Prospective purchasers should take into account not only the purchase price of the property but also the other costs associated with property ownership. For example, there is the cost for any renovations the purchaser plans on making to the property. Additionally, there are the costs of utilities, maintenance, and homeowners' insurance. A prospective purchaser will want to obtain copies of average utility bills from the seller as well as copies of any lawn care or other maintenance-related expenses.

When evaluating the costs of home ownership, the purchaser should also understand that certain tax benefits are associated with home ownership. The loan interest on mortgage loans is tax deductible, as are loan origination fees and real property taxes.

Further, the *Taxpayer Relief Act of 1997* allows property owners to exclude up to $250,000 of gain ($500,000 for married couples filing a joint return) realized on the sale or exchange of a principal residence. This exclusion is allowed each time a property owner sells or exchanges a principal residence (with the caveat that the exclusion may not be claimed more frequently than once every two years). Additionally, the property owner is not required to reinvest the sales proceeds in a new residence to claim this exclusion. In order to be eligible for the exclusion, the property owner must have owned and used the residence as his or her primary residence for a combined period of at least two years out of the five years prior to the sale or exchange.

Location impacts the present and resale values of the property. The prospective purchaser of a home should check to see how close to major roadways and shopping the subject property is located. How close is it to where the purchaser works? Is it located in a good school district? This is important even if the purchaser does not have school-age children because location within a good school district will be a marketing advantage for resale.

Is the property located within or without city limits? This will impact the real property taxes on the property, as each local governing authority may impose real property taxes. Thus, property located within city limits will have both city and county real property tax assessments imposed. The prospective purchaser will want to obtain copies of the real property tax assessments from the seller.

Is the property located within an area that is zoned strictly residential, or is there mixed zoning? Zoning may be a major consideration for a purchaser who plans on using a portion of his or her home for business purposes. Conversely, if the property is located in a mixed zoning area, there may be commercial entities located nearby that adversely affect the noise and traffic conditions in the area. Additionally, the purchaser should consider whether the property is located in a flood-prone area, which would require the obtaining of flood insurance.

The prospective purchaser will be concerned about the condition of the premises. This is always an important consideration, but it is of particular concern if purchasing a foreclosed property. If a homeowner cannot make monthly mortgage loan payments or has abandoned the property, the chances that internal and external aspects of the property have been maintained tend to decrease. Are the plumbing, mechanical, and electrical systems in good condition? What is the condition of the roof? Have termite and mold inspections been done? What are the conditions of the interior and exterior walls?

The prospective purchaser should consider the resale prices of similar properties in the neighborhood. Is the subject property the most expensive property on the street or in the neighborhood? If so, he or she may find it more difficult to sell it down the road. Purchasers often are advised to "purchase the best neighborhood or area they can afford" rather than the best house.

Common-Interest Communities

Many purchasers decide to purchase residences in *common-interest communities*. These communities include condominiums, cooperatives, and planned unit developments. Ownership within these communities entails living in a community environment in which there are certain trade-offs. A purchaser looking to own a residence who wants accessibility of recreational amenities yet does not want the responsibility of maintaining the grounds surrounding his or her living quarters may opt for one of these types of common-interest communities. In doing so, however, the purchaser will be required to pay a proportionate share of the assessments for maintaining the grounds and recreational facilities. Additionally, he or she may face certain restrictions that run the gamut from the way in which he or she may decorate the exterior of the residence to the type of vehicle permitted in the parking lot.

State statutory law governs common-interest communities. Some states have adopted the Uniform Condominium Act, a handful of states have adopted the Uniform Common Interest Ownership Act, and others have statutes not patterned after either of these Acts.

The *Uniform Condominium Act* was originally approved by the National Conference of Commissioners on Uniform State Laws in 1977 and amended in 1980. A *uniform law* is a law in a specific subject area—in this instance, condominium law—that is approved by the National Conference of Commissioners on Uniform States Laws and is adopted in whole or in part by individual states. At the time of this writing, thirteen states have adopted the Uniform Condominium Act. This Act governs the creation, management, and termination of condominium associations and provides certain protections for condominium purchasers. It requires disclosure of the terms of sale, the condition of the condominium properties, the financial condition of the condominium association, and any restrictions imposed. It gives condominium associations a limited lien priority status for unpaid assessments.

Additionally, it provides protections for tenants in residential units that are to be converted to condominiums. Under this Act, tenants must be given notice at least 120 days before they must vacate the property and have a right to purchase for 60 days after notice is given.

At the time of this writing, eight states have enacted the *Uniform Common Interest Ownership Act.* This Act was completed in 1982 and amended in 1994 and 2008. It governs the creation, management, and termination of condominiums, planned unit developments, and cooperatives. It provides for disclosure of important facts pertaining to the property at time of sale to the purchaser and gives the purchaser the right to rescind the contract for purchase and sale. Additionally, it provides for the escrow of deposits.

The following sections discuss the creation and operation of condominiums, cooperatives, and planned unit developments and explain the special factors inherent in these forms of ownership.

Condominiums

A **condominium** is a form of ownership in which the property owner owns the interior of his or her unit, plus an undivided interest, expressed as a percentage interest, in the common elements of the condominium complex. The unit owner is given a deed to the property upon closing and is responsible for his or her own real property taxes.

The **common elements** are those areas that all of the owners use in common, such as the grounds on which the condominium building is located, the roof, the exterior walls and structural components, the parking lot, and any recreational facilities (for example, swimming pools, tennis courts, clubhouses). Areas that benefit less than all of the condominium unit owners (for example, assigned parking spaces, storage facilities) are sometimes referred to as **limited common elements**. The cost of the upkeep of the common elements and the real estate taxes on them is assessed proportionately to each unit owner, who pays condominium assessments monthly, quarterly, semiannually, or annually to the condominium association or its management agent.

Because condominium ownership assumes living in a communal environment, rules and regulations promoting the general good for the condominium as a whole are upheld by a **condominium association,** comprised of members who are unit owners. Should a unit owner fail to abide by these rules, the association may fine the unit owner. Further, should a unit owner fail to pay any assessments, the association may place a lien on the delinquent owner's unit and foreclose on it in a manner similar to the foreclosure of a mortgage.

A condominium is more than just a structure; it is a creature of statute. Every state has statutes that govern both the creation and the operation of condominiums. In addition to state laws, there are federal laws that impact condominiums. If the condominium units are marketed in any state other than the state in which they are located, the sale of the condominiums must comply with the requirements of the Securities Act of 1933 and any other pertinent regulations promulgated by the Securities and Exchange Commission.

Creation. A condominium is legally created when a **declaration of condominium,** sometimes referred to as a *master deed,* is prepared, signed by the developer, and

condominium: A form of ownership in which the property owner owns the interior of a unit, plus an undivided interest, expressed as a percentage interest, in the common elements of the condominium complex.

common elements: Those areas of a condominium development that all of the owners use in common, such as the grounds on which the condominium building is located, the roof, the exterior walls and structural components, the parking lot, and any recreational facilities.

limited common elements: Areas that benefit fewer than all of the condominium unit owners, such as assigned parking spaces or storage facilities.

condominium association: An association comprised of unit owners that sets rules and manages the operation of the condominium.

declaration of condominium: The document that legally creates a condominium.

recorded in the land records for the county in which the condominium is located. Although the statutory requirements for the contents of a declaration vary from state to state, most states require that a declaration include the following:

1. The name of the condominium
2. The name of the county in which the condominium is located
3. The legal description of the condominium
4. A statement of the maximum number of units that will be included in the condominium
5. A description of the boundaries of each unit
6. A description of any limited common elements
7. A description of any development rights reserved by the developer of the condominium (this is particularly pertinent if the developer is building the condominium complex in stages or phases)
8. A statement indicating the allocation of percentage interests in the common elements to each unit
9. A statement indicating the voting rights of each unit
10. Any restrictions on use, occupancy, and transfer of units
11. A plat or plan of the condominium

The plat or plan that is attached as an exhibit to the declaration is a general schematic map of the entire condominium. It shows the location and dimensions of the vertical and horizontal boundaries of each condominium unit and each unit's identifying number, the location and dimensions of all common and limited common elements, and all easements burdening the property (for example, utility easements, cable easements). A sample declaration of condominium is provided in Exhibit 3–2, at the end of this chapter.

The next step is creating a condominium association to oversee the operation of the condominium. The condominium association generally is organized as a not-for-profit corporation and therefore, like other corporations, is not legally created until its articles of incorporation are filed with the state filing authority. The association must be organized no later than the date the first condominium unit is conveyed. If the developer is creating a multiphased condominium, the developer often creates a **master association,** sometimes referred to as an *umbrella association,* that provides management services and decision-making functions to smaller condominiums. The membership of the association consists of all of the unit owners, who elect an executive board of directors to oversee the condominium operations. The Uniform Condominium Act and most state statutes recognize the necessity of allowing the developer, called the *declarant* or *sponsor,* to control the association during the developmental phases of a condominium project. The developer then relinquishes control after all or a certain percentage of the units have been sold.

The powers granted to condominium associations by state statute may vary. However, they usually include the powers set forth in section 3-102 of the Uniform Condominium Act, which provides associations with the power to adopt and amend the bylaws and the rules and regulations, to adopt and amend budgets, to hire and discharge employees, to make contracts and incur liabilities, and to exercise many other powers, including all those necessary for the governance and operation of the association.

master association: An umbrella association that provides management services and decision-making functions to smaller condominiums.

The third requirement is the preparation of condominium bylaws. The bylaws set forth the governing procedures of the condominium. Unlike the articles of incorporation, the bylaws are not recorded in the public records. Because the articles of incorporation become public knowledge when recorded, most attorneys drafting them prefer to keep them skeletal, containing only those provisions required by state statute. All other matters pertaining to the operation of the condominium are set forth in the bylaws. Generally, the bylaws of a condominium association include the following:

1. The number of directors on the executive board and the titles of the officers of the association
2. The election by the executive board of the officers of the association
3. The qualifications, powers, duties, and term of office of the directors on the executive board
4. The manner of electing and removing directors and officers and the manner of filling vacancies
5. Which, if any, of its powers the executive board or officers may delegate to others
6. Which of its officers may prepare, execute, certify, and record amendments to the declaration
7. The method of amending the bylaws
8. Any other matters the association deems necessary and appropriate

Operation. Once the condominium's executive board is elected, its primary duties are twofold: (1) to ensure that all unit owners abide by the association's rules and regulations that have been promulgated for the common good of the condominium community and (2) to oversee the maintenance, repair, and replacement of the common elements. To perform this latter duty, the board must develop a budget that covers the normal, everyday expenses of maintaining the common areas and that also sets aside reserves for those repairs or replacements that occur less often, such as repaving the parking lots, painting the exterior of the buildings, or resurfacing the roof. The association must obtain property insurance on the common elements insuring against all risks of physical damage. Additionally, it must obtain liability insurance covering all occurrences commonly insured against for death, bodily injury, and property damage arising out of, or in connection with, the use, ownership, or maintenance of the common elements. The monies to cover all these expenses come from assessing each unit owner for his or her proportionate share. The budgets on which these assessments are based are devised annually and list each expense, in terms of both monthly cost and annual cost, such as the sample budget provided in Exhibit 3–1.

As noted previously, should a unit owner fail to make an assessment payment, the condominium association may file a lien against the unit and foreclose that lien in a manner similar to a lender foreclosing on a defaulted mortgage loan. The lien may cover not only the delinquent assessment amount but also fees, late charges, fines, and interest. Further, section 3.116(b) of the Uniform Condominium Act provides that the association's lien on a unit takes priority over all other liens and encumbrances except those recorded prior to the recordation of the declaration, those imposed for real estate taxes or other governmental assessments or charges against the unit, and first mortgages recorded before the date the assessment became

Budget for condominium association **EXHIBIT 3–1**

RIVERDALE CONDOMINIUM ASSOCIATION, INC.
A Corporation Not for Profit
2015 BUDGET

		Monthly	Annually
I.	**Expenses for the Association and condominium**		
A.	Administration of Association	$ 225.00	$ 2,700.00
B.	Management fees	1,200.00	14,400.00
C.	Building cleaning and maintenance	248.00	2,976.00
D.	Lawn and property maintenance	750.00	9,000.00
E.	Expenses on Association property		
	(1) Taxes	93.00	1,116.00
	(2) Cleaning and maintenance	90.00	1,080.00
F.	Electricity (common elements)	563.00	6,756.00
G.	Water, sewer and garbage service	1,350.00	16,200.00
H.	Insurance	938.00	11,256.00
I.	Miscellaneous		
	(1) Annual filing fee with Bureau of Condominiums	10.00	120.00
	(2) Professional services (legal and accounting)	400.00	4,800.00
J.	Security provisions	.00	.00
K.	Pest control	203.00	2,436.00
	TOTAL	$6,070.00	$72,840.00
II.	**Reserves**		
A.	Building painting	$ 594.00	$ 7,128.00
B.	Pavement resurfacing	120.00	1,440.00
C.	Roof replacement	450.00	5,400.00
D.	Miscellaneous reserves	113.00	1,356.00
	TOTAL	$1,276.00	$15,324.00

BUDGET NOTES

1. The expenses for individual units are as follows:
   (a) A-type units — $ 269.64
   (b) B-type units — 274.65
   (c) C-type units — 285.75
2. The balance in the reserve accounts of the Association at the beginning of the current budget year is as follows:
   (a) Building painting — $ 42,768.00
   (b) Pavement resurfacing — 12,960.00
   (c) Roof replacement — 43,200.00
   (d) Miscellaneous reserves — 6,750.00
3. The formula for each reserve category is based on the following estimates:
   (a) Building painting to occur every eight years, and one-eighth of the total estimated cost is allocated to each fiscal year. Six of the eight years are currently on deposit.
   (b) Pavement resurfacing to occur every fifteen years, and one-fifteenth of the total estimated cost is allocated to each fiscal year. Nine of the fifteen years are currently on deposit.
   (c) Roof replacement to occur every twenty years, and one-twentieth of the total estimated cost is allocated to each fiscal year. Eight of the twenty years are currently on deposit.
   (d) Miscellaneous items of deferred maintenance and capital expenditures are based upon the need for such expenditures as determined over the previous ten years of the Association and to cover needs not specifically identified in paragraphs (a), (b), and (c).

delinquent. Interestingly, this section of the Act includes a caveat regarding first mortgages. It states that in regard to a prior first mortgage (that is, one given by the unit owner to a lender when financing the purchase of the unit), the condominium association's lien has priority for six months' assessments based on the periodic budget. This means that in those states whose statutes parallel the Uniform Condominium Act, a lender holding a first mortgage on a condominium unit whose owner is delinquent in maintenance payments would have to pay the six months' assessments if it wanted to prevent the foreclosure on the unit by the condominium association. If it did not do so, the association would have priority over the lender with respect to any monies realized from bringing a foreclosure action.

In the recent economic climate, condominium associations and unit owners have struggled due to a sharp increase in maintenance payment delinquencies. When fellow unit owners do not pay maintenance assessments, this causes a ripple effect throughout a condominium community. Condominium associations may have rules that permit the imposition of fines for late payments, but unit owners who cannot make their periodic maintenance assessments cannot pay the fines. The increased costs of using legal counsel to pursue collection and foreclosure measures against these unit owners fall on the shoulders of the entire community. Threatening a delinquent unit owner with a lien against the property and possible foreclosure may be ineffective because in most instances that unit owner already is facing a mortgage foreclosure. Additionally, if the association does foreclose on a unit and take legal title to it, the lien it had on the property is extinguished, and it cannot recover those past-due payments. If a lender forecloses on the property, as mentioned above, there may be a possibility of recouping some of the loss.

Increasing the periodic maintenance assessments to cover legal costs and the loss of income caused by delinquencies may put current paying unit owners in financial jeopardy. If an association chooses instead to cut back on services, repairs, and preventative maintenance to keep assessment costs level, the association's board may be in breach of its fiduciary duties and state statutes.

While some condominium communities do face the difficulties noted, others are financially stable. If the executive board finds there are surplus funds left over at the end of a fiscal year, the board, unless otherwise stated in the declaration, typically uses them for the prepayment of reserves and credits any remaining funds to the accounts of the unit owners to reduce their future assessments.

To aid the executive board in carrying out its activities, the board may create committees to oversee various functions, such as a screening committee to screen potential new owners or a development committee to oversee the addition or expansion of the recreational facilities. The board may hire a real estate management company to oversee the daily operations of the condominium, to collect the assessments, and to hire the contractors and subcontractors to carry out the maintenance and repair work required. If the board hires employees directly to carry out these tasks, it must take care of such matters as workers' compensation and unemployment insurance.

Purchase and Sale. Prior to purchasing a condominium unit, a prospective purchaser will be given a set of condominium documents to review, containing the declaration, the articles of incorporation of the association, and the bylaws. Most states have statutes providing a "cooling off" period that allows a prospective purchaser a statutorily specified number of days after receiving the documents to cancel a contract for sale and purchase without any penalty. During this period, it is advisable for the prospective purchaser also to obtain copies of minutes of past condominium association meetings and bring these and the condominium documents to an attorney for review. A review of the minutes will indicate whether any recent decisions have been made to increase assessments or to amend the condominium documents. The minutes also may contain discussions and statistics regarding the number of foreclosed units in the condominium development. If state law requires association audits, it is advisable to obtain any audited financial statements. These statements should include a section on assessments receivable that will provide valuable information on outstanding maintenance fees. The attorney, in turn, may turn the documents over to you, the paralegal, to scrutinize and prepare a summary of use restrictions, the purchaser's voting rights as a unit owner, and his or her responsibilities for regular and special assessments for the attorney to review with the purchaser.

The prospective purchaser will need to know of any restrictions imposed on his or her use of the property. For example, a unit owner often is prohibited from making any alterations to the exterior of the property, including the addition of porches and/or the addition of decorative elements, without first obtaining association approval. The purchaser may be buying the unit as an investment. In this situation, particular attention should be paid to those sections of the rules and regulations pertaining to rental of the unit. Many condominium associations, to prevent transiency, limit the number of times a unit may be rented each year and may require leases no shorter than a specified period. Further, they often require the submission of the lease to the association for approval. In some instances, to purchase the unit the purchaser must be approved by a screening committee, and should he or she later wish to sell the unit, the screening committee will have to approve any prospective buyer. A number of condominiums impose restrictions on pets or on the types of motor vehicles allowed on the property. These and other use restrictions should be pointed out to the purchaser.

The purchaser of a condominium unit has many of the same concerns as the purchaser of other residential property, including financing, location, and other costs associated with home ownership such as real estate taxes and utilities. The following checklist should aid you in reviewing the matters to be considered when the firm's client is purchasing a condominium.

CONDOMINIUM CHECKLIST

1. Purchase price
2. Location
3. Financing
4. Condominium documents
   a. Receipt of all documents required by state statute
   b. Compliance of contents of documents with state statute
5. Condominium board approval through screening
6. Cost of real estate taxes (obtain prior tax bills from seller if not a new unit)
7. Cost of utilities (obtain prior utility bills from seller if not a new unit)
8. Cost of homeowners' and other insurance

9. Recreational facilities provided
    a. Clubhouse(s)
    b. Swimming pool(s)
    c. Tennis court(s)
    d. Golf course(s)
    e. Other
10. Control of condominium board
    a. Developer-controlled; if so, until when?
    b. Unit owner–controlled
11. Condominium assessments
    a. Current amount for regular assessments
    b. Any anticipated raises in assessments; if so, when and by how much?
    c. Last time special assessments were assessed and whether any are projected in the near future; if so, how much?
    d. Timing of assessment payments (for example, monthly, quarterly)
    e. Any late fees charged for late payment; amount of fee; any grace period
    f. Lien rights of association for delinquent assessments
12. Voting rights
    a. Do all unit owners have an equal vote?
    b. Do unit owners vote on proposed budgets?
    c. Do unit owners vote on amendments to condominium documents?
13. Use restrictions
    a. Restrictions on use of unit (for example, cannot use for business purposes)
    b. Restrictions on pets
    c. Restrictions on parking
    d. Restrictions on vehicles
    e. Restrictions on visitors
    f. Restrictions on transfer of unit
    g. Restrictions on leasing of unit
    h. Restrictions on decorating exterior of unit; balcony or porch usage
    i. Restrictions on right to make improvements
    j. Other
14. Responsibility for other contracts when purchasing, such as cable television contracts
15. Expansion by developer
    a. Timing of additional phases
    b. Number of units in each additional phase
    c. Architecture and aesthetics of building(s) in additional phase(s)
    d. Impact on unit owner's assessments
16. Fixtures included with the unit
17. Easements and other encumbrances

Cooperatives

cooperative: A multiunit building owned by a corporation. One purchases stock in the corporation, which entitles the purchaser of the stock to enter into a long-term lease with the corporation.

A **cooperative** is a multiunit building owned by a corporation. One does not purchase a unit within the building; rather, one purchases stock in the corporation. This entitles the purchaser of stock to enter into a long-term lease with the corporation. Acquiring a larger unit often entails purchasing a larger number of shares. The corporation owns not only the multiunit building but also the land on which it is built, together with all common elements shared by the shareholder-tenants. The law governing cooperatives generally is state corporate law.

As in the case of other corporations, the shareholders are the owners of the corporation. In this instance, the shareholders are owners of the cooperative rather than owners of individual units. Just as in other corporations, shareholders of a cooperative control the corporation indirectly by electing a board of directors to manage the cooperative. Similarly, the shares of stock in the cooperative are transferable, just as stock in any corporation is transferable. A shareholder in a cooperative can increase his or her share of ownership by acquiring additional shares of stock.

Because ownership in a cooperative pertains to the ownership of shares of stock, the cooperative owner is a purchaser of personal property rather than a purchaser of real property. His or her real property interest is a leasehold interest. Thus, the documents involved in this type of transaction differ from those in other real estate transactions. In most real estate transactions, the document evincing ownership is the deed. Here the document allowing use of the premises is a long-term lease, and the documents evincing the ownership interest in the cooperative building are the stock certificates.

Individuals residing in the units are not taxed individually for real property assessments. The building as a whole is assessed and taxed. The shareholders each pay periodic assessments to the corporation to cover the maintenance of the property, the real property taxes, insurance, and the mortgage payments on the building. To purchase the property and construct the cooperative building, the corporation will have given a mortgage to a lending institution, which will be a first mortgage on the property. All shareholders are responsible for this first mortgage. If an individual purchaser of an interest in the cooperative needs to obtain additional financing to purchase his or her shares or to make improvements in his or her unit, the mortgage instrument he or she gives to a lender is considered a second mortgage. As security for this second mortgage, the purchaser pledges his or her long-term lease and shares of stock.

Mortgage liens (in the event of failure to pay by the individual with a second mortgage loan) are liens against the whole building. Therefore, financing is more complicated in this type of transaction. Failure of one or more individuals to pay assessments in a timely manner may cause the corporation to default on its obligations, and the result may be a foreclosure on the corporation that affects all shareholders unless other shareholders pay additional sums to make up for the delinquency. Because the financial viability of the cooperative is so dependent on the communal responsibility of the shareholders, prospective cooperative owners typically face tougher screening committees than prospective condominium owners. As in the case of condominiums, cooperatives have strict rules and regulations by which each tenant must abide.

A client considering cooperative ownership should understand the distinctions between cooperatives and condominiums, particularly the fact that he or she will not own an individual unit and that there is collective responsibility for mortgage and tax payments. Just as in the case of a prospective purchaser of a condominium, the rules and regulations of the cooperative must be scrutinized. The attorney for the prospective purchaser will want to inspect the original prospectus and all amendments to it as well as the corporation's records and financial statements. Inspection of the records includes inspection of the corporation's minutes. The minutes may reveal plans to undertake repairs or refurbishment that translates into increased costs for each member of the corporation. Further, they may reveal delinquencies in assessment payments. These should be thoroughly investigated prior to purchasing shares and signing a lease. The following case illustrates the possible repercussions in cooperative ownership of defaulting on one's financial obligations.

CASE: *Hochman v. 35 Park W. Corp.*

293 A.D.2d 650 (N.Y. 2002)

In an action, inter alia, to recover damages for injury to property rights, the plaintiff Aaron Hochman appeals from an order of the Supreme Court, Kings County (G. Aronin, J.), dated February 23, 2001, which granted the defendant's motion for summary judgment dismissing the complaint.

Ordered that the order is affirmed, with costs.

In 1991 the plaintiff Aaron Hochman (hereinafter the plaintiff) pledged the shares of his cooperative apartment to Citibank as collateral for a business loan. After the plaintiff's company defaulted on its obligations to Citibank, the bank took possession of the collateral pledged to secure the loan, and new stock certificates and a new proprietary lease were issued to Citibank's nominee. In 1996 the plaintiff entered into a stipulation of settlement with Citibank in which he agreed to pay the entire outstanding balance of the business loan. Pursuant to the stipulation, Citibank agreed, inter alia, to reconvey the plaintiff's cooperative shares and proprietary lease back to him. However, the transfer to the plaintiff was conditioned upon the consent of the defendant cooperative corporation. In the event that such consent could not be obtained, Citibank agreed to pay the plaintiff $460,000 for the apartment, less the maintenance and other expenses paid by its nominee. The cooperative's Board of Directors denied the plaintiff's request to approve the transfer of the shares and proprietary lease back to him, due to his alleged former financial difficulties and history of failing to make maintenance payments. According to the plaintiff, the apartment was later sold for $800,000. The plaintiff then commenced this action against the cooperative corporation, seeking, inter alia, damages for its refusal to ratify Citibank's agreement to reconvey the apartment shares and lease back to him. Over three years later, the defendant moved for summary judgment, contending, inter alia, that its decision denying him permission to reacquire his rights to the apartment came within the purview of the business judgment rule. The Supreme Court granted the defendant's motion for summary judgment, and we affirm.

Contrary to the plaintiff's contention, the Supreme Court correctly found that the business judgment rule was the proper standard to apply in reviewing the defendant's decision. Although the plaintiff correctly asserts that he had

a statutory right to redeem his cooperative shares from Citibank until the bank disposed of the shares (see UCC 9-506), it is undisputed that when Citibank took possession of the plaintiff's collateral, new stock certificates and a new proprietary lease were issued to its nominee. Accordingly, the plaintiff's request to have the shares and lease conveyed back to him came within the scope of the provision of the proprietary lease which prohibits assignment of the lease without the written consent of the cooperative board. Thus, the decision whether to permit the requested assignment was within the board's authority.

Furthermore, the defendant's motion for summary judgment was properly granted pursuant to the business judgment rule, which prohibits judicial inquiry into decisions made by cooperative or condominium governing boards which are "taken in good faith in the exercise of honest judgment" (*Matter of Levandusky v. One Fifth Ave. Apt. Corp.*, 75 N.Y.2d 530, 538, quoting *Auerbach v. Bennett*, 47 N.Y.2d 619, 629). Pursuant to the rule, the party seeking review of a governing board's actions has the burden of demonstrating a breach of fiduciary duty, through evidence of unlawful discrimination, self-dealing, or other misconduct by board members (*see Matter of Levandusky v. One Fifth Ave. Apt. Corp.*, supra at 539, *Kleinman v. Point Seal Restoration Corp.*, 267 A.D.2d 430; *Jones v. Surrey Coop. Apts.*, 263 A.D.2d 33, 36). In support of its motion for summary judgment, the defendant made a prima facie showing that the board members acted in good faith and within the scope of its authority in denying the plaintiff's request to have his apartment shares and proprietary lease reconveyed to him. In opposition to the motion, the plaintiff failed to submit any evidence to support his conclusory assertion that board members engaged in misconduct and self-dealing. Thus, the defendant was entitled to summary judgment (*see Kleinman v. Point Seal Restoration Corp.*, supra; *Cooper v. 6 W. 20th St. Tenants Corp.*, 258 A.D.2d 362; *Jones v. Surrey Coop. Apts.*, supra).

The plaintiff's remaining contentions are without merit.

S. Miller, J.P., Krausman, Goldstein and Cozier, J.J., concur.

(continued)

Case Questions

1. Note that in the above case, the plaintiff did not default on a mortgage loan, but rather on a business loan for which he had pledged his shares of his cooperative apartment as collateral. In light of this fact, do you think the cooperative association was within its rights to refuse to ratify Citibank's agreement to reconvey the apartment and lease back to him? Why or why not? Do you think the business judgment rule gives associations too broad an authority? Why or why not?

2. If, instead of living in a cooperative apartment, the plaintiff had purchased a condominium and had pledged the condominium property as collateral for the business loan, then defaulted on the loan, and finally entered into a stipulation of settlement with the bank, how would the outcome differ from the outcome in the above case?

3. In the above case, Citibank agreed in the stipulation agreement to pay the plaintiff $460,000 for the apartment, less the maintenance and other expenses paid by its nominee, should the cooperative association refuse its consent to the transfer of the shares and proprietary lease to the plaintiff. The apartment was later sold for $800,000. Under the circumstances, should the plaintiff have been entitled to all or part of the profits on the sale of the apartment? Why or why not?

Reprinted from Westlaw with permission of Thomson Reuters.

Time Shares

Time share ownership is the purchase of the right to use real property for a limited, specified period of time each year. Other time share owners purchase the right to use the same property for varying time segments during the year. Each time share owner becomes a tenant in common with the other time share owners.

Time share owners usually purchase time shares because they are located in resort areas and the purchasers want assurance of regular, prepaid vacation spots. Should the owner of a time share choose not to use his or her allotted time spot, he or she may lease the property to another for the time period or partake in a time share exchange. For example, Ann might own a time share in Florida, while Roger owns one in Aspen for the same time period. Ann and Roger might swap their time shares for the year so that Roger can get a suntan and Ann can have a ski holiday.

Although one may purchase a time share in a cooperative or a home, most time shares involve condominiums. Many state statutes do not include provisions pertaining to time share ownership. The Uniform Condominium Act, however, provides that, if the declaration of condominium states that ownership or occupancy of any units is or may be in time shares, the condominium documents must include the following information:

1. The number and identity of units in which time shares may be created
2. The total number of time shares that may be created
3. The minimum duration of any time shares that may be created
4. The extent to which the creation of time shares will or may affect the enforceability of the association's lien for assessments

Just as in the case of the purchase of a condominium, the prospective time share purchaser is given a statutorily prescribed period of time in which to review the relevant documents and rescind a contract for sale and purchase.

Planned Unit Developments

A **planned unit development (PUD)** is also referred to as a *planned community* or a *cluster development*. It is a subdivision containing individual lots with common areas controlled by a homeowners' association. Although the association usually

time share: The purchase of the right to use real property for a limited, specified period of time each year.

planned unit development (PUD): A subdivision containing individual lots with common areas controlled by a homeowners' association.

takes the form of a nonprofit corporation, it may be organized as a for-profit entity. The association is comprised of members who are homeowners within the subdivision. The common areas are owned not by the property owners but rather by the association as a distinct entity. Statutes pertaining to planned unit developments have been adopted in many states.

The homes within a planned unit development may be uniform or mixed. For example, one might find attached town houses and large detached homes within the same development. The shared common areas may include some of the same recreational facilities found in condominium developments, such as shared swimming pools, tennis courts, and clubhouses.

A planned unit development is created by the recordation of a subdivision plat in the county in which the subdivision property is located. The subdivision map is a plat map (discussed in detail in Chapter 5) that indicates the property set aside to be dedicated for public use; the location of each lot, with the demarcation of lot size; the location and description of all common areas; and the location and description of all easements and other encumbrances.

In addition, a **declaration of covenants and restrictions** is recorded. This declaration is very similar to the declaration of condominium recorded to create a condominium because it covers such topics as property ownership, land use restrictions, membership and voting rights, and assessments for common expenses. Many homeowners' associations have architectural committees through which plans to renovate, expand, or construct on vacant lots must be submitted and approved. Therefore, the land use restrictions may be relaxed or stringent.

Membership in the homeowners' association usually is automatic upon purchasing a lot in the subdivision. Members are assessed their proportionate share of the expenses for the maintenance of the common areas. As with condominium ownership, should a homeowner within a planned unit development fall delinquent in his or her assessment payments, the homeowners' association may place a lien on his or her property and foreclose.

To limit the homeowners' liability in common areas, the homeowners' association is created as a separate legal entity by the filing of articles of incorporation with the state filing authority. The functions of the association are governed by its bylaws. Unless special state statutes exist, state corporate law governs the association.

The purchaser of a home or vacant lot within a planned unit development has to consider many factors prior to purchase. He or she may hire an attorney to review the declaration of covenants and restrictions to determine whether any of the land use restrictions imposed will be problematic. Figures and payment periods of assessments should be ascertained. If the purchaser is buying a vacant lot, local ordinances must be researched as well as the architectural standards set forth by the association's architectural committee. Further, if all the land is not yet developed within the subdivision, the purchaser will want information concerning future building projects within the community and how the future development will impact the resale value of his or her property as well as the cost of future assessments.

Commercial Property

declaration of covenants and restrictions: A document setting forth the rights and restrictions of property owners within a planned unit development.

Commercial real estate transactions often are more complex procedures than residential transactions. These transactions may require more complicated financing methods than the purchase of a single-family home. (These transactions are discussed in detail in Chapter 14.) Increased government controls regarding zoning, environmental, and energy considerations tend to complicate matters. Items to be taken into consideration in a commercial real estate transaction are enumerated in the following checklist. Many of these items can be addressed as contingencies in the contract for sale and purchase.

COMMERCIAL PROPERTY CHECKLIST

1. Zoning and local ordinances
2. Location for traffic
3. Traffic count
4. Visibility
5. Competition
6. Availability and cost of utilities
7. Water supply facilities
8. Sewage disposal facilities
9. Expansion capability
10. Availability of rail, water, air, and other freight shipping facilities
11. Availability of concomitant or contributing businesses
12. Access for pedestrian patronage
13. Access for vehicular traffic
14. Parking
15. Character of neighborhood as affecting particular businesses
16. Population type and density
17. Source of labor and labor laws
18. Load-bearing qualities of the land
19. Soil conditions of the land
20. Drainage
21. Financing
22. Licenses
23. Taxes

Transportation; Demographics

Although not every one of the factors in the preceding checklist will pertain to every business, most of them are relevant to the purchase of commercial property. Certain factors may be of primary concern. For example, if the property is being sought as the location of an import-export business, transportation facilities will be of primary concern. In such a situation, the attorney for the prospective purchaser of the property should include a clause in the contract for sale and purchase that conditions the obligation to close on obtaining satisfactory agreements with rail-road officials, port officials, and so forth. The cost of fuel, for instance, for water transportation can be a major factor if most of the acquisitions or sales are shipped by water transportation. For other businesses, local demographics may be of utmost concern. If this is the case, the closing on a contract for sale and purchase should be conditioned on a satisfactory report from a professional business survey firm.

Load-Bearing Quality; Drainage

In some parts of the country, some of the factors to be considered in a commercial real estate transaction are of greater importance than others. For example, in parts of the country that contain much filled land, the load-bearing quality of the property is crucial. Commercial buildings generally are large, and the cost to fill in the area of land needed or to construct the building on pilings could be prohibitive. In these parts of the country, drainage also may be of greater concern. It is almost universal in contracts for sale and purchase of land for commercial property to include a provision that the contract is subject to positive results of engineering and soil tests.

Zoning; Local Ordinances

Although zoning and local ordinances play a role in the purchase of residential property, they often play an even greater role in the purchase of commercial property. If the zoning regulations are too restrictive, the plans of the purchaser may never see the light of day. Getting property rezoned is a lengthy and, at times, expensive procedure, as it may require the hiring of attorneys to aid in the process. Certainly, if rezoning would be necessary for the purposes of the purchaser, a contract for sale and purchase should make the sale conditional on the rezoning. Because rezoning can take so much time, the seller may not be willing to tie up a property for that length of time. On the other hand, if the property has been sitting for awhile without other prospects in sight, it is in the seller's best interests to help the purchaser obtain the rezoning required for the nature of the proposed business. A prospective purchaser also must consider local ordinances pertaining to setback requirements, advertising signage, and so forth.

Taxes

Real estate taxes are a consideration for purchasers of both residential and commercial properties, but because the value of the land and the improvements upon it is often greater with commercial properties, the taxes are also proportionately greater. Specialty use business taxes, such as hotel taxes or airport area taxes, may be imposed by state and local governmental authorities. If the property to be purchased is a lot upon which a structure will be built, the real estate tax assessment will indicate the tax only for the land itself and will not give the purchaser any idea about the tax assessment on the building to be constructed. Real property taxes are local taxes, assessed by the city and county and special taxing districts. All other factors remaining the same, a purchaser would be better off taxwise to purchase property that is located outside of city limits because then city taxes would not apply. In reality, this may not be feasible because, depending on the nature of the purchaser's business, the demographics might indicate that prospective customers are located within the city limits and prefer the convenience of shopping close to home. Even if the property desired is located outside of a city, an investigation should be made in regard to whether there is a probability that the unincorporated area will be annexed by the city or will be incorporated to form a new city. In addition to regular real property taxes, the purchaser must consider whether the city or county is planning any improvements in the area in which the property is located, requiring special assessments to be paid by local property owners.

Federal, State, and Local Laws

A thorough investigation prior to the purchase of commercial real estate must include researching state and federal environmental protection laws (discussed in detail in Chapter 4). This is of special concern for properties that will be used for industrial purposes. Further, labor laws must be checked to determine the cost of compliance with state and local laws affecting employees, such as unemployment compensation and workers' compensation.

Traffic Flow

Traffic flow is of greater concern to developers of shopping centers and office buildings than to developers of warehouses and industrial parks. A prospective purchaser who considers traffic flow of major importance should try to determine whether local or state authorities have any future plans that would alter the present traffic patterns surrounding and leading to the subject property. Those plans may include not only a rerouting that would decrease traffic flow but also road improvements that would alter ingress and egress to the property due to the placing of medial strips. Often the best way to obtain this information is by contacting the state department of transportation. The department should have surveys available showing highway design, traffic flow, intersections, interchange patterns, breaks, and crossovers in road patterns. Local police and fire departments may be asked to review and comment on proposed designs regarding traffic flow.

Licensing

Licensing compliance is required. Purchasers planning on constructing restaurants, entertainment establishments, hotels, and motels must check local licensing laws to determine the requirements for obtaining liquor licenses. State statutes and local ordinances regarding the sale of liquor should be checked. If the laws are too restrictive, another site may be more appropriate. Other businesses also require special licenses, including, but not limited to, banks, insurance companies, and cemeteries.

Competition

A further consideration is the competition factor. The purchaser may be looking to purchase a parcel of land that is part of a larger tract. The purchaser needs to consider not only the existing businesses in the vicinity but also the prospective purchasers of the rest of the seller's tract. A purchaser seeking to limit competition may attempt to negotiate with the seller to include a clause in the contract for sale and purchase that prevents the seller from selling the remainder of the parcel to businesses in direct competition with the purchaser. Many sellers are reluctant to do this, not wanting to limit their future sales opportunities.

Expansion

The prospective purchaser must contract with an eye not only to present but also to future needs. Should the purchaser wish to expand in the future, the property under contract should be conducive to this. If the seller owns not only the subject property but also surrounding properties, the purchaser may wish to include in the contract for sale and purchase an option to lease or purchase one or more of the surrounding parcels or a right of first refusal should the seller have prospects for the surrounding property.

Purchasing an Existing Business

Not all transactions involve the purchase of a tract of land for future development of a commercial enterprise. Many commercial transactions involve the purchase of an existing business or commercial structure. If the prospective purchaser is looking to purchase a retail or wholesale business, as well as the property on which the business is located, the purchaser must investigate not only the matters discussed previously but also federal and state commercial law. For example, most states have **bulk transfer laws** that pertain to the sale and purchase of all or substantially all of the inventory of a business. These laws generally require that the seller provide the prospective purchaser with an affidavit (a sworn statement) setting forth the name and address of each of the seller's creditors and the amount owed to each. Notice of the sale of the business must be given to all creditors within a statutorily prescribed time period before the closing of the sale. In some states, a notice must be published in a local newspaper of general circulation as well.

If the prospective purchaser is looking to buy an existing office building or shopping center, there is a great likelihood that there are existing leases for all or a portion of the space contained within the building or center. Before committing to the purchase, the prospective purchaser will want to examine the existing leases, noting the time period of each, the rent amount, and the security deposit paid. (A thorough discussion of commercial leases is found in Chapter 16.) The purchaser of a rented commercial property is purchasing that property for investment purposes. Therefore, in addition to inspecting the individual leases, the purchaser will need to make accurate income projections. In order to do this, the purchaser will need to obtain financial statements from the seller, inspect the seller's financial records, and review copies of any management and service contracts.

Finally, the purchaser of an existing business or commercial structure will want to consider any fixtures and personal property located on the property. As noted in Chapter 2, all personalty and fixtures should be described in great detail on an addendum to be attached to the contract for sale and purchase. Care must be taken here. Whereas in a residential transaction the fixtures and personalty are owned by the seller, the seller in a commercial transaction may be leasing much of the equipment located on the premises. Leased items must be clearly separated from other items.

Special Considerations for Shopping Centers

Shopping centers are distinct from strip centers or the groups of retail stores often found in the downtown business areas of a city. A *shopping center* is an integrated merchandising unit. The developer of a future center or the purchaser of an existing one is very concerned with obtaining the optimal tenant mix of goods and services to create the maximum drawing power from the community.

A primary draw to any shopping center is an anchor store. An **anchor store** is a major lessee—typically, a major department store or a supermarket. A prospective

bulk transfer laws: Laws that pertain to the sale and purchase of all or substantially all of the inventory of a business.

anchor store: A major lessee in a shopping center—typically, a major department store or, in the case of a neighborhood center, a supermarket.

purchaser of land for the development of a shopping center should condition the purchase on obtaining a commitment for occupancy by one or more anchor stores.

Traffic considerations are of great importance to developers of shopping centers as well as to city planners. The developer will be concerned with access to the site from major traffic arteries. City planners will not give site approval of a large shopping center until they are assured that surrounding traffic arteries will be able to absorb the traffic flowing into and out of the site. Additional traffic signals and turning lanes may need to be installed. The developer also must consider the location of interior drives of the shopping center tract. Because of the complexity of traffic concerns, a developer of a shopping center should have a traffic survey prepared by a qualified engineer and make closing on the tract of land contingent upon the approval of the survey by local governmental authorities.

Finally, the developer interested in building a shopping center and acting as lessor must consider the creation of a merchants' association. A purchaser of an existing shopping center must ascertain whether a merchants' association exists and obtain a copy of its bylaws (prior to contracting, if possible). A **merchants' association** is an organization consisting of the merchants of a shopping center whose primary purpose is the promotion of the common good of the center. It will work on joint advertising and special promotions. It will oversee the conduct of its members and ensure that all members are abiding by the policies set forth in its bylaws. The lessor of the center typically is expected to provide a certain percentage of the annual contributions made each year. A lessee's contributions are often proportionate to the square footage rented.

Acreage

Acreage is a tract of undeveloped real property, often purchased for development purposes but at times purchased for cultivation as farmlands, timberlands, groves, orchards, or grazing property. Large tracts are often sold at a specified price per acre rather than at a lump sum figure. A special problem occurs in areas in which large tracts of land include sections of inland water. The purchaser paying a price per acre does not want to pay for the area covered in water, yet he or she will want that area included in the deed conveying the property. The purchaser should negotiate a reduced price per acre for those acres that include inland water.

As in the case of commercial properties, zoning laws and local ordinances relating to the use of the property are of key concern to potential purchasers. A prospective purchaser with an eye toward development of acreage into a residential subdivision may find the ideal tract in an area zoned as agricultural. Having the area rezoned for residential purposes may be a time-consuming and laborious process. Further, land may not be subdivided without first obtaining the requisite subdivision approval from local governmental authorities. As in the case of a commercial purchaser, the purchaser of acreage with future plans for development should make the closing of the transaction contingent upon obtaining the necessary zoning and subdivision approvals.

The purchaser may require that the contract for sale and purchase include a provision whereby the seller must pay or share the costs incurred in preparing the documentation to be submitted to the local governing boards. As with any other

merchants' association: An organization consisting of the merchants of a shopping center whose primary purpose is the promotion of the common good of the center.

acreage: A tract of undeveloped real property.

real estate purchase, the prospective purchaser of acreage should also make closing on the property contingent on obtaining satisfactory financing. Additionally, the purchaser will need to have qualified personnel perform soil and other engineering tests to determine the condition of the property and its suitability for the intended building plans and should make the closing on the property contingent upon satisfactory engineering reports.

Because acreage tracts often are quite large in size, the question of access to public roads may become an issue. The purchaser will want to obtain assurances from the seller that direct access to public roads exists or will be provided. Finally, the purchaser will need to consider water supply facilities, sewage disposal facilities, and utility hookups. Even if water and sewage facilities presently exist, there is the question of whether they will be sufficient for the prospective purchaser's future needs, especially if the tract is to be used for the construction of a large residential development.

CHAPTER SUMMARY

1. The basic categories of residential property include single-family homes (located within or without a planned unit development), condominiums, and cooperatives. Prior to purchasing any of these properties, one should consider such factors as the cost of purchasing the property (the purchase price and all other associated costs), the feasibility of obtaining adequate financing, the location of the property, the condition of the property, and the projected resale value of the property.

2. A condominium is a form of ownership in which the property owner owns the interior of a unit plus an undivided interest in the common elements. A creature of statute, a condominium cannot legally be created until a declaration of condominium is recorded in the county in which the property is located. The overseeing body of the condominium is the condominium association, which elects an executive board to supervise daily operations. The board's primary duties are the policing of the condominium's rules and regulations and the development of annual budgets for the maintenance, repair, and replacement of common elements.

3. Some of the factors to consider when purchasing a condominium are the amount of regular and special assessments, the voting rights of unit owners, the recreational facilities provided, the use restrictions imposed upon unit owners, and any plans for expansion of the condominium development.

4. A cooperative is a multiunit building, together with the property on which it is located, that is owned by a corporation. The purchase of a cooperative is the purchase of personal property rather than real property because one purchases shares in the building rather than an individual unit. Each shareholder owns a percentage of the building and holds a long-term lease to an individual unit.

5. A planned unit development (PUD) is a subdivision created by the recording of a subdivision plat and a declaration of covenants and restrictions in the county in which the subdivision is located. The homeowners within the subdivision are members of a homeowners' association, which assesses the members for the costs of maintaining common areas. Just as in

the case of condominium ownership, use restrictions are enforced to promote the aesthetic sense of the community as well as the character of the community.

6. The purchase of commercial property for use as an office complex, shopping center, or industrial park is more complex than the purchase of residential property. In addition to many of the same concerns confronting a residential purchaser, the purchaser of commercial property must consider factors such as demographics, traffic count, visibility, competition, expansion capability, federal and state environmental laws, labor sources, and licensing procedures.

7. The purchaser of an existing business must investigate federal and state commercial law as well as obtain all relevant financial statements from the seller. The purchaser of an existing commercial structure must obtain and examine any existing leases and management and service contracts. The purchaser of an existing shopping center also must examine the bylaws of any existing merchants' association.

WEB RESOURCES

http://www.uniformlaws.org/

This is the official site of The National Conference of Commissioners on Uniform State Laws. This site provides access to all uniform acts promulgated by the Conference, including those discussed in this chapter. The complete texts of final acts are provided, as are summaries and legislative fact sheets. Drafts of proposed amendments and bill tracking can also be accessed.

http://www.irs.gov/

The website of the Internal Revenue Service provides detailed information on income tax deductions, including those pertaining to home ownership, and capital gains taxes.

http://realestate.findlaw.com/

FindLaw is a general site that links to primary legal sources, government resources, and related FindLaw pages. It also provides overviews of real estate principles, including common-interest communities.

http://www.communityassociations.net/

This site, maintained by the Community Associations Network, contains a wealth of information for people who are on association boards or are thinking about joining an association board. It includes links to state and federal laws, articles, blogs, legal news, and resources pertaining to management, finance, and technology.

http://real-estate-law.freeadvice.com/

This site is designed for consumers who have basic questions regarding commercial real estate. If you access the commercial real estate area of the site, numerous general questions are listed (e.g., What is commercial real estate? What is a lawyer's role in a commercial real estate transaction?). Clicking on a question provides a basic answer easily understood by laypersons. It also contains articles relating to commercial real estate leases and sales. The site is good as an overview of general issues pertaining to commercial real estate transactions.

REVIEW QUESTIONS

1. What factors are of common concern to purchasers of any type of residential property?
2. Explain the purpose of each of the following:
   a. Declaration of condominium
   b. Articles of incorporation of a condominium association
   c. Condominium bylaws
3. Compare and contrast condominium and cooperative ownership.
4. How is a planned unit development created?
5. What factors should be considered when purchasing commercial property?

DISCUSSION QUESTIONS

1. When you purchase a condominium, you also are purchasing a way of life in a communal environment. Considering this, please review the Declaration of Whitehaven Condominium (Exhibit 3–2). Do you think the restrictions imposed by the Whitehaven declaration are reasonable? Why or why not?
2. Suppose you owned a condominium unit and the association wanted to amend the declaration to include a restriction on renting units. The choices are (1) to prohibit all renting of units, (2) to allow owners to rent once per year, (3) to freely allow renting of units, and (4) to allow unit owners to rent their unit only after they have owned the unit for three years. What are the pros and cons of each choice? Which way would you vote and why?
3. Your firm is representing the seller of a condominium unit. The closing is set for March 5. The buyer has to be approved by the screening committee. The buyer is in Europe until three days before the closing. The screening committee meets once a month on the fifteenth day of each month. What is the best way to handle this issue?
4. Your client is a member of the board of a cooperative. The board wants to terminate Mr. Smith's tenancy on the basis of "objectionable conduct." Mr. Smith's proprietary lease contains a provision that authorizes the cooperative to terminate a tenant's lease based on "objectionable conduct" but does not specifically define this term. Mr. Smith has unceasingly made vigorous written complaints about a number of other tenants since he moved into the cooperative. The complaint letters to the board have alleged illegal activities and disruptive conduct on the part of these tenants that, when investigated by the board, were found to be completely false. Indeed, the letters could be considered libelous. In addition, Mr. Smith has made alterations to his unit without board approval and has denied board members the right to inspect these alterations. Based on this situation, do you believe the board has a right to terminate his proprietary lease? On what do you base your conclusion? Would your answer change if Mr. Smith had made no alterations to his unit? Why or why not?

5. A new corporate client, TNP Corporation, is looking to purchase a strip center located diagonally across the street from a major shopping mall. The current tenants are a dry cleaning business, a packaging store, a shoe repair shop, and a printing business. The other three rental spaces currently are vacant. TNP Corporation's president wants to revamp the strip center and turn it into a discount fashion center, with stores carrying name brand and designer clothes and shoes at discount prices. He believes the shoppers currently traveling to the mall would be potential shoppers at such a center. What are the most important issues for consideration that should be raised by your attorney when advising the client on this potential purchase?

ETHICAL QUESTION

You were recently hired by your present law firm. Your supervising attorney concentrates on condominium law and represents many of the major condominium associations in your area. Carl Jackson, president of Shoreham Condominium Association, Inc., has been referred to your firm and has called to set up an appointment with your supervising attorney to discuss the possibility of your firm's representation of Shoreham in a construction defects suit it wants to bring against the developer, Skyline Development Co. After setting the appointment, you recall that when you were with your previous firm, one of the partners (not your then-supervising attorney) represented Skyline Development in several matters. What should you do?

Declaration of condominium	EXHIBIT 3–2

**DECLARATION OF CONDOMINIUM
OF
WHITEHAVEN, A CONDOMINIUM**

A Corporation Not for Profit
Under the Laws of the State of Any State

HORIZON CONSTRUCTION CORPORATION, an Any State corporation, being the owner of record of the fee simple title to the real property situated, lying and being in Any County, Any State, as more particularly described in the Survey Exhibit attached hereto as Exhibit 1, which is incorporated herein by reference, does hereby declare that the realty described in Exhibit 1 under the legend "Whitehaven 1, A Condominium, Phase 1," together with improvements thereon, is submitted to condominium ownership pursuant to the Condominium Act of the State of Any State (Chapter 525 of the Any State Statutes) and does hereby file this Declaration of Condominium.

    1.   PURPOSE; NAME AND ADDRESS; LEGAL DESCRIPTION; EFFECT.
        1.1 PURPOSE. The purpose of this Declaration is to submit the lands and improvements herein described to condominium ownership and use in the manner prescribed by the Laws of the State of Any State.
        1.2 NAME AND ADDRESS. The name of this Condominium is as specified in the title of this document.

EXHIBIT 3–2   *(continued)*

1.3 THE LAND. The real property described in Exhibit 1 is the Condominium Property contemplated to be subject to condominium ownership as provided for herein. Such property is subject to such easements, restrictions, reservations and rights of way of record, together with those contained or provided for in this instrument and the exhibits attached hereto.

1.4 EFFECT. All of the provisions of this Declaration of Condominium and all Exhibits attached hereto shall be binding upon all Unit Owners and are enforceable equitable servitudes running with the Condominium Property and existing in perpetuity until this Declaration is revoked and the Condominium is terminated as provided herein. In consideration of receiving, and by acceptance of a grant, devise or mortgage, all grantees, devisees or mortgagees, their heirs, personal representatives, successors and assigns, and all parties claiming by, through, or under such persons agree to be bound by the provisions hereof. Both the burdens imposed and the benefits granted by this instrument shall run with each Unit as herein defined.

2. SURVEY AND DESCRIPTION OF IMPROVEMENTS.

2.1 SURVEY. On Exhibit 1 is a survey of the land, graphic description, and plot plans of the improvements constituting the Condominium, identifying the Units, Common Elements and Limited Common Elements, and their respective locations and approximate dimensions.

2.2 PHASING. This Condominium is a phase condominium as provided for in Section 525.301 of the Any State Statutes. On Exhibit 1, Sheets two (2) through eight (8), there are representations and descriptions of the land which may become part of the Condominium and upon which each phase is to be built. There are three types of units to be constructed in the Condominium: Type A, approximately 1,025 square feet; Type B, approximately 1,195 square feet; and Type C, approximately 1,500 square feet. Such size is the maximum per unit type.

   The proposed arrangement of the three unit types for each phase of the Condominium appears on Sheets eight (8) and nine (9) of Exhibit 1. The Declarant reserves the right to alter the mix and size of unit types so long as there will be no material or adverse change in the approximate size of the units. The maximum and minimum number of units to be included in each phase is twenty (20) units.

2.3 AMENDMENT. No amendment, notwithstanding anything in the Declaration to the contrary, adding phases to the Condominium shall require the execution of such amendment or any form of consent thereto by Unit Owners, the Association or by any party other than the Declarant. The form of such amendment is attached hereto as Exhibit 2.

2.4 EFFECT OF PHASING. The general effect of phasing a condominium is the submission of a parcel of property to condominium ownership as the initial condominium phase and the addition(s) of subsequent parcels to condominium ownership with such subsequent parcels being part and parcel of the same condominium and governed by the same condominium association. It is not anticipated that the submission of additional phases to the Condominium will have significant impact upon the individual Unit Owner's rights except as set forth in this Declaration. The adding of a subsequent phase to this Condominium, thereby adding additional Units, will reduce the fraction of common elements attributable to each previously created Unit, as specifically set forth in Exhibit 3. The adding of a subsequent phase to this Condominium will not affect the vote of any Unit Owner as a member of the Association. Each Unit Owner shall continue to have one vote for each Unit in the Condominium owned by such Unit Owner, provided, however, that the total number of votes entitled to be cast will increase by the number of Units contained in the phase so added. If Declarant decides not to add any or all of the additional phases to this Condominium, the number of Units in this Condominium will be as created by this Declaration and the Owners thereof shall comprise the complete membership of the Association and thereby be entitled to cast 100% of the votes of the Association. No time shares may be created with respect to Units in any phase. There are no recreation areas and facilities owned as common elements of the Condominium, and therefore, phasing will have no effect on such areas and facilities.

The phases of the Condominium will be completed by the following schedule.

Phase	Completion date	Phase	Completion date
1	April 30, 2015	3	August 31, 2015
2	June 30, 2015	4	October 31, 2015

3. THE UNIT AND COMMON ELEMENTS.

3.1 INTEREST IN COMMON ELEMENTS. Each Unit Owner shall own, as an appurtenance to his or her Unit, an undivided interest in the Common Elements as assigned thereto in Exhibit 3 (subject to the provisions of Paragraph 2.4). The percentage of undivided interest of each Unit shall not be changed without the unanimous consent of all owners of all of the Units except as otherwise provided herein.

3.2 BOUNDARIES. The boundaries of each Unit shall be the horizontal plane of the undecorated finished ceiling, the horizontal plane of the undecorated finished floor, and the vertical planes of the undecorated finished interior walls.

3.3 AUTOMOBILE PARKING AREAS. After the filing of this Declaration, there shall be assigned to each Unit the exclusive right to use at least one automobile parking space. Such assigned parking spaces shall be used only by the owner of such Unit or such owner's guests and invitees. The assignment of such parking spaces shall be made by the Declarant and may be amended by the Community Association at its discretion. Parking spaces shall be assigned by a Designation of Parking Space to be conveyed to each Unit Owner at closing. Said designations shall be retained in the Community Association's files but will not be recorded.

4. EASEMENTS.

4.1 PERPETUAL NONEXCLUSIVE EASEMENT. The Common Elements are hereby declared to be subject to a perpetual nonexclusive easement in favor of all of the Unit Owners in the Condominium for their use and the use of their immediate families, guests, and invitees, for all proper and normal purposes, including the providing of services for the benefit of all Units.

4.2 UTILITY EASEMENTS. Utility easements are reserved and/or granted through the Condominium Property as may be required for utility service (including construction and maintenance) in order to adequately serve the Condominium.

4.3 INGRESS AND EGRESS. A nonexclusive easement for ingress and egress is hereby created for pedestrian traffic over, through and across sidewalks, paths, walks, driveways, passageways and lanes as the same, from time to time, may exist upon the Common Elements; and for vehicular traffic over, through and across such portions of the Common Elements as, from time to time, may be paved and intended for such purposes.

4.4 ADDITIONAL EASEMENTS. Declarant reserves unto itself, or its designee, the unequivocal right to create additional easements over, upon, or through the Condominium Property, at any time, for any purpose without the joinder of the Association or any Unit Owners whomsoever, provided that said easements so created shall not cause a diminution of parking spaces or cause a taking of part or all of the actual building. However, if requested, the Association and Unit Owners shall join in the creation thereof.

EXHIBIT 3–2   *(continued)*

5. COMMON EXPENSE; COMMON SURPLUS.

    5.1 LIABILITY AND METHOD OF SHARING. Each Unit shall share in the Common Surplus and be liable for the Common Expenses in the same percentage as the percentage representing the undivided interest of each Unit in the Common Elements as it may exist at any time. The right to share in the Common Surplus does not include the right to withdraw, or to require payment or distribution thereof, except upon termination and dissolution of the Condominium.

    5.2 DECLARANT'S OBLIGATION. The Declarant shall be excused from payment of the share of Common Expenses in respect to those units owned by Declarant which have not been leased and which are offered for sale during such period of time that Declarant shall have guaranteed that the assessment for Common Expenses of the Condominium imposed upon the Unit Owners other than Declarant shall not increase over a stated dollar amount, and for which period Declarant shall have obligated itself to pay any amount of Common Expenses not produced by the assessments at the guaranteed level receivable from other Unit Owners. Declarant guarantees that monthly assessments shall not exceed the amount per year for each Unit listed on Exhibit 4 during the year of the guarantee period. The time period during which assessments shall be guaranteed at the stated rate shall be in effect for a period for one year from the date of recordation of this Declaration.

6. ADMINISTRATION OF THE CONDOMINIUM.

    6.1 THE ASSOCIATION. The Association shall administer the operation and management of the Condominium Property and undertake and perform all acts and duties incident thereto in accordance with this Declaration, its exhibits and the Condominium Act and join with other corporations or entities in becoming a member of the Community Association to assist same in promoting the health, safety and welfare of the residents of the Whitehaven Community.

    As phases are added to, and become a part of, this Condominium, the Association shall administer the operation and management of the Condominium as it then exists.

    6.2 MEMBERSHIP. Each Unit Owner shall automatically become a member of the Association with full voting rights. No person holding any lien, mortgage or other encumbrance upon any Unit shall be entitled, by virtue thereof, to membership in the Association or Community Association or to any of the rights or privileges of such membership.

    6.3 POWERS OF ASSOCIATION. In the administration of the Condominium, the Association shall have, and is hereby granted, the authority and power to enforce the provisions of this Declaration, to levy and collect assessments in the manner hereinafter provided, and to adopt, promulgate and enforce such Rules and Regulations governing the use of the Units, Common Elements and Limited Common Elements as the Board of the Association may deem to be in the best interest of the Condominium. The Association shall have all of the powers and duties set forth in the Condominium Act except where limited herein or where the exercise of such powers and duties will impair the rights of other parties.

    6.4 VOTING. Each Unit Owner or Owners, including the Declarant, shall be entitled to only one (1) vote for each Unit owned. The vote of each Unit Owner shall be governed by the provisions of the Bylaws.

    6.5 MANAGEMENT AGREEMENT. The Association may enter into an agreement with any person, firm or corporation for the administration, maintenance and repair of the Condominium Property and may delegate to such contractor or manager such of the powers and duties of the Association as the Association and such person, firm or corporation shall agree.

7. USE AND OCCUPANCY.

    7.1 RESIDENTIAL USE

    (a) Each Unit is hereby restricted to residential use as a single-family residence by the owner or owners thereof, their immediate families, guests and invitees but in no event shall there be more than two (2) natural person owners of any Unit or more than one non-natural person owner of any Unit. Guests and invitees may visit and temporarily reside in a Unit no more than twice in any calendar year for a period of time not to exceed thirty (30) days for each visit unless otherwise approved by the Association in cases of extreme personal need or hardship.

    (b) The sidewalks, entrances, and all other Common Elements must not be obstructed, encumbered or used for any purpose other than ingress and egress to and from the premises. No carriages, bicycles, motorcycles, wagons, shopping carts, chairs, benches, tables, furniture, or any other object of similar type and nature shall be stored thereon. No business, service, repair or maintenance for the general public shall be allowed on the Condominium Property at any time.

    7.2 VEHICLES AND PARKING. The parking facilities shall be used in accordance with the regulations adopted by the Board of the Community Association. No vehicle that cannot operate on its own power shall remain on the Condominium Property for more than twelve hours, and no repair, except emergency repair, of vehicles shall be made on the Condominium Property. No commercial vehicle owned or driven by a condominium owner shall be parked on the Condominium Property. No boat, boat trailer, trailer, recreational vehicle, camper, truck, bus, mobile home, tractor, motor coach, commercial vehicle, lettered commercial vehicle or vehicle in excess of 6,000 pounds of gross weight or like vehicle shall be left or stored on the Condominium Property except with the prior, written approval of the Association. Bicycles shall be parked in the areas, if any, provided for that purpose.

    7.3 PETS. Only one (1) walking animal with a weight of not more than forty (40) pounds shall be kept or harbored in a Unit at any time. Walking animals shall be permitted only within a Unit or Privacy Area. No other pets may be kept without the written consent of the Board. Such consent may be given upon such conditions as the Board may prescribe and shall be deemed provisional and subject to revocation at any time. No animal or pet shall be maintained or harbored within a Unit that would create a nuisance to any other Unit Owner. A determination by the Board that an animal or pet maintained or harbored in a Unit creates a nuisance shall be conclusive and binding upon all parties. In no event shall a Unit Owner or any other person allow a walking animal anywhere on the Condominium Property unless carried or held on a leash not to exceed six (6) feet. Each Unit Owner and any other person so walking an animal shall be responsible for the immediate, appropriate and complete removal of all animal excrement.

    7.4 ALTERATIONS AND ADDITIONS. No Unit Owner shall make or permit to be made any internal material alteration, addition or modification to his or her Unit without the prior written consent of the Association and Declarant. No Unit Owner shall cause the balcony or terrace which is abutting, or part of, his or her Unit to be enclosed or cause any improvements or changes to be made therein or to the exterior of the Unit without the written permission of the Association, Declarant and the Architectural Control Committee of the Community Association for so long as at least one (1) unit in the Whitehaven Community remains for sale in the ordinary course of business by Declarant. All improvements or changes which may be permitted shall be uniform in appearance. No Unit Owner shall cause to be made any modification or installation of electrical wiring, satellite dishes,

EXHIBIT 3–2   *(continued)*

television antenna systems or connections whether inside or outside the Unit or in any manner change the appearance of any portion of the Condominium Property. No Unit Owner may cause any material puncture or break in the boundaries of his or her Unit. No Unit Owner shall grow or plant any type of plant, shrub, flower, etc. outside his or her Unit or in his or her Privacy Area without the prior, written consent of the Association and Declarant. The Declarant's consent shall not be unreasonably withheld. All units above ground level shall maintain fully carpeted floors in said units at all times (except in bathrooms and kitchens).

7.5   LEASING. No lease may be made for less than a ninety (90) day period nor shall any transient accommodations be provided. No Owner may lease his or her Unit more than twice a calendar year. A Unit Owner intending to lease his or her Unit shall furnish the Association a copy of said lease. No part of a unit may be leased. All leases of a unit shall be subject to the provisions of the Condominium Documents. Failure of any lessee to comply with the provisions of said documents shall constitute a default under the terms of the lease.

7.6   RULES AND REGULATIONS. All Unit Owners and other persons shall use the Condominium Property in accordance with the Rules and Regulations promulgated by the entity in control thereof and the provisions of this Declaration and the Bylaws of the Association, as applicable.

8.   MAINTENANCE, ALTERATION AND REPAIR OF THE CONDOMINIUM PROPERTY.

8.1   MAINTENANCE BY ASSOCIATION. The Association, at its expense, shall be responsible for and shall maintain, repair and replace all of the Common and Limited Common Elements, except for lawn maintenance which shall be the responsibility of the Community Association. Any exterior painting, repair or replacement requires the prior approval of the Architectural Control Committee of the Community Association.

8.2   MAINTENANCE BY UNIT OWNER. The Unit Owner shall, subject to the other provisions of this Declaration, maintain, repair and replace, at his or her expense, all portions of his or her Unit including, but not limited to, all doors, windows, glass, screens, porch, balcony, screening, electric panels, electric wiring, electric outlets and fixtures, heaters, hot water heaters, refrigerators, dishwashers and other appliances, drains, plumbing fixtures and connection, interior surfaces of all walls, floors and ceilings, and all other portions of his or her Unit. The Unit Owner shall maintain and repair the air-conditioning compressor, refrigerant and electrical line appurtenant to his or her Unit.

8.3   LIABILITY OF UNIT OWNER. Should a Unit Owner undertake additions and modifications to his or her Unit or to his or her Privacy Area(s) without the prior written consent of the Board of Directors and Declarant, or refuse to make repairs as required, or should a Unit Owner cause any damage to the Common Elements, the Association may make such removals, repairs or replacements and have the right to levy a special assessment for the cost thereof against the said Unit Owner. In the event a Unit Owner threatens to or violates the provisions hereof, the Association shall also have the right to proceed in a court of equity for an injunction to seek compliance with the provisions hereof.

8.4   RIGHT OF ENTRY BY ASSOCIATION. Whenever it is necessary to enter any Unit for the purpose of inspection, including inspection to ascertain a Unit Owner's compliance with the provisions of this Declaration, or for performing any maintenance, alteration or repair to any portion of the Common Elements or Unit, the Unit Owner shall permit an authorized agent of the Association and Management Firm to enter such Unit, to go upon the Limited Common Elements, or to go upon the Common Elements, provided that such entry shall be made only at reasonable times and with reasonable advance notice. In the case of emergency such as, but not limited to, fire, flood or hurricane, entry may be made without notice or permission. The Unit Owners acknowledge that the Association has retained a master pass key to all the Units in the Condominium. Each Unit Owner does hereby appoint the Association as his or her agent for the purposes herein provided and agrees that the Association shall not be liable for any alleged property damage or theft caused or occurring on account of any entry.

9. TAX OR SPECIAL ASSESSMENT ASSESSED AGAINST THE CONDOMINIUM PROPERTY. If any taxing authority levies or assesses any Tax or Special Assessment against the Condominium Property as a whole, and not the individual Units, the same shall be paid as a Common Expense by the Association and assessed to the Unit Owners. In such event, the amount due shall constitute a lien prior to all mortgages and encumbrances upon any parcel to the same extent as though such Tax or Special Assessment had been separately levied by the taxing authority upon each unit.

10. INSURANCE PROVISIONS. The insurance which shall be purchased and maintained for the benefit of the Condominium shall be governed by the following provisions.

    10.1 PURCHASE OF INSURANCE. All insurance purchased pursuant to this Paragraph shall be purchased by the Association for the benefit of the Association, the Unit Owners and their respective mortgagees, as their interest may appear, and shall provide for the issuance of certificates of insurance and mortgagee endorsements to any or all of the holders of institutional first mortgages. Said policies and endorsements shall be deposited with the Insurance Trustee who must first acknowledge that the policies and any proceeds thereof will be held in accordance with the terms and conditions hereof.

    10.2 COST AND PAYMENT OF PREMIUMS. The cost of obtaining all insurance hereunder, excluding only the insurance as may be purchased by individual Unit Owners, is declared to be a Common Expense, as are any other fees or expenses incurred which may be necessary or incidental to carry out the provisions hereof.

    10.3 UNIT OWNERS' RESPONSIBILITY. Each Unit Owner may obtain insurance, at his or her own expense, affording coverage upon his or her own property and for his or her own liability and living expenses as he or she deems advisable. All such insurance shall contain the same waiver of subrogation that is referred to herein and shall waive any right to contribution.

    10.4 DETERMINATION TO RECONSTRUCT. If any part of the Condominium Property shall be damaged by casualty, the determination as to whether or not it shall be reconstructed shall be made in the following manner.

        10.4.1 COMMON ELEMENTS. If the damage is only to Common Elements, the damaged property shall be reconstructed unless it is determined in the manner elsewhere provided that the Condominium shall be terminated.

        10.4.2 DAMAGE TO UNITS

            (a) If the damage is to Units to which more than 70% of the Common Elements are appurtenant and the Units are found by the Board of Directors to be untenantable, then the damaged property will not be reconstructed and the Condominium will be terminated without agreement as elsewhere provided, unless within sixty (60) days after the casualty Unit Owners owning 75% or more of the Common Elements agree in writing to such reconstruction.

            (b) If the damage is to Units to which more than 30% of the Common Elements are appurtenant and the Units are found by the Board of Directors to be tenantable, then reconstruction shall be determined on a building-by-building basis.

EXHIBIT 3–2   *(continued)*

11. ASSESSMENTS.

11.1 GENERAL AUTHORITY. The Association, through its Board, shall have the power to make, levy and collect regular and special assessments for Common Expenses and such other assessments as are provided for by the Condominium Act and the provisions of this Declaration and all other expenses declared by the Directors of the Association to be Common Expenses from time to time.

11.2 UNIT OWNERS' GENERAL LIABILITY. All Common Expenses levied against Unit Owners and Units shall be on a uniform basis in the same proportion as the percentages of the undivided shares in the ownership of the Common Elements unless specifically otherwise provided for herein, without increase or diminution for the existence, or lack of existence, of any exclusive right to use a part of the Limited Common Elements. Should the Association be the owner of any Unit(s), the assessment, which would otherwise be due and payable to the Association or others by the owner of such Unit(s), shall be a Common Expense as the same relates to the collection of such sums from the Unit Owners to pay the Association's obligations.

11.3 PAYMENT. The assessments of the Association levied against the Unit Owner and his or her Unit shall be payable in such installments, and at such times, as may be determined by the Board of Directors of the Association and for which the Unit Owner and his or her Unit shall be responsible and liable.

11.4 EMERGENCIES. If statements levied are, or may prove to be, insufficient to pay the costs of operation and management of the Condominium, or in the event of emergencies, the Board of Directors shall have the authority to levy such additional assessment or assessments as it shall deem necessary.

11.5 LIEN. The Association is hereby granted a lien upon each Condominium Unit, together with a lien on all tangible personal property located within said Unit (except that such lien upon the aforesaid tangible personal property shall be subordinate to prior bona fide liens of record), which lien shall secure the payment of all monies from each Unit Owner for which he or she is liable to the Association, including all assessments, interest and expenses provided for in the Declaration and reasonable attorneys' fees incurred as an incident to the enforcement of said lien. The lien granted to the Association may be foreclosed as provided in the Condominium Act. The lien granted to the Association shall further secure such advances for taxes and payments on account of Institutional Mortgages, liens or encumbrances which may be advanced by the Association in order to preserve and protect its lien. The lien shall be effective, have priority and be collected as provided by the Condominium Act, unless by the provisions of this Declaration, such liens would have a greater priority or dignity, in which event, the lien rights in favor of the Association having the highest priority and dignity shall be the lien of the Association. Notwithstanding anything herein to the contrary, any such lien shall be subordinate to any mortgage guaranteed by the Veterans Administration and any first mortgage on the Condominium Unit.

12. TERMINATION. The Condominium may be terminated in the following manner:

12.1 DESTRUCTION. If it is determined in the manner provided above that the Condominium Property as a whole shall not be reconstructed, the Condominium will be terminated.

12.2 AGREEMENT. As provided in Section 525.201 of the Any State Statutes, the Condominium may be terminated at any time by the approval in writing of all Unit Owners and all record owners of mortgages on Units.

12.3 CERTIFICATE. The termination of the Condominium shall be evidenced by a certificate of the Association executed by its President and Secretary certifying the fact of the termination, which shall become effective upon the certificate being recorded in the Public Records.

13. AMENDMENTS. Except as herein or elsewhere provided, this Declaration may be amended in the following manner:

13.1 NOTICE. Notice of the subject matter of a proposed amendment shall be included in the notice of any meeting at which a proposed amendment is to be considered in the form prescribed by Section 525.104 of the Any State Statutes.

13.2 PROPOSAL OF AMENDMENT. An amendment may be proposed by either the unanimous vote of the Board of Directors of the Association, or by fifteen percent (15%) of the members of the Association. Directors and members not present in person or by proxy at the meeting considering the amendment may express their approval in writing, provided such approval is delivered to the Secretary within ten (10) days after the meeting. Except as elsewhere provided, a proposed amendment must be approved by either:

13.2.1 Not less than seventy-five percent (75%) of the entire membership of the Board of Directors and by not less than seventy-five percent (75%) of the votes of the entire membership of the Association. Provided however, in the event said amendments relate to leasing of units, or provisions which are for the express benefit of Institutional Mortgagees, the Association shall furnish said Mortgagees with notice of proposed amendments and must procure fifty-one percent (51%) approval of said Mortgagees to the proposals in addition to the percentage unit owner approval provided for herein.

13.2.2 Until the first election of a majority of the directors by the membership as provided for in Article VII of the Articles of Incorporation, only by all of the directors.

13.3 EXECUTION AND RECORDING. Except as otherwise provided in this Declaration, a copy of each amendment shall be attached to a certificate, executed by the officers of the Association, certifying that the amendment was duly adopted. The amendment shall be effective when the certificate and copy of the amendment are recorded in the Public Records.

14. CONDEMNATION PROCEEDINGS. If condemnation proceedings are successfully litigated against all or any part of the Condominium Property, the entire Association shall secure the condemnation award in accordance with the ratio of ownership herein provided as it pertains to the Common Elements and disburse same to Unit Owners and their mortgagees as their interests appear of record. The Association shall give prompt written notice to each holder of a mortgage of record of any such condemnation procedures, and shall take no action in any such proceedings that will disturb any mortgagee's first lien priority.

The Association shall represent the Unit Owners in any condemnation proceedings or in negotiations, settlements and agreements with the condemning authority for acquisition of the Common Elements or part thereof. Each Unit Owner hereby appoints the Association as its attorney-in-fact for the purposes described herein.

15. CONSTRUCTION. All of the provisions of this Declaration shall be construed in accordance with the Law of the State of Any State. This construction shall govern in all matters, including matters of substantive and procedural law.

16. CAPTIONS. The captions to the paragraphs of this Declaration are intended for convenience only and are not deemed to be all inclusive as to the matters contained in such paragraphs or considered in connection with the construction of any of the provisions of this Declaration.

17. SEVERABILITY. If any terms or provision of this Declaration, or the application thereof to any person or circumstance, shall, to any extent, be determined to be invalid or unenforceable, the remainder of this Declaration, or the application of such term or provision

---

EXHIBIT 3–2   *(continued)*

---

to persons or circumstances other than those to which such term may be held invalid or unenforceable, shall not be affected thereby and each term and provision of this Declaration shall be valid and enforceable to the fullest extent permitted by law.

IN WITNESS WHEREOF, the Declarant has executed this Declaration on this _____ day of _____.

Signed, sealed and delivered   HORIZON CONSTRUCTION CORP.,
in the presence of: an Any State corporation

_____   By: _____ (Seal)
_____   President
                                                        Corporate Seal

STATE OF ANY STATE
COUNTY OF ANY COUNTY

BEFORE ME, the undersigned authority, personally appeared _____ to me well known to be the person described in and who executed the foregoing instrument as President of Horizon Construction Corporation, an Any State corporation, and he acknowledged before me that he executed such instrument as such Officer of said Corporation, and that the Seal affixed thereto is the Corporate Seal of said Corporation, and that it was affixed to said instrument by due and regular Corporate authority, and that said instrument is the free act and deed of said Corporation.

WITNESS my hand and official seal, at the State and County aforesaid, this _____ day of _____.

_____
Notary Public, State of Any State
My commission expires: _____

Slossberg Law Office on CourseMate

Please go to www.cengagebrain.com to log into CourseMate, access the Slossberg Law Office, and work on your client files. Each module corresponds to a chapter in the text. Within each module, you will be provided with instructions by the supervising attorney. You are asked to keep track of time spent on time sheets. The documents produced through working on client files in the law office can then be compiled into a portfolio of final work product.

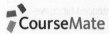 CourseMate

The available CourseMate for this text has an interactive eBook and interactive learning tools, including flash cards, quizzes, and more. To learn more about this resource and access free demo CourseMate resources, including the Slossberg Law Office, go to www.cengagebrain.com, and search for this book. To access CourseMate materials that you have purchased, go to login.cengagebrain.com.

Ownership Restrictions

4

CHAPTER OBJECTIVES

Upon completion of this chapter, the student will:

- Understand the concept of police power and the various ways the exercise of this power by federal, state, and local governments can impact the private property owner

- Know the different types of zoning and the methods by which a private property owner can be relieved from zoning restrictions

- Understand the obligations placed upon property owners by environmental protection and fair housing laws

- Know the steps taken in assessing property for real property tax purposes

- Know the different types of easements, how they are created, and how they may be terminated

Introduction

Earlier in this text, the basic ownership rights of property owners were discussed. Recall that these rights include the right of disposition, the right of possession, the right of exclusion, and the right of use. The property owner, however, is not allowed complete freedom in the exercise of these rights. The truth is that each of these rights may be restricted in some manner by governmental or private restrictions on ownership.

The right of disposition is granted to the holder of a fee simple estate. In theory, this right seems to allow the property owner to choose to whom he or she sells or leases the property. In practice, this right is restricted by state and federal fair housing laws that prohibit certain discriminatory practices in the sale or leasing of private property. The rights of possession and exclusion, in theory, allow the property owner to occupy his or her premises in privacy and to exert total control over entry onto the property. In practice, the property owner may be forced to permit access to others, as is the case with appurtenant easements, or to surrender the property to the government through the government's exercise of eminent domain. The right of use implies the right of a property owner to utilize his or her property in any manner in which he or she sees fit. However, zoning laws, environmental protection laws, and restrictive covenants each place limitations on that use.

As a real estate paralegal, you may be asked to assist your supervising attorney with handling a zoning matter, drafting an easement, or finding an expert to perform an environmental audit in compliance with environmental regulations. This chapter begins with a discussion of zoning and situations in which permission to deviate from zoning ordinances might be obtained. It then moves into a discussion of environmental protection and fair housing laws, followed by a discussion of tax assessments and exemptions and by a look at situations in which a local, state, or federal government may take private property. The chapter concludes with a discussion of private restrictions on ownership, including but not limited to restrictive covenants and easements.

Governmental Restrictions on Ownership

Federal, state, and local governments impose restrictions on the rights of owners of real property through the implementation of their police powers. **Police powers** are those powers given to the federal government and to the states by their constitutions to create laws necessary for the protection of public health, safety, and welfare. State governments may, in turn, vest local governmental bodies with the power to create and enforce local regulations that do not conflict with state statutes. Laws fitting this category include, but are not limited to, those designed to curtail noise, water, and air pollution and to control population density as well as those intended to prevent the use of discriminatory practices in the sale or rental of real property. Real property can be regulated through various means, such as zoning ordinances, subdivision regulations, building codes, and environmental and fair housing legislation. Police powers include the power of taxation as a method of raising revenue for the public welfare.

Zoning

Zoning and land use planning are fundamental methods of government control over real estate development. Local governments are given the authority by state enabling acts to formulate comprehensive plans that are subsequently implemented and enforced through local government zoning ordinances that control density of population, as well as intensity of use, and help stabilize and protect property values in a given area.

Local governmental authorities have the responsibility of identifying and prioritizing the economic, social, and ecological needs within their jurisdiction and then formulating a plan that best meets these needs. A planning commission may be appointed to create a **master plan,** sometimes referred to as a *general plan*. Based on information gleaned from physical, demographic, and economic surveys, a master plan serves two objectives. The first is to present a comprehensive policy statement outlining the goals of the local authorities based on the perceived needs of the community. The second is to present a working plan of how those goals are to be met.

Although master plans vary significantly, most include provisions for land use, conservation, circulation, noise regulation, and public facilities. *Land use* includes the creation of standards for economic and residential development. *Conservation* includes the preservation of natural and historical resources. *Circulation* includes the routing of public roads to prevent traffic congestion and enhance the accessibility of public transportation systems. *Noise regulation* includes the imposition of regulations specifying permissible noise decibel limits and the routing of air and railroad traffic to less populated areas. Planning for *public facilities* includes planning for libraries, courthouses, schools, utility plants, and the like.

police powers: Those powers given to the federal government and to the states by their constitutions to create laws necessary for the protection of public health, safety, and welfare.

master plan: A plan created by a local planning commission that provides for land use, conservation, circulation, noise regulation, and public facilities in a given area.

Zoning is the primary mechanism for implementing the master plan. In so doing, zoning necessarily places restrictions on land use for the sake of the common good. Without the creation and enforcement of zoning ordinances, nothing would prevent a property owner from building a textile factory next to a single-family residence. Zoning can regulate the size and height of physical structures, the purposes for which such structures may be used, the number of persons permitted to occupy the structures, the setback requirements for the structures, and even the appearance of the structures. The zoning specifications of a given area can be found on a *zoning map*. These maps usually use various colors to differentiate different zoning categories.

Because zoning is one of the several police powers afforded to local governments, zoning ordinances must be reasonably related to the promotion of the public welfare in order to be deemed valid. In most states, not only must the ordinance be reasonably related to public welfare, but also it must be exercised in a reasonable and nondiscriminatory manner.

Prior to the passage of any zoning ordinance, due process dictates that members of the public receive notice of the proposed ordinance and be given an opportunity to voice their approval or objections at a public hearing. Notice typically is given through publication in general and legal newspapers. Often, the notice will provide the text of the proposed ordinance as well as the time and date of the hearing. Affected property owners may demand that the zoning board present evidence that the ordinance is valid. Most ordinances provide certain procedures to be followed should a property owner wish to appeal the enforcement of a zoning decision. An example of a notice of public hearing is found in Exhibit 4–1.

Notice of public hearing	**EXHIBIT 4–1**

CITY OF ANY CITY
936 MAIN STREET
ANY CITY, ANY STATE

**NOTICE OF PUBLIC HEARING
ON PETITION TO AMEND MASTER PLAN**

The City Council of the City of Any City will hold a public hearing in the meeting room of the City Hall, 936 Main Street, at 7:00 p.m. or as soon thereafter as practicable, on the dates hereinafter specified. Comments of any interested parties relative to this matter may be submitted in writing and/or presented at the hearing.

PETITIONER/OWNER: Orange Blossom Estates, Inc.

DATE OF CITY COUNCIL HEARING: July 6, 2015

LOCATION DESCRIPTION: Generally located within Orange Blossom Estates

ADDRESS OF SUBJECT PROPERTY: 2500 block of Orange Blossom Drive

REQUEST: Reconsideration of request to amend the PRD Master Plan associated with Ordinance 15-44.

THIS MATTER SHOULD BE REFERRED TO AS ZB 30-3-15. FOR FURTHER INFORMATION, CALL GAIL GRANT IN THE PLANNING AND ZONING DIVISION AT 444-0000. ANY PERSON WISHING TO APPEAL ANY DECISION MADE BY THIS BOARD OR COMMITTEE WITH RESPECT TO ANY MATTER CONSIDERED AT SUCH MEETINGS OR HEARINGS WILL NEED A RECORD OF THE PROCEEDINGS AND, FOR SUCH PURPOSES, MAY NEED TO ENSURE THAT A VERBATIM RECORD OF THE PROCEEDINGS IS MADE, WHICH RECORD INCLUDES THE TESTIMONY AND EVIDENCE UPON WHICH THE APPEAL IS MADE.

June 30, 2015

Once adopted, zoning ordinances usually are enforced through the issuance of *building permits*. Most cities and counties require permits to be obtained before any construction can be done on real property. This can include not only new construction but remodeling and additions as well. Compliance with all zoning ordinances and *building code* regulations is implied in the issuance of a permit. Building inspectors are sent out to the site at various stages of construction to assure compliance, and no one is allowed to occupy a constructed premises until a *certificate of occupancy* is issued.

Should a property owner decide to defy a zoning ordinance, compliance can be enforced through the imposition of fines and the issuance of an *injunction,* which is a court order demanding that a party stop certain activities or be held in contempt of court. For example, if a seamstress operates a clothing alteration business out of her home, which is located in a residential zoning district, she can be prevented from continuing operations and may be subject to fines. If, however, the district is zoned for mixed use, residential and commercial, the seamstress may be permitted to continue her business.

Injunctions and fines also are imposed for failure to obtain a building permit. In some instances, fines are accrued on a daily basis for each day on which noncompliance occurs. For example, suppose Frank Dawson decides to enclose his patio. The city of Any City requires that plans and architectural drawings be submitted for approval and a building permit obtained before work can proceed. Frank does not submit drawings or obtain a permit; instead, he simply proceeds with the construction of the enclosure. A building inspector inspecting other construction in the area passes by Frank's house and notices that work is proceeding without a permit. The city issues Frank a citation, requiring that all work cease and informing him that a fine of $100 per day is imposed for each day work is done in violation of the citation. Ten days have passed since Frank began work on the enclosure. To date, his fines total $1,000. Depending on the wording of the citation, the fines may continue to accrue, even if work is stopped, until such time as Frank obtains a permit.

Types of Zoning. Zoning ordinances divide land use into a number of classifications. These can include the following:

1. *Residential:* permitting single-family or multifamily dwellings or a combination of the two. Residential zoning is designed to regulate population density by limiting the number of dwellings per acre.
2. *Commercial:* permitting office buildings, shopping centers, and other commercial development. Commercial zoning is not as concerned with population density as it is with use intensity. By regulating the commercial enterprises permitted in a particular locality, zoning can indirectly regulate the flow of traffic patterns.
3. *Industrial:* permitting factories and other industrial enterprises that bring employment opportunities into a particular locality. Industrial zoning is similar to commercial zoning in that it is concerned with use intensity. It additionally is concerned with industrial wastes and emissions that can impact the quality of life for the general public.
4. *Agricultural:* permitting crop production and animal farming.

5. *Public:* permitting public facilities such as post offices, libraries, and recreation centers. The placement of these facilities takes into consideration both population density and use intensity. For example, the placement of a large convention center must take into consideration public access to the center, traffic flow to and from the center, and noise levels emanating from the crowds entering and exiting the center.

Some zoning ordinances divide these categories further. For example, a residential zone may be subdivided into areas that permit only certain types of residences, such as detached single-family homes or duplexes, and disallow high-rise buildings. This sometimes is referred to as *exclusive zoning.* Another example would be an industrial zone that permits only one type of industrial activity, such as a paper mill or a textile mill. Conversely, zoning ordinances may provide for *multiple-use zoning,* sometimes referred to as *cumulative zoning* or *cluster zoning.* This zoning facilitates the growth of planned unit developments. The advantages of multiple-use zoning are apparent with the expansion of suburban areas into small cities. An area that is populated sparsely does not require numerous shopping centers or hospitals. As demographics change and certain areas become more densely populated, however, the need for support services in those areas increases. Multiple-use zoning allows residential and commercial growth to complement each other.

Periodically, the need to rezone occurs, as when a formerly agricultural area undergoes economic changes and farming diminishes. The once-productive farmland can be put to better use, for example, by encouraging light industry to build plants in the area. Before this can be done, the area must be rezoned. Additionally, zoning officials are increasingly implementing the use of *buffer zones* to ease the transition between one zoning area and another. For example, a park may be placed as a buffer zone between commercial and residential areas.

In addition to zoning ordinances that classify areas into designated uses, there are ordinances that are concerned primarily with aesthetics. For example, an ordinance may forbid modern-looking office buildings in a historical district or may prohibit billboards in certain areas.

Variances. Property owners desiring to deviate from strict compliance with all or part of a zoning ordinance may apply for a **variance** to the zoning board or other applicable board. In order to be granted a variance, a property owner typically has to show that compliance with the ordinance will create an undue hardship that will either prevent the anticipated benefits to the property or prevent best usage of the property. Additionally, the property owner must show that the variance will not adversely affect the surrounding properties or change the character of the community.

For example, suppose that plans have been approved and a house has been constructed on a lot. If an engineering team comes out to the property to conduct a final survey before the certificate of occupancy can be issued and during the survey discovers that the house has exceeded the back setback by three inches, the property owner will have to apply for a variance from the board. In this case, the variance will most likely be granted, as it would be unconscionable to require that a house in its final stages of construction be torn down for a three-inch variance from the setback requirements. Further, the property owner can show that the three-inch difference will not change the character of the community or adversely

variance: Permission given to a property owner to deviate from strict compliance with all or part of a zoning ordinance.

affect surrounding properties. Another example would be one in which a developer is planning to build a high-rise luxury apartment building on beachfront property. The area in which the apartment building is to be constructed has a height limit of forty feet. If the developer can show that the best usage of the property would be to add an additional story to the building, although this addition may be over the forty-foot limit, the board may be willing to grant a variance.

If the board will not grant a variance, one possible recourse is to attempt to change the zoning ordinance by amendment. The proposed amendment will then be noticed and debated at a public hearing. If successful, the property owner's efforts will change the zoning ordinance for the entire area. If neither a variance nor an amendment to the ordinance is granted, the final recourse available to the property owner is the court system.

Special Exceptions. A property owner may seek a **special exception,** also referred to as a *conditional-use permit,* if the property owner wishes to use property for a use undesignated in that area. For example, suppose there is a large orthodox Jewish population living in a particular residential area. There may be several synagogues in the city; however, building an orthodox synagogue within walking distance in the neighborhood would be beneficial because orthodox Jews are not allowed to drive on the Sabbath. If the residential area is zoned exclusively for residential use, the prospective purchaser who wishes to build the synagogue would have to apply for a special exception.

Nonconforming Use. A different problem confronts the property owner who has built an improvement on land prior to the enactment of a zoning ordinance and now finds that the improvement is in conflict with the ordinance. For example, suppose a property owner built a gasoline station in an area many years ago when the area was relatively undeveloped. Over the years as the population grew, the zoning map was redrawn, and the area is now zoned exclusively residential. The zoning authorities will have to "grandfather" the property in and declare it a permissible **nonconforming use,** in some areas referred to as *preexisting use.* In some jurisdictions, the permitted nonconforming use is phased out over a specified period of time.

If the nonconforming use is permitted, the property owner may not make alterations to the property or change from one type of nonconforming use to another. For example, the gasoline station owner could not add a car wash to the property or tear the station down and replace it with a car dealership. Further, once an owner discontinues a nonconforming use, the owner may not subsequently revive it. If the owner sells the property, the new owner purchases the property with the understanding that he or she must comply with the zoning ordinance, and the permission for nonconforming use will be discontinued.

Environmental Protection Laws

The federal government understood over a century ago the need for federal regulation of real estate development to curtail damage to the nation's natural resources when it enacted the Rivers and Harbors Act of 1899, which prohibited unauthorized construction in navigable waters. Nonetheless, most of the major legislation in the area of environmental protection did not begin until the 1960s, growing in range and complexity in recent years. Environmental legislation imposes restrictions on the development and use of real property as well as imposing affirmative obligations such as waste management and cleanup. Although the greatest initial

special exception: Permission given to a property owner to use property for a use undesignated in that area.

nonconforming use: Also referred to as *preexisting use.* Permission given to a property owner who has built an improvement on land prior to the enactment of a zoning ordinance to continue to use the land in the same manner as before.

impact of environmental legislation was on industrial and commercial developers, today all real property owners are impacted to some extent by federal, state, and local environmental protection laws.

In 1969, Congress passed the National Environmental Policy Act (NEPA), which established the Environmental Protection Agency (EPA) for the purpose of creating environmental standards. In conjunction with the EPA, a Council on Environmental Quality was created, and environmental impact studies became a prerequisite for approval of large federal government projects as well as for federal decisions regarding large private projects. (The council was replaced in the 1990s by the White House Office on Environmental Policy.) The NEPA was shortly followed by the passage of the Clean Air Act, which established national primary and secondary air quality standards—the former for the protection of public health and the latter for the protection of plant and animal life. Further, this Act made it a requirement for states to comply with these standards in two ways: (1) by reviewing preconstruction plans to determine direct (for example, industrial plant emissions) and indirect (for example, traffic congestion) sources of potential air pollution and (2) by developing programs to maintain air quality standards (for example, vehicle emissions inspections).

The Clean Water Act gave the U.S. Army Corps of Engineers control over dredge and fill activities. Section 404 of the Act requires that any party wishing to engage in dredge and fill activities in any body of water, whether publicly or privately owned, first obtain a permit from the Army Corps of Engineers.

Other environmental legislation passed by Congress included the Solid Waste Disposal Act and the Federal Water Pollution Control Act. The Solid Waste Disposal Act was enacted to improve the methods for disposal of solid and hazardous waste by prohibiting open dumping and imposing severe civil and criminal penalties for violations. It also imposes various guidelines for solid waste management on state governments. The Federal Water Pollution Control Act has two objectives: (1) to establish a comprehensive plan to eliminate pollution from navigable waters, making them safe for public recreation, and (2) to provide federal assistance for public waste treatment facilities and waste management programs.

The biggest advance in federal environmental legislation in the 1980s was brought about by passage of the 1980 Comprehensive Environmental Response, Compensation and Liability Act (CERCLA). This legislation imposes liability for hazardous waste cleanup of toxic sites, regardless of cost or degree of responsibility for the presence of hazardous waste on the property. Those parties who may be held responsible for the cleanup of property polluted by hazardous waste include the current owner or operator of a facility on the property, the party that owned or operated a facility when the hazardous wastes were dumped on the property, and the party that selected the site or arranged for the disposal of hazardous waste. Thus, the liability originally imposed under the CERCLA was strict and could be applied retroactively.

To temper this harsh result, the CERCLA was amended in 1986 by the Superfund Amendments and Reauthorization Act (SARA), which allows purchasers a defense to liability if they can prove that proper inquiry into the property's prior ownership and usage was made. To clarify its intentions further, the federal government later issued policy statements indicating that the CERCLA was not meant to impose liability on residential property owners who did not directly contribute to the toxic pollution of the property. Consequently, the SARA encourages prospective property owners, other than residential owners, to research the environmental compliance of previous owners prior to purchase or potentially suffer the consequences for their failure to do so. As a result of the SARA, it has become common for buyers to make a sales contract contingent upon the results of an environmental audit and to demand inclusion in the contract of a hazardous waste indemnification provision.

There are tens of thousands of abandoned hazardous waste disposal sites around the country. Recognizing the urgency for cleanup of these sites and the potential hindrance of cleanup operations due to the great cost, the CERCLA created the Superfund, a congressional appropriation of over a billion dollars to clean up the most polluted sites. Even in instances in which private parties are held liable, they may not have adequate funds to cover the total cost of cleanup; therefore, the Superfund may be used to partially subsidize private cleanup efforts.

The increase in public awareness of the interdependency of ecological systems has led to concern in recent years for the preservation of wetlands. Correspondingly, there has been an increase in federal and state legislation to control development in these ecologically fragile areas. The definition of *wetland* can vary, depending on the federal or state agency reviewing a particular development project. The U.S. Army Corps of Engineers, in section 328.3(b) of Title 33 of the *Code of Federal Regulations,* defines *wetlands* as those areas that are inundated or saturated by surface groundwater at a frequency and duration sufficient to support, and that under normal circumstances do support, a prevalence of vegetation typically adapted for life in saturated soil conditions.

Whether development will be permitted and what types of assurances will be required in order to proceed with development will depend on the role of a particular parcel of land in the structure of the ecosystem. For example, some wetlands play an integral role by providing plant and wildlife habitats, by aiding in the control of erosion and flooding, or by serving as a buffer for upland areas in the event of a hurricane. Section 320.4(b)(2) of Title 33 of the *Code of Federal Regulations* requires an assessment of the effect of development on the following categories of wetlands before development is permitted:

1. Wetlands that serve significant biological functions, including food chain production, general habitat and nesting, spawning, rearing, and nesting sites for aquatic and land species;

2. Wetlands that are set aside for study of the aquatic environment or as sanctuaries or refuges;

3. Wetlands that, if destroyed or altered, would affect detrimentally natural drainage characteristics, sedimentation patterns, salinity, distribution, flushing characteristics, current patterns, or other environmental characteristics;

4. Wetlands that are significant in shielding other areas from wave action, erosion, or storm drainage; such wetlands are often associated with barrier beaches, islands, reefs, and bars;

5. Wetlands that serve as valuable storage areas for storm and flood waters;

6. Wetlands that are groundwater discharge areas that maintain minimum baseflows important to aquatic resources and those that are prime natural recharge areas;

7. Wetlands that serve significant water purification functions; and

8. Wetlands that are unique in nature or scarce in quantity to the region or local area.

A summary of the major federal environmental laws impacting land use is found in Exhibit 4–2.

| Federal environmental laws impacting land use | **EXHIBIT 4–2** |

Act	Purpose
Clean Air Act	Establishes national primary and secondary air quality standards. Requires compliance through review of pre-construction plans to determine direct and indirect sources of air pollution.
Clean Water Act	Requires property owners to obtain permit from Army Corps of Engineers prior to dredge and fill activities in any body of water.
Solid Waste Disposal Act	Prohibits open dumping of solid and hazardous waste and imposes civil and criminal penalties for such activities.
Federal Water Pollution Control Act	Establishes comprehensive plan to eliminate pollution from navigable water and provides federal assistance for public waste treatment facilities and waste management.
Comprehensive Environmental Response, Compensation and Liability Act (CERCLA)	Imposes liability for hazardous waste cleanup of toxic sites, regardless of cost or degree of responsibility for the presence of hazardous wastes on property.
Superfund Amendments and Reauthorization Act (SARA)	Amends CERCLA. Limits liability of residential property owners to those who directly contribute to toxic pollution of the property and encourages others to research environmental compliance of prior owners. Sets up federal fund to clean up the most badly polluted sites.

In addition to federal restrictions on land use, state and local governments have implemented their own conservation regulations. Some states carve out areas designated as Areas of Critical State Concern (ACSC) due to environmental, historical, natural, or archaeological resources located in these areas (for example, the Green Swamp Area in Florida). These areas must meet state land use guidelines.

From the preceding discussion, it is clear that a prospective developer of real property should commission a full environmental audit to identify and resolve any environmental problems prior to closing. Legal counsel should exercise great care in drafting an environmental audit provision for a sales contract. Prior to drafting the provision, legal counsel should identify and review all applicable federal, state, and local environmental laws. The provision should detail all steps to be taken in the environmental audit. These steps may include a public records search, site inspection, and historical review of operations on the property. Additionally, the audit may include a sampling and analysis of soil, air, and groundwater. The prospective buyer should retain all audit records and property appraisals to evince the actions taken in his or her preacquisition inquiry.

Fair Housing Laws

In addition to placing restrictions on how real property owners may use their property, federal and state governments place certain restrictions on how they may dispose of real property. Ironically, although these laws may be interpreted as restrictive of an owner's right to dispose of property freely, the legislative intent was, and continues to be, to make real property available to greater numbers by preventing discriminatory practices.

The first move by the federal government in this direction directly followed the Civil War. The federal Civil Rights Act of 1866 was enacted to prohibit racial discrimination, declaring that "[a]ll citizens of the United States shall have the same right in every state and territory as is enjoyed by white citizens thereof to inherit, purchase, lease, sell, hold and convey real and personal property." Still in force, this Act pertains to the sale or leasing of any real property, whether transacted by the owner of the property or through the use of a real estate broker.

One hundred years passed before the next significant federal measure occurred, again a result of civil struggle—this time, the civil rights movement of the 1960s. The Kennedy administration, noting that little effort had been made to date to enforce the Civil Rights Act of 1866, decided in 1962 to impose an executive order, No. 11063, designed to prevent discrimination in all housing financed by Federal Housing Administration (FHA) and Veterans Administration (VA) loans. This measure was followed by the congressional enactment of the Civil Rights Act of 1964, which prohibited discrimination in any housing program that received whole or partial federal funding.

Shortly thereafter, Congress passed the Civil Rights Act of 1968. Title VIII of the Act, devoted to fair housing legislation, has come to be known as the Federal Fair Housing Act. With it, Congress was attempting to reach out even further by broadening both the types of discriminatory practices prohibited and the types of housing covered by federal antidiscrimination statutes. The Federal Fair Housing Act of 1968 prohibits discrimination not only on the basis of race but also on the basis of color, religion, and national origin. While broadening its range to include housing other than government-subsidized housing, the Act does not pertain to all housing; it covers only the following:

1. With regard to single-family dwellings:
   a. All houses not privately owned,
   b. All privately owned houses if a real estate broker or salesperson is employed to sell or rent the premises,
   c. All houses owned by a person who owns three or more houses, and
   d. Any house owned by a person who, during any two-year period, sells two or more houses belonging to other persons.
2. With regard to multifamily dwellings:
   a. All multifamily dwellings with five or more units and
   b. All multifamily dwellings of four or fewer units if none of the units is owner-occupied.

The Federal Fair Housing Act of 1968 does not preempt the Civil Rights Act of 1866. Thus, racial discrimination is prohibited, regardless of whether the real property owner's premises fit into one of the above housing categories. These categories are relevant with regard to the added protected classes.

The Federal Fair Housing Act of 1968 specifies certain prohibited practices that include, but are not limited to, the refusal to sell or rent to persons in the protected classes. Additionally, quoting different terms or conditions to different people for the rental or sale of real property and engaging in discriminatory advertising are both prohibited. Real estate brokers and salespersons may not use blockbusting or steering practices. **Blockbusting** is the attempt to get homeowners to list their property for sale by stating or implying that minority groups may be moving into the neighborhood. **Steering** is the attempt to guide prospective homeowners into one neighborhood as opposed to another based on the racial, religious, or ethnic composition of a particular neighborhood. Lending institutions are prohibited from **redlining,** which is denying a loan or presenting different terms or conditions

blockbusting: The attempt to get homeowners to list their property for sale by stating or implying that minority groups may be moving into the neighborhood.

steering: The attempt to guide prospective homeowners into one neighborhood as opposed to another based on the racial, religious, or ethnic composition of a particular neighborhood.

redlining: Denying a loan or presenting different terms or conditions for a loan based upon the composition of the neighborhood or other discriminatory reasons.

for a loan based upon the composition of a neighborhood or other discriminatory reasons. Further, denying membership to a member of a protected class in any real estate–related organization or service is prohibited.

The scope of protected classes was expanded to include sex when the Housing and Community Development Act of 1974 was enacted. The Fair Housing Amendments Act of 1988 extended protection to handicapped persons and to persons on the basis of familial status. The term *handicapped* refers to persons with physical and mental impairments, including recovering alcoholics and recovering drug addicts, although current drug addicts are excluded from protection. The 1988 Act also protects persons with AIDS. In reference to blind or deaf persons, the Act prohibits a landlord from refusing to rent, evicting, or charging an increased security deposit because the tenant owns a guide dog. The Act additionally prohibits refusal to permit reasonable modifications of the premises if the modifications are necessary to allow the handicapped person full enjoyment of the premises and are paid for at his or her expense.

The familial status designation in the Act refers to children under the age of eighteen residing with either a parent or another person having legal custody of the children. It also prohibits discrimination against pregnant women and persons seeking custody of a child. In enacting this section of the Act, Congress carved out the following three exceptions in which seniors-only housing is permitted:

1. Housing provided under any federal or state program that is specifically designed and operated to assist elderly persons;
2. Housing intended for and occupied solely by persons sixty-two years of age or older, if existing prior to the amendment; and
3. Housing in which eighty percent or more of the units are occupied by persons fifty-five years of age or older.

All real estate brokers must have an equal housing opportunity poster placed conspicuously in their offices. This poster is available from the U.S. Department of Housing and Urban Development (HUD) and contains the equal housing opportunity logo and a statement supporting the Federal Fair Housing Act. Failure to display the poster may be considered in an investigation of a broker for discriminatory practices.

Federal fair housing laws not only prohibit direct discrimination against persons in the designated protected classes but also prohibit the printing or publishing of notices, statements, or advertisements that discriminate against persons in these classes. Due to continuing confusion over what wording in advertisements would be considered discriminatory and in violation of the law, in 1995 HUD issued some guidelines in a memorandum in an attempt to clarify prohibited versus acceptable advertising. The use of words describing a neighborhood or its residents in ethnic, racial, or religious terms is prohibited. Thus, an advertisement stating "four-bedroom home in Jewish neighborhood" or "no Haitians" is in violation of the law.

A tricky situation occurs when the premises are owned by a religious organization—for example, the Hebrew Home for the Aged. Can an advertisement use the name of the premises without violating fair housing laws? The HUD guidelines indicate that it may as long as a disclaimer is included stating that "This home does not discriminate on the basis of race, color, religion, national origin, sex, handicap or familial status." Advertisements are not allowed to contain words indicating an explicit preference based on sex; however, certain terms that have become common usage, such as *bachelor apartment,* are not considered discriminatory in and of themselves and may be used without violation. Additionally, advertisements cannot contain limitations on the ages or number of children, although a landlord is allowed to deny rental to a family whose numbers exceed any local ordinances regulating the number of persons per unit.

The most recent significant federal legislation in this area is the Americans with Disabilities Act of 1990 (ADA). Although its primary intention is to prevent discrimination in the employment of qualified individuals with disabilities, Title III of the ADA spills over into the area of real estate by requiring the removal of physical barriers in buildings of public accommodation (for example, restaurants, hotels) that impede persons with disabilities. In structures already existing prior to the enactment of the ADA, installation of ramps, accessible toilet stalls, and the like must be added if this can be easily accomplished. In new or remodeled structures, installation of these facilities is required.

Many states have enacted laws similar to the federal laws concerning fair housing. States are permitted to include additional protected classes, and local ordinances generally may be more restrictive than federal and state laws (for example, adding age as a protected class) but are not allowed to be less so.

An individual has one year from the time of an alleged fair housing violation to file a complaint with HUD. An individual also can file a lawsuit in state or federal court. If a complaint is filed with HUD, HUD investigates the matter and then decides whether to drop the complaint or to attempt a conciliation agreement between the parties. If the parties cannot reach an agreement, the matter then goes to an administrative hearing presided over by an administrative law judge.

If one is guilty of a fair housing violation, one can be ordered to:

1. compensate the complainant for actual damages, including humiliation, pain, and suffering;
2. make housing available to the complainant;
3. pay a civil penalty to the federal government, which can run from $10,000 to $50,000 for repeat offenses; and
4. pay the complainant's reasonable attorney's fees and costs.

Two recent cases have highlighted the problems of policing the enforcement of fair housing laws when the Internet is used as a vehicle for advertising properties. In both of these cases, courts were asked to determine the extent to which online services are protected by the Communications Decency Act from liability for advertisements that appear to run afoul of the Federal Fair Housing Act.

In *Fair Housing Council of San Fernando Valley v. Roommates.com, LLC,* 521 F.3d 1157 (9th Cir. 2008), local fair housing councils in California brought legal action against the operator of an Internet roommate-matching website. The site required that subscribers, either posting housing opportunities or searching listings, create profiles by completing a questionnaire using prompts and drop-down menus. The questionnaire included questions pertaining to gender, sexual orientation, and children who would be brought to a household. It also required each subscriber to state roommate preferences relating to these same three criteria. Subscribers could supplement the profile questions by completing an "Additional Comments" section. The majority decision did not determine whether the website operator violated state or federal fair housing laws. It determined that the operator was shielded from potential liability for alleged discriminatory practices by the Communications Decency Act, section 230 of which states: "No provider . . . of an interactive computer service shall be treated as the publisher or speaker of any information provided by another information content provider." Section 230 also states that the immunity applies only if the interactive computer provider is not also an information content provider.

Chief Judge Kozinski, writing for the majority, held that the immunity did not apply to the questionnaire. Although subscribers completed the questionnaire themselves, the website operator, Roommates.com, LLC, was acting as an information content provider by aiding the subscribers in creating allegedly discriminatory profiles when it required responses to prepopulated answers. However, the majority held that the website operator did retain immunity for any comments subscribers entered in the "Additional Comments" section of the profiles. A strong dissenting opinion voiced concerns that the majority decision was attempting to expand the liability of Internet service providers beyond the intentions of Congress.

In the same year, the Seventh Circuit was asked to determine whether the same section of the Communications Decency Act provided immunity to Craigslist for allegedly discriminatory postings. In *Chicago Lawyers' Committee for Civil Rights Under Law, Inc. v. Craigslist, Inc.*, 519 F.3d 666 (7th Cir. 2008), a public interest consortium brought legal action alleging that by permitting discriminatory postings on its site, Craigslist itself was violating the Federal Fair Housing Act. The consortium argued that courts enforce the statutory law against newspapers that publish discriminatory housing advertisements. The majority conceded that online services share certain similarities with newspapers but reasoned that they also share similarities with common carriers such as telephone companies, the latter not being subject to fair housing statutory enforcement because they do not create or publish discriminatory advertisements. In applying section 230 of the Common Decency Act in this context, the court held that Craigslist was immune from potential liability for alleged housing discrimination. It was not an information content provider but simply a messenger.

With the Internet becoming the preferred method for all types of advertising, the enforcement of both state and federal fair housing laws is becoming increasingly problematic. Organizations such as the National Fair Housing Alliance have identified many thousands of discriminatory housing advertisements posted online. Although the Common Decency Act does protect interactive online providers when they do take steps to filter offensive materials, these providers are not mandated to do so and, as noted, are shielded from liability if they simply act as a forum for communication and do not themselves actively play a role in the creation of discriminatory content.

Taxation

County and city governments are permitted to impose ad valorem taxes on real property located within their jurisdictions as well as **special assessments** for shared improvements that enhance the value of real property, such as the installation of sewer lines or sidewalks. State and federal governments do not levy direct property taxes. Income or losses realized from the use of property, however, must be included in state and federal income tax returns.

special assessment: An assessment for shared improvements that enhance the value of real property.

Recall from the discussion of homestead property in Chapter 2 that taxes are imposed on the value of the real property and any improvements thereon; these are referred to as *ad valorem taxes*. Certain designated *tax districts* are permitted to impose ad valorem taxes as well. These districts may include school districts, drainage districts, water districts, and sanitary districts.

County or city taxing authorities have the responsibility of assessing the value of real property for taxation purposes. They also have the authority to establish a tax rate, called a **millage rate,** to be used in computing ad valorem taxes. A mill equals one-tenth of a penny and is written 0.001. Some state legislatures impose tax rate ceilings—for example, a ten-mill cap. The taxable value of the property is multiplied by the millage rate to determine the taxes owed. For example, if the taxable value of the real property is $400,000 and the millage rate is 0.0115000, the taxes owed would be $4,600.

State statutes dictate the tax year for real property taxes. In many states, property taxes are levied on a calendar-year basis. This means that real property taxes are paid in arrears for the period January 1 through December 31 each year. After assessment is completed and the taxes computed, these taxes become a lien against the subject real property until such time as they are paid in full. A real property owner receives a tax bill informing him or her of the taxes owed and the due date, sometimes referred to as the penalty date, for payment of the taxes. Some areas encourage prompt payment by offering discounts. Conversely, penalties may be imposed for late payment. In other areas, taxes may be paid in monthly, quarterly, or semiannual installments. Failure to pay real estate taxes can subject the real property to a tax foreclosure or tax sale. (For a detailed discussion of tax liens, see Chapter 9.)

Budgets and Tax Levies. As noted, there may be many different taxing authorities, including counties, cities, school boards, and special tax districts. Each of these taxing authorities must prepare an operating budget each year that provides for all anticipated expenditures for the upcoming fiscal year. To complicate the task, each taxing authority's budget is really a composite of several departmental budgets. For example, the fire department will submit its budget, which will include the estimated cost of operating every phase of the fire department in the upcoming fiscal year (for example, new fire trucks, additional staff), to the city, which will review the fire department budget and combine it with the budgets submitted by other departments—such as the sheriff's department, social services, and so forth—to create the city's operating budget.

Once each taxing authority has put together an operating budget based on the information provided from each subordinate department, it has to estimate the revenue that can be anticipated from sources other than real property taxes. This revenue may come from a variety of sources, such as occupational license fees, building permit fees, fines for parking and speeding tickets, and state and federal funding for specified programs. Once this figure has been calculated, each taxing authority is in a position to determine how much revenue must be raised through real property taxes. The amount of property taxes received by each taxing authority must come from a **tax base,** which is the total assessed value of all taxable property in that taxing authority's jurisdiction.

Assessments. All real property undergoes the process of assessment. Property taxes are levied against land and all permanent improvements to the land. Often, the assessed value of the land and the assessed value of its improvements are arrived at

millage rate: A rate used in computing ad valorem real property taxes.

tax base: The total assessed value of all taxable real property in a taxing authority's jurisdiction.

separately and then combined in a single tax statement. The assessment is done by a county property appraiser or similar official. The appraiser determines the ownership and value of each parcel of real property placed on an *assessment roll*, sometimes referred to as a *tax list*. Real property is required by law to be assessed at *just value*. Staff members from the property appraiser's office typically go out to assess real property using forms and specific recording procedures. The information obtained through the property inspection is processed through a computer that uses applicable formulas to arrive at the assessment value. Depending on the state statute, appraisers are to take into consideration numerous factors in calculating just value, such as the following:

1. The present value of the property;
2. The location of the property;
3. The quantity or size of the property;
4. The condition of the property;
5. The highest and best use to which the property can be expected to be put in the immediate future (the most profitable use of the land only, not the land and improvements) and the present use of the property;
6. The cost of the property and the replacement value of any improvements thereon;
7. The income from the property; and
8. The net proceeds of the sale of the property, as received by the seller, after deduction of all usual and reasonable fees and costs and allowance for atypical financing.

If real property is sold during the year, the sale price of the property may become a factor for consideration in assessing its value, but generally it is not the controlling factor.

In many parts of the country, residential areas are divided into subdivisions. It is common in community developments within subdivisions to find standard-size lots. In these developments, appraisers often carry out their inspections by making a thorough inspection of a single lot that is selected as a standard lot. Its assessed value can then be applied to all other lots in the subdivision that correspond to that standard lot. Corner lots or lots with unusual features are exceptions and must be inspected individually. While the majority of lots in a subdivision may be similar, the houses or other improvements built on them are different and are assessed on an individual basis.

Once an assessment has been made, the owner is informed of the taxes owed through receipt of a tax statement. Tax statements are mailed to the property owner at the last address of record, and it is the responsibility of the property owner to ensure that a current address is on file in those counties in which he or she owns real property.

Should a real property owner wish to dispute the assessment, he or she must follow statutorily prescribed procedures. In some states, the first step is to seek an *adjustment* by contacting the property appraiser's office within a prescribed time period. The appraiser will then review the request for adjustment. If the appraiser finds that the property owner's arguments are valid, the appraiser is authorized to make an adjustment to the tax statement. Should the appraiser reject the property owner's argument, the next step is often to go before a *board of assessment,* sometimes referred to as an *adjustment board,* and request a review. In some states, the appraiser is not contacted as a first step, and the board review process is the appropriate procedure for filing an assessment protest or complaint. In many states, the members of the board of assessment are elected officials. This allows taxpayers to change the composition of the board should they believe certain members to be biased or unfair. Some states use a *board of equalization,* whose purpose is to determine whether a taxing authority's assessments are in line with those of neighboring areas. Should the board reject the property owner's arguments, the last resort typically is litigation. The property owner may choose to file suit against the appraiser and the tax collector if the real property tax is paid under protest. Most courts, however, are not in a position to make assessments; rather, they can specify the procedures to be used in reassessing the property if they believe the assessment to be improper.

Exemptions. State statutes dictate the categories of real property not included in the tax base as well as the categories and dollar amounts of permissible deductions that may be taken when calculating the amount of real property taxes owed. Although it is a misnomer, all of these categories are commonly classified as *exemptions.* Certain properties are immune from real property taxation. These properties include city, county, state, and federal government properties, which are not taxed unless they are leased or sold to private parties. Other properties may be subject to taxation but wholly or partially released from the obligation. These properties include religious properties, homestead properties, and properties owned by persons with disabilities.

The concept of homestead was discussed at length in Chapter 2. There it was noted that many states allow a statutorily prescribed dollar amount to be deducted from the assessed value of real property before the real property taxes are calculated. In this manner, homestead property is granted a partial tax exemption. Thus, the assessed value of real property is not always the taxable value of the property.

Some states grant partial tax exemptions to widows and widowers. In these states, a widow or widower who is a bona fide resident of the state may claim a specified dollar amount as a partial exemption that will be deducted from the assessed property value before the real property tax is calculated, just as is done with the homestead exemption. For example, if state law permits a $1,000 exemption for widows and widowers, $1,000 will be deducted from the assessed value of the property to get the taxable value. This taxable value will then be multiplied by the tax rate (the millage rate) to ascertain the taxes owed. In states that allow this exemption, the exemption eligibility expires when the widow or widower remarries.

Many states permit a disability tax exemption. In some states, the tax exemption may be partial, while others allow for a total tax exemption for the homestead property of a person who is disabled. The definition of *disabled* varies from state to state. Quadriplegics, paraplegics, hemiplegics, persons whose disabilities necessitate the use of a wheelchair, and persons who are legally blind are often included in statutory definitions. Proof of disability is required before the exemption will be allowed. For those disabled in an armed services–related activity, the proof commonly required is a certificate from the U.S. Department of Veterans Affairs. Some states permit a certificate from state-licensed physicians.

Whole or partial tax exemptions are not automatic but, rather, must be applied for to the taxing authority, and often the initial application must be made in person at the office of the property appraiser or other designated official. In many localities, once the initial application is made and approved, subsequent renewals may be made by mail or, in some instances, are automatic. Because the procedure varies widely, local law must be checked.

Tax Rates. From the discussion thus far, it is clear that the assessed value and taxable value of real property are often different. It is the taxable value and the tax rate that ultimately determine the amount of taxes. Taxing authorities determine the applicable tax rate through the application of formulas. The following is one commonly used formula:

$$Tax\ rate = \frac{Approved\ budget\ minus\ nonproperty\ tax\ revenue}{Total\ assessed\ valuation\ minus\ exemptions}$$

The following example should provide some clarification. Assume that the operating budget of Any County has been approved. This budget projects expenditures of $20,000,000 for the next fiscal year. Based on past experience, it is estimated that $5,000,000 in revenue can be culled from sources other than real property taxes. The assessed value of all real property in Any County is $1,750,000,000. The homestead tax exemption in Any County is $10,000, and 10,000 properties are eligible and have applied for this exemption, so the total exemptions amount to $100,000,000. With these figures and the above formula, the officials of Any County can calculate the required tax rate as follows:

$$Tax\ rate = \frac{\$20,000,000 - \$5,000,000}{\$1,750,000,000 - \$100,000,000}$$

This becomes

$$\frac{\$15,000,000}{\$1,650,000,000} = 0.009$$

Thus, the tax rate to be applied in Any County is nine mills.

Suppose that Angela and Andrew Aronson own a home in Any County. The assessed value of the property is $250,000, and they have applied for a homestead exemption. The calculation of their annual county property taxes is as follows:

Assessed value	$250,000
Homestead exemption	− 10,000
Taxable value	$240,000
County tax rate	× 0.009
County property taxes	$ 2,160

If Angela and Andrew lived within city limits, they would be subject to any city property taxes as well, plus the taxes imposed by any other taxing authorities.

Special Assessments. Finally, taxing authorities may impose *special assessment taxes*. These taxes are not paid annually. Rather, they are paid once, when some improvement in the area or neighborhood is planned that increases the property value of the properties to be assessed. These improvements may include sewer hookup, installation of septic tanks, street lighting, sidewalk paving, and so forth. Special assessment taxes are not ad valorem taxes and therefore are not calculated based upon the value of the property. Typically, these taxes are levied based upon the front footage of the property. Each property benefiting from the improvement will be taxed its pro rata share. An example will help illustrate this concept.

Suppose the City of Any City is installing sewer hookups in a neighborhood that has previously been dependent on septic tanks. Veronica Jackson lives in this neighborhood. Any City is slated to pay 40 percent of the costs involved, and the residents of the neighborhood are to be taxed a special assessment for the remaining 60 percent of the costs. The city officials have calculated that the costs should run $30 per foot. Veronica's lot frontage is 115 feet. Because there is property on both sides of the street, once an initial calculation is made based on the frontage, Veronica will be responsible for only half of that amount:

Lot frontage	115 feet
Cost per foot	× $30
Total cost for 115 feet	$3,450
City's percentage	× 0.40
City's share of cost	$1,380
Total cost for 115 feet	$3,450
City's share of cost	− $1,380
Property owners' share	$2,070

Dividing $2,070 by 2 shows that Veronica's assessment will be $1,035.

In addition to ad valorem taxes and special assessments, other taxes have an impact on real property ownership. Although it is beyond the scope of this chapter, please note that many people and businesses purchase real property for investment purposes. Property owners will be responsible for federal and, when applicable, state income taxes on income received from these properties. Additionally, property owners are allowed certain deductions for expenses when computing taxable income from the operation of investment properties. As the laws in this area are continually revised, it is advisable to consult a tax adviser before acquiring income-producing real estate.

Eminent Domain

The greatest governmental intrusion on private property ownership is the governmental taking of private real property for public use. This is done under the power of **eminent domain,** granted to the federal government by the Fifth Amendment of the U.S. Constitution and applied to the states under the Fourteenth Amendment. Eminent domain is the right of federal, state, and local governments and certain public and quasi-public corporations and utilities, such as railroads and electric companies, to take private property for public use. The process through which the private property is taken is called **condemnation.** Property may be taken by condemnation only after a legislative enactment for public use, payment of *just compensation,* and due process. Therefore, affected property owners receive notice of *suit for condemnation* and are given an opportunity to make objections at a hearing.

eminent domain: The right of federal, state, and local governments and certain public and quasi-public corporations and utilities to take private property for public use.

condemnation: The process by which private property is taken by federal, state, and local governments for public use.

At the hearing, a property owner may attempt to argue that the governmental agency does not need the property for public use or, more often, that the compensation offered is not a fair price for the property. Courts are reluctant to rule on whether the taking of private property is necessary to serve public interests, preferring to leave that determination to government agencies. Rather, a court will consider whether the taking is for public use. In evaluating whether the compensation paid to the property owner is just compensation, a court will determine whether the price paid reflects the value of the property if put to its best usage. For evaluation purposes, it is irrelevant if the property, at the time of suit, is indeed being put to this best usage. If only a portion of the property is condemned, then just compensation is calculated by determining the decrease in value of the entire property by the taking of the portion.

A more difficult situation occurs when governmental authorities rezone areas for conservation or other public welfare purposes. For example, an area that was originally zoned residential may be rezoned into a special conservation area to protect endangered wildlife. This rezoning will dramatically affect the market value of the property in that area. The question becomes whether the rezoning is equivalent to the exercise of eminent domain. If so, the government may be required to pay just compensation to property owners in the area for the difference in the value of their property under the original zoning versus the value of their property under the rezoning. If it is determined that the rezoning does not constitute a "taking," then the property owners will have to live with the newly imposed restrictions without receiving any compensation.

In 2005, the U.S. Supreme Court looked at the power of eminent domain and just how "public" the use must be to justify the taking of private property in the case *Kelo v. City of New London.*

CASE: *Kelo v. City of New London*
545 U.S. 469, 125 S. Ct. 2655 162 L. Ed. 439 (2005)

Justice STEVENS delivered the opinion of the Court.

In 2000, the city of New London approved a development plan that, in the words of the Supreme Court of Connecticut, was "projected to create in excess of 1,000 jobs, to increase tax and other revenues, and to revitalize an economically distressed city, including its downtown and waterfront areas." 268 Conn. 1, 5, 843 A.2d 500, 507 (2004). In assembling the land needed for this project, the city's development agent has purchased property from willing sellers and proposes to use the power of eminent domain to acquire the remainder of the property from unwilling owners in exchange for just compensation. The question presented is whether the city's proposed disposition of this property qualifies as a "public use" within the meaning of the Takings Clause of the Fifth Amendment to the Constitution.

The city of New London (hereinafter City) sits at the junction of the Thames River and the Long Island Sound in southeastern Connecticut. Decades of economic decline led a state agency in 1990 to designate the City a "distressed municipality." In 1996, the Federal Government closed the Naval Undersea Warfare Center, which had been located in the Fort Trumbull area of the City and had employed 1,500 people. In 1998, the City's unemployment rate was nearly double that of the State, and its population of just under 24,000 residents was at its lowest since 1920.

These conditions prompted state and local officials to target New London, and particularly its Fort Trumbull area, for economic revitalization. To this end, respondent New London Development Corporation (NLDC), a private nonprofit entity established some years earlier to assist the City in planning economic development, was reactivated.

(continued)

In January 1998, the State authorized a $5.35 million bond issue to support the NLDC's planning activities and a $10 million bond toward the creation of a Fort Trumbull State Park. In February, the pharmaceutical company Pfizer Inc. announced that it would build a $300 million research facility on a site immediately adjacent to Fort Trumbull; local planners hoped that Pfizer would draw new business to the area, thereby serving as a catalyst to the area's rejuvenation.

*   *   *

The NLDC intended the development plan to capitalize on the arrival of the Pfizer facility and the new commerce it was expected to attract. In addition to creating jobs, generating tax revenue, and helping to "build momentum for the revitalization of downtown New London," *id.*, at 92, the plan was also designed to make the City more attractive and to create leisure and recreational opportunities on the waterfront and in the park.

*   *   *

Petitioner Susette Kelo has lived in the Fort Trumbull area since 1997. She has made extensive improvements to her house, which she prizes for its water view. Petitioner Wilhelmina Dery was born in her Fort Trumbull house in 1918 and has lived there her entire life. Her husband Charles (also a petitioner) has lived in the house since they married some 60 years ago. In all, the nine petitioners own 15 properties in Fort Trumbull—4 in parcel 3 of the development plan and 11 in parcel 4A. Ten of the parcels are occupied by the owner or a family member; the other five are held as investment properties. There is no allegation that any of these properties is blighted or otherwise in poor condition; rather, they were condemned only because they happen to be located in the development area.

In December 2000, petitioners brought this action in the New London Superior Court. They claimed, among other things, that the taking of their properties would violate the "public use" restriction in the Fifth Amendment. After a 7-day bench trial, the Superior Court granted a permanent restraining order prohibiting the taking of the properties located in parcel 4A (park or marina support). It, however, denied petitioners relief as to the properties located in parcel 3 (office space). 2 App. to Pet. for Cert. 343–350.

After the Superior Court ruled, both sides took appeals to the Supreme Court of Connecticut. That court held, over a dissent, that all of the City's proposed takings were valid. It began by upholding the lower court's determination that the takings were authorized by chapter 132, the State's municipal development statute. See Conn. Gen. Stat. § 8–186 *et seq.* (2005). That statute expresses a legislative determination that the taking of land, even developed land, as part of an economic development project

is a "public use" and in the "public interest." 268 Conn., at 18–28, 843 A.2d, at 515–521. Next, relying on cases such as *Hawaii Housing Authority v. Midkiff*, 467 U.S. 229, 104 S.Ct. 2321, 81 L.Ed.2d 186 (1984) and *Berman v. Parker*, 348 U.S. 26, 75 S.Ct. 98, 99 L.Ed. 27 (1954), the court held that such economic development qualified as a valid public use under both the Federal and State Constitutions. 268 Conn., at 40, 843 A.2d, at 527.

Finally, adhering to its precedents, the court went on to determine, first, whether the takings of the particular properties at issue were "reasonably necessary" to achieving the City's intended public use, *id.*, at 82, 843 A.2d, at 552–553, and, second, whether the takings were for "reasonably foreseeable needs," *id.*, at 93, 843 A.2d, at 558–559. The court upheld the trial court's factual findings as to parcel 3, but reversed the trial court as to parcel 4A, agreeing with the City that the intended use of this land was sufficiently definite and had been given "reasonable attention" during the planning process. *Id.*, at 120–121, 843 A.2d, at 574.

*   *   *

Two polar propositions are perfectly clear. On the one hand, it has long been accepted that the sovereign may not take the property of *A* for the sole purpose of transferring it to another private party *B*, even though *A* is paid just compensation. On the other hand, it is equally clear that a State may transfer property from one private party to another if future "use by the public" is the purpose of the taking; the condemnation of land for a railroad with common-carrier duties is a familiar example. Neither of these propositions, however, determines the disposition of this case.

*   *   *

Viewed as a whole, our jurisprudence has recognized that the needs of society have varied between different parts of the Nation, just as they have evolved over time in response to changed circumstances. Our earliest cases in particular embodied a strong theme of federalism, emphasizing the "great respect" that we owe to state legislatures and state courts in discerning local public needs. See *Hairston v. Danville & Western R. Co.*, 208 U.S. 598, 606–607, 28 S.Ct. 331, 52 L.Ed. 637 (1908) (noting that these needs were likely to vary depending on a State's "resources, the capacity of the soil, the relative importance of industries to the general public welfare, and the long-established methods and habits of the people"). For more than a century, our public use jurisprudence has wisely eschewed rigid formulas and intrusive scrutiny in favor of affording legislatures broad latitude in determining what public needs justify the use of the takings power.

Those who govern the City were not confronted with the need to remove blight in the Fort Trumbull area, but their determination that the area was sufficiently distressed

(continued)

to justify a program of economic rejuvenation is entitled to our deference. The City has carefully formulated an economic development plan that it believes will provide appreciable benefits to the community, including—but by no means limited to—new jobs and increased tax revenue. As with other exercises in urban planning and development, the City is endeavoring to coordinate a variety of commercial, residential, and recreational uses of land, with the hope that they will form a whole greater than the sum of its parts. To effectuate this plan, the City has invoked a state statute that specifically authorizes the use of eminent domain to promote economic development. Given the comprehensive character of the plan, the thorough deliberation that preceded its adoption, and the limited scope of our review, it is appropriate for us, as it was in *Berman*, to resolve the challenges of the individual owners, not on a piecemeal basis, but rather in light of the entire plan. Because that plan unquestionably serves a public purpose, the takings challenged here satisfy the public use requirement of the Fifth Amendment.

To avoid this result, petitioners urge us to adopt a new bright-line rule that economic development does not qualify as a public use. Putting aside the unpersuasive suggestion that the City's plan will provide only purely economic benefits, neither precedent nor logic supports petitioners' proposal. Promoting economic development is a traditional and long accepted function of government. There is, moreover, no principled way of distinguishing economic development from the other public purposes that we have recognized.

*   *   *

Petitioners contend that using eminent domain for economic development impermissibly blurs the boundary between public and private takings. Again, our cases foreclose this objection. Quite simply, the government's pursuit of a public purpose will often benefit individual private parties.

*   *   *

Alternatively, petitioners maintain that for takings of this kind we should require a "reasonable certainty" that the expected public benefits will actually accrue. Such a rule, however, would represent an even greater departure from our precedent. "When the legislature's purpose is legitimate and its means are not irrational, our cases make clear that empirical debates over the wisdom of takings— no less than debates over the wisdom of other kinds of socioeconomic legislation—are not to be carried out in the federal courts." *Midkiff*, 467 U.S., at 242, 104 S.Ct. 2321. . . . A constitutional rule that required postponement of the judicial approval of every condemnation until the likelihood of success of the plan had been assured would unquestionably impose a significant impediment to the successful consummation of many such plans.

Just as we decline to second-guess the City's considered judgments about the efficacy of its development plan, we also decline to second-guess the City's determinations as to what lands it needs to acquire in order to effectuate the project. "It is not for the courts to oversee the choice of the boundary line nor to sit in review on the size of the particular project area. Once the question of the public purpose has been decided, the amount and character of land to be taken for the project and the need for a particular tract to complete the integrated plan rests in the discretion of the legislative branch." *Berman*, 348 U.S., at 35–36, 75 S.Ct. 98.

In affirming the City's authority to take petitioners' properties, we do not minimize the hardship that condemnations may entail, notwithstanding the payment of just compensation. We emphasize that nothing in our opinion precludes any State from placing further restrictions on its exercise of the takings power. Indeed, many States already impose "public use" requirements that are stricter than the federal base line. Some of these requirements have been established as a matter of state constitutional law, while others are expressed in state eminent domain statutes that carefully limit the grounds upon which takings may be exercised. As the submissions of the parties and their *amici* make clear, the necessity and wisdom of using eminent domain to promote economic development are certainly matters of legitimate public debate. This Court's authority, however, extends only to determining whether the City's proposed condemnations are for a "public use" within the meaning of the Fifth Amendment to the Federal Constitution. Because over a century of our case law interpreting that provision dictates an affirmative answer to that question, we may not grant petitioners the relief that they seek.

The judgment of the Supreme Court of Connecticut is affirmed. It is so ordered.

*   *   *

Justice O'CONNOR, with whom THE CHIEF JUSTICE, Justice SCALIA, and Justice THOMAS join, dissenting.

Over two centuries ago, just after the Bill of Rights was ratified, Justice Chase wrote:

> "An ACT of the Legislature (for I cannot call it a law) contrary to the great first principles of the social compact, cannot be considered a rightful exercise of legislative authority. . . . A few instances will suffice to explain what I mean. . . . [A] law that takes property from A. and gives it to B: It is against all reason and justice, for a people to entrust a Legislature with SUCH powers; and, therefore, it cannot be presumed that they have done it." *Calder v. Bull*, 3 Dall. 386, 388, 1 L.Ed. 648 (1798) (emphasis deleted).

(continued)

Today the Court abandons this long-held, basic limitation on government power. Under the banner of economic development, all private property is now vulnerable to being taken and transferred to another private owner, so long as it might be upgraded—i.e., given to an owner who will use it in a way that the legislature deems more beneficial to the public—in the process. To reason, as the Court does, that the incidental public benefits resulting from the subsequent ordinary use of private property render economic development takings "for public use" is to wash out any distinction between private and public use of property—and thereby effectively to delete the words "for public use" from the Takings Clause of the Fifth Amendment. Accordingly, I respectfully dissent.

* * *

This case returns us for the first time in over 20 years to the hard question of when a purportedly "public purpose" taking meets the public use requirement. It presents an issue of first impression: Are economic development takings constitutional? I would hold that they are not. We are guided by two precedents about the taking of real property by eminent domain. In *Berman*, we upheld takings within a blighted neighborhood of Washington, D.C. The neighborhood had so deteriorated that, for example, 64.3% of its dwellings were beyond repair. 348 U.S. at 30, 75 S.Ct. 98. It had become burdened with "overcrowding of dwellings," "lack of adequate streets and alleys," and "lack of light and air." *Id.*, at 34, 75 S.Ct. 98. Congress had determined that the neighborhood had become "injurious to the public health, safety, morals, and welfare" and that it was necessary to "eliminat[e] all such injurious conditions by employing all means necessary and appropriate for the purpose," including eminent domain. *Id.*, at 28, 75 S.Ct. 98. Mr. Berman's department store was not itself blighted. Having approved of Congress' decision to eliminate the harm to the public emanating from the blighted neighborhood, however, we did not second-guess its decision to treat the neighborhood as a whole rather than lot-by-lot. *Id.*, at 34–35, 75 S.Ct. 98; see also *Midkiff*, 467 U.S. at 244, 104 S.Ct. 2321 ("it is only the taking's purpose, and not its mechanics, that must pass scrutiny").

* * *

In *Midkiff*, we upheld a land condemnation scheme in Hawaii whereby title in real property was taken from lessors and transferred to lessees. At that time, the State and Federal Governments owned nearly 49% of the State's land, and another 47% was in the hands of only 72 private landowners. Concentration of land ownership was so dramatic that on the State's most urbanized island, Oahu, 22 landowners owned 72.5% of the fee simple titles. *Id.*, at 232, 104 S.Ct. 2321. The Hawaii Legislature

had concluded that the oligopoly in land ownership was "skewing the State's residential fee simple market, inflating land prices, and injuring the public tranquility and welfare," and therefore enacted a condemnation scheme for redistributing title. *Ibid.*

In those decisions, we emphasized the importance of deferring to legislative judgments about public purpose. Because courts are ill-equipped to evaluate the efficacy of proposed legislative initiatives, we rejected as unworkable the idea of courts' "deciding on what is and is not a governmental function and . . . invalidating legislation on the basis of their view on that question at the moment of decision, a practice which has proved impracticable in other fields." *Id.*, at 240–241, 104 S.Ct. 2321. . . .

* * *

The Court's holdings in *Berman* and *Midkiff* were true to the principle underlying the Public Use Clause. In both those cases, the extraordinary, precondemnation use of the targeted property inflicted affirmative harm on society—in *Berman* through blight resulting from extreme poverty and in *Midkiff* through oligopoly resulting from extreme wealth. And in both cases, the relevant legislative body had found that eliminating the existing property use was necessary to remedy the harm. *Berman, supra,* at 28–29, 75 S.Ct. 98; *Midkiff, supra,* at 232, 104 S.Ct. 2321. Thus a public purpose was realized when the harmful use was eliminated. Because each taking *directly* achieved a public benefit, it did not matter that the property was turned over to private use. Here, in contrast, New London does not claim that Susette Kelo's and Wilhelmina Dery's well-maintained homes are the source of any social harm. Indeed, it could not so claim without adopting the absurd argument that any single-family home that might be razed to make way for an apartment building, or any church that might be replaced with a retail store, or any small business that might be more lucrative, if it were instead part of a national franchise, is inherently harmful to society and thus within the government's power to condemn.

In moving away from our decisions sanctioning the condemnation of harmful property use, the Court today significantly expands the meaning of public use. It holds that the sovereign may take private property currently put to ordinary private use, and give it over for new, ordinary private use, so long as the new use is predicted to generate some secondary benefit for the public—such as increased tax revenue, more jobs, maybe even aesthetic pleasure. But nearly any lawful use of real property can be said to generate some incidental benefit to the public. Thus, if predicted (or even guaranteed) positive side-effects are enough to render transfer from one private party to another constitutional, then the words

(continued)

"for public use" do not realistically exclude *any* takings, and thus do not exert any constraint on the eminent domain power.

* * *

I would hold that the takings in both Parcel 3 and Parcel 4A are unconstitutional, reverse the judgment of the Supreme Court of Connecticut, and remand for further proceedings.

Justice THOMAS, dissenting.

Long ago, William Blackstone wrote that "the law of the land . . . postpone[s] even public necessity to the sacred and inviolable rights of private property. 1 Commentaries on the Laws of England 134–135 (1765) (hereinafter Blackstone). The Framers embodied that principle in the Constitution, allowing the government to take property not for "public necessity," but instead for "public use." Amdt. 5. Defying this understanding, the Court replaces the Public Use Clause with a "'[P]ublic [P]urpose'" Clause, *ante,* at 2662–2663 (or perhaps the "Diverse and Always Evolving Needs of Society" Clause, *ante,* at 2662 (capitalization added)), a restriction that is satisfied, the Court instructs, so long as the purpose is "legitimate" and the means "not irrational," *ante,* at 2667 (internal quotation marks omitted). This deferential shift in phraseology enables the Court to hold, against all common sense, that a costly urban-renewal project whose stated purpose is a vague promise of new jobs and increased tax revenue, but which is also suspiciously agreeable to the Pfizer Corporation, is for a "public use."

I cannot agree. If such "economic development" takings are for a "public use," any taking is, and the Court has erased the Public Use Clause from our Constitution, as Justice O'CONNOR powerfully argues in dissent. *Ante,* at 2671, 2674–2677. I do not believe that this Court can eliminate liberties expressly enumerated in the Constitution and therefore join her dissenting opinion. Regrettably, however, the Court's error runs deeper than this. Today's decision is simply the latest in a string of our cases construing the Public Use Clause to be a virtual nullity, without the slightest nod to its original meaning. In my view, the Public Use Clause, originally understood, is a meaningful limit on the government's eminent domain power. Our cases have strayed from the Clause's original meaning, and I would reconsider them.

* * *

. . . In my view, it is "imperative that the Court maintain absolute fidelity to" the Clause's express limit on the power of the government over the individual, no less than with every other liberty expressly enumerated in the Fifth Amendment or the Bill of Rights more generally. *Shepard v. United States,* 544 U.S.----,----, 125 S.Ct. 1254,

1264, 161 L.Ed.2d 205 (2005) (THOMAS, J., concurring in part and concurring in judgment) (internal quotation marks omitted).

* * *

The most natural reading of the Clause is that it allows the government to take property only if the government owns, or the public has a legal right to use, the property, as opposed to taking it for any public purpose or necessity whatsoever.

* * *

Tellingly, the phrase "public use" contrasts with the very different phrase "general Welfare" used elsewhere in the Constitution. See *ibid.* ("Congress shall have Power To . . . provide for the common Defence and general Welfare of the United States"); preamble (Constitution established "to promote the general Welfare"). The Framers would have used some such broader term if they had meant the Public Use Clause to have a similarly sweeping scope.

* * *

The consequences of today's decision are not difficult to predict, and promise to be harmful. So-called "urban renewal" programs provide some compensation for the properties they take, but no compensation is possible for the subjective value of these lands to the individuals displaced and the indignity inflicted by uprooting them from their homes. Allowing the government to take property solely for public purposes is bad enough, but extending the concept of public purpose to encompass any economically beneficial goal guarantees that these losses will fall disproportionately on poor communities. Those communities are not only systematically less likely to put their lands to the highest and best social use, but are also the least politically powerful. If ever there were justification for intrusive judicial review of constitutional provisions that protect "discrete and insular minorities," *United States v. Carolene Products Co.,* 304 U.S. 144, 152, n. 4, 58 S.Ct. 778, 82 L.Ed. 1234 (1938), surely that principle would apply with great force to the powerless groups and individuals the Public Use Clause protects. The deferential standard this Court has adopted for the Public Use Clause is therefore deeply perverse. It encourages "those citizens with disproportionate influence and power in the political process, including large corporations and development firms" to victimize the weak. *Ante,* at 2676 (O'CONNOR, J., dissenting).

* * *

The Court relies almost exclusively on this Court's prior cases to derive today's far-reaching, and dangerous, result. See *ante,* at 2662–2664. . . . When faced with a clash of constitutional principle and a line of unreasoned

(continued)

cases wholly divorced from the text, history, and structure of our founding document, we should not hesitate to resolve the tension in favor of the Constitution's original meaning. For the reasons I have given, and for the reasons given in Justice O'CONNOR's dissent, the conflict of principle raised by this boundless use of the eminent domain power should be resolved in petitioners' favor. I would reverse the judgment of the Connecticut Supreme Court.

Case Questions

1. In writing his opinion for the majority of the Supreme Court, Justice Stevens indicated that "many States already impose 'public use' requirements that are stricter than the federal base line." In reviewing your state's eminent domain statutes, does your

state impose a stricter standard than the Supreme Court applied in this case? If a similar situation arose in your state, how do you think your state courts would rule, based on state law?

2. This case makes mention of prior case law, particularly the *Midkiff* case and the *Berman* case. How would you distinguish the factual scenarios in the *Midkiff* and *Berman* cases from each other and from this case? Do you think the eminent domain power was utilized properly in those cases? Do you believe there are enough similarities in those cases to this case to result in the same decision? Why or why not?

3. Who makes the stronger argument for limitations to be placed on the power of eminent domain, Justice O'Connor or Justice Thomas? Explain your answer.

Escheat to the State

Perhaps the most encompassing power of the state, and sometimes local, governments is the right of reversion of title to private property in their jurisdiction. This right of reversion is exercised when a property owner dies intestate leaving no heirs. In that circumstance, his or her real property will **escheat** to the state. The probate laws of each state determine the point at which real property reverts to the state or, in certain instances, to the city or county in which the property is located. For example, the intestacy laws of some states require that there be no heirs not only of the decedent but also of the decedent's predeceased spouse to claim the property before the property escheats.

Private Restrictions on Ownership

Restrictive Covenants

Restrictive covenants are private restrictions imposed on the use of private property, which may take the form of *subdivision regulations,* restrictions imposed by a developer or a condominium or homeowners' association, or **deed restrictions,** which are restrictive covenants contained in the deed transferring property from seller to buyer. In each of these situations, the restrictions upon which title to the property is taken are recorded in the public records. As is the case with zoning ordinances, most restrictive covenants attempt to preserve or increase the value of the subject parcel and surrounding properties. They may restrict the size of the homes constructed on the property, require committee approvals for alterations, or impose setback requirements. Restrictive covenants are binding on present and future owners of the property.

Similarly, as noted in the previous chapter, a condominium owner takes title to a condominium unit subject to the restrictions contained in the declaration of condominium, which is recorded when the condominium is created. The declaration may include several use restrictions, such as those pertaining to pets, regulating trucks and commercial vehicles, and regulating the sale or lease of a condominium unit. The condominium association is invested with the authority to enforce these restrictions.

escheat: The right of reversion of title to private property in their jurisdictions, given to state and local governments.

restrictive covenants: Private restrictions imposed on the use of private property.

deed restrictions: Restrictive covenants contained in a deed transferring property from seller to buyer.

Other restrictive covenants arise when restrictions are placed in a deed transferring title from one party to another. These restrictions limit the use of the real property described in the deed. The restrictions imposed may be perpetual or for a specified period of time. While in effect, the restrictions are binding on the present owner and all subsequent owners. The courts, however, will not enforce any deed restriction that is discriminatory as to race, ethnicity, sex, or religion.

Easements

An **easement** is the enforceable right to use the real property of another for a particular purpose. Because an easement is considered an encumbrance on the real property on which it is located, it can be considered a nonexclusive limitation of the property owner's full use and enjoyment of his or her property.

Types of Easements. An **easement in gross** is an easement given to benefit a particular individual or entity rather than one given to confer a benefit to real property. Although some easements in gross may be noncommercial, the most common are commercial in nature, such as those granted to utility or cable companies. The granting of the easement permits a company to come onto the grantor's real property to install and repair transmission lines. These easements usually are created by the execution of a *grant of easement,* which contains the names of the grantor and grantee, the date upon which the easement is created, the legal description of the property on which the easement is conferred, and the specific rights of usage conveyed by the easement. The grant of easement is signed by the parties, witnessed and notarized, and recorded in the public records in the county in which the property is located. Because this easement is personal to the easement holder, it is not considered a right that runs with the land. Traditionally, easements in gross were nontransferable for this reason. Today, however, many courts permit the assignment or sale of commercial easements in gross.

An **appurtenant easement** is an easement given to confer a benefit to adjacent real property. This easement typically is created to permit ingress and egress to landlocked property. For example, suppose Sarah Bostwick purchases acreage in an area that has one main access road on the north end of the property. She then decides to keep a parcel (Parcel A) and to sell a parcel located on the south end of the property (Parcel B) to Eric Winters. Prior to purchasing the property, Eric wants assurance of access to the main access road. In granting this access across her property, Sarah's property has become the *servient estate,* sometimes referred to as the *servient tenement.* In other words, Sarah's property "serves" Eric's by providing access. Eric's property becomes the *dominant estate,* sometimes referred to as the *dominant tenement.* Eric's property is "dominant" because it receives the benefit conferred, as illustrated in Exhibit 4–3.

An appurtenant easement runs with the land and thus is transferred to the new owner when the dominant estate is transferred. This is the case even if the deed transferring the real property does not specifically mention the easement. An appurtenant easement may be created by an express grant, such as a grant of easement, but is customarily created by operation of law inasmuch as egress and ingress are considered a necessity.

Another type of appurtenant easement is a **party wall easement.** A party wall is a shared partition wall separating two properties. Each property owner owns that

easement: The enforceable right to use the real property of another for a particular purpose.

easement in gross: An easement given to benefit a particular individual or entity rather than one given to confer a benefit to real property.

appurtenant easement: An easement given to confer a benefit to adjacent real property.

party wall easement: An easement on the part of a shared partition wall between two properties.

EXHIBIT 4–3	Illustration of an appurtenant easement

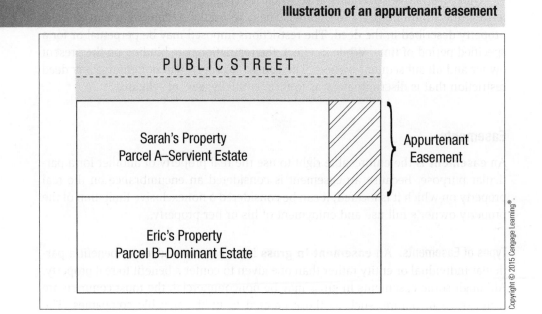

portion of the party wall that is located on his or her property and has an appurtenant easement on the remaining portion. Unlike other appurtenant easements, a party wall easement is not created by operation of law and must be created by an express grant.

A **prescriptive easement,** sometimes referred to as an *easement by prescription,* is created when a person adversely uses the property of another for a statutorily specified time period. Thus, acquiring a prescriptive easement is similar to acquiring property through adverse possession, discussed at length in Chapter 2. In most states, the use must be continuous, uninterrupted, hostile, open, and notorious. Periods of occupation by successive users may be tacked on to meet the statutory time requirements if the successive users are successors in interest—that is, legally related by blood or contract.

Sometimes easements are granted to permit an encroachment on the property. An **encroachment** is an illegal intrusion of a building or appurtenance onto the property of another. For example, suppose Malcolm Gallagher decides to redesign and resurface his driveway. Engineers come out and survey, and the design is approved. After the driveway is completed, it is found that the new driveway extends a few inches over Malcolm's boundary line and onto the property of his neighbor, Gwendolyn Stewart. Legally, if Gwendolyn does nothing and the prescriptive time period passes, Malcolm will acquire a prescriptive easement over those few inches. Before this happens, Gwendolyn can force Malcolm to realign his driveway so that it fits within his boundary lines, but that may be unreasonable and cause hard feelings between neighbors. A third alternative is for Gwendolyn to grant an easement to Malcolm for a specified duration.

Drafting Easements. The drafting of the document that grants an easement is similar to the drafting of other formal real estate documents in that attention to detail is crucial. Prior to drafting, certain matters should be addressed. First, a boundary survey should be done of the easement area. Second, any third-party approvals should be obtained. For example, if the servient estate is mortgaged, the consent of all mortgagees must be obtained. Next, it is important to verify the legal names

prescriptive easement: An easement created when a person adversely uses the property of another for a statutorily specified time period.

encroachment: An illegal intrusion of a building or appurtenance onto the property of another.

of both the grantor and the grantee. The grantor must be of legal age and of sound mind. There is no reciprocal requirement of the grantee. The document must include the legal names of the parties and the legal description of the easement area, the latter to be copied from the boundary survey.

An easement is not necessarily a contract. For example, an appurtenant easement may be granted by the servient estate without requiring remuneration in return. Therefore, a number of states do not require a recital of consideration. However, because some states do require this recital, even if money does not actually change hands, state statutes should be checked.

The term for which the easement is granted should be stated. If the document does not include this, there is a legal assumption that the easement is meant to be perpetual. It can be stated in a certain number of years or until the happening of a certain event. The right of use conveyed should be described with specificity. The grantor may be granting an exclusive or nonexclusive right of use. Any restrictions or limitations imposed on the right of use should be detailed.

Responsibilities for maintenance of the easement should be apportioned between the grantor and grantee. With easements shared equally by the grantor and grantee, such as is the case with party wall easements, it is common for these responsibilities to be apportioned equally. Additionally, the grantor may desire that an indemnification provision be included in the document whereby the grantee indemnifies the grantor from any liability for injury to persons or property arising out of the use of the easement and may require, as a condition of granting the easement, that the grantee carry appropriate liability coverage and provide the grantor with a copy of the policy.

Once these provisions are reviewed, the grant of easement must be signed in front of the statutorily prescribed number of witnesses and, if required, a notary public. Finally, the easement must be recorded with the appropriate recording clerk in the relevant political subdivision (typically, the county) in which the property is located. A sample easement is found in Exhibit 4–4.

Termination of Easements. Easements may be terminated in various ways. An appurtenant easement will terminate should the dominant estate and the servient estate merge into one property. This is called *termination by merger*. For example, suppose the area in which Sarah Bostwick and Eric Winters live is zoned for mixed use, residential and commercial. Recall that Sarah originally owned all the acreage encompassing both properties prior to selling a portion to Eric. Eric was granted an appurtenant easement over Sarah's property for right of ingress and egress to the main access road. Now XYZ Corporation, a developer of shopping malls, wants to purchase both properties, and Eric and Sarah agree to sell. When title to their properties is transferred to XYZ Corporation, the easement granted to Eric by Sarah will terminate by merger.

If a grant of easement provides that an easement shall last for a specified duration of time or until a specified event occurs, when that time period expires or that event occurs, the easement naturally is terminated. In addition, an easement may be terminated by a written release in which the grantee expressly releases the easement right to the grantor. Easements also may be terminated through physical abandonment by the grantee. The intention of the parties is decisive in determining whether an easement has, in fact, been abandoned. For example, suppose The Repertory Theatre Company is located in a seasonal area, and although it has adequate parking for most of the year, during "season" its patrons complain of lack of parking space. George Goodwin owns the vacant lot next to the theatre

EXHIBIT 4–4	Utility easement

THIS UTILITY EASEMENT is made this 6th day of July, 2015, by and between Tresham Development Corporation, an Any State corporation ("Grantor"), and Any City Electric Company ("Grantee").

In consideration of Three Thousand Dollars ($3,000.00) paid by Grantee to Grantor, the receipt and sufficiency of which is hereby acknowledged, Grantor does hereby grant and convey to Grantee, its successors and assigns, a thirty (30) foot permanent easement across and along the tract of land described as Tract 8, Tresham Estates No. 5, as recorded in Plat Book 518, Page 20, of the Public Records of Any County, Any State, the location of said easement is as set forth on the attached survey. By conveyance of this easement, Grantor gives Grantee the right to install, operate, inspect, repair, alter, and extend utility lines upon said land. Further, Grantor gives Grantee the right to trim and clear limbs from any trees that may obstruct or interfere with the operation of said utility lines. Grantee indemnifies Grantor from any liability for injury to persons or property arising out of the use of this easement.

The granting of this easement conveys only those rights and privileges set forth above and does not convey any further rights or interests in the real property herein described.

IN WITNESS WHEREOF, Grantor has set forth its hand and seal, this 6th day of July, 2015.

Signed, sealed and delivered
in the presence of:

TRESHAM DEVELOPMENT CORPORATION,
an Any State corporation

Robin Hobart

By: _Francis Tresham_
President

Terrence Lowell

Attest: _Candace Darcy_
Secretary
[Corporate Seal]

Subscribed and sworn to before me this 6th day of July, 2015, by Francis Tresham, President, and Candace Darcy, Secretary, of Tresham Development Corporation, a corporation organized under the laws of the State of Any State.

Gillian Furniss
Notary Public, State of Any State
My commission expires: _04/20/16._

and grants an easement to The Repertory Theatre Company, permitting the parking overflow onto his lot during specified months of the year. Should The Repertory Theatre Company move across town to a larger location with increased parking, the move would indicate the theatre's intention of abandoning the easement. Additionally, an easement may be terminated by foreclosure on the servient estate by a prior lienholder. Finally, an easement may be terminated by a court in a suit to quiet title against a person claiming an easement.

Licenses

A **license** is the personal right to perform specified activities on the real property of another. A license is often difficult to distinguish from an easement in gross. Perhaps the best way to make the distinction is to say the emphasis with a license is on the right to perform activities, whereas the emphasis with an easement in gross is on the right to use the land. Some licenses are implied. For example, the owner of a supermarket impliedly gives customers a license to enter the premises to shop. However, the owner does not give an implied license to persons to come onto the

license: A personal right to perform specified activities on the real property of another.

premises to hand out political flyers, and if they do so without express permission, they may be required to leave. A license can also be express, either oral or written. For example, an owner of property may grant an express license permitting a charitable organization to hold a weekend carnival on the property to raise money for that particular charity. The charitable organization (the *licensee*) may or may not pay for this right, depending on the agreement it made with the property owner (the *licensor*). Generally speaking, unless consideration is paid for the license privilege, the privilege may be revoked at will by the licensor.

Somewhat similar to a license or easement is **profit à prendre,** sometimes referred to as *profit.* Profit à prendre is the right to remove certain items from another's land or to remove a portion of the land. What generally is removed is a natural resource, such as lumber, minerals, or crops.

Leases

When a buyer purchases income-producing property, that buyer typically takes title to the property subject to the leases executed by the seller/landlord and the tenants. In so doing, the new owner of the income-producing property is restricted in his or her disposal of the rental space by the terms of the leases. Because of this, a prospective buyer will request, prior to closing, *estoppel certificates* from each of the tenants, which state the names of the tenants; their addresses; the terms of their leases; their rental payments and rental due dates; the amounts of any security deposits, other deposits, and advance rents; the condition of any fixtures and/or furniture if rented furnished; statements regarding any options to purchase; and statements pertaining to monies owed by or claims made against the landlord. (Leases are covered in depth in Part III of this text.)

Liens

A **lien** is a claim or charge against property for payment of a debt. The property acts as security for the debt. Should the property owner fail to satisfy the debt, the lienholder may foreclose on the property. If not removed prior to sale of the real property, the buyer takes title to the property subject to the liens and risks foreclosure.

Some liens are *general liens*—that is, they affect any and all property of the debtor, both real and personal. For a general lien to attach against a particular parcel of real property, that lien must be recorded against the property with the records clerk in the county in which the property is located. An example of a general lien is a *judgment lien,* a charge on property owing as the result of a court-awarded judgment, such as a personal injury award by a civil court. Other liens are *specific liens,* attaching only to specific real property. An example of a specific lien is a *mortgage lien,* which attaches only to the mortgaged real property.

Certain liens have priority over others. Therefore, if a lienholder wants to foreclose on real property, the lienholder must first search the title to the property to determine whether there are any lienholders in senior position who have priority. If there are such lienholders, the lienholder is relegated to a junior position and if the lienholder forecloses, all senior lienholders must be paid with the proceeds from the foreclosure sale before the lienholder in the junior position receives any money to partially or wholly satisfy the outstanding debt. (For a detailed discussion of liens, see Chapter 9.)

profit à prendre: The right to remove certain items from another's land or to remove a portion of the land.

lien: A claim or charge against property for payment of a debt.

CHAPTER SUMMARY

1. The federal and state constitutions grant police powers to governmental agencies that allow them to place restrictions on private property owners when deemed necessary for the protection of public health, safety, and welfare. Police power is exercised through the right of taxation given to city and county taxing authorities to levy ad valorem taxes. Further, it is exercised through the creation and enforcement of zoning ordinances, the adoption of environmental protection and fair housing laws, and the ultimate power to take possession of private property through eminent domain and escheat to the state.

2. Zoning ordinances are imposed to implement the goals set forth in the master plans devised by planning commissions. A master plan prioritizes perceived needs in the area of land use, conservation, circulation, noise regulation, and public facilities. Through examination of this plan, zoning maps are designed to delineate zoning areas that best accomplish the plan's objectives. A zoning map divides areas into land use classifications. The typical classifications are residential, commercial, industrial, agricultural, and public use. Some areas may be designated for multiple use.

3. When property owners desire to deviate from strict compliance with zoning ordinances, they may request a variance or permission to be treated as a special exception or nonconforming use. A property owner requests a variance if he or she believes that undue hardship will occur unless he or she is allowed to vary from the requirements of the ordinance. A property owner seeks classification as a special exception if he or she wishes to use the property for a use undesignated in that area. Finally, a property owner may seek to be "grandfathered" in as a nonconforming use if the zoning ordinances change after the property owner has constructed improvements on the property.

4. The 1960s marked a significant stride in the area of environmental protection legislation with the passage of the National Environmental Policy Act (NEPA) and the establishment of the Environmental Protection Agency (EPA). In the years that have followed, Congress has placed increasing emphasis on legislation designed to preserve air and water quality and improve methods for disposal of solid and hazardous wastes, including the establishment of a Superfund to aid in toxic waste cleanup.

5. The Fair Housing Act of 1968 and its amendments prohibit discrimination in the sale or rental of certain properties on the basis of race, color, religion, sex, national origin, handicap, or familial status. The Act prohibits the refusal to sell or lease to members of these protected classes. Further, it prohibits such practices as blockbusting, steering, and redlining. In recent years, the increased use of the Internet to advertise real property sales and rentals has made the process of policing and enforcing fair housing laws more complex.

6. For the purpose of levying ad valorem property taxes, a designated appraiser and staff must assess the value of each parcel of land and any permanent improvements to the land. The assessment process must establish the just value of the property. Factors aiding in determining just value include the present value, location, size, and condition of the property as well as the highest and best use to which the property may be put.

7. An easement is the enforceable right to use the real property of another for a particular purpose. The two major types of easements are easements in gross and appurtenant easements. An easement in gross is considered a personal right given to benefit a particular individual or entity, whereas an appurtenant easement is conferred to benefit real property. An appurtenant easement runs with the land, but an easement in gross does not. Both may be created by execution of a grant of easement. An appurtenant easement also may be created by operation of law. In addition, a prescriptive easement may be created if a claimant adversely uses the property of another for a statutorily prescribed time period. Easements may be terminated by merger, abandonment, foreclosure, expiration of a term, execution of a release, or a suit to quiet title.

WEB RESOURCES

http://www.hud.gov/

This is the site of the U.S. Department of Housing and Urban Development. It provides a wealth of information and covers a multitude of topics, including information on fair housing laws and enforcement activities. It also provides the name, case number, and basis of each complaint filed with HUD. The full text of the complaints can be accessed from this site as PDF files.

http://www.ada.gov/

This is the U.S. Department of Justice home page for the Americans with Disabilities Act (ADA). It provides information pertaining to ADA design standards and code certifications, new or proposed regulations, instructions on filing complaints, and links to federal agencies with ADA responsibilities.

http://www.hss.energy.gov/

This is the site of the U.S. Department of Energy, Office of Health, Safety, and Security. It provides information on federal environmental policies.

http://www.epa.gov/

The website of the U.S. Environmental Protection Agency provides information on the Clean Air Act, the Clean Water Act, and other environmental issues.

http://www.fairhousingfirst.org/

This site, supported by the U.S. Department of Housing and Urban Development, provides information on Fair Housing Act design and construction requirements.

http://www.nationalfairhousing.org/

This is the site of the National Fair Housing Alliance. It is a consortium of individuals; private, nonprofit fair housing organizations; and state and local civil rights agencies throughout the United States. The site provides fair housing resources as well as articles and blogs pertaining to the latest fair housing issues.

http://www.eminentdomaintoday.org/

This site is a forum to discuss issues pertaining to eminent domain. It provides eminent domain news articles as well as links to eminent domain sites, appraisal sites, and legal research materials.

REVIEW QUESTIONS

1. Explain the concept and purpose behind the police powers given to federal, state, and local governments, and describe the various methods of exercising these powers.
2. Explain the process by which real property tax assessments are made.
3. Distinguish among (a) blockbusting, (b) redlining, and (c) steering.
4. What provisions should be included when drafting an easement?
5. Distinguish among (a) an appurtenant easement, (b) a prescriptive easement, and (c) an encroachment.

DISCUSSION QUESTIONS

1. You now know the categories that are exempt from compliance with the Fair Housing Act. Do you agree that these categories should be exempt from compliance? Why or why not?
2. Do you believe that there is a need for adult-only designated communities and that individuals under fifty-five should not be allowed to live in such communities? What purpose does this serve?
3. You are glancing through the local newspaper over the weekend and notice an advertisement for condominium units. The advertisement has three color photographs: one of the exterior of the condominium buildings, one of a Caucasian couple on a tennis court, and one of a Caucasian woman having coffee in a sunlit kitchen. Is this advertisement a violation of the Fair Housing Act? Why or why not?
4. Do you believe that interactive online service providers should be held accountable for any housing advertisements posted to their sites that violate fair housing laws? Why or why not?
5. Suppose there is an eighteen-hole municipal golf course in your neighborhood. The city wants to sell part of the golf course land to a developer and retain a portion of the course as a nine-hole course. The developer wants to build luxury high-rise condominiums on the other portion. Many homes in your neighborhood currently have a view of the golf course. What are the pros and cons of allowing the city to proceed with the sale?
6. In the state of Any State, the homestead tax exemption has been $10,000 for many years. There is a political movement to raise the exemption to $30,000, and the matter will be voted on as a referendum on the next ballot. What are the pros and cons of passing this referendum?

ETHICAL QUESTION

Your cousin is a real estate developer and needs an attorney to represent him in a zoning matter. Your supervising attorney is out of town, but you know she handles zoning matters for several clients, so you tell your cousin she will handle his case. He asks you what her fees are, and you go over the typical fee arrangement she has with regard to handling such matters. Have you acted within your scope of authority?

Slossberg Law Office on CourseMate

Please go to www.cengagebrain.com to log into CourseMate, access the Slossberg Law Office, and work on your client files. Each module corresponds to a chapter in the text. Within each module, you will be provided with instructions by the supervising attorney. You are asked to keep track of time spent on time sheets. The documents produced through working on client files in the law office can then be compiled into a portfolio of final work product.

CourseMate

The available CourseMate for this text has an interactive eBook and interactive learning tools, including flash cards, quizzes, and more. To learn more about this resource and access free demo CourseMate resources, including the Slossberg Law Office, go to www.cengagebrain.com, and search for this book. To access CourseMate materials that you have purchased, go to login.cengagebrain.com.

5

Legal Descriptions of Property

CHAPTER OBJECTIVES

Upon completion of this chapter, the student will:

• Know the three types of legal descriptions and how to draft them

• Know how to review a survey

• Know the minimum technical standards required for surveys

• Know how to prepare a legal description from a survey

Introduction

Every major document pertaining to a real estate transaction contains a legal description of the subject real property. The **legal description** provides the parties with a precise delineation of the specific property involved that sets the property apart from all other parcels of real estate. A legal description is more technical than a street address and sets forth the exact boundaries of the real property, indicating where one parcel of property ends and another begins. A legal description is written in words that also may be used to map out a graphic form on a survey map. Surveys show the boundary lines of the property, improvements on the property, and encroachments or encumbrances. Surveys are discussed in detail later in the chapter.

There are three types of legal descriptions: (1) the metes and bounds description, (2) the government survey description, and (3) the plat description. In certain areas of the country, one of these methods may be in greater use than the others. For example, the government survey method is not used uniformly across the country. In some instances, one method may be precluded because of the nature of the real property involved. For example, the plat method may be used only in a situation in which the parcel of property is located within a subdivision for which a plat map has been drawn and recorded.

Because paralegals prepare most of the documents involved in a real estate transaction, they have to be able to read and understand the three types of legal descriptions utilized in describing property. A paralegal may be asked simply to proofread a lengthy legal description for mistakes, comparing it to previous descriptions. Alternatively, a paralegal may be asked to prepare a written description from a survey map provided. This chapter outlines the three types of legal descriptions, explaining the components of each and the most common situations in which each type of description is used. The chapter then discusses surveys, the parties who may require a survey, the standards that must be met for an acceptable survey, and the process of reviewing a survey.

Types of Legal Descriptions

In many contexts, the use of a street address is sufficient to describe real property. However, in many legal documents and in real estate transactions in which property is being sold, leased, or mortgaged, a more precise identification is required that indicates the exact boundary lines of the real property. A prospective buyer wants to know the exact size of the parcel of property being bought as well as the line at which the property ends and another parcel begins. The boundary lines are important not only to describe size but also to indicate whether any improvements to the property are within the boundary lines or encroaching on another's property and, likewise, to indicate whether any improvements to the neighboring properties are encroaching on the subject property. Further, boundary lines provide a starting point for measuring setback requirements when building on real property.

To meet the needs for a precise description, one of three methods may be used. The first is the **metes and bounds method,** which is the oldest of the three methods and which many consider the most detailed method of describing real property. An alternative method, commonly used in a majority of states in the country, is the **government survey method.** Exhibit 5–1 indicates which states are government survey states and which are not. The third method, undeniably the simplest and only pertinent to certain types of real property, is the **plat method.**

Metes and Bounds Method

A metes and bounds legal description is one that outlines the boundary lines of a parcel of real property by establishing a starting point called the **point of beginning** and describing the *course* (direction) and *distance* each boundary line travels from that point around the perimeters of the property until returning to the point of beginning. The point of beginning must be a readily identifiable point. It may be a street intersection, a lot corner, a monument, or a described course and distance from a monument. A **monument** is a natural or man-made object that is permanent and fixed, such as a boulder, a large tree, a statue, or a building. The term *metes* refers to the distance of a line, and the term *bounds* refers to the direction of a line. The course and distance of each line is broken down into short segments, referred to as **calls.** "South 30° East, a distance of 45.15 feet" is an example of a call. This same call can be written as follows: S30°00'00"E45.15'. Thus, the legal description is comprised of a series of calls. By drawing out the series of calls, the resulting diagram should display a parcel of property with closed borders. If the lines do not result in the description ending at the precise place at which it started, there is a problem with the legal description.

Notice the sample call in the preceding paragraph. The first half of the call provides the direction, or course, of the boundary line. This portion of the call is referred to as the **bearing,** or the *course bearing*. Notice that in the sample bearing, the direction is given as south 30 degrees east. This is the case because a bearing is determined by a compass reading, a compass dividing measurements into 360 degrees to make a full circle. A surveyor takes the 360-degree circle and divides

legal description: A precise delineation of a specific parcel of real property that sets the property apart from other parcels of real estate.

metes and bounds method: A method of legal description that outlines the boundary lines of a parcel of real property by establishing a starting point called the point of beginning and describing the course and distance each boundary line travels from that point around the perimeters of the property until returning to the point of beginning.

government survey method: A method of legal description, established by the U.S. Congress, that works on a grid system.

plat method: A method of legal description that describes real property by making reference to its location on a plat map recorded in the land records in the county in which the property is located.

point of beginning: A readily identifiable point that is the starting point of a metes and bounds legal description of the subject real property.

monument: A natural or man-made object that is permanent and fixed.

call: A short segment providing the course and distance of a line of a metes and bounds legal description.

bearing: That part of a call that provides the direction or course of a boundary line.

EXHIBIT 5–1			Methods used to describe real property in various states		
State	**Metes and Bounds**	**Government Survey**	**State**	**Metes and Bounds**	**Government Survey**
Alabama		X	Montana		X
Alaska		X	Nebraska		X
Arizona		X	Nevada		X
Arkansas		X	New Hampshire	X	
California		X	New Jersey	X	
Colorado		X	New Mexico		X
Connecticut	X		New York	X	
Delaware	X		North Carolina	X	
District of Columbia	X		North Dakota		X
Florida		X	Ohio		X
Georgia	X		Oklahoma		X
Hawaii	X		Oregon		X
Idaho		X	Pennsylvania	X	
Illinois		X	Rhode Island	X	
Indiana		X	South Carolina	X	
Iowa		X	South Dakota		X
Kansas		X	Tennessee	X	
Kentucky	X		Texas	X	
Louisiana		X	Utah		X
Maine	X		Vermont	X	
Maryland	X		Virginia	X	
Massachusetts	X		Washington		X
Michigan		X	West Virginia	X	
Minnesota		X	Wisconsin		X
Mississippi		X	Wyoming		X
Missouri		X			

it into four quadrants, each comprised of 90 degrees. The bearing S30°E is thus located in the southeast quadrant. For more exact measurements, each degree can be divided into 60 minutes. The symbol for minutes is ('). Each minute can be further divided into 60 seconds. The symbol for seconds is ("). Therefore, the bearing N48°27'42" reads as north 48 degrees, 27 minutes, 42 seconds.

The second portion of the call, providing the distance traveled, typically measures distance in feet or in hundredths of a foot. In the sample call S30°00'00" E45.15', the distance this segment of the boundary line travels is 45 and 15/100ths of a foot. In some areas, other forms of measurement are used, such as rods, chains, and yards. Exhibit 5–2 provides a chart setting forth the equivalencies of feet, yards, rods, and chains.

If you are required to draw out a written metes and bounds legal description, you need a compass and ruler. The first step is to break the legal description into a series of calls so that you are working with only one call at a time. Then locate the point of beginning and place the center of the compass circle over the point of beginning so that the compass lines up in a north-south direction. Next, read the first call—for example,

Measurement of equivalencies			EXHIBIT 5-2

Measurement Equivalencies			
Feet	Yards	Rods	Chains
66	22	4	1
132	44	8	2
198	66	12	3
264	88	16	4
330	110	20	5
396	132	24	6
462	154	28	7
528	176	32	8
594	198	36	9
660	220	40	10
726	242	44	11
792	264	48	12
838	286	52	13
924	308	56	14
990	330	60	15
1,056	352	64	16
1,122	374	68	17
1,188	396	72	18
1,254	418	76	19
1,320	440	80	20

South 30°E, a distance of 45.15 feet. Find the southeast quadrant and locate 30 degrees east of the north-south line. Make a mark at the 30-degree point. Then read the rest of the call, which in this example states a distance of 45.15 feet. Taking a ruler, from the point of beginning draw a line to the mark you made at the 30-degree point, and then measure along that angle a straight line equivalent to 45.15 feet.

The term *equivalent* is used here because you are drawing to scale. When drawing to scale, you are making sure that the measurements of the boundary lines in your diagram relate in size to the measurements of the actual boundary lines of the particular parcel of real property. For example, the scale might indicate that 1 mile equals 8 inches. Once this line is drawn, you have drawn your first call. To continue, take the compass and place the center of the compass in a north-south direction at the end of the line just drawn and repeat the procedure with the next call. Once you have drawn each call, the diagram should close at the point of beginning.

The measurements described thus far work well enough when the property in question is perfectly square or rectangular. Many parcels of property, however, contain curved boundary lines. To demarcate curved lines, a surveyor makes reference to the arc distance of the curve, the radius distance of the curve, and the course and distance of the chord. The term **arc** refers to the length of a curved line that makes up a segment of the boundary of the real property. The **radius** refers to the distance between any point on that curved line and the center of an imaginary circle that could be drawn if that curved line was extended to form a full circle. A **chord** is a straight line drawn from the starting point of an arc to the end point of

arc: The length of a curved line that makes up a segment of the boundary of the real property.

radius: The distance between any point on a curved line and the center of an imaginary circle that could be drawn if that curved line was extended to form a full circle.

chord: A straight line drawn from the starting point of an arc to the end point of an arc.

EXHIBIT 5-3   **Metes and bounds description**

SAMPLE METES AND BOUNDS
DESCRIPTION IN PARAGRAPH FORM

Begin at the NW corner of Section X, Thence south along section line 21 feet, Thence east 10 feet to a Point of Beginning, Thence due east a distance of 34 feet, Thence south 62°50′ east a distance of 32 feet, Thence southeasterly along a line forming an angle of 8° to the right with a prolongation of the last described course a distance of 30 feet, Thence south 13° to the left of a prolongation of the last described line a distance of 50 feet, Thence due east a distance of 40 feet, Thence due south a distance of 30 feet to a point of curvature of a curve to the right concave to the northwest having a radius of 20 feet and a central angle of 90°, Thence along the arc of said curve a distance of 31.4 feet to a point of tangency, Thence run due west a distance of 100 feet to a point of curvature of a curve to the right concave to the northeast having a radius of 60 feet and a central angle of 15°, Thence along the arc of said curve a distance of 15.7 feet to a point of tangency, Thence north 30° west a distance of 40 feet, Thence north 40° east a distance of 30 feet, Thence north 42°04′ west a distance of 55.3 feet to the Point of Beginning.

SAMPLE METES AND BOUNDS
LEGAL DESCRIPTION IN LIST FORM

1. Begin at the NW corner of Section X
2. Thence south along the section line 21 feet
3. Thence east 10 feet to a Point of Beginning
4. Thence due east a distance of 34 feet
5. Thence south 62°50′ east a distance of 32 feet
6. Thence southeasterly along a line forming an angle of 8° to the right with a prolongation of the last described course a distance of 30 feet
7. Thence south 13° to the left of a prolongation of the last described line a distance of 50 feet
8. Thence due east a distance of 40 feet
9. Thence due south a distance of 30 feet to a point of curvature of a curve to the right concave to the northwest having a radius of 20 feet and a central angle of 90°
10. Thence along the arc of said curve a distance of 31.4 feet to a point of tangency
11. Thence run due west a distance of 100 feet to a point of curvature of a curve to the right concave to the northeast having a radius of 60 feet and a central angle of 15°
12. Thence along the arc of said curve a distance of 15.7 feet to a point of tangency
13. Thence north 30° west a distance of 40 feet
14. Thence north 40° east a distance of 30 feet
15. Thence north 42°04′ west a distance of 55.3 feet to the Point of Beginning

Reproduced through the courtesy of Attorneys' Title Insurance Fund, Inc.

the arc. A sample call demarcating a curved boundary line reads as follows: "thence run along said curve to the right having a chord bearing of S32°01'E, a radius of 47 feet, and a central angle of 46°50' for an arc distance of 35.17 feet to a point of tangency." This example illustrates the complexity of some metes and bounds descriptions. Exhibit 5-3 provides a sample metes and bounds description, first in paragraph form and then broken down into a list of calls. Exhibit 5-4 provides a diagram of this metes and bounds description.

If you are asked to prepare a written metes and bounds description from a provided survey, the first thing you must do is find the point of beginning and describe it. If you were asked to provide the legal description for the property diagramed in Exhibit 5-4, for example, you would notice that the point of beginning does not

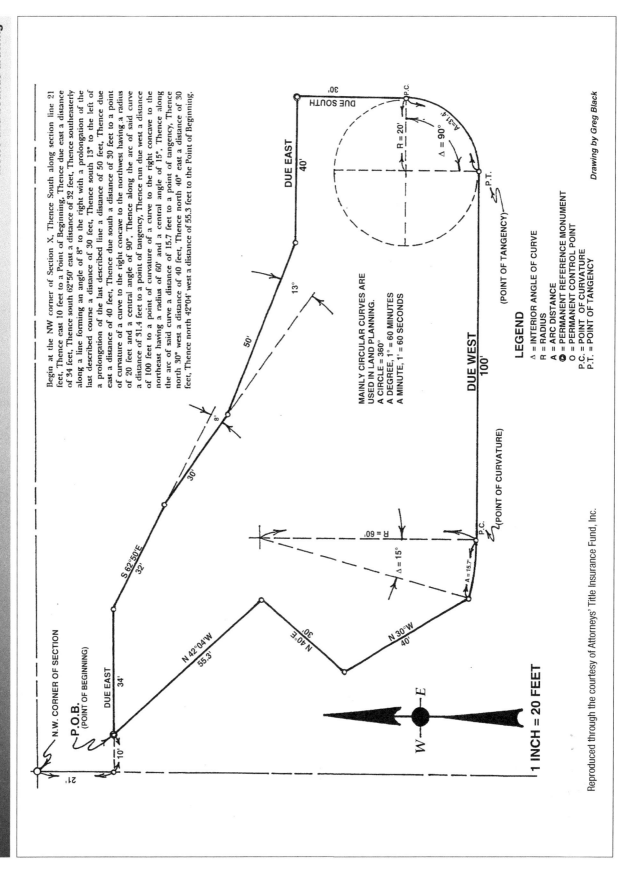

Begin at the NW corner of Section X, Thence South along section line 21 feet, Thence east 10 feet to a Point of Beginning, Thence due east a distance of 34 feet, Thence south 62°50' east a distance of 32 feet, Thence southeasterly along a line forming an angle of 8° to the right with a prolongation of the last described course a distance of 30 feet, Thence south 13° to the left of a prolongation of the last described line a distance of 50 feet, Thence due east a distance of 40 feet, Thence due south a distance of 30 feet to a point of curvature of a curve to the right concave to the northwest having a radius of 20 feet and a central angle of 90°, Thence along the arc of said curve a distance of 31.4 feet to a point of tangency, Thence run due west a distance of 100 feet to a point of curvature of a curve to the right concave to the northeast having a radius of 60' and a central angle of 15°, Thence along the arc of said curve a distance of 15.7 feet to a point of tangency, Thence north 30° west a distance of 40 feet, Thence north 40° east a distance of 30 feet, Thence north 42°04' west a distance of 55.3 feet to the Point of Beginning.

EXHIBIT 5-4   **Metes and bounds drawing**

MAINLY CIRCULAR CURVES ARE
USED IN LAND PLANNING.
A CIRCLE = 360°
A DEGREE, 1° = 60 MINUTES
A MINUTE, 1' = 60 SECONDS

LEGEND

Δ = INTERIOR ANGLE OF CURVE
R = RADIUS
A = ARC DISTANCE
◉ = PERMANENT REFERENCE MONUMENT
O = PERMANENT CONTROL POINT
P.C. = POINT OF CURVATURE
P.T. = POINT OF TANGENCY

1 INCH = 20 FEET

start at the exact northwest corner of Section X. It starts 21 feet south and 10 feet east of the corner. Therefore, the description begins: "Begin at the NW corner of Section X, thence south 21 feet, thence east 10 feet to a Point of Beginning." Then find the first call—in this instance, "Thence due east 34 feet"—and describe each call in turn until you come back to the point of beginning.

As noted earlier, monuments are often referred to in metes and bounds descriptions. What is the result when there is a discrepancy in reference to a monument and a course and distance measurement? This issue was addressed in the following North Carolina case.

CASE: *Baker v. Moorefield*

154 N.C. App. 134, 571 S.E.2d 680 (2002)

WYNN, Judge.

Wade and Lola Baker appeal the Superior Court's judgment establishing a common boundary line between the Bakers' property and adjacent property owned by Clyde and Donna Moorefield. The Bakers present one issue on appeal: Did the trial court err by finding the recorded deed ambiguous and using a monument, instead of course and distance, to establish the common boundary? After a careful review of the record, we conclude the trial court had competent evidence to find ambiguity in the deed. Moreover, our Supreme Court has consistently held that when "there is a conflict between course and distance and a fixed monument, the call for the monument will control." *Cutts v. Casey*, 271 N.C. 165, 170, 155 S.E.2d 519, 522 (1967). Accordingly, we affirm the judgment of the Superior Court, Stokes County.

The facts of this case tend to show that in 1953, the Moorefields and Bakers entered into a land conveyance contract and used the following legal description to describe the property conveyed:

> BEGINNING at an iron stake in the Golden Baker and C.D. Slate line, at a point 54.8 feet, South 79 degrees 51 minutes East of Golden Baker's and C.D. Slate's corner in C.T. McGee's line, *and runs thence South 7-1/2 degrees West, said line being parallel to the brick wall of the store building;* 100 feet to a corner in line of U.S. Highway 52; thence South 79 degrees 57 minutes East 140 feet to a point in the line U.S. Highway 52, thence parallel with the first line, running North 7-1/2 degrees East 150 feet to an iron stake, Golden Baker's corner and Mrs. C.D. Slate's line; thence with her line North 79 degrees 57 minutes West 140 feet to the BEGINNING.

The present controversy arises from the placement of a common boundary line which the deed describes as running "South 7-1/2 degrees West" and "parallel to the brick wall

of the store building." In 1986, the Moorefields tore down the brick wall and store building, and constructed a new structure on the property. In December 1997, the Bakers filed a Petition to Establish Boundaries in Superior Court, Stokes County. The Bakers alleged that the Moorefields' new structure encroached on the 7½ degree boundary arch. In response, the Moorefields alleged that the new structure was parallel to the brick wall of the old store building.

In August 2001, the case was tried without a jury before Superior Court Judge Clarence W. Horton who made the following contested Findings of Fact:

> 8. Location of the first line, which proceeds generally South . . . is the primary focus of the dispute between the parties. The description of the first line . . . describes a course South 7½ degrees West, running parallel to the brick wall of the Store Building. . . . Although the old Store Building has now been removed . . . its exact location was plotted. . . . [However a] course of 7½ degrees West is not parallel with the Store Building, and does not accurately represent the common boundary line . . . as shown by . . . the surveys. 11. [T]he Store Building was a monument, and the description of the line as being parallel to the Store Building would take precedence over the description of the same line as being South 7½ degrees.

Based on these findings of fact, the trial court concluded the "true boundary lines of the [Bakers' Property]" did not run 7½ degrees South, but rather, were parallel to the old store building and brick wall. Accordingly, the trial court affirmed the status quo, and held that the Moorefields were not encroaching on the Bakers' property. The Bakers appeal this judgment.

In a petition to establish boundaries, "where the location of the boundary line . . . is admitted, or evidence is not conflicting . . . the location of the line [is] a question of

(continued)

law for the court." *Young v. Young*, 76 N.C.App. 93, 95, 331 S.E.2d 769, 770 (1985). However, "where the language is *ambiguous* so that the effect of the instrument must be determined by resort to extrinsic evidence . . . the question of the parties' intention becomes one of fact." *Runyon v. Paley*, 331 N.C. 293, 305, 416 S.E.2d 177, 186 (1992) (emphasis in original). "Findings of fact are binding on appeal if there is competent evidence to support them, even if there is evidence to the contrary." *Sessler v. Marsh*, 144 N.C.App. 623, 628, 551 S.E.2d 160, 163, *disc. review denied*, 354 N.C. 365, 556 S.E.2d 577 (2001) (citations omitted).

First, the Bakers contend the trial court erred "in determining the placement of a boundary line" by "inappropriately isolating a single phrase," and giving the phrase too much weight. Essentially, the Bakers argue the trial court erroneously concluded that the deed was ambiguous. We disagree.

The deed specifically provides that the boundary line running "South 7-1/2 degrees West" is "parallel to the brick wall of the store building." Craig Sizemore, a surveyor hired by the Moorefields in 1986, before the present controversy arose, testified that a line drawn 7½ degrees South was not parallel with the location of the brick wall. Marvin Cavenaugh, a surveyor appointed by the Clerk of Court for Superior Court of Stokes County, also testified that a 7½ degree line was not "exactly parallel" with the brick wall. Thus, the court heard testimony from two professional surveyors that the terms in the original deed were inconsistent when applied to the contested boundary. Accordingly, the trial court's finding of ambiguity in the deed is binding on appeal, because there was competent evidence to support the trial court's determination that a "course of 7½ degrees West is not parallel with the Store Building, and does not accurately represent the common boundary line." Therefore, this assignment of error is without merit.

Second, the Bakers contend the trial court erred by using the brick wall of the store building to establish the common boundary instead of using the course and distance description in the deed. We disagree.

In North Carolina, it is well established that: "[w]here there is a conflict between course and distance and a fixed monument, the call for the monument will control." *Cutts. v. Casey*, 271 N.C. 165, 170, 155 S.E.2d 519, 522 (1967); *North Carolina State Highway Commission v. Gamble*, 9 N.C.App. 618, 623–24, 177 S.E.2d 434, 438 (1970); *see also Stephen v. Dortch*, 148 N.C.App. 509, 517, 558 S.E.2d 889, 894 (2002). . . .

Here, as previously noted, the terms in the original deed are inconsistent when applied to the contested boundary. Moreover, the conflict involves a call to course and distance that is inconsistent with a known monument. Accordingly, the trial court correctly applied North Carolina law by resolving the controversy in favor of the monument. Therefore, this assignment of error is without merit.

Affirmed.

Judge BIGGS concurs.

Judge GREENE dissents.

GREENE, Judge, dissenting.

As I disagree with the majority that, in order to determine the common boundary line between the parties in this case, the call in the deed to a monument prevails over a call to a course, I dissent.

Our Supreme Court has held: "'In the construction of deeds, words are not the principal thing . . . and . . . when there are any words in a deed that appear repugnant to the other parts of it, and to the general intention of the parties, they will be rejected.'" *Lumber Co. v. Lumber Co.*, 169 N.C. 80, 93, 85 S.E. 438, 446 (1915) (citation omitted). As a general rule of hierarchy, "'monuments, natural or artificial, referred to in a deed, control its construction, rather than courses and distances; but this rule is not inflexible. It yields whenever, taking all the particulars of the deed together, it would be absurd to apply it.'" *Lumber Co.*, 169 N.C. at 94, 85 S.E. at 446 [quoting *White v. Luning*, 93 U.S. 514, 524, 23 L.Ed. 938, 939–40 (1876)].

While Craig Sizemore (Sizemore), the Moorefields' surveyor, testified a line drawn "South 7-1/2 degrees West" as required by the deed "would have gone up either close to or through the old store building, and definitely not parallel with it," this testimony must be disregarded as Sizemore never considered the deed in surveying the property. Instead, he located iron stakes that were not referenced in the deed but purported by the Moorefields to establish the property boundaries and based his deductions regarding the common boundary line between the Moorefields and the Bakers on the location of these stakes.

Later in the hearing, the parties also stipulated that, contrary to Sizemore's testimony, the line would not have gone through the store building. This stipulation was based on a projection by Marvin Cavenaugh (Cavenaugh), the court-appointed surveyor, who explained the line would not even get close to the building, although it would be "not exactly parallel." In addition, Cavenaugh expressed doubt "[w]hether or not the day [the property] was surveyed [for purposes of the deed the original surveyors] actually went out and located the two corners of the building and created a line parallel."

(continued)

Cavenaugh had prepared several maps with respect to the property in question: (1) a map following the calls in the deed (the deed map), (2) a map (the stake map) reflecting the iron stakes found on the property, (3) a map setting out the Bakers' contentions regarding the boundaries, and (4) a map outlining the Moorefields' contentions. With respect to the deed map, Cavenaugh testified "the deed closed and . . . had a mathematical closure that was proper and acceptable." Comparing the deed map to the stake map, Cavenaugh concluded that "beyond [the northern boundary line of the property] there[] [was] not a whole lot of semblance" between the two maps.

It thus appears that a map based on a survey that closes by following the deed description and accepting a common boundary line as being close to but "not exactly parallel" to the store building is a more accurate reflection of the parties' intentions than a map based on movable iron stakes that hardly has any semblance to the deed description. Upholding the general rule of hierarchy among calls in a deed by taking the word "parallel" literally instead of accepting it as a general reference for the direction of the intended line would make it repugnant to the other parts of the deed and lead to an absurd result. *See Lumber Co.*, 169 N.C. at 93, 85 S.E. at 446. Accordingly, I would agree with the Bakers that the trial court "inappropriately

isolate[d] a single phrase" in the deed and that its judgment must therefore be reversed and remanded for determination of the common boundary line between the parties pursuant to the call in the deed to a course of "South 7-1/2 degrees West."

Case Questions

1. In his decision, Judge Wynn quoted from the *Runyon* case, stating that "where the language is ambiguous so that the effect of the instrument must be determined by resort to extrinsic evidence . . . the question of the parties' intention becomes one of fact." From the information provided in the case, what do you think the parties' intentions were regarding the boundary line of the property conveyed? What evidence would you look at to make this determination?

2. How should the legal description in question be rewritten to make it accurate and unambiguous?

3. Who do you believe presents the stronger argument given the facts in this case, Judge Wynn writing for the majority of the court or Judge Greene in the dissenting opinion? Why?

Reprinted from Westlaw with permission of Thomson Reuters.

Government Survey Method

The second oldest method of legal description is the government survey method, also referred to as the *rectangular survey method*. This is the most widely used method in this country. It was established by the U.S. Congress in 1785 to provide the federal government with a standard method of describing and dividing large tracts of territory west of the original established colonies. The government survey method works on a grid system. The basic grid structure is built around intersecting government survey lines running north-south and east-west. The federal government has established at various points throughout the United States vertical lines running north and south called **principal meridians.** The principal meridians intersect with designated lines running east and west called **base lines.** For example, in Florida, the principal meridian and base line intersect at a point in Tallahassee. There are thirty-five principal meridians in the United States, each of which is identified by a name or a number. Principal meridians and base lines are located by referring to degrees of longitude and latitude. These intersecting lines are the reference points for dividing areas of land into a grid of squares to enable a particular parcel of land to be readily located.

The intersection of a principal meridian and a base line is the starting point for forming a grid. Surveyors have established lines running parallel to each principal meridian at twenty-four-mile intervals both east and west of each principal meridian. They also have established lines running parallel to each base line at twenty-four-mile intervals both north and south of each base line. This forms a grid pattern of squares called **checks.** Each check is twenty-four miles square.

The grid can be further refined by the addition of survey lines every six miles in both directions. These additional survey lines are referred to as *range lines* and

principal meridian: An imaginary line running north and south used in the government survey method of legal description.

base line: An imaginary line running east and west used in the government survey method of legal description.

check: A measurement of land that is twenty-four miles square.

township lines. **Range lines** are located at each six-mile interval running in a north-south direction parallel to the principal meridian. Each range line is identified as being east or west of the principal meridian, and each is numbered sequentially. For example, the third range line from the principal meridian located east of the principal meridian is referred to as Range 3 East, or shortened to R3E. **Township lines** are located at each six-mile interval running in an east-west direction parallel to the base line. Each township line is identified as being north or south of the base line, and like range lines, each is numbered sequentially. Thus, the fourth township line from the base line located south of the base line is referred to as Township 4 South, or shortened to T4S.

The intersections of these lines divide each check into sixteen smaller squares called **townships.** Each township is six miles square (thirty-six square miles). The location of a township is described by making reference first to the township line number and direction and then to the range line number and direction—for example, Township 2 North, Range 3 East (see Exhibit 5–5).

Each township is divided into thirty-six smaller squares, each measuring one mile square and containing 640 acres. These one-mile squares are called **sections.** Each section is given a consecutive number from 1 to 36, with Section 1 always in the northeast corner of the township, Section 6 in the northwest corner, Section 31 in the southwest corner, and Section 36 in the southeast corner (see Exhibit 5–6).

Each section can be divided further into halves and quarters until a particular parcel of real property can be located. Each division of a section can be identified by referring to the direction of the division (that is, north, south, east, west, northeast, northwest, southeast, or southwest) and a fraction indicating the size of the division (that is, 1/2, 1/4)—for example, the Northeast 1/4 of the Northeast 1/4 of Section 8, Township 5 South, Range 3 West of the Any State Principal Meridian. This description also can be written as NE 1/4, NE 1/4 of Section 8, T5S, R3W, of the Any State Principal Meridian. Notice the commas between each division. These commas are synonymous with the word *of.* The location of this property is diagrammed in Exhibit 5–7.

Recall that each section equals 640 acres. To figure out the size of a parcel, you can take the denominators of each fraction in the legal description, multiply them, and then take this number and divide it into 640. For example, the parcel described in the preceding paragraph is forty acres ($4 \times 4 = 16$; $640 \div 16 = 40$).

range lines: Imaginary lines located at each six-mile interval, running in a north-south direction parallel to a principal meridian.

township lines: Imaginary lines located at each six-mile interval running in an east-west direction parallel to a base line.

township: A measurement of land that is six miles square, or thirty-six square miles.

section: A measurement of land that is one mile square and contains 640 acres.

Location of a township

EXHIBIT 5–5

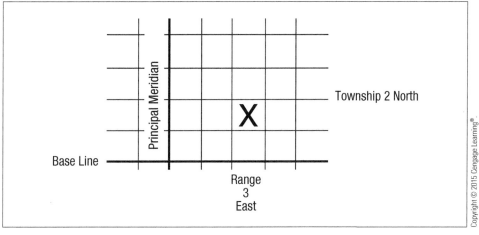

EXHIBIT 5–6   **Section location diagram**

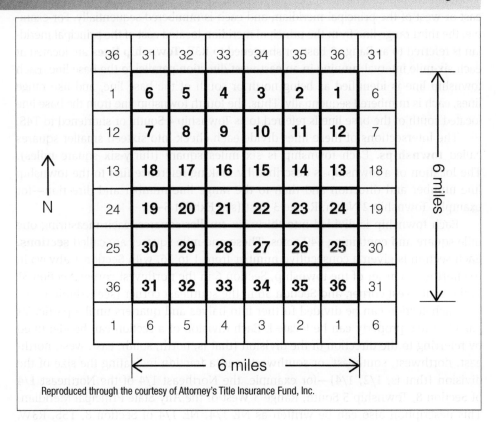

Reproduced through the courtesy of Attorney's Title Insurance Fund, Inc.

EXHIBIT 5–7   **Identifying property within a section**

Section 8

	NW ¼ of NE ¼	NE ¼ of NE ¼
NW ¼	SW ¼ of NE ¼	SE ¼ of NE ¼
SW ¼		SE ¼

It is also possible to combine portions of a section, such as the Northeast 1/4 of the Southwest 1/4 and the North 1/2 of the Northwest 1/4 of the Southeast 1/4 of Section 11. This can also be written as NE 1/4, SW 1/4 and N 1/2, NW 1/4, SE 1/4 of Section 11. To figure out the size of a combined portion of a section such as this one, you must first separate the description into two parts: the part before the word *and* and the part after it. Then you proceed as stated above, treating each part as a separate equation and then adding the results together. The first part of the example—NE 1/4, SW 1/4—equals forty acres. The second part of the example—N 1/2, NW 1/4, SE 1/4—equals twenty acres ($2 \times 4 \times 4 = 32$; $640 \div 32 = 20$). Adding the first forty acres with the second twenty acres provides the size of the property, which is sixty acres.

When drawing a government survey description, always start from the end of the description and work toward the beginning. To illustrate, consider the example N 1/2, NE 1/4, SW 1/4 of Section 29, T8N, R6E of the Any State Principal Meridian. To begin to draw this description, you would start at the end of the description that refers to the southwest quarter. You would divide a square into four parts or quadrants and locate the southwest quadrant. Once you have done this, you will be working in this quadrant and can ignore the others. Next, reading back to front, the description refers to the northeast quarter. Again, you have to divide this quadrant into four parts and find the northeast portion. Finally, you have to take this portion and divide it into halves, as the last part of the description refers to the north half. This description is illustrated in Exhibit 5–8.

Thus far, the discussion of the government survey method has assumed that land masses fit perfectly within a grid system. This assumes a flat earth. The curvature of lines produced by the roundness of the earth means that the range lines (running north-south) would converge. To compensate for this, the government survey method utilizes **correction lines** and **guide meridians.** Every fourth township line above and below the base line has been designated a correction line, and at each correction line, the range lines are remeasured to a distance of six miles apart. Further, every fourth range line east and west of the principal meridian has been designated a guide meridian.

correction lines: Every fourth township line above and below a base line. At each correction line, the range lines are remeasured to a distance of six miles.

guide meridians: Every fourth range line east and west of the principal meridian.

Drawing a description   EXHIBIT 5–8

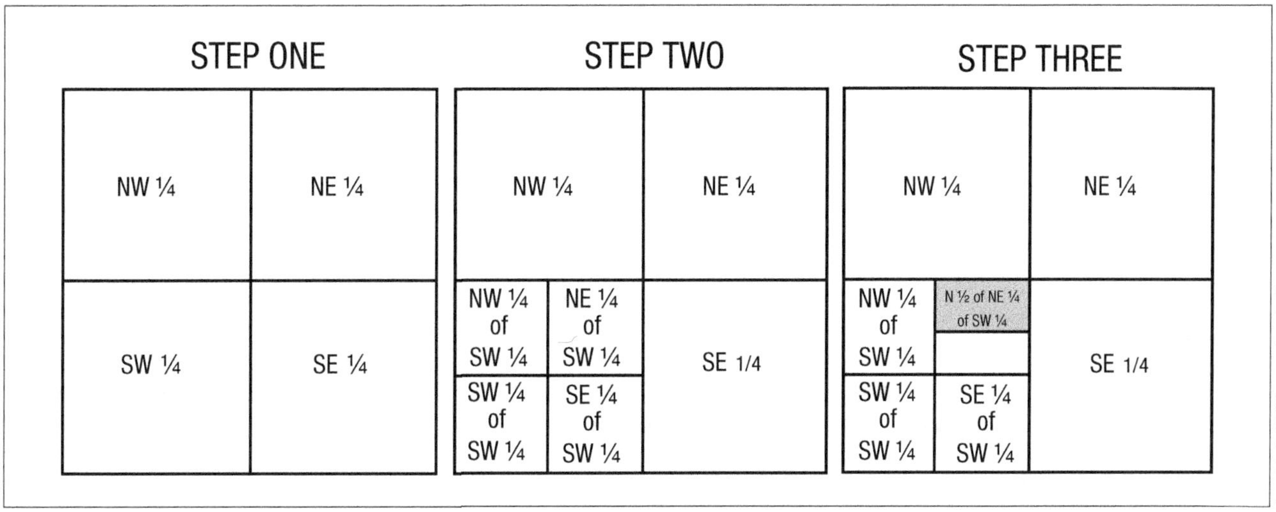

STEP ONE		STEP TWO		STEP THREE	
NW ¼	NE ¼	NW ¼	NE ¼	NW ¼	NE ¼
SW ¼	SE ¼	NW ¼ of SW ¼ / NE ¼ of SW ¼ ; SW ¼ of SW ¼ / SE ¼ of SW ¼	SE 1/4	NW ¼ of SW ¼ / N ½ of NE ¼ of SW ¼ ; SW ¼ of SW ¼ / SE ¼ of SW ¼	SE 1/4

Even with correction lines and guide meridians, the accuracy of the government survey method would be questionable without compensating for irregular tracts of land. These irregularities may be created, for example, by bodies of water such as rivers, lakes, and oceans. Because of these irregularities, sections may end up being undersized or oversized. These sections are referred to as fractional sections and cannot be properly divided by using the customary quartering system. Government surveyors have compensated for these irregular tracts by designating them **government lots** and giving each a number within a section—for example, "Government Lot 1 in the northwest quarter of fractional Section 6, Township 9 South, Range 7 West of the Any State Principal Meridian."

Plat Method

The plat method is also commonly referred to as the *lot and block method* and has its basis in the government survey system. This is the simplest of the three types of legal descriptions, describing a particular parcel of real property by making reference to its location on a plat map recorded in the land records in the county in which the property is located. When a real estate developer purchases a large tract of land with the intention to divide that land into smaller parcels, the real estate developer creates a subdivision. To do this, the real estate developer must get approval from local authorities by submitting a survey called a **plat map,** or *survey plat,* which breaks the tract down into blocks referenced by letter or number.

These blocks are further subdivided into individual lots referenced by sequential number. Lot sizes are indicated and details filled in, such as the locations and names of streets within the subdivision, the location of sewer lines and utility lines, and any land within the subdivision that is to be used for recreation areas or for other community uses. The subdivision name also appears on the plat map. Additionally, the plat map includes the legal description for the entire tract. This description may be a metes and bounds description or a government survey description. Once a plat map is approved, it is recorded in a plat book or official records book in the public records in the county in which the tract is located. A sample recorded plat map is found in Exhibit 5–9.

A proper plat method legal description includes (1) the name of the subdivision, (2) the lot number, (3) the block number or letter, (4) the plat book number or official records book number, (5) the page number in the plat book or official records book, and (6) the county and state in which the plat was recorded. Sometimes a developer divides a tract into sections (not to be confused with the term *section* as it is used in a government survey description). This is particularly common if the subdivision is to be developed in stages. If the subdivision is divided into more than one section, the number of the section also should be included in the legal description. The following is an example of a plat method legal description.

Lot 3, Block 5, of EMERALD ISLES ESTATES, 2ND SECTION according to the plat thereof, recorded in Plat Book 69, Page 16, of the Public Records of Any County, Any State.

The plat method is used for single-family homes within a subdivision, industrial parks, and condominiums. When a prospective condominium owner seeks to purchase a condominium, one of the documents he or she will receive is a declaration of condominium (see Chapter 3 for a detailed discussion). The declaration will include a map showing the location of the condominium units. The declaration

government lot: An irregular-sized tract of land labeled by government surveyors.

plat map: A survey that breaks down a tract of land into blocks referenced by letter or number.

Plat map

EXHIBIT 5-9

is recorded in the county in which the condominium is located. Therefore, a plat method description of a condominium unit differs from a regular plat method description by (1) making reference to a unit number rather than a lot and block number, (2) making reference to the name of the condominium rather than to the name of a subdivision, and (3) making reference to a declaration of condominium rather than to a plat map, such as in the following example.

> *Unit 205, of LYNTON PLACE, a Condominium according to the Declaration of Condominium recorded at Official Records Book 1130, Page 42 of the Public Records of Any County, Any State.*

Surveys

A **survey** is an investigation or examination that determines the boundaries of a parcel of land or locates all improvements on the parcel. Once the examination is completed, the surveyor sets forth the results in a map or *plat of survey*. A surveyor may be a private individual or a local government official, depending on state law. There are many types of surveys. A survey that simply sets forth the boundaries of a parcel is referred to as a *boundary survey*. A survey that sets forth the location of improvements on the parcel, such as buildings, driveways, and fences, is referred to as an *as-built survey, record survey,* or *loan survey*. Other surveys include, but are not limited to, condominium, topographic, and special purpose surveys. Surveys often are required by lending institutions prior to closing a mortgage loan. Title insurance companies may require a current survey prior to issuing a title policy.

Minimum Technical Standards

State statutes, administrative codes, or professional standards prescribe the minimum technical standards for surveys. Although these standards vary from state to state, minimum technical standards typically include the following:

1. A statement of the type of survey depicted in the survey map;
2. The name, address, and certificate of authorization number of the surveying firm;
3. The surveyor's name and license number;
4. The date of the field survey and the date(s) of any revisions;
5. A graphic scale of the map (for example, 1" equals 40');
6. Plotted features supported by accurate survey measurements (distance expressed to nearest hundredth of a foot);
7. Clearly referenced bearings, if applicable (for example, "Bearings are referenced to the South right-of-way line of Route 88, which bears N75°05'30"W as shown on the right-of-way maps for Route 88");
8. A showing of any inconsistencies between the legal description and the map (for example, overlapping descriptions);
9. A description of all monuments;
10. A showing of all fences, walls, and other open, notorious evidence of boundary lines;
11. Indications of any encroachments from or onto neighboring property;
12. The location of recorded private and public rights-of-way and easements; and
13. The location of fixed improvements in reference to the boundaries.

survey: An investigation or examination that determines the boundaries of a parcel of land or locates all improvements on the parcel.

In addition to minimum technical standards mandated by state law, the American Land Title Association (ALTA) and the American Congress on Surveying and Mapping (ACSM) have adopted Minimum Standard Detail Requirements for ALTA/ACSM Land Title Surveys. The National Society of Professional Surveyors (NSPS) also has adopted model standards for surveys. The person ordering a survey should therefore be clear in his or her request as to which standards the survey should meet.

Obtaining a Survey

In a real estate transaction, it is the buyer who typically asks for a survey and pays for it, although this is negotiable. If a survey was done recently, the existing survey may suffice and a new one need not be ordered. Therefore, before ordering a survey, it is good practice to check whether the seller has an existing survey in his or her possession, how old the survey is, and if additions have been made since the survey date as well as checking with the lender and/or title company to determine whether the existing survey will meet its requirements.

If a new survey is to be ordered, it is common practice for the title insurance company or the buyer's attorney to order the survey. The person ordering the survey should contact the surveyor as soon as the contract for sale and purchase is signed to find out how much time it will take to complete the survey. Once this is determined, several days should be tacked on to this time period to take into account unforeseen interruptions, such as inclement weather. The client should be informed of the survey fee prior to ordering the survey, and unless the client has provided the attorney with a retainer to be used for this type of transaction-related expense, the surveyor should be informed that the client, not the law firm, is to be billed for the survey.

Contracts for sale and purchase of real property include clauses pertaining to an inspection period during which the buyer may inspect the property and report any defects or problems to the seller. It is advisable to include in the contract for sale and purchase a stipulation that the seller shall provide the buyer with all existing surveys within a specified time frame and that the buyer shall be granted an extended inspection period (and depending on the length of delay, an extension of the closing date) should the surveys not be delivered within this time frame.

A *title commitment* is a document from a title insurance company indicating the terms and conditions under which it will issue a title insurance policy on the property covered by the contract for sale and purchase. (Title commitments and title examination are discussed in detail in Chapter 11.) If a new survey of the property is required, most attorneys representing buyers want to have this title commitment in hand prior to the receipt of the survey so that they can give the surveyor a copy of the commitment. This enables the surveyor to demarcate all easements and other encumbrances set forth in the commitment on the survey map. When reviewing a contract for sale and purchase, it is imperative to make sure that all deadlines relating to inspection periods, delivery of title documents, and delivery of surveys work with one another.

As a paralegal, should you be asked by your supervising attorney to order the survey for the buyer-client, you should provide the surveyor with the following:

1. A legal description of the real property;
2. A copy of the title commitment;
3. A list of all permitted exceptions included in the contract for sale and purchase (for example, restrictive covenants, utility easements); and

4. Specific instructions regarding the minimum technical standards that must be met, together with any other specific instructions of the lending institution or title insurance company that will be requesting a copy of the survey.

The cover letter should reconfirm the type of survey ordered (a survey providing both boundaries and location of improvements is typically desired), the date the survey will be delivered, and the survey fee as well as the number of copies requested.

Reviewing Surveys

Paralegals may be asked to verify information to ascertain whether any problems exist that must be sorted out prior to the closing of a real estate transaction. In order to do a thorough job, you should have these additional documents at hand: (1) the cover letter requesting the survey, (2) the contract for sale and purchase, and (3) the title commitment. The following checklist is a helpful guide in reviewing a survey.

SURVEY REVIEW CHECKLIST

1. Cover letter
   a. Check the type of survey ordered with the type of survey received.
   b. Check the delivery date stated in the letter with the date the survey is received.
   c. Check the minimum technical standards specified with the survey to ensure they have been met.
   d. Check any special instructions set forth in the cover letter with the survey to ensure they have been followed.
2. Contract for sale and purchase
   a. Check to ensure the survey meets the contract's requirements.
   b. Check the time period within which the buyer must make objections to survey defects and the time period within which the seller must cure defects.
   c. Check the exceptions set forth in the contract (for example, homeowners' association restrictions, utility easement).
3. Title commitment
   a. Check the legal description in the survey with the legal description in the title commitment for discrepancies.
   b. Check the legal description against the drawing shown on the survey for discrepancies.
   c. Check the list of exceptions in the title commitment with the drawing, noting whether all are included and noting any encumbrances shown that do not appear on the commitment.

There will be some exceptions listed in the title policy that will not show up on the survey, such as a current outstanding mortgage. (An explanation of exceptions found in title commitments and policies is provided in Chapter 11.)

Defects Revealed in a Survey

If a prospective seller is hesitant to provide a survey, this may be an indication that there are problems the survey will reveal that the seller does not want to bring up.

If a prospective seller knows of problems indicated on an existing survey (for example, an unrecorded easement or encroachment), the seller should bring these problems to the attention of his or her attorney prior to negotiating a contract for sale and purchase. If the problems are ones that can be cured, they should be cured prior to contracting, if possible. If they can be cured but curing will take time and the seller is anxious to go to contract, the seller may choose to include a clause in the contract that the defect will be cured within a specified period of time. The buyer may choose to include a clause in the contract that, if the survey reveals defects that the seller is unable to cure, resulting in a failure to close the sale on the property, the seller is responsible for reimbursing the buyer for all expenses incurred in association with the transaction (for example, survey fees, inspection fees). In no event should a seller with knowledge of a defect opt to forego informing the buyer, hoping the buyer will neglect to find out on his or her own.

What problems might be revealed by a survey? The most common ones include easements that are not listed as permitted exceptions under the contract of sale and purchase, encroachments, and violations of zoning or land use ordinances or statutes. Another possible problem is the existence of a variation between the legal description in the contract or the existing deed and the actual boundary measurements provided in the survey map. How much of a problem this poses depends on the magnitude of the variation between the description and the survey map. If the variation is slight, the problem can be remedied by having the title company issuing title insurance issue a survey endorsement as well, acknowledging that the real property described in the policy is the same as the property set forth on the survey map. One of the main reasons for requesting a survey is to determine whether there are any defects on the property that would make the title to the property unmarketable. A survey endorsement from a title company in this situation stipulates that any variation between the description and the survey does not affect the quality of the title to the property.

CHAPTER SUMMARY

1. The purpose of a legal description is to provide the exact boundary lines of a specific parcel of real property, indicating where one property ends and another begins. A legal description, rather than simply a street address, is required on many closing documents, such as deeds, title policies, and mortgage loan documents.

2. There are three basic types of legal descriptions: (1) the metes and bounds method, (2) the government survey method, and (3) the plat method. The oldest and most complicated is the metes and bounds method. The government survey method is utilized in a majority of states and is based on government survey lines running north-south and east-west, forming a grid pattern over large areas of the country. The plat method is the newest and simplest type of legal description. It pertains only to real property located within a subdivision for which a plat map has been recorded.

3. A metes and bounds legal description begins at a point certain, referred to as the point of beginning, and proceeds to describe a parcel's boundaries through a series of calls. The calls describe the direction and distance of each boundary line. A proper metes and bounds description must end back at the point of beginning.

4. In a metes and bounds description, the direction of each segment of a boundary line is measured in degrees, minutes, and seconds. The distance of each segment of a boundary line is typically measured in feet and hundredths of a foot.

5. The government survey method, also known as the rectangular survey method, describes a particular parcel of property by its location within a grid system. The grid's infrastructure is built around government survey lines called principal meridians and base lines. Range lines radiate every six miles to the east and west of a principal meridian, and township lines radiate every six miles to the north and south of a base line, forming squares called townships. Each township is divided into thirty-six sections, each section measuring one mile square. Sections can further be divided into halves and quarters until the precise location of a parcel of property is identified.

6. The plat method of legal description describes a parcel of property within a subdivision by referring to the parcel's location on a plat map recorded in the county records. The plat map shows the location of blocks of land and the division of each block into individual lots, numbering each lot and providing its dimensions. A proper plat method description includes the name of the subdivision, the lot and block numbers, the plat book number and page number, and the county and state in which the plat was recorded.

7. A survey is an examination of a parcel of land to establish its exact boundaries and/or the location of any improvements and encumbrances on it. The results are set forth in a survey map. State law prescribes the minimum technical standards a surveyor must observe when preparing a survey. These most often include, but are not limited to, a statement of the type of survey depicted; the name, address, and certificate of authorization number of the surveying firm; the surveyor's name and license number; the date of the field survey; a graphic scale of the map; accurate and clearly referenced survey measurements; the location of all improvements; and the location of any encumbrances. In addition to state statutory standards, ALTA/ASCM minimum technical standards and NSPS model standards exist that surveyors may be requested to follow.

8. When reviewing a survey, a paralegal should refer not only to the survey map but also to the cover letter sent when ordering the survey, the contract for sale and purchase, and the title commitment. The survey should follow the instructions set forth in the cover letter and meet the requirements set forth in the contract. It should match the legal description provided in the title commitment and include the exceptions listed in the title commitment as well as any encumbrances that do not appear in the commitment.

WEB RESOURCES

http://www.alta.org/

This site is set up for the benefit of the public, title insurers, abstractors, and surveyors. From the "Resources" section of the site, if you select "Policy Forms" and then "Related Documents," you can access the Minimum Standard Detail Requirements for ALTA/ACSM Land Title Surveys as adopted by the American Land Title Association (ALTA) and the National Society of Professional Surveyors (NSPS).

http://www.nsps.us.com/

This is the site of the National Society of Professional Surveyors (NSPS). It provides a platform for those in the surveying profession to share thoughts and opinions. The NSPS administers a number of certification programs including Certified Survey Technician, Certified Hydrographer, and Certified Floodplain Surveyor. In the "Resources" section of the site, you can access various model standards of practice, including, but not limited to, the Model Standards for Property Surveys, the Classification and Accuracy Standards for Property Surveys, and the Model Topographic Survey Standards. You can also access the ALTA/ACSM Standards from this site.

REVIEW QUESTIONS

1. Which type of legal description should be used to describe the following real property?
    a. A plot of acreage in Vermont
    b. A plot of acreage in California
    c. A condominium in Florida
2. Explain the procedure that should be used in drafting a written metes and bounds description from a survey map.
3. What is the size of each of the following parcels of real property?
    a. The W 1/2 of the SW 1/4 of Section 2
    b. The S 1/2 of the N 1/4 of the NE 1/4 of Section 4
    c. The SE 1/4 of the SE 1/4 of the SW 1/4 of Section 8
4. How does a plat method legal description for a condominium unit differ from a plat method legal description for a single-family home within a subdivision?
5. List the steps that should be taken when reviewing a survey map.

DISCUSSION QUESTIONS

1. In the case of *Baker v. Moorefield,* which you read earlier in the chapter, the court relied on the principle that in the construction of deeds, monuments rather than courses and distances should control. Do you believe this is a sound rule to follow? Why or why not? Is this principle embraced by the laws of your state?
2. Because parcel identification numbers are used by tax assessors and collectors to identify parcels of property, do you think these parcel identification numbers should be considered valid substitutes for legal descriptions on deeds? Why or why not?
3. Mr. Smith lives in a condominium complex known as 1800 Washington Avenue. He entered into a contract to sell his unit to Mr. White at the agreed purchase price of $260,000. The actual street address for Mr. Smith's unit is 1818 Washington Avenue. The address on the contract for purchase and sale is 1800 Washington Avenue, the address of the entire complex. No legal description is included in the contract. Some time after the signing of the contract, Mr. White changes his mind and wants to get out of the contract. He contends that the

contract is unenforceable because the legal description is insufficient to identify the property to be conveyed. Do you believe, if this case went to court,
Mr. White would win? Why or why not?

4. Do you believe it should be a legal requirement in your state for all contracts for
    purchase and sale to include a full legal description of the property to be con-
    veyed in order to be legally binding on the parties? Why or why not?

5. If a contract for purchase and sale of a residential property contains an errone-
    ous legal description but a correct street address, which should control? Why?

ETHICAL QUESTION

Two months ago, two of the paralegals in your law firm left, one moving out of state
and the other leaving due to a serious illness. Neither has been replaced, and the
real estate files that they handled have become your responsibility. Your office is
crowded with current client files requiring immediate attention. Although you are
usually very organized and on top of things, your present caseload has you juggling
too many real estate closings, and you are afraid that the pressure will cause you to
forget important deadlines. You have been coming in early and leaving late for the
last three weeks, and you still do not feel like you are catching up. Your supervising
attorney has told you that the situation is temporary and that you were given the
extra caseload because you are the most experienced real estate paralegal in the
firm. What should you do?

Slossberg Law Office on CourseMate

Please go to www.cengagebrain.com to log into CourseMate, access the Slossberg
Law Office, and work on your client files. Each module corresponds to a chapter in
the text. Within each module, you will be provided with instructions by the supervising attorney. You are asked to keep track of time spent on time sheets. The documents
produced through working on client files in the law office can then be compiled into
a portfolio of final work product.

CourseMate

The available CourseMate for this text has an interactive eBook and interactive learning tools, including flash cards, quizzes, and more. To learn more about this resource
and access free demo CourseMate resources, including the Slossberg Law Office, go
to www.cengagebrain.com, and search for this book. To access CourseMate materials
that you have purchased, go to login.cengagebrain.com.

Real Estate Brokers

6

CHAPTER OBJECTIVES

Upon completion of this chapter, the student will:

- Understand the respective responsibilities of brokers and attorneys

- Understand the broker's fiduciary duties to the principal

- Know the various types of listing agreements that may be used in the procurement of a broker's services

- Know the terms that should be included in a listing agreement

- Understand the role of a broker in a short sale transaction

Introduction

Working in the area of real estate, paralegals may have as the firm's clients buyers, sellers, developers, and financial institutions. While these persons and entities may comprise the majority of clients, real estate law firms also represent real estate brokers, and, therefore, it is important for a paralegal to understand the function of the real estate broker in a real estate transaction as well as the rights and duties of brokers. Even if a broker is not a client, the chances that a client will procure the services of a broker are considerable, and a paralegal needs to be aware of the various types of contracts a client can enter into with a broker.

A real estate **broker** is a person licensed under state law to facilitate a real estate transaction in return for compensation. The compensation received typically is a commission, which amounts to a certain dollar figure or a percentage of the purchase price of the property. Real estate brokers are governed by federal and state law. In most states, to become licensed, a real estate broker must first become a licensed real estate salesperson and then work under a broker for a specified period of time. Although requirements differ from state to state, most states mandate passing certain courses and a state examination to become a licensed salesperson (also known as sales associate). Additional course work and examinations are required to become a broker. Many states have a continuing education requirement for real estate salespersons and brokers. The course work and examinations usually cover such topics as residential and commercial financing, property valuation, real estate investment, leasing of real property, zoning, brokerage office procedures, ethics, the handling of escrow accounts, and state and federal laws impacting the sale and leasing of real property. Further, salespersons and

broker: A person licensed under state law to facilitate a real estate transaction in return for compensation.

Realtor®: A real estate licensee who voluntarily becomes a member of a local board of Realtors® that is affiliated with the National Association of Realtors®.

real estate agent: A real estate licensee; either a real estate salesperson or a real estate broker.

brokerage: The name given to the business engaged in by real estate brokers.

multiple listing service (MLS): An organization of brokers who agree to publicize their listings to all other broker members through the use of the service.

brokers are instructed in the law of agency relationships (discussed in detail in the following text) because of the agency relationships created between brokers and their salespersons as well as between brokers and their clients.

A **Realtor®** is a real estate licensee who voluntarily becomes a member of a local board of Realtors® that is affiliated with the National Association of Realtors®. Neither brokers nor salespersons may use the term *Realtor®* in their advertisements, stationery, or business cards unless they are members of their local board of Realtors®. A **real estate agent** is a real estate licensee and may be a real estate broker or a real estate salesperson. The term *agent* refers to the agency relationship created between a broker or salesperson and a client that authorizes the broker or salesperson to act on the client's behalf and in the client's best interests. **Brokerage** is the name given to the business engaged in by real estate brokers. A brokerage firm may take the form of any one of the business entities mentioned in Chapter 2.

In most circumstances, it is the seller who procures the services of a real estate broker to find a buyer for a particular property. When the seller hires the broker, he or she gives the broker the right to list his or her property. This is referred to as a *listing*. To aid in the process of procuring buyers for their listings, many real estate brokerage firms belong to a multiple listing service. A **multiple listing service (MLS)** is an organization of brokers who agree to publicize their listings to all other broker members through the use of the service. Thus, each broker who is a member of the service has access to the listings of all other brokers who are members. The information is shared through the use of computerized multiple listing directories. The sharing of this information helps brokers to build up an "inventory" of listings and increases the chances of finding a buyer for the property through the assistance of other brokers who will then share in the commission. Before a property can be listed with a multiple listing service, the broker must procure the consent of the seller. Many brokerage agreements contain a multiple listing clause in which the seller gives his or her consent both to the listing of the property with such a service and to the authority of other broker members to assist in selling the listed property.

This chapter will explore the role of brokers in the real estate transaction, the agency relationship that is created between brokers and their clients as well as between brokers and their subagents, the compensation paid for their services, their ethical duties as fiduciaries, and the various types of contractual relationships that can be created between brokers and their clients.

The Role of the Broker

Responsibilities of the Broker Versus the Attorney

Attorneys and real estate brokers each have responsibilities to their clients in that they occupy positions of trust and confidence with regard to their clients; in addition, each has certain responsibilities to third parties and the general public. Nonetheless, they each have their own areas of expertise, and if the client cannot distinguish between the responsibilities of the broker and those of the attorney, it is the obligation of both the broker and the attorney to do so.

Real estate brokers are hired for their expertise in marketing real property, which includes knowledge of such areas as real estate valuation, financing, and investment. Brokers are allowed by law to make representations regarding the value of a particular property, although it is the seller who must ultimately determine the purchase price of the property. The average seller is less knowledgeable of the property's true value than the broker and therefore relies on the broker to assist in formulating the purchase price. A broker often makes a valuation of a particular property by conducting a **comparative market analysis (CMA),** sometimes referred to as a *competitive market analysis,* which is a comparison of prices of properties similar to the seller's property that have recently been sold. Properties are compared that are similar in size, style, location, and amenities to determine the estimated market value of the seller's property.

Brokers are allowed by law to partake in the preliminary negotiations and the drafting of documents leading to an agreement between the parties to a real estate transaction. Therefore, a broker may draft memoranda, deposit receipts, or even, in some states, contracts for sale and purchase as long as, in so doing, the broker does not engage in the unauthorized practice of law by giving legal advice. No matter how experienced the broker, he or she must not give opinions of title or prepare documents affecting the transfer of title from one party to the other.

In the optimum situation, the attorney and broker will work hand-in-hand to ensure a smooth transaction for their mutual client. This can happen only if both the attorney and the broker respect each other's spheres of expertise and communicate that respect to the client. Neither should assume responsibility in a transaction that is beyond the scope of his or her employment. Further, neither should evaluate the services of the other or quote to the client what he or she thinks is reasonable compensation of the other.

The Broker as Agent and Fiduciary

The relationship between a real estate broker (or real estate salesperson) and the persons the broker represents in a real estate transaction is governed by the *law of agency.* An **agent** is a person authorized to act on behalf of another (the **principal**). The law of agency governs not only the rights and duties of principals and agents to each other but also the obligations of each with respect to third parties.

As soon as a broker's services are procured, an agency relationship may be created. Although the use of a written contract is customary, there is no requirement that a written contract exist in order for the agency relationship to be formed. This is because the contract between the broker and seller is a services contract (hiring the broker's services to market the property and procure a buyer), not a contract for the transfer of an interest in real property. As such, it does not fall under the statute of frauds (discussed in the next chapter). However, state law does require that real estate brokers and salespersons meet state licensing requirements before a legal agency relationship can occur.

Typically, a real estate broker is the agent of the persons the broker is representing in a real estate transaction, regardless of which party pays the broker's commission. An exception exists when a broker is acting as a transaction broker, discussed later in this section. In addition, an agency relationship exists between a real estate broker and the broker's salespersons because a broker is a principal to the salespersons (his or her employees) and these employees are the broker's agents. With regard to this latter relationship, the common law principle of respondeat superior controls. **Respondeat superior** is a Latin term meaning "let the master answer." This legal doctrine holds the principal (here, the broker) legally responsible for the actions of the agent (here, the salesperson).

comparative market analysis (CMA): A comparison of prices of properties similar to the seller's property that have recently been sold.

agent: A person authorized to act on behalf of another.

principal: The person upon whose behalf an agent is authorized to work.

respondeat superior: "Let the master answer." A legal doctrine that holds the principal legally responsible for the actions of the agent.

Types of Agents. There are several types of agents. *A universal agent* is an agent who is authorized to conduct any and all transactions of every nature that may be lawfully delegated by a principal. Real estate brokers are not universal agents. A *general agent* is an agent who is authorized to act by a principal in all matters related to a particular business. A *special agent* is an agent who is authorized to conduct a single transaction, or a finite series of transactions not anticipated to be of an ongoing nature, for a principal. For example, when a broker is hired by a seller to sell the seller's primary residence, a special agency is formed. A **subagent** is someone who is authorized by an agent to aid in a transaction for a principal, if authorized under the original agency agreement. For example, a real estate salesperson is a subagent of a broker. A seller or buyer procures the services of a real estate brokerage firm. The firm thereby becomes the agent. The seller or buyer works with a salesperson of the firm to complete the transaction. The salesperson is the subagent. A subagent is under the control and authority of both the agent (here, the broker) and the principal (here, the seller or buyer).

A subagent may also be another brokerage firm. For example, a seller procures the services of Broker 1. Broker 1 lists the seller's house with a multiple listing service. Broker 2 is a member of the multiple listing service, sees the listing of the seller's house, and finds potential buyers for that house. Broker 2 has become a subagent in this transaction and must interact with the potential buyers on behalf of the seller as an agent of the seller. Should Broker 2's efforts result in the sale of the house, the commission due to Broker 1 will be divided between Broker 1 and Broker 2.

A **single agency** occurs when a broker represents only one principal in a transaction, either the buyer or the seller. Brokers have a **fiduciary duty** (the duty owed by a person holding a special position of trust) to their principals. In a single agency, the broker's fiduciary duty is to one party only. Thus, a broker working as a single agent can be either a seller agent or a buyer agent. Even though brokers work closely with buyers, they are generally seller agents, and their allegiance therefore is to the seller. If a broker is a seller agent, the broker works for the seller but with the buyer. The distinction can often appear blurred in the course of a transaction. Agency policies must be clear and should require the disclosure of the agency relationship to all parties in the transaction at the first available opportunity, including written documentation evidencing the disclosure. Even in the absence of an official firm policy, most state statutes address the issue of agency disclosure. Typically, a broker must disclose his or her agency relationship before showing the property, eliciting confidential information, or executing an offer on the property.

A **dual agency** occurs when a broker represents both the seller and the buyer in a transaction. While disclosed dual agencies are permissible, an undisclosed dual agency (one in which the parties do not know and acknowledge that the broker is working for both parties) is illegal. Because there is a potential conflict of interest in dual agency relationships, most state statutes have strict laws governing them and require the written, informed consent of all parties to the transaction.

Some states permit brokers to act as transaction brokers. A **transaction broker** is a broker who provides limited representation to one or both parties in a transaction and does not represent one of the parties to the detriment of the other. A transaction broker is not considered to be an agent or a fiduciary of either party but simply works to effectuate a real estate transaction. Therefore, transaction brokers

subagent: Someone who is authorized by an agent to aid in a transaction for a principal, if authorized under the original agency agreement.

single agency: A broker who represents only one principal in a transaction.

fiduciary duty: A duty held by a person in a special position of trust (for example, the duty of care, obedience, diligence, and loyalty).

dual agency: An agency situation in which a broker represents both the seller and the buyer in the same transaction.

transaction broker: A broker who provides limited representation to one or both parties in a real estate transaction and does not represent one party to the detriment of the other.

do not owe certain fiduciary duties to the parties, such as complete confidentiality or loyalty. Nonetheless, all brokers are obligated to deal fairly and honestly; to utilize skill, care, and diligence; and to disclose all known material facts pertaining to the property. In most states that permit brokers to act as transaction brokers, written disclosure must be provided to the parties indicating that the broker is acting in this capacity, and consent of all parties to the transaction must be obtained. The parties must be made aware of the fact that the broker is not a fiduciary of either party. Exhibit 6–1 provides an example of a transaction broker notice.

Transaction broker notice

EXHIBIT 6–1

IMPORTANT NOTICE REGARDING REPRESENTATION

THE LAW OF ANY STATE REQUIRES THAT REAL ESTATE LICENSEES PROVIDE THIS NOTICE REGARDING REPRESENTATION TO POTENTIAL SELLERS AND BUYERS OF REAL ESTATE

Do not assume that any real estate broker or sales associate represents you unless you agree to engage a real estate licensee in an authorized brokerage relationship, either as a single agent or as a transaction broker. Do not to disclose any information you want to be held in confidence until you make a decision on representation.

TRANSACTION BROKER NOTICE

THE LAW OF ANY STATE REQUIRES THAT REAL ESTATE LICENSEES OPERATING AS TRANSACTION BROKERS MAKE THE FOLLOWING DISCLOSURES.

As a transaction broker, Atlantis Realty Company and its sales associates provide you a limited form of representation that includes the following duties:

1. The duties of honesty and fair dealing;
2. The duties of skill, care, and diligence in the transaction;
3. The duty to disclose all known facts that materially affect the value of residential real property and are not readily observable to the buyer;
4. The duty of presenting all offers and counteroffers in a timely manner, unless the buyer or seller has previously directed the licensee otherwise in writing;
5. The duty to account for all funds;
6. The duty of limited confidentiality, unless waived in writing by buyer or seller. This limited confidentiality will prevent disclosure that the seller will accept a price less than the asking or listed price, that the buyer will pay a price greater than the price submitted in a written offer, of the motivation of seller for selling or buyer for buying property, that a seller or buyer will agree to financing terms other than those offered, or of any other information requested by buyer or seller to remain confidential; and
7. Any additional duties that are entered into by this or by separate written agreement.

Limited representation means that a buyer or seller is not responsible for the acts of the real estate licensee. It also means that the buyer and seller are giving up their rights to the undivided loyalty of the real estate licensee. This allows a real estate licensee to assist both the buyer and the seller, but a real estate licensee will not work to represent one party to the detriment of the other party when acting as a transaction broker to both parties.

_____   _____
Signature   Date

_____   _____
Signature   Date

The Fiduciary Duties of the Broker. A broker acting in a fiduciary capacity owes his or her principal the duties of care, obedience, loyalty, confidentiality, disclosure, and accounting. The duty of care requires a real estate broker (and salesperson) to exercise reasonable skill and knowledge in representing the principal in a real estate transaction. Although a broker is not expected to, and indeed cannot, give legal advice, a broker is expected to be more knowledgeable than a layperson in the area of real estate and must be acquainted with such areas as financing, zoning, escrow accounts, and certain federal and state laws, such as those relating to fair housing, environmental protection, equal credit, and landlord-tenant rights and obligations. A broker must utilize this knowledge to properly represent the interests of his or her principal. As part of a broker's duty of care, the broker must not bind the principal to actions not specifically authorized by the principal. Thus, the broker must refrain from making unauthorized promises or representations on behalf of the principal. For example, the broker should not tell a prospective buyer that the seller will allow the buyer to move in before closing or that the seller will be willing to partially finance the sale unless the seller authorizes the broker to do so.

The duty of *obedience* requires a broker to follow all instructions given by the principal as long as those instructions are legal. This means that a broker must carry out a legal instruction, even if the broker believes the instruction is not in the best interest of the principal. For example, a broker is required to submit all counteroffers to the seller. If the broker is a seller agent and the seller tells the broker to accept a counteroffer that the broker believes to be unreasonably low, the broker must inform the seller accordingly, but then if the seller insists on accepting, the broker must accept the counteroffer on the seller's behalf.

If a broker finds that he or she is unable to carry out a legal instruction, the broker must withdraw from the transaction. A broker must never obey an illegal instruction and, if asked to do so, must withdraw. For example, a broker may never engage in discriminatory practices in showing a house for a seller. If the seller insists, the broker has no choice but to withdraw as the seller's agent. The National Association of Realtors® has adopted a Code of Ethics and Standards of Practice that must be followed by all members of the association, and discrimination practices are among the actions prohibited by this code. However, discriminatory practices are not the only area in which a broker may be asked to follow an illegal instruction. For example, a broker may be asked to put a false purchase price on a document. Note that there is a difference between naming nominal consideration, such as $10, on a deed, which is a common practice, and naming a false purchase price.

The duty of *loyalty* requires the broker always to act in the best interest of the principal, to the exclusion of all other interests, including those of the broker. Thus, a broker may not act in self-interest without the informed consent of the principal. For example, as per federal law, a broker may not receive a secret commission. Further, a broker may not purchase a property listed with the broker for himself or herself directly or for an entity in which the broker has an interest without disclosing the interest to the seller and receiving the consent of the seller. Disclosure in this instance means not only informing the seller of the broker's interest but also informing the seller of every fact that he or she has knowledge of regarding the property in question that might influence the seller's decision. A broker who fails to do so will be subject to strict disciplinary action that may include suspension or revocation of his or her license. Similarly, a broker may not sell real property he or she owns without disclosing to the prospective buyer his or her interest in the property.

The duty of *confidentiality* requires that a broker preserve the confidences of the principal as long as it is ethically correct to do so. This duty exists both during and after the termination of the agency relationship. Thus, a broker cannot reveal a principal's underlying motives for selling (or purchasing) a particular property, the financial status of the principal, the principal's willingness to accept a lower price, or similar information without the consent of the principal. However, the broker must disclose any intent by the principal to commit a crime, such as intentional falsification of documents to procure a loan. In this respect, a broker's duties regarding confidentiality are quite similar to those of the legal profession.

The duty of *disclosure*, sometimes referred to as *notice*, requires that the broker disclose all material facts, reports, and even rumors that have a bearing on the real estate transaction. In an effort to enable the principal to secure the best price and terms in the transaction, the broker should disclose any information that may be pertinent. Obviously, a broker is obligated to disclose any offers made on the property, regardless of whether the broker believes the offer to be reasonable, but disclosure is not limited to offers. Disclosure includes such subjects as the tax consequences of the sale (the broker may advise the seller or buyer to seek the counsel of a tax expert), rumors of zoning changes (even if the passing of such changes seems unlikely), and financing issues (such as the fact that the buyer may have a problem in making the down payment, if the broker is a seller agent).

The duty of disclosure includes the prohibition of both negligent and intentional misrepresentation to either party in a real estate transaction. Prospective buyers are allowed to rely on any representations made by a broker through the mail as well as any representations regarding construction that are not visibly apparent. Misrepresentation includes misrepresentation by both commission and omission. **Fraudulent misrepresentation** is made with an intent to mislead or deceive. To prove a case of fraudulent misrepresentation, a party must show that (1) the statements made by the broker were misrepresentations, (2) the statements were material to the transaction, and (3) the party reasonably relied on the statements to his or her detriment. If a real estate contract was procured through fraudulent misrepresentation, the contract can be rescinded or canceled. Not only will the broker lose a commission in such an instance, but also the broker may be sued by the parties to the transaction for any damages incurred as a result of the broker's actions. A broker may not, however, be required to make independent investigations of all material facts presented to the broker by the seller. Thus, if the seller misrepresented a fact to the broker who, unaware of the misrepresentation, passed this information on to the buyer, the buyer would be able to rescind the contract, but the seller would still be liable to the broker for the sales commission.

The broker's responsibilities regarding disclosure go beyond the principal and include third parties when the disclosures have a bearing on public protection in the purchase of real property. In addition to the fiduciary duty of disclosure, both brokers and sellers have an affirmative legal duty to make certain disclosures to prospective buyers regarding real property. Although the common law doctrine of *caveat emptor* ("let the buyer beware") is often quoted in common parlance, it does not apply to real estate transactions.

For example, state statutes require brokers and sellers to disclose structural defects concerning the property and to provide inspection reports or allow buyers to have termite, roof, and other inspections made prior to closing on the property. Although the broker may not be required to inspect for latent defects, the broker

fraudulent misrepresentation:
Misrepresentation made with an intent to mislead or deceive.

and seller must both inform a prospective buyer of any known latent defects. If the property is in violation of building codes or city or county ordinances, even if the violation does not result in a structural defect (for example, inadequate smoke detectors, utilization of the property in contravention of zoning ordinances), the prospective buyer must be informed.

In addition to structural concerns, notice must be made regarding the environmental integrity of the property. Because of the Comprehensive Environmental Response, Compensation and Liability Act (CERCLA; see Chapter 4 for a detailed discussion), subsequent owners may be liable for cleanup costs of environmentally contaminated property. Therefore, investigations should be made and all details disclosed. Further, brokers and sellers should investigate any federal, state, or local environmental regulations that may impact the marketability of the property. For example, a commercial buyer may be attracted to the seller's property as a site upon which to build a textile factory. The zoning may be appropriate for such a use, but state or local regulations may prohibit the factory because of the noxious fumes that would emanate from it.

The following California case addresses the potential liability of a broker for misrepresentations and nondisclosure in the sale of residential property.

CASE: *Holmes v. Summer*
188 Cal. App. 4th 1510, 116 Cal. Rptr. 3d 419 (2010)

MOORE, J.

Particularly in these days of rampant foreclosures and short sales, "[t]he manner in which California's licensed real estate brokers and salesmen conduct business is a matter of public interest and concern. [Citations.]" (*Wilson v. Lewis* (1980) 106 Cal.App.3d 802, 805–806, 165 Cal.Rptr. 396.) When the real estate professionals involved in the purchase and sale of a residential property do not disclose to the buyer that the property is so greatly overencumbered that it is almost certain clear title cannot be conveyed for the agreed-upon price, the transaction is doomed to fail. Not only is the buyer stung, but the marketplace is disrupted and the stream of commerce is impeded. When properties made unsellable by their debt load are listed for sale without appropriate disclosures and sales fall through, purchasers become leery of the marketplace and lenders preparing to extend credit to those purchasers waste valuable time in processing useless loans. In the presently downtrodden economy, it behooves us all for business transactions to come to fruition and for the members of the public to have confidence in real estate agents and brokers.

The case before us presents the interesting question of whether the real estate brokers representing a seller of residential real property are under an obligation to the buyers of that property to disclose that it is overencumbered and

cannot in fact be sold to them at the agreed-upon purchase price unless either the lenders agree to short sales or the seller deposits a whopping $392,000 in cash into escrow to cover the shortfall. Here, the buyers and the seller agreed to the purchase and sale of a residential real property for the price of $749,000. Unbeknownst to the buyers, the property was subject to a first deed of trust in the amount of $695,000, a second deed of trust in the amount of $196,000 and a third deed of trust in the amount of $250,000, for a total debt of $1,141,000, and the lenders had not agreed to accept less than the amounts due under the loans in order to release their deeds of trust. According to the buyers, after they signed the deal with the seller, they sold their existing home in order to enable them to complete the purchase of the seller's property. Only then did they learn that the seller could not convey clear title because the property was overencumbered.

In a lawsuit against the seller's brokers, the trial court sustained a demurrer without leave to amend, holding that the brokers owed no duty of disclosure to the buyers. The buyers appeal. We reverse, holding that, under the facts of this case, the brokers were obligated to disclose to the buyers that there was a substantial risk that the seller could not transfer title free and clear of monetary liens and encumbrances.

(continued)

I FACTS

Phil and Jenille Holmes (buyers) made the following allegations in their first amended complaint against Sieglinde Summer and Beneficial Services, Inc. (collectively brokers). Summer is a licensed real estate broker who represented the seller of certain residential real property located in Huntington Beach, California. Summer was employed by Beneficial Services, Inc., which operated a Re/Max office in Huntington Beach.

The brokers listed the property for sale on a multiple listing service, advertising a price of $749,000 to $799,000. The listing noted that the seller was motivated and that Summer would receive a 3 percent commission for the sale. The buyers saw the listing on the multiple listing service Web site and became interested in the property. Summer showed them the property, and made no mention of any encumbrances on the property that might affect the ability of the seller to sell at the advertised price.

The buyers offered to purchase the property for $700,000, free and clear of all monetary liens and encumbrances other than a new loan in the amount of $460,000, escrow to close in 60 days. The brokers prepared a counter offer on the seller's behalf, with a sales price of $749,000 and a 30-day escrow. The buyers accepted the counter offer. The counter offer did not disclose that the property was subject to three deeds of trust totaling $1,141,000. Unbeknownst to the buyers at the time they signed the purchase documents, the property could not be transferred to them free and clear of all monetary liens and encumbrances, other than their own purchase money deed of trust, because the existing debt on the property far exceeded the purchase price. The buyers suffered damage in an amount to be proven at trial.

The first amended complaint asserted causes of action for negligence, for negligent misrepresentation, and for deceit—based on both misrepresentation and the failure to disclose. The brokers filed a demurrer. They argued that the lawsuit was a disguised effort to require the brokers to guarantee the seller's performance. They also asserted that if the seller decided to sell the property at a loss, such that it would have to come up with cash to close the transaction, but then changed its mind, that was a business decision for which the brokers could not be held liable.

In their opposition to the demurrer, the buyers stated that Summer had admitted both that she knew about the excess debt when she listed the property on the multiple listing service and that she did not disclose the excess debt to the buyers. The buyers also alleged that Summer was actually attempting to arrange a "short sale," which would have required the lenders to accept less money than was owing to them in order to retire the debt against the property. In addition, the buyers asserted that, during escrow, the lenders refused to discount the loans and demanded full payment before they would release their liens against the property.

The court sustained the demurrer without leave to amend and ordered the dismissal of the first amended complaint. Judgment was entered accordingly.

II DISCUSSION

*   *   *

C. Brokers' Duty to Buyers

(1) Introduction

The buyers are correct that the fundamental issue is not whether they should have sued the seller. The question, aptly framed by the trial court, is whether the defendants before us—the brokers—owed a duty of disclosure to the buyers. We turn now to that issue. According to the allegations, the brokers represented that the property could be purchased for $749,000, and indeed negotiated a sale for that price, even though they knew that the property was encumbered with $1,141,000 in debt. In other words, the brokers knew that the property could not in fact be sold for the price of $749,000, free and clear of monetary liens and encumbrances, unless either two or more lenders agreed to discount the debt on the property by a total amount of $392,000 or the seller put at least $392,000 in cash into the escrow in order to pay off the lenders. . . . Considering the magnitude of the discrepancy between the sales price and the total debt on the property, the buyers argue the brokers were obligated to disclose the excess debt because it indicated a substantial risk, over and above that inherent in the routine residential sales transaction, that the escrow would not close.

The brokers, on the other hand, argue that they were precluded from disclosing the financial issues affecting the transaction. They say that for them to have made the disclosure in question would have required them to disclose the seller's confidential financial information or its strategy in determining the price at which it would be willing to sell. The brokers assert that it would have required them to disclose that the seller might lose money on the property.

*   *   *

(2) General rule

As the buyers point out, "It is now settled in California that where the seller knows of facts materially affecting the value or desirability of the property which are known or accessible only to him and also knows that such facts are not known to, or within the reach of the diligent attention and observation of the buyer, the seller is under a duty to disclose them to the buyer.

(continued)

[Citations.]"(*Lingsch v. Savage* (1963) 213 Cal.App.2d 729, 735, 29 Cal.Rptr. 201; accord, *Alfaro v. Community Housing Improvement System & Planning Ass'n., Inc.* (2009) 171 Cal.App.4th 1356, 1382, 89 Cal.Rptr. 3d 659 (*Alfaro.*)) When the seller's real estate agent or broker is also aware of such facts, "he [or she] is under the same duty of disclosure." (*Lingsch v. Savage, supra,* 213 Cal. App.2d at p. 736, 29 Cal.Rptr. 201.) A real estate agent or broker may be liable "for mere nondisclosure since his [or her] conduct in the transaction *amounts to a representation of the nonexistence of the facts which he has failed to disclose* [citation]." (*Ibid.*)

According to the buyers, the monetary liens and encumbrances on the property affected both the value and the desirability of the property. Because the brokers were aware of the magnitude of the debt, and should have known that the buyers were not aware of the same, the brokers had a duty to disclose the problem. By their silence, the brokers represented the nonexistence of any impediments to the transfer of title free and clear of monetary liens and encumbrances. The brokers, on the other hand, contend there is no connection between the amount of debt on the property and the value or desirability of the property, at least where, as here, the seller agrees to sell the property free and clear of monetary liens and encumbrances. In other words, the physical characteristics and intrinsic desirability of the property are distinct from the financing.

The latter viewpoint misses the big picture. While a buyer may be harmed by acquiring title to a property with undisclosed defects, such as hazardous waste or soil subsidence problems, a buyer may also be harmed by entering into an escrow to purchase property when it is highly likely that, unbeknownst to the buyer, the escrow will never close. We must bear in mind that the main purposes of the rule expressed in *Lingsch v. Savage, supra,* 213 Cal.App.2d 729, 29 Cal.Rptr. 201, "are to protect the buyer from the unethical broker and seller and to insure that the buyer is provided sufficient accurate information to make an informed decision whether to purchase." (*Easton v. Strassburger* (1984) 152 Cal.App.3d 90, 99, 199 Cal.Rptr. 393.) "Despite the absence of privity of contract, a real estate agent is clearly under a duty to exercise reasonable care to protect those persons whom the agent is attempting to induce into entering a real estate transaction for the purpose of earning a commission. [Citations.]" *Id.* at p. 98, fn. 2, 199 Cal.Rptr. 383.)

Here, the buyers say that they sold their existing home in order to purchase the seller's property and were damaged when the seller failed to convey title. Whether or not the brokers knew the buyers would need to sell their existing home in order to complete the transaction, it should be perfectly foreseeable to an experienced real estate agent

or broker that one who is purchasing a $749,000 residence may need to sell an existing residence in order to make the move.

Although the duty to disclose a physical property defect is not at issue, we observe that real estate agents or brokers have been held to have a duty to disclose matters that do not pertain to physical defects, but otherwise affect the desirability of the purchase. . . .

In addition to arguing that the rule enunciated in *Lingsch v. Savage, supra,* 213 Cal.App.2d 729, 29 Cal.Rptr. 201 is inapplicable because we are not talking about the value or desirability of the property itself, as opposed to the desirability of entering into a contract to purchase the property, the brokers also argue that the rule is inapplicable because the liens were disclosed during escrow and because the buyers failed to protect themselves. However, as to the first point, the allegation here is that the brokers had a duty to disclose the liens *before* the buyers signed the agreement. Only then could the buyers weigh the risks of entering into an agreement and preparing their finances and related affairs to facilitate completion of the purchase, considering there was a significant possibility the transaction would fall through. Disclosing the liens only after the buyers had entered into the escrow failed to protect them in this context.

The brokers' second point goes to the latter portion of the *Lingsch* rule, that is, that the information in question must be unknown to, or outside "the diligent attention and observation of the buyer. . . ." (*Lingsch v. Savage, supra,* 213 Cal.App.2d at p. 735, 29 Cal.Rptr. 201; see also Civ. Code § 2079.5). The argument would be that inasmuch as the encumbrances in question were reflected by deeds of trust of record, a diligent buyer could have done a title search before making an offer on the property, in order to avoid exactly the situation that occurred.

This argument is unpersuasive for two reasons. First, even though a title search might have divulged the existence of recorded deeds of trust against the property, it would not likely have disclosed the current balances of the promissory notes secured by those deeds of trust, unless foreclosure proceedings had been commenced. (See Civ. Code § 2924f.) Second, it is not typical in a residential purchase in California for a buyer to perform a title search on each property of interest before deciding whether to make an offer on one of them. Rather, it is more typically the case that a preliminary title report is provided to the buyer during escrow, so that the buyer can determine, before closing escrow, whether there are any title defects that are unacceptable to the buyer. Moreover, when a buyer makes an offer to purchase the property free and clear of all liens and encumbrances, and the seller agrees to sell on those terms, the seller

(continued)

impliedly represents that he or she expects to be in a position to deliver title free and clear.

* * *

As a final note, we observe that even when a buyer is on constructive notice of matters of record, that does not necessarily mean a cause of action in tort arising out of failure to disclose will not lie. . . .

* * *

(3) Balancing of factors

The brokers, in support of their position, cite *Merrill v. Buck* (1962) 58 Cal.2d 552, 25 Cal.Rptr. 456, 374 P.2d 304. In a case having to do with the duty of a real estate agent to a person with whom she had no privity of contract, the court stated: "'The determination whether in a specific case the defendant will be held liable to a third person not in privity is a matter of policy and involves the balancing of various factors, among which are the extent to which the transaction was intended to affect the plaintiff, the foreseeability of harm to him, the degree of certainty that the plaintiff suffered injury, the closeness of the connection between the defendant's conduct and the injury suffered, the moral blame attached to the defendant's conduct, and the policy of preventing future harm.'[Citations.]" (*Id.* at p. 562, 25 Cal.Rptr. 456, 375 P.2d 304; accord, *Krug, supra*, 220 Cal.App.3d at p. 42, 269 Cal. Rptr. 228.) The brokers argue that, applying these factors, it is clear they owed no duty to the buyers. We disagree.

The brokers do not address the first factor—"'the extent to which the transaction was intended to affect the plaintiff.'" (*Merrill v. Buck, supra*, 58 Cal.2d at p. 562, 25 Cal.Rptr. 456, 375 P.2d 304.) Obviously, the purchase and sale transaction was intended to directly affect the buyers. The first factor is squarely satisfied.

With regard to the foreseeability factor, the brokers contend that to impose a duty upon them in this instance would be to fashion a rule that brokers are required to divine when sellers may breach their agreements and to disclose their forecast to the buyer. Not at all. We agree that it is possible in every transaction that one party may fail to perform. However, to impose a duty to disclose upon the brokers in this case would neither necessitate that they become clairvoyant nor require them to guarantee their seller's performance. Rather, the rule we articulate in this case is simply that when a real estate agent or broker is aware that the amount of existing monetary liens and encumbrances exceeds the sales price of a residential property, so as to require either the cooperation of the lender in a short sale or the ability of the seller to put a substantial amount of cash into the escrow in order to obtain the release of the monetary liens and encumbrances affecting title, the agent or broker has a duty to disclose this state of affairs to the buyer, so that

the buyer can inquire further and evaluate whether to risk entering into a transaction with a substantial risk of failure.

* * *

The third factor set forth in *Merrill v. Buck, supra*, 58 Cal.2d 552 . . . is "'the degree of certainty that the plaintiff suffered injury.'" (*Id.* at p. 562. . . .) The brokers do not address this factor. However, the buyers allege that they were harmed when the sellers failed to convey the property. On the review of the ruling on the demurrer, we assume the truth of the factual allegations. (*Fremont Indemnity Co. v. Fremont General Corp., supra*, 148 Cal. App.4th at p. 111, 55 Cal.Rptr.3d 621.) Consequently, for the purpose of evaluating the third factor, we assume the buyers suffered injury.

With regard to the closeness of the connection between the brokers' conduct and the buyers' injury, the brokers argue that there is no connection at all. They say that the alleged injury was very simply caused by the seller's breach, not by any action of the brokers. However, the brokers could have informed the buyers that in order for the transaction to be consummated at a price of $749,000, either the lenders would have had to agree to accept less money than the amounts owing to them or the seller would have had to deposit cash into escrow to cover the excess debt. Then, the buyers could have protected themselves by making inquiry about the seller's ability to close escrow and then weighing whether to take a risk on an escrow that had a substantial probability of failure.

Turning now to moral blame, we observe that "California cases recognize a fundamental duty on the part of a realtor to deal honestly and fairly with all parties in the sale transaction. [Citations.]"(*Krug, supra*, 220 Cal.App.3d at p. 42, 269 Cal.Rptr. 228) Surely a sense of rudimentary fairness would indicate that buyers in a case such as this should be informed before they open escrow and position themselves to consummate the same that there is a substantial risk that title cannot be conveyed to them.

* * *

General duties notwithstanding, the brokers contend that they were not at liberty to disclose the information at issue in this case because to do so would have required them to violate their duty of confidentiality to the seller. In support of their position, the brokers cite Civil Code section 2079.16 and Standard of Practice 1-9 of the Code of Ethics and Standards of Practice of the National Association of Realtors.

In their discussion of Civil Code section 2079.16, the brokers cite only a single sentence thereof. That sentence provides: "An agent is not obligated to reveal to either

(continued)

party any confidential information obtained from the other party that does not involve the affirmative duties set forth above." . . . The question in this case, then, is whether the information in question was confidential information that did "*not* involve" such duties.

First of all, the information in question, to the extent it involved the disclosure that there were three deeds of trust recorded against the property, was not confidential at all. The existence of the three deeds of trust was a matter of public record and the brokers cannot seek the cloak of confidentiality to protect themselves from the requirement to disclose the mere existence of those deeds of trust. . . . Of course, as noted previously, that does not mean the current loan balances were of record. To the extent the buyers may seek to argue that they were entitled to know the current loan balances, that information could be construed as an element of the seller's personal and confidential information.

Second, as we have said, Civil Code section 2079.16 provides that there is no obligation to disclose confidential information "that does *not* involve the [enumerated] affirmative duties. . . ." (Italics added.) But here, the affirmative duty to treat each party to the transaction honestly and fairly, as expressed in section 2079.16, is involved. Arguably, the duty to disclose known matters materially affecting the desirability of entering into the transaction is also at issue, by analogy to the aforementioned case law.

*   *   *

The brokers seek shelter in the somewhat more restrictive language of Standard of Practice 1-9 of the Code of Ethics and Standards of Practice of the National Association of Realtors (2010). That standard of practice contains the following language: "REALTORS shall not knowingly . . . : [¶] 1) reveal confidential information of clients; or [¶] 2) use confidential information of clients to the disadvantage of clients; or [¶] 3) use confidential information of clients for . . . the advantage of third parties unless: [¶] a) clients consent after full disclosure. . . ." This standard of practice, unlike Civil Code section 2079.16, makes no mention of affirmative duties of disclosure.

We observe that the Code of Ethics and Standards of Practice of the National Association of Realtors (2010), in the introductory words preceding the preamble, states: "While the Code of Ethics establishes obligations that may be higher than those mandated by law, in any instance where the Code of Ethics and the law conflict, the obligations of the law must take precedence." The solution to the conflict between the duty to disclose and the duty to maintain client confidentiality is clear. When the duty of fairness to all parties requires the disclosure to the buyer of confidential information reflecting

a substantial risk that the escrow will not close, then the seller's real estate agent or broker must obtain the seller's permission to disclose such confidential information to the buyer, before the buyer enters into a contract to purchase the property. . . .

The final factor, as noted in *Merrill v. Buck, supra*, . . . to be applied in determining whether a seller's real estate agent or broker owes a duty to the buyer, is the policy of preventing future harm. (*Id.* at p. 562, 25 Cal.Rptr. 456, 375 P.2d 304.) The brokers here say the only thing to prevent is a seller's breach and that they are not responsible for their seller's conduct. The brokers miss the point. If a seller is at substantial risk of breach, due to factors known to his or her agent or broker, the agent or broker is in a position to prevent harm to the buyer by disclosing the risk. If an informed buyer chooses to take the risk, and then suffers harm, he or she cannot blame the agent or broker who made the appropriate disclosure. The policy of preventing harm to an uninformed buyer weighs in favor of imposing a duty of disclosure on a seller's agent or broker in circumstances such as those before us.

*   *   *

III DISPOSITION

The judgment is reversed. The buyers, appellants Phil and Jenille Holmes, shall recover their costs on appeal.

Bedsworth, Acting P.J., and O'Leary, J., concurred.

Case Questions

1. The case indicates that the brokers did not volunteer information regarding the three outstanding deeds of trust on the property. Do you believe the buyers had an affirmative obligation to determine whether there were any outstanding loans against the property during the initial stages of negotiating a purchase price? Why or why not?

2. What information are brokers required to disclose to buyers in your state? Do you believe the outcome would be the same under your state's requirements? Why or why not?

3. The buyers did not include the seller in the lawsuit because the seller's debt obligations ostensibly left the seller with no recoverable assets, yet the seller signed the contract for purchase and sale knowing that it was highly unlikely that he or she would be able to close on the property. Do you think the buyers should be allowed to recover against the brokers without requiring that the seller be held liable in this situation? Why or why not?

The duty of **accounting** refers to the broker's duty in safeguarding any monies, documents, or property held by the broker on behalf of the principal. This includes all deposit monies, deeds, title commitments or abstracts, mortgage instruments, keys to the property, and so forth. All deposits and other monies retained on behalf of a principal must be strictly accounted for and kept in escrow accounts in accordance with state statutory law, as discussed in the next section of this chapter.

Thus far, a broker's duties to his or her principal have been detailed, but note that a principal also owes certain duties to his or her agent/broker. A broker is an agent with limited authority to act on the principal's behalf. Because this authority is limited to the carrying out of the principal's specific instructions, the principal has the duty to make himself or herself available to the agent for consultation. The inaccessibility of a principal prevents the agent from carrying out his or her job. Further, the principal has a duty to supply all necessary information to the agent concerning the property, the principal's requirements, and any other information that has an impact on the transaction.

The principal has the duty to compensate the agent in accordance with the agency agreement entered into by the principal and agent. If the principal is the seller, the agreement will often state that the seller is to pay the agent a specified commission upon the agent's procurement of a ready, willing, and able buyer. Able in this context refers to the buyer's capacity to contract as well as to the buyer's financial ability to meet the seller's price and terms (for example, ability to come up with the purchase price or to procure financing to meet the purchase price). If the agent finds a buyer willing and able to meet the seller's price and terms, the seller cannot then change the price or terms to back out of the deal and refuse to pay the commission. Finally, the principal has the duty to indemnify the agent if the principal's actions result in financial harm to the agent.

Broker's Responsibility for Earnest Money Deposits

A broker will often be the person to first receive an earnest money deposit. **Earnest money** is a sum of money paid by a buyer at the time of entering into a contract to indicate the buyer's intention of carrying out the terms of the contract. These deposits and fees must be placed in an escrow account. An **escrow account** is an account in a bank, savings and loan, credit union, or similar financial institution that is held by a third party called an escrow agent (such as a broker, attorney, or title company), in which funds are deposited to be held until the happening of a certain event (for example, the closing on the real property). A broker may act as an escrow agent or may utilize the services of an attorney or a title company to act as escrow agent for funds received by the broker. Escrow agents are not required to open separate escrow accounts for each client. Escrow accounts can be interest-bearing or noninterest-bearing accounts. Prior to monies being placed in an interest-bearing account, a written agreement should be made by the parties to the real estate transaction as to who is entitled to the earned interest and when the interest must be disbursed. State law may specify a time period (such as twenty-four or forty-eight hours) within which a broker must deposit monies into an escrow account. Commingling of escrow deposits with other business funds is prohibited. An exception generally is made for small personal sums used in opening an escrow account or in keeping the account open or paying service charges on the account.

accounting: A broker's duty in safeguarding any monies, documents, or property held by the broker on behalf of the principal.

earnest money: A sum of money paid by a buyer at the time of entering a contract to indicate the buyer's intention of carrying out the terms of the contract.

escrow account: An account in a bank, savings and loan, credit union, or similar financial institution that is held by a third party and into which funds are deposited to be held until the happening of a stated event.

In addition to earnest money deposits, an agency agreement between the broker and principal may call for the collection of brokerage fees before the real estate transaction closes. Some states have laws regulating the collection of advance fees. State law may require that advance fees be deposited in the common escrow account or in a special escrow account called an **advance fee trust account.** Because the purpose of collecting advance fees usually is to provide the broker with coverage of advertising and other expenses incurred in marketing the property, the broker typically is entitled to use a certain percentage of the advance fees prior to closing. Before withdrawing the allowable sum from the account, the broker must provide the principal with an itemized statement showing the amount of the advance fee and how it is to be spent. Advance fees are not to be used to cover the broker's normal overhead expenses in running the brokerage office. If the property in question has not been sold or a contract for sale and purchase signed within the term of the agency agreement, the broker is required to return all advance fees to the principal.

If a broker handles the above accounts, the broker is required by state law to keep records of monthly statements comparing the broker's trust liability with the reconciled bank balances of all escrow and trust accounts. The trust liability is the total of all deposits that are received, being held by the broker, or pending at any given time. The statement should include such items as the name of the financial institution, the account(s) and the account number(s), the date the reconciliation was done, the account balance(s), outstanding checks, and deposits in transit. The monthly statement should be signed by the broker. In some states, these statements must be sent to the state real estate commission or other similar governmental authority. A sample monthly reconciliation statement is found in Exhibit 6–2.

There are occasions when a real estate broker is faced with conflicting demands for the escrow deposits. Paralegals should be aware of the fact that in most states there are statutes in place that outline the steps to be taken by a broker in the event of such a dispute. In such an instance, the attorneys for the parties may each make an argument to the broker regarding the deposits. These arguments may be based on the interpretation of the terms of the contract for sale and purchase. Nonetheless, the broker must abide by the state statutes, not the contract terms, with regard to the settling of escrow disputes.

State statutes usually outline the notification procedures and deadlines as well as the settlement procedures to be followed in the event of escrow disputes. Often, the state real estate commission or other applicable governmental authority must be notified of the dispute. State statutes may call for mandatory mediation or arbitration within a specified time period from the date the broker notifies the appropriate governmental authority of the dispute. Similarly, if the broker has his or her own good-faith doubt as to whether a party is entitled to escrow funds in a given situation (for example, a situation in which one party has indicated its intentions not to close and the broker has not received instructions, or has received conflicting instructions, with regard to the disbursement of the escrowed funds), the broker must follow state statutes governing the handling of escrow disputes. Should the broker's commission be in dispute, the broker may be allowed to retain the amount of commission in escrow until the dispute is settled through the use of statutorily mandated settlement procedures.

If a buyer makes an earnest money deposit at the time of making an offer to purchase and then revokes the offer prior to its acceptance by the seller, the buyer

Monthly reconciliation statement

EXHIBIT 6-2

MONTHLY STATEMENT RECONCILIATION
ESCROW ACCOUNT OF ATLANTIS REALTY COMPANY
FOR THE MONTH ENDING JULY 31, 2015

I. BANK RECONCILIATION

Patriot Bank, Atlantis Realty Escrow Account

Account Number 100009-000-3356

Reconciliation performed July 31, 2015

   A. Balance as per July 31, 2015: $110,500.00

   B. Escrow Deposits in Transit

Date	Amount
July 31, 2015	$20,000.00
July 31, 2015	$15,000.00
Total deposits in transit:	$35,000.00

   C. Total of A plus B: $145,500.00

   D. Escrow Outstanding Checks Not Included in Bank Statement

Date	Check Number	Amount
July 28, 2015	6102	$10,000.00
July 29, 2015	6103	$12,000.00
Total escrow outstanding checks:		$22,000.00

   E. Reconciled Bank Balance (C minus D): $123,500.00

II. BROKER'S TRUST LIABILITY RECONCILIATION

Comparison of Reconciled Bank Balance with Broker's Trust Liability:

   A. Reconciled Bank Balance: $123,500.00

   B. Broker's Trust Liability: $123,500.00

I, the undersigned, hereby state that the Reconciled Bank Balance and the Trust Liability _____ agree _____ do not agree. (If they do not agree, state the amount of shortage or overage and the reason(s) for same below.)

ATLANTIS REALTY COMPANY

BY:_____
Broker

---

is entitled to return of the deposit. Similarly, if a buyer makes an earnest money deposit at the time of making an offer to purchase and that offer is subsequently rejected by the seller, the buyer is entitled to return of the deposit. A contract may also state that, if there is a default by the seller or buyer, the broker may be able to enforce commission against the defaulting party out of the earnest money deposit.

Broker's Compensation

A real estate broker is compensated for his or her services by the payment of a commission. Only licensed real estate brokers (and salespersons) are entitled to commissions. Further, most state statutes provide that a broker can share commissions only with other licensed brokers and salespersons. The amount to be paid is negotiated between the broker and the principal and usually is reduced to writing in an agency agreement. If the principal is the seller, the agency agreement is called a **listing agreement.** In most transactions, the commission is computed as an agreed-upon percentage of the purchase price of the property and is paid customarily to the broker at closing.

Antitrust laws (laws protecting against unlawful restraints in trade and commerce, such as monopolies and price-fixing) prohibit the imposition by brokerage firms of uniform rates of commission. These laws also prohibit the allocation of markets, which occurs when two or more brokers agree to allocate different market sectors, based on such criteria as geographic location or property price ranges. For example, Broker 1 may be allocated the northern half of the city, while Broker 2 is allocated the southern half of the city, the brokers agreeing not to infiltrate each other's market. Under the **Sherman Act** (a federal antitrust law), brokers engaged in price-fixing or allocation of markets are guilty of a felony punishable by both a fine and a prison sentence.

The date the commission is earned may be different from the date upon which it is paid. The date upon which the commission is earned is crucial to both the principal and the broker because once the commission is earned, the principal is obligated to pay it. In order to earn a commission, a real estate broker (or salesperson) must be the procuring cause of the purchase and sale. The interpretation of "procuring cause" may be found in the wording of the listing agreement. In the case of a seller agent, the seller agent usually is the procuring cause of the purchase and sale of the real property when he or she (or one of his or her subagents) finds a buyer who is ready, willing, and able to purchase the property. A ready, willing, and able buyer is one who is agreeable to and capable of purchasing the property on the seller's terms. If, however, the listing agreement stipulates that the broker must "effect a sale," the broker has not earned his or her commission until there is a written contract executed by both the buyer and the seller.

Once a broker finds a ready, willing, and able buyer or, alternatively, effects a sale by obtaining a contract signed by both parties, the broker has earned the commission, regardless of whether the transaction ever gets to closing. A number of obstacles may appear after the contract is signed that may prevent a closing from taking place. Such obstacles can include, but need not be limited to, title defects that cannot be corrected, inspection reports calling for repairs beyond the amount agreed to be paid by the seller, or simply a change of heart by one of the parties. Although a broker normally will make every effort to see that a transaction is consummated, once the broker's responsibilities under the listing agreement have been met, the principal must honor the agreement.

Types of Listing Agreements

listing agreement: A contract between a seller and a broker.

Sherman Act: A federal antitrust law protecting against unlawful restraints in trade and commerce, such as monopolies and price-fixing.

Paralegals should be aware of the fact that there are several types of listing agreements that may be negotiated between a broker and a seller (recall that a seller, when hiring a broker, "lists" his or her property with that broker). Paralegals may be called upon by their supervising attorneys to draft listing agreements for broker clients or to review such agreements should a dispute arise between the broker and the seller. As noted earlier, there is no requirement for a written contract to establish an agency relationship because the relationship is established the moment the principal confers authority on the agent by delegating responsibilities to the agent. Further, a contract between broker and principal is a contract for services, not a contract for an interest in real property and, therefore, some jurisdictions hold that it does not have to be in writing to be legally valid. Nonetheless, written listing agreements are standard practice. The most common types of listing agreements are the open listing, the exclusive listing, and the exclusive-right-to-sell listing.

Open Listing

An **open listing,** sometimes referred to as a *general listing or a nonexclusive listing,* is the granting of the right to solicit and receive offers on the seller's property. This is a nonexclusive right given to a broker, and the broker shares this right with all other brokers with whom the seller decides to list the property. The broker is entitled to a commission only if he or she (or one of his or her salespeople) finds the buyer or effects the sale. Thus, an open listing can be characterized as a unilateral contract that becomes binding only if and when the broker procures the sale. The broker is not entitled to a commission if another broker procures the sale or if the seller finds a buyer for the property. Although at first glimpse this arrangement may seem advantageous to the seller, the truth is that most brokers expend very little time or energy on open listings and are unwilling to expend considerable money in advertising the property when the chances of procuring a commission are risky. Therefore, an open listing will receive less of a broker's attention than an exclusive or exclusive-right-to-sell listing, and the seller may be stuck with the property for a longer period of time.

Exclusive Listing

An **exclusive listing** is one in which the seller agrees to list the property with no broker other than the listing broker for the term of the listing agreement. As an exclusive agent of the seller, the listing broker is entitled to receive compensation if the listing broker or any other person procures a buyer for the property. However, the seller reserves the right to find his or her own buyer, and if he or she is successful in so doing, no commission is owed to the listing broker.

For example, the seller gives Broker 1 an exclusive listing. Broker 1 proceeds to put the listing in the multiple listing service directory. Broker 2, a member of the multiple listing service, finds a buyer for the property. Broker 1 is called the listing broker or listing agent because the listing agreement was signed with him or her. Broker 2 is called the selling broker or selling agent because he or she procured the sale. Recall the prior discussion of subagency. Broker 2 will be considered a subagent of Broker 1 in this instance, and the commission will be split between the two brokers. If Broker 1 puts the listed property in the multiple service directory but ends up procuring a buyer with his or her own leads and efforts, Broker 1 keeps the entire commission. The only way Broker 1 will not receive a commission is if the seller finds the buyer.

A word of caution is in order here. The wording of an exclusive listing agreement often is very similar to the wording of an exclusive-right-to-sell listing agreement (discussed in the following text), although the rights that are conferred differ. If there is any ambiguity in the language of the contract, contract law dictates that the ambiguity must be construed against the drafter of the contract and in favor of

open listing: The granting of a nonexclusive right to solicit and receive offers on the seller's real property.

exclusive listing: A listing agreement in which the seller agrees to list the property with no broker other than the listing broker for the term of the agreement. As an exclusive agent, the listing broker is entitled to receive compensation if the listing broker or any person other than the seller procures a buyer within the listing term.

the other party. Because the broker (or the broker's attorney) is usually the person responsible for drafting the contract, if there is any ambiguity leading one to question whether the contract is an exclusive listing agreement or an exclusive-right-to-sell listing agreement, the courts most likely will construe the contract to be the former rather than the latter.

Exclusive-Right-to-Sell Listing

All brokers want an **exclusive-right-to-sell listing.** Under this type of listing agreement, the listing broker is entitled to a commission if anyone procures a buyer for the property within the listing term. This means that even if the seller procures his or her own buyer, the listing broker is entitled to a commission. Because the seller is parting with his or her rights to sell the property, some jurisdictions require that an exclusive-right-to-sell listing agreement be in writing, even if the jurisdiction allows for other verbal listing agreements. Brokers are more willing to expend money for advertising and other costs associated with the marketing of real property if they have the property listed under this type of agreement.

Other Listing Arrangements

Net Listing. A **net listing** agreement is one in which the seller specifies the net amount of money he or she must receive in order to sell the property. Under the terms of the agreement, the listing broker receives any monies in excess of this specified amount as commission. Therefore, the broker sets the purchase price, keeping the seller's requirements in mind. Net listing agreements are illegal in a number of states because of the potential for fraud. In those states in which net listing agreements are allowed, however, brokers receive compensation only if the property is sold. Thus, if the broker sets the purchase price prohibitively high in an effort to glean greater compensation, the chances of the property selling are minimal, so it is in the broker's best interests to establish a reasonable purchase price.

Flat-Fee Sales. The **flat-fee sale** has become a popular method of selling property for those sellers who do not mind putting some effort into selling their own property. A flat-fee sales arrangement is one in which, for a flat fee (which is considerably smaller than the average commission), a broker will evaluate and photograph the seller's property, write a description sheet of the property that will be placed in a special online directory, and provide the seller with For Sale signs. The seller is responsible for holding open houses and showing the property to prospective buyers who find out about the property by looking at the online directory or by driving by the property.

Broker's Agreement Checklist and Sample Agreement

As noted earlier, a paralegal may be called upon to draft an agreement for a broker client or to review such an agreement to determine the rights and obligations of a client who is a principal under such an agreement. Just as with any other aspect of real estate practice, a paralegal should obtain as much detailed information as possible. The following checklist will aid in the drafting or reviewing of a broker's agreement.

exclusive-right-to-sell listing: A listing agreement in which the listing broker is entitled to a commission if anyone procures a buyer within the listing term.

net listing: A listing agreement in which the seller specifies the net amount of money he or she must receive in order to sell the property. Under the terms of the agreement, the broker receives any monies in excess of this specified amount as commission.

flat-fee sale: An arrangement in which, for a flat fee, a broker evaluates and photographs a property, places a property description in a special online directory, and provides For Sale signs to the seller.

BROKER'S AGREEMENT CHECKLIST

1. Parties
   a. Names of all parties and marital status of the principal(s)
2. Commencement date of agreement
3. Termination date of agreement
4. Type of agreement established
   a. Open listing
   b. Exclusive listing
   c. Exclusive-right-to-sell listing
   d. Net listing
   e. Flat-fee sale
   f. Other (specify)
5. Listing price of the property
6. Amount of commission
   a. Dollar figure
   b. Percentage of purchase price
7. Property description
   a. Street address
   b. Legal description, if available
   c. Size of the lot
   d. Size and description of the improvements (for example, house, apartment building, shopping center), including the following:
      i. Square footage of the total structure (indicating whether the derived figure is air-conditioned/heated space or includes space that is not air-conditioned/heated)
      ii. Room count
      iii. Square footage of each room within the structure, if possible
      iv. Age of the improvements
      v. Method of construction used
   e. Zoning classification of the property
   f. Fixtures to be sold with the premises
   g. Any personal property to be sold with the premises
8. Seller's warranties with regard to the property
9. Broker's authority
   a. Rights given to broker, including the following:
      i. Permissible types of advertising
      ii. Holding of open houses
      iii. Placement of signs on the property
      iv. Acceptance of earnest money deposits
10. Multiple listing service provision

(continued)

11. Broker's responsibilities
    a. For procuring buyer (if seller agent)
       i. Finding ready, willing, and able buyer
       ii. Effecting a sale
    b. Disclosure of agency relationship
    c. Accounting
12. Renewal of agreement
    a. Automatic renewal
    b. Conditions for renewal
13. Indemnification of broker
14. Termination of agreement
    a. Circumstances under which agreement terminates
    b. Broker protection clause (a clause that states that the broker is entitled to commission within a specified time frame after the expiration of the agreement if the property is sold to a party originally in contact with the broker)
15. Signatures of the parties

Exhibit 6–3 is a sample exclusive-right-to-sell listing agreement.

EXHIBIT 6–3   **Exclusive-right-to-sell listing agreement**

EXCLUSIVE-RIGHT-TO-SELL LISTING AGREEMENT

THIS AGREEMENT is entered into this 9th day of May, 2015, by and between Carl Andrews, a duly licensed real estate broker as representative of Atlantis Realty Company, a real estate brokerage firm duly licensed under the laws of the State of Any State ("Broker"), and Grant Daniels, a single man ("Owner").

I. EXCLUSIVE RIGHT TO SELL. Owner agrees to give Broker an exclusive and irrevocable right to sell the property described below for a period commencing on the date above listed and terminating at midnight on November 9, 2015. There shall be no automatic renewal of this Agreement. Broker agrees to use his best efforts to effect a sale of the property described below, plus all fixtures therein as set forth in Exhibit B attached to and made a part of this Agreement.

II. PROPERTY DESCRIPTION. The Property for which the Broker's services have been procured to effect a sale is described as follows:

> Lot 10, Block 7 of THE PALLADIUM according to the plat thereof, recorded
> in Plat Book 60, Page 7 of the Public Records of Any County, Any State.

The improvements on said Property contain 2,500 square feet under air. A floor plan of said improvements is set forth in Exhibit A attached to and made a part of this Agreement.

III. PRICE. The listing price of the Property shall be $300,000.00 to be paid on terms acceptable to the Owner.

IV. COMMISSION. In effecting a sale during the term of this Agreement, the Broker shall be entitled to a commission equal to Six (6%) Percent of the Purchase Price of the Property. Should the Property be sold within six months from the expiration date of this Agreement to a person or persons who were in contact with Broker prior to the expiration of this Agreement, Broker shall be entitled to the full commission set forth in this paragraph.

(*continued*)

EXHIBIT 6–3

V. BROKER'S ACCESS TO THE PROPERTY. Owner hereby grants Broker and Broker's subagents, together with potential buyers, access to the Property through the installation of a lockbox containing a key to the Property. Broker shall not be held responsible for any loss due to theft, loss or vandalism resulting from any such access, and the Owner shall be solely responsible for obtaining appropriate insurance.

VI. DEPOSITS. Owner authorizes Broker to accept earnest deposits on behalf of Owner and to issue receipts for such deposits.

VII. SIGNAGE. Owner authorizes Broker to place appropriate signage on the Property during the term of this Agreement.

VIII. MULTIPLE LISTING SERVICE. Broker is a member of a local Board of Realtors®. Broker is authorized to disseminate information concerning the Property through a multiple listing service and utilize the assistance of cooperating brokers to effect a sale of the Property.

IX. AGENCY RELATIONSHIP. Broker and Owner hereby acknowledge that an agency relationship is created upon execution of this Agreement and that Broker has the right to inform all prospective buyers of the existence of said agency relationship upon Broker's first contact with the potential buyers.

X. OWNER'S WARRANTIES. Owner represents and warrants that Owner is the owner of record of the Property. Owner further represents and warrants that the roof is in good repair and that the heating, cooling, plumbing and electrical systems and built-in appliances are in good working condition.

XI. INDEMNIFICATION. Owner agrees to indemnify and hold Broker and all other cooperating brokers harmless against any and all claims, liability, damage or loss arising from any misrepresentation or breach of warranty by Owner in this Agreement. Owner further agrees to indemnify and hold Broker and all other cooperating brokers harmless against any incorrect information supplied by Owner relating to adverse conditions or latent defects.

XII. ATTORNEY'S FEES. In connection with any litigation arising out of this Agreement, the prevailing party shall be entitled to recover reasonable attorney's fees and costs.

XIII. ENTIRE AGREEMENT. This Agreement, including all attached Exhibits, shall constitute the entire agreement between Owner and Broker and supersede any other written or oral agreements between them. This Agreement may be modified only by a writing signed by Owner and Broker.

OWNER: BROKER: ATLANTIS REALTY COMPANY

Grant Daniels   BY: *Carl Andrews*
                                                         Representative

The Broker's Role in a Short Sale Transaction

In a depressed or slow real estate market, a broker may find himself or herself working with a client who can no longer afford the mortgage payments on his or her home and is looking for alternatives to foreclosure. One possible option is a short sale transaction. A **short sale** is the sale of a property for a price that is "short," or less than the full amount owed on the property. A short sale also may be referred to as a *pre-foreclosure sale*. For a short sale transaction to occur, the lender (or lenders if there is more than one mortgage lien on the property) must approve the transaction. Before a lender will decide whether to accept less than full payment to release its lien on a property so that a sale can proceed, the lender will require that the borrower/owner provide a **short sale package** for review and consideration.

short sale: The sale of a property for a price that is "short," or less than the full amount owed on the property.

short sale package: A compilation of documentation that a lender reviews to determine the value of the property, the existence of other encumbrances and costs associated with the sale of the property, and the financial situation of the borrower/owner.

The package is a compilation of documentation that the lender will want to review to determine the value of the property, the existence of other encumbrances and costs associated with the sale of the property, and the financial situation of the borrower/owner. Although short sale transactions are discussed in more detail in later chapters, note that a real estate broker plays a key role in compiling the requisite documentation and in the short sale negotiation process.

Real estate brokers, title companies, and attorneys all participate in the preparation and compilation of the documentation required for a short sale transaction. Regardless of who ultimately is responsible for the submission of a completed short sale package to the borrower/owner's lender, the broker will be responsible for providing certain information. One of the documents the lender will require is a copy of the listing agreement. The listing agreement should include a short sale addendum. This addendum (1) explains to the borrower/owner that any sale of the property is contingent on the approval of the lender and other lienholders and that the broker cannot provide any guarantees of this approval; (2) explains that the lender may require modification of various terms prior to approval for approval to be granted; (3) explains that lender approval may not always extinguish all obligations of the borrower/owner to the lender; (4) suggests that the borrower/owner solicit advice from attorneys, accountants, and other professionals regarding the legal, tax, and credit consequences of a short sale; (5) requires the borrower/owner to provide authorization for the lender to provide requisite information to the broker; (6) requires the borrower/owner to provide all requisite documentation for the short sale package; and (7) provides authorization for the broker to market the property as a short sale and indicate in the MLS listing that the sale of the property and the commission to be paid to the broker and any cooperating brokers are subject to the approval of the lender and may be modified. A sample short sale addendum to a listing agreement is provided in Exhibit 6–4.

As mentioned above, the broker will need to communicate with the borrower/owner's lender. A lender cannot provide confidential information to the broker

---

EXHIBIT 6–4   **Short sale addendum to listing agreement**

SHORT SALE ADDENDUM TO LISTING AGREEMENT

This Short Sale Addendum ("Addendum") dated the 19th of June, 2015, is attached to and made a part of the Exclusive-Right-to-Sell Listing Agreement ("Listing Agreement") between Carl Andrews, a duly licensed real estate broker as representative of Atlantis Realty Company, a real estate brokerage firm duly licensed under the laws of the State of Any State ("Broker"), and Marsha Vincent, a single woman ("Seller"), regarding the real property located at 313 Findlay Avenue, Any City, Any State ("Property").

I. ACKNOWLEDGEMENT OF SHORT SALE. The Seller acknowledges that the sale of the Property may result in a short sale. A short sale occurs when the purchase price for the sale of the Property is insufficient to pay in full the costs of the sale, including but not limited to the Seller's closing costs and the outstanding amount of the Seller's loan(s) and other debts against the Property due and owing to one or more lender(s) and/or other lienholder(s) (collectively referred to as "Lienholders"). The Seller acknowledges that the Seller will not receive any net sales proceeds at closing.

II. LIENHOLDERS' APPROVAL AND CONDITIONS. The Seller acknowledges that any contract for sale of the Property shall be contingent upon the written approval of the Lienholders. Seller understands that the Lienholders are not obligated to approve a short sale, are not obligated to release the Seller from further liability even if the Lienholders approve a short sale, and may impose conditions prior to an approval of a short sale.

III. OPTIONS. The Seller understands that there may be disadvantages to a short sale. The Seller is advised to explore other options such as loan modification, a revised payment plan, refinancing, bankruptcy, or a voluntary deed-in-lieu of foreclosure. These options may have adverse consequences to the Seller and should be discussed with appropriate professionals.

IV. CONSEQUENCES OF A SHORT SALE. A short sale may have tax, credit, and legal consequences. It may negatively affect the Seller's credit score or credit rating. A short sale may result in taxable income to the Seller even though the Seller does not receive any cash proceeds from the sale. The Broker has advised the Seller to consult legal counsel and a tax professional concerning the tax, credit, and legal ramifications of a short sale.

V. BROKER AUTHORIZATION. The Seller authorizes the Broker to communicate with the Lienholder(s) throughout the term of the Listing Agreement. The Seller authorizes the Broker to (1) identify the Property listing in the Multiple Listing Service ("MLS") as a short sale, as required by the MLS rules and regulations; (2) disclose to prospective buyers and realtors® that the transaction is a short sale and that the sale terms are subject to the Lienholders' approval; (3) disclose to prospective buyers and realtors® that the commission offered in the MLS listing is subject to the Lienholders' approval and may be modified accordingly; and (4) provide or disclose any requested documentation or information to the Lienholders for the purpose of obtaining approval of the sale of the Property.

VI. INDEMNIFICATION OF BROKER. The Seller acknowledges that the Broker shall have no liability resulting from the Broker's communications with the Lienholder(s) and/or any attempts by the Broker to facilitate the sale of the Property. Furthermore, the Seller acknowledges that the Broker shall have no liability for the decisions of the Lienholder(s).

VII. SELLER'S DUTIES. The Seller agrees to cooperate with the Broker to furnish to the Broker and the Lienholder(s) any and all information and documentation deemed necessary in the short sale process. The Seller may be asked to furnish executed copies of the listing agreement, the contract for purchase and sale, a preliminary closing statement, a hardship letter, proof of assets and liabilities, pay stubs, tax returns, bank statements, homeowner or condominium association lien status letters (if applicable), and other documentation the Lienholder(s) request to determine the need for a short sale.

All other terms of the Listing Agreement not modified by this Addendum shall remain in full force and effect.

SELLER:

Marsha Vincent

BROKER: ATLANTIS REALTY COMPANY

By: *Carl Andrews*
    Representative

without the written authorization of the borrower/owner. Therefore, one of the first documents a broker's client must provide is an authorization letter. An example is provided in Exhibit 6–5.

A broker often will be asked to include a copy of the actual MLS listing as part of the short sale package and may also be asked to submit a comparative market analysis. However, the lender also will have a valuation of the property prepared by an independent party. The independent party submits a document referred to as a **broker price opinion (BPO)** or *broker opinion of valuation (BOV)*. Although the National Association of Realtors® provides a voluntary certification program to become a certified "broker price opinion resource," state laws vary regarding the requirements for someone to provide property valuations. Some states, for example, prohibit anyone other than a duly licensed property appraiser to provide a property valuation for a fee. The information contained in a BPO varies, depending on what

broker price opinion (BPO): A valuation of a property conducted by an independent party that is requested by a lender in a short sale transaction.

EXHIBIT 6–5   **Authorization letter**

June 19, 2015

Century Bank
1100 Main Street
Any City, Any State

Attn: Loss Mitigation Department

RE: Loan #:   990004370
     Property: 313 Findlay Avenue, Any City, Any State
     Borrower: Marsha Vincent
     Last 4 digits of
     Social Security No.:   8081

To whom it may concern:

Please accept this letter as my authorization to discuss and to release any and all information regarding the above-referenced loan to:

Carl Andrews, Licensed Real Estate Broker
Atlantis Realty Company
672 N.E. 23rd Street
Any City, Any State
carlandrews@atlantisrealty.com
Phone: (000) 505-4433
Fax: (000) 505-4430

This authorization shall remain in effect until further written notice is provided. Thank you for your cooperation.

Authorized by:

Marsha Vincent

a lender requests. The lender may ask for a drive-by BPO or an interior BPO, the latter typically providing greater detail regarding the subject property. In addition to information regarding the subject property, most BPOs contain information regarding the neighborhood in which the property is located, a comparison of the property to a certain number of other comparable properties sold within a specified time period, and a comparison of the property to a certain number of other comparable properties currently on the market. A sample BPO is provided in Exhibit 6–6.

If the borrower/owner and a prospective purchaser have signed a contract for purchase and sale (subject to lender approval), the broker will submit this as part of the short sale package, together with the prospective purchaser's proof of preapproval of any financing. Other documentation that will be submitted to the lender in the short sale package includes items that must be obtained from the borrower/owner, such as recent pay stubs, tax returns, bank statements, and a financial information worksheet. A preliminary title search will have to be done to determine any other outstanding liens, and a preliminary HUD-1 closing statement will have to be prepared for lender review, so the broker will need to communicate with a title company and the closing agent or attorney, who provides this information.

Broker price opinion   E X H I B I T   6 – 6

BROKER PRICE OPINION

Inspection Date: August 31, 2015
BPO Type: _____ Drive-By   ____ X ____ Interior
Client: Century Bank
Property Address: 313 Findlay Avenue, Any City, Any State
Parcel Number: 72400580009
Property Type: Detached, single-family home
Loan #:   990004370
Borrower/Owner: Marsha Vincent
Completed By: Erica Dormer, Swinton Realty, Inc.
                     edormer@swintonrealty.com
                     (000) 273-4498

I.   GENERAL MARKET CONDITIONS

Current market condition: _____ Depressed   __ X __ Slow _____ Stable

                              _____ Improving   _____ Excellent

Market price for this
type of property has: __ X __ Decreased _____ Increased

                          _____ Remained stable

in the last __12__ months

II. NEIGHBORHOOD MARKET CONDITIONS

Location: _____ Urban   __ X __ Suburban   _____ Rural

Current number of properties for sale in this area: <u>Subject property is located in Findlay Gardens subdivision. There currently are 42 properties for sale within this subdivision. The subdivision contains condominium units, townhouses, and single-family homes. There currently are 19 single-family homes for sale within this subdivision.</u>

Sales price of properties in the last __ 12 __ months: <u>$285,000</u> to <u>$535,000</u> for <u>single-family homes</u>

Normal marketing time in this area: <u>180 days</u>

Estimated ratio of owner/tenant occupied properties in this area: <u>75/25 ratio</u>

III. SUBJECT PROPERTY

For the neighborhood, the subject property is:

_____ Under-improved   _____ Over-improved   __ X __ Appropriate

Listing status: _____ not yet listed   __ X __ currently listed

                     _____ listing expired

Listing company: <u>Atlantis Realty Company</u>
Listing agent: <u>Carl Andrews</u>
                     <u>carlandrews@atlantisrealty.com</u>
                     <u>(000) 505-4433</u>

Days on the market (DOM): __74__

EXHIBIT 6-6   *(continued)*

IV. COMPETITIVE CLOSED SALES

ITEM	SUBJECT	COMPARABLE #1	COMPARABLE #2	COMPARABLE #3
Address	313 Findlay Avenue	339 Findlay Avenue	503 Parkside Terrace	620 Avon Court
Proximity to subject		same block	two blocks	0.25 miles
Type of sale		Market	Market	Market
Sale price		$370,000	$293,000	$412,500
Price/Liv. Sq. Ft.	$169.57 per sq. ft.	$198.07 per sq. ft.	$137.88 per sq. ft.	$172.09 per sq. ft.
Data source	county tax records 72400580009	MLS 43211553	MLS 43266401	MLS 43344277
Property type	SF Detach	SF Detach	SF Detach	SF Detach
Sale date		May 16, 2015	March 5, 2015	Jan. 11, 2015
DOM	74	169	111	212
Lot size	0.15 acre	0.15 acre	0.16 acre	0.19 acre
Location	Good	Good	Good	Good
View	Garden	Garden	Garden	Lake
Design	Single story	Single story	Single story	Single story
Liv. sq. ft.	2,064	1,868	2,125	2,397
Construction quality	Good	Good	Good	Good
Age	22 yrs	22 yrs	20 yrs	19 yrs
# of bedrooms	3	3	3	3
# of bathrooms	2	2	2	2
Garage	2 attached	2 attached	2 attached	2 attached
Pool	No	No	No	No
Porch/Patio	Patio	Patio	Patio	Patio
Heating/Cooling	Central A/C	Central A/C	Central A/C	Central A/C
Finished basement	No	No	No	No
Special features	None	None	None	None
Value adjustments	$0	$0	$0	$0
Adjusted sales price of comparables		$370,000	$293,000	$412,500

V. COMPETITIVE LISTINGS

ITEM	SUBJECT	COMPARABLE #1	COMPARABLE #2	COMPARABLE #3
Address	313 Findlay Avenue	327 Findlay Avenue	404 Willow Lane	519 Lakeview Dr.
Proximity to subject		same block	two blocks	0.25 miles
Type of listing		Market	Market	Market
List price	$350,000	$394,000	$399,000	$428,000
Price/Liv. Sq. Ft.	$169.57 per sq. ft.	$184.54 per sq. ft.	$187.76 per sq. ft.	$201.41 per sq. ft.
Data source	county tax records 72400580009	MLS 43355117	MLS 43320993	MLS 43511200
Property type	SF Detach	SF Detach	SF Detach	SF Detach
DOM	74	298	236	82

(*continued*)

EXHIBIT 6–6

ITEM	SUBJECT	COMPARABLE #1	COMPARABLE #2	COMPARABLE #3
Lot size	0.15 acre	0.15 acre	0.16 acre	0.19 acre
Location	Good	Good	Good	Good
View	Garden	Garden	Garden	Lake
Design	Single story	Single story	Single story	Single story
Liv. sq. ft.	2,064	2,135	2,125	2,250
Construction quality	Good	Good	Good	Good
Age	22 yrs	22 yrs	21 yrs	23 yrs
# of bedrooms	3	3	3	3
# of bathrooms	2	2	2	2
Garage	2 attached	2 attached	2 attached	2 attached
Pool	No	No	No	No
Porch/Patio	Patio	Patio	Patio	Patio
Heating/Cooling	Central A/C	Central A/C	Central A/C	Central A/C
Finished basement	No	No	No	No
Special features	None	None	None	None
Value adjustments	$0	$0	$0	$0
Adjusted sales price of comparables		$394,000	$399,000	$428,000

VI. REPAIRS

Itemized needed repairs and costs:

Item	Estimated Cost
None noted.	$0

VII. MARKET STRATEGY/VALUE

	As-Is	Repaired
Market Value	$350,000	$350,000
Suggested Listing Price	$350,000	$350,000

Marketing Strategy: Market As-Is. Property is priced in keeping within the range of comparable properties sold in the past eight months.

Short sale transactions can be time-consuming and may not always result in lender approval. Brokers may find that a lender will require a lowering of the brokerage commission as one of the conditions for approval. Brokers who choose to work with such transactions should understand the complexities involved and be prepared for delays and setbacks as well as lender requests for submissions of updated data.

CHAPTER SUMMARY

1. A real estate broker is a person who is duly licensed by the state to negoti-
    ate the sale and purchase of real property for compensation. A broker may
    become a Realtor® by becoming a member of a local board of Realtors® that is
    affiliated with the National Association of Realtors®. Brokers may employ real
    estate salespersons to act as their subagents in providing services for the
    broker's principal. All earned commissions must be paid directly to the
    broker who, in turn, may pay a certain portion of the commission to a
    salesperson.

2. Attorneys and brokers are both professionals who provide valuable services
    for their clients. A broker's expertise is in the area of marketing properties
    and negotiating sales. An attorney's expertise is in the area of examining
    title and drafting the documents necessary to consummate the transaction.
    Neither the broker nor the attorney should assume responsibility beyond the
    scope of his or her employment.

3. A broker may be a single agent, a dual agent, or a transaction broker.
    A broker's role must be disclosed to all parties, and the broker must receive
    their written consent.

4. A broker acting in a fiduciary capacity owes his or her principal the duties of
    care, obedience, loyalty, confidentiality, disclosure, and accounting. A broker
    is expected to exercise his or her knowledge and skill in the diligent service
    of his or her principal. A broker must obey all legal instructions of the
    principal and always act in the principal's best interests. This includes
    keeping confidences and making full disclosure to the principal of all matters
    material to the real estate transaction.

5. Brokers may act as escrow agents. Any deposits and advance fees received
    must not be commingled with other business funds but, rather, must be placed
    in special accounts. Brokers must make an accounting to their principals re-
    garding the keeping of these accounts and any disbursements made from them.

6. A broker and seller may enter into one of several types of listing agreements.
    An open listing provides the seller with the most flexibility because the
    seller gives no one broker the exclusive right to sell the property. However,
    this type of listing is least favored by brokers, and, therefore, brokers are not
    likely to expend much time on an open listing. An exclusive listing makes the
    listing broker the seller's exclusive agent, while allowing the seller to retain
    the right to procure a buyer on his or her own. An exclusive-right-to-sell list-
    ing guarantees the listing broker a commission, regardless of who procures a
    buyer, as long as a buyer is procured within the listing period.

7. A listing agreement should include, but need not be limited to, the following
    terms: the names of the parties, the commencement and termination dates of
    the agreement, a description of the property, a description of the type of list-
    ing established, the amount of commission, the listing price of the property,
    and the rights and responsibilities of the broker.

8. A real estate broker plays a key role in a short sale transaction. The sale of
    the listed property will be subject to lender approval and must be listed as a
    short sale in the multiple listing service (MLS). The broker must submit vari-
    ous documents to the borrower/owner's lender as part of a short sale pack-
    age for lender review and consideration. This documentation includes items

in the hands of the broker, such as the listing agreement with the attached short sale addendum, the MLS listing, a comparative market analysis, and, when applicable, the agreement for purchase and sale with the prospective purchaser's loan preapproval verification. Other documentation must be gathered from the borrower/owner of the property and outside professionals. The lender will have an independent valuation of the property conducted prior to deciding whether to approve the short sale transaction.

WEB RESOURCES

http://www.realtor.org/

This is the site of the National Association of Realtors®. Current real estate news and housing statistics can be accessed at this site. Additionally, the latest edition of the Code of Ethics and Standards of Practice of the National Association of Realtors® can be accessed at this site, as can summaries of relevant ethics cases pertaining to real estate licensees.

http://www.law.cornell.edu/

This is the site of the Legal Information Institute (LII). Under the "Legal Resources" section, you can find your state's statutes and administrative code regulations pertaining to the licensing of real estate brokers and salespersons.

REVIEW QUESTIONS

1. Distinguish among (a) a real estate broker, (b) a Realtor®, and (c) a real estate agent.
2. Explain the fiduciary duties owed by a real estate broker to his or her principal.
3. Compare and contrast the following:
    a. A single agent and a transaction broker
    b. An exclusive listing and an exclusive-right-to-sell listing
4. What are a broker's responsibilities regarding disclosure to (a) parties to the transaction and (b) third parties?
5. What terms should be included in a listing agreement?

DISCUSSION QUESTIONS

1. A real estate broker is showing properties to a prospective buyer. The buyer wants to buy a house only in an area where there are a lot of children. She tells the broker, "I don't want my children to be the only ones in the neighborhood going door to door on Halloween. I want them to have other children to play with when they come home from school without having to drive them around town to other neighborhoods." Go to the website of the National Association of Realtors®, and review the Code of Ethics and Standards of Practice. Based on your review, how would you suggest the broker handle this situation?

2. As noted in this chapter, a transaction broker may provide limited representation to both parties in the same transaction and does not owe the full array of fiduciary duties to his or her client(s) as required in a single agency relationship. Do you think a broker can adequately represent both parties in the same transaction? Why or why not?

3. A real estate broker lists a property for a seller. The broker not only puts the listing into the MLS system but also places a newspaper advertisement for the property in a local paper, indicating that the property is listed with the broker. A prospective buyer sees the newspaper advertisement and calls the broker to set up an appointment to see the property. The prospective buyer indicates that he is not represented by a broker and is seeing the property on his own. After reviewing the Code of Ethics and Standards of Practice of the National Association of Realtors®, what obligations, if any, does the listing broker have to the unrepresented buyer?

4. In most states, sellers of property and brokers representing them are not required to disclose the fact that a property is a stigmatized or psychologically impacted property. A stigmatized or psychologically impacted property is one that has had some undesirable event occur on the premises, such as a murder, suicide, death, or similar event. Do you believe such disclosures should be required by law? Do you consider events such as these to be material factors in making a buying decision? Why or why not?

5. You receive a postcard in the mail from ABC Realty Co. Its header reads: "Sales Are Booming in Greenacres" (your development). Underneath the header, ten addresses in Greenacres are listed, followed by the price at which each of these properties sold. Underneath the list is a photograph of a broker with her name and title and the name, address, and telephone number of ABC Realty Co. It is true that these properties sold for the prices listed, but ABC was the listing broker for only one of the properties and the selling broker for another of the properties. It was not involved in any way with the sale of eight of the ten properties listed on the postcard. After reviewing the Code of Ethics and Standards of Practice of the National Association of Realtors®, is this postcard advertisement a violation of the code? Why or why not?

ETHICAL QUESTION

Your law firm acts as escrow agent for Reed Realty Company and often conducts closings for its clients. This morning Amy Quinn, a real estate agent with Reed Realty, comes to your office and delivers to you an executed contract for sale and purchase and a deposit check from the buyers for a property listed with Reed Realty. Amy has been acting as a transaction broker in this transaction. As she hands you the check and contract, Amy states, "I hope this goes to closing. The buyers have their inspectors scheduled for next week for the home inspection and the routine inspection probably won't pick up the potential mold problem, but if the inspector tells them to conduct an additional mold inspection, we can kiss the deal goodbye." She then leaves the office. What should you do?

Slossberg Law Office on CourseMate

Please go to www.cengagebrain.com to log into CourseMate, access the Slossberg Law Office, and work on your client files. Each module corresponds to a chapter in the text. Within each module, you will be provided with instructions by the supervising attorney. You are asked to keep track of time spent on time sheets. The documents produced through working on client files in the law office can then be compiled into a portfolio of final work product.

CourseMate

The available CourseMate for this text has an interactive eBook and interactive learning tools, including flash cards, quizzes, and more. To learn more about this resource and access free demo CourseMate resources, including the Slossberg Law Office, go to www.cengagebrain.com, and search for this book. To access CourseMate materials that you have purchased, go to login.cengagebrain.com.

7

The Basic Real Estate Contract

CHAPTER OBJECTIVES

Upon completion of this chapter, the student will:

- Know the basic terms found in contracts for sale and purchase

- Know how to draft a basic real estate contract, including a contract for new construction

- Understand the special provisions that may be found in short sale contracts, contracts for the sale and purchase of income-producing property, contracts for the sale and purchase of condominiums, and contracts for the sale and purchase of vacant land

- Know how to draft an option contract

Introduction

The contract for sale and purchase of real property is the most important document in the real estate closing process because a properly drafted contract serves as a map that guides the parties along the winding and sometimes bumpy road to closing. A comprehensive real estate contract will outline all agreements of the parties, detail any conditions placed upon the closing on the property, set forth various deadlines for documents to be exchanged and inspections to be made, and indicate the respective rights and obligations of the parties.

In many residential transactions, parties turn to standard form contracts provided by the state bar association, the state Board of Realtors®, or similar organization rather than hiring an attorney to draft a customized contract. Even in cases in which form contracts are used, an attorney's assistance is needed to review the contracts and make modifications when necessary. In more complex transactions, standard form contracts are insufficient to cover all items the parties must address, and an attorney may be asked to draft a contract tailored to the transaction at hand. At other times, a developer client may hire an attorney to draft a contract to be used as a standard contract for all sales within the development project. In any of these instances, a paralegal's assistance may be required. Additionally, a paralegal will need to know basic contract law and have a thorough knowledge of a client's real estate contract to aid in the closing of the client's transaction.

In order for any valid contract to exist, certain elements must be present. First, there must be mutual assent between the parties. This means that there must be an offer and an acceptance of that offer. Second, there must be consideration. Consideration is something of value that the parties exchange as part of their bargain. In the case of a real estate contract, this would typically (but not always) be money in exchange for real property. Third, the parties must have the legal capacity to enter into the contract. This means that they must have the requisite mental capacity to understand the agreement. Persons held to lack capacity are minors, those adjudicated mentally incompetent, and intoxicated persons. Finally, the obligation(s) undertaken by the parties must be legal. If all of these elements are present, a valid contract ordinarily exists. There are certain contracts, however, in which an additional element must be present—namely, the contract must be in writing in order to be legally enforceable. Contracts for the transfer of an interest in real property are contracts falling under the **statute of frauds,** which is the name given to state statutes indicating which contracts must be in writing and signed by the party to be charged in order to be legally enforceable. The exception in most states is a contract for the lease of real property if the lease term is one year or less.

Parties entering into written contracts for the sale or purchase of a home are often entering into a binding legal agreement for the largest financial transaction of their lives, yet they generally are cognizant of only some of the terms of the contract, such as those pertaining to deposits, the purchase price, financing, and the closing date; they become aware of the other provisions only when a problem arises. Often, a client caught up in the excitement of the sale or purchase of property will sign a real estate contract and only afterward approach an attorney for advice on the transaction, at which point there is little an attorney can do to help. However, if the contract includes a provision making the terms of the contract contingent upon an attorney's approval, the attorney may make suggestions for modifications that can then be incorporated into the contract upon agreement by the parties. Should the parties desire to modify a standard form contract, the altered provisions should be crossed out and the new provisions typed in, either in the body of the contract itself or as an attachment. It is advisable to have each party initial the crossed-out provisions as well as the new provisions to evidence that no unilateral changes have been made.

This chapter explores the provisions found in most contracts for sale and purchase, whether those contracts are form contracts or contracts negotiated and drafted by the parties and their attorneys. This discussion is followed by a look at special contract provisions, such as those for contracts for the purchase of income-producing property and short sales contracts, among others. Finally, the chapter addresses special types of real estate transactions, such as option contracts and installment contracts, that require particular care in drafting.

Common Contractual Terms

The Date

The date of the contract may be found at the beginning or the end of the contract. The date is often referred to as the **effective date,** meaning the date upon which the contract becomes legally binding on all parties. The frequent use of real estate brokers as "middlemen" between buyer and seller often means that the buyer and the seller do not come together and sign a contract at the same time. The broker usually presents the prospective buyer with the seller's asking price, and the prospective buyer may accept the offer or make a counteroffer. Any counteroffers are submitted to the seller

statute of frauds: A state statute indicating which contracts must be in writing and signed by the party to be charged in order to be legally enforceable.

effective date: The date upon which a contract becomes legally binding on all parties.

for acceptance or rejection. When a purchase price is agreed upon, the broker may then ask the prospective buyer to sign a standard contract for sale and purchase, which is then submitted to the seller for signature. If negotiations are handled in this manner, the effective date is the date upon which the last required party signs the contract.

The effective date is only one of many dates that may appear in a real estate contract. Other dates that may appear include the closing date, the date by which the buyer must obtain financing, the date by which evidence of title must be submitted by the seller to the buyer, and the date by which inspections must be made. A paralegal reviewing a real estate contract must be cognizant of all of these dates and their significance.

The Parties

The name and status of each party to the contract should be clearly identified. If, for example, the buyer's name is listed as John Winthrop, care must be taken to determine whether John Winthrop is indeed the buyer's proper legal name (for instance, his legal name may be Jonathan Winthrop or Michael Jonathan Winthrop, and he prefers to be called John Winthrop) and what the buyer's marital status is. If John is a single man, that fact should be designated on the contract. If, on the other hand, John is a married man but is planning to purchase the property in question in his own name, his status as a married man should nonetheless be noted because many states require the joinder of a spouse on mortgage documents and closing documents. Further, if the seller is married, regardless of whether title is held jointly or singly, the seller's spouse should be named in the contract and should sign all closing documents, including the deed, to indicate the spouse's relinquishment of any contingent rights the spouse legally may have in the sold property. (For a detailed discussion of these contingent rights, see Chapter 2.)

Note that assumptions should not be made about spelling. For example, Frances Sterling may really be Francis Stirling. It is advisable to have the seller's name appear on the contract in precisely the manner in which it appears on the present deed to the property and to have the buyer's name appear on the contract precisely as it is to appear on the new deed transferring title.

If either party is not a natural person (for example, if a party is a business entity, such as a corporation or a partnership), a determination must be made as to whether the entity legally exists and whether the person signing the contract on behalf of the entity has the authority to do so. Additionally, care must be taken that the signatory's representative capacity is clearly indicated (for example, Marie Ellison, President, when signing on behalf of Ellison Enterprises, Inc.), or else the signatory may be found to be personally responsible for all contractual obligations. The sale or purchase of real property by a corporation typically requires a resolution of the board of directors or the shareholders to authorize the transaction, and a certified copy of this resolution should be obtained.

Property Description

An accurate description of the real property is required. A street address should be supplemented with a legal description of the property. This legal description may be a metes and bounds description, a governmental survey description, or a plat method description, each of which is discussed in detail in Chapter 5. The best way of ensuring that the property description is accurate is to copy the property description on the current deed or title report. Another method is to attach a copy of the survey of the property to the contract as an exhibit. Attachment of a survey may be particularly appropriate in the case of rural property. The fence lines surrounding a parcel of rural property may not be the true boundary lines of the property, and a prospective buyer reading the legal description may assume that the fence lines he or she inspected on the property match the legal description.

Any personal property to be sold together with the real property should be itemized with particularity, as outlined in Chapter 2. Often, standard form contracts provide inadequate space for a detailed listing of all personal property and fixtures. The natural tendency is to try to fit all items into the space provided. The better method is to refer in the contract to an attachment upon which all personal property and fixtures are listed.

Consideration

As noted earlier, every contract must indicate the true consideration to be provided by each party to the contract. In most real estate contracts, the consideration provided by the seller is the real property, and the consideration provided by the buyer is the payment of the negotiated purchase price. The purchase price, exclusive of closing costs, should be indicated, as should the method of payment of the purchase price so as to avoid confusion or possible delay in the closing procedures. The seller typically requires one or more deposits to be made prior to the closing, and the amount of the deposits will be deducted from the purchase price, with the balance to be paid at closing. The seller may accept personal checks for the payment of deposits but usually will require that the balance be paid by wire transfer, although in some instances the seller may agree to payment by certified check or by cashier's check. If the purchase price is contingent on any conditions, which often is the case when the buyer is seeking financing, these conditions should be stated. These contingencies are discussed in more detail elsewhere in the chapter.

Deposits

The seller often will require an initial deposit from the buyer, usually upon execution of the contract. This initial deposit is referred to as an **earnest money deposit,** a deposit that indicates the good faith of the buyer with regard to his or her intent to purchase the property. In some circumstances, the seller may require additional deposits on specified dates or within a specified time period after the execution of the contract. What happens to these deposits between the time they are paid by the buyer and the date of closing is a matter of state statute or negotiation between the parties. It is common practice for deposits to be held in escrow until the closing. The escrow agent may be an attorney, a bank, a title company, or a real estate broker.

The handling of escrow accounts is strictly regulated by state statute. Recall that monies placed in escrow accounts may not be commingled with other business accounts. An escrow agent need not open an individual account for each earnest money deposit; rather, earnest money deposits from several buyers may be placed in a single escrow account. This system requires meticulous record keeping by the escrow agent. Statutory law may specify that deposits be placed in interest-bearing or in noninterest-bearing accounts, or the law may leave such decisions to negotiation between the parties.

earnest money deposit:
An initial deposit given by the buyer that indicates the good faith of the buyer with regard to his or her intent to purchase the property.

As previously mentioned, state statutes often require that reports on escrow accounts be made to applicable authorities, such as the state bar association for escrow accounts held by attorneys or the state real estate commission for escrow accounts held by real estate brokers. Additionally, state statutes set forth the procedures to be followed by escrow agents in the event that a dispute arises between the parties to the contract over escrowed monies, including the time period for notification of the appropriate governing authorities and the settlement procedures to be used. The real estate contract should outline the amount and due date of each deposit, the type of account in which the deposits will be placed, and the escrow agent's name and contact information, as in the following provision.

> *Deposit to be paid upon signing of*
> *this Agreement.. $15,000.00*
> *Deposit to be paid within fifteen (15)*
> *days of signing this Agreement.. $ 5,000.00*
> *All deposits are to be held in escrow in a noninterest-bearing account with:*
> *Escrow Agent: Terra Nova Title Company*
> *Address: 4500 Commercial Avenue, Any City, Any State*
> *Phone: (000) 284-8400*
> *Fax: (000) 284-8444;*
> *e-mail: jwalters@terranovatitle.com*
> *and shall be applied in accordance with the terms and conditions of this*
> *Agreement.*

Contracts providing that buyers may receive deposits back under certain conditions or that sellers may retain deposits under certain conditions should state with particularity which deposits may be retained or returned if the buyer makes more than one deposit prior to closing.

The Method of Payment and Payment Contingencies

The method of payment provision spells out the method by which the buyer will pay the balance of the purchase price to the seller. The transaction may be a **cash sale,** in which the buyer pays cash for the property and does not acquire financing from a lending institution. More often, the buyer will finance the purchase by acquiring a mortgage loan in return for executing a mortgage instrument and note.

There are four basic financing mechanisms available to the buyer: (1) obtaining a new loan from a lending institution, (2) assuming the seller's existing mortgage, (3) taking the property subject to the seller's existing mortgage, and (4) obtaining a purchase money mortgage (for a detailed discussion of mortgages, see Chapter 10). The first financing mechanism is acquiring a new mortgage loan, the most common method of acquiring primary financing, in which the buyer procures a new loan and the seller's existing loan (if any) is paid off in full with the closing proceeds. A buyer will seek out new financing if the current interest rates and other conditions are more favorable than those in the seller's existing mortgage loan. An example of a method-of-payment clause for new financing follows.

> *If the purchase price or any part of it is to be financed by a third-party loan, this Agreement is conditioned on the Purchaser obtaining a written commitment within sixty (60) days after the Effective Date of this Agreement for a fixed or adjustable rate loan in the principal amount of Two Hundred Twenty-Five Thousand Dollars ($225,000), at an initial interest rate not to exceed five percent (5%) and a term of thirty (30) years. The Purchaser*

cash sale: A sale in which a buyer pays cash for the property and does not acquire financing from a lending institution.

*agrees to use best efforts to make prompt application and to execute dili-
gently and in good faith all necessary papers for the loan set forth above.*

If interest rates are currently high, the buyer may, alternatively, seek an
assumption of mortgage, in which the buyer assumes personal responsibility for
payment of the seller's existing mortgage loan. Should the buyer default on any
mortgage payments under the term of the loan and the lending institution initiate
foreclosure on the property, the buyer will be primarily liable for any deficiency
judgments. An assumption of mortgage is a financing option only if the existing
mortgage is assumable. If the existing mortgage is assumable, the lending institution's approval will be required before an assumption may take place. The lending institution will most likely undertake a thorough financial investigation of the
buyer before giving (or denying) its approval. If the lending institution agrees to the
assumption, it may choose to release the seller from all responsibility for the loan
or to make the buyer primarily liable and the seller secondarily liable for the loan.

A **sale subject to existing mortgage** is one in which the buyer becomes
responsible for the seller's payments under the existing mortgage but the seller
remains primarily liable under the mortgage note. In this situation, if the buyer
defaults in paying the mortgage payments, the lending institution may foreclose on
the property (forcing the buyer out) but must seek out the seller for any deficiency
judgment, not the buyer. The following is an example of a method-of-payment
provision providing for the buyer to either assume or take subject to an existing
mortgage loan.

> *This Agreement is conditioned upon the Purchaser's ability to ____ take
> title subject to or ____ assume the existing first mortgage loan of record with
> an approximate balance of Two Hundred Twenty-Five Thousand Dollars
> ($225,000), payable over a remaining term of twenty-five (25) years, three
> (3) months, with a current fixed interest rate of five percent (5%) per an-
> num. If the Purchaser has agreed to assume a mortgage which requires ap-
> proval of Purchaser by the Mortgagee for assumption, then Purchaser shall
> promptly obtain the necessary application and diligently complete it and
> return it to the Mortgagee. The Purchaser agrees to pay an assumption fee
> not to exceed two (2) points.*

A **purchase money mortgage sale** is one in which the seller finances all or a
portion of the purchase price of the property, with the buyer executing a mortgage
instrument and mortgage note in favor of the seller. A purchase money mortgage may
be either a first or a second mortgage. Purchase money mortgages, especially if they are
second mortgages, usually are of shorter duration than institutional mortgages. A sample provision for a purchase money mortgage loan as a second mortgage loan follows.

> *In addition to the third-party loan set forth above, the balance of the Pur-
> chase Price shall be financed by the Purchaser executing a note and mort-
> gage in the amount of One Hundred Thousand Dollars ($100,000) in favor
> of the Seller secured by the property payable over a term of five (5) years in
> monthly installments of $1,887.12, including interest at a rate of five per-
> cent (5%) per annum from date of closing.*

If the purchase price is being financed, the buyer's obligations under the contract typically are subject to certain contingencies. The buyer will want the purchase of the property to be contingent upon obtaining loan approval. The seller, on
the other hand, will want a strong commitment from the buyer to make diligent efforts to seek loan approval and will want to give a limited time frame within which

assumption of mortgage:
A situation in which a buyer
assumes personal responsibility
for payment of the seller's existing
mortgage loan.

**sale subject to existing mort-
gage:** A situation in which a buyer
becomes responsible for the seller's
payments under an existing mortgage but the seller remains primarily liable under the mortgage note.

**purchase money mortgage
sale:** A sale in which the seller
finances all or a portion of the purchase price of the property, with the
buyer executing a mortgage instrument and mortgage note in favor of
the seller.

to obtain it. If the purchase of the property is contingent upon loan approval, the contract should specify this contingency as well as the type of loan sought and the time frame within which the loan must be approved.

Often implied or expressly included in a financing provision is an appraisal contingency. A lender will not provide a loan commitment unless the property that is serving as collateral for the loan appraises at a valuation that is satisfactory to the lender. Sometimes, as in the case of Federal Housing Administration (FHA) or Veterans Affairs (VA) financing (discussed in detail in Chapter 10), there are specific references to guidelines that must be met, as indicated in the following example.

> *The total purchase price (exclusive of prorations and closing costs as set forth in this Agreement) shall be $200,000.00. It is expressly agreed that, notwithstanding any other provisions of this Agreement, the Purchaser shall not incur any penalty by forfeiture of deposit or down payment or otherwise be obligated to complete the purchase of the property described herein, if the purchase price or cost exceeds the reasonable value of the property established by the Department of Veterans Affairs and/or the Federal Housing Administration.*

Even if the buyer is paying cash or providing sufficient equity in the property to substantially lower the lender's risk, the buyer may choose to include an appraisal contingency to ensure that the purchase price paid for the property is in alignment with the current value of the property. Regardless of the method of payment, if the buyer wants to include an appraisal contingency, the provision should be drafted clearly and comprehensively. The best practice is to set forth the condition that must be met, how the condition can be met, the deadline by which the condition must be met, the notification that must be provided to the other party, and what occurs if the condition is not met. The following case illustrates the issues that can arise when the parties to a contract have opposing interpretations of an appraisal contingency provision.

CASE: *Gibney v. Pillifant*

32 So. 3d 784 (Fla. 2d DCA 2010)

LAROSE, Judge.

The trial court, after a nonjury trial, entered a final judgment ruling that Nigel and Christine Gibney breached a contract to buy a house from Randy and Helen Pillifant. The judgment awards the Gibneys' $124,000 deposit to the Pillifants. The trial court erred in determining that an appraisal contingency in the contract was ambiguous and interpreting that provision in a manner that differed from the written terms. We reverse and remand with directions that the trial court enter judgment for the Gibneys.

By way of background, we note that the Gibneys contracted to buy a house under construction in Naples from the Pillifants. The purchase price was $620,000. The Gibneys

insisted on adding a provision to protect them from a drop in property values. Their language, to which the Pillifants agreed, provided that the contract was "conti[n]gent upon this property appraising for no less than $620,000 to be conducted by a local appraiser." Pursuant to the contract, the Gibneys escrowed a $124,000 deposit.

Before closing, the Gibneys obtained a $560,000 appraisal. Convinced that the property was worth more, the Pillifants secured a $635,000 appraisal. Notwithstanding the second appraisal, the Gibneys refused to close and terminated the contract because the property appraised at less than $620,000. The Pillifants sued for breach of contract and sought to recover the deposit as liquidated damages.

(continued)

The Pillifants argued to the trial court that the appraisal contingency was ambiguous. In their view, it did not specify the parties' respective rights or duties. The Pillifants claimed that the Gibneys drafted the provision; thus, it should be construed against them. *See City of Homestead v. Johnson*, 760 So. 2d 80, 84 (Fla. 2000). The Pillifants contended that any appraisal of $620,000 or more obligated the Gibneys to close. The Gibneys responded that they could terminate the contract if any appraisal valued the property at less than $620,000. The trial court allowed parol evidence about the parties' intent and conduct relating to the contingency.

Ultimately, the trial court rejected the Gibneys' argument, ruling that the Pillifants' $635,000 appraisal satisfied the contingency, that the Gibneys breached the contract by failing to close, and that the Pillifants were entitled to the Gibneys' deposit. The Gibneys appealed. We review the trial court's interpretation of the contract de novo. *Leopold v. Kimball Hill Homes Fla., Inc.*, 842 So. 2d 133, 136 (Fla. 2d DCA 2003).

Absent an ambiguity, "'the actual language used in the contract is the best evidence of the intent of the parties, and the plain meaning of that language controls.'" *Emergency Assocs. of Tampa, P.A. v. Sassano*, 664 So. 2d 1000, 1003 (Fla. 2d DCA 1995) (quoting *Acceleration Nat'l Serv. Corp. v. Brickell Fin. Servs. Motor Club, Inc.*, 541 So. 2d 738, 739 (Fla. 3d DCA 1989)); *see Waksman Enters., Inc. v. Oregon Props., Inc.*, 862 So. 2d 35, 40 (Fla. 2d DCA 2003). Although inartful, the appraisal contingency is not ambiguous. In our view, "appraising for no less than $620,000" means that no appraisal may be less than $620,000. The Pillifants' $635,000 appraisal did not obligate the Gibneys to close; the property also appraised for the lesser value of $560,000. The appraisal contingency allowed the Gibneys to terminate the contract if *any* appraisal valued the property at less than $620,000.

In *Emergency Associates*, we held that the phrase "five (5) square miles," in a provision prohibiting the seller from practicing medicine within a certain area, was not ambiguous, and that the trial court erred in receiving extrinsic evidence to vary the contract terms by interpreting the phrase to mean "within a five-mile radius." 664 So. 2d at 1003. In *Metro Development Group, L.L.C. v. 3D-C & C, Inc.*, 941 So. 2d 11, 12 (Fla. 2d DCA 2006), we held that an option contract requiring payment "on or before the forty-fifth day after the effective date" was not ambiguous as to whether "day" could mean "business day." Here, the trial court erred in receiving extrinsic evidence to vary the contract terms by interpreting the phrase, as urged by the Pillifants, to mean "contingent upon any appraisal of at least $620,000."

Perhaps the Pillifants subjectively thought they were bargaining for their view of the appraisal contingency.

But, they did not reserve a right to a competing appraisal nor did they provide that any such appraisal would be controlling. As the facts establish, the Gibneys' appraisal was less than $620,000. The contingency triggering an obligation to close did not occur. The Gibneys could walk away without penalty. We will not "rewrite a contract or interfere with the freedom of contract or substitute [our] judgment for that of the parties ... in order to relieve one of the parties from the apparent hardship of an improvident bargain." *Beach Resort Hotel Corp. v. Wieder*, 79 So. 2d 659, 663 (Fla. 1955); *Metro Dev. Group*, 941 So. 2d at 14.

Reversed and remanded with directions.

VILLANTI, J. and FULMER, CAROLYN K., Senior Judge, Concur.

Case Questions

1. In the above case, the trial court held that there was an ambiguity in the contract pertaining to the appraisal contingency. The appellate court found no ambiguity. With whom do you agree, and why?

2. The appellate court did state that the appraisal contingency provision was "inartful." How would you rewrite the provision to make it more clearly reflect the interpretation provided by the court? By the Pillifants?

3. In support of its stance that the appraisal contingency provision was not ambiguous and that extrinsic evidence should not be admitted to interpret the provision, the appellate court referenced the decision in *Metro Development Group, L.L.C. v. 3D-C & C, Inc.*, in which the interpretation of "day" was at issue in the phrase "on the forty-fifth day after the effective date of the contract." In *Metro*, an option contract required that payment for an extension of the option be made on or before the forty-fifth day after the effective day of the contract. The forty-fifth day after the effective day of the contract fell on a Saturday. The party making the payment did so on Monday, the next business day. The court held that the payment was not timely. It found no ambiguity in the term "day" and interpreted "day" to mean calendar day rather than business day. The court reasoned that other deadlines in the contract did not specify "business days" and that there was only one specific reference to "business days" in the contract, which was found in the provision pertaining to the extension of the inspection period. Do you believe this case is on point and bolsters the court's decision in *Gibney v. Pillifant*? How might you distinguish the situation in *Metro* from the situation in *Gibney*?

In the case of new construction, in which the seller is a developer or builder who sells a lot and builds a house for the buyer, the seller may require that the purchase price be paid in a series of payments as construction progresses. The amount of each progress payment, together with the corresponding completion stage, should be set forth as exemplified in the following provision.

> *The balance of the purchase price shall be payable in accordance with the schedule of progress payments set forth below. Each progress payment shall be an amount equal to twenty percent (20%) of the balance of the purchase price and shall be payable as follows:*
> *(A) Completion of floor slab; block*
>   *walls up; the beam poured* *$60,000.00*
> *(B) Roof dry-in; interior partitions completed* *$60,000.00*
> *(C) Interior drywall taped and painted;*
>   *stucco finish coat applied; windows*
>   *installed* *$60,000.00*
> *(D) Cabinets and trim complete; painting*
>   *finished; driveway finished* *$60,000.00*
> *(E) Balance due at closing* *$60,000.00*

Another possibility in the case of new construction is that the seller obtains a construction loan to finance the construction of the house and the buyer is made responsible for the balance of the purchase price at closing (said balance to be paid in cash or to be financed by a mortgage loan to the buyer by one of the financing mechanisms discussed earlier). In this instance, the seller may choose to include, under the method-of-payment provision, a statement in which the buyer's rights under the contract are subordinate to the rights of the construction lender. Additionally, the seller may provide that the buyer is responsible for all of the seller's closing costs in connection with the construction loan, such as in the following provision.

> *Seller may borrow construction money from lenders to construct the improvements on the property. Purchaser agrees that any lender advancing construction funds will have a first mortgage on the property until closing. At that time, Seller may use all closing proceeds to release the property from the lien of the construction mortgage. This Agreement and the deposits paid hereunder will not give Purchaser any lien or claim against the property, and Purchaser's rights hereunder will be subordinate to those of any lender holding a mortgage. At closing, Purchaser shall reimburse Seller any and all costs incurred by Seller in connection with the construction mortgage, as reflected on the loan closing statement.*

Quality of Title

The buyer of real property wants to be assured that upon closing, the title to the property is free from all liens, restrictions, and other encumbrances and will require that any unacceptable encumbrance be removed before title is transferred. As noted in Chapter 4, most real property is encumbered in some manner, and not all encumbrances will be unacceptable. For example, if the property in question is located within a large subdivision, it is likely that the property will be subject to utility easements that create a benefit to the property owner. Additionally, title may be subject to homeowners' association restrictions that exist for the benefit of all property owners within the development.

The prospective buyer must be made aware of these restrictions but should be advised by his or her attorney of which encumbrances are benign and which are problematic. This typically is done by inspection of an abstract or title commitment by the buyer's attorney (discussed in detail in Chapter 11). Benign encumbrances do not diminish the marketability of title to the property.

The real estate contract should include a provision pertaining to the inspection of title. The provision should set forth the respective parties' responsibilities for obtaining evidence of title, the time period within which inspection of title must be made, the time within which the seller must cure any defects, the respective parties' responsibilities for procurement and payment of title insurance, and the type of deed to be delivered upon closing. A sample title provision is set forth below.

> *It is understood and agreed that title to the property shall be marketable and insurable. At least forty-five (45) days before the closing date, Seller shall, at Seller's expense, deliver to Purchaser or Purchaser's attorney a title commitment and, after closing, an owner's policy of title insurance. Title shall be conveyed by General Warranty Deed. If, at time of closing, Seller's title does not conform to the provisions hereof, Seller shall have ninety (90) days within which to satisfy its obligations hereunder. If, within such ninety-day period, Seller is unable to cure title so that title conforms to the provisions hereof, all deposits shall be refunded to the Purchaser and this Agreement shall be deemed terminated.*

Possession

The real estate contract should indicate the date, or events upon which, the buyer may take possession of the property. Typically, the buyer takes possession on the closing date. There may be situations, however, in which the buyer desires to take possession prior to closing. For example, the buyer may have sold his or her home sooner than anticipated and may want to move into the new property prior to the closing date, or the buyer may wish to begin certain improvements (for example, new cabinetry or flooring) prior to the closing date. The seller, on the other hand, may not want to allow the buyer to move in (or to have the buyer's subcontractors on the site) and alter or potentially damage the property until the closing funds have cleared. In addition to any potential damage that can be caused by the buyer's subcontractors is the potential of construction liens placed on the property. If the buyer begins improvements on the property before closing and the transaction does not close, the buyer may not pay for the improvements, leaving the seller to do so or to suffer construction liens placed on the property. Difficulties are compounded if the buyer takes possession prior to closing and, during the interval between the buyer's taking possession and closing, a fire or other casualty occurs on the property. An issue may arise as to which party suffers the risk of loss in such a situation. The possession provision should address such concerns, as does the provision that follows.

> *Seller shall deliver exclusive possession to Purchaser upon closing and clearance of all funds due Seller. Should the parties, subsequent to the signing of this Agreement, agree in writing that Purchaser be allowed to take occupancy prior to the closing date, it is hereby agreed by Purchaser that Purchaser assumes all risk of loss to property from the date of occupancy, shall be responsible and liable for maintenance from that date, and shall be deemed to have accepted property in its existing condition as of time of taking occupancy. The Purchaser shall not commence any improvements on the property prior to the closing date.*

Inspections and Warranties

Prior to the signing of the real estate contract, the seller and/or the seller's real estate broker will have made full disclosure, as required by law, of all known defects on the property. Nonetheless, the buyer may be allowed to make inspection of the premises prior to closing, and the seller may be required to repair any defects revealed by these inspections. The most important inspections are roof and termite inspections, but other inspections may also be provided for. A current issue being addressed in thousands of lawsuits across the country is toxic mold. A regular inspection may not be sufficient to detect all mold issues, so the buyer may want to include a mold inspection provision. If such a provision is not included and the regular inspection turns up indications of a potential mold problem, the inspector may advise that an additional mold inspection be conducted within the inspection period time frame.

The seller will want a time limit within which the inspections must take place and adequate time within which to make any warranted repairs and will want to make only those repairs considered "reasonable" and not be obligated to incur repair expenses exceeding a specified cost. Both the buyer and the seller will want to be able to cancel the contract without liability should the inspections show defects in the property. Further, the buyer will want the seller to warrant that full disclosure has been made to the buyer.

If the property in question is new construction, the buyer will want the seller to warranty the construction and the improvements, including all appliances and fixtures placed on the property. With regard to houses built after November 30, 1979, the Federal Trade Commission has mandated that builders include in the sales contract information pertaining to the type of insulation used in the home, its thickness, and its resulting R-value.

State statutes may require that other disclosure provisions be included as a matter of course, such as those pertaining to radon gas, special flood hazards, or hazardous waste. A combined inspection and warranty provision follows.

> *Seller warrants that all heating, cooling, electrical, and plumbing systems are in good working condition as of date of closing. The Purchaser may, within the time period allowed for delivery of evidence of title and examination thereof, have, at Purchaser's expense, roof and termite inspections conducted on the property. If, as a result of said inspections, repairs are deemed necessary, Seller agrees to pay up to two percent (2%) of the purchase price for said repairs, repairs to be undertaken by contractors duly licensed under the laws of the State of Any State.*

In the current housing market, it is common to see contracts containing "as-is" provisions or to see "as-is" contracts. These provisions or contracts specify that the seller is selling the property as is, subject to the buyer's right to inspect. The seller is not obligated to make any repairs to the property. The buyer is given the option of rescinding the contract if the inspection reveals repairs are needed. Sometimes the contract will state a dollar amount of repair costs; if the repairs will cost more than the stated dollar amount, the buyer may choose to pay for the repairs or to rescind the contract. If the repairs do not exceed the stated dollar amount, the buyer will be obligated to pay for the repairs and close on the property. The following is an example of an "as-is" provision.

> *Seller makes no warranties other than marketability of title. Seller will keep the property in the same condition from effective date until closing, except for normal wear and tear, and will convey the property in its "as-is"*

condition with no obligation to make any repairs. Buyer may, at Buyer's expense, conduct professional and walk-through inspections. If Buyer fails to timely conduct any inspection which Buyer is entitled to make under this provision, Buyer waives the right to inspection and accepts the property "as-is." Seller will provide access and utilities for Buyer's inspections. Buyer will repair all damages to the property resulting from the inspections and return the property to its pre-inspection condition. The inspections will be done by a person who specializes in and holds an occupational license (if required by law) to conduct home inspections. Buyer may cancel the contract by written notice to Seller within five (5) days from the end of the inspection period if the estimated cost of treatment and repairs determined to be necessary by Buyer is greater than $ ____ . For the cancellation to be effective, Buyer must include in the written notice a copy of the inspector's written report, if any, and treatment and repair estimates from the inspector or person(s) holding an appropriate license to repair the items inspected. Any conditions not reported in a timely manner will be deemed acceptable to Buyer.

Closing Time and Place

The real estate contract should specify the date, time, and location of the closing. In the case of new construction, the developer/builder will want a provision that specifies an estimated closing date and includes a statement that the seller does not guarantee closing by the specified date. It is common in many real estate contracts to find a statement that "time is of the essence." This statement implies that a party delaying closing is in breach of contract. The inclusion of a "time is of the essence" statement, however, does not conclusively mean that time is of the essence.

Should a dispute arise, courts may look at several factors to determine whether a delay results in breach, including the reasonableness of the date set for performance. Additionally, courts may look at circumstances behind the transaction. For example, a union strike may have delayed construction materials or services due to no fault of the seller, or a bank may be undergoing a merger that delays the approval of the buyer's loan. Nonetheless, if time is indeed of the essence, a clause to this effect should be included in the contract, such as the provision that follows.

Closing shall be held on August 10, 2015 at 2:00 p.m. at the offices of Terra Nova Title Company. Both parties hereby acknowledge that time is of the essence of this Agreement and that delay in closing by either party shall be deemed a default under this Agreement.

Closing Documents

This provision sets forth each party's responsibility for producing certain documents at the closing. Although the parties themselves may find this provision less important than many of the others already discussed, the absence or ambiguous drafting of such a provision can cause confusion and delays with the closing. A paralegal preparing or reviewing a real estate contract will want to pay special attention to this provision because it is the paralegal's responsibility to keep track of all documents that are necessary for the client's transaction, the person responsible for preparing or obtaining each document, and the date of receipt of each document. A sample provision follows.

Seller shall furnish the deed, bill of sale, no-lien affidavit, mortgage estoppel letters, and corrective instruments. Purchaser shall furnish the closing statement, mortgage, mortgage note, security agreement, and financing statements.

Broker's Fee

Although the person procuring a real estate broker will often sign a separate contract with the broker regarding payment of any broker's fee, some contracts include a provision pertaining to the payment of brokers' fees. These provisions should be drafted carefully and should include a statement regarding each party's obligation for payment of the broker's fee should either the seller or the buyer default. For example, the buyer may be obligated to forfeit all or a portion of the deposit as payment to the broker should the buyer fail to perform under the terms of the contract, and the seller may be obligated to pay the broker the full commission earned should the seller fail to perform under the terms of the contract. A sample provision follows.

> The parties agree that the broker named below is the procuring cause of the sale of the property. Seller agrees to pay, at time of closing, from the proceeds of the sale, the broker's commission set forth in the listing agreement between Seller and broker for broker's services in finding a Purchaser ready, willing, and able to purchase the property in accordance with the terms of this Agreement. In the event Purchaser defaults, it is agreed that Seller shall not be obligated to pay the commission and that the Purchaser shall be obligated to pay said commission to the broker. In the event the Seller defaults, the Seller shall pay said commission to the broker on demand.

Closing Costs and Apportionments

Each party will be responsible for certain expenses relating to the transfer of the property. Certain expenses may be assigned to individual parties, while other expenses may be shared. These expenses are commonly referred to as **closing costs.** Closing costs can include, but are not limited to, such items as appraisal fees, attorneys' fees, title fees, recording fees, transfer taxes (sometimes referred to as documentary stamps), and prorations.

Prorations are charges that are apportioned between the parties. For example, if the buyer is taking title to the property on June 1, it is not fair for either the buyer or the seller to pay the entire real property tax bill for the year. Therefore, the amount of the real property tax bill each party must pay will be prorated. Other prorations include hazard and flood insurance, rents (for income-producing property), maintenance fees to condominium or homeowners' associations, and mortgage interest on loans that are taken subject to the existing mortgage or assumed. (Prorations are discussed in detail in Chapter 12.)

A closing cost provision is set forth below.

> Seller shall pay the cost of recording the deed, documentary stamps affixed to the deed, and the cost of furnishing to the Purchaser an owner's policy of title insurance. Purchaser shall pay for all inspections and shall pay all loan fees, all loan closing costs, and all other related sums, including but not limited to escrows for taxes and insurance, recording fees, documentary stamps, intangible tax, and credit report. Each party shall be responsible for their respective attorneys' fees. In addition, real property taxes, insurance, and homeowners' association dues shall be prorated as of the date of closing.

Risk of Loss

The risk of loss provision indicates which party bears the risk of loss should the property be damaged by fire or other casualty prior to closing. State statute may

closing costs: Certain expenses relating to the transfer of real property, including appraisal fees, attorneys' fees, title fees, recording fees, transfer taxes (sometimes referred to as documentary stamps or documentary stamp tax), and prorations.

prorations: Charges that are apportioned between the parties.

govern this provision. If state statutory law is silent on the matter, then the matter may be negotiated by the parties. Often, the risk of loss is borne by the party in possession of the property at the time the loss occurs. A risk of loss provision may provide the seller with an option to restore the property and, if the seller fails to do so, may allow the buyer either to terminate the contract or to accept the property as is and receive any insurance proceeds paid out. Alternatively, the risk of loss provision may provide that the buyer is obligated under the contract if the damage to the property does not exceed a specified amount and that either the purchase price will be adjusted accordingly or the purchase price will remain the same but the buyer will receive applicable insurance proceeds. Another option is to allow the seller a specified time period within which to restore the premises to its original condition, such as in the following provision.

> *If the improvements are damaged by fire or other casualty, the Seller shall have the option to cancel this Agreement and return all deposits to the Purchaser or, if the Seller so chooses, to extend the date of closing for a period not to exceed ninety (90) days and restore the property to substantially its original condition.*

Contract Assignability

If for some reason the buyer cannot perform under the contract, he or she will want the option of assigning his or her obligations under the real estate contract. The seller, however, may be concerned that the buyer will assign the contract to an unqualified individual or undercapitalized corporation to avoid personal liability. In some states, the matter of assignment may be dictated by statute, with the statutory presumption that the contract is assignable unless the contract provides otherwise. A concerned seller may, if statutorily permissible, forbid assignment or may make assignment contingent upon the seller's written consent, such as in the sample provision set forth below.

> *The Purchaser shall not assign this Agreement or any right, interest, or obligation hereunder without the prior written consent of the Seller.*

Default and Remedies

If the buyer defaults, the buyer wants to risk as little as possible. The buyer will want to risk only the deposits paid to the seller prior to the default and will want to prevent the seller from bringing suit to recover damages or specific performance of the buyer's obligations under the contract. Conversely, the seller will want to have as many options as possible should the buyer default. The seller will want the option to retain the deposits or to bring suit either for damages (in which event the measure of damages usually is the difference between the purchase price under the contract and the amount the seller received from the subsequent sale of the property) or for specific performance (in which the seller asks the court to specifically enforce the contract and make the buyer pay the purchase price under the contract).

If the seller defaults, the seller will want to limit his or her damages to the return of any deposits. The buyer, on the other hand, will want the option to accept the return of the deposits and the payment of all expenses incurred by the buyer up to the date of default or to bring suit against the seller for specific performance. A sample default and remedies provision follows.

> *If the Purchaser defaults under the terms of this Agreement, the Seller shall be entitled to retain all deposits paid as liquidated damages, and the Seller shall have no other recourse against the Purchaser. If the Seller defaults under the terms of this Agreement, the Purchaser shall be entitled to the return of all deposits paid as liquidated damages, and the Purchaser shall have no other recourse against the Seller.*

Attorneys' Fees

Under common law, no party to a contract is entitled to attorneys' fees unless the contract so provides. Real estate contracts usually provide either that the prevailing party in litigation shall be entitled to recovery of attorneys' fees and costs from the losing party or, alternatively, that each party shall be responsible for his or her own attorneys' fees. Sometimes a dispute arises that requires intervention of legal counsel but is settled before litigation occurs. In such an event, the party hiring counsel to settle the dispute will want the other party to pay his or her legal fees. A clause such as the following covers both litigation and pre-litigation matters.

> *In the event the Purchaser needs to consult with legal counsel or resort to litigation (including any appellate proceedings) to enforce the terms of this Agreement, then the Purchaser shall be entitled to recover reasonable attorneys' fees and costs. In the event the Seller needs to consult with legal counsel or resort to litigation (including any appellate proceedings) to enforce the terms of this Agreement, then the Seller shall be entitled to recover reasonable attorneys' fees and costs.*

Signature Block

As noted earlier in the chapter, usually the buyer and the seller will not be signing the contract for purchase and sale at the same time. Drafts may go back and forth several times before the parties are in agreement on all points. Although they may be sent as facsimile copies, most often the drafts and the finalized version of the contract will be sent by computer via the Internet. In most states, facsimile and digital contracts are treated the same as originals, and signing them holds the same legal significance as signing an original document. Additionally, the majority of state statutes recognize electronic signatures on contracts. In states that may require notarization of real estate contracts, electronic notarization may also be permissible, so state statutes should be checked.

Special Provisions

Short Sales. In addition to the basic provisions discussed so far, the parties to a real estate contract may have special needs that must be addressed in the contract. As discussed in Chapter 6, if a homeowner can no longer afford the mortgage payments on his or her home, the homeowner may first seek to sell it as an alternative to foreclosure. If the market value of the property is less than the outstanding mortgage and other debts encumbering the property, the homeowner will attempt a short sale transaction. For this transaction to succeed, the lender(s) must agree to accept a sales price less than the full amount owed on the property, and a lender approval contingency must be included either in the contract itself or in a short sale addendum. The contract or addendum should provide that lender approval is not guaranteed and that the lender may make approval contingent upon modification of, or additions to, the terms set forth in the contract. The contract or addendum typically includes a deadline for obtaining the approval and may allow the seller to accept back-up offers. A sample short sale addendum is found in Exhibit 7–1.

| Short sale addendum to contract for purchase and sale | EXHIBIT 7–1 |

SHORT SALE ADDENDUM TO CONTRACT FOR PURCHASE AND SALE

This Short Sale Addendum ("Addendum") is attached to and made a part of the Contract for Purchase and Sale ("Contract") between Marsha Vincent, a single woman ("Seller"), and Oscar and Greta Kemp, Husband and Wife ("Buyers"), for the purchase and sale of the property known as 313 Findlay Avenue, Any City, Any State ("Property").

1. SHORT SALE ACKNOWLEDGMENT. Seller represents to Buyers that this transaction is a short sale transaction in which the purchase price of the Property may be insufficient to cover payment for all liens on the Property and costs of sale.

2. THIRD PARTY APPROVAL CONTINGENCY. This Contract is contingent upon the written approval of Seller's lender(s) and/or other lienholder(s) ("Lienholders") of the purchase price, the terms of the Contract, and the HUD-1 settlement statement. Seller shall use best efforts to obtain the Lienholders' approval and shall submit to the Lienholders all documentation required for review and approval of this transaction. Seller and Buyers acknowledge that no Lienholder is required to accept the terms of the Contract and that the Lienholders may request modifications or additional conditions to the Contract ("Third Party Conditions"). Any Third Party Conditions are not binding upon Seller or Buyers without their mutual written consent. Either party may terminate the Contract if, in that party's sole discretion, the Third Party Conditions are unacceptable by providing written notice to the other within three (3) business days from receipt the Lienholders' approval containing said Third Party Conditions.

3. APPROVAL DEADLINE. If Seller does not deliver written notice to Buyers of Lienholders' approval of the purchase price and terms of the Contract within forty-five (45) days from the Effective Date of the Contract ("Approval Deadline"), either party may cancel the Contract by written notice to the other party, and all deposits shall be returned to the Buyers.

4. OTHER DEADLINES. The Closing Date shall be thirty (30) calendar days from the date of Lienholders' written approval. All other time periods under the Contract shall commence from the Effective Date of the Contract.

5. BACK-UP OFFERS. The parties agree that at any time prior to Lienholders' approval, Seller __ X __ may _____ may not continue to market the Property for sale, accept back-up offers for the purchase of the Property subject to the rights of the Buyers under this Contract, and submit such offers for Lienholders' review.

By signing below, Seller and Buyers acknowledge that they have read, understand, and accept the terms of this Short Sale Addendum.

| *Marsha Vincent* | July 20, 2015 |
| Seller | Date |

| *Oscar Kemp* | July 20, 2015 |
| Buyer | Date |

| *Greta Kemp* | July 20, 2015 |
| Buyer | Date |

Income-Producing Property. The buyer of income-producing property has special concerns that should be addressed in the contract. The buyer will require clauses pertaining to inspection of the seller's books and records regarding the operating costs incurred and income produced by the property. The buyer also will want to examine current and pending lease agreements and will require estoppel certificates from all tenants verifying the terms and status of their leases (discussed in detail in Chapter 14) and an assignment of all lease rights. Sample provisions addressing these concerns are set forth below.

> *Inspection of Books and Records. This Agreement is conditioned upon the Purchaser's inspection and approval of the Seller's books, records, and tax returns pertaining to the subject property. Within ten (10) days from the execution of this Agreement, Seller shall deliver to Purchaser or to Purchaser's named accountant for approval originals or conformed copies of all books, records, and tax returns pertaining to the subject property. Seller warrants that all books and records to be inspected by Purchaser are maintained by the Seller in the ordinary course of business. If the Purchaser does not, with fifteen (15) days of receipt of said books and records, indicate in writing Purchaser's disapproval of the information contained in said books and records, Purchaser shall be deemed to have waived this condition.*

> *Estoppel Certificates. Prior to closing, the Seller shall provide the Purchaser with estoppel certificates from all current tenants. Said certificates shall set forth the name of the tenant, a description of the leased premises, the term of the rental agreement, the total amount owed under the terms of the rental agreement, the amount of any deposits and advance rents paid, any delinquent payments, and any claims the tenant may have against the Seller.*

Contract Subject to Sale of Other Property. Often, a buyer must sell his or her current home in order to afford a new one. The buyer will want to make his or her obligations under the real estate contract contingent upon the buyer's sale of the current residence. The seller usually will be reluctant to tie up the property until the buyer sells the current residence. Therefore, if the seller agrees to the condition, the seller will want the inclusion of an "escape clause," allowing the seller to terminate the contract if the seller receives a bona fide offer from another party, such as the clause included in the following provision.

> *This Agreement is conditioned upon the sale by the Purchaser of the Purchaser's real property located at 125 Jasmine Lane, Any City, Any State, provided, however, that should Seller receive another offer in writing acceptable to Seller, the Purchaser shall have ten (10) days from written notice by Seller to remove this contingency. If the Purchaser fails to remove this contingency within the stated time period, this Agreement shall be terminated, and all deposits paid to date shall be returned to the Purchaser.*

Condominiums. If the property in question is a condominium, the buyer will want an opportunity to inspect the condominium documents before committing to the purchase of the property. In some states, statutory law dictates a specified period within which the buyer may cancel a real estate contract after inspection of these documents. Further, the buyer's obligations under the contract may be contingent upon approval of the buyer by the condominium association. If so, a provision stating this condition should be included. Set forth below are sample provisions covering these areas.

> **Cancellation by Purchaser**. *This Agreement is voidable by Purchaser by delivering written notice of the Purchaser's intention to cancel within fifteen (15) days after the date of execution of this Agreement by the Purchaser and receipt by Purchaser of all condominium documents. In the event the Purchaser voids this Agreement, s/he must return all condominium documents furnished by Seller.*

> **Association Approval**. *This Agreement is contingent upon approval of the Purchaser by the condominium association. The Purchaser shall make application for approval within ten (10) days of execution of this Agreement. Any association fees charged in connection with approval shall be paid by the Purchaser.*

Vacant Land. A buyer may purchase a parcel of vacant land with the objective of building a particular project. The buyer will want the contract to be contingent on zoning permitting the building of the proposed project. Further, the buyer will want the contract to be contingent upon the land's physical suitability for the proposed project and may require satisfactory engineering reports as a condition of the purchase. A provision combining these contingencies is set forth below.

> **Conditions of Sale**. *This Agreement is contingent upon zoning permitting the construction of an industrial park. Further, this Agreement is contingent upon receipt of engineering reports on the subject property satisfactory to Purchaser's designated contractor.*

From the discussion thus far, it is apparent that a paralegal assigned to draft a real estate contract must use a comprehensive checklist or worksheet to ensure that all requisite provisions are included. Such a checklist or worksheet can also aid a paralegal in reviewing a prepared contract. A sample completed worksheet can be found in the Hypothetical Client Matter at the end of the chapter.

Special Types of Real Estate Contracts

Installment Contracts

Traditionally, an **installment contract** was one in which the buyer made a down payment, and the balance of the purchase price was payable in monthly installments over a period of years. At closing, the buyer received possession of the property and became responsible for the payment of real property taxes and all other expenses associated with real property ownership, but the seller retained legal title to the property. This method of sale was sometimes referred to as a *contract for deed* because the buyer received the deed to the property either when all installments had been paid or when the unpaid balance had been reduced to a previously agreed-upon figure. In the latter instance, when the specified figure had been reached and the buyer had built up a certain percentage of equity in the property, the seller would transfer the deed to the buyer, who, in turn, would provide the seller with a purchase money mortgage and note covering the balance of the purchase price.

installment contract: A contract in which at least one payment under the contract is made after the close of the taxable year of sale.

This situation worked well for the buyer who had little money for a down payment and/or had trouble with financing. The seller obtained favorable tax treatment by being able to spread the gain and the income tax on the gain over the period of time in which the payments were being made by the buyer. In order to obtain this favorable tax treatment, however, the sale had to comply with the federal tax laws governing installment sales, which allowed installment sale treatment of gains only if 30 percent or less of the purchase price was received by the seller in the year of the sale.

Changes occurred in 1980 with the implementation of the federal Installment Sales Revision Act of 1980, which deleted the 30-percent-down rule and now treats all sales as installment sales (unless the seller elects otherwise) if at least one payment under the contract is made after the close of the taxable year of sale. Under the Act, the seller pays tax in any taxable year on the gain received in that year. This means that installment sales contracts can now be structured with as many or as few payments as the parties negotiate between themselves as long as there is at least a single deferred payment after the year of sale. Note that some states have statutes governing installment contracts, and these statutes should be researched thoroughly before drafting an installment contract.

Option Contracts

An **option contract** is one in which the seller (*optionor*) gives a potential buyer (*optionee*) the exclusive right within a specified, limited time period to purchase real property. The potential buyer pays the seller for this exclusive right. The money that the potential buyer pays is not considered a deposit because the buyer is not committing himself or herself to the purchase of the property. The potential buyer is paying for time within which to decide whether to purchase the property. The consideration paid by the potential buyer is irrevocable. The parties may agree that, if the option is exercised, the consideration paid under the option will be applied toward the purchase price of the property. If the seller accepts another offer within the specified time period, then the seller is in breach of the option contract.

Although option contracts can be used in many situations, they are most often used in land development transactions (for example, where the developer is working on getting additional investors) and in transactions in which the potential buyer is looking at the property as an investment and is speculating on the increase in value of the property without committing to the purchase of the property (for example, based on the outcome of a voting referendum on gambling for a potential hotel/casino site or of a vote on highway expansion bringing larger populations to the site).

The use of an option contract is a relatively safe way to speculate with real property because the purchase price and terms for the contract of sale are all negotiated and made a part of the option contract. If the potential buyer exercises the option, he or she has "locked in" the purchase price and other terms at the originally negotiated price, regardless of the increase in value of the property. If the value does not increase as the potential buyer anticipated, then he or she has forfeited only the money paid for the option and can walk away from the deal. A checklist for an option contract is provided below, and a sample option contract is shown in Exhibit 7–2.

option contract: A contract in which the seller gives a potential buyer the exclusive right, within a specified, limited time period, to purchase real property. The potential buyer pays the seller for this exclusive right.

OPTION CONTRACT CHECKLIST CHECKLIST

1. Effective date
2. Legal names and addresses of the parties
3. Property description
4. Consideration paid for the option and method of payment
5. Time period of the option, with commencement and termination dates
6. Extension of the option period, if any, and consideration to be paid for the extension
7. Whether the consideration paid for the option is to be applied to the purchase price
8. Manner in which the option is to be exercised
9. Purchase price and terms of payment
10. Right of entry by optionee on the option property to conduct tests, inspections, and surveys
11. Optionor's warranty not to encumber the property during the option period
12. Risk of loss during the option period (if there are improvements on the real property)
13. Assignability of the option
14. Date of closing upon exercise of the option
15. Other applicable basic contract provisions (for example, title, method of payment, prorations)

Option contract for purchase of real property

EXHIBIT 7–2

OPTION CONTRACT FOR PURCHASE OF REAL PROPERTY

THIS AGREEMENT is made and entered into this 10th day of August, 2015, by and between PBD Properties, Inc., an Any State corporation having its principal office at 446 S.W. 10th Avenue, Suite 112, Any City, Any State (hereinafter referred to as "Optionor"), and Shangri-La Land Investments Corp., an Any State corporation having its principal office at 800 Revere Road, Suite 405, Any City, Any State (hereinafter referred to as "Optionee").

I. OPTION PERIOD AND CONSIDERATION. The Optionee hereby agrees to pay to the Optionor the sum of Fifty Thousand Dollars ($50,000.00) evidenced by personal check, receipt of which is hereby acknowledged, for an option to purchase the real property described below, the option period beginning August 10, 2015, and terminating at midnight on October 9, 2015.

II. EXTENSION OF OPTION. Optionor agrees to grant the Optionee the right to extend the original option period set forth above to midnight on November 9, 2015, upon payment by the Optionee of the sum of Twenty Thousand Dollars ($20,000.00) before the expiration of the original option period.

III. PROPERTY DESCRIPTION. The Optionor agrees, upon proper exercise of the option by the Optionee, to sell to the Optionee the real property described as:

SW 1/4 of the NE 1/4 of the SW 1/4, Sec 4, T32S, R23E, Any County, Any State

EXHIBIT 7–2   *(continued)*

IV. CREDIT OF OPTION PAYMENT. Upon proper exercise of the option, the total consideration paid for the option (including the consideration paid for any extension of the option period) shall be applied to the purchase price.

V. PURCHASE PRICE AND METHOD OF PAYMENT. Upon proper exercise of the option by the Optionee, the Optionor agrees to sell the above-described property for the purchase price of Two Million Dollars ($2,000,000.00). The Optionee agrees to use best efforts to secure a Mortgage Loan in the principal amount of One Million Four Hundred Thousand Dollars ($1,400,000.00). Purchase of the property is contingent upon loan approval within ninety (90) days from the exercise of the option by the Optionee, otherwise either party may terminate the Agreement. Should the Agreement be terminated due to failure of the Optionee to secure financing, the Optionor shall retain the total consideration paid by the Optionee for the option period (including any extensions thereof).

VI. OPTIONOR'S WARRANTY. The Optionor hereby agrees not to encumber the above-described property in any manner or grant any contractual or other property rights in the above-described property during the option period.

VII. RIGHT OF ENTRY. During the option period or any extension thereof, the Optionee shall have the right to enter upon the above-described property for the purpose of conducting a survey of said property and to conduct engineering tests. The costs of the survey and the engineering tests shall be borne by the Optionee.

VIII. EXERCISE OF OPTION. The Optionee may exercise this option by delivering notice of said exercise of option to the Optionor during the option period (or any permitted extensions thereof). Notice shall be in writing addressed to the Optionor at the address set forth in this Agreement and shall be (i) hand delivered, (ii) sent by certified or registered mail, postage prepaid, return receipt requested, (iii) sent by Federal Express or similar overnight courier service, or (iv) by telecopy. Notice shall be deemed given when received by the Optionor.

IX. FAILURE TO EXERCISE OPTION. If the Optionee fails to exercise this option in accordance with its terms and within the option period (including any extensions thereof), then this option shall automatically terminate, and Optionor shall retain all consideration paid by the Optionee for the option period (including any extensions thereof).

X. CLOSING DATE. Upon proper exercise of this option, the parties agree that the closing shall take place within thirty (30) days from the date the Optionee receives loan approval.

XI. TITLE. The Optionor shall deliver to the Optionee at the Optionor's expense a preliminary title report within twenty (20) days from the proper exercise of the option and shall deliver, at Optionor's expense, a standard owner's title policy upon closing. The parties agree that title is to be free of liens, easements, and restrictions other than: (i) current property taxes and (ii) covenants, conditions, restrictions, and public utility easements of record, if any. Title shall be transferred upon closing by General Warranty Deed.

XII. CLOSING COSTS, PRORATIONS, AND CLOSING DOCUMENTS. The Optionor shall pay for documentary stamps and recording of deed and recording of corrective instruments. The Optionee shall pay for documentary stamps and any intangible tax on mortgage and all costs associated with the closing of the mortgage loan. The Optionor shall provide, at closing, the General Warranty Deed, no-lien affidavit, mortgage estoppel letter, and corrective instruments. The Optionee shall provide, at closing, the closing statement, mortgage, mortgage note, security agreement and financing statements.

XIII. BROKER'S FEE. Upon execution of this option, the Optionor agrees to pay to Broker the amount agreed upon in the broker's agreement, a copy of which is attached as an exhibit to this Agreement. In the event the Optionee exercises the option, then the Broker shall receive from the Optionor the additional sum indicated in the broker's agreement.

XIV. ASSIGNABILITY. This option is not assignable by Optionee.

XV. ATTORNEYS' FEES. In any action between Optionor and Optionee arising out of this Agreement, the prevailing party shall be entitled to reasonable attorneys' fees and costs.

IN WITNESS WHEREOF, the parties have hereunto set their hands and seals the day and the year first above written.

Signed, Sealed and Delivered
in the presence of:

_____

_____

OPTIONOR: PBD PROPERTIES, INC.,
an Any State corporation
BY: _____
    Paul Davidson, President

OPTIONEE: SHANGRI-LA LAND
INVESTMENTS CORP.,
an Any State corporation

BY: _____
    Kenneth Colby, President

_____

_____

hypothetical client matter

Barbara Hammond is a real estate paralegal who has worked for the law firm of Fisher, Ross, and Simon, P.A., for the past three years. Barbara works most closely with attorney Ava Ross, and over the years, Ava, impressed with Barbara's competency, has provided Barbara with the opportunity to assist in a variety of real estate–related matters. This morning Ava asked Barbara to sit in on a meeting with a client.

The client is a real estate development company, Lyndale Properties, Inc., headed by its president, Craig Newfield. Approximately six months ago, Craig's company purchased a tract of land within a subdivision for the purpose of building a luxury single-family community called Orange Walk Estates. Ava assisted Craig with the closing on the property as well as with other real estate matters. Orange Walk Estates will be offering prospective purchasers five model homes from which to choose. Construction on the first two models has already begun, and Craig's company is in the process of installing a trailer on the property to be used as a temporary sales office.

Craig has asked to meet with Ava to discuss the drafting of a real estate contract that his company can use in negotiations with prospective purchasers. The standard form real estate contract approved by the state bar association and the state Board of Realtors® does not meet the particular needs of parties negotiating a contract for new construction.

The prospective purchaser of a home in Orange Walk Estates must select a lot within the subdivision tract upon which the home will be built. A lot deposit reservation will be required to secure the lot prior to the signing of a sale and purchase contract. The purchaser must then pick one of the models offered. Each model will have a base purchase price, and numerous optional extras will be made available to the prospective purchaser, with the cost of each extra to be added to the base price. The prospective purchaser will be given certain options from which to choose cabinets, countertops, appliances, carpeting, and similar items. Some of these decisions will be made by the prospective purchaser at the time of contracting. Should the purchaser change his or her mind about selections or wish to add other extras not specifically listed in the contract, Craig requires that all change orders and requests for additional extras be made in writing and that payment for them be made at the time they are ordered. Further, Craig requires final decisions to be made within a certain period of time and wants a contract that will allow the developer to make selections for the purchaser if the purchaser does not reply within that time frame.

Some purchasers may not like the selections offered and may choose to install their own flooring, appliances, or other fixtures and receive a "credit" for the items not selected. The credit amount will be deducted from the purchase price. If this is done, however, Craig wants to prevent the purchaser from bringing his or her own subcontractors to the construction site to begin the installation of fixtures or make other improvements to the property until after the closing.

Because each home in Orange Walk Estates will be built as deposits are received and contracts signed, Craig does not want to guarantee a closing date, only to find his company in breach of contract if construction is not completed by that date. Instead, he suggests that the contract provide an estimated closing date but allow some leeway if that date needs to be adjusted. Also, as an experienced builder and developer, Craig realizes that certain modifications may need to be made from the original plans as work

(continued)

progresses. For example, building code specifications may change, or a particular material may no longer be available. Craig wants to be able to make such modifications without first obtaining the purchaser's approval. Further, if such modifications are required by a governmental authority and increase the costs of construction, Craig wants the increased costs to be paid by the purchaser.

It is customary in the building industry in Any State for builders to provide a one-year warranty on new construction and to present the purchaser with a builder's warranty at the closing. Such a warranty usually provides that the builder has completed the construction in substantial conformity with the approved plans and specifications. In addition, most sellers (builders included) provide a no-lien affidavit at closing, stating under oath either that no liens have been placed on the property within the specified time period other than those listed in the affidavit or that those liens placed on the property have been paid off and removed. This document is of great importance to the purchaser, especially in the matter of new construction inasmuch as numerous subcontractors have provided services or materials to the property. Craig will provide both a builder's warranty and a no-lien affidavit at the closing. Apart from providing a general warranty deed upon closing, however, Craig does not want to provide evidence of title or title policies to purchasers unless these items are specifically requested—and then only at the purchasers' expense.

The majority of prospective purchasers will be financing the purchase of their homes. To prevent a lengthy tie-up of a particular lot, Craig wants to give the purchasers a time limit within which they must secure financing. Further, even if a married person is purchasing a home in his or her name only, Craig knows that most lenders require the signatures of spouses on mortgage instruments. Craig wants a financing provision that requires the signatures of spouses on all mortgages and other closing documents.

All deposits are to be kept in a noninterest-bearing escrow account Craig has set up with Patriot Bank. Should his company default under the contract, Craig wants to limit the purchasers' remedies to the return of deposits. Conversely, should a purchaser default, Craig wants the option of retaining the deposits or litigating the matter.

These matters and several others are discussed at length between Craig and Ava, after which Ava suggests that Barbara escort Craig to the conference room to complete a worksheet in which these and other contractual provisions will be detailed. Craig plans on beginning a large advertising campaign for Orange Walk Estates in two weeks and therefore would like to review the drafted contract as soon as possible. Upon completion of her session with Craig, Barbara's worksheet looks as shown in Exhibit 7–3.

From the information provided in this worksheet, Barbara is able to draft a contract tailored to meet her client's needs. In addition to the provisions indicated above, Barbara will include certain boilerplate provisions. A boilerplate provision is a provision found in most standard contracts, such as a provision indicating the applicable law governing the interpretation of the contract or a provision indicating that any section of the contract that may be found to be invalid or illegal will be severed from the contract and the remainder of the contract will remain in full force and effect. Note that even when including such standard provisions, care must be taken that these provisions meet the client's needs and do not contradict other provisions in the contract. With her worksheet as a guide, Barbara drafts the contract shown in Exhibit 7–4 for Ava's review.

EXHIBIT 7–3   **Real estate contract worksheet**

REAL ESTATE CONTRACT WORKSHEET

DATE OF INTAKE:	August 11, 2015
ATTORNEY:	Ava Ross
PARALEGAL:	Barbara Hammond
CLIENT NUMBER:	2007
MATTER NUMBER:	0004
PERSON RESPONSIBLE FOR INTAKE:	Barbara Hammond

1. SELLER(S) (Provide name(s) as appear on deed):
   Lyndale Properties, Inc.
2. ADDRESS(ES):   1800 Coolidge Street, Suite 400
   Any City, Any State
3. E-MAIL ADDRESS: cnewfield@lyndaleproperties.com
4. PHONE NUMBER(S): (000) 233-4991 FAX NUMBER: (000) 233-4909
   CELL: (000) 233-4090
5. SOCIAL SECURITY NUMBER(S):
   EIN #81-9082

6. DESCRIBE MANNER IN WHICH TITLE TO PROPERTY IS
   PRESENTLY HELD: <u>Held in name of Lyndale Properties, Inc., an Any State corporation.</u>

7. BUYER(S) (Provide name(s) as to appear on new deed):
   <u>To be filled in at a later date.</u>

8. ADDRESS(ES): <u>To be filled in at a later date.</u>

9. E-MAIL ADDRESS: <u>N/A</u>

10. PHONE NUMBER(S): <u>N/A</u> FAX NUMBER: <u>N/A</u>
    CELL: <u>N/A</u>

11. SOCIAL SECURITY NUMBER(S):
    <u>To be filled in at a later date.</u>

12. DESCRIBE MANNER IN WHICH TITLE TO PROPERTY WILL BE HELD:
    <u>To be filled in at a later date.</u>

13. ATTORNEY FOR OTHER PARTY:
    <u>To be filled in at a later date.</u>

14. ADDRESS: <u>To be filled in at a later date.</u>

15. E-MAIL ADDRESS: <u>N/A</u>

16. PHONE NUMBER: <u>N/A</u> FAX NUMBER: <u>N/A</u>

17. REAL ESTATE BROKER:
    <u>Seller has sales office on location; any cobrokers to be specified</u>
    <u>at a later date.</u>

18. ADDRESS: <u>To be filled in at a later date.</u>

19. E-MAIL ADDRESS: <u>N/A</u>

20. PHONE NUMBER: <u>N/A</u> FAX NUMBER: <u>N/A</u>

21. COMMISSION: <u>Amount of seller's commission to sales office not to be included</u>
    <u>in this contract.</u>

22. COMMISSION TO BE PAID BY:
    <u>Sales office commission (and cobrokers registering therewith)</u>
    <u>to be paid by seller.</u>

23. ESCROW AGENT: <u>Patriot Bank</u>

24. ADDRESS: <u>2000 Truman Avenue, Any City, Any State</u>

25. E-MAIL ADDRESS: <u>nwright@patriotbank.com</u>

26. PHONE NUMBER: <u>(000) 445-6677</u> FAX NUMBER: <u>(000) 445-6688</u>

27. TYPE OF CONTRACT: __VACANT LAND __ RESIDENTIAL RESALE
    _X_ RESIDENTIAL NEW CONSTRUCTION
    __ CONDOMINIUM/COOPERATIVE
    __ COMMERCIAL PROPERTY
    __ OTHER (SPECIFY): _____

28. STREET ADDRESS OF PROPERTY:
    <u>To be filled in at a later date.</u>

29. LEGAL DESCRIPTION OF PROPERTY:
    <u>Lot , of ORANGE WALK ESTATES, according to the plat thereof, recorded in Plat Book</u>
    <u>71, Page 117, Public Records of Any County, Any State; together with the single-family</u>
    <u>residence to be constructed thereon; and together with all appurtenances thereto.</u>

30. PERSONAL PROPERTY TO BE INCLUDED WITH SALE (Describe with specificity):
    <u>To be filled in at a later date.</u>

31. CLOSING:
    (A) DATE: <u>Estimated closing date to be filled in at a later date. Estimated closing</u>
    <u>date is not guaranteed. Time is not of the essence as to the estimated date. Seller shall</u>
    <u>give buyer not less than 10 days' notice of closing. Permanent Certificate of Occupancy</u>
    <u>shall evidence unit is ready for delivery and shall be the sole condition of closing.</u>
    (B) TIME: <u>To be filled in at a later date.</u>
    (C) PLACE: <u>To be filled in at a later date.</u>

EXHIBIT 7–3   *(continued)*

32. PURCHASE PRICE: To be filled in at a later date.
33. DEPOSITS:
    (A) LOT RESERVATION DEPOSIT (Applicable for new construction):
        1. AMOUNT OF DEPOSIT: To be filled in at a later date.
        2. DUE DATE: Prior to signing of contract.
        3. METHOD OF PAYMENT: Cash or check subject to collection.
        4. __ INTEREST-BEARING ACCOUNT
           X NONINTEREST-BEARING ACCOUNT
        5. IF PLACED IN INTEREST-BEARING ACCOUNT, PROVIDE DETAILS:

    (B) INITIAL DEPOSIT:
        1. AMOUNT OF DEPOSIT: To be filled in at a later date.
        2. DUE DATE: Upon execution of contract.
        3. METHOD OF PAYMENT: Cash or check subject to collection.
        4. __ INTEREST-BEARING ACCOUNT
           X NONINTEREST-BEARING ACCOUNT
        5. IF PLACED IN INTEREST-BEARING ACCOUNT, PROVIDE DETAILS:

    (C) ADDITIONAL DEPOSIT(S):
        1. AMOUNT OF DEPOSIT(S): To be filled in at a later date.
        2. DUE DATE(S): To be filled in at a later date.
        3. METHOD OF PAYMENT(S): Cash or check subject to collection.
        4. __ INTEREST-BEARING ACCOUNT
           X NONINTEREST-BEARING ACCOUNT
        5. IF PLACED IN INTEREST-BEARING ACCOUNT, PROVIDE DETAILS: ·

34. PAYMENT:
    (A) SOURCE OF PAYMENT: __ CASH
                             __ FINANCING
                             __ LENDING INSTITUTION
                             __ SELLER
                             __ OTHER (SPECIFY): Either cash or financing.
    (B) IF FINANCED, SPECIFY: __ NEW CONVENTIONAL MORTGAGE
                             __ NEW FHA MORTGAGE
                             __ NEW VA MORTGAGE
                             __ ASSUMPTION OF EXISTING MORTGAGE
                             __ TAKING SUBJECT TO EXISTING MORTGAGE
                             __ PURCHASE MONEY MORTGAGE
        [Note: To be filled in at a later date.]
    (C) IF FINANCED, SPECIFY:
        1. TIME PERIOD WITHIN WHICH TO OBTAIN FINANCING: 60 days
        2. TERM OF LOAN: To be filled in at a later date.
        3. AMOUNT OF LOAN: To be filled in at a later date.
        4. INTEREST RATE: To be filled in at a later date.
        5. TERMS AND CONDITIONS: To be filled in at a later date.
35. IF NEW CONSTRUCTION, ARE PROGRESS PAYMENTS REQUIRED?
                              YES   X   NO
    IF YES, SUPPLY AMOUNT AND DUE DATE OF EACH PAYMENT.

36. CONSTRUCTION SPECIFICATIONS (Applicable for new construction):
    Seller agrees that construction shall be substantially in accordance with the plans and
    specifications attached to contract. Seller reserves right to make minor modifications
    in plans and to make substitution of materials, fixtures, appliances, and equipment.

provided substitutions are of substantially the same or better quality. If changes are required by any governmental or quasi-governmental authority, buyer shall, at closing, pay any costs incurred by such changes.

37. CHANGE ORDERS AND COLOR SELECTIONS (Applicable for new construction): All change orders must be in writing and paid for at time change is ordered. Seller reserves right to refuse or accept change orders. If extras are ordered, other than those set forth in contract, they shall be paid for by buyer at the time ordered. Buyer shall submit to seller in writing selections of color, materials, and extras, other than those set forth in contract, not later than 15 days from seller's request. If buyer does not comply, seller may make selection in seller's sole discretion, declare buyer in default, or delay closing without seller incurring liability for delay.

38. EVIDENCE OF TITLE: _____ ABSTRACT _X_ TITLE COMMITMENT
    (A) DUE DATE: To be supplied only at request of buyer.
    (B) PAYMENT OBLIGATION: Buyer, if buyer requests evidence of title.
    (C) INSPECTION PERIOD: Within 10 days of closing.
    (D) CURE PERIOD: Seller to use reasonable diligence within reasonable time period.
    (E) ADDITIONAL INFORMATION: If cannot be cured within reasonable time, seller to return all deposits to buyer and contract is terminated. However, buyer can choose to accept title in existing condition. If buyer does so, buyer waives any and all obligations and claims with respect to title.

39. TITLE POLICY:
    (A) TITLE COMPANY: To be determined at a later date.
    (B) AGENT: To be determined at a later date.
    (C) TYPE(S) OF POLICY(IES) TO BE PROVIDED:
        Title commitment or owner's policy only upon request of buyer.
    (D) PAYMENT OBLIGATION: Buyer, if buyer requests policy.
    (E) SPECIAL PROVISIONS: N/A

40. INSPECTIONS:
    (A) TERMITE:
        1. TIME WITHIN WHICH TO MAKE INSPECTION: N/A
        2. TIME WITHIN WHICH TO MAKE OBJECTIONS: N/A
    (B) ROOF:
        1. TIME WITHIN WHICH TO MAKE INSPECTION: N/A
        2. TIME WITHIN WHICH TO MAKE OBJECTIONS: N/A
    (C) APPLIANCES:
        1. TIME WITHIN WHICH TO MAKE INSPECTION: See (E) below.
        2. TIME WITHIN WHICH TO MAKE OBJECTIONS: See (E) below.
    (D) HEATING/COOLING/ELECTRICAL/PLUMBING SYSTEMS:
        1. TIME WITHIN WHICH TO MAKE INSPECTION: See (E) below.
        2. TIME WITHIN WHICH TO MAKE OBJECTIONS: See (E) below.
    (E) OTHER INSPECTIONS (Specify):
        Buyer will be given a reasonable opportunity to examine unit with seller's representative prior to closing and at that time will present seller with an inspection statement setting forth any defects. Seller will be obligated to correct any defects within a reasonable period of time, but neither seller's obligation to correct nor buyer's failure to inspect shall be grounds for deferring closing.

41. WARRANTIES: Seller warrants its workmanship and materials for one year from date the improvements are completed. If manufacturers' warranties exceed one year, these warranties inure to the buyer's benefit. Buyer will receive a builder's warranty at closing that construction is in substantial compliance with approved plans and specifications. Seller will not be obligated to correct, and will not be liable to buyer as a result of, any insubstantial variations from filed building plans or those which are necessitated by site conditions or job requirements provided that (i) the approval of any governmental authority having jurisdiction is obtained, if required, and (ii) the market value of the unit is not substantially diminished.

EXHIBIT 7–3   *(continued)*

42. REPAIRS: <u>New construction, so not applicable except as provided under inspection provision.</u>
43. SURVEY: <u>Seller shall provide if requested by buyer, at buyer's expense.</u>
44. ZONING: <u>Residential, single-family homes.</u>
45. EASEMENTS AND DEED RESTRICTIONS:
    <u>Zoning and regulatory ordinances; restrictions and limitations of record including but not limited to those common to the subdivision; all easements of record; ad valorem real property taxes for the current year; encumbrances assumed or created by buyer.</u>
46. LIENS: <u>At closing, seller shall give buyer a no-lien affidavit.</u>
47. OCCUPANCY: <u>Buyer shall not enter into possession of property or onto construction site until after closing and all funds have cleared. Buyer cannot make any improvements or modifications until closing is completed.</u>
48. RISK OF LOSS: <u>If property is damaged by fire or other casualty before closing and cost of restoration does not exceed 3% of assessed valuation of property, seller shall restore property. If cost of restoration exceeds 3%, buyer can take property as is, together with the 3% or any insurance proceeds, or buyer may terminate contract.</u>
49. TYPE OF DEED TO BE GRANTED: <u>X</u> GENERAL WARRANTY DEED
    ___ SPECIAL WARRANTY DEED
    ___ QUITCLAIM DEED
    ___ OTHER (Specify):
50. CLOSING DOCUMENTS:
    (A) SELLER WILL PROVIDE:
        <u>Deed, no-lien affidavit, builder's warranty, and any corrective instruments.</u>
    (B) BUYER WILL PROVIDE:
        <u>Closing statement, mortgage instrument, mortgage note, security agreement and financing statements.</u>
51. PRORATIONS:
    (A) PRORATED THROUGH THIS DATE: <u>Closing date.</u>
    (B) PRORATION FORMULA: ___ 360-DAY YEAR <u>X</u> 365-DAY YEAR
    (C) TO BE PRORATED:
        <u>X</u> CITY TAXES   ___ SPECIAL ASSESSMENTS
        <u>X</u> COUNTY TAXES   ___ RENT
        ___ OTHER TAXES   ___ INTEREST
        ___ INSURANCE   ___ OTHER (Specify):
52. CLOSING EXPENSES:
    (A) EXPENSES TO BE PAID BY SELLER:
        <u>Documentary stamps on deed and recording of corrective instruments. Also, sales office commissions.</u>
    (B) EXPENSES TO BE PAID BY BUYER:
        <u>Documentary stamps and intangible tax on mortgage and all costs incurred with buyer's mortgage loan.</u>
53. <u>ASSIGNMENT OF CONTRACT:</u> <u>Contract may not be assigned without prior written consent of seller. Seller, in its sole discretion, can withhold consent and contract will remain in full force and effect, or can terminate contract and return buyer's deposits.</u>
54. DEFAULT AND REMEDIES:
    (A) <u>SELLER'S DEFAULT/BUYER'S REMEDIES: If seller defaults, buyer may elect to void contract and all deposits will be returned to buyer within a reasonable period of time upon written demand, allowing for the clearance of any deposits. Upon return of deposits, contract is terminated. Failure by buyer to give notice in writing to seller of any alleged default before seller tenders performance of any omitted act shall constitute a waiver of seller's default.</u>
    (B) <u>BUYER'S DEFAULT/SELLER'S REMEDIES: If buyer fails or refuses to perform any contractual obligation, seller, at its sole option, may terminate contract and retain</u>

(*continued*)

EXHIBIT 7–3

all deposits as liquidated damages. In lieu of termination, seller may elect to institute legal proceedings to specifically enforce the contract.

55. ATTORNEYS' FEES/COSTS: In connection with any litigation, including appellate proceedings, prevailing party shall be entitled to reasonable attorneys' fees and costs. In the event of a dispute or litigation in connection with any alleged default of buyer in which seller deems it advisable to retain counsel, and which is settled prior to litigation by buyer's compliance, seller shall be entitled to recovery of costs and reasonable attorneys' fees incurred in connection therewith at closing.

56. NOTICE:
(A) TO SELLER: At address provided in contract.
(B) TO BUYER: At address provided in contract.

57. ADDITIONAL PROVISIONS: Contract not recordable. Buyer subordinate to any construction loan mortgage. Costs of all construction loan financing to be paid by seller. Insulation disclosure to be included as attachment.

Purchase and sale agreement

EXHIBIT 7–4

PURCHASE AND SALE AGREEMENT

THIS AGREEMENT, made and entered into this _____ day of _____, 20 __, by and between LYNDALE PROPERTIES, INC., an Any State corporation ("Seller"), having its principal office located at 1800 Coolidge Street, Suite 400, Any City, Any State, and the Purchaser(s) named below ("Purchaser").

Purchaser: _____

Address: _____

City: _____

Home Phone Number: _____ Cell Phone Number: _____

Fax Number: _____ Social Security Number(s): _____

I. DESCRIPTION OF PROPERTY. Seller agrees to sell to Purchaser, on terms contained in this Agreement, Lot ____, of ORANGE WALK ESTATES according to the plat thereof, recorded in Plat Book 71, Page 117, Public Records of Any County, Any State; together with the single-family residence to be constructed thereon; and together with all appurtenances thereto. The above-described Lot and improvements thereon ("Dwelling Unit") are referred to in this Agreement as the "Property." The Property address shall be _____, Any City, Any State.

II. PURCHASE PRICE. The type of Dwelling Unit and sale price listed below are followed by a list of changes and extras to be added to this new Dwelling Unit. Purchaser acknowledges that Purchaser understands that the models on view at Orange Walk Estates contain certain optional extra changes which are not included in the total adjusted price unless specifically listed below.

A. Model Type (Base Price) ...._____ $ _____
    (Name of Model)

B. Add ...._____ $ _____

C. Add ...._____ $ _____

D. Add ...._____ $ _____

E. Add ...._____ $ _____

F. Add ...._____ $ _____

TOTAL PURCHASE PRICE $ _____

EXHIBIT 7-4   (*continued*)

The purchase price for the Property, exclusive of any closing costs described in this Agreement, shall be as follows.

A. Lot Reservation Deposit (previously received): $ _____

B. Deposit of ten percent (10%) of the Purchase
   Price less Lot Reservation Deposit, if any
   (received this date): $ _____

C. Additional Deposit to be paid on or before $ _____

D. Balance due at closing (cash, certified check,
   or wire transfer) $ _____

All monies receipted herein are held in escrow in a noninteresting-bearing account, to be applied in accordance with the terms and conditions of this Agreement.

III. FINANCING. The Purchaser agrees to use his or her best efforts to make prompt application and to execute diligently and in good faith all necessary papers for a _____ Mortgage Loan ("Loan") for the principal amount of _____. If the Purchaser is married, and the Purchaser's spouse is not named as a Purchaser herein, Purchaser shall be responsible and liable for such spouse executing the mortgage and other closing documents as required by lender and Seller. Failure of said spouse to do so shall be considered a default of this Agreement and Seller shall be entitled to such remedies as are provided in this Agreement. The Agreement is contingent upon loan approval within sixty (60) days from the execution of this Agreement, otherwise at Seller's option, this Purchase Agreement will be null and void and Seller shall refund all payments made by the Purchaser.

IV. COMPLETION OF CONSTRUCTION AND CLOSING DATE. Completion of the proposed construction, in substantial accordance with plans and specifications approved by appropriate governmental authorities, is estimated, but not guaranteed, on or about _____. The estimated time of delivery set forth in the preceding sentence is made as an accommodation to Purchaser to assist Purchaser in formulating future plans, but such estimated time of delivery shall not be considered as time which is of the essence of this Agreement. Seller shall not be liable to Purchaser for any expense or inconvenience which may directly arise from delay of completion or from delay of delivery of possession. Closing shall be held at such place and on such day and hour as Seller may designate, but not less than ten (10) days from the giving of notice of closing by the Seller to Purchaser. The issuance of a Permanent Certificate of Occupancy as to Purchaser's Dwelling Unit by the Building Department of Any County, Any State, or its equivalent shall evidence that the Dwelling Unit is ready for delivery and shall be the sole condition of closing.

V. CONSTRUCTION SPECIFICATIONS. Seller agrees that the construction of the Dwelling Unit shall be substantially in accordance with the Plans and Specifications attached hereto and incorporated by reference herein. Seller specifically reserves the right to make minor modifications in said Plans and Specifications and to make substitutions of materials, fixtures, appliances and equipment, provided same are of substantially the same or better quality. In the event changes in said Plans, building materials or other items for the Dwelling Unit are required by any governmental or quasi-governmental rule, regulation, code, order, statute or ordinance, Purchaser shall pay Seller at closing any and all costs incurred by Seller in effectuating such changes.

VI. WARRANTIES. Seller shall warrant its workmanship and materials furnished under this Agreement for a period of one (1) year from the date the improvements are completed; provided, however, that manufacturer's warranties which exceed one year shall inure to the Purchaser's benefit. The Purchaser will receive at closing a warranty from Seller of completion of construction in substantial conformity with the approved plans and specifications. Seller will not be obligated to correct, and will not be liable to the Purchaser as a result of, any insubstantial variations from filed Plans or which are necessitated by site conditions or job requirements, provided only that (i) the approval of any governmental authority having jurisdiction thereof is obtained, if required, and (ii) the market value of the Property is not substantially diminished. Further, Seller warrants that the insulation used in the construction of the Dwelling Unit is in conformity with the information provided in the Insulation Exhibit attached to this Agreement.

VII. CHANGE ORDERS AND COLOR SELECTIONS. All change orders must be in writing and paid for at the time the changes are ordered. Seller reserves the right to refuse to accept any change orders after the date hereof. In the event Purchaser orders an option or extra other than those set forth in this Agreement, same shall be paid for at the time such option or extra is ordered. Such order shall not be subject to cancellation by Purchaser, nor shall Purchaser be entitled to a credit or refund therefor.

Purchaser shall submit to Seller in writing selections of color, materials and extras, other than those set forth in this Agreement, not later than fifteen (15) days from Seller's request therefor, which request may be made by telephone, regular mail or other reasonable means of communication. In the event Purchaser fails to comply herewith, Seller may at its option (i) make such selections in its sole discretion, (ii) declare Purchaser in default and exercise any and all remedies set forth in this Agreement, or (iii) delay closing without liability therefor.

VIII. SURVEY. Seller will not furnish a survey to Purchaser except upon request of Purchaser and at Purchaser's expense.

IX. TITLE. Seller will not furnish an owner's title insurance policy or commitment except upon request of Purchaser and at Purchaser's expense. Seller shall convey to Purchaser a good and marketable title by General Warranty Deed subject only to (i) zoning and regulatory ordinances of governmental agencies having jurisdiction; (ii) conditions, restrictions and limitations of record including but not limited to those common to the subdivision in which the Property is located; (iii) all easements of record; (iv) ad valorem real property taxes for the current year which shall be prorated as of date of closing; and (v) encumbrances assumed or created by the Purchaser.

In the event that title shall not be found marketable within ten (10) days of closing, Seller agrees to use reasonable diligence to make the title good and marketable, and shall have a reasonable time to do so. If after reasonable diligence and reasonable time Seller is unable to make said title good and marketable, this Agreement shall be deemed canceled and Seller shall return to Purchaser all deposits paid by Purchaser under this Agreement. Thereupon, each of the parties shall be relieved from any further obligations under this Agreement. Upon request of Purchaser, however, Seller shall deliver the title in its existing condition, whereupon Purchaser shall be deemed to have waived any and all objections and claims with respect to title.

X. LIENS. At closing, Seller shall deliver to Purchaser a Seller's form No-Lien Affidavit in the form attached hereto.

XI. INSPECTION. Purchaser shall be given a reasonable opportunity to examine the Dwelling Unit with Seller's representative prior to closing, and at that time shall present to Seller an Inspection Statement signed by Purchaser setting forth any defects in workmanship or materials. As to any items therein described which are truly defects in workmanship and materials (keeping in mind the construction standards prevalent in Any County relative to the type and price of the subject Dwelling Unit), Seller shall be obligated to correct the same at its cost within a reasonable period of time, but Seller's obligation to correct shall not be a ground for deferring the closing nor the imposition of any condition upon closing. Failure of Purchaser to examine the Dwelling Unit prior to the date established by Seller for closing shall not be a ground for deferring closing or for the imposition of any condition upon closing.

XII. OCCUPANCY. Purchaser shall not enter into possession of the Property or onto the construction site (with the exception of inspection of the Dwelling Unit as provided in paragraph XI) until this transaction has been fully closed and all funds due Seller have cleared. Purchaser shall be prohibited from commencement of any construction, improvement, modification or work with respect to the Property until closing has been completed.

XIII. RISK OF LOSS. If the Property is damaged by fire or other casualty prior to closing and the cost of restoration does not exceed three percent (3%) of the assessed valuation of the Property

EXHIBIT 7–4   *(continued)*

as damaged, the cost of restoration shall be the obligation of the Seller and the closing shall proceed pursuant to this Agreement, with said restoration costs escrowed at closing. Should the restoration costs exceed three (3%) percent of the assessed valuation of the Property as damaged, Purchaser shall have the option of either taking the Property as is, together with either the three (3%) percent or any applicable insurance proceeds payable for said damage, or of canceling this Agreement. Should Purchaser choose the latter option, all received deposits shall be returned to Purchaser.

XIV. CLOSING DOCUMENTS. Seller shall deliver to Purchaser at closing a General Warranty Deed, Seller's form No-Lien Affidavit, Builder's Warranty and any corrective instruments. Buyer shall furnish the closing statement, mortgage, mortgage note, security agreement and financing statements.

XV. PRORATIONS. Proration of real estate taxes shall be made at the date of closing as of the date of closing. Real property taxes will be prorated on the latest information available. If the taxes for the year of closing are not precisely ascertainable, such taxes will be prorated based on estimates and will be adjusted later based on the exact amount of taxes with allowance for full discount. Proration of any and all other proratable items shall be made at the date of closing as of the date of closing.

XVI. CLOSING EXPENSES. Documentary stamps on the General Warranty Deed, recording of any corrective instruments, and commissions owed to the sales office (and any cobroker registered therewith) shall be paid by the Seller. Documentary stamps and intangible tax on mortgage, loan fees, loan closing costs and all other related sums (including but not limited to attorneys' fees, escrows for taxes and insurance, recording fees and credit report) shall be paid by Purchaser. In addition, Purchaser shall be responsible for payment of commission owed to any Buyer's real estate broker(s) according to the terms of such broker agreement.

XVII. ASSIGNMENT. This Agreement is binding on the parties hereto and their heirs, legal representatives, successors and assigns, and this Agreement may not be assigned by the Purchaser without the prior written consent of Seller. A transfer of a legal, equitable or beneficial interest in Purchaser shall be deemed an assignment hereunder. Seller, in its sole discretion, may withhold consent to any attempted assignment of this Agreement and the Agreement shall remain in full force and effect, or may terminate this Agreement and refund all deposits to Purchaser, in which event the parties shall be relieved of further liability hereunder. No assignment of this Agreement shall be effective unless in writing upon such form as Seller shall provide, with the written consent of Seller as noted thereon.

XVIII. DEFAULT AND REMEDIES. If Purchaser fails or refuses to perform any of his or her obligations under this Agreement, Seller, at its sole option, may notify Purchaser in writing that this Agreement is terminated. In the event of such termination, Seller may retain all payments theretofore made by Purchaser as agreed upon liquidated damages which shall not be construed as a penalty; and all further rights and obligations of the parties under this Agreement shall thereupon be terminated. In lieu of such termination, the Seller may elect to institute legal proceedings to specifically enforce this Agreement between the parties and collect damages owing to Purchaser's failure or refusal to perform.

If Seller defaults in the performance of this Agreement, Purchaser may elect to void this Agreement, in which event all sums paid by Purchaser under this Agreement shall be returned to Purchaser within a reasonable period of time upon written demand, allowing for, without limitation, the clearance of any deposits made hereunder, and upon such refund being made to Purchaser, this Agreement shall be terminated and Seller shall be under no obligation or liability whatsoever to Purchaser for any damages that Purchaser may have sustained and neither party will have any claim as against the other under the terms of the Agreement. Failure by Purchaser to give notice in writing to Seller of any alleged default before Seller tenders performance of any omitted act shall constitute a waiver of Seller's default.

XIX. ATTORNEYS' FEES AND COSTS. In connection with any litigation including appellate proceedings arising out of this Agreement, the prevailing party shall be entitled to recover reasonable attorneys' fees and costs. In the event of any dispute or litigation between Seller and Purchaser in connection with any alleged breach or default upon the part of the Purchaser wherein Seller deems it advisable or necessary to retain the services of an attorney, and which is settled prior to litigation by Purchaser otherwise complying with the demands of Seller as to Purchaser's duties and obligations hereunder, Seller shall be entitled to the recovery of costs and reasonable attorneys' fees incurred in connection therewith at closing.

XX. ESCROW AGENT. The escrow agent for all deposits paid hereunder shall be Patriot Bank, 2000 Truman Avenue, Any City, Any State. Purchaser may obtain a receipt for deposits from the escrow agent upon written request.

XXI. AGREEMENT NOT RECORDABLE. This Agreement shall not be recorded and execution hereof shall not create any lien or lien right in favor of the Purchaser, the Purchaser hereby expressly waiving and relinquishing any such lien or lien rights. The Purchaser agrees that all terms and provisions of this Agreement are and shall be subject and subordinate to the lien of any building loan mortgage heretofore or hereafter made, and advances heretofore or hereafter made thereon to the full extent thereof without the execution of any further legal documents by the Purchaser. The costs of all construction loan financing are to be paid by the Seller.

XXII. NOTICES. Except as otherwise provided, whenever a notice is required to be sent, the same shall be in writing addressed to the parties at the addresses set forth in this Agreement and shall be (i) hand delivered; (ii) sent by certified or registered mail, postage prepaid, return receipt requested; (iii) sent by Federal Express or similar overnight courier service; or (iv) by telecopy. Notice given by or to the attorney representing either party shall be effective as if given by or to said party. All notices shall be deemed and considered given upon mailing or telecopying.

XXIII. JOINT AND SEVERAL LIABILITY. Purchasers, if more than one, shall be jointly and severally liable for full performance of all obligations of Purchaser hereunder.

XXIV. SEVERABILITY. If any part, clause, provision or condition of this Agreement is held to be void, invalid or inoperative, the parties agree that such invalidity shall not affect any other part, clause, provision or condition hereof, but that the remainder of this Agreement shall be effective as though such void part, clause, provision or condition had not been contained herein.

XXV. APPLICABLE LAW. This Agreement shall be construed under the laws of the State of Any State.

XXVI. EFFECTIVE DATE. The effective date of this Agreement shall be the date when the last one of the Seller and Purchaser has executed this Agreement.

IN WITNESS WHEREOF, the parties have hereunto set their hands and seals the day and year first above written.

Signed, Sealed and Delivered
in the presence of:

SELLER: LYNDALE PROPERTIES, INC.,
an Any State corporation

_____

BY: _____
    Craig Newfield, President

_____

PURCHASER(S):

_____

_____

_____

_____

Social Security or Federal I.D.
Number(s) of Purchaser(s):

_____

_____

CHAPTER SUMMARY

1. A well-drafted real estate contract is key to achieving the client's goals in the closing of a real estate transaction. The contract should address the responsibilities not only of the parties to the contract but also of the lenders, brokers, escrow agents, title companies, and attorneys. All elements important to the closing of the transaction should be set forth in adequate detail in the real estate contract.

2. To prepare a properly drafted contract, all pertinent information must be gathered, preferably with the aid of a worksheet. Legal names and marital status of the parties should be verified by checking official documents, legal descriptions copied from current deeds, zoning restrictions verified with governmental authorities or zoning maps, and profits and expenses of income-producing property verified by inspection of operating statements.

3. The basic provisions found in a real estate contract for sale and purchase include, but need not be limited to, the naming of the parties, the legal description, the effective date, the closing date, the purchase price, deposits, the method of payment, inspections and warranties, evidence and quality of title, closing costs and apportionments, brokers' fees, defaults and remedies, and attorneys' fees.

4. The purchase of real property may be financed in a number of ways. The buyer may pay cash and take title clear of all mortgage liens. Alternatively, the buyer may seek out a new conventional, FHA, or VA loan; may take the property subject to the existing mortgage; may assume the existing mortgage; or may receive a purchase money mortgage loan from the seller.

5. Most buyers want to make minimum deposits, want ample contingencies included in the contract to provide a means of escape should they wish to back out (for example, contingencies pertaining to attorney approval, financing, zoning, inspection), want as many warranties from the seller as possible, want the right to assign the contract, want to limit the seller's remedies in case of the buyer's default to the retaining of deposits, and want a choice of options in the event the seller defaults.

6. Most sellers want to receive large deposits, want no buyer contingencies, want to give minimum warranties, want to retain deposits as well as seek specific performance or damages should the buyer default, and want to limit the buyer's remedies to the return of deposits in the event the seller defaults. A well-negotiated contract gives neither party everything it wants and yet addresses each party's primary concerns.

7. The contract for purchase and sale of a condominium may be governed by statutory law setting forth a time period within which the buyer may inspect the condominium documents and, upon inspection, cancel the contract. The purchase of a condominium may be subject to approval of the buyer by the condominium association.

8. An option contract is one in which the optionee pays the optionor an agreed-upon price for the privilege of keeping the property off the market for a specified period of time. During this time period, the optionee has the exclusive right to purchase the property. The option price paid is irrevocable. If the optionee chooses to exercise the option, the transaction proceeds in like manner to a regular real estate transaction.

WEB RESOURCES

http://www.findlaw.com/

At the Findlaw site, under the topic "Real Estate" you will find a link to "Buying a Home" that provides various relevant articles, including those pertaining to contracts for purchase and sale. Under the "Home Buying Guide," you also can access a home buying-selling dictionary with definitions for terms most commonly found in real estate contracts.

http://homebuyingabout.com/

This site provides numerous articles that approach a real estate transaction from both a buyer's and a seller's point of view, including articles pertaining to contract negotiation strategies and contract contingencies.

http://www.ilrg.com/

This is the site of the Internet Legal Research Group. It features a large archive of legal forms that may be downloaded for a fee. These forms may be viewed free of charge. If you click on the "ILRG Legal Form Archive" link, you can view various real estate contracts for purchase and sale.

http://www.realtor.com/

At this site, if you click on "Buy" under "Articles," you will find tips for both buyers and sellers of real property. The "Buy" link will take you to useful articles on making offers on homes and what contingencies should be included in an offer to purchase or sell a home.

http://www.realestateabc.com/

At this site, if you click on "Home Buying" under "Articles & Tips," you can access articles on writing offers to purchase.

REVIEW QUESTIONS

1. What are the elements of a valid contract?
2. Why is the contract for sale and purchase considered the most important document in the real estate closing?
3. Distinguish between (a) a sale subject to an existing mortgage and (b) a sale with an assumption of mortgage.
4. What are the basic provisions found in a real estate contract for sale and purchase?
5. What special provisions should be included in the following contracts?
   a. A short sale contract
   b. An option contract
   c. A contract for the sale and purchase of income-producing property
   d. A contract for the sale and purchase of a condominium

DISCUSSION QUESTIONS

1. Why do you think buyers and sellers negotiate very few of the contract terms under which they find themselves obligated?
2. Review the contract found in Exhibit 7–4. What provisions are contained in this contract that would not be appropriate for a contract pertaining to a resale?
3. Review the contract found in Exhibit 7–4. If you were to rewrite certain provisions to make them more favorable to the buyer, which provisions would you rewrite, and why?
4. Review the contract found in Exhibit 7–4. If you were to rewrite certain provisions to make them more favorable to the seller, which provisions would you rewrite, and why?
5. This chapter discusses some of the issues that may arise if the seller permits the buyer to take possession of the property prior to closing. Are there any circumstances under which a seller may want to remain on the premises after closing? Are there any potential problems in allowing a seller to do so? If the seller is allowed to do so, what provisions would you change or add to a contract for sale and purchase to protect the buyer?

ETHICAL QUESTION

Attorney Michael Hogan is acting as escrow agent in several real estate transactions. Michael has been particularly busy with an inordinate number of real estate closings during the past two months, and you have been asked by your supervising attorney to assist him. State law dictates that all earnest money deposits be deposited in escrow accounts within forty-eight hours of receipt. In reviewing a number of files Michael has assigned to you, you come across several earnest money deposit checks dated several weeks ago that have yet to be deposited. What should you do?

Slossberg Law Office on CourseMate

Please go to www.cengagebrain.com to log into CourseMate, access the Slossberg Law Office, and work on your client files. Each module corresponds to a chapter in the text. Within each module, you will be provided with instructions by the supervising attorney. You are asked to keep track of time spent on time sheets. The documents produced through working on client files in the law office can then be compiled into a portfolio of final work product.

CourseMate

The available CourseMate for this text has an interactive eBook and interactive learning tools, including flash cards, quizzes, and more. To learn more about this resource and access free demo CourseMate resources, including the Slossberg Law Office, go to www.cengagebrain.com, and search for this book. To access CourseMate materials that you have purchased, go to login.cengagebrain.com.

Deeds

CHAPTER OBJECTIVES

Upon completion of this chapter, the student will:

- Know the legal requirements of a deed

- Know how to prepare a deed

- Know the differences among a general warranty deed, special warranty deed, bargain and sale deed, and quitclaim deed

- Understand the significance of recording documents and the differences between state recording statutes

- Understand the various methods by which deed fraud is perpetrated and the mechanisms in place to combat its escalation

Introduction

A **deed** is a formal written instrument that conveys title to real property from one party to another. Unlike a contract, which is signed by both parties to a transaction, a deed is signed only by the person(s) conveying the property. It serves as documentary evidence of the transfer, describes the quality of title transferred, and outlines any restrictions regarding the transfer of the property.

Paralegals are often asked to prepare deeds at the direction of their supervising attorney. Therefore, this chapter focuses on the legal requirements for a valid deed, the clauses typically included in a deed, and the drafting of deeds. The most commonly used deeds are discussed, together with a number of special purpose deeds a paralegal may have occasion to draft. The chapter concludes with a discussion of the recording of deeds and other real estate documents.

Legal Requirements of a Deed

The basic requirements for a valid deed are (1) a written instrument (2) signed by a competent grantor, (3) identifying the grantee(s), (4) indicating the date of conveyance, and (5) containing a recital of consideration and (6) words of conveyance of (7) real property described with specificity, which is (8) witnessed (if required by state statute) and (9) acknowledged (if required by state statute) and which is (10) delivered by the grantor to the grantee.

deed: A formal written instrument that conveys title to real property from one party to another.

grantor: The person or entity conveying title of real property to another.

Grantor

A valid deed requires a competent grantor. The **grantor** is the person (or entity) that transfers ownership of the real property. Grantors may be individuals, corporations, partnerships, limited liability companies, trustees, guardians, personal representatives, or governmental authorities or agents. For an individual, competence means being of legal age (in most states, eighteen years of age or older) and being of sound mind (capable of understanding the nature and consequence of the transaction). For a business entity, such as a corporation, competence means being in legal existence (being organized and operating in full accordance with the laws of the state of domicile) and having proper authorization to convey the real property in question (in the case of a corporation, this means having a resolution by the board of directors or shareholders authorizing the president of the corporation to enter the transaction on behalf of the corporation).

If the grantor is an unmarried individual, the deed should so indicate (for example, "Gail Bryce, a single woman" or "Gail Bryce, an unmarried woman"). If the grantor is married, it is advisable that his or her spouse also be named as grantor, even if title to the property is held in only one name (for example, "Martin Compton and Allison Compton, his wife" or "Martin Compton and Allison Compton, husband and wife"). In many states, it is necessary to name both spouses and to have both spouses execute the deed to remove any question concerning homestead rights.

If the grantor is a business entity, the legal name of the business entity should be designated, followed by its state of domicile (for example, "Grantham Properties, Inc., a Nebraska corporation" or "Crowley Associates, a California general partnership"). If the grantor is a fiduciary acting on behalf of a minor or a personal representative acting on behalf of an estate, this should be so indicated (for example, "Millicent Linton, Legal Guardian of Justin Pearce, a minor" or "Brian Tyson, Executor of the Estate of Vernon Tyson, deceased").

It is important that the grantor's name appear precisely the way it is written in the deed by which he or she acquired the property. For example, if Nicole Branston is the owner of the property in question and her present deed reads "Nicole D. Branston, a single woman," her middle initial should be included when entering her name in the new deed as grantor. If she has not married since acquiring the property, the designation "a single woman" should be included as well. If she has married since acquiring the property and has taken the surname "Dickenson," her name on the deed should read "Nicole D. Dickenson, a married woman (formerly known as Nicole D. Branston)," and her husband's name should be included on the deed. It is good practice to obtain the prior deed before drafting a new deed. The prior deed will not only provide the proper spelling of names but also provide the legal description of the property and, usually, any restrictions that should be noted.

Finally, the grantor's name on the signature line of the deed should conform to the grantor's name as it appears in the opening paragraph. If the grantor is a corporation, statutory law should be followed. Typically, the president of the corporation executes the deed, his or her signature is attested to by the secretary of the corporation, and the corporate seal is embossed on the deed. If the grantor is a general partnership or limited liability partnership, all partners should execute the deed. If the grantor is a limited partnership or limited liability limited partnership, all general partners should sign the deed. If the grantor is a limited liability company, depending on state law, either the members or the managers must sign the deed (state law varies, so it should be carefully checked). Statutory law provides authority for fiduciaries to sign deeds on behalf of a trust, ward, or estate. A court order may be required, so refer to state statutes.

Grantee

The next requirement for a valid deed is the inclusion of the name of the grantee. The **grantee** is the person to whom the real property is to be conveyed and therefore does not sign the deed. There is no requirement that the grantee be of sound mind or of the age of majority. The marital status of the grantee should be indicated. In the case of a business entity, the type of entity and its state of domicile should be noted. If there is more than one grantee, the manner by which the grantees take joint title should be clearly indicated. For example, in some states the designation "Frank Potter and Hilda Potter, husband and wife" would raise the legal presumption that the Potters are taking title as tenants by the entirety, while in other states this designation would indicate that the Potters are taking title as tenants in common (recall the detailed discussion of concurrent ownership in Chapter 2). In some states, the words "with right of survivorship" must follow a designation of the parties as joint tenants, or a tenancy in common will be presumed. Nothing should be presumed; the manner in which title is to be held should be discussed with the client and spelled out on the deed.

Date

The date of execution of the deed should appear in the opening paragraph or clause or near the signature. A transfer of ownership is completed when a deed is delivered by the grantor to the grantee. Unless there is contrary evidence, the delivery date is presumed to be the date appearing on the face of the deed.

Consideration

A deed must include a recital of consideration. In most instances, a recital of nominal consideration (for example, ten dollars [$10.00]) is sufficient. The actual consideration paid for the real property must be disclosed to local and/or state tax departments for tax purposes. Real property may be conveyed as a gift, in which case no actual monetary consideration is being exchanged for the real property. There are special circumstances in which the actual sales price must be inserted, as in the case of a deed in which the grantor is acting in a fiduciary capacity on behalf of the owner of the real property (see the discussion that follows).

Words of Conveyance

A deed must include words of conveyance by which the grantor expresses his or her intention to make a present conveyance of title to the property to the grantee. The exact words used vary from state to state and vary depending upon the type of deed used in the conveyance. The words of conveyance also indicate the type of estate being conveyed (for example, a fee simple, a life estate). In some states, the words "and his/her heirs" are used to indicate the conveyance of a fee simple estate. In many states, a fee simple estate will be presumed if there are no words of limitation indicating otherwise.

grantee: The person or entity to whom title to real property is conveyed.

Legal Description

An accurate description of the real property to be transferred must be included in the deed. If personal property is to be sold as well, the listing of personal property should not be included in the deed; rather, it should be listed in a bill of sale (for a discussion of bills of sale, see Chapter 2). The description should meet the requirements for one of the three major types of land descriptions: the metes and bounds description, the government survey description, or the plat description. In most cases, it is good practice to copy the legal description from the prior deed or title policy. However, situations arise in which a grantor may not be granting the entirety of the land owned, or all rights owned, so this information must be checked before drafting the deed.

Witnesses and Acknowledgment

The rules pertaining to the witnessing and acknowledgment of the execution of a deed vary from state to state. In some states, two disinterested witnesses are required to sign the deed. In others, the acknowledgment before a notary public is sufficient. In still other states, witnesses are required only if the deed is to be recorded. Thus, state law should be consulted prior to execution of the deed.

Delivery

The legal transfer of ownership of real property is not complete until the deed is physically delivered by the grantor (or his or her agents) to the grantee and the deed is accepted by the grantee. As long as the deed remains in the possession of the grantor, there is a rebuttable presumption that the transfer of ownership has not taken place. If the deed is physically delivered to the grantee, the grantee's acceptance is presumed. Further, if the deed is recorded in the public records, it is presumed to have been delivered and accepted. The following Missouri case illustrates a situation in which this presumption was successfully rebutted.

CASE: *Greuter v. Wetekamp*

172 S.W.3d 822 (Mo. App. S.D. 2005)

JOHN E. PARRISH, Presiding Judge.

Sharon Dudley appeals a judgment setting aside a deed executed by her mother, Gladys Greuter, in 1981 that purported to convey a 160-acre farm located in Texas County, Missouri, to Gladys Greuter, Sharon Dudley, and Shirley Wetekamp as joint tenants. This court affirms.

This case was tried before the trial judge without a jury. As such, appellate review is undertaken pursuant to Rule 84.13(d). . . .

*   *   *

Sharon Dudley and Shirley Wetekamp are twin daughters of Gladys Greuter. Mrs. Greuter and her husband,

Henry Greuter, who died in 1973, owned the real estate described in the 1981 deed for many years prior to his death. In 1981, Mrs. Greuter requested an attorney, William Gladden, to prepare the deed for the property that is the subject of this action. After the deed was prepared and signed by Mrs. Greuter, she "took it home and rolled it up, put it in a container—it was a metal container, . . . a little metal box." She put the metal box in the bottom of a clothes hamper where she kept her "special papers." The deed was filed for record and recorded in the deed records of Texas County, Missouri, on July 15, 1991.

Mrs. Greuter was asked the following questions and gave the following answers about the recording of the deed:

(continued)

Q. Now, Ms. Greuter, did you, yourself, take the deed out of that box and take it over to the courthouse?
A. No, I never.

. . .

Q. Did you give anyone permission to take the deed and have it recorded?
A. Not unless I had passed away.

Q. Not unless you had passed away. That's going to be my next question. Did you tell your kids that when you died they should take the deed over and record it?
A. Yes.

Q. And why was it that you didn't want it recorded until you died?
A. Well, I just wanted everything in my own possession.

Q. Okay. Did you want to be able to tear that deed up or change your mind if you wanted to?
A. I don't think I had any intentions of ever tearing it up.

Q. But if you wanted to do that, did you—
A. But if I wanted to do that, that was what I would have done.

Q. Okay. Did you want that deed to be put into effect while you were still alive?
A. No.

Q. Who—Do you know who took the deed and recorded it?
A. No, I don't.

Q. And you didn't want it recorded, though?
A. I didn't want it recorded, no.

Mrs. Greuter told the trial court she was "asking the Court to set aside the deed that was recorded, to make it unrecorded, so to speak." She said she wanted to make a different disposition of her property.

The trial court made findings of fact and entered conclusions of law. It found there was no delivery of the deed with the grantor's concurrent intent that the deed operate immediately to convey a present interest in the property. It concluded that Gladys Greuter did not intend for the deed to take effect during her lifetime; that the deed was "void for lack of delivery." The trial court entered judgment setting aside the deed.

Ms. Dudley presents one point on appeal. She contends the trial court erred in setting aside the deed "for want of delivery." She argues "the record of evidence was legally insufficient either to meet the burden of proof as to nondelivery, or overcome the legal presumption of delivery created by recording, in that the grantor was also a co-grantee, the deed was duly recorded pursuant to law and thereafter placed in the possession and control of the remaining co-grantees."

Rhodes v. Hunt, 913 S.W.2d 894 (Mo. App. 1995), explains:

> A deed, to be operative as a transfer of the ownership of land or an interest or estate therein, must be delivered; it is delivery that gives the instrument force and effect. [*Galloway v. Galloway*, 169 S.W.2d 883 (Mo. 1943)] at 888. Delivery signifies that all dominion and control over the deed is passed from the grantor to the grantee, or to someone for him, with the intention of transferring the present ownership of land, or an interest or estate therein. *Id.* The intention of the parties, especially of the grantor, is the essence of delivery. *Id.* Such intention may be manifested by acts, words, or both. *Id.* The burden of proving nondelivery is upon the party who seeks to invalidate the deed because of alleged nondelivery. *Id.* at 900.

"Recording of a deed, even by the grantor, does not in itself operate as delivery of the deed." *Wilkie v. Elmore*, 395 S.W.2d 168, 172 (Mo. 1965). Its recording does, however, create a presumption or a prima facie case of delivery. *Id.* The controlling element, however, in determining delivery of a deed is the intention of the parties, particularly that of the grantor. *Underwood v. Gillespie*, 594 S.W.2d 372, 375 (Mo. App. 1980); *LeMehaute v. LeMehaute*, 585 S.W.2d 276, 280 (Mo. App. 1979).

Mrs. Greuter testified that she did not intend to deliver the deed; that she did not know how it came to be recorded; that she was not the one who recorded it. The trial court heard the testimony. The trial court stated in its findings of fact, "Having reviewed and considered all of the evidence, the Court finds that the evidence is clear, cogent and convincing that Gladys Greuter did not intend for the deed to take effect during her lifetime." It further found, "The evidence is clear, cogent and convincing that there has not been a delivery of the deed with the concurrent intent by grantor Gladys Greuter that it operate immediately to convey a present interest in the property." The trial court concluded, "The 1981 deed is void for lack of delivery. Plaintiff Gladys Greuter is entitled to the equitable relief she has requested."

There was substantial evidence to support these findings. The fact that Mrs. Greuter was, in addition to the grantor, a co-grantee, and the fact that the deed was placed within the possession and control of the remaining co-grantees, does not require a determination adverse to that made by the trial court.

Delivery of a deed to one of several grantees, including a grantee who is also a grantor, operates as a delivery to all of them in the absence of a disclaimer. *LeMehaute, supra.* This rule is applicable only when the intention of the grantor to convey title is not known. *Id.* The controlling factor in

(continued)

determining whether delivery of title occurred is the intention of the parties, particularly that of the grantor. *Id.* Further, "[p]lacing an executed and acknowledged deed in a place where the grantee has access and from which he can, without hindrance, transfer it to his possession, but with the intent that the grantee not take it and have it recorded until after the grantor's death, does not constitute a delivery." *Green v. Stanfill,* 612 S.W.2d 435, 437 (Mo. App. 1981).

There was evidence, which was believed by the trial court, that the intent to effect delivery of the deed was lacking and that the deed was recorded without authority. The judgment is supported by substantial evidence. It is not against the weight of the evidence. This court finds no erroneous declaration or application of law. The Judgment is affirmed.

BATES, C.J. and SHRUM, J., concur.

Case Questions

1. What result was Mrs. Greuter trying to achieve when she deeded the property from herself to herself and her daughters as joint tenants but verbally gave instructions that the deed should not be recorded until after her death?

2. If Mrs. Greuter lived in your state and died prior to bringing this action in court to set aside the deed, how would the property pass?

3. Do you think that recordation of a deed should be deemed conclusive evidence of delivery or should it simply create a rebuttable presumption of delivery? Why?

Other Requirements

In addition to the requirements already discussed, some states require other information to appear in a deed, such as the property appraiser's identification number or the preparer's name and address. Further, state law typically imposes a tax on the transfer of real property called a **documentary stamp tax** or *transfer tax*. The deed cannot be recorded unless the proper amount of documentary stamp tax is paid or the proper statutory exemption noted on the deed. The documentary stamp tax is based on the purchase price of the property and is usually calculated on each $100 or fraction thereof of this purchase price (for example, $.70 per each $100 or fraction thereof).

For example, if the purchase price of the property is $200,000 and the tax imposed is $.50 per each $100 or fraction thereof, the documentary stamp tax would be $1,000. To arrive at this amount, one takes the purchase price of $200,000 and divides it by 100 to arrive at 2,000. This number is then multiplied by the amount of the tax—in this instance, $.50—to arrive at a tax of $1,000.

Deed Clauses

Premises Clause

documentary stamp tax:
A tax imposed on the transfer of real property. It is sometimes referred to as a transfer tax.

premises clause: The opening paragraph of a deed, setting forth the date of execution of the deed, the parties to the deed, and, in states that so require, the addresses of the parties.

The **premises clause** is the opening paragraph of a deed. This clause sets forth the date of execution of the deed, the parties to the deed (together with their designation, either "grantor" and "grantee," or "party of the first part" and "party of the second part"), and, in states that so require, the addresses of the parties. It is common for the opening words of this clause to read, "This Indenture made this . . . day of . . . ," "Know all men by these presents that . . . ," "This deed is made on . . . ," or similar wording. An example of a premises clause follows.

THIS INDENTURE, Made this 12th day of August, 2015, between CLAIRE MASTERSON, an unmarried woman, of the County of Any County, State of Any State, Grantor, and VICTOR DRAPER and DENISE DRAPER, husband and wife, of the County of Any County, State of Any State, Grantees.

Granting Clause

The premises clause is followed by the **granting clause,** which contains the words of conveyance expressing the grantor's intention of transferring the real property. As noted earlier, the precise wording varies from state to state and varies depending upon the type of deed used. Words of conveyance may include any of the following: *grant, bargain, sell, release, convey,* or *remise.* Besides the words of conveyance, the granting clause includes the recital of consideration and the legal description of the real property to be conveyed, such as in the following example.

> WITNESSETH, that the said Grantor, for and in consideration of the sum of Ten Dollars ($10.00), and other good and valuable consideration to said Grantor in hand paid by said Grantee, the receipt of which is hereby acknowledged, has granted, bargained, and sold to the said Grantee, real property in Any County, Any State, described as follows:

> Lot 5 in Block 14 of PINE TREE ESTATES, 1ST SECTION, according to the plat thereof, recorded in Plat Book 61, Page 3, of the Public Records of Any County, Any State.

Encumbrance Clause

When the grantor conveys title, he or she may be conveying title to property that is encumbered by existing mortgages or other liens, leases, easements, or restrictions. These encumbrances should be set forth in the deed in the **encumbrance clause,** sometimes referred to as the *"subject to" clause.* This clause directly follows the legal description of the property. Some attorneys believe the best practice is to list all known encumbrances separately. The encumbrances that are on record should be obtained through a title search. A number of attorneys prefer to use a catchall clause, like the one that follows, to put the grantee on notice that he or she is taking the property subject to all encumbrances on record.

> SUBJECT TO all valid and subsisting restrictions, reservations, covenants, conditions, rights-of-way, and easements properly of record, if any, affecting the above-described property, and taxes for the current year and subsequent years.

Note the reference to taxes in this example. This reference is included because a grantee searching the title of the real property will not come across a written lien filed against the property for currently owed property taxes, and therefore these taxes will not be "of record."

If the grantee is agreeing to take over the grantor's mortgage rather than obtaining a new mortgage to purchase the property, the mortgage lien created when the grantor obtained the mortgage loan will remain on the property and should be noted in the encumbrance clause as follows.

> SUBJECT TO a first mortgage in the original amount of $200,000.00 given by Malcolm Johnson to Patriot Bank, dated March 5, 2011 and recorded on March 5, 2011 in Official Records Book 1213, Page 57 of the Public Records of Any County, Any State, now in the unpaid amount of $188,000.00, which mortgage debt with interest and other lawful charges thereon, from the date hereof, the grantee hereby assumes and agrees to pay in accordance with the terms of the said note and mortgage.

Perhaps the seller is helping to finance the purchase of the subject property through a purchase money mortgage as a second mortgage that is secured by a mortgage note and mortgage lien given to the seller by the buyer. In this case, many

granting clause: A deed clause that contains the words of conveyance expressing the grantor's intention of transferring the real property. It also includes the recital of consideration and the legal description of the property to be conveyed.

encumbrance clause: A deed clause setting forth any encumbrances on the real property conveyed, such as mortgages, leases, liens, easements, or restrictions.

states require that this mortgage be included in the encumbrance clause, as in the following example.

> SUBJECT TO a purchase money second mortgage in the amount of $40,000.00, which said mortgage is to be executed and delivered by the grantee to the grantor as security for a portion of the purchase price of the premises, and which said mortgage is intended to be recorded simultaneously herewith.

Reddendum Clause

The **reddendum clause,** sometimes referred to as the *reserving clause*, reserves some right in the real property for the grantor or imposes a restriction on the use of the property by the grantee. This clause often runs together with the encumbrance clause. The most common use of this clause is to restrict the size or type of structure that can be built on the property to have conformity within a subdivision, such as in the following clause.

> Only one single-family residence of not less than 2,000 square feet of living space may be erected, altered, or placed on the above-described property.

Habendum Clause

The **habendum clause** describes the type of estate being conveyed to the grantee(s). In most instances, the estate conveyed will be a fee simple estate. As noted earlier, the words "in fee simple" may be expressly used; however, the words "to said Grantee, his heirs and assigns forever" also indicate that a fee simple estate is being conveyed. In circumstances of joint ownership, the type of Joint Tenancy in which the property will be held may be included in the granting clause or the habendum clause, or sometimes is found in both. A sample habendum clause follows.

> TO HAVE AND TO HOLD the premises herein granted unto the party of the second part, the heirs or successors and assigns of the party of the second part, forever, in fee simple.

Tenendum Clause

The **tenendum clause** indicates the improvements that are being conveyed together with the land, such as the buildings built on the land. This clause begins with the words *together with* and may appear as a separate clause or as part of the habendum clause. The following wording is commonly found in a tenendum clause.

> TOGETHER with all the tenements, hereditaments, and appurtenances thereto belonging or in anywise appertaining.

Warranty Clause

Some deeds will include a **seisin clause** (sometimes spelled *seizin*), by which the grantor warrants that he or she is the rightful owner of the property in question and thereby has the right and power to convey the property to the grantee. To be "seized" of real property means to own or to have legal and equitable title to real property. This clause may be found in general warranty deeds and special warranty deeds, both of which are discussed later. The following is an example of a seisin clause.

> The said Grantor does covenant, grant, and agree to and with the Grantee that the Grantor, at the time of the sealing and delivery of this deed, is

reddendum clause: A deed clause reserving some right in the real property for the grantor or imposing a restriction on the use of the property by the grantee.

habendum clause: A deed clause describing the type of estate being conveyed to the grantee(s).

tenendum clause: A deed clause indicating the improvements that are being conveyed together with the land, such as the buildings built on the land.

seisin clause: A deed clause by which the grantor warrants that he or she is the rightful owner of the property in question and thereby has the right and power to convey the property to the grantee.

lawfully seized in his own right of a good, absolute, and infeasible estate of inheritance, in fee simple, of the above-granted premises, with the appurtenances.

General warranty deeds include other warranties as well, such as the promise that the property is unencumbered by liens, easements, and restrictions (other than those expressly listed) or the promise that the grantee may enjoy ownership of the property undisturbed by claims of others. These and other warranties, discussed in the following text, may be implied or may be expressly stated, such as in the following clause.

Said Grantor covenants that the said Grantee, her heirs and assigns, may forever hereafter have, hold, possess, and enjoy the said premises without any suit, molestation, or interruption, by any person whatever, lawfully claiming any right therein.

Testimonium Clause

The final deed clause is the **testimonium clause,** in which the deed is executed, witnessed, and acknowledged. The typical language of this clause is "In Witness Whereof, the Grantor has signed and sealed this deed, the day and year first above written."

Common Types of Deeds

The most common types of deeds are (1) the general warranty deed, (2) the special warranty deed, (3) the bargain and sale deed, and (4) the quitclaim deed. In states that have statutory forms of these deeds, the statutory forms should be used.

General Warranty Deeds

A **general warranty deed** is sometimes called a *full covenant and warranty deed* or simply a *warranty deed.* This type of deed provides the greatest degree of protection for the buyer (grantee). With a general warranty deed, the seller (grantor) is stating that the seller has valid title and will defend that title against any defect arising from the actions of the seller or the actions of any of the seller's predecessors. Further, the seller is stating that he or she will defend the buyer's title against any claim made against that title. In essence, when the seller conveys real property through a general warranty deed, the seller is making a number of promises or guarantees, called **covenants,** to the buyer.

 The first covenant contained in a general warranty deed is the *covenant of seisin.* Through this covenant, the seller is guaranteeing the buyer that he or she has good title to convey. A second covenant contained in a general warranty deed is the *covenant against encumbrances,* which guarantees that the title being conveyed is not encumbered by easements, liens, restrictions, or other encumbrances with the exception of those set forth in the deed instrument. A third covenant contained in a general warranty deed is a *covenant of quiet enjoyment.* This covenant guarantees that the buyer may enjoy ownership of the real property undisturbed by claims against his or her title to the property by third parties. Additionally, a general warranty deed contains a *covenant of further assurances,* by which the seller guarantees that if necessary the seller will obtain any and all legal instruments to cure a defective title. Lastly, a general warranty deed contains a *covenant of warranty forever,* by which the seller guarantees that he or she will defend the buyer's good

testimonium clause: A deed clause in which the deed is executed, witnessed, and acknowledged.

general warranty deed: A deed by which the grantor states that he or she has valid title and will defend that title against any defect arising from the actions of the grantor or the actions of the grantor's predecessors. This type of deed provides the greatest degree of protection for the grantee.

covenant: A promise or guarantee.

title to the property forever. If any of these covenants is breached by the seller, the buyer may bring suit for damages against the grantor or former grantors.

In some states, these covenants are set forth explicitly, while in other states the use of certain words implies the existence of these covenants. For example, in many states the use of the words "grants, bargains, and sells" indicates that the instrument conveying title is a general warranty deed. In other states, different words may be used to indicate the same, such as "conveys and warrants" or "grants, sells, and conveys." A sample general warranty deed is provided in Exhibit 8–1.

| **EXHIBIT 8–1** | **General warranty deed** |

GENERAL WARRANTY DEED

THIS INDENTURE, Made this 12th day of August, 2015, Between

HAROLD NICHOLSON and PAULA NICHOLSON, Husband and Wife of the County of Any County, State of Any State, grantors, and

MATTHEW BROMLEY and VICTORIA BROMLEY, Husband and Wife of the County of Any County, State of Any State, grantees;

WITNESSETH, That said grantors, for and in consideration of the sum of Ten Dollars ($10.00), and other good and valuable considerations to said grantors in hand paid by said grantees, the receipt whereof is hereby acknowledged, have granted, bargained, and sold to the said grantees, and grantees' heirs and assigns forever, the following described land, situate, lying and being in Any County, Any State, to wit:

> Lot 9 in Block 10 of ROOKWOOD ESTATES, 1ST SECTION according to the plat thereof, recorded in Plat Book 211, Page 3, of the Public Records of Any County, Any State.
>
> SUBJECT TO taxes for the current year and subsequent years, and the Declaration of Restrictions and Covenants of Rookwood Estates Subdivision as appear of record in Official Records Book 366, Page 28, of the Public Records of Any County, Any State.

and said grantors do hereby fully warrant the title to said land, and will defend the same against the lawful claims of all persons whomsoever.

IN WITNESS WHEREOF, Grantors have hereunto set their hands and seals the day and year first above written.

Signed, sealed and delivered in our presence:

Kelly Kirkland   *Harold Nicholson*
                                                          Harold Nicholson

Claire Haggerty   *Paula Nicholson*
                                                          Paula Nicholson

STATE OF ANY STATE
COUNTY OF ANY COUNTY

I HEREBY CERTIFY that on this day before me, an officer duly qualified to take acknowledgments, personally appeared HAROLD NICHOLSON and PAULA NICHOLSON, Husband and Wife, to me known to be the persons described in and who executed the foregoing instrument, and acknowledged before me that they executed the same.

WITNESS my hand and official seal in the County and State last aforesaid this 12th day of August, 2015.

Rebecca Barclay
Notary Public, State of Any State
My commission expires: 3/25/16

Special Warranty Deeds

From its name, one may be tempted to draw the implication that a **special warranty deed** is somehow superior to a general warranty deed. Just the opposite is the case. A special warranty deed is also known as a *limited warranty deed*. Thus, the guarantees that the seller is making to the buyer and all subsequent purchasers are limited in scope. By using this deed instrument to convey title, the seller is warranting only that he or she has done nothing to encumber the title to the property (with the exception of any encumbrances set forth in the deed itself) but does not provide further assurances or guarantees with regard to the seller's predecessors and therefore will be responsible to the buyer only for any defects caused by his or her own actions.

For example, if the seller had made improvements to the property and failed to pay certain contractors in full, resulting in a construction lien being placed on the property after closing (in many states, contractors have a statutorily prescribed period of time within which to record a lien after completing work on the property, as discussed in detail in the next chapter), the seller would be responsible to the buyer for removing that lien. If the seller's predecessor, however, had encumbered the property in some manner, such as obtaining a second mortgage and failing to secure a release of mortgage evidencing the extinguishment of the debt, that second mortgage would remain an encumbrance on the property, but the buyer would not be able to sue the seller for defective title because that encumbrance was not caused by the seller. Although conveyance by special warranty deed may seem precarious to the buyer, note that in current practice, the process of searching title and the acquisition of title insurance considerably reduce the risk of this method of conveyancing.

The wording that indicates this limited warranty is "by and through the grantor" or "by, through, or under the grantor" in the following covenant: "And the grantor hereby covenants with said grantee that the grantor is lawfully seized of said land in fee simple; that it has good, right and lawful authority to sell and convey said land; that it hereby fully warrants the title to said land and will defend the same against the lawful claims of all persons claiming by, through, or under the said grantor." A special warranty deed commonly is used when real property is sold at public auction, such as in the case of foreclosure on a mortgage or a tax lien, or when real property is conveyed by a personal representative of an estate. However, it may be used in other circumstances, especially in instances when property has changed hands frequently. A sample special warranty deed is found in Exhibit 8–2.

Bargain and Sale Deeds

A **bargain and sale deed** is also sometimes referred to as a *deed of bargain*. When this instrument is used, the seller simply is transferring the real property itself, together with any structures on the property, rather than transferring any particular interest in the property. This deed generally contains no warranties, although the words "grants and conveys" or "grants, bargains, and sells" may be used. The words "conveys and warrants" cannot be used with this deed because the seller is not making any warranties about the title to the property. (Note that in New York, however,

special warranty deed: Also known as a *limited warranty deed*. A deed by which the grantor, in conveying title to real property, warrants only that he or she has done nothing to encumber the property and does not provide further assurances with regard to the grantor's predecessors.

bargain and sale deed: A deed that transfers the real property itself rather than transferring any particular interest in the property.

EXHIBIT 8–2   Special warranty deed

SPECIAL WARRANTY DEED

THIS SPECIAL WARRANTY DEED, Made and executed the 12th day of August, 2015, by WOODARD PROPERTIES, INC., a corporation existing under the laws of Any State, and having its principal place of business at 1539 N.E. 4th Avenue, Any City, Any State, hereinafter called the grantor, to DAVID BOSWORTH, a single man, whose post office address is 135 Union Drive, Any City, Any State, hereinafter called the grantee:

WITNESSETH, That the grantor, for and in consideration of the sum of Ten Dollars ($10.00) and other valuable considerations, receipt whereof is hereby acknowledged, by these presents does grant, bargain, sell, alien, remise, release, convey and confirm unto the grantee, all that certain land situate in Any County, State of Any State, to wit:

> The Southeast one-quarter of the Southeast one-quarter of the Northwest one-quarter of Section 2, Township 32 South, Range 12 West, Any County, Any State.
>
> SUBJECT TO easements, restrictions and limitations of record and taxes for the current year and subsequent years.

TOGETHER, with all the tenements, hereditaments and appurtenances thereto belonging or in anywise appertaining.

TO HAVE AND TO HOLD, the same in fee simple forever.

AND the grantor hereby covenants with said grantee that the grantor is lawfully seized of said land in fee simple; that it has good, right and lawful authority to sell and convey said land; that it hereby fully warrants the title to said land and will defend the same against the lawful claims of all persons claiming by, through, or under the said grantor.

IN WITNESS WHEREOF, the grantor has caused these presents to be executed in its name, and its corporate seal to be hereunto affixed, by its proper officers thereunto duly authorized, the day and year first above written.

[Corporate seal]

ATTEST: *Frances Wheeler*   WOODARD PROPERTIES, INC.
        Secretary

Signed, sealed and delivered in the presence of: By: *George Woodard*
                                                 President

Ruth Barton
Norman Portman

STATE OF ANY STATE
COUNTY OF ANY COUNTY

I HEREBY CERTIFY that on this day before me, an officer duly authorized to administer oaths and take acknowledgments, personally appeared GEORGE WOODARD and FRANCES WHEELER, known to me to be the President and Secretary respectively of WOODARD PROPERTIES, INC., the corporation in whose name the foregoing instrument was executed, and that they severally acknowledged executing the same for such corporation, freely and voluntarily, under authority duly vested in them by said corporation.

WITNESS my hand and official seal in the County and State last aforesaid this 12th day of August, 2015.

                                           Rebecca Barclay
                                           Notary Public, State of Any State
                                           My commission expires: 3/25/16

there are two types of bargain and sale deeds, those with and those without covenants.) In some states, the words "grants and releases" are used, which are the most accurate in describing the conveyance made. Exhibit 8–3 provides an example of a bargain and sale deed.

Bargain and sale deed	EXHIBIT 8–3

BARGAIN AND SALE DEED

THIS INDENTURE, Made this 12th day of August, 2015, Between
CARY KNOWLES, a single man,
whose post office address is 220 S.E. 9th Terrace, Any City, Any State, referred to as the grantor, and
NICOLE QUINN, a single woman,
whose post office address is 980 Chastleton Avenue, Any City, Any State, referred to as the grantee.

WITNESSETH, that said grantor, for and in consideration of the sum of Ten Dollars ($10.00), and other good and valuable considerations, the receipt of which is hereby acknowledged, grants and releases to the said grantee, in fee simple, the following described property, consisting of the land and all the buildings and structures on the land, to wit:

Lot 5 in Block 5 of HEWELL GRANGE, according to to the plat thereof, recorded in Plat Book 1100, Page 13, of the Public Records of Any County, Any State.

SUBJECT TO taxes for the current year and subsequent years, and certain conditions and restrictions of record in Official Records Book 1204, Page 44, of the Public Records of Any County, Any State.

IN WITNESS WHEREOF, grantor has hereunto set his hand and seal the day and year first above written.

Signed, sealed and delivered in our presence:

Sally Griffin

Gene Powell
STATE OF ANY STATE
COUNTY OF ANY COUNTY

Cary Knowles
Cary Knowles

I HEREBY CERTIFY that on this day before me, an officer duly qualified to take acknowledgments, personally appeared CARY KNOWLES, a single man, to me known to be the person described in and who executed the foregoing instrument and acknowledged before me that he executed the same.

WITNESS my hand and seal in the County and State last aforementioned this 12th day of August, 2015.

Rebecca Barclay
Notary Public, State of Any State
My commission expires: 3/25/16

Quitclaim Deeds

More commonly used than the bargain and sale deed to transfer property when the seller does not wish to make any guarantees to the buyer is the **quitclaim deed,** sometimes referred to as a *release deed*. There is a technical distinction that should be made between a bargain and sale deed and a quitclaim deed. A bargain and sale deed transfers land only, not interest in the land. With a quitclaim deed, the grantor is transferring whatever interest he or she may have, without making any warranties regarding the quality of his or her interest. If the title is defective, the grantee has no recourse whatsoever against the grantor. Indeed, the grantor may be uncertain as to whether he or she even has a legitimate interest in the real property in question.

quitclaim deed: A deed in which the grantor transfers whatever interest he or she may have without making any warranties regarding the quality of the title.

What the grantor does, in effect, with the use of a quitclaim deed is convey to the grantee any interest he or she has or *may* have, and no more.

The term *grantor* or *releasor* is used here intentionally, rather than *seller*, because the transferor of the real property is usually not a "seller" when a quitclaim deed is used. In a sales transaction, a buyer will rarely accept a quitclaim deed. These deeds often are used in intrafamily transfers of title, in divorce proceedings when one spouse transfers his or her interest to the other, and in probate proceedings when an heir wishes to give up a claim (present or future) to real property; they are also used to clear any present or potential cloud on the title to real property and to transfer less than fee simple title.

Because no warranties are provided by the grantor, in a quitclaim deed the word *warrant* is omitted, and the words *remise, release, and quitclaim* are found. In some states, such as New Jersey, the conveyance language may be "neutral" (for example, "grant and convey"), but a clause will be inserted to indicate that the deed is a quitclaim deed. A sample quitclaim deed is found in Exhibit 8–4.

EXHIBIT 8–4	**Quitclaim deed**

QUITCLAIM DEED

THIS INDENTURE, Made this 12th day of August, 2015, between AGNES PERKINS, Widow, of the County of Any County, State of Any State, hereinafter referred to as grantor, and PETER PERKINS, a single man, of the County of Any County, State of Any State, hereinafter referred to as grantee.

WITNESSETH that grantor, for and in consideration of the sum of Ten Dollars ($10.00) and other good and valuable considerations, the receipt of which is hereby acknowledged, by these presents does remise, release, and forever quitclaim unto the said grantee the following property:

> Condominium Unit No. 201, in HUDDINGTON COURT CONDOMINIUM, according to the Declaration of Condominium thereof, recorded in Official Records Book 3210, Page 88, of the Public Records of Any County, Any State.

TO HAVE AND TO HOLD the said described premises to grantee, so that neither grantor nor any person or persons claiming under grantor shall at any time have, claim, or demand any right or title to said premises or appurtenances, or any rights thereof.

IN WITNESS WHEREOF, grantor has signed and sealed this deed the day and year first above written.

Signed, sealed and delivered in the presence of:

Jessica McDonnell　　　　　　　　　　*Agnes Perkins*
　　　　　　　　　　　　　　　　　　　　Agnes Perkins

Jason Long

STATE OF ANY STATE
COUNTY OF ANY COUNTY

I HEREBY CERTIFY that on this day before me, an officer duly qualified to take acknowledgments, personally appeared AGNES PERKINS, a widow, to me known to be the person described in and who executed the foregoing instrument, and acknowledged before me that she executed the same.

WITNESS my hand and official seal in the County and State last aforesaid this 12th day of August, 2015.

Rebecca Barclay
Notary Public, State of Any State
My commission expires: 3/25/16

Special-Purpose Deeds

Corrective Deeds

In most circumstances, conveyance of real property will be done through the use of one of the four deed instruments discussed previously. There are times, however, when special circumstances require the use of a particular special-purpose deed. For example, suppose the deed used to transfer title from seller to buyer is later found to contain an error in the spelling of a name, in the marital status of a party, in the legal description, or in the omission of a restriction. To correct such an error, a corrective deed must be prepared, signed, and recorded. The corrective deed relates back to the date of the original deed. Note that documentary stamp taxes need not be paid on corrective deeds because this deed does not represent another conveyance of the property. An example of a corrective deed is found in Exhibit 8–5—in this case, to correct an error transposing the numbers of an official records book in which a mortgage has been recorded. The buyer (grantee), rather than applying for a new mortgage, has agreed to take over the existing mortgage on the property.

Corrective deed	EXHIBIT 8–5

CORRECTIVE DEED

THIS INDENTURE, made this 12th day of August, 2015, between MARK ROSWELL and DONNA ROSWELL, his wife, of the County of Any County, State of Any State, Grantors, and EMILY STRATFORD, a single woman, of the County of Any County, State of Any State, Grantee,

Whereas, by a warranty deed dated the 30th day of July, 2015, and recorded on the 31st day of July, 2015, in Official Records Book 720, Page 23, of the Public Records of Any County, Any State, the Grantors conveyed to the Grantee certain lands therein and hereinafter described; and

Whereas, in the said deed by mistake the words "SUBJECT TO the lien of that certain mortgage to Patriot Bank, dated February 11, 2013, filed of record February 18, 2013, in Official Records Book 689, Page 112 of the Public Records of Any County, Any State, which the Grantee herein assumes and agrees to pay" were written instead of the words "SUBJECT TO the lien of that certain mortgage to Patriot Bank, dated February 11, 2013, filed of record February 18, 2013, in Official Records Book 698, Page 112 of the Public Records of Any County, Any State, which the Grantee herein assumes and agrees to pay," and this deed is executed for the purpose of correcting the said mistake.

WITNESSETH, that the Grantors, for and in consideration of the sum of Ten Dollars ($10.00) and other good and valuable considerations, the receipt whereof is hereby acknowledged, have granted, bargained, and sold to Grantee, and Grantee's heirs and assigns forever, the following described land, situate, lying and being in the County of Any County, State of Any State:

Lot 9 in Block 5 of MAPLE TREE ESTATE, 2ND SECTION, according to the plat thereof, recorded in Plat Book 102, Page 33, of the Public Records of Any County, Any State.

SUBJECT TO the lien of that certain mortgage to Patriot Bank, dated February 11, 2013, filed of record February 18, 2013, in Official Records Book 698, Page 112 of the Public Records of Any County, Any State, which the Grantee herein assumes and agrees to pay.

SUBJECT TO easements, restrictions, and limitations of record and taxes for the current year and subsequent years.

together with all the tenements, hereditaments, and appurtenances thereto belonging or in any wise appertaining.

EXHIBIT 8–5   *(continued)*

TO HAVE AND TO HOLD the same in fee simple forever.

AND said Grantors do hereby fully warrant the title to said land, and will defend the same against the lawful claims of all persons whomsoever.

IN WITNESS WHEREOF, Grantors have hereunto set their hands and seals the day and year first above written.

Signed, sealed and delivered in our presence:

Michael Watson   _Mark Roswell_
Michael Watson   Mark Roswell

Eric Brown   _Donna Roswell_
Eric Brown   Donna Roswell

STATE OF ANY STATE
COUNTY OF ANY COUNTY

I HEREBY CERTIFY that on this day before me, an officer duly qualified to take acknowledgments, personally appeared MARK ROSWELL and DONNA ROSWELL, his wife, to me known to be the persons described in and who executed the foregoing instrument, and acknowledged before me that they executed the same.

WITNESS my hand and official seal in the County and State aforesaid this 12th day of August, 2015.

Rebecca Barclay
Notary Public, State of Any State
My commission expires: 3/25/16

Deeds Conveying Government-Owned Property

Sometimes the grantor of real property is not a private individual or corporation but is a city, county, or state. Prior to the conveyance of government-owned real property, certain procedures must take place. The conveyance must be approved by the appropriate legislative body. This legislative body must, in turn, confer authority upon an official to act on behalf of the city, county, or state in the transaction. If the land is state-owned, the governor, a state agency, or a committee must approve the actions of the state legislature in making the decision to sell the property. The deed must recite the date and number of the bill approving the conveyance, must be signed by the official authorized to act on behalf of the state and by the governor, and must be attested to by the secretary of state (if state-owned property). At times, a legislative body may vote to auction off government-owned land to increase revenue. If this is the case, as it is in the sample deed provided in Exhibit 8–6, the property is sold to the highest bidder.

Fiduciary Deeds

There are circumstances under which the grantor may not be able to sign a deed. For example, the grantor may be under age, the grantor may not have the legal mental capacity because the grantor has been adjudicated incompetent, or the grantor may be deceased. In these and similar circumstances, an appointed fiduciary is given the

Deed	EXHIBIT 8-6

DEED

BY VIRTUE OF the authority conferred upon me by Senate Bill No. 15-108 introduced on June 27, 2015 and approved by the state legislature of Any State on July 3, 2015, I, WILLIAM ELLIS, Director of the Department of Agriculture, duly authorized and acting for and on behalf of the State of Any State, Grantor, do hereby grant, sell, and convey to LFR CORPORATION, Grantee, a corporation duly organized and operating under the laws of the State of Any State, having its principal office in the City of Any City, State of Any State, the following described real property:

> ALL THAT TRACT of land lying and being in the Southeast quarter of the Northeast quarter of the Northwest quarter of Section 10, Township 50 South, Range 41 East, Any County, Any State.

TO HAVE AND TO HOLD the same unto the said Grantee, and Grantee's successors and assigns, in fee simple, together with all appurtenances thereunto belonging, said Grantee having been the highest bidder at public auction held at the location of the above-described real property on the 5th day of August, 2015, at 10:00 A.M., pursuant to notice duly published as required by law.

Given under my hand and official seal, and of the seal of the State of Any State, this 12th day of August, 2015.

State of Any State

By   *William Ellis*_____

Director of the Department of Agriculture

[Seal]

Approved this 12th day of August, 2015.

*Rosemary Maxwell*_____

Governor

Attest:

*Alfred Creighton*_____

Secretary of State

[State Seal]

STATE OF ANY STATE
COUNTY OF ANY COUNTY

I HEREBY CERTIFY on this day that an officer duly authorized in the state and county aforesaid, WILLIAM ELLIS, Director of the Department of Agriculture of the State of Any State, personally known to me to be the same person and official who executed the above and foregoing instrument, appeared before me this day in person and acknowledged that, as such official, he signed, sealed and delivered the above and foregoing instrument on behalf of the Grantor, State of Any State, pursuant to authority conferred on him by law.

IN WITNESS WHEREOF I hereunto set my hand and official seal in the County and State last aforesaid this 12th day of August, 2015.

*Gregory Nicholls*_____

Notary Public, State of Any State

My commission expires: *4/7/16*_____

authority to sign the deed on the grantor's behalf. A fiduciary, such as a personal representative of an estate, a guardian of a minor, or a trustee, ordinarily will convey property not through the use of a general warranty deed but rather through the use of a special warranty deed, guaranteeing that he or she did nothing to encumber the property but not making guarantees to defend the title against liens, claims, or defects arising from the actions of others.

Personal Representatives' Deeds. A personal representative is a person (or entity) who administers the estate of a deceased person. The personal representative operates under the auspices of the probate court. A decedent may have left explicit instructions in a will about how he or she would like to dispose of his or her real property. Unless the will is contested, the probate court, by court order, normally authorizes the personal representative to make the conveyance(s) in accordance with the decedent's express wishes. If the decedent died intestate, the real property of the decedent is passed on according to the intestate statutes of the state in which the real property is located.

Sometimes a will may direct that a personal representative sell certain real property and deliver the proceeds of the sale to named persons in the will. In these circumstances, the recital of nominal consideration is insufficient, and a recital of the actual consideration paid for the real property must be included in the deed to safeguard the interests of the beneficiaries named in the will. If a conveyance is to be made to a named beneficiary in a will and not to a bona fide purchaser, money does not change hands in the transaction, and, therefore, a recital of nominal consideration is appropriate.

Exhibit 8–7 provides an example of a personal representative's deed conveying real property to a beneficiary named in a will. The real property in question here is a condominium unit. Note that in some states, such as Connecticut, a probate court Certificate of Descent/Devise is used to convey title to heirs or devisees, while a personal representative's deed is used to convey real property to others.

Guardians' Deeds. Not as frequently, a minor may be the owner of real property. As noted earlier, a person must be legally competent to convey real property as a grantor but need not be legally competent to receive real property as a grantee. Infancy (minority) makes a party incapable of conveying real property. However, a minor's real property may be sold on the minor's behalf by the minor's guardian acting as the minor's fiduciary.

Another situation in which a guardian's deed may be used to convey real property is when the property owner is an adult who has been adjudicated incompetent to handle his or her own affairs. In such an instance, the court will appoint a guardian to act on that individual's behalf. Often, when such an individual becomes incapable of living on his or her own, it becomes necessary to sell his or her home. The proceeds of the sale may be needed to pay for the costs of an assisted living facility. Because the property owner has been found to be incompetent to handle his or her own affairs, he or she cannot sign a deed transferring title; such a deed must be signed by the guardian.

As in the case of a personal representative, when a guardian sells real property, full disclosure must be made in the deed regarding the actual consideration paid for the property. In most states, the property owner, through his or her guardian, must petition the court for permission to sell the real property, and the court then oversees the transaction. The court may require that the guardian post a bond and may appoint an individual to act as referee during the transaction as an added protection.

Sheriffs' or Referees' Deeds

When real property is foreclosed upon, statutorily prescribed procedures are followed by which title to the real property is passed from the property owner to the highest bidder at a foreclosure sale. Although these procedures differ from

PERSONAL REPRESENTATIVE'S DEED

THIS INDENTURE, made this 13th day of August, 2015, between HENRY MARSHALL, personal representative of the last will and testament of JUDITH STEVENSON, late of the County of Any County, Any State, deceased, as Grantor, and BETH STEVENSON, a single woman, residing at 45 Cotswald Lane, Any City, Any County, Any State, as Grantee.

Whereas, by her last will and testament, dated the 30th day of January 2008, the said JUDITH STEVENSON appointed HENRY MARSHALL as personal representative thereof; and

Whereas, the said JUDITH STEVENSON died on the 11th day of May, 2015, and her last will and testament was duly proved and allowed by the probate court of the County of Any County and State of Any State on the 19th of May, 2015,

WITNESSETH, that in the exercise of the powers to him given by the said last will and testament, and in consideration of the sum of Ten Dollars ($10.00) to him in hand paid by the Grantee, the receipt whereof is hereby acknowledged, the Grantor, personal representative as aforesaid, does hereby grant and convey unto the said Grantee all that real property herein described, to wit:

Unit 202, in BRAMBLEWOOD CONDOMINIUM, according to the Declaration of Condominium thereof, recorded in Official Records Book 4907, Page 78 of the Public Records of Any County, Any State.

SUBJECT TO all valid and existing restrictions, reservations, covenants, conditions, and easements of record.

together with the appurtenances, and also all the estate which the said decedent had at the time of decedent's death in said premises, and also the estate therein, which the Grantor has power to convey;

TO HAVE AND TO HOLD the premises herein granted unto the Grantee in fee simple forever.

AND Grantor covenants that the Grantor has not done or suffered anything whereby the said premises have been encumbered in any way whatever, except as aforesaid.

IN WITNESS WHEREOF, the Grantor has duly executed this deed the day and year first above written.

In presence of:

Jane Harley

HenryMarshall
Henry Marshall as Personal Representative
of the Last Will and Testament of
Judith Stevenson, Deceased

Christina Owens
STATE OF ANY STATE
COUNTY OF ANY COUNTY

I HEREBY CERTIFY that on this day before me, an officer duly authorized in the state and county aforesaid to take acknowledgments, personally appeared HENRY MARSHALL, personal representative of the last will and testament of JUDITH STEVENSON, to me known to be the person described in and who executed the foregoing instrument, and acknowledged before me that he executed the same for the purposes herein expressed.

IN WITNESS WHEREOF I hereunto set my hand and official seal in the County and State last aforesaid this 13th day of August, 2015.

James O'Connell
Notary Public, State of Any State
My commission expires: _10/24/16_

state to state, most commonly a court entering judgment on behalf of the creditor (for example, the lender in a mortgage foreclosure, the city or county in a tax sale) will direct a sheriff or court-appointed referee to oversee the public auction of the real property, after which the real property is conveyed to the highest bidder by a deed called a *sheriff's deed* or a *referee's deed,* which is similar to a special warranty deed. The owner of the property does not sign the deed as grantor; rather, the sheriff or referee signs the deed as grantor. Although the sheriff or referee is not considered a fiduciary, a sheriff's or referee's deed is similar to a fiduciary deed in that the grantor makes no guarantees to the grantee(s) concerning title except for the guarantee that he or she has not encumbered the title. A sheriff's or referee's deed is also similar to a fiduciary deed in that the deed must fully disclose the consideration paid for the real property. In some states, such as Florida, a certificate of title or similar document may be used, rather than a sheriff's deed or referee's deed, to transfer title after a foreclosure sale.

Mention must be made here of other circumstances under which a sheriff's or referee's deed may be used to convey real property. In a situation in which real property is jointly owned, the owners may request the court to partition the real property. This commonly occurs in divorce proceedings where the spouses own real property as tenants by the entirety and wish to have the property sold and the proceeds distributed accordingly. A court may order that the property be partitioned and sold at public auction by a sheriff or referee. Exhibit 8–8 provides an example of a sheriff's deed.

Preparation of Deeds

As a paralegal, you will often be assigned the task of preparing deeds by your supervising attorney. The first step to take, prior to drafting, is to determine whether your state law prescribes a statutory form that must be utilized. Your office may have statutory deed forms that are ready to be customized to the needs of the parties involved in the transaction. The next step is to determine which form of deed is appropriate for the particular transaction. The contract for sale and purchase often specifies the type of deed that will be conveyed upon closing. If the contract is silent, consult the client file notes, or ask your supervising attorney. Generally, if the contract for sale and purchase does not otherwise specify, a general warranty deed is used; however, you should not make any assumptions in this regard.

Once the type of deed to be used is determined, the next step is to ascertain the correct legal names of the parties and their status. As noted earlier, the grantor's current deed or title policy may be consulted to ascertain the correct name of the grantor. Check on whether the grantor's marital status has changed since he or she acquired the property in question. If the grantor was single and is now married or if the grantor took title to the property in his or her sole name although married, ascertain the name of the grantor's spouse. It may be necessary to have the spouse sign the deed as well. The grantee's name will appear on the contract for sale and purchase; however, it is good practice to double-check the spelling, use of middle initials, and so forth.

Inquiry also must be made about the manner in which title is to be held (for example, tenants by the entirety, tenants in common). The contract for sale and purchase should provide the current addresses of the parties, information that should be included in the deed if required by state statute. If your state requires inclusion of the property appraiser's parcel identification number, this can be copied from the grantor's current deed.

SHERIFF'S DEED

THIS INDENTURE, made this 14th day of August, 2015, between ROBERT HANDLER, sheriff of the County of Any County, State of Any State, as Grantor, and MONICA JONES, a single woman, residing at 88 Foxtail Lane, Any City, Any County, Any State, as Grantee.

Whereas, at a hearing of the Circuit Court of the County of Any County held on the 8th day of July, 2015, it was ordered by said court, in a certain action then pending therein between plaintiff and defendant, that the mortgaged premises mentioned in the complaint in said action and in said judgment and hereinafter described be sold at public auction according to statute by or under the direction of the sheriff of the County of Any County; that the sale be made in the county where the premises are situated; that said sheriff give public notice of the time of the sale according to statute; that the sheriff execute to the purchaser or purchasers of said mortgaged premises a good and sufficient deed of conveyance for the same; and

Whereas, the sheriff, pursuant to said judgment, did on the 6th day of August, 2015, sell at public auction the premises, due notice of the time and place of such sale being first given, to the Grantee for the sum of Two Hundred and Forty-Eight Thousand Dollars ($248,000.00), that being the highest sum bid for the sale.

WITNESSETH, that the Grantor, sheriff as aforesaid, pursuant to the order and judgment of said court and in consideration of the sum of money aforesaid being first duly paid by the Grantee, the receipt whereof is hereby acknowledged, has bargained and sold and by these presents doth grant and convey unto the Grantee the following described land, situate, lying and being in Any County, Any State, to wit:

Lot 5 in Block 18 of CRESTWOOD ESTATES, 1ST SECTION, according to the plat thereof, recorded in Plat Book 88, Page 41, of the Public Records of Any County, Any State.

To have and to hold the same unto the Grantee, her heirs and assigns forever.

IN WITNESS WHEREOF, the Grantor, sheriff as aforesaid, has hereunto set Grantor's hand and seal the day and year first above written.

Signed, sealed and delivered in our presence:

Faith Freemont

Gregory Evans

Robert Handler
Robert Handler, Sheriff of
Any County

STATE OF ANY STATE
COUNTY OF ANY COUNTY

I HEREBY CERTIFY that on this day before me, an officer duly qualified to take acknowledgments, personally appeared ROBERT HANDLER, Sheriff of Any County, to me known to be the person described in and who executed the foregoing instrument, and acknowledged before me that he executed the same.

WITNESS my hand and official seal in the County and State last aforesaid this 14th day of August, 2015.

Maria Perez
Notary Public, State of Any State
My commission expires: 5/10/16

Once this information is obtained, you will be able to draft the premises clause of the deed. The date of execution typically is the date set for closing, but last-minute complications often arise, so it is advisable to leave the date blank and fill it in at or directly before closing. A deed should be double-spaced, with the exception of the legal description and any encumbrance or reserving clauses, which are single-spaced and block-indented.

Next, insert a nominal consideration in the granting clause unless your supervising attorney instructs otherwise or unless the deed is a fiduciary deed. Then the grantor's current deed or an updated survey should be reviewed to verify the proper legal description of the real property. If a standard form is used and inadequate space is given for the legal description, make reference in the deed to an attached exhibit and type the description on the exhibit. After typing a legal description, it is always good practice to have someone else review it with you by reading the description from the current deed aloud to the other person and having that person check your typed description for any discrepancies. This is imperative with lengthy metes and bounds legal descriptions.

Unless your supervising attorney prefers you to use a catchall encumbrance clause, such as the one discussed earlier, make sure to list all "subject to" provisions. The encumbrances of record should appear on the title examination. Remember that there may be other encumbrances, such as a second mortgage, that may need to be included, so also review the contract, any addendums, and all other papers in the client's file. Some attorneys, as an extra precaution, list all encumbrances and also include a catchall clause.

Having reviewed state statutes to determine the proper number of witnesses and the required form of acknowledgment, you can draft the testimonium clause, making sure that the grantor's name under the signature line conforms to the grantor's name in the premises clause. If the grantor is a corporation, the name of the corporation should appear above the signature line, the word "By" should appear in front of the signature line, and the name of the signing corporate officer and his or her representative capacity should appear under the signature line (for example, Mildred White, President). Further, be sure to include the attestation of the corporate secretary and the affixation of the corporate seal. The witnesses' names generally do not have to be typed under the signature lines for the witnesses. When typing the acknowledgment, you must include the name and status of the grantor as his or her name appears in the premises clause. If your state statutes require the inclusion of the name and address of the preparer, this appears either at the top or at the bottom of the deed. Your supervising attorney's name should be inserted, together with the law firm's address.

After your attorney reviews the deed, calculate the documentary stamp tax to be paid upon recording. To do this, check the contract for sale and purchase for the actual purchase price and the state statutes for the current documentary stamp tax rate. Check compliance with local and state taxing departments. You must also review the recording fee schedule to determine the correct amount for the recording fee. After recordation, the original deed is returned to the grantee. The deed preparation checklist below will provide a helpful review.

DEED PREPARATION CHECKLIST

1. Review state statutes to determine:
   a. Statutory deed forms.
   b. If no statutory forms, state requirements regarding number of witnesses, form of acknowledgment, inclusion of parties' addresses, and so on.
   c. Documentary stamp tax.

2. Review grantor's current deed for:
   a. Correct spelling of grantor's name and grantor's marital status.
   b. Legal description of the property.
   c. Listing of any encumbrances.
   d. Property appraiser's tax identification number (if required).
3. Review updated title examination for a listing of any encumbrances (check against the grantor's current deed).
4. Review contract for sale and purchase for:
   a. Type of deed required by contract.
   b. Correct spelling of grantee's name and marital status (double-check against other documents or directly with the grantee).
   c. Closing date.
5. Determine manner in which title is to be held by grantee(s).
6. Determine whether additional encumbrances (other than those of record) exist or will be created (for example, a second mortgage). These must be included in the deed.
7. Using the information supplied above, draft:
   a. Premises clause.
      i. Leave date of execution blank.
      ii. Insert appropriate county and state, names and statuses of the parties, manner in which title will be held (this may be included additionally or alternatively in the granting clause), and the addresses of the parties, if applicable.
   b. Granting clause.
      i. Insert the recital of consideration and the manner in which title is to be held by the grantees if this was not included in the premises clause.
      ii. Insert legal description (either type legal description in the body of the deed or include as an exhibit).
   c. Encumbrance and reddendum clauses. Insert all "subject to" provisions and any reserving clauses.
   d. Testimonium clause.
      i. Prepare signature lines for grantor(s) and witnesses.
      ii. Prepare acknowledgment.
8. Before the deed is signed:
   a. Have supervising attorney review it.
   b. Once date of closing is confirmed, insert date, and then make copies for grantor, lending institution, and office file.
9. After the deed is signed:
   a. Conform copies to the original.
   b. Prepare or acquire the check for the documentary stamp tax and recording fee.
   c. Record deed and comply with local and state taxing departments.
   d. Return original deed to the grantee.

Recording Deeds and Other Real Estate Documents

In the preceding discussion, mention was made a number of times of documents in the public record. Documents are placed in the public record through a process called **recording.** When a document is recorded, it is delivered to the appropriate government official for transcription into a plat book, deed book, mortgage book, or official records book. The document may then be perused by anyone who knows the book number and page number. An inquiring person who does not know the book and page number may locate them through one of several indexes, such as a grantor-grantee index or a mortgage index. Many types of documents may be recorded, including but not limited to deeds, mortgages, satisfactions of mortgages, liens, easements, releases of liens, plat maps, and declarations of condominium.

The purpose of recording documents is to put the public on notice regarding the information contained in the document. If the document in question is a deed, the recording of the deed puts the public on notice regarding the contents of the deed, including the identification of the current owner of the real property, the legal description of the property, and the encumbrances on the property. This notice is referred to as **constructive notice,** meaning that the information recorded has been made available to anyone who searches the public records. **Actual notice** refers to direct knowledge a person has about the ownership and condition of title of real property. For example, title to property is conveyed by deed to Janet Ingram. The deed is recorded. Michael Holt drives by the property in question and decides he would like to buy it if it is available. Michael has constructive notice of the owner of the subject property because the deed is recorded in the public records. If Michael conducts a search of the public records, he then has actual notice of the owner of the property and of the encumbrances on the property.

At the time of this writing, most states have either adopted the *Uniform Real Property Electronic Recording Act* (*URPERA*) or introduced it for adoption by their state legislatures. The purpose of the Act is to provide legal authority for the electronic recording of real property documents and to establish the minimum standards for recording offices to follow, with each state retaining the authority to establish additional standards and safeguards on a statewide or countywide basis. The actual timetable for full implementation of the electronic recording of real property documents varies by county, so your local rules must be checked. Regardless of whether a county currently has implemented electronic recording, the public records in many states can be searched electronically for documents recorded manually or electronically.

Recording Statutes

Each state has statutory law, referred to as **recording statutes,** that prescribes the requirements for recording a document and determines the priority of rights to real property if there are conflicting claims. There are three types of recording statutes: (1) race statutes, (2) notice statutes, and (3) race-notice statutes. To understand the differences among these statutes, imagine a situation in which two parties are making a claim to a particular parcel of real property and

recording: Delivering a document to the appropriate government official for transcription into a plat book, deed book, mortgage book, or official records book.

constructive notice: Notice legally presumed because of the recording of documents in the public records.

actual notice: Direct knowledge a person has about the ownership and condition of title of real property.

recording statute: A statute that prescribes the requirements for recording a document and that determines the priority of rights to real property if there are conflicting claims.

both parties acquired the property from the same grantor. Further, imagine that both parties are bona fide purchasers for value. A **bona fide purchaser for value** is someone who purchases property in good faith and for valid consideration.

Race Statutes. Assuming the above scenario, in a state with a **race statute,** priority of claim to title of the property is determined literally by a race to record the deed. The first person to record his or her deed to the property is deemed to have superior title. For example, suppose Stanley is the owner of the subject property and he conveys the property to Karen by a deed on the 4th of January. Karen plans on recording the deed but does not get around to doing so until the 20th of January. In the interim, Stanley conveys the same property to Nicholas by a deed dated the 7th of January. Nicholas records the deed that same day. If both Karen and Nicholas are bona fide purchasers for value in a race statute state, Nicholas would have a superior claim to the property. The first to record the deed wins.

Notice Statutes. In a state with a **notice statute,** the notice a subsequent purchaser has of a previous purchaser's deed is controlling. Assume the same scenario with Stanley, Karen, and Nicholas, but add the fact that Nicholas had actual knowledge of Stanley's prior conveyance to Karen at the time Nicholas accepted delivery of his deed on the 7th of January. Because Nicholas had actual knowledge, in a state with a notice statute he is deemed to have been put on notice of Karen's claim, and Karen's claim is therefore considered superior to that of Nicholas.

Race-Notice Statutes. A **race-notice statute** is the most common form of notice statute, combining aspects of both theories. In a race-notice state, the premise is to protect a bona fide purchaser for value without notice if he or she is the first to record the deed. Thus, if the subsequent purchaser has no notice of a prior purchaser's claim and is the first to record his or her deed, this subsequent purchaser has priority.

The Torrens System

The **Torrens system** was invented by Sir Robert Torrens in the late nineteenth century and provides a unique method for determining title to real property through the institution of a lawsuit. The procedure commences when an applicant files an application with the court in which he or she makes a claim to title of the property and lists any other parties who have any interest in the property. A suit is brought in which all those listed are defendants and must defend their claims to title. If they fail to appear in court to defend their claims or if their claims are found to be inferior, the applicant is considered the proper titleholder, and the court orders the registrar of title to issue a certificate of title called a **Torrens certificate**, presenting title to the applicant. The Torrens certificate is the actual legal title to the property in states that still use this system. This certificate is then registered in the public records. When the property is transferred, the certificate is canceled, and a new certificate is issued to the transferee. Because this system is laborious and time-consuming, it is not widely used.

bona fide purchaser for value: Someone who purchases property in good faith and for valid consideration.

race statute: A recording statute whereby priority of claim to title of real property is determined literally by a race to record the deed.

notice statute: A recording statute whereby the notice a subsequent purchaser has of a previous purchaser's deed is determinative of the priority of title to the real property.

race-notice statute: A recording statute premised on protecting a bona fide purchaser for value without notice if he or she is the first to record the deed to real property.

Torrens system: A method for determining title to real property through the institution of a lawsuit.

Torrens certificate: In states that utilize the Torrens system, a certificate, issued by the registrar of title, that is the actual legal title to the real property.

Deed Fraud

Fraudulent transfers of title to real property have increased significantly nationwide in recent years. Perpetrators of deed fraud are aided by several factors: (1) the ease of access to public records, (2) the rise in identity theft, (3) the increased number of vacant properties, and (4) the lack of verification or authentication systems at time of recording deeds. These factors make it relatively simple to access the requisite information pertaining to the current owner(s) and the legal description of the property, draft a quitclaim deed that conveys the property from the current owner(s) to the perpetrator, and record the fraudulent deed. Often, the true property owners do not know of the fraudulent transfer until they go to sell the property or take out financing on the property. By the time the true property owners do find out, the perpetrator may have used the property to secure a loan or may have transferred title to the property to a third party.

Perpetrators of deed fraud can scout out properties and obtain the addresses of these properties. Then they can access the names of property owners and the legal descriptions of property through the public records. They also can ascertain if the property is encumbered by mortgage liens. Once they have very basic information pertaining to the owners, they can assume the owners' identities and create counterfeit forms of identification. This often is sufficient to then draft a quitclaim deed conveying the property from the "owners" to the grantee(s). As noted earlier in the chapter, grantees do not sign the deed; therefore, the perpetrators sign as the owners and convey the properties to themselves, to a corporation they have created for this purpose, or to "straw buyers." In areas of the country where mineral rights are a considerable component of a property's value, schemes to sell mineral rights to properties have arisen as well, using a fraudulent deed to convey the mineral rights rather than surface rights.

County recording offices may require personnel to run down a checklist of items to ascertain the legal sufficiency of a deed before recording, such as the inclusion of the parties' names, the legal description, the requisite number of witness signatures, and so forth. However, recording offices typically do not have procedures in place to authenticate documents, leaving the issue of authentication to notaries. Notaries must exercise due diligence in verifying the identities of the grantors, requiring that the grantors sign in the notary's physical presence and scrutinizing the presented forms of identification. Another wrinkle can surface when one of the grantors of concurrently owned property presents a power of attorney, purportedly from the other concurrent owner, giving him or her the right to sign the deed on the other owner's behalf. The best practice is to try to reach the other owner and verify that the power of attorney is valid. Notaries also should never notarize a document that has blank spaces that can be filled in after the fact, such as a deed that has a blank space where the legal description should be inserted. Finally, although a notary should exercise vigilance in keeping the notary seal secure from possible theft, some states are allowing the use of notary stamps rather than seals, which may be easier to counterfeit.

Some cities, counties, and states are implementing measures to combat deed fraud. For example, in Philadelphia, the records department has implemented a document notice program that informs real property owners, by mail, whenever a deed or mortgage is recorded against the property. The letter provides details of the transaction and allows the owners to verify the transaction or take action if the transaction is fraudulent. Similarly, in Miami-Dade County in Florida, the clerk of court recorder mails a courtesy letter to a property owner whenever a quitclaim deed is recorded against the property. The New York City Department of Finance has implemented a notice of recorded document program that requires property owners to register with the program. Once registered, the owners receive electronic notification when documents affecting an ownership interest in real property are recorded against the property. McLean County, Illinois, utilizes a combination of the above-mentioned measures. It permits a property owner to register for electronic notification whenever any document related to the property is filed. It also mails a postcard to a property owner when a quitclaim deed is filed.

Another type of deed fraud can occur that is perpetrated by the actual owner of a property. An owner may attempt to transfer legal title to real property to another with the intention of keeping the property out of the hands of creditors. Typically, the owner will transfer title to the property to another family member, a close friend, or a corporate entity out of the reach of creditors. The owner may later re-take title to the property or leave legal title in the name of the grantee but exercise possession of the property. Most states have adopted the *Uniform Fraudulent Transfer Act (UFTA)*. The purpose of this Act is to create a right of action for any creditor against a debtor of another who has received property from the debtor through a fraudulent transfer. A present creditor can recover the property when a debtor has transferred the property to an "insider" if the debtor is insolvent or becomes insolvent as a result of the transfer.

hypothetical client matter

Scott and Theresa Reed are selling their condominium in Fair Isles Village to Warren and Melissa Sloane. The Sloanes have been screened by the condominium association and have been approved. The Reeds have hired attorney Ava Ross to handle the real estate closing. According to the client file, the closing is to take place at the end of the week. Since everything seems to be on schedule, Ava has asked her paralegal, Barbara Hammond, to prepare the deed for review. Ava will be out of the office for the next two days and therefore would like to review the deed as soon as possible. Barbara consults the contract for sale and purchase, which indicates that the property is to be conveyed by general warranty deed. She checks the signatures of the grantees for proper spelling. She then consults a copy of the Reeds' current deed in the client file and notices that Scott's name includes the middle initial "P." She continues to review the deed for the legal description of the property as well as any encumbrances on the property. She notes an easement in favor of the Any State Power and Light Company as well as a reference to the Declaration of Condominium of Fair Isles Village. She then checks the title examination and notes a mortgage in favor of Hamilton Savings and Loan Association

that will be paid off at closing because the Sloanes have opted for a new mortgage loan rather than assuming the outstanding one. Her file notes indicate that the Sloanes are taking title as tenants by the entirety.

With this information in hand, Barbara locates her state's statutory general warranty deed on her computer. The signatures of two witnesses are required. Besides being a paralegal, Barbara is a notary public, and she will notarize the deed. Her completed deed is shown in Exhibit 8–9.

Barbara next refers back to the contract for sale and purchase to determine the purchase price of the condominium, which is stated in the contract as $250,000. The current documentary stamp tax rate in Any County is $.60 per each $100 or fraction thereof. Barbara divides the purchase price by 100 and then multiplies the resulting sum by $.60, arriving at a documentary stamp tax of $1,500. Finally, she pulls up on her computer screen the state department of revenue form and completes it as shown in Exhibit 8–10. This form provides evidence that the proper amount of documentary stamp tax has been calculated and paid.

As a final touch, Barbara places stickers on the sections of the form that must be filled in on the day of closing.

EXHIBIT 8–9   **Warranty deed**

This instrument prepared by:

Ava Ross, Esquire
Fisher, Ross, and Simon, P.A.
1900 N.W. 3rd Avenue
Any City, Any State

WARRANTY DEED

THIS INDENTURE, Made this _____ day of _____, 2015, by and between SCOTT P. REED and THERESA REED, husband and wife, hereinafter called Grantors, and WARREN SLOANE and MELISSA SLOANE, husband and wife, as tenants by the entirety, hereinafter called Grantees.

WITNESSETH, That said Grantors, for and in consideration of the sum of Ten Dollars ($10.00), and other good and valuable considerations to said Grantors in hand paid by said Grantees, the receipt whereof is hereby acknowledged, hereby grant, bargain, and sell to said Grantees the following described land, situate, lying and being in Any County, Any State, to wit:

Unit 301, of FAIR ISLES VILLAGE, a Condominium according to the Declaration of Condominium recorded in Official Records Book 2238, Page 170, of the Public Records of Any County, Any State.

SUBJECT TO an easement to Any State Power and Light Company dated September 6, 1997, recorded September 6, 1997 in Official Records Book 2030, Page 11, of the Public Records of Any County, Any State.

SUBJECT TO the Declaration of Condominium of Fair Isles Village, a Condominium, and Exhibits thereto recorded January 9, 2003 in Official Records Book 3065, Page 40, of the Public Records of Any County, Any State.

SUBJECT TO taxes for the current year and subsequent years.

TO HAVE AND TO HOLD the above described premises, unto the Grantees in fee simple forever, together with all the tenements, hereditaments, and appurtenances thereto belonging or in any wise appertaining.

AND the Grantors hereby covenant with the said Grantees that the Grantors are lawfully seized of said premises in fee simple; that the Grantors have good right and lawful authority to sell and convey said premises; that the Grantors fully warrant the title to said premises and will defend the same against the lawful claims of all persons whomsoever; and that said premises is free of all encumbrances, except those expressly stated herein.

IN WITNESS WHEREOF, the Grantors have signed and sealed these presents the day and year first above written.

Signed, sealed and delivered in our presence:

_____
SCOTT P. REED

_____
THERESA REED

STATE OF ANY STATE
COUNTY OF ANY COUNTY

I HEREBY CERTIFY that on this day before me, an officer duly qualified to take acknowledgments, personally appeared SCOTT P. REED and THERESA REED, husband and wife, to me known to be the persons described in and who executed the foregoing instrument, and they acknowledged before me that they executed the same.

WITNESS my hand and official seal in the County and State last aforesaid this _____ day of _____, 2015.

_____
Notary Public, State of Any State
My commission expires: _____

State department of revenue form   EXHIBIT 8-10

ANY STATE DEPARTMENT OF REVENUE
RETURN FOR TRANSFERS OF INTEREST IN REAL PROPERTY

1. Parcel Identification Number: 91219323455
2. Mark (x) all that apply:
   Multi-parcel transaction? ____ Transaction is a split or cutout from another parcel? ____
   Property was improved with building(s) at time of sale/transfer? _X_
3. Grantor: Scott P. Reed and Theresa Reed
   Mailing Address: 27 Windsor Court, Any City, Any State
   Phone: (000) 121-0908
4. Grantee: Warren Sloane and Melissa Sloane
   Mailing Address: 350 Fair Isles Lane, #301, Any City, Any State (000) 223-3239
5. Date of Sale/Transfer: July 20, 2015 Sale/Transfer Price: $250,000.00
   Property Located In: Any County
6. Type of Document: Warranty Deed _X_ Contract/Agreement for Deed ___
                        Quitclaim Deed ___ Other ___
7. Are there any mortgages on the property? Yes _X_ No ___
   If yes, outstanding mortgage balance: $200,000.00
8. To the best of your knowledge, were there unusual circumstances or conditions to the sale/transfer such as: Forced sale by court order? Foreclosure pending? Distress sale? Title defects? Corrective deed? Mineral rights? Sale of a partial or undivided interest? Related to seller by blood or marriage? Yes ___ No _X_
9. Was the sale/transfer financed? Yes _X_ No ___
   If yes, please indicate type or types of financing:
   Conventional _X_ Seller Provided ___ Agreement or Contract for Deed ___ Other ___
10. Property Type: Mark (x) all that apply:
   Residential _X_ Commercial ____ Industrial ____ Agricultural ____ Institutional/
   Miscellaneous ___ Government ___ Vacant ___ Acreage ___ Timeshare ___
11. To the best of your knowledge, was personal property included in the sale/transfer?
   Yes ___ No _X_
   If yes, please state the amount attributable to the personal property. $ _N/A_
12. Amount of Documentary Stamp Tax: $1,500.00
13. If no tax is due, is deed exempt from Documentary Stamp Tax under Any State statutes?
   Yes ___ No ___

Under penalties of perjury, I declare that I have read the foregoing return and that the facts stated in it are true. If prepared by someone other than the taxpayer, his/her declaration is based on all information of which he/she has any knowledge.
Signature of Grantor or Grantee or Agent: _____ Date: _____

To be completed by the Clerk of the Circuit Court's Office   Clerk's Date Stamp
O.R. Book ____ Page Number ____ File Number ____
Date Recorded _____

CHAPTER SUMMARY

1. A valid deed includes the names and current statuses of the grantor and grantee, the date of execution, a recital of consideration, words of conveyance, a legal description of the property, the signatures of the grantor and witnesses, and an acknowledgment. In addition, some states require the inclusion of other items such as the property appraiser's parcel identification

number and/or the addresses of one or both parties. A deed must be delivered to the grantee for a proper conveyance.

2. Extra care should be taken in the spelling of the parties' names, the typing of the legal description, and the inclusion of all pertinent restrictions. Should an error come to light after a deed is signed and recorded, a corrective deed must be prepared, indicating and correcting the error.

3. Documentary stamp tax must be paid at the time of recording. This is a transfer tax on the transfer of the real property. The tax is based on the purchase price of the property.

4. All deeds contain a premises clause, a granting clause, a habendum clause, and a testimonium clause. These first three clauses specify the parties, the date of execution, the words of conveyance, and the type of estate being conveyed. The testimonium clause includes the signatures of the grantor and the witnesses as well as the acknowledgment. Depending on the type of deed used and the nature of the transaction, other clauses may be added.

5. A general warranty deed provides the greatest protection for the grantee. It includes the covenant of seisin, the covenant against encumbrances, the covenant of quiet enjoyment, the covenant of further assurances, and the covenant of warranty forever. Through conveyance of property by a general warranty deed, the grantor is promising to forever defend the grantee's title against any and all claims.

6. A special warranty deed is limited in the number of covenants made by the grantor to the grantee. The grantor of a special warranty deed is warranting only that he or she has done nothing to encumber the property but makes no statements of warranty regarding the actions of prior titleholders.

7. Neither a bargain and sale deed nor a quitclaim deed contains convenants guaranteeing good title. A bargain and sale deed simply transfers property, not any particular interest in the property. A quitclaim deed transfers only whatever interest the grantor has in the property, if any, and thus makes no representations regarding the quality of title.

8. There are a number of preliminary steps that should be taken prior to drafting a deed. State statutes should be consulted to determine state requirements for the content of the deed and whether the use of statutory deed forms is mandated. The grantor's current deed should be examined for correct spelling of the grantor's name, for the legal description, and for the listing of any encumbrances. An updated title examination should be consulted for encumbrances not listed with particularity in the current deed. Finally, the contract for sale and purchase should be reviewed to ascertain the type of deed required, the closing date, and the correct spelling of the grantee's name.

9. The recording of documents such as deeds, mortgages, and other liens puts the public on constructive notice of the existence of these documents. Each state has its own recording statutes prescribing the requirements for recording documents and determining the priority of adverse claims. State recording statutes are race statutes, notice statutes, or race-notice statutes, each of which has its own method of determining the priority of rights to real property.

10. Deed fraud has increased in recent years, aided by the following factors: (1) the ease of access to public records, (2) the rise in identity theft, (3) the increased number of vacant properties, and (4) the lack of verification or authentication systems at time of recording deeds. Some cities, counties, and states have instituted measures to notify property owners whenever a document affecting title to real property is recorded against their property.

11. Most states have adopted the Uniform Fraudulent Transfer Act (UFTA), which provides creditors with legal remedies if a property owner transfers title to real property to another for the purpose of keeping the property out of the hands of creditors.

WEB RESOURCES

http://www.lectlaw.com/

This is the site of The 'Lectric Law Library.' You can access free, generic quitclaim deed forms by selecting "Free Legal Forms" under "Some Main Rooms" and then selecting "Business & General Forms."

http://www.uniformlaws.org/

This is the site of the National Conference of Commissioners on Uniform State Laws. Here you can access the Uniform Real Property Electronic Recording Act (URPERA) and the Uniform Fraudulent Transfer Act (UFTA).

http://www.ilrg.com/

This is the site of the Internet Legal Research Group. It features a large archive of legal forms that may be downloaded for a fee. These forms may be viewed free of charge. If you click on the "ILRG Legal Forms Archive" link and then choose "Leases and Real Estate," you can review a quitclaim deed and a warranty deed.

http://publicrecords.onlinesearches.com/

This site provides access to various public records. You can search by choosing either the type of record or the state, allowing you to search property information contained in county and state public records.

REVIEW QUESTIONS

1. Distinguish between the following:
   a. A general warranty deed and a special warranty deed
   b. A bargain and sale deed and a quitclaim deed
2. Name and explain each of the covenants contained in a general warranty deed.
3. Outline the steps to be taken:
   a. Prior to the actual drafting of a deed
   b. During the actual drafting of a deed
   c. After the drafting of a deed
4. Compare and contrast a race statute, a notice statute, and a race-notice statute.

DISCUSSION QUESTIONS

1. You have been searching the title of a particular parcel of property as part of the pre-closing procedures and notice that a deed recorded in 1977 indicates in the encumbrance clause that the property can be used only for residential purposes. Back then, the zoning for the area was strictly residential. In 1998, the zoning was changed to mixed usage (residential and commercial). Do you think this deed restriction is still valid? It is not illegal to impose this type of restriction, yet it does limit the usage of the property and thus its potential value. What suggestions do you have for handling this situation?

2. Do you think there should be a requirement of full disclosure of the true purchase price on all deeds? Why or why not?

3. Loretta Long is eighty-seven years of age and has chronic medical problems. She also has frequent memory lapses, although it has not been determined that she has Alzheimer's. She owns a small home but her daughter, Lisa, believes she should be placed in an assisted living facility. Loretta really does not want to move into such a facility and calls them "death houses," but Lisa has scared her into it, saying that there is no money to take care of her at home and she will fall down one day and die with no one hearing her cries for help. Lisa has found a buyer for the house and has discussed this with her mother, but Loretta has a short attention span and sometimes forgets what she has been told. Do you think Loretta should be allowed to sign the deed? Why or why not? If not, is there another solution to moving forward with the sale of the property?

4. Six years ago, Mrs. Patterson entered into a contract to purchase a parcel of real property from Mr. Chase. The contract lists Mrs. Patterson as the sole purchaser. Two months later, at closing, Mrs. Patterson executed, in her name alone, a note payable to ABC, Inc., which had provided the financing for the purchase. The closing attorney informed Mrs. Patterson that her then-estranged husband, Mr. Patterson, would have to sign a mortgage in favor of ABC, Inc., so that his homestead rights would be waived as to the mortgage lien of ABC, Inc. A mortgage instrument was prepared that listed both Mr. and Mrs. Patterson as mortgagors, and both of them signed the instrument. The closing attorney's paralegal, who prepared the deed, inadvertently listed both Mr. and Mrs. Patterson as grantees. The error was not detected until several weeks later when the deed was returned to Mrs. Patterson after being recorded in the county clerk's office. The error was then brought to the attention of Mr. Chase, and a corrective deed was prepared, listing only Mrs. Patterson as grantee. This deed was properly executed and recorded a month after the original deed was recorded. Mrs. Patterson now wants to bring a court action seeking reformation of the original deed, alleging that Mr. Patterson had liens recorded against the property, including a lien in favor of the State Department of Revenue. The Department of Revenue is arguing that during the period while the original deed was recorded, Mr. Patterson had an interest in the property to which the state's tax lien could attach and that the state's tax lien takes priority over any right to reformation. If this goes to court, which party should win, and why?

5. Mrs. Benson's will was admitted to probate five years ago. In her will, she devised a parcel of property to her son, Donald Benson. While her estate was going through the probate process, Donald Benson conveyed the property to

Brenda Conway by a quitclaim deed. The deed was dated June 10 four years ago but was not recorded at that time. Approximately two years later, Donald Benson entered into an option agreement with Mark Ford by which he granted Mark Ford an option to purchase the property. The quitclaim deed to Brenda Conway was recorded on July 18 two years ago at 10:30 a.m., and the option agreement was executed on that same date at 3:30 p.m. Two months later, the personal representative of Donald's mother's estate executed a personal representative's deed prepared by Mark Ford's attorney conveying the property to Donald Benson, the deed stating that Donald's mother died testate, stating the date her estate was admitted to probate, stating that the grantor was appointed personal representative and was acting in that capacity, and stating that the deed was a deed of distribution according to the terms of the will. A week later, Donald Benson executed a deed conveying the property to Mark Ford. The deed was recorded three days later. Assume this all transpired in your state. According to your state's law, who is the legal owner of the property? Why?

6. If your county's recording office was seeking to implement measures to combat deed fraud, what recommendations would you suggest? How effective do you believe the measures taken by the cities and counties mentioned in the text are in combating this problem?

ETHICAL QUESTION

You have just assisted in a closing on a large, commercially zoned tract of land purchased by your firm's client, Talbott Industries, Inc. Talbott Industries is a large pharmaceutical company and is planning on moving its headquarters from its present location to your city. Approximately seven thousand people will be employed at this new location once Talbott constructs its plant on the acquired property. Thus far, the only people with knowledge of these plans are the parties directly involved in the real estate closing transaction. Talbott is planning on making a public announcement after the annual meeting of its shareholders at the beginning of next month.

This afternoon, another client, Jim Campbell, president of Campbell Construction Company, has an appointment with your supervising attorney to discuss a possible land acquisition. Campbell Construction Company specializes in moderately priced residential developments and, at the present time, is considering the acquisition of one of three land tracts for a new development project, each in a different area of the city. One of the tracts being considered is very close to the future Talbott headquarters. You know that a moderately priced residential development would be a great success in that location because of the number of new families that will be transferring from the present Talbott headquarters to its new location. Jim Campbell tells your supervising attorney that he is coming close to signing a contract on one of the other tracts of land, and he wants her to review the seller's proposed contract. What should you do?

Slossberg Law Office on CourseMate

Please go to www.cengagebrain.com to log into CourseMate, access the Slossberg Law Office, and work on your client files. Each module corresponds to a chapter in the text. Within each module, you will be provided with instructions by the supervising attorney. You are asked to keep track of time spent on time sheets. The documents produced through working on client files in the law office can then be compiled into a portfolio of final work product.

CourseMate

The available CourseMate for this text has an interactive eBook and interactive learning tools, including flash cards, quizzes, and more. To learn more about this resource and access free demo CourseMate resources, including the Slossberg Law Office, go to www.cengagebrain.com, and search for this book. To access CourseMate materials that you have purchased, go to login.cengagebrain.com.

Liens on Property

9

CHAPTER OBJECTIVES

Upon completion of this chapter, the student will:

- Understand the distinction between general and specific liens

- Understand the way construction liens work and the various steps that may be required to perfect a construction lien

- Know the priority status of various lien claimants

- Understand the distinction between a lien and a lis pendens

Introduction

A *lien* is a claim against property that secures a debt incurred by the property owner. A lien acts as an *encumbrance* on property because it is an interest in property that diminishes the property's value. A lien allows a *lienholder*, also referred to as a *lienor,* to request a court order to force the sale of property to satisfy, or partially satisfy, the outstanding debt.

Lien rights can be created voluntarily, such as when a prospective purchaser of real property takes out a mortgage loan and, in return for the borrowed money, gives the lending institution a mortgage that attaches to the real property until the borrowed monies plus agreed-upon interest are paid back. The mortgage instrument is considered a voluntary lien because it is created by the purchaser voluntarily entering into the loan transaction and signing the mortgage instrument.

Additionally, lien rights can be created involuntarily, as with *statutory liens* (created by state statute), including construction liens and real property tax liens. The lienor is given a statutory right to attach and foreclose upon certain property if debts are not paid—in this instance, monies due to persons improving real property or monies due to the local government for real property taxes.

Liens can also be categorized as general liens and specific liens. A **general lien** is one that is not secured by any particular parcel of real property and therefore may affect all nonexempt property of a debtor. An example of a general lien is a lien for federal estate taxes. If these taxes are not paid, the U.S. government may go after any nonexempt property of the decedent's estate, wherever it is located, as full or partial satisfaction of the debt. Thus, the government may force the sale of a home, a car, a boat, and so forth.

general lien: A lien that is not secured by any particular parcel of real property and that therefore may affect all nonexempt property of a debtor.

specific lien: A lien that is secured by a particular parcel of real property.

monetary judgment: An award of monies to a plaintiff if he or she wins a lawsuit.

declaratory judgment: A judgment sought when the parties to a lawsuit want a judicial decree on their status and rights with regard to a particular matter.

A **specific lien** is one that is secured by a particular parcel of real property. An example of a specific lien is a special assessment lien. As discussed in detail in Chapter 4, property owners are charged for special improvements in their neighborhood that enhance their property value, such as the installation of sidewalks or sewer hookups. If the charges are not paid, a real property owner may have a special assessment lien recorded against his or her real property. The lienholder cannot go after other property of the debtor, however, because the lien attaches to the real property itself, not to the debtor.

As a paralegal working in the area of real estate law, you may be asked by your supervising attorney to assist in the enforcement of a judgment or construction lien for a firm client, to draft a satisfaction of mortgage or writ of attachment, or to file a notice of lis pendens. This chapter will discuss various general and specific liens that are encumbrances on real property, the manner in which each type of lien attaches, and each lien's priority status in the lien hierarchy. Special focus is placed on construction liens, for they are the most complex of liens in terms of statutory regulation and enforcement. The chapter concludes with a discussion of writs of attachment and notices of lis pendens.

Judgment Liens

A *judgment* is a final decree of a court resolving a dispute and determining the rights and obligations of the respective parties. A court can be asked to award a monetary judgment or a declaratory judgment. A **monetary judgment** is an award of monies to a plaintiff if he or she wins the lawsuit. A **declaratory judgment** is one that is sought when the parties want a judicial decree on their status and rights with regard to a particular matter.

When a money judgment is issued in favor of a plaintiff in a lawsuit, the plaintiff becomes a *judgment creditor* of the defendant (*judgment debtor*), who is now indebted to the plaintiff for the amount stated in the judgment award. If the defendant fails to pay the plaintiff according to the terms of the court award, the plaintiff, as creditor, may have legal recourse to force the sale of the plaintiff's property to satisfy the debt. Because the amount of debt, if any, owed by the defendant to the plaintiff is undetermined prior to a court determination, the plaintiff has no collateral for the alleged debt. Once a judgment has been awarded in the plaintiff's favor, the plaintiff can look to both the real and the personal property of the defendant. Thus, a judgment lien is a general lien.

A judgment award in and of itself is not the lien. For a judgment to become a lien and attach to real property, a certified copy of the judgment must be recorded in a *judgment docket*, a *judgment register*, or, in some counties, the *official records book* in the county in which the real property is located. This is true even if the county in which the property is located is the same county as the one in which the judgment was rendered by the court.

For example, suppose David Holmes brought suit against Jack Alexander in a personal injury action in the County of Any County and was successful. The jury returned a judgment in David's favor in the amount of $100,000. The judgment is recorded in the public records by the clerk of the civil court. Jack has some income property located in Any County. If David wants to proceed against this property to satisfy the $100,000 award, David must obtain a certified copy of the judgment from the clerk and record it as a judgment lien in the judgment docket or register. If a plaintiff wishes to proceed against property located outside the court's jurisdiction, the plaintiff must obtain a certified copy of the judgment and have it recorded in the other counties in which the defendant has property.

To enforce a judgment lien, the plaintiff must have the court issue a **writ of execution** which directs the sheriff to levy upon the property and sell it at a sheriff's sale. The proceeds of the sale are used to pay the plaintiff the monies owed to him or her and to pay for the expenses incurred in the execution process. Any surplus from the sale is returned to the defendant.

State statutes dictate the priority date of judgment liens. In most states, a judgment lien's priority in regard to a particular parcel of real property is established by the date of the recording of the lien in the county in which the parcel is located. In some states, priority status is determined not by the date of recording but rather by the date the court entered the judgment. In still other states, priority status is determined by the date of issuance of the writ of execution. Once a judgment lien is recorded, it remains a lien against real property until the debt is paid or the statute of limitations expires. If the defendant pays the court award, plus any accrued interest, a **satisfaction of judgment** must be recorded to evidence the satisfaction of the debt and the removal of the encumbrance from the property.

In the earlier example, if David records a judgment lien against Jack's income property and Jack then sells the property to Oscar Addison, Oscar takes title to the property subject to the lien. Thus, Oscar must pay off the lien or take the risk of having a writ of execution issued and the property levied against. If Oscar had researched, or had his attorney or a title company research, the title to the property prior to closing on it, he would have been aware of the judgment lien, and he would have elected either to have Jack clear the title by satisfying the debt and recording a satisfaction of judgment or to not proceed with the closing. A sample judgment and satisfaction of judgment are provided in Exhibits 9–1 and 9–2, respectively.

State statutes determine what property is exempt by law from forced sale. In some states, homestead property is exempted totally from forced sale to satisfy a judgment. In other states, a statutorily specified dollar amount of the value of the homestead property, or of the debtor's equity in the homestead property, is exempt from creditors. Therefore, if homestead property was totally exempt in Jack's state, David would be prevented from proceeding against Jack's home, but he would not be prevented from proceeding against other property, such as the income property owned by Jack in the above example.

If a judgment creditor does file a lien against homestead property in a state that provides homestead protection, the owner of the homestead property should file a *notice, declaration,* or *affidavit of homestead,* providing the notice required by state statute. In some states, the judgment creditor then has a statutory period within which to challenge the homestead status of the property, and if no challenge is made within the statutory time period or if the challenge is unsuccessful, the lien is deemed not to attach to the homestead property.

One development that has occurred as a result of the recent real estate market is the renting of homestead property to tenants to aid in defraying the financing costs and forestall foreclosure or to hold onto the property until property values rise. A homestead owner may jeopardize homestead status in so doing, for state statutes may require that the owner live in the premises continuously or during each year in which a homestead exemption is claimed. If a judgment creditor files a judgment lien against the property and the property owner is not living in it, the

writ of execution: A court order that directs the sheriff to levy upon real property and sell it at a sheriff's sale.

satisfaction of judgment: A document recorded to evidence the satisfaction of a debt and the removal of an encumbrance from real property.

EXHIBIT 9–1   **Final judgment**

**IN THE CIRCUIT COURT OF THE NINTH JUDICIAL CIRCUIT,
IN AND FOR ANY COUNTY, ANY STATE**

DAVID HOLMES,   CASE NO. 15-12345 GORDON
   Plaintiff,

vs.

JACK ALEXANDER,
   Defendant.

_____/

FINAL JUDGMENT

THIS CAUSE coming on to be heard before the Honorable Christine Gordon and a jury who, having been first duly sworn according to law, returned in open Court the following verdict, to wit:

"WE, THE JURY, find in favor of the Plaintiff, DAVID HOLMES, and against the Defendant, JACK ALEXANDER, and assess the damages of the Plaintiff, DAVID HOLMES, in the amount of One Hundred Thousand Dollars ($100,000.00).

SO SAY WE ALL.

                                            /s/ James McGee
                                            Foreman

DATE: May 17, 2015"

IT IS, THEREFORE, ORDERED AND ADJUDGED that Final Judgment be, and it is hereby entered, in said cause in favor of the Plaintiff, DAVID HOLMES, and against the Defendant, JACK ALEXANDER; and the Plaintiff, DAVID HOLMES, shall have and recover from said Defendant the sum of ONE HUNDRED THOUSAND DOLLARS ($100,000.00), lawful money of the United States of America, for which sum let execution issue; each party to bear their own costs.

   DONE AND ORDERED in Chambers at Any City, Any County, Any State, this 17th day of May, 2015.

                                         Christine Gordon
                                         Circuit Judge

property may no longer qualify as homestead property, and the lien may attach. Therefore, caution should be exercised before moving out of homestead property and moving renters in.

Note that even in states that provide homestead protection from judgment liens, homestead property is not protected from all types of liens. Many of the liens discussed below, such as tax liens, mortgage liens, construction liens, and any lien to which a property owner agrees by accepting the property subject to codes or covenants and restrictions (i.e., condominium liens or homeowners' association liens) may attach to homestead property.

Tax Liens

Federal, state, and local governments can attach liens to private property if a taxpayer fails to pay taxes in a timely manner. These tax liens can include liens for failure to pay federal and state income taxes, federal and state estate and inheritance taxes, intangible taxes, corporate franchise taxes, business-related taxes, and real property taxes. All of these taxes except the last one, real property taxes, are general liens.

**IN THE CIRCUIT COURT OF THE NINTH JUDICIAL CIRCUIT,
IN AND FOR ANY COUNTY, ANY STATE**

DAVID HOLMES,   CASE NO. 15-12345 GORDON
  Plaintiff,
vs.
JACK ALEXANDER,
  Defendant.

_____/

SATISFACTION OF JUDGMENT

  KNOW ALL MEN BY THESE PRESENTS: That I, DAVID HOLMES, the Plaintiff in the above-styled cause, wherein a judgment was rendered on the 17th day of May 2015, in the above-named court for ONE HUNDRED THOUSAND DOLLARS ($100,000.00) against JACK ALEXANDER, the Defendant therein, and judgment being duly recorded in the minutes of said Court and a copy thereof having been recorded in Official Records Book 147157, Page 288, of the Public Records of Any County, Any State, do hereby acknowledge full payment and satisfaction thereof and hereby consent that the same shall be satisfied of record.

  WITNESS my hand and seal this 15th day of August, 2015.

Signed, sealed, and delivered in the presence of:

_____   _____
Jean Karney   David Holmes

_____
Deborah Portman

STATE OF ANY STATE
COUNTY OF ANY COUNTY

  On this 15th day of August, 2015, personally appeared before me David Holmes and acknowledged that he executed the foregoing Satisfaction of Judgment for the purposes therein expressed.
  WITNESS my hand and seal the day and year last above written

_____
Notary Public, State of Any State
My commission expires: _____

Federal tax liens attach to all property of the debtor, including property that may be exempt from judgment liens, such as homestead property. A federal tax lien's priority is based on the date of its recording. According to federal statute, federal tax liens are valid for ten years and thirty days from the date of assessment unless the lien is refiled during that time period. Note that the date of assessment is different than the date of recording of the lien.

A federal tax lien will indicate the name and address of the delinquent taxpayer, the kind(s) of taxes owing, the pertinent tax period(s), the date(s) of assessment, identifying number(s), and the unpaid balance of the assessment(s). A *tax sale* is held after a notice of tax sale is published in a newspaper of general circulation in the county in which the real property to be sold is located. The purchaser of the property must pay, at a minimum, the amount of the delinquent tax, any accrued penalties, and court costs. The delinquent taxpayer is given the **equitable right of redemption,** which is the right to buy back the property at any time prior to the tax sale by paying the full amount of the tax owed and all additional charges. In some states, the delinquent taxpayer may redeem the property even after a tax sale by paying the amount paid at the tax sale, plus any additional interest and charges. This right, if granted, is a statutory right and is known as the *statutory right of redemption.*

Recall from Chapter 2 that when property is held as a tenancy by the entirety, the law creates a legal fiction that each spouse owns 100 percent of the real property. As such, the property is deemed exempt from the reach of creditors who are creditors of only one spouse. However, in 2002, the U.S. Supreme Court challenged this concept with regard to Internal Revenue Service (IRS) tax liens in the case of *United States v. Craft,* which follows.

equitable right of redemption: The right to buy back real property at any time prior to a forced sale by paying the full amount of the debt owed and all additional charges.

CASE: *United States v. Craft*
535 U.S. 274, 122 S. Ct. 1414, 152 L. Ed. 2d 437 (2002)

Justice O'CONNOR delivered the opinion of the Court.

This case raises the question whether a tenant by the entirety possesses "property" or "rights to property" to which a federal tax lien may attach. 26 U.S.C. §6321. Relying on the state law fiction that a tenant by the entirety has no separate interest in entireties property, the United States Court of Appeals for the Sixth Circuit held that such property is exempt from the tax lien. We conclude that, despite the fiction, each tenant possesses individual rights in the estate sufficient to constitute "property" or "rights to property" for the purposes of the lien, and reverse the judgment of the Court of Appeals.

I

In 1988, the Internal Revenue Service (IRS) assessed $482,446 in unpaid income tax liabilities against Don Craft, the husband of respondent Sandra L. Craft, for failure to file federal income tax returns for the years 1979 through 1986. App. to Pet. for Cert. 45a, 72a. When he failed to pay, a federal tax lien attached to "all property and rights to property, whether real or personal, belonging to" him. 26 U.S.C. §6321.

At the time the lien attached, respondent and her husband owned a piece of real property in Grand Rapids, Michigan, as tenants by the entirety. App. to Pet. for Cert. 45a. After notice of the lien was filed, they jointly executed a quitclaim deed purporting to transfer the husband's interest in the property to respondent for one dollar. *Ibid.* When respondent attempted to sell the property a few years later, a title search revealed the lien. The IRS agreed to release the lien and allow the sale with the stipulation that half of the net proceeds be held in escrow pending determination of the Government's interest in the property. *Ibid.*

Respondent brought this action to quiet title to the escrowed proceeds. The Government claimed that its lien had attached to the husband's interest in the tenancy by the entirety. It further asserted that the transfer of the property to respondent was invalid as a fraud on creditors. *Id.* at 46a–47a. The District Court granted the Government's motion for summary judgment, holding that the federal tax lien attached at the moment of the transfer to respondent, which terminated the tenancy by the entirety and entitled the Government to one-half of the value of the property. No. 1:93-CV-306, 1994 WL 669680, 3 W.D. Mich., Sept. 12, 1994.

Both parties appealed. The Sixth Circuit held that the tax lien did not attach to the property because under Michigan state law, the husband had no separate interest in the property held as a tenant by the entirety. 140 F.3d 638, 643 (C.A.6 1998). It remanded to the District Court to consider the Government's alternative claim that the conveyance should be set aside as fraudulent. *Id.* at 644.

On remand, the District Court concluded that where, as here, state law makes property exempt from the claims of creditors, no fraudulent conveyance can occur. 65 F. Supp. 2d 651, 657–658 (W.D. Mich.999). It found, however, that respondent's husband's use of nonexempt funds to pay the mortgage on the entireties property, which placed them beyond the reach of creditors, constituted a fraudulent act under state law, and the court awarded the IRS a share of the proceeds of the sale of the property equal to that amount. *Id.* at 659.

Both parties appealed the District Court's decision, the Government again claiming that its lien attached to the husband's interest in the entireties property. The Court of Appeals held that the prior panel's opinion was law of the case on that issue. 233 F.3d 358, 363–369 (C.A.6 2000). It also affirmed the District Court's determination that the husband's mortgage payments were fraudulent. *Id.* at 369–375.

(continued)

We granted certiorari to consider the Government's claim that respondent's husband had a separate interest in the entireties property to which the federal tax lien attached. 533 U.S. 976, 122 S.Ct. 23, 150 L.Ed.2d 804 (2001).

II

Whether the interests of respondent's husband in the property he held as a tenant by the entirety constitutes "property and rights to property" for the purposes of the federal tax lien statute, 26 U.S.C. §6321, is ultimately a question of federal law. The answer to this federal question, however, largely depends upon state law. The federal tax lien statute itself "creates no property rights but merely attaches consequences, federally defined, to rights created under state law." *United States v. Bess*, 357 U.S. 51, 55, 78 S.Ct. 1054, 2 L.Ed.2d 1135 (1958); see also *United States v. National Bank of Commerce*, 472 U.S. 713, 722, 105 S.Ct. 2919, 86 L.Ed.2d 565 (1985). Accordingly, "[w]e look initially to state law to determine what rights the taxpayer has in the property the Government seeks to reach, then to federal law to determine whether the taxpayer's state-delineated rights qualify as 'property' or 'rights to property' within the compass of the federal tax lien legislation." *Drye v. United States*, 528 U.S. 49, 58, 120 S.Ct. 474, 145 L.Ed.2d 466 (1999).

*   *   *

III

We turn first to the question of what rights respondent's husband had in the entireties property by virtue of state law. In order to understand these rights, the tenancy by the entirety must first be placed in some context.

*   *   *

A tenancy by the entirety is a unique sort of concurrent ownership that can only exist between married persons. 4 Thomson §33.02. Because of the common-law fiction that the husband and wife were one person at law (that person, practically speaking, was the husband, see J. Cribbet et al., *Cases and Materials on Property* 329 (6th ed. 1990), Blackstone did not characterize the tenancy by the entirety as a form of concurrent ownership at all. Instead, he thought that the entireties property was a form of single ownership by the marital unity. Orth, "Tenancy by the Entirety: The Strange Career of the Common-Law Marital Estate," 1997 B.Y.U. L. Rev. 35, 38–39. Neither spouse was considered to own any individual interest in the estate; rather, it belonged to the couple.

*   *   *

. . . Michigan's version of the estate is typical of the modern tenancy by the entirety. Following Blackstone, Michigan characterizes its tenancy by the entirety as creating no individual rights whatsoever. "It is well settled under the law of this State that one tenant by the entirety has no interest separable from that of the other. . . . Each is vested with an entire title." *Long v. Earle*, 277 Mich. 505, 517, 269 N.W. 577, 581 (1936). And yet, in Michigan, each tenant by the entirety possesses the right of survivorship. Mich. Comp. Laws Ann. §554.872(g) (West Supp. 1997), recodified at §700.2901(2)(g) (West Supp. Pamphlet 2001). Each spouse—the wife as well as the husband—may also use the property, exclude third parties from it, and receive an equal share of the income produced by it. See §557.71 (West 1988). Neither spouse may unilaterally alienate or encumber the property. *Long v. Earle, supra,* at 517, 269 N.W. at 581; *Rogers v. Rogers*, 136 Mich. App. 125, 134, 356 N.W.2d 288, 292 (1984), although this may be accomplished with mutual consent, *Eadus v. Hunter*, 249 Mich. 190, 228 N.W. 782 (1930). Divorce ends the tenancy by the entirety, generally giving each spouse an equal interest in the property as a tenant in common, unless the divorce decree specifies otherwise. Mich. Comp. Laws Ann §552.102 (West 1988).

In determining whether respondent's husband possessed "property" or "rights to property" within the meaning of 26 U.S.C. §6321, we look to the individual rights created by these state law rules. According to Michigan law, respondent's husband had, among other rights, the following rights with respect to the property: the right to use the property, the right to exclude third parties from it, the right to a share of income produced from it, the right of survivorship, the right to become a tenant in common with equal shares upon divorce, the right to sell the property with the respondent's consent and to receive half the proceeds from such a sale, the right to place an encumbrance on the property with the respondent's consent, and the right to block respondent from selling or encumbering the property unilaterally.

IV

We turn now to the federal question of whether the rights Michigan law granted to respondent's husband as a tenant by the entirety qualify as "property" or "rights to property" under §6321. The statutory language authorizing the tax lien "is broad and reveals on its face that Congress meant to reach every interest in property that a taxpayer might have." *United States v. National Bank of Commerce*, 472 U.S., at 719–720, 105 S.Ct. 2919. "Stronger language could hardly have been selected to reveal a purpose to assure the collection of taxes." *Glass City Bank v. United States*, 326 U.S. 265, 267, 66 S.Ct. 108, 90 L.Ed. 56 (1945). We conclude that the husband's rights in the entireties property fall within this broad statutory language.

Michigan law grants a tenant by the entirety some of the most essential property rights: the right to use the property, to receive income produced by it, and to exclude others from it. See *Dolan v. City of Tigard*, 512 U.S. 374, 384, 114 S.Ct. 2309, 129 L.Ed.2d 304 (1994). . . .

The husband's right in the estate, however, went beyond use, exclusion, and income. He also possessed the right

(continued)

to alienate (or otherwise encumber) the property with the consent of the respondent, his wife. *Loretto, supra,* at 435, 102 S.Ct. 3164 (the right to "dispose" of an item is a property right). It is true, as respondent notes, that he lacked the right to unilaterally alienate the property, a right that is often in the bundle of property rights. See also *post*, at 1429–1430 (THOMAS, J., dissenting). There is no reason to believe, however, that this one stick—the right of unilateral alienation—is essential to the category of "property."

This Court has already stated that federal tax liens may attach to property that cannot be unilaterally alienated. In *United States v. Rodgers*, 461 U.S. 677, 103 S.Ct. 2132, 76 L.Ed.2d 236 (1983), we considered the Federal Government's power to foreclose homestead property attached by a federal tax lien. Texas law provided that "the owner or claimant of the property claimed as homestead [may not], if married, sell or abandon the homestead without the consent of the other spouse." *Id.*, at 684–685, 103 S.Ct. 2132 (quoting Tex. Const., Art. 16 §50). . . .

Excluding property from a federal tax lien simply because the taxpayer does not have the power to unilaterally alienate it would, moreover, exempt a rather large amount of what is commonly thought of as property. It would exempt not only the type of property discussed in *Rodgers*, but also some community property. Community property states often provide that real community property cannot be alienated without the consent of both spouses. . . .

*   *   *

That the rights of respondent's husband in the entireties property constitute "property" or "rights to property" "belonging to" him is further underscored by the fact that if the conclusion were otherwise, the entireties property would belong to no one for the purposes of §6321. Respondent had no more interest in the property than her husband; if neither of them had a property interest in the entireties property, who did? This result not only seems absurd, but would also allow spouses to shield their property from federal taxation by classifying it as entireties property, facilitating abuse of the federal tax system. Johnson, "After *Drye*: The Likely Attachment of the Federal Taxation Lien to Tenancy-by-the-Entireties Interests," 75 Ind. L.J. 1163, 1171 (2000).

*   *   *

We therefore conclude that respondent's husband's interest in the entireties property constituted "property" or "rights to property" for the purposes of the federal tax lien statute. We recognize that Michigan makes a different choice with respect to state law creditors: "[L]and held by husband and wife as tenants by the entirety is not subject to levy under execution on judgment rendered against either husband or wife alone." *Sanford v. Bertrau*, 204 Mich. 244, 247, 169 N.W. 880, 881 (1918). But that

by no means dictates our choice. The interpretation of 26 U.S.C. §6321 is a federal question, and in answering that question we are in no way bound by state courts' answers to similar questions involving state law. As we elsewhere have held, "'exempt status under state law does not bind the federal collector.'" *Drye v. United States*, 528 U.S., at 59, 120 S.Ct. 474. See also *Rodgers, supra*, at 701, 103 S.Ct. 2132 (clarifying that the Supremacy Clause "provides the underpinning for the Federal Government's right to sweep aside state-created exemptions").

V

We express no view as to the proper valuation of respondent's husband's interest in the entireties property, leaving this for the Sixth Circuit to determine on remand. We note, however, that insofar as the amount is dependent upon whether the 1989 conveyance was fraudulent, see *post*, at 1426, n.1 (THOMAS, J., dissenting), this case is somewhat anomalous. The Sixth Circuit affirmed the District Court's judgment that this conveyance was not fraudulent, and the Government has not sought certiorari review of that determination. Since the District Court's judgment was based on the notion that, because the federal tax lien could not attach to the property, transferring it could not constitute an attempt to evade the Government creditor, 65 F. Supp. 2d, at 657–659, in future cases, the fraudulent conveyance question will no doubt be answered differently.

The judgment of the United States Court of Appeals for the Sixth Circuit is accordingly reversed, and the case is remanded for proceedings consistent with this opinion.

It is so ordered.

Justice SCALIA, with whom Justice THOMAS joins, dissenting.

I join Justice THOMAS's dissent, which points out (to no relevant response from the Court) that a State's decision to treat the marital partnership as a separate legal entity, whose property cannot be encumbered by the debts of its individual members, is no more novel and no more "artificial" than a State's decision to treat the commercial partnership as a separate legal entity, whose property cannot be encumbered by the debts of its individual members.

I write separately to observe that the Court nullifies (insofar as federal taxes are concerned, at least) a form of property ownership that was of particular benefit to the stay-at-home spouse or mother. She is overwhelmingly likely to be the survivor that obtains title to the unencumbered property; and she (as opposed to her business world husband) is overwhelmingly unlikely to be the source of the individual indebtedness against which a tenancy by the entirety protects. It is regrettable that the Court has eliminated a large part of this traditional protection retained by many States.

(continued)

Justice THOMAS, with whom Justice STEVENS and Justice SCALIA join, dissenting.

The Court today allows the Internal Revenue Service (IRS) to reach proceeds from the sale of real property that did not belong to the taxpayer, respondent's husband, Don Craft, because, in the Court's view, he "possesse[d] individual rights in the [tenancy by the entirety] estate sufficient to constitute 'property' or 'rights to property' for the purposes of the lien" created by 26 U.S.C. §6321. *Ante*, at 1419. The Court does not contest that the tax liability the IRS seeks to satisfy is Mr. Craft's alone, and does not claim that, under Michigan law, real property held as a tenancy by the entirety belongs to either spouse individually. Nor does the Court suggest that the federal tax lien attaches to particular "rights to property" held individually by Mr. Craft. Rather, borrowing the metaphor of "property as a bundle of sticks"—a collection of individual rights which, in certain combinations constitute property," *ante*, at 1420, the Court proposes that so long as sufficient "sticks" in the bundle of "rights to property" "belong to" a delinquent taxpayer, the lien can attach as if the property itself belonged to the taxpayer, *ante*, at 1424.

This amorphous construct ignores the primacy of state law in defining property interests, eviscerates the statutory distinction between "property" and "rights to property" drawn by §6321, and conflicts with an unbroken line of authority from this Court, the lower courts, and the IRS. Its application is all the more unsupportable in this case because, in my view, it is highly unlikely that the limited individual "rights to property" recognized in a tenancy by the entirety under Michigan law are themselves subject to lien. I would affirm the Court of Appeals and hold that Mr. Craft did not have "property" or "rights to property" to which the federal tax lien could attach.

I

A

If the Grand Rapids property "belong[ed] to" Mr. Craft under state law prior to the termination of the tenancy by the entirety, the federal tax lien would have attached to the Grand Rapids property. But that is not the case. As the Court recognizes, pursuant to Michigan law, as under English common law, property held as a tenancy by the entirety does not belong to either spouse, but to a single entity composed of the married persons. See *ante*, at 1421–1422. . . .

The Court does not dispute this characterization of Michigan's law with respect to the essential attributes of the tenancy by the entirety estate. However, relying on *Drye v. United States*, 528 U.S. 49, 59, 120 S.Ct. 474, 145 L.Ed.2d 466 (1999), which in turn relied upon *United States v. Irvine*, 511 U.S. 224, 114 S.Ct. 1473, 128 L.Ed.2d 168 (1994), and *United States v. Mitchell*, 403 U.S. 190,

91 S.Ct. 1763, 29 L.Ed.2d 406 (1971), the Court suggests that Michigan's definition of the tenancy by the entirety estate should be overlooked because federal tax law is not controlled by state legal fictions concerning property ownership. *Ante*, at 1420–1421. But the Court misapprehends the application of *Drye* to this case.

Drye, like *Irvine* and *Mitchell* before it, was concerned not with whether state law recognized "property" as belonging to the taxpayer in the first place, but rather with whether state laws could disclaim or exempt such property from federal tax liability after the property interest was created. *Drye* held only that a state-law disclaimer could not retroactively undo a vested right in an estate that the taxpayer already held, and that a federal lien therefore attached to the taxpayer's interest in the estate. 528 U.S. at 61, 120 S.Ct. 474. . . . Similarly, in *Irvine*, the Court held that a state law allowing an individual to disclaim a gift could not force the Court to be "struck blind" to the fact that the transfer of "property" or "property rights" for which the gift tax was due had already occurred; *"state property transfer rules* do not transfer into federal taxation rules." 511 U.S. at 239–240, 114 S.Ct. 1473 (emphasis added). . . .

Extending this Court's "state law fiction" jurisprudence to determine whether property or rights to property *exist* under state law in the first place works a sea change in the role States have traditionally played in "creating and defining" property interests. By erasing the careful line between state laws that purport to disclaim or exempt property interests after the fact, which the federal tax lien does not respect, and state laws' definition of property and property rights, which the federal tax lien does respect, the Court does not follow *Drye*, but rather creates a new federal common law of property. This contravenes the previously settled rule that the definition and scope of property is left to the States. . . .

B

That the Grand Rapids property does not belong to Mr. Craft under Michigan law does not end the inquiry, however, since the federal tax lien attaches not only to "property" but also to any "rights to property" belonging to the taxpayer. While the Court concludes that a laundry list of "rights to property" belonged to Mr. Craft as a tenant by the entirety, it does not suggest that the tax lien attached to any of these particular rights. Instead, the Court gathers these rights together and opines that there were sufficient sticks to form a bundle, so that "respondent's husband's interest in the entireties property constituted 'property' or 'rights to property' for the purposes of the federal tax lien statute." *Ante*, at 1425, 1424.

But the Court's "sticks in a bundle" metaphor collapses precisely because of the distinction expressly drawn by the statute, which distinguishes between "property" and "rights to property." The Court refrains from ever stating

(continued)

whether this case involves "property" or "rights to property" even though §6321 specifically provides that the federal tax lien attaches to "property" and "rights to property" "belonging to" the delinquent taxpayer, and not to an imprecise construct of "individual rights in the estate sufficient to constitute 'property' or 'rights to property' for the purposes of the lien." *Ante*, at 1419.

Rather than adopt the majority's approach, I would ask specifically, as the statute does, whether Mr. Craft had any particular "rights to property" to which the federal tax lien could attach. He did not. Such "rights to property" that have been subject to the §6321 lien are valuable and "pecuniary," *i.e.*, they can be attached, and levied upon or sold by the Government. *Drye*, 528 U.S. at 58–60, and n.7, 120 S.Ct. 474. With such rights subject to lien, the taxpayer's interest has "ripen[ed] into a present estate" of some form and is more than a mere expectancy, *id.* at 60, n.7, 120 S.Ct. 474, and thus the taxpayer has an apparent right "to channel that value to [another]," *id.*, at 61, 120 S.Ct. 474.

In contrast, a tenant in a tenancy by the entirety not only lacks a present divisible vested interest in the property and control with respect to the sale, encumbrance, and transfer of the property, but also does not possess the ability to devise any portion of the property because it is subject to the other's indestructible right of survivorship. *Rodgers v. Rodgers*, 136 Mich. App. 125, 135–137, 356 N.W.2d 288, 293–294 (1984). . . .

It is clear that some of the individual rights of a tenant in entireties property are primarily personal, dependent upon the taxpayer's status as a spouse, and similarly not susceptible to a tax lien. For example, the right to use the property in conjunction with one's spouse and to exclude all others appears particularly ill suited to being transferred to another, see *ibid.*, and to lack "exchangeable value," *id.*, at 56, 120 S.Ct. 474.

Nor do other identified rights rise to the level of "rights to property" to which a §6321 lien can attach, because they represent, at most, a contingent future interest, or an "expectancy" that has not "ripen[ed] into a present estate." *Id.* at 60, n.7, 120 S.Ct. 474. . . .

II

That the federal tax lien did not attach to the Grand Rapids property is further supported by the consensus among the lower courts. For more than 50 years, every federal court reviewing tenancies by the entirety in States with a similar understanding of tenancy by the entirety as Michigan has concluded that a federal tax lien cannot attach to such property to satisfy an individual spouse's tax liability. This consensus is supported by the IRS's consistent recognition, arguably against its own interest,

that a federal tax lien against one spouse cannot attach to property or rights to property held as a tenancy by the entirety. That the Court fails to so much as mention this consensus, let alone address it or give any reason for overruling it, is puzzling. While the positions of the lower courts and the IRS do not bind this Court, one would be hard pressed to explain why the combined weight of these judicial and administrative sources—including the IRS's instructions to its own employees—do not constitute relevant authority.

III

Finally, while the majority characterizes Michigan's view that the tenancy by the entirety property does not belong to the individual spouses as a "state law fiction," *ante*, at 1419, our precedents, including *Drye*, 528 U.S. at 58–60, 120 S.Ct. 474, hold that state, not federal, law defines property interests. Ownership by "the marriage" is admittedly a fiction of sorts, but so is a partnership or a corporation. There is no basis for ignoring this fiction so long as federal law does not define property, particularly since the tenancy by the entirety property remains subject to lien for the tax liability of *both* tenants.

* * *

Just as I am unwilling to overturn this Court's longstanding precedent that States define and create property rights and forms of ownership, *Aquilno*, 363 U.S. at 513, n.3, 80 S.Ct. 1277, I am equally unwilling to redefine or dismiss as fictional forms of property ownership that the State has recognized in favor of an amorphous federal common-law definition of property. I respectfully dissent.

Case Questions

1. Justice O'Connor, in writing her opinion, placed emphasis on the concept of a "bundle of rights" that she maintained state law provided each tenant in property held as a tenancy by the entirety in the state of Michigan. Based upon this reasoning, she stated that the husband held property rights to which a federal tax lien could attach. Looking at the laws of your state, what property rights does a tenant have in property held as a tenancy by the entirety?

2. In reviewing the opinion of Justice O'Connor and the dissenting opinion of Justice Thomas, whom do you believe makes the stronger argument? Why?

3. If Justice O'Connor's reasoning is correct, should other creditors have the right to attach liens to properties held as tenancies by the entirety in situations in which only one spouse is the debtor? Why or why not?

To aid taxpayers who have fallen behind with payments due to recent economic difficulties, the IRS has increased the dollar threshold for unpaid taxes before liens are filed. At the time of this writing, the IRS also has modified its procedures for taxpayers who have unpaid assessments of $25,000 or less and who enter into direct debit installment agreements. In most instances, liens are withdrawn for taxpayers who meet these criteria.

State tax liens, such as those for state estate and inheritance taxes, intangible taxes, corporate franchise taxes, and business-related taxes, are governed by state statute. *Estate and inheritance tax liens* are encumbrances on a decedent's real and personal property and are normally satisfied as part of the probate proceedings of a decedent's estate. **Intangible taxes** are taxes imposed in certain states for the right to issue, execute, sell, assign, trade in, or receive income from intangible property, such as stocks and bonds. *Corporate franchise taxes* are taxes imposed for the right to exist and do business as a corporation in a certain state.

Real property tax liens may be enforced only against the real property that is the subject of the tax. They have priority over all other liens and need not be recorded to be enforced. Real property tax liens may be imposed for failure to pay ad valorem real property taxes or special assessment taxes. As with other tax liens, the real property can be sold at a tax sale to satisfy the outstanding tax bill, penalties, and costs. The owner of the real property must be given notice of the proposed sale, and notice is also published in a newspaper of general circulation in the county in which the real property is located. (See Exhibit 9–3 for a sample notice of sale.) In some states, prior to giving public notice of the sale, the taxing authority must file a *bill of complaint* in the appropriate court in the county in which the property is located, naming itself as complainant and the property as defendant. After a tax sale, the purchaser of the property receives a *tax deed*. If the real property is not sold at a tax sale because of lack of interest, the real property may be forfeited to the state.

Mortgage Liens

A *mortgage* instrument is one of two documents given by the *mortgagor* (the person or entity receiving the loan) to the *mortgagee* (the lender). Although financing instruments, including mortgage instruments, are discussed in great detail in the next chapter, a word concerning mortgage instruments is necessary here to illustrate how one works as a lien on real property.

When an individual or business entity takes out a loan to purchase real property, the lender requires a promissory note and a mortgage. The *promissory note* is a document in which an individual or business entity, called the *maker,* promises to repay a loan to the lender. If a default on the loan occurs, the promissory note permits the lender to proceed against the maker personally and any property, real or personal, owned by the maker. The mortgage instrument is a specific lien, attaching only to the particular real property that is purchased with the loan proceeds. A mortgage becomes a lien against the real property when recorded in the public records in the county in which the real property is located.

A mortgage lien's priority status is determined by the date of its recording. As noted, real property tax liens are superior to all other liens, including mortgage liens. Because of this, many lenders include in their calculation of monthly mortgage payments the amount of annual real property taxes and escrow this sum until the tax bill is issued. The original tax bill is then forwarded to the lender rather than the

intangible tax: A tax imposed for the right to issue, execute, sell, assign, trade in, or receive income from intangible property.

EXHIBIT 9–3   **Notice of sale**

IN THE CIRCUIT COURT OF THE SEVENTH JUDICIAL CIRCUIT, IN AND FOR ANY COUNTY, ANY STATE

CITY OF ANY CITY,
    Complainant,
vs.
CERTAIN LANDS UPON WHICH SPECIAL ASSESSMENTS ARE DELINQUENT,
    Defendants.

CASE NO. 6000830
Phase III, Parcel 65B

NOTICE

TO ALL PERSONS AND CORPORATIONS INTERESTED IN OR HAVING ANY LIEN OR CLAIM UPON ANY OF THE LANDS DESCRIBED HEREIN:

You are hereby notified that the CITY OF ANY CITY has filed its Bill of Complaint in the above-named court to foreclose delinquent special assessments, with interest and penalties, upon the parcel of land set forth below. The aggregate amounts of such special assessments, including accelerated principal balance, with interest and penalties through August 15, 2015, against said parcel of land, as set forth in said Bill of Complaint, are set forth below:

DESCRIPTION OF LAND
Phase III, Parcel 65B

A portion of Section 18, Township 49 South, Range 41 East, more particularly described as follows:

The South 112.00 feet of the Northeast one-quarter of the Southwest one-quarter of the Southeast one-quarter of said Section 18, less therefrom the East 332.90 feet thereof, together with:

The Southeast one-quarter of the Southwest one-quarter of the Southeast one-quarter of said Section 18, less therefrom the South 577.00 feet and the East 332.90 feet thereof.

Said lands situate, lying and being in the City of Any City, Any County, Any State, and contain 1.0424 acres, more or less. Said parcel being a portion of PINERIDGE INDUSTRIAL PARK, PARCEL 65, as recorded in Plat Book 126, Page 28, of the Public Records of Any County, Any State.

Amount Due: $49,922.18 (plus per diem interest and penalty after August 15, 2015).

In addition to the amount set forth herein, interest and penalties, as provided by law, on such delinquent special assessments, together with the costs and expenses of this suit are sought to be enforced and foreclosed in this suit. You are hereby notified to appear and make your defenses to said Bill of Complaint on or before the date of August 26, 2015, and if you fail to do so on or before said date, the bill will be taken as confessed by you, and you will be barred from thereafter contesting said suit, and said respective parcel of land will be sold by decree and said Court for nonpayment of said assessment lien, interest and penalties thereon, and the costs of this suit.

IN WITNESS WHEREOF, I have hereunto set my hand and affixed the official seal of said Court, this date of August 15, 2015.

NINA HORNSBY
Clerk of said Court
By: Steven Lockridge
Deputy Clerk
A True Copy
Circuit Court Seal

Helen Douglas
Assistant City Attorney
Attorney for Complainant
CITY OF ANY CITY
1500 N.W. 10th Street
Any City, Any State
(000) 444-1111

property owner, and the lender pays the taxes due with the escrowed sum. Most lenders want to maintain priority status over all other liens. To accomplish this, they may require subordination agreements to be executed by other lienors. A **subordination agreement** is one in which a party agrees that his or her interest in real property should have a lower priority than the interest to which it is being subordinated.

Should a mortgagor default on a loan, the mortgagee may foreclose on the property. Mortgage foreclosures are discussed in detail in Chapter 19. Once a mortgage loan is paid in full—when the real property is sold, when the term expires, or at some earlier date—a **satisfaction of mortgage,** such as the one provided in Exhibit 9–4, must be recorded to remove the lien as an encumbrance on the real property.

subordination agreement:
An agreement by which one party agrees that his or her interest in real property should have lower priority than the interest to which it is being subordinated.

satisfaction of mortgage: A document recorded to evidence the payment in full of a mortgage loan.

Satisfaction of mortgage	EXHIBIT 9–4

LOAN NO. 1302-762724 33

This instrument was prepared by:

AMERICAN SECURITY BANK
6008 South Commercial Avenue
Any City, Any State

SATISFACTION OF MORTGAGE

KNOW ALL MEN BY THESE PRESENTS:

That AMERICAN SECURITY BANK, a corporation organized and existing under the laws of the United States of America, the owner and holder of a certain mortgage executed by

EDWARD S. TURNER and EVELYN C. TURNER, his wife

to AMERICAN SECURITY BANK, bearing date of the 12th day of October, 2012, and recorded on the 13th day of October, 2012, in Official Records Book 14501, Page 306, of the Public Records of Any County, Any State, given to secure the sum of

- - - - - - -TWO HUNDRED TWENTY-FIVE THOUSAND AND NO/100 - - - - - - -

Dollars evidenced by a certain promissory note, has received full payment of said indebtedness and does hereby acknowledge satisfaction of said mortgage, and hereby directs the Clerk of the Circuit Court of Any County, Any State, to cancel the same record.

IN WITNESS WHEREOF, AMERICAN SECURITY BANK has caused these presents to be executed in its name this 15th day of August, 2015.

SIGNED, SEALED AND DELIVERED
IN THE PRESENCE OF:

AMERICAN SECURITY BANK

By _____
_____
Tamara St. James   Ann Marcus, Vice President

_____
Gerald Randall

STATE OF ANY STATE
COUNTY OF ANY COUNTY

I HEREBY CERTIFY that on this day before me, an officer duly authorized in the state and county aforesaid to take acknowledgements, personally appeared Ann Marcus, well known to me to be the Vice President of American Security Bank, and that she acknowledged executing the same in the presence of two subscribing witnesses freely and voluntarily under the authority duly vested in them.

WITNESS my hand and official seal in the county and state last aforesaid this 15th day of August, 2015.

_____
Notary Public, State of Any State
My commission expires: _____

Construction Liens

In General

A **construction lien,** often referred to as a *mechanic's lien* or *materialman's lien,* is a *statutory lien*. It allows certain persons and entities who provide labor or materials for the improvement of real property and who are not paid the statutory right to place a claim of lien on and ultimately foreclose on specific real property and any improvements thereon. Construction liens are based on the principle of *unjust enrichment,* preventing a party from being unjustly enriched by receiving the services, labor, or materials of another without full reimbursement. Construction liens can be placed on both commercial and residential properties, although some states prohibit the placement of construction liens on owner-occupied residential real property.

Because a construction lien is statutory in nature, there generally is no requirement that the lien claimant be in privity of contract with the property owner. The persons or entities entitled to a construction lien are specified by state statute and typically include general contractors, subcontractors (and in some states, more remote subcontractors, such as subsubcontractors), laborers, and suppliers of materials. Many state statutes include lessors of equipment, architects, interior designers and decorators, professional engineers, and land surveyors as parties entitled to construction liens. In states that do require an express or implied contract with the property owner or an authorized representative of the owner in order for a person to be entitled to place a construction lien on property, a general contractor who has a contract with the owner may be considered the owner's authorized representative, carrying the authority to hire anyone necessary to complete the construction job, including subcontractors, laborers, and material suppliers.

In a number of states, a claimant, in order to be entitled to file a construction lien, must supply services, labor, or material that results in a fixture or "permanent benefit" to the real property. Although state statutes may be vague in defining this term, court cases seem to indicate that the improvement must be one that prepares the structure for occupancy, including site preparation such as excavation and grading, or that incorporates materials in the structure or land (for example, planting of landscaping materials, installation of flooring).

This requirement is not difficult for certain lien claimants, such as a plumber or an electrician, to meet, but it may be tricky for certain suppliers who sell materials to subcontractors or to owners over the counter without knowing the particular job site in which the materials are to be incorporated. If the materials are delivered to a particular construction site, most courts hold that there is a presumption that they are to be used at that site. Nonetheless, it is advisable for the supplier to have a delivery receipt signed by the person ordering the materials to evidence the drop-off location. If the materials are sold over the counter, it is advisable that the supplier have the buyer fill out a form indicating the location of the site at which the materials will be used, the name and address of the owner of the site, and other relevant information.

If the materials furnished are customized, the supplier generally has a right to file a construction lien, even if the materials are not ultimately used on the site. For example, if a supplier is asked to customize a tub to meet specified size requirements not found in standard tubs, the supplier, if not paid, may file a claim of lien against the property on which the tub was supposed to be installed, even if the owner does not install the tub.

construction lien: A statutory lien placed on real property by persons or entities providing labor or materials for the improvement of real property.

In states that require an express or implied contract with the owner or the owner's authorized representative, the owner may avoid responsibility for unauthorized work done or unauthorized materials furnished by completing a **notice of nonresponsibility,** which then is posted on the construction site and recorded in the public records in the county in which the property is located.

A lien claimant is entitled to his or her claim only once work is done or materials are furnished to the real property. To establish a claim of lien, a lien claimant must record a claim of lien within a statutorily specified time period with the recording clerk in the county in which the real property is located. In some states, the lien claimant, upon first beginning work or furnishing materials, must send a notice to the owner of the property indicating that the claimant is providing goods or services to improve the property (see the discussion of notice to owner later in this chapter). This notice makes the owner aware of all parties involved with the improvements to the real property. This is important to the owner because often the owner only contracts with the general contractor and leaves it to the general contractor to hire the necessary subcontractors, laborers, and suppliers for the job. In states requiring a notice to owner, failure to provide one will negate the lien rights of the claimant.

The amount of monies a lien claimant is entitled to is determined by state statute. In some states, a lien claimant is entitled to the entire amount owed and outstanding, regardless of whether the owner of the real property has made payment to the general contractor. In these states, it is especially important for the owner to know how many subcontractors, laborers, and suppliers are involved with the job and the amounts owing to each at each stage of the construction.

To ensure that the monies paid to the general contractor are being paid, in turn, to parties hired by the general contractor, the owner may insist that the general contractor supply the owner with **lien waivers,** or *lien releases,* from the subcontractors and others at various stages before further payment is made. These waivers show that the subcontractors have been paid and will not be subjecting the property to liens. Subcontractors also can be asked to sign partial lien waivers specifying the amount paid to date and indicating that the owner's potential liability for payment is reduced by the amount stated.

Some states require that lien waivers be witnessed and notarized. The signatory of a lien waiver should be an agent of the company duly authorized to sign. A president of a company typically is authorized to bind a company and therefore may sign a lien waiver, while a secretary of a company may or may not be so authorized. A lien waiver absent a duly authorized signature will not bind the company, so authorization must be checked. A right to claim a lien may not be waived in advance. A lien right may be waived only to the extent of labor, services, or material furnished. A sample partial lien waiver is provided in Exhibit 9–5.

In some states, a lien claimant is limited by the contract price as set forth in a contract between the general contractor and the owner, and the owner will not be held liable beyond that amount. For example, suppose the owner and general contractor enter into a contract for a patio enclosure to be constructed on an already existing house. The contract price is $30,000, to be paid in three installments of $10,000 each; the first installment is to be paid upon the signing of the contract, the second is to be paid halfway through the job, and the third is to be paid at the completion of the job. The general contractor hires a drywall company to put up walls for the enclosure for $15,000. At the time of completion of the work, the

notice of nonresponsibility: A notice posted on a construction site by the owner of the property to avoid legal responsibility for unauthorized work done or unauthorized materials furnished.

lien waiver: A document indicating that a subcontractor has been paid and will not be subjecting real property to liens.

PARTIAL WAIVER OF LIEN

KNOW ALL MEN BY THESE PRESENTS, that JENSEN & JASPERS LANDSCAPING, in consideration of the sum of Fifteen Thousand Seven Hundred ($15,700.00) Dollars, receipt whereof is hereby acknowledged, does hereby partially waive, release and quitclaim all lien rights, claims or demands of every kind whatsoever which the undersigned now has, or may hereafter have, against that certain real property and the improvements thereon situated in Any County, Any State located at 254 Granville Drive, Any City, Any County, Any State and legally described as:

Lot 50 in Block 12 of GRANVILLE MANOR ESTATES, according to the plat thereof recorded in Plat Book 75, Page 201 of the Public Records of Any County, Any State

on account of work and labor performed and/or materials furnished in, to, or about the construction of any building or buildings situated thereon, or in improving the above-described property or any part thereof, all invoices that were due for payment on or before the below-written date having been paid in full.

The undersigned expressly agrees to indemnify and hold harmless NATHANIEL TAYLOR and GAIL TAYLOR, owners of record of the above-described property, from any and all costs and expenses including reasonable attorney's fees, arising out of claims by laborers, subcontractors, or materialmen who might claim that they have not been paid for services or materials furnished by or through the undersigned in connection with the work performed, at the property through April 11, 2015.

Dated: April 11, 2015   JENSEN & JASPERS LANDSCAPING

By: *Henry Jensen*
                      Henry Jensen, Partner

owner has paid $20,000 to the general contractor, and the general contractor has not paid the drywall company.

In states that limit the construction lien to the contract price between the owner and the general contractor, the drywall company can claim only $10,000 against the property of the owner, which is the difference between the contract price of $30,000 and the amount owed on the contract—namely, $10,000. In states imposing no such limitation, the drywall company can record a claim of lien for the entire $15,000.

Construction liens generally attach to property retroactively, so their priority is not established by the date upon which the lien was recorded. In some states, priority of the lien dates back to the date upon which the claimant completed work on or last furnished supplies to the premises; in other states, it dates back to the first date the lien claimant entered the property; and in still other states, the lien, once recorded, dates back to the first date work began on or supplies were furnished to the property. In the latter instance, state statute requires that the owner of the real property record a **notice of commencement** indicating the first date upon which construction began. In applicable states, once this notice is filed and recorded, all construction liens properly filed and recorded date back to the date of the notice.

For example, suppose an owner files a notice of commencement dated February 1. A roofing company hired by the general contractor will not come onto the premises for the first time until a good portion of the construction is completed—for example, starting work on May 1 and finishing on May 18. If the roofing company is not paid

notice of commencement: A document recorded by a property owner indicating the date upon which construction began on the property.

and files a claim of lien against the property on July 1, in states that require owners to record a notice of commencement, the roofing company's lien will date back to February 1. Suppose further that the paving company installing the driveway begins work on June 1, completes work on June 6, and files a claim of lien on August 1. Although the two lien claimants, the roofing company and the paving company, commenced work and completed work on different dates, neither is superior to the other in lien priority in this instance because both liens date back to February 1.

In states with statutes that date construction liens back to the date upon which the claimant first furnished labor or services, the roofing company's lien would date back to May 1, and the paving company's lien would date back to June 1; therefore, the roofing company's lien would be superior. In states with statutes that date construction liens back to the date the claimant completed work or the last date materials were supplied, the roofing company's lien would again be superior inasmuch as the roofing company completed work on May 18, whereas the paving company completed work on June 6. Many states treat liens recorded by architects, engineers, land surveyors, and other hired professionals differently than other construction liens, establishing their lien priority by the date upon which the lien was recorded rather than the date upon which work was first furnished.

A construction lien is similar to the other liens previously discussed in the manner of its enforcement. Construction liens are enforced through foreclosure suits. Although state statutes of limitations vary in setting the time limit for bringing a foreclosure action on a construction lien, the time period typically is of short duration (for example, one year). In some states, the statute of limitations may run from the date of the recording of the claim of lien, whereas in other states it may run from the last furnishing of labor or materials to the construction site. If the lien claimant fails to file a foreclosure suit within this time period, he or she cannot thereafter recover on the claim of lien. At that point, the lien claimant's best alternative would be to file a breach of contract action against the party with whom he or she was in privity of contract.

If full payment is made, either after the recording of a claim of lien or after the filing of a foreclosure action, a release of lien must be recorded to remove the lien as an encumbrance on the property. Some states permit an owner to file a *notice of contest of lien,* in which the owner states that he or she disputes the lien claim. The filing of a notice of contest of lien may statutorily shorten the time period within which a lien claimant may file suit to enforce the lien. In most states, should a foreclosure action accrue, the owner of the real property has a right of redemption in the same manner as is provided for mortgage foreclosures.

Notice of Commencement

In states that make a notice of commencement a statutory requirement, the recording of such a notice serves as notification to third parties that the owner of the specified real property has authorized certain improvements to be undertaken on the property. In these states, a notice of commencement is executed and recorded by the owner after a building permit is issued allowing construction on the property.

Recall from the earlier discussion that construction liens in some states date back to the recording of the notice of commencement. Lending institutions providing construction loans typically require that the notice of commencement be recorded after their mortgage deed is recorded in order to preserve their lien priority. Often, to ensure that documents are recorded in a certain order, the lending institution will have the owner execute a notice of commencement and give it to the lending institution to record after the mortgage deed is recorded. State statutes may mandate that a notice of commencement automatically expires after a specified time period (for example, one year) unless the notice of commencement provides otherwise.

In addition to providing notice that improvements to real property are to commence, a notice of commencement contains information helpful to potential lien claimants. Although the contents may vary from state to state, a notice of commencement usually contains the following information:

1. The legal description of the real property
2. A description of improvements to be made
3. The owner's name and address
4. The owner's interest in the real property
5. The general contractor's name and address
6. If the project is bonded, the name and address of the surety company and the amount of the bond
7. The lending institution's name and address
8. The name and address of all persons other than the owner who are designated to receive notices
9. The expiration date for the notice of commencement if the project completion date is expected to be after the statutorily prescribed expiration date
10. The signature of the owner
11. Notarization

Once the notice of commencement is signed by the owner and notarized, it is recorded in the clerk's office in the county in which the property is located. In some states, recording alone is insufficient, and there is the additional requirement of posting a certified copy of the notice of commencement in a conspicuous place on the real property. In these states, the posting of the notice may be a prerequisite to obtain a first inspection approval for work on the property. Once recorded, the improvements described in the notice of commencement must begin within a specified time period (for example, ninety days) or else the notice becomes void and a new notice must be recorded.

Suppose Austin Moore purchased a parcel of land and hired a general contractor, Prestige Builders, Inc., to build a custom home on the property. All applicable plans are approved, and the building permit has been issued. According to state statute, Austin must record a notice of commencement and post a certified copy on the property. His notice of commencement may read like that provided in Exhibit 9–6.

Notice to Owner

In many states, a potential lien claimant must comply with the state's **notice to owner** requirements in order to enforce a construction lien. Some states do not require that parties in privity of contract with the owner, such as the general contractor, file a notice to owner as a prerequisite to the later filing of a claim of lien; rather, they require this step only from subcontractors, laborers, and material suppliers who are not in privity of contract with the owner.

notice to owner: A document that puts a property owner on notice of those parties expecting payment for work or materials incorporated into the owner's real property.

NOTICE OF COMMENCEMENT

STATE OF ANY STATE
COUNTY OF ANY COUNTY

THE UNDERSIGNED hereby gives notice that improvement will be made to certain real property, and in accordance with Section 893.07 of the Statutes of Any State, the following information is provided in this Notice of Commencement.

1. Description of property: Lot 56 in Block 18, BLACKWELL ESTATES, according to the plat thereof, recorded in Plat Book 12, Page 27, of the Public Records of Any County, Any State.

2. General description of improvement: Construction of a two-story, single-family residence.

3. Owner information:
   (a) Name and address: Austin Moore
   127 Palliser Drive, Any City, Any State
   (b) Interest in property: Fee simple

4. Contractor's name and address: Prestige Builders, Inc.
   633 Kennedy Avenue, Any City, Any State

5. Surety information:
   (a) Name and address: Not applicable
   (b) Amount of bond: $

6. Lender's name and address: American Security Bank
   6008 South Commercial Avenue, Any City, Any State

7. Expiration date of Notice of Commencement: April 10, 2015

_____
Austin Moore, Owner

Sworn to and subscribed before me by Austin Moore on this 10th day of April, 2015.

_____
Notary Public, State of Any State
My commission expires: _____

A notice to owner puts an owner on notice of those parties expecting payment for work or materials incorporated into the owner's property. Without this requirement, the owner may not be aware of all parties providing services, labor, and materials because the owner typically does not enter into individual contracts with each of these parties. As noted earlier, once the owner has knowledge of these parties, the owner can demand that the general contractor provide lien waivers indicating payment of each subcontractor, laborer, or supplier as work progresses.

State statutes may specify the time period within which a notice to owner must be served on the owner and any other indicated parties (for example, within forty-five days from first furnishing services, labor, or materials). In states requiring a *contractor's final affidavit* at completion of a construction project, a notice to owner should be served prior to the presentation of the affidavit. In most states, a notice to owner is considered properly served when hand delivered or mailed to the owner's address provided on the notice of commencement. It is advisable to mail the notice to owner by certified mail, return receipt requested. If service cannot be made by either mail or hand delivery, it may be permissible to post the notice to owner at the project site. If there is more than one owner of the real property, serving a notice to owner on one owner may legally suffice as service on all.

In some states, the notice to owner must be served not only upon the owner but also upon everyone higher up in the construction chain, such as the general contractor, the surety company posting bond on the property, if applicable, and the lending institution. The potential lien claimant often is not required to serve a notice to owner on the party with whom he or she is in privity of contract. Thus, for example, a supplier of sod and planting materials providing these materials under contract with a landscape architect would not have to serve a notice to owner on the landscape architect because the landscape architect is well aware of the supplies to be furnished and the amount owed under the terms of the contract.

Continuing the example above, suppose the general contractor hired by Austin Moore, in turn, hires various subcontractors, including a plumbing contractor, S & G Plumbing, Inc. S & G Plumbing, Inc., enters into a contract with Ellison Plumbing Supplies, Inc., to provide plumbing fixtures for the residence under construction. Ellison Plumbing Supplies, Inc., furnishes most of the plumbing fixtures on May 25; however, some plumbing fixtures are on special order and will not be available for several weeks. Nonetheless, Ellison Plumbing Supplies, Inc., wants to serve a notice to owner as soon as the first materials are furnished. It may serve a notice to owner such as the one provided in Exhibit 9–7.

EXHIBIT 9–7	Notice to owner

NOTICE TO OWNER

DATE: May 25, 2015

TO: Austin Moore
127 Palliser Drive
Any City, Any State

The undersigned hereby informs you that he/she has furnished, or is furnishing, service or materials as follows:

plumbing fixtures

for the improvement of the real property identified as:

Lot 56 in Block 18, BLACKWELL ESTATES, according to the plat thereof recorded in Plat Book 12, Page 27, of the Public Records of Any County, Any State.

under an order given by:
S & G Plumbing, Inc.
310 N.E. 10th Street
Any City, Any State

Ellison Plumbing Supplies, Inc.

By_____
Noel Ellison, President

Copies furnished to:

Prestige Builders, Inc.
633 Kennedy Avenue
Any City, Any State

American Security Bank
6008 South Commercial Avenue
Any City, Any State

Claim of Lien

If full payment is not received for services, labor, or materials furnished for the improvement of real property, a lien claimant may, after following all statutorily mandated prerequisites, such as serving a notice to owner, record a claim of lien against the real property. This lien will remain an encumbrance on the property until full payment is made, settlement is reached, or the time period for bringing suit has expired. State statutes specify the time period within which a claim of lien must be recorded.

A claim of lien must be executed under oath, and it usually contains the following information:

1. The state and county in which the lien is executed
2. The name and position of the lienor
3. The address of the lienor
4. The name of the person or entity with whom the lienor contracted
5. The name of the owner of the real property
6. The legal description of the real property
7. The total value of labor, services, or materials
8. The amount owing
9. The date of service of notice to owner (including return receipt certified mail numbers, if applicable)
10. The names of witnesses (if required by state statute)
11. Signature of the lienor
12. Notarization

Some states require that the lienor serve a copy of the recorded claim of lien on the owner and all others listed on the notice of commencement and notice to owner within a specified time period (for example, within fifteen days after recording). Again, if served by mail, it is advisable to send the copies by certified mail, return receipt requested.

Suppose Ellison Plumbing Supplies, Inc., delivered the last of the plumbing fixtures on special order to the project site on June 18 and the fixtures were accepted by S & G Plumbing, Inc. Although its contract states that payment in full is due within ten business days after the last of the plumbing fixtures are furnished, by July 2, only half of the monies owed to Ellison Plumbing Supplies, Inc., have been paid. State statute requires that a construction lien be recorded within ninety days from the date of last furnishing services, labor, or supplies. Noel Ellison waits until July 30 before recording a claim of lien, having decided that the sooner the lien is recorded, the better are the chances of being paid. The lien he files is found in Exhibit 9–8.

If Ellison Plumbing Supplies, Inc., is paid in full prior to filing a foreclosure action on the property, a release and satisfaction of recorded claim of lien must be recorded with the clerk's office in the county in which the property is located to remove the lien as an encumbrance on the property. Thus, if Noel Ellison receives the remaining $5,000 owed from whatever source, be it S & G Plumbing, Inc., Austin Moore, or Prestige Builders, Inc., a release, such as the one provided in Exhibit 9–9, must be recorded.

EXHIBIT 9-8   **Claim of lien**

CLAIM OF LIEN

STATE OF ANY STATE
COUNTY OF ANY COUNTY

BEFORE ME, the undersigned authority, personally appeared Noel Ellison who, being duly sworn, says that he is the President of Ellison Plumbing Supplies, Inc., whose address is 675 S.W. Parkway Avenue, Any City, and that pursuant to a contract with S & G Plumbing, Inc., Lienor furnished labor, services or materials consisting of plumbing fixtures on the following described real property in Any County, Any State:

Lot 56 in Block 18, BLACKWELL ESTATES, according to the plat thereof recorded
in Plat Book 12, Page 27, of the Public Records of Any County, Any State.

owned by Austin Moore for a total of $10,000.00, of which there remains unpaid $5,000.00 and furnished the first of the same on May 25, 2015, and the last of the same on June 18, 2015, and that Lienor served its Notice to Owner on May 25, 2015, by U.S. Certified Mail, Return Receipt No. P244 615 899, on the general contractor by U.S. Certified Mail, Return Receipt P244 615 900, and on the lender by U.S. Certified Mail, Return Receipt P244 615 901.

Signed, sealed and delivered   Ellison Plumbing Supplies, Inc.
in the presence of:

                                                By _____
_____
Lisa Gray   Noel Ellison, President

_____
Simon Larkin

Sworn to and subscribed before me by Noel Ellison on this 30th day of July, 2015.

                                                _____
                                                Notary Public, State of Any State
                                                My commission expires: _____

Copies furnished to:

Austin Moore
127 Palliser Drive
Any City, Any State

Prestige Builders, Inc.
633 Kennedy Avenue
Any City, Any State

American Security Bank
6008 South Commercial Avenue
Any City, Any State

Other Liens

In addition to the most common liens already discussed, there are several other liens that can attach to real property. One such lien is a *vendor's lien*. A vendor is a seller, and more specifically in this instance, a seller of real property. Often a mortgage loan will not cover the full purchase price of real property. The buyer then must make up the difference between the loan amount and the purchase price. The buyer may do this by paying the difference with accumulated savings, by taking out a second mortgage loan, or by owing the difference to the seller. In the last instance, the difference between the purchase price and the mortgage loan is seller-financed by a *purchase*

| Release and satisfaction of recorded claim of lien | EXHIBIT 9-9 |

RELEASE AND SATISFACTION OF RECORDED CLAIM OF LIEN

STATE OF ANY STATE
COUNTY OF ANY COUNTY

The undersigned, having filed a Claim of Lien in the amount of $5,000.00 against the property of Austin Moore, on the 30th day of July, 2015, in Official Record Book 1720, at Page 743, in the Office of the Clerk of the Circuit Court of Any County, State of Any State, against the following described real property in Any County, Any State:

> Lot 56 in Block 18, BLACKWELL ESTATES, according to the plat thereof recorded in Plat Book 12, Page 27, of the Public Records of Any County, Any State.

NOW, THEREFORE, the Lienor, for TEN DOLLARS ($10.00) and other good and valuable consideration, does hereby acknowledge having received full payment and satisfaction of the Claim of Lien and does direct the Clerk of the Circuit Court to cancel and discharge the Claim of Lien in accordance with Section 893.12 of the Statutes of Any State.

Signed, sealed and delivered this 25th day of August, 2015.

Signed, sealed and delivered   Ellison Plumbing Supplies, Inc.
in the presence of:

_____   By _____
Lisa Gray   Noel Ellison, President

_____
Simon Larkin

Before me personally appeared Noel Ellison, the President of Ellison Plumbing Supplies, Inc., who did take an oath and acknowledged to and before me that he executed this instrument for the purposes therein expressed on behalf of said company, this 25th day of August, 2015.

_____
Notary Public, State of Any State
My commission expires: _____

money mortgage, through which the seller obtains a specific lien on the real property. Unless a written mortgage deed is properly executed and recorded, a vendor's lien is enforceable only against the original purchaser, not subsequent purchasers.

Other specific liens are *condominium liens, homeowners' association liens,* and *Uniform Commercial Code (UCC) liens.* As discussed in Chapter 3, property owners living in condominiums and developments run by condominium and homeowners' associations are required to make regular maintenance payments (for example, monthly, quarterly, semiannually) to meet the common expenses, such as maintenance of common areas, security guard services, and the like. Condominium associations and homeowners' associations are required annually to prepare a budget of common expenses covering their financial affairs. From these budgets, each condominium owner's or homeowner's share of expenses is determined. Additionally, these associations occasionally require special assessments to be paid for certain expenses that do not occur on a regular basis, such as the repaving of parking lots or roof repairs. The right to impose liens on the condominium units or homes of individuals failing to make their required payments is found in the declaration of condominium or the declaration of restrictions and covenants for the subdivision that is governed by a homeowners' association. As noted in Chapter 2, UCC liens cover personal property used as collateral to secure a loan. The filing of a UCC-1 financing statement with the secretary of state acts as a notice to the public of the creditor's interest in the personal property set forth in the financing statement. The priority of all of these liens is determined by date of recording.

Lien Priority

As can be gleaned from the discussion so far, the priority of most liens (except real property tax liens) typically is established by date of recording under the principle of first in time, first in right. As also observed, exceptions to this rule do exist. Priority becomes important in the case of foreclosure on real property. Recall that when foreclosure occurs, the real property is sold under court order to pay debts. The proceeds from the sale are taken to pay all lienors if the sale procures enough money to go around. However, this is not always the case.

Suppose Warren Masterson purchases real property with the proceeds of a mortgage loan from American Security Bank, and a mortgage deed is recorded on February 4. Warren then takes out a second mortgage loan from Roosevelt Bank to finance certain home improvements; the second mortgage deed is recorded on April 2. Next, Warren hires a contractor to add an extra bathroom onto the house. Warren records a notice of commencement on May 5. Warren then has the misfortune of being named a defendant in a lawsuit and loses the case, the court awarding the plaintiff, Rosemary Wright, a judgment award. Rosemary records a certified copy of the judgment in the county in which Warren's property is located on May 25. Faced with cash flow problems, Warren fails to pay the tile installer, who records a construction lien on June 28, having served a notice to owner on May 11 and completed work on May 13. Finally, Warren fails to pay his monthly maintenance payments to the homeowners' association, which records a lien against his property on August 6.

In order of priority, American Security Bank is first, followed by Roosevelt Bank. If Warren's property is located in a state in which construction liens date back to the date of the notice of commencement or the date the lienor completed work on the property, then the tile installer is third in line because, although he did not record his lien until June 28 (after the recording of Rosemary's judgment lien on May 25), the notice of commencement is dated May 5 and work was completed on May 13. However, if Warren's property is located in a state in which the priority of construction liens is based on the date of recording, then Rosemary is third in line, followed by the tile installer. The homeowners' association, having recorded its lien on August 6, is last.

If Warren defaults on his first mortgage with American Security Bank, American Security Bank, which in this example is in a superior position to that of the other lienors, can foreclose on the property by suing Warren and all subordinate lienors (that is, Roosevelt Bank, Rosemary, the tile installer, and the homeowners' association). If there are insufficient proceeds from the foreclosure sale to pay all lienors, American Security Bank must be paid in full (that is, the total amount of the loan, plus any penalties, additional charges, and costs) before any of the other lienors are paid. If there are proceeds remaining to pay some but not all of the remaining lienors, the lienor next in priority must be fully paid before any subordinate lienor can receive anything. In this instance, the next in line is Roosevelt Bank because it recorded its lien prior to the recording of the judgment lien, the construction lien, or the homeowners' association lien. Thus, lienors are not paid off on a pro rata basis.

If, instead of defaulting on his first mortgage, Warren defaulted on his second mortgage, Roosevelt Bank could bring action to foreclose, but any proceeds from the sale would first go to pay off American Security Bank, because of its superior position, before Roosevelt Bank would receive anything from the sale. In both examples, before either American Security Bank or Roosevelt Bank is paid, all real property taxes must be paid because they are superior to any other liens. Recall from an earlier discussion that real property tax liens do not have to be recorded to be enforced.

Attachment

A **writ of attachment** prevents a party to a lawsuit from conveying title to property, real or personal, while the suit is pending. The property need not be the subject matter of the suit. Litigation attorneys adhere to the adage that a lawsuit is only as good as its collectibility. Prior to commencing suit, a plaintiff's attorney will seek to determine if the defendant has any nonexempt assets. If not, the plaintiff may choose to reconsider bringing suit, for even if the court awards judgment in the plaintiff's favor, the plaintiff may never be able to collect on the judgment. If, however, the defendant owns sufficient nonexempt property, the plaintiff may seek a writ of attachment to ensure that the defendant does not transfer title to that property to someone else prior to the conclusion of the suit. In most instances, a court will require that a plaintiff post a surety bond or deposit with the court a sum of money to cover any possible loss in value of the attached property the defendant may sustain pending the outcome of the suit. An example of a writ of attachment is found in Exhibit 9–10.

writ of attachment: A court order that prevents a party to a lawsuit from conveying title to property, real or personal, while the suit is pending.

Writ of attachment   **EXHIBIT 9–10**

IN THE CIRCUIT COURT OF THE FIFTH JUDICIAL CIRCUIT, IN AND FOR ANY COUNTY, ANY STATE

THOMAS JOHNSON,   CASE NO. 15-22018 WOLF
   Plaintiff,
VS.
ELEANOR FISHER,
   Defendant.
_____/

WRIT OF ATTACHMENT

THE STATE OF ANY STATE:

To Each Sheriff of the State:

   YOU ARE COMMANDED to attach and take into custody so much of the lands, tenements, goods and chattels of Defendant, ELEANOR FISHER, as is sufficient to satisfy the sum of Fifty Thousand Dollars ($50,000.00) and costs.

   ORDERED in Any County, Any State, on August 16, 2015.

                                  *Franklin Wolf*_____
                                    CIRCUIT COURT JUDGE

*Ava Ross*_____
Attorney for the Plaintiff
Any State Bar No. 123456

Fisher, Ross, and Simon, P.A.
1900 N.W. 3rd Avenue
Any City, Any State
(000) 555-2000

Lis Pendens

Unlike a writ of attachment, a notice of **lis pendens** (Latin for "litigation pending") is a notice recorded when a lawsuit affects title to a particular parcel of real property. The lawsuit can be a suit to foreclose on the property, a suit to quiet title to the property, a suit to partition the property, a bankruptcy proceeding, or any other suit in which a court judgment can affect the property. The notice is recorded in the public records in the county in which the property is located. A notice of lis pendens is not a lien. Its purpose is to put third parties on notice that the property is the subject matter of litigation. The notice of lis pendens cuts off the rights of any party whose interest in the real property arises after the notice is filed. State statutes dictate the expiration date of the notice. The court may require that a bond be posted to maintain the lis pendens or to renew it after the expiration date. Should a lien later result as an outcome of the litigation, the lien's priority is established by the date the notice of lis pendens is recorded.

To illustrate a situation in which the recording of a notice of lis pendens would be appropriate, suppose Neil and Annette Adams are having marital problems and Neil decides to file for a divorce. If Neil and Annette do not reach an amicable agreement about the division of property, that matter will have to be determined by the judge presiding in the divorce action.

If Neil moves out of the house and Annette decides to put the house on the market, there is nothing in the public records to indicate that title to the house may

lis pendens: A notice recorded when a lawsuit affects title to a particular parcel of real property.

EXHIBIT 9–11   Notice of lis pendens

**IN THE CIRCUIT COURT OF THE FOURTH JUDICIAL CIRCUIT,
IN AND FOR ANY COUNTY, ANY STATE**

NEIL ADAMS,   CASE NO. 15-22019 MURPHY
  Petitioner,   FAMILY DIVISION
VS.
ANNETTE ADAMS,
  Respondent.

_____/

NOTICE OF LIS PENDENS

TO RESPONDENT ANNETTE ADAMS, AND ALL OTHERS WHOM IT MAY CONCERN:

  YOU ARE NOTIFIED of the institution of this action by the petitioner against you seeking a divorce and relief concerning the following property in Any County, Any State:

    Lot 22 in Block 4, VINTAGE ESTATES, a subdivision according to the plat thereof as recorded in Plat Book 78, Page 11, of the Public Records of Any County, Any State.

DATED on August 16, 2015.

                                                       Ava Ross
                                                Attorney for the Petitioner
                                                Any State Bar No. 123456

                                                Fisher, Ross, and Simon, P.A.
                                                  1900 N.W. 3rd Avenue
                                                Any City, Any State
                                                  (000) 555-2000

be affected by the judgment of the divorce court. The court may award the house to one party or the other or may order it sold and the proceeds split. However, if a notice of lis pendens is recorded by either Neil's attorney or Annette's attorney, a prospective purchaser will have fair warning that title may be affected by court proceedings. If, instead of selling the house, Annette wants to take out a home equity loan, the notice of lis pendens warns the potential lender that its lien may be inferior to any lien arising out of the lawsuit for which the notice has been recorded. A sample notice of lis pendens is provided in Exhibit 9–11.

CHAPTER SUMMARY

1. Liens are encumbrances on the title to real property. General liens, such as judgment liens and federal income tax liens, are not secured by any particular parcel of real property. Therefore, the lienholder of a general lien is free to proceed against all nonexempt property of the debtor, both real and personal, wherever located. A specific lien, on the other hand, is one that attaches only to specific real property. Specific liens include mortgage liens, construction liens, real property tax liens, condominium association liens, and homeowners' association liens.

2. Tax liens include liens for federal and state income taxes, estate and inheritance taxes, intangible taxes, corporate franchise taxes, and real property taxes. Although the priority of most liens (including most tax liens) is established by date of recording, real property tax liens have a superpriority and thus are superior to all other liens.

3. Construction liens are specific liens that attach to a particular property on which improvements are made by contractors, subcontractors, laborers, suppliers of materials, and certain professionals. Construction liens typically attach retroactively. In this regard, they are distinct from any other lien.

4. The statutory procedures for establishing and enforcing construction liens vary considerably from state to state. Depending on state statute, a property owner may be required to record a notice of commencement to begin construction on real property. As each potential lienor commences work on the property, he or she serves a notice to owner on the property owner and persons in positions superior to the potential lienor in the construction chain. If a potential lienor is not paid, or is not paid in full, he or she may record a claim of lien against the real property. The lienor then must file suit to foreclose before the statute of limitations expires.

5. A notice of lis pendens is recorded when a lawsuit is pending that affects the title of real property. The notice is not a lien; rather, it puts third parties on notice of pending litigation and cuts off the rights of any party whose interest in the real property arises after the notice is recorded.

WEB RESOURCES

http://publicrecords.onlinesearches.com/

This site provides access to various public records. You can search by choosing either the type of record or the state. Among other options, the site provides links to each state's online database to search UCC filing records.

http://www.nationallienlaw.com/

At this site, one can access each state's construction lien laws. Click on your state under "Mechanics Lien Law, Time Deadlines & Forms." The timetables that pertain to each state's statutory requirements are free; the forms must be purchased.

REVIEW QUESTIONS

1. Explain the distinction between the following liens:
   a. General liens and specific liens
   b. Voluntary liens and statutory liens
2. Once a plaintiff is awarded a judgment in a lawsuit, what steps must be taken before he or she can enforce the judgment and have the defendant's real property sold to pay off the debt?
3. How is lien priority typically established? What are the exceptions to the rule?
4. Explain the steps that may be required to perfect a construction lien.
5. Explain the difference between a lien and a notice of lis pendens.

DISCUSSION QUESTIONS

1. ABC Corp. brought a lawsuit against Mr. and Mrs. Morgan, won the suit, and obtained a judgment for monetary damages in the amount of $53,000. ABC Corp. recorded a judgment lien against the Morgans' homestead property. The homestead property is located in Any County, Any State. The Morgans then filed for Chapter 7 bankruptcy relief and included the judgment lien as a dischargeable debt on their bankruptcy forms. Under the laws of Any State, the homestead exemption cap is $40,000 of equity in homestead property. The bankruptcy petition was granted, and the judgment was discharged by the bankruptcy court. The Morgans are maintaining that a satisfaction of judgment should be recorded, removing the lien from the homestead property. ABC Corp. argues that recording a satisfaction of judgment would result in a windfall for the Morgans because state law permits only a $40,000 homestead exemption and the judgment amount is $53,000. Should a satisfaction of judgment be recorded? Why or why not?
2. Under the laws of Any State, a construction lien must be filed within four months of final performance on a single-family residence and within eight months of final performance on a multifamily residence. Mr. Hill resides in apartment 10C in a cooperative apartment building at 500 Main Street. He contracted with JKL Corp. to undertake renovations in his unit. JKL subcontracted with XYZ Electric Corp. to perform the electrical work that amounted to $30,000. XYZ performed work in the unit from February 25 to May 21. It claimed that $10,000 of its bill remained unpaid after all of its work was performed, and it filed a construction lien on October 27. The lien therefore was filed more than four months and less than eight months after completion of work in Mr. Hill's unit. The lien lists 500 Main Street Owners Corp. as the owner of the property and lists 10C as the location of the improvements performed.

Mr. Hill seeks to have the lien removed, arguing that this unit is a single-family residence and thus XYZ waited too long to file the lien. XYZ maintains that the building is a multifamily residence and therefore that it filed the lien within the appropriate time frame. What is the appropriate result in this circumstance?

3. For the purposes of this question, assume that XYZ Electric Corp. waited too long to record its construction lien. Are there any other remedies available to XYZ Electric Corp.?

4. For the purposes of this question, assume that Mr. Hill's unit, 10C, is a condominium unit rather than a cooperative unit. What would XYZ have to do to file a valid construction lien in Any State?

5. Mrs. Anderson owned a house at 420 Adams Street in Your City, Your County, Your State. At the time of her death, she was delinquent on her real property taxes. She was a ward of a public guardian. Upon her death, the public guardian, Medicaid, two hospitals, and a utility company all filed claims against her estate. In addition, the estate incurred administrative costs and attorney's fees. The personal representative of Mrs. Anderson's estate moved to declare the estate insolvent and to determine the priority of creditors. Under the laws of your state, would the tax lien be the first debt to be paid? Why or why not?

ETHICAL QUESTION

You are the paralegal in your law firm with the most experience in the area of construction lien law. You have assisted your supervising attorney with numerous client matters in this area and have kept up-to-date on changes in state statutory law regarding construction liens. Your firm has just hired some new associates, and your supervising attorney has asked you to prepare a procedure manual on the steps to take to perfect a construction lien that is intended for use by the new associates and other paralegals in the firm. May you prepare the manual?

Slossberg Law Office on CourseMate

Please go to www.cengagebrain.com to log into CourseMate, access the Slossberg Law Office, and work on your client files. Each module corresponds to a chapter in the text. Within each module, you will be provided with instructions by the supervising attorney. You are asked to keep track of time spent on time sheets. The documents produced through working on client files in the law office can then be compiled into a portfolio of final work product.

CourseMate

The available CourseMate for this text has an interactive eBook and interactive learning tools, including flash cards, quizzes, and more. To learn more about this resource and access free demo CourseMate resources, including the Slossberg Law Office, go to www.cengagebrain.com, and search for this book. To access CourseMate materials that you have purchased, go to login.cengagebrain.com.

10

Financing

CHAPTER OBJECTIVES

Upon completion of this chapter, the student will:

- Understand the differences between deeds of trust and mortgages

- Know the various types of loans available to a prospective purchaser of real property

- Understand the loan application process

- Understand the underlying causes of the recent real estate recession and the resulting federal legislative reforms

- Know how to draft deeds of trust, mortgages, and promissory notes

Introduction

The purchase of real property is often the largest financial expenditure in a person's life. The purchaser looks at the real property both as a form of security and stability and as a major investment. Similarly, lenders look at the financing of real property as a stable investment. A loan to purchase real property will be collateralized by the real property that is to be purchased. Real property has been considered choice collateral because it is physically fixed in terms of location and thus cannot be removed from the lender's reach should the purchaser default on the loan payments. It historically also was considered choice collateral because, with proper upkeep, it was more likely to increase in value over the loan term than most other types of collateral.

When a purchaser enters into a loan agreement with a lender, the lender essentially is "selling" the purchaser money at a specified interest rate. The lender requires two things: (1) a promise to repay the debt on agreed-upon terms and conditions evidenced in a written **promissory note** and (2) a written financing or security instrument that pledges the real property as collateral for the loan debt. The security instrument generally will take one of two forms: (1) a mortgage or (2) a deed of trust, both of which are discussed in detail in this chapter. The note is the legal evidence of the borrower's intentions to repay the debt. It is a personal obligation, which means that, if the borrower defaults on the loan, the lender may come after the borrower personally wherever the borrower may be located and seek a court judgment against the borrower. The judgment allows the lender to seize, through legal measures, any of the borrower's assets for repayment of the debt.

Most often, the lender will choose, rather than going after the borrower personally, to go after the real property that is the collateral for the loan, which is the borrower's greatest asset. In some states, the lender must initiate a court action to foreclose on the real property, sell it at public auction, and use the proceeds as repayment for the debt. In other states, the lender does not have to bring a court action, and the foreclosure procedures are simplified. In either situation, if the proceeds from the sale of the real property are insufficient to cover the total outstanding loan obligation, plus fees and costs associated with the foreclosure, the lender may seek a **deficiency judgment** against the borrower, on the basis of the note, looking to the borrower personally to make up the difference between the sales price and the outstanding debt. If the borrower cannot pay the deficiency judgment and it is forgiven, the borrower is considered to have incurred income for that taxable year (the amount of the debt that is forgiven). Some states have antideficiency statutes that preclude the lender from looking to the borrower for the deficiency.

This chapter discusses the primary sources for financing, the types of loans available, the lending process, and the governmental regulations surrounding it. If you, as a paralegal, are working with the in-house counsel of a lender, you may be asked to monitor and review loan files, which will require knowledge of the loan application process. Further, whether working for a lender or in a real estate law firm, you may be asked to prepare promissory notes and security instruments. This chapter discusses the differences between a deed of trust and a mortgage and outlines the steps to take to prepare each of these instruments.

Legal Theories of Financing Instruments

As in most other aspects of American law, imported English practices have had an impact in the development of the law relating to financing instruments. Two separate legal theories pertaining to financing instruments developed in England: the **title theory** and the **lien theory.** The theories differ regarding whether a financing instrument transfers conditional title in the secured real property to the lender, as the title theory claims, or whether a financing instrument simply serves as a lien on the real property, similar to other types of liens, as the lien theory maintains. Some states have adopted the title theory, while other states have adopted the lien theory.

In states that have adopted the title theory, when a borrower gives the lender a financing instrument as security for the promise to repay the loan obligation outlined in the promissory note, the title to the real property vests in the lender or in a third party acting as an escrow agent. That third party may be a title company, an escrow company, or a trust company. The borrower retains possession of the real property and remains in possession as long as the borrower conforms to the terms of the loan agreement. When the loan is paid off, the legal title to the property then transfers to the borrower. In some title theory states, this arrangement allows the lender, in the event of a default by the borrower, to take possession and sell the property to satisfy the outstanding debt obligation without commencing a foreclosure lawsuit.

In states that have adopted the lien theory, when the borrower gives the lender a financing instrument, such as a mortgage, as security for the promise to repay the loan obligation, the borrower is giving the lender only a lien on the real property. The borrower obtains legal title to the property. The lender perfects its lien by recording it in the recording office in the county in which the real property is

promissory note: A written promise to repay a debt on agreed-upon terms and conditions. The note is the legal evidence of the borrower's intentions to repay the debt.

deficiency judgment: A court judgment for the difference between the proceeds from the sale of real property in a foreclosure action and the outstanding loan debt.

title theory: A legal theory pertaining to financing instruments under which a financing instrument transfers conditional title in the secured real property to the lender.

lien theory: A legal theory pertaining to financing instruments under which a financing instrument serves as a lien on the secured real property.

located. The lender, as a lienholder, has the right to enforce this lien by bringing a foreclosure action should the borrower default. The lender may not take possession of the property until the foreclosure action is completed. A detailed discussion of foreclosure is found in Chapter 19.

Financing Sources

A prospective purchaser of real property has a variety of sources with which to finance the acquisition. As noted in Chapter 7, the purchaser may pay all cash, although this is rare. If the seller has an outstanding loan, the purchaser may attempt to assume that loan or take the property subject to that loan.

Recall that an *assumption of a loan* occurs when the purchaser takes over the seller's loan. A purchaser may want to do this if the current interest rates are high and the seller has a low-interest loan. In order to assume the loan, the seller's existing loan documents must not contain a nonassumption clause. Further, the lender must approve the assumption. The lender typically will check out the purchaser's financial situation as thoroughly as if the purchaser were applying for a new loan. Should the assumption be approved, the purchaser becomes primarily liable for the loan obligation. Additionally, lenders have the right to charge an assumption fee, and if the original loan documents have a due-on-sale clause, the lender has the right to raise the interest rate, which may defeat the purchaser's objective in assuming the loan. A **due-on-sale clause** is a clause that states that, should the real property securing the loan obligation be sold, the total amount outstanding on the loan becomes immediately due.

As noted in Chapter 7, when a purchaser buys real property *"subject to" an existing loan,* the seller remains primarily liable for the debt obligation. The loan remains in the seller's name. The purchaser makes the loan payments, and if the purchaser defaults, the lender can move to foreclose on the property. However, the purchaser is not personally liable for the debt and therefore cannot be personally sued. Should the value of the real property prove to be less than the amount of the outstanding debt obligation, the lender may sue for a deficiency judgment against the seller, who still is primarily liable for the loan.

More commonly, a prospective purchaser will seek to obtain new financing. The source of the new financing may be a fiduciary lender. A **fiduciary lender** is a lender that has a fiduciary duty to its principals. A fiduciary lender's principals may be its depositors, as in the case of commercial banks and savings and loan institutions, or its premium payers, as in the case of insurance companies. In safeguarding their principals' monies, fiduciary lenders have the responsibility of making careful and prudent choices in accepting loan applications through scrupulous screening of loan applicants.

Commercial Banks

Commercial banks are a major source of construction loans, short-term loans, and home improvement loans. They generally choose not to tie up their resources in long-term loans because a large portion of their deposits are demand deposits rather than savings deposits. A **demand deposit** is exactly what the term suggests, an account in which the depositor may take out his or her money on demand—for example, a checking account. Depositors' accounts are insured by the **Federal Deposit Insurance Corporation (FDIC)** through the **Bank Insurance Fund (BIF)**.

due-on-sale clause: A clause in a loan document that states that, should the real property securing the loan obligation be sold, the total amount outstanding on the loan becomes immediately due.

fiduciary lender: A lender that has a fiduciary duty to its principals.

commercial bank: A lender that is a major source of construction loans, short-term loans, and home improvement loans.

demand deposit: An account in which the depositor may take out his or her money on demand, such as a checking account.

Federal Deposit Insurance Corporation (FDIC): An institution that insures depositors' accounts.

Bank Insurance Fund (BIF): A fund that insures depositors' accounts.

Commercial banks are either state chartered or federally chartered. Commercial banks may make conventional loans or governmentally backed loans, such as Federal Housing Administration (FHA) and Department of Veterans Affairs (VA) loans, which are discussed later in this chapter.

Savings and Loan Associations

Like commercial banks, **savings and loan associations** are either federally or state chartered. They primarily make conventional loans but on occasion make FHA or VA loans. Unlike commercial banks, however, savings and loan associations specialize in residential, long-term loans. In the 1980s, many savings and loan associations closed as a result of defaults on high-risk loans. In response to the perceived crisis in the savings and loan industry, the federal government enacted the **Financial Institutions Reform, Recovery and Enforcement Act of 1989 (FIRREA).** Under the FIRREA, the savings and loan regulatory and insurance systems were restructured. Now, insurance funds for savings and loan associations are managed, like commercial banks, by the FDIC, which insures savings and loan deposits through the **Savings Association Insurance Fund (SAIF).**

Mutual Savings Banks

Mutual savings banks are found primarily in the Northeast. They are owned by their depositors, who are their investors. Their depositor-investors receive a return on their investments through the payment of interest on their savings accounts. Mutual savings banks operate similarly to savings and loan associations in that they offer only limited checking account services. They differ from savings and loan institutions, however, in the types of loans they make. Unlike savings and loan associations, which focus on residential loans, mutual savings banks make loans for both residential and income-producing properties. Mutual savings banks also gravitate to FHA and VA loans more than do savings and loan associations.

Insurance Companies

Insurance companies invest a large portion of the premiums paid to them by policyholders in real estate loans. They invest primarily in large commercial and industrial loans. Additionally, they often purchase blocks of residential FHA and VA loans from secondary markets, such as the Federal National Mortgage Association, which is discussed later in this chapter. Some insurance companies become partners or joint venturers in commercial real estate projects and thereby not only receive interest on the monies loaned for these projects but also share in the appreciation of value of the properties.

Other Financing Sources

Other financing sources are also available to prospective borrowers. One such source is a **credit union.** Credit unions are cooperative associations in which members make savings deposits. Credit unions pay interest on the savings accounts and permit members to borrow money for both short-term loans, such as home improvement loans, and long-term residential loans.

savings and loan association: A lending institution that primarily makes residential, conventional loans but that on occasion makes FHA and VA loans.

Financial Institutions Reform, Recovery and Enforcement Act (FIRREA): A federal law that restructured the savings and loan regulatory and insurance systems, giving management of insurance funds for savings and loans to the FDIC.

Savings Association Insurance Fund (SAIF): A fund that insures savings and loan deposits.

mutual savings bank: A lending institution found primarily in the Northeast that is owned by the depositors, who are the investors. The depositor-investors receive a return on their investment through the payment of interest on their savings accounts. Mutual savings banks make loans for both residential and income-producing properties.

credit union: A cooperative association in which members make savings deposits. Credit unions pay interest on the savings accounts and permit members to borrow money for both short-term and long-term residential loans.

Retirement and pension plans accumulate large sums that are invested on behalf of the plan participants. A portion of these sums is invested in real estate financing activities. Retirement and pension plan funds typically are invested in both residential and commercial loans, often through the services of mortgage brokers.

Mortgage banking companies are private corporations that originate loans for other lenders and investors, such as those mentioned above, for which they receive a servicing fee. They make a variety of loans rather than specializing in a particular type of loan. Some mortgage banking companies borrow money to make loans. These loans are then sold to investors.

Mortgage brokers, on the other hand, are licensed individuals who act as middlemen in financing transactions. They bring lenders and borrowers together, similar to the manner in which real estate brokers bring sellers and buyers together. State statutes regulate their licensing requirements. Mortgage brokers are agents of their principals, whether the principal is the lender or the borrower. They differ from mortgage bankers in two respects. First, they do not service a loan. Rather, they locate potential borrowers (if their principal is the lender) or potential lenders (if their principal is the borrower) and process the initial loan application. In return, they receive a placement fee. Second, they are not lenders themselves; they simply act as intermediaries.

As mortgage markets become more competitive, the services of mortgage brokers become more popular. They have access to wholesale capital markets and pricing discounts, and they can be competitive because they can reduce their profit margin in ways that large lenders often cannot use. They typically are aware of niche markets for loans that are not readily discovered by laypersons. They are particularly helpful in obtaining financing if the property to be purchased is unusual or if the borrower has a difficult credit history.

The services performed by mortgage brokers include:

1. Assessing a client's credit history
2. Finding a mortgage product that is appropriate for the client
3. Completing the lender's preapproval paperwork
4. Collecting the documentation required by the lender
5. Completing the lender's application form and submitting all materials to the lender
6. Explaining all documents to the client

Title insurance companies recently have become active in the real estate investment market. Title companies prefer to invest in subdivision developments. In addition to receiving interest on the loan, the title company becomes the exclusive title insurer on the subdivision project and therefore also makes money on the title policies written for each lot. Further, the title company may act as closing agent for all real estate closings within the subdivision and receive a closing agent's fee.

Real Estate Investment Trusts (REITs) provide another source of funds for borrowers. REITs accumulate funds by selling beneficial interests in the trusts to members of the public. Through the utilization of mortgage bankers, the trusts invest in various types of loans—typically, construction loans and loans for larger real estate projects.

Finally, individuals may provide a source of financing. A seller may agree to accept a certain percentage of the sale price in cash and finance the remainder by

mortgage banking company: A private corporation that originates loans for other lenders and investors, for which it receives a servicing fee.

mortgage broker: A licensed individual who acts as a middleman in a financing transaction, bringing lenders and borrowers together in return for a placement fee.

Real Estate Investment Trust (REIT): A trust that accumulates funds by selling beneficial interests in the trust to members of the public. The trust then invests in various types of loans—typically, construction loans and loans for larger real estate projects.

accepting a purchase money mortgage and accompanying note from the buyer. Alternatively, the buyer may take out a first mortgage loan with a financial institution and still need another loan in order to meet the purchase price. The seller may be agreeable to taking a second mortgage and accompanying note to make up the difference. Purchase money mortgages generally are short-term loans (for example, five or ten years) as opposed to long-term loans (for example, twenty-five or thirty years).

Types of Financing Instruments

Mortgages

Some states in this country utilize mortgages as their primary security device, while others utilize deeds of trust. A **mortgage** is a two-party instrument. The parties to a mortgage are the **mortgagor** (the borrower) and the **mortgagee** (the lender). The mortgage instrument includes a description of the real property that serves as collateral for the loan as well as all pertinent information included in the promissory note, such as the loan amount, the interest rate, the monthly payments, and so forth. The mortgage sets forth the rights of the mortgagee should the mortgagor default on the loan payments. The **acceleration clause** permits the mortgagee, at its option, upon default by the mortgagor, to accelerate the entire loan amount, making the full outstanding balance, plus interest and penalties, immediately due. Should the mortgagor fail to cure his or her default, the mortgagee may bring a court action to foreclose on the real property and sell it at public auction. An example of a short form of mortgage instrument is found in Exhibit 10–5 in the Hypothetical Client Matter section at the end of the chapter. Mortgage instruments and deeds of trust are similar in most of their provisions, and most of the provisions found in the sample deed of trust in Exhibit 10–1 would be applicable to mortgage instruments as well.

Deeds of Trust

A **deed of trust** (sometimes referred to as a *mortgage trust deed* or *trust deed*), unlike a mortgage, is a three-party instrument. The three parties to this instrument are (1) the trustor (the borrower), (2) the beneficiary (the lender), and (3) the trustee (an escrow or a title or trust company). The borrower, as trustor, deeds legal title to the real property in question to the trustee as collateral for the loan, while the borrower remains in physical possession of the property. The trustee holds legal title to the property on behalf of the lender-beneficiary. The lender is the holder of the promissory note that outlines the loan terms. Upon payment in full of the loan obligation, the trustee reconveys the real property to the borrower. By deeding over legal title through the execution of a deed of trust, the borrower gives the trustee, through a **power-of-sale clause,** the power to sell the property at public auction if the borrower defaults on his or her loan obligation. State statute dictates who can serve as trustee as well as the procedures to be followed in the foreclosure of the real property. Generally, the foreclosure process is faster and the procedures are less complex under a deed of trust than under a mortgage instrument.

Exhibit 10–1 provides an example of a deed of trust instrument.

mortgage: A two-party security instrument between the mortgagor/borrower and the mortgagee/lender that describes the property serving as collateral for the loan and sets forth the rights of the lender should the borrower default.

mortgagor: The borrower.

mortgagee: The lender.

acceleration clause: A clause in a financing instrument that permits the lender, at its option, upon default by the borrower, to accelerate the entire loan amount, making the full outstanding balance, plus interest and penalties, immediately due.

deed of trust: A three-party financing instrument between the trustor/borrower, beneficiary/lender, and trustee. The borrower, as trustor, deeds legal title to the real property in question to the trustee as collateral for the loan, while the borrower remains in physical possession of the property.

power-of-sale clause: A clause in a deed of trust that gives the trustee the power to sell the real property serving as collateral for a loan at public auction if the borrower defaults on his or her loan obligation.

EXHIBIT 10–1   Deed of trust

DEED OF TRUST

THIS DEED OF TRUST ("Security Instrument") is made on August 17, 2015. The Grantor is SARAH MORGAN ("Borrower"). The Trustee is ANY CITY TRUST COMPANY of Any City, Any State. The Beneficiary is COMMERCE BANK, which is organized and existing under the laws of Any State, and whose address is 500 Commercial Avenue, Any City, Any State ("Lender"). Borrower owes Lender the principal sum of Two Hundred and Sixty-Eight Thousand Dollars ($268,000.00). This debt is evidenced by Borrower's note dated the same date as this Security Instrument ("Note"), which provides for monthly payments, with the full debt, if not paid earlier, due and payable on September 17, 2045. This Security Instrument secures to Lender: (a) the repayment of the debt evidenced by the Note, with interest, and all renewals, extensions and modifications; (b) the payment of all other sums, with interest, advanced under paragraph 7 to protect the security of this Security Instrument; and (c) the performance of Borrower's covenants and agreements under this Security Instrument and the Note. For this purpose, Borrower irrevocably grants and conveys to Trustee, in trust, with power of sale, the following described property located in Any County, Any State:

Lot 12 in Block 4 of CUMBERLAND ESTATES, a subdivision, according to the plat thereof, as recorded in Plat Book 101, Page 14, of the Public Records of Any County, Any State.

which has the address of 725 St. Ives Road, Any City, Any State ("Property Address");

TOGETHER WITH all the improvements now or hereafter erected on the property, and all easements, rights, appurtenances, rents, royalties, mineral, oil and gas rights and profits, water rights and stock and all fixtures now or hereafter a part of the property. All replacements and additions shall also be covered by this Security Instrument. All of the foregoing is referred to in this Security Instrument as the "Property."

BORROWER COVENANTS that Borrower is lawfully seized of the estate hereby conveyed and has the right to grant and convey the Property and that the Property is unencumbered, except for encumbrances of record. Borrower warrants and will defend generally the title to the Property against all claims and demands, subject to any encumbrances of record.

THIS SECURITY INSTRUMENT combines uniform covenants for national use and nonuniform covenants with limited variations by jurisdiction to constitute a uniform security instrument covering real property.

UNIFORM COVENANTS. Borrower and Lender covenant and agree as follows:

1. **Payment of Principal and Interest; Prepayment and Late Charges.** Borrower shall promptly pay when due the principal of and interest on the debt evidenced by the Note and any prepayment and late charges due under the Note.
2. **Funds for Taxes and Insurance.** Subject to applicable law or to a written waiver by Lender, Borrower shall pay to Lender on the day monthly payments are due under the Note, until the Note is paid in full, a sum ("Funds") equal to one-twelfth of: (a) yearly taxes and assessments which may attain priority over this Security Instrument; (b) yearly leasehold payments or ground rents on the Property, if any; (c) yearly hazard insurance premiums; and (d) yearly mortgage insurance premiums, if any. These items are called "escrow items." Lender may estimate the Funds due on the basis of current data and reasonable estimates of future escrow items.

The Funds shall be held in an institution the deposits or accounts of which are insured or guaranteed by a federal or state agency (including Lender if Lender is such an institution). Lender shall apply the Funds to pay the escrow items. Lender may not charge for holding and applying the Funds, analyzing the account or verifying the escrow items, unless Lender pays Borrower interest on the Funds and applicable law permits Lender to make such a charge. Borrower and Lender may agree in writing that interest shall be paid on the Funds. Unless an agreement is made or applicable law requires interest to be paid, Lender shall not be required to pay Borrower any interest or earnings on the Funds. Lender shall give to Borrower, without charge, an annual accounting of the Funds showing credits and debits to the Funds and the purpose for which each debit to the Funds was made. The Funds are pledged as additional security for the sums secured by this Security Instrument.

If the amount of the Funds held by Lender, together with the future monthly payments of Funds payable prior to the due dates of the escrow items, shall exceed the amount required to pay the escrow items when due, the excess shall be, at Borrower's option, either promptly repaid to Borrower or credited to Borrower on monthly payments of Funds. If the amount of the Funds held by Lender is not sufficient to pay the escrow items when due, Borrower shall pay to Lender any amount necessary to make up the deficiency in one or more payments as required by Lender.

Upon payment in full of all sums secured by this Security Instrument, Lender shall promptly refund to Borrower any Funds held by Lender. If under paragraph 19 the Property is sold or acquired by Lender, Lender shall apply, no later than immediately prior to the sale of the Property or its acquisition by Lender, any Funds held by Lender at the time of application as a credit against the sums secured by this Security Instrument.

3. **Application of Payments.** Unless applicable law provides otherwise, all payments received by Lender under paragraphs 1 and 2 shall be applied: first, to late charges due under the Note; second, to prepayment charges due under the Note; third, to amounts payable under paragraph 2; fourth, to interest due; and last, to principal due.

4. **Charges; Liens.** Borrower shall pay all taxes, assessments, charges, fines and impositions attributable to the Property which may attain priority over this Security Instrument, and leasehold payments or ground rents, if any. Borrower shall pay these obligations in the manner provided in paragraph 2, or if not paid in that manner, Borrower shall pay them on time directly to the person owed payment. Borrower shall promptly furnish to Lender all notices of amounts to be paid under this paragraph. If Borrower makes these payments directly, Borrower shall promptly furnish to Lender receipts evidencing the payments.

Borrower shall promptly discharge any lien which has priority over this Security Instrument unless Borrower: (a) agrees in writing to the payment of the obligation secured by the lien in a manner acceptable to Lender; (b) contests in good faith the lien by, or defends against enforcement of the lien in, legal proceedings which in the Lender's opinion operate to prevent the enforcement of the lien or forfeiture of any part of the Property; or (c) secures from the holder of the lien an agreement satisfactory to Lender subordinating the lien to this Security Instrument. If Lender determines that any part of the Property is subject to a lien which may attain priority over this Security Instrument, Lender may give Borrower a notice identifying the lien. Borrower shall satisfy the lien or take one or more of the actions set forth above within 10 days of the giving of notice.

5. **Hazard Insurance.** Borrower shall keep the improvements now existing or hereafter erected on the Property insured against loss by fire, hazards included within the term "extended coverage" and any other hazards for which Lender requires insurance. This insurance shall be maintained in the amounts and for the periods that Lender requires. The insurance carrier providing the insurance shall be chosen by Borrower subject to Lender's approval which shall not be unreasonably withheld.

All insurance policies and renewals shall be acceptable to Lender and shall include a standard mortgage clause. Lender shall have the right to hold the policies and renewals. If Lender requires, Borrower shall promptly give to Lender all receipts of paid premiums and renewal notices. In the event of loss, Borrower shall give prompt notice to the insurance carrier and Lender. Lender may make proof of loss if not made promptly by Borrower.

Unless Lender and Borrower otherwise agree in writing, insurance proceeds shall be applied to restoration or repair of the Property damaged, if the restoration or repair is economically feasible and Lender's security is not lessened. If the restoration or repair is not economically feasible or Lender's security would be lessened, the insurance proceeds shall be applied to the sums secured

EXHIBIT 10-1   *(continued)*

by this Security Instrument, whether or not then due, with any excess paid to Borrower. If Borrower abandons the Property, or does not answer within 30 days a notice from Lender that the insurance carrier has offered to settle a claim, then Lender may collect the insurance proceeds. Lender may use the proceeds to repair or restore the Property or to pay sums secured by this Security Instrument, whether or not then due. The 30-day period will begin when the notice is given.

Unless Lender and Borrower otherwise agree in writing, any application of proceeds to principal shall not extend or postpone the due date of the monthly payments referred to in paragraphs 1 and 2 or change the amount of the payments. If under paragraph 19 the Property is acquired by Lender, Borrower's right to any insurance policies and proceeds resulting from damage to the Property prior to the acquisition shall pass to Lender to the extent of the sums secured by this Security Instrument immediately prior to the acquisition.

6. **Preservation and Maintenance of Property; Leaseholds.** Borrower shall not destroy, damage or substantially change the Property, allow the Property to deteriorate or commit waste. If this Security Instrument is on a leasehold, Borrower shall comply with the provisions of the lease, and if Borrower acquires fee title to the Property, the leasehold and fee title shall not merge unless Lender agrees to the merger in writing.

7. **Protection of Lender's Rights in the Property; Mortgage Insurance.** If Borrower fails to perform the covenants and agreements contained in this Security Instrument, or there is a legal proceeding that may significantly affect Lender's rights in the Property (such as a proceeding in bankruptcy, probate, for condemnation or to enforce laws or regulations), then Lender may do and pay for whatever is necessary to protect the value of the Property and Lender's rights in the Property. Lender's actions may include paying any sums secured by a lien which has priority over this Security Instrument, appearing in court, paying reasonable attorneys' fees and entering on the Property to make repairs. Although Lender may take action under this paragraph 7, Lender does not have to do so.

Any amounts disbursed by Lender under this paragraph 7 shall become additional debt of Borrower secured by this Security Instrument. Unless Borrower and Lender agree to other terms of payment, these amounts shall bear interest from the date of disbursement at the Note rate and shall be payable, with interest, upon notice from Lender to Borrower requesting payment.

If Lender required mortgage insurance as a condition of making the loan secured by this Security Instrument, Borrower shall pay the premiums required to maintain the insurance in effect until such time as the requirement for the insurance terminates in accordance with Borrower's and Lender's written agreement or applicable law.

8. **Inspection.** Lender or its agent may make reasonable entries upon and inspections of the Property. Lender shall give Borrower notice at the time of or prior to an inspection specifying reasonable cause for the inspection.

9. **Condemnation.** The proceeds of any award or claim for damages, direct or consequential, in connection with any condemnation or other taking of any part of the Property, or for conveyance in lieu of condemnation, are hereby assigned and shall be paid to Lender.

In the event of a total taking of the Property, the proceeds shall be applied to the sums secured by this Security Instrument, whether or not then due, with any excess paid to Borrower. In the event of a partial taking of the Property, unless Borrower and Lender otherwise agree in writing, the sums secured by this Security Instrument shall be reduced by the amount of the proceeds multiplied by the following fraction: (a) the total amount of the sums secured immediately before the taking, divided by (b) the fair market value of the Property immediately before the taking. Any balance shall be paid to Borrower.

If the Property is abandoned by Borrower, or if, after notice by Lender to Borrower that the condemnor offers to make an award or settle a claim for damages, Borrower fails to respond to

(*continued*)

EXHIBIT 10-1

Lender within 30 days after the date the notice is given, Lender is authorized to collect and apply the proceeds, at its option, either to restoration or repair of the Property or to the sums secured by this Security Instrument, whether or not then due.

Unless Lender and Borrower otherwise agree in writing, any application of proceeds to principal shall not extend or postpone the due date of the monthly payments referred to in paragraphs 1 and 2 or change the amount of such payments.

10. **Borrower Not Released; Forbearance by Lender Not a Waiver.** Extension of the time for payment or modification of amortization of the sums secured by this Security Instrument granted by Lender to any successor in interest of Borrower shall not operate to release the liability of the original Borrower or Borrower's successors in interest. Lender shall not be required to commence proceedings against any successor in interest or refuse to extend time for payment or otherwise modify amortization of the sums secured by this Security Instrument by reason of any demand made by the original Borrower or Borrower's successors in interest. Any forbearance by Lender in exercising any right or remedy shall not be a waiver of or preclude the exercise of any right or remedy.

11. **Successors and Assigns Bound; Joint and Several Liability; Cosigners.** The covenants and agreements of this Security Instrument shall bind and benefit the successors and assigns of Lender and Borrower, subject to the provisions of paragraph 17. Borrower's covenants and agreements shall be joint and several. Any Borrower who cosigns this Security Instrument but does not execute the Note: (a) is cosigning this Security Instrument only to mortgage, grant and convey that Borrower's interest in the Property under the terms of this Security Instrument; (b) is not personally obligated to pay the sums secured by this Security Instrument; and (c) agrees that Lender and any other Borrower may agree to extend, modify, forbear or make any accommodations with regard to the terms of this Security Instrument or the Note without that Borrower's consent.

12. **Loan Charges.** If the loan secured by this Security Instrument is subject to a law which sets maximum loan charges, and that law is finally interpreted so that the interest or other loan charges collected or to be collected in connection with the loan exceed the permitted limits, then: (a) any such loan charge shall be reduced by the amount necessary to reduce the charge to the permitted limit; and (b) any sums already collected from Borrower which exceeded permitted limits will be refunded to Borrower. Lender may choose to make this refund by reducing the principal owed under the Note or by making a direct payment to Borrower. If a refund reduces principal, the reduction will be treated as a partial prepayment without any prepayment charge under the Note.

13. **Legislation Affecting Lender's Rights.** If enactment or expiration of applicable laws has the effect of rendering any provision of the Note or this Security Instrument unenforceable according to its terms, Lender, at its option, may require immediate payment in full of all sums secured by this Security Instrument and may invoke any remedies permitted by paragraph 19. If Lender exercises this option, Lender shall take the steps specified in the second paragraph of paragraph 17.

14. **Notices.** Any notice to Borrower provided for in this Security Instrument shall be given by delivering it or by mailing it first-class mail unless applicable law requires use of another method. The notice shall be directed to the Property Address or any other address Borrower designates by notice to Lender. Any notice to Lender shall be given by first-class mail to Lender's address stated herein or any other address Lender designates by notice to Borrower. Any notice provided for in this Security Instrument shall be deemed to have been given to Borrower or Lender when given as provided in this paragraph.

EXHIBIT 10–1 *(continued)*

15. **Governing Law; Severability.** This Security Instrument shall be governed by federal law and the law of the jurisdiction in which the Property is located. In the event that any provision or clause of this Security Instrument or the Note conflicts with applicable law, such conflict shall not affect other provisions of this Security Instrument or the Note which can be given effect without the conflicting provision. To this end the provisions of this Security Instrument and the Note are declared to be severable.

16. **Borrower's Copy.** Borrower shall be given one conformed copy of the Note and of this Security Instrument.

17. **Transfer of the Property or a Beneficial interest in Borrower.** If all or any part of the Property or any interest in it is sold or transferred (or if a beneficial interest in Borrower is sold or transferred and Borrower is not a natural person) without Lender's prior written consent, Lender may, at its option, require immediate payment in full of all sums secured by this Security Instrument. However, this option shall not be exercised by Lender if exercise is prohibited by federal law as of the date of this Security Instrument.

If Lender exercises this option, Lender shall give Borrower notice of acceleration. The notice shall provide a period of not less than 30 days from the date the notice is delivered or mailed within which Borrower must pay all sums secured by this Security Instrument. If Borrower fails to pay these sums prior to the expiration of this period, Lender may invoke any remedies permitted by this Security Instrument without further notice or demand on Borrower.

18. **Borrower's Right to Reinstate.** If Borrower meets certain conditions, Borrower shall have the right to have enforcement of this Security Instrument discontinued at any time prior to the earlier of: (a) 5 days (or such other period as applicable law may specify for reinstatement) before sale of the Property pursuant to any power of sale contained in this Security Instrument; or (b) entry of a judgment enforcing this Security Instrument. Those conditions are that Borrower: (a) pays Lender all sums which then would be due under this Security Instrument and the Note had no acceleration occurred; (b) cures any default of any other covenants or agreements; (c) pays all expenses incurred in enforcing this Security Instrument, including, but not limited to, reasonable attorneys' fees; and (d) takes such action as Lender may reasonably require to assure that the lien of this Security Instrument shall continue unchanged. Upon reinstatement by Borrower, this Security Instrument and the obligations secured hereby shall remain fully effective as if no acceleration had occurred. However, this right to reinstate shall not apply in the case of acceleration under paragraphs 13 or 17.

NONUNIFORM COVENANTS. Borrower and Lender further covenant and agree as follows:

19. **Acceleration Remedies.** Lender shall give notice to Borrower prior to acceleration following Borrower's breach of any covenant or agreement in this Security Instrument (but not prior to acceleration under paragraphs 13 and 17 unless applicable law provides otherwise). The notice shall specify: (a) the default; (b) the action required to cure the default; (c) a date, not less than 30 days from the date of the notice given to Borrower, by which the default must be cured; and (d) that failure to cure the default on or before the date specified in the notice may result in acceleration of the sums secured by this Security Instrument and sale of the Property. The notice shall further inform Borrower of the right to reinstate after acceleration and the right to bring a court action to assert the nonexistence of a default or any other defense of Borrower to acceleration and sale. If the default is not cured on or before the date specified in the notice, Lender at its option may require immediate payment in full of all sums secured by this Security Instrument, without further demand, and may invoke the power of sale and any other remedies permitted by applicable law. Lender shall be entitled to collect all expenses incurred in pursuing the remedies

provided in this paragraph 19, including, but not limited to, reasonable attorneys' fees and costs of title evidence.

If Lender invokes the power of sale, Lender or Trustee shall give to Borrower (and the owner of the Property, if a different person) notice of sale in the manner prescribed by applicable law. Trustee shall give public notice of sale by advertising, in accordance with applicable law, once a week for two successive weeks in a newspaper having general circulation in the county or city in which any part of the Property is located, and by such additional or any different form of advertisement the Trustee deems advisable. Trustee may sell the Property on the eighth day after the first advertisement or any day thereafter, but not later than 30 days following the last advertisement. Trustee, without demand on Borrower, shall sell the Property at public auction to the highest bidder at the time and place and under the terms designated in the notice of sale in one or more parcels and in any order Trustee determines. Trustee may postpone sale of all or any parcel of the Property by advertising in accordance with applicable law. Lender or its designee may purchase the Property at any sale.

Trustee shall deliver to the purchaser Trustee's deed conveying the Property with special warranty of title. The recitals in the Trustee's deed shall be prima facie evidence of the truth of the statements made therein. Trustee shall apply the proceeds of the sale in the following order: (a) to all expenses of the sale, including, but not limited to, Trustee's fee of 10% of the gross sale price and reasonable attorneys' fees; (b) to the discharge of all taxes, levies and assessments on the Property, if any, as provided by applicable law; (c) to all sums secured by this Security Instrument; and (d) any excess to the person or persons legally entitled to it. Trustee shall not be required to take possession of the Property prior to the sale thereof or to deliver possession of the Property to the purchaser at the sale.

20. **Lender in Possession.** Upon acceleration under paragraph 19 or abandonment of the Property, Lender (in person, by agent or by judicially appointed receiver) shall be entitled to enter upon, take possession of and manage the Property and to collect the rents of the Property including those past due. Any rents collected by Lender or the receiver shall be applied first to payment of the costs of management of the Property and collection of rents, including, but not limited to, receiver's fees, premiums on receiver's bonds and reasonable attorneys' fees, and then to the sums secured by this Security Instrument.

21. **Release.** Upon payment of all sums secured by this Security Instrument, Lender shall request Trustee to release this Security Instrument and shall surrender all notes evidencing debt secured by this Security Instrument to Trustee. Trustee shall release this Security Instrument without charge to Borrower. Borrower shall pay any recordation costs.

22. **Substitute Trustee.** Lender, at its option, may from time to time remove Trustee and appoint a successor trustee to any Trustee appointed hereunder. Without conveyance of the Property, the successor trustee shall succeed to all the title, power and duties conferred upon Trustee herein and by applicable law.

23. **Identification of Note.** The Note is identified by a certificate on the Note executed by any Notary Public who certifies an acknowledgment hereto.

24. **Riders to This Security Instrument.** If one or more riders are executed by Borrower and recorded together with this Security Instrument, the covenants and agreements of each such rider shall be incorporated into and shall amend and supplement the covenants and agreements of this Security Instrument as if the rider(s) were a part of this Security Instrument.

___ Adjustable Rate Rider   ___ Condominium Rider
___ Graduated Payment Rider   ___ Planned Unit Development Rider
___ 2-4 Family Rider   ___ Other(s) [Specify]

EXHIBIT 10–1 *(continued)*

NOTICE: THE DEBT SECURED HEREBY IS SUBJECT TO CALL IN FULL OR THE TERMS THEREOF BEING MODIFIED IN THE EVENT OF SALE OR CONVEYANCE OF THE PROPERTY CONVEYED.

BY SIGNING BELOW, Borrower accepts and agrees to the terms and covenants contained in this Security Instrument and in any rider(s) executed by Borrower and recorded with it.

_____
Sarah Morgan

STATE OF ANY STATE
COUNTY OF ANY COUNTY

The foregoing instrument was acknowledged before me this 17th day of August, 2015, by SARAH MORGAN.

_____
Notary Public, State of Any State
My commission expires: _____

Types of Loans

Overview of Conventional Loans

A **conventional loan** is a loan made by a private lender in which the lender usually does not have any insurance or guarantee from a third party, such as a government agency, backing the loan should the borrower fail to meet his or her loan obligations. Traditionally, this meant that a lower percentage of the property value was loaned to correspondingly lower the risk to the lender, so that if the borrower defaulted and the lender had to foreclose and sell the property, the value of the property would meet or exceed the amount of the outstanding debt obligation.

The correspondence between the value of the property to serve as collateral for a loan and the amount of the loan is called the **loan-to-value ratio** (sometimes symbolized as L/V). Traditionally, the loan-to-value ratio for a conventional loan has been 80/20. For example, if the real property value is $300,000, the lender will provide an 80 percent loan—in this instance, $240,000—requiring the borrower to contribute $60,000. Thus, when considering a loan, a conventional lender not only qualifies the borrower and the property to serve as collateral for the loan but also commonly wants to see the borrower put down a sizeable amount of cash, evidencing the borrower's equity in the property. The lower the loan-to-value ratio, the higher the down payment required of the borrower.

The loan-to-value ratio of conventional loans generally is lower than that of FHA and VA loans. In order to make conventional loans more competitive, however, the Mortgage Guaranty Insurance Corporation, in 1951, introduced the concept of **private mortgage insurance (PMI).** Private mortgage insurance is available from private insurance providers. The purpose of the private mortgage insurance is to insure the portion of the loan that exceeds the typical conventional loan-to-value ratio. If the borrower defaults, the insurer buys the loan from the lender and then proceeds to enforce the debt obligation against the borrower. A borrower may pay

conventional loan: A loan made by a private lender in which the lender usually does not have any insurance or guarantee from a third party, such as a government agency, backing the loan should the borrower fail to meet his or her loan obligations.

loan-to-value ratio: The correspondence between the value of the real property to serve as collateral for a loan and the amount of the loan.

private mortgage insurance (PMI): Insurance from private insurance providers that insures the portion of a loan that exceeds the typical conventional loan-to-value ratio.

the total private mortgage insurance premium at closing or, alternatively, a certain percentage with the rest factored into the balance of the loan.

Historically, conventional loans were all straight loans. A **straight loan** is one in which the borrower makes periodic interest payments, with the entire principal paid at the end of the loan term. Today, one sees a similar payment structure in a **balloon mortgage,** which is a loan calling for periodic payments that are less than the amount required to pay off the loan completely at the end of the loan term. The remaining balance of the principal thus "balloons" into a single, large payment at the end of the loan term. Balloon mortgages generally are used for short-term, second mortgage loans.

Most conventional loans are now fully amortized loans. An **amortized loan** is one in which level payments are made throughout the life of the loan. In the early years of the loan, the greater portion of each payment goes to pay off the interest on the loan. As years go by, although the monthly payments remain level, the portion of the payment applied to interest decreases, and the portion of the payment applied to principal increases until, at the end of the loan term, all of the interest and principal is paid off.

Conventional loans often take less time to process than governmentally backed loans. They involve less paperwork and fewer federal restrictions. Additionally, there are no set maximum amounts that may be borrowed, and conventional loans are available to the widest range of borrowers and properties.

Conventional lenders usually charge a **loan origination fee** to process the loan application, normally 1 percent of the loan amount. They may also charge **points** (sometimes referred to as *discount points*). Each point is equal to 1 percent of the loan amount. Thus, if the loan amount is $200,000 and the lender is charging two points, the points equal $4,000. The charging of points is a method of increasing the lender's yield, while not increasing the interest rate. Remember that lenders are in the money business and are making money by lending it. The lender will make a certain amount on a loan, be it by charging points, increasing the interest rate, charging prepayment penalties, or using a combination of these methods. In addition, prior to closing on a loan, the lender will require a property appraisal and current credit reports. The property tax records will have to be reviewed, so often there will be a tax service fee. These loan closing costs, as well as the loan origination fee and any points charged, can either be paid at closing or be financed into the loan. If they are financed, the borrower is paying interest on these costs each time he or she makes a loan payment.

FHA Loans

In the aftermath of the great stock market crash in 1929 and subsequent Depression, the federal government sought a means for stimulating the national economy, particularly the real estate sector. In 1934, the Federal Housing Administration (FHA) was established to entice reluctant lenders to finance residential loans. The FHA operates under the Department of Housing and Urban Development (HUD) and does not make loans itself; rather, it insures loans made by approved lenders. Lenders that are members of the Federal Reserve System or the FDIC are automatically approved to make FHA-insured loans.

The FHA insures loans for owner-occupied one- to four-family dwellings. It sets maximum loan amounts, which vary from area to area, as well as the minimum

straight loan: A loan in which the borrower makes periodic interest payments, with the entire principal paid at the end of the loan term.

balloon mortgage: A loan calling for periodic payments that are less than the amount required to pay off the loan completely at the end of the loan term. The remaining balance of the principal "balloons" into a single, large payment at the end of the loan term.

amortized loan: A loan in which level payments are made throughout the life of the loan.

loan origination fee: A fee charged by lenders to process a loan application.

points: A lending charge, sometimes referred to as *discount points*. Each point is equal to 1 percent of the loan amount.

down payment to be made by the borrower. Before the FHA will insure a loan, both the borrower and the property to serve as collateral for the loan must qualify. The subject real property must be appraised. The borrower is provided with a notice stating that the purpose of the appraisal is to estimate the value of the property and not to serve as a warranty of its condition. With regard to homes constructed before 1978, borrowers must be given a notice pertaining to lead-based poisoning.

In addition to the lender's own loan application, a HUD addendum and a mortgage credit analysis worksheet are completed for the borrower seeking an **FHA loan.** The lender takes all of the loan application documents and forwards them to the FHA for approval. The FHA looks at many of the same factors that influence conventional lenders in accepting or rejecting loan applications. It looks at both the quality and the quantity of the borrower's income. While quantity is self-explanatory, quality refers to the stability of the income source (for example, long-term employment, stocks and bonds). It also looks at the other demands on the borrower's income (for example, car loan payments, credit card debt). Although the FHA looks at many of the same factors conventional lenders consider, the FHA tends to have a more relaxed standard for qualifying a borrower than that used by conventional lenders. If the results of the examination indicate that the borrower is a good prospect, the FHA will insure the loan.

Lenders always make FHA loans in even $50 increments, and if the loan amount does not come out evenly, the amount is rounded down rather than rounded up. Thus, if the permissible maximum loan amount is $196,343.25, the actual amount loaned would be $196,300.

FHA loans may be written for a term of up to thirty years. FHA loans allow prepayment privileges, and they generally are assumable. The FHA does not set interest rates; the lenders do. The FHA does require that borrowers pay **mortgage insurance premiums,** which are collected into the FHA's Mutual Mortgage Insurance Fund. The FHA uses this fund to insure lenders against bad loans. The borrower pays a portion of the mortgage insurance premium at closing and then pays an annual premium based on the unpaid principal balance of the loan. In addition to mortgage insurance premiums, lenders that make FHA loans are allowed to charge a 1 percent loan origination fee and may charge points as well. Further, included in each monthly payment is one-twelfth of the annual real property taxes on the property and hazard insurance premiums. This type of loan payment is often referred to as **PITI** (principal, interest, taxes, insurance).

VA Loans

Ten years after the Federal Housing Administration was established, the Servicemen's Readjustment Act (commonly referred to as the GI Bill of Rights) was passed to help returning World War II veterans purchase homes. This act gave birth to the **VA loan.** "VA" originally stood for Veterans Administration and now stands for the U.S. Department of Veterans Affairs. The VA guarantees loans made to veterans by approved lenders. Unlike conventional loans and FHA loans, there is no requirement that an eligible veteran make a down payment. The VA does collect a funding fee, which may be paid by the borrower at closing or added into the total loan amount. As is the case with FHA loans, VA loans require PITI payments, the maximum loan term is thirty years, residential property must be owner-occupied, and the borrower is allowed to prepay the loan without suffering

FHA loan: A loan insured by the Federal Housing Administration. The FHA insures loans for owner-occupied one- to four-family dwellings.

mortgage insurance premium: An insurance premium charged on FHA loans. These premiums are collected into the FHA's Mutual Mortgage Insurance Fund to insure lenders against bad loans.

PITI: A loan payment that is comprised of principal, interest, taxes, and insurance.

VA loan: A loan made to veterans by approved lenders for residential, owner-occupied property and guaranteed by the U.S. Department of Veterans Affairs.

a penalty. The same HUD addendum is added to the loan package of both FHA and VA loans. Unlike the FHA, the VA does not establish maximum loan amounts; however, it does set a limit on the amount it will guarantee, or pay the lender should the veteran default on the loan.

A veteran applying for a VA loan must first complete a Request Pertaining to Military Records and a Request for Certificate of Veteran Status, which allow the lender to receive a copy of the veteran's military records. Next, the veteran must apply for a **certificate of eligibility.** The certificate states the maximum available loan guaranty entitlement for the veteran. Additionally, application must be made for a **certificate of reasonable value** for the property to be purchased. The certificate sets forth the current market value of the property based on a VA-approved appraisal and thus establishes the maximum allowable loan on the property. In addition to these forms and the lender's customary loan application forms, the VA requires the completion of its own loan analysis, a debt questionnaire, and a verification of VA benefit–related indebtedness.

Service members must be counseled, using the Counseling Checklist for Military Homebuyers. This checklist states that the VA is not responsible for the condition of the residential property or for the appreciation or depreciation of the value of the property. Applicants who knowingly purchase a home when they are aware that they have to go on active duty or leave the area within twelve months of purchasing the property are deemed to have acted in bad faith.

Lenders must obtain specific approval from the VA to use imaged documents. The VA will submit a *certificate of commitment* to the lender evidencing approval of the loan. The lender must report the closing on the loan within sixty days of its occurrence. If all is in order, the VA will then issue a *loan guaranty certificate* to the lender.

Unmarried widows and widowers of veterans are also eligible for VA loans. VA loans can be assumed by nonveterans; however, the veteran originating the loan will remain primarily liable on the loan unless the VA issues a release from liability.

Adjustable-Rate Loans

A loan can be either a fixed-rate loan or an **adjustable-rate loan** (referred to as an *adjustable-rate mortgage,* or ARM). Which type of loan is preferable to a borrower depends on the prevailing interest rates at the time the loan is made. Under an adjustable-rate loan, the interest rate typically starts lower than that under a fixed-rate loan and then periodically changes in relation to an index rate, such as the rate on Treasury securities or the national average of cost of funds to savings and loan associations. The period between one rate change and the next is called the **adjustment period.** Thus, a loan with a one-year adjustment period is often referred to as a one-year ARM.

The **margin** is the number of percentage points the lender adds to the index rate to come up with the ARM interest rate (for example, two or three percentage points). The margin usually remains constant for the duration of the loan term.

ARMs have **interest rate caps** that limit the amount the interest rate can increase. Interest rate caps may take the form of periodic caps, which limit the interest rate increase from one adjustment period to the next, or they may take the form of overall caps, which limit the interest rate increase over the life of the loan. Federal law requires that lenders provide borrowers with a disclosure statement when a borrower applies for an adjustable-rate loan.

certificate of eligibility: A certificate that states the maximum available loan guaranty entitlement for a veteran.

certificate of reasonable value: A certificate that sets forth the current market value of the property to be purchased.

adjustable-rate loan: A loan in which the interest rate typically starts lower than that of a fixed-rate loan and then periodically changes in relation to an index rate, such as the rate on Treasury securities.

adjustment period: The period between one rate change and the next for an adjustable-rate loan.

margin: The number of percentage points a lender adds to the index rate to come up with an ARM interest rate.

interest rate cap: A limitation on the amount an interest rate can increase on an adjustable-rate loan.

The Lending Process

The Loan Application and Related Documents

The lending process begins with a loan application and an interview between the prospective borrower and a loan officer. A prospective borrower should realize that he or she should bring certain documents to the initial interview to assist the loan officer in finalizing the loan application documents. The borrower should have ready at the initial interview:

1. Borrower's Social Security number.
2. The contract for sale and purchase with closing date or a construction contract.
3. The names and addresses of all financial institutions in which the borrower has accounts, together with the account numbers.
4. If divorced, a copy of the divorce decree and separation agreement, including evidence of income or payment resulting from the divorce action.
5. The names and addresses of all employers for the past two years; if self-employed, copies of federal income tax returns for the past two years.
6. Borrower's annual gross salary, together with last year's W-2 form. If overtime or bonuses were paid, these should be listed separately.
7. List of all assets, together with their current market value (including monthly or quarterly statements, if applicable).
8. Name of life insurance company and policy number of life insurance policy.
9. A complete list of all outstanding debt obligations, including the names and addresses of creditors and the amount owed to each (for example, department stores, student loans, car loans; each credit card creditor should be listed separately). If the borrower has an outstanding mortgage loan, the name and address of the lending institution, the original loan amount, the current balance, and the account number.

With this information in hand, the borrower can effectively complete a standard loan application. The loan officer will also ask the borrower to sign certain request forms, such as a request for credit reports, a request for verification of employment, a request for verification of deposits (to verify monies in bank accounts), and, if the borrower presently is a renter, a request for verification of rent. The borrower may also be asked to sign a general certification and authorization form, certifying that the information provided to the lender is accurate and complete and authorizing the release of pertinent information to the lender.

The loan officer can determine the amount of a loan the borrower qualifies for from the loan application information. The first step is determining the borrower's monthly income. The gross monthly income generally is multiplied by a percentage up to 28 percent to arrive at the borrower's allowable monthly payment for principal and interest. There will be additional payments that must be figured, such as monthly real estate taxes (one-twelfth the annual real property tax) and monthly homeowners' insurance.

Before completing the loan application forms, the loan officer will discuss with the borrower the types of loans available. The loan officer also will order an appraisal to be done on the real property to verify its value and request a credit report verifying the borrower's credit. After the loan officer receives responses to all these information requests, a determination will be made on the loan application package.

If the borrower's loan application is accepted, the borrower will receive a **loan commitment,** which is a document outlining the terms under which the lender will loan the specified amount to the borrower. The loan commitment is an offer by the lender; when it is accepted by the borrower, it becomes a contract between the parties.

In this tangle of information, what are lenders truly looking for? First, they are looking for a favorable income ratio, one indicating that the majority of the borrower's income will not be devoted to the payment of principal, interest, taxes, and insurance. Second, lenders are looking at the borrower's overall debt load. They will set a ceiling on what percentage of the borrower's income can acceptably be apportioned to the payment of ongoing expenses. Third, lenders are looking at the borrower's employment history, preferring steady employment and a consistent pattern of upward income growth over a particular salary amount. Fourth, lenders are looking at the borrower's overall net worth. Fifth, lenders are looking at the borrower's credit history.

In looking at credit history, lenders rely very heavily on credit scoring, which uses statistical samples to predict the likelihood that a borrower will pay back a loan. The scoring methodology assigns a weight to various characteristics that serve as predictors. The most commonly used credit scoring system at the time of this writing is known as FICO, which stands for the Fair Isaac Corporation, the company that provides the formula and software for the scoring system. FICO scores range from approximately 300 to 850. The higher the score number, the better risk the borrower is, and the greater the chance that the borrower will receive favorable terms from a lender.

Each of the three major credit bureaus—Transunion, Experian, and Equifax—has its own credit scoring system based on the FICO model, but none are identical; thus, a borrower's credit score can differ from one credit bureau to the next. The three bureaus recently have formed a new entity, VantageScore Solutions, LLC, to market a different credit scoring system, VantageScore. VantageScore uses a larger range of scores than FICO, with its scores ranging from 500 to 990.

The most common reasons for refusal of loan applications are lack of financial earning ability, lack of financial resources, frequent changes in employment, poor credit history, and excessive installment purchases.

Secondary Markets

A **secondary market** is a market for the purchase and sale of existing mortgages. The lenders who originate loans comprise the primary market. Once a loan closing has been completed, that loan can be bought or sold in the secondary market. A loan is an investment. The return on the investment for a lender in the primary market is the interest paid on the loan. However, lenders can also profit by selling the loan to investors in the secondary market. Even after the loan is sold, the lender may continue to service the loan by collecting the loan payments from the borrower and passing them on to the investor. The lender receives a servicing fee for servicing the loan.

The secondary market takes all these purchased loans, "warehouses" them, and packages them to resell to investors. The three major secondary lenders are

loan commitment: A document outlining the terms under which the lender will loan a specified amount to the borrower. Once accepted by the borrower, it becomes a contract.

secondary market: A market for the purchase and sale of existing mortgages.

(1) the Federal National Mortgage Association (FNMA), referred to colloquially as Fannie Mae; (2) the Government National Mortgage Association (GNMA), referred to colloquially as Ginnie Mae; and (3) the Federal Home Loan Mortgage Corporation (FHLMC), referred to colloquially as Freddie Mac.

The **Federal National Mortgage Association (FNMA)** was established in 1938 as an agency of the federal government to create a secondary market for loans. In 1968, the FNMA became a private, though governmentally regulated, corporation. The FNMA buys and services conventional, FHA, and VA residential loans that meet its specified guidelines. The **Government National Mortgage Association (GNMA)** was established in 1968 as a division of HUD to provide special assistance for disadvantaged residential borrowers as well as to manage a large portfolio of mortgages. The GNMA works in tandem with the FNMA in the secondary market to assist lending institutions with low-income housing projects. The GNMA provides these institutions with a commitment to purchase the low-income housing loans at a fixed rate. The GNMA then receives a commitment from the FNMA to buy these loans at the current market rate.

The **Federal Home Loan Mortgage Corporation (FHLMC)** was established in 1970 to provide a secondary market, primarily for conventional loans. Its main purpose is to provide liquidity to lenders, such as savings and loan associations, which can sell qualified loans for cash to the FHLMC and then use the cash proceeds to make new loans.

The Real Estate Recession and Mortgage Fraud

The Recent Real Estate Recession

From the mid-1990s through 2006, the U.S. housing market experienced a phenomenon commonly referred to as a "housing bubble." Interest rates were low, so the incentive to save also was correspondingly low and the incentive to obtain loans at advantageous rates to purchase residential housing was high. The demand for housing increased prices until they were spiraling out of control. The "bubble" ultimately burst, leading to a deflated real estate market and, following on its heels, an economic recession.

One of the underlying causes for this dramatic downturn was the offering of creative lending packages to make home-owning more affordable. In addition to making **prime mortgage loans** to high-quality borrowers at prime rates, traditional lenders, as well as financial intermediaries, started offering loans to those borrowers who could not qualify for prime mortgage loans. **Subprime mortgage loans** were available to borrowers with a higher-than-average risk of default due to factors such as poor credit history and lack of steady income. These borrowers obtained financing but were charged a higher interest rate to compensate the lender for the higher risk. Borrowers with credit profiles that were not as dire as those of the subprime borrowers but that did raise issues (for example, a higher loan-to-value or debt-to-revenue ratio or inadequate income verification) qualified for **ALT-A mortgage loans,** which carried an interest rate higher than prime mortgage loans but lower than subprime mortgage loans.

Borrowers of subprime and ALT-A mortgage loans were enticed to enter into loan agreements because the initial terms appeared to be manageable. For example, many of these borrowers obtained ARMs with very low initial payments ("teaser rates").

Federal National Mortgage Association (FNMA): A governmentally regulated corporation that buys and services conventional, FHA, and VA residential loans that meet its specific guidelines.

Government National Mortgage Association (GNMA): A division of HUD that works in tandem with the FNMA in the secondary market to assist lending institutions with low-income housing projects.

Federal Home Loan Mortgage Corporation (FHLMC): A corporation established to provide a secondary market, primarily for conventional loans.

prime mortgage loan: A loan given at the prime rate to a high-quality borrowers.

subprime mortgage loan: A loan given to a borrower who has a higher-than-average risk of default and who pays a higher interest rate to compensate the lender for the higher risk.

ALT-A mortgage loan: A loan given to a borrower whose credit profile presents some issues that disqualify him or her from obtaining a prime mortgage loan. The borrower pays an interest rate higher than a prime mortgage loan and lower than a subprime mortgage loan.

Although the loans were scheduled to reset at much higher rates, borrowers believed they could either refinance before the higher rates took effect or sell their homes at a profit because housing prices kept climbing. Once residential market values started to plummet, neither option was viable, and these borrowers owed more than their homes were worth on the market. Indeed, even those borrowers with prime mortgage loans who bought their properties at the height of the real estate bubble found themselves with loan obligations exceeding the much reduced market value of residential properties.

Lenders were willing to originate a large volume of loans, including higher-risk loans, because they did not retain these loans. They packaged the loans and sold them to investors as mortgage-backed securities. In doing this, the loan-originating lenders passed along the repayment risk. Because the interest rates charged on subprime and ALT-A loans provided a higher rate of return for investors than more traditional investments, these mortgage-backed securities were attractive, and demand for them grew.

Housing prices eventually reached their peak, stalled, and then sharply declined. Borrowers who purchased and financed during the housing bubble found themselves with a debt obligation higher than the value of their properties. A number of borrowers also had acquired home equity lines of credit when the market value of their properties was high and thus were burdened with that financial obligation in addition to their first mortgage loans. Many saw no viable way to extricate themselves from these obligations other than foreclosure. The increased number of foreclosed properties on the market led to an even greater decline in housing prices.

The federal government's response to the real estate crash has been a series of mortgage relief measures geared toward aiding current homeowners, coupled with financial reform measures discussed in the government regulation section of this chapter.

Mortgage Fraud

The economic climate that set the stage for the real estate bubble and its aftermath also produced an environment conducive to mortgage fraud and related fraudulent activity, such as distressed homeowner fraud. The FBI's Financial Institution Fraud Unit (FIFU), in its investigations of these activities, works cooperatively with numerous organizations such as HUD's Office of the Inspector General; the Financial Crimes and Enforcement Network (FinCEN); the Mortgage Bankers Association (MBA); the Department of Justice's Fraud Section; the United States Attorney's Office; and the Internal Revenue Service's Criminal Investigation Section—as well as other federal, state, and local enforcement agencies. In recent years, these agencies have dedicated increased resources to combating a wide variety of fraudulent schemes.

The primary aim of some of these schemes is to acquire housing in which to live. These are loan origination schemes in which the perpetrators are borrowers who have the intent to repay their mortgage loans. Fraudulent activity falling into this category includes misrepresentation of income and asset information. It also includes borrowing money for the down payment on the purchase of property without disclosing this second mortgage to the primary lender. The primary lender agrees to give the borrower a first mortgage loan under the mistaken belief that the borrower invested his or her own money in the down payment.

Other schemes are intended to realize profit through fraudulent activity. These often involve several participants and may include industry professionals such as mortgage brokers, loan officers, appraisers, and others. The fraudulently inflated appraisal of real property is an example of one such scheme. Appraisal documents are falsified to artificially raise the value of a property. This may also involve reporting artificially inflated values of comparable properties in the area of the property to be purchased. Other loan origination schemes for profit include paying industry professionals to falsify a borrower's financial information to qualify the borrower for a loan and participating in illegal property flipping. Another area of fraudulent activity for profit is settlement fraud. This activity often involves title agents and attorneys and includes embezzlement of escrowed funds and funds received at closing, failure to record deeds, and falsification of deeds.

Distressed homeowner fraud and short sale schemes have become more prevalent in recent years. One type of distressed homeowner fraud is an advance fee scheme in which perpetrators purporting to be foreclosure rescue, loan modification, or debt elimination companies charge up-front fees for services that never are provided. Short sale schemes typically involve fraudulent statements made to lenders regarding the absence of hidden agreements between the buyer and seller.

Government Regulation

Dodd-Frank Wall Street Reform and Consumer Protection Act. In response not only to the housing crisis but also to the general economic recession, in July 2010 Congress passed the **Dodd-Frank Wall Street Reform and Consumer Protection Act** (commonly referred to as the **Dodd-Frank Act**). This all-encompassing legislative act, over 2,000 pages in length, created new regulations reforming the financial services industry as well as amending existing federal legislation pertaining to lending practices. In relation to consumer mortgage loans, the Dodd-Frank Act (1) prohibits unfair lending practices, (2) requires additional disclosures for consumer mortgage loans, (3) requires lenders to make more responsible lending decisions pertaining to consumers' abilities to repay these loans, (4) holds lenders responsible for violations, and (5) increases consumer protection on high-cost mortgages. Additionally, it created the Office of Housing Counseling and the Consumer Financial Protection Bureau (CFPB).

Federal Truth in Lending Act. The **Federal Truth in Lending Act (TILA)** and Regulation Z went into effect in 1969. The purpose of these laws is to inform consumers of the exact costs incurred when obtaining a loan. Lenders must make full disclosure of all costs incurred in obtaining credit. Further, lenders are required to disclose to borrowers the annual percentage rate applied to the loan. The **annual percentage rate (APR)** is the true interest rate, which includes charges added such as points and mortgage insurance. These disclosures must be provided within three business days from the date of the loan application. The TILA was revised in 1987 to require complete disclosures regarding ARMs.

As part of the broad reforms in the *Housing and Economic Recovery Act of 2008*, enacted by the federal government in response to the economic and housing crisis, the TILA was amended to include the *Mortgage Disclosure Improvement Act* (*MDIA*), which went into effect in July 2009. This Act expands the coverage of disclosure requirements to transactions that were not originally covered and mandates

Dodd-Frank Wall Street Reform and Consumer Protection Act (Dodd-Frank Act): A broad federal law enacted to reform the financial services industry. In relation to consumer mortgage loans, it establishes increased protections for consumers with respect to mortgage lending practices, including the expansion of consumer disclosures and the implementation of penalties for lender violations.

Federal Truth in Lending Act (TILA): A federal law requiring lenders to make full disclosure of all costs incurred in obtaining credit.

annual percentage rate (APR): The true interest rate on a loan, which includes charges added such as points and mortgage insurance.

waiting periods between disclosures and closings. The MDIA applies to any extension of credit secured by the dwelling of a consumer, including a home refinance loan. There is no requirement that the dwelling be the consumer's principal dwelling. The disclosure statement must contain language that informs consumers that they are not obligated to complete the loan transaction simply because disclosures were provided or because they applied for a loan. A seven-business-day mandatory waiting period is imposed between the time the consumer receives an initial disclosure and the closing of the loan. If the final annual percentage rate differs from the initial rate by more than one-eighth of a percentage point (0.125 percent), the lender is required to re-disclose and then wait an additional three business days before closing on the transaction. Under the MDIA, the only fee that the lender may collect from a consumer prior to providing a disclosure statement is a credit report fee. Additionally, the lender is required to provide a copy of the real estate appraisal at least three business days prior to the closing on the loan. Violation of the TILA (including the amendments contained in the MDIA) can result in both civil and criminal penalties.

Home Ownership and Equity Protection Act (HOEPA). In 1994, the TILA was amended by the **Home Ownership and Equity Protection Act (HOEPA)** to address deceptive practices occurring in home equity lending. The law primarily affects refinances and home equity installment loans. Certain disclosures are required pertaining to loans with high interest rates and/or high fees, and certain lending practices are prohibited regarding these loans. These loans are referred to as *Section 32 mortgages,* referencing Section 32 of Regulation Z, and more commonly as high-cost loans. The Dodd-Frank Act amended the HOEPA by increasing the threshold for transactions requiring HOEPA disclosures. Loans considered high-cost loans by this Act are (1) first mortgage loans on property in which the APR exceeds the rates on Treasury securities by more than eight percentage points, (2) second (or junior) mortgage loans in which the APR exceeds the rates on Treasury securities by more than ten percentage points, and (3) loans in which the total fees and points paid by the borrower exceed 8 percent of the loan amount.

If a loan qualifies, the lender must provide the borrower with several disclosures at least three business days prior to finalizing the loan. In addition to the disclosure requirements under the TILA, the HOEPA requires that lenders give borrowers a written notice that they do not have to complete the loan process and that they have three business days to decide whether they want to consummate the loan transaction. Borrowers of high-cost loans must be warned that they can lose their residence if they fail to make payments. The lender must disclose the APR, the regular payment amount, the loan amount, and any credit insurance premiums included. If the borrower has opted for an adjustable-rate loan, the lender must disclose that the rate and monthly payment may increase and must provide the amount of the maximum monthly payment.

Under the HOEPA, prohibited practices pertaining to high-cost loans include (1) balloon payments, (2) most prepayment penalties, and (3) negative amortization. Due-on-demand clauses cannot be exercised unless the borrower has committed fraud or a material misrepresentation regarding the loan, fails to repay according to the terms of the loan, or takes action that adversely affects the lender's security.

Home Ownership and Equity Protection Act (HOEPA): A federal law, primarily affecting refinancing and home equity installment loans, that requires additional disclosures and prohibits certain practices when a borrower obtains a high-cost loan.

Real Estate Settlement Procedures Act. The **Real Estate Settlement Procedures Act** (commonly referred to as **RESPA**) complements the Truth in Lending Act. The RESPA was enacted to prevent kickbacks and to ensure that borrowers receive full disclosure of all charges they are to pay at closing. The RESPA requires the use of a uniform settlement statement issued by the U.S. Department of Housing and Urban Development (HUD) called a HUD-1 statement in all nonexempt loan transactions. (The HUD-1 statement is discussed in detail in later chapters.) The RESPA also requires that lenders provide all prospective borrowers with an information booklet entitled *Settlement Costs: A HUD Guide.* Further, lenders are to provide borrowers with a **Good Faith Estimate (GFE)**, which is a summary of loan terms and an estimation of closing costs incurred by borrowers. Lenders are required to provide a GFE within three days from the date the loan application is submitted. As a result of the Dodd-Frank Act, changes were made to the RESPA in 2010, and the RESPA regulatory responsibilities were transferred from HUD to the CFPB. One of the major changes pertains to the GFE form, which was expanded to provide greater detail and more transparency of costs and options for consumers, enabling consumers to comparison shop for financing. This form is provided in Exhibit 10–2.

The top of the three-page GFE form sets forth the contact information for the borrower and for the lender originating the mortgage loan as well as the date of the GFE. The terms outlined on the GFE are valid for ten business days. The first page also specifies other important dates such as the lock-in date for the interest rate. It provides a summary of the loan terms, including the initial loan amount, duration of the loan, interest rate, any prepayment penalty, and any balloon payment. If the lender is requiring escrows for real property taxes, insurance, or both, this information is detailed. The bottom of the first page of the GFE summarizes the estimated closing (settlement) charges. These charges are itemized on the second page of the GFE.

Section A on the second page of the GFE itemizes the adjusted charges pertaining to the loan origination. Any loan origination fee, typically calculated as a percentage of the loan amount, will appear here. If points are being charged in connection with the loan, this information also appears in section A. Any points charged are described on the form as a charge incurred for the interest rate quoted. Section B itemizes all other closing costs, including but not limited to charges for title work, government recording charges, and transfer taxes (for a detailed discussion of closing costs, see Chapter 12).

The third page of the GFE describes the three main categories of settlement (closing) charges that can appear on the HUD statement the borrower will receive at closing. These are expressed as limits or tolerances. The first category pertains to charges that cannot increase from those set forth on the GFE. These are the loan origination charge, any credit or points connected to the interest rate, and transfer taxes. The second category pertains to those charges that can increase up to 10 percent from those outlined in the GFE. These are government recording charges and charges for services provided by companies selected or identified by the lender. For example, if the company providing title insurance either is selected by the lender or appeared in a list of title insurance providers identified by the lender, then the actual charges for title insurance charged at closing cannot be more than 10 percent of the estimated cost of title insurance set forth on the GFE. The final category of settlement charges pertains to those that can change (with no specified cap). These include required services provided by companies not selected or identified by the

Good faith estimate form   **EXHIBIT 10-2**

OMB Approval No. 2502-0265

Good Faith Estimate (GFE)

Name of Originator		Borrower	
Originator Address		Property Address	
Originator Phone Number			
Originator Email		Date of GFE	

Purpose

This GFE gives you an estimate of your settlement charges and loan terms if you are approved for this loan. For more information, see HUD's *Special Information Booklet* on settlement charges, your *Truth-in-Lending Disclosures,* and other consumer information at www.hud.gov/respa. If you decide you would like to proceed with this loan, contact us.

Shopping for your loan

Only you can shop for the best loan for you. Compare this GFE with other loan offers, so you can find the best loan. Use the shopping chart on page 3 to compare all the offers you receive.

Important dates

1. The interest rate for this GFE is available through [   ]. After this time, the interest rate, some of your loan Origination Charges, and the monthly payment shown below can change until you lock your interest rate.

2. This estimate for all other settlement charges is available through [   ].

3. After you lock your interest rate, you must go to settlement within [ ] days (your rate lock period) to receive the locked interest rate.

4. You must lock the interest rate at least [ ] days before settlement.

Summary of your loan

Your initial loan amount is	$
Your loan term is	years
Your initial interest rate is	%
Your initial monthly amount owed for principal, interest, and any mortgage insurance is	$ per month
Can your interest rate rise?	☐ No ☐ Yes, it can rise to a maximum of %. The first change will be in
Even if you make payments on time, can your loan balance rise?	☐ No ☐ Yes, it can rise to a maximum of $
Even if you make payments on time, can your monthly amount owed for principal, interest, and any mortgage insurance rise?	☐ No ☐ Yes, the first increase can be in and the monthly amount owed can rise to $. The maximum it can ever rise to is $.
Does your loan have a prepayment penalty?	☐ No ☐ Yes, your maximum prepayment penalty is $
Does your loan have a balloon payment?	☐ No ☐ Yes, you have a balloon payment of $ due in years.

Escrow account information

Some lenders require an escrow account to hold funds for paying property taxes or other property-related charges in addition to your monthly amount owed of $[   ].
Do we require you to have an escrow account for your loan?
☐ No, you do not have an escrow account. You must pay these charges directly when due.
☐ Yes, you have an escrow account. It may or may not cover all of these charges. Ask us.

Summary of your settlement charges

A	Your Adjusted Origination Charges *(See page 2.)*	$
B	Your Charges for All Other Settlement Services *(See page 2.)*	$
A + B	Total Estimated Settlement Charges	$

Good Faith Estimate (HUD-GFE) 1

EXHIBIT 10–2   *(continued)*

Understanding your estimated settlement charges

Some of these charges can change at settlement. See the top of page 3 for more information.

Your Adjusted Origination Charges

1. Our origination charge This charge is for getting this loan for you.	
2. Your credit or charge (points) for the specific interest rate chosen ☐ The credit or charge for the interest rate of [＿＿] % is included in "Our origination charge." (See item 1 above.) ☐ You receive a credit of $ [＿＿＿] for this interest rate of [＿＿] %. This credit **reduces** your settlement charges. ☐ You pay a charge of $ [＿＿＿] for this interest rate of [＿＿] %. This charge (points) **increases** your total settlement charges. The tradeoff table on page 3 shows that you can change your total settlement charges by choosing a different interest rate for this loan.	
A Your Adjusted Origination Charges	$

Your Charges for All Other Settlement Services

3. Required services that we select These charges are for services we require to complete your settlement. We will choose the providers of these services. *Service* *Charge*	
4. Title services and lender's title insurance This charge includes the services of a title or settlement agent, for example, and title insurance to protect the lender, if required.	
5. Owner's title insurance You may purchase an owner's title insurance policy to protect your interest in the property.	
6. Required services that you can shop for These charges are for other services that are required to complete your settlement. We can identify providers of these services or you can shop for them yourself. Our estimates for providing these services are below. *Service* *Charge*	
7. Government recording charges These charges are for state and local fees to record your loan and title documents.	
8. Transfer taxes These charges are for state and local fees on mortgages and home sales.	
9. Initial deposit for your escrow account This charge is held in an escrow account to pay future recurring charges on your property and includes ☐ all property taxes, ☐ all insurance, and ☐ other [＿＿＿＿＿＿＿＿].	
10. Daily interest charges This charge is for the daily interest on your loan from the day of your settlement until the first day of the next month or the first day of your normal mortgage payment cycle. This amount is $[＿＿＿] per day for [＿＿] days (if your settlement is [＿＿＿＿＿]).	
11. Homeowner's insurance This charge is for the insurance you must buy for the property to protect from a loss, such as fire. *Policy* *Charge*	
B Your Charges for All Other Settlement Services	$
A + **B** Total Estimated Settlement Charges	$

 Good Faith Estimate (HUD-GFE) 2

Instructions

Understanding which charges can change at settlement

This GFE estimates your settlement charges. At your settlement, you will receive a HUD-1, a form that lists your actual costs. Compare the charges on the HUD-1 with the charges on this GFE. Charges can change if you select your own provider and do not use the companies we identify. (See below for details.)

These charges **cannot increase** at settlement:	The total of these charges **can increase up to 10%** at settlement:	These charges **can change** at settlement:
■ Our origination charge ■ Your credit or charge (points) for the specific interest rate chosen (*after you lock in your interest rate*) ■ Your adjusted origination charges (*after you lock in your interest rate*) ■ Transfer taxes	■ Required services that we select ■ Title services and lender's title insurance (*if we select them or you use companies we identify*) ■ Owner's title insurance (*if you use companies we identify*) ■ Required services that you can shop for (*if you use companies we identify*) ■ Government recording charges	■ Required services that you can shop for (*if you do not use companies we identify*) ■ Title services and lender's title insurance (*if you do not use companies we identify*) ■ Owner's title insurance (*if you do not use companies we identify*) ■ Initial deposit for your escrow account ■ Daily interest charges ■ Homeowner's insurance

Using the tradeoff table

In this GFE, we offered you this loan with a particular interest rate and estimated settlement charges. However:

■ If you want to choose this same loan with **lower settlement charges,** then you will have a **higher interest rate.**

■ If you want to choose this same loan with a **lower interest rate,** then you will have **higher settlement charges.**

If you would like to choose an available option, you must ask us for a new GFE.

Loan originators have the option to complete this table. Please ask for additional information if the table is not completed.

	The loan in this GFE	The same loan with lower settlement charges	The same loan with a lower interest rate
Your initial loan amount	$	$	$
Your initial interest rate[1]	%	%	%
Your initial monthly amount owed	$	$	$
Change in the monthly amount owed from this GFE	No change	You will pay $ **more** every month	You will pay $ **less** every month
Change in the amount you will pay at settlement with this interest rate	No change	Your settlement charges will be **reduced** by $	Your settlement charges will **increase** by $
How much your total estimated settlement charges will be	$	$	$

[1] For an adjustable rate loan, the comparisons above are for the initial interest rate before adjustments are made.

Using the shopping chart

Use this chart to compare GFEs from different loan originators. Fill in the information by using a different column for each GFE you receive. By comparing loan offers, you can shop for the best loan.

	This loan	Loan 2	Loan 3	Loan 4
Loan originator name				
Initial loan amount				
Loan term				
Initial interest rate				
Initial monthly amount owed				
Rate lock period				
Can interest rate rise?				
Can loan balance rise?				
Can monthly amount owed rise?				
Prepayment penalty?				
Balloon payment?				
Total Estimated Settlement Charges				

If your loan is sold in the future

Some lenders may sell your loan after settlement. Any fees lenders receive in the future cannot change the loan you receive or the charges you paid at settlement.

Good Faith Estimate (HUD-GFE) 3

Source: U.S. Department of Housing and Urban Development; http://www.hud.gov/content/releases/goodfaithestimate.pdf

lender, the initial escrow deposit, the daily interest charges, and homeowner's insurance. The third page of the GFE also includes a trade-off table and a chart to aid a borrower in comparing GFEs received by multiple lenders.

Related to the change in the GFE form, the RESPA changed the form of the HUD-1 statement to tie settlement charges itemized on the HUD statement to those on the GFE. As of January 2010, the HUD-1 statement used in residential transactions is a three-page form, the third page containing a chart comparing the estimated settlement charges on the GFE to the actual settlement charges as of the date of closing itemized on the HUD-1 statement. The third page also provides a summary of the loan terms. The CFPB has been charged with developing new mortgage disclosure forms that will merge the TILA and RESPA forms. As of the date of this writing, some prototypes have been created, but none have been officially adopted and mandated. As it is likely that new forms will be forthcoming, federal regulations should be checked.

Other changes the Dodd-Frank Act made to the RESPA include mandates placed on servicers of federally related mortgage loans. They must respond in a timely fashion to a borrower's request to correct errors pertaining to payments and balances. They must respond, within ten business days, to a borrower's request for contact information of the owner or assignee of the borrower's loan. Additionally, these servicers cannot obtain force-placed hazard insurance unless there are reasonable grounds for believing that the borrower has not complied with property insurance requirements stated in the loan agreement. Before force-placed insurance can go into effect, a loan servicer must send written notification about the insurance to the borrower. A second written notice must be sent at least thirty days after the sending of the first notification. The borrower, upon receipt of notification, can send written confirmation of existing hazard insurance to the servicer, and if proper insurance is in place, the servicer must terminate any force-placed insurance and refund the borrower.

In keeping with the intention of federal reforms to protect borrowers and increase accountability, the **Secure and Fair Enforcement for Mortgage Licensing Act (S.A.F.E. Act)** was enacted in 2008. It requires mortgage loan originators (MLOs) employed by institutions regulated by various federal agencies to complete a federal registration process with the Nationwide Mortgage Licensing System and Registry. Mandatory registration began in 2011. The twofold aim is to achieve more transparency by providing consumers with access to background information on MLOs and to reduce mortgage fraud.

Mortgage Assistance Relief Services Rule. The **Mortgage Assistance Relief Services Rule (MARS),** promulgated by the Federal Trade Commission (FTC), went into effect in January 2011. The rule applies to any person or entity that provides, offers to provide, or arranges for others to provide any mortgage assistance relief service. It defines *mortgage assistance relief service* as a service, plan, or program that is represented, either expressly or impliedly, in exchange for consideration, to help consumers with negotiating and obtaining mortgage relief, such as loan modifications, forebearance agreements, short sales, deeds-in-lieu of foreclosure, and other similar types of relief. The purpose of the rule is to protect consumers from false or misleading claims made by providers of mortgage assistance relief services. It requires that specific information be disclosed regarding services in advertisements geared to a general audience, in communications with prospective customers, and

Secure and Fair Enforcement for Mortgage Licensing Act (S.A.F.E. Act): A federal law requiring mortgage loan originators employed by institutions regulated by various federal agencies to register on a nationwide registry to provide consumers with access to their background information.

Mortgage Assistance Relief Services Rule (MARS): A federal regulation that prohibits the making of false and misleading claims by providers of mortgage assistance relief services. It sets forth mandatory disclosure, record-keeping, and compliance requirements for the providers of these services.

in offers of mortgage relief from a lender or loan servicer. Fees may not be collected from a customer until an offer of mortgage relief is made by the customer's lender or loan servicer, that offer is communicated in writing to the customer, and the customer accepts the offer. Additionally, the MARS imposes record-keeping and compliance requirements pertaining to advertising and promotional materials, sales records, communications with customers, and agreements with customers.

Clients who are in need of mortgage relief may seek legal advice from attorneys, raising the question of whether attorneys can be categorized as providing mortgage assistance relief services and thus subject to the MARS requirements. According to the FTC, attorneys are not subject to the MARS requirements if (1) they provide mortgage assistance relief services as part of the practice of law, (2) they are licensed to practice law in the state where their client or their client's home is located, and (3) they comply with all relevant state laws concerning attorney conduct.

Equal Credit Opportunity Act. The **Equal Credit Opportunity Act (ECOA) of 1974** was enacted to prevent discrimination in making credit available to consumers. Under the ECOA, no lender may discriminate against a borrower on any of the following bases: race, color, religion, national origin, sex, marital status, age, or receipt of income from public assistance programs. The Dodd-Frank Act created an Office of Fair Lending and Equal Opportunity to coordinate the efforts of the CFPB to enforce fair lending laws, and it amended the ECOA to transfer rule-making authority from the Board of Governors of the Federal Reserve System to the CFPB.

Lenders must have borrowers sign an Equal Credit Opportunity Notice, verifying that the borrower is aware of the discrimination prohibition. A sample Equal Credit Opportunity Notice is provided in Exhibit 10–3.

When evaluating an applicant's qualifications, lenders must consider the following:

1. Reliable public assistance income
2. Reliable income from part-time employment, Social Security, pensions, and annuities
3. Reliable alimony, child support, or separate maintenance payments
4. Income, regardless of the sex or marital status of the applicant

> **Equal Credit Opportunity Act (ECOA):** A federal law enacted to prevent discrimination in making credit available to consumers.

Equal credit opportunity notice	EXHIBIT 10–3

EQUAL CREDIT OPPORTUNITY NOTICE

THE FEDERAL EQUAL CREDIT OPPORTUNITY ACT PROHIBITS CREDITORS FROM DISCRIMINATING AGAINST CREDIT APPLICANTS ON THE BASIS OF RACE, COLOR, RELIGION, NATIONAL ORIGIN, SEX, MARITAL STATUS, AGE (PROVIDED THE APPLICANT HAS THE CAPACITY TO ENTER A BINDING CONTRACT); BECAUSE ALL OR PART OF THE APPLICANT'S INCOME DERIVES FROM ANY PUBLIC ASSISTANCE PROGRAM; OR BECAUSE THE APPLICANT HAS IN GOOD FAITH EXERCISED ANY RIGHT UNDER THE CONSUMER CREDIT PROTECTION ACT. THE FEDERAL AGENCY THAT ADMINISTERS COMPLIANCE WITH THIS LAW CONCERNING THIS CREDITOR IS THE CUSTOMER ASSISTANCE GROUP, COMPTROLLER OF THE CURRENCY, 1301 MCKINNEY STREET, SUITE 3710, HOUSTON, TX 77010-3031.

Both the ECOA and the Fair Credit Reporting Act (discussed below) require a creditor to notify a credit applicant when it has taken adverse action against the applicant. The term *creditor* includes lenders, and, therefore, lenders must not only notify loan applicants when they deny a loan request but also provide specific disclosures.

Fair Credit Reporting Act (FCRA). Enacted in 1970, the **Fair Credit Reporting Act** (FCRA) gives individuals the right to examine their own credit history. It enables consumers to contact credit bureaus and find out what credit information is being provided by the bureaus. Additionally, it allows consumers to dispute the wrongful use or interpretation of their information. The FCRA was amended in 2003 by the *Fair and Accurate Transaction Act* (*FACTA*). The FACTA provides for more accurate credit reporting, measures to prevent identity theft, and restrictions on the use of client-sensitive information in marketing. It also gives consumers the right to one free credit report per year from each bureau. Under the FACTA, both the credit bureau and the information provider must correct any inaccurate or incomplete information in a credit report brought to their attention by the consumer. Further, consumers are entitled to obtain a list of everyone who has requested a report within the past year (within the past two years for an employment-related request).

The FCRA was amended again by the Dodd-Frank Act. One significant amendment pertains to the information that must be provided if a lender takes adverse action against a borrower or potential borrower. ECOA-FCRA adverse action notices must disclose credit scores and related information if a credit score is used in whole or in part to deny a loan request. The following information must be included:

1. A numerical credit score used in making the credit decision;
2. The range of possible scores under the model used;
3. Up to four key factors that adversely affected the credit score (or up to five factors if the number of inquiries made is a key factor);
4. The date on which the credit score was created; and
5. The name of the person or entity that provided the credit score.

Homeowner's Protection Act (HPA). The **Homeowner's Protection Act (HPA) of 1998** was enacted to establish rules for homeowners who wish to cancel their private mortgage insurance (PMI). Under the Act, borrowers can cancel their PMI after they have paid off 20 percent of their home's cost as long as they:

1. Request cancellation in writing,
2. Have a good payment history, and
3. Have not permitted devaluation of the property securing the loan.

Automatic cancellation of PMI occurs when 22 percent of the home's value has been paid off.

Gramm-Leach-Bliley Act. The **Gramm-Leach-Bliley Act** went into effect on July 1, 2001. It requires financial institutions to establish safeguards to ensure the confidentiality of customer records and nonpublic personal information. Financial institutions must have privacy policies and disclose these policies to their customers at the commencement of the customer relationship and thereafter at least once a year. Additionally, customers must be given the option to opt out before any nonpublic information

Fair Credit Reporting Act (FCRA): A federal law enacted to give individuals the right to examine their own credit history.

Homeowner's Protection Act (HPA): A federal law that establishes rules for homeowners who wish to cancel their private mortgage insurance.

Gramm-Leach-Bliley Act: A federal law requiring financial institutions to establish safeguards to ensure the confidentiality of customer records and nonpublic personal information.

is disclosed to an unaffiliated third party. The Act provides that the FTC is to enforce the privacy provisions on mortgage brokers and lenders not affiliated with banks. In accordance with this mandate, the FTC promulgated the *Financial Privacy Rule* and the *Safeguards Rule,* which must be followed by these brokers and lenders.

Preparation of Financing Instruments

Promissory Notes

As noted in the introduction to this chapter, a promissory note is a document evidencing a promise to pay a specified amount of money over a specified period of time. The parties to the note are the borrower, referred to as the **maker,** and the lender, referred to as the **payee** or *holder*. A promissory note is signed only by the maker and usually is not witnessed, notarized, or recorded. There are some exceptions, however, such as in New York, where promissory notes are witnessed and sometimes notarized. In certain situations, the lender may require additional assurance that the loan will be paid and may require a guarantor. This is especially true when a corporation or limited liability company is the borrower. The owners of these businesses are not personally responsible under ordinary circumstances for business debts. Thus, if a corporation obtains a loan and then defaults, the lender cannot look to the individual shareholders to repay the debt. When the maker is a corporation or limited liability company, the lender will almost always require a key individual in the business, such as the president of the corporation, to personally guarantee the repayment of the loan by signing personally, not as the maker, but as a guarantor. This may be accomplished in a separate document. If this is done and the corporation defaults, the lender may look to the president personally to repay the debt obligation.

As a real estate paralegal, there may be many occasions on which you will be asked to prepare a promissory note. In order to prepare a note, you must know the names of the parties, the date, the place at which the note is made, the amount of the loan, the interest rate, the payment terms, the rights of the parties upon default, and the prepayment provisions. Some lenders allow prepayment without penalty. Recall that in both FHA and VA loans, for example, the borrower is allowed to prepay without paying any penalty charges. Some lenders institute a lock-in period, such as the first two or three years of the loan, during which time prepayment is prohibited. Other lenders may prohibit all prepayment unless stiff prepayment penalties are paid. In preparing a promissory note, the checklist found below may prove helpful. A sample note is provided in Exhibit 10–4 in the Hypothetical Client Matter section at the end of the chapter.

maker: The borrower signing a promissory note.

payee: The lender as receiver of a promissory note.

NOTE PREPARATION CHECKLIST

1. Date
2. City and state in which note is made
3. Parties
   a. Name of maker
   b. Name of payee
   c. Name of guarantor(s), if any

4. Amount of loan
5. Interest rate, fixed or adjustable. If adjustable, specify:
   a. Adjustment period
   b. Periodic cap
   c. Overall cap
   d. Index to which interest rate is tied
6. Total amount of payments
7. Maturity date
8. Amount of each payment and what is included in each payment
   a. Principal
   b. Interest
   c. Taxes
   d. Insurance
9. When payments are to be made
10. Where payments are to be made
11. Late charges, if any
12. Security for note
13. Prepayment privileges or penalties
14. Parties' rights in event of default
15. Waiver of homestead or other debtor's rights
16. Signature(s) of maker and guarantor

Mortgages and Deeds of Trust

Some attorneys use preprinted forms for mortgages and deeds of trust, while others prepare their own forms for the most common types of loans. Lenders may require their own printed forms, and FNMA and FHLMC documents are often used so that the loans can then be sold in secondary markets.

There will be two or three parties to a financing instrument, depending on whether the instrument is a mortgage or a deed of trust. If the borrower is married, his or her spouse must also join as a party in order to relinquish all homestead and inchoate rights in the property that is the collateral for the loan in states that recognize these rights. In addition to the names of the parties, a financing instrument must include the date, an accurate legal description of the property that is the security for the debt, a description of all personal property that is included as collateral for the loan, and a description of the debt terms (this should be taken directly from the note).

The financing instrument should include an agreement to pay the debt; a maintenance clause in which the borrower agrees to maintain the property in good condition and to allow the lender to take over maintenance and charge the borrower accordingly if the borrower defaults on this provision; a tax clause in which the borrower agrees to pay all real property taxes and to allow the lender to make the requisite tax payments and charge the borrower accordingly if the borrower defaults on this provision; an assignment of rents clause, if applicable; a receivership clause permitting the lender to have a receiver appointed to oversee income-producing property if it is necessary to preserve the income value of the property; and a clause permitting the lender to inspect the property. The name and address of the preparer of the instrument should be included if state statute so requires. The signature of the borrower must be witnessed and notarized. State law specifies the number of witnesses and form of notarization.

After delivery to the lender or trustee, the financing instrument must be recorded in the jurisdiction in which the real property securing the debt is located. The checklist found below should prove helpful in the preparation of deeds of trust and mortgages. A sample deed of trust can be found in Exhibit 10–1, while a sample short-form mortgage is provided in Exhibit 10–5 in the Hypothetical Client Matter section at the end of this chapter.

FINANCING INSTRUMENT PREPARATION CHECKLIST

1. Date
2. Parties
   a. If deed of trust:
      i. Trustor
      ii. Trustee
      iii. Beneficiary
   b. If mortgage:
      i. Mortgagor
      ii. Mortgagee
3. Legal description of the real property
4. Description of all personal property serving as additional collateral
5. Description of the loan debt terms (take this from the note)
6. Agreement by trustor/mortgagor to pay debt on above terms
7. Tax clause
8. Maintenance clause
9. Inspection clause
10. Assignment of rents clause, if applicable
11. Receivership clause, if applicable
12. Duties of trustor/mortgagor
13. Due-on-sale clause, if applicable
14. Rights of parties in event of default
15. Signature of trustor/mortgagor
16. Signatures of witnesses
17. Notarization
18. Name and address of preparer of instrument

hypothetical client matter

In consulting her tickler file this morning, Barbara notices that she has scheduled the drafting of certain documents in preparation for an upcoming residential closing. The clients in question are Karen and Henry Lipton, who have contracted to sell their house to Marilyn and Richard Olson. In the clients' file, Barbara reviews the financing arrangements for the purchase of the Lipton residence and notes that $125,000 of the purchase price is to be seller-financed by the Liptons. The interest to be charged on the $125,000 principal is 5 percent, the note to be payable in monthly installments over a period of ten years. The monthly payments under this arrangement work out to $1,326.00, comprising principal and interest. Taking note of other pertinent information, such as the street address and legal description of the property, Barbara proceeds to prepare the promissory note and mortgage instrument.

Barbara prepares the note first because a substantial portion of the note's contents must be repeated in the mortgage instrument. The closing is scheduled to take place on August 18, so the monthly payments would begin September 18 (recall that loan payments are paid in arrears). When completed, the promissory note reads as shown in Exhibit 10–4.

Barbara next turns her attention to the mortgage instrument. The mortgage will be executed on the same day as the note and will be recorded when the deed transferring title is recorded. The mortgage must include the legal description of the property, which Barbara copies from the contract for sale and purchase. The mortgage will contain a recital of the major provisions of the note as well as an acceleration clause, tax clause, and maintenance clause. Under state law, the mortgage must be witnessed by two witnesses for each signatory and must be notarized. Upon completion, the mortgage reads as shown in Exhibit 10–5.

EXHIBIT 10–4   **Promissory note**

PROMISSORY NOTE

$125,000.00   Any City, Any State
                                                                     August 18, 2015

FOR VALUE RECEIVED, the undersigned, jointly and severally, promise to pay to HENRY LIPTON and KAREN LIPTON, his wife (hereinafter referred to as "Holders"), in the manner hereinafter specified, the principal sum of ONE HUNDRED AND TWENTY-FIVE THOUSAND DOLLARS ($125,000.00) with interest from date at the rate of five percent (5%) per annum on the unpaid balance, payable in lawful money of the United States of America at 55 Durham Lane, Any City, Any State, or at such place as may hereafter be designated by written notice from the Holders to the Makers hereof, on the date and in the manner following:

> Payable in equal monthly installments of One Thousand Three Hundred and Twenty-Six Dollars ($1,326.00), principal and interest inclusive, for 120 months, commencing on the 18th day of September, 2015, and continuing on the 18th day of each month thereafter, until fully paid. Prepayment in full or a portion of the principal balance may be made at any time.

This note with interest is secured by a mortgage on real estate, of even date herewith, made by the Makers hereof in favor of the Holders, and shall be construed and enforced according to the laws of the State of Any State.

If default be made in the payment of any of the sums or interest herein mentioned or in said mortgage for a period of 30 days, the Holders may, at their option, declare the entire principal sum and interest at once due and collectible. Failure to exercise this option shall not constitute a waiver of the right to exercise the same in the event of any subsequent default.

In the event of default in the making of any payments herein provided and in the event the Holders exercise the option to declare the entire principal sum and interest at once due and collectible, said principal sum and accrued interest shall both bear interest from such time until paid at the highest rate allowable under the laws of the State of Any State. Makers hereby agree to pay all costs, including a reasonable attorney's fee, whether suit be brought or not if, after maturity of this note or default hereunder, or under said mortgage, counsel shall be employed to collect this note

EXHIBIT 10–4

or to protect the security of said mortgage. Makers further waive demand, protest and notice of demand, protest and nonpayment.

GIVEN under the hand and seal of each party, the day and year first above written.

_____
Richard Olson

_____
Marilyn Olson

Mortgage

EXHIBIT 10–5

This instrument prepared by:
Ava Ross, Esquire
Fisher, Ross, and Simon, P.A.
1900 N.W. 3rd Avenue
Any City, Any State

MORTGAGE

Executed the 18th day of August, 2015, by RICHARD OLSON and MARILYN OLSON, his wife (hereinafter the "Mortgagors") to HENRY LIPTON and KAREN LIPTON, his wife (hereinafter the "Mortgagees"). In consideration of the principal sum specified in the promissory note hereafter described, the Mortgagors hereby mortgage to the Mortgagees the real property in Any County, Any State, described as follows:

Lot 7 in Block 3, DUMBARTON ESTATES, a subdivision according to the plat thereof, as recorded in Plat Book 206, Page 9, of the Public Records of Any County, Any State

as security for the payment of the promissory note herein substantially copied, to-wit:

$125,000.00

Any City, Any State
August 18, 2015

FOR VALUE RECEIVED, the undersigned, jointly and severally, promise to pay to HENRY LIPTON and KAREN LIPTON, his wife (hereinafter referred to as "Holders"), in the manner hereinafter specified, the principal sum of ONE HUNDRED AND TWENTY-FIVE THOUSAND DOLLARS ($125,000.00) with interest from date at the rate of five percent (5%) per annum on the unpaid balance, payable in lawful money of the United States of America at 55 Durham Lane, Any City, Any State, or at such place as may hereafter be designated by written notice from the Holders to the Makers hereof, on the date and in the manner following:

Payable in equal monthly installments of One Thousand Three Hundred and Twenty-Six Dollars ($1,326.00), principal and interest inclusive, for 120 months, commencing on the 18th day of September, 2015, and continuing on the 1st day of each month thereafter, until fully paid. Prepayment in full or a portion of the principal balance may be made at any time.

If default be made in the payment of any of the sums or interest herein mentioned or in said mortgage for a period of 30 days, the Holders may, at their option, declare the entire principal sum and interest at once due and collectible. Failure to exercise this option shall not constitute a waiver of the right to exercise the same in the event of any subsequent default.

EXHIBIT 10–5   *(continued)*

In the event of default in the making of any payments herein provided and in the event the Holders exercise the option to declare the entire principal sum and interest at once due and collectible, said principal sum and accrued interest shall both bear interest from such time until paid at the highest rate allowable under the laws of the State of Any State. Makers hereby agree to pay all costs, including a reasonable attorney's fee, whether suit be brought or not if, after maturity of this note or default hereunder, or under said mortgage, counsel shall be employed to collect this note or to protect the security of said mortgage. Makers further waive demand, protest and notice of demand, protest and nonpayment.

GIVEN under the hand and seal of each party, the day and year first above written.

/s/ Richard Olson
Richard Olson

/s/ Marilyn Olson
Marilyn Olson

The Mortgagors agree that this purchase money mortgage is given and intended to be recorded simultaneously with a deed executed and delivered by the Mortgagees to the Mortgagors, in order to secure a portion of the purchase price of the above-described real estate.

The Mortgagors further agree to pay promptly when due the principal and interest provided for in said note and this mortgage.

The Mortgagors agree to pay all taxes, assessments, liens and encumbrances on the above-described real estate promptly when due. Should the Mortgagors fail to pay them promptly, the Mortgagees may pay them, without waiving any rights of foreclosure, and such payments, with interest accruing from the date of payment at the same rate as specified in the note, shall also be secured by this mortgage.

The Mortgagors agree to permit no waste, impairment or deterioration of the above-described real property or the improvements thereon at any time, and to keep the building on said property insured in an amount of not less than eighty percent (80%) of full insurable value of the improvements, with a company acceptable to the Mortgagees, the policy or policies to be held by, and payable to, the Mortgagees. In the event any sum of money becomes payable by virtue of such insurance, the Mortgagees have the right to receive and apply the same to the indebtedness hereby secured, accounting to the Mortgagors for any surplus.

The Mortgagors agree to pay all expenses reasonably incurred by the Mortgagees because of Mortgagors' failure to comply with the agreements contained in the note or in this mortgage, including reasonable attorneys' fees. Such sums for expenses, with interest thereon from the date of payment at the same rate as specified in the note, shall also be secured by this mortgage.

If any sum of money herein referred to is not promptly paid within thirty (30) days after the same becomes due, or if any of the agreements, stipulations, conditions or covenants contained within the note or this mortgage are not fully complied with, the entire unpaid balance of the note shall, upon the option of the Mortgagees, become due and payable, and the Mortgagees may foreclose this mortgage in the manner provided by law and have the mortgaged property sold to satisfy the indebtedness hereby secured. Failure of the Mortgagees to exercise any of the rights or options herein provided shall not constitute a waiver of any rights or options under the note or this mortgage.

IN WITNESS WHEREOF, the said mortgage has been hereunto signed and sealed on the day and year first above written.

Signed, sealed and declared in the presence of:

_____   _____
                                          Richard Olson

_____   _____
                                          Marilyn Olson

STATE OF ANY STATE
COUNTY OF ANY COUNTY

I HEREBY CERTIFY that on this day before me, an officer duly authorized in the State aforesaid and in the County aforesaid to take acknowledgments, personally appeared RICHARD OLSON and MARILYN OLSON, his wife, to me known to be the persons described in and who executed the foregoing instrument, and they acknowledged before me that they executed the same.

WITNESS my hand and official seal in the County and State aforesaid this _____ day of _____, 2015.

_____
Notary Public, State of Any State
My commission expires: _____

CHAPTER SUMMARY

1. When a borrower enters into a loan transaction with a lender, the borrower, in return for the money loaned, gives the lender a promissory note, evidencing the borrower's pledge to repay the loan on specified terms. The borrower also gives the lender a security instrument in the form of either a deed of trust or a mortgage, which pledges the real property as collateral for the debt.

2. A mortgage is a two-party instrument. The parties are the borrower (mortgagor) and lender (mortgagee). The mortgage sets forth the legal description of the real property pledged as collateral, a description of the debt terms as provided in the note, various agreements by the borrower to maintain the property and pay all taxes and insurance, and the rights and remedies available should a default occur. In the latter instance, the lender is given the right to accelerate the loan. Should the borrower fail to pay the outstanding sum, the lender can initiate a foreclosure action.

3. A deed of trust is a three-party instrument. The parties are the borrower (trustor), the lender (beneficiary), and a third-party trustee. The terms of a deed of trust are similar to those found in a mortgage. In a deed of trust, however, the trustee is given a power of sale whereby, upon the borrower's default, the trustee can publish a notice of public sale of the property without bringing a court action.

4. There are a variety of financial sources from which a prospective borrower may seek financing. The two most common sources are commercial banks and savings and loan associations. Commercial banks generally provide construction loans, short-term loans, and home improvement loans. Savings and loan associations specialize in residential, long-term loans. Both commercial banks and savings and loan associations make conventional, FHA, and VA loans. Commercial banks, however, make a greater number of FHA and VA loans than do savings and loan associations. Other loan sources include insurance companies, mutual savings banks, credit unions, mortgage banking companies, REITs, and individuals.

5. A conventional loan typically has a lower loan-to-value ratio than an FHA or VA loan. The lender wants assurance that the borrower is committed to repayment of the debt through the borrower's equity investment in the property. FHA loans require a minimum down payment from the borrower, while VA loans may require no down payment at all.

6. FHA and VA loans are made for owner-occupied residential dwellings. In applying for either an FHA or a VA loan, both the borrower and the property must qualify. FHA loans are available to all borrowers, whereas VA loans are available to eligible veterans and to their widows and widowers. The FHA insures loans made by approved lenders, whereas the VA guarantees loans made by approved lenders. The FHA charges the borrower a mortgage insurance premium. Both FHA and VA loans require the borrower to make PITI payments.

7. Loans can be either fixed-rate loans or adjustable-rate loans. Adjustable-rate loans start out with a lower interest rate than fixed-rate loans. The interest rate is tied to an index and is altered each adjustment period. Adjustable-rate loans have both periodic and overall caps.

8. The lending process begins with an initial interview between the prospective borrower and a loan officer. The borrower provides the loan officer with the requisite information to complete the loan application forms. An appraisal is ordered on the real property to verify its value, and a credit report check is run on the borrower. Considerable time is spent on verifying the information supplied by the borrower. Should both the borrower and the property qualify, the lender provides the borrower with a loan commitment.

9. The recent real estate recession, caused in part by creative lending practices, has led both to an increase in mortgage-related fraud and to legislative reforms aimed at consumer protection and transparency in lending practices. These reforms have led to the creation of new federal regulations, such as the Mortgage Assistance Relief Services Rule, as well as amendments to long-standing legislative acts, such as the Fair Credit Reporting Act, the Truth in Lending Act, and the Real Estate Settlement Procedures Act.

WEB RESOURCES

http://www.hud.gov/

This is the site of the U.S. Department of Housing and Urban Development (HUD). If you select "About HUD" and then "Programs of HUD," you can access information on federal statutory laws pertaining to lending as well as information on various government assistance programs and Ginnie Mae mortgage-backed securities. Under the "Resources" tab, you can access FHA mortgage limits and HUD handbooks. State-specific information can be accessed under the "State Info" tab.

http://www.ftc.gov/

This is the site of the Federal Trade Commission (FTC). Information pertaining to credit and loans can be obtained at this site.

http://www.fdic.gov/

This is the site of the Federal Deposit Insurance Corporation (FDIC). If you select "Regulations & Examinations," you can review the laws and regulations that govern FDIC-insured institutions.

http://www.fha.com/

This site provides information on various FHA loan types, FHA loan lending limits for each state, and FHA loan requirements. It also provides an FHA mortgage calculator.

http://www.benefits.va.gov/

This site provides an overview of the VA home loan program and the eligibility requirements.

http://www.ginniemae.gov/

This is the official site of the Government National Mortgage Association (Ginnie Mae). It explains what Ginnie Mae is and what it does, and under "Inside Ginnie Mae," it provides a link to Ginnie Mae statutes and regulations.

http://www.fanniemae.com/

This site explains the background of Fannie Mae. Under "Homeowners & Community," a homeowner can determine whether Fannie Mae owns his or her loan. The site also has information pertaining to predatory lending and provides a mortgage calculator.

http://www.freddiemac.com/

This site provides an overview of the Federal Home Loan Mortgage Corporation, commonly known as "Freddie Mac," and its role in the secondary market. A homeowner can determine whether Freddie Mac owns his or her loan. Information pertaining to HARP and other programs aimed at assisting homeowners can be accessed at this site.

http://www.bankrate.com/

This site gives you daily mortgage rates on fixed-rate and adjustable-rate mortgage loans so you can compare rates. Additionally, it provides mortgage calculators, news, articles, and advice.

http://www.mbaa.org/

This is the site of the Mortgage Bankers Association. In addition to current mortgage loan rates, under the "Community Outreach" section, you will find a home loan learning center, providing information on mortgage basics and related brochures. You can access various mortgage calculators, news articles, research, and forecasts on mortgage finance and the economy.

http://www.fbi.gov/

This is the site of the Federal Bureau of Investigation (FBI). You can access its mortgage fraud reports by selecting "About Us" and then selecting "Reports and Publications."

http://www.respanews.com/

This site provides the latest news pertaining to the RESPA, TILA, and industry news. It also has a glossary of RESPA terminology.

REVIEW QUESTIONS

1. What major differences exist between a deed of trust and a mortgage?
2. Explain the loan application process.
3. What are the primary reasons for refusal of a loan application?
4. What information must be provided on a Good Faith Estimate?
5. Compare and contrast FHA and VA loans.
6. What information must be included in the following?
    a. A promissory note
    b. A deed of trust or mortgage

DISCUSSION QUESTIONS

1. Two years ago, Mary Cutler executed a mortgage note and mortgage instrument with a private individual, Donald Easton. According to the note, Mary was obligated to repay Donald a principal amount of $100,000 plus stated interest in 180 monthly installments. The note stated that there were no prepayment penalties, but it also stated that any prepayment would be subject to the approval of the holder of the note (Donald Easton). A house at 250 Briarwood Lane served as collateral for the loan. Mary now wants to sell the house and has a buyer for it. She wants to pay off the note, but Donald will not give his approval. If the matter ended up in litigation, which party would prevail? Why?
2. Under what circumstances would it be advisable to use the services of a mortgage broker?
3. Tim Lindstrom has been shopping for mortgage loans. He is looking for a fixed-rate loan. ABC Bank is offering a thirty-year fixed-rate loan at 5 percent with two points. XYZ Bank is offering a thirty-year fixed-rate loan at 5.5 percent with no points. What factors should Tim take into consideration in determining which of these loans is the better option for him?
4. Sandra Baker has contracted to buy a house and is working with a mortgage broker. Sandra is concerned about meeting the monthly payment obligations of a loan, and the mortgage broker suggests she go with an adjustable-rate mortgage loan. Sandra knows that with the lower starting interest rate on an adjustable-rate loan, the initial monthly payments will be easier for her to meet. She is concerned about what will happen down the line when that rate increases. The mortgage broker says to her, "Oh, you can always refinance later." Do you believe the mortgage broker is giving her sound advice? Why or why not?
5. Raymond Steele entered into a contract with Michelle Findley to purchase a parcel of property for $175,000. The contract contained a mortgage contingency clause that provided that the contract was contingent upon the buyer obtaining a first mortgage commitment from a lending institution in the amount of $140,000 within four weeks from the signing of the contract. The clause further stated that the buyer agreed to make a good faith application for the mortgage loan and that, if approval was not obtained in the four-week period, either party could terminate the contract by providing written notice. Raymond obtained a conditional mortgage commitment letter for $180,000 from ABC Bank within the time frame specified in the contract. The letter contained closing conditions

and a list of approval conditions, including an appraisal report indicating the value of $195,000 for the property. (The purchase price was $175,000.) Upon expiration of the four-week deadline, Michelle's attorney sent Raymond a letter stating that Michelle elected to terminate the contract. She then entered into another contract with a new prospective buyer. Has Michelle breached the contract with Raymond? Why or why not?

ETHICAL QUESTION

The law firm receptionist transfers a telephone call for your supervising attorney, Deborah Sanders, to your office. The caller is Mark Farnsworth, a prospective client. Mark is behind on his loan payments and has received a demand letter from his lender, Metropolitan Bank. He wants to meet with Deborah to discuss his options in responding to the letter. You set up an appointment for tomorrow morning. You then follow your usual routine of doing a conflict of interest check. Your law firm has offices in three counties of your state. Upon doing your search, you discover that Allen Mitchell, an attorney working out of another of your law firm's offices, represents Metropolitan Bank in several legal matters. May Deborah represent Mark? Why or why not?

Slossberg Law Office on CourseMate

Please go to www.cengagebrain.com to log into CourseMate, access the Slossberg Law Office, and work on your client files. Each module corresponds to a chapter in the text. Within each module, you will be provided with instructions by the supervising attorney. You are asked to keep track of time spent on time sheets. The documents produced through working on client files in the law office can then be compiled into a portfolio of final work product.

CourseMate

The available CourseMate for this text has an interactive eBook and interactive learning tools, including flash cards, quizzes, and more. To learn more about this resource and access free demo CourseMate resources, including the Slossberg Law Office, go to www.cengagebrain.com, and search for this book. To access CourseMate materials that you have purchased, go to login.cengagebrain.com.

11

Title Examination and Title Insurance

CHAPTER OBJECTIVES

Upon completion of this chapter, the student will:

- Understand the function of title insurance
- Know how to examine an abstract of title
- Know how to prepare a title commitment
- Know how to prepare title policies

Introduction

As noted in earlier chapters, when one purchases a parcel of land, one is purchasing not only the land itself but also the legal rights inherent in real property ownership. In addition to the individual rights held by the owner, others may have legal rights that have an impact on the owner's rights. These other rights may stem from the creation of easements on the property; liens recorded against the property; restrictions on usage imposed by homeowners' associations or condominium associations; or local, state, or federal regulations that affect the title of the owner of the property.

When purchasing real estate, the buyer wants assurance that the title to the property being conveyed is good and marketable. This does not necessarily mean that the property is free and clear of all encumbrances. For example, there may be an easement across a small portion of the property that was created to benefit the property, such as a utility easement. However, good and **marketable title** does mean a title that is free from encumbrances that would bring down the value of the property or threaten foreclosure against the property, such as an encroachment on the property or a construction lien filed against the property.

Prior to closing a real estate transaction, the purchaser must determine the quality of the title he or she will receive. In order to make this determination, a **title search** must be conducted. A title search is the search of the public records to determine if title to real property is marketable. All instruments that affect the title of the parcel of real property in question must be examined. This typically is done through the use of electronic databases that may be free of charge or fee-based. The records must be searched first to determine what recorded instruments exist that affect the property. Instruments affecting title to real property include, but are not limited to, mortgage instruments; deeds; judgment, tax, and other liens; divorce decrees;

declarations of condominium; and homeowners' association declarations of covenants and restrictions.

Once the documents themselves are located, their legal sufficiency must be determined. For example, a deed recorded forty years ago conveying the property from a previous seller may not have been notarized. If notarization was required by state statute at the time the deed was recorded in the public records, this lack of notarization may be a defect in the title to the property unless statutory law presently exists that allows for correction of this defect. Similarly, if a mortgage instrument had been recorded but no satisfaction of mortgage was found canceling that obligation prior to or after the property passed to the grantee, that mortgage instrument remains on the record as a still-existing lien and thus is considered a defect in the title unless it can be removed.

From these illustrations, one can understand that title examination is a very detailed and scrupulous process that the average purchaser is not equipped to undertake on his or her own. Thus, the responsibility of title examination has fallen on attorneys, who are in the position to provide a prospective purchaser with a written legal opinion on the condition of the title to the real property in question. When a client hires an attorney to represent him or her in a real estate transaction, the client is hiring the attorney to perform a myriad of tasks: (1) to prepare the necessary documents needed for the real estate closing and ensure that they are properly recorded, (2) to examine the title to the property and prepare an opinion on the title, (3) to supervise the closing process, and (4) to provide title insurance to protect the purchaser and lender.

An attorney's legal opinion on the title of the property covers only those items that are contained in the public records. The attorney cannot give an opinion regarding matters that are not revealed by an examination of the records, such as a neighbor's encroachment, adverse possession, or forged signatures on crucial documents. Therefore, while an attorney's legal opinion letter regarding the title is important, it does not, and cannot, cover all matters that may affect the title. The purpose of title insurance is to cover those matters that are not readily identifiable.

Title insurance is insurance obtained by an owner of real property or another having an interest in the real property (such as the lender-mortgagee) against loss brought about by encumbrances, defective titles, invalidity, or adverse claims to the title. While the attorney's role is to ascertain what the more obvious risks might be through an examination of the records, a title insurance policy is a contract to indemnify the property owner (or lender) against loss in value due to the more unlikely risks, such as forged deeds, recording mistakes, claims of undisclosed heirs, and so forth.

Title companies that issue title insurance are regulated by state statute and the insurance departments of their respective states. Prior to issuing title policies in a given state, title companies must submit both their policy forms and their rates for approval by the state's insurance department. Title insurance agents are licensed according to state regulations. In addition to issuing title insurance policies and collecting premiums, they may act as closing agents. In this capacity, they may be responsible for escrowing funds such as real estate commissions, closing costs, and mortgage loan payoffs.

The title company attorney conducts a title examination and then issues a title report called a **title commitment,** or *title binder*. The title commitment sets forth the status of the title of a particular parcel of real property and states the terms

marketable title: Title to real property that is free from encumbrances that would bring down the value of the real property or create reasonable doubt or controversy.

title search: The search of the public records to determine if title to real property is marketable.

title insurance: Insurance obtained by an owner of real property or another having an interest in the real property against loss brought about by encumbrances, defective titles, invalidity, or adverse claims to the title.

title commitment: A document that sets forth the status of the title of a particular parcel of real property and the terms under which a title policy for the property will be issued.

under which a title policy for the property will be issued. The title commitment also may be used by the seller as evidence of marketable title prior to closing.

Because title companies issue title insurance policies based on attorneys' opinions, most title companies employ their own in-house counsel as title examiners. In some states, title insurers have been created specifically for attorneys. Attorneys become members by contributing a portion of the fee from real estate transactions to a statewide fund. The membership funding provides the monies to underwrite the title property.

The **American Land Title Association (ALTA)** is an organization that was created to meet the demands for uniform title insurance protection nationwide. The ALTA has devised title commitment and title policy forms that are used in many parts of the country. Most title insurers utilize the ALTA forms in their original form or in a modified form.

As a real estate paralegal, you may be working at a title insurance company that employs in-house counsel, at a law firm that utilizes the services of outside title insurance companies, or at a law firm that has attorney-members acting as title agents of an attorney-owned underwriter. In any of these situations, a knowledge of title examination and preparation is crucial. Your supervising attorney may call upon you to examine an abstract of title, to review or prepare a title commitment and/or title policies, or to conduct or update a title search. This chapter explains the function of title insurance and the process of title examination. It also details the procedures for writing title commitments and title policies and explains the most commonly used endorsements attached to title policies.

The Function of Title Insurance

Title insurance, like other forms of insurance, is a contract in which the insurer agrees to pay for loss or damage arising from an event in return for the insured's payment of a premium. However, title insurance differs from other forms of insurance in several important aspects.

Most types of casualty insurance provide for coverage of loss arising from the occurrence of an event within a contractually prescribed time period beginning from the effective date of the policy, such as one year. The event covered must occur within this time period. Title insurance, on the other hand, provides coverage for loss in value to the real property from a defect in title that existed prior to the effective date of the policy. For example, suppose a title search mistakenly overlooks a mortgage lien placed on the property prior to the issuance of a title insurance policy. That mortgage lien is a defect that existed prior to the issuance of the policy. The title insurance company will cover the risk of such a happening.

Casualty insurance must be renewed continuously to keep the coverage effective. This is done through the periodic payment of premiums. At the end of each policy period, the insurer may reevaluate the cost of the insurance and adjust the premium payments accordingly. Title insurance, on the other hand, is purchased by the insured once through the payment of a single premium. The premium is based strictly on the amount of coverage provided. An owner's policy generally covers the purchase price of the real property. The insured is then covered against risks for as long as the insured retains title to the property. Note, however, that a title insurance policy may not be assigned from the existing property owner to a new purchaser.

American Land Title Association (ALTA): An organization that was created to meet the demands for uniform title insurance protection nationwide. It has devised title commitment and title policy forms that are used in many parts of the country.

Casualty insurers evaluate the risk they are taking by looking at the statistics showing the probability of a certain event (for example, a hurricane or flood) happening in a particular location within the contractual period. Title insurers evaluate marketable title determined from a search of the records of the subject property. Items affecting the quality of title must be either cleared up prior to the issuance of the policy (for example, the payment in full of the seller's existing mortgage loan on the property) or noted as exceptions to the coverage of the policy. By instituting these measures, the insurer greatly reduces its risk.

Title insurance provides coverage for risks of possible defects undiscovered because the title search was incomplete, because the title examiner misinterpreted the records, or because the defects could not be ascertained by a regular examination of the documents (for example, forgery or lack of legal capacity of a party to an instrument). Although these risks seem unlikely to occur, they have occurred.

The cost of title insurance is modest compared to many of the other closing costs incurred in a real estate transaction. In addition to any owner's coverage that might be purchased, banking laws require lending institutions to obtain from a mortgagor title insurance covering the mortgagee's lien priority up to the loan amount. The mortgagee's coverage decreases as the loan balance is reduced. In some states, both the owner and the lender-mortgagee are covered on the same title policy. In other states, when title insurance is issued, two policies typically are issued: an owner's policy and a mortgagee's policy.

Who pays for title insurance is negotiated and is a matter of contract. Sellers must provide proof of marketable title. The contract for sale and purchase should indicate what proof is acceptable, who is required to do the title search, the date upon which the search must be completed and the results provided to the purchaser, who will issue the policy(ies), and who will pay for the policy(ies).

The Examination Process

In General

A title examination may be conducted by an attorney or delegated to the attorney's paralegal. It may also be conducted by a title company or an abstract company. The examination process begins by a search of the public records to find all recorded documents pertaining to the subject real property. The public records books to be inspected often are located with the clerk of the court in the county in which the real property is located or in separate land records facilities. In some states and/or counties, recorded documents may be amassed in one set of books called official records books. In other states and/or counties, the documents are sorted and recorded according to type. In these places, several books must be inspected, such as deed books, mortgage books, and so forth. As noted above, public records searches typically can be conducted online.

When examining the public records, the title examiner attempts to establish a chain of title for the property in question. A **chain of title** is the genealogy of the property. It is a listing of all instruments affecting the property, from the first recorded instrument to the most recent, and indicates (1) the kind of instrument, (2) the date recorded, (3) the place recorded, (4) the maker of the instrument, (5) the person for whose benefit the instrument was made, and (6) the interest(s) created by the instrument.

chain of title: The genealogy of a particular parcel of real property.

A title examiner may search the actual records or, when available, may utilize an abstract (discussed later). When searching the records, the title examiner begins with a set of indices, commonly the *grantee index* and the *grantor index*, and begins with the present owner and works backward. For example, if the present owner of the property is Theodore Warner, the title examiner would start with the grantee index because the last deed to the property was deeded to Theodore Warner. If Erica Lanson deeded the property to Theodore, then the grantee index for Erica Lanson must be consulted to determine who deeded the property to her. This process is repeated until the earliest public records have been found. After completing this procedure, the title examiner has a chronological list of grantors and grantees. Next, the title examiner must consult the grantor index, looking up the name of each grantor, to determine whether any of the grantors listed delivered more than one deed to the property or encumbered the property in any way during their periods of ownership.

Another way in which a title examiner may commence a search of the public records is by starting with a **tract index.** Whereas the grantor and grantee indices are compiled by the names of the parties in a real estate conveyance, the tract index is compiled by a description of parcels of property. Thus, rather than starting with the name of the present owner of the property in question, the examiner starts with the legal description of the property. The examiner first refers to that portion of the legal description that sets forth the record or plat book number and page. Turning to that page, the plat or tract map to locate the parcel of real property is reviewed. The map should provide a parcel identification number for each parcel of property within the tract, which can then be used to find all other recorded documents directly pertaining to the property.

The search of the grantee and grantor indices, or the tract index, is just the start. There may be other matters affecting the title to the property in court records, such as a probate, divorce, or a mortgage foreclosure, that must be checked. Additionally, the current or previous owners of the property may have pledged personal property, as well as the real property in question, as security for a mortgage loan. To determine this, the examiner must research the Uniform Commercial Code financing statement index for recorded financing statements.

The examination of the indices is a laborious, time-consuming process. Therefore, title companies and abstract companies conveniently put together the "history" of properties in abstracts of title. An **abstract of title** is a copy or condensed version of each document pertaining to a particular parcel of property. Title examiners rely on the work of prior abstractors and update existing abstracts when the title to the property is to change hands. (Abstract examination is discussed in detail in the following text.)

Some states allow a title examiner to utilize the work of prior examiners to streamline the procedure by using a previous title policy issued on the subject property in place of a search of the records up to that date. The policy issuance date is the date until which the search is current. The title examiner must then do a search from that date until the present to bring the search up-to-date.

In addition to inspection of the records, a physical inspection of the property must be done to ascertain any encumbrances to the land that do not appear in the record. Many lending institutions require that a survey be done as a condition of financing. (For a detailed discussion of surveys, see Chapter 5.) The title examiner will want to review the survey for the location of easements mentioned in the

tract index: An index compiled by a description of parcels of real property.

abstract of title: A copy or condensed version of each document pertaining to a particular parcel of real property.

recorded documents to note where the easements are located in relation to the improvements on the property. The title examiner will also look for encroachments and any discrepancy between the legal description provided by the surveyor and the legal description in the previous title policy.

Examination of Documents

Once the title examiner finds all of the documents pertaining to the subject real property, each document must be examined, in turn, to ascertain its legal sufficiency. This process is called *chaining title*. With each document, the examiner must make a notation of (1) the type of document (for example, a deed or mortgage), (2) the contents of the document, (3) the names of the parties to the document, (4) the date of the document, (5) the date of recording of the document, (6) the signatures and acknowledgments, and (7) any other information affecting interests or rights to the property mentioned in the document.

The type of document will indicate the type of interest the document conveys (for example, a deed conveying ownership rights or a mortgage lien conveying lien rights). A deed may convey the entire property or a portion of it. It may convey a fee simple or a life estate. The deed may contain restrictions as to usage. It may refer to other encumbrances on the property. The type of deed may indicate what claims the grantor is making regarding the title (for example, a warranty deed, giving the greatest number of assurances, or a quitclaim deed, giving no assurances).

The names of the parties to each document must be examined to determine whether the granting party has the legal right to convey an interest in the real estate. For example, if a prior deed was granted by Marjory Williams to James M. Douglas and the next deed in chronological order was granted by Jim Douglas, Jr., to Alice Fairchild, there is a question about whether James M. Douglas and Jim Douglas, Jr., are the same person. The use of "Jr." indicates that there is more than one James Douglas, and the matter must be researched to determine whether the grantor in the second deed was indeed the grantee in the first. Examination of the parties to a document also includes examination of their marital status. As noted earlier in the text, spouses must be included as grantors in a deed to relinquish any dower, curtesy, or homestead rights they may have in states that recognize these rights.

The date the document was signed and the date the document was recorded should be checked. The date the document was recorded establishes record title in the property. The date the document was signed may be relevant in determining the legal sufficiency of the instrument. For example, state statutes may require that all documents executed after a statutorily specified date be witnessed by two witnesses. If the document in question is signed by only one witness, the date of the document will determine whether it is defective.

Finally, the signatures on the document must be reviewed to determine legal sufficiency. The signatures must match the names of the granting parties. If a corporation is the grantor, the document must be signed by the officer(s) given the authority to act on behalf of the corporation by statute or by the corporation's board of directors. This information may be checked by looking at the corporate resolution giving the officer(s) the authority to sell the property on behalf of the corporation. If acknowledgments are required, they must meet your state statute's requirements.

Abstract Examination

An abstract of title is a condensed history of each document affecting the title of a particular parcel of real property prepared by a licensed and bonded abstractor. The abstractor develops the chain of title and "abstracts" each document, which means that he or she writes out a synopsis of each document, setting forth only the information that directly pertains to the title of the subject property. In addition, most abstract or title companies now make a copy of every document in the public record pertaining to the property. Each document is marked by an entry number and compiled into one instrument, the abstract of title.

An abstract of title contains (1) a caption setting forth the legal description of the real property and the name of the person or title company preparing the abstract, (2) each document in chronological order from the earliest to the most recent, and (3) an **abstractor's certificate,** which states the records the abstractor has examined, any records not examined, and the dates covered by the search. The abstract is then updated each time ownership of the property is transferred.

As a real estate paralegal, you may be asked to review an abstract of title and report your findings to your supervising attorney. This is most easily done if you have a pad and a pen or pencil handy. To begin, you should first compare the legal description in the caption of the abstract of title with the legal description of the property as set forth in the current owner's title policy or in the current deed. Next, you should write down at the top of the pad (1) the client file and matter number, (2) the name(s) of the purchaser(s), (3) the name(s) of the seller(s), (4) the legal description of the property, and (5) the abstract(s) reviewed, noting the number on the abstract(s), the name of the company preparing the abstract(s), the person from whom the abstract(s) was obtained, the dates covered by the abstract(s), and the number of entries in the abstract(s).

The next step is to divide your page into three columns. In one column, you will put your chain of title, commencing with the first entry in the abstract. In the middle column, you will put any encumbrances, such as mortgages or liens, as well as any satisfactions. In the third column, you will note any problems detected in a particular document entry, such as lack of witnesses, lack of spousal joinder, or lack of notarization. In the column in which you commence your chain of title, start by noting the entry number, and then indicate the following: (1) the grantor, (2) the type of document (you may use abbreviations, such as W.D. for warranty deed), (3) the date of the instrument, (4) the date of recording, and (5) the book and page number of the recorded document, such as is found in the example provided in Exhibit 11–1.

abstractor's certificate: A certificate that states the records the abstractor has examined, any records not examined, and the dates covered by the search.

EXHIBIT 11–1   **Sample chain of title entry**

> **Mark Hampton and Susan Hampton**
> **Husband and Wife**
>
> W.D.
> 3-17-15
> 3-19-15
> O.R.B. 107/25

If, in your review of the entry, you find anything affecting the validity of the document or title, note it in the appropriate column. Mortgages should be noted in the encumbrance column. When noting a mortgage, set forth (1) the name of the mortgagee, (2) the date of execution, (3) the date of recording, and (4) the book and page number of the recorded instrument. Likewise, when a satisfaction of mortgage entry is found, put it in the encumbrance column, with a line connecting the mortgage and the satisfaction of mortgage. You can put an "X" through each, indicating that they cancel each other out.

For a better understanding of abstract examination, a small, sample abstract is provided in Exhibit 11–2, followed by a review of the contents of the abstract. Note that most abstracts contain more entries than those provided in this sample.

Working one's way through the abstract chronologically, the first entry appears to be in order. It sets forth that the conveyance was made by a warranty deed; it gives the pertinent information pertaining to date executed and recorded; it gives the deed book and page numbers. The legal description is correct. The deed was signed in the presence of two witnesses. Assuming that two witnesses are required in the state of Any State, the deed meets this specification. The deed was also notarized. The notary public's commission was still in force at the time of notarization, and the notary's seal appears on the deed.

In the second entry, the grantor is Cynthia Adams, the widow of Benjamin Adams. The title examiner would need to obtain proof of death for Benjamin Adams and to determine that Cynthia was the only heir, as her name did not appear on the prior deed, so she and Benjamin did not take title to the property together as tenants by the entirety. The title examiner would also have to ascertain that Cynthia was single at the time of the conveyance to Jonathan Baker. If she was not, then the joinder of her spouse was necessary to convey any curtesy rights and/or homestead rights in the property. (For a detailed discussion of homestead and dower and curtesy rights and a discussion of the various types of tenancies, see Chapter 2.)

The third entry is a mortgage lien securing a loan in the amount of $35,000. Because a mortgage lien is an encumbrance, a notation of this would be put in the encumbrance column rather than in the chain of title column when writing out a review of the abstract.

The fourth entry is a satisfaction of the mortgage loan in the third entry. A notation of the satisfaction would be put in the encumbrance column, with a line connecting it to the mortgage. An "X" can then be placed over each, indicating that one cancels out the other.

The fifth entry indicates that this deed was witnessed by only one witness. If the state of Any State required only one witness at the time, there is no problem here. The title examiner would have to research the relevant statute operating at the time of conveyance rather than the current statute. Thus, it is the statutory law of 1971 that controls. If it is found that two witnesses were indeed required, then the title examiner must research to determine whether there are any state corrective statutes that will cure the lack of witnesses.

In the sixth entry, there is a notation that the expiration date of the notary public's commission was not stated. This means that from looking at the information on the deed, one cannot determine whether the notary public's commission was still in force at the time the deed was notarized. The title examiner in this instance would have to research the relevant state statutes regarding notarizations to

EXHIBIT 11–2   **Sample abstract**

SAMPLE ABSTRACT

No. 2222
LOT 5, BLOCK 4 of
CEDARCREEK ESTATES

According to the plat thereof recorded in Plat Book 12, Page 50, of the Public
Records of Any County, Any State
(Caption lies in the SE 1/4 of NW 1/4 of Section 9, Township 3 North, Range 5
West, Any County, Any State)
Compiled by
Any State Title Company

ENTRY 1

Edward Rodgers and	
Helen Rodgers, his wife	W.D.
to	Dated: March 1, 1945
	Filed: March 9, 1945
Benjamin Adams	Deed Book 30, Page 40

Grant, bargain, sell and convey to party of second part the following property in Any County, Any State, to wit:

The SE 1/4 of NW 1/4 of Section 9, Township 3 North, Range 5 West.

Signed and sealed by Edward Rodgers and Helen Rodgers, his wife, in the presence of two witnesses.

Acknowledged by grantors March 1, 1945, before Notary Public, Any County, Any State. Notary's commission expired June 1, 1947—Notary's Seal.

ENTRY 2

Cynthia Adams, widow of Benjamin Adams	W.D.
to	Dated: April 5, 1955
	Filed: April 8, 1955
Jonathan Baker	Deed Book 60, Page 70

Grants, bargains, sells and conveys the SE 1/4 of NW 1/4 of Section 9, Township 3 North, Range 5 West.

Signed and sealed by grantor in presence of two witnesses. Acknowledged by grantor April 5, 1955, before Notary Public, Any County.

Notary's commission expired September 31, 1956—Notary's Seal.

ENTRY 3

Jonathan Baker and	
Louise Baker, his wife	Mortgage: $35,000.00
	Dated: April 5, 1955
to	Filed: April 8, 1955
Cynthia Adams	Mortgage Book 20, Page 55

Encumbers property in Any County, Any State, the SE 1/4 of NW 1/4 of Section 9, Township 3 North, Range 5 West.

Secures one note of even date in amount of $35,000 bearing interest at 7% per annum, payable five years after date.

Signed and sealed by Jonathan Baker and Louise Baker, his wife, in presence of two witnesses. Acknowledged by mortgagors April 5, 1955. Notary's commission expired November 1, 1957—Notary's Seal.

ENTRY 4

Cynthia Adams, widow

to

The Public

Satisfaction of Mortgage
Dated: March 2, 1960
Filed: March 4, 1960
Mortgage Book 24, Page 13

Recites payment in full of mortgage indebtedness secured by mortgage executed by Jonathan Baker and Louise Baker, his wife, to Cynthia Adams dated April 5, 1955, recorded in Mortgage Book 20, page 55, Any County Records, and directs Clerk to cancel same of record.

Signed and sealed by Cynthia Adams. Acknowledged by Cynthia Adams, March 2, 1960. Notary's commission expired May 10, 1961—Notary's Seal.

ENTRY 5

Jonathan Baker and
    Louise Baker, his wife

to

Joan Grant, a single woman

W.D.
Dated: July 17, 1971
Filed: July 20, 1971
Deed Book 70, Page 14

Grants, bargains, sells and conveys the SE 1/4 of the NW 1/4 of Section 9, Township 3 North, Range 5 West.

Signed and sealed by grantors in presence of only one witness, before Notary Public, Any County, Any State, July 17, 1971. Notary's commission expired October 1, 1973—Notary's seal.

ENTRY 6

Joan Grant, a single woman

to

Jay Davidson and
    Alice Davidson, his wife

W.D.
Dated: September 20, 1983
Filed: September 25, 1983
Deed Book 80, Page 22

Grants, bargains, sells and conveys the SE 1/4 of the NW 1/4 of Section 9, Township 3 North, Range 5 West.

Signed and sealed by grantors in presence of two witnesses. Acknowledged by grantors September 20, 1983. Expiration of Notary's commission not stated—Notary's Seal.

ENTRY 7

IN THE CIRCUIT COURT OF THE 5TH JUDICIAL CIRCUIT, IN AND FOR
ANY COUNTY, ANY STATE, CASE NO. 84-1000

Martha Kent

v.

Jay Davidson

Dated: February 11, 1984
Filed: February 11, 1984
(Certified copy)
Official Records Book 902, Page 40

It is considered, ordered and adjudged that Plaintiff to have and recover from the Defendant, Jay Davidson, the sum of $21,000, together with interest at 8% per annum, from January 3, 1983, and costs of Court taxes at $90.00 for which let execution issue.

Done and ordered at Any City, Any County, Any State, this 11th day of February, 1984.

Gregory M. Hall
Circuit Judge

EXHIBIT 11–2   *(continued)*

ENTRY 8

IN RE:

    Estate of Jay Davidson,

      deceased

In Circuit Judge's Court

Any County, Any State Probate

No. 5555, Petition filed, May 3, 1993

Petition for Letters of Administration filed by Alice Davidson recites that Jay Davidson died intestate April 20, 1993; that at the time of his death, he was domiciled in Any City, Any State; that the approximate value of his estate was $400,000; that the residence and post office address of the petitioner is 450 Cedarcreek Drive, Any City, Any State.

That the petitioner, aged 62, was the wife of the decedent and that the only other heir is Angela Davidson, daughter, aged 27, residing at 325 N.W. 16th Street, Any City, Any State. Prays for Letters of Administration to Petitioner.

Sworn by petitioner May 2, 1993. Orders for Letters of Administration entered May 3, 1993, no bond required. Oath of Administration filed May 3, 1993. Letters of Administration to Alice Davidson May 3, 1993. Administrator discharged November 10, 1995.

ENTRY 9

Angela Davidson, a single woman

    to

Alice Davidson

Q.C. Deed

Dated: November 15, 1995

Filed: November 18, 1995

Deed Book 90, Page 34

Remises, releases and quitclaims the SE 1/4 of the NW 1/4 of Section 9, Township 3 North, Range 5 West.

Signed and sealed by grantor in presence of two witnesses. Acknowledged by grantor November 15, 1995. Notary commission expired February 20, 1996—Notary's Seal.

ENTRY 10

Alice Davidson

    to

GEM Development Corp.

(an Any State corporation)

W.D.

Dated: June 6, 2001

Filed: June 8, 2001

Deed Book 97, Page 55

Grants, bargains, sells and conveys the SE 1/4 of the NW 1/4 of Section 9, Township 3 North, Range 5 West. Signed by grantor in presence of two witnesses.

Acknowledged by grantor June 6, 2001, before Notary, Any County, Any State. Notary's commission expired December 31, 2001—Notary's Seal.

ENTRY 11

GEM Development Corp.

(an Any State corporation)

    to

Lawrence Miller and

    Donna Miller, his wife

W.D.

Dated: August 14, 2010

Filed: August 15, 2010

Deed Book 105, Page 23

Grants, bargains, sells and conveys the SE 1/4 of the NW 1/4 of Section 9, Township 3 North, Range 5 West. Signed in the name of the corporation by Bruce Stewart as President. Corporate seal affixed and attested by Ann Evans as Secretary in the presence of two witnesses.

Acknowledged August 14, 2010, by Bruce Stewart as President and Ann Evans as Secretary of the corporation before a Notary Public, Any County. Notary's commission expired March 5, 2011.

NO. 2222
CERTIFICATE
OF
ANY STATE TITLE COMPANY

Any State Title Company hereby certifies that the foregoing Abstract of Title comprising Entries numbered 1 to 11, inclusive, correctly exhibits or recites all matters affecting Title to, or encumbering the property described in the caption hereof (except zoning and other Governmental Regulations and matters expressly excepted therein), which were filed for Public Record during the period of time set out hereinbelow.

The period of time covered by this Abstract extends from the earliest public records to and including February 20, 2015, at 6:00 o'clock p.m.

IN WITNESS WHEREOF, Any State Title Company has caused this Certificate to be signed in its name and its corporate seal to be affixed this 21st day of February, 2015.

ANY STATE TITLE COMPANY
By: *Diane Barclay*

(Corporate Seal)   President

determine whether a statement of the expiration date of commission was required. If it was required, then the title examiner would have to research state statutes to determine the existence of a curative statute to correct this defect.

The seventh entry is a judgment lien against Jay Davidson, one of the grantees in the prior deed. Like the mortgage lien, the judgment lien is an encumbrance against the property and should be noted in the applicable column. Here the question of tenancy is relevant. The prior deed indicates the grantees to be "Jay Davidson and Alice Davidson, his wife." The title examiner would need to determine whether this language would be sufficient in the state of Any State to create a tenancy by the entirety. If a tenancy by the entirety was created by the prior deed, the judgment would not create a lien on the property because a judgment against one spouse cannot encumber tenancy by the entirety property. Recall from earlier discussions that this form of tenancy gives a 100 percent interest in the property to each spouse. Because the judgment is only against Jay, Alice's property interest cannot be affected, and she owns 100 percent of the property, as does Jay.

If the language of the deed is found not to create a tenancy by the entirety, then the title examiner would have to see if any subsequent documents satisfy the judgment. If so, the lien is removed, as was the case with the mortgage lien noted earlier. If no satisfaction of judgment is recorded, the title examiner would research state statutes to determine how long a judgment lien remains a lien on the property. This lien was recorded in 1984. The abstract was completed in 2015. This is a span of thirty-one years. It is likely that the statute of limitations pertaining to enforcement of the judgment lien has expired. If this is the case, the judgment lien is no longer an encumbrance.

If you are asked to review an abstract, you would continue to work through each entry in this fashion through the final entry. In each instance, you would note any concerns, such as those mentioned in the preceding text, and research your state's *curative statutes* (statutes designed to remedy legal defects in previous transactions), statute of limitations, and other relevant statutes to determine whether any title problems can be remedied.

Computerized Title Searches

In most states, title records can be obtained through computerized systems. An attorney-owned title insurance underwriter may have its own computerized system that it makes available to its agent-members. Exhibit 11–3 provides an example of part of a printout from the Attorneys' Title Information Data System (ATIDS), a computer data system made available to members of the Attorneys' Title Insurance Fund, Inc., a Florida title insurance underwriter. If an attorney wanted to update an abstract or obtain updated information since the last title policy was written for a particular property, he or she might utilize a similar system.

The information at the top of Exhibit 11–3 indicates the date of the title search, February 19, 2007; the county in which the search was conducted, Palm Beach County; and the time the computer printout was produced, 8:14 a.m. The printout next indicates that the information provided is certified from December 14, 1977, through February 1, 2007, at 11:00 p.m. This is followed by a file number and a description of the search; in this instance, the description provided is the name of a party to the real estate transaction. Note that the legal description of the property can be found in Plat Book 29, Page 196. This title search covers from June 15, 2000, through January 31, 2007. Next to this information, on the right, the code "ID" appears. It pertains to restricted searches. If a special, restricted search was done, the ID code for the type of documents searched would be shown here.

The next section provides information concerning the plat. The name of the platted subdivision is La Mancha 2. The plat was recorded in the public records on September 5, 1972. The "LB" following "authorized levels" indicates that the legal designation of the property is by lot and block number. The "T" stands for "tract." The printout is certified through February 1, 2007, at 11:00 p.m. The number of instruments found for the search data provided is fourteen. From this point on in the printout, data are provided for each instrument found through the search. The printout is fourteen pages in length. Only a portion is provided in Exhibit 11–3.

The instruments appear in the printout in reverse chronological order, the most recently recorded instrument appearing at the bottom of the first page of the printout. "DOF" refers to the date of recording of the instrument; in this instance, September 18, 2006. The primary reference (PR) for this first entry is Official Records Book Number 20863, Page 85. The secondary reference (SR) is to the clerk's file number—here 2006 for the year filed, followed by file number 0535346. The date of the instrument (DOI) is September 11, 2006. The type of instrument (TOI) is noted by abbreviation. Here the abbreviation "AFF" appears, indicating an affidavit. The first party to this instrument is the clerk of the circuit court. In this instance, there is no second party to the instrument. In the comments section,

ATIDS printout

EXHIBIT 11–3

```
ATID AEG@        **** ATTORNEYS' TITLE INSURANCE FUND, INC. ****      02/19/2007
                      ATTORNEY TITLE INFORMATION DATA SYSTEM            08:14:32
                            FOR COUNTY OF PALM BEACH
                  * * * * * * * * * CERTIFIED PRINTOUT * * * * * * * * *
                    DATA FOR:
              CUSTOMER NO.:  899976
    FUND BRANCH INFORMATION:  CERTIFIED THROUGH 02/01/2007 AT 1100 PM
                              CERTIFIED THROUGH BOOK 21369   PAGE 1777
                              CERTIFIED FROM    12/14/1977
               FILE NUMBER:  04-0045
               DESCRIPTION:  LEBLANC
                             H CO., FL

                    OPENED:  01/24/2006
                    CLOSED:  01/31/2007

ATID AEG@        **** ATTORNEYS' TITLE INSURANCE FUND, INC. ****      02/19/2007
                            FOR COUNTY OF PALM BEACH                    08:14
      SP- PB  BK-     29    PG-      196    FILE/ORDER REF: 04-0045
      SEARCH  FROM- 06152000     THRU- 01312007     ID-
      --L1-- --L2-- --L3--     --L1-- --L2-- --L3--     --L1-- --L2-- --L3--
  ->       9      V
  ->
  ->
  ->
      PLAT NAME:
       LA MANCHA 2
      DATE OF PLAT- 09/05/1972    AUTHORIZED LEVELS- LB /T /
      PLAT CERTIFIED - ALL POSTINGS CONFORM TO AUTHORIZED LEGALS.
      FUND BRANCH CERTIFIED THROUGH 02/01/2007 AT 11:00 PM

                   ********* RETRO DATA CERTIFIED *********
    14 INSTRUMENTS FOUND FOR SEARCH ARGUMENTS
```

```
    ATID           **** ATTORNEYS' TITLE INSURANCE FUND, INC. ****PAGE 0001 OF 0014
    DOF: 09182006    PR: OR 20863       85   SR: CN 2006 0535346    DOI: 09112006
    TOI: AFF  DESC:                            MIN:        -         -
    1ST PARTY:   CLERK CIRCUIT COURT
    2ND PARTY:
      AMOUNT:                NAME:                              TYPE:
    REFERENCE:
       LEGAL:   PB 29/196

     COMMENTS:    *DMK
    1ST PG-SEARCHD      9/     V/    PB     29 /   196 06/15/2000-01/31/2007
```

EXHIBIT 11-3   (*continued*)

```
ATID              **** ATTORNEYS' TITLE INSURANCE FUND, INC. ****  PAGE 0002 OF 0014
 DOF: 12302005    PR: OR 19736      1301   SR:  CN 2005 0795202   DOI: 01011900
 TOI: M   DESC:                                       MIN:         -          -
 1ST PARTY: JEAN LUC LEBLANC  FRANCINE  LEBLANC
 2ND PARTY:    WA MUTUAL BK F A 2273 N GREEN VALLEY PKWY STE 14 HENDERSON NV 890
14
     AMOUNT:    135000.00 NAME: WA MUTUAL BK                       TYPE: EQTY
 REFERENCE:
      LEGAL: LT 9 BLK V PB 29/196

   COMMENTS:
         SEARCHD     9/    V/    PB     29 /    196 06/15/2000-01/31/2007


ATID              **** ATTORNEYS' TITLE INSURANCE FUND, INC. ****  PAGE 0003 OF 0014
 DOF: 10042005    PR: OR 19345      1424   SR:  CN 2005 0624042   DOI: 09212005
 TOI: SM  DESC:                                       MIN:         -          -
 1ST PARTY: CITIMORTGAGE INC
 2ND PARTY: JEAN LUC LEBLANC  FRANCINE  LEBLANC H/W
    AMOUNT:            NAME:                           TYPE:
 REFERENCE: OR 12940/346
      LEGAL: LT 9 BLK V PB 29/196

   COMMENTS:
         SEARCHD     9/    V/    PB     29 /    196 06/15/2000-01/31/2007


ATID              **** ATTORNEYS' TITLE INSURANCE FUND, INC. ****  PAGE 0004 OF 0014
 DOF: 10212004    PR: OR 17664      583    SR:  CN 2004 0598521   DOI: 08242004
 TOI: AGR DESC:                                       MIN:         -          -
 1ST PARTY: PALM BCH CTY
 2ND PARTY: VILLAGE ROYAL PALM BCH
    AMOUNT:            NAME:                           TYPE:
 REFERENCE:
      LEGAL: POB BEING PT INTERSEC S R/W LINE S BLVD (SR 80/US 98) WITH E LINE SE
C 36-43-41, NLY ALG E LINE SEC 36 25 24 13 12 & 1-43-41 TO NE COR SAID SEC 1-43-
41 BEING ALSO SE COR SEC 12-42-41, NLY ALG E LINE SAID SEC (INC)

   COMMENTS: SURVEY ATTACHED*JR
         SEARCHD     9/    V/    PB     29 /    196 06/15/2000-01/31/2007


ATID              **** ATTORNEYS' TITLE INSURANCE FUND, INC. ****  PAGE 0005 OF 0014
 DOF: 11122002    PR: OR 14379      990    SR:  CN 2002 0594832   DOI: 10212002
 TOI: AM  DESC:                                       MIN:         -          -
 1ST PARTY: OH SAV BK F/K/A/ OH SAV BK F S B
 2ND PARTY: CITIMORTGAGE INC
    AMOUNT:            NAME:                           TYPE:
 REFERENCE: OR 12940/346
      LEGAL: NONE

   COMMENTS:
         SEARCHD     9/    V/    PB     29 /    196 06/15/2000-01/31/2007
```

Form reproduced through the courtesy of Attorneys' Title Insurance Fund, Inc.

"DMK" appears. These are the initials of the person who signed the affidavit for the clerk of the court.

The second entry, found at the top of the second page of the printout, is a mortgage instrument. Note that the type of mortgage is indicated next to "Type" as a home equity mortgage loan. Although the date of filing of the instrument is December 30, 2005, the date of the instrument is unknown. In such a situation, a code is inserted next to "DOI." Here the code is 01011900. The third entry is a satisfaction of mortgage provided by Citimortgage, the mortgagee, to the LeBlancs, the mortgagors. The fourth entry is an agreement entered into between the Village of Royal Palm Beach and the county of Palm Beach. The fifth entry is an assignment of mortgage, in which Ohio Savings Bank is assigning the mortgage to Citimortgage.

The proper reading of a computer printout title search necessarily requires familiarity with the format used by each particular data system. The example provided in Exhibit 11–3 is simply illustrative of one such system. A thorough reading also requires knowledge of the abbreviations used, which also may vary considerably from one system to the next.

A proper title examination includes not only a review of the recorded documents but also a search of the current parties to the transaction to comply with the Patriot Act. A thorough search includes a determination of whether the names of the current property owners, the proposed buyers, and any private lender involved in the transaction match those that appear on the list of "Specially Designated Nationals and Blocked Persons" (the SDN list), which is published by the Office of Foreign Assets Control (OFAC). The Patriot Act prohibits transactions with individuals and organizations on this list.

From this discussion, it should be clear that title examination is very detailed work. A paralegal should not attempt to perform a title examination without using a checklist to keep track of the various matters to consider. If your law firm has not developed a checklist for such use, the checklist provided below may be utilized.

TITLE EXAMINATION CHECKLIST

1. Preliminary information obtained
    a. Legal description of the property
    b. Name of present owner of the property
    c. Copies of
        i. Current deed and/or survey
        ii. Current title insurance policy
2. Period of search
    a. Full search (going back fifty years or whatever is required by statute)
    b. Limited search (going back to last search or last policy issued)
3. Title information reviewed
    a. Public records
    b. Abstract of title (note the dates covered)
    c. Prior policy
    d. Computer search printout

4. Items to be checked for each instrument
   a. Names of the parties to the instrument
   b. Type of instrument and interest in property provided
   c. Contents of the instrument, particularly those setting forth restrictions, conditions, and encumbrances on the property
   d. Date of the instrument
   e. Date of recording of the instrument
   f. Signatures and acknowledgments
   g. Other interests or rights
5. Title matters considered
   a. Ad valorem taxes
   b. Assessment liens
   c. Bankruptcy proceedings
   d. Construction liens
   e. Corporate status
   f. Creditors' rights issues
   g. Declaration of condominium
   h. Divorce proceedings
   i. Easements
   j. Encroachments
   k. Foreclosure proceedings
   l. Homestead
   m. Judgment liens
   n. Lis pendens
   o. Matters shown on plat map
   p. Mortgages
   q. Probate or guardianship proceedings
   r. Reservations
   s. Restrictions
   t. Tax liens
   u. UCC financing statements
   v. Other
6. SDN search

Title Insurance Preparation

Once a thorough title examination has been conducted, a title agent can prepare a document called a *title commitment,* sometimes referred to as a *title binder* or *title report.* As noted earlier, a title commitment assures the purchaser and the lending institution that the title to the subject real property has been examined to the date specified on the commitment and discloses the status of the title as of that date. It further creates an obligation on the insurer to write a title policy based on the stipulations set forth in the commitment. As a paralegal, you may be asked to review and/or draft title commitments, so a thorough knowledge of their components is necessary. Sample completed schedules for a title commitment, an owner's title policy, and a mortgagee's title policy are found in the Hypothetical Client Matter at the end of the chapter.

The Commitment

Commitment Jacket. The cover, or jacket, of the title commitment stipulates the standard terms under which the title insurance company commits to issue a title policy. The front of the commitment jacket will contain a serial number that represents the commitment number. This serial number should be inserted where indicated on the schedules of the title commitment. The back of the commitment jacket lists the standard exceptions to insurance coverage. They are as follows:

1. Taxes for the year of the effective date of the commitment and taxes or special assessments that are not shown as existing liens by the public records

2. Rights or claims of parties in possession not shown by the public records

3. Encroachments, overlaps, boundary line disputes, and any other matters that would be disclosed by an accurate survey and inspection of the premises

4. Easements, or claims of easements, not shown by the public records

5. Any lien, or right to a lien, for services, labor, or material furnished, imposed by law and not shown by the public records

To understand the first exception, recall the manner in which real property owners are taxed. The ad valorem taxes are assessed upon a parcel of property as of January 1 of a particular year. However, they do not become due and payable until some later date, stipulated by statute. This exception for taxes may be waived by the insurer for the year in which the taxes are due if they have been paid and evidence of payment is provided to the insurer.

The second exception refers to the possibility of someone in possession of the real property other than the present owner who may have some claim to an interest in the property. This exception may be waived by the insurer if the owner provides adequate evidence that there is no one physically on the property who may claim such an interest. To do this, the owner may have to provide a survey and allow a personal physical inspection of the property. The insurer additionally may want an affidavit from the owner that no other person is in possession.

The third exception refers to possible encroachments and other matters that may be determined only by an actual survey of the real property. To waive this exception, the insurer will require that a survey be obtained and reviewed by one of its agents. The same is true of the fourth exception, pertaining to easements. With regard to this fourth exception, the insurer also may require an affidavit from the owner stating that no easements or claims to easements exist.

The fifth exception relates to construction liens. Recall from prior discussions that construction liens work retroactively in terms of date of priority. Thus, a construction lien may be placed on the property after the sale, yet attach as of the date the first work was done on the property. State statutes dictate the time period within which a construction lien must be filed. To waive this exception, the insurer will require that the owner provide an affidavit stating that no goods, services, or materials were provided within that statutory period. If, in fact, work has been done, the insurer will require a waiver of lien signed by all parties who performed services or provided materials. Additionally, the owner and general contractor may have to sign an affidavit indicating that all parties with potential claims have signed and agreeing to indemnify the insurer.

Schedule A. Schedule A indicates (1) the effective date of the commitment, (2) the type(s) of policy(ies) to be issued, (3) the amount(s) of coverage, (4) the name(s) of the proposed insured(s), (5) the name(s) of the party(ies) in whom title to the property is presently vested, and (6) the legal description of the real property.

At the top of Schedule A, one inserts the commitment number found on the front cover of the commitment jacket. Next, one inserts the effective date of the policy. The effective date is the month, day, year, and time through which the title of the property has been examined, *not* the date on which the commitment is prepared. The agent's file reference number (the number the title agent has assigned to this transaction) typically is included.

If more than one policy will be issued simultaneously (that is, an owner's policy and a mortgagee's policy), both must be noted on Schedule A. The proposed amount of insurance for an owner's policy is the full insurable value of the property. This most often is the purchase price. The proposed amount of insurance for a mortgagee's policy most often is the full principal amount of the debt, although state statutes may allow a stipulated percentage in excess of this to cover interest and foreclosure costs.

The name(s) of the present owner(s) of the property and the legal description of the property must be provided. The name of the title agent issuing the policy is inserted at the bottom of the page, together with the agent's number (assigned by the title insurance company, not the attorney's bar number if the agent is an attorney) and address, if this information is required by the title insurance underwriter.

Schedule B. Schedule B contains two parts, Part I and Part II. Part I specifies the requirements that must be complied with in order for the title insurer to issue the policy(ies). The first requirement typically listed under Part I requires that full payment be made for the property. Next, one lists the items to be obtained and recorded before the issuance of the policy(ies), such as the deed from the seller to the purchaser, the mortgage instrument from the mortgagor to the mortgagee, and the satisfaction of mortgage for a mortgage loan that is in existence but that is not being assumed by the purchaser.

Part II of Schedule B is where the exceptions to the insurance coverage are listed. The standard exceptions are incorporated by reference here. Excluded from coverage are any defects in title that appear in the public records in the **gap period.** This refers to items appearing in the public record in the period between the effective date of the commitment and the recording date of the instruments giving rise to the interest being insured (for example, the recording of the deed and mortgage). The title insurer may delete the gap period exception if certain

gap period: The period between the effective date of the commitment and the recording date of the instruments giving rise to the interest being insured.

conditions are met. The title examination would need to be updated again just prior to the disbursement of funds at closing. Further, most title insurers require that the funds be disbursed through one of their agents in order to delete this exception.

In addition, one must insert in this section all liens, encumbrances, and other defects of record that have been discovered through inspection of the property. Items to be inserted here include, but are not limited to, deed restrictions, items contained in a declaration of condominium, and easements.

Under usual circumstances, upon closing of a property a title insurance company will issue policies based on the terms stated in the title commitment if all conditions in the title commitment have been met. The case below considers whether title commitment conditions are satisfied (thus obligating a title insurer to issue title policies) when a necessary document is forged.

CASE: *Fidelity National Title Insurance Co. v. Keyingham Investments, LLC*
288 Ga. 312, 702 S.E.2d 851 (2010)

NAHMIAS, Justice.

We granted certiorari in this case to consider whether a condition of a title insurance commitment was satisfied when the borrower who executed a security deed, it is later discovered, was an imposter who forged the true owner's name on the deed. The Court of Appeals held that the condition was satisfied, see *Keyingham Investments v. Fidelity Nat. Title Ins. Co.*, 298 Ga.App. 467, 680 S.E.2d 442 (2009), and we affirm.

1. The Court of Appeals's opinion contains a detailed account of the facts, see *Keyingham*, 248 Ga.App. at 468-469, 680 S.E.2d 442, and they will only be reiterated here as necessary. The title commitment condition at issue was as follows:

> Documents satisfactory to the Company creating the interest in the land and/or mortgage to be insured must be signed, delivered and recorded:
>
> a) Execution, recording and delivery of a Security Deed in the original amount of [$]106000, in favor of [the lenders], to secure subject property.

Relying on *Glass v. Stewart Title Guaranty Co.*, 181 Ga.App. 804, 354 S.E.2d 187 (1987), Fidelity National Title Insurance Company ("Fidelity") contends that a forged deed is void ab initio and does not create an interest in the property and that, without such interest, no title insurance can issue. *Glass* stated this proposition but cited only cases addressing whether someone who unknowingly buys property based on a forgery holds superior title to the true owner, not cases addressing whether

title insurance purchased by the unknowing buyer covers the risk of a forgery. See id. at 805, 354 S.E.2d 187.

As properly recognized by the Court of Appeals in this case, Fidelity's argument "ignores that one of the very purposes of title insurance is to protect a party from the consequences of forgery in the chain of title, which necessarily results in the party not receiving an interest in the land." *Keyingham*, 298 Ga.App. at 471, 680 S.E.2d 442 (citing numerous authorities) (emphasis omitted). See also *FTC v. Ticor Title Ins. Co.*, 504 U.S. 621, 626, 112 S.Ct. 2169, 119 L.Ed.2d 410 (1992) (explaining that title insurance protects an insured from "losses resulting from title defects not discoverable from a search of the public records, such as forgery, missing heirs, previous marriages, impersonation, or confusion in names"); Michael Braunstein, *Structural Change and Inter-Professional Competitive Advantage: An Example Drawn From Residential Real Estate Conveyancing*, 62 Mo. L. Rev. 241, 248 (1996) ("[T]itle insurance provides coverage against hidden risks. Thus, title insurance protects the purchaser against such defects as a forged, stolen or undelivered deed").

Title insurance protects against "defective titles," OCGA § 33-7-8, and a forged deed conveys a defective title, see *Brock v. Yale Mortgage Corp.*, 287 Ga. 849, 852, 700 S.E.2d 583 (2010) ("[E]ven a bona fide purchaser for value without notice of a forgery cannot acquire good title from a grantee in a forged deed . . ., because the grantee has no title to convey."). Exclusions from coverage are to be strictly construed, and " '[i]t is the understanding of the average policyholder which is to be accepted as a court's guide to the meaning of words, with the help of the established rule that ambiguities and uncertainties are to

(continued)

be resolved against the insurance company.'" *Cunningham v. Middle Ga. Mut. Ins. Co.*, 268 Ga.App. 181, 185, 601 S.E.2d 382 (2004). We therefore conclude that, in the absence of language in a title insurance commitment that plainly excludes coverage for a forgery, a commitment must be construed to provide coverage for forgeries. *Glass* is disapproved to the extent that it stands for the contrary proposition.

2. Fidelity also contends that the condition that "[d]ocuments satisfactory to the Company creating the interest in the land and/or mortgage to be insured must be signed, delivered and recorded" is plain and specific enough to exclude coverage for forgeries, because the condition requires that the documents must create an interest in land. Again, we disagree. First, as explained by the Court of Appeals, this phrase can be read as requiring that the "documents" that purport to create the insured interest, here the security deed, be satisfactory to Fidelity, not that they actually create an unassailable interest in the land. See *Keyingham*, 298 Ga.App. at 470, 680 S.E.2d 442. Indeed, the phrase is nonsensical if interpreted to mean that a perfected interest in the land must be created by the deed alone, which could not create such an interest before it is "signed" and "delivered."

Moreover, the phrase should be read not in isolation but in the context of the title insurance commitment as a whole. See *Cunningham*, 268 Ga.App. at 185, 601 S.E. 382. Immediately following the phrase on which Fidelity relies is the phrase "Execution, recording and delivery of a Security Deed in the original amount of [$]106000, in favor of [the lenders]." An insured could reasonably read the latter phrase as setting forth the specific document that had to be signed, recorded, and delivered to obtain the title insurance, and that phrase did not specify that the security deed had to create a perfected interest in the property. Indeed, as discussed above, title insurance is fundamentally designed to protect against title defects, and a forged deed creates such a defect. These provisions could lead the average policyholder to conclude that, if a security deed between the lenders and the borrower was executed, recorded, and delivered in a form satisfactory to Fidelity and its agent—and, here, Fidelity's closing attorney verified, accepted, and recorded the security deed—the commitment would cover forgeries.

For these reasons, the phrase on which Fidelity relies did not require that the security deed in this case create a perfected interest in the property in order to obtain coverage.

3. Accordingly, we conclude that the Court of Appeals properly ruled that Fidelity was required to issue the title insurance policy in question.

Judgment affirmed.

All the Justices concur.

Case Questions

1. What steps, if any, could have been taken prior to the recording of the security deed to prevent this situation?

2. Does the recording of the forged security deed affect the title of the true property owner? If not, why not? If so, then what steps should be taken to clear title?

3. In this case, after the documents were executed and reviewed, the law firm acting as Fidelity's agent disbursed the funds from the closing, including payment to Fidelity of the insurance premium for the title policy to be issued. The document was then sent for recording. Would the outcome of this case be different if the forgery had been detected after the premium was issued but before the document was recorded? Would the outcome have been different if the forgery had been detected after the document had been recorded but before any premium was issued?

Owner's Policy

In 2006, ALTA made a number of changes to its owner's and mortgagee's policy forms. Title insurance companies have the choice of utilizing the 1992 version of the policy forms or the 2006 version. Differences will be noted in the discussion below.

Policy Jacket. An owner's policy is not issued until the purchaser becomes the owner of the real property. Therefore, the policy generally is issued after the closing. The policy jacket sets forth the coverage provided. It typically states that the policy insures the owner for any damages sustained by reason of the following:

1. Title to the estate or interest described in Schedule A being vested other than as stated therein

2. Any defect in or lien or encumbrance on the title

3. Unmarketability of the title

4. Lack of a right of access to and from the land

The first item indicates that the title insurer insures that the owner holds the type of interest in the property set forth in Schedule A of the policy. The second item states that apart from those items listed as exceptions to coverage in Schedule B, the title insurer insures against any other defects in title to the property. The third item insures against unmarketability of the title, meaning that the insurer insures that the owner holds superior title. The fourth item insures that the owner has access to the public roads from his or her property.

The 2006 ALTA forms include a number of additional covered risks. The reference to "any defect in or lien or encumbrance on title" has been expanded specifically to include:

- Forgery, fraud, undue influence, duress, incompetency, incapacity, or impersonation
- Lack of authority of any person executing on behalf of the true owner
- Failure of proper creation, execution, witnessing, acknowledgment, notarization, or delivery of any document affecting title
- Failure to properly create a document by electronic means authorized by law
- Execution under a power of attorney that is invalid because it has expired or was falsified
- Failure to properly file, record, or index a document in the public records or to perform those acts by electronic means authorized by law
- Any defect in any judicial or administrative proceeding through which title or the lien of the insured mortgage is derived
- Real estate tax or assessment liens that are due but unpaid
- Any encroachment, encumbrance, violation, or adverse circumstance affecting title that would have been disclosed by a complete survey

Also included as covered risks under the ALTA 2006 forms are the violation or enforcement of any governmental laws and/or regulations pertaining to (1) the occupancy, use, or enjoyment of the property; (2) the character, dimensions, or location of any improvement on the property; (3) the subdivision of the property; or (4) environmental protection. These situations are covered if a notice is recorded in the public records describing the property (or any part of it) and setting forth the violation or intention to enforce the law or regulation.

The back of the jacket itemizes the exclusions from coverage. In summary, these items usually include the following:

1. Governmental police power, laws, ordinances, or governmental regulations

2. Rights of eminent domain

3. Defects, liens, and encumbrances created by the insured, known to the insured but not to the insurer, that are created subsequent to the date of the policy or that result in no damage to the insured

4. Title defects that are created after the effective date of the policy

5. Matters resulting in loss or damage that would not have occurred if the insured had paid value for the insured's interest in the property

Schedule A. Schedule A of the owner's policy contains many similarities to Schedule A of the commitment. At the top of the page, one inserts the policy number, which is taken from the front cover of the policy jacket. The effective date of the policy is the month, day, year, and time through which the title has been examined, which must be through the time of recording of the instrument that the policy insures—in this case, through the date of the recording of the deed conveying ownership. The agent's file number also is inserted.

Unlike the commitment schedule, Schedule A of the owner's policy only makes reference to the owner of the property as the insured. The amount of the insurance indicated in the commitment to cover the owner, usually the purchase price, is inserted on this schedule as well as the name(s) of the insured(s). The name(s) of the insured(s) should appear in the manner in which they appear on the deed.

Recording information for the deed and the legal description of the property are also included on this schedule.

Schedule B. Schedule B of the owner's policy contains a listing of the specific exceptions to insurance coverage. As discussed earlier, exceptions may be waived if the conditions of the title insurer have been satisfied. In addition to the preprinted exceptions, one must list on this schedule all matters discovered through title examination that are encumbrances on the title, such as easements, restrictions, and so forth. Note that, if the purchasers have obtained a mortgage loan to finance the purchase of the property, the mortgage instrument securing the loan will be recorded against the property and may appear on this schedule.

Mortgagee's Policy

Policy Jacket. Just as is the case with the owner's policy, the mortgagee's policy may not be issued until after the closing, when mortgage instruments have been executed and recorded. The cover page of the policy jacket sets forth the risks covered by the policy. Some of these items will be the same as those appearing on the cover of the owner's policy. The items will vary, depending on whether the 1992 or 2006 version of the forms is utilized. If the 2006 ALTA form is used, the mortgagee's policy will contain added covered risks, such as those found in the owner's policy. However, the mortgagee policy also protects against items of specific interest to the lender. The policy protects against the unenforceability of the lien of the mortgagee. It also protects the priority of the insured mortgage over any other lien not shown on Schedule B of the policy, including construction liens for work begun prior to the date of the policy.

The back of the jacket sets forth the exclusions from coverage. Many of these exclusions are the same as those found in the owner's policy. In addition, the mortgagee's policy excludes from coverage any loss resulting from the unenforceability of the mortgagee's lien due to the mortgagee's failure to comply with the applicable "doing business" laws of the state in which the property is located.

Schedule A. Although Schedule A of the mortgagee policy is similar to Schedule A of the owner's policy, there are some differences. The amount of the insurance listed on this schedule will be the amount of the insurance listed by the mortgagee's name on the commitment—typically, the full amount of the loan. The name(s) of the owner(s) of the property are included as well as the legal description of the property. Additionally, one must insert mortgage recording information, indicating (1) who the mortgage is given by, (2) to whom the mortgage is given, (3) the date the mortgage instrument was executed, (4) the date the mortgage instrument was recorded, (5) the record book and page numbers and the county and state of recording, and (6) the original principal sum of the loan.

Schedule B. Schedule B contains a listing of all items the policy does not insure against. There are differences in the owner's policy and the mortgagee's policy. The mortgagee's policy does not include a listing of the standard exceptions found in the owner's policy. It does, however, include an item pertaining to real estate taxes, which may be deleted if the insurer waives this exception upon receipt of evidence that the current taxes have been paid. Unless the other standard exceptions have been waived (that is, easements not shown by the public records, encroachments that would be disclosed by a survey), one must insert them here. Additionally, one must list all restrictions and encumbrances that appear on record from the title examination.

Other Mortgagee Policies

In addition to the standard mortgagee's policy discussed above, paralegals working in the area of residential real estate may also be asked to review or prepare two other types of mortgagee policies. One is a *short form residential loan policy*. This policy contains no cover jacket; the complete policy consists of a Schedule A and a Schedule B. This form of policy can be used only if the following criteria are met: (1) the property must be a one- to four-family residence; (2) the improvements on the property must be complete (no ongoing construction); (3) the property must be located within a planned unit development (PUD), or it must be a property of less than five acres described by a metes and bounds legal description; (4) the loan amount must not be greater than $500,000; and (5) the seller must sign an affidavit stating that no major improvements have been made since the seller obtained title (the title company often will ask for a copy of the old survey to verify this).

Another type of residential mortgagee's policy is the *residential limited coverage junior loan policy*. As its name implies, this policy covers a junior lienholder, such as a holder of a second mortgage loan or the holder of a secured line of credit. It can be used if the property is a one- to four-family residence. It provides more limited coverage than a standard mortgagee's policy. It insures the policy holder against loss due to any monetary lien affecting the title that has been recorded in the public records and is not listed as an exception on Schedule B of the policy. It also protects the policy holder from any loss due to real estate taxes or assessments that appear in the real estate records on the date of the policy.

Endorsements

An **endorsement** is a form provided by the title insurer that is used for the amendment of any information that has appeared as part of a title commitment or title policy. It often provides special coverage not contained in the standard title policy. The most commonly used endorsements pertain to a mortgagee's policy. An assignment of mortgage endorsement is used when the note and the mortgage instrument are assigned by the holder to someone else—typically, when an institutional mortgagee assigns a mortgage to the secondary market. A variable-rate mortgage endorsement assures the mortgagee that the mortgagee's lien position will not be impaired in the event of negative amortization.

A condominium endorsement is another commonly used endorsement. It provides affirmative coverage for matters specific to condominiums, such as those pertaining to the valid creation of the condominium, present violations of any restrictive covenants contained in the condominium documents that restrict the use of the unit and its common elements, and any charges or assessments unpaid as of the policy date that are provided for by statute or by the condominium documents. A PUD endorsement is used when the subject property is located in a PUD. It insures against loss or damage sustained by reason of situations such as present violations of any restrictive covenants, any charges or assessments unpaid as of the policy date to the homeowners' association, and the enforced removal of any structure existing on the property as of the policy date that encroaches on adjoining property or on any easement. A survey endorsement acknowledges that the property described in Schedule A is the same as that described in an identified survey. This endorsement comes into play when there are minor discrepancies between the legal description in the survey and that provided in the policy.

Special Title and Closing Issues

Due to the recent real estate downturn, title companies are dealing with unusual situations relating to the closing of real estate transactions and the issuance of policies. There has been an increase in short sales transactions, which have required that closing agents pay particular attention to lienholders' conditions and instructions. Prior to the closing of a short sale, a lender will provide the closing agent with a *short sale estoppel letter*. This letter will indicate any conditions that the lender has mandated in connection with the satisfaction of the seller's outstanding mortgage loan. In some instances, these conditions may include the right to revoke approval or reinstate the mortgage loan *after* the closing of the transaction if it is discovered that the property was acquired by fraudulent means or if the property is "flipped" shortly after the closing of the transaction. The Internal Revenue Service may also submit an estoppel letter containing conditions. For example, an estoppel letter may provide that the Internal Revenue Service will not release an outstanding lien if it is determined after closing that the value of the property was greater than the IRS initially was informed. Some title insurance companies have notified their agents that they are not authorized to close transactions in which a lienholder has submitted a short sale estoppel letter containing the above-mentioned or similar conditions.

endorsement: A form provided by the title insurer that is used for the amendment of any information that has appeared as part of a title commitment or title policy. It often provides special coverage not contained in the standard title policy.

A different issue presents itself when a lender agrees to accept a *deed-in-lieu of foreclosure* and releases the owner/borrower from his or her loan obligations (deeds-in-lieu of foreclosure are discussed in detail in Chapter 19). Here the borrower is conveying title to the property to the lender, and the lender becomes the owner. Under these circumstances, the lender should obtain a new owner's policy. Prior to issuance, a title insurance company should obtain an appraisal of the property to determine its current value.

As a real estate paralegal, your supervising attorney may ask you to prepare title commitments and/or title policies. A checklist of those items to be included in the various schedules of title commitments and policies is provided below.

TITLE POLICY PREPARATION CHECKLIST

1. Title commitment
   a. Schedule A
      i. Commitment number
      ii. Effective date (date through which title examination was conducted)
      iii. Agent's file number
      iv. Type of policy(ies)
      v. Amount of coverage
          (a) Owner's policy—purchase price
          (b) Mortgagee's policy—loan amount
      vi. Name and estate or interest of current owner
      vii. Legal description of property
      viii. Agent's name (address and number, if required) and signature
   b. Schedule B
      i. Part I—listing of all conditions that must be met prior to issuance of policy
      ii. Part II—listing of all liens, encumbrances, and defects to be exceptions from coverage
2. Owner's policy
   a. Schedule A
      i. Policy number
      ii. Effective date (date through which title examination was conducted)
      iii. Agent's file number
      iv. Name(s) of insured(s)
      v. Amount of coverage—purchase price
      vi. Recording information for deed
      vii. Legal description of property
      viii. Agent's certification statement
      ix. Agent's name (address and number, if required) and signature
   b. Schedule B—listing of all liens, encumbrances, and defects to be exceptions from coverage

3. Mortgagee's policy
   a. Schedule A
      i. Policy number
      ii. Effective date (date through which title examination was conducted)
      iii. Agent's file number
      iv. Name(s) of insured(s)
      v. Amount of insurance—loan amount
      vi. Name and estate or interest of owner
      vii. Legal description of property
      viii. Mortgage recordation information
      ix. Agent's name (address and number, if required) and signature
   b. Schedule B—listing of all liens, encumbrances, and defects to be exceptions from coverage
4. Endorsements
   a. Condominium endorsement
   b. Planned unit development, or PUD, endorsement
   c. Variable rate mortgage endorsement
   d. Assignment of mortgage endorsement
   e. Mortgage modification endorsement
   f. Environmental protection lien endorsement
   g. Covenants, conditions, and restrictions endorsement
   h. Survey endorsement
   i. Other

hypothetical client matter

Paralegal Barbara Hammond is assisting her supervising attorney, Ava Ross, with the Swanson real estate closing. Ava Ross is a title agent and a member of the Any State Title Insurance Fund. She is representing the sellers, Timothy and Karen Swanson, who have contracted with Charles and Erica Kelly. The closing took place last week, and all of the requisite documents have been recorded. Ava has asked Barbara to prepare the owner's and mortgagee's title policies.

Barbara first reviews the title commitment that has been issued to the Kellys (see Exhibit 11–4). Note that under Part I of Schedule B, the title insurer requires the recording of a warranty deed executed by the Swansons to the Kellys before it will issue an owner's title policy to the Kellys. Similarly, the title insurer requires the recording of a mortgage instrument executed by the Kellys in favor of Patriot Bank before it issues a mortgagee's policy to Patriot

Bank. Additionally, the satisfaction of the current outstanding loan given to the Swansons by their lender is listed as a condition prerequisite to the issuing of the policies. Some title agents choose not to include this, as it is not technically an instrument creating an estate or interest to be insured.

Barbara notes the effective date of the commitment and conducts a computerized title search from that date to the present date. The only new encumbrance indicated on the printout is the mortgage given to Patriot Bank in the amount of $340,000. The mortgage loan given to the Swansons by Any State First National Bank has been satisfied, and a satisfaction of mortgage has been recorded. Using the printout and the title commitment, Barbara prepares the owner's and mortgagee's policy schedules for review by Ava (see Exhibits 11–5 and 11–6).

FUND COMMITMENT FORM

SCHEDULE A

Commitment No.: 1111111

Member's
File Reference: 1235.001

Effective Date: 06/29/15 at 5:00 p.m.

1. Policy or Policies to be issued   Proposed Amount of Insurance:

OWNER'S: OPM $425,000.00

Proposed Insured:

     CHARLES KELLY and ERICA KELLY, his wife

MORTGAGEE: MP $340,000.00

Proposed Insured:

     PATRIOT BANK and its successors and/or assigns as their interest may appear

2. The estate or interest in the land described or referred to in this commitment is a fee simple and title thereto is at the effective date hereof vested in:

     TIMOTHY SWANSON and KAREN SWANSON, his wife

3. The land referred to in this commitment is described as follows:

     Lot 6 in Block 1 of PINEHURST ESTATES, according to the plat thereof recorded in Plat Book 70, Page 35, of the Public Records of Any County, Any State.

Fisher, Ross, and Simon, P.A. 1900 N.W. 3rd Avenue, Any City, Any State	2222 Agent No	_Ava Ross_ Agent's Signature

Form reproduced through the courtesy of Attorneys' Title Insurance Fund, Inc.

EXHIBIT 11–4   *(continued)*

FUND COMMITMENT FORM

SCHEDULE B-I

Commitment No. #:1111111
Member's File No. #: 1235.001

I. The following are the requirements to be complied with:

1. Payment of the full consideration to, or for the account of, the grantors or mortgagors.

2. Instruments creating the estate or interest to be insured which must be executed, delivered and filed for record:

    (a) Warranty Deed to be executed by Timothy Swanson and Karen Swanson, his wife, to Charles Kelly and Erica Kelly, his wife.

    (b) Satisfaction of Mortgage in favor of Any State First National Bank dated November 8, 2007 and recorded November 9, 2007 at O.R. Book 5700, Page 81 of the Public Records of Any County, Any State.

    (c) Mortgage to be executed by Charles Kelly and Erica Kelly, his wife in favor of Patriot Bank given to secure the principal sum of $340,000.00.

FUND COMMITMENT FORM

SCHEDULE B-II

Commitment No. #: 1111111
Member's File No. #: 1235.001

II. Schedule B of the policy or policies or guarantee to be issued will contain exceptions to the following matters unless the same are disposed of to the satisfaction of The Fund:

1. Defects, liens, encumbrances, adverse claims or other matters, if any, created, first appearing in the public records or attaching subsequent to the effective date hereof but prior to the date the proposed Insured acquires for value of record the estate or interest or mortgage thereon covered by this commitment.

2. Any owner and mortgagee policies issued pursuant hereto will contain under Schedule B the standard exceptions set forth at the inside cover hereof unless an affidavit of possession and a satisfactory current survey are submitted, an inspection of the premises is made, it is determined the current year's taxes or special assessments have been paid, and it is determined there is nothing of record which would give rise to construction liens which could take priority over the interest(s) insured hereunder (where the liens would otherwise take priority, submission of waivers is necessary).

3. Easement from Any State Power and Light Company dated February 20, 1994, recorded March 2, 1994 at O.R Book 4007, Page 48 of the Public Records of Any County, Any State.

4. Restrictive covenants of Pinehurst Estates Subdivision, dated April 10, 1998, recorded April 12, 1998 at O.R. Book 4012, Page 90 of the Public Records of Any County, Any State.

Form reproduced through the courtesy of Attorneys' Title Insurance Fund, Inc.

EXHIBIT 11–5   **Kelly owners' policy**

FUND OWNER'S FORM

SCHEDULE A

Policy No: 4444444   Effective Date: 08/18/15 at 1:30 p.m.   Amount of Insurance: $425,000.00

Agent's File Reference: 1235.001

1. Name of Insured:

    CHARLES KELLY and ERICA KELLY, his wife

2. The estate or interest in the land described herein and which is covered by this policy or guarantee is a fee simple and is at the effective date hereof vested in the named insured as shown by instrument recorded in Official Records Book 6200, Page 103, of the Public Records of Any County, Any State.

3. The land referred to in this Policy is described as follows:

    Lot 6 in Block 1 of PINEHURST ESTATES, according to the plat
    thereof recorded in Plat Book 70, Page 35 of the Public Records of
    Any County, Any State.

Fisher, Ross, and Simon, P.A. 1900 N.W. 3rd Avenue., Any City, Any State	<u>2222</u> Agent No	*Ava Ross* Agent's Signature

FUND OWNER'S FORM

SCHEDULE B

Policy or
Guarantee No. 4444444   File No.#: 1235.001

This policy does not insure against loss or damage by reason of the following exceptions:

1. Taxes for the year of the effective date of this policy or guarantee and taxes or special assessments which are not shown as existing liens by the public records.

2. Rights or claims of parties in possession not shown by the public records.

3. Encroachments, overlaps, boundary line disputes, and any other matters which would be disclosed by an accurate survey and inspection of the premises.

4. Easements or claims of easements not shown by the public records.

5. Any lien, or right to a lien, for services, labor or material heretofore or hereafter furnished, imposed by law and not shown by the public records.

6. Mortgage from Charles Kelly and Erica Kelly, his wife to Patriot Bank dated August 11, 2015, and recorded on August 12, 2015 in Official Records Book 6200, Page 104, of the Public Records of Any County, Any State, securing the original principal sum of $340,000.00.

7. Easement from Any State Power and Light Company dated February 20, 1994, recorded March 2, 1994 at O.R. Book 4007, Page 48 of the Public Records of Any County, Any State.

8. Restrictive covenants of Pinehurst Estates Subdivision, dated April 10, 1998, recorded April 12, 1998 at O.R. Book 4012, Page 90 of the Public Records of Any County, Any State.

EXHIBIT 11–6   Patriot Bank's mortgagee policy

FUND MORTGAGEE FORM

SCHEDULE A

Policy No.: 5555555   Amount of Insurance: $340,000.00   Agent's File Reference: 1235.001
                                   Effective Date: 08/18/15 at 1:30 p.m.

1. Name of Insured:

   PATRIOT BANK, and its successors and/or assigns as their interest may appear

2. The estate or interest in the land described herein and which is encumbered by the insured mortgage is a fee simple and is at the effective date hereof vested in:

   CHARLES KELLY and ERICA KELLY, his wife

3. The land referred to in this Policy is described as follows:

   > Lot 6 in Block 1 of PINEHURST ESTATES, according to the plat thereof recorded in Plat Book 70, Page 35 of the Public Records of Any County, Any State.

4. The mortgage, herein referred to as the insured mortgage, and the assignments thereof, if any, are described as follows:

   Mortgage from Charles Kelly and Erica Kelly, his wife to Patriot Bank, dated August 11, 2015, and recorded on August 12, 2015, in Official Records Book 6200, Page 104, of the Public Records of Any County, Any State, securing the original principal sum of $340,000.00.

Fisher, Ross, and Simon, P.A.   2222   _Ava Ross_
1900 N.W. 3rd Avenue, Any City, Any State   Agent No   Agent's Signature

FUND MORTGAGEE FORM

SCHEDULE B

Policy No.: 5555555

File No.#: 1235.001

This policy does not insure against loss or damage by reason of the following:

1. The lien of all taxes for the year 2015 and thereafter which are not yet due and payable.

2. Rights or claims of parties in possession not shown by the public records.

3. Encroachments overlaps, boundary line disputes, and any other matters which would be disclosed by an accurate survey and inspection of the premises.

4. Easements or claims of easements not shown by the public records.

5. Easement from Any State Power and Light Company dated February 20, 1994, recorded March 2, 1994 at O.R. Book 407, Page 48 of the Public Records of Any County, Any State.

6. Restrictive covenants of Pinehurst Estates Subdivision dated April 10, 1998, recorded April 12, 1998 at O.R. Book 4012, Page 90 of the Public Records of Any County, Any State.

Form reproduced through the courtesy of Attorneys' Title Insurance Fund, Inc.

CHAPTER SUMMARY

1. When a purchaser buys a parcel of real property, the purchaser wants to be assured that he or she is receiving marketable title—that is, a title free from encumbrances that would diminish its market value. To determine the marketability of title, a title examiner is hired to conduct a title examination. The title examination is composed of a search of all documents in the public records as well as a physical inspection of the property.

2. To examine documents thoroughly, a title examiner must note (1) the type of document, (2) the contents of the document, (3) the names of the parties to the document, (4) the date of the document, (5) the date of recording of the document, and (6) the signatures and acknowledgments. Should a problem with a document appear, the title examiner must research the state statutes to determine whether a curative statute exists that can negate the defect.

3. Numerous matters must be considered when conducting a title search. They include, but are not limited to, assessment liens; construction liens; judgment liens; divorce, probate, and bankruptcy proceedings; deed restrictions; easements; encroachments; and restrictive covenants.

4. An abstract of title is a condensed history of each document affecting the title of a particular parcel of real property. An abstractor creates a chain of title for the property as well as a synopsis of each recorded document pertaining to the property. The abstractor's certificate indicates the dates covered by the title search. The abstract is updated each time ownership of the property is transferred.

5. Title insurance is insurance provided to an owner or mortgagee to protect against loss brought about by encumbrances or defects in the title. A title insurance policy insures against losses due to hidden defects such as recording errors, forged deeds, and undisclosed claims.

6. A title commitment sets forth the status of the title of a particular parcel of real property. It also states the condition under which a title policy will be issued. The commitment jacket sets forth the standard exceptions to insurance coverage. Schedule A sets forth the effective date of the commitment, the type(s) of policy(ies) to be issued, the amount(s) of coverage, the name(s) of the party(ies) in whom title is presently vested, and a legal description of the property. Schedule B indicates the conditions that must be complied with prior to issuance of the policy. It also sets forth all exclusions from coverage.

7. An owner's policy insures marketable title, while a mortgagee's policy insures the mortgage lien the lender is acquiring. An owner's policy covers the market value or purchase price of the property, whereas the mortgagee's policy covers the debt amount.

WEB RESOURCES

http://www.alta.org/

This is the site of the American Land Title Association, which is the national trade association of the abstract and title insurance industry. Title industry news and resources, as well as the ALTA/ACSM Standards, can be accessed here.

http://www.homeclosing101.org/

This site provides consumer information relating to title insurance, closing costs, and real estate resources. A real estate glossary is provided. The site contains information pertaining to types of title insurance, how title rates are set, and rate terminology.

REVIEW QUESTIONS

1. Explain the ways in which title insurance differs from other forms of insurance.
2. List the records that should be searched when conducting a title examination.
3. List the information contained in the following:
   a. Schedule A of a title commitment
   b. Schedule B of a title commitment
4. What are the most common exclusions from coverage under an owner's title policy?
5. Explain the purpose of endorsements, and provide an example of an endorsement one might find pertaining to an owner's policy.

DISCUSSION QUESTIONS

1. This chapter provided examples of some of the potential title defects that are covered by title policies. What are some other potential defects that may not be discovered through an examination of recorded documents?
2. Do you think buyers/borrowers should be required to purchase a new lender's policy if they refinance with the same lender? Why or why not?
3. Annette Suskind purchased residential property in Any County, Any State, intending that the property be used not only for her residence but also for the construction of a freestanding garage/office space for her business. She applied for a loan with Platinum Bank to purchase the property, informing the bank of the property's planned use. ABC Title Company issued a title commitment naming Annette Suskind and Platinum Bank as proposed insureds. The title commitment provided that both policies would contain a comprehensive endorsement without exceptions. The commitment did not indicate that there were any restrictive covenants recorded against the property. After the real estate closing, both an owner's policy and a mortgagee's policy were issued by ABC Title Company. Neither policy indicated any restrictive covenants. After construction on the garage/office began, Annette Suskind and Platinum Bank discovered that a restrictive covenant had been recorded against the land several decades ago providing that no part of the property may be used for business or commercial purposes. Because she could not use the property as she intended, Annette Suskind defaulted on her loan. Platinum Bank foreclosed on the property but could not recoup the full value of the loan. Platinum Bank is now suing ABC Title Company in a declaratory judgment action seeking to hold ABC Title Company liable on the mortgagee's policy of title insurance. In addition, it is bringing suit for negligent

misrepresentation. Do you think Platinum Bank can win under the theory of negligent misrepresentation? Why or why not?

4. You are examining title to a parcel of property and notice that in 1987 George and Valerie Green sold the property to Brian Dearborn. No marital status for Brian is indicated. Brian sold the property in 1993 to Monica Fairbanks, a single woman. From there on, all documents indicate the marital status of buyers and sellers. Does the lack of indication of Brian's marital status create a title defect? Why or why not?

5. Do you believe it is appropriate for states to set rates for all carriers issuing title policies within state boundaries? Why or why not?

ETHICAL QUESTION

Your firm has been hired to represent the buyer, Janet Monroe, in a real estate closing. You have been asked by your supervising attorney to examine the abstract sent to your office by the seller. It is a long document; you have reviewed most of it but have not completed it. While your supervising attorney is out of the office, you receive a telephone call from Janet. She has heard that the seller was involved in major litigation a number of years ago, and she wants to know if there are any judgment liens recorded against the property that remain unpaid. She believes the litigation occurred about seven years ago. You have completed your review of abstract documents up to five years ago and have not come across any judgment liens, so you tell Janet that none appear that would correspond with the information she has received. Later in the afternoon, you resume your review and come across a judgment lien dated four years ago that has not been satisfied. What should you do?

Slossberg Law Office on CourseMate

Please go to www.cengagebrain.com to log into CourseMate, access the Slossberg Law Office, and work on your client files. Each module corresponds to a chapter in the text. Within each module, you will be provided with instructions by the supervising attorney. You are asked to keep track of time spent on time sheets. The documents produced through working on client files in the law office can then be compiled into a portfolio of final work product.

CourseMate

The available CourseMate for this text has an interactive eBook and interactive learning tools, including flash cards, quizzes, and more. To learn more about this resource and access free demo CourseMate resources, including the Slossberg Law Office, go to www.cengagebrain.com, and search for this book. To access CourseMate materials that you have purchased, go to login.cengagebrain.com.

PART **II**

The Closing: Residential and Commercial Closings

12

An Introduction to the Closing

CHAPTER OBJECTIVES

Upon completion of this chapter, the student will:

- Know how to set up and manage a real estate closing file

- Understand the preclosing, closing, and postclosing tasks to be performed by a paralegal

- Know how to calculate prorations

- Understand the closing costs associated with a typical real estate transaction

- Understand the various sections of a HUD-1 Uniform Settlement Statement

- Know the special concerns when working on the closing of a short sale transaction

Introduction

The term **closing** (also called *settlement*) refers to the process of transferring documents and monies to complete a real estate transaction in accordance with the contract for sale and purchase executed by the parties. Often, there are two types of closings occurring simultaneously. The first is the loan closing, whereby the purchaser executes the promissory note and related financing instruments in exchange for the lender's loan to cover a certain amount of the purchase price. The second closing is the closing on the contract for sale and purchase, whereby the seller executes the deed and any other requisite documents to transfer marketable title to the purchaser in exchange for the sales proceeds.

There are a number of interested parties in any given closing. They include the seller and purchaser, the purchaser's lender, the seller's lender (if the seller has an outstanding loan on the property), the real estate broker(s), the title company, and the insurance companies. If the property in question is income-producing property, the tenants must be considered as well. If the property is a condominium or is located within a development that has a homeowners' association, the condominium association or homeowners' association may have to approve the prospective buyer.

The closing agent, sometimes referred to as the escrow agent or settlement agent, has the responsibility of pulling these diverse parties together and organizing the necessary paperwork and disbursements to have a smooth-running closing. The closing agent may be a title company, law firm, attorney for the lender, or escrow agent. Similarly, a paralegal working on a real estate closing file may be working for the lender's in-house counsel, a title company, or a law firm that handles real estate transactions.

It is the paralegal's task to maintain control over a transaction that at times may seem to take on a life of its own. The paralegal must draft and organize correspondence and closing documentation, order surveys, and keep tabs on incoming inspection reports, information requests, expense receipts, or other documentation from third parties. The paralegal must keep track of all deadlines specified in the contract for sale and purchase, the loan commitment, and other relevant documents. Additionally, the paralegal must verify all computations on the closing statement for accuracy and make sure that all parties are able to close on the specified closing date so there is no breach of contract.

This chapter introduces the paralegal to the opening and managing of a real estate file. It walks the paralegal through the steps to be taken prior to closing, during closing, and after closing. It details the closing costs associated with the typical residential closing and explains the HUD-1 Uniform Settlement Statement section by section.

> **closing:** The process of transferring documents and monies to complete a real estate transaction in accordance with the contract for sale and purchase executed by the parties.

Opening and Managing a Real Estate File

Meticulous organization and attention to detail are the keys to managing a real estate file. The primary aid will be a closing worksheet. The following chapters provide closing worksheets for residential and commercial closings. The worksheet should be kept at the front of the client file for easy access because it will give the paralegal quick reference to the names, addresses, and telephone numbers of the parties, the lenders, the real estate broker(s), the title company, and so forth. It will also contain the legal description of the property, the parcel identification number of the property, and a thorough list of items to be ordered, obtained, prepared, and reviewed. The worksheet will indicate which party has the responsibility for each item, the date by which the item must be completed or obtained, and which party is to be charged. The worksheet therefore becomes an invaluable reference source and allows the paralegal quickly to surmise the status of the real estate file.

Your supervising attorney may have his or her own preference for the manner in which the physical file is to be organized, in which case you should follow those instructions accordingly. If the file organization is left to you, as is often the case, it is advisable to have separate folders for each document. This makes retrieval of a particular document effortless in a file that will be quickly expanding from the time the contract for sale and purchase is signed until the date of closing. Thus, you would set up a separate folder for the contract, for the deed, for the financing instrument, and so forth. All correspondence may be kept in the same folder. It is customary to arrange correspondence in reverse chronological order, with the most recent letter on top. The correspondence can be fastened to the right-hand side of the folder, with each letter tabbed. The index to the correspondence can be placed on the left-hand side, with item numbers corresponding to the tabs.

Your client may be bringing in original documents, such as a deed or title policy, if the client is a seller. Originals should never be hole-punched. One method is to affix a document-sized envelope to a folder and then insert the original document in the envelope. Another method is to staple an index card to the document and then hole-punch the index card and fasten it to a folder. Any original documents that you or your supervising attorney prepares should not be defaced by hole-punching. Copies of documents, such as a copy of the contract for sale and purchase, may be fastened directly to a folder.

Electronic files should be organized so that any document can be accessed with ease. When sending a document electronically to a third party—whether it is a lender, a Realtor®, or counsel representing the other party in the real estate transaction—be sure to follow the ethical guidelines set forth by your state bar association regarding the handling of metadata.

As soon as you are assigned a file, you should set up a tickler system to keep track of all the various deadlines. Your worksheet can provide you with a rudimentary system by noting the dates items are due. From this, you will want to enter due dates in a computerized or manual tickler system, providing first, second, and third reminders. This gives you enough lead time to follow through. Some of the real estate closing software programs discussed later in the chapter have tracking programs that work like tickler systems to keep track of closing-related tasks.

When beginning to set up a tickler system and worksheet for a real estate file, the best place to start is with the contract for sale and purchase. A thorough contract acts as a blueprint for the future closing, providing not only the closing date but also other due dates and specifying the parties responsible for preparing various documents. Go through the contract line by line, and mark down on your worksheet the tasks or items and due dates as they appear for your tickler system.

Next, scrutinize the names of the parties and titles of the parties. Verify the correct spellings as they are to appear on the deed and other closing documents. If either the seller or the purchaser is married, this information is important for the preparation of documents. A lender customarily will want both spouses to sign the note and financing instrument. Further, the marital status of the purchasers is important in preparing the deed, for the manner in which title is held has many legal ramifications, as noted in Chapter 8. Similarly, if the seller is married, even if the seller holds title to the property in his or her name only, the seller's spouse may be required to sign the deed conveying title. This is important, as it relates to issues of homestead and inchoate rights, as discussed in Chapter 2.

If either party is a corporation, verification of its corporate standing is required. This is done by requesting a certificate of good standing from the secretary of state's office. Some corporations keep up-to-date certificates in their corporate records book, in which case a copy can be obtained from the party itself. Additionally, the purchase or sale of real property is a matter that must be approved by a corporation's board of directors. Therefore, you will want to obtain a certified copy of the corporate resolution approving the purchase or sale. If a party is some other entity, such as a partnership, limited partnership, limited liability partnership, limited liability limited partnership, limited liability company, or trust, you will need to obtain copies of the relevant documents to ascertain whether the entity is in good standing (if applicable), whose authorization is necessary for the transaction, and who is to sign the closing documents on behalf of that party. With regard to any business entity, you should review the entity's organizational documents (for example, articles of incorporation and bylaws of a corporation) to determine that all requisite procedures required by these documents have been followed.

Although the contract will often provide the addresses of the parties, it will not always supply their telephone numbers. You can obtain this information from your client and from the real estate broker (if any) involved in the transaction.

The contract will also specify the commission to be paid to the broker(s) or indicate that a separate listing brokerage agreement was signed. If the latter is the case, you will want to obtain a copy of the agreement and review it to ascertain not only the amount of the commission but also the conditions precedent to be met by the broker before he or she is entitled to commission. (For a thorough discussion of this matter, refer to Chapter 6.) The contract will also indicate any earnest money deposits paid and whether there are subsequent deposits to be made.

The legal description of the subject property may appear on the contract. Sometimes an abbreviated description is used. It is important to obtain a full description from the seller's deed, current title policy, or survey. You will want to obtain these items as soon as possible. Make sure to copy the legal description accurately onto the worksheet. This will shortcut efforts later, when you can simply refer to the worksheet rather than sorting through a pile of documents. If the description is lengthy, type it on a separate sheet of paper, make numerous copies, and put them in a file folder labeled "Legals" or "Legal Description." In this way, you can make an exhibit out of the legal description to be attached to various documents, such as the deed and seller's affidavit.

It is important to document everything. Although this may seem time-consuming initially, it will save time later in the closing process by preventing confusion. Confirm each party's responsibility by letter. The contract may not indicate who is to act as closing agent. This should be agreed upon by the parties as soon as possible and confirmed in writing. Correspondence, either a traditional letter or an e-mail, should be sent to the other party, or his or her attorney if legally represented, to confirm the identity of the closing agent. If a lending institution is involved, correspondence should be sent to the lender, confirming the documentation the lender is to prepare. Correspondence should be sent to your client as well, outlining the matters for which he or she is responsible.

As documentation comes in, review it thoroughly before checking it off on the worksheet as completed. There may be errors in a document, and you do not want to wait until the date of closing to make this discovery. Once documents are approved and/or tasks completed, be sure to put a check by the corresponding items on the worksheet. All closing documents should be in finalized form prior to the day of closing, as all parties to the transaction will want to review them in advance of closing. Never send originals for review. Keep them in your files, and send photocopies or forward the documents in electronic format. In the event it is imperative to send an original document, be sure to send it by certified mail, return receipt requested, or by overnight courier. Never let a document leave the file until a copy of it is made and inserted in its place.

Preclosing

The contract will indicate whether the purchaser is looking to obtain institutional financing as a condition for closing on the property. This is known as a financing contingency. If so, the contract will indicate how long the purchaser has to make a loan application as well as how long he or she has to obtain a loan commitment. The purchaser will be required to submit not only an application form but also various and sundry other items to the lender prior to obtaining loan approval, as noted in Chapter 10. Once a loan commitment is obtained, it generally will be valid only for a short duration. Therefore, it is important to review the loan commitment to determine its period of validity and make sure this period does not expire prior to the closing date. If there is a problem, the closing date may need to be changed, and this should be arranged by the parties as quickly as possible. An amendment to the contract may be required to change the closing date.

The loan commitment usually mandates that an appraisal of the property be done prior to the date of closing. The appraisal is the lending institution's assurance that the loan amount is not greater than the value of the property. This becomes important if the purchaser/borrower defaults and the lending institution has to foreclose on the property. The appraisal gives the lender assurance that it will most likely recoup the amount of the loan if it becomes necessary to foreclose on the property. The lender typically arranges for the appraisal, but the cost of the appraisal is charged to the purchaser.

If your firm is representing the seller, it may fall upon your party to provide an updated abstract or title commitment within the time period stipulated in the contract. (Note that in some states, such as New York and New Jersey, the purchaser's attorney usually arranges for the title work.) You will want to find out from your client whether a current survey of the property exists. If your firm does not prepare title work in-house, make sure that the title company hired to prepare the commitment can do so within the contract deadlines. Notify the purchaser or his or her attorney as soon as the abstract or title commitment has been ordered. If there is a delay and the abstract or commitment cannot be completed within the contractually specified time frame, send the purchaser a copy of your client's current title policy for review in the interim period, as many of the exceptions to coverage on the current policy will appear in the upcoming commitment.

If your firm is representing the purchaser, once the title commitment is received, examine it to make sure that all information is set forth correctly. The current owner listed on the commitment should be the seller. Make sure that the coverage amounts listed for the owner's policy and mortgagee's policy are correct. Check the legal description against the legal description in the contract for sale and purchase. Review the requirements to be satisfied prior to issuance of the policies and the exceptions to coverage. If any title problems exist, notify the seller immediately in writing. The contract for sale and purchase typically indicates the time period within which the seller must cure title defects. It also indicates the time period within which the purchaser must notify the seller of such defects, so review this portion of the contract carefully.

If the seller has one or more existing outstanding loans on the subject property, this loan must either be assumed by the purchaser or be paid off at closing. Assuming the latter is the case, the firm representing the seller must send a written request to the appropriate lending institution asking for a **mortgage estoppel letter** (also referred to as a *payoff statement*), which specifies the amount to be paid to satisfy the debt. The mortgage estoppel letter will include (1) the outstanding balance of the loan as of a specified date; (2) the per diem interest on the loan from a specified date; (3) prepayment penalties, if any; (4) escrow amounts, if any; and (5) any other requirements to satisfy the loan. When writing to request a mortgage estoppel letter, include not only the seller's name and the property address but also the loan number. The seller should be able to provide you with this information.

If the purchaser is assuming the existing loan or taking title to the property subject to the existing loan, the seller's financing instruments must be reviewed to determine whether the loan may indeed be assumed or whether the instrument

mortgage estoppel letter:
A letter specifying the amount to be paid to satisfy an outstanding loan debt.

contains a due-on-sale clause. If assumption is permitted, the purchaser may still have to qualify with the lender, and the contract should indicate the time period within which this must be accomplished. Just as in the case of new financing, the lending institution will charge the purchaser certain processing and other fees. If there is an escrow account for interest reserves, escrowed taxes, and/or insurance, the seller must assign the escrow account to the purchaser. In turn, the purchaser must credit the seller on the closing statement for the amount the lender is holding in escrow.

The seller's most current tax bill for the property should be obtained, as the taxes must be apportioned between the seller and the purchaser. If the seller cannot find the bill, a copy should be obtained by making a written request to the tax collector's office. Depending on the time of year, the seller may or may not have received the tax bill for the current year. If not, the current year's taxes will be estimated based on the most recent bill. Any adjustments can be made after the new bill is received. Additionally, the amount of the maintenance assessment paid to any condominium association or homeowners' association must be confirmed by requesting this information in writing from the association. If the property purchased is located within a condominium development or a development governed by a homeowners' association, it may be necessary to obtain approval by the association of the purchaser prior to closing. Check both state statutes and the governing condominium or homeowners' association documents to determine whether this is required.

The contract for sale and purchase will indicate the inspections to be made by the purchaser and the deadlines for these inspections. It will also indicate which party is to pay for the inspections. Should an inspection reveal a problem, such as termites or structural damage to the roof, the contract should be reviewed to determine the seller's responsibility to cure such problems or to determine if the property is being sold "as is." If the property is not being sold "as is," the contract usually will state that the seller has a specified time period within which to cure the defect. It may also state that the seller is responsible for repairs only up to a stated dollar amount or a percentage of the purchase price. The inspection dates should be monitored, and the purchaser should obtain inspection reports and receipts. Copies of these should be provided to the seller.

Lenders will have specific requirements for hazard and flood insurance to be effective on the day of closing. Some lenders will require that funds be escrowed for hazard and flood insurance premiums. If the property purchased is a condominium, it will be covered under a master policy held by the condominium association. A portion of the maintenance assessment pays for the unit owner's share of the master policy premiums. The lender will require a copy of the master policy. For other residential properties, a certificate of insurance should be obtained that specifies the amount of insurance, the type of coverage, and the dates of coverage.

If fixtures and/or personal property is included in the sale of the property, the Uniform Commercial Code (UCC) records must be searched to determine whether any financing statements have been filed that affect these items. Further, UCC-1 forms must be prepared to be filed for any fixtures and/or personal property that the lending institution has included in the financing instrument as security for the purchaser's loan. (Recall the example in Chapter 2.)

Schedule a final walk-through of the premises by the purchaser prior to closing so that, if there is a problem, the seller can attempt to correct it prior to the scheduled closing date. If a cure cannot be accomplished prior to closing, a post-closing agreement and/or escrow may be established to address the problems identified at the walk-through. If the electricity has been turned off, arrange to have it turned on prior to the walk-through. When conducting the walk-through, the purchaser should have an itemized list of the fixtures and personal property (if any) that are to be transferred together with the real property. These items should be compared with the fixtures and personal property found on the property.

Most contracts for sale and purchase mandate that the purchaser pay the balance of the funds required to close and transfer title by cashier's check or wire transfer of funds. This means that the purchaser will need to obtain the check or arrange for the wire transfer before the date of closing. Therefore, the closing statement should be prepared in advance of closing so that the purchaser may be notified of his or her total costs.

Confirm the date of closing with all parties, the real estate broker(s), and the lending institution. The closing agent should arrange for checks to be disbursed or wire transfers to be made in accordance with the closing statement.

If the closing pertains to a short sale transaction, additional steps must be taken. As noted in Chapter 6, lender approval must be obtained for such a transaction, and the lender will require the submission of a short sale package before making its determination. The compilation of the requisite documentation for this package may be done by a real estate broker, a title company, or an attorney. Although the contents of a short sale package will vary, depending upon each lender's requirements, the package typically is comprised of the following components:

1. A short sale proposal letter
2. The seller's hardship letter and all supporting documentation
3. The seller's financial information statement and all supporting documentation
4. The real estate broker's listing agreement
5. The real estate broker's comparable market analysis
6. An estimate of the cost of needed repairs to the property
7. The MLS listing
8. The marketing history
9. The signed contract for purchase and sale (this should contain a short sale addendum—see Chapter 7)
10. Written documentation verifying the purchaser's ability to purchase the property
11. An affidavit signed by the parties affirming that the transaction is an "arm's length" transaction
12. A preliminary title examination
13. A detailed, preliminary HUD-1 Uniform Settlement Statement

If your firm is representing the seller in a short sale transaction, you may be required to assist in the compilation of the above documentation. If more than one lender is involved or if there are other lienholders who must approve the transaction, you will need to determine the requirements of each and be certain that all documentation is in order. You also will need to have the seller sign an authorization form, giving permission for the lender to disclose financial information to your firm. Once you have the signed authorization, the first step is to contact the lender's loss mitigation department to ask whether there are lender-specific forms that must be used and to discuss the lender's checklist for the short sale package. Some items on the list you can obtain from your client, but others you may need to obtain from third parties, such as real estate brokers.

Even if the real estate broker has compiled most of the items on the lender's list, it most likely will be the seller's attorney or the title company that prepares the HUD-1 Uniform Settlement Statement (the closing statement or HUD-1 statement). The preparation of this document is detailed below. However, note that there are additional items that must be included on a HUD-1 statement for a short sale that usually do not appear on a HUD-1 statement for a regular residential transaction. Remember that the seller typically is seeking a short sale transaction as a method of avoiding foreclosure. This means that there is a great likelihood that the seller is past due on various obligations related to the property. These may include past due amounts due to the lender, past due condominium association or homeowners' association fees, past due property taxes, past due water and sewer fees, and so forth. All of these must be itemized on the HUD-1 statement.

Document Preparation and Execution

As noted, the contract for sale and purchase outlines the responsibilities of each party for document preparation. Although this, like most other items, is negotiable, in many states it is customary for the seller's attorney to prepare the majority of the closing documents, particularly those necessary for transferring marketable title to the purchaser. These documents include the deed, the bill of sale (if personal property is transferred with the real property), the seller's affidavit (or no-lien affidavit), and the satisfaction of mortgage if the seller has an outstanding loan that is to be paid off at closing. Additionally, the contract may stipulate that the seller is to provide the title commitment and title policies. The seller's attorney may also prepare the closing statement.

The contract for sale and purchase should indicate the type of deed to be delivered by the seller upon closing. If no type of deed is specified, state law in most states indicates that a general warranty deed should be used. If your state has statutorily prescribed forms for deeds, these should be used. As noted in Chapter 8, you should check your state statutes to determine the requirements for a valid deed in your state. The statutes should specify the number of witnesses necessary and the form of acknowledgment, if any, that is required. The marital status of the grantor(s), as well as the manner in which title will be held by the grantee(s), should be clearly stated on the deed. Some state statutes require that the deed also include the property parcel identification number.

The legal description of the property, as well as the exceptions affecting title, must be inserted. Some attorneys prefer to list each exception separately, while others prefer to use a blanket statement such as "all easements, restrictions, and covenants of record." The deed restrictions should match the exceptions listed in the title commitment.

If the deed is to be executed by a corporation, you should check state statutes to determine the proper method of execution. Typically, deeds may be executed by the corporation's president or vice president in the presence of two subscribing witnesses. Alternatively, the deed may be signed by the president or vice president and embossed with the corporate seal.

As noted in Chapter 2, the bill of sale should include all items of personal property that are to be transferred with the real property, described with as much particularity as possible. The actual purchase price need not be indicated. It is customary to insert a nominal consideration, such as $10.00. Some attorneys prepare a bill of sale even if only fixtures are to be transferred and no personal property is being sold. If the property is a condominium unit in which the fixtures transferred with the property are standard, then the description of the fixtures may be a general description.

The **seller's affidavit** (also referred to as a *no-lien affidavit*) is a sworn statement signed by the seller stating that there are no existing liens on the property that would encumber the purchaser's title. It includes (1) the legal description of the property; (2) a statement that the property is clear of all taxes, liens, encumbrances, and claims except those listed on the affidavit; (3) a statement that no improvements have been made on the property within the statutorily prescribed time frame (for example, thirty or ninety days) that could give rise to a statutory construction lien; (4) a statement that the seller is in exclusive possession of the property and that there are no leases or options pertaining to the property except those listed on the affidavit; and (5) a statement as to the purpose of executing the affidavit (for example, to induce the purchaser to purchase or the title company to issue a title policy).

The seller may also prepare a **nonforeign certification** (discussed later) to certify that the seller is not a *foreign person* as that term is defined in section 1445 of the Internal Revenue Code and that monies need not be withheld from the sale for tax purposes.

If the seller has an outstanding loan that is to be paid off, the seller should prepare a satisfaction and release of mortgage to be signed by the seller's lender. As discussed in Chapter 10, the satisfaction and release of mortgage nullifies the mortgage lien on the real property. It is recorded when the new deed and new financing instrument are recorded. The satisfaction sets forth (1) the name of the holder of the financing instrument, (2) the person who executed the financing instrument, (3) the principal amount of the loan, (4) the records book and page number in which the financing instrument was recorded, (5) the legal description of the real property securing the note, and (6) a statement that full payment and satisfaction of the note and financing instrument has been made. Check your state statutes to determine your state's particular requirements. It is a common requirement that the signator's signature be witnessed and acknowledged for recording purposes.

If the seller(s) is/are married, a **continuous marriage affidavit** is sometimes prepared, which is a sworn statement verifying the marital status of the seller(s). It includes (1) the legal description of the property, (2) the date of marriage, and (3) a statement that the affiants have lived together as husband and wife from that date, that the marriage was never dissolved, and that at the present time they are husband and wife. This affidavit also may be required if a spouse dies and the surviving spouse wants to convey title to the property. In this situation, a certified copy of the death certificate of the deceased spouse also should be obtained, and state requirements should be checked to determine whether any other forms, such as state department of revenue forms, will be needed to be completed before title to the property can be transferred.

If your firm is acting as the closing agent, it will have to fill out a 1099-S reporting form, which reports the transaction to the Internal Revenue Service (discussed

seller's affidavit: A sworn statement signed by the seller stating that there are no existing liens on the property that would encumber the purchaser's title.

nonforeign certification: A statement certifying that the seller is not a foreign person as that term is defined in section 1445 of the Internal Revenue Code and that monies need not be withheld from the sale for tax purposes.

continuous marriage affidavit: A sworn statement verifying the marital status of the sellers.

later in the text) unless the transaction falls under a reporting exception. Additionally, many states require a state department of revenue form to be filed.

If your firm is representing the lender in the transaction, you will have to prepare the promissory note and financing instrument to be executed by the purchaser at closing. (These documents are discussed in detail in Chapter 10.) Once the note is drafted, it must be executed by the borrower exactly as the borrower's name appears on the deed. The note may be executed on the reverse side by the guarantors (if applicable). Alternatively, the guarantors may execute a separate guaranty document. The note should be drafted with care, as no markings for corrections or additions should appear on the face of the note.

The financing instrument, be it a deed of trust or a mortgage instrument, should include the name(s) of the borrower(s) exactly as they appear on the deed. If any riders are to be attached to the instrument (for example, a condominium rider or a planned unit development, or PUD, rider), these should be executed in addition to the financing instrument. Witnessing and acknowledgment should be in compliance with your state statutes. Make sure that the date on the note and the date on the financing instrument are identical. It is common for lenders to require the signature of a spouse on the note and financing instrument even if that spouse is not included in the title to the deed.

The type of closing statement to be prepared will depend on the type of closing in question. Most residential transactions require that a HUD-1 Uniform Settlement Statement be used. (This type of closing statement is discussed in great detail later in the chapter.). A HUD-1 statement need not be used for commercial transactions. In addition to the closing statement, the parties may ask for separate buyer's and seller's statements, each detailing the debits and credits of the respective party. The HUD-1 statement must be signed by all parties and the closing agent. The buyer's and seller's statements are signed by each respective party.

Closing Costs

In addition to the purchase price, the buyer will have to pay for a number of other items associated with closing on the loan and closing on the property as set forth in the contract. The seller also will have certain items deducted from the purchase price. Recording fees, brokerage charges, and attorneys' fees are some of the items considered closing costs associated with a real estate transaction. Items owed *by* a party will appear in the debit column of the closing statement; items owed *to* a party will appear in the credit column of the closing statement. Items that are paid in advance or arrears and are to be apportioned *between* the parties are referred to as *prorations*. The chart found in Exhibit 12–1 sets forth the common closing costs charged to the parties. Note that which party is charged for each item may vary, depending on the terms of the contract, state law, or what is customary in a particular locale. For example, in some areas, it is more common for the seller to pay for such items as the title commitment, owner's title policy, and/or survey, while in other areas it is more common for the purchaser to bear these costs. To make the determination, always look to the contract for sale and purchase first and then to statutory law and custom.

Reviewing the chart, it is customary for the purchaser to pay all costs associated with obtaining a loan. Lenders may charge loan origination fees (a percentage of the loan amount, such as 1 percent) and discount points (a percentage of the

EXHIBIT 12–1   **Common closing costs**

COMMON CLOSING COSTS			
Item	Purchaser's Cost	Seller's Cost	Prorated
Loan fees (e.g., discount points, loan origination fees)	X		
Attorneys' fees	X	X	
Hazard and flood insurance (new)	X		
Hazard and flood insurance (assigned to purchaser)			X
Title commitment	X		
Title insurance:			
(a) owner's policy	X		
(b) mortgagee's policy	X		
Termite inspection	X		
Roof inspection	X		
Survey	X		
Recording of financing instruments	X		
Recording of deed	X		
Recording of satisfaction of mortgage		X	
Documentary stamps on deed		X	
Documentary stamps on financing instruments	X		
Intangible tax on new financing	X		
Broker's commission		X	
Real property taxes			X
Utilities			X
Condo maintenance			X
HOA maintenance			X
Special assessments			X
Rent (if income-producing property)			X
Interest on loan (if loan assumed by purchaser)			X

loan amount, such as 1.5 percent). If the loan is a VA loan, however, the seller must pay for any discount points charged. Lenders may also charge appraisal fees, credit report fees, inspection fees for sending their own inspectors out to the property, fees for processing the mortgage insurance application, tax service fees, assumption fees if the existing loan is to be assumed by the purchaser, and so forth. All or some of these fees may be paid at closing. If they are to be paid outside of closing, the closing statement typically will indicate this by the insertion of P.O.C. (Paid Outside Closing) next to the item.

If the seller is paying off an existing loan at closing, there may be certain charges accruing to the seller. For example, if the seller's financing instrument specifies that a prepayment penalty charge is to be paid if the loan is paid off before a specified time period, a penalty charge may be required of the seller. Therefore, it is important to review the seller's loan instruments prior to closing.

In addition to the items payable in connection with the loan, the lender may require that the purchaser pay certain items in advance, such as interest. Interest on loans is paid in arrears. This means that the mortgage interest payment made in April pays the interest owed for March. If the closing is to take place on May 15, the purchaser would not be paying the interest for May until June. The lender may request that the interest owed from May 15 until the end of May be paid at closing. If a mortgage insurance premium is to be charged in connection with the loan, the lender may request that the premium for a specified number of months be paid in advance at closing. Hazard insurance and flood insurance are other items that the lender may require to be paid in advance upon closing.

The lender may require the purchaser to prepay hazard insurance and show proof of policy effective as of date of closing with the lender as a loss payee, or it may require that the hazard, flood, or mortgage insurance premiums for a specified number of months be held in reserve by the lender. The same may be true with real property taxes. Many mortgage payments are PITI (principal, interest, taxes, and insurance) payments, whereby each monthly mortgage payment includes not only a payment of interest and a portion of the principal but also one-twelfth of the annual real property taxes and insurance on the property. In this manner, the lender guarantees that a real property tax lien with priority over the mortgage will not accrue on the property. The lender also is assured that the insurance coverage is paid to protect the collateral. In such a situation, when the tax bill is sent out, the original bill goes directly to the lender, who pays the real property taxes out of the escrow held in reserve for taxes. The same is true for the insurance.

The seller or purchaser may pay for the title examination. The party paying for the policies may differ from county to county, as noted earlier. In addition to the policy premiums, title agents usually charge extra for each endorsement attached to the policy. Thus, if the purchaser is buying a condominium, for example, a condominium endorsement may be attached to the title policy, and an additional charge will be added for this endorsement. (For a discussion of title endorsements, see Chapter 11.)

Each party is responsible for paying for his or her own attorneys' fees. Because the seller's attorney often is responsible for the majority of the document preparation and the lender prepares the loan documentation, many purchasers choose not to be represented by an attorney in simple residential transactions. As noted, the closing agent may be a title company, a lender, an escrow agent, or a law firm. An additional charge may be added for serving as closing agent. This may be paid by one or the other of the parties, or it may be split between the two parties.

The seller is responsible for the broker's commission unless the broker is a buyer's broker (discussed in Chapter 6). The broker's fee may be a flat fee or may be a specified percentage of the sales price. If more than one broker is involved in the transaction, the commission is split between the brokers. Note that the commission is not always split evenly; therefore, the contract between the seller and listing broker must be consulted.

If the purchaser has put down an earnest money deposit that is being held in escrow by the broker, the broker's fee may be deducted from the escrowed amount, and any remaining monies from the deposit are credited to the seller. In some areas, this is handled differently, however, with the broker giving the lender's attorney a check and the lender's attorney cutting the broker a check for the commission amount. If no deposit was made or if the deposit is held in escrow with someone other than the broker, a check will have to be disbursed (or wire transfer made) at closing to the broker(s) for the commission owed.

Governmental agencies charge fees for the recording of documents. The fees charged vary from county to county. They usually are a specified amount per page recorded (for example, $10.00 per page). The documents to be recorded include the deed, the satisfaction of mortgage for the seller's paid-off loan, and the new financing instruments.

City, county, and/or state authorities may charge documentary stamp taxes, also referred to as *transfer taxes,* on the deed and financing instrument. As noted in Chapter 8, the documentary stamp tax on the deed is calculated using the purchase price of the property. For example, the tax may be $.60 per each $100. If the purchase price is $300,000, you would divide this amount by 100, which would equal 3,000. You would then multiply 3,000 by $.60 to arrive at the documentary stamp tax of $1,800.

The documentary stamp tax on the financing instrument is calculated using the principal amount of the loan. If the tax is $.32 per each $100 and the principal loan amount is $200,000, you would divide this amount by 100, which would equal 2,000. You would then multiply 2,000 by $.32 to arrive at the documentary stamp tax of $640. In some jurisdictions, you are required to round up to the next increment of 100 before calculating the tax. For example, if the amount of the loan is $169,935, you would round up to $170,000 before dividing by 100 and then multiplying by the tax amount. Some governmental authorities charge an intangible tax on new loans (assumed loans would not be subject to the tax in this instance). The tax charged is multiplied by the principal amount of the loan. For example, if the loan amount is $230,000 and the intangible tax charged is two mills ($.002), you would multiply 230,000 by $.002 to arrive at the intangible tax of $460.

Certain items must be prorated between the purchaser and the seller. These items include, but are not limited to, real property taxes, rents paid or owed (if the property is rented to tenants), utility bills, loan interest if the existing loan is assumed by the purchaser, condominium maintenance fees, homeowners' association maintenance fees, special assessments, and hazard and flood insurance if the seller is assigning an existing policy to the purchaser. For example, if the closing is taking place on June 6, it is not fair for either the purchaser or the seller to pay the tax bill for the entire year. Each must pay his or her share of the tax bill. To prorate an item, there are several steps involved, as noted in Exhibit 12-2.

Consider the following example. The closing is taking place on March 10. The taxes for the year have not yet been paid. The tax bill is $4,000. The hazard insurance policy owned by the seller is to be assigned to the purchaser. It is a two-year policy. The premium is $1,000. The property is a condominium unit for which maintenance assessments are paid monthly. The monthly assessment is $250. Finally, the purchaser is assuming the seller's loan. The annual interest is $9,000. Each of these items will have to be prorated prior to closing. The parties are using a 365-day year (note that in a leap year, one would use a 366-day year). The actual days in the month are used to calculate monthly prorations. The day of closing is to be the proration date, and the day of closing is given to the purchaser.

EXHIBIT 12-2

PRORATION STEPS

1. Determine the proration year used (365 or 366 days).
2. Determine the proration month used (actual days in the month or 30-day months).
3. Determine the proration date (for example, the date of closing, the day before closing, or some other date).
4. Determine to whom the day of closing belongs if the closing date is used as the proration date. (Does the closing day belong to the seller or the purchaser?)
5. Divide the amount of the bill accordingly (for example, by the number of days in the year for an annual bill such as taxes, by the number of days in the month for a monthly bill such as interest).
6. Determine how many days in the time frame (for example, month, year, quarter) belong to the seller and how many days belong to the purchaser.
7. Determine whether the amount is paid in arrears or in advance. If paid in advance, use the number of days of the year assigned to the purchaser to calculate, and then credit the seller and debit the purchaser. If paid in arrears, use the number of days of the year assigned to the seller to calculate, and then credit the purchaser.

To calculate the portion of the annual tax bill owed by each of the parties, you must first divide the bill by 365. The tax bill is $4,000, so dividing 4,000 by 365, you get $10.9589. You then determine how many days in the year belong to each of the parties. January has 31 days, February has 28 (except in a leap year), and the seller has 9 days in March, so the seller's days are 68. The remaining days—namely, 297—belong to the purchaser. The taxes have not been paid in advance; the purchaser must pay for them when the bill comes. Therefore, the seller owes the purchaser. You take 68 (the number of seller's days) and multiply it by $10.9589 (the daily rate or *per diem* rate) to get $745.2052. This is rounded up to $745.21. This is the amount of the bill owed by the seller. This amount would be debited the seller and credited to the purchaser at closing.

The next proration is the hazard insurance premium. The total amount of the policy is $1,000. The premium is for two years, so to break it down to a daily rate, you would divide not by 365, but by 730. Thus, $1,000 divided by 730 equals $1.3698. If the policy was purchased at the beginning of this year, the purchaser owes for the remainder of the year—namely, 297 days—and for the number of days in the second year, 365. Added together, the number of days owed by the purchaser is 662. This amount, 662, multiplied by the daily rate of $1.3698 equals $906.8076, which is rounded to $906.81. This is the amount that would be debited the purchaser and credited to the seller.

The third proration is for the monthly condominium maintenance fee, which is paid in advance. The monthly charge is $250. There are 31 days in March. The seller has 9 days in the month, and the purchaser has 22 days. The monthly charge is divided by 31 to arrive at a daily rate of $8.0645. Because the fee was paid in advance, the purchaser owes the seller, so you take 22 (the number of days allocated to the purchaser) and multiply it by $8.0645 to arrive at $177.419, which is rounded to $177.42. This amount is debited the purchaser and credited to the seller.

The final proration is for the interest on the loan. Interest is paid in arrears. This means that the interest owed for the month of closing, March, will not be paid until

April. Therefore, the seller owes the purchaser for the seller's portion of the March interest payment. The annual interest is $9,000. This is divided by 12 to arrive at a monthly interest of $750. This amount is then divided by the number of days in the month—in this case 31—to arrive at a daily rate of $24.1935. The seller owes the purchaser, so the seller's days are used in the calculation. Thus, 9 multiplied by $24.1935 equals $217.7415, which rounded equals $217.74. This amount is debited the seller and credited to the purchaser.

The HUD Uniform Settlement Statement

As noted in Chapter 10, the Real Estate Settlement Procedures Act of 1974 (RESPA) was enacted to ensure that residential borrowers receive full disclosure of all charges they are to pay at closing. This Act requires that a uniform settlement statement, or closing statement, be utilized in all nonexempt closing transactions. This closing statement, the HUD-1 Uniform Settlement Statement, is often referred to as a "HUD-1 statement" or simply as a "HUD-1." HUD stands for the Department of Housing and Urban Development. (Note that a HUD-1A statement is used for refinancing transactions.) The current HUD-1 Uniform Settlement Statement is a three-page document, tying closing costs listed on the statement to those provided to the purchaser/borrower on the Good Faith Estimate (GFE). This allows the borrower to compare the closing costs as originally quoted with the actual costs allocated on the closing statement. As noted in Chapter 10, the Consumer Financial Protection Bureau has been charged with developing new mortgage disclosure forms that will merge the Truth in Lending Act and RESPA forms. Such a merger will affect the HUD-1 statement, so federal regulations should be checked. As of the date of this writing, some prototypes have been created, but none have been officially adopted and mandated. Therefore, the following discussion of the HUD-1 statement pertains to the form that went into effect as of January 2010.

The HUD-1 statement gives a detailed account of all charges connected with a residential transaction. The purchaser, seller, and lender each receive a copy of the statement at closing. The statement is signed by the seller, the purchaser, and the closing agent. The purchaser is referred to as the "borrower" on the statement. A copy of a blank HUD-1 statement is provided in Exhibit 12–3. This statement is mandated when the transaction includes a federally related loan that is used, in whole or in part, to finance the purchase of residential property—more particularly, one- to four-family dwellings. Condominiums and cooperatives are included in this definition. Transactions that are exempt from RESPA are all-cash transactions, transactions involving commercial loans, sales in which the existing loan is taken subject to or assumed (unless an assumption fee of more than $50 is charged), and transactions involving loans on vacant land or loans to purchase property consisting of twenty-five acres or more. Although RESPA does not mandate the use of the HUD-1 statement for these exempt transactions, parties may want to use a HUD-1 statement in any transaction.

As noted above, the HUD-1 is currently a three-page document. The first two pages are divided into alphabetical sections, from A through L. Section A is simply the title of the closing statement. Section B pertains to the specifics of the loan: the type of loan, the file number, the loan number, and the mortgage insurance case number are inserted in this section. Section C is a note pertaining to items paid outside of closing. Section D requires the name(s) and address(es) of the borrower(s).

HUD-1 Uniform Settlement Statement

OMB Approval No. 2502-0265

A. **Settlement Statement (HUD-1)**

B. Type of Loan

1. ☐ FHA	2. ☐ RHS	3. ☐ Conv. Unins.	6. File Number:	7. Loan Number:	8. Mortgage Insurance Case Number:
4. ☐ VA	5. ☐ Conv. Ins.				

C. Note: This form is furnished to give you a statement of actual settlement costs. Amounts paid to and by the settlement agent are shown. Items marked "(p.o.c.)" were paid outside the closing; they are shown here for informational purposes and are not included in the totals.

D. Name & Address of Borrower:	E. Name & Address of Seller:	F. Name & Address of Lender:
G. Property Location:	H. Settlement Agent:	I. Settlement Date:
	Place of Settlement:	

J. Summary of Borrower's Transaction		**K. Summary of Seller's Transaction**	
100. Gross Amount Due from Borrower		**400. Gross Amount Due to Seller**	
101. Contract sales price		401. Contract sales price	
102. Personal property		402. Personal property	
103. Settlement charges to borrower (line 1400)		403.	
104.		404.	
105.		405.	
Adjustment for items paid by seller in advance		**Adjustment for items paid by seller in advance**	
106. City/town taxes to		406. City/town taxes to	
107. County taxes to		407. County taxes to	
108. Assessments to		408. Assessments to	
109.		409.	
110.		410.	
111.		411.	
112.		412.	
120. Gross Amount Due from Borrower		**420. Gross Amount Due to Seller**	
200. Amount Paid by or in Behalf of Borrower		**500. Reductions In Amount Due to seller**	
201. Deposit or earnest money		501. Excess deposit (see instructions)	
202. Principal amount of new loan(s)		502. Settlement charges to seller (line 1400)	
203. Existing loan(s) taken subject to		503. Existing loan(s) taken subject to	
204.		**504. Payoff of first mortgage loan**	
205.		505. Payoff of second mortgage loan	
206.		506.	
207.		507.	
208.		508.	
209.		509.	
Adjustments for items unpaid by seller		**Adjustments for items unpaid by seller**	
210. City/town taxes to		510. City/town taxes to	
211. County taxes to		511. County taxes to	
212. Assessments to		512. Assessments to	
213.		513.	
214.		514.	
215.		515.	
216.		516.	
217.		517.	
218.		518.	
219.		519.	
220. Total Paid by/for Borrower		**520. Total Reduction Amount Due Seller**	
300. Cash at Settlement from/to Borrower		**600. Cash at Settlement to/from Seller**	
301. Gross amount due from borrower (line 120)		601. Gross amount due to seller (line 420)	
302. Less amounts paid by/for borrower (line 220)	( )	602. Less reductions in amounts due seller (line 520)	( )
303. Cash ☐ From ☐ To Borrower		**603. Cash** ☐ To ☐ From Seller	

The Public Reporting Burden for this collection of information is estimated at 35 minutes per response for collecting, reviewing, and reporting the data. This agency may not collect this information, and you are not required to complete this form, unless it displays a currently valid OMB control number. **No confidentiality is assured; this disclosure is mandatory.** This is designed to provide the parties to a RESPA covered transaction with information during the settlement process.

Previous edition are obsolete   Page 1 of 3   HUD-1

Source: U.S. Department of Housing and Urban Development, http://www.hud.gov/offices/
adm/hudclips/forms/files/1.pdf

EXHIBIT 12-3   *(continued)*

L. Settlement Charges			
700. Total Real Estate Broker Fees		Paid From Borrower's Funds at Settlement	Paid From Seller's Funds at Settlement
Division of commission (line 700) as follows :			
701. $ to			
702. $ to			
703. Commission paid at settlement			
704.			
800. Items Payable in Connection with Loan			
801. Our origination charge	$ (from GFE #1)		
802. Your credit or charge (points) for the specific interest rate chosen	$ (from GFE #2)		
803. Your adjusted origination charges	(from GFE #A)		
804. Appraisal fee to	(from GFE #3)		
805. Credit report to	(from GFE #3)		
806. Tax service to	(from GFE #3)		
807. Flood certification to	(from GFE #3)		
808.			
809.			
810.			
811.			
900. Items Required by Lender to be Paid in Advance			
901. Daily interest charges from to @ $ /day	(from GFE #10)		
902. Mortgage insurance premium for months to	(from GFE #3)		
903. Homeowner's insurance for years to	(from GFE #11)		
904.			
1000. Reserves Deposited with Lender			
1001. Initial deposit for your escrow account	(from GFE #9)		
1002. Homeowner's insurance months @ $ per month $			
1003. Mortgage insurance months @ $ per month $			
1004. Property Taxes months @ $ per month $			
1005. months @ $ per month $			
1006. months @ $ per month $			
1007. Aggregate Adjustment -$			
1100. Title Charges			
1101. Title services and lender's title insurance	(from GFE #4)		
1102. Settlement or closing fee	$		
1103. Owner's title insurance	(from GFE #5)		
1104. Lender's title insurance	$		
1105. Lender's title policy limit $			
1106. Owner's title policy limit $			
1107. Agent's portion of the total title insurance premium to	$		
1108. Underwriter's portion of the total title insurance premium to	$		
1109.			
1110.			
1111.			
1200. Government Recording and Transfer Charges			
1201. Government recording charges	(from GFE #7)		
1202. Deed $ Mortgage $ Release $			
1203. Transfer taxes	(from GFE #8)		
1204. City/County tax/stamps Deed $ Mortgage $			
1205. State tax/stamps Deed $ Mortgage $			
1206.			
1300. Additional Settlement Charges			
1301. Required services that you can shop for	(from GFE #6)		
1302.	$		
1303.	$		
1304.			
1305.			
1400. Total Settlement Charges (enter on lines 103, Section J and 502, Section K)			

Previous edition are obsolete   Page 2 of 3   HUD-1

Source: U.S. Department of Housing and Urban Development, http://www.hud.gov/offices/ adm/hudclips/forms/files/1.pdf

Comparison of Good Faith Estimate (GFE) and HUD-1 Charrges		Good Faith Estimate	HUD-1
Charges That Cannot Increase	**HUD-1 Line Number**		
Our origination charge	# 801		
Your credit or charge (points) for the specific interest rate chosen	# 802		
Your adjusted origination charges	# 803		
Transfer taxes	# 1203		

Charges That In Total Cannot Increase More Than 10%		Good Faith Estimate	HUD-1
Government recording charges	# 1201		
	#		
	#		
	#		
	#		
	#		
	#		
	#		
	Total		
Increase between GFE and HUD-1 Charges		$ or	%

Charges That Can Change		Good Faith Estimate	HUD-1
Initial deposit for your escrow account	# 1001		
Daily interest charges $ /day	# 901		
Homeowner's insurance	# 903		
	#		
	#		
	#		

Loan Terms

Your initial loan amount is	$
Your loan term is	years
Your initial interest rate is	%
Your initial monthly amount owed for principal, interest, and any mortgage insurance is	$ includes ☐ Principal ☐ Interest ☐ Mortgage Insurance
Can your interest rate rise?	☐ No ☐ Yes, it can rise to a maximum of **%. The first change will be on** and can change again every after . Every change date, your interest rate can increase or decrease by %. Over the life of the loan, your interest rate is guaranteed to never be **lower** than % or **higher** than %.
Even if you make payments on time, can your loan balance rise?	☐ No ☐ Yes, it can rise to a maximum of $
Even if you make payments on time, can your monthly amount owed for principal, interest, and mortgage insurance rise?	☐ No ☐ **Yes, the first increase can be on** and the monthly amount owed can rise to $. The maximum it can ever rise to is $.
Does your loan have a prepayment penalty?	☐ No ☐ Yes, your maximum prepayment penalty is $
Does your loan have a balloon payment?	☐ No ☐ Yes, you have a balloon payment of $ due in years on .
Total monthly amount owed including escrow account payments	☐ You do not have a monthly escrow payment for items, such as property taxes and homeowner's insurance. You must pay these items directly yourself. ☐ You have an additional monthly escrow payment of $ that results in a total initial monthly amount owed of $. This includes principal, interest, any mortagage insurance and any items checked below: ☐ Property taxes ☐ Homeowner's insurance ☐ Flood insurance ☐ ☐ ☐

Note: If you have any questions about the Settlement Charges and Loan Terms listed on this form, please contact your lender.

Previous edition are obsolete   Page 3 of 3   HUD-1

Source: U.S. Department of Housing and Urban Development, http://www.hud.gov/offices/adm/hudclips/forms/files/1.pdf

Section E requires the name(s) and address(es) of the seller(s). Section F requires the name and address of the lender. Section G is where the property location is inserted. This is typically a street address, although one can insert a legal description. The county and parcel identification number may be inserted as well. Section H is for the insertion of the name and address of the settlement agent. The closing date is inserted in section I.

Section J is a summary of the borrower's transaction, with the 100s relating to the borrower's debits and the 200s relating to the borrower's credits. Inserted in the 100s would be the contract price (line 101), the price of any personal property sold to the borrower (line 102), the closing costs to be paid by the borrower (line 103, based on the itemization in section L), and prorated items for which the seller has paid in advance (lines 106 through 112). Line 120 totals the items to be debited the borrower. The 200s cover items paid by or on behalf of the borrower. These include any earnest money deposit paid (line 201), the amount of the financing (lines 202 and 203), the amount of any purchase money mortgage to be held by the seller (lines 204–209), and prorated items unpaid as yet by the seller (lines 210 through 219). The borrower's credits are totaled on line 220. The 300s subtract the borrower's credits from the borrower's debits to arrive at the amount of money owed by the borrower at closing.

Section K is a summary of the seller's transaction, with the 400s relating to the seller's credits and the 500s relating to the seller's debits. The seller's credits include the sales price of the property (line 401), the sales price for any personal property involved in the transaction (line 402), and prorated items paid in advance by the seller (lines 406 through 412). The seller's credits are totaled on line 420. The seller's debits include the closing costs charged to the seller (line 502, based on the itemization in section L), the payoff of the existing loan (line 504), and any prorated items for which the seller has not yet paid (lines 510 through 519). If the seller is providing a purchase money mortgage loan to the borrower, this amount is debited the seller on lines 506–509. The seller's debits are totaled on line 520. The 600s subtract the seller's debits from the seller's credits to arrive at the sum of money to be received by the seller at closing.

Section L itemizes the closing costs charged to each party. The 700s relate to brokerage commissions. Lines 701 and 702 will show any commission split. Line 703 is where the commission is charged to the seller. This assumes that the earnest money deposit made by the borrower is held by someone other than the broker. If the deposit has been retained by the broker in escrow, the broker will subtract the commission amount from the deposit and give the seller a check for any excess. If there is any excess from the deposit, this amount should be inserted on line 501 with an indication that the excess is to be paid outside closing (P.O.C.), and the total amount of the commission is inserted on line 703.

The 800s pertain to items payable in connection with the loan. Note that a number of the items listed in this section are referenced back to the GFE. Line 801 pertains to the lender's loan origination charge. This fee will be inserted by the internal dollar sign on this line. Line 802 pertains to any credit or charge for the interest rate paid on the loan. Points are considered a charge for obtaining a lower ("discounted") interest rate. This amount will be inserted by the internal dollar sign on this line. On line 803, one adds the figures on lines 801 and 802 to derive the adjusted origination charge. This adjusted figure should be inserted in the borrower's column on line 803. Lines 804–807 pertain to various items that the lender may require as part of the loan process, such as appraisals, credit reports, flood certifications, and so forth. These itemized costs are borrower's costs in connection with obtaining the loan. Any other similar items (for example, an HOA certification fee) should be inserted in blank lines within the 800s.

The 900s pertain to items required by the lender to be paid in advance. Again, these items are referenced back to items that may have appeared on the GFE. These include interest on the loan (line 901) and various insurance premiums (lines 902–904). The 1000s pertain to reserves deposited with the lender for insurance, taxes, and assessments. The total charges for this section will appear on line 1001 in the borrower's column. The charge for each item will be noted by the internal dollar signs.

The 1100s pertain to title charges. As with prior sections, certain references to the GFE are noted. Included in this section are any fees charged by the settlement (closing) agent as well as charges for title services and title policies. Notary fees and attorneys' fees may appear either in the 1100s or in the 1300s. Line 1101 pertains to the portion of the settlement fee paid by the purchaser and the charge for the lender's title insurance. The total settlement fee is noted on line 1102, and any portion the seller is required to pay should appear in the seller's column. The fee for the owner's title policy appears on line 1103. On line 1104, the fee for the lender's policy appears by the internal dollar sign. Lines 1105 and 1106 set forth the policy limits for the owner's and the lender's coverage. Lines 1107 and 1108 separate the portion of the title insurance premium that is paid to the title agent and the portion that is paid to the underwriter. Any endorsements issued in connection with the policies also will appear in the 1100s.

Government-related fees, such as those charged for the recording of documents, documentary stamp taxes, and intangible taxes, are found in the 1200s. The 1300s are for miscellaneous charges, such as pest inspections, surveys, and so forth. These two sections also relate back to the GFE. The total closing cost charges for each party are inserted on line 1400 and then also entered on lines 103 and 502 in sections J and K, respectively, on the first page of the HUD-1.

On the third page of the HUD-1, the purchaser is provided a side-by-side comparison of the borrower's closing costs as they appear on the GFE and the actual closing costs set forth on the HUD-1. The costs are divided into the same categories, or tolerances, as appear on the GFE: (1) those charges that cannot change, (2) those charges that cannot increase more than 10 percent from the figures provided on the GFE, and (3) those charges that can change (no limit designated) from those quoted on the GFE. The second portion of the third page is a summary of the borrower's loan terms.

Real Estate Closing Software

At times, the paperwork involved in the average real estate closing may seem endless, and the task of putting together a final closing package may seem daunting. Fortunately, many real estate law firms, title companies, and lending institutions are taking advantage of an array of real estate closing software programs that simplify the documentation process.

The software programs presently on the market differ in pricing, specialized features, and interfacing capabilities with other programs, but they have a number of common aspects. They all can print out the HUD-1 Uniform Settlement Statement and the basic closing documents, and they can automatically calculate prorations—and recalculate should last-minute changes occur. Most of the programs are used nationwide. While the primary function of these programs is to prepare the HUD-1 statement, they are capable of doing much more. They can print checks, loan amortization schedules, disbursement summaries, separate buyer's and seller's statements, and 1099 forms for filing with the Internal Revenue Service. (See a discussion of 1099 reporting requirements in the following text.) The key to these software programs is the single-entry concept: Once information is input, the relevant data will appear in each document. For example, after typing in the legal description of a property once, it will appear in the deed, the seller's affidavit, the title commitment, and so forth. This is particularly useful because it can cut down not only on time but also on the possibility of error. If the legal description is input accurately, it will be reproduced accurately in all of the documents.

Most of the closing software can be customized to be state- and county-specific, which makes calculations effortless. Besides prorations, the systems can accurately and automatically calculate your county's recording fees, documentary stamp taxes, and intangible taxes. If the closing date changes, one need only input the new date once, and it will appear on all corresponding documents. Additionally, the program will automatically recalculate all prorations on the closing statement.

Some of the software programs have scheduling and calendar functions. They keep track of multiple closings on closing calendars, and they act as tickler files, tracking the parties responsible for various closing tasks.

Many of the programs have user-friendly main menus from which one can choose to enter or change closing data; print documents, checks, or amortization schedules; or prepare various reports. A number of programs use a look-alike HUD-1 statement for the initial input of data. Almost all systems interface with WordPerfect, Microsoft Word, or both. A number of the programs interface with Quicken for escrow accounting. Many of the programs also are available as completely Web-based ("cloud") systems.

Some of the real estate software programs are sold as complete systems, while others are sold in modules. One purchases the modules that one uses most often. Thus, if a firm never prepares title work, the firm would not purchase the module for preparing title policies. The licensing fee charged will depend on whether the system is to support single or multiple users. It may also vary depending on the number of closing files open at any one time. Most software companies charge an annual maintenance fee, although the amount of the fee varies.

Many attorneys have their paralegals research the available real estate closing software programs on the premise that the paralegal will be using the program on a daily basis. Besides the cost factor, both the paralegal and the attorney should consider several other factors. The first factor to consider is whether a Web-based system is desirable or whether other formats should be considered. With the latter option, one must check to see if the system is compatible with the firm's current computer hardware capabilities. The training and technical support provided by the software company are crucial. The length of time during which free technical support is offered varies considerably from company to company. Some companies will provide on-site training for no extra cost, while others charge for this service. Additionally, the system must be user-friendly and conducive to working with speed and accuracy. A busy real estate firm can have several closings scheduled daily, and the software system purchased should allow the paralegal to prepare the requisite documentation quickly enough to meet the needs of the firm.

It is advisable to obtain demonstration copies of various software programs prior to purchasing one of them. Some companies provide demonstration disks that can be used for a specified time period (for example, thirty days or six months). These disks may or may not limit the number of closing files that may be available at a given time. Many companies now provide the option of trial versions that can be downloaded from their websites.

The Closing

The closing date, time, and place must be confirmed with all parties, including the lender, in advance. Each party will want to review the closing documents and closing statement prior to the date of closing. Assuming all is in order, the paralegal should make a list of those parties signing original documents and those parties receiving original documents. For example, the seller signs the original deed, but once that original deed is back from recording, the purchaser receives it. Similarly, the purchaser signs the original note and financing instrument, but the lender receives the originals, while the purchaser receives copies.

If the parties are going to be present at the closing and will not be signing documents in advance, the paralegal must also make sure that a notary will be available to notarize documents at closing; that the requisite number of witnesses, if required, are available to sign necessary documents; and that the corporate secretary is available to attest to signatures if a party to the transaction is a corporation. For example, grantees (purchasers) cannot be witnesses on deeds, so in jurisdictions requiring two witnesses for a valid deed, two nonparties must be available to witness the document. The paralegal should have a complete set of unexecuted copies of documents for the client file prior to closing.

If institutional financing is involved in the transaction, that portion of the closing often occurs first, with the purchaser executing the financing instruments before the other closing documents are executed. The parties should not be rushed through this process. Although the purchaser may have seen copies of the financing instruments prior to closing, the lender's representative (if present) should highlight the salient points once again prior to execution of the note and financing instrument. If the purchaser has any last-minute questions, the appropriate time to ask them is before, not after, signing the loan documentation. Once the loan portion of the closing has taken place, the loan amount may be transferred by wire transfer into the closing agent's trust account as part of the funds to be paid to the seller.

Next, the closing agent should review each closing document with the parties prior to execution and make certain that each document is executed, witnessed, and notarized (when applicable) in full before moving on to the next. For example, the purchaser should review the deed to determine whether the exceptions listed match those in the title commitment. The names of the parties should be rechecked to ensure that they are spelled properly and that they conform throughout the set of documents. The parties should bring along forms of identification, as the notary will require proper identification prior to notarization.

Once all documents are properly executed, the closing agent should retrieve them so that the appropriate documents may be recorded. If the seller's address is to change as a result of the transaction, the seller's new address must be obtained.

Although, depending on the terms of the contract, the parties may have cashier's checks made out to the closing agent to be deposited into the escrow account to cover the closing costs, it is common to have the monies sent by wire transfer. The paralegal must ensure that separate disbursements in the appropriate sums are made from the account for brokerage commissions, title company fees, and so forth. A disbursement summary should be prepared and provided to the parties. In some states, all documents must be recorded prior to disbursing closing proceeds, so state law should be checked.

Finally, the keys and any other pertinent items (for example, garage door openers or appliance warranties) must be given to the purchaser.

Postclosing

The paralegal's responsibilities do not end with the closing. There are a number of postclosing matters that need attention. No documents should leave the office until copies have been made for the parties and the file. Certain disbursements will be made at the closing itself, while others will be made after closing. These latter disbursements include the payoff of the seller's existing loan as well as recording fees and documentary stamp taxes. Further, if your firm has acted as escrow agent, you must send interest statements to the party who received the interest on the deposit(s) at closing.

The original satisfaction of mortgage and payoff check or wire transfer must be sent immediately to the seller's lender. Examples of a satisfaction and corresponding cover letter are found in the next chapter. Once the executed satisfaction is received, it should be sent, together with the original deed and original financing instrument, to the recording clerk's office, along with the appropriate fees. In some jurisdictions, it is possible to record these documents electronically.

After the original documents are recorded, the paralegal must provide the recording information to the title company so that the owner's and mortgagee's policies can be prepared. If the paralegal's supervising attorney is a title agent, the paralegal may take part in the preparation of the policies. Prior to issuance of the policies, the title search must be updated.

Once the title policies are prepared, they should be reviewed for accuracy. The legal description should be checked, the coverage amounts should be checked, and the exceptions should be compared with a copy of the marked-up title commitment. If an abstract of title was used for the title examination, it should be sent to the purchaser or the purchaser's lender (whichever is indicated by the parties).

Next, closing packages must be organized for the purchaser, seller, and lender. The paralegal must organize the documents in chronological order, providing originals and copies as appropriate. The document packages should include a closing binder index. (Closing package organization and closing binder indices are discussed in detail in the next chapter.) In the interim between the recordation of the closing documents and the preparation of the final closing binders, the attorneys representing the respective parties may correspond with their clients, describing the documents to be received. The clients can then check the closing binder packages against the attorneys' letters to make sure that all documentation has been provided. Once all these tasks are completed, the client file can be closed.

The following South Carolina case illustrates the potential pitfalls when a closing agent with a lack of experience and poor attention to detail meets up with an unethical party in the closing process.

CASE: *In Re Boulware*

366 S.C. 561, 623 S.E.2d 652 (2005)

PER CURIAM.

The Office of Disciplinary Counsel (ODC) and respondent have entered into an Agreement for Discipline by Consent pursuant to Rule 21, RLDE, Rule 413, SCACR, in which respondent admits misconduct and agrees to imposition of an admonition, public reprimand, or definite suspension not to exceed thirty (30) days. We accept the agreement and issue a public reprimand. The facts, as set forth in the agreement, are as follows.

FACTS

In February 2002, respondent approached Amy Cook, the principal of Carolina Title Services, Inc., (CTS) in hopes of obtaining some of its real estate business.[1] CTS was an agent for Chicago Title Insurance Company (Chicago Title) and had an ongoing business relationship with attorney William J. McMillan III for the closing of real estate transactions. Respondent sought to be a closing attorney for CTS, but Cook only needed a lawyer to fill in for McMillan at closings when he was unavailable. After seeking and obtaining Chicago Title's approval and speaking with McMillan by telephone, respondent agreed to the arrangement.

Respondent represents that, during her telephone conversation with McMillan, he assured her that, other than attending the actual closing, he would be supervising all aspects of the transactions.[2] Respondent never met McMillan and did not communicate with him again until after terminating her relationship with CTS.

From February through April 2002, respondent attended approximately twenty-four real estate closings. Respondent was asked only to attend the closings and be responsible for the review and execution of the closing documents. Respondent represents she was under the good faith impression that McMillan would attend to or supervise all other aspects of the real estate transactions; however, McMillan did not do so and it is now known that he took no part in these transactions.

The closings took place at CTS's offices. Respondent received all files and instructions from Cook or her employees and, after the closing, she left all closing documents and monies with Cook or her employees. Most of the closings at issue were relatively uncomplicated. On the few occasions when a question or problem arose, respondent stopped the closing and Cook rescheduled it for a later date. Respondent is now advised and does not dispute that the title abstracts and closing documents were prepared by Cook and CTS employees without the supervision of any lawyer, that disbursement of funds and recordation of documents were handled by Cook and CTS employees without the supervision of any lawyer, and that McMillan's only involvement in the transactions consisted of allowing Cook unlimited and unsupervised use of his trust accounts.

Respondent represents she verbally informed the parties to each closing that her role was limited to explaining and executing the documents and that CTS and its lawyer were responsible for all other aspects of the closing. However, on several occasions, respondent supervised the buyer's execution of an attorney preference form during which buyers selected respondent to represent them in all aspects of the transaction. On these occasions, respondent filled in her own name as the selected attorney on the form prior to its execution by the buyer.

On thirteen occasions, the HUD-1 Settlement Statements included a $12 wire fee payable to respondent even though respondent never incurred a wire fee in any transaction with CTS. ODC is informed and believes that, in each of these closings, a wire fee was incurred by CTS or McMillan's trust account under Cook's control. Because respondent had requested Cook increase her fee, Cook offered to give respondent the $12 wire fee as a way to increase her fee without turning away clients who might object to an overt fee increase. Respondent consented to this arrangement. Respondent now recognizes that the HUD-1 statement was not completely accurate and that the arrangement resulted in respondent receiving a portion of her fee from someone other than her client.

On one occasion, respondent closed a transaction in which the buyers were personal friends of Cook. Cook had agreed not to charge the buyers an attorney fee and the HUD-1 Settlement Statement reflected no fee to any lawyer. However, Cook and respondent agreed that Cook would pay respondent a fee outside the closing and not disclose the fee to anyone. Respondent now recognizes that closing the transaction in this manner and accepting an undisclosed fee violated the Rules of Professional Conduct and federal law.

In most of the transactions respondent closed, respondent's name or her firm name were shown on the HUD-1 as "Settlement Agent," but respondent did not act as settlement agent as she neither held nor disbursed the closing proceeds. Due to her inexperience, respondent was not aware of all the implications made by the statements on the HUD-1 form. Respondent now recognizes that, by forwarding inaccurate HUD-1 forms to clients and other

(continued)

parties, she misrepresented her role to all parties relying on the HUD-1 Settlement Statements, particularly lenders who were not present at the closings. Her misrepresentation is most pronounced in those closings in which the HUD-1 Settlement Statements indicated that respondent incurred a wire fee, as the statements implied to lenders and subsequent assignees that respondent was disbursing the loan proceeds, including making payoffs of prior mortgages and liens.

On two occasions, a lender delivered closing funds to respondent's trust account rather than to McMillan's trust account for transactions in which respondent was to act as closing attorney for CTS. Respondent endorsed the first check to CTS based on information from Cook that the lender wanted Cook to disburse the money. The second check was a wire transfer into respondent's trust account, which respondent initially refused to endorse to Cook but, when a CTS employee refused to give respondent a disbursement summary, respondent relented and wrote a trust account check to CTS for the funds so that the transaction could close without the borrower losing a favorable interest rate.

On one occasion, a buyer brought funds to the closing in the form of a check payable to respondent. Due to a title issue, the closing was delayed until a time when respondent would not be available. As a result, respondent endorsed the buyer's check to CTS and gave it to Cook. Respondent now recognizes she should not have given the client funds to a non-lawyer.

On two occasions, respondent signed a loan confirmation or "First Lien Letter" several days after closing. These letters advised the lender and title insurance company that the transaction was closed and completely disbursed, that all prior liens were satisfied, and that the lender's mortgage was a valid first lien on the property. Respondent represents she believed those statements were true but admits that such a belief was merely an assumption, that she had no actual knowledge of the truth or falsity of the statements, and that she did not verify the information with anyone outside of CTS before executing the letters.

It is now known that in most, if not all, of the transactions closed by respondent for CTS, Cook diverted closing proceeds from McMillan's trust accounts to her personal accounts and did not disburse money to the parties as indicated on the HUD-1 Settlement Statements. Respondent had no knowledge of this activity at the time.

Since 2002, Chicago Title and its counsel have worked to correct the title problems caused by Cook's defalcation in transactions involving respondent and other lawyers. Chicago Title has spent approximately $250,000 to resolve title issues in closings in which respondent was involved. In addition, several holders of unpaid prior mortgages compromised their debts in settling with Chicago Title and, therefore, remain financially prejudiced; Chicago Title denied coverage in several other cases, leaving the holders of those unpaid prior liens and mortgages with no recourse but foreclosure. Respondent has resolved through settlement each lawsuit in which she was a named defendant.

In addition to the transactions in which respondent served as closing attorney, on numerous occasions respondent received checks written on McMillan's trust account and signed by Cook as payment of attorney fees for closing in which respondent had no involvement. In at least three of these transactions, Cook had used respondent's name as the settlement agent on closing documents but, as with other transactions, Cook had stolen the lender's money and did not make the disbursements as indicated in the HUD-1 Settlement Statements. Respondent had no knowledge of these transactions or of Cook's defalcations until being so advised by ODC. Nevertheless, respondent and her staff deposited these fee checks into respondent's operating account, incorrectly assuming that they related to transactions in which she had served as closing attorney.

Respondent maintained no office procedure for matching incoming payments to closing work performed and, therefore, unwittingly received payments for the use of her name and law license by a non-lawyer.

On three occasions in March 2002, a lender wired closing funds totaling $197,285.99 to respondent's trust account. Respondent closed two of those transactions, not knowing funds were wired to her account, but assuming they were wired to McMillan's account as usual. Cook closed the third transaction without respondent's knowledge. In all three of the transactions, the funds were not disbursed as indicated in the HUD-1 Settlement Statements. Respondent attempted to reconcile her trust account on a monthly basis, but her reconciliations did not alert her to the excess funds in her trust account.

Several months after respondent terminated her relationship with CTS she sought an agency relationship with Stewart Title Company pursuant to which Stewart Title conducted an audit of respondent's trust account. The audit alerted respondent to the excess funds in July 2002 and respondent immediately took steps that resulted in delivery of those funds to the appropriate parties. Until the audit, respondent had no knowledge of the three wires into her trust account. Respondent now recognizes that, in order to comply with Rule 417, SCACR, on a monthly basis she must reconcile the trust account balance according to the bank's records with the balance according to her records of account activity and that, if she had complied with Rule 417, she would have been immediately alerted to the improper deposits.

After closing approximately two dozen transactions between February and April 2002, respondent became aware that Cook or a CTS employee had forged her name on a

(continued)

HUD-1 Settlement Statement and on a closing proceeds check from a lender and that checks written by CTS were being dishonored for insufficient funds. Upon learning this information, respondent severed her relationship with CTS. Respondent then sent a letter to the Commission on Lawyer Conduct (Commission) purporting to be an anonymous report of Cook's and McMillan's actions. The letter sought the advice of the Commission and offered respondent's assistance in stopping the ongoing defalcation.

In mitigation, respondent states she was under the good faith impression that McMillan was performing or supervising all aspects of the real estate transaction that required attorney participation. She further states she was unaware that Cook was engaged in the unauthorized practice of law, that she was unaware that Cook had unsupervised access to and use of McMillan's trust accounts, and that she in no way intentionally contributed to the defalcation in these transactions

LAW

Respondent admits that, by her misconduct, she has violated the following provisions of the Rules of Professional Conduct, Rule 407, SCACR: Rule 1.1 (lawyer shall provide competent representation); Rule 1.4(b) (lawyer shall explain a matter to the extent reasonably necessary to permit the client to make informed decisions regarding the representation); Rule 1.8(f) (lawyer shall not accept compensation for representing a client from one other than the client unless the client consents after consultation); Rule 1.15 (lawyer shall safe keep client funds); Rule 4.1(a) (in course of representing a client, lawyer shall not make a false statement of material fact to a third person); Rule 5.5(b) (lawyer shall not assist a person in the unauthorized practice of law); Rule 8.4(a) (it is professional misconduct for lawyer to violate Rules of Professional Conduct); and Rule 8.4(d) (it is professional misconduct for lawyer to engage in dishonesty, fraud, deceit, or misrepresentation). Respondent acknowledges that her misconduct constitutes grounds for discipline under the Rules for Lawyer Disciplinary Enforcement, Rule 413, SCACR, specifically Rule 7(a)(1) (it shall be ground for discipline for lawyer to violate Rules of Professional Conduct).

CONCLUSION

We find that respondent's misconduct warrants a public reprimand. Accordingly, we accept the Agreement for Discipline by Consent and publicly reprimand respondent for her misconduct.

PUBLIC REPRIMAND.

TOAL, C.J., MOORE, BURNETT and PLEICONES, JJ., concur. WALLER, J., not participating.

Case Questions

1. What steps could Boulware have taken initially, prior to agreeing to the arrangement with CTS, that could have altered the ultimate outcome of this situation for her?

2. Considering her inexperience, do you think it was appropriate for Boulware to conduct the closings? What could she have done to better prepare herself?

3. Which of her transgressions do you believe is the most serious in nature? Why? How could this have been prevented?

1. Respondent was admitted to the Bar in November 1999. At the time she contacted Cook, respondent had recently opened her own office and was seeking to build her practice.

2. McMillan's statements to ODC contradict respondent's representation.

Tax-Related Items

In 1985, an amendment to the Foreign Investment in Real Property Tax Act (FIRPTA) went into effect. Section 1445 of the Internal Revenue Code requires any individual or entity that purchases property from a foreign person to withhold 10 percent of the purchase price for the Internal Revenue Service. (An exception is made for the purchase of property for use as a home if the sales price is not more than $300,000.) The code defines *foreign persons* as foreign nationals who do not hold permanent resident visas. This definition includes both individuals and business entities. If the stipulated 10 percent is not withheld, real estate agents may be held liable to the extent of their commission, and purchasers are liable for the balance. The purchaser is responsible for determining the seller's citizenship status. Most attorneys prepare a nonforeign certification (sometimes referred to as a FIRPTA affidavit) to be signed by the seller, verifying that the seller is not a foreign person and therefore monies need not be withheld. The affidavit also includes the seller's address and federal taxpayer's identification number.

In addition to the withholding requirements of section 1445 of the FIRPTA, the Tax Reform Act of 1986 mandates that real estate transactions be reported to the Internal Revenue Service by the closing agent. As noted earlier in the chapter, the closing agent may be a title company, a lending institution, an escrow company, or an attorney. The person handling the closing has the legal responsibility for reporting. The transaction is reported on a **1099-S form.** The form must be completed with the following information: (1) the closing agent's name, address, and taxpayer's identification number; (2) the seller's name, address, and taxpayer's identification number; (3) the closing date; (4) the sales price; (5) the type of transaction; (6) the property's address; and (7) the parcel identification number. The Internal Revenue Service makes a reporting exception for the sale or exchange of a residence for $250,000 ($500,000 if married, filing joint tax returns) if the closing agent has received an acceptable written assurance from the seller that the property being sold is the seller's principal residence and the full amount of the gain on the sale is excludable from gross income under section 121 of the Internal Revenue Code. The closing agent must obtain a seller certification (or one from each seller if joint sellers). The certification must be signed under penalties of perjury. If the certifications are not obtained, then the 1099-S must be filed, even if the sale meets the monetary qualification for this exception. A sample seller certification is found in Exhibit 12–4.

Certain real estate–related costs are tax deductible for income tax purposes. These items include interest paid on a promissory note, loan origination fees charged by the lender, and real property taxes. Other costs may be capitalized by adding them to the price paid for the property. By so doing, these costs become a part of the base for capital gains tax purposes when the property is later sold. Items that may be capitalized include attorneys' fees, appraisal fees, title insurance premiums, recording fees, notary fees, escrow fees, and transfer taxes.

Escrow Closings

The description of the actual closing provided in the preceding text presumes that the parties are able to meet face-to-face at the closing agent's office. Alternatively, instead of a face-to-face encounter, an **escrow closing** may be held (also referred to as a closing in escrow). In some states, such as California, escrow closings are common practice. In an escrow closing, a third party, such as a title company, law firm, or escrow company, acts as the escrowee or escrow holder. Both parties deposit their closing documents with the escrowee, and the escrowee proceeds to close the transaction as an impartial agent, attending to the requirements of each party.

If the parties know at the time of contracting that an escrow closing will be required, the contract for sale and purchase may indicate the name of the person or firm to act as escrowee. The parties and the escrowee would then sign an escrow agreement. The escrow agreement stipulates the responsibilities of each signatory as well as the documents each party must prepare and deposit with the escrowee prior to the date of closing. The escrow agreement should also provide for interpleader in the event of a dispute and provide indemnification for the escrowee. Sometimes, instead of signing a separate escrow agreement, all of the terms for an escrow closing are included in the contract for sale and purchase, and the escrowee, as well as the purchaser and seller, signs the contract to indicate his or her agreement with the escrow terms.

1099-S form: A federal tax reporting form for the reporting of real property sales transactions.

escrow closing: A closing in which a third party acts as escrowee and receives closing documents deposited by each party, whereupon the escrowee proceeds to close the transaction.

SELLER CERTIFICATION

Part I. Seller Information

Name:
Kimberly Jamison

Address/legal description of property:
389 St. Michaels Drive
Any City, Any State

Taxpayer Identification Number:
xxxxx0109

Part II. Seller Assurances

Check "True" or "False" for assurances (1) through (5) and "True," "False," or "Not Applicable (N/A)" for assurance (6).

True | False |
--- | --- | --- | ---
[X] | [ ] | (1) | I owned and used the residence as my principal residence for periods aggregating 2 years or more during the 5-year period ending on the date of the sale or exchange of the residence.
[X] | [ ] | (2) | I have not sold or exchanged another principal residence during the 2-year period ending on the date of the sale or exchange of the residence.
[X] | [ ] | (3) | I (or my spouse or former spouse, if I was married at any time during the period beginning after May 6, 1997, and ending today) have not used any portion of the residence for business or rental purposes after May 6, 1997.
[X] | [ ] | (4) | At least one of the following three statements applies: The sale or exchange is of the entire residence for $250,000 or less.
OR
I am married, the sale or exchange is of the entire residence for $500,000 or less, and the gain on the sale or exchange of the entire residence is $250,000 or less.
OR
I am married, the sale or exchange is of the entire residence for $500,000 or less, and (a) I intend to file a joint return for the year of the sale or exchange, (b) my spouse also used the residence as his or her principal residence for periods aggregating 2 years or more during the 5-year period ending on the date of the sale or exchange of the residence, and (c) my spouse also has not sold or exchanged another principal residence during the 2-year period ending on the date of the sale or exchange of the principal residence.
[X] | [ ] | (5) | During the 5-year period ending on the date of the sale or exchange of the residence, I did not acquire the residence in an exchange to which section 1031 of the Internal Revenue Code applied.

True | False | N/A |
--- | --- | --- | --- | ---
[ ] | [ ] | [X] | (6) | If my basis in the residence is determined by reference to the basis in the hands of a person who acquired the residence in an exchange to which section 1031 of the Internal Revenue Code applied, the exchange to which section 1031 applied occurred more than 5 years prior to the date I sold or exchanged the residence.

Part III. Seller Certification

Under penalties of perjury, I certify that all the above information is true as of the end of the day of the sale or exchange.

Kimberly Jamison	9/3/15
Seller	Date

STATE OF ANY STATE
COUNTY OF ANY COUNTY

The foregoing instrument was acknowledged before me this 3rd day of September, 2015, by Kimberly Jamison, who [X] is personally known to me or [ ] produced _____ as identification.

Daniel Clark
Notary Public

Daniel Clark
Printed Notary Name

My Commission Expires: 5/30/16

The purchaser deposits any earnest money with the escrowee, and later the cash balance needed to close the transaction. The financing instruments are deposited with the escrowee by the lender to be sent to the purchaser for signature. The seller deposits with the escrowee the executed deed, the seller's affidavit, and any other documents required to transfer marketable title.

Once all the documentation is deposited, the escrowee examines it to ensure that it is in order. The escrowee checks to see that the documents are executed legally and that the necessary witnessing and acknowledgments are completed. The parties should provide the escrowee with copies of photo identification to compare with the signatures on the documents. The escrowee conducts a final title check to make sure that there are no encumbrances on the title to be transferred. If all is in order, the escrowee disburses the funds according to a set of escrow instructions signed by both parties, records the documents, and sends originals and copies to the respective parties.

Although electronically signed contracts for purchase and sale are widely accepted, at the time of this writing the concept of conducting entire closings electronically is moving at a slower pace. Nonetheless, just as electronic recording of documents and electronic filing of pleadings has gained acceptance in both state and federal arenas, there is a growing movement to encourage e-closings. Therefore, paralegals should make themselves aware of state regulations pertaining to electronic signatures and electronic notarizations.

CHAPTER SUMMARY

1. A closing is the process of transferring title documents and monies to complete a real estate transaction. The process requires the participation not only of the seller and the purchaser but of third parties as well. These third parties include, but are not limited to, real estate brokers, lenders, title companies, and insurance companies, each with a specific set of criteria to be met.

2. The key to organization of a real estate file is attention to detail. The use of a closing worksheet puts information that is important and referred to repeatedly at ready access. The worksheet itemizes the tasks to be done, specifies the party responsible for each task, sets due dates, and indicates the party to be charged. A tickler system should be set up to work in conjunction with the worksheet.

3. Short sale transactions require special attention to preclosing matters. Checklists should be followed and lender-specific instructions reviewed in the compilation and review of short sale packages. The HUD-1 Uniform Settlement Statement required by the lender as part of the preclosing process includes items not typically found in other transactions. These items include, but are not limited to, past due amounts owed to the lender and those owed for taxes and association fees.

4. All closing documents should be prepared for final review prior to closing. The closing statement figures must be made available to the purchaser at least two or three days prior to the closing date because the purchaser will have to pay all sums due with a cashier's check or wire transfer.

5. Prior to closing, a purchaser pursuing institutional financing will make a loan application and provide the prospective lender with all pertinent financial

records. If accepted, a loan commitment will be issued that will be valid for a short duration. The closing must take place within this time frame, or an extension on the commitment must be sought. The commitment sets forth items that must be complied with to the lender's satisfaction prior to the closing of the loan. The fees for such items as appraisals, credit reports, and lender's inspections comprise part of the purchaser's closing costs.

6. Prior to closing, the seller must provide the purchaser with an updated abstract of title or title commitment. Any defects in title indicated by these instruments must be cured by the seller within the contractually stipulated time frame. If the seller has an outstanding loan encumbering the property, a mortgage estoppel letter must be obtained from the seller's lender providing the payoff amount. The seller must provide the most recent real property tax bill. Each party's share of the property taxes will be apportioned on the closing statement. Similarly, the seller must obtain official statements from his or her condominium or homeowners' association (if applicable) regarding regular and special assessments. These items will also be prorated on the closing statement.

7. The seller's attorney typically prepares the deed, seller's affidavit, bill of sale, nonforeign certification (if applicable), continuous marriage affidavit (if applicable), satisfaction of mortgage, and any other document necessary to transfer marketable title. The lender's attorney prepares the promissory note and financing instruments, including UCC-1 forms if personal property is to serve as part of the collateral for the loan.

8. Items owed *by* a party will appear in the debit column of a closing statement, and items owed *to* a party will appear in the credit column of a closing statement. Items that are paid in advance or arrears and are to be apportioned *between* the parties are referred to as prorations. Items that may be prorated include, but are not limited to, hazard and flood insurance, property taxes, rent, utilities, maintenance fees, and interest on an assumed loan.

9. Certain disbursements, such as the payoff of the seller's loan, the documentary stamp and intangible taxes, and recording fees, are made after closing. Recorded documents include the deed, satisfaction of mortgage, and financing instruments. Once documents are recorded, title policies can be issued and closing binders prepared for the seller, purchaser, and lender.

WEB RESOURCES

http://www.hud.gov/

This is the main site of HUD. If you select "Resources" and then select "HUD Handbooks, Forms and Publications," you can access the HUD-1 Uniform Settlement Statement and instructions for its completion.

The following are sites for some of the real estate software systems in use at the time of this writing. Some are available as Web-based options.

http://www.landtechdata.com/

This is the site of Landtech Data Corporation, which provides Landtech real estate settlement software. The software provides graphical HUD-1 and HUD-1A closing statements; full automatic calculations and prorations; amortization schedules;

checks, disbursements, and full trust accounting; and digital signatures; it works with Microsoft Word, WordPerfect, Quicken, and Quickbooks.

http://www.softprocorp.com/

This is the site of SoftPro Corporation, which provides applications including ProForm (closing and title insurance forms), ProTrust (a trust account management and reconciliation tool), Pro1099 (IRS 1099-S forms), ProIndx (an electronic title indexing tool), ProMort (amortization calculations and schedules), ProDesign (custom forms designer), SoftPro EC (advanced electronic escrow exchange), GreatDocs (state documents), and SoftPro SQL (provides additional networking and remote computing functionality). You can download a SoftPro demo from this site.

http://www.ramquest.com/

This is the site of RamQuest Software, Inc., which provides land title closing and escrow accounting software. The site provides a guided online demonstration.

http://www.displaysoft.com/

This is the site of DisplaySoft, which provides DisplaySoft closing software. The software modules available include a module that generates HUD and other settlement statements; a module that generates seller documents; a module that generates commitments, policies, and endorsements; a module that generates lender documents; a module that generates amortization schedules; a module for escrow accounting; a module for postclosing matters; a module that generates reports; a module for 1099-S reporting; and a link to Quicken and QuickBooks.

http://www.thefund.com/

This is the site of Attorneys' Title Fund Services, LLC, which provides DoubleTime closing software.

http://www.iwanttss.com/

This is the site of TSS Software Corporation, which provides TitleExpress software, a title and settlement system. It provides HUD-1 preparation, document preparation, check writing, escrow account reconciliation, and management reporting. It also is available as TitleExpress Cloud and TitleSphere, which are Web-based formats.

http://www.e-closing.com/

This is the site of E-Closing, a completely Web-based closing and title processing suite. It provides the ability to prepare documents, track the closing process, print checks, reconcile escrow accounts, and electronically record documents.

REVIEW QUESTIONS

1. What real estate–related costs are
   a. Tax deductible for income tax purposes?
   b. Capitalized?
2. What information is included in the following?
   a. Mortgage estoppel letter
   b. Seller's affidavit
   c. Satisfaction of mortgage

3. What closing costs are typically paid by (a) the seller and (b) the purchaser?
4. What items are prorated on a closing statement?
5. A closing is to take place on May 17. The parties are using a 365-day year and an actual month for the calculations. The proration date is the day of closing, and the day of closing is given to the purchaser. Prorate the following items:
   a. Monthly homeowners' association assessment fee of $400 per month (already paid by the seller)
   b. Annual real property tax bill of $3,000 (not yet paid by the seller)
   c. Monthly utility bill of $500 (not yet paid by the seller)

DISCUSSION QUESTIONS

1. You are in charge of the White–Green closing, which is scheduled to take place in two weeks. Your firm is representing the sellers, the Whites. The house has been on the market for awhile. The Whites went to contract with prior prospective purchasers (the White–Black contract), but the contract fell through due to an inability to obtain the desired financing. While waiting to hear word on the financing, the Blacks had an inspection done, and the inspector came up with a short list of items to be taken care of prior to closing. These were never attended to because that contract fell through. The Greens have now had an inspection done with a different inspector, and this inspector has a longer list of items to be fixed prior to closing. The Whites do not want to take care of everything on this list and do not know why they need to take care of items that did not appear on the first list. They would prefer to simply reduce the monies to be received by them by the projected cost of the repairs listed on the first inspection report and have the Greens take care of the repairs. The Greens currently are residing out of state, do not know any repair personnel in the area, and do not want to take care of the repairs themselves. They are purchasing the property because it is a "turn-key" property and they will be able to just walk in and begin enjoying it. What should be done in this situation?

2. Your firm is representing the buyer in a real estate closing. The buyer has twenty days from the effective date of the contract to secure financing. The buyer has been shopping lenders and finally found a suitable lender eight days before the deadline. The property being purchased is a condominium, and the lender is requiring a copy of the condominium's master policy of insurance coverage before it will approve the loan. The president of the condominium association is in Europe for two weeks and will not be back until after the deadline. What should be done?

3. You are representing the seller in a real estate closing. The buyer is a corporation, ABC, Inc. As part of your preclosing tasks, you have requested a verification of corporate status to determine if the corporation is in good standing in its state of incorporation, and you also have requested a copy of the corporate resolution authorizing this transaction and setting forth the officers authorized to act on behalf of the corporation in this matter. The buyer provides these documents to you three days before closing. You have reviewed the resolution and notice that the president is authorized to act on behalf of the corporation. The contract

for purchase and sale was signed by the vice president of the corporation. What should you do?

4. A common complaint is that documents are not available until just before closing, which makes a timely and careful review of the documents difficult. The closing agent typically is blamed, but the usual reason for the delay is that the closing package has not been completed by the lender. Why do you think this occurs, and what suggestions do you have for resolving this situation?

5. What aspect of the closing process do you consider the most daunting? Why? What could you do to make it less so?

ETHICAL QUESTION

Martha Patton and Audrey Edwards, two elderly sisters who are both widowed, have decided to purchase together a house listed with Hanson Realty. The sisters have not obtained an attorney to represent them. Brent Hanson, the real estate broker in charge of the listing, offers to complete the contract for sale and purchase by filling in the blanks on an approved, standardized contract form commonly used for residential transactions. If Brent completes the form, is he guilty of the unauthorized practice of law?

Brent has been a real estate broker for twenty years and has, over the course of the years, become familiar with the legal consequences attendant upon the manner in which title is held. He suggests to Martha and Audrey that they take title to the house as joint tenants with right of survivorship, since this would allow the unit to pass to the survivor upon the death of the other without the imposition of state death taxes. Is Brent engaging in the unauthorized practice of law by making this suggestion?

Slossberg Law Office on CourseMate

Please go to www.cengagebrain.com to log into CourseMate, access the Slossberg Law Office, and work on your client files. Each module corresponds to a chapter in the text. Within each module, you will be provided with instructions by the supervising attorney. You are asked to keep track of time spent on time sheets. The documents produced through working on client files in the law office can then be compiled into a portfolio of final work product.

CourseMate

The available CourseMate for this text has an interactive eBook and interactive learning tools, including flash cards, quizzes, and more. To learn more about this resource and access free demo CourseMate resources, including the Slossberg Law Office, go to www.cengagebrain.com, and search for this book. To access CourseMate materials that you have purchased, go to login.cengagebrain.com.

Residential Real Estate Closings

13

CHAPTER OBJECTIVES

Upon completion of this chapter, the student will:

- Know how to prepare the closing documents utilized most often in a residential real estate closing

- Know how to prepare the necessary correspondence utilized for requesting information from lenders and parties to the closing transaction

- Know how to prepare a HUD-1 Uniform Settlement Statement

- Know how to prepare a residential closing binder index

Introduction

In the last chapter, we examined the procedures for opening a real estate closing file, the matters that must be attended to prior to closing, the types of documents that must be drafted, the items that must be prorated, and postclosing matters. In this chapter, we will focus on a sample residential real estate closing to illustrate how the procedures looked at individually in the last chapter come together.

As can be surmised from the previous chapter, there are a myriad of tasks and documents to keep track of between the time a contract for sale and purchase is signed and the time a closing actually occurs. It is imperative that each party understand his or her own obligations to perform such tasks as obtaining information, approvals, and inspections and preparing the requisite documents. The paralegal's task is to keep track of each party's responsibilities and due dates. In order to do so, a checklist or worksheet is crucial. A completed residential closing worksheet is found in the hypothetical closing in the following text.

The closing of a condominium unit was chosen for illustration purposes because virtually all of the documents required in the closing of a single-family home are also required in the closing of a condominium unit. Further, the closing of a condominium unit requires additional items not included in the closing of a single-family home, such as approval of the purchaser by the condominium association. Other items included in the purchase and sale of a condominium unit are similar to those encountered in the purchase and sale of a house located within a development controlled by a homeowners' association. These include documents that must be provided to the purchaser for review, such as the declaration of condominium, bylaws, and related documents, or in the case of the homeowners' association, the declaration of restrictive covenants. Additionally, in both instances, there will be prorations of certain assessments, such as maintenance payments.

Besides organizing the file and drafting closing documents, the paralegal must prepare the correspondence to his or her own clients; to the other party or his or her attorney, if so represented; and to title companies, lenders, condominium associations, homeowners' associations, records clerks, and so forth. The sample closing here provides examples of some of the most commonly drafted correspondence. Although the examples provided are formatted as traditional letters, the contents would also pertain to correspondence sent via e-mail.

Finally, the paralegal must present the parties with packets of the final documentation. Each party, including the lender, receives a packet of documents pertinent to the transaction. The paralegal must sort out who receives originals of certain items and who receives copies and then put the documents in a coherent order for each recipient. One way to do this is to prepare a residential closing binder index for each party, which serves as a table of contents for the final closing package. Each document is tabbed and numbered for quick and easy reference.

Hypothetical Client Closing

Barbara Hammond, Ava Ross's paralegal, has set aside some time this afternoon to prepare the last of the documents needed for an upcoming closing. The client is the seller, Parker Properties, Inc., the owner of a condominium development called Kingsfield Estates. Hugh Parker, president of Parker Properties, has hired Ava to handle all of its closings for units in Kingsfield Estates. Parker Properties is selling units directly from its sales office, so in many instances a real estate broker is not involved. The purchaser for the subject closing is Patricia Wallis, who is single. She has chosen not to hire an attorney to represent her in this matter. Parker Properties, according to the contract for sale and purchase, is responsible for preparing the requisite closing documents, including the closing statement.

When Hugh Parker called Ava's office to set up an appointment, Barbara advised him to bring along certain documents, such as the contract and survey. To reconfirm the meeting, she sent the letter found in Exhibit 13–1.

The client file was opened by Barbara on June 29, the date the client came into the office with the signed contract. In opening the file, Barbara reviewed the contract to assist her in completing the residential closing worksheet her firm utilizes for all of its residential real estate closings. From the contract, Barbara was able to ascertain such information as the names and addresses of the parties, the legal description of the property, the anticipated closing date, other due dates stipulated in the contract, and the responsibilities of each party. Unless otherwise stipulated, the effective date of the contract is the date upon which the parties signed the contract. If the parties sign on different dates, as is often the case, it is the date upon which the last of the parties signs. A copy of the contract, together with its exhibits, is found in Exhibits 13–2, 13–3, 13–4, and 13–5.

Because the sale in question is the sale of a condominium unit, the purchaser is entitled, by law, to receipt of all pertinent condominium documents for review. The documents provided are listed in Exhibit 13–3. Under the state statutes of Any State, a prospective purchaser of a condominium unit has fifteen days within which to inspect the documents. If, within this time frame, the prospective purchaser decides not to go ahead with the purchase of the condominium, he or she is entitled to a

Confirmation of meeting letter	EXHIBIT 13–1

June 25, 2015

Mr. Hugh Parker
Parker Properties, Inc.
700 Commercial Blvd., Suite 360
Any City, Any State

Re: Parker Properties, Inc. to Patricia Wallis
       Unit 305, Bldg. 2550, Kingsfield Estates II

Dear Mr. Parker:

   This will confirm the meeting to be held in our office at 9:30 a.m. on June 29, 2015. Please bring the original signed contract for sale and purchase, together with either the original or a copy of the deed, survey, and other closing papers you received when you closed on the property now comprising Kingsfield Estates Condominium. This documentation will be of help to us in preparing the documentation for the above-referenced transaction.
   Should you have any questions, please feel free to call our office.

Sincerely,

Barbara Hammond
Paralegal to Ava Ross

Purchase and sale agreement	EXHIBIT 13–2

PURCHASE AND SALE AGREEMENT

Seller: PARKER PROPERTIES, INC., an Any State corporation
         700 Commercial Boulevard, Suite 360
         Any City, Any State

   Name: Patricia Wallis, a single woman
   Address: 235 Crestview Drive, Apt. 205
   City: Any City   State: Any State
   Phone: (000) 010-0009
(hereinafter called "Purchaser").

1.   **DESCRIPTION.** Subject to the provisions of this Agreement, Seller agrees to sell and Purchaser agrees to purchase the condominium parcel known as:
       Unit 305, Building 2550, of KINGSFIELD ESTATES II, A CONDOMINIUM, according to the DECLARATION OF CONDOMINIUM thereof, recorded in Official Records Book 4676, Page 1342, of the Public Records of Any County, Any State; together with the undivided share of the Common Elements of the Condominium declared in the Declaration of Condominium to be appurtenant thereto; and use of Parking Space No. 300, which space shall be assigned to Purchaser at closing.

EXHIBIT 13–2   *(continued)*

2.   **PURCHASE PRICE AND TERMS OF PAYMENT.**

   (a) Base Purchase Price $325,000.00

   (b) Additions to Purchase Price, if any $ -0-

   (c) TOTAL PURCHASE PRICE $325,000.00

PAYMENT:

   (d) Deposit due to Seller upon execution of this Agreement $ 32,500.00

   (e) Additional Deposit due _____ $ -0-

   (f) Institutional First Mortgage, if any $260,000.00

   (g) Balance due at closing (subject to adjustments and prorations) $ 32,500.00

3.   **DEPOSITS.** All deposit monies shall be paid to Seller and shall be held by Seller in escrow in accordance with the terms of this Agreement. Purchaser shall not be entitled to any interest earned on the Deposit.

4.   **TITLE INSURANCE.** Seller shall, at Purchaser's expense, cause a reputable title insurer or an agent thereof, designated by Seller, to issue to Purchaser a standard form of commitment for an Owner's Title Insurance Policy ("Title Policy"). The commitment shall show title in Seller subject to those exceptions customarily found in such commitments, and subject also to all matters affecting title to the Unit, none of which shall prohibit Purchaser's use of the Unit as a residence. Purchaser acknowledges that Seller may select, in Seller's sole discretion, the title company and the title insurance agent for the title company upon which the Title Policy shall be issued, and such agent may or may not be affiliated with Seller.

5.   **FIXTURES.** Appliances, personal property, and/or fixtures displayed in models, if any, are not included in the Purchase Price unless they have been installed in the Unit as of the Effective Date of this Agreement. Models, if any, are for display purposes only and do not constitute a representation of items contained in the Purchase Price. All representations of dimensions are approximate.

6.   **FINANCING.** If the Purchase Price or any part of it is to be financed by an institutional third-party loan, this Agreement is conditioned upon the Purchaser obtaining a written commitment for (CHECK (1) or (2) or (3)): (1) _____ a fixed, (2) _____ an adjustable, or (3) __X__ a fixed or adjustable rate loan within _30_ days after the Effective Date at prevailing interest rates, for a term of _30_ years and for the principal amount of $260,000.00. Purchaser will make application within _10_ days after Effective Date and use reasonable diligence to obtain the loan commitment and, thereafter, to meet the terms and conditions of the commitment and close the loan. Purchaser shall pay all loan expenses. If Purchaser fails to obtain the commitment or after diligent effort fails to meet the terms and conditions of the commitment, then either party thereafter by prompt written notice to the other may cancel this Agreement, and Purchaser shall be refunded the deposit(s).

7.   **CONDOMINIUM ASSOCIATION.** Upon closing, Purchaser shall become a member of Kingsfield Estates Association, Inc. (hereinafter called the "Condominium Association") and will be bound by the terms and conditions of the Declaration of Condominium of this Condominium, the Articles and Bylaws of the Condominium Association, and any rules and regulations enacted pursuant thereto, including without limitation, the obligation to pay assessments and other exactions. Purchaser agrees to pay his/her proportionate share of the Common Expenses of the Condominium Association in accordance with the Association's documents. Purchaser acknowledges that the Condominium Association has a lien upon the Unit pursuant to its governing documents to secure payment by Purchaser of the applicable assessments and other exactions.

8.   **CLOSING DATE AND POSSESSION.** The "Closing" is the conveyance of the Unit as evidenced by the delivery of the deed transferring title to Purchaser, which shall be at such office in Any County as designated by Seller. Closing shall take place (hereinafter called the "Closing Date") on or before August 19, 2015. Purchaser will be in default of this Agreement if he/she fails to close as scheduled. The Closing Date may be changed

and rescheduled by mutual written agreement of the parties. Purchaser shall be given possession of his/her Unit as of the Closing Date. Until the Closing has been completed, Purchaser shall not be permitted to occupy the Unit or store any property therein.

As of the Closing Date, Purchaser, when so requested by Seller, hereby agrees to execute a separate document as to the Unit wherein he/she acknowledges, assumes, and accepts the Condominium Documents and confirms the lien thereunder upon the Unit, acknowledges approval of same, and/or authorizes release to Seller of any escrowed deposits. The Closing of this transaction and acceptance of the deed by Purchaser shall be conclusive evidence of the compliance by Seller with Seller's obligations under this Agreement.

9. <u>**EXPENSES OF CLOSING.**</u> The following expenses will be paid by the Purchaser at time of closing: SEE RIDER ATTACHED HERETO AND MADE A PART HEREOF.

10. <u>**TITLE AND CONVEYANCE.**</u> Seller will convey insurable title by Warranty Deed, subject only to (1) the Declaration of Condominium and all Exhibits attached thereto; (2) utility easements, easements for vehicular rights-of-way and all other easements pertaining to the Condominium Property; (3) any mortgage executed by Purchaser encumbering the Condominium Unit; (4) taxes (including, but not limited to, those imposed by Any County) for the current year and subsequent years attributable to Purchaser's Unit; (5) zoning, restrictions, prohibitions and other requirements imposed by governmental authority; (6) matters shown on any recorded Plats of Condominium Property (as defined in the Declaration of Condominium); (7) such other easements, covenants, conditions and restrictions as Seller may reasonably consider necessary or expedient to hereafter impose on the Condominium Property, provided that the same do not prevent the use of the Condominium Property for residential purposes; (8) the standard printed exceptions contained in an Owner's Title Insurance Policy; and (9) all covenants, conditions and limitations, restrictions, reservations and easements of record.

If Seller is unable to deliver title as provided herein, Seller shall not be obligated to cure any objections or defects, but shall be afforded a reasonable time (not less than ninety [90] days) to do so if Seller so elects. If not cured within such period, or if Seller elects not to so cure, Purchaser may accept title in its then existing condition, but without any reduction in the Purchase Price, or may rescind this Agreement by providing written notice thereof to Seller, and thereafter receive a return of his/her Deposit, at which time this Agreement shall be null and void, and this shall be Purchaser's sole remedy at law and in equity.

11. <u>**NO RIGHT TO PURCHASER'S LIEN.**</u> Neither any rights of a Purchaser hereunder nor any deposits made hereunder shall constitute a lien upon the Condominium Property or any portion thereof, and in the event of a dispute between the parties involving this Agreement, Purchaser waives his/her right to file a Lis Pendens against the Unit.

12. <u>**RECEIPT OF DOCUMENTATION.**</u> Prior to the execution of this Agreement, Seller has provided to Purchaser copies of the documents described in Exhibit A attached to this Agreement, the receipt of which is acknowledged by Purchaser by the execution of this Agreement.

Notwithstanding anything to the contrary in this Agreement, Seller shall have the right to make such changes in the above documents as are necessary to meet the requirements of a lender, governmental entity, title insurer or for such other reasons as Seller, in its sole discretion, may determine. If Seller elects to exercise that right, Seller shall furnish to Purchaser a copy of the revised documents. If the modified documents materially alter or modify the documentation in a manner adverse to the Purchaser, Purchaser shall have the immediate right of cancellation of this Agreement on notice furnished to Seller within fifteen (15) days from Purchaser's receipt of said revised documents, and upon such cancellation, Seller shall return any deposit money paid to Seller or Escrow Agent under this Agreement. Failure to so notify the Seller of intent to cancel within the time provided shall be deemed a waiver of that right.

EXHIBIT 13-2   (*continued*)

13. **BINDING EFFECT.** This Agreement is binding upon the parties hereto and their heirs, legal representatives, successors and assigns. This Agreement will supersede any and all understandings and agreements between the parties, and it is mutually understood and agreed that this Agreement represents the entire agreement between the parties. No amendment, supplement or rider to this Agreement shall be binding unless in writing and signed by both Purchaser and Seller. No employee, agent, broker, salesperson, officer or other representative of Seller has authority to make or has made any statement, representation, warranty, undertaking, agreement or promise (either oral, written, express or implied) in connection with this Agreement or the Unit, supplementing or amending the provisions of this Agreement.

14. **PURCHASER'S DEFAULT.** Purchaser shall be in default under this Agreement in the event that:

    (a)   Purchaser fails or refuses to complete and execute all the instruments required of Purchaser under this Agreement promptly or when requested to do so by Seller or Purchaser's Mortgagee, if any; or

    (b)   Purchaser fails or refuses to make timely payment of any payments required under this Agreement; or

    (c)   Purchaser in any other manner fails or refuses to perform his/her obligations under this Agreement.

    In the event of any such default by Purchaser, Seller shall give Purchaser written notice of such default and allow five (5) calendar days from the date of such notice for Purchaser to cure such default. If Purchaser shall fail to cure such default within such five (5) day period, Seller shall, and does hereby have the unrestricted option to: (1) consider Purchaser in default under this Agreement; (2) retain all sums paid to it hereunder plus any interest accruing thereon, as agreed upon and liquidated damages, and (3) terminate all rights of Purchaser under this Agreement.

    Purchaser and Seller recognize the impossibility of measuring Seller's damages if Purchaser defaults. The provision herein contained for agreed upon and liquidated damages is a bona fide provision for such damages and is not a penalty. The Purchaser understands that by reason of the withdrawal of the Unit from sale to the general public at a time when other prospective purchasers would be interested in purchasing it, the Seller will have sustained damages if the Purchaser defaults, which damages will be substantial but not capable of being determined with mathematical precision. Purchaser agrees that if he/she defaults in this Agreement, he/she will not file any action against Seller seeking the return of any portion of said liquidated and agreed upon damages, nor seeking any reduction in the amount of liquidated and agreed upon damages.

15. **SELLER'S DEFAULT.** If Seller defaults in the performance of this Agreement, Purchaser shall give Seller written notice of such default, and Seller shall have seven (7) calendar days from receipt of such written notice within which to begin to take such action as would cure the default within a reasonable period of time. In the event Seller fails to begin to take such action within such seven (7) day period, then Purchaser, upon having performed all of his/her obligations hereunder, shall have the right to either (1) seek specific performance, or (2) elect to receive a return of his/her Deposit, and/or right to seek damages from Seller by reason of such default.

16. **ATTORNEYS' FEES AND COSTS.** In connection with any litigation including, but not limited to, appellate proceedings, arising out of this Agreement, the prevailing party shall be entitled to recover reasonable attorneys' fees and costs.

17. **DELINQUENT PAYMENT.** If Purchaser is delinquent in the payment of any sums due under this Agreement, including the balance of the purchase money payable at the closing, and Seller has not elected to cancel this Agreement and declare a forfeiture of deposits pursuant to Paragraph 14 above, Purchaser shall pay to Seller interest on all

delinquent sums at a rate of eighteen percent (18%) per annum or at the then highest rate allowed by law, whichever is less. Furthermore, if Purchaser is delinquent in closing the transaction, prorations for taxes, assessment charges, and other proratable items may, at the option of Seller, be calculated based on the scheduled Closing Date set forth above rather than the actual Closing Date.

18. **CLOSING DOCUMENTS.** Seller shall be responsible for providing the Warranty Deed, the Closing Statement, and any other documents necessary for transferring good and marketable title to Purchaser at Seller's expense. Seller shall, at Purchaser's expense, provide a Title Commitment in accordance with Paragraph 4 of this Agreement and, at Purchaser's expense, provide the Title Policy after closing.

19. **RECORDING.** Purchaser shall not record this Agreement nor any notice thereof in the Public Records of Any County, Any State, or in any other Public Records.

20. **NOTICES.** Any notice, request, demand, instruction or other communication to be given to either party, except where required by the terms of this Agreement to be delivered at the closing, shall be in writing and shall be sent by registered or certified mail, return receipt requested, or by express overnight courier, to the noticed party at the address herein set forth at the beginning of this Agreement or to such other address as either Seller or Purchaser shall designate by notice in accordance with this Paragraph. Notice shall be deemed given if forwarded by certified or registered mail through the facilities of the United States Post Office on the day following the date that the notice in question is deposited in the facilities of the United States Postal Service. If notice is forwarded by express overnight courier, it shall be deemed given on the day following the date that the notice in question is deposited in the facilities of an express overnight courier, but only if deposited in time for the courier to give next-day delivery service.

21. **CAPTIONS.** The captions contained herein are included solely for the convenience of the parties and do not, in any way, modify, amplify or give full notice of any of the terms, covenants or conditions of this Agreement.

22. **WAIVER.** Seller's waiver of any condition or provision of this Agreement shall not be construed as a waiver of any other application of that same condition or provision, nor as a waiver of any other condition or provision herein.

23. **GOVERNING LAW.** Purchaser certifies that Purchaser is executing this Agreement while in the State of Any State on Purchaser's own volition and that this purchase was not solicited either by telephone or mail in another state. The obligations under this Agreement shall be performed in the State of Any State and this Agreement shall be governed by Any State law. In the event any court of competent jurisdiction determines any provision of this Agreement to be invalid or unenforceable, no other provision shall be affected by such invalidity but shall remain in full force and effect according to its original terms.

24. **TIME OF ESSENCE.** Time is of the essence with respect to each provision of this Agreement which requires performance by either party upon a specified date or within a specified period, except where otherwise specifically provided for herein.

25. **REAL ESTATE BROKERS/SELLING AGENT.** Seller and Purchaser represent and warrant that there is no real estate broker involved in this transaction who is entitled to a commission except _____N/A_____ (the "Broker"), who shall be paid a commission pursuant to a separate written agreement between Broker and Seller. If the name of the Broker is not written in the forgoing line and initialed by Seller, then it is absolutely presumed that there are no brokers involved in this transaction.

26. **ASSIGNMENT.** This Agreement may not be assigned by the Purchaser except with the express written permission of Seller which may be withheld at the sole discretion of Seller or which may be granted subject to those conditions specified by Seller, including but not limited to the payment to Seller of any assignment fee as assessed by Seller.

EXHIBIT 13-2   (*continued*)

27. **ADDENDUM TO AGREEMENT.** The parties shall be bound by any addendum or addenda to this Agreement in the same manner as they are bound under this Agreement, provided that said addendum has been signed by all of the parties hereto.

28. **EFFECTIVE DATE.** The Effective Date of this Agreement shall be the date when the last of the Purchaser and Seller has signed this Agreement.

29. **DISCLOSURE.** THIS AGREEMENT IS VOIDABLE BY PURCHASER BY DELIVERING WRITTEN NOTICE OF THE PURCHASER'S INTENTION TO CANCEL WITHIN 15 DAYS AFTER THE DATE OF EXECUTION OF THIS AGREEMENT BY THE PURCHASER, AND RECEIPT BY PURCHASER OF ALL OF THE ITEMS REQUIRED TO BE DELIVERED TO HIM/HER BY THE SELLER UNDER SECTION 415.101, ANY STATE STATUTES. THIS AGREEMENT IS ALSO VOIDABLE BY PURCHASER BY DELIVERING WRITTEN NOTICE OF THE PURCHASER'S INTENTION TO CANCEL WITHIN 15 DAYS AFTER THE DATE OF RECEIPT FROM THE SELLER OF ANY AMENDMENT WHICH MATERIALLY ALTERS OR MODIFIES THE OFFERING IN A MANNER THAT IS ADVERSE TO THE PURCHASER. ANY PURPORTED WAIVER OF THESE VOIDABILITY RIGHTS SHALL BE OF NO EFFECT. PURCHASER MAY EXTEND THE TIME FOR CLOSING FOR A PERIOD OF NOT LESS THAN 15 DAYS AFTER THE PURCHASER HAS RECEIVED ALL OF THE ITEMS REQUIRED. PURCHASER'S RIGHTS TO VOID THIS AGREEMENT SHALL TERMINATE AT CLOSING

30. There is no land or recreational lease associated with this Condominium.

31. This Unit is not being conveyed subject to a lease.

IN WITNESS WHEREOF, the undersigned have executed this Agreement on the dates below.

SELLER: PURCHASER:

PARKER PROPERTIES, INC.,   *Patricia Wallis*
an Any State corporation

By: *Hugh Parker*
    President

Date: June 23, 2015   Date: June 23, 2015

full return of his or her deposit, and the contract is terminated. Purchasers in some states do not have such expansive rights. The other two exhibits to the contract explain the closing costs connected with the transaction.

Under the terms of the contract, the seller, at the purchaser's expense, provides a title commitment and subsequent title policies. Because Ava Ross is a title agent, Parker Properties has hired her to conduct the title search, examination, and preparation of the commitment and policies. Title work costs will show up as charges separate from the attorneys' fees charged for preparing the closing documents and acting as escrow/closing agent. Although the terms of this contract stipulate that the purchaser is responsible for the title work costs, the party who typically pays for these items is often a matter of custom in the jurisdiction in which the property is located. In some instances, the seller pays for the owner's policy, and the purchaser pays for the mortgagee's policy. To ensure the avoidance of a conflict of interest, Barbara prepared a letter pertaining to the title work and had both parties sign it. It may be found in Exhibit 13–6.

EXHIBIT A
RECEIPTS FOR CONDOMINIUM DOCUMENTS

The undersigned acknowledges that the documents checked below have been received or, as to plans and specifications, made available for inspection.

Name of Condominium: KINGSFIELD ESTATES II, A CONDOMINIUM
Address of Condominium: 2500 Kingsfield Drive
Any City, Any State

Place an "X" in the column by each document received or, for the plans and specifications, made available for inspection. If an item does not apply, place "N/A" in the column.

DOCUMENT	RECEIVED
Prospectus Text	X
Declaration of Condominium	X
Articles of Incorporation	X
Bylaws	X
Current Operating Budget	X
Form of Agreement for Sale or Lease	X
Rules and Regulations	X
Ground Lease	N/A
Management and Maintenance Contracts for More than One Year	N/A
Renewable Management Contracts	X
Lease of Recreational and Other Facilities to Be Used Exclusively by Unit Owners of Subject Condominium	N/A
Phase Development Description	X
Plot Plan	X
Floor Plan	X
Survey of Land and Graphic Description of Improvements	X

THE PURCHASE AGREEMENT IS VOIDABLE BY PURCHASER BY DELIVERING WRITTEN NOTICE OF THE PURCHASER'S INTENTION TO CANCEL WITHIN FIFTEEN (15) DAYS AFTER THE DATE OF EXECUTION OF THE PURCHASE AGREEMENT BY THE PURCHASER AND RECEIPT BY THE PURCHASER OF ALL OF THE DOCUMENTS REQUIRED TO BE DELIVERED TO HIM/HER BY THE SELLER. THE AGREEMENT IS ALSO VOIDABLE BY THE PURCHASER BY DELIVERING WRITTEN NOTICE OF THE PURCHASER'S INTENTION TO CANCEL WITHIN FIFTEEN (15) DAYS AFTER THE DATE OF RECEIPT FROM THE SELLER OF ANY AMENDMENT WHICH MATERIALLY ALTERS OR MODIFIES THE OFFERING IN A MANNER THAT IS ADVERSE TO THE PURCHASER. PURCHASER MAY EXTEND THE TIME FOR CLOSING FOR A PERIOD OF NOT MORE THAN FIFTEEN (15) DAYS AFTER THE PURCHASER HAS RECEIVED ALL OF THE DOCUMENTS REQUIRED. PURCHASER'S RIGHT TO VOID THE PURCHASE AGREEMENT SHALL TERMINATE AT CLOSING.

Executed this _23rd_ day of June, 2015.

Patricia Wallis
Purchaser

In a similar vein to the payment allocations made for the title work, this contract has the purchaser paying the documentary stamp tax on the deed, as well as on the mortgage instrument. Often, the seller pays the documentary stamp tax on the deed. Custom notwithstanding, these matters, like so many others, are subject to negotiation between the parties.

EXHIBIT 13–4   **Notice to purchaser of costs**

EXHIBIT B
NOTICE TO PURCHASER OF COSTS

You are hereby notified that you, as Purchaser at KINGSFIELD ESTATES II, A CONDOMINIUM, may be required to pay additional costs in connection with your purchase. The additional costs to be paid by the Purchaser at KINGSFIELD ESTATE II, A CONDOMINIUM, include the following:

		Estimated Amount (not included if unknown)
1.	Prorated Association Assessments for the Month of Closing	$ 100.65
2.	Documentary Stamps Affixed to Deed	$ 2,275.00
3.	Cost of Recording Deed	$ 18.50
4.	Title Examination and Commitment	$ 150.00
5.	Title Insurance	$ 2,050.00
6.	Ad Valorem Real Estate Taxes	$ to be prorated
7.	Purchaser's Attorneys' Fees	$
8.	Assessments	$
9.	Solid Waste Authority	$ to be prorated
10.	Mortgage Closing Costs, if applicable (including discount points and escrow fees)	$ see Lender

I have read the above and understand it. I acknowledge receipt of a copy of this notice this _23rd_ day of June, 2015, before signing the Purchase and Sale Agreement.

Purchaser: _Patricia Wallis_

Barbara takes a moment to review the closing worksheet to determine what steps must be taken next. The closing worksheet is found in Exhibit 13–7.

The closing worksheet indicates several dates. According to the contract, Patricia has ten days from the signing of the contract to make a loan application, so the date indicated on the worksheet is July 3, ten days from the date of signing, June 23. In fact, Patricia filled out a loan application with Millennium Bank on June 27, well within the contractual requirements.

The closing worksheet shows a due date for a loan commitment of July 23. Millennium Bank issued a loan commitment to Patricia on July 20, as shown in Exhibit 13–8. Note that the commitment expires on August 20, so if the closing is delayed for any reason and does not occur on August 19, Patricia will need to obtain an extension of the commitment. It is the responsibility of the purchaser's attorney to review the loan commitment to make sure that the commitment truly binds the lender. Some loan commitments contain numerous contingencies that swallow up the commitment.

Certain condominium-related items are noted on the worksheet. The date of July 8 is indicated as the date by which Patricia must review the condominium document she received upon signing the contract. In order to transfer title of the condominium unit to Patricia, certain condominium transfer information is required, including information pertaining to maintenance payments, special assessments, transfer fees, and an interview of the prospective purchaser prior to

EXPENSE RIDER

THIS EXPENSE RIDER ("Rider") is attached to and made a part of that certain Purchase and Sale Agreement ("Agreement") by and between PARKER PROPERTIES, INC., an Any State corporation ("Seller"), and <u>Patricia Wallis</u> ("Purchaser") under which Agreement Purchaser agrees to buy and Seller agrees to sell Unit <u>305</u>, Building <u>2550</u>, located in KINGSFIELD ESTATES II ("Property"). The Agreement and this Rider are sometimes collectively hereinafter referred to as the "Agreement."

1.   In the event of any conflict between the terms and conditions of this Rider and the terms and conditions of the Agreement, the terms and conditions of this Rider shall control.

2.   **EXPENSES OF CLOSING.** Purchaser shall pay, in addition to the Purchase Price, the following costs at the closing:

   A.   The costs of recording the Deed, Any State Documentary Stamp Taxes required to be affixed to the Deed and the premium for an Owner's Policy of Title Insurance to be issued to Purchaser at closing by a title insurance agent to be selected by Seller, together with the abstracting fee charged by such title insurance agent, which abstracting fee shall not exceed $150.00.

   B.   Purchaser's pro rata share of the maintenance assessments charged by the Condominium Association for the assessment period in which the closing occurs.

   C.   An amount equal to any capital contribution that may from time to time be assessed by the Condominium Association, if any.

   D.   In the event Purchaser chooses to obtain financing to complete this transaction, Purchaser shall pay to Lender all closing costs imposed by Lender, including, but not limited to, points, origination fees, prepaid loan interest, escrow account balances and private mortgage insurance premium, if required. The obligations of Purchaser under this Agreement are not contingent upon Purchaser qualifying for financing or obtaining a written loan commitment unless Paragraph 6 of this Agreement entitled "Financing" is completely filled in and initialed by the Seller.

   E.   A pro rata share of real property taxes for the year of closing. Real property taxes will be prorated on the latest information available. If the taxes for the year of closing are not precisely ascertainable, such taxes will be prorated based upon estimates and will be later adjusted based upon the exact amount of taxes, with allowance for full discount. Certified special assessment liens as of the date of closing shall be paid by Seller. Pending special assessment liens as of the date of closing shall be assumed by Purchaser. Purchaser shall also pay all utility deposits or similar fees applicable to the Unit which may have been advanced by Seller on behalf of Purchaser.

IN WITNESS WHEREOF, the parties have hereunto set their hands and seals this <u>23rd</u> day of <u>June, 2015.</u>

SELLER: PURCHASER:

PARKER PROPERTIES, INC.,
an Any State corporation   *Patricia Wallis*

By: *Hugh Parker*
      President

obtaining condominium association approval. As stated in Chapter 3, condominium association approval of a sale is not always required, so this must be checked on a case-by-case basis. The worksheet indicates that Barbara sent a request for condominium transfer information on June 29. The request form, as completed by the condominium association, is found in Exhibit 13–9.

EXHIBIT 13-6	Letter pertaining to title work

June 29, 2015

Seller: Parker Properties, Inc.   Purchaser: Patricia Wallis

Property: Unit 305, Bldg. 2550, Kingsfield Estates II

Re: Services rendered to Seller and Purchaser

We, the undersigned Seller and Purchaser, hereby acknowledge that the law firm of FISHER, ROSS, AND SIMON, P.A. represents the Seller in the above transaction. We have prior knowledge of and consent to the firm also preparing and issuing a title insurance policy for the Purchaser. This title policy shall be prepared and issued for a fee as a convenience, and not as counsel for the Purchaser.

Seller: Parker Properties, Inc.   Purchaser: Patricia Wallis

         By: *Hugh Parker*   *Patricia Wallis*
             President

EXHIBIT 13-7	Residential closing worksheet

RESIDENTIAL CLOSING WORKSHEET

DATE FILE OPENED: 6/29/15
ATTORNEY: Ava Ross
PARALEGAL: Barbara Hammond
CLIENT NUMBER: 15432
MATTER NUMBER: 0001
CLIENT: _____ BUYER __X__ SELLER _____ LENDER

1.   SELLER NAME(S):   Parker Properties, Inc., an Any State corporation
2.   ADDRESS(ES):   700 Commercial Boulevard, Suite 360
                        Any City, Any State
3.   E-MAIL ADDRESS: hparker@parkerproperties.com
4.   PHONE NUMBER(S):   (000) 012-3333, CELL: (000) 012-3131
     FAX NUMBER(S):   (000) 012-3335
5.   SOCIAL SECURITY NUMBER(S) [IF A BUSINESS ENTITY, FEDERAL TAX
     I.D. NO.]:   000998888
6.   BUYER NAME(S):   Patricia Wallis, a single woman
7.   ADDRESS(ES):   235 Crestview Drive, Apt. 205
                        Any City, Any State
8.   E-MAIL ADDRESS: pwallis@xyz.com
9.   PHONE NUMBER(S):   (000) 010-0009, CELL: (000) 010-0128
     FAX NUMBER(S):   N/A
10. SOCIAL SECURITY NUMBER(S) [IF A BUSINESS ENTITY, FEDERAL TAX
     I.D. NO.]:   000-50-5555
11. BUYER'S LENDER: Millennium Bank
12. ADDRESS: 1750 Wellington Avenue
                        Any City, Any State
13. E-MAIL ADDRESS: djamison@millenniumbank.com

14. PHONE NUMBER: (000) 041-4000
    FAX NUMBER: (000) 041-4100
15. LOAN OFFICER ASSIGNED TO LOAN FILE: Derek Jamison
16. LOAN NUMBER: 677377
17. SELLER'S LENDER (IF SELLER HAS EXISTING MORTGAGE ON
    PROPERTY):   Century Bank
18. ADDRESS: 1100 S. Main Street
                         Any City, Any State
19. E-MAIL ADDRESS: mclark@centurybank.com
20. PHONE NUMBER: (000) 099-0020
    FAX NUMBER: (000) 099-0030
21. LOAN NUMBER: 540031
22. ATTORNEY FOR: __X__ BUYER   _____ SELLER
23. ATTORNEY NAME: N/A
24. ADDRESS: _____

25. E-MAIL ADDRESS: _____
26. PHONE NUMBER: _____
    FAX NUMBER: _____
27. REAL ESTATE
    BROKER #1:   N/A
28. ADDRESS: _____

29. E-MAIL ADDRESS: _____
30. PHONE NUMBER: _____
    FAX NUMBER: _____
31. REAL ESTATE
    BROKER #2:   N/A
32. ADDRESS: _____

33. E-MAIL ADDRESS: _____
34. PHONE NUMBER: _____
    FAX NUMBER: _____
35. COMMISSION: N/A
    HOW SPLIT: N/A
36. ESCROW AGENT: Fisher, Ross, and Simon, P.A.
37. ADDRESS: 1900 N.W. 3rd Avenue
                         Any City, Any State
38. E-MAIL ADDRESS: aross@fisherrossandsimon.com
39. PHONE NUMBER: (000) 555-2000
    FAX NUMBER: (000) 555-2020
40. TITLE COMPANY: In-house
41. ADDRESS: _____

42. E-MAIL ADDRESS: _____
43. PHONE NUMBER: _____
    FAX NUMBER: _____
44. STREET ADDRESS OF PROPERTY:
                         2550 Kingsfield Drive, Apt. 305
                         Any City, Any State

EXHIBIT 13-7   (*continued*)

45. LEGAL DESCRIPTION OF PROPERTY:
Unit 305, Building 2550, of KINGSFIELD ESTATES II, A CONDOMINIUM, according to the DECLARATION OF CONDOMINIUM thereof, recorded in Official Records Book 4676, Page 1342, of the Public Records of Any County, Any State; together with the undivided share of the Common Elements of the Condominium declared in the Declaration of Condominium to be appurtenant thereto.

46. PARCEL IDENTIFICATION
NUMBER: 7989594939

47. CLOSING:
(A) DATE: August 19, 2015
(B) TIME: 10:00 a.m.
(C) PLACE: our offices

48. PURCHASE PRICE: $325,000.00

49. DEPOSITS:	AMOUNT	DATE DUE	DATE RECEIVED
(A) LOT:			
(B) INITIAL:	$32,500.00	6/23/15	6/23/15
(C) ADDITIONAL:			

50. ITEM	DONE BY SELLER	DONE BY BUYER	DATE DUE	CHARGE TO
Title Search	X			Buyer
Order Survey				
Title Examination	X			Buyer
Title Commitment	X		7/21/15	Buyer
Remedy Defects				
Issue Policy(ies):				
(a) Owner's	X			Buyer
(b) Mortgagee's	X			Buyer
(c) Endorsements:				
ALTA 4.1	X			Buyer
Property Appraisal				
Loan Application		X	7/3/15	Buyer
Loan Commitment		Lender	7/23/15	Buyer
Promissory Note		Lender	8/19/15	Buyer
Mortgage/Deed of Trust		Lender	8/19/15	Buyer
UCC Forms				
Mortgage Estoppel Letter	X		8/5/15	Seller
Satisfaction of Mortgage/ Deed of Trust	X		8/19/15	Seller
Insurance Coverage				
Request for Condo Transfer Information	X		6/29/15	Seller
Approval of Condo Documents		X	7/8/15	
Condo Ass'n Approval	X		7/19/15	Seller
HOA Approval				
Termite Inspection				
Roof Inspection				
Appliance Inspection				
Heating/Cooling/Elec./ Plumbing Inspection				

ITEM	DONE BY SELLER	DONE BY BUYER	DATE DUE	CHARGE TO
Verification of Corporate Status	X		7/10/15	Seller
Verification of Marital Status				
Corporate Resolution	X		5/9/15	Seller
Tax Receipts	X		8/1/15	
City Tax Prorated				
County Tax Prorated	X		8/17/15	Buyer
Special Assessments Prorated				
Maintenance Assessments Prorated	X		8/17/15	Buyer
Other Prorations:				
Solid Waste Authority	X		8/17/15	Buyer
Bill of Sale	X		8/19/15	Seller
Seller's Affidavit	X		8/19/15	Seller
Deed	X		8/19/15	Seller
Continuous Marriage Affidavit				
FIRPTA Affidavit	X		8/19/15	Seller
Closing Statement	X		8/17/15	Seller
Final Walk-Through		X	8/19/15	
Keys	X		8/19/15	
Recordation of Deed	X			Buyer
Recordation of Financing Instrument	X			Buyer
Recordation of UCC Forms				
Recordation of Satisfaction of Mortgage/Deed of Trust	X			Seller
Doc. Stamps on Deed	X			Buyer
Doc. Stamps on Financing Instrument	X			Buyer
Intangible Tax on New Financing Instrument	X			Buyer
1099S Filed	X			
State Revenue Form Filed	X			
Disbursement to Seller			8/19/15	
Disbursement to Seller's Lender			8/19/15	
Disbursement to Brokers				
Disbursement to Title Company			8/19/15	
Residential Closing Binder Index Prepared	X			
Documents Mailed to Buyer	X			
Other:				

_____

File Closed _____

EXHIBIT 13-8   Conventional mortgage loan commitment

CONVENTIONAL MORTGAGE LOAN COMMITMENT

BORROWER: Patricia Wallis
DATE: July 20, 2015
MORTGAGE COMMITMENT NUMBER: 677377

WE ARE PLEASED TO OFFER YOU A LOAN COMMITMENT WITH THE FOLLOWING TERMS AND CONDITIONS:

LOAN TYPE: __X__ Fixed Rate
                                       _____ Adjustable Rate
                                             ( ) 1 Year ARM
                                             ( ) 3 Year ARM
                                             ( ) Other

LOAN AMOUNT: $ 260,000.00
POINTS: N/A OF LOAN AMOUNT: N/A
TERM OF LOAN: 30 years
CURRENT INTEREST RATE: 5.000%
PRINCIPAL & INTEREST PAYMENT: $ 1395.74

Payable on the first day of each month,
plus Taxes and Insurance

PURPOSE OF LOAN: Purchase
CLOSING AGENT: Fisher, Ross, and Simon, P.A.

PROPERTY ADDRESS: 2550 Kingsfield Drive, #305
                                       Any City, Any State

CLOSING COSTS: You will be responsible for all out-of-pocket expenses incurred by the Bank in processing your request including, but not limited to, credit report(s), appraisal fees, abstract continuations, surveys, and the designated closing agent's fees. It is understood that any costs arising out of the proposed transaction shall be borne by you whether or not the loan is closed.

LOAN APPROVAL: Final loan approval is contingent upon items required for your loan in accordance with the following additional requirements.

CONTINGENCIES: Applicable if the following is checked including the attached "additional closing contingencies."

_____   Tax returns: Tax returns to be signed with original signatures at closing. Those pages requiring signatures will be sent to the designated closing agent for execution at closing.

_____   Private mortgage insurance: Approved by _____.You shall pay the cost of all subsequent private mortgage insurance policies which shall be included in your monthly escrow payments.

__X__   Condominium: This commitment is subject to approval by our designated closing agent of the Declaration of Condominium and related documents and approval by the condominium association if required.

__X__   Payoff(s): Subject to paying off existing mortgage with Century Bank. Payment of any outstanding taxes, liens or other outstanding obligations on the property.

_____   Sale of real estate: Prior to closing, evidence must be presented that your property located at _____ has been sold and closed.

_____   Completion of construction: This loan is subject to satisfactory completion of construction. Certificate of occupancy and soil treatment certificate are required at or prior to closing.

_____   Other: This commitment is subject to the following items as listed below. Final acceptance by the Lender must be obtained prior to scheduling the loan closing.

(continued)   **EXHIBIT 13–8**

It is imperative that we receive this signed commitment letter as soon as possible to ensure a timely closing of your loan. Subject to the conditions hereof, this commitment shall expire on August 20, 2015, and thereafter be of no further force and effect.

The undersigned acknowledge and accept the terms of this commitment.

LENDER: BORROWER:

MILLENNIUM BANK

By: *Derek Jamison*   *Patricia Wallis*
    Vice President

Date: July 20, 2015   Date: July 20, 2015

Request for condominium transfer information   **EXHIBIT 13–9**

REQUEST FOR CONDOMINIUM TRANSFER INFORMATION

Date: 6/29/15
Our File: 15432
Seller: Parker Properties, Inc.   Buyer: Patricia Wallis
Seller's Unit: Unit 305, Bldg. 2550   Unit Address: 2550 Kingsfield Drive
                                                                    Any City, Any State

To: Kingsfield Estates Condominium Association

Our firm is representing the Seller of the above-described unit. Please fill out this form and return to our office as soon as possible.

  I.   Condominium Maintenance Payments.
      1. Payment installments: __X__ Monthly   _____ Quarterly
                                      _____ Semi-Annually   _____ Annually
      2. Amount of each installment: $251.63
      3. Date upon which last installment payment was made: 6/27/15
      4. Amount of penalty for late payment, if any: $25.00
      5. Is there a change in the maintenance expected? No
         If so, when? _____ What will be the new payment? _____
 II. Special Assessments.
      1. Are there any special assessments against the above-described unit? If so, please state the amount and when due: None
      2. Are there any special assessments anticipated within the next twelve months? If so, please describe: None
III. Transfer Fee.
     Is there a transfer fee charged upon transfer of title of the abovedescribed unit? If so, please state the amount: N/A
IV. Interview for Condominium Association Approval.
     Please state the name and telephone number of the individual(s) that must be contacted to set up an interview: Joyce McCarthy (000) 032-0078

Dated: July 5, 2015
Kingsfield Condominium Association, Inc.

By: *Harold Lipson*
    Vice President

Note that the maintenance payments will include the seller's portion of hazard and/or flood insurance. The condominium association insures the structure of the building but not the interior of the unit or its contents. The maintenance payments include the cost of the insurance, the routine maintenance of the building, and any other items specified in the budget as allocated to such payments.

Patricia has already met with the appropriate condominium association committee for an interview and has been approved. The condominium's Certificate of Approval is found in Exhibit 13–10.

Because one of the parties is a corporate entity—in this instance, the seller—Barbara must verify that the corporation is still in good standing with the secretary of state's office in Any State. She has done so. She must further obtain a certified copy of a corporate resolution in which the board of directors of Parker Properties, Inc., permits the sale of the subject property. She has obtained a copy of the client's articles of incorporation and bylaws and reviewed them to ensure that all procedures have been correctly followed. The corporate resolution was signed in May, and Barbara has obtained the certified copy for the file shown in Exhibit 13–11.

EXHIBIT 13–10   **Certificate of approval**

CERTIFICATE OF APPROVAL

KINGSFIELD CONDOMINIUM ASSOCIATION, INC., an Any State corporation not for profit, the association which administers KINGSFIELD ESTATES Condominium, does hereby certify that the Association has approved the following sale:

Condominium Unit Number:	Unit 305, Building 2550
Seller:	Parker Properties, Inc.
Purchaser:	Patricia Wallis
Date of Approval:	July 19, 2015

KINGSFIELD CONDOMINIUM ASSOCIATION, INC.

By: *Lillian Keller*
President

(Corporate Seal)

Attest: *Daniel Lamott*
Secretary

STATE OF ANY STATE
COUNTY OF ANY COUNTY

BEFORE ME, the undersigned authority, personally appeared LILLIAN KELLER and DANIEL LAMOTT, as President and Secretary respectively of KINGSFIELD CONDOMINIUM ASSOCIATION, INC., an Any State corporation not for profit, who acknowledged before me that they executed the above certificate as such officers of the Corporation and the above certificate is the act and deed of the Corporation.

IN WITNESS WHEREOF, I have hereunto set my hand and official seal this 19th day of July, 2015.

Roberta Hodge
Notary Public
My commission expires: 4/30/16

Resolution of the board of directors	EXHIBIT 13–11

RESOLUTION OF THE BOARD OF DIRECTORS OF PARKER PROPERTIES, INC.

I, the undersigned Secretary of Parker Properties, Inc., a corporation duly organized and existing under the laws of the State of Any State, hereby certify that the following is a true copy of a resolution duly adopted by the Board of Directors at a special meeting held on May 9, 2015.

RESOLVED, that the officers of the Corporation and each of them be, and they hereby are, authorized to sell that certain real property as legally described on Exhibit A attached hereto and to execute on behalf of the Corporation all requisite documents and take all other action on behalf of the Corporation as may be necessary or required in connection therewith.

I DO FURTHER CERTIFY that neither the Articles of Incorporation nor the bylaws of the Corporation require any consent of the shareholders for the execution of the documents by the Corporation and that this resolution is not in conflict with any provision of the Articles of Incorporation or the bylaws of the Corporation.

IN WITNESS WHEREOF, I have affixed my name as Secretary and have caused the corporate seal of the Corporation to be hereunto affixed this 9th day of May, 2015.

(Corporate Seal)

Kenneth Ellington
Secretary

The contract does not specify a due date for the preparation of a title commitment. Barbara already has obtained the survey from the seller. From the information gleaned from a title search and examination, as well as the information provided in the survey, Barbara has prepared a title commitment and has submitted it to Patricia. The date indicated on the worksheet is the effective date of the commitment. Schedules A and B of the commitment may be found in Exhibit 13–12.

The closing worksheet indicates that the client has an existing mortgage on the property in favor of Century Bank. Because Patricia has opted to secure new financing rather than assuming the existing loan, the existing note and mortgage will be paid off at closing. In order to determine what must be paid, Barbara has sent a request for a mortgage estoppel letter regarding certain payoff information to the servicing department of Century Bank. The due date set forth on the worksheet indicates the target date by which Barbara should either receive a response to the letter or, failing that, call to confirm the items set forth in the letter. A copy of the letter appears in Exhibit 13–13.

The closing is taking place in August. This being the case, the client has not yet received the annual tax bill for the property and therefore has not paid it. The client has forwarded a copy of its tax bill for the previous year to Barbara on the date indicated on the worksheet. The taxes for the current year will be prorated as of the date of closing. Because the closing is taking place prior to the client's actual receipt of the current tax bill, Barbara will use the last tax bill for prorating purposes and will make any required adjustments after receipt of the current bill. Note that in some places real estate taxes are paid quarterly rather than annually. In such a situation, whether the seller has paid the taxes depends on when during the quarter the closing takes place.

The closing worksheet indicates that other items must be prorated as well. Although the closing does not take place until August 19, the worksheet states the due dates for the prorations as August 17. This allows all parties to review the

EXHIBIT 13–12   **Title commitment**

FUND COMMITMENT FORM

SCHEDULE A

Commitment No.: **1449898**

Agent's
File Reference: 15432.001

Effective Date: 7/21/15 at 9:00 a.m.

1. Policy or Policies to be issued   Proposed Amount of Insurance:

OWNER'S: $325,000.00

Proposed Insured:

Patricia Wallis, a single woman

MORTGAGEE: $260,000.00

Proposed Insured:

Millennium Bank its successors and/or assigns as their interest may appear

2. The estate or interest in the land described or referred to in this commitment is a Fee Simple and title thereto is at the effective date hereof vested in:

Parker Properties, Inc., an Any State corporation

3. The land referred to in this commitment is described as follows:

Unit 305, Building 2550, of KINGSFIELD ESTATES II, A CONDOMINIUM, according to the Declaration of Condominium thereof, recorded in Official Records Book 4676, Page 1342 of the Public Records of Any County, Any State; together with an undivided share of the Common Elements of the Condominium declared in the Declaration of Condominium to be appurtenant thereto.

Fisher, Ross, and Simon, P.A. 1900 N.W. 3rd Avenue, Any City, Any State	2222 Agent No	*Ava Ross* Agent's Signature

Reproduced through the courtesy of Attorney's Title Insurance Fund, Inc.

FUND COMMITMENT FORM

SCHEDULE B-I

Commitment No. #: 1449898
Agent's File No. #: 15432.001

I. The following are the requirements to be complied with:

1. Payment of the full consideration to, or for the account of, the grantors or mortgagors.

2. Instruments creating the estate or interest to be insured which must be executed, delivered and filed for record:

    (a) Warranty Deed to be executed by Parker Properties, Inc., an Any State corporation, to Patricia Wallis, a single woman.

    (b) Satisfaction of Mortgage in favor of Century Bank dated March 10, 2011 and recorded March 11, 2011, at O.R. Book 4678, Page 905, of the Public Records of Any County, Any State.

    (c) Mortgage to be executed by Patricia Wallis, a single woman to Millennium Bank; given to secure the principal sum of $260,000.00.

Reproduced through the courtesy of Attorney's Title Insurance Fund, Inc.

EXHIBIT 13–12   (*continued*)

FUND COMMITMENT FORM

SCHEDULE B-II

Commitment No. #: 1449898
Agent's File No. #: 15432.001

II. Schedule B of the policy or policies or guarantee to be issued will contain exceptions to the following matters unless the same are disposed of to the satisfaction of The Fund:

1. Defects, liens, encumbrances, adverse claims or other matters, if any, created, first appearing in the public records or attaching subsequent to the effective date hereof but prior to the date the proposed Insured acquires for value of record the estate or interest or mortgage thereon covered by this commitment.

2. Any owner and mortgagee policies issued pursuant hereto will contain under Schedule B the standard exceptions set forth at the inside cover hereof unless an affidavit of possession and a satisfactory current survey are submitted, an inspection of the premises is made, it is determined the current year's taxes or special assessments have been paid, and it is determined there is nothing of record which would give rise to construction liens which could take priority over the interest(s) insured hereunder (where the liens would otherwise take priority, submission of waivers is necessary).

3. Restrictions, dedications, conditions, reservations, easements, and other matters set out on the Plat of Kingsfield Estates recorded in Plat Book 37, Page 13, which includes, but is not limited to, easement for utilities, drainage, limited access; drainage right-of-ways; private access easements; restrictions against building or planting on easements; and setbacks of the Public Records of Any County, Any State.

4. Terms, provisions, covenants, restrictions and easements contained in the Declaration of Condominium of Kingsfield Estates II, a Condominium, recorded at Official Records Book 4676, Page 1342 of the Public Records of Any County, Any State.

Request for mortgage estoppel letter	EXHIBIT 13–13

July 20, 2015

Mortgage Servicing Department

Century Bank
1100 S. Main Street
Any City, Any State

RE: Borrower: Parker Properties, Inc.

       Purchaser: Patricia Wallis
       Property: Unit 305, Building 2550, Kingsfield Estates II
       Street Address: 2550 Kingsfield Drive, #305
                                     Any City, Any State

       Loan No: 540031

Dear Sir/Madam:

Please forward to the undersigned a Mortgage Loan Payoff Letter for the above-referenced loan as of August 19, 2015. Our firm has been retained by the Seller of the subject property to conduct the closing on August 19, 2015. In your letter, please indicate the following:

1. Principal balance
2. Annual interest rate and per diem interest
3. Escrow balance and escrow shortage, if any
4. Total payoff amount as of August 19, 2015

Thank you for your assistance in this matter, and should you have any questions, please do not hesitate to contact us.

Sincerely,

Ava Ross, Esquire

closing statement before the closing date and provides Patricia with advance notice of the exact amount she will need to pay at closing, either by wire transfer or with a cashier's check. Thus, Barbara's first task this afternoon is to complete a closing statement to be signed by the parties that itemizes each party's expenses and indicates the balance due from the purchaser.

Because Barbara has input information into her real estate closing software as it has been received, completing the HUD-1 Uniform Settlement Statement (HUD-1 statement) should not take much time. The completed HUD-1 statement is found in Exhibit 13–14.

The software automatically calculates the prorations for condominium maintenance and waste management based on the dates input by Barbara. Both items have been paid in advance by the client, so they will appear in the 100s and 400s on the HUD-1 statement. The condominium maintenance assessments are paid in advance each month, so Patricia owes Parker Properties her share from the date of closing until September 1. The waste management bill has been paid through the end of the year, so Patricia owes Parker Properties her portion of the bill from the date of closing through the last day of the year.

EXHIBIT 13-14

HUD-1 Uniform Settlement Statement

OMB Approval No. 2502-0265

A. Settlement Statement (HUD-1)

B. Type of Loan				
1. ☐ FHA 2. ☐ RHS 3. ☒ Conv. Unins. 4. ☐ VA 5. ☐ Conv. Ins.	6. File Number 15432001	7. Loan Number 677377	8. Mortgage Insurance Case Number	

C. Note: This form is furnished to give you a statement of actual settlement costs. Amounts paid to and by the settlement agent are shown. Items marked "(p.o.c.)" were paid outside the closing; they are shown here for information purposes and are not included in the totals.

D. Name and Address of Borrower	E. Name and Address of Seller	F. Name and Address of Lender
Patricia Wallis, a single woman 235 Crestview Drive, Apt. 205 Any City, Any State	Parker Properties, Inc. 700 Commercial Boulevard, Suite 360 Any City, Any State	Millennium Bank 1750 Wellington Avenue Any City, Any State

G. Property Location	H. Settlement Agent ((000) 555-2000)	
2550 Kingsfield Drive, Unit 305 Any City, Any State	Fisher, Ross, and Simon, P.A.	
	Place of Settlement 1900 N.W. 3rd Avenue Any City, Any State	I. Settlement Date 08/19/15

J. SUMMARY OF BORROWER'S TRANSACTION:		K. SUMMARY OF SELLER'S TRANSACTION:	
100. GROSS AMOUNT DUE FROM BORROWER		**400. GROSS AMOUNT DUE TO SELLER**	
101. Contract sales price	325,000.00	401. Contract sales price	325,000.00
102. Personal property		402. Personal property	
103. Settlement charges to borrower (line 1400)	8,973.06	403.	
104.		404.	
105.		405.	
Adjustments for items paid by seller in advance		*Adjustments for items paid by seller in advance*	
106. City/town taxes to		406. City/town taxes to	
107. County taxes to		407. County taxes to	
108. Assessments to		408. Assessments to	
109. Condo Assn. Maintenance 08/19 to 09/01	105.52	409. Condo Assn. Maintenance 08/19 to 09/01	105.52
110. Solid Waste Authority 08/19 to 01/01	60.29	410. Solid Waste Authority 08/19 to 01/01	60.29
111.		411.	
112.		412.	
120. GROSS AMOUNT DUE FROM BORROWER	334,138.87	**420. GROSS AMOUNT DUE TO SELLER**	325,165.81
200. AMOUNTS PAID BY OR IN BEHALF OF BORROWER		**500. REDUCTIONS IN AMOUNT TO SELLER**	
201. Deposit or earnest money	32,500.00	501. Excess Deposit (see instructions)	
202. Principal amount of new loan(s)	260,000.00	502. Settlement charges to seller (line 1400)	1,010.00
203. Existing loan(s) taken subject to		503. Existing loans taken subject to	
204.		504. Payoff of first mortgage loan	131,982.19
205.		505. Payoff of second mortgage loan Magna Bank	
206.		506.	
207.		507. Deposit being disbursed as proceeds (32,500.00)	
208.		508.	
209.		509.	
Adjustments for items unpaid by seller		*Adjustments for items unpaid by seller*	
210. City/town taxes to		510. City/town taxes to	
211. County taxes 01/01 to 08/19	1,951.06	511. County taxes 01/01 to 08/19	1,951.06
212. Assessments to		512. Assessments to	
213.		513.	
214.		514.	
215.		515.	
216.		516.	
217.		517.	
218.		518.	
219.		519.	
220. TOTAL PAID BY / FOR BORROWER	294,451.06	**520. TOTAL REDUCTION AMOUNT DUE SELLER**	134,943.25
300. CASH AT SETTLEMENT FROM OR TO BORROWER		**600. CASH AT SETTLEMENT TO OR FROM SELLER**	
301. Gross amount due from borrower (line 120)	334,138.87	601. Gross amount due to seller (line 420)	325,165.81
302. Less amounts paid by/for borrower (line 220)	294,451.06	602. Less reduction amount due to seller (line 520)	134,943.25
303. CASH FROM BORROWER	39,687.81	**603. CASH TO SELLER**	190,222.56

Form reproduced through the courtesy of Landtech Data Corporation

(continued)

EXHIBIT 13-14

		PAID FROM BORROWER'S FUNDS AT SETTLEMENT	PAID FROM SELLER'S FUNDS AT SETTLEMENT
L. SETTLEMENT CHARGES:	File Number: 15432001		
700. Total Real Estate Broker Fees	0.00		
Division of commission (line 700) as follows:			
701. $ to			
702. $ to			
703. Commission paid at Settlement			
704.			
705.			
800. Items Payable in Connection with Loan	P.O.C.		
801. Our origination charge (Includes Origination Point(s) 1% or $2,600.00) $ 2,600.00 (from GFE#1)			
802. Your credit or charge (points) for the specific interest rate chosen $ (from GFE#2)			
803. Your adjusted origination charges (from GFE A)		2,600.00	
804. Appraisal fee Millennium Bank (from GFE#3) 395(B*)			
805. Credit report Millennium Bank (from GFE#3) 45(B*)			
806. Tax service Millennium Bank (from GFE#3) 50(B*)			
807. Flood certification (from GFE#3)			
808.			
809.			
810.			
811.			
812.			
813.			
814.			
900. Items Required by Lender to Be Paid in Advance			
901. Daily interest charges from 08/19/15 to 09/01/15 @$ 35.62 /day (from GFE#10) 13 day(s)		463.06	
902. Mortgage insurance premium for to (from GFE#3)			
903. Homeowner's insurance for to (from GFE#11)			
904.			
905.			
1000. Reserves Deposited with Lender			
1001. Initial deposit for your escrow account (from GFE#9)			
1002. Homeowner's insurance mo. @ $ per mo. $			
1003. Mortgage insurance mo. @ $ per mo. $			
1004. City property taxes mo. @ $ per mo. $			
1005. County property taxes mo. @ $ per mo. $			
1006. Annual Assessments mo. @ $ per mo. $			
1007. mo. @ $ per mo. $			
1008. mo. @ $ per mo. $			
1009. Aggregate Adjustment $			
1100. Title Charges			
1101. Title services and lender's title insurance (from GFE#4)		400.00	
1102. Settlement or closing fee			
1103. Owner's title insurance Fisher, Ross, and Simon, P.A. (from GFE#5)		1,700.00	
1104. Lender's title insurance Fisher, Ross, and Simon, P.A. $ 350.00			
1105. Lender's title policy limit 260,000.00 --- 350.00			
1106. Owner's title policy limit 325,000.00 --- 1,700.00			
1107. Agent's portion of the total title insurance premium Fisher, Ross, and Simon, P.A. $ 1,525.00			
1108. Underwriter's portion of the total title insurance premium Regional Title Corporation $ 525.00			
1109. Endorsements ALTA 4.1 and ALTA 8.1 $ 50.00 (from GFE#4)			
1110. Attorney's fees Fisher, Ross, and Simon, P.A.			1,000.00
1111.			
1112.			
1113.			
1200. Government Recording and Transfer Charges			
1201. Government recording charges (from GFE#7)		105.00	
1202. Deed $ 18.50 Mortgage $ 86.50 Releases $ 10.00			10.00
1203. Transfer taxes (from GFE#8)		3,705.00	
1204. City/county tax/stamps Deed $ Mortgage $			
1205. State tax/stamps Deed $ 2,275.00 Mortgage $ 910.00			
1206. Intangible Tax Deed $ Mortgage $ 520.00 (from GFE#8)			
1207. (from GFE#8)			
1208. (from GFE#8)			
1300. Additional Settlement Charges			
1301. Required services that you can shop for (from GFE#6)			
1302.			
1303.			
1304.			
1305.			
1306.			
1307.			
1308.			
1400. Total Settlement Charges (enter on lines 103, Section J and 502, Section K)		8,973.06	1,010.00

Paid Outside Closing: B* by Borrower

Form reproduced through the courtesy of Landtech Data Corporation

EXHIBIT 13–14   (*continued*)

Comparison of Good Faith Estimate (GFE) and HUD-1 Charges		File Number: 15432001	Good Faith Estimate	HUD-1
Charges That Cannot Increase		HUD-1 Line Number		
Our origination charge	$ 2,600.00 # 801		2,600.00	2,600.00
Your credit or charge (points) for the specific interest rate chosen	# 802			
Your adjusted origination charges	# 803		2,600.00	2,600.00
Transfer taxes	# 1203		3,705.00	3,705.00
State tax/stamps - Deed	$ 2,275.00 # 1205			
State tax/stamps - Mortgage	$ 910.00 # 1205			
Intangible Tax - Mortgage	$ 520.00 # 1206			
Charges That in Total Cannot Increase More Than 10%			Good Faith Estimate	HUD-1
Government recording charges	# 1201		110.00	105.00
Government recording charges - Deed	$ 18.50 # 1202			
Government recording charges - Mortgage	$ 86.50 # 1202			
Appraisal fee	# 804		395.00	395.00
Credit report	# 805		45.00	45.00
Tax service	# 806		50.00	50.00
Title services and lender's title insurance	# 1101		500.00	400.00
Owner's title insurance	$ 1,700.00 # 1103		1,850.00	1,700.00
		TOTAL	2,950.00	2,695.00
		Increase between GFE and HUD-1 Charges $	0.00 or	0.00 %
Charges That Can Change			Good Faith Estimate	HUD-1
Initial deposit for your escrow account	# 1001			
Daily interest charges	# 901 $ 35.62 /day		463.06	463.06
Homeowner's insurance	# 903			

Loan Terms

Your initial loan amount is	$ 260,000.00
Your loan term is	30 years
Your initial interest rate is	5 %
Your initial monthly amount owed for principal, interest, and any mortgage insurance is	$ 1,395.74 includes ☒ Principal ☒ Interest –>$ 1,395.74 ☐ Mortgage Insurance
Can your interest rate rise?	☒ No. ☐ Yes, it can rise to a maximum of %. The first change will be on and can change again every after . Every change date, your interest rate can increase or decrease by %. Over the life of the loan, your interest rate is guaranteed to never be lower than % or higher than %.
Even if you make payments on time, can your loan balance rise?	☒ No. ☐ Yes, it can rise to a maximum of $.
Even if you make payments on time, can your monthly amount owed for principal, interest, and mortgage insurance rise?	☒ No. ☐ Yes, the first increase can be on and the monthly amount owed can rise to $ The maximum it can ever rise to is $
Does your loan have a prepayment penalty?	☒ No. ☐ Yes, your maximum prepayment penalty is $.
Does your loan have a balloon payment?	☒ No. ☐ Yes, you have a balloon payment of $ due in years on
Total monthly amount owed including escrow account payments	☒ You do not have a monthly escrow payment for items, such as property taxes and homeowner's insurance. You must pay these items directly yourself. ☐ You have an additional monthly escrow payment of $ that results in a total initial monthly amount owed of $ 1,395.74 . This includes principal, interest, any mortgage insurance and any items checked below: ☐ Property taxes ☐ Homeowner's Insurance ☐ Flood Insurance ☐ ☐ ☐

Note: If you have any questions about the Settlement Charges and Loan Terms listed on this form, please contact your lender.

Page 3 of 3   HUD-1

Form reproduced through the courtesy of Landtech Data Corporation

---

The contract and worksheet indicate that Patricia made an earnest money deposit of $32,500, which is being held in escrow by Barbara's firm. This figure appears on line 201 of the HUD-1 statement. Line 202 states the principal amount of the loan as reflected in the loan commitment. Using the payoff information received from Century Bank, Barbara inserts the payoff amount of the existing mortgage on line 504.

Parker Properties, Inc., has not yet received the tax bill for the year of closing, so Patricia will pay the bill when it arrives. Therefore, Barbara needs to credit

Patricia for the portion of the taxes owed by Parker Properties under the section of the HUD-1 statement labeled "Adjustments for items unpaid by the seller." Barbara uses the software to prorate the taxes based on the annual bill for the prior year's taxes, crediting Patricia for the number of days Parker Properties owned the property during the year of closing (thus, from the first day of the year until the day of closing). Although the condominium has a city address, it is physically located outside the city limits, and, therefore, no city taxes accrue. Only county taxes are prorated. They appear on lines 211 and 511.

Barbara moves to the second page of the settlement statement. No real estate broker took part in the transaction, so the 700s, pertaining to brokers' commissions, are left blank. Millennium Bank, Patricia's lender, is charging a loan origination fee of 1 percent. When Barbara inserts this number, the software calculates the dollar amount of the loan origination fee automatically. Because no points are being charged in connection with Patricia's loan, the origination fee and the adjusted origination fee are the same. The appraisal fee paid to Millennium Bank is to be paid outside of closing. Because it is paid outside of closing, no dollar amount will appear in the borrower's column. The same is true of the credit report fee and the tax service fee. "B*" appears by the cost for each of these items; the explanation of this marking provided at the bottom of the page.

Millennium wants Patricia to pay in advance the interest on the loan from the date of closing to the beginning of the following month. The software calculates the dollar amount of the advance interest to be $463.06, which appears on line 901. Because the property in question is a condominium, and thus the hazard and flood insurance payments comprise part of each unit owner's monthly maintenance assessments, Millennium Bank is not escrowing sums for the payment of the insurance. Costs for the owner's and lender's title policies are calculated at $1,700 for the owner's policy and $350 for the lender's policy, both of which are being paid by Patricia. In addition to the standard coverage, a condominium endorsement and an environmental endorsement are being issued for an additional fee of $25 each. The $50 for these endorsements is noted on line 1109 and is added to the $350 for the lender's title policy, totaling $400 on line 1101. Some attorneys note only the cost of the lender's policy on line 1104, while others note the total cost of the lender's policy plus any lender-required endorsements on this line. Although the estimated closing costs provided to Patricia included $150 for the title commitment, Ava Ross, acting as title agent, has decided not to charge for this service and only charge for the policies. If she had elected to include this charge, it would be added to the $400 appearing on line 1101. The agent's and underwriter's portions of the total premiums are specified on lines 1107 and 1108, respectively. Again, some firms add in the endorsement costs to the policy costs and include this in the breakdown of the agent's and underwriter's portions of the premiums. Parker Properties is paying for the attorneys' fees. These fees are noted in the 1100s; however, some attorneys choose to note them in the 1300s.

The recording fees in Any County are $10 for the first page and $8.50 for each additional page per document. Patricia is paying for the recording of the deed and mortgage instrument, while Parker Properties is paying for the recording of the satisfaction of mortgage for the old loan. When setting up the software defaults, the formulas for calculating the documentary stamp taxes and intangible tax can be set so that the calculations are performed automatically. The documentary stamp taxes on the deed and mortgage appear on line 1205, and the intangible tax appears on line 1206. The third page of the HUD-1 statement compares Patricia's estimated closing costs as provided in the Good Faith Estimate she received from Millennium Bank with the actual costs she has to pay at closing. A summary of her loan terms also is provided on this page.

Having completed the HUD-1 statement, Barbara can inform Patricia that she will need to either arrange a wire transfer or obtain a cashier's check for $39,687.81 on the date of closing. In addition to the HUD-1 statement, Barbara prints out separate buyer's and seller's closing statements, which itemize each party's debits and credits in list form. These statements are found in Exhibits 13–15 and 13–16.

Barbara next turns her attention to the preparation of the deed. Her software will automatically insert the names and addresses of the parties, the identity of the preparer of the deed, the parcel identification number, and the legal description. If Barbara had needed to include customized "subject to" provisions, she would have typed them into the software file, and they would have appeared under the legal description. Instead, she has chosen to use the standard "subject to" language, indicating Patricia's title is subject to all restrictions, reservations, and limitations that appear on record as well as all future real property taxes. Once signed, witnessed, and acknowledged at closing, the warranty deed will read as shown in Exhibit 13–17.

Although the unit is new and sold unfurnished, it does come with standard appliances, lighting fixtures, window screens, and wall-to-wall carpeting. These items are commonly considered fixtures that "go with" the unit. It is common practice in Barbara's firm, however, to complete a bill a sale covering such items to prevent any misunderstandings. The bill of sale, as signed by Hugh Parker on the date of closing, is found in Exhibit 13–18.

Barbara next turns her attention to completing the seller's affidavit, also referred to as a "no lien" affidavit. The state statutes in Any State give a laborer or supplier of materials up to ninety days from the date the last work was completed or the last materials were furnished to the property to file a construction lien. This affidavit verifies that no work was done or materials furnished within the last ninety days. The affidavit, as it will appear when signed by Hugh Parker at the closing, is found in Exhibit 13–19.

Because both the client and Patricia want the existing mortgage lien removed from the property as soon as possible after closing, Barbara prepares a satisfaction of mortgage to be signed by an officer of Century Bank. She will send the document, together with the check for the loan payoff, by courier the same day so she can have the document returned immediately for recording. A copy of the satisfaction of mortgage, as signed by an officer of the bank, appears in Exhibit 13–20.

The new mortgage note and mortgage instrument securing the property are prepared not by Barbara but by Millennium Bank. Patricia is taking out a loan in the amount of $260,000, with a fixed interest rate of 5 percent for a period of thirty years. The mortgage instrument prepared by Millennium Bank has a condominium rider attached to it, by which Patricia promises to abide by the terms of the

Buyer's closing statement

EXHIBIT 13–15

Buyer(s)/Borrower(s) Closing Statement

Prepared by

Fisher, Ross, and Simon, P.A.
1900 N.W. 3rd Avenue
Any City, Any State
(000) 555-2000

File Number: 15432001   **Settlement Date:** 08/19/15   **Proration Date:** 08/19/15

SELLER(S):
Parker Properties, Inc.

PURCHASER(S):
Patricia Wallis, a single woman

LENDER:
Millennium Bank
Loan Number: 677377

PROPERTY:
2550 Kingsfield Drive, Unit 305, Any City, Any State

Description		Charges	Credits
Sales Price		325,000.00	
Country taxes: 01/01-08/19			1,951.06
Condo Assn. Maintenance 08/19 to 09/01		105.52	
Solid Waste Authority 08/19 to 01/01		60.29	
Deposit			32,500.00
New Loan and Note	Millennium Bank		260.000.00
Our origination charge	Millennium Bank	2,600.00	
Daily interest charge 08/19/15 to 09/01/15	Millennium Bank	463.06	
Owner's title insurance	Fisher, Ross, and Simon, P.A.	1,700.00	
Lender's title insurance	Fisher, Ross, and Simon, P.A.	350.00	
Endrosements	ALTA 4.1 and ALTA 8.1	50.00	
Record Deed	Board of County Commissioners	18.50	
Record Trust Deed/Mortgage	Board of County Commissioners	86.50	
Deed Documentary Stamps	Board of County Commissioners	2,275.00	
Mortgage Doc Stamps	Board of County Commissioners	910.00	
Intangible Tax	Board of County Commissioners	520.00	

	Charges	Credits
CASH DUE FROM PURCHASER(S)		39,687.81
TOTAL CHARGES/CREDITS	334,138.87	334,138.87

Form reproduced through the courtesy of Landtech Data Corporation

EXHIBIT 13–16   Seller's closing statement

Seller(s) Closing Statement
Prepared by

Fisher, Ross, and Simon, P.A.
1900 N.W. 3rd Avenue
Any City, Any State
(000) 555-2000

File Number: 15432001   **Settlement Date:** 08/19/15   **Proration Date:** 08/19/15

SELLER(S):
Parker Properties, Inc.

PURCHASER(S):
Patricia Wallis, a single woman

LENDER:
Millennium Bank
Loan Number: 677377

PROPERTY:
2550 Kingsfield Drive, Unit 305, Any City, Any State

Description		Charges	Credits
Contract Sales Price			325,000.00
County taxes: 01/01-08/19		1,951.06	
Condo Assn. Maintenance 08/19 to 09/01			105.52
Solid Waste Authority 08/19 to 01/01			60.29
Loan Payoff #1	Magna Bank	131,982.19	
Attorney's Fees	Fisher, Ross, and Simon, P.A.	1,000.00	
Releases	Board of County Commissioners	10.00	
CASH DUE TO SELLER(S)		190,222.56	
TOTAL CHARGES/CREDITS		325,165.81	325,165.81

Form reproduced through the courtesy of Landtech Data Corporation

THIS INSTRUMENT PREPARED BY AND RETURN TO:

Fisher, Ross, and Simon, P.A.
1900 N.W. 3rd Avenue
Any City, Any State
Property Appraisers Parcel Identification (Folio) Number: 7989594939

_____SPACE ABOVE THIS LINE FOR RECORDING DATA_____

WARRANTY DEED

THIS WARRANTY DEED, made the 19th day of August, 2015, by **Parker Properties, Inc., an Any State corporation**, herein called the Grantor, to **Patricia Wallis, a single woman,** hereinafter called the Grantee:
(Wherever used herein the terms "Grantor" and "Grantee" include all the parties to this instrument and the heirs, legal representatives and assigns of individuals, and the successors and assigns of corporations)

W I T N E S S E T H: That the Grantor, for and in consideration of the sum of TEN AND 00/100'S ($10.00) Dollars and other valuable considerations, receipt whereof is hereby acknowledged, hereby grants, bargains, sells, aliens, remises, releases, conveys and confirms unto the Grantee all that certain land situate in Any County, State of Any State, to wit.:

> **Unit 305, Building 2550, of KINGSFIELD ESTATES II, A CONDO-MINIUM, according to the Declaration of Condominium thereof, recorded in Official Records Book 4676, Page 1342 of the Public Records of Any County, Any State; together with the undivided share of the Common Elements of the Condominium declared in the Declaration of Condominium to be appurtenant thereto.**

> **Subject to easements, restrictions and reservations of record and taxes for the current year and subsequent years.**

TO HAVE AND TO HOLD the same in fee simple forever.

AND, the Grantor hereby covenants with said Grantee that the Grantor is lawfully seized of said land in fee simple; that the Grantor has good right and lawful authority to sell and convey said land, and hereby warrants the title to said land and will defend the same against the lawful claims of all persons whomsoever; and that said land is free of all encumbrances, except taxes accruing subsequent to December 31, 2014.

IN WITNESS WHEREOF, the said Grantor has signed and sealed these presents the day and year first above written.

Signed, sealed and delivered in the presence of:

_____*Barbara Hammond*_____
Witness Signature

_____Barbara Hammond_____
Witness Printed Name

_____*Mitchell Wood*_____
Witness Signature

_____Mitchell Wood_____
Witness Printed Name

PARKER PROPERTIES, INC.,
an Any State corporation

By: _____*Hugh Parker*_____
                                President

Form reproduced through the courtesy of Landtech Data Corporation

EXHIBIT 13-17   *(continued)*

STATE OF ANY STATE
COUNTY OF ANY COUNTY

The foregoing instrument was acknowledged before me this 19th day of August, 2015, by Hugh Parker in his representative capacity as president of PARKER PROPERTIES, INC., an Any State corporation, who [X] personally known to me or [ ] produced _____ as identification.

SEAL

_____
Ellen Dunning
Notary Public

_____
Ellen Dunning
Printed Notary Name

My Commission Expires: 3/31/16

Form reproduced through the courtesy of Landtech Data Corporation

condominium documents. Additionally, the rider states that Patricia's obligation to maintain hazard insurance is satisfied by the blanket coverage afforded under the condominium association's policy. The rider to the mortgage instrument is found in Exhibit 13–21.

Both state and federal tax authorities require notification when a sale of real property takes place. Barbara prepares a Department of Revenue of Any State Return for Transfers of Interest in Any State Real Property that will be filed when the deed is recorded. This form is found in Exhibit 13–22. Note that in the form in Exhibit 13–22, the address given for Patricia Wallis is the street address for the property purchased because this will be her primary residence once the closing takes place. Note also that some states may provide exceptions to the requirements for reporting of a real property transaction, so state law should be checked. Barbara also prepares a nonforeign certification (a sample of a nonforeign certification can be found in the next chapter).

Barbara must attend to one more tax matter. As noted in the previous chapter, federal law requires that the person, firm, or company handling the real estate closing report the sale to the Internal Revenue Service. This is done on a 1099-S form. The form includes the name, address, and tax identification number of the filer; the name, address, and tax identification number of the transferor (seller); the address or legal description of the property; the date of closing; the sales price; and the purchaser's portion of the real estate tax. The Internal Revenue Service does provide an exception to the requirement for reporting if the sale or exchange of a residence is $250,000 or less for a single person or $500,000 or less for married sellers filing jointly. The closing agent must receive an acceptable written certification from the seller(s) for the exception to apply.

After closing, Barbara will send the deed, satisfaction of mortgage from Century Bank, and mortgage instrument in favor of Millennium Bank for recording. She will include a trust account check to cover the recording costs as well as the documentary stamp tax on the deed and mortgage note and the intangible tax on the

BILL OF SALE, ABSOLUTE

This Instrument was prepared by
Fisher, Ross, and Simon, P.A.
1900 N.W. 3rd Avenue
Any City, Any State

KNOW ALL MEN BY THESE PRESENTS:

***That* Parker Properties, Inc., an Any State corporation,** transferor, for and in consideration of the sum of Ten Dollars ($10.00), lawful money of the United States, to be paid by **Patricia Wallis, a single woman,** transferee, the receipt whereof is hereby acknowledged, has granted, bargained, sold, transferred and delivered, and by these presents does grant, bargain, sell, transfer and deliver unto the transferee, her heirs, successors and assigns, the following good and chattels located at 2550 Kingsfield Drive, Unit 305, Any City, Any State:

> All fixed equipment; all window screens, treatments and hardware all wall-to-wall floor coverings, attached wall coverings and attached lighting fixtures as now installed on the property.

To Have and to Hold the same unto the transferee, her heirs, successors and assigns forever.

And the transferor, for itself and transferor's successors and assigns, covenants to and with the transferee, her heirs, successors and assigns, that it is the lawful owner of the said goods and chattels; that they are free from all encumbrances; that it has good right to sell the same aforesaid, and that it will warrant and defend the sale of the said property, goods and chattels hereby made, unto the transferee, her heirs, successors and assigns, against the lawful claims and demands of all persons whomsoever.

In Witness whereof, the transferor has hereunto set its hand and seal this 19th day of August, 2015.

Signed, sealed and delivered in the presence of us:

_____*Barbara Hammond*_____	PARKER PROPERTIES, INC.,
Witness Signature	an Any State corporation
_____Barbara Hammond_____	
Witness Printed Name	
_____*Mitchell Wood*_____	By: _____*Hugh Parker*_____
Witness Signature	President
_____Mitchell Wood_____	
Witness Printed Name	

STATE OF ANY STATE
COUNTY OF ANY COUNTY

The foregoing instrument was acknowledged before me this 19th day of August, 2015, by Hugh Parker in his representative capacity as president for PARKER PROPERTIES, INC., an Any State corporation who [X] is personally known to me or [ ] produced _____ as identification.

SEAL

_____*Ellen Dunning*_____
Notary Signature

_____Ellen Dunning_____
Printed Notary Signature
My Commission Expires: 3/31/16

Form reproduced through the courtesy of Landtech Data Corporation

EXHIBIT 13–19   Seller's affidavit

AFFIDAVIT

STATE OF ANY STATE
COUNTY OF ANY COUNTY

BEFORE ME, the undersigned authority, duly authorized to administer oaths and take acknowledgments, personally appeared this day, **Hugh Parker, President of Parker Properties, Inc., an Any State corporation**, (Affiant) who, after being duly sworn, deposes and says as follows:

1. That the Affiant has personal knowledge of all matters set forth herein, warranting the accuracy of same and that Parker Properties, Inc. the fee simple title holder of the real property described as follows:

   > Unit 305, Building 2550, of KINGSFIELD ESTATES II, A CONDOMINIUM, according to the Declaration of Condominium thereof, recorded in Official Records Book 4676, Page 1342 of the Public Records of Any County, Any State; together with the undivided share of the Common Elements of the Condominium declared in the Declaration of Condominium to be appurtenant thereto.

2. That there are no unresolved contractual disputes, outstanding contracts for the sale of the property, unrecorded deeds, mortgages, easements, leases, options or other conveyances which could affect title to the property.

3. That there are no liens, encumbrances, mortgages, claims, demands or security interests in or against the property or any appliances, fixtures or equipment installed or affixed to the property; and that there are no unpaid taxes, municipal liens, levies, assessments, special assessments, paving liens or utility liens against the property (other than real estate taxes for the current year).

4. The there are no improvements and/or repairs or contracts for improvements and/or repairs made upon the property within the past ninety (90) days for which there remain any outstanding and/or unpaid bills for labor, materials, supplies, or services for which a lien or liens have or could attach to the property.

5. There are no matters pending against the Affiant which could give rise to a lien that could attach to the property during the period of time between the effective date of the title insurance commitment and the time of recording of the deed of conveyance; and that the Affiant has not and will not execute any instrument that would adversely affect the title to the property from the effective date of the title insurance commitment through the date of recording the deed of conveyance.

6. There are no actions, proceedings, judgments, claims, disputes, demands or other matters pending against Affiant in any State or Federal Court that could attach to the property including but not limited to tax liens, bankruptcy, receivership or insolvency proceedings.

7. That Affiant is in exclusive, complete and undisputed possession of the property and no other person or entity has any right to possession of the property, or asserts any claim of title or other interests which could affect title to the property.

8. That there are no violations of governmental laws, sales tax laws, zoning regulations or ordinances pertaining to the use of the property, or any violations of any enforceable covenants, restrictions, declarations, easements or conditions, pertaining to the property, nor do any improvements on the property violate municipal, subdivision or platted building setback lines.

9. Affiant understands that the figures set forth on the settlement statement relating to mortgage fees, payoffs, assumptions, taxes, utilities, rental prorations, maintenance fees, special assessments, and/or other charges are based on the best information available to Affiant and in the event said figures differ from the actual figures, Affiant agrees to promptly pay all additional sums rightfully owing by Affiant to said respective parties which are necessary to fully pay said outstanding balances.

Form reproduced through the courtesy of Landtech Data Corporation

10.   This Affidavit is made for the purpose of inducing PATRICIA WALLIS, a single woman, to purchase the above-described property from PARKER PROPERTIES, INC. and for the purpose of inducing FISHER, ROSS, AND SIMON, P.A., as title agent, to issue a title policy covering such property.

FURTHER AFFIANT SAYETH NAUGHT.

_____*Barbara Hammond*_____
Witness Signature

PARKER PROPERTIES, INC., an
Any State corporation

_____*Mitchell Wood*_____
Witness Signature

By_____*Hugh Parker*_____
President

STATE OF ANY STATE
COUNTY OF ANY COUNTY

The foregoing instrument was acknowledged before me this 19ᵗʰ day of August, 2015 Hugh Parker in his representative capacity as president for PARKER PROPERTIES, INC., an Any State corporation who [X] is personally known to me or [   ] produced _____ as identification.

_____*Ellen Dunning*_____
Printed Name: Ellen Dunning
Notary Public

My Commission Expires: 3/31/16

Form reproduced through the courtesy of Landtech Data Corporation

new mortgage. The cover letter she sends is found in Exhibit 13–23. As mentioned previously in the text, a number of jurisdictions permit the electronic recording of documents, so local rules should be reviewed.

Once the documents are returned from recording, Barbara prepares the title policies for Patricia and for Millennium Bank. She attaches the ALTA 4.1 endorsement, which is a condominium endorsement insuring the policyholder against loss or damage by reason of such circumstances as the failure of the condominium documents to comply with state statutes and any charges or assessments provided for in the condominium statutes and condominium documents that are due and unpaid at the date of the policy. She also attaches the ALTA 8.1 endorsement, which is an environmental protection lien endorsement. This endorsement insures the policyholder against loss or damage occurring by reason of lack of priority of the mortgage lien over any environmental protection lien provided by state statute in effect on the date of the policy.

EXHIBIT 13-20   **Satisfaction of mortgage**

THIS INSTRUMENT WAS PREPARED BY
AND RETURN TO:
Fisher, Ross, and Simon, P.A.
1900 N.W. 3rd Avenue
Any City, Any State
Property Appraisers Parcel Identification (Folio) Number: 7989594939

_____SPACE ABOVE THIS LINE FOR RECORDING DATA _____

SATISFACTION OF MORTGAGE

Know All Men By These Presents: That **Century Bank** is the owner and holder of a certain mortgage deed executed by **Parker Properties, Inc.,** an Any State corporation, bearing the date March 10, 2011, recorded on March 11, 2011 in Official Records Book 4678, page 905, of the Public Records of Any County, Any State, securing that certain note in the principal sum of $140,000.00 Dollars, and certain promises and obligations set forth in said mortgage, upon the property situate in said State and County described as follows, to-wit:

> Unit 305, Building 2550, of KINGSFIELD ESTATES II, A CONDOMINIUM, according to the Declaration of Condominium thereof, recorded in Official Records Book 4676, Page 1342 of the Public Records of Any County, Any State; together with the undivided share of the Common Elements of the Condominium declared in the Declaration of Condominium to be appurtenant thereto.

Century Bank hereby acknowledges full payment and satisfaction of said note and mortgage, and surrender the same as canceled, and hereby direct the Clerk of said Circuit Court to cancel the same of record.

In Witness Whereof, the owner and holder has executed this Satisfaction of Mortgage the 19th day of August, 2015.

Signed, Sealed and Delivered in Presence of:

                                                                    CENTURY BANK

_____*Eleanor Jacobs*_____   By: _____*Mark Jansen*_____
Witness Name   Vice President
_____*Eleanor Jacobs*_____
Printed Name
_____*Robert Spence*_____
Witness Name
_____*Robert Spence*_____
Printed Name

STATE OF ANY STATE
COUNTY OF ANY COUNTY

The foregoing instrument was acknowledged before me this 19th day of August, 2015, by Mark Jansen in his representative capacity as vice president for CENTURY BANK who [X] is personally known to me or [ ] produced _____ as identification.

                                        _____*Alice Tompkins*_____
                                        Notary Public
                                        _____*Alice Tompkins*_____
                                        Printed Notary Name

My Commission Expires: 4/20/16

Form reproduced through the courtesy of Landtech Data Corporation

Condominium rider   **EXHIBIT 13–21**

CONDOMINIUM RIDER

THIS CONDOMINIUM RIDER is made this 19th day of August, 2015, and is incorporated into and shall be deemed to amend and supplement the Security Instrument of same date given by the undersigned ("Borrower") to secure Borrower's Note to MILLENNIUM BANK ("Lender") of the same date and covering the Property described in the Security Instrument and located at: 2550 Kingsfield Drive, Unit 305, Any City, Any State. The Property includes a unit in, together with an undivided interest in the common elements of, a condominium project known as Kingsfield Estates II ("Condominium Project").

Borrower shall perform all of Borrower's obligations under the Condominium Project's Constituent Documents. The "Constituent Documents" are the: (1) Declaration or any other document which creates the Condominium Project; (2) bylaws; (3) code of regulations; and (4) equivalent documents. Borrower shall promptly pay, when due, all dues and assessments imposed pursuant to the Constituent Documents.

So long as the Owners' Association maintains, with a generally accepted insurance carrier, a "master" or "blanket" policy on the Condominium Project which is satisfactory to Lender and which provides insurance coverage in the amounts, for the periods and against the hazards Lender requires, then Lender waives the provision in paragraph 2 of the Security Instrument for the monthly payment to Lender of one-twelfth of the yearly premium installments for hazard insurance on the Property.

If Borrower does not pay condominium dues and assessments when due, then Lender may pay them. Any amounts disbursed by Lender under this paragraph shall become additional debt of Borrower secured by the Security Instrument. Unless Borrower and Lender agree to other terms of payment, these amounts shall bear interest from the date of disbursement at the Note rate and shall be payable, with interest, upon notice from Lender to Borrower requesting payment.

BY SIGNING BELOW, Borrower accepts and agrees to the terms and provisions contained in this Condominium Rider.

Patricia Wallis
Borrower

Barbara then sends the lender, Millennium Bank, the original recorded financing instrument, the original mortgagee's title policy, and a copy of the warranty deed. The cover letter sent with these documents is found in Exhibit 13–24.

Barbara then turns her attention to the preparation of a residential closing binder index of documents to be provided to Patricia. The index essentially tells the chronology of the closing, starting with the contract through the issuance of the owner's title policy. Each item is numbered, and the corresponding documents are provided in order, separated by dividers that are tabbed and numbered. The completed closing binder index for the documents to be sent to Patricia is found in Exhibit 13–25.

ANY STATE DEPARTMENT OF REVENUE
RETURN FOR TRANSFERS OF INTEREST IN REAL PROPERTY

1. Parcel Identification Number: 7989594939
2. Mark (x) all that apply:
   Multi-parcel transaction?_____ Transaction is a split or cutout from another parcel?_____
   Property was improved with building(s) at time of sale/transfer? __X__
3. Grantor: Parker Properties, Inc.
   Mailing Address: 700 Commercial Blvd., Suite 360, Any City, Any State
   Phone: (000) 012-3333
4. Grantee: Patricia Wallis
   Mailing Address: 2550 Kingsfield Drive, Unit 305, Any City, Any State
                          (000) 010-0009
5. Date of Sale/Transfer: August 19, 2015   Sale/Transfer Price: $325,000.00
   Property Located In: Any County
6. Type of Document: Warranty Deed __X__ Contract/Agreement for Deed_____
                          Quitclaim Deed_____ Other_____
7. Are there any mortgages on the property? Yes __X__ No_____
   If yes, outstanding mortgage balance: $260,000.00
8. To the best of your knowledge, were there unusual circumstances or conditions to the sale/
   transfer such as: Forced sale by court order? Foreclosure pending? Distress sale? Title
   defects? Corrective deed? Mineral rights? Sale of a partial or undivided interest? Related to
   seller by blood or marriage? Yes_____ No__X__
9. Was the sale/transfer financed? Yes __X__ No_____
   If yes, please indicate type or types of financing:
   Conventional__X__ Seller Provided_____ Agreement or Contract for Deed_____
   Other_____
10. Property Type: Mark (x) all that apply:
    Residential__X__ Commercial_____ Industrial_____ Agricultural_____
    Institutional/Miscellaneous_____ Government_____ Vacant_____ Acreage_____
    Timeshare_____
11. To the best of your knowledge, was personal property included in the sale/transfer?
    Yes_____ No__X__
    If yes, please state the amount attributable to the personal property. $
12. Amount of Documentary Stamp Tax: $2,275.00
13. If no tax is due, is deed exempt from Documentary Stamp Tax under Any State statutes?
    Yes_____ No_____

Under penalties of perjury, I declare that I have read the foregoing return and that the facts stated
in it are true. If prepared by someone other than the taxpayer, his/her declaration is based on all
information of which he/she has any knowledge.

Signature of Grantor or Grantee or Agent: _____ Date: _____

To be completed by the Clerk of the Circuit Court's Office   Clerk's Date Stamp
O.R. Book_____ Page Number_____ File Number_____
Date Recorded_____

Sample cover letter to recording clerk	EXHIBIT 13–23

August 20, 2015

Recording Clerk
Circuit Court of Any County
Any County Courthouse
500 Courthouse Road
Any City, Any State

Re: Recording of Documents

Dear Clerk:

Enclosed is our trust account check number 3044, made payable to Clerk, Circuit Court of Any County, Any State, in the amount of $3,820.00 for the recording of the following documents:

1.	Recording Warranty Deed	$ 18.50
	Documentary Stamps on Deed	$2,275.00
2.	Recording Mortgage	$ 86.50
	Documentary Stamps on Mortgage	$ 910.00
	Intangible Tax on Mortgage	$ 520.00
3.	Recording Satisfaction of Mortgage	$ 10.00

If you have any questions with regard to the above, please do not hesitate to contact me. Please return all recorded documents to my office in the enclosed, self-addressed, stamped envelope. Thank you for your assistance in this matter.

Sincerely,

Barbara Hammond
Paralegal to Ava Ross, Esquire

Enc.

Barbara next prepares a residential closing binder index for Parker Properties, Inc., as shown in Exhibit 13–26.

After making copies of all documentation for the office file, Barbara will send these settlement packets to the respective parties and close the file.

EXHIBIT 13–24   **Sample cover letter to lender**

September 1, 2015

Mortgage Loan Closing Department
Millennium Bank
1750 Wellington Avenue
Any City, Any State

Re: Patricia Wallis
         2550 Kingsfield Drive, #305
         Any City, Any State

         Loan Number: 677377

Dear Sir/Madam:

In connection with the mortgage loan closing for the above-referenced customer, enclosed are the following items for your files:

1.   Copy of deed conveying title to the subject property to Patricia Wallis, a single woman, from Parker Properties, Inc., dated 8/19/15, and recorded on 8/24/15 in Official Records Book 5120, Page 1003, of the Public Records of Any County, Any State.

2.   Original Mortgage encumbering the subject property in favor of Millennium Bank, dated 8/19/15, and recorded on 8/24/15 in Official Records Book 5120, Page 1005 of the Public Records of Any County, Any State.

3.   Original Mortgagee Title Insurance Policy Number 698006 issued 9/1/15, providing $260,000.00 of lender's coverage.

The receipt of the enclosed documents should complete your file on this closing. Should you have any further questions, however, please do not hesitate to contact us.

Sincerely,

Barbara Hammond
Paralegal to Ava Ross, Esquire

Enc.

EXHIBIT 13-25

RESIDENTIAL CLOSING BINDER INDEX
PARKER PROPERTIES, INC.—WALLIS CLOSING
Property: Unit 305, 2550 Kingsfield Drive
Any City, Any State
Closing Date: August 19, 2015

1. Copy of Contract for Purchase and Sale dated June 23, 2015, between Patricia Wallis, a single woman (Purchaser) and Parker Properties, Inc., an Any State corporation (Seller).
2. Copy of Title Commitment, dated July 21, 2015 (Original previously provided).
3. Copy of Mortgage Instrument by Patricia Wallis, a single woman, in favor of Millennium Bank, dated August 19, 2015.
4. Copy of Note in the amount of $260,000.00 by Patricia Wallis, a single woman, in favor of Millennium Bank, dated August 19, 2015.
5. Original Warranty Deed from Parker Properties, Inc., an Any State corporation, to Patricia Wallis, a single woman, dated August 19, 2015.
6. Original Bill of Sale from Parker Properties, Inc, an Any State corporation, to Patricia Wallis, a single woman, dated August 19, 2015.
7. Original Seller's Affidavit from Parker Properties, Inc., an Any State corporation, to Patricia Wallis, a single woman, dated August 19, 2015.
8. HUD-1 Uniform Settlement Statement, dated August 19, 2015.
9. Purchaser's Closing Statement, dated August 19, 2015.
10. Original Owner's Title Insurance Policy No. 739119, issued September 1, 2015.

EXHIBIT 13-26

RESIDENTIAL CLOSING BINDER INDEX
PARKER PROPERTIES, INC.—WALLIS CLOSING
Property: Unit 305, 2550 Kingsfield Drive
Any City, Any State
Closing Date: August 19, 2015

1. Copy of Contract for Purchase and Sale dated June 23, 2015, between Patricia Wallis, a single woman (Purchaser) and Parker Properties, Inc., an Any State corporation (Seller).
2. Copy of Warranty Deed from Parker Properties, Inc., an Any State corporation, to Patricia Wallis, a single woman, dated August 19, 2015.
3. Copy of Bill of Sale from Parker Properties, Inc., an Any State corporation, to Patricia Wallis, a single woman, dated August 19, 2015.
4. Copy of Seller's Affidavit from Parker Properties, Inc., an Any State corporation, to Patricia Wallis, a single woman, dated August 19, 2015.
5. HUD-1 Uniform Settlement Statement, dated August 19, 2015.
6. Seller's Closing Statement, dated August 19, 2015.
7. Original Satisfaction of Mortgage from Century Bank, dated August 19, 2015.

CHAPTER SUMMARY

1. The key to a successful real estate closing is organization. To aid in organizing a residential closing file, a worksheet is a must. A residential closing worksheet should allow the paralegal to have all pertinent information at his or her fingertips. It should include the names, addresses, telephone numbers, fax numbers, and tax identification numbers of each party. It should contain all relevant information pertaining to lenders, real estate brokers, title companies, and escrow agents. Finally, it should specify the dates and detail all steps that must be taken prior to, during, and following the closing, indicating which party is responsible for each step and which party will be paying for each item.

2. A paralegal will be called upon to prepare not only the closing documents but also the correspondence to be sent to parties, their attorneys, lenders, brokers, condominium or homeowners' associations, and so forth. The first correspondence to be sent, either by traditional letter or by e-mail, should confirm the initial appointment with the client. If the client is the seller, he or she should be requested to bring a copy of the contract for sale and purchase (unless your office will be drafting it) and all documentation he or she received at the closing of his or her purchase of the property. If the seller has a survey, he or she should bring that as well. If the client is the buyer, he or she should be asked to bring a copy of the contract for sale and purchase (unless your office is drafting it) and any other documentation provided by the seller at the time of contracting, such as condominium documents.

3. Other correspondence that a paralegal may draft during the course of a real estate closing includes letters or e-mail (1) requesting mortgage payoff or estoppel information, (2) requesting the transfer of mortgage papers if the mortgage is to be assumed, (3) requesting condominium transfer information, (4) pertaining to prorations of taxes if there is the possibility that the prorations will need to be readjusted after closing, and (5) containing transmittal information. Letter and e-mail correspondence signed by paralegals should be accurate as to facts and contain no legal advice.

4. Once all parties have signed the required documents at closing, funds have been disbursed, and documents have been recorded, the paralegal must prepare professional packages of the closing documents to be given to the parties. The purchaser is provided with a copy of the contract, a copy of the title commitment (he or she should already have received the original), copies of the financing instrument and note, and the originals of the deed, bill of sale, seller's affidavit, and any other instruments executed by the seller in favor of the purchaser. The purchaser also receives a HUD-1 Uniform Settlement Statement and an owner's title policy.

5. After closing, the seller is provided with a copy of the contract; copies of the deed, bill of sale, seller's affidavit, and any other instruments executed by the seller in favor of the purchaser; and the original satisfaction of mortgage, if applicable. The seller also receives a HUD-1 Uniform Settlement Statement.

WEB RESOURCES

http://www.irs.gov/

You can order 1099-S forms at this site.

http://www.hud.gov/

This is the main site of the Department of Housing and Urban Development. If you select "Resources" and then select "HUD Handbooks, Forms and Publications," you can access the HUD-1 Settlement Statement and instructions for its completion.

http://www.ilrg.com/

This is the site of the Internet Legal Research Group. Its legal forms archive provides a basic form for a warranty deed.

REVIEW QUESTIONS

1. Assume that in the hypothetical closing presented in this chapter, city taxes are assessed as well as county taxes. Assume further that the annual calendar-year city taxes are in the amount of $3,012.40 and that this tax bill is not paid by the seller before the date of closing. Factoring this in, how much cash will be paid by the buyer and how much cash will be due to the seller at closing?
2. Assume that in the hypothetical closing presented in this chapter, the closing date is moved from August 19 to August 10. The due dates of which items on the closing worksheet must be changed?
3. After a closing, the purchaser receives originals of which documents?
4. After a closing, the seller receives originals of which documents?
5. After a closing, the lender receives originals of which documents?

DISCUSSION QUESTIONS

1. Your clients, Mr. and Mrs. Rodriguez, purchased two homes in the Green Hills Estates development. It is a new, large development, and approximately half of the homes within the development were sold when your clients made their purchase. The Declaration of Covenants and Restrictions has a regulation that allows only one home per purchaser. This regulation is in place to discourage investors from buying them and flipping them, thus competing with the developer. Your clients, to get around this rule, purchased one home in their names and one in the name of Mrs. Rodriguez's mother, Mrs. Perez, who is a Venezuelan citizen. She has never lived in the home. Your clients are now selling both properties and have found buyers for both. The title company is acting as closing agent. The title company makes one check for the sellers' proceeds for one of the sales in the name of Mr. and Mrs. Rodriguez. The company makes out the other check for the seller's proceeds to Mrs. Perez. Your clients then tell you that they do not want the check to Mrs. Perez to show as income to her because of tax issues and that the money really is not to go to her. What should be done in this situation?
2. Your clients are Mr. and Mrs. Stanford. They are the sellers in this transaction. The closing is taking place today. You were informed in advance that

Mr. Stanford travels constantly for business and would be out of state on the day of closing. Thus, you prepared a power of attorney for him to sign giving Mrs. Stanford the right to sign the requisite documents for him. You gave the power of attorney to Mrs. Stanford a couple of weeks ago, and she promised that her husband would sign it and have it notarized. She handed the power of attorney to you a few minutes before closing. You are in the conference room ready to begin the closing. You notice that the signature for Mr. Stanford on the power of attorney does not look like his signature on other papers you have in the closing file. It looks like the signature of Mrs. Stanford. What should you do?

3. Suppose you are working on the Smith–Brown closing and your firm is representing the buyers, Jane and John Brown. They are purchasing a condominium from Sally and Steve Smith. The Smiths have never lived in the condominium. They bought it as an investment property. The closing is taking place this afternoon at 3:00 p.m., and you are conducting the closing. Your supervising attorney is out of the office and is not expected back until 3:00 p.m. She cannot be reached until then. Jane Brown calls you, very upset. It is 11:00 a.m. She and her husband have completed the walk-through of the unit and found out that, although the refrigerator has an automatic ice dispenser on the door, there is no hookup for the ice dispenser. There was an inspection two weeks ago. The inspector brought his son, who is new to the business. While the inspector was looking at the air conditioning unit, he asked his son to check out the kitchen. His son stated that everything was fine. Mrs. Brown cannot recall whether he moved the refrigerator to check the hookups.

   The Smiths are taking the position that the contract states that the unit comes with a refrigerator. It does not state what type of refrigerator and does not refer to hookups. They have never lived in the unit, so they never bothered to look to see if there was an ice dispenser or hookup. They are willing to replace the refrigerator with one that does not have a door ice dispenser but are not going to pay what it would cost to rip up the walls to insert the hookup. The Browns are insisting that the Smiths do so or else they are not going to close this afternoon. The Smiths told the Browns that, if they do not close, they are in breach of contract. They believe the Browns are making a mountain out of a molehill. What should you say to the Browns? Is there any way to save this closing? Do you side with the Browns or the Smiths? Why?

4. Suppose the refrigerator and ice dispenser hookups are not the issue in the above question. Suppose instead that, when the Browns first looked at the unit, they noticed a closet that had hookups for a washer and dryer. Mrs. Smith told them that there would be no problem fitting a piggyback washer–dryer combo in the closet.

   When the Smiths first bought the unit as an investment, there were no hookups in the closet. A few months after the Smiths closed, they were told by the management company for the condominium association that no washers were allowed because of potential plumbing issues in the building. It is an older building, and management feared the existing plumbing would not be able to handle the additional burden of multiple units with washers. The condominium documents do not specifically prohibit washers. Subsequent to the discussion with the management company, Mrs. Smith installed the hookups but never installed a washer or dryer.

   It is now the morning of the Smith–Brown closing, and the Browns just found out from another unit owner about the prohibition on washers. They are very upset. The Smiths have told them that, if they do not close this afternoon, they are in breach of contract. What should you say to the Browns? Is there any way to save this closing? Do you side with the Browns or the Smiths? Why?

5. You are conducting the Miller–Morrison closing. You have prepared the closing documents, including the HUD-1 statement. The closing software you use has been customized to default to the customary practices in your county. In your county, it is customary for the seller to pay for the owner's title policy. You and your supervising attorney have reviewed the closing documents, and you are now in the closing reviewing the HUD-1 statement with the parties. When you get to the title policy line item, the seller objects to the figure in the seller's column, stating that the contract specifies that the buyer pays for the owner's policy. You pull out the contract and find that the seller is correct. You realize that you neglected to override the default in the software and charged the seller rather than following the contract and charging the buyer. The buyer expected to be charged for the owner's policy but has to come to the closing with a cashier's check covering the amount of cash due from buyer stated on the HUD-1 statement. Thus, the cashier's check is short by the amount charged for the owner's title policy. How should this situation be handled?

ETHICAL QUESTION

Assume that your state bar association conducts random audits of law firms' client trust accounts. Your supervising attorney has informed you that your firm's client trust fund accounts for the last three years are being audited. You have been asked to assist the firm's bookkeeper in preparing for the audit. During this process, you review bank deposit receipts and discover that numerous deposits are not identified in any manner and that you cannot match these deposits to specific clients. You find out that Tom, a relatively new paralegal, has been working on real estate transactions with another attorney in the firm. Tom's procedure for handling client trust fund deposits for the last four months has consisted of removing the bank deposit slip relative to a client matter from the deposit book and placing it in the client file. How should this situation be handled?

Slossberg Law Office on CourseMate

Please go to www.cengagebrain.com to log into CourseMate, access the Slossberg Law Office, and work on your client files. Each module corresponds to a chapter in the text. Within each module, you will be provided with instructions by the supervising attorney. You are asked to keep track of time spent on time sheets. The documents produced through working on client files in the law office can then be compiled into a portfolio of final work product.

CourseMate

The available CourseMate for this text has an interactive eBook and interactive learning tools, including flash cards, quizzes, and more. To learn more about this resource and access free demo CourseMate resources, including the Slossberg Law Office, go to www.cengagebrain.com, and search for this book. To access CourseMate materials that you have purchased, go to login.cengagebrain.com.

14

Commercial Real Estate Closings

CHAPTER OBJECTIVES

Upon completion of this chapter, the student will:

- Understand the advantages and disadvantages of investing in commercial property

- Understand the data that must be evaluated prior to purchasing commercial property

- Know the paperwork that must be compiled prior to a commercial closing

- Know how to draft an assignment of leases, commercial closing statement, and other commercial closing documents

Introduction

Individuals and companies looking for avenues of investment have a plethora of possibilities, including savings certificates, stocks and bonds, commodities, and real estate. The investor seeks the highest rate of return on his or her investment. Although the commercial real estate market has been adversely affected in recent years due to the economic downturn, at the time of this writing the effects have not been as dramatic as they have been in the residential real estate market. Additionally, not all sectors of commercial real estate have been affected equally. For example, in some parts of the country retail investments have seen challenges in terms of both declining rents and increasing vacancies, while investors in apartment buildings have seen increasing rents and decreasing vacancies in recent years as purchases of residential properties have declined. When construction activity slows, an adjustment in the supply-and-demand dynamic occurs that favors the investment potential in the commercial real estate market for both local and foreign investors.

Although there is risk involved, a smart investor can estimate his or her anticipated return on an investment. The commercial real estate market can be divided into submarkets, such as office buildings or retail. Depending on location, number of units, and so forth, the investor can find comparable projects, research the rents and costs, and from this information make an objective decision about the profitability of the investment.

Real estate investment also allows more tax flexibility than most other investments. In purchasing a commercial property, the investor is allowed depreciation allowances and deductions for operating expenses. **Operating expenses** are those expenses incurred in maintaining and managing the property. They include, but are not limited to, real property taxes, insurance premiums, and management and service contracts.

operating expenses: Expenses incurred in maintaining and managing property.

sale–leaseback: A situation in which an owner of real property sells the property to an investor and then leases the property back.

In addition to the advantages of investing in commercial real estate, there are some attendant disadvantages. The capital requirements for property acquisition are quite high. Lending institutions often require a larger cash down payment from the purchaser than they do in residential transactions, usually from 20 to 40 percent. This ties up a large portion of the investor's capital in an investment with poor liquidity because it is harder to turn real property into ready cash than it is with most other investments.

Further, there are management concerns with commercial real estate. The investor must be ready to manage the property or hire someone to do so. There is continuous property maintenance. In addition, because the investor becomes a landlord, unless he or she turns the property over quickly, there is more personal involvement and time investment required in a commercial real estate investment. There are tenants to be found, contracts to be negotiated, complaints to be handled, and evictions to be dealt with. Although a property manager can be hired to deal with these issues on a daily basis, the investor nonetheless must be involved at some level.

The financing sources for commercial transactions generally are commercial banks and life insurance companies. Savings and loan institutions tend to concentrate their loans in the single-family residential market. Another possible arrangement for a commercial property is the **sale–leaseback.** In this situation, the owner of a property sells the property to an investor and then leases the property back. The rents are established to provide a prearranged return on the investment over the period of the lease. In this manner, the investor receives a guaranteed return on the investment. Additionally, the seller has the advantage of receiving the cash proceeds to invest in other projects, while deducting the rental amount paid to the investor as an operating expense.

A third possibility is seller "take-back" financing, in which the buyer of the property looks not to a lending insitution but to the seller to finance a portion of the transaction, and the buyer executes a promissory note and mortgage in favor of the seller.

As noted in earlier chapters, when one purchases commercial real estate, one must consider numerous factors. A market analysis must be done to determine whether the location and economic climate are conducive to realizing a profit. The investor obtains all data pertaining to the physical site such as surveys and plans, obtains copies of pertinent zoning ordinances, has engineering reports compiled, and so forth. The investor also looks at competitive rental prices currently charged in the locale and comparable occupancy rates.

In addition to looking at the current leases of the prospective seller of a property, the investor must be able to predict whether future occupancy levels will rise or fall. If the seller's current rent prices appear low in comparison to those of the competition, the investor will be concerned with the length of the lease terms. If the rents are high, the investor will look to see if the tenants are contractually committed on long leases. In looking at occupancy rates, the investor will take into consideration the under- or oversupply of rental space in the locale.

The investor will want to analyze the property owner's financial records. In addition to the income the property produces, the investor will look at the operating expenses. The investor will need to take reserve requirements into account.

Reserve requirements are monies set aside for the replacement of items over and above regular maintenance requirements. Reserves may be used to replace a roof or an elevator, for example. The investor is most concerned with determining the **break-even point,** which is the point at which gross income equals the total of fixed costs and variable costs. When a property's gross income exceeds the break-even point, the property begins to realize a profit. **Fixed costs** are costs that remain constant and do not vary according to the income generated. They include such items as real property taxes, insurance premiums, and loan payments. **Variable costs,** on the other hand, are costs that vary according to the income generated. They include such items as advertising costs and managerial fees. The higher the occupancy rate needed to break even on the property, the poorer the investment. For example, if a break-even analysis indicates that a 98 percent occupancy rate is necessary to break even, the profitability of the property is virtually nonexistent.

Once an investor contracts to purchase a commercial property, the real estate attorney hired to handle the closing must keep track of numerous documents and deadlines. Of special importance is the deadline by which all **due diligence** must be completed. This encompasses all requisite inspections, investigations, and review of items that impact the decision to move forward to closing. During the due diligence period, the purchaser will want confirmation that the property and any buildings on it comply with applicable zoning and building codes. The purchaser may need to schedule environmental testing of the property to determine any environmental concerns, such as contamination by hazardous materials. Specific inspections also may be conducted for asbestos, radon, or mold. The purchaser will need to determine whether the property is in compliance with the Americans with Disabilities Act requirements for accessibility to persons with disabilities. Additionally, if the purchaser will be buying any personal property together with the real property, the purchaser will need to have a Uniform Commercial Code (UCC) lien search conducted to determine whether any liens exist that affect that purchase.

The seller must supply the purchaser with the most current list of leases and rent roll. The purchaser will require a list of security deposits held by the seller. Further, the seller will need to obtain tenant estoppel certificates prior to closing. A **tenant estoppel certificate** verifies the terms and conditions of each tenant's lease. Both the purchaser and the purchaser's lender will require these certificates. Additionally, an assignment of leases must be drafted, assigning the current leases between the seller and tenants to the purchaser.

If there are existing service contracts for a commercial property such as an office building or an apartment complex, the purchaser may want to keep them in place after the closing, in which case assignments of these contracts must be drafted. Typical service contracts that are assigned include landscaping services and elevator maintenance. Most commercial properties are managed by property management companies. The purchaser may choose to hire a new property management company or may want to continue to utilize the services of the property management company under contract with the seller. In the latter instance, this contract must be assigned as well.

If there is personal property to be sold together with the real property, a bill of sale must be drafted. In addition to including any equipment, appliances, fixtures, and inventory (if applicable), the bill of sale is the appropriate document to convey title to any assignable warranties, licenses, and permits.

reserve requirements: Monies set aside for the replacement of items over and above regular maintenance requirements.

break-even point: The point at which gross income equals the total of fixed costs and variable costs.

fixed costs: Costs that remain constant and do not vary according to the income generated.

variable costs: Costs that vary according to the income generated.

due diligence: The process of investigating, inspecting, and reviewing matters within a certain time framework.

tenant estoppel certificate: A document that verifies the terms and conditions of a tenant's lease.

Often, the title work involved in a commercial transaction will include special endorsements requested by the purchaser, the purchaser's lender, or both. One commonly requested endorsement is a zoning endorsement: either an American Land Title Association (ALTA) 3 endorsement for vacant land or an ALTA 3.1 endorsement for improved property (i.e., property with a structure affixed to it, such as an office building or strip center). This endorsement protects against loss if the structures on the property do not comply with zoning code provisions. Before a zoning endorsement will be provided, the title insurer will require an ALTA survey. Certification from the applicable zoning department regarding the zoning classification and authorized use must be obtained. Additionally, special use permits and variances, if applicable, must be provided and reviewed.

Other endorsements commonly requested in commercial transactions are an extended coverage endorsement, an access endorsement, and a contiguity endorsement. An extended coverage endorsement deletes the general exceptions to coverage that appear on an owner's title policy and may be provided if the parties can supply satisfactory documentation to warrant the deletion of these exceptions. An access endorsement provides assurances of proper vehicular access to public streets. A contiguity endorsement may be requested when the commercial property being purchased is comprised of multiple parcels. This endorsement assures that these parcels are contiguous and that there are no gaps between them.

The paperwork involved in a commercial closing is considerable, and it will be your responsibility, as paralegal, to keep track of papers submitted by both parties as well as to draft the closing documents. This chapter sets forth a hypothetical commercial closing, providing samples of most documents found in these transactions. As in the case of residential closings, a worksheet should be used as soon as a commercial closing file is opened to help you keep organized.

A commercial closing worksheet will be similar in some respects to a residential closing worksheet, addressing such items as the parties, lenders, brokers, title company, escrow agent, deposits, title work, loan applications, and so forth. Certain items included in a residential closing worksheet, however, will be omitted (for example, condominium association approval and homeowners' association approval), while others will be added. For example, a commercial closing worksheet should include the preparation and execution of tenant estoppel certificates, rent rolls, security deposit lists, schedules of prepaid and delinquent tenants, occupancy/ vacancy analysis reports, and the assignment of tenant leases. In addition to tax and other prorations, rents must be prorated between the parties. A commercial closing worksheet is found in the hypothetical closing that follows.

Hypothetical Client Closing

Mansart Corporation owns several commercial properties in town. One of these properties is Tavistock Commercial Plaza, a group of three warehouse buildings. Mansart Corporation wants to get out of the industrial side of commercial properties and focus primarily on apartment complexes; therefore, it listed Tavistock Commercial Plaza with Jean Farrell of Farrell Realty. Jean procured a purchaser for the property, WFD Corporation, which recently sold one of its commercial properties and has been looking for another investment to purchase with the sales proceeds.

Gretchen Mansart, president of Mansart Corporation, has hired Ava Ross to represent the company in the transaction. Ava drafted the contract for sale and purchase, and her firm is acting as escrow/closing agent in the transaction. Barbara Hammond, Ava's paralegal, is assisting with the transaction. Upon first opening the client file, Barbara reviewed the contract, which is found in Exhibit 14–1. The exhibits to the contract are found in Exhibits 14–2, 14–3, 14–4, and 14–5.

EXHIBIT 14–1   **Agreement for sale and purchase**

AGREEMENT FOR SALE AND PURCHASE

THIS AGREEMENT is entered by MANSART CORPORATION, an Any State Corporation (the "Seller"), and WFD CORPORATION, an Any State Corporation (the "Buyer").

WHEREAS, the Seller is currently the owner of certain warehouse buildings located in the City of Any City, Any State, known as Tavistock Commercial Plaza, and which are legally described in Exhibit A to this Agreement ("Property"), the parties to this Agreement have agreed to the sale and purchase of the Property on the terms hereinafter set forth.

1. **Purchase and Sale.** Subject to all of the terms and conditions of this Agreement, the Seller will sell to the Buyer, and the Buyer will purchase from the Seller, the Property, together with all appurtenances, rights, easements and rights-of-way incident thereto.

2. **Purchase Price.** The purchase price to be paid by the Buyer to the Seller for the Property shall be Two Million Seven Hundred Thousand Dollars ($2,700,000.00) ("Purchase Price").

3. **Deposit.** Upon the execution of this Agreement, the Buyer has deposited with Fisher, Ross, and Simon, P.A. ("Escrow Agent") the sum of Fifty Thousand Dollars ($50,000.00) to be held as an earnest money deposit ("Deposit"), which shall be applied in accordance with the terms of this Agreement. The Deposit shall be placed into an interest-bearing account. Upon closing, any interest earned on the Deposit shall be paid to the Buyer. If this transaction does not close, the interest shall be paid to the party entitled to retain the Deposit under the terms of this Agreement.

4. **Payment of Purchase Price.** At the closing of this transaction, the Buyer will pay to Seller the Purchase Price as follows:
   (a) The Buyer shall deliver a cashier's check to the order of the Seller in the amount of $2,650,000.00.
   (b) The Escrow Agent shall deliver a cashier's check to the order of Seller in the amount of $50,000.00.

5. **Title.** Within ten (10) days of the execution of this Agreement, the Seller shall deliver a Commitment for an Owner's Title Policy in respect of the Property. The Commitment shall obligate the title company to issue to Buyer a title insurance policy in the amount of the Purchase Price, insuring Buyer's title to the Property. If the Commitment reveals any title matters other than the "Permitted Exceptions" enumerated in Exhibit C which render the title other than good and marketable, Buyer shall, within ten (10) days from receipt of the Commitment, notify Seller in writing, specifying the defect(s). Seller shall have thirty (30) days after receipt of such notice in which to cure such defects and furnish to Buyer evidence that all such defects have been cured. If such defects are cured within that time, the sale and purchase shall be closed in accordance with the terms of this Agreement. If Seller cannot cure all such defects within the thirty (30) day period, Buyer shall have the option, to be exercised in its sole discretion, to complete the purchase and to accept title to the Property subject to such defects or to notify Seller in writing that Buyer elects not to complete the purchase, and thereupon, all rights and liabilities of the parties each to the other shall end.

6. **Leases.** None of the leases identified in Exhibit D attached hereto and made a part hereof shall be modified or amended in any material respect after the date hereof without the consent of the Buyer, which consent will not be unreasonably withheld.

At closing, Seller shall provide Buyer with executed originals of all leases and shall assign all leases to Buyer. Seller shall credit Buyer (together with such certificates of insurance from tenants as may be in Seller's possession) the amount of all deposits and prepaid rent held under the leases. Seller covenants and agrees with Buyer that both Seller and Buyer shall be responsible for the negotiation and execution of each new lease affecting the Property, and no lease shall be executed after the date hereof without the prior written approval of Buyer, which shall not be unreasonably withheld or delayed.

7. **Inspection.** From and after the effective date of this Agreement, the Buyer shall have thirty (30) days in which to examine all aspects of the Property to determine whether or not the Property is acceptable and whether the Buyer will conclude the transaction contemplated by this Agreement. Buyer may extend the Inspection Period for ten (10) additional days if Buyer has not received its engineering report, environmental report and appraisal within the thirty (30) day period. During such "Inspection Period," the Seller shall cooperate fully with the Buyer and shall make available to the Buyer copies of all leases and service contracts, together with such building plans, surveys, financial records, operating statements and schedules from tax returns, pertaining to the Property as may be in the Seller's possession and control. The Buyer shall be permitted to conduct a physical inspection of the Property including the performance of testing for environmental or termite problems. By 5:00 p.m. on the final day of the Inspection Period, the Buyer shall notify the Seller in writing whether or not it intends to proceed with the purchase of the Property. If the Buyer fails to notify the Seller of its intention, the Buyer shall be deemed to have elected to proceed with this transaction. If the Buyer elects not to proceed, the Deposit, together with interest thereon, will be returned to the Buyer and this Agreement will be terminated.

8. **Governmental Compliance.** Notwithstanding the Buyer's inspection rights as set forth in Paragraph 7 above, if the Buyer's inspection discloses any condition or situation which is a violation of any governmental law, ordinance, code, zoning or environmental restriction applicable to the Property, the Seller shall be obligated to proceed diligently to cure such condition following receipt of notice from Buyer. The date of closing shall be postponed by the number of days required by Seller to effectuate such cure. However, if the cost to cure such condition exceeds Twenty-Seven Thousand Five Hundred Dollars ($27,500.00), the Seller shall notify the Buyer of such excess cost, and the Buyer shall elect whether or not to pay such cost in excess of Twenty-Seven Thousand Five Hundred Dollars ($27,500.00). If the Buyer does not elect to pay such excess cost, the Buyer may elect to terminate this Agreement. In the event of such termination, the Deposit, together with interest thereon, shall be refunded to the Buyer and the parties shall have no further obligations under this Agreement.

9. **Closing.** The purchase and sale contemplated by this Agreement shall be closed on September 1, 2015. Closing shall occur in the offices of Fisher, Ross, and Simon, P.A., 1900 N.W. 3rd Avenue, Any City, Any State, commencing at 2:00 p.m. Time is of the essence with respect to the parties' obligations to close this transaction.

10. **Seller's Representations and Warranties.** As a material inducement for Buyer to enter into this Agreement and to consummate the closing hereunder, Seller makes the following representations and warranties to Buyer, which shall survive closing for a period of one year:

    (a) Seller has full power and authority to execute and deliver this Agreement and all documents now or hereafter to be delivered by it pursuant to this Agreement ("Seller's Documents") and to perform all obligations arising under this Agreement and under Seller's Documents;

    (b) Seller is the owner of fee simple title to the Property, and no other person or entity has or claims any interest therein except as reflected in the Title Commitment;

EXHIBIT 14–1 *(continued)*

    (c)   The Property is free and clear of all obligations for taxes except for ad valorem taxes for the current year, not yet due and payable, and for all subsequent years;

    (d)   The Property is or at the time of Closing will be free and clear of all encumbrances other than those described in the Title Commitment;

    (e)   Seller has no knowledge of any pending or contemplated condemnation proceedings affecting the Property or any part thereof;

    (f)   Seller is not aware of any litigation affecting the Property;

    (g)   There will be no construction liens against the Property at Closing except liens for which adequate security and bonding have been provided by Seller;

    (h)   All structures upon the Property are being sold "as is." The Seller specifically disclaims any and all warranties or representations (whether express or implied) concerning the physical condition of the Property;

    (i)   The Rent Roll attached as Exhibit D is true and correct in all material respects;

    (j)   Except as reflected on the Exhibit D Rent Roll, Seller is aware of no defaults of any tenants under the leases, nor is Seller aware of any claims by a tenant that Seller is in default under any leases;

    (k)   Seller is unaware of any violations of rules, ordinances and codes of any governmental authority with jurisdiction over the Property;

    (l)   Seller has received no requests to increase its insurance coverage of the Property;

    (m)   There has been no rent strike or organized action of the tenants against the Seller during the past twelve (12) months;

    (n)   The Property is not located within an officially designated historic district.

11.   **Buyer's Representations.** As a material inducement for Seller to enter into this Agreement and to consummate the Closing hereunder, Buyer makes the following representations to Seller, which representations shall be true and correct at Closing, as though such representations and warranties were made at and as of the date of Closing:

    (a)   Buyer has full power and authority to execute and deliver this Agreement and all documents now or hereafter to be delivered by it pursuant to this Agreement ("Buyer's Documents") and to perform all obligations arising under this Agreement and under Buyer's Documents;

    (b)   This Agreement and Buyer's Documents do not and will not contravene any provision of Buyer's Articles of Incorporation, any present judgment, order, decree, writ or injunction, or any provision of any currently applicable law or regulation.

12.   **Seller's Deliveries.** Seller shall deliver to Buyer at Closing the following documents, dated as of the closing date, the delivery and accuracy of which shall be a condition to the consummation of the purchase and sale:

    (a)   <u>Deed.</u> A special warranty deed in recordable form, duly executed by Seller, conveying to the Buyer good and marketable and insurable fee simple title to the Property, subject only to the Permitted Exceptions.

    (b)   <u>Affidavit.</u> A no-lien affidavit in form and content customarily used in Any County, Any State, relating to any activity of Seller at the Property within the period that a lien can be filed based on such activity prior to the closing.

    (c)   <u>Closing Statement.</u> A Closing Statement setting forth the purchase price, deposits, deductions, prorations, fees, recording costs and other items customarily reflected on a Closing Statement in Any County.

    (d)   <u>Assignment of Leases.</u> An assignment of all leases relating to the Property, together with the originals of such leases. Such assignment shall provide for the assumption by Buyer of all obligations under the leases from and after the date of Closing.

    (e)   <u>Estoppel Letters.</u> Estoppel letters in a form substantially similar to Exhibit B from all those tenants who have completed an estoppel letter. Prior to Closing, Seller will mail estoppel letters to all tenants by certified mail, postage prepaid, return receipt requested, and will instruct them to sign and return the estoppel letters.

(f) Certified Resolutions. Certified resolutions of the Seller authorizing the entering into and execution of this Agreement and the consummation of each and every transaction contemplated herein.

(g) Other Documents. Such other documents as Buyer or its counsel may reasonably require in order to effect the closing of this transaction, together with keys, alarm codes (if any), warranties (if any) and operating manuals (if any).

13. **Buyer's Deliveries.** At Closing, and after the Seller has complied with all of the terms and conditions of this Agreement and has delivered the documents required, Buyer shall:

(a) Purchase Price. Pay to the Seller by cashier's check or wire transfer the cash portion of the Purchase Price. Seller consents to the use of its closing proceeds to pay off the existing mortgages encumbering the Property.

(b) Certified Resolutions. Deliver certified resolutions of the Buyer authorizing the entering into and execution of this Agreement and the consummation of each and every transaction contemplated herein.

14. **Closing and Recording Costs.** Seller shall pay the cost of documentary stamps to be affixed to the deed. Seller shall also pay the cost of the Title Commitment and the cost of an Owner's Title Insurance Policy, together with the cost of recording any documents necessary to render title as required under this Agreement. Buyer shall pay the cost of recording the financing instrument, all intangible tax (if any) pertaining to the Note, and the cost of a Mortgagee's Title Insurance Policy.

15. **Tax Proration and Adjustments.**

(a) Adjustments. The following adjustments shall be made between the parties at the Closing: (i) Buyer shall be credited and Seller charged with security deposits or advance rentals in the nature of security deposits made by tenants under the Leases; (ii) Buyer shall be credited and Seller charged with the aggregate amount of rental abatement, concessions or build-out allowances (if any) under the leases, attributable to the period commencing on the date of the Closing and extending to the date when full rental becomes payable thereunder; and (iii) Seller shall be credited and Buyer charged with transferable deposits under service contracts assumed by Buyer, if any, provided Seller delivers to Buyer at the Closing a letter from the other party to each such service contract, confirming the amount of such deposit and the transferability thereof.

(b) Prorations. The following shall be prorated between the parties as of the date of the Closing: real estate taxes for the calendar year in which the Closing occurs, water and sewer charges, rent payments under the Leases to the extent actually received by Seller prior to the Closing, charges and fees paid or payable under service contracts which are assigned to Buyer and such other items of income and expense as are customarily prorated in a transaction of this nature.

(c) Real Estate Taxes and Liens. At Closing, taxes on the Property shall be prorated between the parties on the basis of the taxes paid for the most recent tax year that has been assessed and billed. If the actual taxes for the year of Closing are not determinable at the closing date, the parties agree to reprorate taxes promptly upon issuance of the tax bill for the year of Closing. Special assessment liens certified as of Closing shall be paid by Seller. Pending liens shall be assumed by Buyer.

(d) Utilities. Seller shall endeavor to have all meters read and final bills rendered for all utilities servicing the Property, including, without limitation, water, gas and electricity, for the period to and including the day preceding the Closing, and

EXHIBIT 14-1 *(continued)*

Seller shall pay such bills where appropriate, except in the case of utility charges paid or payable by any tenants directly to the utility companies.

(e) Rent Arrears. At the Closing, Seller shall deliver to Buyer a list of all tenants who are delinquent in the payment of rent, which list shall set forth the amount of each such delinquency, the period to which each such delinquency relates and the nature of the amount due, itemizing separately fixed monthly rent and any additional charges. If the tenant under the lease is in arrears in the payment of rent on the date of Closing, rents received by Buyer from such tenant after the Closing shall be applied in the following order of priority: (i) first to the month in which such rents are received; (ii) then to any rent arrearages for months subsequent to the month in which the Closing occurs; (iii) then to any rent arrearages for the month in which the Closing occurs; and (iv) then to the period for which the tenant in question was in arrears prior to the month in which the Closing occurs. If all or part of any rents, or any escalation charges for real estate taxes, insurance, operating expenses or other charges of a similar nature, received by Seller or Buyer after the Closing are payable to the other party by reason of this allocation, the appropriate sum, less a proportionate share of any reasonable attorneys' fees and other costs and expenses of collection thereof, shall be promptly paid to the other party.

(f) Proration of Additional Rents. To the extent Seller has received payments from tenants under the Leases for real estate taxes, operating expenses or other charges of a similar nature, including all amounts noted in Paragraphs 15(b) and 15(d) hereof ("Additional Rents"), and Seller has not expended these monies for the operation of the Property, Seller shall deliver to Buyer (or Buyer's property manager, if so directed by Buyer) the balance of said monies. This delivery shall be in lieu of the prorations provided for in Paragraphs 15(b) and 15(d) except, to the extent any tenant under a Lease is in default in the payments of any Additional Rent, Seller shall deliver an amount to Buyer at the Closing equal to the amount which said tenant is in default in paying. If any Additional Rents are collected by Buyer after the Closing which are attributable in whole or in part to any period prior to the date of the Closing, the Buyer shall pay Seller's proportionate share thereof to Seller within five (5) business days after receipt, less any reasonable attorneys' and accountants' fees and other costs and expenses incurred by Buyer in connection with the collection thereof. Nothing in this Paragraph 15(f) shall be construed as limiting the provisions of Paragraph 15(g) hereof.

(g) Postclosing Adjustment Procedures. Seller and Buyer acknowledge that it may be impossible to make all necessary adjustments at the Closing. Therefore, Seller and Buyer agree that subject to the provisions of Paragraphs 15(c), 15(d), 15(e) and 15(f), all operating revenues, including rental payments, from the Property which relate to the Period prior to the date of the Closing (the "Preclosing Period") shall belong to Seller, including all accrued but unpaid rental payments; and all such revenues applicable to the period on or after the date of the Closing shall belong to Buyer.

(h) Errors. If any errors or omissions are made at the Closing regarding adjustment or prorations, the parties shall make the appropriate corrections promptly after the discovery thereof.

The provisions of this Article 15 shall survive the Closing until all such adjustments and payments have been made.

16. Possession. Buyer shall be granted possession of the Property as of the date of Closing, subject, however, to the possessory interests of the tenants under the Leases.

17. **Real Estate Commissions.** Seller hereby warrants to Buyer that Seller has not engaged any broker or agent with respect to the purchase and sale of the Property as contemplated by this Agreement other than Farrell Realty and Cromwell Realty. Seller shall indemnify and hold Buyer harmless against any and all liability, cost, damage and expense (including, but not limited to, attorneys' fees and costs of litigation, including appeals) that Buyer shall ever suffer or incur because of any claim by any other broker or agent claiming to have dealt with Seller, whether or not meritorious, for any commission or other compensation with respect to this Agreement or to the purchase and sale of the Property in accordance with this Agreement.

18. **Condemnation.** In the event of the institution against the record owner of the Property of any proceedings, judicial, administrative or otherwise, relating to the taking, or to a proposed taking, of any portion of the Property by eminent domain, condemnation or otherwise, prior to Closing, then Seller shall notify Buyer promptly and Buyer shall have the option, in its sole and absolute discretion, of either (a) terminating this Agreement, or (b) closing in accordance with the terms of this Agreement, but at such Closing Seller shall assign to Buyer all of its right, title and interest in and to any net awards that have been or may be made with respect to such eminent domain proceeding or condemnation. Such election must be made by the Buyer within thirty (30) days of the notice furnished by Seller. If Buyer fails to make an election in writing, Buyer shall be deemed to have elected to close in accordance with the terms of this Agreement.

19. **Loss or Damage.** Any loss or damage to the Property between the date of this Agreement and Closing shall not void this Agreement or modify the provisions hereof, provided that Seller at its sole cost and expense shall maintain fire and extended coverage insurance upon the Property to the full insurable value thereof with a loss payable provision endorsement in favor of Seller. Any and all insurance proceeds shall be received by Seller and Seller shall apply such insurance proceeds to the repair or loss of damage to the Property.

20. **Default.** If this transaction does not close solely due to a refusal or default on the part of Buyer, the Deposit placed under this Agreement, together with the interest thereon, shall be delivered by Escrow Agent to Seller as liquidated and agreed upon damages, and thereafter, Buyer shall be relieved from all further obligations under this Agreement; or Seller, at its option, may proceed at law or in equity to enforce its legal rights under this Agreement.

   If this transaction fails to close due to a default on the part of the Seller, then at the option of Buyer, the Deposit, including all interest thereon, shall be returned by Escrow Agent to Buyer, or Buyer may proceed against the Seller only for specific performance of this Agreement. In no event shall the Seller be liable to the Buyer for money damages.

21. **Entire Agreement.** This Agreement constitutes the entire agreement between the parties with respect to the transaction contemplated herein, and it supersedes all prior understandings or agreements between the parties.

22. **Binding Effect.** This Agreement shall be binding upon and inure to the benefit of the parties hereto and their respective successors and assigns.

23. **Survival of Warranties.** No representations, warranties, covenants and agreements specified in this document shall survive the closing, other than those set forth in Paragraphs 16 and 18.

24. **Waiver; Modification.** The failure by Buyer or Seller to insist upon or enforce any of their rights shall not constitute a waiver thereof, and nothing shall constitute a waiver of Buyer's right to insist upon strict compliance with the terms of this Agreement. Either party may waive the benefit of any provision or condition for its benefit which is contained in this Agreement. No oral modification of this Agreement shall be binding upon the parties; any modification must be in writing and signed by the parties.

25. **Government Law; Venue.** This Agreement shall be governed by and construed under the laws of the State of Any State. In the event of any litigation concerning this Agreement, venue shall be in the Eleventh Judicial Circuit of Any State.

EXHIBIT 14-1   *(continued)*

26. **Headings.** The paragraph headings as set forth in this Agreement are for convenience of reference only and shall not be deemed to vary the content of this Agreement or limit the provisions or scope of any paragraph herein.

27. **Notices.** Any notice, request, demand, instruction or other communication to be given to either party, except where required by the terms of this Agreement to be delivered at Closing, shall be in writing and shall be sent by registered or certified mail or by private overnight delivery service, as follows:

If to Buyer: WFD Corporation
                 c/o Walter F. Davidson
                 1200 N.W. 30th Street, Suite 200
                 Any City, Any State

with copy to: Emily Griffin, Esquire
                 Griffin, Hill, and Colson, P.A.
                 504 S.E. 6th Avenue, Suite 302
                 Any City, Any State

If to Seller: Mansart Corporation
                 c/o Gretchen Mansart
                 705 N.E. 12th Street, Suite 100
                 Any City, Any State

with copy to: Ava Ross, Esquire
                 Fisher, Ross, and Simon, P.A.
                 1900 N.W. 3rd Avenue
                 Any City, Any State

If forwarded by overnight delivery service, notice shall be effective when received. If forwarded by certified or registered mail, notice shall be effective upon delivery, or, if delivery is refused, upon the first delivery attempt.

28. **Assignment.** This Agreement may be assigned by Buyer. Notwithstanding any assignment, Buyer shall continue to remain responsible for the performance of this Agreement.

29. **Indemnification.** The Seller hereby indemnifies and holds harmless the Buyer from any loss, cost or liability it may incur (including reasonable attorneys' fees) based on any claim arising from the ownership or operation of the Property prior to the date of Closing. Conversely, the Buyer hereunder indemnifies and holds harmless the Seller from any loss, cost or liability it may incur (including reasonable attorneys' fees) based on any claim arising from the ownership or operation of the Property from and after the date of Closing.

30. **Effective Date.** The date of this Agreement shall be the date upon which the last party to sign has executed this Agreement.

The parties have executed this Agreement on the respective dates set forth below.

BUYER:

ATTEST: WFD CORPORATION, an Any State
                           Corporation

Mitchell Maynard
Secretary   By: *Walter F. Davidson*
(Corporate Seal)   President
                           DATE: July 5, 2015

                           SELLER:
ATTEST: MANSART CORPORATION, an Any State
                           Corporation

Dean Slater
Secretary   By: *Gretchen Mansart*
(Corporate Seal)   President
                           DATE: July 5, 2015

The undersigned agrees to act as Escrow Agent in accordance with the terms of this Agreement.

Fisher, Ross, and Simon, P.A.

By: *Ava Ross*_____

The undersigned brokers agree that only upon the closing of the transaction set forth in the forgoing Agreement, they shall each be entitled to receive a commission, payable by the Seller, in the respective amounts described below.

FARRELL REALTY, INC.

By: *Jean Farrell*_____
    Vice President

Amount: $67,500.00_____

SELLER:

MANSART CORPORATION

By: *Gretchen Mansart*_____
    President

CROMWELL REALTY, INC.

By: *George Cromwell*_____
    President

Amount: $67,500.00_____

The property description is a rather lengthy metes and bounds description, so rather than including it in the body of the contract, it is attached as an exhibit (Exhibit 14–2). The contract lists a purchase price of $2,700,000. Glaringly missing from the contract is a financing provision. This is because WFD Corporation is reinvesting capital from the recent sale of a property and is not obtaining outside financing. According to the contract terms, the seller has ten days from the execution of the contract to provide the purchaser with a title commitment. The seller is to pay for the title examination, the title commitment, and the owner's policy. No mortgagee policy need be prepared, as there is no mortgagee involved. This also means that no financing instrument will be recorded, and no accompanying fees for recording, documentary stamp tax, and intangible tax will be assessed to the purchaser.

The contract stipulates that the purchaser has a thirty-day inspection period. In this time period, the purchaser may conduct engineering tests and other physical inspections. During this time period, the seller must provide the purchaser with building plans, surveys, and financial records pertaining to the property, such as operating statements and tax return schedules. Should problems arise during the course of the inspections related to governmental codes, ordinances, zoning, environmental restrictions, and so forth, the purchaser must immediately inform the seller, and the seller must take steps to cure the defects. Realizing that the costs to remedy these problems may be steep, a dollar limitation is set on the seller's obligation of $27,500. Should the cost to cure the problems exceed this amount, the purchaser may choose to pay the excess or to cancel the contract.

The contract details the steps that may and may not be taken regarding leases between the time of contracting and date of closing. Leases cannot be modified without the consent of the purchaser. Any new leases entered into during this period must be negotiated by both the seller and the purchaser. Upon closing, the seller is to provide the purchaser with all original leases, the security deposits, and prepaid rents as well as a list of delinquent rents. When and if recovered, the delinquent rents are to be applied in a specified order. Additionally, the seller is to provide the purchaser with tenant estoppel certificates or letters in a format similar to that found in Exhibit 14–3.

EXHIBIT 14–2   **Legal description of property**

EXHIBIT A
LEGAL DESCRIPTION

A parcel of land being described as Lot 21 and a portion of Lot 4, Block 9, of the PLAT OF SOUTHERN HILLS, SECTION 4, according to the plat thereof recorded in Plat Book 20, Pages 101 through 105, of the Public Records of Any County, Any State, said parcel being more particularly described as follows:

Beginning at the Southeast corner of Lot 10, Block 9, of the aforementioned plat, thence Northerly along the Easterly lines of Lots 10, 11, 12, 13, 14, 15, and 16, Block 9, a distance of 680.68 feet to a point; thence Northerly with a deflection of 4°47'30" to the right along the Easterly lines of Lots 16 and 17, Block 9, a distance of 178.15 feet to a point; thence Easterly along the South line of Lots 19 and 20, Block 9, a distance of 158.43 feet to a point; thence Northerly along the Westerly line of Lot 21, Block 9, a distance of 160.00 feet to a point, said point being the Southeast corner of Lot 21; thence Southerly with a deflection to the left of 13°33'40", a distance of 20.57 feet to a point; thence Easterly with a deflection to the left of 76°26'20", a distance of 53.08 feet to a point; thence Southerly with a deflection to the right of 76°26'20", a distance of 805.66 feet to a point; thence Westerly at right angles to the preceding course, a distance of 72.50 feet to a point; thence Northerly at right angles to the preceding course, a distance of 42.50 feet to a point; thence Westerly at right angles to the preceding course, a distance of 143.56 feet to a point; thence Southerly with a deflection of 89°54'09" to the left, a distance of 118.33 feet to the Northeast corner of Parcel 10 of the City of Any City as recorded in Deed Book 760, Page 301, Public Records of Any County, Any State; thence Westerly along the North line of said Parcel 10, a distance of 70.01 feet to the Northwest corner of Parcel 10; thence Northerly along the East line of Lot 8, Block 9, a distance of 15.83 feet to a point; thence Westerly along the North line of Lot 8, a distance of 36.26 feet to the Southeast corner of Lot 9, Block 9; thence Northerly along the East line of Lot 9, Block 9, a distance of 102.50 feet more or less back to the Point of Beginning.

EXHIBIT 14–3   **Tenant's estoppel certificate**

EXHIBIT B
TENANT'S ESTOPPEL CERTIFICATE

Date: _____

TO:
RE: Lease (the "Lease") dated _____ by and between MANSART CORPORATION, an Any State corporation, as Landlord and _____, as Tenant, with respect to Tavistock Commercial Plaza, Suite _____, 1400 S.E. 19th Avenue, Any City, Any State.

To Whom it May Concern:

As Tenant under the above-referenced Lease, the undersigned hereby acknowledges for the benefit of WFD CORPORATION, or its assigns, which has or is about to purchase the above-referenced property, the truth and accuracy of the following statements pertaining to said Lease:

1. The copy of the Lease attached hereto is a true, complete and correct copy, and includes all modifications, amendments or other terms of the Lease.
2. Except as otherwise set forth in Paragraph 7 below, Tenant is paying the full rent stipulated in said Lease, and to the best of its knowledge Tenant is in good standing and not in default or breach of any of its obligations under the Lease.

3. Current monthly base rent under the Lease is $ _____, the rent is fully paid through _____, and no monies have been paid to Landlord in advance of the due date except as follows:

Current Operating Expense Reimbursements or other rent due in addition to the current monthly base rent is payable as follows:

Monthly Real Estate Tax and Electricity Charges of $ _____
Monthly Other Operating Expense Charges of $ _____
and is fully paid through: _____.

The Landlord is presently holding a security deposit in the amount of $ _____.

4. The current term of the Lease commenced on _____. Landlord has satisfactorily complied with all of the requirements and conditions precedent to the commencement of the term of the Lease as specified therein. The current term ends on _____ and there are no remaining renewal or extension options except:

5. The Landlord is not, as of the date of this certificate, in default in the performance of the Lease, nor are there any circumstances which, with the passage of time, the giving of notice, or both, would result in a breach or default under the Lease by Landlord, nor are there any existing setoffs, counterclaims, or credits against rentals due or to become due under the Lease, nor are there existing defenses against the enforcement of the Lease by Landlord.

6. Tenant hereby acknowledges that (a) there have been no modifications or amendments to said Lease other than as specifically stated herein; (b) it has no notice of a prior assignment, hypothecation or pledge of rents or of the Lease; and (c) notice of the proposed assignment of Landlord's interest in said Lease may be given it by certified or registered mail, return receipt requested, at the premises.

7. The Tenant has not been granted any options to purchase or unused concession of free rent except:

TENANT:

_____
(Print name)

By: _____

Name: _____

Title: _____

Other exhibits attached to the contract are the permitted exceptions (Exhibit 14–4) and the lease/rent roll of current tenants (Exhibit 14–5).

The contract indicates that two real estate brokers were involved in the transaction: Farrell Realty as the listing broker and Cromwell Realty as the selling broker. They will split a 5 percent commission.

As both the seller and the purchaser are corporate entities, each must provide the other with certified resolutions from their boards of directors that authorize the sale and purchase of the property in question. Under the terms of the contract, the seller is to prepare the closing statement as well as the seller's affidavit, an assignment of

EXHIBIT 14-4   **Permitted exceptions**

EXHIBIT C
PERMITTED EXCEPTIONS

A.   Taxes for the current year and subsequent years, which are not yet due and payable.
B.   Public utilities and building lines as shown on the plat of SOUTHERN HILLS, SECTION 4, recorded in Plat Book 20, Pages 101 to 105, Public Records of Any County, Any State.
C.   Covenant creating private road dated March 26, 2001, recorded March 31, 2001, in Official Records Book 2444, Page 58, Public Records of Any County, Any State.
D.   Declaration Not to Relocate, Modify, Terminate or Cancel Ingress-Egress Easement dated March 26, 2001, recorded March 31, 2001, in Official Records Book 2444, Page 59, Public Records of Any County, Any State.
E.   Declaration of Parking Easement dated March 26, 2001, recorded March 31, 2001, in Official Records Book 2444, Page 60, Public Records of Any County, Any State.
F.   Parties in possession under Leases.

Copyright © 2015 Cengage Learning®.

leases, and the deed. The deed to be delivered is a special warranty deed. Because the property is encumbered with an existing mortgage, the seller must pay off the seller's lender and record a satisfaction of mortgage. Note that the lender in this instance is an insurance company, Scarborough Life Insurance Company.

The scheduled closing date is September 1. If the closing takes place as scheduled, rents will not have to be prorated. Real estate taxes, however, will be prorated. The seller has not yet received the tax bill for the current year, and, therefore, the parties will need to sign a tax proration agreement whereby they agree to readjust the tax proration according to the tax bill when it is received.

From this initial review of the contract, Barbara filled in the preliminary information on a commercial closing worksheet; other information will be added as it is received. The worksheet appears in Exhibit 14–6. Note that the file date is July 1, before the contract was signed, because Ava drafted the contract. The due dates listed for the closing statement and various other documents to be prepared by Barbara's firm are two days before the date of closing. As mentioned in the last chapter, the closing statement figures must be provided to the purchaser prior to the date of closing because the purchaser will have to obtain a cashier's check to deliver at closing. Further, both parties need to review the closing documents prior to closing so that, if corrections need to be made, they will not delay the closing.

As the closing date is nearing, Barbara reviews the worksheet shown in Exhibit 14–6 to determine what has already been done and what she must tackle next. She has already prepared a title commitment and delivered it to Emily Griffin, WFD Corporation's attorney, for review.

Barbara has prepared a cover letter for Mansart Corporation to deliver with the tenant estoppel certificate forms to each tenant. Barbara has instructed the client to attach a copy of each tenant's lease to that tenant's certificate form. The purchaser will receive the original leases at a later time. The cover letter is found in Exhibit 14–7. Although the certificates do not have to be presented until closing, the cover letter requests that the tenants return them no later than August 10, providing some lead time.

She has sent a letter to her client's lender, Scarborough Life Insurance Company, requesting the payoff figures for a September 1 closing. In return, she has received the payoff statement from Scarborough found in Exhibit 14–8.

Lease/rent roll

EXHIBIT 14–5

EXHIBIT D
LEASE/RENT ROLL

BUILDING I UNITS	TENANT	SQ. FT.	DATE OF LEASE	TERM	MONTHLY RENT
101, 103	Daltrey Designs	4145	1/1/13	5 yr	2,103.57
105, 107, 109	Red Carpet Motors	4523	5/1/15	1 yr	2,453.12
111, 113	Weller Marble	2010	6/25/14	2 yr	910.34
115, 117	Colber Creations	1507.5	5/1/15	1 yr	821.16
119	Brian Buchanan	502	6/1/15	1 yr	288.51
121, 123	Naturescape, Inc.	1507.05	6/14/15	2 yr	833.86
125	----------------	1005	-----------	--------	------------
127	----------------	1005	-----------	--------	------------
129	Vittorio Furniture	3015	2/22/15	1 yr	1,433.38
131	----------------	1005	-----------	--------	------------
133, 135	Holms Carpet	1005	9/1/13	40 mo.	477.00
137, 139	Lance Glass	2010	12/1/13	3 yr	1,575.75
141	Gordon's Lawn Co.	1005	7/1/15	1 yr	503.50
143, 145	Stevenson Interiors	2010	8/1/14	2 yr	1,639.37
147	AVH Builders, Inc.	1005	4/1/15	1 yr	530.00
149, 151	Mulligen Linens	2760	10/9/13	5 yr	1,220.77
153, 155	Palladium Cable	2010	4/1/14	3 yr	1,614.54
157, 159	----------------	3800	-----------	--------	------------
BUILDING II UNITS					
200, 202, 204	WWP Tire, Inc.	5400	2/3/14	3 yr	2,981.25
206, 208, 210	Car Doctor, Inc.	4420	6/1/15	2 yr	2,217.85
212, 214, 216	Wincott Enterprises	3315	7/15/14	3 yr	1,485.62
218, 220	Murillo Accessories	2210	6/1/15	1 yr	1,001.46
222	J.C. Howell	1005	12/1/14	13 mo.	585.65
224, 226, 228	Rollins Sprinkler	3210	1/1/15	3 yr	1,598.09
230, 232, 234	Flynn Corp.	4972.5	1/15/15	3 yr	2,659.81
236, 238	Jeffrey Long	1657.5	1/15/14	3 yr	736.91
240, 242	Newton Technology	1455	4/1/15	2 yr	835.41
244	Mansart Corp.	285	-----------	--------	------------
BUILDING III UNITS					
300	----------------	800	-----------	--------	------------
302, 304	Marilyn Callahan	3100	8/1/13	5 yr	1,631.90
306, 308	Beverly Enterprises	3100	7/13/14	2 yr	2,141.50
310, 312	T.J. McCarthy	3100	2/1/14	3 yr	1,554.00
314, 316	Madison Furniture	1982	11/1/14	2 yr	1,218.00
318, 320, 322	LPR Stucco, Inc.	1080	12/14/14	3 yr	551.20
324	Stockwell, Inc.	3600	9/13/14	3 yr	1,855.00
326	VMV, Inc.	2360	6/24/15	3 yr	1,414.04
328	James Reilly	800	9/22/14	3 yr	551.20
330	Ritter Labs	3660	11/3/14	3 yr	1,542.30
332, 334, 336	Dunmore Systems	1680	3/21/14	2 yr	808.78
338, 340, 342	Garrett Pool Care	1920	10/1/13	3 yr	968.84
344	----------------	1005	-----------	--------	------------

EXHIBIT 14–6   Commercial closing worksheet

COMMERCIAL CLOSING WORKSHEET

DATE FILE OPENED: July 1, 2015
ATTORNEY: Ava Ross
PARALEGAL: Barbara Hammond
CLIENT NUMBER: 15480
MATTER NUMBER: 0001
CLIENT: _____ BUYER X SELLER _____ LENDER

1. SELLER NAME(S): Mansart Corporation, an Any State corporation
2. ADDRESS(ES): 705 N.E. 12th Street, Suite 100
   Any City, Any State
3. E-MAIL ADDRESS: gmansart@mansartcorp.com
4. PHONE NUMBER(S): (000) 004-2090 CELL: (000) 004-2091
   FAX NUMBER(S): (000) 004-2095
5. SOCIAL SECURITY NUMBER(S) [IF A BUSINESS ENTITY, FEDERAL TAX
   I.D. NO.]: 000625425
6. BUYER NAME(S): WFD Corporation, an Any State corporation
7. ADDRESS(ES): 1200 N.W. 30th Street, Suite 200
   Any City, Any State
8. E-MAIL ADDRESS: wdavidson@wfdcorp.com
9. PHONE NUMBER(S): (000) 471-7200 CELL: N/A
   FAX NUMBER(S): (000) 471-7230
10. SOCIAL SECURITY NUMBER(S) [IF A BUSINESS ENTITY, FEDERAL TAX
    I.D. NO.]: 000644461
11. BUYER'S LENDER: Not applicable
12. ADDRESS: _____

13. E-MAIL ADDRESS: _____
14. PHONE NUMBER: _____
    FAX NUMBER: _____
15. LOAN OFFICER ASSIGNED TO LOAN FILE: _____
16. LOAN NUMBER: _____
17. SELLER'S LENDER (IF SELLER HAS EXISTING MORTGAGE ON
    PROPERTY): Scarborough Life Insurance Company
18. ADDRESS: 500 Chamberlain Street Any City, Any State
19. E-MAIL ADDRESS: bcarter@scarborough.com
20. PHONE NUMBER: (000) 203-6500
    FAX NUMBER: (000) 203-6550
21. LOAN NUMBER: 560816
22. ATTORNEY FOR: X BUYER _____ SELLER _____ LENDER
23. ATTORNEY NAME: Emily Griffin, Esq., Griffin, Hall, and Colson, P.A.
24. ADDRESS: 504 S.E. 6th Avenue, Suite 302
    Any City, Any State
25. E-MAIL ADDRESS: egriffin@griffinhallandcolson.com
26. PHONE NUMBER: (000) 154-0500
    FAX NUMBER: (000) 154-0550
27. REAL ESTATE BROKER #1: Farrell Realty (Jean Farrell)
28. ADDRESS: 786 Wisteria Street
    Any City, Any State
29. E-MAIL ADDRESS: jfarrell@farrellrealty.com
30. PHONE NUMBER: (000) 367-2952
    FAX NUMBER: (000) 367-2953
31. REAL ESTATE BROKER #2: Cromwell Realty (George Cromwell)
32. ADDRESS: 481 Tunbridge Drive
    Any City, Any State

(continued)　　　　　　　　　　　　　　　　　　　　　　　　　　　　**EXHIBIT 14-6**

33.	E-MAIL ADDRESS:	gcromwell@cromwellrealty.com
34.	PHONE NUMBER:	(000) 259-1778
	FAX NUMBER:	(000) 259-1779
35.	COMMISSION:	5%　　HOW SPLIT: 50/50
36.	ESCROW AGENT:	Fisher, Ross, and Simon, P.A.
37.	ADDRESS:	1900 N.W. 3rd Avenue
		Any City, Any State
38.	E-MAIL ADDRESS:	aross@fisherrossandsimon.com
39.	PHONE NUMBER:	(000) 555-2000
	FAX NUMBER:	(000) 555-2020
40.	TITLE COMPANY:	Fisher, Ross, and Simon, P.A.
41.	ADDRESS:	
42.	E-MAIL ADDRESS:	
43.	PHONE NUMBER:	
	FAX NUMBER:	

44. STREET ADDRESS OF PROPERTY:
　　　Tavistock Commercial Plaza, 3082 Tavistock Drive
　　　Any City, Any State

45. LEGAL DESCRIPTION OF PROPERTY:
　　　See attached Exhibit

46. PARCEL IDENTIFICATION NUMBER: 7321483300

47. CLOSING:
　　(A)　DATE:　　9/1/15
　　(B)　TIME:　　2:00 p.m.
　　(C)　PLACE:　our offices

48. PURCHASE PRICE:　$2,700,000.00

49. LOAN AMOUNT:　Not applicable

50.	**DEPOSITS:**	**AMOUNT**	**DATE DUE**	**DATE RECEIVED**
	(A)　LOT:			
	(B)　INITIAL:	$50,000.00	7/5/15	7/5/15
	(C)　ADDITIONAL:			

51. **ITEMS**	**DONE BY**	**DATE DUE**	**CHARGE TO**
Title Search	Seller	7/10/15	Seller
Order Survey	Seller	7/5/15	P.O.C.
Title Examination	Seller	7/10/15	Seller
Title Commitment	Seller	7/15/15	Seller
Remedy Defects			
Issue Policy(ies):			
(a)　Owner's	Seller		Seller
(b)　Mortgagee's			
(c)　Endorsements:			
_____	____	____	____
Property Appraisal	Seller		P.O.C.
Engineer's Report	Buyer	7/25/15	P.O.C.
Zoning Information	Seller	7/10/15	
Environmental Information	Seller	7/10/15	
Warranty Information	Seller	7/10/15	
Inspections	Buyer	7/25/15	P.O.C.
Loan Application			
Loan Commitment			
Promissory Note			

EXHIBIT 14-6   (*continued*)

ITEMS	DONE BY	DATE DUE	CHARGE TO
Mortgage/Deed of Trust			
UCC Financing Forms			
Lease List/Rent Roll	Seller	7/10/15	
Security Deposits List	Seller	7/25/15	
Vacancy Summary	Seller	7/25/15	
Tenant Estoppel Certificates	Seller	8/10/15	
Assignment of Leases	Seller	8/30/15	
Schedule of Prepaid Tenants	Seller	8/30/15	
Schedule of Delinquent Tenants	Seller	8/30/15	
Tenant Notice Letter	Seller	8/30/15	
Assignment/Termination of			
Management/Service Contracts	Seller	7/31/15	
Mortgage Estoppel Letter	Seller	8/10/15	
Satisfaction of Mortgage/Deed of Trust	Seller	8/30/15	
Insurance Coverage	Buyer		P.O.C.
Verification of Corporate Status	B and S	S-7/20/15	
Corporate Resolution	B and S	S-6/25/15	
Tax Receipts	Seller	8/30/15	
City Tax Prorated	Seller	8/30/15	
County Tax Prorated	Seller	8/30/15	
Rents Prorated	Seller	8/30/15	
Special Assessments Prorated			
Maintenance Assessments Prorated			
Other Prorations:			
_____	_____	_____	_____
_____	_____	_____	_____
Deed	Seller	8/30/15	
FIRPTA Affidavit	Seller	8/30/15	
Bill of Sale			
Seller's Affidavit	Seller	8/30/15	
Marriage Affidavit			
Closing Statement	Seller	8/30/15	
Recordation of Deed	Seller		Buyer
Recordation of Financing Instrument			
Recordation of UCC Forms			
Recordation of Satisfaction of			
Mortgage/Deed of Trust	Seller		Seller
Doc. Stamps on Deed	Seller	8/30/15	Seller
Doc. Stamps on Financing Instrument			
Intangible Tax on New Mortgage			
1099S Filed	Seller		
State Revenue Form Filed	Seller		
Disbursement to Seller		9/1/15	
Disbursement to Seller's Lender		9/1/15	
Disbursement to Brokers		9/1/15	
Disbursement to Title Company		9/1/15	
Commercial Closing Binder			
Index Prepared	Seller		
Documents Mailed to Buyer			
Other:			
Tax Proration Agreement	Seller	8/30/15	
Tax Reproration Letter			
File Closed _____			

Sample cover letter

EXHIBIT 14–7

July 15, 2015

Dear Tenant:

We are asking that you complete the enclosed Tenant's Estoppel Certificate, which is attached to a copy of your lease, as soon as possible and return it to us at your earliest convenience. We would appreciate it if you could complete and return the form to us by August 10, 2015.

We appreciate your help and thank you for your kind cooperation.

Sincerely,

Mansart Corporation

Payoff statement

EXHIBIT 14–8

PAYOFF STATEMENT

Investor: SCARBOROUGH LIFE INSURANCE COMPANY

Loan #:   560816
Date: August 5, 2015

Borrower Name/Address:
    Mansart Corporation
    705 N.E. 12th Street, Suite 100
    Any City, Any State

Sent to:
Fisher, Ross, and Simon, P.A.
Interest Rate: 7.5%
Interest Paid Through: 7/31/15

Property Address:
    3082 Tavistock Drive
    Any City, Any State

Statement of amount necessary to pay loan in full on September 1, 2015:

Present Balance:	$948,717.49
Interest through August 1, 2015:	$ 5,904.77
Prepayment Penalty (Waived):	$ 0.00
Late Charges Due:	$ 0.00
TOTAL TO PAY LOAN IN FULL:	$954,622.26

Funds received after September 1, 2015, will require the addition of $196.83 interest per day.

Please wire the funds to the following:

Wexford Bank
100 Kettering Place
Any City, Any State
Attn: Peter Fowler

For Credit to:
Scarborough Life Insurance Company
Account #000-7-890778

Please notify our office once the wire has taken place. The Satisfaction of Mortgage will be forwarded after required funds have been received and processed by the investor.

Sincerely,

Shirley Hayes
Loan Service Administrator

Mansart Corporation has already provided WFD Corporation with financial records, including a list of security deposits and a vacancy summary, indicating the percentages of space occupied and vacant. It has submitted a schedule of the tax bills for the last two years, as the current tax bill is as yet unavailable. The vacancy summary and schedule of tax bills are found in Exhibits 14–9 and 14–10, respectively.

Having reviewed all of the items discussed so far, Barbara is ready to draft the closing statement. She will not be using the HUD-1 Uniform Settlement Statement, as this is not a residential closing. Prior to drafting the closing statement and closing documents, Barbara makes several photocopies of certain exhibits attached to

EXHIBIT 14–9   **Vacancy summary**

VACANCY SUMMARY

Building I		**Building II**	
Total units:	29	Total units:	23
Total sq. feet:	35,925	Total sq. feet:	26,930
Units occupied:	25	Units occupied:	22
Sq. feet occupied:	29,110	Sq. feet occupied:	26,645
Units vacant:	4	Units vacant:	1*
Sq. feet vacant:	6,815	Sq. feet vacant:	285*
Vacancy rate (based on # of units):	16%	Vacancy rate (based on # of units):	4%*
Vacancy rate (based on # sq. ft.):	19%	Vacancy rate (based on # sq. ft.):	1%*

Building III	
Total units:	23
Total sq. feet:	27,297
Units occupied:	21
Sq. feet occupied:	25,492
Units vacant:	2
Sq. feet vacant:	1,805
Vacancy rate (based on # of units):	8%
Vacancy rate (based on # sq. ft.):	7%

* Unit/sq. feet is presently occupied by Mansart Corporation as a leasing office.

EXHIBIT 14–10   **Schedule of tax bills**

Real Estate Taxes—Warehouse Buildings				
Building #	Assessed	Square feet	2013	2014
Building I	$1,240,377.00	35,925	$27,620.52	$28,344.11
Building II	$ 856,481.00	26,645	$19,139.14	$19,644.46
Building III	$1,016,143.00	27,297	$22,702.20	$23,301.34

the contract—specifically, the legal description, the permitted exceptions, and the lease list/rent roll—because one or more of these items will be attached to various documents. The closing statement, as executed by the parties at closing, is found in Exhibit 14–11.

Settlement statement	EXHIBIT 14–11

SETTLEMENT STATEMENT

DATE OF CLOSING:	September 1, 2015
SELLER:	MANSART CORPORATION, an Any State corporation
BUYER:	WFD CORPORATION, an Any State corporation
PROPERTY:	See Exhibit A attached hereto

	Credit Seller	Credit Buyer
PURCHASE PRICE (REAL PROPERTY)	$ 2,700,000.00	
DEPOSIT: Held by Fisher, Ross, and Simon, P.A.		$ 50,000.00
TAX PRORATION: Based on $71,289.91 per year; $194.3418 per day × 243 days		$ 47,225.06
SECURITY DEPOSIT LIABILITY: See Schedule Attached.		$ 45,341.98
PREPAID RENT: See Schedule Attached		$ 2,797.72
SUBTOTALS.	$ 2,700,000.00	$145,691.76
CREDIT SELLER LESS CREDIT BUYER.	145,691.76	
CASH DUE BEFORE EXPENSES.	$ 2,554,308.24	

BUYER'S EXPENSES:

Engineering Report	$	628.00
Record Deed	$	44.00
TOTAL BUYER'S EXPENSES	$	672.00

SELLER'S EXPENSES:

Payoff of Outstanding Mortgage.	$	954,622.26
Record Satisfaction of Mortgage	$	10.00
Documentary Stamps	$	18,900.00
Title Insurance.	$	10,175.00
Title Search	$	150.00
Real Estate Commissions.	$	135,000.00*
TOTAL SELLER'S EXPENSES	$ 1,118,857.26	

BUYER'S RECAP:

CASH DUE BEFORE EXPENSES.	$ 2,554,308.24
PLUS BUYER'S EXPENSES	$ 672.00
NET CASH DUE FROM BUYER.	**$ 2,554,980.24**

SELLER'S RECAP:

CASH DUE BEFORE EXPENSES.	$ 2,554,308.24
PLUS DEPOSIT.	$ 50,000.00
LESS SELLER'S EXPENSES	($ 1,118,857.26)
NET CASH DUE TO SELLER.	**$ 1,485,450.98**

*Farrell Realty.	$	67,500.00
Cromwell Realty.	$	67,500.00

EXHIBIT 14-11   *(continued)*

Buyer and Seller hereby acknowledge that the terms of the Agreement for Sale and Purchase between Buyer and Seller (the "Contract") provide that certain obligations of the parties shall survive the Closing (the "Closing") of the sale and purchase contemplated thereby and, to the extent necessary, Buyer and Seller hereby ratify and confirm all such obligations to which the survival language in the Contract is applicable and agree that the provisions of the Contract in which such obligations are stated have survived the Closing and the delivery of the documents at Closing.

The undersigned Buyer and Seller, having read the foregoing Settlement Statement, do hereby acknowledge and approve the disbursements set forth herein and do hereby authorize and direct Closing Attorney and the Title Agent, as applicable, to disburse the funds in accordance herewith.

APPROVED:

MANSART CORPORATION,   WFD CORPORATION,
an Any State corporation   an Any State corporation

By: *Gretchen Mansart*   By: *Walter F. Davidson*
    President   President

The purchase price of the property, $2,700,000, is listed on the first line of the settlement statement shown in Exhibit 14–11. The purchaser put down a $50,000 deposit when it executed the contract, which was put in escrow with Barbara's firm. To prorate the taxes, Barbara took the latest figures for each building, added them together, and then divided by 365 to get a daily rate. She then multiplied by the number of days owed by the seller, as the taxes have not yet been paid for the current year. Next, she totaled the security deposit figures to determine the amount to be credited the purchaser, with the security deposit list to be attached to the closing statement. Having received a list from the client of those tenants who have prepaid rent, she credited the purchaser accordingly. The schedule of prepaid rents, to be attached as an exhibit to the closing statement, is found in Exhibit 14–12.

The purchaser has only two expenses that will be paid at closing: the fee for recording the deed and the cost of the engineering report. The deed is five pages long, as the lengthy legal description and list of permitted exceptions will

EXHIBIT 14-12   **Schedule of prepaid rents**

Schedule of Prepaid Rents			
Building	**Unit**	**Tenant**	**Amount paid**
I	115,117	Colber Creations	$ 821.16 (September)
I	119	Brian Buchanan	$ 288.51 (September)
II	220	J.C. Howell	$ 585.65 (September)
III	328	James Reilly	$1,102.40 (September and October)
		TOTAL	$2,797.72

be attached to it. The list of seller's expenses is longer. As noted earlier, the seller is to pay for all the title work costs, the documentary stamp tax on the deed, the recording of the satisfaction of mortgage, and the real estate commissions. From the payoff statement provided by Scarborough Life Insurance Company, Barbara has inserted the payoff amount to satisfy the seller's outstanding loan obligation.

Barbara next turns her attention to the drafting of the assignment of leases, by which the client assigns all current leases to WFD Corporation. By assigning the leases, the seller is transferring its rights and obligations under the leases to the purchaser. Once completed and reviewed by Ava, Barbara will attach the legal description and lease list/rent roll as exhibits. As noted earlier, in some circumstances the sellers of commercial property assign their current management or service contracts to the purchaser as well. In this instance, however, the contracts will be terminated, as they expire at the end of July, and Mansart Corporation will take responsibility for providing these services for the month of August.

The assignment of leases, as executed by the parties at closing, appears in Exhibit 14–13.

Barbara has received the list of delinquent tenants to provide to the purchaser at closing. At such time as these rents are paid (if at all), the rent proceeds will be applied first to the month in which the rents are received, then to any rent arrearages for months subsequent to the month in which the closing takes place, then to any rent arrearages for the month of closing, and finally to any rent arrearages for the months prior to the month of closing. This being the case, there may be a situation in which the delinquent rents will have to be apportioned between the seller and the purchaser. The schedule of delinquent tenants appears in Exhibit 14–14.

Barbara next turns her attention to the drafting of the deed. The contract stipulates that a special warranty deed is to be delivered. The legal description

Assignment of leases	EXHIBIT 14–13

ASSIGNMENT OF TENANT LEASES AND ASSUMPTION AGREEMENT

THIS ASSIGNMENT OF TENANT LEASES AND ASSUMPTION AGREEMENT is executed by and between MANSART CORPORATION, an Any State corporation ("Assignor"), whose post office address is 705 N.E. 12th Street, Suite 100, Any City, Any State, and WFD CORPORATION, an Any State corporation ("Assignee"), whose post office address is 1200 N.W. 30th Street, Suite 200, Any City, Any State.

WITNESSETH:

Assignor has entered into certain tenant leases with tenants covering leased premises located in the buildings located on a certain tract of land situated in Any County, Any State (the "Property"), more particularly described on Exhibit A attached hereto and made a part hereof for all purposes.

Attached hereto as Exhibit B and made a part hereof for all purposes is a true and correct copy of the list of the tenant leases presently in force (the "Leases").

Assignee desires to purchase from Assignor, and Assignor desires to sell and assign to Assignee, the lessor's interest in the Leases and the leasehold estates created thereby.

NOW, THEREFORE, for and in consideration of the sum of Ten and No/100 Dollars ($10.00) and other good and valuable consideration this day paid and delivered by Assignee to Assignor, Assignor does hereby assign, transfer and deliver to Assignee all of Assignor's right, title and interest in and to all Leases pertaining to the warehouse project located on the Property and the leasehold

EXHIBIT 14-13 *(continued)*

estates created thereby, and all of the rights, benefits and privileges of the lessor thereunder, including without limitation an amount of cash equal to all refundable security, damage or other deposits and unapplied prepaid rentals made under the Leases as shown on the rent roll attached as Exhibit B (the "Rent Roll"), but subject to all terms, conditions, reservations and limitations set forth in the Leases, except Assignor reserves all rights in and to any unpaid rent or other sums due to the Assignor under the Leases attributable to the period of time prior to the date hereof.

TO HAVE AND TO HOLD all and singular the Leases unto Assignee, its successors in interest and assigns, and Assignor does hereby bind itself and its successors to warrant and forever defend all and singular the Leases unto Assignee, its successors in interest and assigns, against every person whomsoever lawfully claiming or attempting to claim the same, or any part thereof, by, through or under Assignor, but not otherwise.

1. It is specifically agreed that Assignor shall not be responsible to the lessees under the Leases for the discharge and performance of any and all duties and obligations to be performed and/or discharged by the lessor thereunder from and after the date hereof. By accepting this Assignment of Tenant Leases and Assumption Agreement and by its execution hereof, Assignee hereby assumes and agrees to perform all of the terms, covenants and conditions of the Leases on the part of the lessor therein required to be performed from and after the date hereof.

2. Assignor hereby certifies that the Rent Roll set forth as Exhibit B attached hereto is a true and correct list of the Leases in effect on the date hereof.

3. All of the covenants, terms and conditions set forth herein shall be binding upon and shall inure to the benefit of the parties hereto and their respective heirs, executors, personal representatives, successors and assigns.

Assignor and Assignee have executed this Assignment of Tenant Leases and Assumption Agreement to be effective as of the 1st day of September, 2015.

WITNESSES:

Alison Simons

Vincent Morris

ASSIGNOR:
MANSART CORPORATION,
an Any State corporation

By: *Gretchen Mansart*
     President

Kevin Smith

ASSIGNEE:
WFD CORPORATION,
an Any State corporation

Carol Burton

By: *Walter F. Davidson*
     President

STATE OF ANY STATE
COUNTY OF ANY COUNTY

The forgoing instrument was acknowledged before me this 1st day of September, 2015, by Gretchen Mansart, President of Mansart Corporation, an Any State corporation, and Walter F. Davidson, President of WFD Corporation, an Any State corporation, who are personally known to me and who acknowledged executing the forgoing document.

WITNESS, my hand and official seal in the State and County last aforesaid this 1st day of September, 2015.

Ellen Dunning
Notary Public
My commission expires: 3/31/16

(Notary Seal)

Schedule of delinquent tenants				EXHIBIT 14-14

Schedule of Delinquent Tenants			
Building	Unit	Tenant	Amount due
I	145	Stevenson Interiors	$514.37 (August $489.37 & Late Fee)
II	236–238	Jeffrey Long	$756.91 (August $731.91 & Late Fee)
III	332–336	Dunmore Systems	$833.78 (August $808.78 & Late Fee)
		TOTAL	$2,105.06

and permitted exceptions will be attached as exhibits to the deed. She also prepares the seller's affidavit and the nonforeign certification, all to be executed by the seller. The deed and nonforeign certification appear in Exhibits 14–15 and 14–16, respectively. (A sample seller's affidavit was provided in the hypothetical found in the previous chapter. The format of such an affidavit used for a commercial closing would be similar to that for the affidavit used in a residential closing and therefore is not included here.) As the purchaser is buying warehouse buildings, no personal property such as appliances or equipment is being purchased as part of the transaction. Furthermore, there are no assignable warranties or guaranties applicable in this transaction. Therefore, Barbara is not preparing a bill of sale.

As mentioned previously, the tax proration set forth on the closing statement is an estimate of the taxes owed, based on the most current tax bill in the seller's possession. It is unlikely that the tax amounts will remain the same in the bill for the current year's taxes; thus, the parties agree to a reproration when the new tax bill becomes available. The seller and the purchaser therefore will sign a tax proration agreement consenting to the adjustment. The agreement prepared by Barbara, as executed by the parties at closing, is found in Exhibit 14–17.

The tenants must be informed that the sale has been completed and be told where to send their rent checks. Barbara prepares a letter of attornment, sometimes referred to as a tenant notice letter, to be sent to all tenants of Tavistock Commercial Plaza. The letter, as signed by both parties, is found in Exhibit 14–18.

Barbara then proceeds to prepare the tax filing forms. Upon closing, she will send a trust account check for the amount of the loan payoff to the bank indicated on Scarborough Life Insurance Company's payoff statement for deposit in Scarborough's account. Barbara has prepared the satisfaction of mortgage for Scarborough to execute and send back to her. Along with a cover letter, she encloses a courier envelope with a self-addressed label to be returned immediately to her firm. The cover letter appears in Exhibit 14–19.

After closing, Barbara will also update the title examination and prepare the owner's policy. When that is done and the deed and satisfaction of mortgage are recorded, she will prepare a closing binder index for each party and send them their set of closing documents. When the tax bill arrives, the necessary adjustment will be made. Exhibit 14–20 provides the letter sent to Mansart Corporation requesting that a check for the tax reproration be sent to WFD Corporation.

EXHIBIT 14–15   Special warranty deed

Prepared by and return to:

Ava Ross, Esquire
Fisher, Ross, and Simon, P.A.
1900 N.W. 13th Avenue
Any City, Any State

SPECIAL WARRANTY DEED

MANSART CORPORATION, an Any State corporation ("Grantor"), whose post office address is 705 N.E. 12th Street, Suite 100, Any City, Any State, for and in consideration of the sum of TEN AND NO/100 DOLLARS ($10.00) paid to Grantor and other good and valuable consideration, the receipt and sufficiency of which are hereby acknowledged, has GRANTED, SOLD and CONVEYED and by these presents does hereby GRANT, SELL and CONVEY unto WFD CORPORATION, an Any State corporation ("Grantee"), whose post office address is 1200 N.W. 30th Street, Suite 200, Any City, Any State, that certain land located in Any County, Any State, and being more particularly described in Exhibit A attached hereto and incorporated herein by reference, together with all improvements located on such land (such land and improvements being collectively referred to as the "Property").

This conveyance is made and accepted subject to all matters (the "Permitted Exceptions") set forth in Exhibit B, attached hereto and incorporated herein by reference.

TO HAVE AND TO HOLD the Property, together with all and singular the rights and appurtenances pertaining thereto, including all of Grantor's right, title and interest in and to adjacent streets, alleys and rights-of-way, subject to the Permitted Exceptions, unto Grantee and Grantee's successors in interest and assigns forever; and Grantor does hereby bind itself and its successors in interest to warrant and forever defend the Property unto Grantee and Grantee's successors in interest and assigns, against every person whomsoever claiming or to claim the same or any part thereof or interest therein, by, through or under Grantor, but not otherwise, subject, however, to the Permitted Exceptions.

EXECUTED as of the 1st day of September, 2015.

WITNESSES: MANSART CORPORATION,
                                                   an Any State corporation

Alison Simons

                                                   By: *Gretchen Mansart*
Vincent Morris   President

STATE OF ANY STATE
COUNTY OF ANY COUNTY

The forgoing instrument was acknowledged before me this 1st day of September, 2015, by Gretchen Mansart, President of Mansart Corporation, an Any State corporation, who is personally known to me and who acknowledged executing the aforesaid document.

WITNESS, my hand and official seal in the State and County last aforesaid this 1st day of September, 2015.

Ellen Dunning
Notary Public
My commission expires: 3/31/16

(Notary Seal)

NONFOREIGN CERTIFICATION

Section 1445 of the Internal Revenue Code provides that a transferee of a United States real property interest must withhold tax if the transferor is a foreign person. To inform the transferee that withholding of tax is not required upon the disposition of a United States real property interest by MANSART CORPORATION, an Any State corporation, the undersigned hereby certifies the following:

1. MANSART CORPORATION, an Any State corporation, is the fee owner of the real property located in Any County, Any State, more particularly described in Exhibit A attached hereto.
2. MANSART CORPORATION is conveying the aforedescribed property to WFD CORPORATION, an Any State corporation.
3. MANSART CORPORATION is not a foreign entity (as that term is defined in the Internal Revenue Code and Income Tax Regulations).
4. The Federal Tax Identification Number for MANSART CORPORATION is 000625425.
5. The address of MANSART CORPORATION is 705 N.E. 12th Avenue, Suite 100, Any City, Any State.
6. The officers of MANSART CORPORATION understand that this certification may be disclosed to the Internal Revenue Service by the transferee and that any false statement contained herein could be punished by fine, imprisonment, or both.
7. That this Affidavit is being given for the purpose of providing an exception from the withholding requirements of Internal Revenue Code Section 1445.

Under penalties of perjury, I declare that I have examined this certification and to the best of my knowledge and belief it is true, correct and complete.

ATTEST: MANSART CORPORATION,
                                                      an Any State corporation

Dean Slater
Secretary   By: _Gretchen Mansart_
                                                      President

(Corporate Seal)

STATE OF ANY STATE
COUNTY OF ANY COUNTY

I HEREBY CERTIFY that on this day before me, an officer duly authorized in the State and County aforesaid to take acknowledgments, personally appeared Gretchen Mansart as President of Mansart Corporation, an Any State corporation, and Dean Slater, as Secretary of Mansart Corporation, an Any State corporation, who are personally known to me and who acknowledged executing and attesting to the aforesaid document.

WITNESS, my hand and official seal in the State and County aforesaid this 1st day of September, 2015.

Ellen Dunning
Notary Public
My commission expires: 3/31/16

(Notary Seal)

EXHIBIT 14–17   **Tax proration agreement**

TAX PRORATION AGREEMENT

Date: September 1, 2015
Seller: Mansart Corporation
Purchaser: WFD Corporation
Property: Tavistock Commercial Plaza
             3082 Tavistock Drive
             Any City, Any State

Seller and Purchaser agree as follows:

1. The closing on the above-described property took place on the above date.
2. The real estate taxes for the current year were estimated because the tax bill for the current year was not available at the time of closing.
3. The real estate taxes shown on the closing statement of the above date are an estimate only.
4. At the time the tax bill for the current year is available, the real estate taxes shall be reprorated, and any adjustment will be promptly paid by the Seller to the Purchaser.
5. The parties, upon review of the closing statement, shall make readjustments for any typographical or mathematical error(s), and any adjustment made shall promptly be paid as applicable.

SELLER: PURCHASER:

MANSART CORPORATION,   WFD CORPORATION,
an Any State corporation   an Any State corporation

By: _Gretchen Mansart_   By: _Walter F. Davidson_
    President   President

EXHIBIT 14–18   **Letter of attornment**

LETTER OF ATTORNMENT

September 1, 2015

RE: NOTICE TO TENANTS OF SALE OF THE TAVISTOCK COMMERCIAL PLAZA, ANY CITY, ANY STATE, TO WFD CORPORATION

Notice is hereby given to the tenants of the Tavistock Commercial Plaza, Any City, Any State (the "Property"), that MANSART CORPORATION, an Any State corporation ("Seller"), has, effective September 1, 2015, sold and conveyed the Property to WFD CORPORATION, an Any State corporation ("Purchaser"), who has assumed all of the obligations of landlord under your lease of a warehouse unit at the Property, accruing after the date hereof, and is responsible for any security deposits delivered by you under the terms of your lease.

Tenants are hereby directed to pay all future rental payments due under the terms of your lease and direct all future inquiries as specified below:

TO: WFD Corporation
        1200 N.W. 30th Street, Suite 200
        Any City, Any State

SELLER: PURCHASER:

MANSART CORPORATION,   WFD CORPORATION,
an Any State corporation   an Any State corporation

By: _Gretchen Mansart_   By: _Walter F. Davidson_
    President   President

Sample cover letter	EXHIBIT 14–19

September 1, 2015

HAND DELIVERED BY COURIER

Wexford Bank
Attn: Peter Fowler
100 Kettering Place
Any City, Any State

RE: Property: Tavistock Commercial Plaza
                   3082 Tavistock Drive
                   Any City, Any State

      Loan No.:   560816

Dear Mr. Fowler:

Enclosed you will find our trust account check in the amount of $954,622.26 representing the amount necessary to pay off the above-described loan as set forth in Scarborough Life Insurance Company's payoff statement dated August 5, 2015. A copy of the payoff statement is enclosed. I have also enclosed a Satisfaction of Mortgage for execution by Scarborough Life Insurance Company, to be returned to our offices for recording. A Federal Express envelope with self-addressed mailing label is provided for your convenience.

If you have any questions, please do not hesitate to contact our offices.

Very truly yours,

Barbara Hammond
Paralegal to Ava Ross, Esquire

Enc.

cc: Mansart Corporation

Letter requesting a check for tax reproration	EXHIBIT 14-20

October 15, 2015

Mansart Corporation
705 N.E. 12th Street, Suite 100
Any City, Any State

Attn: Gretchen Mansart, President

Re: Request for Funds After Tax Reproration

Dear Ms. Mansart:

Enclosed is a copy of the current tax bill for Tavistock Commercial Plaza, which has been forwarded to our offices by the Purchaser.

EXHIBIT 14–20   *(continued)*

At the time of the closing, the real estate taxes were estimated, since the current tax bill was not available. Now that the actual figures are known, the following is a breakdown of the reprorations:

Amount of Actual Tax Bill:	Building I:	$28,950.20
	Building II:	$20,116.40
	Building III:	$23,976.80
	TOTAL	$73,043.40

Actual Tax Proration ($200.1189 per day × 243 days):	$48,628.89
Estimated Tax Proration:	$47,225.06
Difference Due (Please pay this amount):	$ 1,403.83

Please make the check for the difference due payable to and send to the following:

WFD Corporation
1200 N.W. 30th Street, Suite 200
Any City, Any State

Thank you for your prompt attention to this matter. Should you have any questions, please do not hesitate to contact our offices.

Very truly yours,

Ava Ross, Esquire

Enc.

CHAPTER SUMMARY

1. Commercial real estate can be a good investment for those seeking a high rate of return. Although there are risks involved, the investor can minimize those risks by conducting a thorough market analysis and researching comparable projects. The investor must also look at all data pertaining to the subject property, including engineering reports, surveys, plans and specifications, governmental regulations, and the property owner's financial records.

2. When considering the purchase of a commercial property, the investor is most concerned with the break-even point, the point at which gross income equals the total of fixed costs and variable costs. The higher the occupancy rate needed to break even on the property, the poorer the investment.

3. A purchaser of commercial real estate enjoys certain tax advantages in the form of depreciation allowances and deductions for operating expenses.

4. In purchasing commercial real estate, one must expend large amounts of capital. The cost of commercial projects is high, and lending institutions require larger cash down payments than they require when purchasing residential property. The purchaser's capital is tied up in an investment with poor liquidity, as real estate is harder to convert into ready cash than many other forms of investment.

5. The documentation provided by the seller to the purchaser in a commercial transaction includes, but is not limited to the following: (a) a current list of leases and rent roll; (b) a vacancy analysis; (c) surveys, plans, and specifications; (d) a list of security deposits; (e) tenant estoppel certificates; (f) a list of prepaid tenants; (g) a list of delinquent tenants; (h) an assignment of leases; and (i) an assignment of contracts (when applicable).

6. Tenant estoppel certificates verify the terms and conditions of each tenant's lease. They usually state (a) the term of the lease, (b) the current monthly base rent, (c) any monies paid in advance, (d) current operating expense reimbursements or other rent due in addition to the current monthly base rent, (e) the amount of the security deposit held by the landlord, (f) any free rent concessions, and (g) any options to purchase or renew granted the tenant.

7. On a commercial closing statement, the purchaser must be credited for any earnest money deposits, the security deposits held by the seller, and prepaid rents. Rents for the month of closing must be prorated between the parties. A list of the security deposits, a schedule of prepaid tenants, and a schedule of delinquent tenants should accompany the closing statement.

8. In addition to the special documentation provided by the seller in a commercial closing, the seller provides (a) a deed transferring title, (b) a seller's affidavit verifying that there are no outstanding construction or other liens on the property, (c) a bill of sale if there is personal property transferred together with the real property, and (d) a nonforeign certification informing the purchaser that withholding of tax is not required.

WEB RESOURCES

http://real-estate-law.freeadvice.com/

This site is designed for consumers who have basic questions regarding real estate. Numerous general questions are listed, such as "What is commercial real estate?" and "If I am buying commercial real estate, what should go into my contract?" Clicking on a question provides a basic answer easily understood by laypersons. The site is good as an overview of general issues pertaining to commercial real estate transactions.

http://www.irei.com/

This is the site of Institutional Real Estate, Inc., a company that provides information to institutional real estate investors. It provides a glossary of fundamental terms used in connection with commercial real property transactions.

http://www.tannedfeet.com/

This site provides various legal forms used in business and real estate transactions. If you select "Legal Forms," you can access a sample tenant estoppel letter or certificate in Word format that can be customized for a client's transaction.

REVIEW QUESTIONS

1. What are the advantages and disadvantages of investing in commercial real estate?
2. Provide examples of the following:
   a. Operating expenses
   b. Fixed costs
   c. Variable costs
3. What advantages are there to a seller in a sale–leaseback situation?
4. What documentation must be prepared for a commercial closing that is not prepared for a closing of a single-family residence?
5. What clauses are included in a commercial real estate sales contract that do not appear in a residential real estate sales contract?

DISCUSSION QUESTIONS

Questions 1–3 pertain to the following fact pattern. Sellers Tony and Mary Spencer entered into a commercial real estate transaction in which they agreed to sell a commercial property to buyer Henry Sloan for $800,000. Your firm is representing the buyer. The contract calls for a down payment of $40,000, with an additional $40,000 to be deposited in escrow within 90 days of the effective date of the contract, which is May 22. The closing date specified in the contract is November 30. The contract includes a "time is of the essence" clause. The financing clause reads as follows:

3. THIRD-PARTY FINANCING: Within 60 days from Effective Date ("Application Period") Buyer will, at Buyer's expense, apply for third-party financing in the amount of $640,000 . . . to be amortized over a period of 25 years . . . with a fixed interest rate not to exceed 7.5 percent. . . . Buyer will notify Seller immediately upon obtaining financing or being rejected by a lender. If Buyer, after diligent effort, fails to obtain a written commitment within 90 days from Effective Date ("Financing Period"), Buyer may cancel the Contract by giving prompt notice to Seller and Buyer's deposit(s) will be returned to Buyer.

The contract also contains the following provision:

4. TITLE. . . . (a) Evidence of Title: Seller will, at . . . Seller's expense and within 10 days. . . . from date Buyer meets or waives financing contingency in Paragraph 3, deliver to Buyer . . . a title insurance commitment. . . .

In May and again in June, Henry Sloan contacted a bank with which he had a pre-existing relationship to secure financing. Because the closing was not scheduled until the end of November, he was informed by a loan officer that it was too early to submit a loan application, as the bank does not accept loan applications more than 90 days prior to the closing date. On August 7, Henry informed the Spencers that he could not yet obtain a loan commitment because it was too early to apply for a loan but that he intended to go forward with the transaction. Three days later, the Spencers' attorney wrote to your firm, indicating that the Spencers were canceling the contract because the buyer had not yet applied for financing. Your client, Henry Sloan, wants to move forward with this transaction.

1. According to the contract terms, can the sellers cancel the contract? Why or why not?

2. Based on the sellers' decision to cancel the contract, should your client make the second deposit? Why or why not?

3. Does the contract's "time is of the essence" clause play a role in this issue? Why or why not?

4. ABC Corp. is selling an office building to XYZ, Inc. The contract was signed one month ago, and the closing is scheduled to take place next month. The rent rolls for the property indicated that 85 percent of the rental space is rented, with tenant leases running from three to ten years. Many of the leases contain an option to renew. Tenant Jerry Neville, a plastic surgeon, originally signed a five-year lease with an option to renew for an additional five years. The original lease also gave him the right of first refusal should the landlord decide to sell the building. When it came time to renew the lease, Dr. Neville renewed it, and that lease has three more years before it terminates. The president of ABC Corp. did not consider Dr. Neville's first right of refusal when he negotiated the contract to sell the building because the original lease with Dr. Neville was signed seven years ago and he simply forgot about that provision. Now the tenant estoppel certificates are being prepared, and the issue has arisen. Dr. Neville has found out about the sale, and he is angry that he was not given the right of first refusal. He wants to purchase the property, but it is already under contract. How should this matter be resolved?

5. Dr. Leary, a veterinarian, entered into a contract to purchase a commercial building for his veterinary practice. The building is located in an area that is going through a transition period. The current zoning ordinance does not permit use of the property as a veterinary clinic. The seller and the seller's real estate broker both have assured Dr. Leary that they will be able to get the zoning board to permit the clinic, as the clinic would be in line with the redevelopment vision for the area. The contract, containing a zoning contingency, was signed by the parties, and the closing is scheduled to take place at the end of the week. The seller has now informed Dr. Leary that the zoning board did not meet last month as scheduled and that it is not scheduled to meet again until the middle of next month. He again has assured Dr. Leary that obtaining permission of the zoning board to use the property as a clinic should not be a concern because he has discussed the issue informally with a couple of members of the zoning board. Dr. Leary's current loan commitment for financing this transaction is set to expire the day after the scheduled closing date. How should this situation be handled?

ETHICAL QUESTION

Your state's rules of professional conduct include the following rule:

> A lawyer shall not give anything of value to a person for recommending the lawyer's services, except that a lawyer may pay the reasonable cost of advertising or written communication permitted by this rule and may pay the usual charges of a not-for-profit lawyer referral service or other legal service organization.

Your supervising attorney is often asked by real estate clients to recommend a good title insurance company. She always suggests Premium Title Company. In return for this favor, the title agents at Premium always suggest your supervising attorney when their customers ask for the name of a good real estate lawyer. Has your supervising attorney violated the above rule by participating in this arrangement?

Slossberg Law Office on CourseMate

Please go to www.cengagebrain.com to log into CourseMate, access the Slossberg Law Office, and work on your client files. Each module corresponds to a chapter in the text. Within each module, you will be provided with instructions by the supervising attorney. You are asked to keep track of time spent on time sheets. The documents produced through working on client files in the law office can then be compiled into a portfolio of final work product.

CourseMate

The available CourseMate for this text has an interactive eBook and interactive learning tools, including flash cards, quizzes, and more. To learn more about this resource and access free demo CourseMate resources, including the Slossberg Law Office, go to www.cengagebrain.com, and search for this book. To access CourseMate materials that you have purchased, go to login.cengagebrain.com.

Landlord/Tenant Law

15

Residential Leases

CHAPTER OBJECTIVES

Upon completion of this chapter, the student will:

- Understand the various rights and obligations of residential landlords and tenants
- Know the basic provisions to be included in a residential lease
- Know how to draft a residential lease

Introduction

A **lease** serves two functions. First, a lease operates as a contract, expressing the terms and conditions mutually agreed upon by the lessor and lessee. Second, a lease operates as an instrument of conveyance, similar to a deed, conveying from the lessor to the lessee a leasehold estate that includes the right of exclusive possession, but not ownership, in real property for a period of time in return for the payment of rent. The lessor retains a reversionary right in the real property.

Residential leases are governed not only by the common law of contracts but also by state statutes. In addition to state statutes that apply to general real property law, a number of states have adopted the Uniform Residential Landlord and Tenant Act (URLTA). The URLTA, originally approved by the National Conference of Commissioners on Uniform State Laws in 1972 and amended in 1974, was created in recognition of the trend in state law to move away from the English common law treatment of residential leaseholds.

Under English common law, the landlord–tenant relationship was treated primarily as a conveyance of a leasehold rather than as a contractual relationship. Therefore, the covenants made by each party were considered independent covenants, and, as such, the failure of the lessor to abide by his or her covenants did not release the lessee from his or her covenants (or vice versa). Over the years, state laws have recognized that the obligations arising under a residential landlord–tenant relationship should be treated as interdependent obligations.

The URLTA embodies this principle and attempts to treat both parties evenhandedly, covering such issues as the landlord's obligation to maintain the premises, the tenant's obligation to maintain the premises, landlord remedies, tenant remedies, and a tenant's protection against retaliation by the landlord for complaints. At the time of this writing, the URLTA has been adopted by twenty-one states.

Many states allow for the recording of long-term leases in the county in which the leased premises are located. In some states, a **memorandum of lease** may be recorded rather than the actual lease, the memorandum providing only such skeletal information as the names of the lessor and lessee and a description of the leased premises to put others on notice of a transfer of physical possession of the property. However, neither the actual lease nor a memorandum is recorded in most instances. The lessee's physical presence on the property puts third parties on notice of the lessee's leasehold interest in the property.

Paralegals working in the area of real estate law are often asked by their supervising attorneys to review or prepare residential leases. It is important therefore that you understand the rights and duties of both lessor and lessee in a residential tenancy. This chapter focuses on these rights and duties, from the standpoint of both general real property law and the URLTA. The chapter continues with a discussion of common lease provisions and ends with a look at how a lease might be drafted to meet a hypothetical client's needs.

Rights and Duties of the Landlord

Historically, a landlord (the *lessor*) had no duties to provide a tenant (the *lessee*) with a habitable premises unless a lease so provided. It was the lessee's responsibility to inspect the premises, and the lessee was assumed to take the premises as he or she found them under the doctrine of *caveat emptor* (let the buyer beware). A lessor had no common law duty to make needed repairs to the leased premises. Indeed, it could be stated that it was in the lessor's best interests not to repair, for if the lessor was negligent in the manner in which repairs were made, the lessor could be held liable for resulting injuries. On the other hand, if the lessor neither agreed to make nor actually made repairs, the lessor could not be held liable for injuries suffered by the lessee or third parties as a result of dangerous conditions on the leased premises unless those conditions could not have been discovered by reasonable inspection of the premises.

However, because a lessor retained exclusive control over *common areas*, such as hallways, sidewalks, and stairwells, the lessor did have the duty to keep those areas safe, and neglect of a dangerous condition in a common area would lead to potential liability. The lessor's responsibility for common areas has carried over to current law and has been extended to include all fixtures and equipment located in common areas, such as laundry appliances in a common laundry room and exercise equipment in a common exercise room.

The law has expanded over time to increase the nature of a residential lessor's duties. Most states now require that the landlord be held responsible for maintaining the premises in a habitable condition. For example, Alabama, one of the states that has adopted the URLTA, provides in Section 35-9A-204(a) of its statutes that a landlord shall:

(1) comply with the requirements of applicable building and housing codes materially affecting health and safety;

(2) make all repairs and do whatever is necessary to put and keep the premises in a habitable condition;

(3) keep all common areas of the premises in a clean and safe condition;

(4) maintain in good and safe working order and condition all electrical, plumbing, sanitary, heating, ventilating, air-conditioning, and other facilities and appliances, including elevators, supplied or required to be supplied by the landlord;

lease: A document that conveys a leasehold interest in real property that includes the right of possession, but not ownership, for a period of time in return for the payment of rent.

memorandum of lease: A document providing skeletal information of a lease, such as the names of the lessor and lessee and a description of the leased premises. This document is recorded in the county in which the leased premises are located to put others on notice of a transfer of physical possession of the property.

(5) provide and maintain appropriate receptacles and conveniences for the removal of garbage, rubbish, and other waste incidental to the occupancy of the dwelling unit and arrange for their removal; and

(6) supply running water and reasonable amounts of hot water at all times and reasonable heat except where the building that includes the dwelling unit is not required by law to be equipped for that purpose, or the dwelling unit is so constructed that heat or hot water is generated by an installation within the exclusive control of the tenant and supplied by a direct public utility connection.

What constitutes compliance with applicable building, health, and safety codes can vary considerably from state to state. Statutory law or local ordinances may require that the lessor provide pest control services and/or smoke detection devices. Subsection (c) of section 2.104 of the URLTA provides that, if the leased premises are a single-family residence, the lessor and lessee may agree in writing that the lessee will be responsible for trash removal; for the supply of running water, hot water, and heat; and for specified repairs. Further, subsection (d) provides that a lessee and a lessor of leased premises other than a single-family residence may enter into a written lease in which the lessee is responsible for specific repairs—but only if the repair work is not necessary to cure the lessor's noncompliance with applicable building, health, and safety codes.

A lease may expand upon the maintenance duties listed above. A lessor, however, cannot negate his or her statutory responsibilities by inclusion of a lease provision in which the lessee waives the right to a warranty of habitability. Such a provision is unconscionable. In some states, a lessor, while responsible for maintaining and repairing the premises, is allowed to charge the lessee for such services.

Should a lessor fail to maintain the leased premises in a habitable condition, most states allow the lessee legal recourse. Some states require that the lessee provide the lessor with written notice of the lessor's material noncompliance and provide an opportunity to cure before terminating the lease. The lessee may be allowed to make the necessary repairs, or hire someone qualified to do so, and then deduct the cost of the repairs against rent owed. Alternatively, the lessee may be allowed to remain in the premises but *abate* the rent. **Abatement of rent** is a deduction from the rent owed for the diminishment in value of the premises caused by the lack of maintenance.

If the lessor's noncompliance is so egregious as to render the premises uninhabitable by local building, health, or safety code standards, the lessee may not be able to remain on the premises due to the defective conditions. Under these circumstances, the lessor is said to have *constructively evicted* the lessee. Should constructive eviction occur, a lessee is entitled to move out of the premises and will not be held responsible for the rent due for the remainder of the lease term. Constructive eviction is discussed in Chapter 17.

Section 4.101 (a) of the URLTA provides that a lessee may deliver written notice to the lessor specifying the acts or omissions constituting noncompliance and indicating that the lease will terminate if the acts or omissions are not cured within a statutorily prescribed time period. Illustrative of this point, Kentucky, another state that has adopted the URLTA, provides in Section 383.625(1) of its statutes that a lease may be terminated, in compliance with notice requirements, subject to the following:

(a) If the breach is remediable by repairs, the payment of damages or otherwise and the landlord adequately remedies the breach before the date specified in the notice, the rental agreement shall not terminate by reason of the breach.

abatement of rent: A deduction from the rent owed for the diminishment in value of the premises caused by the lack of maintenance.

(b) If substantially the same act or omission which constituted a prior noncompliance covered by subsection (1) of which notice was given recurs within six (6) months, the tenant may terminate the rental agreement upon at least fourteen (14) days' written notice specifying the breach and the date of termination of the rental agreement.

(c) The tenant may not terminate for a condition caused by the deliberate or negligent act or omission of the tenant, a member of his family, or other person on the premises with his consent.

In addition to any remedies available to a lessee for the lessor's failure to maintain and repair the premises, city and county ordinances may impose fines on the lessor for noncompliance.

Most states prohibit the lessor from interrupting essential services, such as electricity, gas, heat, and water. If these services are willfully or negligently interrupted and the interruption is not corrected after proper notice is given, a lessee may be allowed an abatement of rent, may take measures to reinstall the services and deduct the cost from rent owed, or may move out temporarily until such time as the services are reinstalled. In the last instance, the lessee will not be liable for rent during the period in which the services are interrupted and may recover the cost of reasonably suitable housing.

For the protection and preservation of the leased and surrounding property as well as the welfare of the lessee and third parties, a lessor may impose reasonable rules and regulations regarding the use of the leased premises. It is not uncommon, for example, for a lessor to disallow pets, particularly in furnished premises, or to require additional security deposits to cover any potential damage. A lessor may prohibit the playing of loud music before or after certain hours for the welfare of other tenants or may prohibit barbecuing on a balcony. Section 3.102(a) of the URLTA allows a lessor to impose rules and regulations upon the use of leased premises upon the certain conditions. Kansas, which has adopted the URLTA, provides in Section 58-2556 of its statutes that a lessor may enforce a rule or regulation against a lessee only if:

(a) Its purpose is to promote the convenience, safety, peace or welfare of the tenants in the premises, preserve the landlord's property from abusive use or make a fair distribution of services and facilities held out for the tenants generally;

(b) it is reasonably related to the purpose for which it is adopted;

(c) it applies to all tenants in the premises equally;

(d) it is sufficiently explicit in its prohibition, direction or limitation of the tenant's conduct to fairly inform the tenant of what such tenant must or must not do to comply;

(e) it is not for the purpose of evading the obligations of the landlord; and

(f) the tenant has notice of it at the time such tenant enters into the rental agreement.

After the tenant enters into the rental agreement, if a rule or regulation which effects a substantial modification of the rental agreement is adopted, such rule or regulation is not enforceable against the tenant unless such tenant consents to it in writing.

To ensure the protection of the premises and the lessee's compliance with reasonably imposed rules and regulations, state law allows a lessor to inspect the premises periodically. As noted in the lease provisions section in the following text, these inspections must be made at reasonable times and with the consent of the lessee, whose consent cannot be unreasonably withheld.

Most states have case law and/or statutory law that dictates the extent of a lessor's duties to protect lessees from criminal acts of third parties or other lessees. The scope of these duties varies but typically hinges upon the foreseeability of harm caused by the criminal conduct of others on the premises and the ability of a lessor to take measures to prevent its occurrence. If a lessor knows or has reason to know of prior criminal incidents on the premises or in the neighborhood and fails to implement prudent security measures or warn lessees, a lessor may be held civilly liable. Additionally, lessors are expected to take at least minimum precautions to protect their lessees, so if insufficient lighting, faulty locks, or nonexistent security systems facilitate a criminal act on the premises that results in injury, a lessor may be held liable.

In the following Georgia case, the issue of lessor liability rested on whether the lessor had knowledge superior to that of the lessee of any danger.

CASE: *Dolphin Realty v. Headley*

271 Ga. App. 479, 610 S.E.2d 99 (2005)

ANDREWS, Presiding Judge.

Pursuant to our grant of its interlocutory application for appeal, Dolphin Realty d/b/a Riverside House Apartments (Riverside) appeals from the trial court's denial in part of its motion for summary judgment and the trial court's deferral of a ruling on part of the motion on Denise Headley's premises liability claim.

In reviewing the grant or denial of summary judgment, we apply a de novo standard of review and consider the evidence with all reasonable inferences therefrom in favor of the party opposing summary judgment. *Goring v. Martinez*, 224 Ga. App. 137, 138(2), 479 S.E.2d 432 (1996). . . .

So viewed, the undisputed evidence was that Headley rented an apartment at Riverside in August 1997. Riverside is a residential complex of 220 units located approximately a mile north of I-285 in metro Atlanta. Headley's apartment was located on the ground floor, directly across the parking lot from the laundromat of the complex. Headley felt "safe on the ground floor" because she "never heard" of any crime on the property. Betty Head, the resident manager of Riverside for ten years, was also unaware of any serious crimes on the property prior to the incidents involving Headley.

On Friday evening, February 9, 2001, Headley went back and forth to the laundromat while doing her laundry. As was her habit, she left her front door unlocked because the laundromat was so close. During her first several trips, she noticed nothing out of the ordinary. Upon her return to her apartment with a load of clothes, Headley walked into her bedroom and was attacked by an unidentified man. The man put a sharp object to her neck and held his hand over her mouth. During the assault, the man told Headley he would give her some advice—"not to go out after dark and not to do the laundry after dark." Then he said, "you didn't see me in the dark; did you?" After subduing Headley, the man forced her to remove her clothes and perform oral sodomy on him. Following the sexual assault, the man left her on the bed, blindfolded, with her ankles and hands tied. The man then removed numerous items from Headley's apartment, including a television, stereo, alcohol, and money from her purse. Headley freed herself after the man left and the police were called.

Headley also reported the assault to resident manager Head, who was "horrified" and "shocked" because this was the first time a resident had been attacked and sexually assaulted on the property.

The day following the assault, Headley prepared and circulated a flyer to residents of the complex, telling them about the incident and asking for any information they might have about the assailant. After reporting the incident to William Keappler, her superior, Head also drafted a Crime Awareness Letter and distributed it to residents on February 12. In that letter, she advised of the attack, including a description of the attacker, and warned residents to be as "cautious as possible with respect to your property and surroundings." It advised not walking alone around the complex at night, locking the door upon leaving the apartment and immediately contacting law enforcement upon the occurrence of any incident. Finally, it stated that "[a]s you realize, no one can guarantee your safety. We remind you that your security is the responsibility of the local law enforcement and yourself. We

(continued)

believe that by taking an active role in your own security you can help avoid any unnecessary problems." Keappler directed Head to have maintenance make sure that all outside lights on the property were working and to check and see if any trees needed to be cut back or pruned. At least one tree near a light was trimmed back.

No one on behalf of Dolphin Realty had ever conducted a general survey of crimes for the area where Riverside was located, nor was a lighting survey ever conducted of the apartment complex. There were no formal security manuals or policies in place for the complex and no security officer.

Headley decided to remain at Riverside following this assault because she "felt like it was still a good location" and "wasn't a bad crime area otherwise." Following this assault, Headley stopped doing the laundry after dark for a period of time. At some point prior to December, however, she began doing laundry after dark again.

On the evening of December 3, 2001, Headley was doing her laundry after dark. As she returned to her apartment from the laundromat, she heard running footsteps coming down the breezeway as she was closing her front door, which she had locked before going to the laundromat. The same man who had assaulted her in February pushed his way into the apartment and held a sharp object to her neck. Headley recognized the man because he had on the same exact outfit he wore in February, including the tennis shoes. There was no sexual assault, but the man took a television and VCR.

Headley moved from Riverside shortly after this attack, stating at the time that she did not believe the police had been very active in helping her.

Headley claimed that Riverside was negligent in failing to protect her from two attacks by the same assailant based on Riverside's "superior knowledge of the dangerous and defective condition of [the] premises because of prior, substantially similar incidents," because of which Riverside "had reason to anticipate a criminal act would occur on its premises."

Riverside sought summary judgment based on the absence of any legal duty to protect Headley from third-party criminal conduct. Regarding the first attack, the trial court determined, without citing any authority, that police reports and computer printouts indicating property crimes at Riverside's premises provided a sufficient basis upon which to defer ruling on any duty on Riverside regarding the first attack. Regarding the second attack, the trial court denied the motion based upon Riverside's knowledge of the first attack.

1. Dolphin Realty argues, and we agree, that on the record before us, it was entitled to summary judgment regarding the lack of duty owed to Headley prior to the February 2001 assault.

A landlord's duty to its tenants arises under OCGA §51-3-1. In Georgia that duty extends to protecting tenants from third-party criminal acts under certain circumstances. *Doe v. Prudential-Bache, & c. Realty Partners, L.P.*, 268 Ga. 604, 492 S.E.2d 865 (1997); *Sturbridge Partners v. Walker*, 267 Ga. 785, 786, 482 S.E.2d 339 (1997). While the general rule is that a landlord is not an insurer of his tenant's safety, the landlord does have a duty to exercise ordinary care to prevent foreseeable third-party criminal attacks upon tenants. The duty to guard against crime generally arises when, due to prior experience with substantially similar types of crime, the landlord has reason to anticipate criminal acts. A tenant will be precluded from recovery, even where such prior acts are known to the landlord, however, as a matter of law, when he or she has equal or superior knowledge of the risk and fails to exercise ordinary care for his or her own safety. *Johnson v. Atlanta Housing Auth.*, 243 Ga. App. 157, 532 S.E.2d 701 (2000); *Jackson v. Post Properties*, 236 Ga. App. 701-702, 513 S.E.2d 259 (1999); *Habersham Venture v. Breedlove*, 244 Ga. App. 407, 409-410(1), 535 S.E.2d 788 (2000).

Here, the only record of previous property crimes in the area was a computer printout used by Headley's expert showing dates and addresses of various area crimes and numerous copies of crime reports in the area. Pretermitting the issue of the lack of showing of the required similarities, no showing was made of any knowledge on behalf of Dolphin Realty of these crime statistics. In fact, Head and Keappler both affirmatively stated that no such search of crime statistics had been made.

It has repeatedly been held that "[t]here is no authority in this State imposing a duty upon a property owner to investigate police files to determine whether criminal activities have occurred on its premises[.]" *Sun Trust Banks v. Killebrew*, 266 Ga. 109, 464 S.E.2d 207 (1995). See also *Johnson v. Atlanta Housing Auth.*, supra at 159(1), 532 S.E.2d 701.

Therefore, exercising our de novo review, we conclude that Dolphin Realty was entitled to summary judgment regarding the February 2001 assault because Headley failed to come forward and demonstrate knowledge of prior similar crimes that would have put Dolphin Realty on notice and imposed a duty. *Johnson v. Atlanta Housing Auth.*, supra; see *Spear v. Calhoun*, 261 Ga. App. 835, 837-838(1), 584 S.E.2d 71 (2003).

(continued)

2. Regarding the December 2001 assault, we agree with Dolphin Realty that it had no knowledge superior to that of Headley of any danger, pretermitting the issue whether the first incident was sufficient to impose a duty upon Dolphin Realty.

As discussed above, a tenant is precluded from recovery when, as here, she has equal or superior knowledge of the risk and fails to exercise ordinary care for her own safety. E.g., *Habersham Venture*, supra.

Here, after being told by the assailant not to continue to do laundry after dark, Headley proceeded to do just that, knowing her belief, as alleged here, that the lighting was insufficient and foliage interfered with some lighting.

Therefore, Dolphin Realty was entitled to summary judgment on this basis. E.g., *Rice v. Six Flags, & c*, 257 Ga. App. 864, 572 S.E.2d 322 (2002); *Johnson v. Atlanta Housing Auth.*, supra.

Additionally, there was [in]sufficient evidence that the claimed inadequacy of the lighting was the cause in fact of the assailant's ability to gain access to her apartment. For instance, there is no indication that the assailant was not a resident of the complex with equal access to all common areas, regardless of lighting. Therefore, Dolphin Realty was also entitled to summary judgment on this basis. *Brown v. All-Tech Investment Group*, 265 Ga. App. 889, 894(1), 595 S.E.2d 517 (2004); *Niles v. Bd. of Regents, &c, of Ga.*, 222 Ga. App. 59, 61(2), 473 S.E.2d 173 (1996); see also *Fallon v. Metro. Life Ins. Co.*, 238 Ga. App. 156, 158(2), 518 S.E.2d 170 (1999) (physical precedent only); *Post Properties v. Doe*, 230 Ga. App. 34, 37, 495 S.E.2d 573 (1997) (physical precedent only).

Judgment reversed.

ELLINGTON, J., concurs.

MILLER, J., concurs in the judgment only.

Case Questions

1. Does your state impose a statutory requirement on landlords to protect tenants from third-party criminal acts? If it does, applying your state's statutory law to the facts presented in the above case, which party would win if the matter were tried in your state? Why?

2. Do you believe there should be a legal duty imposed upon landlords to investigate police files and/or other statistical data to determine whether criminal activities have occurred on their premises or within a certain geographic parameter of their premises? Why or why not?

3. In the above case, the court stated that a tenant is precluded from recovery when he or she has equal or superior knowledge of the risk and fails to exercise ordinary care for his or her own safety. What do you think of this principle? Do you think the court would have ruled the same way if the second incident was perpetrated by a different assailant? If the second incident occurred during daylight hours? If the second incident occurred at night when Ms. Headley was walking to her car in the parking lot rather than to the laundry room?

If a lessee defaults or breaches a lease agreement, a lessor's remedies may include money damages or injunctive relief. Often, a lease will include a remedies provision. Section 4.201 of the URLTA specifies the remedies available to the lessor for a lessee's noncompliance with a rental agreement. Under this section, should the lessee breach the lease or fail to maintain the leased premises, the lessor may send written notice to the lessee specifying the acts or omissions constituting the breach and notifying the lessee that the lease will terminate if violations are not corrected within a statutorily prescribed time period. It further states that, if the lessee has previously committed the same violation, the lessor need not give the lessee a second opportunity to cure and instead may simply provide written notice that the lessor is terminating the lease within a specified time period.

Neither those states adopting the URLTA nor any other state allows a lessor to evict a lessee without following some degree of due process of law. At common law, a lessor had the right to forcibly remove a lessee for failure to pay rent as well as a right to *distress*, also referred to as *distraint for rent*. **Distress** is the right to seize a lessee's goods to satisfy a rent arrearage. The present statutory trend is away from self-help measures and toward court-supervised proceedings. Section 4.205(b) of the URLTA abolishes distraint for rent. Although some states do consider personal

distress: The right to seize a lessee's goods to satisfy a rent arrearage.

property left behind in a leased premises to be abandoned when the lessee abandons the property and therefore allow the lessor to dispose of the personal property as he or she sees fit, most states consider it unconstitutional to seize personal property by forcible entry to satisfy an outstanding rent obligation without going through formal notice and hearing procedures.

To remove a lessee lawfully, due process typically requires that a lessor bring a *suit for possession*. This procedure, known as *actual eviction*, is covered at length in Chapter 17 of the text. Prior to evicting a lessee, a lessor must serve notice upon the lessee. State statutes dictate the prescribed notice period and the manner in which such notice is to be served. Once proper notice has been served, the lessor files a complaint with the court requesting permission to evict the lessee and retake possession of the leased premises. The lessee is allowed to respond to the complaint. Should the lessee fail to do so, a court may award judgment in favor of the lessor, which judgment will be executed by the sheriff or other court-appointed official. Whether contested or not, until the court renders judgment, the lessor is not entitled to harass the lessee or to interrupt the lessee's essential services. Once the judgment is rendered, the sheriff will oversee the removal of the lessee and the lessee's property from the premises.

In addition to evicting the lessee, the lessor may claim back rents owed. Once the lessee is evicted, however, the lease is terminated, and many states will not allow the lessor to recover future rents unless the lease contains a provision for their collection. Even so, state statute may require that the lessor attempt to mitigate damages by finding another lessee for the premises.

Rights and Duties of the Tenant

A lessee is responsible for more than the prompt payment of rent. State law imposes minimum duties on the conduct of lessees, consistent with local health and safety codes. A lessee must maintain the interior of the leased premises in a clean and safe condition and must use all appliances in a reasonable manner. Although normal wear and tear is expected when one leases property, a lessee must not negligently or willfully destroy property or allow others invited onto the premises to do so. Connecticut's statutes provide an example of a lessee's obligations. Connecticut has adopted the URLTA and Section 47a-11 of its statutes requires a lessee to:

(a) comply with all obligations primarily imposed upon tenants by applicable provisions of any building, housing or fire code materially affecting health and safety;

(b) keep such part of the premises that he occupies and uses as clean and safe as the condition of the premises permits;

(c) remove from his dwelling unit all ashes, garbage, rubbish and other waste in a clean and safe manner to the place provided by the landlord . . .;

(d) keep all plumbing fixtures and appliances in the dwelling unit or used by the tenant as clean as the condition of each fixture or appliance permits;

(e) use all electrical, plumbing, sanitary, heating, ventilating, air conditioning and other facilities and appliances, including elevators, in the premises in a reasonable manner;

(f) not wilfully or negligently destroy, deface, damage, impair or remove any part of the premises or permit any other person to do so;

(g) conduct himself and require other persons on the premises with his consent to conduct themselves in a manner that will not disturb his neighbors' peaceful enjoyment of the premises or constitute a nuisance . . .

Under the URLTA, there is no affirmative duty placed upon a lessee to repair the premises; instead, there is an affirmative duty to use the premises in such a manner as to preserve their condition. Nonetheless, a lease may include a provision obligating the lessee to make specific repairs. A lessee may not make alterations or improvements to a leased premises unless the lease so provides. Further, most states hold the lessee liable for unsafe conditions caused by the lessee that injure the lessee or a third party.

If a lessee fails to maintain the premises in a proper manner, many states allow the lessor, after providing written notification of the violation and having given the lessee the statutorily prescribed time period within which to cure, to enter the premises and make any necessary repairs, which may then be charged to the lessee. In some states, or if the lease so provides, failure to maintain the premises may be considered a material breach of the lease and grounds for termination.

Upon taking lawful possession of the leased premises, a lessee is entitled to a covenant of quiet enjoyment of the premises. This covenant pertains not only to intrusions by third parties but also to unreasonable intrusions or harassment by a lessor. Most states allow a lessee to seek injunctive relief against a lessor's unlawful entry and may additionally allow recovery of attorneys' fees. Further, many states, including those adopting the URLTA, protect a lessee from retaliatory conduct by the lessor. Section 5.101 of the URLTA prohibits a lessor from increasing rent, decreasing services, or threatening eviction in retaliation for complaints lodged against the lessor by the lessee. Further, this section allows a legal presumption of retaliatory conduct if the lessee's complaint was made within a statutorily specified time period prior to the resulting conduct.

Many states have recognized **tenant unions** as a proper means for lessees to find strength in numbers. Lessees forming tenant unions believe that retaliatory conduct is minimized in the face of structured grievance procedures and the requirement of negotiating through elected representatives. Tenant unions may, through their representatives, consolidate tenant complaints, negotiate favorable rent agreements, and ensure compliance with maintenance requirements.

The rights of prospective tenants have been strengthened by the Dodd–Frank Wall Street Reform and Consumer Protection Act's amendment to the Fair Credit Reporting Act (FCRA). Prior to the amendment, landlords had been required to provide rental applicants with an adverse action notice if adverse action was taken regarding the applicant due to information obtained from the applicant's credit report. Adverse action can include denying an applicant or requiring the applicant to pay a higher security deposit. Effective July 21, 2011, landlords are required to disclose an applicant's credit score if the credit score played some role in adverse action taken against the applicant. The notice must include the following disclosures: (1) the numerical credit score used, (2) the range of possible credit scores under the model used, (3) the date on which the credit score was created, (4) the name of the person or entity that provided the credit score, and (5) the top four factors that adversely affected the applicant's credit score. If the number of inquiries made is a key factor, then this must be included.

Most tenants are renting premises that are subject to one or more mortgage loans. The recent dramatic increase in real estate foreclosures has caused legitimate

tenant unions: Organizations that elect representatives to consolidate tenant complaints, negotiate favorable rent agreements, and assure compliance with maintenance requirements.

concern for residential tenants. These residential tenants' concerns were noted and their rights addressed by federal legislation with the passage of the Helping Families Save Their Homes Act of 2009 and, more specifically, Title VII of this Act, which is known as the *Protecting Tenants at Foreclosure Act of 2009.* This Act pertains to foreclosures on federally related mortgage loans on any dwelling or residential real property. It protects tenants under a bona fide lease. A lease is considered bona fide if (1) the tenant is not the mortgagor or a child, spouse, or parent of the mortgagor; (2) the lease is the product of an arm's-length transaction; and (3) the rental price must either be at least fair market value or be government subsidized.

Under the Protecting Tenants at Foreclosure Act of 2009, bona fide leases entered into prior to a notice of foreclosure must be honored until the end of the lease term. An exception is permitted if the purchaser of the foreclosed property will be using the property as his or her primary residence or if the lease is terminable at will under state law. In these circumstances, prior to terminating the existing lease, the purchaser is required to provide the tenant with a ninety-day notice to vacate. Regarding other bona fide tenants, the Act requires a ninety-day notice prior to requiring that they vacate the leased premises. At the time of this writing, this Act is scheduled to sunset on December 31, 2014.

Section 8 Rental Programs

In the current economic climate, some landlords have shown a heightened interest in participating in **Section 8 rental programs.** Section 8 refers to the pertinent section of the United States Housing Act of 1937. Section 8 programs, managed by the U.S. Department of Housing and Urban Development (HUD), subsidize rental payments for qualified low-income families. Both the rental property and the tenants must qualify.

Section 8 assistance is available to families (1) whose members are either U.S. citizens or who have eligible immigration status and (2) whose family income is categorized as "very low income," which HUD defines as a family income that does not exceed 50 percent of the median income for the area. Each year HUD updates its income data, which can be accessed on its income limits documentation system. Data compiled for each county in each state include the median income for the county and the income limits based on the number of individuals in a family unit for each of three categories: low income (80 percent of the median income), very low income (50 percent of the median income), and extremely low income (30 percent of the median income). For example, according to HUD's data for fiscal year 2013, the median family income in Fulton County, Georgia (which includes the Atlanta metropolitan area), was $66,300. For a four-person family, a low family income (80 percent of the median family income for the county) was $53,050, a very low family income was $33,150, and an extremely low family income was $19,900.

Qualified families receive Section 8 vouchers from local public housing authorities. These families then are free to find suitable rental housing. The public housing authority pays the housing subsidy directly to the landlord, and the family pays the difference between the rental amount and the subsidy allowance.

The rental property must meet certain qualifications. The rental price must match the amount HUD calculates as the fair market rent for the geographic location.

Section 8 rental program: A program, managed by HUD, to subsidize rental housing for qualified low-income families.

The property must be inspected prior to contract to assure that it meets the program's housing quality standards.

If all requirements are met, the landlord enters into both a contract with the public housing authority and a separate lease with the tenants. The public housing authority conducts annual income reviews and property inspections to assure continued compliance.

Lease Provisions

A lease is a contract and, as such, must meet the four basic criteria for a contract in order to be legally binding: (1) offer and acceptance, (2) consideration, (3) capacity to contract, and (4) a legal subject matter. The first criterion, offer and acceptance, implies that the parties, the lessor and lessee, have mutually agreed to the terms of the contract. The second criterion, consideration, implies that each party has provided something of legal value—typically, the payment of rent in exchange for the occupation of the leased premises and the accompanying *covenant of quiet enjoyment,* which is the right to possession free from interference. The third criterion, capacity to contract, implies that all parties are of legal age and sound mind when entering into the contract. The fourth criterion, a legal subject matter, implies that the objectives of the contract are legal. To ensure that this last criterion is met, most written contracts include a *severability* provision, discussed later, stating that should any provision in the contract be invalid, it is severed from the remaining provisions, which will continue in force.

Not all leases have to be in writing in order to be legally binding on the parties in the majority of states. In most states, however, the statute of frauds requires that contracts for a term of more than one year be in writing.

As is the case with other contracts, a residential lease may be customized to suit the objectives of the parties to the agreement. While some lessors choose to use standardized lease forms for their expediency and low cost, this is not always suitable. Even if standard leases are used, the parties must understand each provision in terms of their rights and obligations and should be informed that standard lease forms may, and should, be modified to achieve the objectives of both parties.

Standard leases are not always drafted with evenhandedness; many of their provisions are drafted in favor of the lessor. A prospective lessee often feels he or she has unequal bargaining power. Nonetheless, the use of a standardized lease form is not unconscionable in and of itself, so both prospective lessees and prospective lessors should review the lease with an attorney before signing. Ideally, the parties to a lease should have an attorney draft the agreement. Although the specifics will vary, most residential leases contain similar components.

Parties

The *parties* to the lease should be indicated. The lessee may be dealing directly with the lessor or may be dealing with an agent. The lessor's legal name should appear on the lease. If the lessor is a corporation, the lease may need to be approved by the directors or stockholders of the corporation by adoption of a corporate resolution (a formal expression of the decision of a group, adopted by vote). If the lessor is an individual and that individual is married, it is advisable that the names of both the individual and his or her spouse appear on the lease as lessors.

The rental of a condominium or a cooperative may require the approval of a committee of condominium or cooperative owners. Some condominium documents limit the number of times a unit may be rented in a year (for example, only once per year), and some specify the minimum rental periods (for example, three months or longer). If the lessor is the owner of a condominium or cooperative unit, approval procedures and applicable rules should be checked.

The lease should list as lessees all adults who will be living in the leased premises. For example, if Amy Anderson wants to rent a two-bedroom apartment with her good friend Carla Carrington, both names should appear as lessees on the lease. This way, the lessor may hold both Amy and Carla, or either of them, legally responsible for the entire rental payment. The lease should also specify the *number* of parties occupying the premises, indicating separately the number of adults and the number of children. Many zoning ordinances limit the number of persons per square footage.

Use of the Premises

Zoning ordinances may limit the use of the premises to single-family residential purposes, and the lease should acknowledge that the premises will be used only for such purposes. For example:

> *The premises shall be used and occupied by Lessee exclusively as a private, single-family residence, and no part thereof shall be used at any time during the term of this lease by Lessee for the purpose of carrying on any business, profession, or trade of any kind. Lessee shall comply with all laws, ordinances, rules, and orders of appropriate governmental authorities affecting the occupancy, preservation, and cleanliness of the leased premises.*

Description of the Premises

An adequate *description* of the premises should be included. If a single-family house is being leased, the street address often will be adequate. If an apartment is being leased, the street address of the building together with the apartment number should be sufficient. Some states may require the inclusion of a legal description of the premises, so state statutes should be checked. Apartment units are often provided with designated parking spaces. If applicable, designated parking spaces should be noted on the lease.

Lease Term and Renewal

The *lease term* provision should indicate the date the lease commences and the date the lease terminates. If the lessor intends to give the lessee the right to *renew* the lease at the expiration of the lease term, a provision should be included specifying the notice required for election to renew and the terms of renewal. The renewal terms may be included in the original lease or in an addendum to be attached to the original lease. A renewal provision may read as follows.

> *Lessor grants to Lessee the option to renew this lease at the expiration thereof, provided said option is exercised by written notification given by Lessee to Lessor at least ninety (90) days prior to the expiration of this lease. Said renewal shall be accomplished by the execution of an addendum to this lease.*

In addition to or in place of a renewal provision, a lease may give a lessee the option to purchase the premises, usually at a predetermined price, the option to be kept open for a specified time period. This *option to purchase* provision may provide added incentive by crediting rent paid toward the purchase price.

Rent

It is advisable to include in the *rent* provision the total amount of rent due for the entire term of the lease as well as the number of periodic installments, the amount of each, the date they are to commence, and the date each subsequent installment is due (for example, the first of each month). If some or all utilities are included as part of the rent payment, this should be specified. Where the rental payment is to be made may be included in the rent provision or in the *notice* provision of the lease. The following is a sample rent provision.

> *Lessee agrees to pay Lessor, without demand, as rent for the premises the total amount of Twelve Thousand Dollars ($12,000.00), payable in twelve installments of One Thousand Dollars ($1,000.00) per month in advance on the first day of each calendar month beginning May 1, 2015, at the following address: 4500 Commercial Drive, Any City, Any State.*

Some longer leases contain a built-in mechanism for incremental rent increases during the lease period. One type of lease that does this is an **index lease,** which ties the rent to the government cost-of-living index or some similar index and requires periodic changes in the rent amount as determined by the index. It should be noted that, if a lease is calculated this way, there is a chance of a cost-of-living decrease, which will then be translated into a rent decrease. Another type of lease that accomplishes similar results is a **graduated lease,** which provides for rent increases on specified dates in predetermined amounts.

The lessor may wish to include certain penalties for late rent or returned rent checks. These penalties may be part of the rent provision or may be put into a separate provision. For example:

> *Lessee agrees to pay a late charge fee of five percent (5%). If the rental payment is made by check and said check is refused by the designated bank for any reason, Lessee shall be required to redeem said check from Lessor with a money order or cashier's check for rent covered by said check plus a Twenty-Five Dollar ($25.00) service charge and to make all future payments by money order or by certified or cashier's check.*

Deposits

Most lessors will require a *security deposit* from the lessee, either when signing the lease or when first moving into the leased premises. This deposit cannot be treated as rent. The amount of the security deposit may equal one month's rent or may be some other amount. Statutory law prohibits placement of the security deposit in the lessor's personal bank account; rather, it should be kept in a separate account similar to an escrow or trust account. State statutes may include detailed rules regarding security deposits.

Many states set maximum limits on the amount that may be collected (for example, one month's rent), as does section 2.101 of the URLTA. Some statutes give the lessor the choice of placing security deposits in either interest-bearing or noninterest-bearing accounts. If placed in an interest-bearing account, who receives

index lease: A lease that contains a built-in mechanism for incremental rent adjustments during the lease period, tying the rent to the governmental cost-of-living index or some similar index.

graduated lease: A lease that provides for rent increases on specified dates in predetermined amounts.

the interest? Statutory law may dictate that the lessee receives the interest, or it may be silent on the matter, making the payment of interest a point of negotiation between the parties. In either case, a security deposit provision in a lease should specify not only the amount of the deposit but also the type of account in which it will be placed; who receives the interest, if any; when the interest will be paid; the conditions under which the security deposit will be returned; and when it will be returned. For example:

> Upon execution of this lease, Lessee shall pay a security deposit in the amount of One Thousand Dollars ($1,000.00). Said security deposit shall be placed in an interest-bearing account bearing an interest rate of five percent (5%). Accrued interest shall be paid to Lessee at the end of each year in which the lease remains in force. Said security deposit shall be returned in full within ten (10) days after termination of this lease if Lessee returns the premises in good condition, normal wear excepted.

Statutory law may provide that security deposits must be returned within a prescribed time period as well as providing procedures that must be followed if they are retained. For example, some statutes provide that the lessor has a specified number of days within which to return the security deposit with interest, if any, or to give the tenant written notice of the lessor's intention to impose a claim on the deposit and the reason for imposing the claim. Upon receipt of this notice, the lessee is then given a specified number of days within which to object to the claim. Failure of the landlord to abide by the governing law may mean the imposition of punitive or double damages in some states.

In addition to requiring ordinary security deposits, many lessors will require a *pet deposit* if the lease allows the lessee to bring a pet onto the premises. Here again, the lease should indicate the amount of the pet deposit; the conditions under which it will be returned, if refundable; and when it will be returned. If there are any size limitations or other restrictions imposed on the keeping of a pet, these should also be indicated. For example:

> One pet under twenty-five pounds will be allowed. A Five Hundred Dollar ($500.00) pet fee (nonrefundable) must be paid upon the signing of the lease. Pets must be leashed when outside.

Although state statutes cover security deposits, many do not cover pet deposits, so the deposit is left as a point of negotiation between the parties. Further, if pets are not allowed, a statement to that effect should be included, such as the following.

> By the execution of this lease, the Lessee warrants to the Lessor that the Lessee does not have a pet, and further, the Lessee understands that it cannot harbor a pet in this unit during the term and/or extension of this lease.

The Fair Housing Amendments of 1988 prohibit discrimination against individuals with disabilities, and, therefore, persons who are blind or deaf may not be charged additional deposits or be evicted because they have service dogs.

Advance Rent

It is common to request *advance rent* upon execution of a lease. A lessor may require payment of the first month's rent, the last month's rent, or both. It is important that the lease clearly distinguish between monies collected as deposits and monies collected as advance rent. If the monies collected from the lessee are deemed a security deposit, the lessor may not apply those monies to the last month's rent. Additionally, security and other deposits are not considered taxable income to the lessor, unlike advance rents, which are considered as such.

Personalty

It is not uncommon to lease furnished premises. The lease should indicate whether the leased premises are furnished or unfurnished. If furnished, an exhibit should be attached to the lease listing all items contained in the leased premises, preferably room by room, and indicating the condition of each item. This exhibit should be signed by both the lessor and the lessee acknowledging the accuracy of the list.

As a further precaution, the lessor may choose to photograph or videotape the items prior to turning the premises over to the lessee. The photographs or videotape can then serve as a record of the contents and their condition should a dispute later arise. Even when the premises are leased unfurnished, it is good practice for the lessor to do a "walk-through" with the lessee, taking note of the condition of all appliances, cabinetry, plumbing fixtures, floor coverings, and window treatments and signing a statement acknowledging their condition.

Insurance

Insurance coverage is another provision to be included in the lease. It is common for state statutes to require lessors of apartment complexes to carry fire, windstorm, and public liability insurance. However, the personal contents of a rented unfurnished apartment or home are not covered by this insurance, and the lessee must obtain renter's insurance to protect his or her personal property, as in the following provision.

> *It is the Lessee's responsibility to insure all personal property. The Lessee acknowledges and accepts that the Lessor will not be responsible for any loss, theft, or damage to the Lessee's property resulting from any act, occurrence, or event.*

Indemnity

A lease may include an *indemnity* provision, sometimes called an *injury or loss* provision, which safeguards the lessor from any potential liability as a result of personal injury or losses suffered by the lessee or any other person on the leased premises. For example:

> *Unless caused by the willful conduct of Lessor or Lessor's agents, Lessee hereby indemnifies and holds Lessor harmless from any and all suits, actions, damages, liability, and expenses in connection with the loss of life, bodily injury, or property damage arising from or out of any occurrence in, upon, at, or from the premises or the occupancy or use by Lessee of said premises or any part thereof, or occasioned wholly or in part by any act or omission of Lessee, Lessee's agents, contractors, servants, invitees, or licensees.*

A word of caution is warranted here. In a number of states, including those that have adopted the URLTA, provisions exculpating the lessor entirely from all wrongdoing or limiting any liability of the lessor arising under law are illegal (see section 1.403(a)(4) of the URLTA). Therefore, state statutes should be checked prior to drafting an indemnification provision, and great care should be taken in its drafting.

Maintenance and Repairs

A *maintenance/repairs* provision should outline the responsibilities of each party for maintaining and/or repairing the premises. If the lease is silent, many state statutes indicate the duties of the parties. In most states, the lessor is responsible for structural and exterior repairs, and the lessee is responsible for the maintenance of the interior of the premises unless the lease provides otherwise. Nonetheless, including a maintenance/repairs provision in the lease allows the parties to elaborate on and clarify these obligations. For example:

> Lessor will maintain the exterior of the apartment, including but not limited to the exterior walls, doors, windows, and other exterior features, in good condition. Lessee will maintain the interior of the apartment in good and clean condition and in a state of good repair at all times, and shall use and maintain all mechanical equipment, to wit: kitchen appliances, plumbing fixtures and air-conditioning equipment, strictly in accordance with the suggestions and requirements of the manufacturer thereof, and regulations that may from time to time be promulgated by Lessor.

As noted earlier, the lessor upon notice is allowed by state law to enter the leased premises for *inspection* and repair purposes. In a number of states, a lessor may enter at any time for protection of the premises and at a reasonable time and upon reasonable notice to the lessee for the purpose of repairing the premises. Further, some state statutes provide that a lessor may enter when necessary (1) with the consent of the lessee, (2) in case of emergency, (3) when the lessee unreasonably withholds consent, and (4) if the lessee is absent from the premises for a statutorily prescribed time period. The lessor also will desire entry toward the expiration of the lease term in order to show the premises to prospective new lessees, potential purchasers, or mortgagees. A sample entry and inspection provision follows.

> At reasonable times during the term of this lease and any renewal thereof the Lessor and Lessor's agents shall have the right to enter the premises to inspect and to protect the condition of the premises and to repair or to alter the premises and all of Lessor's property contained therein. Lessor reserves the right, at reasonable times during the last sixty (60) days of the term of this lease, to show the premises to prospective lessees.

Alterations

A lessee may desire to make certain *alterations* or *improvements* to the interior of the leased premises. It is advisable that the lease contain a provision requiring that any and all alterations and/or improvements be made only with the written consent of the lessor. This is of particular importance because of the issue of construction liens. If the lessee fails to pay a wallpaper hanger, for example, the wallpaper hanger may, depending on state law, have a statutory right to file a construction lien against the lessor's property. While it is difficult for a lessor to protect himself or herself from such a happening, the lessor should be aware of this possibility.

The lessor could include a provision stating that the tenant has no power or authority to create liens on the property. However, while this provision will be binding on the tenant, it will not be binding on subcontractors or laborers who are third parties. Thus, the lessor could sue the tenant for breach of contract if a construction lien is filed against the property but would still have to deal with the lienor. Additionally, the lessor runs the risk of injury to a subcontractor or an employee of the subcontractor. To guard against this liability, any written consent should require, as a prerequisite to work commencing, that the lessee supply the lessor with written evidence that all persons performing work on the premises carry workers' compensation and any other necessary insurance.

The characterization of these improvements is important. Depending on the nature of the improvements, they may be considered fixtures. The question then becomes whether they are affixed in such a manner that they remain with the premises upon the expiration of the lease. The alterations provision may indicate that all alterations and improvements remain on the premises. The following is a typical example of an alterations and improvements provision.

> *Without the prior written consent of Lessor, Lessee shall make no altera-tions or improvements to the premises including, but not necessarily lim-ited to, interior painting and wallpapering. The Lessee shall have no power or authority to create any lien or allow any lien to attach to the premises. If any such lien attaches, the Lessor shall have the option of paying or discharging the lien, and the Lessee agrees to reimburse the Lessor for all expenses incurred. All alterations, changes and improvements in and about the premises made by Lessee with the exception of Lessee's movable personal property and Lessee's fixtures, removable without damage to the premises, shall become the property of Lessor and remain on the premises at the expiration of the lease.*

Casualty

Unforeseen events happen and often leave damage in their wake. Therefore, a lease should include a provision stipulating how the parties will treat *casualty* or *destruc-tion* to the premises caused through no fault of either party. In the event of a fire, flood, or other casualty that renders the total premises uninhabitable, it is customary that the lease is terminated.

Sometimes even severe damage, although less than total destruction, may be cause for terminating a lease. What are the options if the leased premises are par-tially destroyed? Some provisions allow abatement of all or a portion of the rent until repairs are completed. Other provisions allow a choice between abatement of rent and termination of the lease, the choice given to one or both parties. If repairs are possible but the premises are rendered uninhabitable while the repairs are in progress, who pays for the lessee's temporary accommodation? Again, this is something that must be negotiated by the parties. The following sample provision provides one option.

> *If the premises, or any part thereof, shall be partially damaged by fire or other casualty not due to Lessee's negligence or willful act or that of Lessee's agents, family, or visitors, Lessor shall have the option of promptly repairing the premises or of terminating this lease. In the event that Lessor elects to repair the premises, Lessor and Lessee acknowledge and agree that Lessee's sole remedy, if any, against Lessor, shall be a reasonable abatement of rent, the computation of said abatement to be based upon the extent to which the premises are rendered uninhabitable.*

Subordination

Often, the leased premises will be mortgaged. As a condition for obtaining financ-ing, a lessor may have had to agree to obtain *subordination agreements* from all present and future lessees. A subordination agreement states that the lessee's interests in the premises legally are inferior to those of the financial institution, the mortgagee. Instead of executing a separate subordination agreement, the lessor may choose to include a subordination provision in the lease, such as the following one.

> *This lease and Lessee's interest hereinunder are and shall be subordinate to any liens or encumbrances now or hereinafter placed upon the premises by Lessor, all advances made under any such liens or encumbrances, the interest payable upon any of such liens or encumbrances, and any and all renewals or extensions of such liens or encumbrances.*

Even absent wording to the effect, if a mortgagee or some other person or entity with title superior to that of the lessee should evict the lessee from the premises, the lessee will not be held responsible for the remaining rent owed on the lease.

Assignment and Subletting

Most leases include a provision pertaining to *assignment* and *subletting* of the premises by the lessee. The terms *assignment* and *subletting* are not synonymous. A lessee who transfers all of his or her interest in a lease has *assigned* the lease. A lessee who transfers less than all of his or her interest in a lease has *sublet* the leased premises.

In either circumstance, the original lessee remains legally liable to the lessor for all rents owed under the lease unless the lessor agrees to work a *novation*, which is a substitution of an original party to a contract with a new party, the substitution relieving the substituted party of all legal obligations under the contract. With an assignment, the assignee typically makes rental payments to the lessor, but with a sublet, the sublessee makes rental payments to the original lessee, who, in turn, makes rental payments to the lessor. A lessor generally allows either the assignment of the lease or the subletting of the premises only with his or her prior written consent. A provision that prohibits assignment but is silent with regard to subletting (or vice versa) will be narrowly construed by the courts and will not be read to prohibit both. A typical assignment and subletting provision reads as follows.

> *Without the prior written consent of Lessor, Lessee shall not assign this lease or sublet the premises or any part thereof. An assignment or sublet without the prior written consent of Lessor shall be void and shall, at Lessor's option, constitute a default under this lease.*

Default

A crucial provision in a lease is the *default* provision. This provision specifies the circumstances or actions constituting default by one or both parties. It is not uncommon in residential leases to find that, although this clause emphasizes conduct of the lessee constituting grounds for default, it may tend to omit breaches in performance by the lessor. A lessee's remedies in the event of default or breach by the lessor, however, are governed by state statutory law, and the omission of such remedies in the lease does not negate them.

If the lessee defaults, the lessor usually is required to provide written notice to the lessee of the default and to specify a time period within which the lessee may attempt to cure. If the lessee has defaulted on the lease by failure to pay rent, provision may be made for interest on the rent after default. This provision may include a listing of remedies available to the nonbreaching party, or the available remedies may be set forth in a separate provision. For example:

> *If Lessee defaults in the payment of rent, or any part, or if Lessee breaches or defaults in performance of or in compliance with, or violates any term or condition of this lease, at the option of the Lessor, the lease shall termi-nate, and Lessor may take action for eviction as provided by state statute, re-enter the premises and retake possession, recover damages, including court costs incurred and attorneys' fees, and take any further action pro-vided under law. Lessee shall be given five (5) days' written notice of any default in rental payment and seven (7) days' written notice of any viola-tion of this lease.*

In the event the lessor breaches or defaults, the usual remedy available to the lessee is money damages. Should the lessor default by failing to provide services required under either the lease or state statute, the provision may allow the lessee to hire contractors to supply the necessary services and then charge back the cost of the services against the amount of rent due under the lease. In most states, the pre-vailing party in a breach of contract action is not entitled to attorneys' fees and costs unless the contract so specifies. Therefore, it is necessary to include a statement to that effect in any remedies provision if that intention is desired by the parties.

Abandonment

It is common for a lease to include an *abandonment* provision separate from a de-fault provision, indicating the actions that may be taken by a lessor should a lessee abandon the leased premises. Statutory law typically dictates the actions a lessor may and may not take under these circumstances, and an abandonment provision should be in accordance with state statutory law. As stated earlier in this chapter, some states allow the lessor to lay claim to any personal property the lessee leaves behind in the leased premises, such as in the following sample provision, and may make a distinction between forcible entry for seizure of property and the claiming of abandoned property.

> *If Lessee abandons the premises, Lessor may, at Lessor's option, take posses-sion of the premises without becoming liable to Lessee for damages. If Lessor's right of re-entry is exercised following abandonment of the premises by Lessee, Lessee agrees that Lessor may consider any personal property belonging to Lessee that is left in the premises to also have been abandoned, in which case Lessee agrees that Lessor may dispose of all such personal property in any manner Lessor deems proper, and Lessee hereby relieves Lessor of all liability for doing so.*

Miscellaneous Provisions

All leases contain a *notice* provision, indicating the manner in which and the address to which written notification should be sent to the parties. Additionally, leases usu-ally include several *boilerplate* provisions, which are standard provisions found in most contracts. These may include a clause specifying that this lease is meant to represent the *entirety of the agreement* between the parties and that no prior writ-ten or oral understandings apply. Additionally, the lease may contain a *severability* provision, which states that an invalid portion of the lease shall be severed from the remainder, which shall otherwise remain in full force and effect. Further, the lease may indicate that the law of a certain state controls if any matter concerning the lease is litigated by the parties.

Finally, care should be taken in the execution of a lease. If the lease is to be signed by an agent of either party, that agent's authority must be verified, and the agent's representative capacity should be indicated beneath the appropriate signature line. Similarly, if the lessor is a corporation, only an officer with the requisite authority to bind the corporation may sign the lease. Usually, the corporate resolution approving the lease will indicate which corporate officials have the authority to sign. If not, then the corporation's bylaws or state statutes may specify who may sign contracts on behalf of the corporation.

If the lessor is a partnership, many state statutes provide that the actions of any partner may bind the partnership unless a partnership agreement provides otherwise. A lessee may request either that all partners in the partnership sign the lease or that the lessee be given written verification that the signing partner has the authority to bind the partnership to the lease.

If the parties will record the lease, state statutory law should be followed for the recording of instruments. Many states require that recorded instruments be both witnessed and notarized.

Paralegals may be actively involved in drafting or reviewing residential leases. They may be involved in gathering information by interviewing clients, or they may be asked to draft a lease from the attorney's notes. Even if the law firm has a standard residential lease agreement in its computer files, a paralegal must, as with any other contract, customize the lease to obtain the desired results for the client. If the law firm has a residential lease worksheet, this will prove invaluable in ensuring that all necessary information is obtained prior to drafting the lease. It is advisable, as stated earlier, to include, as an attachment to the lease, a listing of the items found in each room of the premises, providing a description of each item and an assessment of its condition. A sample worksheet and lease attachment are found in the hypothetical client matter that follows.

hypothetical client matter

Checking her tickler file as soon as she arrives at the office this morning, Barbara notices that she has scheduled the drafting of the Munson lease. Michael and Mary Munson are new clients, referred to Ava Ross by another client. Michael Munson's company is transferring him to a position with a subsidiary company located in Washington, D.C. His company has found a house for them to rent just outside of D.C. in Arlington, Virginia, and will paying the moving costs to move their furniture. Because Michael is uncertain at this stage whether the position in D.C. will be permanent or he will be returning to the company's main office in Any State, the Munsons decided to rent out their house in Any State rather than sell it. They have found prospective tenants, the Russells. Raymond and Robin Russell have just moved to Any State and are currently staying with Raymond's brother. They want to rent for a year before making a commitment to purchase a home. They have a six-month-old baby, a two-year-old, and a golden retriever. Many potential lessors

will not allow pets, but the Munsons are agreeable to leasing to pet owners. The Russells also like the fact that a four-bedroom house will allow Robin to have a home office. The Russells have provided references to the Munsons, and, having checked the references, the Munsons are ready to have a lease drafted.

They met yesterday afternoon with attorney Ava Ross, who asked Barbara to sit in on the meeting. After a preliminary discussion, Ava asked Barbara to take the Munsons into the conference room to obtain the necessary information to draft the lease. Barbara used her residential lease worksheet to guide her as she worked with the Munsons. The Munsons are requiring a $1,000 security deposit and a $500 pet deposit to be paid upon the signing of the lease, but they have decided not to ask for the first or last month's rent based on the strength of the Russells' references. At this point, because of the uncertainty of the length of their stay in the D.C. area, the Munsons do not

(continued)

want to give the Russells an automatic renewal option or an option to buy. However, they do want to leave open the possibility of negotiating an extension of the lease should they stay in D.C. longer than a year.

Ava has discussed with them the applicable law in Any State regarding such topics as repairs, indemnification for injury or loss, and eviction. The statutory law of Any State prohibits provisions attempting to exculpate or indemnify lessors from all wrongdoing, and, therefore, Ava has advised the clients against including such an indemnification provision in their lease. However, the statutory law of Any State does allow for distraint of a tenant's property in the case of abandonment, and Ava has suggested that the lease contain a provision that parallels state law on this issue. Ava has also advised the Munsons to make a videotape of the premises prior to turning the premises over to the Russells. This videotape will provide evidence of the condition of the premises prior to leasing should a dispute later arise.

Barbara now pulls out the Munsons' folder and reviews the completed worksheet, which reads as shown in Exhibit 15–1.

Having reviewed the worksheet, Barbara is ready to proceed with the drafting of the lease. She has a skeletal form for a residential lease in her computer files; it contains some of the provision headings she will incorporate into the clients' lease as well as many of the boilerplate provisions found in standard contracts. (Even boilerplate provisions must be scrutinized to make sure they are applicable in each client's situation.) Using this form and her worksheet as guides, she drafts the agreement shown in Exhibit 15–2.

When meeting with the Munsons yesterday afternoon, Barbara worked with them on a list of fixtures that will remain in the house during the lease term. These fixtures included floor, lighting, and window treatments as well as kitchen, bathroom, and laundry appliances. Using this list, Barbara drafts an exhibit to be attached to the lease and signed by all parties (see Exhibit 15–3). This exhibit assures that all parties understand what will remain in the premises and that all parties agree that the items are delivered at the commencement of the lease in the condition indicated on the exhibit.

EXHIBIT 15–1   **Residential lease worksheet**

RESIDENTIAL LEASE WORKSHEET

DATE OF INTAKE: September 17, 2015
ATTORNEY: Ava Ross
PARALEGAL: Barbara Hammond
CLIENT NUMBER: 2231
MATTER NUMBER: 0001
PERSON RESPONSIBLE
FOR INTAKE: Barbara Hammond

1. LESSOR: Michael and Mary Munson
2. ADDRESS: 813 Ridge Lake Boulevard
                           Any City, Any State
3. E-MAIL ADDRESS: mmmunson@xyz.com
4. TELEPHONE: (000) 445-7896   FAX: not applicable
                           CELL: (000) 445-7888
5. LESSEE: Raymond and Robin Russell
6. ADDRESS: 250 Wilcox Street
                           Any City, Any State
7. E-MAIL ADDRESS: rrrussell@xyz.com
8. TELEPHONE: (000) 888-3333   FAX: not applicable
                           CELL: (000) 888-3344
9. ADDRESS OF LEASED PREMISES (Include legal description if
   applicable):   813 Ridge Lake Boulevard
                           Any City, Any State

10. PREMISES ARE ____ FURNISHED   X UNFURNISHED
     (complete contents sheet and
     attach to lease as exhibit)

11. NUMBER OF OCCUPANTS: __2__ ADULTS   __2__ CHILDREN

12. PETS: X ALLOWED   ____ NOT ALLOWED
     IF ALLOWED, SPECIFY NUMBER, TYPE, SIZE, AND ANY CONDITIONS:
     One dog. Lessee shall pay additional deposit for pet upon execution of lease, deposit
     to be returned with security deposit if premises returned in good condition.

13. ASSIGNED PARKING SPACE (If applicable): not applicable

14. LEASE TERM:
     (A) BEGINNING DATE: October 1, 2015
     (B) ENDING DATE: September 30, 2016

15. USE OF PREMISES: Premises are to be used for single-family residential
     purposes only.

16. RENT:
     (A) TOTAL AMOUNT: $21,600.00
     (B) PAID IN 12 INSTALLMENTS OF $1,800.00
     (C) COMMENCEMENT DATE: October 1, 2015
     (D) DUE DATE EACH INSTALLMENT: First of each month

17. SECURITY DEPOSIT FOR PREMISES:
     (A) AMOUNT: $1,000.00
     (B) PLACED IN: ____ INTEREST-BEARING ACCOUNT
          X NONINTEREST-BEARING ACCOUNT
     (C) IF PLACED IN INTEREST-BEARING ACCOUNT, SPECIFY PROCEDURE
          FOR PAYMENT OF INTEREST: not applicable
     (D) RETURN OF SECURITY DEPOSIT (Specify conditions, time period after
          termination of lease, etc.): Security deposit to be returned in full within
          15 days after termination of lease if premises returned in good condition,
          normal wear excepted.

18. OTHER REQUIRED DEPOSITS (Pets, etc.): $500.00 pet deposit to be returned in full
     within 15 days after termination of lease if no evidence of damage to premises
     by pet.

19. ADVANCE RENTS: ____ FIRST MONTH   ____ LAST MONTH
     ____ BOTH   TOTAL: $ N/A

20. UTILITIES PAID BY LESSOR: All utilities to be paid by Lessees.

21. UTILITIES PAID BY LESSEE: Lessees are responsible for paying all utilities.

22. INSURANCE: Lessors shall obtain and continue in force for the duration of the lease
     term an insurance policy covering loss or damages to the premises by fire or other
     perils up to full replacement value. Lessors shall not be responsible for loss or
     damages to any furniture or other contents belonging to the Lessees. It is the
     responsibility of the Lessees to obtain renters' insurance covering such losses.

23. REPAIRS TO BE DONE BY LESSOR: Lessors shall be responsible for all repairs to
     exterior walls, windows, doors, roof, and any other exterior features of the premises.
     Lessors shall also be responsible for all repairs to air-conditioning and heating units.

EXHIBIT 15–1   (*continued*)

24. REPAIRS TO BE DONE BY LESSEE: Lessees shall be responsible for all repairs to the interior of the premises, including plumbing and electrical repairs. Lessees shall be responsible in addition for the upkeep of the front, side, and back yards of the premises.

25. ALTERATIONS/IMPROVEMENTS BY LESSEE: Upon obtaining the written consent of the Lessors, the Lessees may make alterations or improvements to the interior of the premises at Lessees' expense. Any alterations and/or improvements so made shall remain the property of the Lessors at the termination of the lease. Prior to any alterations or improvements made to the interior of the premises, Lessees shall provide Lessors with written evidence that all laborers are covered by workers' compensation and any other necessary insurance. Lessees additionally warrant that the premises of Lessors shall not be subject to any liens for improvements contracted for by Lessees.

26. FIXTURES: The fixtures supplied by Lessors on Exhibit A to the lease shall remain the property of the Lessors at the termination of the lease. Any furniture, appliances, and other personal property supplied by the Lessees that may be removed without damage to the premises shall remain the property of the Lessees at the termination of the lease.

27. OPTION TO RENEW: Should the Lessees desire to extend the lease, they shall provide the Lessors with at least 60 days' written notice prior to the termination of the lease. If the Lessors are agreeable to extending the lease, an addendum to the lease shall be executed by the parties.

28. ASSIGNMENT: Lessees shall not assign this lease without first obtaining the written consent of the Lessors. Lessors may sell, transfer or assign all or any part of their interest in the premises without the consent of the Lessees.

29. SUBLETTING: Lessees shall not sublet all or any portion of the premises without first obtaining the written consent of the Lessors.

30. PENALTIES:
    (A) LATE RENT: Rent received after the 8th of each month shall be considered late rent and a $25.00 late fee shall apply. If rent is not received by the 20th of the month, the Lessees shall be considered in default of this lease and the default provision shall apply.
    (B) RETURNED CHECKS: A $25.00 fee shall be charged for the first returned check. Should any subsequent check be returned for any reason, the Lessees shall be considered in default of this lease and the default provision shall apply.
    (C) OTHER: not applicable

31. SUBORDINATION: This lease and the Lessees' interest hereunder are and shall be subordinate to any liens or encumbrances now or hereinafter placed upon the premises by the Lessors, all advances made under any such liens or encumbrances, the interest payable upon any such liens or encumbrances, and any and all renewals or extensions of such liens or encumbrances.

32. DESTRUCTION OF PREMISES: In the event the premises are destroyed by fire, flood, earthquake, or other act of God, or any other casualty not caused by the Lessees, the lease shall be considered terminated as of the date of the happening of such event. The Lessees shall be responsible for any rents due up to that date, and the Lessors shall refund any rents paid for occupancy beyond that date. Should only part of the premises be destroyed, the rent shall be adjusted accordingly in proportion to the

percentage of the premises so destroyed. If more than 25% of the premises are destroyed, the Lessees shall have the option of paying the adjusted rent or terminating the lease.

33. INDEMNIFICATION: not to be included

34. DEFAULT:
    (A) SPECIFY CONDITIONS CONSTITUTING DEFAULT: Failure by Lessees to pay rent or the payment of rent after the 20th of the month shall be considered default. Failure to maintain the plumbing and electrical systems in good condition or failure to make necessary repairs to said systems or other necessary repairs to the interior of the premises shall be considered default. Failure to maintain the front, side, and back yards of the premises, or using the premises for any purpose other than as a single-family residence, shall be considered default. Having any persons or animals living at the premises other than those specified in the lease shall be considered default. Failure to comply with applicable health codes shall be considered default.
    (B) TIME PERIOD IN WHICH TO CURE: Lessees shall be given written notice of any default and shall be given five days from receipt of such notice to correct. If Lessees have, since the commencement of the lease, received prior written notice from the Lessors of the same or a similar violation, the Lessors, at their option, may choose to give the Lessees five days from receipt of written notice to correct or may choose to pursue those remedies for default available to the Lessors under the terms of this lease.

35. REMEDIES: Should the Lessees be in default of the lease and fail to cure the default, having been properly notified of such default as provided above, the Lessors may declare the lease terminated; enter and retake possession of the premises; remove all persons, animals, and property from the premises; and may sue for any outstanding balance and any damages sustained, including attorneys' fees and costs. Should the Lessors unlawfully terminate the lease, the Lessees may sue for any money damages sustained, including attorneys' fees and costs.

36. ABANDONMENT: If Lessees abandon the premises, Lessors may, at their option, take possession of the premises without becoming liable to the Lessees for damages. If the Lessors' right of re-entry is exercised following abandonment of the premises by the Lessees, the Lessees agree that the Lessors may consider any personal property belonging to the Lessees that is left in the premises to also have been abandoned, in which case the Lessees agree that the Lessors may dispose of all such personal property in any manner the Lessors deem proper, and the Lessees hereby relieve the Lessors of all liability for doing so.

37. NOTICES:
    (A) TO LESSOR: Michael and Mary Munson
        1203 S.E.14th Court
        Arlington, Virginia
    (B) TO LESSEE: Raymond and Robin Russell
        813 Ridge Lake Boulevard
        Any City, Any State

38. ADDITIONAL PROVISIONS: Entry of Lessors: Lessors or their authorized agents may enter premises at reasonable times to inspect. Also, unless an addendum has been executed extending the term of the lease, the Lessors or their authorized agents may show the premises to prospective tenants at reasonable times during the last sixty days of the lease term.

EXHIBIT 15–2   Residential lease agreement

RESIDENTIAL LEASE AGREEMENT

BY THIS LEASE, made and entered into this _____ day of _____, 2015, by and between MICHAEL AND MARY MUNSON (LESSORS) and RAYMOND AND ROBIN RUSSELL (LESSEES), the LESSORS agree to lease an unfurnished, single-family residence located at 813 Ridge Lake Boulevard, Any City, Any State, to the LESSEES under the following terms and conditions.

   I.   **LEASE TERM.** The lease term shall commence on October 1, 2015 and end on September 30, 2016.

   II.   **NUMBER OF OCCUPANTS.** During the term of this lease, the premises shall be occupied by no more than two adults and two children.

   III.   **USE OF PREMISES.** The premises are to be used for single-family residential purposes only.

   IV.   **RENT.** The total amount of rent due under the terms of this lease is Twenty-One Thousand Six Hundred Dollars ($21,600.00), to be paid in monthly installments of One Thousand Eight Hundred Dollars ($1,800.00); payment to commence on October 1, 2015 and to continue to be due on the first day of each month until the expiration of this lease.

   V.   **SECURITY DEPOSITS.** The LESSEES agree, upon the signing of this lease, to pay a security deposit in the amount of One Thousand Dollars ($1,000.00). Said deposit shall be placed by the LESSORS in a noninterest- bearing account and shall be returned in full within fifteen (15) days after the termination of this lease if LESSEES return the premises in good condition, normal wear excepted.

   VI.   **PETS.** LESSEES shall be allowed one dog in or about the premises and, upon the signing of this lease, shall pay a Five Hundred Dollar ($500.00) pet deposit, said deposit to be returned in full within fifteen (15) days after the termination of this lease if there is no evidence of damage to the premises caused by the dog.

   VII.   **UTILITIES.** LESSEES are responsible for paying all utilities, including but not limited to telephone, gas, and electricity.

   VIII.   **INSURANCE.** LESSORS shall obtain and continue in force for the duration of the lease term an insurance policy covering loss or damages to the premises by fire or other perils up to full replacement value. LESSORS shall not be responsible for loss or damages to any furniture or other personal property belonging to the LESSEES. It is the responsibility of the LESSEES to obtain renters' insurance covering such losses.

   IX.   **REPAIRS BY LESSORS.** LESSORS shall be responsible for all repairs to exterior walls, windows, doors, roof, and any other exterior features of the premises. LESSORS shall also be responsible for all repairs to air-conditioning and heating units.

   X.   **REPAIRS BY LESSEES.** LESSEES shall be responsible for all repairs to the interior of the premises, including plumbing and electrical repairs. In addition, LESSEES shall be responsible for the upkeep of the front, side, and back yards of the premises.

   XI.   **ALTERATIONS AND IMPROVEMENTS.** Upon obtaining the written consent of the LESSORS, the LESSEES may make alterations or improvements to the interior of the premises at LESSEES' expense. Any alterations and/or improvements so made shall remain the property of the LESSORS at the termination of the lease. Prior to the commencement of any alterations or improvements, Lessees shall provide the Lessors with written evidence that all laborers are covered by workers' compensation insurance and any other necessary insurance. The Lessees warrant that the premises of the Lessors shall not be subject to any liens for improvements contracted for by the Lessees.

   XII.   **FIXTURES.** The fixtures supplied by LESSORS on Exhibit A to the lease shall remain the property of the LESSORS at the termination of the lease. Any furniture, appliances, and other personal property supplied by the LESSEES that may be removed without damage to the premises shall remain the property of the LESSEES at the termination of the lease.

XIII.   **RENEWAL OPTION.** Should the LESSEES desire to extend the lease, they shall provide the LESSORS with at least sixty (60) days' written notice prior to the termination of the lease. If the LESSORS are agreeable to extending the lease, an addendum to the lease shall be signed by the parties.

XIV.   **ASSIGNMENT.** The LESSEES shall not assign this lease without first obtaining the written consent of the LESSORS. LESSORS may sell, transfer, or assign all or any part of their interest in the premises without the consent of the LESSEES.

XV.   **SUBLETTING.** The LESSEES shall not sublet all or any part of the premises without first obtaining the written consent of the LESSORS.

XVI.   **ENTRY BY LESSORS.** The LESSORS or their authorized agents may enter at reasonable times to inspect the premises. Unless an addendum has been signed by the parties extending the term of the lease, the LESSORS or their authorized agents may show the premises to prospective tenants at reasonable times during the last sixty (60) days of the lease term.

XVII.   **PENALTIES.**
(A)   Rent received after the 8th of each month shall be considered late rent and a Twenty-Five Dollar ($25.00) late fee shall apply. If rent is not received by the 20th of the month, the LESSEES shall be considered in default of this lease and the default provision shall apply.
(B)   A Twenty-Five Dollar ($25.00) fee shall be charged for the first returned rent check. Should any subsequent rent check be returned for any reason, the LESSEES shall be considered in default of this lease and the default provision shall apply.

XVIII.   **SUBORDINATION.** This lease and the LESSEES' interest hereunder are and shall be subordinate to any liens or encumbrances now or hereinafter placed upon the premises by the LESSORS, all advances made under any such liens or encumbrances, the interest payable upon any of such liens or encumbrances, and any and all renewals or extensions of such liens or encumbrances.

XIX.   **DESTRUCTION OF PREMISES.** In the event the premises are destroyed by fire, flood, earthquake, or other act of God or any other casualty not caused by the LESSEES, the lease shall be considered terminated as of the date of the happening of such event. The LESSEES shall be responsible for any rents due up to that date, and the LESSORS shall refund any rents paid for occupancy beyond that date. Should only part of the premises be destroyed, the rent shall be adjusted accordingly in proportion to the percentage of the premises so destroyed. If more than twenty-five percent (25%) of the premises are destroyed, the LESSEES shall have the option of paying the adjusted rent or terminating the lease.

XX.   **DEFAULT.** The LESSEES shall be considered in default of this lease if they:
(A)   fail to pay rent or pay rent after the 20th of the month;
(B)   fail to maintain the plumbing and electrical systems in good condition or fail to make necessary repairs to these systems or other necessary repairs to the interior of the premises;
(C)   fail to maintain the front, side, and back yards of the premises;
(D)   use the premises for any purpose other than as a single-family residence;
(E)   have any persons or animals living in or about the premises other than those specified in the lease; or
(F)   fail to comply with applicable health codes.
The LESSEES shall be given written notice of any default and shall be given five (5) days from receipt of such notice to correct. If LESSEES have, since the commencement of the lease, received prior written notice from the LESSORS of the same or similar violation, the LESSORS, at their option, may choose to give the LESSEES five (5) days from receipt of written notice to correct or may choose to pursue those remedies for default available to the LESSORS under the terms of the lease.

EXHIBIT 15–2 *(continued)*

XXI. **REMEDIES.** Should the LESSEES be in default of the lease and fail to cure such default, having been properly notified of such default as provided above, the LESSORS may declare the lease terminated; enter and retake possession of the premises; remove all persons, animals, and property from the premises; and may sue for any outstanding balance and any damages sustained, including attorneys' fees and costs. Should the LESSORS unlawfully terminate the lease, the LESSEES may sue for any money damages sustained, including attorneys' fees and costs.

XXII. **ABANDONMENT.** If the LESSEES abandon the premises, the LESSORS may, at their option, take possession of the premises without becoming liable to the LESSEES for damages. If the LESSORS' right of re-entry is exercised following abandonment of the premises by the LESSEES, the LESSEES agree that the LESSORS may consider any personal property belonging to the LESSEES that is left in the premises to also have been abandoned, in which case the LESSEES agree that the LESSORS may dispose of all such personal property in any manner the LESSORS deem proper, and the LESSEES hereby relieve the LESSORS of all liability for doing so.

XXIII. **NOTICES.** All rental payments and written notices to the LESSORS shall be sent to the following address: Michael and Mary Munson
                                                              1203 S.E. 14th Court
                                                              Arlington, Virginia
All written notices to the LESSEES shall be sent to the following address:
                                                              Raymond and Robin Russell
                                                              813 Ridge Lake Boulevard
                                                              Any City, Any State

XXIV. **WAIVER.** No waiver of any breach by any party of the terms of this lease shall be deemed a waiver of any subsequent breach.

XXV. **GOVERNING LAW.** This lease shall be construed and governed in accordance with the laws of the State of Any State.

XXVI. **ENTIRE AGREEMENT.** This lease shall constitute the entire agreement between the parties, and any understanding or representation of any kind prior to the date of this lease shall not be binding upon the parties.

XXVII. **MODIFICATION.** Any modification to this lease shall be enforceable only by a written document signed by each party.

XXVIII. **SEVERABILITY.** If, for any reason, any provision of this lease is held invalid, the other provisions of this lease shall remain in effect, insofar as is consistent with law.

IN WITNESS WHEREOF, the parties have executed this lease on the day and year first above written.

LESSORS:

_____
Michael Munson

_____
Mary Munson

LESSEES:

_____
Raymond Russell

_____
Robin Russell

EXHIBIT A

The following items are considered fixtures that shall remain with the LESSORS at the termination of the lease:

ROOM	CONDITION
I. KITCHEN	
kitchen cabinets	good
terracotta tile floor	good
recessed lighting	good
almond miniblinds	good
almond Amana side-by-side refrigerator	good
almond Amana stove and self-cleaning oven	good
almond Amana microwave oven	good
almond Amana dishwasher	good
II. DEN	
terracotta tile floor	good
track lighting	good
almond vertical blinds	good
built-in wall unit	good
III. LIVING ROOM	
off-white wall-to-wall carpeting	good
track lighting	good
off-white damask draperies	good
IV. DINING ROOM	
off-white wall-to-wall carpeting	good
brass chandelier	good
off-white damask draperies	good
V. MASTER BEDROOM	
off-white wall-to-wall carpeting	good
rose damask draperies	good
VI. MASTER BATH	
off-white tile floor	good
off-white cabinets	good
recessed lighting	good
off-white American Standard pedestal sink	good
off-white American Standard toilet	good
stall shower	good
off-white American Standard jacuzzi tub	good
VII. BEDROOM #2	
off-white wall-to-wall carpeting	good
off-white miniblinds	good

ROOM	CONDITION
VIII. BEDROOM #3	
rose wall-to-wall carpeting	good
rose miniblinds	good
IX. BEDROOM #4	
light blue wall-to-wall carpeting	good
light blue miniblinds	good
X. BATHROOM #2	
off-white tile floor	good
recessed lighting	good

EXHIBIT 15–3   *(continued)*

	off-white sink/cabinet combination	good
	off-white American Standard toilet	good
	off-white American Standard tub/shower combination	good
XI.	BATHROOM #3	
	off-white tile floor	good
	recessed lighting	good
	off-white sink/cabinet combination	good
	off-white American Standard toilet	good
XII.	LAUNDRY ROOM	
	terracotta tile floor	good
	fluorescent lighting	good
	white Kenmore clothes washer	good
	white Kenmore clothes dryer	good

The parties hereby acknowledge that the above fixtures are in the condition above stated as of _____, 2015.

LESSORS: LESSEES:

_____   _____
Michael Munson   Raymond Russell

_____   _____
Mary Munson   Robin Russell

CHAPTER SUMMARY

1. Residential leasing is governed by the common law of contracts and real property as well as by federal, state, and local statutory law. The modern trend, reflected in the Uniform Residential Landlord and Tenant Act (URLTA) and in many state statutes, is to provide an equitable distribution of rights and obligations between lessors and lessees.

2. Although historically a lessee took possession of the leased premises under the theory of caveat emptor, present state law requires that a lessor maintain the premises in a habitable condition. Failure to do so could give rise to suit under the possible theories of breach of contract, negligence, and/or strict liability.

3. Lessors may impose reasonable restrictions on the use of the leased premises for the protection of the premises and the welfare of others. A lessor may also enter the leased premises after notice and at reasonable times for the purpose of inspection or repair.

4. Upon breach of a lease by the lessee, a lessor may avail himself or herself of contractual or statutory remedies, which may include injunctive relief, money damages, and/or termination of the lease. However, a lessor may not evict a lessee without following statutorily prescribed procedures.

5. State statutes require that a lessee maintain the leased premises in a clean and safe condition. A lessee is responsible not only for his or her actions in the leased premises but also for the actions of third parties invited onto the premises.

6. Upon taking possession of the leased premises, a lessee is entitled to a covenant of quiet enjoyment, which provides protection from intrusions by third parties as well as unreasonable intrusions by the lessor. The URLTA and many state statutes protect the lessee from retaliatory conduct on the part of the lessor.

7. Should the lessor breach a lease agreement, a variety of remedies may be available to the lessee, depending on the terms of the agreement and state law. A lessee may be entitled to rent abatement, rent withholding, lease termination, money damages, or injunctive relief, based on the nature of the lessor's breach.

8. Families that meet HUD's income qualifications are eligible for governmental assistance with rental housing under Section 8 of the United States Housing Act of 1937. The family unit must qualify as "very low income." Additionally, the rental property must meet physical quality standards and must be rented at fair market rent, as determined by HUD.

9. At a bare minimum, a residential lease should include the names of the parties, a description of the leased premises, the lease term, and the rent amount. A well-drafted lease will include other provisions as well, such as provisions governing security deposits, advance rents, utilities, insurance, repairs, alterations or improvements, assignment and subletting, and default.

WEB RESOURCES

http://www.law.cornell.edu/

This is the site of the Legal Information Institute (LII). It provides an overview of landlord/tenant law.

http://www.lectlaw.com/

This is the site of the 'Lectric Law Library. If you select "Real Estate, Landlord/ Tenant," you can access the full text of the URLTA, with annotations.

http://www.huduser.org/portal/

This is the site of the U.S. Department of Housing and Urban Development's Office of Policy Development and Research. Here you can access income limitation data for Section 8 housing assistance qualifications.

http://www.rentlaw.com/

From this site, you can obtain information on each state's landlord/tenant laws. You also can search each state's eviction laws and find information on security deposits, tenant screening, late fees, and more.

http://www.landlordassociation.org/

This site is geared toward providing resources for landlords. It links to termination notice requirements for each state, landlord/tenant statutes for each state, and HUD guidelines for fair market rents.
Sample residential leases can be found at the following sites:

http://www.ilrg.com/

This is the site of the Internet Legal Research Group (ILRG) Legal Forms Archive. If you choose "Leases and Real Estate" and then select "Agreement to Lease (Residential Lease)," you can view residential leases for each state.

http://www.legaldocs.com/

At this site, you can preview for free a sample residential lease by selecting "Leases" and then clicking on the example of a residential lease (this and other forms at this site must be purchased if you want to download the form).

REVIEW QUESTIONS

1. Explain the duties of a landlord regarding the maintenance of residential leased premises.
2. Explain the duties of a tenant regarding the maintence of residential leased premises.
3. What legal recourse does a residential tenant have if the landlord fails to maintain the leased premises?
4. What remedies are available to a landlord if a residential tenant breaches the lease?
5. What basic provisions should be included in a residential lease?

DISCUSSION QUESTIONS

1. Brian Sullivan and his two children reside in a rental unit at Parkland Apartments. Prior to their moving into the unit, a roach problem had existed in the rental building, and the landlord hired a professional pest control service to treat the entire building for roaches. Brian was not made aware of the problem at the time he signed the lease. A few months after moving into the unit, he received a notice stating that the pest control service would be performing an inspection of the property and requesting that tenants inform the property manager of any insect issues. Brian told the manager that he did see some roaches, and the pest control service subsequently treated his unit. Two months later, Brian again reported a roach problem, and the pest control service returned and retreated the unit. Roaches continued to present an issue, and the treatment was performed for a third time. The cause of the problem turned out to be a single unit within the building that had been improperly maintained by a tenant; the unit's unclean state had caused a roach population to develop. The landlord evicted the tenant and has now changed pest control companies. Brian wants to sue the landlord for violation of the right to quiet enjoyment of his tenancy. Do you think he will be successful with his suit? Why or why not?
2. Based on the fact scenario presented in the previous question, do you believe Brian would have a stronger basis for a lawsuit if he sued on the allegation of breach of the implied warranty of habitability? Why or why not?
3. Timothy Dunn suffers from a disability that confines him to a wheelchair. He receives a housing choice voucher that verifies his eligibility for federal assistance and verifies that money is being set aside to assist him in paying his rent. Timothy submitted an application to rent a one-bedroom apartment in the Oxford Apartments complex. The complex has over 400 rental

units, 15 of which are occupied by tenants who receive federal financial assistance with rent. Timothy also provided Oxford Apartments with copies of his housing voucher and verification of his income from Social Security Disability Insurance (SSDI) and Supplemental Security Income (SSI). The voucher covers approximately 85 percent of the monthly rent, and Timothy is responsible for payment of the remaining 15 percent. Oxford Apartments has a written policy to obtain credit checks and criminal background checks on all applicants. It also imposes minimum income requirements but exempts recipients of federal financial assistance from its minimum income requirements because it may not discriminate against such applicants based on the source of their income.

Oxford Apartments conducted a credit history check on Timothy and found that he has a poor credit history. In addition to unpaid medical, utility, and credit card bills, he owes rent to a prior landlord. Timothy asserts that these credit issues arose between the time of the onset of his disability and subsequent loss of employment and the award of SSDI and SSI benefits and that he is now trying to improve his credit report. Oxford Apartments denied Timothy's rental application based on his poor credit history.

Timothy is now bringing suit against Oxford Apartments for discrimination. In an attempt to rebut poor credit history as the reason for his application denial, Timothy is asserting that Oxford Apartments accepted two tenants with poor credit histories who receive federal financial assistance. Oxford Apartments asserts that one of those tenants has a poor credit history due to medical bills and a child support collection account. The other tenant has been employed by the same company for over twenty years and has a poor credit history due to a bankruptcy filed with her husband many years ago. Do you think the fact that Oxford Apartments made exceptions with these two tenants hurts or helps Timothy's case?

4. In the above fact pattern, Oxford Apartments has a policy of setting minimum income requirements for rental applicants but waives this requirement for recipients of federal financial assistance. Do you think this is a fair practice? Why or why not?

5. Suppose your state legislature was drafting policy guidelines for landlords to follow when screening rental applicants. What guidelines would you impose?

ETHICAL QUESTION

Your supervising attorney has met with client Christa Connolly, who needs a residential lease drafted. After taking down the pertinent information, your supervising attorney turns the task over to you. Christa needs the lease no later than the end of the week. You drafted the lease and put it on your supervising attorney's desk for review three days ago. It is now Friday, and you notice the lease has not yet been reviewed. The client has already phoned twice to check on its progress. When you mention this, your supervising attorney says that she has been too busy to get around to it, that she trusts your work, and that she does not need to look at it. She tells you to call the client and tell her the lease is prepared and ready to be picked up. What should you do?

Slossberg Law Office on CourseMate

Please go to www.cengagebrain.com to log into CourseMate, access the Slossberg Law Office, and work on your client files. Each module corresponds to a chapter in the text. Within each module, you will be provided with instructions by the supervising attorney. You are asked to keep track of time spent on time sheets. The documents produced through working on client files in the law office can then be compiled into a portfolio of final work product.

CourseMate

The available CourseMate for this text has an interactive eBook and interactive learning tools, including flash cards, quizzes, and more. To learn more about this resource and access free demo CourseMate resources, including the Slossberg Law Office, go to www.cengagebrain.com, and search for this book. To access CourseMate materials that you have purchased, go to login.cengagebrain.com.

Commercial Leases

16

CHAPTER OBJECTIVES

Upon completion of this chapter, the student will:

- Know the basic provisions to be included in a commercial lease

- Understand the differences among a gross lease, a graduated lease, a percentage lease, a net lease, and a ground lease

- Understand the special requirements of shopping center, office building, and warehouse leases

- Know how to draft a commercial lease

Introduction

Commercial leases are those leases designed to rent space for business purposes. Although, at the time of this writing, no commercial equivalent to the Uniform Residential Landlord and Tenant Act exists, state statutes typically address the respective responsibilities of commercial landlords and tenants. In many states, commercial statutes parallel residential statutes, with their focus on the handling of security deposits, landlord and tenant obligations regarding maintenance and repair, right of possession upon default, distress for rent, and tort liability, all of which were discussed in detail in the last chapter.

Because a commercial tenant's bargaining power is considered to be on a more even footing with that of a landlord than is the bargaining power of a residential tenant, some state statutes allow more latitude for parties to negotiate their own terms in a commercial lease than would be allowed in a residential lease. For example, landlords may be permitted, by agreement, to allocate more maintenance and repairs to the tenant than would normally occur in residential leases. Additionally, indemnification provisions are found more often in commercial leases than in residential leases. Conversely, commercial landlords may provide more services for their tenants than are provided by residential landlords. For example, a commercial lease may stipulate that the landlord is to provide janitorial and security services over and above those found in a residential building.

As a paralegal working in the area of real estate, you may be called upon by your supervising attorney to review or draft commercial leases. To perform these tasks competently, you need to know the distinctions among various types of commercial leases as well as the provisions found in most commercial leases. This chapter begins with a discussion of the most common types of commercial leases: the gross lease, the graduated lease, the ground lease, the percentage lease, the net lease, and the triple net lease. The chapter then introduces you to provisions generally found in commercial leases and ends with a discussion of those provisions particular to shopping center, office, and warehouse leases, respectively.

Types of Commercial Leases

The Gross Lease

A **gross lease** is a lease in which the lessee pays a fixed amount as basic rent and is not required to pay any portion of the lessor's operating expenses. A gross lease is used most often in less complex transactions, such as in the case of warehouse and executive office suite leases. The following is a sample rent provision for a gross lease.

> *Tenant shall pay unto Landlord a total rent of Nine Thousand Six Hundred Dollars ($9,600.00) per annum, together with any applicable use tax, commencing on March 1, 2015 until the end of the Lease Term. Said rent shall be paid without demand, in equal monthly installments, in advance, on the first day of each calendar month of the Lease Term.*

The Graduated Lease

Commercial leases usually are long-term, requiring the lessor to take into consideration the role of inflation, adjustable mortgage rates, and other factors that may raise the lessor's costs over the lease term. A **graduated lease** is a lease that contains a rent adjustment clause, allowing for the increase and, less often, the decrease of the rent to be paid over the term of the lease. This clause may be tied to the Consumer Price Index or some other commonly used index. The Consumer Price Index typically is used because it is adjusted annually and is tied to the concept of purchasing power. In some cases, a lessor may simply provide that the rent will be increased by a specified percentage each year of the lease term, regardless of whether the lessor's actual costs increase, decrease, or remain the same. A typical rent adjustment provision follows.

> *The base rent shall be Twenty-Five Thousand Dollars ($25,000.00), plus any applicable sales or use tax, for the first year of the Lease Term, said base rent to be adjusted on the first day of each subsequent year of the Lease Term in the same percentage as any increase in the Consumer Price Index.*

The Percentage Lease

A **percentage lease,** commonly used by retail centers, is a lease in which, in addition to the base rent, the lessee is obligated to pay a specified percentage of the lessee's sales receipts to the lessor. Although the percentage may be negotiated by the parties to the lease, the National Association of Realtors® publishes a listing of the percentages used most often with various types of retail and service businesses. Many variations of this form of lease are possible.

Some percentage leases base computations on gross sales figures, while others base computations on net sales figures. A definition of *gross sales* or *net sales* should be included in the lease to avoid ambiguity. The stated percentage of sales

gross lease: A lease in which the lessee pays a fixed amount as basic rent and is not required to pay any portion of the lessor's operating expenses.

graduated lease: A lease that contains a rent adjustment clause, allowing for the increase and, less often, the decrease of the rent to be paid over the term of the lease.

percentage lease: A lease in which, in addition to the base rent, the lessee is obligated to pay a specific percentage of the lessee's sales receipts to the lessor.

receipts may be required to be paid, regardless of the total amount of gross (or net) sales accrued, or it may "kick in" only after sales reach a stated level.

The lessor will require access to the financial records of each lessee to verify that the correct amounts are paid. These records usually are provided to the lessor for inspection quarterly, semiannually, at the end of the lessee's fiscal year, at the end of a calendar year, or at the end of each year of the lease term. Similarly, the lessee may be required to pay the stated percentage at the end of the year (fiscal, calendar, or otherwise) or may be required to make monthly, quarterly, or semi-annual estimated payments, adjusting the payment amounts accordingly at the end of the lessee's fiscal year. The following provides an example of a percentage provision.

> Tenant shall pay unto Landlord the base rent of Thirty-Six Thousand Dol-lars ($36,000.00) per annum, plus any applicable sales and use tax, said base rent to be paid without demand in equal monthly installments. In addition to the base rent, Tenant shall pay unto Landlord Three Percent (3%) of Tenant's annual gross sales for all annual gross sales over the ag-gregate sum of Five Hundred Thousand Dollars ($500,000.00). "Gross sales" is herein defined to include all sales made on the leased premises, including those sales made to employees.

The Net Lease

A **net lease** is a lease in which the lessee, in addition to the base rent, is obligated to pay a pro rata share of some of the lessor's operating expenses. The targeted operat-ing expenses may include, but need not be limited to, real property taxes, utilities, insurance, and maintenance charges. Under a **triple net lease,** a lessee pays a pro rata share of all of the lessor's expenses. A net lease or triple net lease provision should define the term *operating expenses* very clearly. Because the lessee is paying a portion of the operating expenses, the lessee may request inspection of the lessor's records with respect to such expenses, including tax assessments from the property appraiser's office, utility bills, and contracts with insurance and maintenance com-panies. A triple net provision is set forth below.

> This Lease is a triple net lease. Landlord is not responsible for any Operat-ing Expenses arising from or relating to the Premises. Tenant shall pay Ten Percent (10%) of all Operating Expenses as said Expenses are defined in this Lease. Tenant shall pay estimated Operating Expenses in equal quar-terly installments as such amounts shall be estimated from time to time by Landlord, adjustments to be made accordingly at the end of each year of the Lease Term. For the purposes of this Lease "Operating Expenses" shall mean any amounts paid or payable, whether by Landlord or by others on behalf of Landlord, arising out of Landlord's ownership, maintenance, operation, repair, replacement, and administration of the Office Building.

The Ground Lease

A **ground lease** is a lease for a parcel of vacant real property. The lease period may be for up to ninety-nine years or some similar exceedingly lengthy period. The leased property is then used for the construction of a commercial structure, be it a shopping center, office building, or industrial complex. The purpose of the ground lease is to defray the costs of purchasing the real property upon which the structure

net lease: A lease in which the lessee, in addition to the base rent, is obligated to pay a pro rata share of some of the lessor's operating expenses.

triple net lease: A lease in which the lessee, in addition to the base rent, is obligated to pay a pro rata share of all of the lessor's expenses.

ground lease: A lease for a parcel of vacant real property.

is built. A lessee may deduct the entirety of the rent payments on the land as a business expense. If the lessee purchased the land, only a portion of the mortgage payments would be deductible—specifically, that portion allocated to interest. This tax advantage might very well make a vacant parcel more attractive to a business looking to build on a large scale. Additionally, since a lessee is not buying the land, but only leasing it, a ground lease will decrease the amount of financing required because the lessee will require a loan only for the construction of improvements (for example, the office building, the shopping center), not for the purchase of the land upon which the improvements will be located.

The lending institution, on the other hand, may disfavor a ground lease because upon default of the construction loan by the lessee and subsequent foreclosure, the lending institution will step into the shoes of the lessee, acquiring only a leasehold, rather than a freehold, interest in the land itself. The lending institution, as mortgagee, therefore will want to include, in any construction loan agreement, provisions protecting its position. For example, the mortgagee might require that the lessor subordinate its title to the land in favor of the mortgagee. Barring such a provision, the mortgagee may require a provision that allows the mortgagee to cure any default by the lessee under the lease and seek repayment from the lessee.

Basic Elements of a Commercial Lease

Parties

Many of the basic provisions of a commercial lease are quite similar to those provisions found in a residential lease. The opening paragraph of the lease names the *parties* to the lease and often includes the date upon which the lease is signed by the parties. Unlike a residential lease, in which one party, the lessor, is often a business entity entering into the lease with an individual tenant, a commercial lease typically is an agreement entered into by two business entities.

The lessor is often a corporation, partnership, limited partnership, limited liability partnership, limited liability limited partnership, or limited liability company and must be identified as such on the lease (for example, Prestige Commercial Enterprises, Inc., an Any State corporation, or Prestige Commercial Group, an Any State partnership). Likewise, the lessee is often a business entity renting office or retail space, and the lessee's proper legal name should appear on the lease.

It is common for an individual to enter into a commercial lease on behalf of a yet-to-be-created corporation. For example, Arlene Tyson may scout out potential retail space for a new business selling household accessories. She may want to secure a lease in a prime location before the space is taken by someone else, even if the articles of incorporation for the new business, Panache Accessories, Inc., have yet to be drafted and filed with the secretary of state's office. If Arlene enters into a commercial lease agreement before the corporation is legally created, she is signing the lease as a promoter, not as an officer, of the corporation. This means that she is individually liable for payment of the rent and the observance of all conditions of the lease. Therefore, the lease requires a clause allowing Arlene to assign her interest in the leased premises to the new corporation, once the corporation is legally created by the filing of the articles of incorporation and the issuing of a certificate of incorporation by the secretary of state.

If the lessee is a corporation, a limited liability company, limited liability partnership, or limited liability limited partnership, the lessor may want certain personal guarantees with regard to the rent. In these businesses, the owners are not personally liable for business debts. If this business entity is a lessee and fails to pay rent, the lessor's only recourse is to seek a judgment against the business assets, which may be insufficient; the lessor cannot recover from the owners personally.

To guard against this contingency, the lessor will want to investigate the potential lessee's financial status. Further, the lessor may require that the individual owners be parties to the lease as well as entering into the lease as officers of the corporation. Or, instead of having the owners be parties, the lessor may require that the corporation be the named party and the individual owners sign as personal guarantors. Another option is to require sufficient deposits and advance rents (including last month's rent) to make it costly for the lessee to abandon the premises.

Description of the Premises

The introductory paragraph setting forth the parties to the lease is followed by a provision *describing the leased premises*. This provision will include the street address, the square footage of the leased space, the suite number for office space or the bay number for warehouse space, and the fixtures provided. This provision may also include a description of designated parking, or the designated parking may be contained in a separate provision. The following provisions are examples of premises and parking provisions.

> **Premises.** *Landlord does lease unto Tenant the retail premises located in the retail center known as Magnolia Plaza, 2300 Independence Avenue, Any City, Any State, consisting of approximately 2,000 square feet, including all plumbing, electrical, sewerage, heating, air-conditioning, and other utility fixtures thereof, together with the use of all common areas.*

> **Parking.** *The Tenant shall use the parking spaces that extend immediately in front of and/or immediately to the rear of the demised premises.*

Lease Term and Renewal

The *lease term* provision in a commercial lease usually provides for a longer rental period than is found in residential leases. One reason for this is that a commercial tenant often invests a great deal of money in improvements, alterations, and trade fixtures to conform the rental space to the needs of the business. For example, a restaurant renting space in a mall or strip center may spend considerable time and money outfitting the space with the kitchen equipment and decor necessary to create just the right ambience. Another reason for the lengthier lease terms found in commercial leases is the fact that, unless the business is a well-recognized chain name, it will need to remain in one location for an extended period before it becomes well known. An example of a lease-term provision follows.

> *The term of this Lease shall be thirty-six (36) months commencing upon January 1, 2015 ("Commencement Date") and ending December 31, 2018 ("Expiration Date"). At the expiration of this Lease, Tenant will vacate and surrender the Premises to Landlord in accordance with the terms hereof and said Premises shall be in a broomclean condition.*

If the lessor intends to give the lessee the right or option to *renew* the lease, the terms and conditions for the renewal should be set forth either as a provision within the lease or as an addendum to the lease. The lease renewal period may be for the same length or for a different length than the original lease term, and, typically, it will be at a higher base rent price. A renewal provision may read as follows.

> *Provided that Tenant is in good standing and has performed all of the terms and conditions under this Lease, the Tenant shall have the option to extend the Lease for an additional thirty-six (36) months on the same terms and conditions of this Lease by giving Landlord three (3) months' advance written notice of its intent to exercise this option. Said notice shall be delivered by certified mail, return receipt requested. The base rent for the renewal period will be:*
>
> > Year 1: $30,000.00
> > Year 2: $31,500.00
> > Year 3: $33,000.00
>
> *Except as otherwise provided herein, the terms and conditions of the Lease remain in full force and effect.*

Early Termination

Conversely, the lease may include a provision permitting the lessee to *terminate the lease* prior to the lease's expiration date. For new businesses, this is a particularly attractive provision because of the risk involved with new business ventures. Most businesses do not realize profits until their second or third year, and many new entrepreneurs find they do not have the capital resources to hold out for the duration. A provision permitting early termination may provide for the payment of a penalty in exchange for release from the lease obligations; nonetheless, the penalty required usually is much less than what the lessee would contractually be obligated to pay under the full lease term.

If the commercial building or center is mortgaged, the lending institution's approval may be required for early termination. The lending institution's loan to the lessor is secured by the real property and the improvements thereon (for example, the building or center). The value of the improvements increases proportionately with the percentage of space rented. In order to safeguard the value of its collateral, the lending institution may, as part of the loan agreement, prohibit early termination of leases. The following is an example of an early termination provision.

> *Provided that the Tenant shall have been in good standing and has performed all of the terms and conditions under this Lease, the Tenant shall have the option to shorten the term of the Lease to eighteen (18) months by giving the Landlord three (3) months' advance written notice of its intent to exercise this option. Said notice shall be delivered by certified mail, return receipt requested. The Tenant agrees to pay the Landlord one (1) month's rent as a penalty for the early termination of this Lease Agreement. Payment of the penalty must be tendered at the same time as the notice to exercise this option.*

Use of the Premises

The *use of the premises* should be clearly stated. This provision should specify that the tenant's use of the premises must comply with all state, county, and city regulations, including occupational licensing and zoning regulations. This provision may also state that the lessee cannot use the premises in such a manner as to cause an increase in the payments of, or invalidate, the lessor's insurance policies. The following is a sample use provision.

> *Tenant shall use the Premises solely for the purpose of selling retail clothing and accessories and for no other use or purpose whatsoever. Tenant shall comply with all laws, ordinances, rules, and regulations of applicable governmental authorities respecting the use, operation, and activities of the Premises. Tenant shall not make any use of the Premises that would make void or voidable any policy of fire or extended coverage insurance covering the Premises.*

Rent

The drafting of the *rent* provision is dependent on the type of commercial lease agreement. As noted earlier, the lease may be a gross lease, a percentage lease, a net lease, a triple net lease, a graduated lease, or a lease combining several different characteristics, such as a triple net lease with a graduated rent schedule for the minimum base rent. Because commercial leases customarily are long-term leases, the lessor will want to include a rent adjustment mechanism in the lease to hedge against inflation and increased costs, including the costs of any adjustable-rate mortgage on the property.

The rent provision should specify the total base rent, the amount to be paid in each installment, the date upon which each installment is due, and any costs to be paid in addition to the base rent. In many states, the lessor is required to collect applicable sales and use tax. The lessor may impose in the rent provision or in a separate provision a penalty for the *late payment of rent.*

> *Tenant agrees to pay to Landlord rent at the annual rate of Twenty-Four Thousand Dollars ($24,000.00) plus any sales and use tax which Tenant covenants to pay to Landlord in equal monthly installments of Two Thousand Dollars ($2,000.00) plus applicable sales and use tax in advance of the first day of each calendar month of each year of the term, without prior demand. Upon Tenant's failure to pay rent when the same is due, Tenant shall pay to Landlord, as liquidated damages for such failure, six percent (6%) of the delinquent sum per day for each day such payment of rent is delinquent.*

Taxes

Apart from sales and use taxes, a commercial lease should cover the payment of any and all other applicable *taxes,* setting forth each party's responsibility for payment. In a triple net lease, for example, the lessee is responsible for its pro rata share of the lessor's real estate taxes on the property. Even in gross leases, a lessor may tie payment of additional rent to the lessor's increased real estate taxes and assessments. Additionally, the personal property and trade fixtures of the lessee have a bearing on the assessed value of the lessor's shopping center or office building, and the lessor may desire to include a provision in which the lessee is required to pay for any increase in taxes resulting from such a situation, as in the following sample provision.

> *Landlord shall pay all real estate taxes and insurance relating to Trident Towers. Tenant shall be liable for all insurance premiums and taxes levied against personal property and trade fixtures placed by Tenant in and about the demised premises. If any such taxes are levied against Landlord*

or Landlord's property and Landlord pays same or if the assessed value of Landlord's property is increased by the inclusion thereof, Tenant, upon demand, shall pay to Landlord the taxes resulting from such increase in assessment.

Security Deposit

Just as in the case of residential leases, commercial leases contain a provision setting forth the amount of the *security deposit* to be paid by the lessee, the type of account in which the deposit will be held, the conditions under which the deposit will be returned, and the time at which the deposit will be returned. Some state statutes specify the time period within which a lessor must return a security deposit.

Upon execution of this Lease, Tenant shall pay Landlord a security deposit in the amount of one (1) month's rent. The security deposit shall not constitute the payment of Minimum Rent, or any portion thereof, but shall be returned to Tenant within ten (10) business days following the expiration of the Lease Term and the observance and performance by Tenant of all conditions and obligations stated in this Lease. The security deposit shall not bear interest.

Advance Rents

The lessor will want to collect any *advance rents* upon the signing of the commercial lease, usually the first and last month's rent. Note that inasmuch as most commercial leases have a duration of several years and include a rent adjustment provision, the last month's rent often is greater than the first month's rent.

Upon execution of this Lease, Tenant shall pay to Landlord the first and last month's rent (plus the security deposit provided elsewhere in this Lease), which amounts are as follows:

First month's rent: $2,088.00 plus sales tax
Last month's rent: $2,313.00 plus sales tax

Utilities

A commercial lease may provide that the lessee is responsible for all *utilities*, that the lessor is responsible for all utilities, that each party is responsible for a specified percentage of the utility costs, or that each party is responsible for specified utility charges. If the lessee is a tenant in an executive office suite, for example, the lessor often pays for all utilities during normal business hours. In a retail shopping center, on the other hand, it is common for the lessee to be responsible for all utilities. A lessor may agree to pay utility charges as long as such charges do not exceed a certain amount and may charge the lessee for any increased amount, such as in the following provision.

Landlord at its expense will furnish electricity (that consumed by normal office equipment), water, and sewer for Tenant. Air conditioning and heating will be provided Monday through Friday from 8:00 a.m. to 5:30 p.m., excluding legal holidays. If, in any calendar year during the Lease Term or any renewal or extension thereof, the annual electrical or water/sewer rates are greater than the same charges for the prior calendar year, tenant shall pay, in addition to the rent herein fixed, a pro rata amount, equal to that ratio of the amount of gross square feet in the Trident Towers to the gross square feet of Tenant, of said increase for said utility services.

Signs and Advertising

The lessee will want to advertise its business in a manner that will attract the most customers. The lessor will want to ensure uniformity in signage and will want to make sure that all signage complies with local ordinances. A commercial lease should contain a provision pertaining to *signs and advertising* that clearly specifies the type of signage and advertising permitted, those types not permitted, and the allocation of costs for signage, such as the following provision.

Tenant will not exhibit, inscribe, paint or affix any sign, advertisement, notice or other lettering on any part of the outside of the Premises, or inside the Premises if visible from the outside, without first obtaining Landlord's prior approval thereof, which approval shall not be unreasonably withheld or delayed. Tenant shall present to the Landlord plans and specifications for such signage at the time the approval is sought. Tenant shall install only signs that conform with applicable codes of the city of Any City, and said signs shall be in conformance with Landlord's criteria for signage. Tenant shall pay all costs of installation and maintenance of the sign, and the cost of obtaining all necessary government permits and approvals.

Insurance

The lessor normally carries fire insurance and public liability insurance. However, the lessor may require that the lessee carry certain types of *insurance* as well. The lessee may be required to carry public liability insurance for the leased premises as well as workers' compensation and employer's liability insurance to cover employees.

Tenant shall, at its sole expense, provide and maintain in force during the entire term of this Lease, and any extension or renewal hereof, public liability insurance with limits of coverage not less than One Million Dollars ($1,000,000.00) for death or bodily injury for any one occurrence and One Million Dollars ($1,000,000.00) for any property damage or loss from any one accident. Each such policy of insurance shall name as the insured thereunder both the Landlord and the Tenant. Further, Tenant shall maintain, at all times during the term of the Lease, workers' compensation at legally required levels.

Further, should the lessee remodel the leased premises, the lessor will require that the lessee or the lessee's contractor carry builder's risk insurance.

Additionally, the lessee may choose to carry insurance covering the lessee's personal property. This is quite common in the lease of warehouse space, particularly in instances where the lease expressly states that the lessor relinquishes all responsibility for any loss to personal property caused by theft or damage to the leased premises.

The Personal Property of Tenant shall be kept, stored, or maintained in and on the Premises at Tenant's sole risk, and Landlord shall have no liability for any loss or damage caused to the Personal Property from any source whatsoever. If Tenant desires insurance coverage for said Personal Property, it must be obtained by Tenant at Tenant's sole cost and expense.

Indemnity

Although *indemnity* provisions may be found in both residential and commercial leases, these provisions are more common in commercial leases. Recall from the last chapter that an indemnity provision safeguards the lessor from any potential liability as a result of personal injury or losses suffered by the lessee or any other person on the leased premises. Some states frown upon indemnity provisions that exculpate the lessor from all liability (for example, the lessor's own negligence as well as the lessee's negligent acts), so state statutes must be checked carefully before drafting an indemnity provision. A typical indemnity provision reads as follows.

> *Tenant shall protect, indemnify, and hold harmless Landlord, Landlord's agents, employees, licensees, and invitees from and against any and all claims of loss or damage to property and of injury to or death of persons arising out of or in connection with the acts or negligence of Tenant, its agents, employees, licensees, or invitees in or about the Premises.*

Maintenance and Repairs

The *maintenance and repairs* provision should address the responsibilities of each party for maintaining and/or repairing the premises. As is the case with residential leases, state statutes require the lessor to comply with the requirements of all applicable building and health codes and to maintain the structural components of the leased premises in good repair. Some state statutes make it the obligation of the lessor to keep the plumbing in reasonable condition, while others designate this responsibility to the lessor only with regard to residential leases.

In some situations, the lessor provides all maintenance, but the costs are passed on to the lessee. In other situations, the lessor provides maintenance of all structural components and common areas (at the cost of either the lessor or the lessee, as designated in the lease), and the lessee is responsible for the maintenance (and all costs thereof) of the interior of the premises unless the lease provides otherwise. If the potential lessee is to be charged a pro rata share of the common maintenance costs, it is advisable that the lessee ask to see the maintenance fees charged to lessees over the past few years before signing the lease. The following provisions exemplify a common delegation of maintenance duties.

> *Maintenance and Repairs by Landlord. Landlord covenants to keep the following in good order, repair, and condition: (i) the structure of the Office Building; (ii) the mechanical, electrical, and other base building systems (except as may be installed by or be the property of Tenant); and (iii) the entrances, sidewalks, corridors, parking areas, and other facilities from time to time comprising the Common Areas. So long as Landlord is acting in good faith, Landlord shall not be responsible for any damages caused to Tenant by reason of failure of equipment or facilities serving the Office Building or delays in the performance of any work for which Landlord is responsible pursuant to this Lease.*

> *Maintenance and Repairs by Tenant. Tenant shall, at its sole cost, maintain the Premises, in good order, condition, and repair, exclusive of base building, mechanical, plumbing, and electrical systems, all to a standard consistent with a first-class office building, with the exception only as to those which are the obligation of Landlord as set forth above. All repairs and maintenance performed by Tenant in the Premises shall be performed by contractors designated or approved by Landlord.*

Lessor's Access to Premises

Even if the lessor is not responsible for repairs to the interior of the leased premises, the lessor may need access in order to carry out structural or mechanical repairs. Further, the lessor will require access to the leased premises to show the premises to potential mortgagees, interested purchasers, or, toward the end of the lease term, prospective lessees. In most states, the lessor can enter the leased premises at any time for the protection of the premises. In nonemergency situations, the lessor may enter at reasonable times to repair, make alterations, or show the premises. A standard *inspection* provision follows.

> Tenant agrees that Landlord, its agents, and representatives may enter upon the Premises from time to time to inspect the same and to make such repairs, alterations, and improvements to the Premises as may be necessary in Landlord's judgment. Tenant agrees further that Landlord, its agents, and representatives may show the Premises to prospective purchasers or mortgagees of the Premises from time to time during the Term.

Alterations

Commercial lessees typically want to make *alterations* or improvements to the leased space over and above the installation of trade fixtures. This can be arranged in several ways. The lessor can make such alterations for the tenant as a *build-out* (discussed later under special provisions), and the cost of the alterations can be factored into the annual rent or be charged separately. This type of arrangement may be preferable to the lessor. The lessor may own several commercial properties and have experienced, licensed contractors working for the lessor who can move the project along quickly.

Additionally, the lessor may prefer to handle the alterations to prevent potential problems with construction liens. Contractors and subcontractors can attach construction liens on real property for the costs of improvements and, if payment is not forthcoming, foreclose on the property to collect monies owed. If a lessee hires contractors to make alterations to the leased premises and fails to pay them, the lessor's property can be thus encumbered.

The lessor's mortgagee may have reservations about the alterations provision. In many states, the priority of construction liens works retroactively, meaning that the priority of the lien is determined not by the date of recording but by the day the first work was done or the first materials were supplied by the contractor to the site. If the lending institution's mortgage was recorded after this date, the contractor's lien would be superior to that of the lending institution.

Even if the lending institution has no such concerns because its mortgage was recorded before the construction of the building or center commenced, it may be wary of alterations clauses that delegate the responsibility for the alterations work to the lessor. If the lessor fails to perform the alterations work, does the work improperly, or causes undue delay in the performance of the work, the lessee may be entitled, under the terms of the lease, to cancel the lease.

If the lessor does not want to undertake the alterations, a provision can be drafted to require the lessor's approval of all plans, including the requirement that the lessor be provided with all drawings and specifications; the lessor's approval of all contractors performing the alterations; and the lessor's indemnification against all liens.

Tenant's Alterations. Tenant shall have the right to make nonstructural interior alterations to the Premises which are not visible from outside the Premises (excluding electrical, mechanical, and HVAC alterations). Tenant shall submit to Landlord details of the proposed work including drawings and specifications prepared by qualified architects or engineers conforming to good engineering practice. All such alterations shall be performed at the sole cost of Tenant, and in accordance with drawings and specifications approved in writing by Landlord.

Liens. Tenant shall promptly pay for all materials supplied and work done in respect of the Premises so as to ensure that no lien is recorded against any portion of the real property upon which the Office Building is erected or against Landlord's or Tenant's interest therein.

Trade Fixtures

In addition to or as part of remodeling and alterations, commercial tenants install *trade fixtures* in the leased premises. Although the law in most states allows the tenant to remove and take trade fixtures as long as the premises are restored to their original condition, the trade fixtures provision should clearly spell out what may be removed and what must remain on the premises. The lease should delineate leasehold improvements and trade fixtures. Leasehold improvements, such as partitions, usually become the property of the lessor, whereas trade fixtures, such as display cases in a retail store, remain the property of the lessee.

All Leasehold Improvements, other than trade fixtures listed on Exhibit A, shall immediately upon their placement in the Premises become Landlord's property without compensation to Tenant. Tenant may, during the Term, in the usual course of its business, remove its trade fixtures, provided that Tenant is not in default under this Lease.

Casualty

Most commercial leases contain a *casualty* provision setting forth the rights of the parties in the event of a fire or other damage to the premises. If the damage makes the premises untenantable, the lessor typically has the option of terminating the lease or rebuilding. The lessor will be concerned about the adequacy of the insurance proceeds to cover all costs of rebuilding and therefore will desire a casualty provision that does not obligate the lessor to rebuild. Should the lessor choose to rebuild, the question of whether the rent is abated while rebuilding is in progress is material to both parties. If the lessee has business interruption insurance, rent abatement may not apply.

If the option of rebuilding is chosen by the lessor, the time period within which the lessor must rebuild should be specified. Additionally, the question of whether the lessor is responsible for rebuilding the lessee's leasehold improvements should be addressed in the casualty provision, such as in the following provision.

In the event any improvements on the Office Building site are rendered untenantable by fire or other casualty, Landlord shall have the option of terminating this Lease or rebuilding, and in such event, written notice of the election by Landlord shall be given to Tenant within thirty (30) days after the occurrence of such casualty. In the event Landlord elects to rebuild, Landlord shall not be obligated to rebuild the Tenant's Improvements.

Rules and Regulations

The lessor of commercial premises often promulgates *rules and regulations* that must be followed by all lessees (and often the lessees' employees, licensees, invitees, and customers). These regulations usually include, but need not be limited to, rules pertaining to the common areas of the premises, including the passages, stairways, and elevators; rules pertaining to safety concerns; rules pertaining to signage; rules pertaining to defacement of the premises; rules pertaining to storage and to disposal of discarded materials; and rules pertaining to delivery and moving of freight.

The lessor will want to include a statement that the lessor may alter the rules enumerated if in the best interests of the building or center or may add reasonable and appropriate rules to those specifically enumerated. If the regulations are lengthy, they may be attached to the lease as an addendum.

> *Tenant covenants that the rules and regulations attached as an addendum to this Lease, and such other and further rules and regulations as Landlord may make, being in the Landlord's judgment needful for the safety, care, and cleanliness of the Office Building and Premises or for the comfort of tenants, shall be observed by Tenant and by the agents, clerks, servants, and visitors of Tenant.*

In addition to ordinary rules and regulations, the lessor wants to make certain that the lessees comply not only with licensing and zoning laws but also with state and federal environmental laws. The owners of real property can face both civil and criminal penalties for disposal of hazardous substances and other prohibited practices. The lessor therefore may want to attract the lessee's attention to the necessity for compliance by setting forth the lessee's covenant of compliance in a separate provision, such as the following.

> *Tenant hereby covenants that it will strictly comply with any and all local, state and federal environmental rules, regulations, ordinances, and statutes. In the event Tenant violates any such rules, regulations, ordinances, or statutes, Landlord may terminate this Lease. Tenant shall be liable for all cleanup costs and any other costs connected with any such violation, including any and all imposed fines and penalties.*

Subordination

As noted earlier, commercial premises are often mortgaged. As a condition for obtaining financing, the lessor may be required to have all present and future lessees subordinate their rights in the leased premises to the rights of the lending institution.

From the lessee's perspective, the lessee is seeking protection in the event of a foreclosure on the lessor's property. The lessee will seek assurances that it may remain in possession. The lessee may be concerned that in the event of the lessor's default on a loan, the lending institution may seek to set aside existing leases in the hope of obtaining higher rents. From the lending institution's perspective, it is seeking continued income generation from the property and, unless a current lessee is paying a rental rate considerably lower than the prevailing rate for similar properties, will most likely want to be certain that the lessee continues to honor the existing lease terms and makes payments directly to the lending institution or its successor in interest in the event of the lessor's loan default.

subordination, non-disturbance, and attornment (SNDA) agreement: A contract that establishes the rights and obligations of a tenant and and a lessor's lender in the event of the lessor's default of a loan agreement and subsequent foreclosure.

To address all of these interests, a **subordination, non-disturbance, and attornment agreement** (also referred to as an **SNDA agreement**) may be executed. This is a contract that establishes the rights and obligations of a tenant and a lessor's lender in the event of the lessor's default of a loan agreement and subsequent foreclosure. The agreement serves three basic objectives: (1) it subordinates all leases to any mortgage, (2) it maintains the lessee's right to possession after a foreclosure, and (3) it requires the lessee to "attorn" rent payments to the lending institution in the event of a foreclosure. A sample SNDA agreement is shown in Exhibit 16–1.

EXHIBIT 16–1   **Subordination, non-disturbance and attornment agreement**

SUBORDINATION, NON-DISTURBANCE AND ATTORNMENT AGREEMENT

This Subordination, Non-Disturbance and Attornment Agreement ("Agreement") is dated as of the 1st day of March, 2015, between Century Bank ("Lender") located at 1630 Eastbrook Avenue, Any City, Any State, and Greenfield Carpet & Tile, Inc. ("Tenant"), located at 4000 N. W. 35th Street, Any City, Any State.

RECITALS

Whereas, Tenant has leased from DSN Commercial Properties, Corp. ("Landlord") the Premises ("Premises") which comprises a portion of the Real Property ("Property") described in the attached Lease ("Lease") under the terms and conditions described therein, and

Whereas, Lender and Landlord are entering into a mortgage loan agreement ("Loan") secured by a First Mortgage Instrument on the Property ("Security Instrument"), as well as an Assignment of Leases and Rents on the Property (together, the Security Instrument and Assignment referred to as "Security Documents"),

NOW, THEREFORE, the parties, for mutual consideration, the receipt and sufficiency of which are hereby acknowledged, have agreed to the following provisions.

I. **DEFINITIONS:** The term "Lender" as used herein shall include any successor or assign of the named Lender, including but not limited to, any co-lender at the time of making the Loan. The terms "Tenant" and "Landlord" as used herein shall include any successor or assign of the named Tenant and Landlord respectively, provided, however, that any such reference to either Tenant's or Landlord's successors and assigns shall not be construed as constituting Lender's consent to assignment or other transfer by Tenant or Landlord.

II. **SUBORDINATION:** Tenant agrees that the Lease is and shall be subject and subordinate to the Security Documents and to all present and future obligations secured thereby to the full extent of all amounts secured by the Security Documents. Tenant further agrees that the Lease is and shall be subject to all renewals, amendments, modifications, consolidations, replacements, and extensions of the secured obligations and Security Documents.

III. **ATTORNMENT:** Tenant agrees that, in the event of a foreclosure of the Security Instrument by the Lender or the Lender's acceptance of a deed-in-lieu of foreclosure by Lender or any other succession of Lender to fee ownership, Tenant shall attorn to Lender as its landlord for the remaining term of the Lease, including any extension periods permitted thereunder, upon the same terms and conditions as are set forth in the Lease and shall make all required Lease payments to the Lender.

IV.   **NON-DISTURBANCE:** If Lender succeeds to the interest of the Landlord under the Lease, Lender and Tenant hereby agree to be bound under all of the terms and conditions of the Lease for the remainder of the lease term and Lender shall not disturb Tenant's possession of the Premises as long as Tenant complies with and performs all obligations under the Lease.

V.   **LENDER'S OBLIGATIONS:** In the event Lender succeeds to the interest of the Landlord, Tenant agrees that Lender shall not be:

(A)   liable for any act or omission of any prior Landlord (including the above-stated Landlord), or

(B)   subject to any defense or offsets which Tenant may have against any prior Landlord (including the above-stated Landlord), or

(C)   bound by any payment of rent or additional rent Tenant may have paid to any prior Landlord (including the above-stated Landlord) in advance of the due date under the Lease, or

(D)   accountable for any monies, including security deposits, deposited with any prior Landlord (including the above-stated Landlord), except for monies Lender actually receives in segregated cash amounts identified in writing at time of receipt, or

(E)   bound by any termination, amendment, or modifications of any terms of the Lease made without Lender's consent, or

(F)   liable for any representations or warranties made by any prior Landlord (including the above-stated Landlord), whether set forth in the Lease or otherwise made in written or oral form.

VI.   **ASSIGNMENTS:** The Lease shall not be assigned by Tenant without the Lender's prior written consent. Tenant hereby consents to the Assignment of Leases and Rents from Landlord to Lender executed in connection with the Loan, which document serves as security for the purposes specified therein. Tenant agrees that upon written notification by Lender of Landlord's default under the Loan, Tenant will pay rent to Lender in accordance with the Lease terms.

VII.   **NOTICES:** All notices relating to this Agreement shall be in writing and shall be deemed duly made if (a) mailed by certified mail, return receipt requested, or (b) sent via a recognized commercial courier service providing a receipt, to the following addresses:

If to Tenant: Greenfield Carpet & Tile, Inc,
                  4000 N.W. 35th Street
                  Any City, Any State
                  Attn: Theodore Greenfield, President

If to Lender: Century Bank
                  1630 Eastbrook Avenue
                  Any City, Any State
                  Attn: Mark Jansen, Vice President

VIII.   **MODIFICATION:** Any modification of this Agreement shall be enforceable only by a written document signed by each party.

IX.   **SEVERABILITY:** If, for any reason, any provision of this Agreement is held invalid, the other provisions of this Agreement shall remain in effect, insofar as is consistent with law.

X.   **GOVERNING LAW:** This Agreement shall be construed and governed in accordance with the laws of the State of Any State.

EXHIBIT 16–1   *(continued)*

IN WITNESS WHEREOF, the parties hereby execute this Agreement as of the date first above written.

TENANT: GREENFIELD CARPET & TILE, INC.

Pamela Fisher	By: *Theodore Greenfield*
Witness Signature	President
Pamela Fisher	
Printed Name	
Jeremy Knowles	
Witness Signature	
Jeremy Knowles	
Printed Name	

STATE OF ANY STATE
COUNTY OF ANY COUNTY

The foregoing instrument was acknowledged before me this 1st day of March, 2015, by Theodore Greenfield in his representative capacity as president for GREENFIELD CARPET & TILE, INC., who [ ] is personally known to me or [X] produced Any State Driver's License #G11223344 as identification.

Steven Barnes
Notary Public

Steven Barnes
Printed Notary Name

My Commission Expires: July 12, 2016

LENDER: CENTURY BANK

Eleanor Jacobs	By: *Mark Jansen*
Witness Signature	Vice President
Eleanor Jacobs	
Printed Name	
Robert Spence	
Witness Signature	
Robert Spence	
Printed Name	

STATE OF ANY STATE
COUNTY OF ANY COUNTY

The foregoing instrument was acknowledged before me this 1st day of March, 2015, by Mark Jansen in his representative capacity as vice president for CENTURY BANK, who [X] is personally known to me or [X] produced _____ as identification.

Alice Thompkins
Notary Public

Alice Thompkins
Printed Notary Name

My Commission Expires: 4/20/2016

The commercial lease may include a provision stating that the lessee agrees to sign such an agreement. A lessee should be aware that a lease provision that simply references a "subordination agreement," such as the sample provision below, does not necessarily protect the lessee's interests; such a provision only requires that the lessee sign an agreement subordinating its rights to those of the lending institution and does not, by itself, ensure the lessee's continued rights of possession of the premises.

> *It is specifically understood and agreed by and between the Landlord and the Tenant that the Landlord may, from time to time, secure a construction and/or first mortgage on the demised premises from a recognized lending institution, and that this Lease is and shall be subordinate to the lien of said construction and/or first mortgage, and the Tenant agrees that it will execute such subordination or other documents or agreements as may be requested or required by such lending institution.*

Estoppel Certificates

The lending institution typically requires the lessor/mortgagor to provide estoppel certificates signed by all lessees verifying the terms and conditions of their leases. Thus, a commercial lease may contain an *estoppel certificate* provision, similar to the following one.

> *At any time and from time to time, upon not less than ten (10) days' prior notice by Landlord or Landlord's Mortgagee (the "Requesting Party"), Tenant shall comply with, execute, acknowledge, and deliver in writing to the Requesting Party an estoppel certificate certifying the terms of this Lease, including a statement that this Lease is unmodified and in full force and effect, or if there have been modifications, that the Lease is in full force and effect as modified, and stating the modifications and such further information with respect to the Lease or the Premises as the Requesting Party may reasonably request.*

Assignment and Subletting

The *assignment or subletting* of the leased premises is of concern to both parties, as well as to any mortgagee of the leased premises. The lessee wants a way out of paying rent without defaulting on the lease if business is slow. In such a situation, the lessee would ultimately like the ability to terminate the lease early or, failing that, the ability to assign the lease to another party, making that other party, the assignee, primarily liable under the lease and the original lessee only secondarily liable.

The lessor, on the other hand, entered the lease with the lessee based on the financial status of the lessee and that of any guarantors executing the lease. The lessor may not want to negate the lessee's primary liability and that of any guarantors by approving an assignment unless the lessor believes, after thorough investigation, that the prospective assignee is a better business risk than the lessee. The lessor certainly will not agree to a provision allowing assignment of the lease without the lessor's prior written approval.

The lessor might be more willing to allow the lessee to sublet the leased premises. In this way, the lessee remains obligated to the lessor, while the sublessee is obligated to the lessee. Even if the lessor consents to subletting, the lessor will want to be assured that the sublessee agrees to abide by all terms and conditions of the original lease.

> *Tenant shall not enter into, consent to, or permit any transfer of this Lease without the prior written consent of Landlord in each instance, which consent shall not be unreasonably withheld, but shall be subject to Landlord's rights hereunder. Landlord shall, within thirty (30) days after having received such notice and all requested information, notify Tenant either that it consents or that it does not consent to the transfer. If Landlord fails to give any timely notice, Landlord shall be deemed to have refused consent to the transfer.*

Default and Remedies

Most *default and remedies* provisions in commercial leases focus on the lessee's default and the lessor's available remedies. If the lessee defaults, the lessor wants a swift resolution, either a timely cure by the lessee or the lessee's vacating of the premises, together with acceleration of all rent for the entire lease term. State law may severely restrict the remedies available to the lessor, so state statutes should be checked carefully prior to drafting this provision.

This provision should specify the actions constituting a default by the tenant, the time period in which to cure, and the default remedies. Should the lessor default, the typical remedies available to the lessee are the termination of the lease and money damages, where applicable. The lessor will be concerned with the prospect of having property encumbered by a judgment lien and may seek to include a provision limiting the lessee's remedies. Again, state statutes should be checked to determine whether the desired limitations are permitted. Sample default and remedies provisions follow.

> *Default. A default by Tenant shall be deemed to have occurred hereunder if and whenever: (A) any Minimum Rent is in arrears by the fifth of the month, whether or not any notice or demand for payment has been made by Landlord; (B) any Additional Rent is in arrears and is not paid within five (5) days after written demand by Landlord; or (C) Tenant has breached any of its obligations under this Lease (other than payment of Rent), and Tenant fails to remedy such breach within fifteen (15) days (or such shorter period as may be provided in this Lease).*

> *Default Remedies. In the event of any default hereunder by Tenant, then without prejudice to any other rights that may be exercised by Landlord: (A) Landlord may terminate this Lease by notice to Tenant and retake possession of the Premises for Landlord's account; (B) Landlord may enter the Premises as Agent of Tenant to take possession of any property of Tenant on the Premises, to store such property at the expense and risk of Tenant or sell or otherwise dispose of such property in such manner as Landlord may see fit without notice to Tenant, which shall be credited toward any Rent owed Landlord pursuant hereunder; (C) Landlord may accelerate all Rent for the entire Term.*

Be aware that state statutory law may require that a lessor attempt to mitigate damages incurred due to a lessee's breach of a lease. A lessor typically is required to make a good-faith attempt to relet the premises.

At times, the parties may try to anticipate future damages that may be difficult to calculate with certainty and insert a liquidated damages provision in the lease to cover the cost of these damages to the nonbreaching party. Liquidated damages provisions are scrutinized to ascertain whether they truly are a good-faith determination of future damages or whether they are disguised punitive penalty provisions. The following California case addresses a dispute over a liquidated damages provision between a commercial landlord of a shopping center and one of its tenants.

CASE: *El Centro Mall, LLC v. Payless ShoeSource, Inc.*
94 Cal. Rptr. 3d 43 (2009)

ARONSON, J.

Defendant Payless ShoeSource, Inc. (Payless) ceased operations at a shopping center owned by plaintiff El Centro Mall, LLC (ECM) before the end of its lease term. Per a lease provision, ECM charged Payless liquidated damages of 10 cents per square foot of leased space for each day Payless did not operate, totaling $98,010. Payless refused to pay, alleging the liquidated damages provision in the lease was an unenforceable penalty under Civil Code section 1671.[1]

Payless contends the trial court erred when it determined the provision did not constitute an unlawful penalty. Payless argues the evidence demonstrates the liquidated damages provision was arbitrarily applied to the tenants at ECM's shopping center and therefore could not be a reasonable estimate of potential damages at the time the lease was signed. ECM asserts its evidence demonstrates the liquidated damages clause was intended to reimburse ECM for the loss in synergy, goodwill, and patronage the shopping center and other tenants would lose if Payless ceased operation.

We conclude substantial evidence supports the trial court's judgment. Under section 1671, subdivision (b), the liquidated damages clause was presumptively enforceable and Payless had the burden to demonstrate otherwise. Although Payless's evidence may have given rise to an inference the clause was arbitrary, this evidence was not conclusive, and was countered by expert testimony introduced by ECM. Accordingly, we affirm.

I FACTUAL AND PROCEDURAL BACKGROUND

In 1990, Payless entered into a written commercial lease with ECM's predecessor-in-interest to lease 3,300 square feet of retail space in a shopping center for a term of ten years, commencing on January 1, 1991, and ending on December 31, 2000 (lease). In 2000, ECM's predecessor-in-interest and Payless executed a "Lease Amendment/Extension Agreement" (amendment) extending the lease for five years, commencing January 1, 2001, and expiring

December 31, 2005. ECM purchased the shopping center, assuming the lessor's rights under the agreement.

Under the lease terms, as amended, the base monthly rent for the period of January 1, 2005, through December 31, 2005, was $4,950. In addition to the base monthly rent, Payless also agreed to pay ECM "Percentage Rental" on a monthly basis, in a sum equal to Payless's gross sales times six percent, minus the aggregate amount of the minimum annual rent. Payless's rental obligations further also included "Additional Rent," which covered all other costs or charges required under the lease, such as common area maintenance (CAM), costs, and taxes.

The lease also contains a covenant of "Continuous Operation." Section 17.1 provides that Payless will continuously operate and conduct business on the premises: "Tenant covenants and agrees that, continuously and uninterruptedly . . . it will operate and conduct within the premises the business which it is permitted to operate and conduct . . . ." Section 17.2 sets Payless's required hours of operation: "Tenant agrees that commencing with the opening for business by Tenant in the premises and for the remainder of the term of this Lease, Tenant shall be open[ed] for business daily from 10:00 A.M. to 9:00 P.M., Monday through Friday, 10:00 A.M. to 6:00 P.M. Saturday, 12:00 noon to 5:00 P.M. Sunday. . . ."

Section 17.3 provides that if Payless fails to operate within the lease terms, including failing to stay open for business, the lessor, five days after the first breach, "shall be entitled to collect (in addition to the minimum annual rent, Percentage Rental and Additional Rent) an additional charge at the daily rate of Ten Cents ($0.10) per square foot of the Floor Area of the premises or One Hundred Dollars ($100.00), whichever is greater, for each and every day or partial day the Tenant fails to commence to do or to carry on business as herein provided, such additional charge is a liquidated sum representing the minimum damages which Landlord is deemed to have suffered, including damages as a result of Landlord's failure to receive Percentage Rental, if any, under this Lease

(continued)

[and] is without prejudice to Landlord's right to claim and prove a greater sum of damages. . . ."

Payless closed its business operations from March 4, 2005 to December 31, 2005. On March 29, 2005, ECM sent Payless a letter, notifying Payless of its default and of Payless's contractual obligation to stay open for business. ECM also notified Payless of its obligation to pay the additional charge. Payless continued to pay the required based monthly rent, CAM charges, and taxes during this time period, but did not pay the liquidated damage amount called for by section 17.3 of the lease. Due to lagging sales, Payless had not paid any percentage rental since 1999, and ECM did not assert Payless owed any percentage rental for the period during which Payless discontinued business operations.

The parties stipulated that in lieu of trial with live testimony, the trial court could decide the case pursuant to a noticed briefing schedule with written evidence. The parties stipulated to a number of facts, including alternative calculations of the damages owed, which depended on whether the trial court enforced the liquidated damages provision. The trial court ruled in ECM's favor, finding Payless did not overcome the presumption of validity with respect to the liquidated damages clause in the parties' lease agreement. The trial court awarded ECM damages of $90,226.80, based on the parties' agreed calculation of $98,000 in liquidated damages ($330 per day times 279 days), less a $7,783.20 credit owed Payless after a reconciliation of CAM charges and real property taxes for the 2005 lease term.

II STANDARD OF REVIEW

Where the facts are undisputed, we review the question of whether a liquidated damages clause is enforceable de novo. (*Harbor Island Holdings v. Kim* (2003) 107 Cal. App. 4th 790, 794, 132 Cal, Rptr. 2d 406.) Where, as here, there is a conflict in the evidence, we review the trial court's ruling for substantial evidence supporting it. . . .

III DISCUSSION

In 1977, the Legislature revised section 1671 by deleting the presumption that a liquidated damages clause in a commercial context is invalid, and replacing it with a presumption of validity. (*Californians for Population Stabilization v. Hewlett-Packard Co.*, (1997) 58 Cal. App. 4th 273, 289, 67 Cal. Rptr. 2d 621.) As revised, section 1671, subdivision (b) now provides: "[A] provision in a contract liquidating the damages for the breach of the

contract is valid unless the party seeking to invalidate the provision establishes that the provision was unreasonable under the circumstances existing at the time the contract was made."

The Law Revision Commission comment to section 1671 explains: "In the cases where subdivision (b) applies, the burden of proof on the issue of reasonableness is on the party seeking to invalidate the liquidated damages provision. . . .

"Unlike subdivision (d), subdivision (b) gives the parties considerable leeway in determining the damages for breach. All the circumstances existing at the time of the making of the contract are considered, including the relationship that the damages provided in the contract bear to the range of harm that reasonably could be anticipated at the time of the making of the contract. Other relevant considerations in the determination of whether the amount of liquidated damages is so high or low as to be unreasonable include, but are not limited to, such matters as the relative equality of the bargaining power of the parties, whether the parties were represented by lawyers at the time the contract was made, the anticipation of the parties that proof of actual damages would be costly or inconvenient, the difficulty of proving causation and foreseeability, and whether the liquidated damages provision is included in a form contract." (Cal. Law Revision Com. com., 9 West's Ann. Civ. Code (2001 ed.) foll. § 1671, p. 498.)

The objective of a liquidated damages clause is to "stipulate[] a pre-estimate of damages in order that the [contracting] parties may know with reasonable certainty the extent of liability" in the event of breach. (*ABI, Inc. v. City of Los Angeles* (1984) 153 Cal. App. 3d 669, 685, 200 Cal. Rptr. 563.) Courts perform a "'reasonable endeavor test'" to determine the validity of the liquidated damages provision measured at the time of contracting: "The amount set as liquidated damages 'must represent the result of a reasonable endeavor by the parties to estimate a fair average compensation for any loss that may be sustained.'" (*Ridgley v. Topa Thrift & Loan Assn.* (1998) 17 Cal. 4th 970, 977, 73 Cal. Rptr. 2d 378, 953 P.2d 484.)

In determining whether the liquidated damages provision is enforceable, we consider the purposes stated in the provision itself, which provides the liquidated damages specified "represent[s] the minimum damages which the Landlord is deemed to have suffered, including damages as a result of Landlord's failure to receive Percentage Rental." Payless counters by citing section 23.5 of the lease, which provides that the amount of percentage

(continued)

rental to be paid as damages if the lessor terminates the lease based on a tenant's default "shall be computed on the basis of the average monthly amount thereof accruing during any preceding twelve (12) month period selected by the Landlord occurring within the preceding five (5) year period, except that if it becomes necessary to compute such rental before such a twelve (12) month period has occurred then such rental shall be computed on the basis of the average monthly amount hereof accruing during such shorter period."

We conclude the liquidation provision, to the extent considered only as a basis for estimating percentage rental damages, is an unenforceable penalty. Section 23.5 of the lease provides a readily ascertainable basis for calculating damages for loss of percentage rental, rendering the additional liquidated damages provision unnecessary, except to penalize Payless.

ECM, however, contends other damages included in the liquidated damages provision also include the anticipated loss of the synergy, goodwill, and patronage Payless provides by continuing to operate in the retail center. ECM introduced the declaration of an expert witness who explained that stores such as Payless are viewed as a "National tenant" because it conducts retail business throughout the United States, often supported by national and regional advertising campaigns. This allows such stores to generate significant patronage or "foot traffic" in a retail center. In recognition of this fact, retail centers customarily require a covenant of continuous operations. Because it is difficult to estimate the amount of damages from the loss of synergy, goodwill, and patronage accompanying the breach of the continuous operations covenant by a national tenant such as Payless, the landlord will typically require a reasonable liquidated damage calculation. "The rationale for such a liquidated calculation is based upon the theory that the amount of business that a retail tenant may prospectively generate in patronage, synergy or goodwill to the retail center, and in sales, is directly proportional to the amount of space the retail tenant utilizes to conduct business in the retail center. By way of example, a shoe store with a floor area of 100 square feet (a shoe 'kiosk'), or a small coffee hut or 'kiosk,' will not generate as many shoes sales or coffee sales as a full retail shoe store with a floor-area of 3,300 square feet, such as the Payless store here, or as a 'Starbucks' coffee store. The larger stores would be able to carry more styles, brands, and shoes, or coffee and coffee-related supplies than [the] smaller counterpart. As a result, the larger store is likely to conduct more business, generate more goodwill to the retail center, generate more patronage to the retail center, generate more and better complementary tenants at increased rents and also generate more percentage rent."

In opposition, Payless produced evidence that ECM allowed Sears, an anchor tenant in the shopping center, to escape from its lease obligations for a 65,000 square foot space without the payment of any damages for loss of synergy, goodwill, or patronage. Payless also notes that other tenants lacking Payless's national stature were required to pay similar liquidated damages. Specifically, ECM's leases with General Nutrition Corporation, which leases 1,200 square feet, Sports Image, which leases 2,000 square feet, and The Locker, which leases 1,200 square feet, have lease provisions identical to the liquidated damage provision in section 17.3. Moreover, ECM's lease with Nail Trix, Inc., requires liquidated damages for cessation of operations of $250 per day, despite leasing only 1,000 square feet.

Payless contends the foregoing evidence demonstrates the lease's liquidated damage provision is arbitrary and does not represent a reasonable attempt to estimate future damages for breach of the continuous operation provision. Although we agree Payless's evidence may give rise to an inference the provision is arbitrary, it does not conclusively prove the point. Significantly, Payless provides little or no evidence allowing any detailed analysis of the circumstances surrounding the other leases. For example, ECM may have let Sears out of its lease because an event may have occurred giving Sears the right to terminate under a lease provision. Alternatively, ECM may have agreed not to include a liquidated damages provision to persuade Sears to become an anchor tenant. Moreover, Nail Trix, Inc. may be paying a higher cost per square foot because it generates more customers, and thus has more foot traffic, per square foot, than a typical retail business. Finally, Payless presented no evidence of whether GNC, Sports Image, or the Locker were or were not national tenants, like Payless.

Payless also failed to present evidence, usually presented through expert testimony, that showed a charge of 10 cents per square foot did not represent a reasonable estimate of the actual damages a retail center would suffer if a tenant like Payless ceased operations. Payless had the burden of proof to demonstrate the liquidated damages provision in section 17.3 of the lease was not intended by the parties to be a reasonable estimate of damages, but was instead a penalty. The trial court determined Payless did not meet its burden. Because the trial court's decision is supported by substantial evidence, we do not disturb it here.

(continued)

IV DISPOSITION

The judgment is affirmed. ECM is entitled to its costs of this appeal.

WE CONCUR: RYLAARSDAM, Acting P.J. and MOORE, J.

Case Questions

1. In the above case, the court noted that the California legislature amended section 1671 of the California Civil Code, changing the statute's original presumption of invalidity of liquidated damages clauses in commercial leases to the current presumption of validity. What is the applicable rule regarding liquidated damages provisions in your state? Applying that rule to the facts in this case, what result would be reached?

2. ECM's expert witness posited the theory that "the amount of business that a retail tenant may prospectively generate in patronage, synergy or goodwill to the retail center, and in sales, is directly proportional to the amount of space the retail tenant utilizes to conduct business in the retail center." Apply this theory to a large shopping center located near you. Do you believe this theory would hold true? Why or why not?

3. Payless maintained that the liquidated damages clause was an unenforceable penalty as applied because it was applied arbitrarily. Do you believe that arbitrary application of a liquidated damages provision should have any bearing on whether the provision is valid if it can be shown that, at the time of its drafting, it was a reasonable attempt to estimate future damages? Why or why not?

[1]All statutory references are to the Civil Code.

Reprinted from Westlaw with permission of Thomson Reuters.

Should the lessee remain in the leased premises after the expiration of the lease term, some state statutes provide that a month-to-month tenancy is created and that the parties are entitled to such rights and notice as are applicable under such a tenancy. However, if permitted under state law, the holding over of a commercial lessee may be considered by the parties to create only a tenancy at sufferance. State law should be consulted before drafting a *holding-over* provision.

> *If Tenant remains in possession of the Premises after the end of the Term hereof, there shall be no tacit renewal of this Lease, and Tenant shall be deemed to be under a month-to-month tenancy. Tenant shall pay to Landlord an amount equal to the last monthly installment paid under the Lease for each month or portion thereof Tenant remains on the Premises. All other obligations of Tenant under this Lease shall be applicable to Tenant during the period in which Tenant is a month-to-month tenant.*

Miscellaneous Provisions

Finally, a commercial lease will contain many of the boilerplate provisions found in most contracts, albeit altered where necessary to suit the needs of the parties. These provisions include a *notice* provision, specifying the manner in which parties are required to give notice to each other. A *waiver* provision typically is included, specifying that the excusal by one party of any default by the other shall not be a waiver with respect to any continuing or subsequent defaults. A *governing law* provision specifies the state law under which the lease shall be construed, while a *severability* provision provides that should any provision in the lease be found to be invalid, that provision shall be severed from the lease and the rest of the lease shall remain in full force and effect. Additionally, a provision will be included that indicates the lease, plus any addendums or exhibits attached to it, constitutes the *entire agreement* between the parties and that no modification of this lease can be made except by a writing executed by the lessor and the lessee. The next section of this chapter discusses the special concerns or provisions specifically found in shopping center leases, executive office suite leases, and warehouse leases.

Special Provisions

Shopping Centers

When retail space is rented out to a shopping center lessee, the lessee rarely moves into the space without alterations. If the lessee is a restaurant, it typically will require more extensive alterations to the interior space than will a boutique; therefore, interior build-out should be addressed by the parties.

The commencement date of the lease term may be the date of signing the lease, the date the work on alterations commences, or the date on which the alterations are completed. Sometimes these alterations are undertaken by the lessee, but often they are undertaken by the lessor. The cost of alterations may be factored into the rent or may be charged separately. If the lessor undertakes the alterations, the architectural plans and drawings should be attached to the lease as an exhibit. Likewise, any alterations for which the lessee is responsible should be approved by the lessor and attached as a lease exhibit. All agreed-upon alterations should then be referred to in a provision within the text of the lease, such as the following.

> *Landlord will, at its sole expense, perform all work specified to be performed by Landlord, more specifically set forth in Exhibit A attached hereto and entitled "Landlord Improvements." Tenant will, at its sole expense, perform all other work necessary to complete the Premises for its business purposes, more specifically set forth in Exhibit B attached hereto and entitled "Tenant Improvements."*

Parking is another major concern of shopping center lessees. Lessees want to be assured that their customers will have adequate parking space with easy access to their stores and may require a minimum number of guaranteed parking spaces per store or per square footage of rental space. They will also be concerned with the safety of their customers and will desire proper lighting in the parking lot if the center will be open at night as well as possible security patrols. The costs for security, lighting, and parking lot maintenance often are factored into the operating costs to be paid by the lessees. An example of a shopping center parking provision follows.

> *Tenant shall be allotted four (4) reserved parking spaces for its customers in the front parking area. In addition, Tenant's customers shall have the nonexclusive use of all nonreserved parking areas. Landlord shall provide one (1) roaming security patrol guard in the front and rear parking areas during the hours of 5:00 p.m. to 9:00 p.m. on those evenings the shopping center is open for business. The parking areas in front of the shopping center are intended primarily for customers of the center. Tenant and Tenant's employees are to park in the rear parking area.*

A more controversial area of concern is that of competing businesses within the shopping center. The lessee usually desires an exclusivity provision in the lease, acknowledging that the lessor shall not rent out space to stores in competition with the lessee. The lessee will argue that to succeed in a particular location, and thus to be a lucrative tenant, the lessee requires such a provision. Under certain circumstances, this may make sense, such as in the instance of a florist located in a small strip center. Two or more competing florists in the strip center would most likely have a difficult time sustaining business, and one of the florists might find it could not survive and move out, leaving the lessor with vacant space.

On the other hand, a larger shopping center may be able to incorporate two or more similar businesses; for example, a large shopping mall often contains several men's, children's, and women's boutiques as well as several department stores and restaurants. Even in a smaller shopping center, the lessor's conception for the center may include similar businesses; for example, a center for high-fashion designer clothing boutiques necessarily will include more than one such boutique; likewise, a center for home furnishings and home accessories necessarily will include more than one furniture store. Additionally, the lessor's mortgagee may prohibit the inclusion of an exclusivity provision in the lease, since the mortgagee will want to provide as much flexibility in rentals as possible.

If an exclusivity provision is included in the lease, it should be drafted carefully. The lessor should not prohibit other stores from selling the same goods (for example, jewelry); rather, the lessor should agree not to rent space to another business that is in direct competition with the lessee or that is in the same primary business as the lessee. The lessor would not want to be prohibited, for example, from renting space to a clothing boutique that also sold costume jewelry as accessories when the lessor signed a contract containing an exclusivity provision with a store selling gold and other fine jewelry. A sample exclusivity provision follows.

> *Landlord agrees not to rent other space in the shopping plaza, during the term of this Lease and any extensions thereof, to others whose primary business is the sale of exercise equipment. The term "exercise equipment" is defined for the purposes of this Lease as treadmills, stair machines, rowing machines, bench presses, free weights, and similar equipment. It does not include the sale of exercise clothing or footwear. The term "primary business" is defined for the purposes of this Lease as a business in which fifty percent (50%) or more of the inventory of the business comprises exercise equipment.*

Stores in shopping centers often are required to keep uniform store hours. If a lessee fails to abide by the required hours, this breach of contract not only affects the contracting parties but also may have an impact on other tenants. For example, if the center is closed on Sundays but a lessee keeps its store open on Sunday, this causes confusion among shopping center customers and could breed resentment among the tenants. Conversely, a lessee may not want to stay open on evenings designated as evening shopping center hours. The shopping center's advertising and marketing may depend on uniformity. Further, city and county ordinances may regulate business hours. The center's policy on store hours should be set forth clearly in the lease.

> *Tenant's business shall remain open during designated store hours, namely: Monday, Tuesday, and Thursday, 10:00 a.m. to 9:00 p.m.; Wednesday, Friday, and Saturday, 10:00 a.m. to 6:00 p.m.; Sunday, 12:00 p.m. to 5:00 p.m. The shopping plaza shall be closed for business on the following holidays: Christmas Day and Easter Sunday. Should Tenant desire to close the Premises for the taking of inventory, Tenant must first obtain the permission of Landlord. Failure of Tenant to abide by the terms of this provision shall be considered a default under this Lease.*

Finally, a lessor may require lessees to contribute to the promotion of the shopping center. This is commonly done by the formation of merchants' associations, which develop advertising budgets and allocate expenses for the advertising costs on a pro rata basis. The lessor typically contributes a specified percentage of the designated budget and reserves approval rights for all advertising copy and promotions.

Executive Office Suites

An executive office suite lessee usually is a short-term tenant as compared with a lessee in a shopping center. The lessees of an executive office suite are looking for ways in which to minimize their overhead costs. They do not want to hire secretarial support staff or spend money on conference rooms or reference libraries. In keeping overhead to a minimum, they are not interested in extensive alterations to the rented space. They are looking for space in an office building that provides secretarial support services, access to common business facilities, and, occasionally, furnished premises.

The costs of certain services, such as switchboard services, are included in the monthly rent. Other services, such as photocopying and keyboarding, may be included in the monthly rent or, more often, may be available to the lessee who will be charged per transaction. The services to be provided should be outlined in the text of the lease or should appear as an exhibit attached to the lease.

> *Landlord shall provide a switchboard operator to answer incoming calls of Tenant during the workday hours of 8:30 a.m. to 5:30 p.m., Mondays through Fridays. Tenant shall have access to the Secretarial Support Center. The charges for Secretarial Support services are listed on Exhibit A attached to this Lease.*

Executive suite buildings may provide conference rooms that may be reserved by lessees. Some buildings may also include professional libraries, such as law libraries, that may be shared by attorneys who are sole practitioners and who would find the cost of a creating and maintaining a law library prohibitive. Rules for the use of common facilities should be included in the lease or as an exhibit to the lease, such as the following provisions.

> *Use of the switchboard system for advertising, promotion, or toll-free numbers that solicit a high volume of calls is strictly prohibited. The additional volume of these calls and messages places extraordinary pressures on the system and detrimentally impacts the timely response to all Tenants. If it is discovered that the switchboard number is being employed for these purposes, Management will forward all calls to the Tenant's voicemail.*

> *Use of the conference room is on a reservation basis, usually at least twenty-four (24) hours in advance. If the telephone in the conference room is to be used in connection with a meeting to be conducted therein, it is necessary that arrangements for use of the phone be made at the same time the room is reserved.*

Additionally, any furniture, furnishings, and equipment to be supplied in the leased space by the lessor should be inventoried, and each item should be set forth, including but not limited to such items as telephone equipment, desks, desk chairs, side chairs, credenzas, file cabinets, and pictures.

Warehouses

Warehouse or storage space leases often are less complex than shopping center or office leases. The amount of rent paid is small and the rental term short in comparison. No alterations are made to the premises, and maintenance is minimal. Unlike in a retail or office situation, the lessee of warehouse space may be located out of state, giving rise to a concern on the part of both parties.

The lessor wants assurances that out-of-state checks will pass muster. The lessee wants assurances that a delayed rent check will not result in the sale of the stored property as damages. To minimize these concerns, the lessor may require the lessee to open an account in a local bank, may charge a fee for returned checks, or may simply charge a high security deposit. Further, the lessee may be given a specified grace period for late rent (with penalties, if desired by the lessor) before a default occurs. The lease may also require that the lessor provide notice before taking advantage of any rights of distraint afforded by state statute.

A major concern of the lessor is the storage of dangerous or illegal items on the premises. Most warehouse leases include provisions forbidding the storage of hazardous or toxic substances, illegal substances, and animals on the premises, such as the following.

> *Tenant shall not keep anything within the Premises that would increase the insurance premium costs or invalidate any insurance policy carried by Landlord on the Premises, including, but not limited to, petroleum products, explosives, firearms, volatile or flammable chemical products, any toxic products, or any domesticated animals or pets.*

Sometimes a lessee will rent warehouse space and attempt to operate a business, such as automobile repairs or customizing, out of the rented space. If the zoning allows for such use, the lessor may be amenable to renting the space for this or similar purposes. In this instance, employees and customers of the lessee will be entering the premises, and the lessor should require employers' liability, public liability, and workers' compensation insurance as well as requiring an indemnity provision. Under no circumstances should a lessee conduct a business on the premises without the prior knowledge and approval of the lessor. A lessor may include a provision forbidding the conduct of any business, such as the following.

> *The Premises may be used and occupied by Tenant only for the purpose of storing and removing the personal property of Tenant. Tenant shall perform no other labor or service, or conduct any business of any kind whatsoever thereon. Tenant shall comply with the requirements of all constituted public authorities and with the terms of all laws, statutes, ordinances, rules, regulations, and orders of all federal, state, county, and city authorities, commissions, departments, and agencies exercising jurisdiction over the Premises.*

Paralegals may actively be involved with the drafting or reviewing of any of the leases discussed here. Commercial leases usually are negotiated more vigorously than residential leases, and lease forms found in office supply stores often will not suffice. A paralegal should use a commercial lease worksheet in both the drafting and the reviewing of a lease. In drafting a lease, the worksheet will assure the paralegal that all important provisions are discussed with the client. In reviewing a lease, the worksheet will serve as a checklist of provisions that should be included, or at least considered, before signing a lease. A sample completed worksheet is provided in the hypothetical client matter that follows.

hypothetical client matter

Sandor Commercial Group, Inc., is a client of attorney Ava Ross specializing in buying and revitalizing commercial properties. In the past, Ava has drafted retail and warehouse leases as well as handling several commercial closings for this client. Yesterday Ava met with Robert Sandor, president of Sandor Commercial Group, Inc., to discuss a leasing matter. Barbara Hammond, her paralegal, was asked to sit in on the meeting. Having recently acquired a downtown office building, Robert plans to turn the building into executive suites and needs an executive suite lease drafted that can be used as a standard lease form for prospective tenants.

Robert has prepared a list of rules and regulations to be attached to the lease as an exhibit, and he has asked Ava to review the list to ensure that the rules are not in contravention of state law. He has also provided Ava with a tenant cost sheet to be attached to the lease as an exhibit, itemizing the breakdown of amenity costs, such as switchboard services, as well as move-in costs, such as switchboard programming and required deposits.

After Ava discussed the particulars of the executive suite lease with Robert, she asked Barbara to take Robert into the conference room to complete a commercial lease worksheet to be used in the drafting of the lease. This morning Barbara pulls the client file to begin drafting the executive suite lease. She reviews the worksheet, which reads as shown in Exhibit 16–2.

From a review of the worksheet, Barbara knows that the lease is to be a gross lease. This particular building has an underground garage secured by electronic gates. This garage will be used by the tenants, with parking lot spaces allotted to clients and customers of the tenants. The tenants will access the garage by using a garage door opener. Therefore, in addition to the security deposit, the landlord is requiring a garage door opener deposit.

The landlord will provide varied switchboard services; each tenant may select the option that best suits the tenant's needs. The offices will come equipped with basic office furnishings. These furnishings will be inventoried on an attached exhibit. Tenants will have access to a conference room and will be allowed to use it for eight hours each month at no additional cost. Tenants will not be allowed to offer secretarial, administrative, or support services that directly compete with those provided by the landlord.

Although Any State's residential landlord and tenant statutes prohibit provisions attempting to exculpate and indemnify lessors from all wrongdoing, Any State's commercial landlord and tenant statutes permit indemnification provisions as long as such provisions are not unconscionable. Therefore, a standard commercial indemnification provision will be included in this lease. Additionally, according to state statutes, a month-to-month tenancy is created automatically should a commercial tenant hold over after a lease term expires unless the term is renewed by an agreement of the parties. Thus, the holding-over provision in this lease will parallel state law. From this worksheet, Barbara drafts the lease shown in Exhibit 16–3.

Once the lease is reviewed by Ava and approved by the client, three exhibits will be attached to it: (1) an inventory of each suite's furnishings, (2) the rules and regulations of the office building, and (3) the new tenant move-in cost breakdown; these are shown in Exhibits 16–4, 16–5, and 16–6, respectively.

Commercial lease worksheet

EXHIBIT 16–2

COMMERCIAL LEASE WORKSHEET

DATE OF INTAKE:		September 19, 2015
ATTORNEY:		Ava Ross
PARALEGAL:		Barbara Hammond
CLIENT NUMBER:		2150
MATTER NUMBER:		0009
PERSON RESPONSIBLE		
FOR INTAKE:		Barbara Hammond
1.	LANDLORD:	Sandor Commercial Group, Inc.
2.	ADDRESS:	1600 Adams Avenue, Suite 300
		Any City, Any State
3.	TELEPHONE:	(000) 223-4455; CELL: (000) 223-4457
		FAX: (000) 223-4776
4.	E-MAIL ADDRESS:	rsandor@scg.com
5.	TENANT:	Not applicable; preparation of standard lease form.
6.	ADDRESS:	Not applicable
7.	TELEPHONE:	N/A CELL: N/A FAX: N/A
8.	E-MAIL ADDRESS:	N/A

EXHIBIT 16–2   *(continued)*

9. TYPE OF LEASE: (A) _X_ GROSS   ___ NET   ___ TRIPLE NET
                               ___ PERCENTAGE   ___ OTHER
                          (B) ___ RETAIL   ___ WAREHOUSE
                               ___ OFFICE   _X_ EXECUTIVE SUITE
                               ___ OTHER

10. ADDRESS OF LEASED PREMISES (Include legal description if applicable):
                               3100 Commercial Boulevard
                               Any City, Any State

11. ASSIGNED PARKING SPACE (If applicable): Tenant will have use of parking garage and
    will be given a garage door opener for the security gate at entrance to the garage
    ($50.00 deposit on opener). The use of the garage shall be at the sole risk of the
    Tenant or person owning the automobile parked in the garage.

12. LEASE TERM:
    (A) BEGINNING DATE: leave open
    (B) ENDING DATE: leave open

13. RENT:
    (A) TOTAL AMOUNT: leave open
    (B) PAID IN monthly INSTALLMENTS OF $: leave open
    (C) COMMENCEMENT DATE: leave open
    (D) DUE DATE EACH INSTALLMENT: 1st day of each month

14. SECURITY DEPOSIT FOR PREMISES:
    (A) AMOUNT: One month's rent
    (B) PLACED IN: ___ INTEREST-BEARING ACCOUNT
                        _X_ NONINTEREST-BEARING ACCOUNT
    (C) IF PLACED IN INTEREST-BEARING ACCOUNT, SPECIFY PROCEDURE FOR
         PAYMENT OF INTEREST:
                       Not applicable
    (D) RETURN OF SECURITY DEPOSIT: (Specify conditions, time period after termination
         of lease, etc.): Tenant shall notify Landlord in writing no later than 30 days prior
         to the expiration of lease of Tenant's intention to vacate. If Tenant fails to do so or
         if Tenant vacates prior to expiration of lease, security deposit is forfeited. If all is
         in order, security deposit will be returned within 10 business days from Tenant's
         vacating the premises.

15. OTHER REQUIRED DEPOSITS: Garage door opener deposit of $50.00. This and other
    costs, not considered deposits, to be included on exhibit "New Tenant Move-In Cost
    Breakdown" to be supplied by client.

16. ADVANCE RENTS: _X_ FIRST MONTH   ___ LAST MONTH
                        ___ BOTH   TOTAL: $_____
                        ___ OTHER

17. CONSTRUCTION OF PREMISES (Build-out by Landlord or Tenant):
                       Not applicable

18. TENANT'S COVENANTS AS TO USE AND OCCUPANCY:
    Tenant agrees to occupy the premises only as a business office for one or two
    principal persons and shall not underlet the premises without the prior written
    consent of Landlord. Tenant also agrees not to commit waste of the premises, nor
    make any unlawful, improper, or offensive use of same, and shall not disturb the
    business activities of other Tenants.

19. BUILDING HOURS: 8:30 a.m. to 5:30 p.m. Mondays through Fridays, and 8:30 a.m.
    to 12:00 noon on Saturdays. Building to be closed on holidays observed by national
    banks in Any County, Any State.

20. SIGNS: This provision is included in exhibit "Rules and Regulations" provided by client.

21. DELIVERY FACILITIES: This provision is included in exhibit "Rules and Regulations"
    provided by client.

22. OPERATING COSTS: Not applicable

23. UTILITIES PAID BY LANDLORD: Landlord to provide air conditioning and heating for the leased premises and common areas in Landlord's judgment sufficient to reasonably cool or heat the building and electric current for common areas and the leased premises (for details, see provision 29).

24. UTILITIES PAID BY TENANT: All other utilities not included under provision 29 below.

25. INSURANCE: Tenant shall maintain, at all times during the term of the lease, workers' compensation and employer's liability insurance at legally required levels for the benefit of all employees entering the building. Tenant shall maintain at its sole cost and expense any and all insurance covering contents owned by Tenant.

26. REPAIRS TO BE DONE BY LANDLORD: All repairs to be done by Landlord, as Landlord deems necessary for safety, preservation or convenience of Tenant or other occupants.

27. REPAIRS TO BE DONE BY TENANT: None

28. ALTERATIONS TO PREMISES: Tenant shall have no right to alter, modify or improve the premises in any fashion.

29. LANDLORD SERVICES: (a) Landlord shall furnish the following services during workday hours of 8:30 a.m. to 5:30 p.m. on Mondays through Fridays, and 8:30 a.m. to 12:00 noon on Saturdays, inclusive on normal business days, except holidays observed by national banks in Any County, Any State: (i) elevator service in common with other Tenants; (ii) air conditioning and heating for the leased premises and the common areas in Landlord's judgment sufficient to reasonably cool or heat the leased premises; (iii) water for ordinary lavatory purposes; (iv) common use restrooms; (v) janitorial services during nonbusiness hours, except Saturdays and Sundays; and (vi) electric current for common areas and leased premises.
    (b) Landlord shall furnish the following services during workday hours of 8:30 a.m. to 5:15 p.m. on Mondays through Fridays on normal business days, except holidays observed by national banks in Any County, Any State: (i) receive, sort and distribute mail; (ii) switchboard (Tenant will select one of the following): switchboard operator to answer all incoming calls, Tenant to answer incoming calls when Tenant is on premises, Tenant to answer all incoming calls. There shall be no abatement, set-off or apportionment of rent payable by Tenant relative to the failure of Landlord to furnish any of the services in paragraph (a) or the making of any repairs or maintenance.

30. RULES AND REGULATIONS: Tenant agrees that it, and its agents, representatives, officers, guests, clients and customers will comport themselves in a businesslike manner so as not to disrupt other Tenants and will abide by the Landlord's rules and regulations as set forth in an exhibit attached to the lease (exhibit to be supplied by client).

31. LANDLORD'S RIGHT OF ACCESS: Landlord shall have the right to enter the premises at reasonable hours to examine the premises and for the purpose of making such repairs, additions and alterations as Landlord shall deem necessary for the safety, preservation or convenience of Tenant or other occupants. No entry by the Landlord shall constitute a breach of the covenant of quiet enjoyment, nor a retaking of possession by the Landlord.

32. HOLDING OVER: If Tenant remains in possession of the premises after the lease term, there shall be no tacit renewal of the lease, and Tenant shall be deemed a month-to-month tenant.

33. OPTION TO RENEW: This provision is not to be included in the standard lease form; client will negotiate this on an individual basis.

34. ASSIGNMENT: Not permitted without prior written consent of Landlord.

35. SUBLETTING: Not permitted without prior written consent of Landlord.

36. PENALTIES:
    (A) LATE RENT: If Tenant has not paid rent by the 5th day after it is due and payable, then Tenant agrees to pay an administrative late charge of $10.00 per day to Landlord.
    (B) RETURNED CHECKS: This provision not to be included.
    (C) OTHER: Not applicable

EXHIBIT 16–2 *(continued)*

37. SUBORDINATION: This provision not to be included.

38. DESTRUCTION OF PREMISES: This provision not to be included.

39. INDEMNIFICATION: Tenant shall indemnify, defend and hold harmless Landlord against any expense, loss or liability paid, suffered or incurred, including attorneys' fees (at both the trial and appellate levels) as a result of any breach by Tenant, its agents, customers or visitors of any agreement in this lease or as a result of Tenant's use or occupancy of the premises, or the carelessness, negligence or improper conduct of Tenant, its agents, customers or visitors.

40. DEFAULT:

    (A) SPECIFY CONDITIONS CONSTITUTING DEFAULT: Default in payment of rent or if Tenant violates any covenant in the lease or rules and regulations set forth in the attached exhibit.

    (B) TIME PERIOD IN WHICH TO CURE: Tenant immediately becomes a Tenant at sufferance and Landlord shall be entitled to re-enter and retake possession immediately.

    (C) REMEDIES: In the event that legal action is necessary to recover possession of premises, rental payments, damages, or to enforce the provisions of this lease, Tenant agrees to pay to Landlord reasonable attorneys' fees (including the cost of any appeal), and all court costs and other incidental costs. If Landlord fails to perform any covenant, term or condition of this lease, Tenant shall recover a money judgment against Landlord, such judgment to be satisfied only out of the proceeds of sale received upon execution of judgment and levy thereon against the right, title and interest of Landlord in the office complex located at 3100 Commercial Boulevard, Any City, Any State, as the same may then be encumbered and the Landlord shall not be otherwise liable for any deficiency. In no event shall Tenant have the right to levy execution against any property of Landlord other than the office complex described above.

41. ABANDONMENT: It shall be a default if Tenant abandons the premises. Such abandonment shall not release Tenant from the future obligation to pay rent for the duration of the lease, even if Landlord shall retake the premises.

42. NOTICES:

    (A) TO LANDLORD: Sandor Commercial Group, Inc.
        1600 Adams Avenue, Suite 300
        Any City, Any State

    (B) TO TENANT: At the premises

43. ADDITIONAL PROVISIONS: (A) Condition of Premises: Tenant acknowledges that it has inspected the premises and all furniture, fixtures and equipment contained therein and further acknowledges that they are in satisfactory condition and accepts the premises, furniture, fixtures and equipment in their current condition "as is" without requiring Landlord to make any repairs or replacement thereof. (B) Personal Property: Tenant agrees that any personal property brought onto the premises is done so at Tenant's own risk and if any loss or damage occurs, Landlord is not liable. (C) Noncompetitive Office Equipment Use: Tenant shall be allowed to place a computer system, facsimile machine and file cabinet in the premises for the sole use of its business, and said equipment shall not be used to offer services to other Tenants in such manner as to be deemed competitive with the Executive Office Support Services Center. (D) Conference Room: Use of the conference room is on a reservation basis, usually at least 24 hours in advance. For the first 8 hours of use each month there is no charge to the Tenant; for each hour beyond that, per month, the charge is $15.00 per hour. (E) Furniture/Equipment: Landlord has supplied Tenant with furniture and equipment for Tenant's exclusive use during the lease term, as set forth on an attached exhibit. At the expiration of the lease term, Tenant shall surrender all furniture and equipment in the same condition as when the lease commenced and be responsible for any damage, normal wear and tear excepted.

EXECUTIVE SUITE LEASE

THIS LEASE is made this _____ day of _____, 20 ___, between _____, hereinafter referred to as "Landlord," and _____, hereinafter referred to as "Tenant."

WITNESSETH:

That Landlord hereby lets unto Tenant for a term commencing on _____, and ending _____, the following described premises: Executive Suite(s) _____ located at 3100 Commercial Boulevard, Any City, Any State, hereinafter referred to as the "Leased Premises"; the terms and conditions of this Lease being set forth below:

    I.   **RENT.** The monthly rent for the term of the Lease is $_____ per month, being due and payable without demand on the first (1st) day of each month. In addition, Tenant shall pay any state sales tax or use tax, together with each payment of rent. If Tenant has not paid the rent by the fifth (5th) day after it is due and payable, then Tenant agrees to pay an administrative late charge of $10.00 per day to Landlord. Tenant shall also pay the following to Landlord:

        $_____ paid the execution hereon as rent for the month(s) of _____, including sales tax;

        $_____ security deposit;

        $_____ one (1) garage door opener deposit;

        $_____ total deposit.

    II. **SERVICES.**

      (A) Landlord shall furnish the following services during workday hours of 8:30 a.m. to 5:30 p.m. on Mondays through Fridays, and 8:30 a.m. to 12:00 noon on Saturdays, inclusive (except where otherwise specified) on normal business days, except holidays observed by national banks in Any County, Any State:

      (i)   elevator service in common with other tenants;

      (ii) air conditioning and heating for the Leased Premises and the common areas in Landlord's judgment sufficient to reasonably cool or heat the Leased Premises;

      (iii) water for ordinary lavatory purposes;

      (iv) common use restrooms;

      (v) janitorial services during nonbusiness hours, except Saturdays and Sundays; and

      (vi) electric current for common areas and the Leased Premises.

      (B) Landlord shall furnish the following services during workday hours of 8:30 a.m. to 5:15 p.m. on Mondays through Fridays on normal business days, except holidays observed by national banks in Any County, Any State:

      (i)   receive, sort and distribute mail;

      (ii) switchboard (select one):

        _____ switchboard operator to answer incoming calls

        _____ Tenant to answer incoming calls when Tenant is on the Leased Premises

        _____ Tenant to answer all incoming calls

Tenant agrees to follow and abide by the Rules for the Communication System as attached hereto in Exhibit B and made a part hereto.

      (C) There shall be no abatement, set-off or apportionment of rent payable by Tenant relative to the failure of Landlord to furnish any of the services listed in Paragraph (A) above or the making of any repairs or maintenance.

    III. **USE.** The Tenant agrees to occupy the Leased Premises only as a business office for one or two principal persons and shall not underlet the same or any part thereof, or assign this Lease, without the prior written consent of the Landlord. Tenant also agrees

EXHIBIT 16-3   (*continued*)

not to suffer or commit any waste of the Leased Premises, nor make any unlawful, improper or offensive use of same, and shall not disturb the business activities of Landlord or other tenants.

IV. **CONDITION OF PREMISES.** Tenant acknowledges that it has inspected the Leased Premises and all furniture, fixtures and equipment contained therein, and further acknowledges that they are in satisfactory condition and accepts the Leased Premises, furniture, fixtures and equipment in their current condition, "as is," without requiring Landlord to make any repairs or replacement thereof.

V. **ABANDONMENT.** It shall be a default if Tenant abandons the Leased Premises. Such abandonment shall not release Tenant from the future obligation to pay rent for the duration of the Lease, even if Landlord shall retake the Leased Premises. Tenant shall, at the termination of said tenancy, quietly yield up the Leased Premises, together with Landlord's furnishings, if any, in as good and tenantable condition in all respects as the same were at the beginning of the Lease Term.

VI. **DEFAULT.** It is agreed that if any default is made in the payment of rent as above set forth, or if Tenant violates any covenant of the Lease, Tenant shall forthwith become a tenant at sufferance, and the Landlord shall be entitled to re-enter and retake possession immediately. In the event that legal action is necessary to recover possession of the Leased Premises, rental payments, damages, or to enforce the provisions of this Lease, the Tenant agrees to pay to Landlord reasonable attorney's fees (including the cost of any appeal), and all court costs and other incidental costs.

VII. **RULES AND REGULATIONS.** This Lease is subject to rules, regulations and control of Landlord, and Tenant agrees to comply with same as adopted from time to time. Tenant agrees that it and its agents, representatives, officers, guests, clients and customers shall at all times comport themselves in a businesslike manner so as not to disrupt, interfere or impair the ability of the Landlord and other tenants to conduct their business affairs. Continued violation of this provision after written notice from the Landlord shall constitute a default of this Lease. Tenant agrees to follow and abide by the Rules and Regulations as attached hereto in Exhibit B and made a part hereof.

VIII. **REPAIRS AND ALTERATIONS.** Tenant shall have no right to alter, modify or improve the Leased Premises in any fashion. Landlord shall have the right to enter the Leased Premises at reasonable hours to examine the same and for the purpose of making such repairs, additions and alterations as Landlord shall deem necessary for safety, preservation or convenience of Tenant or other occupants of the building. No entry by the Landlord or its agents pursuant to a right granted in this Lease shall constitute a breach of the covenant of quiet enjoyment, nor a retaking of possession by the Landlord.

IX. **SUBLETTING AND ASSIGNMENT.** Tenant shall not sublet, assign or transfer its rights under this Lease without the prior written consent of the Landlord. In the event of a permitted transfer, all covenants and agreements herein contained shall extend to and bind the heirs, personal representatives, successors and assigns of each party hereto.

X. **INDEMNIFICATION.** Tenant shall indemnify, defend and hold harmless Landlord against any expense, loss or liability paid, suffered or incurred, including attorneys' fees (at both trial and appellate levels) as a result of any breach by Tenant, its agents, customers or visitors of any agreement in this Lease, or as a result of the carelessness, negligence or improper conduct of Tenant, its agents, customers or visitors.

XI. **PERSONAL PROPERTY.** Tenant agrees that any personal property brought onto the Leased Premises is done so at Tenant's own risk and if any loss or damage occurs, Landlord is not liable.

XII. **INSURANCE.** Tenant shall maintain, at all times during the term of this Lease, workers' compensation and employer's liability insurance at legally required levels for the benefit of all employees entering the building as a result of or in connection with their employment by Tenant. Tenant shall maintain at its sole cost and expense any and all insurance covering contents owned by Tenant, if any.

XIII. **TENANT'S REMEDIES FOR LANDLORD'S BREACH.** If Landlord shall fail to perform any covenant, term or condition of the Lease upon Landlord's part to be performed and, as a consequence of such default, Tenant shall recover a money judgment against Landlord, such judgment shall be satisfied only out of the proceeds of sale received upon execution of such judgment and levy thereon against the right, title and interest of Landlord in the office complex located at 3100 Commercial Boulevard, Any City, Any State, as the same may then be encumbered, and the Landlord shall not be otherwise liable for any deficiency. It is understood that in no event shall Tenant have any right to levy execution against any property of Landlord other than its interest in the office complex as described above. In the event of the sale or other transfer of Landlord's rights, title and interest in the Premises of the office complex, Landlord shall be released from all liability and obligations hereunder.

XIV. **SUPPORT SERVICES/RULES AND REGULATIONS.** The Executive Suite Support Services and Rules and Regulations are attached hereto by separate schedule and are incorporated into this Lease by reference.

XV. **NONCOMPETITIVE OFFICE EQUIPMENT USE.** Tenant shall be allowed to place a computer system, facsimile machine and file cabinet in the Leased Premises for the sole use of its business and said equipment shall not be used to offer services to other Tenants in such manner as to be deemed competitive with the Executive Office Support Services Center.

XVI. **CONFERENCE ROOM.** Use of the conference room is on a reservation basis, usually at least twenty-four (24) hours in advance. For the first eight (8) hours of use each month, there is no charge to the Tenant; for each hour beyond that, per month, the charge is $15.00 per hour.

XVII. **HOLDING OVER.** If Tenant remains in possession of the Premises after the Lease Term, there shall be no tacit renewal of this Lease, and Tenant shall be deemed to be under a month-to-month tenancy. Tenant shall pay to Landlord an amount equal to the Monthly Rent stated in the Lease for each month or portion thereof Tenant remains on the Premises. All other obligations of Tenant under this Lease shall be applicable to Tenant during the period in which Tenant is a month-to month tenant.

XVIII. **PARKING.** Use of the parking garage shall be at the sole risk of the Tenant or the person owning any automobile parked in the underground garage. The Landlord shall in no event be liable for any loss, destruction, theft or damage to said automobiles or property contained therein.

XIX. **VACATION OF PREMISES.** Tenant shall notify Landlord, in writing no later than thirty (30) days prior to the Lease expiration, of its intentions to vacate the Leased Premises. If Tenant fails to notify Landlord in writing as specified or vacates the Leased Premises prior to the Lease expiration, Tenant's security deposit will be forfeit. If, upon inspection by management, the Leased Premises is in good condition and all other provisions of this Lease have been met by Tenant, Tenant's security deposit shall be returned to Tenant within ten (10) business days after the vacation of the Leased Premises by Tenant.

XX. **FURNISHINGS AND EQUIPMENT.** Landlord has supplied Tenant with furnishings and equipment for Tenant's exclusive use during the term of this Lease as attached hereto in Exhibit A and made a part hereof. At the expiration of the term of this Lease, Tenant

EXHIBIT 16–3   (*continued*)

shall surrender all furnishings and equipment listed in Exhibit A in the same condition as when the Lease commenced and be responsible for any damage, normal wear and tear excepted.

XXI.   NOTICES. Any notice, consent or other instrument required or permitted to be given under this Lease shall be in writing and shall be delivered in person, or sent by certified mail, return receipt requested, postage prepaid, or by Federal Express or similar overnight courier service, address (a) if to Landlord, Sandor Commercial Group, Inc., 1600 Adams Avenue, Suite 300, Any City, Any State; (b) if to Tenant, at the Leased Premises.

IN WITNESS WHEREOF, the parties have hereunto set their hands of the date first above written.

WITNESSES: LANDLORD:
                                                        Sandor Commercial Group, Inc.

_____   BY: _____
                                                        Agent/Owner

_____   Title: _____
                                                        TENANT:

_____   BY: _____

_____   Title: _____

EXHIBIT 16–4   **Suite inventory**

EXHIBIT A

SUITE _____ INVENTORY

The following is a list of the items contained in the above-referenced suite.

Description	Quantity
Executive desk(s)	_____
Executive chair(s)	_____
Credenza(s)	_____
Telephone(s)	_____
Waste basket(s)	_____
Side chair(s)	_____
Picture(s): list name,	_____

artist's name, and picture
number for each picture below:

_____
_____
_____
_____
_____
_____

Tenant agrees not to nail, pin, or tape any items on office walls that have been wallpapered.

_____   _____
Tenant   Owner/Agent

EXHIBIT B
RULES AND REGULATIONS

1. Tenant, its officers, agents, servants and employees shall not block or obstruct any of the entries, passages, doors, elevators, elevator doors, hallways or stairways of building or garage, or place, empty or throw any rubbish, litter, trash or material of any nature into such areas, or permit such areas to be used at any time except for ingress and egress of Tenant, its officers, agents, employees, patrons, licensees, customers, visitors or guests.

2. The movement of furniture, equipment, machines, merchandise or materials within, into or out of the leased premises or building shall be restricted to time, method and routing of movement as determined by Landlord upon request from Tenant, and Tenant shall assume all liability and risk to property, leased premises and building in such movement. Tenant shall not move furniture, machines, equipment, merchandise or materials within, into or out of the building or leased premises without having first obtained a written permit from Landlord twenty-four (24) hours in advance.

3. No signs, door plaques, advertisements or notices shall be displayed, painted or affixed by Tenant, its officers, servants, employees, patrons, licensees, customers, visitors or guests in or on any part of the outside or inside of the building or leased premises without prior written consent of Landlord, and then only of such color, size, character, style and material and in such places as shall be approved and designated by Landlord. Signs on doors and entrances to leased premises shall be placed thereon by a contractor designated by Landlord and paid for by Tenant.

4. Landlord will maintain an alphabetical Directory Board on the ground floor lobby of the building containing one name of each Tenant. Additional listings will be limited to only those required by law.

5. Landlord will not be responsible for lost or stolen personal property, equipment, money or any articles taken from the leased premises or the building regardless of how or when loss occurs.

6. Tenant, its officers, agents, servants and employees shall not install or operate any refrigerating, heating or air-conditioning apparatus or carry on any mechanical operation or bring onto the leased premises or the building any inflammable fluids or explosives without written permission of Landlord.

7. Tenant, its officers, agents, servants or employees shall not use the leased premises or the building for housing, lodging or sleeping purposes or for the cooking or preparation of food without the prior written consent of the Landlord.

8. No additional locks shall be placed on any door in the building without the prior consent of Landlord. Landlord will furnish two keys to each lock on doors in the leased premises, and Landlord, upon the request of Tenant, shall provide additional duplicate keys at Tenant's expense. Landlord may at all times keep a pass key to the leased premises. All keys shall be returned to the Landlord upon termination of the Lease.

9. No space in the building shall, without the prior written consent of the Landlord, be used for manufacturing, public sales, the storage of merchandise or the sale or auction of merchandise, goods or property of any kind.

10. Canvassing, soliciting and peddling in the building are prohibited, and each Tenant shall cooperate to prevent the same. In this respect, Tenant shall promptly report such activities to the Property Manager's office.

11. The work of Landlord's janitors or cleaning personnel shall not be hindered by Tenant after 6:00 p.m., and such work may be done at any time when the offices are vacant. The windows, doors and fixtures may be cleaned at any time. Tenant shall provide adequate waste and rubbish receptacles, cabinets, bookcases, map cases, etc., necessary to prevent unreasonable hardship to Landlord in discharging its obligation regarding cleaning services. In this regard, Tenant shall also empty all glasses, cups and other containers holding any type of liquid whatsoever.

EXHIBIT 16–5   *(continued)*

12. Tenant will be responsible for any damage to the leased premises, including carpeting and flooring, as a result of rust or corrosion of file cabinets, roller chairs, metal objects or spills of any type of liquid.
13. Tenants employing laborers or others outside of the building shall not have their employees paid in the building but shall arrange to pay their payrolls elsewhere.
14. Tenant shall not make or permit any use of the leased premises or building facilities which, directly or indirectly, is forbidden by law, ordinance or governmental or municipal regulations, code or order or which may be disreputable or dangerous to life, limb or property.
15. Tenant shall permit Landlord or its agents to enter the leased premises to make inspection, repairs, alterations or additions in or to the leased premises or the building and at any time in the event of any emergency shall permit Landlord to perform any acts related to the safety, protection, preservation, reletting or improvement of the leased premises or building.
16. Landlord shall have the right to exclude any person from the building other than during customary business hours, and any person in the building will be subject to identification by the employees and agents of Landlord. All persons in or entering the building shall be required to comply with the security policies of the building. If Tenant desires any additional security for the premises, Tenant shall have the right (with the advance written consent of the Landlord) to obtain such additional service at Tenant's sole cost and expense.
17. In keeping with the Clean Air Act of Any State, Management requests that there be no smoking in the leased premises, the lobby, the elevators, the restrooms or any of the other Common Areas.

Initials:

_____
Tenant

_____
Landlord

EXHIBIT 16–6   New tenant move-in cost breakdown

EXHIBIT C
NEW TENANT MOVE-IN COST BREAKDOWN

I. AMENITY COST BREAKDOWN

Furniture	$ 0
Switchboard	$ 75.00 per month
One phone line	$ 0
Second phone line	$ 35.00 per month
Voicemail	$ 0
Parking	$ 30.00 per month, secured covered garage
A/C after hours and weekends	Available
Secretarial services	$ 0
Conference room	8 hours per month free; $15.00 each extra hour per month

_____

Amenities	$ 95.00
Rent for Suite _____	$ _____
Total Package	$ _____

II. MOVE-IN COST BREAKDOWN

Switchboard programming	$140.00
Keys	$ 0
Directory listing	$ 0
Door signage	$ 0 (suite number and company name)
Security deposit	One month's rent
Garage door opener deposit	$ 50.00

One time move-in costs	$140.00
Garage opener deposit	$ 50.00
Security deposit	$ _____
First month's rent	$ _____
Total move-in costs	$ _____

Initials:

_____
Tenant

_____
Landlord

CHAPTER SUMMARY

1. A gross lease is a lease in which the tenant pays a fixed basic rent and the landlord remains responsible for all operating expenses, whereas under a net lease, the tenant, in addition to paying a fixed basic rent, incurs a proportionate share of some or all of the landlord's operating costs.

2. A graduated lease is a lease that allows for rent adjustment (typically upward) over the term of the lease by tying the rent provision to the Consumer Price Index or by providing an increase of a specified percentage of the annual rental payment.

3. A percentage lease, quite popular in retail rentals, requires that the tenant, in addition to paying a fixed basic rent, pay the landlord a stated percentage of the tenant's sales receipts (gross or net). A percentage lease provision should include the requisite percentage figure, a definition of the term *sales,* the conditions under which the provision goes into effect (for example, after annual gross sales exceed a stated figure), and the manner of payment (for example, quarterly or annually).

4. A ground lease is a lease of vacant land for an exceptionally lengthy period of time, allowing the tenant to construct a commercial building on the leased land. The result of a ground lease is the separation of ownership of the land and the improvements to the land.

5. The basic provisions of a commercial lease are similar to those found in a residential lease. The parties, leased premises, rental term, security

deposit, and advance rent should all be specified clearly. The responsibility for utilities, repairs, maintenance, and insurance should be allocated. The conditions constituting default and the applicable remedies should be noted. In addition to these common provisions, commercial leases often include more complex rent payment and alterations provisions as well as provisions pertaining to business hours, signage, delivery facilities, parking, and rules and regulations of the building or center.

6. If the property is mortgaged or may, in the future, be subject to mortgage loans, the lessor's lender typically requires that all lessees subordinate their interests in the property to that of the lender. To protect the interests of both a lessee and the lessor's lender in the event of the lessor's default and subsequent foreclosure, a subordination, non-disturbance, and attornment (SNDA) agreement may be executed. Such an agreement not only subordinates the lessee's interests to the lender but also maintains the lessee's rights to remain on the premises under the terms of the existing lease as well as the lender's right to receive rental payments directly from the lessee should a foreclosure occur.

7. Of particular concern in shopping center leases are the build-out, parking, exclusivity (competing business), and business hours provisions. The parties should designate clearly the nature of the build-out work to be done, the party responsible for performing the work, and the allocation of expenses for the work. The parking provision should specify the number of allocated parking spaces per tenant and any parking restrictions. The exclusivity provision, if included, should be carefully worded to protect the tenant from direct competition, while allowing complementary businesses. The business hours provision should emphasize uniformity of hours within the center and conformity with city and county ordinances.

8. An executive office suite provides a tenant with a professional atmosphere and minimal overhead costs. Rather than hiring full- or part-time support staff, the tenant has access to support services provided by the lessor. The lease should designate the proferred services and indicate whether the cost of such services is included in the monthly rent or is charged separately. Rules and regulations for the use of common business facilities should be included, and any furniture, furnishings, and equipment provided by the lessor should be inventoried.

9. Although warehouse leases typically are less complex than other commercial leases, certain provisions should be of concern to the parties. If the lessee is located out of state, a provision should be included in the lease to safeguard the lessor against bad checks, while, at the same time, protecting the lessee (in the event of a late or lost check) from the lessor's self-help remedies. Further, the lease should include provisions prohibiting the storage of hazardous materials and, unless otherwise agreed, prohibiting the conduct of any business on the leased premises.

WEB RESOURCES

http://www.retailtenants.org/

This is the site of the National Retail Tenants Association (NRTA). It is a nonprofit organization that provides resources and education for commercial and retail real estate lease professionals.

Sample commercial leases can be found at the following sites:

http://www.ilrg.com/

This is the site of the Internet Legal Research Group (ILRG). If you go to the "Legal Forms Archive," choose "Leases and Real Estate," and then select "Agreement to Lease (Commercial Lease)," you can view commercial leases for each state.

http://www.legaldocs.com/

At this site, you can preview for free a sample office lease by selecting "Leases" and then clicking on the example of an office lease.

http://www.freefranchisedocs.com/

This site allows you to view numerous sample documents for various franchises. It also lets you view a sample commercial lease by clicking on "Contracts" and then scrolling down to "Sample Other Agreements."

REVIEW QUESTIONS

1. Distinguish between the following:
   a. A net lease and a triple net lease
   b. A graduated lease and a percentage lease
2. What operating expenses incurred by a lessor might a lessee be obliged to pay under a triple net lease?
3. What advantages, if any, are there to signing a ground lease rather than purchasing a parcel of real property for the construction of commercial premises?
4. What basic provisions should be included in a commercial lease?
5. What special provisions should be included in the following?
   a. A shopping center lease
   b. An executive office suite lease
   c. A warehouse lease

DISCUSSION QUESTIONS

1. ABC, Inc., leased commercial space to Roy and Barbara Wilson for a restaurant. The lease provided for assignment of the lease by the lessees with prior written consent of the lessor, which consent could not be unreasonably withheld. The Wilsons attempted to sell their restaurant business and assign their interest in the lease to the prospective purchaser. They asked ABC, Inc., to approve the assignment and indicated that time was of the essence. ABC, Inc., requested personal and financial information on the prospective assignee, which the Wilsons supplied. It then requested more detailed information, which was also supplied. The information provided indicated that the prospective assignee had an excellent credit score. ABC, Inc., deferred making a decision regarding the assignment until, finally, the prospective assignee withdrew his offer. The Wilsons are suing ABC, Inc., for breach of contract and intentional interference with a prospective business advantage. The Wilsons claim that ABC, Inc., deliberately withheld its consent due to animosity over a prior lawsuit between them. ABC, Inc., contends that it did not refuse consent but merely delayed giving the Wilsons an answer until additional information was obtained. What additional information, beyond

a credit history, could be considered reasonable grounds for a lessor to withhold consent to an assignment?

2. Assume the same fact scenario as presented in Question 1. ABC, Inc., is attempting to distinguish between delaying consent and refusing consent. Do you believe this is a valid argument?

3. Many commercial leases contain assignment clauses identical or similar to the one found in the above fact scenario—a simple clause indicating that the premises may not be assigned without the prior written consent of the lessor, which consent shall not be unreasonably withheld. Do you find this assignment clause vague? Why or why not? If so, what changes would you make?

4. Barton, as lessor, signed a preprinted commercial lease with Stone, as lessee. The property in question was described in the lease as "premises located at a strip mall at 123 Main Street" to be used solely as a health spa. The lease term was five years. An annual square footage rate of $0.90 per square foot and a commencement date were included in the lease. When the parties signed the lease, the strip mall was still under construction. After signing the lease, Barton recommended a contractor to Stone to construct the desired improvements in the space. The contractor recommended an architect. Based on the architectural plans, the contractor prepared an estimate of the costs of the build-out of the space. Stone, in turn, presented the estimate to Barton to discuss payment for the improvements. Barton believed that the lease obligated him to deliver only a building shell, and he refused to pay for the improvements. Stone, on the other hand, believed that Barton was obligated under the lease to provide premises complete with tenant improvements. As a result, the improvements were not made, and Stone never took physical possession of the premises and never paid rent. Barton eventually found another tenant. He alleges that Stone breached the contract and that the breach resulted in over $100,000 in damages. Both parties admit that the first discussion about who would pay for the improvements occurred after the cost estimates were received, which occurred after the lease was signed. If this matter goes to trial, how should the court rule? Why?

5. XYZ, Inc., leased commercial premises to Crystalline Lighting on a month-to-month basis under an oral lease agreement. Crystalline Lighting rented the premises on an "as is" basis and was in exclusive control of the premises. XYZ, Inc., had responsibility for roof repairs and any structural damages. The leased premises at one time had been two separate spaces, but a partition wall had been removed, some time prior to the commencement of the lease, to open the space up and make it one space. Because it originally had been two separate spaces, there was a slight difference in floor levels in the premises. Crystalline Lighting was aware of the difference in floor levels and posted signs alerting patrons of the floor change. Gail Nelson, a patron of the store, did not notice the discrepancy in floor levels and fell, injuring herself. If Gail brings a personal injury suit, who is liable in this instance, XYZ, Inc., or Crystalline Lighting? Why?

ETHICAL QUESTION

Sandra Gordon, an associate with your law firm, graduated from law school one year ago. Tim Benton, a senior partner of the firm, had originally placed Sandra in the family law department of the firm because of Sandra's experience with the family law clinic for legal aid clients that was run by her law school. Tim now believes Sandra should gain experience in other departments and has asked Sandra to work in the real estate department. Sandra loves family law and has neither experience nor interest in real estate; however, she wants to continue to work for this law firm, so she grudgingly accepts the reassignment.

You have been asked to work with Sandra as well as with your present supervising attorney. This morning Sandra met with a client who just purchased a small warehouse and wants a lease drafted for use with future lessees. Sandra hands you a copy of a retail center percentage lease and a legal pad on which Sandra has scratched a few notes, including the name of the client, the address of the warehouse, the size of the warehouse units, the required deposits, and the average monthly rent. She asks you to copy the retail lease verbatim and just insert the information on the legal pad. You inform Sandra that you have several warehouse leases on file that would be more appropriate than the retail center percentage lease. Sandra very sharply insists that you follow her instructions. You know that Sandra's inexperience will become apparent to the client if you follow her instructions and that the document will not best serve the client's needs. What should you do?

Slossberg Law Office on CourseMate

Please go to www.cengagebrain.com to log into CourseMate, access the Slossberg Law Office, and work on your client files. Each module corresponds to a chapter in the text. Within each module, you will be provided with instructions by the supervising attorney. You are asked to keep track of time spent on time sheets. The documents produced through working on client files in the law office can then be compiled into a portfolio of final work product.

CourseMate

The available CourseMate for this text has an interactive eBook and interactive learning tools, including flash cards, quizzes, and more. To learn more about this resource and access free demo CourseMate resources, including the Slossberg Law Office, go to www.cengagebrain.com, and search for this book. To access CourseMate materials that you have purchased, go to login.cengagebrain.com.

17 Eviction Procedures

CHAPTER OBJECTIVES

Upon completion of this chapter, the student will:

- Understand the difference between constructive eviction and actual eviction
- Know the steps to take in an eviction of a tenant
- Know how to draft an eviction complaint
- Understand the concept of distress for rent

Introduction

The last two chapters have focused on the rights and obligations of parties to residential and commercial leases, both as set forth in statutory law and as set forth in the agreements made between the parties themselves. Should the landlord or tenant fail to perform as required by state statute or as agreed, certain remedies are available. Leases very rarely address the issue of a landlord's breach, yet a tenant may have a legal remedy available to him or her, should a landlord fail to maintain the leased premises, through the filing of a lawsuit for constructive eviction. A landlord has several more remedies available should a tenant breach a lease. A landlord may sue the tenant for breach of contract, may terminate the lease and evict the tenant, and in some states may, through an action for distress for rent, have the tenant's personal property sold to reimburse the landlord for back rent owed.

This chapter addresses each of these remedies. As a paralegal, you may be asked by your supervising attorney to research your state's statutes regarding the legal remedies available to either a tenant or a landlord, or you may be asked to draft a notice of termination, an eviction complaint, a complaint for distress for rent, or a stipulation of settlement between the parties. This chapter emphasizes the procedural steps to be taken in securing a legal remedy for a default under a lease.

Constructive Eviction

To evict a tenant is to deprive the tenant of the possession of the leased premises. Eviction can occur through the bringing of a suit for possession of the leased premises by the landlord because of a breach of the lease by the tenant or because of the retention of possession of the premises by the tenant after the expiration of the lease. The bringing of a suit for possession is called

actual eviction, and the procedures through which actual eviction is accomplished are discussed in detail in the following text.

An actual eviction is distinguishable from *abandonment* or a *voluntary surrender* by the tenant. If the tenant abandons the premises, the tenant is considered to have voluntarily surrendered the leased premises. State statutory law may provide guidelines for the legal presumption of a tenant's abandonment (for example, if a residential tenant is renting month-to-month and has been gone from the premises for fifteen days, half of the rental period). Additionally, state law may provide different notice requirements with which a landlord must comply for the presumed abandonment of commercial and residential premises. Regardless of whether the property is residential or commercial, if the tenant is current with rent payments, absent an actual knowledge of tenant abandonment of the premises, most state laws will forbid a landlord to retake possession. Further, if the landlord asks the tenant to leave the premises and the tenant agrees to do so, removing himself or herself together with his or her belongings from the premises, a voluntary surrender has occurred rather than an actual eviction. If a landlord simply is seeking possession and is not seeking monetary damages from the tenant, a landlord should first determine whether a tenant may be amenable to voluntary surrender of the premises before moving forward with an actual eviction. This can save time and money for both parties. It is advisable to obtain the tenant's agreement to this in writing.

In contrast to actual eviction, eviction of a tenant can occur through constructive eviction. **Constructive eviction** happens when the landlord breaches the lease in such a manner as to make the leased premises unusable for the purpose(s) stated in the lease. Through such a breach, the landlord, although not forcibly ejecting the tenant from the premises, is depriving the tenant of the enjoyment of the premises for which the tenant contracted. Constructive eviction can occur through either an act or an omission by the landlord directly or by one of the landlord's agents. In a case of constructive eviction, the tenant may bring suit against the landlord for money damages. In order for a tenant to claim a constructive eviction, the landlord's actions (or omissions) must appear to have been intentionally done (or omitted) to deprive the tenant of possession or permanently to interfere with the tenant's beneficial use or enjoyment of the whole or a part of the leased premises. A mere act or default on the part of the landlord without the requisite accompanying intent is not sufficient to constitute a constructive eviction. The intention to evict may be indicated by the nature and character of the landlord's actions.

In order for a tenant to claim a constructive eviction, the tenant must leave the leased premises within a reasonable time after the occurrence of the wrongful act. The timing of the vacating of the premises can be tricky. For example, if the landlord's breach is a failure to repair and the tenant vacates the leased premises before giving the landlord a reasonable opportunity to make the required repair, it is difficult to prove constructive eviction. The landlord may have had every good intention to repair the premises. On the other hand, if the tenant waits too long in vacating the premises, there is the problem of proving that the landlord's breach made the premises uninhabitable. After all, the tenant continued to reside in the premises after the breach! The burden of showing that the leaving of the premises took place within a reasonable period of time is on the tenant. What constitutes a reasonable period of time therefore depends on the circumstances of each case. The question is a question of fact to be decided by the finder of fact (a judge in a bench trial, a jury in a jury trial). Delay in vacating the leased premises may be excused by showing that the

actual eviction: The bringing of a suit for possession of leased premises.

constructive eviction: The breach by a landlord of a lease in such a manner as to make the leased premises unusable.

tenant relied upon the promises of the landlord to correct the defects complained of. A tenant loses the right to vacate the premises if, before carrying out the intention to vacate, the cause for the constructive eviction has ceased to exist.

What actions or omissions may warrant the bringing of an action for constructive eviction? The interference by a landlord with the tenant's right of ingress and egress to the leased premises, such as by changing the locks or using a bootlock or similar device, may constitute a constructive eviction. It may also lead to a tenant suit for civil theft, alleging that the landlord has taken personal property belonging to the tenant (i.e., the contents of the leased premises) with the intent to deprive the tenant of that property. The termination or continued interruption of water, gas, heat, or other utility service by the landlord, even if the utility service is under the control of the landlord, may constitute eviction. Failure of the tenant to pay for these services does not permit the landlord to terminate the services.

In those states that follow the Uniform Residential Landlord and Tenant Act (URLTA), a tenant may, in an action for constructive eviction against a landlord for these violations, recover treble (triple) damages, plus attorneys' fees and costs. For example, Alabama, a state that has adopted the URLTA, provides in Section 35-9A-407 of its statutes:

> If a landlord unlawfully removes or excludes the tenant from the premises or willfully diminishes services to the tenant by interrupting or causing the interruption of heat, running water, hot water, electric, gas, or other essential service, the tenant may recover possession or terminate the rental agreement and, in either case, recover an amount equal to not more than three months' periodic rent or the actual damages sustained by the tenant, whichever is greater, and reasonable attorney's fees. If the rental agreement is terminated under this section, the landlord shall return all security recoverable under Section 35-9A-201 and all unearned prepaid rent.

The URLTA also has safeguards in place to prevent a landlord from taking retaliatory action against a tenant who complains about a landlord's violation of a statutory or contractual obligation. Illustrative of this point, Rhode Island, another state that has adopted the URLTA, states in Section 34-18-46 (a–c)of its statutes:

> (a) Except as provided in this section, a landlord may not retaliate by increasing rent or decreasing services or by bringing or threatening to bring an action for possession because:
> > (1) The tenant has complained to a governmental agency charged with the responsibility for enforcement of a building or housing code of a violation applicable to the premises materially affecting health and safety; or
> > (2) The tenant has complained to the landlord of a violation under Section 34-18-22; or
> > (3) The tenant has organized or become a member of a tenants' union or similar organization; or
> > (4) The tenant has availed himself or herself of any other lawful rights and remedies.
> (b) If the landlord acts in violation of subsection (a), the tenant is entitled to the remedies provided in Section 34-18-34 and has a defense in any retaliatory action against him or her for possession. In an action by or against the tenant, evidence of a complaint within six (6) months before the alleged act of retaliation creates a presumption that the landlord's conduct was in retaliation. The presumption does not arise if the tenant made the complaint after notice of a proposed rental increase or diminution of services. "Presumption" means that the trier of fact must find the existence of the fact presumed unless and until evidence is introduced which would support a finding of its nonexistence.

(c) *Notwithstanding subsections (a) and (b), a landlord may bring an action for possession if:*

(1) *The violation of the applicable building or housing code was caused primarily by lack of reasonable care by the tenant, a member of his or her family, or other person on the premises with his or her consent; or*

(2) *The tenant is in default in rent; or*

(3) *Compliance with the applicable building or housing code or other public action such as eminent domain, requires alteration, remodeling, or demolition which would effectively deprive the tenant of use of the dwelling unit, and the relocation requirements have been met by the municipality.*

If the landlord makes every attempt to comply with his or her contractual obligations regarding the maintenance of the leased premises and finds that compliance within a reasonable period of time is beyond his or her control (such as in the case of fire or natural disaster), the landlord and tenant may agree to terminate the lease, or, in the case of a commercial tenant with a long-term lease, the landlord and tenant may agree that the tenant will vacate and cease paying rent until such time as the premises are returned to a usable condition.

Eviction Procedures

A landlord may not retake possession of a leased premises unless the tenant abandons or voluntarily surrenders the premises or unless suit for eviction is brought and a writ of possession is issued by a court. The procedure for evicting a tenant varies significantly from state to state. The time it takes to complete an eviction procedure varies as well, depending on several factors, such as the presence or absence of state statutes providing for **summary proceedings** (short and simple proceedings) and the actions taken by the tenant to defend his or her right to possession.

As noted in Chapter 15, the Protecting Tenants at Foreclosure Act (which, at the time of this writing, is scheduled to sunset on December 31, 2014) requires the purchaser of a foreclosed property to honor a residential tenant's lease. The purchaser may not evict the tenant unless the purchaser will occupy the property as his or her primary residence. In that event, the purchaser must comply with the ninety-day notice requirement.

Holdover Tenants

Before a landlord can evict a tenant and retake the premises, the lease must be legally terminated. If neither party breaches the lease, then the lease ordinarily terminates at the expiration of the lease term unless the lease is renewed by the parties. If the lease is indefinite as to the term of duration or if the parties have agreed that the tenant may continue on at the expiration of the written lease but have not entered into another lease agreement, then the tenancy created is a tenancy at will (recall the earlier discussion of this concept in Chapter 2). Either the landlord or the tenant may terminate a tenancy at will if proper notice of termination is given as required by statute (usually thirty days for a month-to-month tenant). The time required for the notice varies in length, depending on the rental period involved. As a practical matter, the notice should be written, and service of the notice should be made by personal delivery, by registered or certified mail with return receipt requested, or by posting on the premises. State statutes may dictate the form or contents of this type of notice. An example of a notice of termination of a tenancy at will is found in Exhibit 17–1. If a tenant in a tenancy at

summary proceedings: Short and simple proceedings used to dispose of certain controversies.

EXHIBIT 17-1 **Notice of termination of tenancy at will**

September 25, 2015

CERTIFIED MAIL #P223274556
RETURN RECEIPT REQUESTED

TO: Andrew Atkins
     Apt. 203, Camelot Apartments
     525 Lancelot Drive
     Any City, Any State

Notice is hereby given that your tenancy at will in the premises located at Apt. 203, Camelot Apartments, 525 Lancelot Drive, Any City, Any State, shall be terminated as of November 1, 2015, or thirty days after service of this notice on you, whichever is later in time.

Demand is made that you surrender the premises by 12:01 a.m. on that date.

Excaliber Luxury Rentals, Inc.
450 N.W. 9th Street, Suite 500
Any City, Any State

By: _Gerald Hargreaves_
     President, Excaliber Luxury
     Rentals, Inc.

will is being evicted by the purchaser of a foreclosed property, the Protecting Tenants at Foreclosure Act must be followed until the date on which the act "sunsets." Although a tenancy at will is considered an exception to the Act's requirement that tenants be permitted to stay in the residence until the end of the lease, the Act still requires that the tenant receive a ninety-day notice before the tenant may be evicted under these circumstances.

More commonly, an original or renewed lease will have a definite expiration term. If the tenant remains in the premises after the expiration of the lease term without the consent of the landlord, the tenant is considered to have "held over." If an eviction proceeding is brought against a tenant who has held over, a landlord may not be required to provide notice of termination prior to filing a complaint for eviction. Nonetheless, it is good practice for a landlord to send a certified letter to the tenant prior to the expiration of the lease, indicating the landlord's intent not to renew (see Exhibit 17–2). In this way, should the tenant hold over after the expiration of the lease term, the landlord has written evidence that the tenant is not continuing on with the consent of the landlord.

In some states, a landlord may collect double rent from a tenant who holds over after the expiration of the lease. In states allowing collection of double rent, the landlord must give the tenant notice of his or her intention to collect the double rent. The double rent may be requested as money damages as part of the eviction proceeding. If, however, the landlord accepts payment from the tenant in the amount agreed upon in the lease after the lease expires, double rent may not be collected.

Once the lease is terminated, a holdover tenant may be removed from the premises by initiating an eviction proceeding in compliance with state statutes.

Notice of landlord's intention not to renew lease	EXHIBIT 17–2

September 25, 2015

CERTIFIED MAIL #P312100448
RETURN RECEIPT REQUESTED

TO: Dean and Pamela Hendricks
     Apt. 400, Ocean Breeze Apartments
     702 Wavecrest Drive
     Any City, Any State

Dear tenants:

This letter serves as a reminder that your lease of Apt. 400, Ocean Breeze Apartments located at 702 Wavecrest Drive, Any City, Any State, expires on November 30, 2015. Please be advised that Seaside Properties, Inc., does not intend to renew or extend your lease. The keys to your apartment should be delivered to the property manager on or before November 30, 2015, together with your forwarding address for return of your security deposit if the premises are returned in satisfactory condition. Should an inspection reveal any damages to the premises, the cost of repairs will be deducted from your security deposit and the balance of the deposit, if any, shall be returned accordingly.

Sincerely,

Michelle St. John, President
Seaside Properties, Inc.
800 Blue Water Drive, Suite 100
Any City, Any State

The process for bringing an eviction suit against a holdover is similar to that for bringing an eviction suit against a tenant who has breached the lease agreement. This process is discussed in the next subsection.

Eviction for Breach of Lease

In most states, a landlord must give a tenant the opportunity to cure a breach of the lease before the landlord can terminate the lease and begin eviction proceedings. The landlord's first step is to provide the tenant with a notice of the breach and a demand that the breach be cured within a specified time period. The time given within which to cure will vary from state to state and may vary depending on the type of action constituting the breach (for example, nonpayment of rent; failure to abide by the rules of the apartment building regarding pets, loud music, parking, or subleasing; and so forth). The lease itself should be reviewed, for its provisions may provide the tenant with a cure period that is longer than the period prescribed by statute.

If the breach is something other than nonpayment of rent, a typical notice will inform the tenant of the violation of the lease; will demand that the breach be cured within the time period specified in the statute or in the lease, if longer; will inform the tenant that, if the breach is not cured within that time period, the lease will be terminated; and will warn the tenant that, if the same or a similar wrongful

EXHIBIT 17–3   Notice of breach

TO: Lydia Richards
        Apt. 303, Jefferson Park Apartments
        1000 Jefferson Street
        Any City, Any State

You are hereby notified that you have breached your duties to maintain the leased premises located at 1000 Jefferson Street, Apt. 303, being occupied by you, as is required by Section 70.70 of the state statutes as follows:

1.   Failure to remove all garbage from the dwelling unit in a clean and sanitary manner
2.   Failure to use and operate plumbing and electrical facilities in a reasonable manner

In addition, you have materially breached paragraphs seven and twelve of the rental agreement. If these defaults are not remedied within seven days after the date of delivery of this notice, the rental agreement shall terminate on that date. If you remain in possession of the premises after termination, you will be charged double rent for any holdover period, as permitted by Section 70.102 of the state statutes.

                        Franklin Residential Leasing, Inc.
                        400 Franklin Avenue, Suite 105
                        Any City, Any State

CERTIFICATE OF SERVICE

I HEREBY CERTIFY that a copy of the above notice was delivered to the above-named tenant by posting on the premises on the 25th day of September, 2015.

                        Alice Franklin
                        President, Franklin Residential Leasing, Inc.

action occurs within a year, the lease will automatically terminate without a further opportunity provided for cure. State statutes commonly provide that the notice be mailed, hand delivered, or posted on the leased premises. If the notice is mailed, the tenant may be entitled to extra days to offset the time it takes for notice to reach the tenant. An example of this type of notice is provided in Exhibit 17–3.

If the breach is not cured within the time period set forth in the notice, a second notice normally follows, informing the tenant that the lease is terminated and demanding that the tenant vacate the premises. State statutes may require that the tenant be given a specified period of time within which to vacate once the tenant is formally notified of the termination of the lease, such as in the sample notice provided in Exhibit 17–4.

If the tenant's breach of the lease agreement is the nonpayment of rent, the notice procedure is similar, but state statutes should be checked because the notice period may be different. For example, the notice period in California is three days, both for the nonpayment of rent and for breaches other than nonpayment of rent; however, in Florida the notice period is three days for nonpayment of rent and seven days for breaches other than the nonpayment of rent. When counting out the days of the notice period, most states do not include the date of delivery of the notice in the calculation, nor do they include weekends and holidays. In many states, "holidays" refers to court holidays only and does not include other holidays.

TO: Lydia Richards
       Apt. 303, Jefferson Park Apartments
       1000 Jefferson Street
       Any City, Any State

You are hereby notified that your lease is terminated effective immediately. You have seven days from delivery of this notice of termination to vacate the premises. This action is taken because of your failure to cure your breach of Section 70.70 of the state statutes and your failure to cure your breach of paragraphs seven and twelve of the rental agreement within the seven-day period allotted.

If you remain in possession of the premises after seven days from delivery of this notice of termination, you will be charged double rent for any holdover period, as permitted by Section 70.102 of the state statutes.

> Franklin Residential Leasing, Inc.
> 400 Franklin Avenue, Suite 105
> Any City, Any State

CERTIFICATE OF SERVICE

I HEREBY CERTIFY that a copy of the above notice was delivered to the above-named tenant by posting on the premises on the 5th day of October, 2015.

> *Alice Franklin*
> President, Franklin Residential Leasing, Inc.

If the tenancy is residential and the tenant's breach is the nonpayment of rent, then compliance with the *Fair Debt Collection Practices Act* may be required. Back rent owed to a landlord by a residential tenant can be characterized as a consumer debt owed. Therefore, an attempt to collect the back rent may be treated by the courts as an attempt to collect a debt falling under the Act. An attorney working on behalf of his or her client to collect the back rent by preparing and serving the notice of nonpayment may be deemed to be acting as a debt collector in this context, particularly if the attorney's practice regularly includes assisting landlords with delinquent tenants.

When preparing the notice for nonpayment of rent, be certain that the delinquent "rent" referred to in the notice includes only what is defined as "rent" in the lease and in state statutes. It is particularly common for commercial leases, for example, to include other "fees" and "additional rents" as tenant obligations that do not fall under "rent" as defined in the lease. State statutory law may prohibit the inclusion of charges other than rent in a demand for back rent owed. This may pertain not only to the charges noted above but also to attorneys' fees and late fees. If this is the case and the notice makes demand for these items, the notice may be deemed defective.

If the tenant receives a notice and cures the breach within the time period specified in the notice, the landlord may not evict the tenant.

The following Indiana case addresses the issues of substantive and procedural due process in an eviction action against a public housing tenant who violated the terms of his lease.

CASE: *Lowery v. Housing Authority of the City of Terre Haute*
826 N.E.2d 685 (2005)

OPINION

BAILEY, Judge.

Case Summary

Appellant-Defendant James Lowery ("Lowery") appeals an order of eviction, upon petition by Appellee-Plaintiff Housing Authority of the City of Terre Haute ("Housing Authority"). We affirm.

Issues

Lowery presents two issues for review, which we restate as the following:

   I. Whether Lowery was denied procedural due process in the termination of his tenancy and rent subsidy; and

   II. Whether Lowery was denied substantive due process because the Housing Authority failed to show good cause for eviction.

Facts and Procedural History

Lowery, the custodial parent of two minor children, is disabled. He and his minor children previously resided in the Morton Lewis Court Community, a public housing complex owned by the Housing Authority. Lowery's rent was $51.00 per month. The one-year lease was executed on November 6, 2003, and listed Lowery and his two minor children as the only members of the household. The Low Income Housing Act of 1937, §8, as amended, 42 U.S.C.A. §1437 ("the Act"), dictated the terms of the lease, which prohibited unlisted tenants or boarders and criminal activity.

On March 30, 2004, Detective Wallace of the Terre Haute Police Department investigated a complaint that Lowery's eighteen-year-old stepson, Joshua Peak ("Peak") caused a disturbance at Oubache Elementary School, which was located adjacent to the Morton Lewis complex. Detective Wallace advised Housing Authority property manager Patricia McGee ("McGee") that Peak appeared to be living at Lowery's apartment. On March 31, 2004, McGee verbally warned Lowery that Peak was not allowed to reside in Lowery's apartment. That same day, McGee sent Lowery a letter summarizing the conversation. On April 8, 2004, Lowery met with McGee and discussed the situation. According to McGee, Lowery stated that he didn't know how to make Peak leave.

On April 27, 2004, Detective Wallace again contacted McGee to apprise her of another disturbance involving Peak and students at the elementary school, and

informed her that Peak was living at Lowery's apartment. That same day, McGee advised Lowery in writing that Peak was not permitted at Lowery's apartment, and that Lowery's lease would be terminated if Peak was found on the premises. The letter was dispatched to Lowery via certified mail, and Lowery signed the postal service receipt on April 28, 2004. The letter provided in pertinent part as follows:

> Mr. Joshua Peak is not allowed on the premises. He is not a tenant and I am warning you that if he is found on the Terre Haute Housing Authority's property, the Terre Haute Police Department will be called to remove him if necessary. I have informed investigators of this. If at any time I receive verification that you are again allowing Mr. Peak or any other unauthorized boarders, your lease will immediately terminate and I will inform the proper agencies of my intent to evict you.

(Appellee's App. 6). On the same day that Lowery received the certified letter, McGee witnessed an altercation in which several young men were threatening Peak, who was standing outside Lowery's apartment. McGee called the police, and also spoke with Lowery. When McGee questioned Lowery as to why Peak was there, Lowery indicated, "he had let him stay there at his apartment." (Tr. 20.)

At McGee's initiation, the Housing Authority sent Lowery a Notice of Lease Termination, dated April 28, 2004, citing Lowery's non-compliance with paragraph X of the lease, which provides in pertinent part as follows:

> Tenant shall be obligated
> (b) Not to give accommodation to boarders or lodgers;
>   To act, and cause household members or guests to act in a manner that will:
>   a. Not disturb other residents' peaceful enjoyment of their accommodations; and
>   b. Be conducive to maintaining all properties in a decent, safe, and sanitary condition.
>
> (o) To assure that Tenant, any member of the household, a guest, or another person under Tenant'[s] control, shall not engage in:
>   a. Any criminal activity that threatens the health, safety, or right to peaceful enjoyment of the housing premises by other residents or employees of the Landlord and/or Management Agent[.]

(Appellee's App. 7.)

(continued)

On May 3, 2004, Lowery met with McGee and advised her that he had "gotten rid of" his unauthorized boarder. (Tr. 24.) McGee informed Lowery that he had a right to request a hearing before a hearing officer and that his request for a hearing should be made within ten days of receiving his notice of termination (which was dated April 28, 2004). On May 18, 2004, the Housing Authority received Lowery's letter requesting a hearing. McGee's supervisor, Kevin Wells, advised Lowery that his request was untimely.

On July 15, 2004, the Housing Authority filed a Complaint for Possession of Real Estate in small claims court. A hearing was held on August 31, 2004. On October 14, 2004, the trial court granted an Order of Eviction, stating in pertinent part:

> Defendant had ample notice that his stepson was not to be on Housing Authority property and that he could not or would not comply with that requirement which was a valid and reasonable term of his occupancy.

Lowery now appeals.

Discussion and Decision

I. Standard of Review

The claim was tried before the bench in small claims court. We review for clear error. *Flint v. Hopkins,* 720 N.E.2d 1230 (Ind.Ct.App.1999). A judgment in favor of a party having the burden of proof will be affirmed if the evidence was such that a reasonable trier of fact could conclude that the elements of the claim were established by a preponderance of the evidence. *Id.* We presume the trial court correctly applied the law. *Barber v. Echo Lake Mobile Home Comm.,* 759 N.E.2d 253, 255 (Ind.Ct.App. 2001) . . . .

B. Analysis—Procedural Due Process

Initially, Lowery asserts that he had a right to reasonable accommodation of visitors, but was denied procedural due process when his stepson was placed on a list of persons banned from entering the public housing complex, without a hearing. The letter from McGee barring Peak from the apartment was not accompanied by notice of hearing procedures. Lowery claims he had a right to a formal hearing, and should have been informed in writing as to how he could request a formal hearing. 24 C.F.R. §966.53(c) provides as follows:

> "Elements of due process" shall mean an eviction action or a termination of tenancy in a State or local court in which the following procedural safeguards are required:
> (1) adequate notice to the tenant of the grounds for terminating the tenancy and for eviction;
> (2) Right of the tenant to be represented by counsel;
> (3) Opportunity for the tenant to refute the evidence presented by the PHA including the right to confront and cross-examine witnesses and to present any affirmative legal or equitable defense which the tenant may have;
> (4) A decision on the merits.

Lowery appears to argue that the full panoply of procedural safeguards was triggered by the Housing Authority management decision to ban Peak, as opposed to the action for termination of tenancy. However, Lowery did not timely request a grievance hearing following his notice of lease termination as permitted by the Act, which would presumably have afforded him the opportunity to challenge the predicate actions of the Housing Authority. Moreover, while Lowery testified at trial that he wasn't given the opportunity to appeal the decision to ban Peak as a visitor, he did not offer any authority for his claimed entitlement to specific notice and hearing in regard to visitation rights as opposed to tenancy rights.

Lowery did not timely avail himself of his right to an administrative hearing prior to the initiation of eviction proceedings in state court. The Housing Authority filed a petition for possession of premises, and Lowery pursued no claim against the Housing Authority. As such, the sole issue actually tried in small claims court was whether Lowery must surrender his leased premises because he breached his lease. Lowery has not established that he was denied procedural due process in the eviction.

II. Substantive Due Process Claim—Good Cause for Eviction

Due process under the Fourteenth Amendment requires a determination of good cause to support termination of public housing tenancy during the term of the lease. *Numme v. Lemon,* 191 Misc.2d 133, 741 N.Y.S.2d 384 (2002). When a housing authority decides to terminate a tenancy or subsidy, it must provide the tenant a written notice stating the specific grounds for termination. 24 C.F.R. 966.4(*l*)(2). Grounds for termination include "serious or repeated violation of material terms of the lease[.]" 24 C.F.R. 966.4(*l*)(2)(i). Also included is criminal activity. 24 C.F.R. 966.4(*l*)(2)(B)(iii)(A).

Pursuant to 24 C.F.R. 966.4(*l*)(5)(ii)(A), a public housing lease must provide that "any criminal activity by a covered person that threatens the health, safety, or right to peaceful enjoyment of the premises by other residents . . . is grounds for termination of tenancy." 24 C.F.R. 5.100 defines a "covered person" as a "tenant, any member of the tenant's household, a guest or another person under the tenant's control."

Although Lowery did not admit that Peak engaged in criminal activity, Lowery admitted that he allowed his stepson

(continued)

to board with him for "probably about a month." (Tr. 93.) However, Lowery argues that he could not control Peak's behavior, and thus the eviction of himself and his dependent children is punitive rather than "for good cause." Too, he claims he evicted Peak as soon as he was made aware it was in violation of his lease. Lowery further contends that he should not be held strictly liable for behavior of another adult whom he could not control, and that the Housing Authority management defined criminal activity too expansively.

Lowery claims it is "debatable" whether or not Congress intended to impose a strict liability standard making tenants liable for the actions of covered persons. Reply Br. at 10. His argument is apparently predicated upon the decision in *Delaware Co. Housing Authority v. Bishop*, 749 A.2d 997 (Pa.Comm.2000), to which he directed the trial court's attention. Therein, a county housing authority sought to evict a public housing tenant whose adult sons had committed rape and possessed drugs. The commonwealth court "refuse[d] to hold a tenant strictly liable for unforeseeable criminal acts committed, without the tenant's knowledge, by family members who are not under the tenant's control." *Id.* at 1002. In part, the commonwealth court relied upon *Charlotte Housing Auth. v. Patterson*, 120 N.C.App. 552, 464 S.E.2d 68 (1995), wherein the Court observed that 42 U.S.C. §1437d(*l*)(requiring a lease term that criminal drug activity by household member or guest under tenant's control is cause for termination of tenancy) was not intended to impose a type of strict liability whereby the tenant is responsible for all criminal acts regardless of knowledge and ability to control them. However, in *Dep't of Housing and Urban Develop. v. Rucker*, 535 U.S. 125, 122 S.Ct. 1230, 152 L.Ed.2d 258 (2002), the Court held that 42 U.S.C. §1437d(*l*)"unambiguously requires lease terms that vest local public housing authorities with the discretion to evict tenants for the drug-related activity of household members and guests whether or not the tenant knew, or should have known, about the activity." *Id.* at 130, 122 S.Ct. 1230. A "household member or guest" is one to whom "access to the premises has been granted by the tenant." *Id.* at 131, 122 S.Ct. 1230.

It does not appear that Peak's problems are drug-related, arguably invoking the strict liability implications of *Rucker*. Moreover, it is not apparent from the record that Lowery could exert physical control over Peak. It may be unduly burdensome to expect a physically infirm individual to restrain a young and able-bodied individual from entering any part of the Housing Authority premises. In this case, the Housing Authority apparently expected Lowery to do so, although the Housing Authority admittedly

failed to seek a restraining order despite breaches of the peace. Nevertheless, regardless of whether Peak engaged in criminal activity or Lowery was able to prevent Peak's alleged criminal activity, the record reveals an alternative basis for Lowery's eviction.

Lowery admittedly permitted Peak to remain in Lowery's apartment for about a month, despite the prohibition against boarders, and did not seek to add Peak as a named tenant. Lowery's generous rent subsidy was calculated upon the assumption that he was the only adult in the household. Moreover, there is evidence from which the trial court could infer that Lowery allowed or invited Peak to return to the apartment despite his protestations to McGee. We will affirm a general judgment on any legal theory supported by the evidence introduced at trial. *D.A.X., Inc. v. Employers Ins. of Wausau*, 659 N.E.2d 1150, 1155 (Ind.Ct.App. 1996), trans. denied. Accordingly, the Housing Authority presented sufficient evidence to establish its claim for eviction by a preponderance of the evidence.

Affirmed.

Case Questions

1. In the above case, Mr. Lowery asserted that he should have been informed in writing as to how he could request a formal hearing. 24 C.F.R. §966.53(c) as cited by the court does not specifically require this. Do you believe that the inclusion of such a requirement is necessary to ensure due process in eviction proceedings? Why or why not?

2. The court stated that Mr. Lowery "appears to argue that the full panoply of procedural safeguards was triggered by the Housing Authority management decision to ban Peak, as opposed to the action for termination of tenancy." Do you believe that tenants should be entitled to specific notice and hearing in regard to visitation rights and the banning of visitors prior to the serving of a notice of termination of lease? Why or why not?

3. The court discussed the strict liability standard that makes tenants liable for the actions of "covered persons"; yet the court indicated that in this case there was insufficient evidence to deduce criminal activity on the part of Peak. It stated that the proper grounds for termination of Mr. Lowery's lease was the boarding of his stepson as an unlisted person on the lease. Do you think it is reasonable to expect Mr. Lowery to prevent his stepson from continually appearing at his apartment? Could this matter have been resolved in any other manner?

Preparation of the Eviction Complaint

Should a tenant fail to cure a breach of the lease, the next step is to begin an eviction suit. A suit is initiated by filing a complaint with the clerk of court. A landlord may hire an attorney to bring suit or may represent himself or herself in the matter. Many landlords believe that the expense of attorneys' fees will negate or exceed a judgment for back rent owed by the tenant. In turn, many attorneys choose not to handle evictions because the fees they can reasonably charge for such cases do not warrant the time spent.

Some attorneys charge a nominal fee to advise a client on the proper procedures to follow in an eviction, and the client then proceeds with self-representation. If the landlord believes that the tenant will fight the eviction, the case may become more complex and may be best handled by an attorney. Note also that, if the landlord is a corporation, the landlord must be represented by legal counsel because a corporation is a legal entity separate and apart from its shareholders, directors, and officers and therefore cannot be represented by them in court.

State statutes may provide a statutory form for the complaint and summons to be used in eviction proceedings and will indicate the court in which the complaint must be filed (for example, county court, circuit court). Therefore, when you are preparing an eviction complaint for a client, check state statutes first. Proper jurisdiction may depend on whether the landlord is seeking only possession or whether the landlord is seeking both possession and monetary damages. Typically, if the landlord is seeking the latter, then one complaint will be filed with separate counts (see below), and proper jurisdiction may be determined by the amount of monetary damages sought. The complaint should be filed in the county in which the leased property is located. The complaint begins with the caption, naming the court in which the case will be heard, the case number, and the parties involved. The case number will be assigned by the clerk of court when the complaint is filed at the courthouse. Following the caption is the pleading designation, indicating that the pleading is a complaint for tenant eviction.

The body of the complaint should be double-spaced and may include one or more counts. The removal of the tenant from the leased premises and the retaking of the premises by the landlord is one count. If the landlord is also asking for back rent, this would be an additional count in the complaint. If the landlord is evicting a holdover tenant, the first count of the complaint would be a count for the eviction of the tenant, and the second count would be for money damages for the holdover period (for example, rent for each day the tenant remains on the premises after the termination of the lease—or double rent in states that so allow).

In closing, the complaint must include a prayer for relief that tells the court what relief is requested by the landlord/plaintiff. The prayer for relief typically includes a request for possession of the property, rent owed (if any), and court costs. If the lease agreement stipulates that a prevailing party in litigation is entitled to attorneys' fees, then attorneys' fees may be included in the prayer for relief as well. If a jury trial is desired, it must be requested. The complaint will be signed by either the landlord/plaintiff or the attorney representing the landlord. A copy of any notice(s) delivered to the tenant and a copy of the lease agreement (if written) should be attached as exhibits to the complaint. Some states require eviction complaints to be verified complaints. A **verified complaint** is a complaint that is signed and sworn to by the plaintiff, attesting that all allegations within the complaint are true to the plaintiff's best knowledge and belief. Have your attorney review the complaint prior to asking the client for his or her signature. Before filing the complaint, make a copy for the client file; a copy for the client; and a copy to provide, together with the original, to the clerk's office. Exhibit 17–5 provides an example of a verified complaint to evict a tenant for breach of a lease other than nonpayment of rent.

verified complaint: A complaint that is signed and sworn to by the plaintiff, attesting that all allegations within the complaint are true to the plaintiff's best knowledge and belief.

EXHIBIT 17–5   **Complaint for tenant eviction**

IN THE COUNTY COURT FOR ANY COUNTY, ANY STATE
CASE NO.

WENDY S. MANNING,
    Plaintiff,

vs.

GLENN MURRAY,
_____ Defendant. /   **COMPLAINT FOR TENANT EVICTION**

Plaintiff, WENDY S. MANNING, sues Defendant, GLENN MURRAY, and alleges:

1. This is an action to evict Defendant from real property located in Any County, Any State.
2. Plaintiff owns the real property described as Apt. 301, Madison Apartments, 211 Greentree Lane, Any City, Any County, Any State.
3. Defendant has possession under a written lease agreement, a copy of which is attached hereto and made a part hereof as Exhibit A.
4. Defendant failed to comply with the terms of the rental agreement as follows:

    Defendant is operating a business on the real property in contravention of county zoning regulations and in contravention of the lease agreement.

5. Plaintiff served Defendant with a notice on September 13, 2015, demanding that Defendant cure the breach, but Defendant failed to do so. A copy of the notice is attached hereto and made a part hereof as Exhibit B.
6. Plaintiff served Defendant with a notice of termination on September 24, 2015, but Defendant has failed to vacate the premises. A copy of the notice of termination is attached hereto and made a part hereof as Exhibit C.

WHEREFORE, Plaintiff demands judgment against Defendant for possession of the real property and costs.

DATED: October 6, 2015.

                                       Wendy S. Manning
                                       Plaintiff
                                       607 Centennial Drive
                                       Any City, Any State
                                       (000) 444-9988

STATE OF ANY STATE
COUNTY OF ANY COUNTY

BEFORE ME, the undersigned authority, personally appeared WENDY S. MANNING, who after being duly sworn deposes and says she has read the foregoing complaint and it is true and correct to her best knowledge and belief.

SWORN TO AND SUBSCRIBED before me this 6th day of October, 2015.

                                        Beth Williams
                                       Notary Public, State of Any State
                                       My commission expires: 6/10/17

The next step is to prepare the summons. As noted, state statute may dictate the form of the summons. The summons will inform the tenant/defendant of the suit filed against him or her and specify the time period within which he or she must file an answer. An original summons must be prepared for each defendant. The summons will be signed by the clerk of the court. All states require filing fees to be paid before a complaint is processed. Have a check for the appropriate amount cut, together with any sheriff's fees that may be required for the service of the complaint.

Most states allow a complaint to be served by either a sheriff or a private, court-approved process server. Ordinarily, the complaint must be served on the tenant personally, but posting of the complaint and summons on the premises may be permitted if several attempts at personal service have failed. Again, state statutes should be checked in this regard. Once service is made, the server of process must complete a return of service and file it with the clerk of court's office.

The time period within which the tenant has to respond to the eviction complaint varies from state to state. In states that permit summary proceedings, the time period in which to respond to an eviction complaint may be considerably shorter than the time period allotted for responses to other types of complaints. Again, as noted above, in some states the time period may also differ for individual claims made in the complaint.

Once the tenant is properly served, one of several things may occur. The first possibility is that the tenant will contact the landlord or the landlord's attorney and try to negotiate. If the tenant's breach is for nonpayment of rent and the landlord believes the tenant is both willing and able to correct the breach, the parties may be able to reach an agreement and avoid eviction.

If an agreement is reached, it should be formalized in a **stipulation.** A stipulation is an agreement made by opposing sides in a lawsuit regulating a matter pertaining to the suit. From the landlord's perspective, the stipulation should include an acknowledgment by the tenant of the amount owed, set out an agreed-upon payment schedule for the back rent, and set forth the payments required to be made in the future until the expiration of the lease. The stipulation should further provide that, if all payments are made according to this schedule, the landlord will dismiss the suit; however, if the payments are not made, the tenant agrees that the landlord may proceed with the suit. If state law allows, the stipulation should provide that, if the tenant fails to make payment, the tenant waives the right to a court hearing and allows the landlord to proceed to summarily evict and retake possession. An example of a stipulation is found in Exhibit 17–6.

A second possibility is that after receiving the summons and complaint, the tenant will fail to respond within the allotted time or fail to appear at the hearing. Should this occur, the next step is to prepare a motion for default, requesting that the clerk of court enter a default judgment or order of judgment against the tenant. Once a default judgment or order is entered, state statutes typically allow the landlord to obtain a final judgment against the tenant as well as a writ of possession. A **writ of possession** is a court order issued to the sheriff ordering the sheriff to remove the tenant from the property. A sheriff's fee commonly is charged to have the sheriff execute the writ. State law may require that the writ be posted for a specified number of days before the sheriff can carry out the instructions in the writ.

A third possibility, especially if the tenant has other debts owing in addition to the back rent owed the landlord, is that the tenant will file a bankruptcy petition.

stipulation: An agreement made by opposing sides in a lawsuit regulating a matter pertaining to the suit.

writ of possession: A court order issued to the sheriff ordering the sheriff to remove a tenant from leased property.

EXHIBIT 17–6   **Stipulation**

IN THE COUNTY COURT FOR ANY COUNTY, ANY STATE

CASE NO. 15-1303

MADELINE GRAYSON,
       Plaintiff,

vs.

PAULINE MILLER,
       Defendant.   **STIPULATION**

_____/

The parties to this action hereby stipulate as follows:

1. The Defendant acknowledges the sum of Two Thousand Four Hundred Dollars ($2,400.00) to be due and owing to the Plaintiff.

2. In partial payment of the above sum, the Defendant agrees to immediately pay the Plaintiff the amount of One Thousand Two Hundred Dollars ($1,200.00), and the balance of the above sum will be paid as follows: $400.00 due on October 13, 2015; $400.00 due on October 20, 2015; and $400.00 due on October 30, 2015.

3. Further, the Defendant agrees to pay the Plaintiff the sum of One Thousand Two Hundred Dollars ($1,200.00) on the first day of each month as provided in the lease agreement. Defendant agrees to make these monthly installments in cash.

4. If all of the above-stated sums are paid as per this stipulation, this action shall be dismissed by the Plaintiff. If any of the above-stated sums are not paid as per this stipulation, the Plaintiff shall, upon the filing with the court of an Affidavit of Nonpayment, be entitled to a Writ of Possession and shall be entitled to a money judgment for any such payments as are in default. Defendant agrees to waive her right to a hearing on Plaintiff's application for said writ and application for money judgment.

Dated this 6th day of October, 2015.

Madeline Grayson   _Pauline Miller_
Plaintiff   Defendant

If the tenant files either a Chapter 7 or a Chapter 13 bankruptcy petition before the landlord obtains a final judgment for eviction and possession, the tenant, as bankruptcy petitioner, receives an *automatic stay*. The automatic stay is a court order from the bankruptcy court that automatically suspends all proceedings against the petitioner until the bankruptcy petition is dismissed, the petitioner's debts are discharged, or a repayment plan is established. In this situation, the landlord must request a removal or lifting of the stay from the federal bankruptcy court. If the stay is lifted, the landlord can proceed.

Under the Bankruptcy Abuse Prevention and Consumer Protection Act of 2005, a landlord can proceed with the eviction process without going to federal court and requesting a lifting of the stay if the tenant files for bankruptcy after the landlord obtains a final judgment for eviction and possession. Note, however, that state statutes must be checked because some states permit tenants to take certain actions within thirty days after filing for bankruptcy to prevent eviction, even if the landlord had obtained a final judgment before the bankruptcy petition was filed. In these states, tenants must file a certification with the court and serve it on the landlord certifying that state law allows a tenant to avoid eviction, even after a final judgment, by paying rent owed. The tenant also must deposit with the clerk of the bankruptcy court any rent that would be due thirty days from the date the bankruptcy petition was filed and must certify to the bankruptcy court that he or she has paid back rent. This certification must also be served on the landlord. If the landlord files an objection to the certifications, a hearing will be held to determine the veracity of the tenant's certifications. If the certifications are not true or the tenant fails to take all actions required within the requisite time frame, the bankruptcy court will lift the stay, and the landlord will be permitted to take possession of the premises.

A fourth possibility is that the tenant will file an answer in response to the complaint. In the answer, the tenant may include any applicable defenses. For example, the tenant may say that the landlord accepted the rent after serving the notice or filing the complaint, or the tenant may say that the landlord failed to maintain the premises and the tenant was withholding rent until the landlord made the required repairs. If the tenant raises the latter defense, the tenant must be able to show that notice of noncompliance with maintenance requirements was provided by the tenant to the landlord and that the landlord was given an opportunity to make the necessary repairs.

In some states, the tenant is required to pay into the court registry the rent owed before the tenant will be allowed to defend himself or herself in court. If the tenant disputes the amount owed, the tenant may pay the amount the tenant believes is owed into the registry. Once the complaint is answered, the suit will proceed to hearing and possibly to trial. If the tenant has paid money into the registry, the landlord may request those funds by motioning for a release of funds.

As in the case of a default judgment, should the landlord win the suit, a final judgment will be ordered in favor of the landlord and a writ of possession issued. A tenant is given the right to appeal; state statutes specify the time period within which a tenant must file a notice of appeal. If a tenant files such a notice, a landlord may file a motion for a supersedeas bond. A **supersedeas bond** is a bond required when one is appealing a judgment. The amount of the bond may be set by the court to cover the amount owed to the landlord.

If back rent is owed, state law may permit a landlord to collect interest on the owed rent running from the date the rent became due until the date of judgment. To collect back rent, the landlord has several options; however, none of them may prove adequate. State law, while permitting the garnishment of wages to satisfy a money judgment, may also place restrictions on the wages that may be garnished. For example, in many states, the wages of the "head of household" are exempt from garnishment. *Head of household* may be broadly defined to include anyone who provides a specified amount of support to one or more dependents. If the tenant owns real property, a lien may be placed against the property. To do so, the landlord must obtain a certified copy of the judgment from the clerk of court and then record that judgment in every county in which the tenant owns real property.

Another method of attempting to collect back rent is to assert the **landlord's lien** on the personal property that the tenant has brought onto the leased premises and have the tenant's property sold to satisfy the judgment. Landlords, by statute, are given a lien on certain personal property of the tenant as soon as the tenant moves property onto the premises. The property covered by the lien may vary, depending on whether the tenant was a residential or a nonresidential tenant. In residential tenancies, it is common for the lien to cover only property actually on the premises, and even then, some states may mandate that there are certain

supersedeas bond: A bond required when one is appealing a court judgment.

landlord's lien: A lien given by statute to a landlord on certain personal property of a tenant.

items that are exempt from collection (for example, personal property owned by the tenant up to the value of $1,000, or beds and bedclothes). It often is difficult to ascertain what property falls within the category of property "usually kept on the premises."

The property must belong to the tenant before it is subject to a lien at all, and the landlord's lien does not attach until its title is in the tenant's name. For example, if the tenant has possession of property under a conditional sales contract, the lien does not exist. In nonresidential tenancies, state statute may permit the lien to cover all nonexempt personal property, whether located on or off the leased premises. Further, the general rule is that, if the personal property is subject to a perfected security interest or lien before it is brought onto the leased property, the landlord's lien will be inferior to that lien, but it will be superior to those perfected or accruing after the property is brought onto the premises.

Distress for Rent

In some states, a landlord's lien is enforced by a summary proceeding known as *distress for rent* (also referred to as *distraint*). This is not part of an eviction proceeding but, rather, is a separate action to which some landlords resort rather than resorting to eviction. In common law, this term applied to the right of a landlord to seize a tenant's goods in a nonjudicial proceeding to satisfy the nonpayment of rent. Today, distress for rent procedures are regulated by state statute and require the posting of a bond before a sheriff will levy upon a tenant's property and prohibit the tenant from moving his or her property. In some of the states that do permit distraint, this remedy pertains only to nonresidential leases and has been specifically abolished with regard to residential leases.

As in an eviction proceeding, the initial pleading in distress proceedings is a complaint filed by the landlord or the landlord's attorney. The complaint is similar to an eviction complaint. It sets forth allegations of ownership of the property by the plaintiff, existence of a lease agreement, the amount of rent owed by the tenant/defendant, and a prayer for relief for damages. Once the complaint has been filed, the clerk of court will require the landlord to post a **distress bond** before issuing a distress writ. The bond must be made payable to the defendant, often in a sum at least double the sum demanded, and conditioned to pay all costs and damages the defendant may sustain should the landlord's suit be found to be improper. The bond must be in a form approved by the clerk and, unless a cash bond is posted, must be with surety. An example of a distress bond is found in Exhibit 17–7.

Once the distress complaint and bond have been filed by the landlord, the court issues a **distress writ,** commanding the sheriff to summon the defendant to answer the complaint. The court also instructs the sheriff either to collect from the tenant the amount claimed by the landlord as unpaid rent or to take custody of a sufficient amount of the tenant's nonexempt property to satisfy the claim if the tenant does not move for dissolution of the writ. The distress writ requires the tenant to serve written defenses to the complaint within the statutorily prescribed time period after service. The writ also enjoins the tenant from damaging, disposing of, secreting, or removing any property liable to distress from the leased premises from the time of service of the writ until the sheriff levies on the property, the writ is vacated, or the court otherwise orders. Exhibit 17–8 provides an example of a distress writ.

distress bond: A bond posted by a landlord in a distraint proceeding.

distress writ: A court order commanding the sheriff to summon the defendant to answer the complaint in a distraint proceeding.

Distress bond

EXHIBIT 17–7

IN THE COUNTY COURT OF ANY COUNTY, ANY STATE
CASE NO. 15-1310

HOWARD ROWLAND,
    Plaintiff,

vs.

JOAN KING,
    Defendant.   **DISTRESS BOND**

_____/

    We, HOWARD ROWLAND as principal, and AAA SURETY COMPANY, as surety, are bound to Defendant, JOAN KING, in the sum of Two Thousand Eight Hundred Dollars ($2,800.00) for the payment of which we bind ourselves, our heirs, personal representatives, successors and assigns, jointly and severally.

    THE CONDITION OF THIS BOND is that if the Plaintiff shall pay all costs and damages that the Defendant sustains in consequence of the Plaintiff's improperly suing out the distress writ in this action, then this bond is void; otherwise it remains in force.

    SIGNED AND SEALED ON this 7th day of October, 2015.

                                _Howard Rowland_____
                                As Principal

                                _Kenneth Alpert_____
                                President of AAA Surety Company
                                as Surety

Approved on October 7, 2015.

_____
Deputy Clerk of Court

Distress writ

EXHIBIT 17–8

IN THE COUNTY COURT OF ANY COUNTY, ANY STATE
CASE NO. 15-1310

HOWARD ROWLAND,
    Plaintiff,

vs.

JOAN KING,
    Defendant.   **DISTRESS WRIT**

_____/

THE STATE OF ANY STATE:

To the Sheriff of Any County, Any State:

    YOU ARE COMMANDED to serve this writ and a copy of the complaint on Defendant, Joan King.

    This distress writ subjects all property liable to distress for rent on the following property in Any County, Any State: Apt. 205, Huntley Manor Apartments, 880 Guildford Street, Any City, Any County, Any State.

EXHIBIT 17-8   *(continued)*

The Defendant is enjoined from damaging, disposing of, secreting, or removing any property liable to be distrained from the rented property after the service of this writ until the sheriff levies on the property or this writ is vacated or the court otherwise orders. If the Defendant does not move for dissolution of the writ, the court may order the sheriff to levy on the property liable to distress forthwith after twenty (20) days from the time the complaint in this action is served. The amount claimed in the complaint is the sum of $1,400.00, with interest and costs.

DATED: October 7, 2015.

                                               _____

                                               County Judge

It is common for state statutes to allow a tenant to recover distrained property by posting a bond with the sheriff. Should a tenant fail to respond to the complaint, resulting in a default judgment, or should the matter be brought to trial, resulting in a verdict in favor of the landlord, the sheriff will be instructed to levy on the tenant's nonexempt property and sell it at a public sheriff's sale. The proceeds will be applied toward the payment of the judgment against the tenant.

hypothetical client matter

When Barbara Hammond enters her office this morning, she checks her tickler file to determine the priority of her tasks. She finds a reminder to call Jack Cameron, president of Cameron Properties, Inc., the firm's client, to find out whether a tenant delinquent in rent payments has paid in full or whether eviction procedures should be initiated. Cameron Properties, Inc., is one of the largest developers of residential rental properties in the state and a long-time client of Fisher, Ross, and Simon, P.A. Barbara's supervising attorney, Ava Ross, does not ordinarily handle evictions herself; rather, she advises clients wishing to initiate eviction procedures on how to handle an eviction themselves. However, the client in this instance is a corporation, Cameron Properties, Inc., which is considered a legal entity separate and apart from its owners and managers. Because individuals may represent only themselves in court, a corporate officer such as Jack Cameron, as president, is not allowed to represent the corporation in court. Further, Cameron Properties is an important, long-standing client; therefore, Ava has agreed to handle evictions for Cameron Properties whenever the need arises.

Jack Cameron had contacted the law office several days ago after receiving information from one of his property managers that a tenant, Lee Jeffries, was now two months delinquent in rent payments. When Mr. Jeffries was delinquent on one month's rent, the property manager attempted to contact him, only to find out that Mr. Jeffries was in the hospital for minor surgery. The property manager was informed that Mr. Jeffries would be bringing a check for the delinquent rent to the property manager's office as soon as

he was out of the hospital. Mr. Jeffries failed to do so, and when the next month's rent became due, the property manager went over to Mr. Jeffries's apartment. Mr. Jeffries was not at home, but neighboring tenants confirmed that he was out of the hospital and that they had seen him recently. The apartment did not appear to be abandoned.

The statutory laws of Any State allow for summary eviction proceedings against residential tenants. The first step is the delivery of a three-day notice of termination, demanding payment in full of all rent owed or surrender of the premises. In Any State, delivery of this notice may be made in person or by posting the notice on the premises. Barbara had prepared such a notice, which was signed by Jack Cameron and posted on the door of Mr. Jeffries's apartment. A copy of the notice in the client file reads as shown in Exhibit 17–9.

Neither Barbara nor Ava has heard from the client since the notice was posted, so Barbara calls the client's office and is informed that Mr. Jeffries has not paid the delinquent rent or surrendered the premises and that the client wishes to proceed with the eviction. Barbara, in turn, informs Ava of the situation, who asks Barbara to prepare the necessary eviction documents. According to the file notes, the amount of back rent owed by Mr. Jeffries is $3,000. In Any State, eviction matters typically are heard in the county courts unless the amount in dispute is over $15,000. Because the property in question is located in Any County, the eviction complaint must be filed in Any County (the concepts of jurisdiction and venue are discussed in detail in the next chapter, which covers real estate litigation). The forms accompanying the Rules of Civil Procedure in Any State provide forms for an eviction summons and an eviction complaint. These statutory forms are on file on Barbara's computer. She proceeds to access the form for a residential eviction summons and completes it as shown in Exhibit 17–10.

A case number will be assigned to the matter when the complaint and summons are filed with the clerk of court. The clerk will sign the summons and have it, together with the complaint, served upon Mr. Jeffries by a sheriff. Note that because the laws of Any State allow for summary proceedings for evictions, the amount of time the defendant/tenant has to respond to the summons and complaint is shorter than it would be in other types of litigation. In Any State, the defendant/tenant must respond within five days (excluding weekends and holidays).

Barbara next pulls up the statutory form for an eviction complaint on her computer screen and proceeds to customize it accordingly. This complaint has two separate counts, or causes of action. The first count is for eviction of Mr. Jeffries from the premises and the return of the premises to Cameron Properties, Inc. The second count is for money damages in the amount of rent owed to date, plus the costs of bringing the proceeding.

In Any State, before an eviction is allowed, the court must be satisfied that the defendant/tenant is not a member of any branch of the military services of the United States. The court requires assurance that the defendant/tenant is not

being deprived of an opportunity to come into court and defend himself or herself because he or she is away on a military assignment. Therefore, the complaint must include a statement that the landlord has knowledge that the defendant/tenant is not a member of the armed services. After the complaint is reviewed and signed by Ava, Barbara will make photocopies of the notice of termination and the lease to be attached to the complaint as exhibits. The complaint and summons will be filed with the clerk of court, together with the appropriate filing fees and sheriff's fees. The completed complaint reads as shown in Exhibit 17–11.

If Mr. Jeffries fails to respond to the complaint within five days of service, the client can proceed with a motion for default against him, requesting that a default be entered by the clerk of court. Barbara prepares the motion for default and default shown in Exhibit 17–12, which will be kept in the file until the statutory time for a response from Mr. Jeffries has expired.

If Mr. Jeffries fails to respond and a default is entered against him, the court will sign a final judgment order, ordering the payment of the back rent and the surrender of the apartment. The court will also issue a writ of possession, giving the sheriff's department the authority to remove Mr. Jeffries from the premises. Barbara prepares the final judgment order and the writ of possession the client wishes the court to sign after entry of default, which are shown in Exhibits 17–13 and 17–14, respectively.

Three-day notice of termination

EXHIBIT 17–9

THREE-DAY NOTICE

TO: Lee Jeffries
       350 Jacaranda Street, Apt. 201
       Any City, Any State

YOU ARE HEREBY NOTIFIED that you are indebted to the undersigned in the sum of $3,000, for the rent and use of the premises known as Apartment 201, Cameron Apartments, 350 Jacaranda Street, Any City, Any County, Any State, now occupied by you and that the undersigned demands payment of said rent or that you surrender possession of said premises within three (3) days (excluding Saturdays, Sundays, and legal holidays) from the date of delivery of this notice, to wit: on or before the 13th day of September, 2015.

                                        Cameron Properties, Inc.
                                        1200 Commercial Avenue, Suite 300
                                        Any City, Any State
                                        (000) 222-8888

CERTIFICATE OF SERVICE

I HEREBY CERTIFY that a copy of the above notice was delivered to the abovenamed tenant by posting on the premises on the 10th day of September, 2015.

                                        Jack Cameron
                                        President, Cameron Properties, Inc.

EXHIBIT 17–10

Residential eviction summons

IN THE COUNTY COURT OF ANY COUNTY, ANY STATE

CASE NO.

CAMERON PROPERTIES, INC.,
an Any State corporation,
    Plaintiff,

vs.

LEE JEFFRIES,
    Defendant.

_____/

EVICTION SUMMONS/RESIDENTIAL

TO: LEE JEFFRIES, Defendant
        350 Jacaranda Street, Apt. 201
        Any City, Any State

PLEASE READ CAREFULLY

You are being sued by CAMERON PROPERTIES, INC. to require you to move out of the place where you are living for the reasons given in the attached complaint.

You are entitled to a trial to decide whether you can be required to move, but you MUST do ALL of the things listed below. You must do them within FIVE (5) days (not including Saturday, Sunday, or any legal holiday) after the date these papers were given to you or to a person who lives with you or were posted at your home.

THE THINGS YOU MUST DO ARE AS FOLLOWS:

(1)   Write down the reason(s) why you think you should not be forced to move. The written reason(s) must be given to the court clerk at Any County Courthouse, 2000 Justice Avenue, Any City, Any County, Any State.

(2)   Mail or take a copy of your written reason(s) to:
        Ava Ross, Esquire
        Plaintiff's Attorney
        Fisher, Ross, and Simon, P.A.
        1900 N.W. 3rd Avenue
        Any City, Any State

(3)   Give the court clerk the rent that is due. You MUST pay the clerk the rent each time it becomes due until the lawsuit is over. Whether you win or lose the lawsuit, the judge may pay this rent to the landlord.

(4)   If you and the landlord do not agree on the amount of rent owed, give the court clerk the money you say you owe. Then before the trial you must ask the judge to set up a hearing to decide what amount should be given to the court clerk.

IF YOU DO NOT DO ALL OF THESE THINGS WITHIN 5 WORKING DAYS, YOU MAY BE EVICTED WITHOUT A HEARING OR FURTHER NOTICE.

THE STATE OF ANY STATE

To Each Sheriff of the State: You are commanded to serve this summons and a copy of the complaint in this lawsuit on the above-named defendant.

DATED on _____.

                          Clerk of the County Court

                          By: _____

                          Deputy Clerk

EXHIBIT 17–11

IN THE COUNTY COURT FOR ANY COUNTY, ANY STATE

CASE NO.

CAMERON PROPERTIES, INC.,
an Any State corporation,
      Plaintiff,

vs.

LEE JEFFRIES,
      Defendant.   **COMPLAINT FOR TENANT EVICTION**

_____/

Plaintiff, CAMERON PROPERTIES, INC., sues Defendant, LEE JEFFRIES, and alleges:

COUNT I

1. This is an action to evict Defendant from real property in Any County, Any State.
2. Plaintiff owns the following described real property in said county: Apartment 201, Cameron Apartments, 350 Jacaranda Street, Any City, Any County, Any State.
3. Defendant has possession of the property under a written agreement to pay rent of One Thousand Five Hundred Dollars ($1,500.00) per month, a copy of which is attached as Exhibit A.
4. Defendant failed to pay rent due August 1, 2015 and September 1, 2015.
5. Plaintiff served Defendant with a notice on September 10, 2015 to pay the rent or deliver possession, but Defendant refuses to do either. A copy of said notice is attached as Exhibit B.
6. Defendant is not in the military service of the United States.

COUNT II

7. This is an action for rent which is past due.
8. Defendant owes Plaintiff the sum of ThreeThousand Dollars ($3,000.00) for past due rent plus rent accruing during the pendency of this action.

    WHEREFORE, Plaintiff demands judgment for possession of the property, damages for back rent against Defendant, and costs.

DATED: _____

                         FISHER, ROSS, AND SIMON, P.A.
                         1900 N.W. 3rd Avenue
                         Any City, Any State
                         (000) 555-2000
                         Attorneys for Plaintiff

                         By: _____
                            Ava Ross, Esquire
                            Any State Bar No.123456

EXHIBIT 17–12

Motion for default and default

IN THE COUNTY COURT OF ANY COUNTY, ANY STATE

CASE NO.

CAMERON PROPERTIES, INC.,
an Any State corporation,
　　　Plaintiff,

vs.

LEE JEFFRIES,
　　　Defendant.

**MOTION FOR DEFAULT
AND DEFAULT**

_____/

　　Plaintiff, CAMERON PROPERTIES, INC., moves for entry of a Default by the Clerk of Court against the Defendant, LEE JEFFRIES, for failure to serve any paper on Plaintiff or file any paper as required by law.

　　I HEREBY CERTIFY that no copy of answer or other pleading of the Defendant in the above-styled cause has been served upon the Plaintiff.

FISHER, ROSS, AND SIMON, P.A.
1900 N.W. 3rd Avenue
Any City, Any State
(000) 555-2000
Attorneys for Plaintiff

By: _____
　　Ava Ross, Esquire
　　Any State Bar No. 123456

DEFAULT

　　A Default is entered in this action against the Defendant named in the foregoing motion for failure to serve or file any paper as required by law.

　　DONE AND ORDERED at Any City, Any County, Any State, this _____ day of _____, 2015.

Clerk of the County Court

By: _____
　　Deputy Clerk

Final judgment   **EXHIBIT 17–13**

IN THE COUNTY COURT FOR ANY COUNTY, ANY STATE
CASE NO.

CAMERON PROPERTIES, INC.,
an Any State corporation,
      Plaintiff,

vs.

LEE JEFFRIES,
      Defendant.   **FINAL JUDGMENT**
_____/

    This cause came on to be heard before me upon the Plaintiff's verified complaint, and default having been duly entered herein, it is
ORDERED AND ADJUDGED

    1.   That Final Judgment be entered in favor of the Plaintiff against the Defendant for possession of the premises located at Apt. 201, Cameron Apartments, 350 Jacaranda Street, Any City, Any County, Any State, for which let Writ of Possession issue forthwith.

    2.   That the Plaintiff recover from the Defendant back rent in the amount of $3,000.00, together with costs in the amount of $125.00, for which sums let execution issue forthwith.

    DONE AND ORDERED at Any City, Any County, Any State on this _____ day of _____, 2015.

                                        _____
                                           County Judge

Writ of possession   **EXHIBIT 17–14**

IN THE COUNTY COURT FOR ANY COUNTY, ANY STATE
CASE NO.

CAMERON PROPERTIES, INC.,
an Any State corporation,
      Plaintiff,

vs.

LEE JEFFRIES,
      Defendant.   **WRIT OF POSSESSION**
_____/

THE STATE OF ANY STATE:

To All Sheriffs of said State:

    YOU ARE HEREBY COMMANDED, in accordance with the Final Judgment entered herein, forthwith to remove all persons from the following described premises located in Any County, Any State: Apt. 201, Cameron Apartments, 350 Jacaranda Street, Any City, Any State; and to put the Plaintiff or its agent in full and immediate possession thereof, and to take with you the force of the County if same is required, after twenty-four hours notice conspicuously posted on the premises.

    WITNESS my hand and seal of said Court this _____ day of _____, 2015.

                                      Clerk of the County Court

                                    By: _____
                                          Deputy Clerk

CHAPTER SUMMARY

1. Actual eviction refers to a lawsuit brought by a landlord for repossession of the leased premises after the termination of a lease. Constructive eviction refers to a lawsuit brought by a tenant for wrongful dispossession of the leased premises caused by the landlord's failure to maintain the premises in a habitable condition.

2. In order to be successful in a suit for constructive eviction, a tenant must first vacate the premises and then show that the landlord's actions were intentionally done to deprive the tenant of possession or enjoyment of the premises.

3. Landlords may not avail themselves of self-help remedies to remove a tenant from the leased premises. A landlord must follow statutory procedures for eviction. A tenant may be evicted only after the lease is legally terminated. A tenant may be evicted for holding over after the expiration of the lease, for failure to pay rent, or for breach of any provision of the lease agreement.

4. Until such time as the Protecting Tenants at Foreclosure Act expires, a purchaser of a foreclosed property must permit residential tenants to stay (absent a breach by the tenant) until the end of the tenant's lease. An exception is made if the purchaser will be occupying the premises as his or her primary residence; in this circumstance, the purchaser is required to provide the tenant with a ninety-day notice to vacate the premises.

5. In situations other than one involving a holdover tenant, the landlord must give the tenant an opportunity to cure the breach prior to terminating the lease and bringing suit for eviction. The time period within which to cure is set by state statute.

6. Landlords and tenants, if individuals (not corporations), may represent themselves in court or may choose to hire an attorney. If the lease agreement so stipulates, a landlord or tenant represented by an attorney may be awarded attorneys' fees as part of the damages award should he or she prevail in the suit. Court costs also are awarded to the prevailing party.

7. Eviction complaints are similar to other types of complaints and include the court caption, separate counts for each cause of action, and a prayer for relief. Copies of notices sent to a tenant and a copy of the lease agreement should be attached to the complaint as exhibits. Some states require that eviction complaints be verified complaints.

8. To collect back rent, a landlord who is successful in an eviction suit may (1) attempt to garnish the tenant's wages, (2) attempt to execute judgment against any real property owned by the tenant by recording a certified copy of the judgment in each county in which the tenant owns real property, or (3) attempt to execute judgment by selling that portion of the tenant's personal property that is subject to a landlord's lien.

9. A distress for rent proceeding is a summary proceeding permitted in some states as a remedy for collecting rent owed. The landlord files suit, posts a bond, and obtains a distress writ ordering the sheriff to levy upon the personal property of the tenant, sell it, and distribute the proceeds to the landlord.

WEB RESOURCES

http://www.rentlaw.com/

At this site, you can select "Eviction" to access a short overview of the eviction process. This site also has links to state-specific eviction laws and procedures.

http://www.landlord.com/

At this site, you can learn about your state's landlord/tenant laws by selecting "Landlord Law" and then clicking on your state.

http://www.expertlaw.com/

At this site, you can access articles on eviction by selecting "Legal Information," then selecting "Real Estate" and then clicking on the relevant article.

http:// www.law.cornell.edu/

This is the site of the Legal Information Institute (LII). It provides an overview of eviction law.

REVIEW QUESTIONS

1. What actions by a landlord constitute a constructive eviction?
2. What remedies are available to a tenant in a suit for constructive eviction?
3. Under what circumstances may a landlord retake possession of leased premises?
4. List the steps to be taken to evict a tenant for breach of a lease agreement.
5. How does a distress for rent proceeding differ from an eviction proceeding?

DISCUSSION QUESTIONS

1. Review your state's eviction statutes. Do you believe they reflect a fair balance between the rights of landlords and tenants? Why or why not?
2. Barker Auto Company (lessee) leases commercial space in a building owned by ABC Motors, Inc. (lessor). The lease provides for a fixed rent of $1,800 per month plus the payment of a portion of real estate taxes as additional rent. The roof of the leased premises has leaked periodically during the lessee's occupancy, and the leak has become worse in recent months. A few months ago the lessee began withholding rent. Through its legal counsel, it sent a letter to the lessor, indicating that it would continue to withhold rent until the roof was properly repaired and rain ceased to come into the leased premises. The lessee also stopped paying the real estate taxes. It placed the rent due in an escrow account. The lessor has served notice of termination of lease for nonpayment of rent and is now bringing an eviction action under your state statutes for possession. The eviction complaint does not include a claim for money damages for unpaid rent. In defending the action, the lessee is claiming that the lessor's failure to repair the roof after repeated verbal demands to do so, followed by the attorney letter, amounts to a breach of warranty of

habitability justifying the withholding of rent. Under your state statutes, will this defense be successful? Why or why not?

3. Assume the same scenario as in Question 2. The lessee is defending the action by claiming it may avoid eviction by paying the unpaid rent offset by damages caused by the roof leak. Under your state's statutes, will this defense be successful? Why or why not?

4. Assume the same scenario as in Question 3; however, the lessor, in addition to seeking possession of the premises, also is seeking monetary damages for unpaid rent. Would your answer change? Why or why not?

5. Denise Long (lessee) was a tenant of the Dorsey Place Apartments (lessor), a government-subsidized housing complex. The lessor sought to evict her, claiming that she violated a condition of her lease that prohibits, under pain of lease termination, criminal activity on the premises that threatens the health, safety, or right to peaceful enjoyment of other tenants. Undisputed evidence indicates that the lessee's cousin entered her apartment after drinking and began a fight with the lessee's boyfriend, who was on the premises. The fight escalated, and the cousin pulled out a gun and fatally shot the boyfriend. The next day the police, executing a search warrant, found a loaded gun under the seat cushions of the lessee's couch. The lessor, through a process server, served a Notice to Quit on the lessee by posting the notice on her door after two unsuccessful attempts to serve her personally. The notice stated the nature of the violation and required her to quit the premises by a specified date. It did not state that she had an opportunity to cure the lease violation. The cousin was later acquitted of the murder charge, the jury finding that he acted in self-defense, but he was convicted of the lesser charge of possessing an illegal firearm. At trial on the eviction suit, the judge granted the lessor's suit for possession. The lessee is now appealing, claiming that the notice should have provided her with an opportunity to cure the lease violation. Do you think the lessee will be successful on appeal? Why or why not?

ETHICAL QUESTION

While your supervising attorney is out of the office, Tom Hanson, another attorney with your law firm, knowing that you are a notary public, enters your office and asks you to notarize a document that he says needs to be filed immediately at the courthouse. You look at the document and see that it is a verified complaint to be signed by Donald Reid. Donald Reid's signature already appears on the signature line, and the client is nowhere in sight. You ask Tom where Mr. Reid is because you need to verify the signature before notarizing the document. Tom informs you that Mr. Reid is out of town on vacation and that the complaint needs to be filed today to prevent the statute of limitations from running out on his cause of action, so Tom signed the document in his place and now needs it notarized. He tells you the client will not mind. What should you do?

Slossberg Law Office on CourseMate

Please go to www.cengagebrain.com to log into CourseMate, access the Slossberg Law Office, and work on your client files. Each module corresponds to a chapter in the text. Within each module, you will be provided with instructions by the supervising attorney. You are asked to keep track of time spent on time sheets. The documents produced through working on client files in the law office can then be compiled into a portfolio of final work product.

CourseMate

The available CourseMate for this text has an interactive eBook and interactive learning tools, including flash cards, quizzes, and more. To learn more about this resource and access free demo CourseMate resources, including the Slossberg Law Office, go to www.cengagebrain.com, and search for this book. To access CourseMate materials that you have purchased, go to login.cengagebrain.com.

PART IV

Real Estate Litigation

18

Overview of Real Estate Litigation

CHAPTER OBJECTIVES

Upon completion of this chapter, the student will:

- Know the various remedies available in an action pertaining to a contract for sale and purchase

- Know how to draft complaints for monetary damages, breach of implied warranty, fraudulent inducement, and specific performance in a contract action

- Know how to draft a complaint for a breach of a brokerage agreement

- Know how to draft a complaint for partition of real property

Introduction

People enter real estate transactions with the best intentions. A couple may be buying their first home and, in so doing, may be engaging in the largest financial commitment they have made to date; they sign the contract for sale and purchase with positive expectations. A seller and broker enter into a brokerage agreement, both having the expectation that the broker will quickly find a buyer ready, willing, and able to purchase the property on terms most favorable to the seller. A partnership may purchase income-producing property as part of its business plan for increased economic growth, never imagining future disputes that could bring about a dissolution of the business and the necessity to partition property.

In previous chapters, great emphasis has been placed on careful, scrupulous drafting of documents with an eye toward preventive medicine, clarifying the obligations and rights of each party to avoid the possibility of future disputes. Nonetheless, occasions arise when parties clash, and attempts to settle disputes amicably fail. In such instances, one or both parties may choose the route of litigation, and you, as a real estate paralegal, will be asked by your supervising attorney to assist in drafting or answering complaints, drafting motions, conducting legal research and discovery, and participating in all aspects of bringing the case to a successful resolution for the client.

This chapter does not attempt to address all stages of the litigation process, which is best left to a civil litigation course; nor does it attempt to address all areas of real estate litigation. Instead, it focuses on three areas real estate attorneys and paralegals come across most often: (1) litigation of contracts for sale and purchase and construction contracts, (2) litigation of broker-age agreements, and (3) partition of real property. A fourth area, mortgage foreclo-sure, is covered separately in the next chapter. This chapter discusses each of the litigation matters stated above by looking at the remedies available to the respective parties involved in the dispute and the steps to be taken in drafting a complaint on behalf of a client.

Actions Pertaining to Contracts for Sale and Purchase

Actions for Monetary Damages for Breach of Contract

The terms of a contract for sale and purchase typically specify the amount recover-able by the nonbreaching party. Damages for breach by the buyer may be the reten-tion of the deposit; liquidated damages agreed upon in the contract for sale and purchase; a suit for monetary damages, the calculation of which will be the difference between the contract price and the fair market value of the property (this remedy is known as the **benefit of the bargain**); or a suit for specific performance (this last remedy is discussed later in this section). Should the buyer's actions indicate bad faith or actions constituting a tort (for example, fraud), separate causes of action may be brought in addition to the cause of action for breach of contract, and additional damages may be awarded.

Damages for breach by the seller may be the return of the deposit; liquidated damages agreed upon in the contract for sale and purchase; a suit for monetary damages, the calculation of which includes the deposit(s) paid by the buyer together with interest, the expenses of investigating title (if any), and the cost of improvements made by the buyer with the approval of the seller in contemplation of the conveyance; or a suit for specific performance.

As noted in Chapter 7, care and attention must be paid to the drafting of a contract for sale and purchase because the contract dictates the procedures for the rest of the real estate transaction. Poorly drafted provisions may come back to haunt a client and his or her counsel should the client find the other party has breached the contract. For example, the parties to the contract may have agreed that retention (or, conversely, return) of the deposit will be the sole remedy of the parties in the event of breach. Suppose, in this instance, that the contract requires an initial deposit upon signing the contract and an additional deposit fifteen days later. Suppose further that the buyer breaches the contract and refuses to make the additional deposit. Is the seller entitled to the additional deposit as damages for breach, or is the seller entitled to only that portion of the deposit that has already been paid?

The answer to this question can sometimes be determined by the wording of the remedies provision of the contract for sale and purchase. However, where the remedies provision simply mentions "deposit" and does not provide greater detail, it is quite possible for the court to find that the seller is entitled to only that portion of the deposit that has been paid by the buyer.

Similarly, great care must be given to the drafting of a liquidated damages provision to prevent a court from interpreting it as a penalty provision that is

benefit of the bargain: A mon-etary remedy in a breach of contract action calculated as the difference between the contract price and the fair market value of the property.

unenforceable against the breaching party. **Liquidated damages** are stipulated damages, the amount of which represents a reasonable sum to be paid to the nonbreaching party for damages suffered as a result of the breach of contract for sale and purchase. For a liquidated damages provision to be upheld, the first requirement is that the damages suffered must be difficult to compute with any degree of certainty, thus causing the parties to agree upon the stipulated sum. For example, suppose the seller is a developer and the contract calls for a particular model of home to be built on the real property within a specified period of time. It may be difficult to calculate with any degree of certainty the amount of damages suffered by a buyer if the construction is delayed, so the parties may agree to a stipulated sum as liquidated damages for each day of delay.

The second requirement for upholding a liquidated damages provision is that the stipulated sum must not be grossly disproportionate to the amount of damages that one would reasonably expect to result from the breach. Take note that if the remedies provision of a contract for sale and purchase includes both a liquidated damages clause and a clause that allows the nonbreaching party to bring suit for monetary damages, there is great likelihood that the liquidated damages clause will be construed as a penalty because the inclusion of the option of bringing suit for monetary damages implies that the parties believe actual monetary damages can be ascertained. It follows, then, that if actual monetary damages can be determined, there is no need for a liquidated damages provision, which implies that actual damages are difficult to ascertain.

In circumstances in which a suit to recover monetary damages is a viable option, a court generally awards a successful seller-plaintiff the difference between the contract price for the real property and the current fair market value of the property. Current fair market value ordinarily is determined by the testimony of a property appraiser who will evaluate the property in question against the recent selling price of other comparable properties. For example, suppose an appraiser testifies that properties comparable to the property in question have recently sold for $365,000. Suppose further that the buyer, under contract, agreed to a purchase price of $410,000. A court finding for the seller would award the seller a sum of $45,000, even though the property may be worth only $365,000 on today's market, because the court will give the seller the benefit of the bargain agreed upon by the parties. If the buyer made a bad bargain and agreed to pay a sum now found to be higher than the current fair market value, that is the buyer's loss. The seller is entitled to that for which he or she bargained.

A successful plaintiff-buyer in a suit for monetary damages will be awarded the return of any deposits paid, together with interest, and the costs for expenses incurred. For example, suppose a buyer contracted with a seller and paid the seller a $20,000 deposit at the time of executing the contract. Suppose further that the buyer hired an attorney to conduct a title examination (the attorney charges $250 for this service), hired a landscape architect (with the express approval of the seller) to prepare a landscape plan (the landscape architect charges $150 for this service, with this charge to be applied toward the actual landscaping should the buyer hire the landscape architect for the job), and so forth. The buyer would be able to recover the $20,000 deposit, plus accrued interest at the current rate of interest, the title examination fee, the landscape architect fee, and any other costs and expenses reasonably incurred in reliance on the seller's contractual promise

liquidated damages: Stipulated damages, the amount of which represents a reasonable sum to be paid to the nonbreaching party for damages suffered as a result of a breach of contract.

to close the transaction. **Punitive damages** (damages designed to punish or to serve as an example) generally are not recoverable in a breach of contract action except in special circumstances (for example, fraud).

In addition to monetary damages, the plaintiff may be entitled to attorneys' fees as the prevailing party. An attorneys' fees provision is often included in a contract for sale and purchase. Under contract law, attorneys' fees may not be recovered by the prevailing party from the losing party unless the contract so provides. If attorneys' fees are recoverable according to the contract, the complaint for breach of contract should include a statement that the plaintiff had to hire counsel as a result of the defendant's breach and therefore the plaintiff is entitled to attorneys' fees. For recovery of these fees, the court may require testimony from expert witnesses as to the reasonableness of the fees. Once a judgment is obtained in favor of the plaintiff, an affidavit of proof of fees will be submitted by the plaintiff's counsel.

Prior to drafting a complaint for breach of contract for sale and purchase, proper jurisdiction must be determined. **Jurisdiction** refers to the authority of a court to hear a matter. Courts must have proper **subject matter jurisdiction** (jurisdiction over the subject matter of the litigation—in this instance, money) as well as *personal jurisdiction,* also referred to as **in personam jurisdiction** (jurisdiction over the persons involved in the litigation). In some states, jurisdiction for contract rights affecting title to real property may be in the county in which the real property is located.

Lawsuits for monetary damages are lawsuits for **legal remedies,** brought in courts of law, whereas lawsuits for **equitable remedies** (remedies administered according to fairness, such as injunctions and actions for specific performance) are brought in courts of equity. In determining which court of law has proper subject matter jurisdiction over the suit, the amount of the damages in question typically is central. Courts of law are divided into a hierarchy of levels, determined by jurisdictional amount. For example, a small claims court in a particular state may hear cases that do not exceed $5,000, the county court may hear cases that exceed $5,000 but do not exceed $15,000, and the circuit court may hear cases that exceed $15,000. To determine proper subject matter jurisdiction, the contract must be reviewed to determine the purchase price and any amounts already paid by the buyer as deposits.

A court has personal jurisdiction over the plaintiff because the plaintiff, by initiating the lawsuit, gives the court power over him or her. A court acquires personal jurisdiction over a defendant by **service of process** (the serving of a summons and the complaint upon the defendant by a sheriff or court-approved process server).

The next step is to determine appropriate venue. **Venue** refers to the proper location to bring the suit. State statutes dictate appropriate venue for various types of lawsuits. In breach of contract actions, proper venue ordinarily is the county in which the defendant resides, the county in which the contract was executed, or the county in which the contract was breached. Since venue statutes vary from state to state, however, your state's statutes should be checked.

The terms of the contract for sale and purchase should be scrutinized to determine the obligations of the parties, the timing of those obligations, and any conditions placed on those obligations. For example, a contract may stipulate that the buyer's

punitive damages: Damages designed to punish or serve as an example.

jurisdiction: The authority of a court to hear a matter.

subject matter jurisdiction: Jurisdiction over the subject matter of the litigation.

in personam jurisdiction: Jurisdiction over the persons involved in litigation.

legal remedies: Remedies awarded in courts of law, such as monetary damages.

equitable remedies: Remedies administered according to fairness, such as injunctions and actions for specific performance.

service of process: The serving of a summons and complaint upon the defendant by a sheriff or court-approved process server.

venue: The proper location to bring a lawsuit.

obligations are subject to the buyer obtaining a mortgage loan of a specified amount at a specified fixed rate within a specified period of time. The contract may further state that, if the buyer fails to acquire a mortgage loan meeting these specifications, the buyer may be released from the contract, and all deposits are to be returned. If the provision says nothing about the buyer having to use his or her "best efforts" to acquire financing or does not specify that the buyer has to make application for a mortgage loan within a specified number of days after the signing of the contract, the buyer's exact obligations are uncertain. How much effort must the buyer make to secure financing? If the buyer goes through the motions but makes little effort, the buyer, under the terms of this provision, may not be in breach if the buyer fails to obtain financing within the specified time period.

In another example, suppose a title examination shows red flags such as judgment liens and construction liens against the property. If the contract states that the seller has a specified period of time after being informed of such defects to correct the same, the buyer must allow the seller the opportunity to cure, even if it delays closing, as long as such delay is within the time period specified for cure of title defects. If the buyer does not do so and refuses to close, the buyer will be in breach of contract. Thus, every provision must be scrutinized in this manner. A copy of the contract for sale and purchase should be attached to the complaint as an exhibit. If a jury trial is desired, this must be specifically requested.

A complaint for breach of contract of sale and purchase contains the following:

1. Jurisdictional facts
2. The existence of a contract for sale and purchase (attach a copy as an exhibit to the complaint)
3. Breach of the contract by the defendant
4. Allegations establishing the plaintiff's full performance under the contract or a statement that the plaintiff is ready, willing, and able to perform under the contract
5. Damages sustained by the plaintiff as a result of the defendant's breach
6. If attorneys' fees are recoverable, that the plaintiff had to employ legal counsel to bring this action
7. Prayer for relief
8. Signature of the attorney

Please note that when drafting any complaint, including all complaints for which samples are provided in this chapter, state law should always be consulted to ensure the cause of action elements are properly pleaded.

Just as in any other type of litigation, when drafting a complaint, a summons form should also be prepared for the clerk of court's signature when the complaint is filed. Payment of the appropriate filing fees must be included when filing the complaint. A case number will be assigned to the case by the clerk of the court. When a lawsuit is brought for monetary damages, a notice of lis pendens should not be filed. Recall from Chapter 9 that a notice of lis pendens is a document that is recorded when a lawsuit affects title to a particular parcel of property, putting third parties on notice that the property is the subject matter of litigation. The notice is recorded in the jurisdiction (most typically, the county) in which the real property is located. In a suit for monetary damages, the title to the real property contracted for is not affected. The only dispute is whether money is owed to one party and, if so, how much. Exhibit 18–1 provides an example of a complaint for breach of a contract for sale and purchase.

In his or her answer to the complaint, the defendant may attempt to raise one or more defenses to the action. If the plaintiff has waited too long to file suit, the defendant may raise the *statute of limitations* as a defense. The statute of

---

Complaint for breach of contract for sale and purchase　　　**EXHIBIT 18–1**

IN THE CIRCUIT COURT OF THE FOURTH JUDICIAL CIRCUIT
IN AND FOR ANY COUNTY, ANY STATE
CASE NO. 15-1350

PAUL GRANT and
CAROLINE GRANT,
　　　Plaintiffs,

vs.

SIMON PAYSON and
FELICIA PAYSON,
　　　Defendants.　　　　　　　　**COMPLAINT**
_____/

COME NOW the Plaintiffs, PAUL GRANT and CAROLINE GRANT, by and through their undersigned counsel, and sue the Defendants, SIMON PAYSON and FELICIA PAYSON, and allege as follows:

1. This is an action for damages in excess of Fifteen Thousand Dollars ($15,000.00).
2. On or about the 6th day of June, 2015, in Any County, Any State, Plaintiffs and Defendants entered into and executed a written contract for sale and purchase of real property located in Any City, Any State, a copy of which is attached hereto and made a part hereof as Exhibit A.
3. All conditions precedent to bringing this cause of action have occurred.
4. On or about September 15, 2015, the Plaintiffs tendered a deed to the subject real property to the Defendants and requested them to make the payments required of them according to the terms of said contract, which Defendants refused to do.
5. As a result of the failure of the Defendants to close and accept the deed, the Plaintiffs have been damaged in an amount in excess of Fifteen Thousand Dollars ($15,000.00).
6. As a result of the failure of the Defendants to close and accept the deed, the Plaintiffs have been forced to hire an attorney to bring this action and to pay their attorney a reasonable fee for her services herein.

WHEREFORE, Plaintiffs demand judgment against the Defendants for a sum in excess of $15,000.00 together with court costs and a reasonable attorney's fee.

DATED: October 8, 2015.

　　　　　　　　　　　　　　FISHER, ROSS, AND SIMON, P.A.
　　　　　　　　　　　　　　1900 N.W. 3rd Avenue
　　　　　　　　　　　　　　Any City, Any State
　　　　　　　　　　　　　　(000) 555-2000
　　　　　　　　　　　　　　Attorneys for Plaintiffs

　　　　　　　　　　　　　　By: _____
　　　　　　　　　　　　　　　　Ava Ross, Esquire
　　　　　　　　　　　　　　　　Any State Bar No. 123456

limitations places limits on the time period in which suit may be brought on various matters. Each state has its own statute, and, thus, state law should be checked. The statute of limitations is an absolute defense, regardless of the worthiness of the plaintiff's cause.

Another possible defense is that the contract is unenforceable. Suppose, for example, the plaintiff and the defendant had an oral contract for the sale and purchase of the real property. An oral contract would be unenforceable because, as noted in Chapter 7, the statute of frauds dictates that a contract pertaining to an interest in real property must be supported by a writing in order to be enforceable. Another defense that might be raised is that certain conditions precedent have not been met by the opposing party and therefore the defendant is not yet obligated to perform under the contract.

A defendant may also include in his or her answer to the complaint a counterclaim for breach of contract against the plaintiff, alleging that the plaintiff, not the defendant, breached the contract. The counterclaim must include all of the allegations found in a breach of contract suit.

Actions for Fraudulent Inducement

When a prospective buyer approaches a seller or a seller's agent (for example, a real estate broker) for information concerning the real property for sale, a buyer is entitled to full disclosure of any defects or other pertinent information regarding the property. Intentional misrepresentation or even omission of relevant facts concerning the real property constitutes fraud.

If the buyer is induced to purchase the property because of intentional misrepresentations or omissions, the buyer has grounds to bring suit for fraudulent inducement. The buyer may choose to rescind a fraudulently induced sale of real property and sue for recovery of the purchase price paid. Alternatively, the buyer may continue to hold title to the real property and bring an action against the seller or the seller's agent who has induced the fraudulent sale and recover the damages the buyer has suffered as a consequence of the fraud. Those damages are the difference between the actual value of the property at the time of the contract and the value the property would have had if the representations of the seller had been true.

Prior to bringing an action for fraudulent inducement, the proper court should be determined. Because this action is one for monetary damages, which court has jurisdiction will be determined by the amount of the damages incurred. Proper venue typically is the county in which the defendant resides, the county in which the real property is located, or the county in which the agreement was made.

Next, a determination should be made regarding who made the misrepresentations. Did the broker representing the seller make the misrepresentations, or were they made directly by the seller? If they were made directly by the seller and the broker was unaware of these fraudulent statements, the appropriate party to bring suit against is the seller. If the misrepresentations were made by the broker, both the broker and the seller should be brought into the suit as defendants. The seller is the broker's principal and thus is responsible for representations made by the broker.

The misrepresentations (or omissions) should be described with specificity in the complaint. If the misrepresentations were made in written form, the document containing the misrepresentations should be attached to the complaint as an exhibit. The complaint must include allegations that the misrepresentations were material to the transaction, that they were intentional, that they were made to induce the buyer to purchase the property, and that the buyer relied on the misrepresentations to his or her detriment. As noted, if a jury trial is desired, this must be specifically stated in the prayer for relief.

In summary, a complaint for fraudulent inducement sets forth the following:

1. Jurisdictional facts
2. Ownership of the real property by the defendant at the time of contracting
3. Description of the real property
4. Agreement made between the plaintiff and the defendant
5. Allegations of fraudulent misrepresentations (or omissions) made by the defendant
6. Allegations that the misrepresentations were made to induce the plaintiff to purchase the property
7. Allegations that the misrepresentations relate to material facts
8. Allegations that the misrepresentations were false and the defendant knew them to be false at the time of making the misrepresentations
9. The plaintiff's reliance on the misrepresentations
10. Damages suffered by the plaintiff as a result of the fraudulent misrepresentations
11. If attorneys' fees are recoverable, that the plaintiff had to employ legal counsel to bring this action
12. Prayer for relief
13. Signature of the attorney

Exhibit 18–2 sets forth a sample complaint for fraudulent inducement.

Complaint for fraudulent inducement	**EXHIBIT 18–2**

IN THE CIRCUIT COURT OF THE SECOND JUDICIAL CIRCUIT
IN AND FOR ANY COUNTY, ANY STATE
CASE NO. 15-1362

EDWARD FULLER and
WENDY FULLER,
     Plaintiffs,

vs.

KURT HARRINGTON,
     Defendant.   **COMPLAINT**
_____/

COME NOW the Plaintiffs, EDWARD FULLER and WENDY FULLER, by and through their undersigned counsel, and sue the Defendant, KURT HARRINGTON, and allege as follows:

    1.   This is an action for damages in excess of Fifteen Thousand Dollars ($15,000.00).

    2.   On June 18, 2015, Defendant was the owner of the following described real property:

        ALL THAT TRACT of land lying and being situated in the Northeast quarter of the Northwest quarter of the Southwest quarter of Section 3, Township 15 North, Range 5 East, Any County, Any State.

EXHIBIT 18-2   *(continued)*

3. Plaintiffs and Defendant entered into negotiations for the sale of the above-described real property and a structure on it under which the Plaintiffs agreed to pay to the Defendant the sum of Four Hundred Thousand Dollars ($400,000.00). During the negotiations that resulted in the sale to the Plaintiffs, Defendant represented to the Plaintiffs that the property was properly zoned for both residential and commercial uses.

4. The representation was made by the Defendant with the intention that the Plaintiffs rely on such representation.

5. The representation relates to an existing, material fact.

6. Defendant knew the representation was false.

7. Plaintiffs, believing the Defendant's representation to be true, relied on it and as a result entered into a contract for sale and purchase with the Defendant on June 18, 2015, and thereafter concluded the sale by payment to the Defendant of the purchase price of Four Hundred Thousand Dollars ($400,000.00). The Defendant then conveyed the property to the Plaintiffs.

8. Defendant's fraudulent representation became known to the Plaintiffs on September 28, 2015, when the Plaintiffs went to apply for an occupational license for their business which they planned on conducting from the above-described property and were told by the clerk at City Hall that the above-described property was zoned for residential use only.

9. As a result of being fraudulently induced to purchase the real property from the Defendant, the Plaintiffs have suffered damages in excess of Fifteen Thousand Dollars ($15,000.00).

10. As a result of being fraudulently induced to purchase the real property from the Defendant, the Plaintiffs have been forced to hire an attorney to bring this action and to pay their attorney a reasonable fee for her services herein.

WHEREFORE, the Plaintiffs demand judgment against the Defendant for damages in excess of Fifteen Thousand Dollars ($15,000.00), together with court costs and a reasonable attorney's fee.

DATED: October 8, 2015.

FISHER, ROSS, AND SIMON, P.A.
1900 N.W. 3rd Avenue
Any City, Any State
(000) 555-2000
Attorneys for Plaintiffs

By: _____
　　Ava Ross, Esquire
　　Any State Bar No. 123456

The defendant in a fraudulent misrepresentation action may raise one or more defenses in his or her answer to the complaint. First, just as in the case of a breach of contract action, if the plaintiff has waited too long to bring suit, the defendant may raise the statute of limitations as an absolute defense. Alternative defenses are that the misrepresentation was not intentional and that the misrepresentation did not go to a material fact that would have induced the plaintiff to enter into, or not enter into, the contract.

Actions for Breach of Implied Warranty

When a buyer purchases a product, such as a television, a lawnmower, or an automobile, there is an implied warranty that the product is fit for the particular purpose for which it was bought. This is called an **implied warranty of fitness and merchantability.** This implied warranty also pertains to the purchase of a house or building and the contents therein. This implied warranty survives after the closing on the property. If an item in the purchased premises is defective, the buyer may have an action for breach of implied warranty.

To be successful in an action for breach of implied warranty, the buyer must be able to show damage on account of the breach. Further, this damage must result in a decrease of the value of the property as a whole, not simply of the item complained of. For example, if the water heater is found to be defective, that in and of itself may not be enough for a successful action under breach of implied warranty, for it is doubtful that the defective water heater would result in a diminution of the value of the property. This is especially the case if the current appraised value of the property is greater than the purchase price contracted for. If, however, there is a serious structural defect in the property, such as cracks in the foundation walls or floors that are not level, it is quite likely that these defects would result in a diminution of the value of the property.

An action for breach of implied warranty is one that requests monetary damages for the devaluation of the property. The calculation of damages is the difference between the purchase price of the property and the value of the property in its present, defective condition. Alternatively, if the plaintiff has hired contractors to repair the damages, the monetary damages are the costs that have been incurred for the repairs that have been done and those that will be incurred for the repairs that will need to be done in the future.

Jurisdiction for a breach of implied warranty action is based on the amount of monetary damages sought. Proper venue typically is the county in which the defendant resides, the county in which the contract for sale and purchase was executed, or the county in which the property is located (where the breach occurred). The complaint should set forth allegations concerning the execution of the contract for sale and purchase, the delivery of the property, specific details regarding the defects amounting to breach of implied warranty, a request for repairs to be made, a refusal to make necessary repairs, and damages to the plaintiff as a result of the breach, as noted in the following checklist:

1. Jurisdictional facts
2. The plaintiff's ownership of the property
3. Existence of a contract for sale and purchase (attach a copy as an exhibit)
4. Allegations of implied warranty that the defendant was to deliver property in condition of fitness
5. Allegations of breach of implied warranty
6. Allegations of demands for repair made by the plaintiff and the defendant's refusal to make repairs
7. Damages sustained by the plaintiff as a result of the defendant's breach
8. If attorneys' fees are recoverable, that the plaintiff had to employ legal counsel to bring this action

implied warranty of fitness: An implied warranty that a product is fit for the particular purpose for which it was bought.

9. Prayer for relief

10. Signature of the attorney

Breach of implied warranty actions happen most commonly (but not exclusively) in construction contract situations. Often, a construction contract will contain a warranty clause stating that the contractor/developer warrants that the house/building being constructed meets specified standards. Further, the warranty clause may provide that the contractor/developer gives the buyer a warranty on the structure, heating, air conditioning, and appliances for a specified time period (often one year). A written warranty is an express warranty rather than an implied warranty, and if an express warranty is included in the contract for sale and purchase and is not honored, the plaintiff has grounds to bring an additional cause of action for breach of express warranty. A sample complaint for breach of implied warranty is found in the hypothetical lawsuit section at the end of this chapter.

In answer to a complaint for breach of implied warranty, a defendant may resort to the statute of limitations, if applicable. If the defect is structural, the defendant may state that the structure was built in exact accordance with approved plans and specifications. Lenders often require inspection of the property prior to closing. For example, if a Federal Housing Administration (FHA) loan was obtained to finance the purchase, the FHA requires submission of plans and specifications for inspection and, before closing, makes a final inspection report to ensure that construction is in compliance with these plans and specifications. If the plaintiff financed the purchase of the property through an FHA loan, the defendant may raise the FHA inspections as a defense.

The following Washington case raises two interesting issues: (1) whether an "as is" provision in a contract for new construction of a house acts as a waiver of an implied warranty of habitability and (2) whether purchasers are deemed third-party beneficiaries to contracts between construction companies and their subcontractors, thus permitting purchasers to sue subcontractors for breach of implied warranty of workmanlike construction.

CASE: *Warner v. Design and Build Homes, Inc.*

128 Wash. App. 34, 114 P.3d 664 (2005)

QUINN-BRINTNALL, C.J.

1. After Curtis and Ana Warner discovered structural defects and significant mold growth in their new home, they sued Design and Build Homes, Inc. (Design) and Omega Pacific Lath & Plaster, Inc. (Omega). The Warners asserted that Design, as the builder-vendor, had breached the implied warranty of habitability. As to Omega, the subcontractor, the Warners maintained that they were third-party beneficiaries under the contract between Omega and Design, therefore entitled them to bring a claim for breach of an implied warranty of workmanlike construction. The trial court granted Design and Omega's motion for summary judgment and the Warners appeal. Because the Warners are not third-party beneficiaries to the contract between Design and Omega and because they disclaimed all implied warranties when they purchased the property "as is," we affirm.

FACTS

2. In March 1999, the Warners entered into a purchase and sale agreement with Design for the sale of a new home. The agreement, drafted by the Warners' real estate agent, included a clause stating that the Warners had inspected the property and agreed to purchase the

(continued)

property "in its present 'as is' condition." Clerk's Papers (CP) at 25. An addendum to the agreement also stated that the sale was conditioned on the Warners' approval of a general building inspection report. The addendum provided that the Warners could decline to purchase "on the basis of any condition identified in the inspection report that the inspector recommends be corrected." CP at 28. If the inspector recommended further evaluation of the home by a specialist, then the addendum gave the Warners additional time to complete this further evaluation. The addendum also gave Design the option to preserve the contract for sale by correcting any condition disapproved by the Warners.

3. The Warners had the home inspected. The inspection report contained the following findings and recommendations: (1) "[e]xterior wall cracks" and "bulging in the stucco" on the rear wall, which "should be further evaluated to verify that a problem does not exist, and what correction is needed to repair/seal the cracks;" (2) "evidence of past water in the crawl space at the north wall," which should be monitored; and (3) the "flashing at the front wall . . . should be checked, due to the potential of water leaking into the stucco." CP at 415–16. The inspection report recommended that a certified professional engineer complete a further evaluation "where there are structural concerns about the building" because "[a]ssessing the structural integrity of a building is beyond the scope of a typical home inspection." CP at 415.

4. The Warners declined to have a further evaluation completed, but they did request that Design repair certain conditions identified in the inspection report. These conditions included the exterior wall cracks and defects in the flashing and stucco. After these conditions were repaired, the Warners completed a walk-through inspection and closed the sale of the property.

5. In September 2001, the Warners began noticing leaks and water damage inside the home. They hired a professional stucco consultant who concluded that the water intrusion was due to defective stucco installation. The Warners also hired an industrial hygienist to evaluate mold contamination in the interior of the home. The hygienist concluded that the water intrusion had led to a significant presence of "several potentially toxic species of airborne fungi" throughout the house. CP at 247.

6. The Warners moved out of the home when it became apparent that Ana Warner and the Warner children were having allergic reactions to the mold. The Warners then hired an engineer and construction company to repair and replace the exterior siding as well as damaged structural components. The engineer eventually concluded that "substantial water intrusion [had] . . . resulted

in substantial rot and fungal growth" which had caused "structural damage to the sheathing and framing components of the Residence." CP at 352–53. The engineer opined that if the water intrusion, rot, and fungus had been allowed to continue, the home would have collapsed within a reasonably foreseeable period.

7. In November 2001, the Warners sued Design and Omega. Design had subcontracted with Omega to install the stucco siding. The Warners alleged that Design had breached the implied warranty of workmanlike construction implicit in the contract between Omega and Design, to which the Warners claimed damages as third-party beneficiaries. The trial court granted Design and Omega summary judgment against the Warners. The Warners appeal.

ANALYSIS

8. The Warners assert that the trial court erred in granting summary judgment to Design and Omega. This appeal turns on two issues: (1) whether the "as is" clause in the Warners' purchase and sale agreement waived all implied warranties, including the warranty of habitability; and (2) whether the Warners are third-party beneficiaries to the contract between Omega and Design. These are questions of law which we review de novo. CR 56(c); *Dep't of Labor & Indus. v. Fankhauser*, 121 Wash. 2d 304, 308, 849 P.2d 1209 (1993).

*"As Is" Clause and Waiver of the Implied
Warranty of Habitability*

9. The contract between the Warners and Design required the Warners' approval of a general building inspection report. If this report listed problems with the home, Design could correct them. If the report recommended further evaluation, the Warners could delay closing on the property so that the evaluation could be completed. Under the purchase and sale agreement, the Warners agreed to purchase the property "as is" if (1) no conditions were identified in the report and a further evaluation was not recommended; or (2) Design repaired any conditions, identified in either the report or the further evaluation, which the Warners wanted fixed. Satisfaction of one of these two alternatives was a condition precedent to the Warners' agreement to purchase the home "as is."

10. Although the inspection report recommended further structural evaluations of the home, the Warners did not conduct them. The Warners did request that certain conditions in the inspection report be fixed. It is undisputed that Design honored the Warners' request. These decisions triggered the purchase and sale agreement's "as is" clause.

(continued)

11. An "as is" clause means that the buyer is purchasing property in its present state or condition. *Olmstead v. Mulder*, 72 Wash. App. 169, 176, 863 P.2d 1355 (1993), *review denied*, 123 Wash. 2d 1025, 875 P.2d 635 (1994). "The term ['as is'] implies that the property is taken with whatever faults it may possess and that the seller or lessor is released of any obligation to reimburse the purchaser for losses or damages that result from the condition of the property." *Olmstead*, 72 Wash. App. at 176, 863 P.2d 1355. Because a warranty disclaimer is not favored in the law, it must meet two conditions to be effective: (1) it must be explicitly negotiated or bargained for, and (2) it must set forth with particularity what is being disclaimed. *Puget Sound Fin., L.L.C. v. Unisearch, Inc.*, 146 Wash. 2d 428, 438, 47 P.3d 940 (2002). An "as is" clause is generally inserted in a contract by the seller and the negotiation and particularity requirements are designed to protect a buyer who, not being in a position of equal bargaining power, is forced into signing a contract prepared by the seller that may contain fine print and boilerplate language. *Olmstead*, 72 Wash. App. at 176, 863 P.2d 1355; *Lyall v. DeYoung*, 42 Wash. App. 252, 257, 711 P.2d 356 (1985), *review denied*, 105 Wash. 2d 1009 (1986).

12. Here, the Warners do not assert that they were either unaware of the "as is" clause or in a position of bargaining power which was grossly disproportionate to Design; either contention would be undercut by the fact that the Warners' real estate agent drafted the purchase and sale agreement. As such, the "negotiation" element is satisfied. *See Olmstead*, 72 Wash. App. at 176–77, 863 P.2d 1355; *Miller v. Badgley*, 51 Wash. App. 285, 294, 753 P.2d 530, *review denied*, 111 Wash. 2d 1007 (1988). But the Warners maintain that the "as is" clause is ambiguous and, therefore, ineffective and unenforceable, because it does not explicitly state the warranties being disclaimed. We disagree.

13. "[U]nless the circumstances indicate otherwise, all implied warranties are excluded by expressions like 'as is', 'with all faults' or other language *which in common understanding* calls the buyer's attention to the exclusion of warranties and makes plain that there is no implied warranty." RCW 62A.2-316(3)(a) (emphasis added); *see also Ltd. Flying Club, Inc. v. Wood*, 632 F.2d 51, 56 (8th Cir. 1980) ("It is fairly clear that ['as is'] . . . operates to disclaim implied warranties."). As the just quoted language indicates, an "as is" clause is unambiguous: the seller makes no warranties regarding the item sold. It is thus unnecessary to list warranties, none of which are being made.

14. Inexplicably, the Warners' agent drafted an agreement containing an "as is" clause which a reasonable person would understand to waive all implied warranties, including the warranty of habitability. Moreover, before the agreement became binding, the Warners were told about existing defects in the stucco and were advised that they should pursue further inspection and evaluation of potential nonvisible stucco and structural deficiencies. The Warners chose not to pursue these further inspections. As our Supreme Court has stated: "They had ample opportunity to inspect. They had their own [real estate agent and inspector]. The extent to which they inspected . . . was their choice. The contractual language is clear. This court not only should not, but it cannot, rewrite the clear agreement of the parties." *Frickel v. Sunnyside Enters., Inc.*, 106 Wash. 2d 714, 721, 725 P.2d 422 (1986). The trial court did not err in giving effect to the Warners' "as is" clause by granting Design and Omega summary judgment.

Third-Party Beneficiary

15. The Warners next assert that they were third-party beneficiaries to the stucco contract between Design and Omega and are therefore entitled to bring a claim against Omega for breach of that contract's implied warranty of workmanlike construction. *See generally Frickel*, 106 Wash. 2d at 726, 725 P.2d 422 (Pearson, J., dissenting) (discussing and distinguishing between implied warranties arising in contracts for the construction of a dwelling, e.g., workmanlike construction, and those arising in contracts for the sale of a new house by a builder-vendor, e.g., habitability). We disagree.

16. The Warners do not cite a single Washington case recognizing an implied warranty for workmanlike performance. Moreover, both Divisions One and Three of this court have concluded that such an implied warranty does not exist in a construction contract. *Anderson Hay & Grain Co. v. United Dominion Indus. Inc.*, 119 Wash. App. 249, 261, 76 P.3d 1205 (2003); *Urban Dev. Inc. v. Evergreen Bldg. Prods. LLC*, Wash. App. 639, 646, 59 P.3d 112, *aff'd sub nom. Fortune View Condo. Ass'n v. Fortune Star Dev. Co.*, 151 Wash. 2d 53, 90 P.3d 1062 (2004). As Division One has noted: "Contracting parties have their remedies for breach and can negotiate for warranties if they so choose. An action for implied warranty of workmanlike performance in construction contracts would be strikingly similar to a cause of action for negligent construction, which is not recognized in Washington." *Urban Dev. Inc.*, 114 Wash. App. at 646, 59 P.3d 112 (citing *Stuart v. Coldwell Banker Commercial Group, Inc.*, 109 Wash. 2d 406, 417, 745 P.2d 1284 (1987). But we need not address whether an implied warranty of workmanlike performance existed in the contract between Omega and Design, for even if it did, the Warners are not third-party beneficiaries to that contract.

(continued)

17. A third-party beneficiary contract exists when the contracting parties, at the time they enter into the contract, intend that the promisor will assume a direct obligation to the claimed beneficiary. *Postlewait Constr. Inc. v. Great Am. Ins. Cos.*, 106 Wash. 2d 96, 99, 720 P.2d 805 (1986). The test of intent is an objective one: Whether performance under the contract necessarily and directly benefits the third party. *Postlewait Constr. Inc.*, 106 Wash. 2d at 99, 720 P.2d 805. An incidental, indirect, or inconsequential benefit to a third party is insufficient to demonstrate an intent to create a contract directly obligating the promisor to perform a duty to a third party. *Del Guzzi Constr. Co. v. Global Northwest Ltd.*, 105 Wash. 2d 878, 886, 719 P.2d 120 (1986).

18. In the construction context, the prevailing rule is that a property owner is generally not a third-party beneficiary of a contract between the general contractor and a subcontractor. Such contracts [between a principal contractor and subcontractors] are made to enable the principal contractor to perform; and their performance by the subcontractor does not in itself discharge the principal contractor's duty to the owner with whom he has contracted. The installation of plumbing fixtures or the construction of cement floors by a subcontractor is not a discharge of the principal contractor's duty to the owner to deliver a finished building containing those items; and if after their installation the undelivered building is destroyed by fire, the principal contractor must replace them for the owner, even though he must pay the subcontractor in full and has no right that the latter shall replace them. It seems, therefore, that the owner has no right against the subcontractor, in the absence of clear words to the contrary. The owner is neither a creditor beneficiary nor a donee beneficiary; the benefit that he receives from performance must be regarded as merely incidental. . . . The Restatement (Second) of Contracts endorses the same rule by way of an illustration: "A contracts to erect a building for C. B then contracts with A to supply lumber needed for the building. C is an incidental beneficiary of B's promise, and B is an incidental beneficiary of C's promise to pay A for the building." Restatement (Second) of Contracts §302 cmt. e, illus. 19 (1979).

19. The facts of this case mirror those posed by the Restatement (Second) of Contracts and closely parallel those in *McDonald Construction Co. v. Murray*, 5 Wash. App. 68, 485 P.2d 626, *review denied*, 79 Wash. 2d 1009 (1971). In *Murray*, a construction company undertook construction of an addition to a commercial building. The construction contract provided that the work was to be completed within a certain period because the owner had found a tenant for the premises. When the construction company failed to meet the deadline, the prospective tenant brought suit, seeking lost profits from the construction company under the theory that it was a third-party beneficiary to the construction contract. In affirming the trial court's dismissal of the tenant's claim, Division One concluded that the tenant derived no direct benefit from the construction contract and "[a]ny benefit which [the tenant] could assert would be derived from the intervening tenancy agreement which it had with the [owner]." 5 Wash. App. at 70–71, 485 P.2d 626.

20. Like the tenant in *Murray*, any benefit the Warners could assert arises out of their contract with Design to purchase the home. The Warners were not third-party beneficiaries to the construction contract between Design and Omega and consequently had no right of action against Omega for any breach of the sub-contract. Thus, even if there were a cause of action for breach of the implied warranty of workmanlike construction, which we do not hold that there is, the Warners were not third-party beneficiaries to the contract and had no right to bring such a claim against Omega.

21. Affirmed.

We concur: MORGAN and BRIDGEWATER, J.J.

Case Questions

1. In the above case, the court stated that a warranty disclaimer must meet two conditions in order to be effective: (1) It must be explicitly negotiated or bargained for, and (2) it must set forth with particularity what is being disclaimed. The court maintained that both elements were met in this instance. Do you agree with the court's reasoning? Why or why not?

2. Do you believe "as is" clauses should be upheld when the contract in question is one for new construction? Why or why not?

3. In discussing the issue of whether the Warners were third-party beneficiaries to the contract between Design and Omega, the court relied on the prevailing rule that a property owner is generally not a third-party beneficiary of agreements between the general contractor and a subcontractor. It further stated that the test to be applied is whether performance under the contract necessarily and directly benefits the third party. Do you think the test was appropriately applied in this instance? Do you think the prevailing rule is sound in general? Why or why not?

In recent years, the most widespread litigation pertaining to breach of express and implied warranties in construction has related to the issues surrounding Chinese drywall. The shortage of domestic drywall, particularly from 2004 to 2006 with the impact of Hurricane Katrina and other storms, coupled with other conditions of the housing market of that time, led to the increased importation and use of Chinese drywall for new construction, restorations, and renovations. Problems with the drywall have been related to both structural and health issues. Defective Chinese drywall has been found to corrode electrical wiring, air-conditioning coils, and copper tubing. It also gives off a noxious odor, and inhabitants of homes containing the defective drywall have complained of a variety of physical ailments. Areas most dramatically impacted have been the Gulf Coast and Florida, although other areas of the country also have been affected. Thousands of incidents have been reported, which has led to multiple class action suits. A recent suit was settled for multiple millions of dollars, setting up an uncapped remediation fund for the damages to the properties and a separate, capped fund for other types of sustained losses, including those related to health problems.

Actions for Specific Performance

An action for **specific performance** is a suit whereby the plaintiff asks the court to order the defendant to do a specific act under the terms of the contract. If the breaching party is the buyer, the seller typically asks the court to order the buyer to pay the purchase price stated in the contract. If the breaching party is the seller, the buyer typically asks the court to order the seller to deliver title to the real property in return for the buyer's payment of the purchase price.

In order to bring an action for specific performance of a real estate contract, two requirements must be met. The first requirement is that the real estate contract must be supported by a writing in compliance with the statute of frauds. An exception to this requirement is carved out by the courts in permitting an oral contract to be specifically enforced if partially performed. Partial performance occurs when (1) payment (full or partial) of consideration is made by the buyer, (2) possession of the property is taken by the buyer, and (3) valuable improvements to the property are made by the buyer with the consent of the seller. The buyer has the burden of proving the existence and partial performance of an oral contract for the sale and purchase of real property by evidence that is "definite and certain," clearly a higher burden of proof than the "preponderance of the evidence" standard used in most civil cases.

The second requirement that must be met in order to bring an action for specific performance is a showing that the plaintiff has no adequate remedy at law. If the contract contains a liquidated damages provision, the inclusion of this provision indicates that the parties to the contract agreed to a stipulated monetary sum to be awarded in the event of breach. A proper liquidated damages provision (one that is not a disguised penalty) provides for monetary damages calculated in a manner agreed upon by the parties at the time of contracting. In this situation, the courts will deem that an adequate remedy at law is indeed available to the complaining party. Further, should the contract provide for alternate remedies—for example, a stipulated sum as liquidated damages or, in the alternative, suit for specific performance—the courts will again find that inasmuch as the parties themselves came up with an alternative to specific performance, the parties concede that

specific performance: A suit whereby the plaintiff asks the court to order the defendant to do a specific act under the terms of the contract.

monetary damages (for example, the liquidated damages sum) can be considered an adequate remedy for breach.

Note that should the courts allow an action for specific performance, this decision does not preclude the courts from awarding monetary damages in addition to specific performance if the monetary damages are necessary in order to restore the parties to their respective positions prior to the breach. For example, the seller may have problems in clearing title defects. If the buyer is willing to accept the property with the title defects, the seller cannot use the title defects as an excuse to back out of the transaction. If the seller does so, the buyer may sue for specific performance, and if specific performance is awarded, the courts may additionally reduce the price of the property accordingly to reflect the diminished value of the title to the property.

The first step in initiating a suit for specific performance, as is the case in a suit for monetary damages, is determining which court has proper jurisdiction. Because an action for specific performance is an equitable action, only courts of equity may hear the case. In most states, the equity courts are the circuit courts. Therefore, a statement that the action is one for specific performance in and of itself is a statement of jurisdiction. Equitable actions are tried by a judge without a jury; therefore, a jury trial is not requested.

Applicable venue statutes must also be checked. Proper venue most commonly will be in any one of three places: (1) where the defendant resides, (2) where the property in question is located, or (3) where the breach of contract occurred.

Once proper jurisdiction and venue are determined, attention must be turned to the contract itself. Just as in a breach of contract action for monetary damages, all of the terms of the contract must be scrutinized, together with any addendums and modifications, to ascertain the exact obligations of each party and to determine whether the plaintiff has fulfilled all of his or her obligations. The obligations of the seller or buyer under the contract and the actions taken by him or her must be specifically pleaded in a complaint for specific performance. Therefore, if a buyer seeks specific performance of a contract for sale and purchase, the buyer must allege in the complaint that payment under the contract has been made or tendered by him or her, or that he or she has been ready, willing, and able to pay, or that he or she has been excused from performance. Once the contract has been reviewed, a notice of lis pendens should be prepared to be filed in the public records of the county in which the property is located, together with any bond that may be required by state law to maintain the lis pendens on the property. A notice of lis pendens is appropriate in an action for specific performance because the relief sought affects title to the property.

A complaint for specific performance must include the following:

1. Jurisdictional facts
2. Allegations setting forth the ownership of the real property (by the plaintiff or the defendant) and the description of the property
3. The existence of a contract for sale and purchase (attach copy as an exhibit to the complaint)
4. Breach of the contract for sale and purchase by the defendant
5. Allegations establishing the plaintiff's full performance under the contract or a statement that the plaintiff is ready, willing, and able to perform under the contract

6. Lack of any adequate remedy at law

7. Damages sustained by the plaintiff as a result of the defendant's breach

8. If attorneys' fees are recoverable, that the plaintiff had to employ legal counsel to bring this action

9. Prayer for relief

10. Signature of the attorney

Exhibit 18–3 provides an example of a notice of lis pendens. Exhibit 18–4 provides an example of a complaint for specific performance.

As a defensive matter, the defendant in an action for specific performance may choose to attack the validity of the contract being sued upon. If the plaintiff delays in bringing suit, the defendant may raise the **doctrine of laches.** This doctrine, similar to the statute of limitations, is premised on the principle of vigilance and propounds that equity aids those who are vigilant, not those who "sleep" on their rights. Therefore, if a plaintiff neglects to assert a claim for an unreasonable length

---

EXHIBIT 18–3　　　　　　　　　　　　　　　　　　　　**Notice of lis pendens**

IN THE CIRCUIT COURT OF THE FIFTH JUDICIAL CIRCUIT
IN AND FOR ANY COUNTY, ANY STATE

CASE NO. 15-1534

LYLE SEATON and
ELAINE SEATON,
　　　　Plaintiffs,

vs.

EVERGREEN PROPERTIES, INC.,
an Any State corporation,
　　　　Defendant.　　　　　　　　　　　**NOTICE OF LIS PENDENS**
_____/

TO DEFENDANT EVERGREEN PROPERTIES, INC., AND ALL OTHERS WHOM IT MAY CONCERN:
YOU ARE NOTIFIED of the institution of this action by Plaintiffs against you seeking specific performance of that certain written real estate contract for sale and purchase of the following described property located in Any County, Any State:

> Lot 18, Block 9, EVERGREEN ESTATES subdivision, a subdivision of a
> portion of Section 17, Township 4 South, Range 20 East, Any County,
> Any State, according to the plat of said subdivision recorded in Plat
> Book 30, Page 11 of the Public Records of Any County, Any State.

DATED: October 10, 2015.

　　　　　　　　　　　　　　　　　　FISHER, ROSS, AND SIMON, P.A.
　　　　　　　　　　　　　　　　　　1900 N.W. 3rd Avenue
　　　　　　　　　　　　　　　　　　Any City, Any State
　　　　　　　　　　　　　　　　　　(000) 555-2000
　　　　　　　　　　　　　　　　　　Attorneys for Plaintiffs

　　　　　　　　　　　　　　　　　　By: _____
　　　　　　　　　　　　　　　　　　　　Ava Ross, Esquire
　　　　　　　　　　　　　　　　　　　　Any State Bar No. 123456

Complaint for specific performance   EXHIBIT 18–4

IN THE CIRCUIT COURT OF THE FIFTH JUDICIAL CIRCUIT
IN AND FOR ANY COUNTY, ANY STATE
CASE NO. 15-1534

LYLE SEATON and
ELAINE SEATON,
          Plaintiffs,

vs.

EVERGREEN PROPERTIES, INC.,
an Any State corporation,   **COMPLAINT FOR SPECIFIC**
          Defendant.   **PERFORMANCE**
_____/

COME NOW the Plaintiffs, LYLE SEATON and ELAINE SEATON, by and through their undersigned counsel, and sue the Defendant, EVERGREEN PROPERTIES, INC., and allege as follows:

1. This is an action for specific performance of a contract for the sale of real estate in Any County, Any State.
2. At all material times, Defendant was and is now the owner of the following-described real property:

    Lot 18, Block 9, EVERGREEN ESTATES subdivision, a subdivision of a portion of Section 17, Township 4 South, Range 20 East, Any County, Any State, according to the plat of said subdivision recorded in Plat Book 30, Page 11 of the Public Records of Any County, Any State.

3. On or about July 14, 2015, Plaintiffs as buyers and Defendant as seller entered into and executed a written contract for sale and purchase pertaining to the above-described real property, a copy of which is attached hereto and is made a part hereof as Exhibit A.
4. Plaintiffs have been and are now ready, willing and able to comply with the terms of said contract by paying the purchase price set forth in said contract to the Defendant and have indicated same to the Defendant.
5. Notwithstanding this, the Defendant has failed to perform and continues to refuse to perform the Defendant's obligations under the terms of said contract.
6. As a result of Defendant's failure to perform, the Plaintiffs have been forced to hire an attorney to bring this action and to pay their attorney a reasonable fee for her services herein.

WHEREFORE, Plaintiffs demand judgment requiring the Defendant to specifically perform the Defendant's obligations under the terms and conditions of said contract, together with court costs and a reasonable attorney's fee.
DATED: October 10, 2015.

FISHER, ROSS, AND SIMON, P.A.
1900 N.W. 3rd Avenue
Any City, Any State
(000) 555-2000
Attorneys for Plaintiffs

By: _____
      Ava Ross, Esquire
      Any State Bar No. 123456

of time, this neglect, together with other circumstances causing prejudice to the defendant, will bar relief by a court of equity. Whether or not a defense of laches will be sustained in any case will depend upon all of the relevant circumstances surrounding the contract for sale and purchase and the period between the making of the contract and the filing of the action for specific performance.

Breach of a Construction Contract

A construction contract is similar to an ordinary contract for sale and purchase. The contractor hired to build a house or building may also be the developer from which the buyer purchased the lot, or the buyer may have purchased the lot from one party (entering into a contract for sale and purchase with that party for the real property) and then entered into a separate contract with another party (the contractor) to build a structure on the property. For this reason, the term *owner* will be used in this discussion rather than *buyer* when referring to the party acquiring the contractor's services. Every state has its own statutes regarding the qualifications and licensing of contractors. Research on qualifications and licensing becomes important in a situation in which suit is brought based on the contractor's negligence. If the contractor fails to meet state qualifications and licensing requirements, most states allow recovery of punitive damages (for example, three times the actual damages) plus attorneys' fees and costs.

An action pertaining to a construction contract normally involves disputes regarding (1) performance by the contractor according to the requirements of the plans and specifications (or noncompliance therewith), (2) changes in the plans and specifications, (3) failure of the owner or the owner's agent (for example, an architect or engineer) to provide something upon which the contractor's performance depends, (4) failure of the contractor to complete performance for the maximum guaranteed costs, (5) incomplete performance, (6) time of completion, or (7) time or amount of payment.

A contractor will sometimes do more work than the construction contract calls for. Under certain circumstances, compensation may be allowed for this extra work. The terms specified in the construction contract should address the issue of whether a contractor is entitled to payment for certain work in addition to the contract price. The general rule is that when parties enter into a construction contract and when during the course of construction alterations or changes are requested by the owner in the form of extras and otherwise, the owner has an obligation to pay the reasonable cost of such extras in addition to the stipulated sum named by the parties in the original contract.

As an added protection to both parties, it is common for a construction contract to include a provision stating that the contractor will not execute any extra work or make any modifications or alterations in the work described in the specifications and plans unless ordered in writing by the owner or the owner's named agent and will not claim pay for extra work, modifications, or alterations unless the written order is produced. There are situations, however, where alteration of plans and specifications is made necessary by the requirements of a city or county ordinance. In these situations, compensation is adjusted to include the additional costs incurred by compliance with the ordinance.

An owner is not required to pay the agreed-upon contract price for defective work. If full payment has not yet been made to the contractor, the owner may deduct the difference between the contract price and the value of the inferior work, plus the amount of any direct damages caused by existing defects. If the defects are not discovered until after the work is completed and full payment is made, the owner, as noted earlier in the discussion of breach of implied warranty, is entitled to bring suit for the difference between the contract price paid and the value of the structure in its defective condition. If, however, a contractor builds the structure in strict conformance with the plans and specifications given to him or her, the contractor is not liable for defects in the work due to the plans and specifications, and the contractor is entitled to receive the agreed-upon contract price for his or her services. In this instance, suit must be brought against the drafter of the plans and specifications.

If a contractor breaches the contract in such a manner as to make it necessary for the owner to hire another contractor to complete the work, the breaching contractor may not recover the value of his or her services if the owner spent more than the original contract price to complete the job properly. In a situation in which the breaching contractor fails to complete the work, he or she may recover the value of his or her services only for the work completed, and not in excess of the contract price. Note that, if the contractor has failed to complete the construction, the owner has a duty to mitigate his or her damages.

It is common for construction contracts to contain a provision mandating that disputes between the parties be referred to professionals, such as architects or engineers, for arbitration. If the parties have agreed to arbitration, the arbitrators, rather than the courts, determine the rights of the parties.

A complaint for breach of a construction contract includes the following:

1. Jurisdictional facts
2. The existence of a construction contract (attach a copy as an exhibit to the complaint)
3. Breach of the construction contract by the defendant
4. Allegations establishing the plaintiff's full performance under the contract or a statement that the plaintiff is ready, willing, and able to perform under the contract
5. Damages sustained by the plaintiff as a result of the defendant's breach
6. If attorneys' fees are recoverable, that the plaintiff had to employ legal counsel to bring this action
7. Prayer for relief
8. Signature of the attorney

All states have statutes of limitations pertaining to construction defect litigation. Additionally, some states have *statutes of repose* pertaining to this litigation. While statutes of limitation typically run from the time an injury has been or reasonably should have been discovered, statutes of repose run from the time an act is completed. Once the statute of repose has run, the cause of action has been extinguished completely, regardless of whether the statute of repose was ever raised by the defendant as an affirmative defense. For example, in California, the statute of limitations for a construction defect suit is three years from discovery of the defect, and the statute of repose is ten years.

Additionally, many states have adopted *"right to cure"* statutes. These statutes require that a property owner provide written notice to the contractor before filing a lawsuit and provide the general contractor and his or her subcontractors with an opportunity to cure defects within a prescribed period of time. Some states require mandatory mediation prior to setting a case for trial, even if the contract between the parties does not explicitly provide for alternative dispute resolution.

Exhibit 18–5 provides an example of a complaint for breach of a construction contract in which the contractor failed to complete performance of his or her contractual obligations for the maximum guaranteed costs, requiring the owner to hire another contractor to complete the job.

EXHIBIT 18–5   **Complaint for breach of a construction contract**

IN THE CIRCUIT COURT OF THE SEVENTH JUDICIAL CIRCUIT
IN AND FOR ANY COUNTY, ANY STATE
CASE NO. 15-1566

LISA S. OWENS,
    Plaintiff,

vs.

PETERSON CONSTRUCTION COMPANY,
    an Any State corporation,
    Defendant.   **COMPLAINT**
_____/

COMES NOW the Plaintiff, LISA S. OWENS, by and through her undersigned counsel, and sues the Defendant, PETERSON CONSTRUCTION COMPANY, and alleges as follows:

1. This is an action for damages that exceed Fifteen Thousand Dollars ($15,000.00).
2. Plaintiff is an individual residing at 711 Cardinal Drive, Any City, Any County, Any State.
3. At all times mentioned in this complaint, Defendant was a corporation organized and existing under the laws of Any State, with its principal place of business located at 305 S.W. 5th Avenue, Any City, Any County, Any State.
4. On June 9, 2015, Plaintiff and Defendant entered into a contract for the construction of a house for Plaintiff to be located at 711 Cardinal Drive, Any City, Any County, Any State. Construction was to be completed for a maximum sum of Three Hundred and Seventy-Five Thousand Dollars ($375,000.00). A copy of this contract is attached hereto and made a part hereof as Exhibit A.
5. Plaintiff has at all times been ready, willing, and able to perform her part of the contractual obligations. Plaintiff has paid or tendered payment to Defendant in the amount of Three Hundred Thousand Dollars ($300,000.00). The balance due on the contract, the sum of Seventy-Five Thousand Dollars ($75,000.00), has been retained by the Plaintiff until such time as the Defendant fully performs the contractual agreement between the parties by completing the following items: (i) completion of the driveway, (ii) installation of the landscaping in the front and back of the house, and (iii) installation of the swimming pool.
6. Defendant has breached the contract between the parties as a result of Defendant's failure to complete the contractual agreement as set forth above.
7. In addition, Defendant represented to the Plaintiff that construction of the house, including landscaping and swimming pool, could be completed for a maximum of Three Hundred and Seventy-Five Thousand Dollars ($375,000.00). Defendant now refuses to accept the Plaintiff's tender of the sum of Seventy-Five Thousand Dollars ($75,000.00) as payment in full and is instead attempting to charge amounts in excess of the agreed maximum contractual price.

8. As a result of the Defendant's breach, the Plaintiff has been forced to hire another contractor to complete the work in an amount in excess of the balance due on the above-described contract, causing the Plaintiff to pay in excess of the agreed maximum contract price for the work for which the parties originally contracted.

9. As a result of the Defendant's breach, the Plaintiff has been forced to hire an attorney to bring this action and to pay her attorney a reasonable fee for her services herein.

WHEREFORE, Plaintiff requests judgment against the Defendant for damages in excess of Fifteen Thousand Dollars ($15,000.00), together with court costs and a reasonable attorney's fee.

DATED: October 10, 2015.

> FISHER, ROSS, AND SIMON, P.A.
> 1900 N.W. 3rd Avenue
> Any City, Any State
> (000) 555-2000
> Attorney for Plaintiff
>
> By: _____
> Ava Ross, Esquire
> Any State Bar No. 123456

Actions by Real Estate Brokers

Although an action by a real estate broker to recover earned commissions is not an action for breach of the contract for sale and purchase per se, the action does relate to the sale and purchase of real property and may stem from a breach of that agreement by the buyer or seller. The real estate broker, for example, might have found a buyer ready, willing, and able to purchase the seller's property, and at some point after the contract for sale and purchase was executed by both the buyer and the seller, the buyer may have attempted to back out of the transaction. The broker, having met his or her obligations to his or her principal (in most cases, the seller) believes he or she is entitled to the agreed-upon commission. The seller, on the other hand, disgruntled to find himself or herself with an unclosed transaction, may be unwilling to pay the commission.

A cause of action available to a broker seeking to recover commissions due will be brought against the broker's employer/principal. The most common situations giving rise to a cause of action against the employer/principal are failure to pay a commission because the sale was never consummated due to the fault of either buyer or seller and the employer's simple refusal to pay a commission on a consummated transaction. Occasionally, an action may be brought against another party, such as a buyer who, by making fraudulent representations, induced the seller who employed the broker to breach the brokerage agreement.

In a real estate brokerage action, jurisdiction will be determined by the amount of monetary damages claimed, as is the case in a breach of contract for sale and purchase in which the plaintiff is seeking monetary damages rather than specific performance. An action for specific performance is not available in a real estate brokerage action because the broker agreement is a contract for services for which a remedy at law, monetary damages, is available. Proper venue is the same in an action for commission as it is in any other contract action. A broker does not have the right to file a notice of lis pendens against the real property because the lawsuit does not concern title to the real property but, rather, concerns the payment of a commission. Neither can the broker file a lien against the real property for payment of his or her commission prior to filing suit. The broker did not perform labor or furnish material in the improvement of real property. Should the broker be successful in the lawsuit and obtain a judgment against the employer/principal, the broker will then be able to file a judgment lien, as is the case in any successful lawsuit brought by a plaintiff against a defendant.

State statutes require that a broker allege and prove his or her licensing under the laws of the state. Only properly licensed brokers (or properly licensed real estate salespersons) may be paid a commission. For example, if the broker's license was up for renewal prior to entering into the brokerage agreement with the employer/principal and the broker's license had expired at the time of contracting and was renewed at a later date, the broker was not properly licensed at the time he or she entered the agreement, and, thus, the agreement would be invalid.

The complaint must also allege the precise nature of the employment in question. When drafting this section of the complaint, the drafter should take into consideration whether the employment was procured by the seller or buyer; whether the contract was oral or written; whether it was an open listing, an exclusive listing, or an exclusive-right-to-sell; whether under the contract the broker was to procure a prospect on terms subject to negotiation or on terms specifically prescribed by the employer; and whether the payment of the commission was conditioned on the consummation of the real estate transaction (that is, conditioned on the transaction closing rather than on simple procurement of a ready, willing, and able buyer). If the contract is a written contract, a copy should be attached to the complaint as an exhibit.

If the employer acted through an agent, as in the case of a corporate employer acting through one of its officers, directors, or shareholders, the complaint should indicate the relationship between the agent and the employer. Further, the complaint should allege that the agent was authorized to act on behalf of the corporation. Real estate brokers do not typically ask to see corporate resolutions authorizing this agency relationship prior to entering into a brokerage agreement (the existence or nonexistence of such a resolution will be determined through the discovery period prior to trial). Nonetheless, the complaint should allege that the agent at all times mentioned was duly authorized to act on behalf of the principal and employ real estate brokers to procure a buyer for the real property, to agree to the compensation to be paid the broker, and to agree on the terms for sale.

The next step in drafting the complaint is to allege full performance by the broker. Performance is the broker's consideration in return for the commission. When a broker is employed to find a buyer ready, willing, and able to purchase the property, the broker simply must allege that he or she did so and does not have to allege that the real estate transaction was completed. If, however, the broker is employed to procure a buyer on specific terms dictated by the seller, the complaint must allege that the broker procured a buyer in accordance with those terms.

In outline form, the complaint contains the following elements:

1. Jurisdictional facts
2. Licensing of the broker under state statute

3. Allegations setting forth ownership of the real property

4. If the defendant is a corporation, allegations of an agency relationship between the defendant and the defendant's agent

5. Existence of a contract for brokerage services (attach copy as an exhibit)

6. Allegations establishing the amount of the agreed-upon commission

7. Allegations setting forth the conditions of performance by the plaintiff

8. Allegations of breach of contract by the defendant

9. Allegations establishing the plaintiff's full performance

10. Allegations of damages sustained by the plaintiff as a result of the defendant's breach

11. If attorneys' fees are recoverable, that the plaintiff has to employ legal counsel to bring this action.

12. Prayer for relief

13. Signature of the attorney

Exhibit 18–6 provides an example of a complaint for breach of a brokerage agreement.

Complaint for breach of a brokerage agreement	EXHIBIT 18–6

IN THE CIRCUIT COURT OF THE FOURTH JUDICIAL CIRCUIT
IN AND FOR ANY COUNTY, ANY STATE
CASE NO. 15-1581

JAY MONROE,
      Plaintiff,

vs.

BDA INVESTMENT PROPERTIES, INC.,
      an Any State Corporation,   **COMPLAINT**
      Defendant.
_____/

COMES NOW the Plaintiff, Jay Monroe, by and through his undersigned counsel, and sues Defendant, BDA INVESTMENT PROPERTIES, INC., and alleges as follows:

1. This is an action for damages that exceed $15,000.00.
2. At all times hereinafter mentioned, Plaintiff was and still is a duly licensed real estate broker under the laws of the State of Any State.
3. At all times hereinafter mentioned, Defendant was and still is a domestic corporation duly organized and existing under the laws of the State of Any State.
4. At all times hereinafter mentioned, Defendant was and still is the owner of a parcel of real property described as:

> ALL THAT TRACT of land lying and being in the Southwest quarter of the Southwest quarter of Section 2, Township 33 South, Range 10 East, Any County, Any State

5. At all times hereinafter mentioned, Christopher Ryan was an officer, shareholder, and director of Defendant and was authorized to act for and on behalf of Defendant to employ real estate brokers to procure a buyer for the above-described property and to agree to the terms and conditions upon which the above-described property was to be sold.

EXHIBIT 18-6   *(continued)*

6. On or about July 19, 2015, Defendant, acting by or through the duly authorized agent named above, employed Plaintiff to procure a ready, willing and able buyer for the above-described property upon the terms and conditions set forth in the exclusive-right-to-sell listing agreement, a copy of which is attached hereto and made a part hereof as Exhibit A.

7. Defendant agreed to pay the Plaintiff the sum of six per cent (6%) of the purchase price of the above-described property as commission.

8. On August 3, 2015, Plaintiff procured a buyer, Reilly Development Corp., ready, willing and able to purchase the property at a price and on terms and conditions satisfactory to Defendant, said purchase price being One Million Dollars ($1,000,000.00), and Defendant agreed to enter into a formal written contract for sale and purchase of the above described property.

9. Defendant thereafter wrongfully and without justification failed and refused to enter into the formal written contract and failed and refused to sell the property to the buyer procured by Plaintiff.

10. Plaintiff has duly performed all of the terms and conditions to be performed by Plaintiff under Plaintiff's contract with Defendant.

11. There is now due and owing from Defendant to Plaintiff the sum of Sixty Thousand Dollars ($60,000.00), with interest, no part of which has been paid, although payment has been demanded.

12. As a result of Defendant's breach of its contract with Plaintiff, Plaintiff has been forced to hire an attorney to bring this action and to pay his attorney a reasonable fee for her services herein.

WHEREFORE, Plaintiff demands judgment for damages against Defendant, together with court costs and a reasonable attorney's fee.

DATED: October 10, 2015.

FISHER, ROSS, AND SIMON, P.A.
1900 N.W. 3rd Avenue
Any City, Any State
(000) 555-2000
Attorneys for Plaintiff

By: _____
   Ava Ross, Esquire
   Any State Bar No. 123456

Actions for Partition of Real Property

The term **partition** refers to the dividing of real property held by joint tenants or by tenants in common, or held jointly by business partners in a tenancy in partnership, into separate and distinct parcels so that each joint owner may hold his or her portion in severalty. Recall from Chapter 2 that ownership in severalty refers to property ownership by an individual owner taking title in fee simple, with the according rights to use and ultimately dispose of the property in any manner the individual owner chooses. Property held as tenancy by the entirety (with each spouse owning 100 percent of the property) cannot be partitioned. Upon dissolution of marriage, however, the spouses become tenants in common, at which point the property may be partitioned if one of the parties so requests. If properly pleaded, the property may

partition: An action by the court dividing real property held by joint tenants, tenants in common, or tenants in partnership.

be partitioned as a part of the dissolution proceedings. When an action for partition is properly brought, all controversies about the title to the real property or other matters relating to the property should be settled in that action.

For example, suppose an income-producing property is held as a tenancy in partnership by the partners of a general partnership. A dispute arises about the managing partner's handling of the accounts regarding the income from the property. This, as well as other problems within the partnership, leads to an action to partition the property. As part of the action to partition, the court may order that an accounting be carried out regarding the partnership's accounts. Similarly, a mortgage held by one owner against part of the real property may be foreclosed in a partition action. If one co-owner has made improvements to the jointly held real property, that co-owner cannot charge the other co-owner(s) for the improvements. However, the co-owner who made the improvements may, in a partition action, have set off to him or her that portion of the real property on which the improvements were made, leaving the other co-owners portions of the remaining property equal in value to the portion given to him or her, without taking into account the value of the improvements.

Partition is available only when the plaintiff has possession or a right to immediate beneficial possession of the real property. It cannot be enforced if there is a life estate outstanding. For example, in a situation where a testator, survived by his second wife and by adult children from his first marriage, devises a life estate to a parcel of land to his wife, naming his children as remaindermen, his children cannot bring an action for partition of the property during the wife's lifetime. They have no standing to do so because they have no right to immediate beneficial possession of the real property. Once the wife dies, however, the children, as joint owners in fee simple, may, if they so choose, bring an action to partition.

It is necessary when drafting a complaint for partition to have complete title information on the property in question. There may be outstanding mortgages against a fractional interest, conveyances of fractional interests among the co-owners or to third parties, or judgment liens against a co-owner. If all parties having interests in or liens upon the land in question are not brought into the partition action as necessary parties, a second action may be necessary. If the only parties with an interest in the real property are the co-owners, only the co-owners are necessary parties to the action. Proper jurisdiction for a partition action is typically in the county in which the real property is located.

A complaint for partition should allege the following:

1. Statement that this is an action for partition
2. Jurisdictional facts
3. A description of the real property
4. The names and places of residence of other persons interested in the land
5. The manner in which title is held by the owners and the quantity held by each
6. Any other matters necessary to enable the court to adjudicate the rights and interests of the parties
7. Statement regarding the divisibility or indivisibility of the real property
8. Prayer for relief
9. Signature of the attorney

If the complaint seeks other incidental relief, it should be alleged. In addition, if the plaintiff seeks some particular equity, such as consideration for improvements placed by him or her on the common property, the circumstances entitling the special treatment should be included.

If the real property is divisible, a court typically appoints commissioners, a special master, or the clerk of the court to partition the property. The court-appointed official will determine the proper share to be allotted to each owner and will employ a surveyor to draw up a survey showing the property as it is to be partitioned. The official will then file a report with the clerk of court that describes the real property divided and the share allotted to each party.

If the real property is indivisible, the court will appoint a special master or the clerk of the court to sell the real property at a private or public sale. Once a purchaser is procured, the sale must be approved by the court before the conveyance of title to the purchaser is made. It is generally the clerk of the court who issues a certificate of sale. The proceeds of the sale of the real property are deposited with the court for disbursement to the parties. If the plaintiff wants the property sold at a private sale, a statement to this effect must be included in the complaint. Each party to the action is bound by the judgment of the court to pay his or her proportionate share of the costs, including attorneys' fees. In a case involving indivisible property in which the property is sold, the court may order costs and fees retained out of the proceeds from the sale. All taxes due at the time of sale also are paid out of the purchase price. If state statute so provides, the reasonable fees and expenses of the commissioners, special masters, surveyors, and such usually are considered costs.

A sample complaint for partition is provided in Exhibit 18–7. A sample judgment for partition is provided in Exhibit 18–8.

EXHIBIT 18–7	**Complaint for partition**

IN THE CIRCUIT COURT OF THE THIRD JUDICIAL CIRCUIT
IN AND FOR ANY COUNTY, ANY STATE

CASE NO. 15-1590

ROBERTA M. PRESCOTT,
    Plaintiff,

VS.

LAWRENCE T. PRESCOTT,
    Defendant   **COMPLAINT FOR PARTITION**
_____/

COMES NOW the Plaintiff, ROBERTA M. PRESCOTT, by and through her undersigned counsel, and sues the Defendant, LAWRENCE T. PRESCOTT, and alleges as follows:

1. This is an action for partition of real property.
2. The property sought to be partitioned is in Any County, Any State and is described as follows:

> Lot 6 in Block 8 of WEDGWOOD ESTATES, 2ND SECTION,
> according to the plat thereof, recorded in Plat Book 1099,
> Page 5, of the Public Records of Any County, Any State.

3. The property was acquired by Bertram C. Prescott by deed dated November 4, 1996, who died testate on June 15, 2008, leaving surviving him a widow, Marjory E. Prescott, since deceased, and two children: Plaintiff, ROBERTA M. PRESCOTT, and Defendant,

LAWRENCE T. PRESCOTT. In and by his last will and testament, Bertram C. Prescott devised the above-described real property to his wife, Marjory E. Prescott, as a life estate, naming his two children, the Plaintiff and the Defendant, as remaindermen.

4. The probate of the estate of Bertram C. Prescott decreed the parties to this action are equal owners of the real property. Their places of residence are set beneath their respective names.

ROBERTA M. PRESCOTT
29 Willow Lane
Any City, Any State
LAWRENCE T. PRESCOTT
621 N.E. 17th Avenue
Any City, Any State

5. The property is indivisible and is not subject to partition in kind without prejudice to its owners.

WHEREFORE, the plaintiff respectfully demands that a partition of the property be ordered.

DATED: October 11, 2015.

> FISHER, ROSS, AND SIMON, P.A.
> 1900 N.W. 3rd Avenue
> Any City, Any State
> (000) 555-2000
> Attorneys for Plaintiff
>
> By: _____
> Ava Ross, Esquire
> Any State Bar No. 123456

Judgments for partition

EXHIBIT 18–8

IN THE CIRCUIT COURT OF THE THIRD JUDICIAL CIRCUIT
IN AND FOR ANY COUNTY, ANY STATE
CASE NO. 15-1590

ROBERTA M. PRESCOTT,
Plaintiff,

vs.

LAWRENCE T. PRESCOTT,
Defendant.

_____/

JUDGMENT FOR PARTITION

This action was heard before the court. On the evidence presented, the court finds that the property sought to be partitioned is indivisible and is not subject to partition in kind without prejudice to its owners, and it is ADJUDGED that:

1. ROBERTA M. PRESCOTT and LAWRENCE T. PRESCOTT are equal owners of real property located in Any County, Any State, described as follows:

> Lot 6 in Block 8 of WEDGWOOD ESTATES, 2ND SECTION, according to the plat thereof, recorded in Plat Book 1099, Page 5, of the Public Records of Any County, Any State.

EXHIBIT 18–8 *(continued)*

> 2. The property is indivisible and none of it is subject to partition without prejudice to its owners.
>
> 3. Patricia Andrews, a practicing attorney of this court, is appointed special master to sell the premises in the manner provided for sales in such cases by state statute. The sale, if public, shall be made within the legal hours of sale, at public auction, to the highest bidder, on the steps of the Any County Courthouse, at Any City, Any State, after publishing notice once each week for four consecutive weeks prior to the sale, in a newspaper regularly published and in general circulation in Any County, Any State. If the special master can secure an offer of a fair price for the premises at a private sale, prior to the date of public sale, she shall report such offer, with her recommendations, to this court.
>
> 4. This court retains jurisdiction of this action to enforce this judgment.
>
> ORDERED on this 14th day of October, 2015, at Any County, Any State.
>
> ————————————————
> Circuit Judge

hypothetical client matter

This afternoon Ava Ross met with clients Amanda and Brad Hartley, who are distressed and frustrated over problems with the house constructed for them fifteen months ago in Royalton Estates, a community developed by RBR Construction Company. Full payment of the contract price was made at the time of completion of the work. In the past couple of months, the Hartleys have found cracks in the foundation walls with resulting leakage causing further structural damage, cracks in the tiles and walls of the bathrooms, window sills separating from the walls, baseboards splitting, and the sliding glass doors separating from the facings, leaving space between the doors.

The Hartleys made several unsuccessful attempts within the past month and a half to contact Roger Robinson, the president of RBR Construction Company, over the phone. They then sent him a demand letter by certified mail, return receipt requested, specifying the repairs to be made. Roger Robinson replied by phone, telling the Hartleys that more than a year has passed since the work was completed and that it is RBR Construction Company's policy to make necessary repairs only within the first year after completion. Roger Robinson further stated that a certain degree of "settling" of a house is to be expected. The Hartleys consulted with another contractor who gave them an estimation of the costs for repairing the defects and has begun work in making the repairs. The Hartleys wanted to know if there was any recourse they could take against RBR Construction Company. They brought with them a photocopy of the original contract, the demand letter with the return receipt, and copies of the repair bills to date, together with the estimated costs of completion of the repair work. Ava discussed the possibility of a lawsuit and explained what would be entailed if suit was brought. The Hartleys decided to go ahead with the litigation.

After meeting with the Hartleys, Ava turns over their file, containing notes of the meeting and photocopies of the documents received from the Hartleys, to Barbara Hammond and asks her to draft a complaint for breach of implied warranty of a construction contract. The statute of limitations for bringing a breach of implied warranty action in Any State is three years and there is no statute of repose in Any State, so there is no bar to the Hartleys' action. Barbara first reads through the construction contract carefully to determine whether it contains any express warranties from the contractor because such warranties could be the basis for an additional cause of action. Seeing no express warranty language, she then notes that the business address of the defendant is located in Any County. Further, she sees that the property in question (the location of the breach) is located in Any County. Therefore, the complaint should be filed in Any County.

Barbara next looks at the repair bills accrued and the estimated costs of future repair work. The total costs exceed $15,000, which is the threshold requirement for bringing suit in circuit court in Any State. In addition to asking for the costs of these repairs, the Hartleys will be asking for damages for the diminution of the value of the property. With the information gathered together in the client file, Barbara proceeds to draft the complaint shown in Exhibit 18–9 for Ava's review and signature.

Barbara next prepares a summons to be served on RBR Construction Company. Once Ava reviews and signs the complaint, Barbara will make copies of the summons and complaint, arrange for the filing fees and sheriff's fees, and submit the complaint, summons, and appropriate fees to the clerk of the court.

IN THE CIRCUIT COURT OF THE FOURTH JUDICIAL CIRCUIT
IN AND FOR ANY COUNTY, ANY STATE

CASE NO.

BRAD HARTLEY and
AMANDA HARTLEY,
     Plaintiffs,

vs.

RBR CONSTRUCTION COMPANY,
an Any State corporation,
       Defendant   /   **COMPLAINT**

COME NOW the Plaintiffs, BRAD HARTLEY and AMANDA HARTLEY, by and through their under-signed counsel, and sue the Defendant, RBR CONSTRUCTION COMPANY, and allege as follows:

1. This is an action for damages that exceed Fifteen Thousand Dollars ($15,000.00).
2. Plaintiffs are now, and at all times mentioned in this complaint were, the owners of real property located at 65 Baron Court, Any City, Any County, Any State.
3. At all times relevant to the events described in this complaint, Defendant was a professional building contractor, having its principal office located at 901 State Street, Suite 205, Any City, Any County, Any State.
4. On February 1, 2014, the Plaintiffs entered into a written contract with the Defendant for the construction by the Defendant of a residential house, for use by the Plaintiffs and their family. A copy of the contract, containing the plans and specifications for the house, is attached hereto and made a part hereof as Exhibit A.
5. An implied term of the contract was that the Defendant would construct the house in a manner that meets ordinary standards reasonably to be expected of living quarters of comparable kind and quality. Plaintiffs relied on the Defendant to construct a house meeting these standards of fitness.
6. On or about June 4, 2014, the Defendant informed the Plaintiffs that construction of the house was completed and executed and delivered to the Plaintiffs a warranty deed.
7. On or about July 16, 2015, the Plaintiffs discovered that the Defendant had failed to construct the house in a reasonable manner in that the foundation walls have cracked resulting in leakage and other structural damage, the tiles and walls of the bathrooms have cracked, the window sills have separated from the walls, the baseboards have split, and the sliding glass doors have separated from the facings, leaving space between the doors.
8. On September 3, 2015, the Plaintiffs sent the Defendant a written demand letter, certified mail, return receipt requested, demanding that the Defendant repair the deficiencies in construction of the house. A copy of the demand letter and the return receipt are attached hereto and made a part hereof as Exhibit B. The Defendant, how-ever, has refused to make such repairs.
9. As a result of the Defendant's failure to honor the Plaintiffs' request, the Plaintiffs have employed contractors to repair the damage at a cost to date of Twenty-Eight Thousand Dollars ($28,000.00).
10. Plaintiff is reasonably certain to suffer additional damages in the future in the sum of Thirty Thousand Dollars ($30,000.00) for the repair of defects caused because of the Defendant's breach of the implied warranty of fitness in failing to properly construct the Plaintiffs' house. Such repairs are necessary to make the house a safe and suitable place for housing the Plaintiffs and their family.
11. The Plaintiffs have suffered additional damage for diminution of the value of the house because it is constructed in an improper manner.

12. The Defendant should have foreseen that all of the items of damage would occur due to the Defendant's failure to construct the house in a manner that meets ordinary standards reasonably to be expected of living quarters of comparable kind and quantity.

13. As a result of the Defendant's breach of the implied warranty of fitness, the Plaintiffs have been forced to hire an attorney to bring this action and to pay their attorney a reasonable fee for her services herein.

WHEREFORE, the Plaintiffs respectfully demand judgment against the Defendant for damages in excess of Fifteen Thousand Dollars ($15,000.00), together with costs of suit, court costs and a reasonable attorney's fee.

DATED: _____

FISHER, ROSS, AND SIMON, P.A.
1900 N.W. 3rd Avenue
Any City, Any State
(000) 555-2000
Attorneys for Plaintiffs

By: _____
   Ava Ross, Esquire
   Any State Bar No. 123456

CHAPTER SUMMARY

1. The possible remedies available to a buyer or seller in an action for breach of contract for sale and purchase are the return (or retention) of the deposit(s), liquidated damages, a suit for monetary damages, and a suit for specific performance.

2. A liquidated damages provision will be upheld by a court only if the actual damages incurred by a party are difficult to calculate and thus a reasonably agreed-upon sum has been arrived at in the contract. If a contract for sale and purchase gives the nonbreaching party the option of recovering liquidated damages or bringing suit for monetary damages, the liquidated damages provision will not be upheld. Similarly, if the contract gives the nonbreaching party the option of recovering monetary damages or bringing suit for specific performance, the court will not allow specific performance because the contract provides an adequate remedy at law.

3. In a suit brought by the seller for monetary damages, a court typically allows the seller the benefit of the bargain for which the seller contracted by awarding the seller the difference between the contract price for the real property and the current fair market value of the property. In a suit brought by a buyer for monetary damages, a court typically awards the return of any deposits, together with interest, and the costs for expenses incurred by the buyer in reliance on the contract. Attorneys' fees are recoverable by the prevailing party only if the contract for sale and purchase so stipulates. Punitive damages ordinarily are not recoverable.

4. Separate causes of action may be brought for fraudulent inducement and breach of implied warranty, if applicable. Fraudulent inducement occurs if the first party is induced, through intentional misrepresentations or omissions of material facts by the second party or the second party's agent, to enter into a contract for sale and purchase. A breach of implied warranty occurs if some aspect of the property is defective, resulting in a decrease of value of the property.

5. Actions pertaining to construction contracts typically involve disputes over the quality of the work performed by the contractor, changes requested or required by law, failure to complete the contracted work, the timing of completion, or the timing or amount of payment. If the work performed by a contractor is defective, the owner may deduct the difference between the contract price and the value of the inferior work. If another contractor has to be employed to complete the work, the breaching contractor may not recover the value of his or her services if the owner spent more than the original contract price to complete the job properly.

6. In an action for breach of a brokerage agreement by the broker's employer/principal, a broker must allege compliance with state licensing requirements, the precise nature of the employment in question including the conditions of performance by the broker, and the broker's full performance of his or her obligations under the contract.

7. Partition is the dividing of real property held by joint tenants, tenants in common, or tenants in partnership. Through a partition action, divisible property is divided so that each joint owner can hold his or her respective share in severalty. Indivisible property is sold by court order and the proceeds from the sale distributed proportionately.

WEB RESOURCES

http://realestate.findlaw.com/

This is the site of FindLaw's Real Estate Center. If you select "Construction Defects," you can click on several construction defect litigation topics.

http://constructiondefectjournal.com/

This is the site of *Construction Defect Journal*. At this site, you can access articles pertaining to the latest issues in construction defect law and litigation.

http://www.jurispro.com/

This site provides a free online directory of expert witnesses, including expert witnesses for real estate litigation.

REVIEW QUESTIONS

1. Distinguish between the concept of legal remedies and the concept of equitable remedies.
2. List the items that must be included in an action for breach of contract for sale and purchase.

3. What defenses might a defendant raise in an action for breach of contract for sale and purchase?
4. What remedies are available to a party fraudulently induced into entering a contract for sale and purchase?
5. Explain the procedure by which a court partitions real property.

DISCUSSION QUESTIONS

1. The Forresters and Walter Kent were neighbors. Shortly after Walter Kent bought his house, he had a survey done of the property, which revealed that a substantial portion of the Forresters' front yard and a portion of their driveway were encroaching on his property. He informed the Forresters of the situation, but no resolution was reached. When the Forresters decided to sell their property, Walter Kent told them that they needed to disclose the boundary issue to prospective purchasers. He also mentioned this to the Forresters' real estate agent, and he prepared a disclosure statement setting forth the information pertaining to the encroachments, which he gave to the real estate agent.

    Alice Miller, a prospective purchaser, looked at the Forresters' property and asked Mrs. Forrester about the property boundary lines. Mrs. Forrester pointed out boundaries that did not accurately correspond to the true boundary lines. Alice Miller subsequently made an offer to purchase the property and was given a disclosure statement signed by the Forresters that stated that they were not aware of any encroachments, unrecorded easements, or boundary line disputes pertaining to the property. The parties then signed a contract for purchase and sale that gave the purchaser the right to have the property surveyed and that contained a merger clause providing that no representation, promise, or inducement not included in the contract is binding on the parties. Additionally, the contract contained a clause indicating that the purchaser has not relied upon any advice, representations, or statements of the real estate brokers and that the brokers are not responsible to advise the purchaser on any matter that could have been revealed through a survey of the property.

    Prior to closing, Alice Miller had a title search performed. The search produced a deed that accurately described, in metes and bounds, the property lines. The closing took place, and shortly afterward Alice Miller, in a discussion with her new neighbor Walter Kent, was informed about the true boundary lines and the encroachments. Assume the property in question is located in your county and state. If Alice Miller brings suit against the Forresters for fraudulent inducement, which party would prevail? Why?
2. Assume the same facts as set forth in Question 1. If Alice Miller brings suit against the Forresters' real estate agent (and the agent's employing broker), would she prevail? Why or why not?
3. Robert Hargrove, as purchaser, brought an action against developer Maynard Development Company for specific performance of a contract for construction and sale of property. When filing suit, he also filed a notice of lis pendens on

the property. He did not post bond for the lis pendens. Maynard Development has submitted a motion to dissolve the lis pendens, contending that because the lis pendens in this situation is not founded on a recorded instrument or a construction lien, bond is absolutely required. If this motion were heard in your county and state, which party would prevail? Why? Would the defendant be required to submit any evidence at the hearing?

4. Philip Bradshaw purchased a condominium unit at Greenfield Estates. The declaration of condominium for Greenfield Estates contains the following provision:

> 5.01 In the event any unit owner wishes to sell, transfer, rent or lease his unit, the Association shall have the option to purchase, rent, or lease said unit, upon the same conditions as are offered by the unit owner to a third person. . . . Any attempt to sell, rent, or lease said unit without prior approval of the Association shall be considered a breach of this Declaration, shall be wholly null and void, and shall confer no title or interest whatsoever upon any purchaser, tenant, or lessee; provided, however, any deed or lease may be validated by subsequent approval of the Association in the event of a sale or lease without prior approval as herein provided.

The declaration further provides that, if a unit owner wishes to sell, transfer, or lease his/her unit, he must deliver a written notice to the board of directors of the condominium association containing the terms of the offer. The board then has ten days to either consent to the transaction or, by written notice, designate the association or particular persons other than unit owners who are willing to purchase or rent the unit on the same terms. The association or its stated designee then has fourteen days to make a binding offer to buy or rent on the same terms. The unit owner then can accept the offer or withdraw and/or reject the offer.

A few years after he purchased his unit, Philip Bradshaw quitclaimed his interest in the condominium unit to his parents, Stuart and Audrey Bradshaw. The deed recited a nominal consideration of ten dollars. Philip never notified the association's board of the transfer or sought its approval. Several months after the transfer, the association notified Philip that he had violated the declaration of condominium and brought suit against Philip and his parents. The Bradshaws reconveyed the unit back to Philip by quitclaim deed, reciting a nominal consideration of ten dollars. The association subsequently acknowledged the initial conveyance from Philip to his parents but did not approve the reconveyance and is now amending its complaint to state that the reconveyance was null and void. The complaint seeks specific performance to enforce the association's right of first refusal to purchase the unit. Assume that this action has been filed in your county and state. Can a court enforce the condominium documents, requiring Philip's parents to convey the condominium unit to the association? Why or why not?

5. Assume the same facts as in Question 4. Assume further that a court determines that the association can enforce its right to first refusal. Under these circumstances, how should the purchase price to be paid by the association be determined?

ETHICAL QUESTION

In the past several months, you have noticed a number of articles in paralegal journals discussing the practice of double billing. Double billing is billing more than one client for the same billable time. These articles indicate that this practice happens quite often. For example, a paralegal may be asked to interview a witness in the next county and, on the drive to and from the office, make follow-up calls to several other clients using a cell phone with hands-free capability provided by the law office. Is it appropriate to bill the client whose witness you interviewed for the time spent in traveling to see the witness and also to bill the clients telephoned during that time? The American Bar Association published an opinion on this matter, stating that it is unethical to charge more than one client for the same hours of work.

You have drafted a complaint for breach of a construction contract and have been asked by your supervising attorney to take the complaint, summons, and filing fee down to the courthouse for filing. You have also been asked, while there, to do some research on a title matter for another client. Is it inappropriate to do both? What if only one client is billed for the time spent?

Slossberg Law Office on CourseMate

Please go to www.cengagebrain.com to log into CourseMate, access the Slossberg Law Office, and work on your client files. Each module corresponds to a chapter in the text. Within each module, you will be provided with instructions by the supervising attorney. You are asked to keep track of time spent on time sheets. The documents produced through working on client files in the law office can then be compiled into a portfolio of final work product.

CourseMate

The available CourseMate for this text has an interactive eBook and interactive learning tools, including flash cards, quizzes, and more. To learn more about this resource and access free demo CourseMate resources, including the Slossberg Law Office, go to www.cengagebrain.com, and search for this book. To access CourseMate materials that you have purchased, go to login.cengagebrain.com.

Mortgage Foreclosures

CHAPTER OBJECTIVES

Upon completion of this chapter, the student will:

- Understand the various alternatives to foreclosure

- Understand the various methods of foreclosure

- Know the key documents in a nonjudicial foreclosure and how to draft them

- Know the key documents in a judicial foreclosure and how to draft them

Introduction

In the best of all possible worlds, a loan transaction is advantageous to both lender and borrower. The borrower obtains the funds necessary to purchase property he or she could not otherwise afford, while the lender makes a profit by "selling" money to the borrower at a specified interest rate. If the borrower makes each payment on time, the parties can continue a satisfactory relationship. Unfortunately, borrowers can find themselves in situations where they default on one or more payments, which cause problems for both parties. The lender becomes anxious about its investment and may seek to accelerate the loan and/or foreclose on the collateral property to prevent a loss. The borrower becomes anxious both about keeping his or her real property and about keeping a good credit rating.

This chapter begins by looking at arrangements that may be worked out between the borrower and lender to prevent foreclosure. It then explores the various foreclosure methods available, focusing on the documents a paralegal working in a real estate law firm or in the legal department of a lending institution may be asked to prepare by his or her supervising attorney, including but not limited to demand letters, notices of default, notices of lis pendens, complaints, various motions, and affidavits.

Arrangements to Prevent Foreclosure

A borrower in default and a lender may work out an arrangement short of foreclosure. One possibility is a **reinstatement of loan.** This is particularly applicable if the loan is secured by a standard Federal National Mortgage Association/Federal Home Loan Mortgage Corporation (FNMA/FHLMC) mortgage instrument. This instrument provides for the borrower's right to reinstate a loan if certain conditions are met. The borrower is required to pay all delinquent sums and late charges as well as take any reasonable actions

reinstatement of loan: An arrangement in lieu of foreclosure, whereby a borrower pays all delinquent sums and late charges and takes any reasonable actions the lender may require to ensure both that the lender's interest in the real property is protected and that the borrower's obligation to pay under the terms of the note and mortgage remains unimpaired.

forbearance agreement: A contract in which the lender agrees to refrain from foreclosing on the real property and also permits the borrower to postpone or reduce payments for a specified period of time, in return for which the borrower agrees to a plan that will bring him or her current on his loan obligations.

deed in lieu of foreclosure: A deed to mortgaged property given by a borrower to the lender in order to prevent foreclosure.

the lender may require to ensure that the lender's interest in the real property is protected and the borrower's obligation to pay under the terms of the note and mortgage remains unimpaired.

If the borrower is facing challenges of a temporary nature, such as a health issue or temporary unemployment that is causing financial difficulties, the borrower may be able to work out a **forbearance agreement** with the lender. A forbearance agreement, sometimes referred to as a *standstill agreement*, is a contract in which the lender agrees to refrain from foreclosing on the real property and also permits the borrower to postpone or reduce payments for a specified period of time, in return for which the borrower agrees to a plan that will bring him or her current on the loan obligations. The borrower will remain liable for interest that will continue to accrue during the period in which payments are suspended or reduced. The agreement may set forth various conditions that must be met under this arrangement. For example, the lender may require that the borrower sign a deed conveying the property to the lender, the deed to be held by a trustee and recorded only if the borrower does not meet the terms of the forbearance agreement. Exhibit 19–1 provides a sample forbearance agreement that includes this provision.

The lender may require additional provisions to protect its interests as well. For example, the lender may be concerned that the borrower may file for bankruptcy. If this is of concern, the lender may include a provision in the forbearance agreement in which the borrower agrees to protect the lender's interests in such a circumstance. The agreement may state that the borrower will consent to the lender's motion for relief from the automatic stay and will take all necessary steps to provide the lender complete relief from the stay.

EXHIBIT 19–1	Forbearance agreement

AGREEMENT

THIS AGREEMENT, dated this 15th day of October, 2015, by and between Melinda Ferrera (referred to as "the Debtor") and Platinum Bank, N.A., a National Banking Association (referred to as "the Bank"),

WITNESSETH:

WHEREAS, on June 8, 2009, the Bank extended to the Debtor certain credit in the form of a loan in the original principal amount of $250,000 evidenced by a promissory note of same date (referred to as "the Loan"); and

WHEREAS, the Loan is secured by a valid and enforceable first mortgage recorded on June 9, 2009, in Official Records Book 458, Page 33 in the public records of Any County, Any State encumbering certain real property (referred to as the "Real Property") located in Any County, Any State, and described as follows:

> Lot 14 in Block 4 of PADDINGTON ESTATES, SECOND SECTION, according to the plat thereof, recorded in Plat Book 903, Page 17 of the Public Records of Any County, Any State

and

WHEREAS, there are certain outstanding sums owed to the Bank by the Debtor, and the Bank has agreed to postpone any collection activities with respect to the Loan in return for certain promises and covenants from the Debtor, all upon the terms and conditions set forth hereinafter,

EXHIBIT 19–1

NOW, THEREFORE, in consideration of the mutual covenants contained herein, as well other good and valuable consideration, the parties hereto agree as follows:

I.   ACKNOWLEDGMENT OF INDEBTEDNESS.
   (A)   The Debtor acknowledges that she has failed to make the following payments to the Bank as required by the promissory note (referred to as "the Note") and the Loan:
      (1)   July 1, 2015, payment in the amount of $1,342.05
      (2)   August 1, 2015, payment in the amount of $1,342.05
      (3)   September 1, 2015, payment in the amount of $1,342.05
      (4)   October 1, 2015, payment in the amount of $1,342.05
      (5)   All aggregate late charges accruing on the above sums
   (B)   The Debtor acknowledges that, having failed to make payment due July 1, 2015, and all subsequent payments, she currently is in default under the Note. The Debtor further acknowledges that the Bank, in the proper execution of its rights, has accelerated all sums due under the Note and that she is now indebted to the Bank in the principal sum of $223,207.20 with interest from June 2015, and late charges. Additionally, the Debtor acknowledges that she is indebted to the Bank for all costs and attorneys' fees associated with the Bank's efforts to enforce its rights with respect to the Loan, that all indebtedness owed under the Loan is now due and payable, that she has no valid setoff to said indebtedness, and that she has no defense or counterclaim against the Bank.

II.   TERMS AND CONDITIONS OF LOAN MODIFICATION.
   The Debtor's obligation for the repayment of the Loan is hereby modified as follows:
   (A)   The Debtor agrees to pay all aggregate late charges that have accrued as of the date of this Agreement and to make all monthly payments called for under the Note as they come due. She further agrees that before November 15, 2015, she shall make the July 1, 2015, August 1, 2015, and November 1, 2015, payments. Additionally, the Debtor agrees that she shall make all future payments as they fall due and that she shall pay to the Bank the September 1, 2015, and October 1, 2015, payments and all late charges before March 1, 2016. Commencing March 1, 2016, payments shall be owed and paid under the Loan based on the original terms of the Note.
   (B)   The Debtor shall be in default of the Loan if either or both of the following occurs:
      (1)   The Debtor's failure to pay the amounts required to be paid under the Note in the amounts and on the dates as set forth above.
      (2)   The Debtor's failure to carry out any covenant or condition under this Agreement.
   (C)   Except as expressly modified by the terms and provisions of this Agreement, all events of default as set forth in any other loan document, including the Note and the mortgage, shall remain events of default, and the Debtor's default thereunder shall constitute an event of default under the Loan, entitling the Bank to notify the Trustee to take those steps as more particularly described in provision IV below.

III.   DEFAULT REMEDIES. If any event of default referred to in provision II occurs, the Bank, at its election, may take any one or more of the following remedial steps:
   (A)   Declare all amounts payable under the Note to be immediately due and payable.
   (B)   Take whatever action at law or in equity it deems necessary to collect the amounts then due and thereafter becoming due under the Note, or to enforce performance or observance of any obligation, agreement, or covenant of the Debtor under this Agreement, the Note, or the other loan documents.

EXHIBIT 19-1

(continued)

(C) Exercise any other right available to it as a remedy on default as set forth under the provisions of any other loan document, including, but not limited to, the right to foreclose the mortgage by judicial proceedings in the manner provided by state law.

(D) Notify Ava Ross, Esquire, of Fisher, Ross, and Simon, P.A., acting the capacity of Trustee, of the default, as set forth in provision IV below.

IV. **RECONVEYANCE OF REAL PROPERTY.** In consideration for the covenants contained in this Agreement, the Debtor has, on October 15, 2015, executed and delivered to Ava Ross, Trustee, a deed conveying to Ava Ross, Trustee, title to the Real Property. The parties agree that this deed shall not be recorded absent the Debtor's default under the terms and conditions of this Agreement. In the event of the Debtor's default under the terms and conditions of this Agreement, the Bank may deliver a written notification to Ava Ross, Trustee, notifying her of the default. Upon this event, Ava Ross, Trustee, shall file in the public records of Any County, Any State, the deed without further notice to the Debtor. Upon such recording, Ava Ross, Trustee, shall hold title to the property for the Bank's benefit and shall act at the Bank's sole direction in the management and sale of the property. The Debtor agrees that, upon any recording of the deed pursuant to this paragraph, she shall vacate the Real Property within fifteen (15) days of the recording.

V. **APPRAISAL.** The Debtor agrees that the Bank, its agents, or its employees may perform an appraisal of the Real Property, at the Debtor's cost, and shall cooperate fully in the performance of the appraisal.

VI. **BANKRUPTCY.** The Debtor acknowledges that, should she file any bankruptcy action during the life of the Loan, she shall provide the Bank with a consent to any motion for relief from the automatic stay filed by the Bank as to the Real Property and shall further sign all documents and take all steps necessary to provide the Bank with complete and total relief from the automatic stay as to the Real Property without delay. The Debtor's signature on this Agreement shall be deemed to constitute such consent.

VII. **ATTORNEYS' FEES AND COSTS.** In the event of any litigation arising out of this Agreement, the prevailing party shall be entitled to recover all reasonable costs incurred, including reasonable attorneys' fees.

VIII. **BINDING EFFECT.** This Agreement shall be binding on the parties and their respective heirs, successors, assigns, and personal representatives.

IN WITNESS WHEREOF, the parties hereto have executed this Agreement on the year and date first above stated.

Signed, sealed and delivered
in our presence as witnesses:

Witnesses as to the Debtor:

Marion Whittaker
Printed Name: Marion Whittaker

By: *Melinda Ferrera*
Melinda Ferrera

Harold Strauss
Printed Name: Harold Strauss

Witnesses as to the Bank:

Platinum Bank, N.A.

Marion Whittaker
Printed Name: Marion Whittaker

Steven Harcourt
By: Steven Harcourt, Vice President

Harold Strauss
Printed Name: Harold Strauss

A forbearance agreement should specifically set forth the standstill or suspension period. In some instances, the due dates of all delinquent payments will be suspended until a certain date; alternatively, the payments may be scheduled on an installment plan. The lender may choose to charge the borrower a forbearance fee as consideration for refraining from enforcing its rights under the loan documents.

The agreement also should specify the events that will constitute a default of the agreement and the consequences of such default. Some forbearance agreements provide that a triggering default event results in automatic termination of the agreement, while others require the lender to provide notice to the borrower before termination.

When the borrower has low equity and is unable to cure default on the loan, yet wants to prevent the expense of defending a foreclosure action, the borrower may sign over to the lender a **deed in lieu of foreclosure.** A lender may save itself the expense of bringing a foreclosure suit by accepting this arrangement. Prior to such acceptance, the lender must consider a number of factors, including the value of the property as well as the tax consequences. On the one hand, if the appraised value of the property is less than the outstanding debt owed to the lender, the lender may not accept a deed in lieu of foreclosure because by accepting the deed, the lender may be relinquishing rights to pursue a deficiency judgment against the borrower for the difference between the value of the real property and the amount of the remaining outstanding debt. On the other hand, if the appraised value is less than the outstanding debt, the lender realizes a financial loss that will act as a federal income tax reduction.

If there are junior liens against the real property, the lender, by accepting the deed in lieu of foreclosure, will have to satisfy those junior lienholders before the lender can deliver clear title to a prospective purchaser of the property. Typically, the lender will not accept a deed in lieu of foreclosure under these circumstances. Tenant-occupied property may also pose a problem for the lender. As noted in Chapter 17, until such time as the Protecting Tenants at Foreclosure Act expires, a purchaser of a foreclosed property must permit residential tenants to stay (absent a breach by the tenant) until the end of the tenant's lease if the tenant took possession prior to the initiation of a foreclosure action. A lender receiving legal title under a deed in lieu of foreclosure is in the same position as a third-party purchaser and must honor a lease. This would prevent the lender from taking title and then selling the property. The lender would have to wait until the expiration of the lease. Additional considerations for the lender in determining whether to accept a deed in lieu of foreclosure are outstanding homeowners' association and condominium fees and the possibility that the borrower has viable defenses against the lender if an actual foreclosure proceeding is initiated.

If the lender agrees to take title to the property, the lender may take title under either a quitclaim deed or a warranty deed (the lender often will prefer the latter). The lender also may require that the borrower sign an estoppel affidavit. This document verifies that the borrower understands the consequences of the transaction, that the consideration received by the borrower in return for transferring title to the lender is the cancellation of any and all debt owed, and that the borrower agrees that this is sufficient consideration. A sample deed in lieu of foreclosure and a sample estoppel affidavit are found in Exhibits 19–2 and 19–3, respectively.

EXHIBIT 19-2

Deed in lieu of foreclosure

THIS INSTRUMENT PREPARED BY AND RETURN TO:

Fisher, Ross, and Simon, P. A.

1900 N.W. 3rd Avenue

Any City, Any State

Tax Parcel I.D. No.: 8129004473

WARRANTY DEED IN LIEU OF FORECLOSURE

THIS INDENTURE, made this 24th day of October, 2015, between Kevin Hale ("Grantor"), whose post office address is 1201 Claridge Court, Any City, Any State, and Century Bank ("Grantee"), whose post office address is 670 N.E. 46th Avenue, Any City, Any State.

WITNESSETH, that Grantor, for valuable consideration, receipt of which is hereby acknowledged does convey to Grantee and Grantee's successors and assigns the following described property located in Any County, Any State:

> Lot 16 in Block 2 of CLARIDGE ESTATES, 3RD SECTION, according to the plat thereof, recorded in Plat Book 504, Page 3 of the Public Records of Any City, Any State.

> Subject to the taxes for the current year and subsequent years.

This deed is an absolute conveyance of title and is not intended as a mortgage or trust conveyance of any kind, the Grantor having conveyed said land to the Grantee for fair and valuable consideration; said consideration being that the Grantee agrees not to bring a personal action on the debt against the Grantor as related to the obligations of the note and mortgage executed by Grantor on the 9th day of March, 2011, in the principal sum of Three Hundred Twenty-Five Thousand Dollars ($325,000.00); which mortgage was recorded on March 11, 2011, in Official Records Book 1105, Page 44 in the Public Records of Any County, Any State.

Grantor fully warrants the title to the land, and will defend the same against the lawful claims of all persons whomsoever.

Grantor declares that this conveyance is free and fairly made pursuant to conditions set forth in the Estoppel Affidavit recorded concurrently with this conveyance.

IN WITNESS WHEREOF, Grantor has signed and sealed these presents on the date and year first above written.

Signed, sealed, and delivered
in the presence of:

Brenda Hughes	*Kevin Hale*
Witness signature	Grantor
Brenda Hughes	
Witness printed name	
Glenn Rodgers	
Witness signature	
Glenn Rodgers	
Witness printed name	

STATE OF ANY STATE

COUNTY OF ANY COUNTY

The foregoing instrument was acknowledged before me this 24th day of October, 2015, by Kevin Hale who [X] is personally known by me or [ ] produced _____ as identification.

Janet Livingston

Printed name: Janet Livingston

Notary Public

My commission expires: 5/16/2017

Estoppel affidavit

EXHIBIT 19-3

ESTOPPEL AFFIDAVIT

STATE OF ANY STATE
COUNTY OF ANY COUNTY

BEFORE ME, the undersigned authority, duly authorized to administer oaths and take acknowledgments, personally appeared this day Kevin Hale ("Affiant") who, after being duly sworn, deposes and says as follows:

1. Affiant executed and delivered the certain Warranty Deed in Lieu of Foreclosure ("Deed") to Century Bank on the same date as this document, which conveyed the interest in real property commonly known as 1201 Claridge Court, Any City, Any State and more particularly described as:

    Lot 16 in Block 2 of CLARIDGE ESTATES, 3RD SECTION, according to the plat thereof, recorded in Plat Book 504, Page 3 of the Public Records of Any City, Any State.

2. The Deed is an absolute conveyance of title and is not intended as a mortgage, trust conveyance, or security of any kind;

3. That as a condition precedent to recording the Deed and this Affidavit, the Grantor has vacated the property and surrendered possession to the Grantee;

4. That the consideration for said Deed is that the Grantee agrees not to bring a personal action on the debt against the Affiant Grantor as related to the obligations of the note and mortgage executed by the Affiant Grantor on the 9th day of March, 2011, in the principal sum of Three Hundred Twenty-Five Thousand Dollars ($325,000.00); which mortgage was recorded on March 11, 2011, in Official Records Book 1105, Page 44 in the Public Records of Any County, Any State;

5. That the Affiant believes that the consideration given is adequate for the real property so deeded in that the fair market value of the property is not in excess of the indebtedness of Grantor as of the date hereof;

6. That the Affiant was solvent at the time of executing said Deed;

7. That this Affidavit is made for the benefit of the Grantee in said Deed, Century Bank, its successors and assigns, and all other parties hereafter dealing with or who may acquire any interest in the property herein described and particularly for the benefit of the title insurer that insures the title to said property in reliance thereon;

8. That in the execution and delivery of said Deed the Affiant was not acting under any misapprehension as to the effect thereof, and acted freely and voluntarily, not under coercion or duress;

9. That the undersigned will testify, declare, depose, or certify before any competent tribunal, officer, or person, in any case now pending or which may hereafter be instituted, to the truth of the particular facts set forth herein.

FURTHER AFFIANT SAYETH NAUGHT.

Brenda Hughes
Witness signature

Brenda Hughes
Witness printed name

Glenn Rodgers
Witness signature

Glenn Rodgers
Witness printed name

Kevin Hale
Affiant

EXHIBIT 19-3   *(continued)*

The foregoing instrument was acknowledged before me this 24th day of October, 2015, by Kevin Hale who [X] is personally known by me or [ ] produced _____ as identification.

Janet Livingston
Printed name: Janet Livingston
Notary Public

My commission expires: 5/16/2017

Often, a lender will want to see evidence that the borrower has made a good faith attempt to sell the property before the lender will agree to accept a deed in lieu of foreclosure. Therefore, a borrower usually will attempt a short sale transaction before resorting to deeding the property over to the lender. As noted in prior chapters, a short sale transaction is one in which the property is sold for less than the amount that will cover the outstanding loan obligation as well as any costs and fees. At closing, the borrower will not walk away with any proceeds from the transaction. The mortgage lien will be released, and, in most circumstances, the borrower will be released from the obligations under the note as well. A short sale package must be compiled, and all lender conditions must be met. For a detailed discussion of short sales and the documentation required, refer to Chapters 6, 7, and 12.

The Concept of Foreclosure and Lien Priority

If none of these remedies is applicable or acceptable, the lender will move to foreclose on the real property. **Foreclosure** is the legal procedure whereby real property is sold to repay a debt to a creditor who has a lien on the real property. The sale may be made to the creditor bringing the foreclosure action, another creditor, or a third party. In this chapter, the creditor in question is the lending institution that has a senior lien on the real property. In practice, the lienholder bringing a foreclosure action, however, may also be a judgment creditor, the holder of a construction lien, the holder of a second mortgage, the U.S. government as holder of a tax lien, or another lienholder.

In many circumstances, a junior lienholder may bring a foreclosure action before action is taken by a senior lienholder. The reason for this lies in the manner in which payment is made in the event of foreclosure. When property is sold in a foreclosure sale, there is a priority in which lienholders are paid from the foreclosure proceeds. The lienholder with the highest priority, often the holder of a first mortgage, is paid first. Junior lienholders receive proceeds only after the senior lienholder's debt is paid in full. If there are no funds left over to pay the lienholder with the second highest priority, neither that lienholder nor lienholders of lesser priority receive anything from the foreclosure sale. This commonly is the case because the foreclosed property is sold to the highest bidder. The senior lienholder will bid the full amount of its outstanding debt obligation. If there are no other bidders, the senior lienholder acquires the property for that amount, which leaves nothing remaining for the other lienholders.

foreclosure: The legal procedure whereby real property is sold to repay a debt to a creditor who has a lien on the real property.

If a junior lienholder wants to protect its interests, it will foreclose and buy the property, usually for the amount of the outstanding debt obligation under the second mortgage, and take title to the property subject to the existing first mortgage. Because the value of the real property will be greater than the outstanding debt obligation under the second mortgage, the junior lienholder will sell the property and pay off all senior lienholders.

Types of Foreclosure

The type of foreclosure method applicable in a given situation generally will depend on whether the state in which the real property is located is a state that uses deeds of trust or one that uses mortgages as the primary security instrument. In lien theory states, mortgages are the primary security instruments. The lender-mortgagee is given a lien against, rather than title to, the real property and therefore must bring a judicial action of foreclosure to perfect its lien. In title theory states, deeds of trust are the primary security instruments. The trustee has title rights to the real property and therefore, under the power-of-sale clause contained in the deed of trust, is allowed to sell the real property in a nonjudicial foreclosure. Additionally, a few states have special foreclosure methods, which are discussed in the following text.

Nonjudicial Foreclosure

Recall from the discussion of deeds of trust in Chapter 10 that there are three parties to a deed of trust: (1) the trustor (borrower), (2) the trustee, and (3) the beneficiary (lender). The trustee is an independent party—normally a title, trust, or escrow company. When a borrower obtains a loan, the borrower signs a deed of trust as trustor to the trustee for the benefit of the lender-beneficiary. This deed allows the trustee to sell the property in question if the borrower fails to meet his or her loan obligations. Additionally, the borrower signs a promissory note, which is given to the lender, setting forth the terms for paying back the loan. If the borrower fails to meet his or her obligations under the note, the lender-beneficiary notifies the trustee. The trustee then proceeds to sell the property under the powers granted to the trustee in the deed of trust.

Before initiating the foreclosure process, the lender may be required, under state law, to send a letter to the borrower informing the borrower of the default and making demand for payment. As this is not a prerequisite to bringing a nonjudicial foreclosure action in all states, state statutes must be checked. The demand may be for the delinquent payment, penalty charges, and attorneys' fees (if an attorney has been hired to handle the matter); or the demand may be for the total sum outstanding on the note, together with interest according to rights granted in an acceleration clause in the deed of trust. A sample demand letter appears in Exhibit 19–4. A discussion of demands for payment and required procedures under the Fair Debt Collection Practices Act is provided in the section of this chapter pertaining to judicial foreclosures.

If a demand letter is sent and the borrower fails to respond, the trustee will begin the foreclosure process. The first step in the nonjudicial foreclosure process is the preparation of a notice of default. The **notice of default** typically is recorded in the recorder's office in the county in which the property is located. A notice of default ordinarily includes the following information: (1) the name of the trustee, (2) the name of the trustor, (3) the name of the beneficiary, (4) the legal description

notice of default: A notice informing a borrower that he or she is in default, setting forth the amount and date of the default, the period within which to respond, and the consequences if he or she does not act within the prescribed period.

July 15, 2015

CERTIFIED MAIL #P432163445
RETURN RECEIPT REQUESTED

Mr. Thomas Trent
423 Grasemere Terrace
Any City, Any State

RE: Loan No. 511884

Dear Mr. Trent:

Please be informed that you are in default under the above-referenced loan as you have failed to make your monthly payment of $1,330.60, which was due on the first day of July. As a result of this default, the lender, Any County First National Bank, declares the entire indebtedness due and payable and demands that you make immediate payment by cashier's check of the outstanding principal balance of $188,263.18, together with interest of $7,747.45. Failure to pay the above-cited sum by August 5, 2015, may result in foreclosure and sale of the following property:

Lot 9 in Block 33, MANSFIELD PARK ESTATES, a subdivision according to the plat thereof as recorded in Plat Book 58, Page 18, of the Public Records of Any County, Any State.

Unless you dispute the validity of this debt within thirty (30) days of your receipt of this notice, the debt shall be assumed valid. Should you notify us in writing within the thirty (30) day period that the debt is in dispute, steps will be taken to verify the debt, and verification shall be forwarded to you.

Sincerely,

Ava Ross, Esquire
Fisher, Ross, and Simon, P.A.

cc: Any County First National Bank, N.A.

of the property, (5) the amount and date of the default, (6) the statutorily prescribed time period within which to respond, (7) the recording information pertaining to the deed of trust, (8) the recording information pertaining to the notice of default, (9) the party to contact for payment to stop foreclosure, and (10) a statement that the property may be sold without court action and that the borrower may lose legal rights if he or she does not act within the time period stated. A sample notice of default is provided in Exhibit 19–5.

Once a notice of default has been recorded and a copy sent to the borrower, a statutorily prescribed waiting period (for example, three months) commences, usually referred to as a **redemption period.** Most states in which deeds of trust are used provide for a redemption period. During this period, the borrower may prevent foreclosure by paying the amounts owed plus interest and penalties or by negotiating an agreement with the lender. If one of these avenues is taken by the borrower or if the borrower has made all required payments prior to the filing and recording of a notice of default, the borrower will request that a **notice of rescission** (sometimes referred to as a *satisfaction of default notice*) be recorded.

redemption period: A statutorily prescribed period of time within which a borrower may prevent foreclosure by paying the amount(s) owed, plus interest and penalties, or by negotiating an agreement with the lender.

notice of rescission: A notice that rescinds a notice of default in a nonjudicial foreclosure.

RECORDING REQUESTED BY:
Any City Trust Company

AND WHEN RECORDED MAIL TO:

Any City Trust Company
669 N.W. 10th Street
Any City, Any State

Attn: Valerie Winslow   Reference No.: 123456

IMPORTANT NOTICE

IF YOUR PROPERTY IS IN FORECLOSURE BECAUSE YOU ARE BEHIND IN YOUR PAYMENTS, IT MAY BE SOLD WITHOUT ANY COURT ACTION, and you may have the legal right to bring your account in good standing by paying all of your past due payments plus permitted costs and expenses within three months from the date this Notice of Default was recorded. This amount is $2,661.20 as of August 1, 2015, and will increase until your account becomes current. You may not have to pay the entire unpaid portion of your account, even though full payment was demanded, but you must pay the amount stated above. After three months from the date of recordation of this document (which date of recordation appears hereon), unless the obligation being foreclosed upon permits a longer period, you have only the legal right to stop the foreclosure by paying the entire amount demanded by your creditor. To find out the amount you must pay, or to arrange for payment to stop the foreclosure, or if your property is in foreclosure for any other reason, contact:

ANY COUNTY FIRST NATIONAL BANK
1000 COMMERCIAL AVENUE
ANY CITY, ANY STATE

If you have any questions, you should contact a lawyer or the government agency which may have insured your loan.

Remember, YOU MAY LOSE LEGAL RIGHTS IF YOU DO NOT TAKE PROMPT ACTION.

> THE FOLLOWING COPY OF "NOTICE," THE ORIGINAL OF WHICH WAS FILED FOR RECORD ON AUGUST 8, 2015, IN THE OFFICE OF THE RECORDER OF ANY COUNTY, ANY STATE, IS SENT TO YOU INASMUCH AS AN EXAMINATION OF THE TITLE TO SAID TRUST PROPERTY SHOWS YOU MAY HAVE AN INTEREST IN THE TRUSTEE'S SALE PROCEEDINGS.

NOTICE OF DEFAULT

NOTICE IS HEREBY GIVEN: THAT ANY CITY TRUST COMPANY is duly appointed Trustee under a Deed of Trust dated October 8, 2011, executed by THOMAS TRENT as Trustor, to secure certain obligations in favor of ANY COUNTY FIRST NATIONAL BANK, N.A. as beneficiary recorded October 9, 2011, as Instrument No. 947 in Book 455, Page 107, of Official Records in the Office of Recorder of Any County, Any State, describing land therein as:

> Lot 9 in Block 33, MANSFIELD PARK ESTATES, a subdivision according to the plat thereof as recorded in Plat Book 58, Page 18, of the Public Records of Any County, Any State

EXHIBIT 19-5 *(continued)*

said obligations including a note for the total sum of $200,000.00 that a breach of, and default in, the obligations for which such Deed of Trust is security has occurred in that payment has not been made of:

$2,661.20

that by reason thereof, the present beneficiary under such Deed of Trust has deposited with said duly appointed Trustee, such Deed of Trust and all documents evidencing obligations secured thereby, and the undersigned does hereby declare all sums secured thereby immediately due and payable and does hereby elect to cause the trust property to be sold to satisfy the obligations secured thereby.

Any City Trust Company

By: _____
Valerie Winslow, President

Dated: August 8, 2015.

A notice of rescission normally includes the following information: (1) the name of the trustee, (2) the name of the trustor, (3) the name of the beneficiary, (4) the legal description of the property, (5) the recording information pertaining to the deed of trust, (6) the recording information pertaining to the notice of default, (7) a statement that the notice of default is rescinded, (8) a statement that such rescission does not amount to a waiver of any breach or default or impair any rights to remedies available to the trustee, and (9) a statement that all obligations under the deed of trust are reinstated.

If the borrower's default payment amount is not in dispute and the borrower fails to satisfy the default obligation or fails to reach an agreement with the lender to extend the payment date or otherwise work out negotiated terms for paying off the debt within the statutorily prescribed period after the notice of default is recorded, the next step is the publication of a **notice of trustee's sale.** The publication requirements vary from state to state. Publication typically is made in a newspaper of general circulation in the county in which the property is located, or it may be made in a newspaper that primarily carries legal notices. State law also may require the recording of the notice of trustee's sale.

A notice of trustee's sale ordinarily includes the following information: (1) the name of the trustee; (2) the name of the trustor; (3) the name of the beneficiary; (4) a legal description of the property and the street address; (5) the date of the sale; (6) the time of the sale; (7) the location of the sale; (8) the recording information pertaining to the deed of trust; (9) the recording information pertaining to the notice of default; (10) the party conducting the sale; (11) the unpaid balance, together with advances, costs, and expenses; (12) the manner in which payment for the property is to be made (for example, cashier's check, cash); and (13) a disclaimer regarding warranty of title of the property. An example of a notice of trustee's sale is provided in Exhibit 19–6.

During the publication period of the notice of trustee's sale, the borrower may attempt to prevent foreclosure by paying the entire outstanding balance, plus

notice of trustee's sale: A notice published in a newspaper of general circulation in the county in which the real property is located announcing the details of the sale of the real property in a nonjudicial foreclosure action.

RECORDING REQUESTED BY:
Any City Trust Company

AND WHEN RECORDED MAIL TO:
Any City Trust Company
669 N.W. 10th Street
Any City, Any State

Attn: Valerie Winslow
     TS#654321   SPACE ABOVE THIS LINE FOR RECORDER'S USE

NOTICE OF TRUSTEE'S SALE

NOTICE

YOU ARE IN DEFAULT UNDER A DEED OF TRUST DATED OCTOBER 8, 2011. UNLESS YOU TAKE ACTION TO PROTECT YOUR PROPERTY, IT MAY BE SOLD AT, A PUBLIC SALE. IF YOU NEED AN EXPLANATION OF THE NATURE OF THE PROCEEDING AGAINST YOU, YOU SHOULD CONTACT A LAWYER.

ON October 29, 2015, at 10:00 A.M., ANY CITY TRUST COMPANY, as duly appointed Trustee under and pursuant to Deed of Trust executed by THOMAS TRENT as Trustor for the benefit and security of ANY COUNTY FIRST NATIONAL BANK, N.A. as Beneficiary, dated October 8, 2011, and recorded as Instrument No. 947, Book 455, Page 107, on October 9, 2011, Any County, Any State

WILL SELL AT PUBLIC AUCTION TO HIGHEST BIDDER FOR CASH, A CASHIER'S CHECK DRAWN ON A STATE OR NATIONAL BANK, A STATE OR FEDERAL CREDIT UNION, OR A STATE OR FEDERAL SAVINGS AND LOAN ASSOCIATION DOMICILED IN THE STATE OF ANY STATE (payable at time of sale in lawful money of the United States) at

ANY COUNTY COURTHOUSE
400 MARSHALL AVENUE
ANY COUNTY, ANY STATE

all right title and interest conveyed to and now held by it under said Deed of Trust in the property situated in said County and State described as:

Lot 9 in Block 33, MANSFIELD PARK ESTATES, a subdivision according to the plat thereof as recorded in Plat Book 58, Page 18, of the Public Records of Any County, Any State

The street address and other common designation, if any, of the real property above is purported to be:

423 Grasemere Terrace, Any City, Any State

THE UNDERSIGNED TRUSTEE DISCLAIMS ANY LIABILITY FOR INCORRECT INFORMATION FURNISHED.

THAT said sale is made without covenant or warranty regarding title, possession, or encumbrances, or as to insurability of title.

THE total amount of the unpaid balance of said obligations, together with advances and estimated costs and expenses, is $197,325.00.

EXHIBIT 19–6   *(continued)*

THAT notice of breach of said obligation and election to sell real property was recorded as Instrument No. 936 in Book 612, Page 4, on October 6, 2015, of the Official Records of the County Recorder of Any County, State of Any State.

Trustee or party conducting Sale

ANY CITY TRUST COMPANY
669 N.W. 10TH STREET
ANY CITY, ANY STATE

ANY CITY TRUST COMPANY

By: _____

Dated: October 8, 2015.   Valerie Winslow, President

---

interest, penalties, costs, and expenses, or by reaching a negotiated agreement with the lender. Alternatively, the borrower may forestall foreclosure by filing for bankruptcy. Should the borrower fail to avail himself or herself of these alternatives, the public auction and sale of the property will proceed. In most deed of trust states, the redemption period ends prior to or on the date of the sale. However, some state statutes may allow a redemption period to continue even after the sale, so state statutes should be checked carefully. The lender, the borrower, or a third party may purchase the property at the foreclosure sale. After the sale, the purchaser of the property receives a trustee's deed, similar to the example provided in Exhibit 19–7.

EXHIBIT 19–7   **Trustee's deed**

RECORDING REQUESTED BY:
Any City Trust Company

AND WHEN RECORDED MAIL TO:
Any City Trust Company
669 N.W. 10th Street
Any City, Any State

Attn: Valerie Winslow

SPACE ABOVE THIS LINE FOR RECORDER'S USE
_____

MAIL TAX STATEMENTS TO:
Robert Pearson
519 S.W. 6th Avenue
Any City, Any State

Trustee's Deed Upon Sale
Trustee Sale No. 654321

The undersigned Grantor declares:
    (1)   The Grantee herein was not the foreclosing beneficiary.
    (2)   The amount of the unpaid debt together with costs was $197,325.00.
    (3)   The amount paid by the Grantee at the trustee sale was $198,500.00.
    (4)   The documentary transfer tax is $1,389.50.
    (5)   The survey fee is $125.00.

(continued)

EXHIBIT 19-7

(6) Said property is in the City of Any City, and ANY CITY TRUST COMPANY (herein called Trustee), as the duly appointed Trustee under the Deed of Trust hereinafter described, does hereby grant and convey, but without warranty, express or implied, to

ROBERT PEARSON, a single man

(herein called Grantee), all of its right, title and interest in and to that certain property situated in the City of Any City, County of Any County, State of Any State, described as follows:

Lot 9 in Block 33, MANSFIELD PARK ESTATES, a subdivision according to the plat thereof as recorded in Plat Book 58, Page 18, of the Public Records of Any County, Any State

TRUSTEE STATES THAT:

This conveyance is made pursuant to the powers conferred upon Trustee by that certain Deed of Trust dated October 8, 2011, and executed by THOMAS TRENT as trustor, and recorded on October 9, 2011, in Book 455, Instrument No. 947, Page 107, of Official Records of Any County, Any State, and after fulfillment of the conditions specified in said Deed of Trust authorizing this conveyance.

Default occurred as set forth in a Notice of Default and Election to Sell which was recorded in the office of the Recorder of said County.

All requirements of law regarding the mailing and recording of copies of notices and the posting and publication and recording of copies of the Notice of Sale have been complied with.

Said property as sold by said Trustee at public auction on October 29, 2015, at the place named in the Notice of Sale, in the County of Any County, Any State, in which the property is situated, Grantee being the highest bidder at such sale, became the purchaser of said property and paid therefor to said Trustee the amount bid, being $198,500.00, in lawful money of the United States, or by the satisfaction, pro tanto, of the obligations then secured by said Deed of Trust.

IN WITNESS WHEREOF, said ANY CITY TRUST COMPANY, as Trustee, has this day, caused its corporate name and seal to be hereunto affixed by its President and Secretary, thereunto duly authorized by resolution of its Board of Directors.

Dated: November 3, 2015.

ANY CITY TRUST COMPANY

By: _____
    Valerie Winslow, President

By: _____
    Curtis Emerson, Secretary

(corporate seal)

STATE OF ANY STATE
COUNTY OF ANY COUNTY

On this 3rd day of November, 2015, before me, the undersigned, a Notary Public in and for the County and State aforesaid, personally appeared VALERIE WINSLOW known to me to be the President and CURTIS EMERSON known to me to be the Secretary of the corporation that executed the within instrument, and known to me to be the persons who executed the within instrument on behalf of the corporation therein named, and acknowledged to me that such corporation executed the same, pursuant to its laws, or a resolution of its Board of Directors.

_____

Notary Public, State of Any State
My commission expires:

As a paralegal working in the legal department of a trust, title, or escrow company; in the legal department of a lending institution; or in a law firm, you may be called upon to prepare any or all of the documents discussed in the preceding text if you work in a deed of trust state. In assisting an attorney in a deed of trust foreclosure, the following checklist should prove helpful.

DEED OF TRUST FORECLOSURE CHECKLIST

1. Review deed of trust and note carefully, noting:
   a. The proper names of all parties
   b. The legal description of the property
   c. The total amount of the debt obligation
   d. The payment terms
   e. The rights conferred upon each party in the event of default
   f. The recording information pertaining to the deed of trust
2. Determine whether a demand letter is required (or desired) to be sent prior to filing and recording a notice of default. If required or desired, include:
   a. The name of the lender
   b. The amount of the default and date it was due
   c. The demand terms (for example, default amount plus penalties, acceleration of the total outstanding obligation)
   d. Date by which default must be corrected
   e. Legal description of the property
   f. Date by which to notify lender or trustee in the event the borrower disputes the default amount
3. Prepare notice of default.
4. Ascertain recording fee for recording notice of default and send original notice, together with applicable recording fee, to county recorder's office.
5. Mail copy of notice of default to borrower and to lender.
6. If borrower corrects default prior to or after recording of notice of default:
   a. Prepare a notice of rescission.
   b. Ascertain recording fee for recording notice of rescission and send original notice, together with applicable recording fee, to county recorder's office.
7. If borrower fails to correct default within redemption period:
   a. Prepare notice of trustee's sale.
   b. Publish notice of trustee's sale according to state statutory requirements.
   c. If required by state statute, record notice of trustee's sale.
   d. Arrange for public auction and sale of the property.
   e. Prepare trustee's deed.
   f. After receiving proceeds from purchaser, record the trustee's deed and provide to purchaser.

Judicial Foreclosure

A judicial foreclosure is a court proceeding in which (1) the court awards judgment against the borrower on the promissory note and (2) all title rights in the secured real property held by the borrower are foreclosed and the property is sold to pay the debt. Mortgages typically are foreclosed through judicial foreclosure.

Prior to initiating a judicial action, the lender's attorney may send a demand letter to the delinquent borrower specifying the nature and amount of the default, the action required to cure the default, the date by which the default must be cured, and the actions that may be taken by the lender should the borrower fail to cure the default by the specified date. Although a demand letter may not be required by state law in all states, a lender may choose to send one even if not mandated. The loan documents themselves may require that a letter be sent; alternatively, the letter may be used to preserve various options open to the lender.

Communications for the collection of a debt incurred for personal, family, or household purposes (such as a residential mortgage loan) must comply with the *Fair Debt Collection Practices Act* (*FDCPA*). The Act requires that, within five days after an initial communication with the debtor (unless the debtor pays the debt within this time period or unless this information was included in the initial communication), the creditor provide the debtor (in this instance, the borrower) with a written notice containing (1) the amount of the debt; (2) the name of the creditor to whom the debt is owed; (3) a statement that unless the debtor, within thirty days after receipt of the notice, disputes the validity of all or any portion of the debt, the debt will be deemed valid; (4) a statement that, if the debtor does provide notification of a dispute within the prescribed time period, the creditor (here the lender) will obtain verification of the debt and provide this to the debtor; and (5) a statement that upon the debtor's written request within the prescribed time period, the creditor will provide the debtor with the name and address of the original creditor, if different from the current creditor. A sample demand letter referencing the thirty-day dispute period, together with samples of the basic documents pertaining to judicial foreclosures, may be found in the hypothetical foreclosure suit provided at the end of this chapter.

Mediation may be attempted before the lender decides to proceed with a judicial foreclosure. In some states, mediation may be a mandatory requirement prior to setting a trial date or entering a default judgment, while in other states mediation may be voluntarily pursued.

Should any attempted mediation be unsuccessful or should no mediation occur and the borrower fails to meet the lender's terms, a judicial foreclosure will be initiated by the filing of a complaint in the trial court in the county in which the real property is located. A judicial foreclosure generally is a lengthier procedure than a nonjudicial foreclosure. The borrower is a defendant in the suit and has the right to raise defenses against the foreclosure action.

Prior to initiating a foreclosure action, one should thoroughly review the loan documents and all other documentation in connection with the transaction. One must determine whether the original mortgage instrument and promissory note are available. In judicial foreclosure actions, the courts often require that these documents be provided before granting a plaintiff the right to foreclose. Additionally, one must ascertain the identity of the appropriate plaintiff. The current holder of the mortgage and note may not be the originator of the loan (as discussed in prior chapters). The sale of loans and the use of loan servicers other than loan originators have complicated the foreclosure process. Because of the frequency with which residential mortgage loans have been sold or assigned, establishing the chain of ownership is an important initial step. The fact that a loan may have changed hands frequently also increases the possibility that the current holder of the mortgage loan is not in possession of the original mortgage instrument and promissory note. If this is the case, the attorney representing the plaintiff may need to take additional steps and include appropriate counts in the complaint to prove that the plaintiff has the standing to bring the foreclosure action. In some instances, the plaintiff may not be a lender but may actually be a company created to act as a collection and litigation agent for the owner of the mortgage loan. The most well-known of these companies is *Mortgage Electronic Registrations Systems, Inc.* (*MERS*). If such a company is acting in this capacity, it may have legal standing to foreclose on behalf of the lender, As one can see, these preliminary undertakings can be quite complex.

The next step is to determine the borrower's military status. If one is uncertain about a borrower's military status, certificates of service should be obtained. Federal law provides special protections for active-duty military personnel under the *Servicemembers Civil Relief Act of 2003* (formerly known as The Soldiers' and Sailors' Civil Relief Act of 1940). The Act applies to active-duty military personnel who had a mortgage obligation prior to enlistment or prior to being ordered to active duty (and in some limited circumstances, it also applies to dependents of service members). These protections include limits on interest rates that may be charged and protections against foreclosures. Under the Act, lenders may not foreclose upon or seize real property for a failure to pay a mortgage debt while a service member is on active duty or within ninety days after the period of military service without court approval. In a court proceeding against a member of the military services, the lender is required to show that the borrower's ability to repay the loan was not affected by his or her military service.

Prior to the filing of a complaint, one must determine all necessary parties to the suit. All necessary parties are those individuals or entities having an interest in the real property inferior (lesser in priority) to the interest of the lender. This includes the borrower and all junior lienholders. To determine the identity of any and all junior lienholders, the title work on the real property should be updated by obtaining a partial abstract from the date the lender's mortgage was recorded to the present date (see Chapter 11 for a detailed discussion of abstracts). The holders of any junior liens must be named as defendants in the suit. If the property in question is rental property, tenants are considered parties having a leasehold interest in the property and therefore must be joined in the action.

Next, state statutes must be checked to determine if court rules require that a particular form of complaint be used in the action. A foreclosure complaint should include a count for foreclosure and a separate count for money damages. If there is a risk that the property's value may diminish because the property has been abandoned or poorly maintained or if the property is rental property, an additional count should be included in the complaint requesting the appointment by the court of a *receiver*. A receiver will protect the lender's interests by maintaining the property and, if applicable, by generating appropriate rents from income-producing property. A copy of the note and a copy of the mortgage should be attached to the complaint as exhibits. Some states require that the filed complaint be a verified complaint.

A notice of lis pendens (discussed in Chapter 18) should be filed at the same time the complaint is filed, putting third parties on notice that the real property is the subject matter of pending litigation. The methods of effectuating service of process upon all parties are set out in state civil procedure statutes. In general, service of process is carried out by serving a summons and a copy of the foreclosure complaint on each defendant. In the event a borrower cannot be personally served, state statute may permit *constructive service* (service by publication or other methods). In these instances, an affidavit of diligent search and inquiry may be required to be filed, setting forth the steps taken by the plaintiff-lender to attempt to find and personally serve the defendant-borrower.

The summons, served personally or constructively, states the statutorily prescribed time period within which the defendants must respond to the complaint. All defendants, not only the borrower, must be properly served. Statutory law may set forth different service requirements and response periods for various defendants. For example, if the borrower is delinquent in paying federal income taxes and there is a federal tax lien on the property, the United States of America is included as a defendant in the action. The appropriate party to serve with actual service of process in this instance is the United States Attorney for the district in which the real property is located, and once service is effectuated, an affidavit indicating compliance should be filed. Additionally, the Attorney General of the United States of America is mailed a copy of the summons and complaint. The United States of America has sixty days to respond to the complaint. Should a defendant in a foreclosure action fail to respond within the required time period, the plaintiff's attorney will move for a default judgment against the defendant.

If a defendant-borrower was served by publication, state law may require the appointment of an **attorney ad litem** to represent the defendant's interests. If this is the case, a motion for appointment of attorney ad litem should be prepared, together with a court order appointing an attorney ad litem before the case proceeds further. If an attorney ad litem is appointed, it is his or her task to attempt to ascertain the whereabouts of the defendant-borrower and to determine the defendant-borrower's military status.

If a defendant-borrower fails to respond to the complaint and it is determined that the defendant-borrower's failure to respond is not due to his or her military posting, a motion for default and an affidavit as to nonmilitary service are prepared. Additionally, if permitted by state statute and court rules, a motion for summary final judgment may be prepared, together with supporting affidavits establishing the sums owed to the plaintiff-lender on the loan, the sums owed for court costs, and the sums owed for attorneys' fees.

A final hearing is then scheduled, and notice of the hearing is sent to the parties. At the hearing, the plaintiff's attorney will present the court with a final judgment order for the judge to sign authorizing a judicial sale. State statute dictates the prescribed form for a notice of sale and the requisite publication period of the notice.

In the event that a defendant-borrower does file an answer to the foreclosure complaint within the statutorily prescribed time period, the answer may contain defenses to the action. One possible defense is that the lender failed to provide written notice of a breach of the loan terms if notice is required either under state law or under the terms of the loan agreement itself. Another possible defense is that the borrower tendered payment prior to the acceleration of the loan. Similarly, a defense may be raised that other necessary conditions precedent to filing a foreclosure action have not been met. The borrower may raise FDCPA violations or violations of other federal consumer protection acts. The borrower may allege mortgage fraud or predatory lending practices. As with any civil action, if appropriate, the borrower may raise the statute of limitations as a defense.

attorney ad litem: An attorney appointed by the court to protect a defendant-borrower's interests.

If a default judgment is in order or if the case is brought to trial and a final judgment for foreclosure is granted, the next step is to proceed with the judicial sale of the property. The final judgment order typically specifies the date and location of the public auction. In a number of local jurisdictions, auctions may be conducted online rather than in a physical locale. Local rules will provide instructions for bidding and may require the payment of deposits as a precondition to place a bid. Often, a plaintiff will be allowed to receive a credit against the bid for the amount owed to the plaintiff (including interest and costs) as set forth in the final judgment. Documentary stamp or transfer taxes must be paid on the accepted bid price. The following case illustrates the problems that can arise if bidding procedures are mishandled. This case also addresses the consequences of bids deemed to be too low in relationship to the value of the property in question.

CASE: *Long Beach Mortgage Corp. v. Bebble*
985 So. 2d 611 (Fla. 4th DCA 2008)

GROSS, J.

We reverse an order refusing to set aside a foreclosure sale where a $500,000 property sold for $1,000.

Long Beach Mortgage Corporation held a mortgage on certain real property. The property went into foreclosure. After negotiating with other mortgagees over priority, Long Beach secured a final judgment in foreclosure giving it a credit bid of $716,139.60 plus interest and setting a foreclosure sale for May 22, 2007 at 10:00 a.m.

Two law firms represented Long Beach in the foreclosure litigation—the Law Offices of Marshall Watson and Fox, Wackeen, Dungey, et. al. Long Beach's title insurer retained Fox, Wackeen to litigate the priority of various mortgages. Although Marshall Watson controlled the foreclosure part of the case, Fox, Wackeen handled the notice of the sale and its publication.

At the foreclosure sale, no one placed a bid on behalf of Long Beach. The property was sold to Aqua-Terra, Inc., a disinterested third party, on its bid of $1,000. The property was appraised at $500,000.

On May 25, 2007, Long Beach moved to set aside the sale to Aqua-Terra on the grounds of its inadvertence, mistake, or accident or that of its agents in failing to attend the sale. At a hearing on the motion, Long Beach presented a scenario of miscommunication and mishaps.

First, the posture of the case was different than the usual foreclosure. Typically Marshall Watson had designated people to handle sales packages; they obtained the final judgment, ordered the sales agent to appear and provided bidding instructions to the sales agent at the sale. Generally, the agent was authorized to bid up to the judgment amount, or less if warranted by the economics of the situation.

In this case, Maxine Housen was the Marshall Watson employee handling the sale package for the foreclosure sale. She reviewed the file and noticed that Long Beach was not listed as a plaintiff in copies of court documents. As a result, Housen was unsure how to proceed, since the firm did not have bidding funds from the client on hand. She contacted an attorney in the firm, Laura Carbo, who explained that Long Beach had been initially named as a defendant junior mortgagee.

On May 21, 2007, the day before the sale, Housen advised the sales agent to bid at the sale on behalf of Long Beach. The agent confirmed that she would attend the sale. Following normal practice in Martin County, the sales agent went to the office of *The Stuart News* to obtain the original proof of publication of sale, but discovered that no original proof of publication was available. Since she could not find the proof of publication at the newspaper office, the sales agent believed that the sale would not proceed.

At 5:00 p.m. on May 21, the Fox, Wackeen firm faxed attorney Carbo the proof of publication of sale. Carbo received the fax on May 22 at 9:00 a.m. Carbo referred the faxed copy to Housen, but Housen did not arrive at the office until 10:00 a.m. Housen immediately began to prepare a sales package for the agent to attend the sale, which she mistakenly believed was scheduled for 11:00 a.m., the time for foreclosure sales in many locales. Housen was unfamiliar with Martin County procedures.

A Fox, Wackeen attorney delivered the original proof of publication to the Martin County clerk of court the morning of the sale. The clerk conducted the sale at 10:00 a.m., and Aqua-Terra made the only bid. Later that morning, the sales agent contacted Housen and told her that the sale had occurred. The agent was present at the sale, but did not participate because she did not have bidding instructions.

(continued)

At the hearing, Aqua-Terra contended it was an innocent purchaser, but conceded that it had paid an inadequate price for the property. Aqua-Terra emphasized that Long Beach's sales agent was present at the sale, but failed to bid. It also argued that the attorney from Fox, Wackeen who attended the sale, corrected the clerk about the amount of the judgment prior to the commencement of bidding. Aqua-Terra took the position that Long Beach and its attorneys committed a unilateral mistake through a failure of "internal procedures."

The trial judge found that the problem at the sale was "not the fault of the purchaser." The trial judge "exercised [his] discretion" and denied the motion to vacate.

"Whether the complaining party has made the showing necessary to set aside a [foreclosure] sale is a discretionary decision by the trial court, which may be reversed only when the court has grossly abused its discretion." *United Cos. Lending Corp. v. Abercrombie*, 713 So. 2d 1017, 1018 (Fla. 2d DCA 1998). In *Arlt v. Buchanan*, 190 So. 2d 575 (Fla. 1966), our supreme court summarized 75 years of case law:

> The general rule is, of course, that standing alone mere inadequacy of price is not a ground for setting aside a judicial sale, But where the inadequacy is gross and is shown to result from any mistake, accident, surprise, fraud, misconduct or irregularity upon the part of either the purchaser or other person connected with the sale, with resulting injustice to the complaining party, equity will act to prevent the wrong result.

Id. at 577. *Arlt* is consistent with the view that an equity judge considering whether to set aside a foreclosure sale "has a large discretion which will only be interfered with by the appellate court in a clear case of injustice." *Mitchell v. Mason*, 75 Fla. 679, 682, 79 So. 163, 164 (1918).

The policy behind this standard of review is to ensure a competitive market in the foreclosure sale process. "Bidders and buyers" at such sales "usually bid and buy to make a profit." *City of Sanford v. Ashton*, 131 Fla. 759, 763, 179 So. 765, 767 (1938). To establish a precedent that encourages the easy setting aside of foreclosure sales "would be to destroy an incentive which prompts bidding at [a] sale and thereby work a hardship on both debtors and creditors." *Id.*

One line of Florida supreme court cases preceding *Arlt* took the view that where there was a gross inadequacy in price, an irregularity in the process of the foreclosure sale could be a basis for setting the sale aside. For example, *Lawyers' Co-operative Publishing Company v. Bennett*, 34 Fla. 302, 308–310, 16 So. 185, 187–88 (1894), held that a mistake by the sheriff conducting a sale, which prevented a judgment creditor from attending it, justified setting the sale aside. In *Macfarlane v. Macfarlane*, 50 Fla. 570, 580,

39 So. 995, 998 (1905), the notice of sale was published in a way that prevented "a fair sale of the property," creating "an element of unfairness in the method of advertising and selling the property, which, coupled with the inadequate price, demand[ed] that the order confirming the sale . . . be reversed." Cf. *Ruff v. Guaranty Title & Trust Co.*, 99 Fla. 197, 126 So. 383 (1930) (court refused to set aside foreclosure sale where the "record reveal[ed] no irregularity in connection with the sale"); *Mitchell*, 79 So. at 165 (affirming order refusing to set aside sale where irregularity in sale procedure caused by the party attacking the sale).

In addition to those cases involving a problem with the mechanics of a foreclosure sale, the supreme court also approved the setting aside of a sale where the "mistake" or "accident" that occurred was a unilateral one, the fault of the person seeking to set aside the sale. In *Florida Fertilizer Manufacturing Company v. Hodge*, 64 Fla. 275, 60 So. 127 (1912), a mortgagor "with little education and no knowledge of legal proceedings" went to a lawyer for advice after "learning of the institution of foreclosure proceedings" on his farm. *Id.* at 128. He "understood the attorney to say that no further proceedings would be taken, and that it would not be necessary for [the mortgagor] to appear in court in the cause." *Id.* Without the mortgagor's knowledge, his property was sold at a foreclosure sale for $110, when it was reasonably worth "$800 to $1,000." *Id.* The supreme court affirmed an order vacating confirmation of the sale, finding that it was "inequitable under the circumstances" for the buyer at the foreclosure sale to take advantage of a "grossly inadequate price." As the law has developed over time, "even a unilateral mistake which results in a grossly inadequate price is legally sufficient to invoke the trial court's discretion to consider setting the sale aside." *Abercrombie*, 713 So. 2d at 1018; *see Fernandez v. Suburban Coastal Corp.*, 489 So. 2d 70 (Fla. 4th DCA 1986); *Van Delinder v. Albion Realty & Mortgage, Inc.*, 287 So. 2d 352 (Fla. 3d DCA 1973).

In two decisions factually similar to this case, this court affirmed orders setting aside foreclosure sales. *Fernandez* involved a mortgagee's agent who failed to attend a sale, resulting in the sale of property for $100, an "unconscionably inadequate" price given the $54,300 value of the property. 489 So. 2d at 71. The agent's failure to attend the sale, caused by a calendaring error, "resulted in the inadequate bid price." *Id.* In *Alberts v. Federal Home Loan Mortgage Corp.*, 673 So. 2d 158, 159 (Fla. 4th DCA 1996), "a mistake in communication" between the lender's counsel and the sale agent resulted in the agent making too low a bid, which the buyer at the sale trumped by bidding $5 more. The property was sold for $19,000; the amount of the foreclosure judgment was $118,955, and the buyers knew that the residence was worth at least $100,000. *Id.* at 159.

(continued)

If *Fernandez* and *Alberts* demonstrate the permissible exercise of judicial discretion, we find that the trial court in this case grossly abused its discretion in failing to set aside the foreclosure sale. This was a case where equity should have acted "to prevent the wrong result," to remedy a "clear case of injustice." *Arlt*, 190 So. 2d at 577; *Mitchell*, 79 So. at 164. As in *Fernandez* and *Alberts*, Long Beach was the innocent victim of the mistakes of its attorneys and agents. The property was sold for $1,000, .02% of its value. Long Beach acted promptly to set aside the sale by filing its motion three days later. The purpose of the law in this area is to promote the viability of the foreclosure sale process, to encourage good faith offers for foreclosed properties, not to protect outrageous windfalls to buyers who make *de minimis* bids. Finally, judicial economy favors resolving a case so that a fair price is realized in this proceeding, instead of inviting a second lawsuit to allocate the losses between Long Beach, Marshall Watson, and Fox, Wackeen.

We distinguish this case from *John Crescent, Inc. v. Schwartz*, 382 So. 2d 383 (Fla. 4th DCA 1980), where the defendants ignored foreclosure suit papers, leading to a default final judgment and foreclosure sale that the defendants made no provisions to attend. It is one thing for a mistake in communications to result in the failure of the mortgagee's agent to attend a sale, and another for properly served parties to ignore a lawsuit altogether. Nor is this case like *Action Realty and Investments, Inc. v. Grandison*, 930 So. 2d 674 (Fla. 4th DCA 2006) and *Esque Real Estate Holdings, Inc. v. C.H. Consulting, Ltd.*, 940 So. 2d 1185 (Fla. 4th DCA 2006), which both involved no irregularity connected with the foreclosure sale.

We also distinguish this case from *Wells Fargo Credit Corp. v. Martin*, 605 So. 2d 531 (Fla. 2d DCA 1992).

There the second district affirmed an order denying a motion to set aside a sale where the mortgagor's agent misread her bidding instructions, leading her to bid $15,000 instead of $115,500, the tax appraised value of the property after deducting the homestead exemption. The property was sold for $20,000. Such a sales price is not as unconscionably inadequate as the $100/$54,300 disparity in *Fernandez* or the $1,000/$500,000 difference in this case.

Reversed.

STEVENSON and MAY, JJ., concur.

Case Questions

1. In the above case, two law firms were representing Long Beach in a foreclosure action, yet no bid was placed on the property on behalf of Long Beach due to mishaps and miscommunication. If you were a paralegal working for either of these firms, what steps, if any, might you have taken to prevent this situation?

2. Some local jurisdictions have instituted online foreclosure auction procedures. If your jurisdiction uses online auctions, review your local rules, and indicate whether you believe the circumstances that occurred in this case could be prevented under these rules.

3. Aqua-Terra, the successful bidder in this case, placed a bid that was determined to be an inadequate price for the property. Do you believe a court should be given judicial discretion to set aside a low bid placed by a bona fide bidder? Why or why not?

After the sale is completed, the clerk of the court typically issues a certificate of sale. Title to the property will be transferred to the buyer by a sheriff's deed, a referee's deed, or a certificate of title. Transfer of title to the real property may be delayed, however, pending the closure of the permitted redemption period, during which the borrower may redeem the property by repaying the amount of the loan plus court costs, interest, and penalties. In addition to the borrower, some lienholders may be granted the right of redemption. For example, the Internal Revenue Service is entitled to redeem the property up to 120 days after the date of the sale. Other lienholders also have certain rights of redemption, so state statutes should be researched before an attempt is made to resell the property.

A paralegal working in a real estate law firm or in the legal department of a lending institution may be asked to prepare any or all of the documents just mentioned. In assisting an attorney with a judicial foreclosure, the following checklist may prove helpful.

MORTGAGE FORECLOSURE CHECKLIST

1. Review mortgage and note carefully, noting:
   a. The proper names of all parties
   b. The legal description of the property
   c. The total amount of the debt obligation
   d. The payment terms
   e. The rights conferred upon each party in the event of default, including any preconditions prior to instituting a foreclosure action
   f. The recording information pertaining to the mortgage
2. Prepare a demand letter that includes:
   a. The name of the lender
   b. The amount of the default and date it was due
   c. The demand terms (for example, default amount plus penalties, acceleration of the total outstanding obligation)
   d. The date by which the default must be corrected
   e. The legal description of the property
   f. The date by which to notify the lender in the event the borrower disputes the default amount
   g. The consequences should borrower fail to act within the specified time period
3. Obtain updated partial abstract to determine junior lienholders.
4. If income-producing property, ascertain names of all tenants.
5. Prepare complaint, including counts for foreclosure, money damages, and, if applicable, appointment of a receiver. Attach copies of note and mortgage as exhibits.
6. Prepare a summons for each defendant.
7. Make the appropriate number of copies of complaint for the clerk and a copy of each summons for office file.
8. Prepare a notice of lis pendens.
9. File the complaint and notice of lis pendens with the applicable filing fee and sheriff's fee. Have clerk sign summonses.
10. Obtain certificates of military status of defendant-borrower from each branch of service by sending a letter with requisite information and fee.
11. If personal service fails, prepare affidavit of diligent search and inquiry, and serve by publication.
12. If required by state statute, prepare motion for appointment of attorney ad litem to represent defendant-borrower served by publication, together with order appointing attorney ad litem.
13. Should defendant-borrower fail to respond to complaint, prepare and file:
    a. Motion for default
    b. Motion for summary final judgment
    c. Affidavit as to nonmilitary service
    d. Affidavit of indebtedness
    e. Affidavit of costs
    f. Affidavit as to attorneys' fees

14. Schedule final hearing.
15. Obtain original note and mortgage.
16. Prepare final judgment order.
17. Prepare notice of sale and publish as per state statutory requirements.

strict foreclosure: A foreclosure method available in a few states in which a court hearing is held to determine the mortgagee's right to foreclose. If the mortgagee's right is authorized, the court awards the real property to the mortgagee without requiring the mortgagee to bid for the property at a public sale.

entry foreclosure: A foreclosure method used in only a few states in which the lender forecloses by taking possession of the real property for a specified time period, after which legal title to the property passes to the lender.

affidavit of indebtedness: A sworn statement attesting to the amounts owed to the affiant by a party.

Strict Foreclosure

Strict foreclosure is a foreclosure method available in a few states. It differs from judicial foreclosure in that the real property serving as collateral for the loan is not sold. A court hearing is held to determine the mortgagee's right to foreclose. If the mortgagee's right is authorized, the court simply awards the real property to the mortgagee without requiring the mortgagee to bid for the property at a public sale. In a judicial foreclosure, should proceeds be left over after the plaintiff and junior lienholders are paid, the remaining proceeds are handed over to the defendant-borrower. In a strict foreclosure, the defendant-borrower receives nothing because no sale has taken place.

Entry Foreclosure

Entry foreclosure is another foreclosure method that is used in only a few states. It is similar to strict foreclosure in that no sale of the real property takes place. Instead, upon default by the borrower, the lender forecloses by taking possession of the real property and holding possession for a specified time period, after which legal title to the property passes to the lender.

hypothetical client matter

Barbara Hammond has set aside some time this afternoon to work on a foreclosure file. The client is Any County First National Bank. Any County First National Bank made a residential mortgage loan to Leonard and Joyce Dryden. The Drydens became delinquent on their monthly payments, and Any County First National Bank contacted attorney Ava Ross to initiate proceedings against the Drydens. The demand letter shown in Exhibit 19–8 was sent to the Drydens, demanding cure of their default.

The demand letter was received, but the Drydens did not respond to the letter, and upon Ava's instruction, Barbara prepared and filed the complaint shown in Exhibit 19–9.

The notice of lis pendens shown in Exhibit 19–10 was filed with the complaint shown in Exhibit 19–9.

Personal service upon the Drydens was perfected, but they have failed to file a responsive pleading. The statutory time period for filing a response has expired, and Ava has asked Barbara to prepare the appropriate motions and supporting affidavits to proceed with the foreclosure. The first document Barbara prepares is a motion for default (see Exhibit 19–11). The top half of the document embodies the motion, while the bottom half contains the default to be signed by the clerk of the court.

Barbara next prepares a motion for final summary judgment (see Exhibit 19–12). This motion will be accompanied by numerous

supporting affidavits to establish the sums owed to Any County First National Bank for the outstanding debt obligation plus interest and penalties, the amount expended on costs, and the amount expended on attorneys' fees in pursuing this action.

Barbara next checks the file to make sure all certificates of military status have been received. Because personal service was perfected on the Drydens, there was no necessity for having an attorney ad litem appointed. Therefore, the responsibility for obtaining the requisite certificates fell upon Barbara. The certificates verify that neither Leonard nor Joyce Dryden is an active member of the military. Barbara proceeds to prepare an affidavit as to nonmilitary service (see Exhibit 19–13), which will be signed by Vincent Gray, the loan officer assigned to the Dryden loan file.

Barbara then prepares an **affidavit of indebtedness** (see Exhibit 19–14), also to be signed by Vincent. This affidavit sets forth the date of execution of the note and mortgage, the date of recording of the mortgage, the Official Records book and page numbers at which the mortgage was recorded, and a breakdown on the amounts owed to the client.

In addition to the sums listed in the affidavit of indebtedness, certain sums were expended as costs incurred in bringing the foreclosure proceeding. In this instance, the costs incurred were the filing fee for filing the complaint, the sheriff's fee, and the cost of obtaining the partial abstract from a title company to ascertain whether any liens were filed against the property since the recording of the client's mortgage. With these costs noted, Barbara prepares an affidavit as to costs (see Exhibit 19–15).

Finally, Barbara refers to the applicable rule in the Any State Bar Code of Professional Responsibility pertaining to the factors to consider when awarding attorneys' fees. The factors set forth in the rule help the court determine whether the attorneys' fees presented are reasonable. Factors commonly considered are the difficulty of the matter, the rates customarily charged for similar matters, and the rates the attorney charges similar clients for such services. Some states require an additional affidavit from an attorney outside the firm, corroborating that the fees charged in the case before the court are reasonable, but no such additional affidavit is required by the courts in Any State. The affidavit as to attorneys' fees prepared by Barbara is shown in Exhibit 19–16.

Demand letter EXHIBIT 19–8

September 7, 2015

CERTIFIED MAIL #P332261355
RETURN RECEIPT REQUESTED

Mr. and Mrs. Leonard Dryden
894 Colonial Avenue
Any City, Any State

RE: Loan No. 655344

Dear Mr. and Mrs. Dryden:

The undersigned law firm has been retained to represent Any County First National Bank, N.A. We have been informed that you presently are in default under the above-referenced loan by failing to make payment due August 1, 2015, and all subsequent payments. You are required, in order to cure this default, to forward to Any County First National Bank certified funds in the total amount of $4,095.70. This amount consists of the following: payments due August 1, 2015, and September 1, 2015, totaling $3,725.70; late charges in the amount of $70.00; and attorneys' fees in the amount of $300.00. If the funds are forwarded after October 1, 2015, then you must add an additional $1,862.85 to the above total sum. The above total sum must be paid no later than October 10, 2015, in order to cure the default. Failure to do so may result in acceleration of the total outstanding balance of your loan secured by your mortgage and judicial foreclosure and sale of the following described real property:

Lot 18 in Block 6, LONGFORD ESTATES, a subdivision according to the plat thereof as recorded in Plat Book 103, Page 59, of the Public Records of Any County, Any State.

According to the terms of the mortgage securing the above-referenced loan, you have the right to reinstate after acceleration, as well as the right to raise any applicable defense in any foreclosure proceeding. Should you fail to cure the default as specified above, the terms of your promissory note hold you responsible for the costs and fees incurred by Any County First National Bank for any further legal proceedings in this matter.

Unless you dispute the validity of this debt within thirty (30) days of your receipt of this letter, we will assume that the debt is valid. Should you notify us in writing within the thirty (30) day period that you are disputing this debt, we will proceed to obtain verification of the debt from Any County First National Bank and forward the verification to you.

Sincerely,

Ava Ross, Esquire

cc: Any County First National Bank, N.A.

EXHIBIT 19-9

Complaint for mortgage foreclosure

IN THE CIRCUIT COURT OF THE THIRD JUDICIAL CIRCUIT
IN AND FOR ANY COUNTY, ANY STATE

CASE NO. 15-4011

ANY COUNTY FIRST NATIONAL BANK, N.A.,
a national banking association,
　　　　　Plaintiff,

vs.

LEONARD DRYDEN and JOYCE DRYDEN,
　　　　　Defendants.
_____/

COMPLAINT FOR MORTGAGE FORECLOSURE

Plaintiff, ANY COUNTY FIRST NATIONAL BANK, N.A., by and through its undersigned counsel, sues Defendants, LEONARD DRYDEN and JOYCE DRYDEN, and alleges:

COUNT I—ACTION FOR MORTGAGE FORECLOSURE

1. This is an action to foreclose a mortgage on real property in Any County, Any State.
2. On May 10, 2012, Defendants executed and delivered a Promissory Note and a Mortgage securing payment of the Note to Plaintiff. The Mortgage was recorded on May 11, 2012, in Official Records Book 1190 at page 15, of the public records of Any County, Any State, and mortgaged the property described in the Mortgage then owned by and in possession of the mortgagor, a copy of the Mortgage and a copy of the Note being attached hereto and made a part hereof as Exhibits A and B.
3. Plaintiff owns and holds the Note and Mortgage.
4. The property is now owned by Defendants who hold possession.
5. Defendants have defaulted under the Note and Mortgage by failing to pay the payment due August 1, 2015, and all subsequent payments.
6. Plaintiff declares the full amount payable under the Note and Mortgage to be due.
7. Defendants owe Plaintiff $267,328.73 that is due on principal on the Note and Mortgage, interest from July 1, 2015, and title search expense for ascertaining necessary parties to this action.
8. Plaintiff is obligated to pay Plaintiff's counsel a reasonable fee for services rendered.

WHEREFORE, Plaintiff demands judgment foreclosing the Mortgage and, if the proceeds of the sale are insufficient to pay Plaintiff's claim, a deficiency judgment.

COUNT II—DAMAGES

9. This is an action for damages that exceed Fifteen Thousand Dollars ($15,000.00).
10. Plaintiff realleges and incorporates herein the allegations contained in paragraphs 2 through 8 above.
11. Defendants owe Plaintiff those sums of money set forth in paragraph 7 above.

WHEREFORE, Plaintiff demands judgment for damages against Defendants.

EXHIBIT 19–9

(continued)

DATED: September 12, 2015.

FISHER, ROSS, AND SIMON, P.A.
1900 N.W. 3rd Avenue
Any City, Any State
(000) 555-2000
Attorneys for Plaintiff

By: _____
Ava Ross, Esquire
Any State Bar No. 123456

EXHIBIT 19–10

Notice of lis pendens

IN THE CIRCUIT COURT OF THE THIRD JUDICIAL CIRCUIT
IN AND FOR ANY COUNTY, ANY STATE

CASE NO. 15-4011

ANY COUNTY FIRST NATIONAL BANK, N.A.,
a national banking association,
       Plaintiff,

vs.

LEONARD DRYDEN and JOYCE DRYDEN,
       Defendants.
_____/

NOTICE OF LIS PENDENS

TO DEFENDANTS LEONARD DRYDEN AND JOYCE DRYDEN, AND ALL OTHERS WHOM IT MAY CONCERN:

YOU ARE NOTIFIED of the institution of this action by Plaintiff against you seeking to foreclose a mortgage on the following property in Any County, Any State:

> Lot 18 in Block 6, LONGFORD ESTATES, a subdivision according to the plat thereof as recorded in Plat Book 103, Page 59, of the Public Records of Any County, Any State.

DATED on September 12, 2015.

FISHER, ROSS, AND SIMON, P.A.
1900 N.W. 3rd Avenue
Any City, Any State
(000) 555-2000
Attorneys for Plaintiff

By: _____
Ava Ross, Esquire
Any State Bar No. 123456

EXHIBIT 19-11   Motion for default

IN THE CIRCUIT COURT OF THE THIRD JUDICIAL CIRCUIT
IN AND FOR ANY COUNTY, ANY STATE

CASE NO. 15-4011

ANY COUNTY FIRST NATIONAL BANK, N.A.,
a national banking association,
      Plaintiff,

vs.

LEONARD DRYDEN and JOYCE DRYDEN,
      Defendants.
_____/

MOTION FOR DEFAULT

    Plaintiff, ANY COUNTY FIRST NATIONAL BANK, N.A., by and through its undersigned counsel, moves for entry of Default by the Clerk against Defendants LEONARD DRYDEN and JOYCE DRYDEN for their failure to serve any paper on the undersigned since the filing of the complaint.

DATED: _____.

                        FISHER, ROSS, AND SIMON, P.A.
                        1900 N.W. 3rd Avenue
                        Any City, Any State
                        (000) 555-2000
                        Attorneys for Plaintiff

                        By: _____
                           Ava Ross, Esquire
                           Any State Bar No. 123456

DEFAULT

    A Default is entered in this action against the Defendants named in the above Motion, for their failure to serve or file any paper as required by law.

DATED: _____.

                        ROSEMARY HIGGINS
                        Clerk of the Court

                        By: _____
                           Deputy Clerk

Copies furnished to:
Ava Ross, Esquire
Leonard Dryden
Joyce Dryden

IN THE CIRCUIT COURT OF THE THIRD JUDICIAL CIRCUIT
IN AND FOR ANY COUNTY, ANY STATE

CASE NO. 15-4011

ANY COUNTY FIRST NATIONAL BANK, N.A.,
a national banking association,
      Plaintiff,

vs.

LEONARD DRYDEN and JOYCE DRYDEN,
      Defendants.

_____/

MOTION FOR SUMMARY JUDGMENT OF FORECLOSURE

COMES NOW the Plaintiff, ANY COUNTY FIRST NATIONAL BANK, N.A., by and through its under-signed counsel, and hereby moves this Court for entry of a Summary Final Judgment of Foreclosure and for attorneys' fees and costs in this cause, and as grounds therefore would show as follows:

1. This is an action to foreclose a Mortgage on real property located in Any County, Any State.
2. There is no material issue of law or fact in this cause, and Plaintiff is entitled to entry of a Summary Final Judgment of Foreclosure in its favor as a matter of law.
3. Service of process has been properly perfected upon the Defendants.
4. Plaintiff has an interest superior to any interest of the Defendants in and to the real property more particularly described as follows:

    Lot 18 in Block 6, LONGFORD ESTATES, a subdivision
    according to the plat thereof as recorded in Plat Book 103,
    Page 59, of the Public Records of Any County, Any State

5. Plaintiff attaches to this Motion the following supporting affidavits:
    (a) Affidavit as to Nonmilitary Service
    (b) Affidavit of Indebtedness
    (c) Affidavit as to Costs
    (d) Affidavit as to Attorneys' Fees

WHEREFORE, Plaintiff requests entry of a Summary Final Judgment of Foreclosure and for attorneys' fees and costs in this cause.

      FISHER, ROSS, AND SIMON, P.A.
      1900 N.W. 3rd Avenue
      Any City, Any State
      (000) 555-2000
      Attorneys for Plaintiff

      By: _____
         Ava Ross, Esquire
         Any State Bar No. 123456

EXHIBIT 19–13   **Affidavit as to nonmilitary service**

IN THE CIRCUIT COURT OF THE THIRD JUDICIAL CIRCUIT
IN AND FOR ANY COUNTY, ANY STATE

CASE NO. 15-4011

ANY COUNTY FIRST NATIONAL BANK, N.A.,
a national banking association,
          Plaintiff,

vs.

LEONARD DRYDEN and JOYCE DRYDEN,
          Defendants

_____/

AFFIDAVIT AS TO NONMILITARY SERVICE

STATE OF ANY STATE
COUNTY OF ANY COUNTY

    BEFORE ME, the undersigned authority, personally appeared VINCENT GRAY who, being first duly sworn, says as follows:

1. Affiant is an employee of Plaintiff in this matter and is authorized to make this affidavit on its behalf.
2. The statements made herein are made upon Affiant's own personal knowledge.
3. To the best of Affiant's knowledge and belief, Defendants, LEONARD DRYDEN and JOYCE DRYDEN, are over eighteen years of age.
4. To the best of Affiant's knowledge and belief, Defendants have not been on active duty in the military service of the United States since the filing of this action.

    FURTHER AFFIANT SAYETH NOT.

_____
Vincent Gray, Affiant

    Sworn to and subscribed before me this _____ day of _____, 2015, by VINCENT GRAY, personally known to me.

_____
Notary Public, State of Any State
My commission expires:

IN THE CIRCUIT COURT OF THE THIRD JUDICIAL CIRCUIT
IN AND FOR ANY COUNTY, ANY STATE

CASE NO. 15-4011

ANY COUNTY FIRST NATIONAL BANK, N.A.,
a national banking association,
        Plaintiff,

vs.

LEONARD DRYDEN and JOYCE DRYDEN,
        Defendants.
_____/

AFFIDAVIT OF INDEBTEDNESS

STATE OF ANY STATE
COUNTY OF ANY COUNTY

BEFORE ME, the undersigned authority, this day personally appeared VINCENT GRAY who, being first duly sworn, says as follows:

1. Affiant is an employee of the Plaintiff in this matter and is authorized to make this affidavit on its behalf.
2. The statements made herein are made upon Affiant's own personal knowledge.
3. On May 10, 2012, Defendants executed and delivered to Plaintiff a Promissory Note. The Mortgage was recorded on May 11, 2012, in Official Records Book 1190, Page 15, of the public records of Any County, Any State. A copy of the Note and Mortgage are attached as Exhibits A and B.
4. The Plaintiff is the holder and owner of said Note and Mortgage.
5. The real property is owned by Defendants, who have possession of the property.
6. Defendants have defaulted under said Note and Mortgage by failing to make the payment due August 1, 2015, and all subsequent payments.
7. Defendants owe Plaintiff the following amounts:

(a)	Principal due on Note and Mortgage	$267,328.73
(b)	Interest from July 1, 2015, to November 12, 2015	6,816.48
	(Interest after the above date at the rate of $51.64 per day)	
(c)	Late charges	140.00
(d)	Taxes and insurance	. 0
	TOTAL	$274,285.21

8. Plaintiff has retained the services of Fisher, Ross, and Simon, P.A. to represent it in this action and is obligated to pay said law firm a reasonable fee for services rendered.

FURTHER AFFIANT SAYETH NOT.

                                      _____
                                      Vincent Gray, Affiant

   Sworn to and subscribed before me this _____day of _____, 2015, by VINCENT GRAY, who is personally known to me.

                                        _____
                                      Notary Public, State of Any State
                                      My commission expires:

EXHIBIT 19–15   **Affidavit as to costs**

IN THE CIRCUIT COURT OF THE THIRD JUDICIAL CIRCUIT
IN AND FOR ANY COUNTY, ANY STATE

CASE NO. 15-4011

ANY COUNTY FIRST NATIONAL BANK, N.A.,
a national banking association,
        Plaintiff,

vs.

LEONARD DRYDEN and JOYCE DRYDEN,
        Defendants.
_____/

AFFIDAVIT AS TO COSTS

STATE OF ANY STATE
COUNTY OF ANY COUNTY

BEFORE ME, the undersigned authority, this day personally appeared Ava Ross, Esquire who, being first duly sworn, deposes and says as follows:

1. She is the attorney for the Plaintiff in this action and is familiar with the costs expended by, or on behalf of, the Plaintiff.
2. The costs expended by the Plaintiff in this action are as follows:
   (a) Clerk of the Court, Any County $100.00
   (b) Sheriff, Any County   45.00
   (c) Any City Title Company   250.00
               TOTAL $395.00

FURTHER AFFIANT SAYETH NOT.

_____
Ava Ross, Affiant

Sworn to and subscribed before me this _____day of _____, 2015, by AVA ROSS, ESQUIRE, who is personally known to me.

_____
Notary Public, State of Any State
My commission expires:

IN THE CIRCUIT COURT OF THE THIRD JUDICIAL CIRCUIT
IN AND FOR ANY COUNTY, ANY STATE

CASE NO. 15-4011

ANY COUNTY FIRST NATIONAL BANK, N.A.,
a national banking association,
        Plaintiff,

vs.

LEONARD DRYDEN and JOYCE DRYDEN,
        Defendants.

_____/

AFFIDAVIT AS TO ATTORNEYS' FEES

STATE OF ANY STATE
COUNTY OF ANY COUNTY

BEFORE ME, the undersigned authority, this day personally appeared AVA ROSS, ESQUIRE of Fisher, Ross, and Simon, P.A., who after being first duly sworn, deposes and says to the best of her knowledge and belief as follows:

1. She is the attorney for the Plaintiff in this action and has been practicing law in the State of Any State since 1990.
2. The following time at the following rates has been expended on this action:
   (a) 3.00 hours by attorney at the rate of $300.00 per hour
   (b) 4.00 hours by paralegal at the rate of $100.00 per hour
   The above hourly rates represent Affiant's fee arrangement with her client.
3. The above-mentioned hourly rate is a rate which is customarily charged for similar matters and one which the Affiant customarily charges similar clients for such services.
4. The hours expended as set forth on the attached Statement for Services are a reasonable amount of time to have spent on this action.

FURTHER AFFIANT SAYETH NOT.

                                _____
                                Ava Ross, Affiant

Sworn to and subscribed before me this _____ day of _____, 2015, by AVA ROSS, ESQUIRE, who is personally known to me.

                                _____
                                Notary Public, State of Any State
                                My commission expires:

CHAPTER SUMMARY

1. When a borrower is in default on a loan, the borrower may seek various remedies to prevent foreclosure on the real property securing the loan. The borrower may attempt to sell the property in a short sale transaction, may attempt to reinstate the loan under the currently existing loan terms, may attempt to enter into a forbearance agreement, may give the lender a deed in lieu of foreclosure, or, as a final measure, may file for bankruptcy.

2. Foreclosure is the process whereby the real property securing a loan is sold and the proceeds used to pay the outstanding debt. However, two types of foreclosure methods exist in which no sale takes place. The first is strict foreclosure, in which a court hearing determines a lender's right to foreclose, after which the property is transferred to the lender. The second is entry foreclosure, in which the lender simply takes possession of the property and, after a stipulated time period, receives title to the property. Strict foreclosure and entry foreclosure are used in only a few states.

3. Nonjudicial foreclosure primarily occurs in deed of trust states. Rather than filing a lawsuit, the trustee records a notice of default setting forth the particulars of the default and notifying the borrower that the property may be sold without court action if the borrower does not act within the stated time period. After the prescribed waiting period expires, a notice of trustee's sale is published, and a public auction is held.

4. In assisting an attorney with a nonjudicial foreclosure, a paralegal may be called upon to prepare the following: (1) a demand letter, (2) a notice of default, (3) a notice of trustee's sale, and (4) a trustee's deed.

5. Mortgages typically are foreclosed through judicial foreclosure. Although the actual procedure varies from state to state, a judicial foreclosure begins with the filing of a complaint naming the borrower, and all other parties with interests inferior to those of the plaintiff, as defendants in the suit. Should the borrower fail to respond to the complaint, a default judgment may be entered against him or her. Upon final hearing, the court will authorize the public sale of the real property. Most states allow a redemption period after the sale, during which time the borrower can redeem the property by paying off the loan plus all penalties, costs, and attorneys' fees.

6. In assisting an attorney with a judicial foreclosure, a paralegal may be called upon to prepare the following: (1) a demand letter, (2) a complaint, (3) a notice of lis pendens, (4) a motion for default, (5) a motion for summary final judgment, and (6) various supporting affidavits.

WEB RESOURCES

http://portal.hud.gov/

This is the site of the U.S. Department of Housing and Urban Development (HUD). If you select "Avoid Foreclosure," you will find information pertaining to federal programs aimed at assisting homeowners who are at risk of foreclosure.

http://www.law.cornell.edu/

This is the site of the Legal Information Institute (LII). If you select "U.S. Code" and then "Title 12," you can access Chapter 38, Multifamily Mortgage Foreclosure, and Chapter 38A, Single Family Mortgage Foreclosure.

http://www.nclc.org/

This is the site of the National Consumer Law Center. If you select "Issues," you will find a section entitled "Foreclosures & Mortgages." Here you will find state foreclosure laws and foreclosure mediation programs. You also will find information pertaining to current mortgage servicing litigation.

http://www.realtytrac.com/

This site provides statistics and trends in the current real estate market, including foreclosure trends. The "Foreclosure" tabs provide a foreclosure overview, foreclosure laws by state, and access to numerous articles pertaining to foreclosure.

REVIEW QUESTIONS

1. What remedies might a borrower seek to prevent foreclosure?
2. Outline the steps to be taken in a nonjudicial foreclosure.
3. Outline the steps to be taken in a judicial foreclosure.
4. Explain the manner in which lienholders are paid in the event of a foreclosure.
5. Distinguish between (a) strict foreclosure and (b) entry foreclosure.

DISCUSSION QUESTIONS

1. Christine Guthrie owned a condominium unit in Bromwell Estates condominium development. ABC Bank held a first mortgage on the unit, and Forsythe Funding Corporation held a second mortgage on the unit. Several years after securing a second mortgage on the unit, Forsythe Funding Corporation assigned the second mortgage to XYZ Bank. Six months later, Christine defaulted on her loans. She also had not paid her condominium assessments for the last three months, and the Bromwell Estates Condominium Association filed a lien against her unit. ABC Bank, the first mortgagee, instituted a judicial foreclosure proceeding. In its complaint, it named Christine, Forsythe Funding Corporation, and Bromwell Estates Condominium Association as defendants. Christine and the condominium association answered the complaint; Forsythe Funding Corporation never responded to the complaint and thus defaulted. A summary judgment of foreclosure was ordered by the court, and the condominium unit was sold to a third party. The sale produced excess funds. The condominium association motioned the court for distribution of the excess funds, and the court ordered that 40 percent of the excess funds be disbursed to the condominium association to cover the unpaid assessments and attorneys' fees incurred by the association and ordered that the remaining 60 percent of the excess funds

be disbursed to Christine. XYZ Bank is now coming forward to challenge the court's distribution. It has submitted proof that it holds the unsatisfied second mortgage. Christine maintains that because Forsythe Funding Corporation, the original junior lienholder, defaulted, XYZ Bank cannot come forward now to claim the surplus funds. Who has the superior right in this situation, and why?

2. Keith Moreland took out a mortgage loan with Sentinel Bank. Years later he defaulted on his mortgage payments. Letters were sent out to him by Sentinel Bank, indicating that foreclosure proceedings would be commenced if the unpaid balance of the loan was not paid within thirty days. The letters were sent to the purported address of the mortgaged property and to a commercial mailing agency that Keith Moreland had designated to receive such notices. Keith failed to repay the balance of the loan within the thirty-day period, and a process server delivered process to Keith's wife at the address to which the post office delivered his mail. The process server also mailed a copy of process to Keith at that street address but designated the wrong town and zip code on the mailed copy. The foreclosure took place, and Keith is now coming forward with an order to show cause to vacate the judgment of foreclosure and sale. He maintains that the service of process was invalid and thus personal jurisdiction was not properly obtained. If this action were brought in your state, would the above service of process be valid? Why or why not?

3. Assume the same facts as set forth in Question 2 above. Suppose further that Keith Moreland maintains that he and his wife are estranged and that although he does receive mail at that address, he has not lived there for several years. Would this change your answer regarding valid service of process? Why or why not?

4. Todd and Charlotte Gilbert (the trustors) owned a house that was encumbered by a deed of trust securing a loan. The lender-beneficiary is Magna Bank, and the trustee is American Trustee Company (American). The Gilberts missed payments on the loan, and the loan went into default. Magna Bank directed American to record a Notice of Default and Election to Sell Under Deed of Trust and a Notice of Trustee's Sale. Four days prior to the sale, the Gilberts tendered a payment at a branch of Magna Bank. Payment was accepted by a branch employee, who then reinstated the loan. Magna Bank never notified American that the loan had been reinstated, and, therefore, American proceeded with the foreclosure, and the property was sold to a third party, Kincade Property Group (Kincade). Kincade received and recorded a trustee's deed. A few days after the deed was recorded, American informed Kincade that a mistake had been made. It recorded a Notice of Rescission of Trustee's Deed and tendered a refund check to Kincade. Kincade has refused to accept the tender of the refund check. Magna Bank has filed an action against Kincade, seeking cancellation of the trustee's deed. Kincade has filed a cross-complaint for slander of title, requesting cancellation of the Notice of Rescission of Trustee's Deed, and the Gilberts have filed an action against Magna, American, and Kincade. How should this matter be resolved?

5. Jay Montgomery conveyed a parcel of property to Philip Burnett by general warranty deed in exchange for a down payment, a promissory note, and a deed of trust. Both the note and the deed of trust contained an acceleration clause

stating that, if all or any part of the property or interest therein was sold or transferred by the note maker without the payee's prior written consent, excluding the creation of a lien or encumbrance subordinate to the deed of trust, then the payee could, at his option, declare all sums secured by the deed of trust immediately due and payable.

Several years after the execution of the promissory note and deed of trust, Philip granted a twenty-five-foot drainage easement across the back of the property to a third party. When Jay found out about the easement, he invoked the acceleration clause and demanded full payment of the balance due on the promissory note. Philip did not pay the full balance within the time specified in the demand letter, and Jay instructed the trustee to foreclose on the property. Philip is suing Jay, seeking an injunction to prevent the foreclosure sale. Which party should prevail? Why?

ETHICAL QUESTION

You spent two hours on your computer preparing foreclosure documents for a lending institution client. This is the first time your supervising attorney has been asked to file a foreclosure, so you were preparing the documents from scratch. As you were completing the documents, a sudden power outage occurred, and when the power came back on, you found that you had lost all of the prepared documents and that you had to start all over again, a task that took an additional two hours. You are now preparing a time slip for the hours spent on this task. How many hours should you bill the client for?

Slossberg Law Office on CourseMate

Please go to www.cengagebrain.com to log into CourseMate, access the Slossberg Law Office, and work on your client files. Each module corresponds to a chapter in the text. Within each module, you will be provided with instructions by the supervising attorney. You are asked to keep track of time spent on time sheets. The documents produced through working on client files in the law office can then be compiled into a portfolio of final work product.

CourseMate

The available CourseMate for this text has an interactive eBook and interactive learning tools, including flash cards, quizzes, and more. To learn more about this resource and access free demo CourseMate resources, including the Slossberg Law Office, go to www.cengagebrain.com, and search for this book. To access CourseMate materials that you have purchased, go to login.cengagebrain.com.

Glossary

A

ABA Model Rules of Professional Conduct: Model rules for the regulation of the ethical conduct of legal professionals that have been adopted by state bar associations.

abatement of rent: A deduction from the rent owed for the diminishment in value of the premises caused by the lack of maintenance.

abstract of title: A copy or condensed version of each document pertaining to a particular parcel of real property.

abstractor's certificate: A certificate that states the records the abstractor has examined, any records not examined, and the dates covered by the search.

acceleration clause: A clause in a financing instrument that permits the lender, at its option, upon default by the borrower, to accelerate the entire loan amount, making the full outstanding balance, plus interest and penalties, immediately due.

accounting: A broker's duty in safeguarding any monies, documents, or property held by the broker on behalf of the principal.

accretion: The addition of land by the gradual deposit of waterborne materials on shore.

acreage: A tract of undeveloped real property.

actual eviction: The bringing of a suit for possession of leased premises.

actual notice: Direct knowledge a person has about the ownership and condition of title of real property.

adjustable-rate loan: A loan in which the interest rate typically starts lower than that of a fixed-rate loan and then periodically changes in relation to an index rate, such as the rate on Treasury securities.

adjustment period: The period between one rate change and the next for an adjustable-rate loan.

advance fee trust account: A special escrow account in which advance fees paid to a broker are deposited. These fees may be used for advertising and other expenses incurred in marketing real property.

adverse possession: The acquisition of title to real property through taking possession of land that belongs to another without the owner's consent and retaining possession for a statutorily prescribed period of time.

affidavit of indebtedness: A sworn statement attesting to the amounts owed to the affiant by a party.

agent: A person authorized to act on behalf of another.

ALT-A mortgage loan: A loan given to a borrower whose credit profile presents some issues that disqualify him or her from obtaining a prime mortgage loan. The borrower pays an interest rate higher than a prime mortgage loan and lower than a subprime mortgage loan.

ameliorative waste: The alteration of property through addition of improvements by a life estate holder that increase the value of the property.

American Land Title Association (ALTA): An organization that was created to meet the demands for uniform title insurance protection nationwide. It has devised title commitment and title policy forms that are used in many parts of the country.

amortized loan: A loan in which level payments are made throughout the life of the loan.

anchor store: A major lessee in a shopping center—typically a major department store or, in the case of a neighborhood center, a supermarket.

annual percentage rate (APR): The true interest rate on a loan, which includes charges added such as points and mortgage insurance.

appurtenant easement: An easement given to confer a benefit to adjacent real property.

arc: The length of a curved line that makes up a segment of the boundary of the real property.

assumption of mortgage: A situation in which a buyer assumes personal responsibility for payment of the seller's existing mortgage loan.

attorney ad litem: An attorney appointed by the court to protect a defendant-borrower's interests.

attorney-client privilege: A rule of evidence law that prevents a court from compelling the revelation of communications between lawyer and client.

avulsion: The loss of land bordering water as a result of a sudden or violent natural disturbance.

B

balloon mortgage: A loan calling for periodic payments that are less than the amount required to pay off the loan completely at the end of the loan term. The remaining balance of the principal "balloons" into a single, large payment at the end of the loan term.

Bank Insurance Fund (BIF): A fund that insures depositors' accounts.

bargain and sale deed: A deed that transfers the real property itself rather than transferring any particular interest in the property.

base line: An imaginary line running east and west used in the government survey method of legal description.

bearing: That part of a call that provides the direction or course of a boundary line.

benefit of the bargain: A monetary remedy in a breach of contract action calculated as the difference between the contract price and the fair market value of the property.

bill of sale: A document that transfers title to personal property.

blockbusting: The attempt to get homeowners to list their property for sale by stating or implying that minority groups may be moving into the neighborhood.

bona fide purchaser for value: Someone who purchases property in good faith and for valid consideration.

break-even point: The point at which gross income equals the total of fixed costs and variable costs.

broker: A person licensed under state law to facilitate a real estate transaction in return for compensation.

brokerage: The name given to the business engaged in by real estate brokers.

broker price opinion (BPO): A valuation of a property conducted by an independent party that is requested by a lender in a short sale transaction.

bulk transfer laws: Laws that pertain to the sale and purchase of all or substantially all of the inventory of a business.

C

call: A short segment providing the course and distance of a line of a metes and bounds legal description.

cash sale: A sale in which a buyer pays cash for the property and does not acquire financing from a lending institution.

certificate of eligibility: A certificate that states the maximum available loan guaranty entitlement for a veteran.

certificate of reasonable value: A certificate that sets forth the current market value of the property to be purchased.

chain of title: The genealogy of a particular parcel of real property.

check: A measurement of land that is twenty-four miles square.

Chinese Wall: A situation in which an attorney or paralegal is isolated from a client case for conflict of interest reasons.

chord: A straight line drawn from the starting point of an arc to the end point of an arc.

client trust fund account: An account separate from the law firm's regular business account in which fee advances, deposit money, closing proceeds, and/or escrowed funds are placed.

closing: The process of transferring documents and monies to complete a real estate transaction in accordance with the contract for sale and purchase executed by the parties.

closing costs: Certain expenses relating to the transfer of real property, including appraisal fees, attorneys' fees, title fees, recording fees, transfer taxes (sometimes referred to as documentary stamps or documentary stamp tax), and prorations.

commercial bank: A lender that is a major source of construction loans, short-term loans, and home improvement loans.

common elements: Those areas of a condominium development that all of the owners use in common, such as the grounds on which the condominium building is located, the roof, the exterior walls and structural components, the parking lot, and any recreational facilities.

community property: All property, both real and personal, acquired during marriage by either spouse, in states that recognize this concept.

comparative market analysis: A comparison of prices of properties similar to the seller's property that have recently been sold.

competence: Having the necessary legal skill to perform a given task and devoting the requisite time to that task to do a thorough job for the client.

condemnation: The process by which private property is taken by federal, state, and local governments for public use.

condominium: A form of ownership in which the property owner owns the interior of a unit, plus an undivided interest, expressed as a percentage interest, in the common elements of the condominium complex.

condominium association: An association comprised of unit owners that sets rules and manages the operation of the condominium.

confidentiality: An ethical concept prohibiting a lawyer and others in a law firm from voluntarily disclosing information about a client matter.

conflict of interest: A situation in which a lawyer's professional judgment might be affected because of business or personal interests.

construction lien: A statutory lien placed on real property by persons or entities providing labor or materials for the improvement of real property.

constructive eviction: The breach by a landlord of a lease in such a manner as to make the leased premises unusable.

constructive notice: Notice legally presumed because of the recording of documents in the public records.

contingency fee: An attorney's fee that is contingent upon the client reaching settlement or winning in court. The payment the attorney receives is set forth as a percentage of the settlement or court award.

continuous marriage affidavit: A sworn statement verifying the marital status of the sellers.

conventional loan: A loan made by a private lender in which the lender usually does not have any insurance or guarantee from a third party, such as a government agency, backing the loan should the borrower fail to meet his or her loan obligations.

cooperative: A multiunit building owned by a corporation. One purchases stock in the corporation, which entitles the purchaser of the stock to enter into a long-term lease with the corporation.

correction lines: Every fourth township line above and below a base line. At each correction line, the range lines are remeasured to a distance of six miles.

covenant: A promise or guarantee.

credit union: A cooperative association in which members make savings deposits. Credit unions pay interest on the savings accounts and permit members to borrow money for both short-term and long-term residential loans.

curtesy: The provision the law makes for a widower to lay legal claim to an interest in his deceased wife's real property.

D

declaration of condominium: The document that legally creates a condominium.

declaration of covenants and restrictions: A document setting forth the rights and restrictions of property owners within a planned unit development.

declaratory judgment: A judgment sought when the parties to a lawsuit want a judicial decree on their status and rights with regard to a particular matter.

deed: A formal written instrument that conveys title to real property from one party to another.

deed in lieu of foreclosure: A deed to mortgaged property given by a borrower to the lender in order to prevent foreclosure.

deed of trust: A three-party financing instrument between the trustor/borrower, beneficiary/lender, and trustee. The borrower, as trustor, deeds legal title to the real property in question to the trustee as collateral for the loan, while the borrower remains in physical possession of the property.

deed restrictions: Restrictive covenants contained in a deed transferring property from seller to buyer.

defeasible estate: A fee simple estate in which the grantor conveys property with conditions attached that may, upon the occurrence or breach of the condition, divest the grantee of ownership of the property.

deficiency judgment: A court judgment for the difference between the proceeds from the sale of real property in a foreclosure action and the outstanding loan debt.

demand deposit: An account in which the depositor may take out his or her money on demand, such as a checking account.

diligence: Attentiveness and care.

distress: The right to seize a lessee's goods to satisfy a rent arrearage.

distress bond: A bond posted by a landlord in a distraint proceeding.

distress writ: A court order commanding the sheriff to summon the defendant to answer the complaint in a distraint proceeding.

doctrine of imputed disqualification: A doctrine that provides that the entire body of lawyers in a firm is treated as one for conflict of interest purposes.

doctrine of laches: A doctrine similar to the statute of limitations, premised on the principle of vigilance; it states that, if a plaintiff neglects to assert a claim for an unreasonable length of time, that neglect, together with other circumstances causing prejudice to the defendant, will bar relief by a court of equity.

documentary stamp tax: A tax imposed on the transfer of real property. It is sometimes referred to as a transfer tax.

Dodd-Frank Wall Street Reform and Consumer Protection Act (Dodd-Frank Act): A broad federal law enacted to reform the financial services industry. In relation to consumer mortgage loans, it establishes increased protections for consumers with respect to mortgage lending practices, including the expansion of consumer disclosures and the implementation of penalties for lender violations.

dower: The provision the law makes for a widow to lay legal claim to an interest in her deceased husband's real property.

dual agency: An agency situation in which a broker represents both the seller and the buyer in the same transaction.

due diligence: The process of investigating, inspecting, and reviewing matters within a certain time framework.

due-on-sale clause: A clause in a loan document that states that should the real property securing the loan obligation be sold, the total amount outstanding on the loan becomes immediately due.

E

earnest money: A sum of money paid by a buyer at the time of entering a contract to indicate the buyer's intention of carrying out the terms of the contract.

earnest money deposit: An initial deposit given by the buyer that indicates the good faith of the buyer with regard to his or her intent to purchase the property.

easement: The enforceable right to use the real property of another for a particular purpose.

easement in gross: An easement given to benefit a particular individual or entity rather than one given to confer a benefit to real property.

effective date: The date upon which a contract becomes legally binding on all parties.

elective share: A spouse's statutory right to a fractional share of real and personal property owned by the deceased spouse at the date of death.

eminent domain: The right of federal, state, and local governments and certain public and quasi-public corporations and utilities to take private property for public use.

encroachment: An illegal intrusion of a building or appurtenance onto the property of another.

encumbrance clause: A deed clause setting forth any encumbrances on the real property conveyed, such as mortgages, leases, liens, easements, or restrictions.

endorsement: A form provided by the title insurer that is used for the amendment of any information that has appeared as part of a title commitment or title policy. It often provides special coverage not contained in the standard title policy.

entry foreclosure: A foreclosure method used in only a few states in which the lender forecloses by taking possession of the real property for a specified time period, after which legal title to the property passes to the lender.

Equal Credit Opportunity Act (ECOA): A federal law enacted to prevent discrimination in making credit available to consumers.

equitable remedies: Remedies administered according to fairness, such as injunctions and actions for specific performance.

equitable right of redemption: The right to buy back real property at any time prior to a forced sale by paying the full amount of the debt owed and all additional charges.

erosion: The gradual washing away of land from the shore by tides or currents.

escheat: The right of reversion of title to private property in their jurisdictions, given to state and local governments.

escrow account: An account in a bank, savings and loan, credit union, or similar financial institution that is held by a third party and into which funds are deposited to be held until the happening of a stated event.

escrow closing: A closing in which a third party acts as escrowee and receives closing documents deposited by each party, whereupon the escrowee proceeds to close the transaction.

estate for years: A tenancy that continues for a designated period.

exclusive listing: A listing agreement in which the seller agrees to list the property with no broker other than the listing broker for the term of the agreement. As an exclusive agent, the listing broker is entitled to receive compensation if the listing broker or any person other than the seller procures a buyer within the listing term.

exclusive-right-to-sell listing: A listing agreement in which the listing broker is entitled to a commission if anyone procures a buyer within the listing term.

F

Fair Credit Reporting Act (FCRA): A federal law enacted to give individuals the right to examine their own credit history.

Federal Deposit Insurance Corporation (FDIC): An institution that insures depositors' accounts.

Federal Home Loan Mortgage Corporation (FHLMC): A corporation established to provide a secondary market, primarily for conventional loans.

Federal National Mortgage Association (FNMA): A governmentally regulated corporation that buys and services conventional, FHA, and VA residential loans that meet its specific guidelines.

Federal Truth in Lending Act (TILA): A federal law requiring lenders to make full disclosure of all costs incurred in obtaining credit.

fee simple absolute: An estate that grants the property owner each of the four basic property rights.

fee simple determinable: A fee simple estate that will terminate automatically upon the occurrence of a condition or event, at which point the estate reverts back to the grantor or the grantor's estate.

fee simple on a condition subsequent: A fee simple estate in which the grantor has the power of termination upon the occurrence of a condition or event.

fee simple subject to executory limitation: A fee simple estate that will terminate upon the happening of an occurrence or event, at which point the rights to the property will vest in a third party.

FHA loan: A loan insured by the Federal Housing Administration. The FHA insures loans for owner-occupied one- to four-family dwellings.

fictitious name: A name other than one's legal name under which one operates a business.

fiduciary duty: A duty held by a person in a special position of trust (for example, the duty of care, obedience, diligence, and loyalty).

fiduciary lender: A lender that has a fiduciary duty to its principals.

Financial Institutions Reform, Recovery and Enforcement Act (FIRREA): A federal law that restructured the savings and loan regulatory and insurance systems, giving management of insurance funds for savings and loans to the FDIC.

fixed costs: Costs that remain constant and do not vary according to the income generated.

fixture: An object that at one time was personal property but that has, through the process of attachment to real property, become part of the real property.

flat fee: An attorney's fee set forth as a sum certain for the performance of a specified task.

flat-fee sale: An arrangement in which, for a flat fee, a broker evaluates and photographs a property, places a property description in a special online directory, and provides For Sale signs to the seller.

forbearance agreement: A contract in which the lender agrees to refrain from foreclosing on the real property and also permits the borrower to postpone or reduce payments for a specified period of time, in return for which the borrower agrees to a plan that will bring him or her current on his loan obligations.

foreclosure: The legal procedure whereby real property is sold to repay a debt to a creditor who has a lien on the real property.

fraudulent misrepresentation: Misrepresentation made with an intent to mislead or deceive.

freehold estate: An estate of indeterminable duration.

G

gap period: The period between the effective date of the commitment and the recording date of the instruments giving rise to the interest being insured.

general lien: A lien that is not secured by any particular parcel of real property and that therefore may affect all nonexempt property of a debtor.

general warranty deed: A deed by which the grantor states that he or she has valid title and will defend that title against any defect arising from the actions of the grantor or the actions of the grantor's predecessors. This type of deed provides the greatest degree of protection for the grantee.

Good Faith Estimate (GFE): A summary of loan terms and an estimation of closing costs incurred by borrowers.

government lot: An irregular-sized tract of land labeled by government surveyors.

Government National Mortgage Association (GNMA): A division of HUD that works in tandem with the FNMA in the secondary market to assist lending institutions with low-income housing projects.

government survey method: A method of legal description, established by the U.S. Congress, that works on a grid system.

graduated lease: A lease that contains a clause that adjusts the rent at predetermined intervals.

Gramm-Leach-Bliley Act: A federal law requiring financial institutions to establish safeguards to ensure the confidentiality of customer records and nonpublic personal information.

grantee: The person or entity to whom title to real property is conveyed.

granting clause: A deed clause that contains the words of conveyance expressing the grantor's intention of transferring the real property. It also includes the recital of consideration and the legal description of the property to be conveyed.

grantor: The person or entity conveying title of real property to another.

gross lease: A lease in which the lessee pays a fixed amount as basic rent and is not required to pay any portion of the lessor's operating expenses.

ground lease: A lease for a parcel of vacant real property.

guide meridians: Every fourth range line east and west of the principal meridian.

H

habendum clause: A deed clause describing the type of estate being conveyed to the grantee(s).

Home Ownership and Equity Protection Act (HOEPA): A federal law, primarily affecting refinancing and home equity installment loans, that requires additional disclosures and prohibits certain practices when a borrower obtains a high-cost loan.

Homeowner's Protection Act (HPA): A federal law that establishes rules for homeowners who wish to cancel their private mortgage insurance.

homestead property: The primary dwelling house or residence of the head of household plus adjoining land.

hourly fee: An attorney's fee based upon the amount of time the attorney spends on a client matter.

I

implied warranty of fitness: An implied warranty that a product is fit for the particular purpose for which it was bought.

index lease: A lease that contains a built-in mechanism for periodic adjustments to the rent that is tied to the governmental cost-of-living index or similar index.

in personam jurisdiction: Jurisdiction over the persons involved in litigation.

installment contract: A contract in which at least one payment under the contract is made after the close of the taxable year of sale.

intangible tax: A tax imposed for the right to issue, execute, sell, assign, trade in, or receive income from intangible property.

interest rate cap: A limitation on the amount an interest rate can increase on an adjustable-rate loan.

J

joint tenancy: A form of concurrent ownership in which two or more persons have undivided interests in property, with right of survivorship.

jurisdiction: The authority of a court to hear a matter.

L

landlord's lien: A lien given by statute to a landlord on certain personal property of a tenant.

lease: A document that conveys a leasehold interest in real property that includes the right of possession, but not ownership, for a period of time in return for the payment of rent.

leasehold estate: An estate of determinable duration.

legal description: A precise delineation of a specific parcel of real property that sets the property apart from other parcels of real estate.

legal remedies: Remedies awarded in courts of law, such as monetary damages.

license: A personal right to perform specified activities on the real property of another.

lien: A claim or charge against property for payment of a debt.

lien theory: A legal theory pertaining to financing instruments under which a financing instrument serves as a lien on the secured real property.

lien waiver: A document indicating that a subcontractor has been paid and will not be subjecting real property to liens.

life estate: An estate in which the grantor conveys title to real property to another for a period of time measured by somebody's life.

life estate pur autre vie: A life estate granted for the lifetime of someone other than the grantee.

limited common elements: Areas that benefit fewer than all of the condominium unit owners, such as assigned parking spaces or storage facilities.

liquidated damages: Stipulated damages, the amount of which represents a reasonable sum to be paid to the nonbreaching party for damages suffered as a result of a breach of contract.

lis pendens: A notice recorded when a lawsuit affects title to a particular parcel of real property.

listing agreement: A contract between a seller and a broker.

littoral rights: Water rights pertaining to a landowner whose property abuts a lake, ocean, or sea.

loan commitment: A document outlining the terms under which the lender will loan a specified amount to the borrower. Once accepted by the borrower, it becomes a contract.

loan origination fee: A fee charged by lenders to process a loan application.

loan-to-value ratio: The correspondence between the value of the real property to serve as collateral for a loan and the amount of the loan.

M

maker: The borrower signing a promissory note.

margin: The number of percentage points a lender adds to the index rate to come up with an ARM interest rate.

marketable title: Title to real property that is free from encumbrances that would bring down the value of the real property or create reasonable doubt or controversy.

master association: An umbrella association that provides management services and decision-making functions to smaller condominiums.

master plan: A plan created by a local planning commission that provides for land use, conservation, circulation, noise regulation, and public facilities in a given area.

memorandum of lease: A document providing skeletal information of a lease, such as the names of the lessor and lessee and a description of the leased premises. This document is recorded in the county in which the leased premises are located to put others on notice of a transfer of physical possession of the property.

merchants' association: An organization consisting of the merchants of a shopping center whose primary purpose is the promotion of the common good of the center.

metes and bounds method: A method of legal description that outlines the boundary lines of a parcel of real property by establishing a starting point called the point of beginning and describing the course and distance each boundary line travels from that point around the perimeters of the property until returning to the point of beginning.

millage rate: A rate used in computing ad valorem real property taxes.

monetary judgment: An award of monies to a plaintiff if he or she wins a lawsuit.

monument: A natural or man-made object that is permanent and fixed.

mortgage: A two-party security instrument between the mortgagor/borrower and the mortgagee/lender that describes the property serving as collateral for the loan and sets forth the rights of the lender should the borrower default.

Mortgage Assistance Relief Services Rule (MARS): A federal regulation that prohibits the making of false and misleading claims by providers of mortgage assistance relief services. It sets forth mandatory disclosure, record-keeping, and compliance requirements for the providers of these services.

mortgage banking company: A private corporation that originates loans for other lenders and investors, for which it receives a servicing fee.

mortgage broker: A licensed individual who acts as a middle-man in a financing transaction, bringing lenders and borrowers together in return for a placement fee.

mortgagee: The lender.

mortgage estoppel letter: A letter specifying the amount to be paid to satisfy an outstanding loan debt.

mortgage insurance premium: An insurance premium charged on FHA loans. These premiums are collected into the FHA's Mutual Mortgage Insurance Fund to insure lenders against bad loans.

mortgagor: The borrower.

multiple listing service: An organization of brokers who agree to publicize their listings to all other broker members through the use of the service.

mutual savings bank: A lending institution found primarily in the Northeast that is owned by the depositors, who are the investors. The depositor-investors receive a return on their investment through the payment of interest on their savings accounts. Mutual savings banks make loans for both residential and income-producing properties.

N

National Association of Legal Assistants (NALA): A voluntary national paralegal association. It lists among its goals working to improve the quality of the delivery of legal services.

National Federation of Paralegal Associations (NFPA): A voluntary national paralegal association. It lists among its goals advancing the paralegal profession through strategic alliances and promoting regulation and educational standards for the paralegal profession.

net lease: A lease in which the lessee, in addition to the base rent, is obligated to pay a pro rata share of some of the lessor's operating expenses.

net listing: A listing agreement in which the seller specifies the net amount of money he or she must receive in order to sell the property. Under the terms of the agreement, the broker receives any monies in excess of this specified amount as commission.

nonconforming use: Also referred to as *preexisting use.* Permission given to a property owner who has built an improvement on land prior to the enactment of a zoning ordinance to continue to use the land in the same manner as before.

nonforeign certification: A statement certifying that the seller is not a foreign person as that term is defined in section 1445 of the Internal Revenue Code, and that monies need not be withheld from the sale for tax purposes.

notice of commencement: A document recorded by a property owner indicating the date upon which construction began on the property.

notice of default: A notice informing a borrower that he or she is in default, setting forth the amount and date of the default, the period within which to respond, and the consequences if he or she does not act within the prescribed period.

notice of nonresponsibility: A notice posted on a construction site by the owner of the property to avoid legal responsibility for unauthorized work done or unauthorized materials furnished.

notice of rescission: A notice that rescinds a notice of default in a nonjudicial foreclosure.

notice of trustee's sale: A notice published in a newspaper of general circulation in the county in which the real property is located announcing the details of the sale of the real property in a nonjudicial foreclosure action.

notice statute: A recording statute whereby the notice a subsequent purchaser has of a previous purchaser's deed is determinative of the priority of title to the real property.

notice to owner: A document that puts a property owner on notice of those parties expecting payment for work or materials incorporated into the owner's real property.

O

open listing: The granting of a nonexclusive right to solicit and receive offers on the seller's real property.

operating expenses: Expenses incurred in maintaining and managing property.

option contract: A contract in which the seller gives a potential buyer the exclusive right, within a specified limited time period, to purchase real property. The potential buyer pays the seller for this exclusive right.

ownership in severalty: Ownership of real property in one's own name as a sole owner.

P

partition: An action by the court dividing real property held by joint tenants, tenants in common, or tenants in partnership.

party wall easement: An easement on the part of a shared partition wall between two properties.

payee: The lender as receiver of a promissory note.

percentage lease: A lease in which, in addition to the base rent, the lessee is obligated to pay a specific percentage of the lessee's sales receipts to the lessor.

permissive waste: The diminishment of the value of property when a life estate holder fails in the upkeep of the property.

personal property: All property that is not considered real property.

PITI: A loan payment that is comprised of principal, interest, taxes, and insurance.

planned unit development (PUD): A subdivision containing individual lots with common areas controlled by a homeowners' association.

plat map: A survey that breaks down a tract of land into blocks referenced by letter or number.

plat method: A method of legal description that describes real property by making reference to its location on a plat map recorded in the land records in the county in which the property is located.

point of beginning: A readily identifiable point that is the starting point of a metes and bounds legal description of the subject real property.

points: A lending charge, sometimes referred to as *discount points.* Each point is equal to 1 percent of the loan amount.

police powers: Those powers given to the federal government and to the states by their constitutions to create laws necessary for the protection of public health, safety, and welfare.

power-of-sale clause: A clause in a deed of trust that gives the trustee the power to sell the real property serving as collateral for a loan at public auction if the borrower defaults on his or her loan obligation.

premises clause: The opening paragraph of a deed, setting forth the date of execution of the deed, the parties to the deed, and, in states that so require, the addresses of the parties.

prescriptive easement: An easement created when a person adversely uses the property of another for a statutorily specified time period.

prime mortgage loan: A loan given at the prime rate to high-quality borrowers.

principal: The person upon whose behalf an agent is authorized to work.

principal meridian: An imaginary line running north and south used in the government survey method of legal description.

private mortgage insurance (PMI): Insurance from private insurance providers that insures the portion of a loan that exceeds the typical conventional loan-to-value ratio.

profit à prendre: The right to remove certain items from another's land or to remove a portion of the land.

promissory note: A written promise to repay a debt on agreed-upon terms and conditions. The note is the legal evidence of the borrower's intentions to repay the debt.

prorations: Charges that are apportioned between the parties.

punitive damages: Damages designed to punish or serve as an example.

purchase money mortgage sale: A sale in which the seller finances all or a portion of the purchase price of the property, with the buyer executing a mortgage instrument and mortgage note in favor of the seller.

Q

quitclaim deed: A deed in which the grantor transfers whatever interest he or she may have without making any warranties regarding the quality of the title.

R

race-notice statute: A recording statute premised on protecting a bona fide purchaser for value without notice if he or she is the first to record the deed to real property.

race statute: A recording statute whereby priority of claim to title of real property is determined literally by a race to record the deed.

radius: The distance between any point on a curved line and the center of an imaginary circle that could be drawn if that curved line was extended to form a full circle.

range lines: Imaginary lines located at each six-mile interval, running in a north-south direction parallel to a principal meridian.

real estate agent: A real estate licensee; either a real estate salesperson or a real estate broker.

Real Estate Investment Trust (REIT): A trust that accumulates funds by selling beneficial interests in the trust to members of the public. The trust then invests in various types of loans—typically, construction loans and loans for larger real estate projects.

Real Estate Settlement Procedures Act (RESPA): A federal law requiring the lender to provide the borrower with a summary of loan terms and an estimate of closing costs incurred by borrowers within three days from the date the loan application is submitted. It also requires the use of a uniform settlement statement for all nonexempt transactions.

real property: Property comprised of land and all things affixed to it, as well as natural objects on or growing on the land.

Realtor®: A real estate licensee who voluntarily becomes a member of a local board of Realtors® that is affiliated with the National Association of Realtors®.

recording: Delivering a document to the appropriate government official for transcription into a plat book, deed book, mortgage book, or official records book.

recording statute: A statute that prescribes the requirements for recording a document and that determines the priority of rights to real property if there are conflicting claims.

reddendum clause: A deed clause reserving some right in the real property for the grantor or imposing a restriction on the use of the property by the grantee.

redemption period: A statutorily prescribed period of time within which a borrower may prevent foreclosure by paying the amount(s) owed, plus interest, and penalties, or by negotiating an agreement with the lender.

redlining: Denying a loan or presenting different terms or conditions for a loan based upon the composition of the neighborhood or other discriminatory reasons.

reinstatement of loan: An arrangement in lieu of foreclosure, whereby a borrower pays all delinquent sums and late charges and takes any reasonable actions the lender may require to ensure both that the lender's interest in the real property is protected and that the borrower's obligation to pay under the terms of the note and mortgage remains unimpaired.

reliction: The gradual drying up of water, resulting in the addition of uncovered land.

reserve requirements: Monies set aside for the replacement of items over and above regular maintenance requirements.

respondeat superior: "Let the master answer." A legal doctrine that holds the principal legally responsible for the actions of the agent.

restrictive covenants: Private restrictions imposed on the use of private property.

retainer agreement: A contract between an attorney and a client that sets forth the manner in which the client will be billed for the attorney's work.

right of disposition: The right to dispose of one's property by transferring rights to the property during one's lifetime or at time of death.

right of exclusion: The right to exercise control over one's property.

right of possession: The right to occupy one's property in privacy.

right of use: The right to use one's property in any lawful manner or to give a general or limited right of use of the property to another.

riparian rights: Water rights pertaining to a landowner whose property abuts a river, stream, or similar watercourse.

S

sale–leaseback: A situation in which an owner of real property sells the property to an investor and then leases the property back.

sale subject to existing mortgage: A situation in which a buyer becomes responsible for the seller's payments under an existing mortgage, but the seller remains primarily liable under the mortgage note.

satisfaction of judgment: A document recorded to evidence the satisfaction of a debt and the removal of an encumbrance from real property.

satisfaction of mortgage: A document recorded to evidence the payment in full of a mortgage loan.

savings and loan association: A lending institution that primarily makes residential, conventional loans but that on occasion makes FHA and VA loans.

Savings Association Insurance Fund (SAIF): A fund that insures savings and loan deposits.

secondary market: A market for the purchase and sale of existing mortgages.

section: A measurement of land that is one mile square and contains 640 acres.

Section 8 rental program: A program, managed by HUD, to subsidize rental housing for qualified low-income families.

Secure and Fair Enforcement for Mortgage Licensing Act (S.A.F.E. Act): A federal law requiring mortgage loan originators employed by institutions regulated by various federal agencies to register on a nationwide registry to provide consumers with access to their background information.

seisin clause: A deed clause by which the grantor warrants that he or she is the rightful owner of the property in question and thereby has the right and power to convey the property to the grantee.

seller's affidavit: A sworn statement signed by the seller stating that there are no existing liens on the property that would encumber the purchaser's title.

separate property: Property that is (1) acquired by a spouse prior to marriage, (2) income from property acquired by a spouse prior to marriage unless commingled in a manner that makes it community property, (3) acquired solely through separate funds, or (4) acquired by gift, will, or descent unless the gift or will clearly indicates that the property is given to both husband and wife.

service of process: The serving of a summons and complaint upon the defendant by a sheriff or court-approved process server.

Sherman Act: A federal antitrust law protecting against unlawful restraints in trade and commerce, such as monopolies and price-fixing.

short sale: The sale of a property for a price that is "short," or less than the full amount owed on the property.

short sale package: A compilation of documentation that a lender reviews to determine the value of the property, the existence of other encumbrances and costs associated with the sale of the property, and the financial situation of the borrower/owner.

single agency: A broker who represents only one principal in a transaction.

special assessment: An assessment for shared improvements that enhance the value of real property.

special exception: Permission given to a property owner to use property for a use undesignated in that area.

special warranty deed: Also known as a *limited warranty deed*. A deed by which the grantor, in conveying title to real property, warrants only that he or she has done nothing to encumber the property and does not provide further assurances with regard to the grantor's predecessors.

specific lien: A lien that is secured by a particular parcel of real property.

specific performance: A lawsuit whereby the plaintiff asks the court to order the defendant to do a specific act under the terms of the contract.

statute of frauds: A state statute indicating which contracts must be in writing and signed by the party to be charged in order to be legally enforceable.

statute of limitations: A statute indicating the time period within which a suit must be brought or be forever barred.

steering: The attempt to guide prospective homeowners into one neighborhood as opposed to another based on the racial, religious, or ethnic composition of a particular neighborhood.

stipulation: An agreement made by opposing sides in a lawsuit regulating a matter pertaining to the suit.

straight loan: A loan in which the borrower makes periodic interest payments, with the entire principal paid at the end of the loan term.

strict foreclosure: A foreclosure method available in a few states in which a court hearing is held to determine the mortgagee's right to foreclose. If the mortgagee's right is authorized, the court awards the real property to the mortgagee without requiring the mortgagee to bid for the property at a public sale.

subagent: Someone who is authorized by an agent to aid in a transaction for a principal, if authorized under the original agency agreement.

subject matter jurisdiction: Jurisdiction over the subject matter of the litigation.

subordination agreement: An agreement by which one party agrees that his or her interest in real property should have lower priority than the interest to which it is being subordinated.

subordination, non-disturbance, and attornment (SNDA) agreement: A contract that establishes the rights and obligations of a tenant and and a lessor's lender in the event of the lessor's default of a loan agreement and subsequent foreclosure.

subprime mortgage loan: A loan given to a borrower who has a higher-than-average risk of default and who pays a higher interest rate to compensate the lender for the higher risk.

subscription: A special billing rate for certain types of ongoing tasks.

summary proceedings: Short and simple proceedings used to dispose of certain controversies.

supersedeas bond: A bond required when one is appealing a court judgment.

survey: An investigation or examination that determines the boundaries of a parcel of land or locates all improvements on the parcel.

T

tax base: The total assessed value of all taxable real property in a taxing authority's jurisdiction.

tenancy at sufferance: A tenancy occurring after the expiration of a lease, in which a tenant remains in possession of the property without the landlord's consent.

tenancy at will: A tenancy that begins as an estate for years, with the tenant remaining on the property by agreement with the landlord after the estate for years expires.

tenancy by the entirety: A form of concurrent ownership by husband and wife in which each spouse has an undivided interest and right of survivorship.

tenancy from period to period: A tenancy that continues for successive intervals until one party to the agreement provides the other party with notice of termination of the tenancy.

tenancy in common: A form of concurrent ownership in which two or more persons have undivided interests in property but which does not confer the right of survivorship.

tenant estoppel certificate: A document that verifies the terms and conditions of a tenant's lease.

tenant unions: Organizations that elect representatives to consolidate tenant complaints, negotiate favorable rent agreements, and assure compliance with maintenance requirements.

tenendum clause: A deed clause indicating the improvements that are being conveyed together with the land, such as the buildings built on the land.

1099-S form: A federal tax reporting form for the reporting of real property sales transactions.

testimonium clause: A deed clause in which the deed is executed, witnessed, and acknowledged.

tickler system: A method of keeping track of priorities and deadlines.

time share: The purchase of the right to use real property for a limited, specified period of time each year.

title commitment: A document that sets forth the status of the title of a particular parcel of real property and the terms under which a title policy for the property will be issued.

title insurance: Insurance obtained by an owner of real property or another having an interest in the real property against loss brought about by encumbrances, defective titles, invalidity, or adverse claim to the title.

title search: The search of the public records to determine if title to real property is marketable.

title theory: A legal theory pertaining to financing instruments under which a financing instrument transfers conditional title in the secured real property to the lender.

Torrens certificate: In states that utilize the Torrens system, a certificate, issued by the registrar of title, that is the actual legal title to the real property.

Torrens system: A method for determining title to real property through the institution of a lawsuit.

township: A measurement of land that is six miles square, or thirty-six square miles.

township lines: Imaginary lines located at each six-mile interval running in an east-west direction parallel to a base line.

tract index: An index compiled by a description of parcels of real property.

transaction broker: A broker who provides limited representation to one or both parties in a real estate transaction and does not represent one party to the detriment of the other.

triple net lease: A lease in which the lessee, in addition to the base rent, is obligated to pay a pro rata share of all of the lessor's expenses.

U

UCC-1 financing statement: A document filed in the public records that perfects a security interest in personal property.

unbundled services: A fee arrangement in which the attorney handles only specific aspects of a legal matter or transaction.

V

VA loan: A loan made to veterans by approved lenders for residential, owner-occupied property and guaranteed by the U.S. Department of Veterans Affairs.

variable costs: Costs that vary according to the income generated.

variance: Permission given to a property owner to deviate from strict compliance with all or part of a zoning ordinance.

venue: The proper location to bring a lawsuit.

verified complaint: A complaint that is signed and sworn to by the plaintiff, attesting that all allegations within the complaint are true to the plaintiff's best knowledge and belief.

voluntary waste: The active use of property by a life estate holder in a manner that reduces its market value.

W

writ of attachment: A court order that prevents a party to a lawsuit from conveying title to property, real or personal, while the suit is pending.

writ of execution: A court order that directs the sheriff to levy upon real property and sell it at a sheriff's sale.

writ of possession: A court order issued to the sheriff ordering the sheriff to remove a tenant from leased property.

Index